CLINICAL HANDBOOK OF COUPLE THERAPY

CLINICAL HANDBOOK OF COUPLE THERAPY

Third Edition

Edited by
ALAN S. GURMAN
NEIL S. JACOBSON

THE GUILFORD PRESS
New York   London

© 2002 The Guilford Press
A Division of Guilford Publications, Inc.
72 Spring Street, New York, NY 10012
www.guilford.com

Printed in the United States of America

This book is printed on acid-free paper.

Last digit is print number: 9 8 7 6 5 4 3 2 1

Library of Congress Cataloging-in-Publication Data
is available from the Publisher

ISBN 1-57230-758-7

About the Editors

Alan S. Gurman, PhD, is a Professor of Psychiatry and Director of Family Therapy at the University of Wisconsin Medical School. He has edited or written many influential books, including *Theory and Practice of Brief Therapy* (with S. Budman), the *Handbook of Family Therapy* (with D. Kniskern), and *Essential Psychotherapies* (with S. Messer). A past Editor of the *Journal of Marital and Family Therapy*, and past President of the Society for Psychotherapy Research, Dr. Gurman has received numerous awards for his contributions to marital and family therapy, including an award for "Distinguished Contribution to Research in Family Therapy" from the American Association for Marriage and Family Therapy, and for "Distinguished Achievement in Family Therapy Research" from the American Family Therapy Academy. A pioneer in the development of integrative approaches to couple therapy, Dr. Gurman maintains an active clinical practice in Madison, Wisconsin.

Neil S. Jacobson, PhD (deceased), was a Professor of Psychology at the University of Washington. A prolific contributor to the literature of both psychology and couple therapy, he published numerous influential books, including—in the marital area—*Marital Therapy: Strategies Based on Social Learning and Behavior Exchange Principles* (with G. Margolin), *Integrative Couple Therapy: Promoting Acceptance and Change* (with A. Christensen), and *Reconcilable Differences* (with A. Christensen). A past President of the Association for Advancement of Behavior Therapy (AABT) and Master Lecturer for the American Association for Marriage and Family Therapy (AAMFT), Dr. Jacobson received many awards for his contributions to marital and family therapy, including an award for "Distinguished Contribution to Research in Family Therapy" from the AAMFT, and for "Distinguished Achievement in Family Therapy Research" from the American Family Therapy Academy. Dr. Jacobson was a pioneer not only in the development of behavioral couple therapy, but also in the treatment of depression and domestic violence.

Contributors

Carl Bagnini, MSW, BCD, Chair, Couple, Child and Family Therapy Program, International Institute of Object Relations Therapy, Chevy Chase, Maryland; Faculty, St. John's University Postdoctoral Program in Couple and Family Therapy, Queens, New York; Faculty, Suffolk Institute of Psychoanalysis and Psychotherapy, Port Washington, New York

Donald H. Baucom, PhD, Professor and Director, Clinical Psychology Program, Department of Psychology, University of North Carolina, Chapel Hill, North Carolina

Thomas N. Bradbury, PhD, Professor, Department of Psychology, University of California–Los Angeles, Los Angeles, California

Andrew Christensen, PhD, Professor, Department of Psychology, University of California–Los Angeles, Los Angeles, California

Rebecca M. Cobb, MA, PhD Candidate, Department of Psychology, University of California–Los Angeles, Los Angeles, California

Gene Combs, MD, Co-Director, Evanston Family Therapy Center, Evanston, Illinois

Jill S. Compton, PhD, Assistant Clinical Professor, Department of Psychiatry, Duke University Medical Center, Durham, North Carolina

Wayne Denton, MD, PhD, Associate Professor and Director, Marital and Family Therapy Program, Department of Psychiatry and Behavioral Medicine, Wake Forest University School of Medicine, Winston-Salem, North Carolina

Sona Dimidjian, MSW, Research Assistant, Department of Psychology, University of Washington Center for Clinical Research, Seattle, Washington

Janice Driver, BS, PhD Candidate, Department of Psychology, University of Washington, Seattle, Washington

Robert E. Emery, PhD, Professor of Psychology and Director of the Center for Children, Families and the Law, Department of Psychology, University of Virginia, Charlottesville, Virginia

Elizabeth E. Epstein, PhD, Associate Research Professor, Clinical Division, Center of Alcohol Studies, Rutgers–The State University of New Jersey, Piscataway, New Jersey

Norman Epstein, PhD, Professor, Department of Psychology, University of Maryland, College Park, Maryland

Victoria M. Follette, PhD, Professor, Department of Psychology, and Associate Dean, University of Nevada, Reno, Nevada

Jill H. Freedman, MSW, Co-Director, Evanston Family Therapy Center, Evanston, Illinois

Michael A. Friedman, PhD, Assistant Professor, Department of Psychology, Rutgers—The State University of New Jersey, Piscataway, New Jersey

Elizabeth L. George, PhD, Research Associate, Colorado Family Project, Department of Psychology, University of Colorado, Boulder, Colorado

Shirley P. Glass, PhD, ABPP, Private Practice, Owings Mills, Maryland

Jackie K. Gollan, PhD, Clinical Instructor, Department of Psychiatry, Pritzker School of Medicine, The University of Chicago, Chicago, Illinois

John M. Gottman, PhD, A. Mifflin Professor, Department of Psychology, University of Washington, Seattle, Washington; Director, The Gottman Institute, Seattle, Washington

Robert-Jay Green, PhD, Professor and Director, Family and Child Psychology Doctoral Training Program, California School of Professional Psychology, Alliant International University, San Francisco Bay Campus, Alameda, California

Alan S. Gurman, PhD, Professor and Director of Family Therapy Training, Department of Psychiatry, University of Wisconsin Medical School, Madison, Wisconsin

W. Kim Halford, PhD, Professor of Clinical Psychology and Head, School of Applied Psychology, Griffith University, Brisbane, Queensland, Australia

Kenneth V. Hardy, PhD, Senior Faculty, Ackerman Institute for the Family, New York, New York; Adjunct Clinical Professor, Family Therapy Program, Syracuse University, Syracuse, New York

Amy Holtzworth-Munroe, PhD, Professor, Department of Psychology, Indiana University, Bloomington, Indiana

Michael F. Hoyt, PhD, Senior Staff Psychologist, Department of Psychiatry, Kaiser Permanente Medical Center, San Rafael, California; Clinical Faculty, University of California School of Medicine, San Francisco, California

Neil S. Jacobson (deceased), PhD, Professor, Department of Psychology, University of Washington, Seattle, Washington

Matthew Johnson, PhD, Assistant Professor, Department of Psychology, State University of New York—Binghamton, Binghamton, New York

Susan M. Johnson, EdD, Professor, Departments of Psychology and Psychiatry, University of Ottawa, Ottawa, Ontario, Canada; Director, Ottawa Couple and Family Institute, Ottawa, Ontario, Canada

James Keim, MSW, LCSW, Threat Assessment Specialist and Student—Family Support Therapist, Poudre School District, Fort Collins, Colorado

Jay Lappin, MSW, LCSW, Director of Family Therapy, Comprehensive Psychotherapy and Consulting Associates, Marlton, New Jersey, and Philadelphia, Pennsylvania

Tracey A. Laszloffy, PhD, Associate Professor and Director, Marriage and Family Therapy Program, Seton Hill College, Greensburg, Pennsylvania

Jaslean J. LaTaillade, PhD, Postdoctoral Research Fellow, Department of Psychology, University of North Carolina, Chapel Hill, North Carolina

Erika Lawrence, PhD, Assistant Professor, Department of Psychology, University of Iowa, Iowa City, Iowa

Amy D. Marshall, BA, PhD Candidate, Department of Psychology, Indiana University, Bloomington, Indiana

Christopher R. Martell, PhD, Clinical Assistant Professor, Department of Psychology, University of Washington, Seattle, Washington; Private Practice, Seattle, Washington

Barry W. McCarthy, PhD, Professor, Department of Psychology, American University, Washington, DC; Private Practice, Washington, DC

Barbara S. McCrady, PhD, Professor II, Department of Psychology, and Clinical Director, Center of Alcohol Studies, Rutgers—The State University of New Jersey, Piscataway, New Jersey

Susan H. McDaniel, PhD, Professor, Departments of Psychiatry (Psychology) and Family Medicine, and Director, Wynne Center for Family Research, University of Rochester School of Medicine and Dentistry, Rochester, New York

Jeffrey C. Meehan, AB, PhD Candidate, Department of Psychology, Indiana University, Bloomington, Indiana

David J. Miklowitz, PhD, Professor, Department of Psychology, University of Colorado, Boulder, Colorado

Ivan W. Miller, PhD, Professor and Director of Psychiatric Research, Department of Psychiatry and Human Behavior, Brown University Medical School, Providence, Rhode Island

Valory Mitchell, PhD, Professor of Psychology and Coordinator, Gender Studies Emphasis, California School of Professional Psychology, Alliant International University, San Francisco Bay Campus, Alameda, California

Elizabeth N. Moore, BA (Psych), Research Officer, School of Applied Psychology, Griffith University, Brisbane, Queensland, Australia

Cheryl Rampage, PhD, Senior Therapist, The Family Institute at Northwestern University, Evanston, Illinois

Uzma Rehman, BA, PhD Candidate, Department of Psychology, Indiana University, Bloomington, Indiana

Laura Roberto-Forman, PsyD, Professor, Department of Psychiatry and Behavioral Sciences, Eastern Virginia Medical School, Norfolk, Virginia

Ronald D. Rogge, MA, PhD, United States Navy, San Diego, California

Michael J. Rohrbaugh, PhD, Professor, Departments of Psychology and Family Studies, University of Arizona, Tucson, Arizona

Nancy B. Ruddy, PhD, Clinical Assistant Professor, Departments of Family Medicine and Psychiatry, University of Rochester School of Medicine and Dentistry/Highland Hospital, Rochester, New York

David A. Sbarra, MEd, PhD Candidate, Department of Psychology, University of Virginia, Charlottesville, Virginia

Jill Savege Scharff, MD, Co-Director, International Institute of Object Relations Therapy, Chevy Chase, Maryland; Clinical Professor of Psychiatry, Georgetown University, Washington, DC; Teaching Analyst and Associate Supervising Analyst, Washington Psychoanalytic Institute, Washington, DC

W. Joel Schneider, MS, PhD Candidate, Department of Psychology, Texas A & M University, College Station, Texas

Varda Shoham, PhD, Professor and Director of Clinical Training, Department of Psychology, University of Arizona, Tucson, Arizona

Douglas K. Snyder, PhD, Professor and Director of Clinical Training, Department of Psychology, Texas A & M University, College Station, Texas

Amber Tabares, BS, PhD Candidate, Department of Psychology, University of Washington, Seattle, Washington

Daniel B. Wile, PhD, Private Practice, Oakland, California

Preface

The seeds for this *Handbook* were sown in December 1975, when I met Neil Jacobson at the annual meeting of the Association for Advancement of Behavior Therapy in San Francisco. It was just a brief conversation, following someone's paper presentation. (Earlier at that conference, I had led a workshop entitled "Misuses of Behavioral Exchange Programs in Couples Therapy." To my knowledge, Neil was not in the audience.) As a postdoctoral fellow at the University of Wisconsin Medical School, I had recently published "The Effects and Effectiveness of Marital Therapy: A Review of Outcome Research" (Gurman, 1973) in *Family Process*, and Neil, still a graduate student at the University of North Carolina, would soon publish "Behavorial Marital Therapy: Current Status" (Jacobson & Martin, 1976) in the *Psychological Bulletin*. Both of these articles attracted a good deal of attention in the marital/couple field, because they were the first to systematically examine the extant research literature on couple therapy. Our overlapping interest in the empirical side of things in couple therapy was the basis for our initial mutual academic attraction.

Our next encounter was in May 1977 at the landmark Butler Hospital/Brown University Marital Therapy Conference (Paolino & McCrady, 1978) in Providence, Rhode Island, at which we were both main speakers. Neil, still a predoctoral clinical psychology intern at Brown, reviewed what we knew about research on couple therapy; I, now a junior faculty member at Wisconsin, offered a critical and comparative analysis of the dominant theoretical approaches to marital therapy. As rewarding as that conference was professionally and intellectually, it was more rewarding personally. Neil and I actually had the opportunity to spend some social time together. We discovered that we had different, but equally quirky and complementary, senses of humor, and that we definitely shared a distaste for received wisdom and reflexive acceptance of mainstream ideas.

About a year later, our provocative debate appeared in *Family Process* (Gurman & Kniskern, 1978; Gurman & Knudson, 1978; Gurman, Knudson, & Kniskern, 1978; Jacobson & Weiss, 1978), about the then just-emerging behavioral approach to marital therapy. Although a zealous and passionate exchange such as that might have driven many people in opposite directions, it actually seemed paradoxically to have increased our mutual respect and curiosity about each other.

Then, in June 1981, I visited Neil in Seattle at the University of Washington, to spend a couple of days with him and his graduate students. The focus was much more on clinical matters than in our earlier meeting and occasional correspondence. We found during this visit that we did a lot of things similarly with couples, but that we thought and talked about what we did quite differently. Although our differences were not surprising, given our earlier *Family Process* debate, I think we were both very pleased by our complementariness, not to mention our insatiable needs to banter. We thought we could make a pretty good team on a joint project. Thus the original *Clinical Handbook of Marital Therapy* (Jacobson & Gurman, 1986) was conceived.

At the time the original *Handbook* was published, we noted in the preface that there were "few detailed guides to clinical practice and even fewer that were comprehensive in their scope" about marital therapy. We optimistically referred to this *Handbook* as "the first comprehensive guide to the clinical practice of marital therapy." Evidently our optimism was not born of mere grandiosity, as workaday clinicians seem consistently to have found the *Clinical Handbook of Marital Therapy* and its second edition, the *Clinical Handbook of Couple Therapy* (Jacobson & Gurman, 1995), to address the central topics in this area of psychotherapy, and teachers and students of couple therapy have made these first two editions the most widely adopted texts in the field.

As pleased as Neil and I were with these results, our original intent was not to add still another "successful" book to the myriad texts on psychotherapy. We hoped not merely to reflect what was happening in the field, but also to influence it. In this third edition of the *Handbook*, it was our plan once again to continue to be comprehensive, in the sense that we tried hard to comprehend just what of significance was going on in the field of couple therapy, and what was also at the cutting edge. As before, we were not content simply to organize a standard 14-chapter textbook (one for each week of a semester). We hoped that with our biased, joint quadocular vision, we could perhaps see just over the horizon to some exciting developments that had not yet received "household name" recognition. Although we certainly wanted to reflect important refinements and advances within established couple treatment methods, we also wanted to provide a forum for new methods that had emerged since the first two editions of the *Handbook* were published. We also wanted to present newer applications of couple therapy that, in our finite wisdom, we considered truly significant because of their empirical warrant, public policy implications, or conceptual and clinical sophistication and creativity. Before Neil's untimely death in June 1999, we devoted a great deal of time and thought about how best to fashion a new edition that would achieve such comprehensive aims.

THE PRESENT EDITION

This third edition of the *Handbook* retains its central core and topical structure from earlier editions, and yet it is quite different in many particulars. About half the chapter topics are either entirely new or reflect major substantive alterations from the earlier editions, and fully two-thirds of the present authors join us here for the first time. Two-thirds of the chapters involve either a new author for an "old" topic or a new topic altogether. Compared to the widely (if only implicitly) known rule of thumb that revising a professional book or textbook usually means it is changed about 30%, this is quite a contrast. And yet, with all that is new to this third edition, there continues in it a fundamental coherence and integrity with the earlier editions.

In addition, in part because the *Handbook* is commonly used for teaching, Neil and I decided to try to make it more structurally consistent from chapter to chapter. We felt that this would facilitate comparative study of different models of couple therapy, as well as recent advances in the applications of couple therapy. Thus we instructed all our contributors to follow a common set of expository "guidelines." (In those few cases where an author's style just could not be meaningfully accommodated to our format, we let the structure of the chapter loosen, but still insisted that the core areas about the treatment approach be attended to.) These guidelines represent a revised version of similar guidelines originally set forth in the Gurman and Kniskern (1981, 1991) *Handbook of Family Therapy*, and more recently in the Gurman and Messer (1995) introductory psychotherapy text. Teachers and students of psychotherapy in particular have found these authors' guidelines to be useful learning tools. Readers already familiar with the *Handbook* will especially note that this edition includes a good deal more illustrative case material than the earlier editions. Here, then, are our authors' guidelines.

I. Background of the approach
    Purpose: To place the approach in historical perspective both within the field of psychotherapy in general and within the area of couple/family therapy in particular.
    Possible points to include:
    (1) The major influences contributing to the development of the approach (e.g., people, books, research, theories, conferences).
    (2) The therapeutic forms, if any, that were forerunners of the approach.
    (3) Types of couples with which the approach was initially developed, and speculations as to why.
    (4) Brief description of early theoretical principles and/or therapy techniques.
II. The healthy/well-functioning versus pathological/dysfunctional couple/marriage
    Purpose: To describe typical relationship patterns and other factors that differentiate healthy/well-functioning and pathological/dysfunctional couples/marriages.
    Possible points to include:
    (1) What interaction patterns, or other characteristics, differentiate healthy/satisfied from unhealthy/dissatisfied couples? (Consider such relationship areas as problem solving, communication, expression of affect, sexuality, the balance of individual and couple needs, and the role of individual psychological health.)
    (2) How do problematic relationship patterns develop? How are they maintained? Are there reliable risk factors for couple functioning and/or couple longevity?
    (3) How do gender factors influence couples' relationship satisfaction and functioning?
    (4) What role do sociocultural factors such as ethnicity, class, and race play in couple satisfaction and functioning?
    (5) How do healthy versus dysfunctional couples handle life cycle transitions, crises, and the like? How do they adapt to the inevitable changes of both individuals and relationships?
III. The assessment of couple functioning and dysfunction
    Purpose: To describe the methods, whether formal or informal, used to understand a couple's clinically relevant patterns of interaction, symptomatology, and adaptive resources.
    Possible points to include:
    (1) Briefly describe any formal or informal system (including tests, questionnaires) for diagnosing or assessing couples, in addition to the clinical interview.
    (2) Describe any characteristics of the clinical interview that are particularly reflective of your approach.
    (3) At what unit levels is assessment made (e.g., individual, dyadic, family system)?
    (4) At what psychological levels is assessment made (e.g., intrapsychic, behavioral)?
    (5) What is the temporal focus of assessment—that is, present or past? For example, is the history of partner/mate selection useful in treatment planning?
    (6) Is assessment separate from treatment or integrated with it? For instance, what is the temporal relation between assessment and treatment?
    (7) To what extent are issues involving gender, ethnicity, and other sociocultural factors included in your assessment? Developmental/life cycle changes?
    (8) Are couple strengths/resources a focus of your assessment?
IV. Goal setting
    Purpose: To describe the nature of the therapeutic goals established and the process by which they are established.

Possible points to include:
(1) Are there treatment goals that apply to all or most cases for which the treatment is appropriate, regardless of between-couple differences or of presenting problems? Relatedly, does a couple's marital status influence your goal setting?
(2) Of the number of possible goals for a given couple, how are the central goals selected for this couple? How are they prioritized?
(3) Do you distinguish between intermediate (or mediating or process) goals and ultimate goals?
(4) Who determines the goals of treatment? Therapist, couple, other? How are differences in goals resolved? To what extent and in what ways are therapist values involved in goal setting?
(5) Is it important that treatment goals be discussed with the couple explicitly? If yes, why? If no, why not?
(6) At what level of psychological experience are goals established with the couple (e.g., are they described in overt, motoric terms, in affective–cognitive terms, etc.)?

V. The structure of the therapy process
   Purpose: To describe the treatment setting, frequency, and duration of treatment that are characteristic of your approach.
   Possible points to include:
   (1) How are decisions made about whom to include in therapy?
   (2) Are psychotropic medications ever used within your method of couple therapy? What are the indications–contraindications for such use?
   (3) How many therapists are usually involved? From your perspective, what are the advantages (or disadvantages) of using cotherapists?
   (4) What is the spatial arrangement within the therapy room? Is it a significant structural aspect of therapy?
   (5) Is therapy typically time-limited or unlimited? Why? Ideal models aside, how long does therapy typically last? How often are sessions typically held?

VI. The role of the therapist
   Purpose: To describe the stance the therapist takes with the couple.
   Possible points to include:
   (1) What is the therapist's essential role? Consultant? Teacher? Healer?
   (2) What is the role of the therapist–couple alliance? How is a working alliance fostered?
   (3) To what degree does the therapist overtly control sessions? How active/directive is the therapist? Relatedly, how is responsibility for bringing about change divided between the therapist and the couple?
   (4) Do the partners talk predominantly to the therapist or to each other?
   (5) Does the therapist use self-disclosure? What limits are imposed on therapist self-disclosure?
   (6) Does the therapist's role change as therapy progresses? As termination approaches?
   (7) What are the clinical skills or other therapist attributes most essential to successful therapy in your approach?

VII. Techniques of couple therapy
   Purpose: To describe techniques and strategies always or frequently used in your approach to couple therapy, and their tactical purposes.
   Possible points to include:
   (1) How structured are therapy sessions? Is there an ideal (or typical) pacing or rhythm to sessions?
   (2) What techniques or strategies are used to join the couple or to create a treatment alliance? How are "transference" and "countertransference" rections dealt with?
   (3) What techniques or strategies lead to changes in structure or transactional patterns? Identify, describe, and illustrate major commonly used techniques.

(4) How is the decision made to use a particular technique or strategy at a particular time? Are some techniques more or less likely to be used at different stages of therapy? With different types of couples or individuals?

(5) Are "homework" assignments or other out-of-session tasks used?

(6) What are the most commonly encountered forms of resistance to change? How are these dealt with?

(7) What are both the most common and the most serious technical errors a therapist operating within your therapeutic approach can make?

(8) On what basis is termination decided, and how is termination effected? What characterizes "good" versus "bad" termination?

VIII. Curative factors in couple therapy/mechanisms of change

Purpose: To describe the factors (i.e., mechanisms of change) that lead to change in couples, and to assess their relative importance.

Possible points to include:

(1) Do patients need insight or understanding in order to change? (Differentiate between historical–genetic insight and interactional insight.)

(2) Are interpretations of any sort important, and if so, do they take history into account? If interpretations are used, are they seen as reflecting a psychological "reality," or are they viewed rather as pragmatic tools for effecting change?

(3) Is the learning of new interpersonal skills seen as important? If so, are these skills taught in didactic fashion, or are they shaped as approximations occur naturalistically in treatment?

(4) Does the therapist's personality or psychological health play an important part?

(5) What other therapist factors influence the course and outcome of the treatment? Are there certain kinds of therapists who are ideally suited to work according to this approach; are there others for whom the approach is probably a poor "fit"?

(6) How important are techniques compared to the patient–therapist relationship?

(7) Must each member of the couple change? Is change in an "identified patient" (where relevant) possible without interactional or systemic change? Does systemic change necessarily lead to change in symptoms? Or vice versa?

(8) What factors or variables enhance or limit the probability of successful treatment in your approach?

(9) What aspects of your therapy are not unique to your approach (i.e., characterize all effective couple therapy)?

IX. Treatment applicability

Purpose: To describe those couples for whom your approach is particularly relevant.

Possible points to include:

(1) For what couples is your approach particularly relevant?

(2) For what couples is your approach either not appropriate or of uncertain relevance? For example, is it less relevant for severely disturbed couples or couples with a seriously disturbed member, or for couples with nontraditional relationship structures? Why?

(3) When, if ever, would a referral be made either for another (i.e., different) type of couple therapy, or for an entirely different treatment (e.g., individual therapy, drug therapy)?

(4) When would no treatment (of any sort) be recommended?

(5) Do any aspects of your approach raise particular ethical issues that are different from those raised by psychotherapy in general?

(6) How is the outcome, or effectiveness, of therapy in this model evaluated in clinical practice? Is there any empirical evidence of the efficacy or effectiveness of your approach? If so, briefly summarize.

X. Case illustration

Purpose: To illustrate the clinical application of this model of couple therapy by detailing the major assessment, structural, technical, and relational elements of the process of treating a couple viewed as typical, or representative, of the kinds of couples for whom this approach is appropriate.

Possible points to include:

(1) Relevant case background (e.g., presenting problem, referral source, previous treatment history).

(2) Description of relevant aspects of your clinical assessment: couple functioning, dysfunctional interaction, resources, individual dynamics/characteristics.

(3) Description of the process and content of goal setting.

(4) Highlighting of the major themes, patterns, and so on, in this couple's therapy over the whole course of treatment. Description of the structure of therapy, the techniques used, the role and activity of the therapist, and so forth.

Note: Do *not* describe the treatment of a "star case," in which therapy progresses perfectly. Select a case that, while successful, also illustrates the typical course of events in your therapy.

CONCLUDING THOUGHT

My good friend Neil Jacobson cared very deeply about this *Handbook*, and saw it as one of his most cherished professional involvements. He held out great hope for the role this edition of the *Handbook* might play in the continuing development of the field of couple therapy. I trust he would not have been disappointed.

ALAN S. GURMAN, PhD
Madison, Wisconsin

REFERENCES

Gurman, A. S. (1973). The effects and effectiveness of marital therapy: A review of outcome research. *Family Process, 12*, 145–170.

Gurman, A. S., & Kniskern, D. P. (1978). Behavioral marriage therapy: II. Empirical perspective. *Family Process, 17*, 139–148.

Gurman, A. S., & Kniskern, D. P. (Eds.). (1981). *Handbook of family therapy.* New York: Brunner/Mazel.

Gurman, A. S., & Kniskern, D. P. (Eds.). (1991). *Handbook of family therapy* (Vol. 2). New York: Brunner/Mazel.

Gurman, A. S., & Knudson, R. M. (1978). Behavioral marriage therapy: I. A psychodynamic–systems analysis and critique. *Family Process, 17*, 121–138.

Gurman, A. S., Knudson, R. M., & Kniskern, D. P. (1978). Behavioral marriage therapy: IV. Take two aspirin and call us in the morning. *Family Process, 17*, 165–180.

Gurman, A. S., & Messer, S. B. (Eds.). (1995). *Essential psychotherapies: Theory and practice.* New York: Guilford Press.

Jacobson, N. S., & Gurman, A. S. (Eds.). (1986). *Clinical handbook of marital therapy.* New York: Guilford Press.

Jacobson, N. S., & Gurman, A. S. (Eds.). (1995). *Clinical handbook of couple therapy.* New York: Guilford Press.

Jacobson, N. S., & Martin, B. (1976). Behavioral marriage therapy: Current status. *Psychological Bulletin, 83*, 540–566.

Jacobson, N. S., & Weiss, R. L. (1978). Behavioral marraige therapy: III. The contents of Gurman et al. may be hazardous to our health. *Family Process, 17*, 149–163.

Paolino, T. J., & McCrady, B. (Eds.). (1978). *Marriage and marital therapy: Psychoanalytic, behavioral and systems theory perspectives.* New York: Brunner/Mazel.

Contents

PART II   APPLICATIONS TO SPECIAL POPULATIONS AND PROBLEMS

Section A   Violence, Trauma, Infidelity, and Divorce

Section B   Gender, Sexual Orientation, Race, and Culture

Section C   Selected Psychiatric Disorders and Medical Illness

Part I

MODELS OF COUPLE THERAPY

Section A

Traditional Approaches

Chapter 1

Brief Strategic Couple Therapy

VARDA SHOHAM
MICHAEL J. ROHRBAUGH

In this chapter we describe applications and extensions to couples of the "brief problem-focused therapy" developed over 25 years ago by Richard Fisch, John Weakland, Paul Watzlawick, and their colleagues at the Mental Research Institute (MRI) in Palo Alto (Weakland, Watzlawick, Fisch, & Bodin, 1974; Watzlawick, Weakland, & Fisch, 1974; Fisch, Weakland, & Segal, 1982; Weakland & Fisch, 1992). This parsimonious therapy approach is based on identifying and interrupting the "ironic processes" that occur when repeated attempts to solve a problem keep the problem going or make it worse. Although Fisch, Weakland, and their colleagues did not themselves use the term "ironic process," it captures well their central assertion that problems persist as a function of people's well-intentioned attempts to solve them, and that focused interruption of these solution efforts is sufficient to resolve most problems.[1]

The hallmark of the Palo Alto (or MRI) approach is conceptual and technical parsimony. The aim of therapy is simply to resolve the presenting complaint as quickly and efficiently as possible, so clients can get on with life: Goals such as promoting personal growth, working through underlying emotional issues, or teaching couples better problem solving and communication skills are not emphasized. Theory is minimal and nonnormative, guiding therapists to focus narrowly on the presenting complaint and relevant solu-

tions, with no attempt to specify what constitutes a normal or dysfunctional marriage. Because the "reality" of problems and change is constructed more than discovered, the therapist attends not only to what clients *do*, but also to how they *view* the problem, themselves, and each other. Especially relevant is clients' "customership" for change and the possibility that therapy itself may play a role in maintaining (rather than resolving) problems. Finally, in contrast to most other treatments for couples, therapists working in the Palo Alto tradition often see the partners individually, even when the focus of intervention is a complaint about the marriage itself.

The Palo Alto model is sometimes called "strategic" because the therapist intervenes to interrupt ironic processes deliberately, on the basis of a case-specific plan that sometimes includes counterintuitive suggestions (e.g., to "go slow" or engage in behavior a couple wants to eliminate). Calling this approach "strategic therapy" alone, however, risks confusing the Palo Alto model with a related but substantially different approach to treating couples and families developed by Jay Haley (who coined the term "strategic") and his associate Cloe Madanes (Haley, 1980, 1987; Madanes, 1981, 1991).[2] More importantly, the "strategic" label gives undue emphasis to intervention style and detracts attention from the more fundamental principle of ironic problem maintenance on which the Palo Alto brief therapy model is based.

5

Our chapter deals primarily with application of brief problem-focused therapy to *couple* complaints, but this is a somewhat arbitrary delimitation. As a general model of problem resolution, this therapy approaches couple problems in essentially the same way it does other complaints. Furthermore, because practitioners of this therapy are inevitably concerned with social interaction, they often focus on couple interaction when working with "individual" problems—for example, depression (Watzlawick & Coyne, 1980; Coyne, 1986a), anxiety (Rohrbaugh & Shean, 1986), and addictions (Fisch, 1986; Rohrbaugh, Shoham, Spungen, & Steinglass, 1995; Rohrbaugh et al., 2001)—and for tactical reasons they may avoid calling this "couple therapy" in dealings with the clients. This, and the predilection of MRI-style therapists to treat couple problems nonconjointly (by seeing individuals), make it difficult to distinguish between what is and is not "couple therapy."

BACKGROUND

The Palo Alto brief therapy model is a pragmatic embodiment of the "interactional view" (Watzlawick & Weakland, 1978), which explains behavior—especially problem behavior—in terms of what happens between people rather than within them. The interactional view grew from attempts by members of Bateson's research group (which included Weakland, Haley, and MRI founder Don D. Jackson) to apply ideas from cybernetics and systems theory to the study of communication. After the Bateson project ended, Watzlawick, Beavin, and Jackson (1967) brought many of these ideas together in *Pragmatics of Human Communication*. At about the same time, Fisch, Weakland, Watzlawick, and others formed the Brief Therapy Center (BTC) at MRI to study ways of doing therapy briefly. Their endeavors were also influenced by the uncommon therapeutic techniques of Arizona psychiatrist Milton Erickson, whom Haley and Weakland visited many times during the Bateson project (Haley, 1967). In retrospect, it is striking how discordant this early work on brief therapy was with the psychodynamic *Zeitgeist* of the late 1960s and early 1970s, when therapies were rarely designed with brevity in mind. Even today, as Gurman (2001) points out, most brief therapies represent abbreviated versions of longer therapies—and most family therapies are brief by default. In its commitment to parsimony, the Palo Alto model was probably the first family-oriented therapy to be brief by design.

Since 1966, the BTC has followed a consistent format in treating nearly 500 cases. Under Fisch's leadership, the staff meets weekly as a team to treat unselected cases, representing a broad range of clinical problems, for a maximum of 10 sessions. One member of the team serves as a primary therapist, while the others consult from behind a one-way mirror. After treatment (at roughly 3 and 12 months following termination), another team member conducts a telephone follow-up interview with the client(s) to evaluate change in the original presenting problem and to determine whether clients have developed additional problems or sought further treatment elsewhere. The BTC's pattern of practice has remained remarkably consistent, with its three core members (Fisch, Weakland, and Watzlawick) all participating regularly until Weakland's death in 1995.

From the work of the Palo Alto BTC emerged a model of therapy that focuses on observable interaction in the present, makes no assumptions about normality or pathology, and remains "as close as possible to practice." The first formal statement of this model appeared in a 1974 *Family Process* paper by Weakland et al., titled "Brief Therapy: Focused Problem Resolution." At about the same time, Watzlawick et al., (1974) also published *Change: Principles of Problem Formation and Problem Resolution*, a more theoretical work that distinguished between first- and second-order change and provided many illustrations of ironic processes. Eight years later, Fisch et al., (1982) offered *The Tactics of Change: Doing Therapy Briefly*, essentially a how-to-do-it manual that remains the most comprehensive and explicit statement to date of the BTC's clinical method. In 1992, Weakland and Fisch concisely described the MRI model in a book chapter; most recently Fisch and Schlanger (1999) have provided another concise outline of the model, along with illustrative clinical material, in *Brief Therapy with Intimidating Cases: Changing the Unchangeable*. Although these sources do not deal with marital therapy per se, couple complaints figure prominently in the clinical principles and examples. Other applications to couples, especially when one of the partners is depressed, can be found in the work of former MRI affiliate James Coyne (1986a, 1986b, 1988). Coyne's papers highlight the significance of the interview in strategic marital therapy, particularly how the therapist works to (re)frame the couple's definition of the problem in a way that sets the stage for later interventions.

In addition to the Palo Alto model's historical connection to the "strategic family therapy" of Haley (1980, 1987) and Madanes (1981), we should mention its close and sometimes confusing connection to "solution-focused therapy" (Berg & Miller, 1992; de Shazer, 1991; de Shazer et al., 1986). Inspired by the Palo Alto group, de Shazer et al. (1986) initially took Weakland et al.'s (1974) "focused problem resolution" as a starting point for a complementary form of brief therapy emphasizing "focused solution development." Subsequently, however, solution-focused therapy has undergone progressive revision (de Shazer, 1991; Miller & de Shazer, 2000) and now has a substantially different emphasis than the parent model (for a detailed comparison, see Shoham, Rohrbaugh, & Patterson, 1995). One of the main points of disconnection is that de Shazer and his colleagues now avoid characterizing their therapy as "strategic," preferring to describe it instead as "collaborative," "co-constructivist," and (by implication) not so manipulative. This (re)characterization aligns solution-focused therapy with the narrative, postmodern tradition that rejects the model of therapist-as-expert-strategist in favor of therapist-as-collaborative-partner (Nichols & Schwartz, 2000). We suspect that this distinction may be more semantic than substantive. In any case, calling one's therapy "strategic" is today probably not a very strategic thing to do.

Finally, although research at the MRI has been mainly qualitative, it is noteworthy that the original description of brief problem-focused therapy by Weakland et al. (1974) included tentative 1-year outcome percentages for the first 97 cases seen at the BTC. Eight years ago, in collaboration with BTC staff member Karin Schlanger, we updated the archival tabulation of outcomes for BTC cases seen through 1991 and attempted to identify correlates of success (Rohrbaugh, Shoham, & Schlanger, 1992). For 285 cases with interpretable follow-up data, problem resolution rates of 44%, 24%, and 32% for success, partial success, and failure, respectively, were very similar to the figures reported by Weakland et al. (1974) more than 15 years earlier. Thus at least two-thirds of the MRI cases reportedly improved, and the average length of therapy was six sessions. To investigate correlates of outcome more closely, we identified subgroups of "clear success" cases (*n* = 39) and "clear failure" cases (*n* = 33) for which 1-year follow-up

data were complete and unambiguous. Then, after coding clinical, demographic, and treatment variables from each case folder, we compared the success and failure groups and found surprisingly few predictors of outcome. Interestingly, however, it appears that about 40% of the cases seen over the years at the BTC have involved some form of marital or couple complaint, and we touch on some findings from the archive study in sections to follow.

A NON-NORMATIVE VIEW OF COUPLE FUNCTIONING

The Palo Alto model makes no assumptions about healthy or pathological functioning. In this sense the theory is non-normative and complaint-based: In fact, if no one registers a complaint, there is no problem (Fisch & Schlanger, 1999). At the relationship level, this means that patterns such as quiet detachment or volatile engagement may be dysfunctional for some couples but adaptive for others. What matters is the extent to which interaction patterns based on attempted solutions keep a complaint going or make it worse—and the topography of relevant problem–solution loops can vary widely from couple to couple.

At the heart of brief problem-focused therapy are two interlocking assumptions about problems and change:

> Regardless of their origins and etiology—if, indeed, these can ever be reliably determined—the problems people bring to psychotherapists persist only if they are maintained by ongoing current behavior of the client and others with whom he interacts. Correspondingly, if such problem-maintaining behavior is appropriately changed or eliminated, the problem will be resolved or vanish, regardless of its nature, or origin, or duration. (Weakland et al., 1974, p. 144)

This implies that how a problem persists is much more relevant to therapy than how the problem originated, and that problem persistence depends mainly on social interaction, with the behavior of one person both stimulated and shaped by the response of others (Weakland & Fisch, 1992). Moreover—and this is the central observation of the Palo Alto group—the continuation of a problem revolves precisely around what people currently and persistently do (or don't do) in order to control, prevent, or eliminate their complaint. That is, how people go about trying to solve a problem usually plays a crucial role in perpetuating it.

A problem, then, consists of a vicious cycle involving a positive feedback loop between some behavior someone considers undesirable (the complaint) and some other behavior(s) intended to modify or eliminate it (the attempted solution). Given that problems persist because of people's current attempts to solve them, therapy need consist only of identifying and deliberately interdicting these well-intentioned yet ironic "solutions," thereby breaking the vicious cycles (positive feedback loops) that maintain the impasse. If this can be done—even in a small way—"virtuous cycles" may develop, in which less of the solution leads to less of the problem, leading to less of the solution, and so on (Fisch et al., 1982).

Such an ironic feedback loop can be seen in the following passage from *Pragmatics of Human Communication* (Watzlawick et al., 1967), which highlights the familiar demand–withdraw cycle common to many marital complaints:

> Suppose a couple have a marital problem to which he contributes passive withdrawal while her 50% is nagging and criticism. In explaining their frustrations, the husband will state that withdrawal is his only *defense against* her nagging, while she will label this explanation gross and willful distortion of what "really" happens in their marriage: namely, that she is critical of him *because* of his passivity. Stripped of all ephemeral and fortuitous elements, their fights consist in a monotonous exchange of the messages, "I will withdraw because you nag" and "I nag because you withdraw." (p. 56; emphasis in original)

Watzlawick et al. (1974) elaborated a similar pattern in *Change*:

> In marriage therapy, one can frequently see both spouses engaging in behaviors which they individually consider the most appropriate reaction to something wrong that the other is doing. That is, in the eyes of each of them the particular corrective behavior of the other is seen as that behavior which needs correction. For instance, a wife may have the impression that her husband is not open enough for her to know where she stands with him, what is going on in his head, what he is doing when he is away from home, etc. Quite naturally, she will therefore attempt to get the needed information by asking him questions, watching his behavior, and checking on him in a variety of other ways. If he considers her behavior as too intrusive, he is likely to withhold from her information which in and by itself would be quite

harmless and irrelevant to disclose—"just to teach her that she need not know everything." Far from making her back down, this attempted solution not only does not bring about the desired change in her behavior but provides further fuel for her worries and her distrust—"if he does not even talk to me about these little things, there *must* be something the matter." The less information he gives her, the more persistently she will seek it, and the more she seeks it, the less he will give her. By the time they see a psychiatrist, it will be tempting to diagnose her behavior as pathological jealousy—provided that no attention is paid to their pattern of interaction and their attempted solutions, which *are* the problem. (pp. 35–36; emphasis in original)

The "solutions" of demand and withdrawal in these examples make perfectly good sense to the participants, yet their interactional consequences serve only to confirm each partner's unsatisfactory "reality." How such a cycle began is likely to remain obscure, and what causes what is a matter of more or less arbitrary punctuation: From the perspective of the Palo Alto group, the problem-maintaining system of interaction is its own explanation.

ASSESSMENT

The main goals of assessment are to (1) define a resolvable complaint; (2) identify solution patterns (problem–solution loops) that maintain the complaint; and (3) understand the clients' unique language and preferred views of the problem, themselves, and each other. The first two provide a template for where to intervene, while the third is relevant to how.

The therapist's first task is to get a very specific, behavioral picture of what the complaint is, who sees it as a problem, and why it is a problem now. Since the problem is not assumed to be the tip of a psychological or relational iceberg, the aim is simply to be clear about who is doing what. A useful guideline is for the therapist to have enough details to answer the question "If we had a video of this, what would I see?" Later the therapist also tries to get a clear behavioral picture of what the clients will accept as a minimum change goal. For example, "What would he [or she, or the two of you] be doing differently that will let you know this is taking a turn for the better?"

The next step requires an equally specific inquiry into the behaviors most closely related to the problem: namely, what the clients (and any other people concerned about it) are doing to handle, prevent, or resolve the complaint, and what happens after these attempted solutions. From this emerges a formulation of a problem–solution loop, and particularly of the specific solution behaviors that will be the focus of intervention. The therapist (or team) can then develop a picture of what "less of the same" will look like—that is, of what behavior, by whom, in what situation, will suffice to reverse the problem-maintaining solution. Ideally, this strategic objective constitutes a 180° reversal of what the clients have been doing. Although interventions typically involve prescribing some alternative behavior, the key element is stopping the performance of the attempted solution (Weakland & Fisch, 1992). Understanding problem-maintaining solution patterns also helps the therapist be clear about what positions and suggestions to avoid—what the Palo Alto group calls the "mine field." Thus, if a husband has been persistently and unsuccessfully exhorting a wife to eat or spend less, the therapist would not want to make any direct suggestions that the wife change in these ways, so as not to perpetuate "more of the same" problem-maintaining solution. A more helpful "less of the same" stance might entail wondering with the wife about reasons why she *shouldn't* change, at least in the present circumstances, and about how she will know whether or when these changes are actually worth making.

The most relevant problem-maintaining solutions are current ones (what one or both partners continue to do about the complaint *now*), but the therapist investigates solutions tried and discarded in the past as well, since these give hints about what has worked before—and may again. In one of our alcohol treatment cases (Rohrbaugh et al., 1995), a wife who in the past had taken a hard line with her husband about not drinking at the dinner table later reversed this stance because she did not want to be controlling. As his drinking problem worsened, he further withdrew from the family and she dealt with it less and less directly, by busying herself in other activities or retreating to her study to meditate. Careful inquiry revealed that the former hard-line approach, though distasteful, had actually worked: When the wife had set limits, the husband had controlled his drinking. By relabeling her former, more assertive stance as caring and reassuring to the husband, the therapist was later able to help the wife reverse her stance in a way that broke the problem cycle.

Along these lines, we have found it useful to distinguish ironic solution patterns that involve action (commission) from those that involve inaction (omission). The solution of pressuring one's partner to change, as in the demand–withdraw cycle described above, exemplifies a commission pattern, whereas the indirect stance of the wife in the case just mentioned illustrates problem maintenance based on omission. While commission patterns are more salient, ironic solutions of omission are surprisingly common, especially among couples coping with health problems. One such pattern involves "protective buffering," where one partner's attempts to avoid upsetting a physically ill spouse sometimes inadvertently lead to more distress (Coyne & Smith, 1991). Similar solution efforts by a husband (H) contributed to continued smoking by a wife (W) with heart disease:

> H, who valued greatly his 30-year "conflict-free" relationship with W, avoids expressing directly his wish for W to quit smoking. Although smoke aggravates H's asthma, he fears that showing disapproval would upset W and create stress in their relationship. W confides that she sometimes finds H's "indirect (non-verbal) messages" disturbing, though she too avoids expressing this directly—and when he holds back this way she feels more like smoking. (Rohrbaugh et al., 2001, p. 20)

The distinction between these two types of ironic processes again underscores the principle that no given solution pattern can be uniformly functional or dysfunctional: What works for one couple may be precisely what keeps things going badly for another—and a therapist's strategy for promoting "less of the same" should respect this heterogeneity.

The last assessment goal—grasping clients' unique views, or what Fisch et al. (1982) call "patient position"—is crucial to the later task of framing suggestions in ways clients will accept. Assessing these views depends mainly on paying careful attention to what people say. For example, how do they see themselves and want to be seen by others? What do they hold near and dear? At some point, the therapist will usually also ask for their best guess as to *why* a particular problem is happening—and why they handle it the way they do. We also find it helpful to understand how partners view themselves as a couple, and typically ask questions such as "If people who know you well were describing you two as a couple, what would they say?" or "What words or phrases capture the strength of your relationship—its values, flavor, and unique style?"

Finally, some of the most important client views concern "customership" for therapy and readiness for change. Although much will be known from how clients initially present themselves, direct questions such as "Whose idea was it to come?" (His? Hers? Both Equally?), "Why now?", and "Who is most optimistic that therapy will help?" should make this crucial aspect of client position clearer. It is also important to understand how (if at all) the clients sought help in the past, what they found helpful or unhelpful, how the helper(s) viewed their problems, and how the therapy ended.

GOAL SETTING

Goal setting in this approach serves several key functions. First, having a clear, behavioral picture of what clients will accept as a sign of improvement helps to bring the complaint itself into focus. Without a clear complaint, it is difficult to have a coherent formulation of problem maintenance (or, for that matter, a coherent therapy). Second, setting a *minimum* goal for outcome supports the therapist's tactical aim of introducing a small but strategic change in the problem–solution patterns, which can then initiate a ripple or domino effect leading to further positive developments. In this sense, the Palo Alto approach emphasizes what some clinicians would call "intermediate" or "mediating" goals rather than ultimate outcomes. For some couples, a spinoff benefit of this strategy may be the implicit message that even difficult problems can show some improvement in a relatively short period of time.

Before setting specific goals, it is usually necessary to inquire in detail about the clients' complaint(s) and, if there are multiple complaints, to establish which are most pressing. As the complaint focus becomes clear, the therapist will at some point ask questions like these: "How will you know the situation is improving? What kinds of change will you settle for? What will need to happen (or not happen) to let you know that, even if you're not out of the woods entirely, you're at least on the right path? What will each of you settle for?" As clients grapple with these questions, the therapist presses for specific signs of improvement (e.g., having a family meal together without someone's getting upset and leaving the table; a spouse's showing affection without its seeming like an obligation). It is easy in such a discussion

to confuse means with ends, and the therapist aims to keep clients focused on the latter (what they hope to achieve) rather than on the former (how to pursue it). Important assessment information does come from queries about what partners think they should do to make things better, but this is much more relevant to formulating problem–solution loops than to goal setting.

THE STRUCTURE OF THERAPY

The basic template for MRI-style brief therapy can be summarized as follows: (1) Define the complaint in specific behavioral terms; (2) set minimum goals for change; (3) investigate solutions to the complaint; (4) formulate ironic problem–solution loops (how "more of the same" solution leads to more of the complaint, etc.); (5) specify what "less of the same" will look like in particular situations; (6) understand clients' preferred views of themselves, the problem, and each other; (7) use these views to frame suggestions for less-of-the-same solution behavior; and (8) nurture and solidify incipient change (Rohrbaugh & Shoham, 2001). Sessions are not necessarily scheduled on a weekly basis, but are allocated in a manner intended to maximize the likelihood that change will be durable. Thus, when the treatment setting formally imposes a session limit (e.g., both the BTC and our own clinic limit treatment to 10 sessions), the meetings may be spread over months or even a year. A typical pattern is for the first few sessions to be at regular (weekly) intervals, and for later meetings to be less frequent once change begins to take hold. Therapy ends when the treatment goals have been attained and change seems reasonably stable. Termination usually occurs without celebration or fanfare, and sometimes clients retain "sessions in the bank" if they are apprehensive about discontinuing contact.

Although two (co)therapists are rarely in the room together, practitioners of this approach usually prefer to work as a team. At the BTC and in most of our own work, a primary therapist sees the clients, with other team members observing (and participating) from behind a one-way mirror. Team members typically phone in suggestions to the therapist during the session, and the therapist sometimes leaves the room to consult briefly with the team. A typical time for such a meeting is late in the session, when the team can help the therapist plan the particulars of a homework assignment or framing intervention.

The team format also opens the possibility of clients' having contact with more than one therapist. As if to downplay the sanctity of "therapeutic relationship factors," the Palo Alto group has historically had no reservations about one BTC therapist's substituting for another who cannot be present—and in fact, about 25% of the BTC cases in the first 3 years of the project did see more than one therapist, but this proportion fell to 11% in the early 1970s and to under 5% by the late 1980s (Rohrbaugh et al., 1992). In our own manual-guided treatments for couples with drinking or smoking problems in one or both members, we routinely hold brief individual meetings with the partners in the second session and use different members of the team to do this (Rohrbaugh et al., 1995, 2001).

As a treatment for couples, the MRI approach differs from most others in that the therapist is willing, and sometimes prefers, to see one or both partners individually. The choice of individual versus conjoint sessions is based on three main considerations: customership, maneuverability, and adequate assessment. First, a Palo Alto-style therapist would rather address a couple complaint by seeing a motivated partner alone than by struggling to engage a partner who is not a "customer" for change. In theory, this should not decrease the possibility of successful outcome, since the interactional view assumes that problem resolution can follow from a change by any participant in the relevant interactional system (Hoebel, 1976; Weakland & Fisch, 1992). Another reason to see partners separately, even when both are customers, is to preserve maneuverability. If the partners have sharply different views of their situation, for example, separate sessions give the therapist more flexibility in accepting each viewpoint and framing suggestions one way for her and another way for him. The split format also helps the therapist avoid being drawn into the position of referee or possible ally. The goal, however, remains to promote change in what happens between the partners.

A third reason for interviewing spouses separately is to facilitate assessment. Some couples relentlessly enact their arguments and conflicts in the therapy room, and others lapse into silence and withdrawal. As Coyne (1988) points out, seeing such patterns at least once is useful, but their repetition can easily handicap the therapist's efforts to track important problem–solution loops that occur outside the therapy session. Strategic therapists often make a point of seeing the partners alone at least once to inquire about their commitment to

the relationship; if either is pessimistic, the therapist may request a moratorium on separation long enough to give treatment a chance to make a difference. In no case, however, does the therapist express more commitment to saving the relationship or to the likely success of therapy than the client being interviewed does (Coyne, 1988). Individual sessions are also used to assess the possibility of spousal abuse or intimidation (Rohrbaugh et al., 1995). This assessment is especially important in cases where there is domestic violence, but the abused partner is too intimidated to state it as a complaint in the conjoint interview.

In the BTC archive study (Rohrbaugh et al., 1992), cases with marital or couple complaints were more likely to be successful when at least two people (the two partners) participated in treatment. This finding would not seem to fit well with the MRI view that such complaints can be treated effectively by intervening through one partner. On the other hand, we did not evaluate the potentially confounding role of customership in these cases, or the possibility that the absent partners were as uncommitted to the relationship as they apparently were to therapy. In any case, the BTC's own data do little to undermine Gurman, Kniskern, and Pinsof's (1986) empirical generalization: "When both spouses are involved in therapy conjointly for marital problems, there is a greater chance of positive outcome than when only one spouse is treated" (p. 572).

A related historical footnote from the archives project bears on the question of brevity itself. In the mid-1970s, the BTC undertook an experiment to test the feasibility of shortening treatment to 5 sessions and, for nearly a year, randomly assigned new cases to either a 5-session limit ($n = 13$) or the usual 10-session limit ($n = 14$). It turned out that cases treated with the 5-session limit fared substantially *worse* than the "control" cases ($p < .01$)—and when this pattern became clear clinically, the BTC abandoned this experiment. Thus, although the MRI group found that most problems could be resolved in fewer than 10 sessions, they surmised that attempting to enforce further brevity could itself become a problem-maintaining solution.

ROLE OF THE THERAPIST

The essential role of the therapist, as explained above, is to persuade at least one participant in the couple (or most relevant interactional system) to do "less of the same" solution that keeps the complaint going. This does not require educating clients, helping them resolve emotional issues, or even working with both members of a couple. It does, however, require that the therapist "work with the customer" and "preserve maneuverability." The customership principle means simply that the therapist works with the person or persons most concerned about the problem (the "sweater" or "sweaters"). Thus a therapist treating a marital complaint would not require or even encourage the participation of a reluctant spouse, especially if this is what the principal complainant has been doing. To preserve maneuverability means that the therapist aims to maximize possibilities for therapeutic influence—which in this model is his/her main responsibility. In *The Tactics of Change*, Fisch et al. (1982) make plain the importance of control: "The therapist, to put it bluntly, needs to maintain his own options while limiting those of the patients" (p. 23); they outline tactics for gaining (and regaining) control, even in initial phone contacts, since "treatment is likely to go awry if the therapist is not in control of it" (p. xii). Preserving maneuverability also means that the therapist avoids taking a firm position or making a premature commitment to what clients should do, so that later, if they *don't* do what is requested, alternative strategies for achieving "less of the same" will still be accessible.

Despite this apparent preoccupation with controlling the course of therapy, an MRI-style therapist rarely exerts control directly in the sense of offering authoritative prescriptions or assuming the role of an expert. Much more characteristic of this approach is what Fisch et al. (1982) call "taking a one-down position." Early in therapy, for example, a Columbo-like stance of empathic curiosity might be used to track behavioral sequences around the complaint (e.g., "I'm a little slow on the uptake here, so could you help me understand again what it is you *do* when John raises his voice that way?"); later, when intervening to promote "less of the same," a therapist might soft-sell a specific suggestion by saying something like "I don't know if doing this when he walks through the door will make much difference, but if you could try it once or twice this week, at least we'll have an idea what we're up against." One purpose of these tactics is to promote client cooperation and avoid the common countertherapeutic effects of overly direct or prescriptive interventions (cf. Shoham, Rohrbaugh, Stickle, & Jacob, 1998).[3]

Empathic restraint, exemplified by the "go slow" messages discussed below under "Techniques," is a related stance characteristic of this approach. Here, too, the therapist aims to avoid apprehension and resistance by conveying that only the client(s) can decide whether and when to change. When the therapist and team are ready to make a specific "less of the same" suggestion, they do so cautiously, without assuming customership (i.e., assuming that clients are ready to change). Once change begins, continued gentle restraint helps the therapist respect the clients' pace and avoid pushing for more change than they can handle. A typical response to clear progress would be for the therapist to compliment clients on what they have done, yet caution them against premature celebration and suggest again that a prudent course might be to "go slow." Similarly, when clients fail to follow a suggestion, a common response is for the therapist to take the blame on him-/herself (e.g., "I think I suggested that prematurely") and seek alternative routes to the same strategic objective, often within the framework of intensified overt restraint. Nevertheless, even this general stance of restraint is applied judiciously and guided by ongoing assessment of the clients' customership, position, and progress.

Although the writings of the Palo Alto group attach little importance to the therapeutic relationship, this does not mean that strategic therapists come across as cold, manipulative, or uncaring. On the contrary, most of the MRI-style therapists we have known and seen in action would be likely to receive high ratings on client rapport and "therapeutic alliance." A reason may be that practicing this approach requires very close attention to clients' unique language, metaphors, and world views—and that communicating effectively within the framework of someone else's construct system (if only to frame an intervention) usually entails a good deal of empathy. In fact, if asked what clinical skills or attributes are most essential to successful therapy in this approach, we would put something akin to this conceptual (or constructivist) empathy high on the list. The stance required is not for everyone, because a strategic therapist becomes

more a chameleon than a firm rock in a sea of trouble. And it is at this point that many therapists dig in behind the retort, "Anything except that," while for others the necessity of ever new adaptations to the world images of their clients is a fascinating task. (Watzlawick, 1978, p. 141)

TECHNIQUES

The Palo Alto group distinguishes *specific* interventions, designed to interdict ironic, case-specific problem–solution loops, from *general* interventions that tend to be applicable across most cases (Fisch et al., 1982). Most of this section is devoted to illustrating specific interventions for common couple complaints, particularly those involving demand–withdraw interaction. First, however, we will comment briefly on more general aspects of this therapy.

Because interrupting an ironic problem-solution loop usually requires persuading clients to do less or the opposite of what they have been committed to doing, it can be crucial to frame suggestions in terms compatible with the clients' own language or world view—especially with how they prefer to see themselves. Indeed, grasping and using clients' views—what Fisch et al. (1982) call "patient position"—is almost as fundamental to the Palo Alto model as are the behavioral prescriptions that interdict problem-maintaining solutions. Some partners, for example, will be attracted to the idea of making a loving sacrifice, but others may want to teach their mates a lesson. The MRI-style therapist is careful to speak the clients' language, use their metaphors, and avoid argumentation. Strategic therapists not only elicit clients' beliefs, but also shape and structure those beliefs to set the stage for later interventions. For example, a therapist might accept a wife's view that her husband is uncommunicative and unemotional, then extend this view to suggest that his defensiveness indicates vulnerability. The extension paves the way for suggesting a different way of dealing with a husband who is vulnerable, rather than simply withholding (Coyne, 1988). A less direct way to break an ironic pattern is to redefine what one partner is doing in a way that stops short of prescribing change, yet makes it difficult for them to continue (e.g., "I've noticed that your reminding him and telling him what you think seems to give him an excuse to keep doing what he's doing without feeling guilty—he can justify it to himself simply by blaming you").

In addition to interventions that target specific problem–solution loops, the MRI group uses several general interventions applicable to a broad range of problems and to promoting change in all stages of therapy. General interventions include telling clients to go slow, cautioning them about dangers of improvement, making a U-turn, and giving instructions about how to make the problem worse (Fisch et al., 1982). Most of these tactics are variations of therapeutic restraint, as described in the previous section. The most common is the injunction to "go slow," given with a credible rationale such as "change occurring slowly and step by step makes for a more solid change than change which occurs too suddenly" (Fisch et al., 1982, p. 159). This tactic is used to prepare clients for change, to convey acceptance of reluctance to change, and to solidify change once it begins to occur. Fisch et al. (1982) suggest two reasons why "go slow" messages work: They make clients more likely to cooperate with therapeutic suggestions, and they relax the sense of urgency that often fuels clients' problem-maintaining efforts at solution.

Coyne (1988) describes several other general interventions that he uses in the first or second session with couples. One involves asking the couple to collaborate in performing the problem pattern (e.g., an argument) deliberately, for the ostensible purpose of helping the therapist better understand how they get involved in such a no-win encounter, and specifically how each partner is able to get the other to be less reasonable than he/she would be normally. This task is more than diagnostic, however, because it undercuts negative spontaneity, creates an incentive for each partner to resist provocation, and sometimes introduces a shift in the usual problem–solution pattern.

In terms of Bateson's (1958) distinction between complementary and symmetrical interaction patterns (cf. Watzlawick et al., 1967),[4] some of the most common foci for specific interdiction of ironic problem–solution loops involve complementary patterns like the familiar demand–withdraw sequence described above. For example, one partner may press for change in some way, while the other withdraws or refuses to respond; one partner may attempt to initiate discussion of some problem, while the other avoids discussion; one partner may criticize what the other does, while the other defends his/her actions; or one may accuse the other of thinking or doing something that the other denies (Christensen & Heavey, 1993). Each of these variations—demand–refuse, discuss–avoid, criticize–defend, accuse–deny—fits the problem-solution loop formula, since more demand leads to more withdrawal, which leads to more demand, and so on. Although the MRI group avoids (normative) a priori assumptions about adaptive or maladaptive family relations, the clinical relevance of demand–withdraw interaction appears well established by research indicating that this pattern is substantially more prevalent in divorcing couples and clinic couples than in nondistressed couples (Christensen & Shenk, 1991). Interestingly, many authors have described the demand–withdraw pattern and speculated about its underlying dynamics (e.g., Fogarty, 1976; Napier, 1978; Wile, 1981), but few have been as concerned as the MRI group with practical ways to change it.

To the extent that the partner on the demand side of the sequence is the main customer for change, intervention will focus on encouraging that person to do less of the same. In the demand–refuse cycle, one spouse may press for change by exhorting, reasoning, arguing, lecturing, and so on—a solution pattern Fisch et al. (1982) call "seeking accord through opposition." If the wife is the main complainant,[5] achieving less of the same usually depends on helping her suspend overt attempts to influence the husband—for example, by declaring helplessness or in some other specific way taking a one-down position, or by performing an observational/diagnostic task to find out "what he'll do on his own" or "what we're really up against." How the therapist frames specific suggestions depends on what rationale the customer will buy. An extremely religious wife, for example, might be amenable to the suggestion that she silently pray for her husband instead of exhorting him. Successful solution interdiction in several MRI cases (Watzlawick & Coyne, 1980; Fisch et al., 1982) followed from developing the frame that behavior seen by one partner as stubbornness was actually motivated by the other's pride. Since proud people need to discover and do things on their own, without feeling pressed or believing that they are giving in, it makes sense to encourage such a person's partner by discouraging (restraining) the partner. A demand-side partner who follows suggestions for doing this will effectively reverse the former solution to the stubborn behavior.

For some couples, the demand–withdraw cycle involves one partner's attempting to initiate discussion (e.g., to get the other to open up, be more expressive, etc.) while the other avoids it. One of us (VS) had the experience of being the primary therapist for one such couple during her training at MRI. The wife, herself a therapist and the main complainant, would repeatedly encourage her inexpressive husband to get his feelings out, especially when he came home from work "looking miserable." When the husband responded to this with distraught silence, the wife would encourage him to talk about his feeling toward her and the marriage (thinking this would bring out positive associations). In a typical sequence, the husband would then begin to get angry and tell the wife to back off. She, however, encouraged by his expressiveness, would continue to push for meaningful discussion, in response to which—on more than one occasion—the husband stormed out of the house and disappeared overnight. The intervention that eventually broke the cycle in this case came from Fisch, who entered the therapy room with a suggestion: In the next week, at least once, the husband was to come home, sit at the kitchen table, and pretend to look miserable. The wife's task, when she saw this look, was to go to the kitchen, prepare chicken soup, and serve it to him *silently* with a worried look on her face. The couple came to the next session looking anything but miserable. They reported that their attempt to carry out the assignment had failed because she—and then he—could not keep a straight face; yet they were delighted that the humor so characteristic of the early days of their relationship had "resurfaced." Although the intervention served to interdict the wife's attempted solution of pursuing discussion, it also interrupted the heaviness and deadly seriousness in the couple's relationship.[6]

When the demand–withdraw pattern involves criticism and defense, both partners are more likely to be customers for change, so change can be introduced through either partner or both. One strategy, noted above, is to develop a rationale for the criticizing partner to observe the behavior he/she is criticizing without commenting on it. Another is to get the defending partner to do something other than defending—for example, simply agreeing with the criticism, or helping the criticizer "lighten up" by not taking the criticism seriously ("I guess you're probably right—therapy is helping me see I'm not much fun and probably too old to change," or "You're right—I don't know if I inherited this problem from my parents or our kids"). In *Change*, Watzlawick et al. (1974) also describe a more indirect interdiction of a wife's attempts to avoid marital fights by defending herself. As homework, the therapist asked the combative husband to pick a fight deliberately with someone outside the marriage. In the next session, the husband recounted in detail how his attempts to do this had failed, because he had not been able to get the other person to lose his temper. In Watzlawick et al.'s view, hearing this "made the wife more aware of her contribution to the problem than any insight-oriented explanation or intervention could have done" (p. 120).

Another approach to interdicting accusation–denial cycles is an intervention the MRI group calls "jamming" (Fisch et al., 1982, pp. 156–158). When one partner accuses the other of something both agree is wrong (e.g., dishonesty, infidelity, insensitivity), and the other partner's denial seems only to confirm the accuser's suspicions, leading to more accusations and more denials, the jamming intervention aims to promote less of the same by both parties. After disavowing any ability to determine who is right or wrong in the situation, the therapist proposes to help the partners improve their communication (which obviously has broken down), particularly the accuser's perceptiveness about the problem. Achieving this, the therapist continues (in a conjoint session), will require that the defender deliberately randomize the behavior of which he/she is accused (e.g., sometimes acting "as if" she is attracted to other people and sometimes not), while the accuser tests his/her perceptiveness about what the defender is "really" doing. Each should keep a record of what they did or observed, they are told in a conjoint session, but they must not discuss the experiment or compare notes until the next session. The effect of such a prescription is to free the defender from (consistently) defending and the accuser from accusing; the circuit is thus "jammed," because verbal exchanges (accusations and denial) now have less information value.

Sometimes a problem cycle is characterized by indirect demands related to the paradoxical form of communication Fisch et al. (1982) call "seeking compliance through voluntarism." For instance, a wife may complain that her husband not only ignores her needs, but should know what to do without her having to tell him, since otherwise he would be doing it only because she asked him and not because he really wanted to. Or a husband may be reluctant to ask his wife to do something because he thinks she may not really want to do it. The brief therapy strategy recommended in these situations is to get the person who is asking for something to do so directly, even if arbitrarily. If clients want to appear benevolent, the therapist can use this position by defining their indirection as unwittingly destructive; for example, "a husband's reticence to ask favors of his wife can be redefined as an 'unwitting deprivation of the one thing she needs most from you, a sense of your willingness to take leadership'" (Fisch et al., 1982, p. 155). Intervening through the nonrequesting partner may also be possible if that person can be persuaded to take the edge off the paradoxical "be spontane-

ous" demand by saying something like "I'm willing to do it and I will, but let's face it, I don't enjoy cleaning up."

In other complaint-maintaining complementary exchanges, one partner may be domineering or explosive and the other placating or submissive. Here, less of the same usually requires getting the submissive, placating partner to take some assertive action. This was the approach taken in a controversial case reported by Bobele (1987), who describes the interactional analysis and successful interdiction of a cycle of violence involving a woman and her boyfriend. (Woody & Woody [1988] criticized Bobele's approach on legal and ethical grounds, but see the rejoinders by Bobele [1988] and Weakland [1988].)

Symmetrical patterns of problem-maintaining behavior are less common but often offer more possibilities for intervention, because customership too is balanced. For combative couples embroiled in symmetrically escalating arguments, the strategy could be to get at least one partner to take a one-down position, or to prescribe the argument under conditions likely to undermine it (Coyne, 1988). Another symmetrical solution pattern stems from miscarriage of the (usually sensible) belief that problems are best solved by talking them through. Yet some couples—including some whose members are very psychologically minded—manage to perpetuate relationship difficulties simply by trying to talk about them. In a case treated at MRI, for example, a couple's problem-solving "talks" about issues in their relationship usually escalated into full-blown arguments. Therapy led them to a different, more workable solution: When either partner felt the need to talk about their relationship, they would first go bowling (R. Fisch, personal communication, 1992).

Interestingly, despite the emphasis on interaction, the MRI group acknowledges a "self-referential" aspect of complaints such as anxiety states, insomnia, obsessional thinking, sexual dysfunction, and other problems with "being spontaneous." These complaints

> can arise and be maintained without help from anyone else. This does not mean that others do not aid in maintaining such problems; often they do. We simply mean that these kinds of problems do not need such "help" in order to occur and persist. (Fisch et al., 1982, pp. 136–137)

Treatment of such problems in a couple context may involve simultaneous interdiction of both interactional and self-referential problem–solution loops. For example, with a woman who experienced difficulty reaching orgasm, the MRI team targeted two problem–solution loops: one self-referential (the harder she tried, the more she failed) and one interactional (the more the husband inquired how aroused she was and whether she had an orgasm, the harder she tried to perform). One strand of the intervention was a prescription that for the wife to become more aware of her feelings during intercourse, she should "notice her bodily sensations, *regardless of how much or how little* pleasure she may experience" (Fisch et al., 1982, p. 158; emphasis in original). The second (interactional) strand was a version of jamming: In the wife's presence, the therapist asked the husband not to interfere with this process by checking her arousal—but if he did, the wife was simply to say, "I didn't feel a thing." Other strategies aimed at combined interdiction of interactional and self-referential solution patterns have been applied in the treatment of such "individual" complaints as depression (Coyne, 1986a, 1988) and anxiety (Rohrbaugh & Shean, 1988).

Interventions for marital/couple complaints usually focus on one or both members of the couple; yet there are circumstances in which other people (relatives, friends, or even another helper) figure prominently in MRI-style couple therapy, especially when the third party is a key customer for change. For example, a mother understandably concerned about her daughter's marital difficulties may counsel or console the daughter in a way that unwittingly amplifies the problem or makes the young husband and wife less likely to deal with their differences directly. In this case brief therapy might focus first on helping the mother—an important complainant—reverse her own solution efforts, and take up later (if at all) the interaction between the young spouses, which is likely to change when the mother becomes less involved. Brief therapists have also found ways to involve third parties who may *not* be customers for change, particularly for problems related to marital infidelity (Teisman, 1979; Green & Bobele, 1988).

Finally, for a small subset of marital complaints, the goal of brief therapy is to help couples reevaluate their problem as "no problem," or a problem they can live with; strategies for achieving this typically involve some sort of reframing. Indeed, marriage is fertile ground for what Watzlawick et al. (1974) call the "utopia syndrome":

Quite obviously, few—if any—marriages live up to the ideals contained in some of the classic marriage manuals or popular mythology. Those who accept these ideas about what a marital relationship should "really" be are likely to see their marriage as problematic and to start working toward its solution until divorce do them part. Their concrete problem is not their marriage, but their attempts at finding the solution to a problem which in the first place is not a problem, and which, even if it were one, could not be solved on the level on which they attempt to change it. (p. 57)

Published case reports notwithstanding, the outcome of brief therapy rarely turns on a single intervention. Much depends on how the therapist nurtures incipient change and manages termination. When a small change occurs, the therapist acknowledges and emphasizes the clients' part in making it happen, but avoids encouraging further change directly. The most common stance in responding to change consists of gentle restraint (e.g., "go slow") and continuation of the interdiction strategy that produced it. Special tactics may be used with clients who are overly optimistic or overly anxious (e.g., predicting or prescribing a relapse) or who minimize change or relapse (e.g., exploring "dangers of improvement"). Termination occurs without celebration or fanfare. If change is solid, the therapist acknowledges progress, inquires about what the clients are doing differently, suggests that they anticipate other problems, and implies that they will be able to cope with whatever problems do arise. Otherwise, various restraining methods may be used. If clients ask to work on other problems, the therapist suggests taking time out to adapt to change and offers to reassess the other problems later (Fisch et al., 1982; Rosenthal & Bergman, 1986).

Before leaving this section on technique, we should add that the MRI approach has been criticized as "manipulative" because the therapist does not usually make the rationale for particular interventions explicit to clients (Wendorf & Wendorf, 1985), and may say things he/she does not truly believe in order to achieve an effective framing (Solovey & Duncan, 1992). Proponents of strategic therapy counter that responsible therapy is inherently manipulative (Fisch, 1990), that therapeutic candor can be disrespectful (Haley, 1987), and that good therapy shows profound respect for clients' subjective "truths" (Cade & O'Hanlon, 1993).

CURATIVE FACTORS

The central (and, purists would say, *only*) curative factor in this approach is interruption of ironic processes. As we have emphasized, this depends, first, on accurate identification of the particular solution efforts that maintain or exacerbate the problem; second, on specifying what less of those same solution behaviors might look like; and third, on designing an intervention that will persuade at least one of the people involved to do less or the opposite of what they have been doing. To demonstrate such a process empirically, it is not enough to document changes in the target complaint. One needs to show that changes in attempted-solution behavior precede and actually relate to changes in the complaint. Evidence of such sequential dependencies in couples is at this point limited to case reports, though we are optimistic that quantitative methods can illuminate these processes as well.

A closely related curative factor is avoidance of ironic *therapy* processes—as can occur, for example, when "working through" a couple complaint in supportive individual therapy makes it possible for the partners to avoid resolving the problem directly, or when pushing one partner to change recapitulates a problem-maintaining solution applied by the clients themselves. The latter pattern is illustrated by a recent study comparing two treatments for couples in which the husband abused alcohol (Shoham et al., 1998). The two treatments—cognitive-behavioral therapy (CBT) and family systems therapy (FST)—differed substantially in the level of demand they placed on the drinker for abstinence and change. Although drinking was as a primary target for change in both approach, CBT took a firm stance about expected abstinence from alcohol, using adjunctive Breathalyzer tests to ensure compliance; whereas FST employed less direct, MRI-style strategies to work with clients' resistance. Before treatment began, we obtained observational measures of how much each couple engaged in demand–withdraw interaction, focusing on the pattern of wife's demand and husband's withdrawal during a discussion of the husband's drinking. The retention and abstinence results were striking: When couples high in this particular demand–withdraw pattern received CBT, they attended fewer sessions and tended to have poorer drinking outcomes—whereas for FST, levels of this pattern made little difference. Thus, for couples high in this problem-maintaining pattern, CBT may have replicated the pattern by providing "more of the same" ineffective solution: The alcoholic husbands appeared to resist a demanding therapist in the same way they resisted their demanding wives.[7]

For better or worse, the Palo Alto model attaches little importance to curative factors such as alliance, understanding, skill acquisition, and emotional catharsis, which are central to other therapies. The focus is entirely on interrupting ironic processes in the present, with no assumption that insight or understanding is necessary for this to happen. History may be relevant to clients' views, which are in turn relevant to how a therapist encourages "less of the same" solution behavior; however, "interpretations" (or frames) offered in this context are pragmatic tools for effecting change, rather than attempts to illuminate any psychological "reality."

A common criticism, of course, is that the MRI approach oversimplifies—either by making unrealistic assumptions about how people change, or by ignoring aspects of the clinical situation that may be crucial to appropriate intervention. Some critics find implausible the rolling-snowball idea that a few well-targeted interventions producing small changes in clients' cognitions or behavior can kick off a process that will lead to significant shifts in the problem pattern; others grant that brief interventions sometimes produce dramatic changes, but doubt that those changes last (Wylie, 1990). Not surprisingly, therapists of competing theoretical persuasions object to the fact that these brief therapies pointedly ignore personality and relationship dynamics that, from other perspectives, may be fundamental to the problems couples bring to therapists. For example, Gurman (quoted by Wylie, 1990) has suggested that "doing no more than interrupting the sequence of behaviors in marital conflict may solve the problem, but not if one spouse begins fights in order to maintain distance because of a lifelong fear of intimacy" (p. 31). Defenders of the brief therapy faith reply that such "iceberg" assumptions about what lies beneath a couple's complaint serve only to complicate the therapist's task and make meaningful change more difficult to achieve. Unfortunately, it is unlikely that research evidence will soon resolve these arguments one way or the other.

APPLICABILITY

In principle, the Palo Alto model is applicable to any couple that presents a clear complaint and at least one customer for change. In practice, however, this approach may be particularly relevant for couples that seem *resistant* to change. Published case reports imply that strategic therapy is most indicated when other, more straightforward approaches are unlikely to work (see Fisch & Schlanger's [1999] *Brief Therapy with Intimidating Cases*). Even advocates of other treatment methods have recommended using MRI principles and techniques at points of impasse— either sequentially, when other methods fail (e.g., O'Hanlon & Weiner-Davis, 1989; Stanton, 1981), or as a therapeutic detour to take before resuming an original treatment plan (Spinks & Birchler, 1982). In addition, controlled studies of both individual problems (Shoham, Bootzin, Rohrbaugh, & Urry, 1996; Shoham-Salomon, Avner, & Neeman, 1989; Shoham-Salomon & Jancourt, 1985) and couple problems (Goldman & Greenberg, 1992) suggest that strategic interventions are more effective than straightforward affective or skill-oriented interventions when clients are more rather than less resistant to change.

Of particular note is Goldman and Greenberg's (1992) study of couple therapy, which compared a "systemic" treatment based on the Palo Alto model to Greenberg's own emotion-focused couple therapy and a wait-list control condition. The systemic treatment employed a team format (with a one-way mirror) and "focused almost exclusively on changing current interactions, [positively] reframing patterns of behavior, and prescribing symptoms" (p. 967). Both of the active treatments were superior to the control condition at termination, but at a 4-month follow-up the couples that had received systemic therapy reported better marital quality and more change in their target complaint than those that had received emotion-focused therapy. This finding, coupled with their clinical observations, led the authors to conclude that the strategic approach may be well suited for change-resistant couples with rigidly entrenched interaction patterns. Goldman and Greenberg's conclusion fits well with the results of our alcohol treatment study, described above, where couples embroiled in demand–withdraw interaction appeared to do better with an MRI-style therapy than with CBT (Shoham et al., 1998).[8]

The Palo Alto model is probably *least* applicable to couples whose concern is relationship enhancement, prevention, or personal growth. This is because therapy requires a complaint and will rarely continue more than a few sessions without one. Sometimes a discussion of growth-oriented goals such as "improved communication" will lead

to specification of a workable complaint, but short of this, the therapist would *not* want to suggest or imply that clients could benefit from therapy. In fact, the concept of ironic processes cautions us against therapeutic excess, and the possibility of therapy itself's becoming a problem-maintaining solution. In this framework, intervention should be proportionate to the complaint—and when in doubt, "less is best."

At the same time, because this approach is so complaint-focused, critics have pointed out that therapists may ignore problems such as partner abuse and substance use disorders if clients do not present them as overt complaints in the first session (Wylie, 1990). Although couple therapists working in this tradition explore complaint patterns in great detail, and some (like us) routinely meet with partners separately to allow an intimidated partner to raise a complaint (Rohrbaugh et al., 1995), the focus of intervention remains almost exclusively on what clients say they want to change. The non-normative, constructivist premise of brief therapy, which rejects the idea of objective standards for what is normal or abnormal or good or bad behavior, may too easily excuse the therapist from attempting to "discover" conditions such as alcoholism or partner abuse. According to Fisch (as cited by Wylie, 1990), an MRI therapist would inquire about suspected partner abuse only if it is in some way alluded to in the interview. Thus, while brief therapists no doubt respect statutory obligations to report certain kinds of suspected abuse and warn potential victims of violence, they clearly distinguish therapy from social control and reserve the former for customers with explicit complaints.

Other ethical dilemmas in couple therapy concern dealing with the (often conflicting) agendas of two adults rather than one. In the MRI approach, a further complication arises when a therapist intervenes through only one member of a couple with the implicit or explicit goal of changing not only the behavior of the motivated client, but also that of the nonparticipating spouse (Watzlawick & Coyne, 1980; Hoebel, 1976): What responsibility, if any, does the therapist have to obtain informed consent from other people likely to be affected by an intervention? Such questions have no easy answer.

CASE ILLUSTRATION: MARIA AND HAROLD

The following case, seen in a university psychology clinic, illustrates essential elements of the MRI approach to couple problems: (1) specification of a complaint and minimum acceptable change goals; (2) formulation of an ironic problem-solution loop, including what less of the same solution would look like behaviorally; (3) focused interruption of the ironic loop in a specific situation; and (4) use of a client's own views and experiences to frame, or sell, the suggestion for less of the same. Because the therapist saw only the female member of the couple, this case also illustrates the Palo Alto group's willingness to intervene in a relational system unilaterally, without conjoint sessions. (The man in the couple felt he had good reasons for not coming to the clinic, and we respected this; he did, however, give consent for therapy to address his *partner's* difficulties, including her concerns about the relationship, and he was ultimately pleased by the results.) The case may also be of interest because of what the therapist did *not* do in terms of exploring or dealing with the bread-and-butter issues of other therapies.

Maria, a 26-year-old graduate student in biology, came to the clinic for "personal counseling." When initially asked about the problem, Maria said "I just don't feel good about myself, especially the way I am with men." She went on to talk at length about her contributions to the demise of two earlier relationships (including one in which she had been engaged), and her worries that she might soon spoil a third, with Harold, whom she lived with and cared for very much. Maria saw herself following a pattern with these men— one she didn't much like, because it was reminiscent of how her mother had been with her father: She simply could not succeed in pleasing or sustaining intimacy with a man she loved, no matter what or how hard she tried. At the same time, she resented feeling that she *should* please a man, and very much wanted to avoid the kind of traditional, subservient relationship her mother had had with her Mexican American father. Despite her feminist sympathies, Maria felt that "old tapes from childhood" about woman-man relationships had contributed to her difficulties with men. Later in the session, she contrasted her failures in love with successes in other parts of her life: Not only was she beginning to publish in her chosen academic specialty; she felt "less anxious" and "more grounded psychologically" than she had several years earlier, when she entered graduate school. Maria attributed this mainly to her practice of "mindfulness meditation," which she had taken up during her first year in graduate school, shortly after breaking off her brief engagement to Carlos (who

she felt was becoming emotionally abusive), and about six months before she became seriously involved with Harold. At the time of the first interview, Maria and Harold had been romantically involved for nearly a year and had lived together (in his house) for 5 months. However, they had not yet discussed long-term plans, and Maria's earlier hopes that marriage would be in the offing were beginning to dim.

After listening attentively to Maria's historical account of problems with men, the therapist[9] asked how these difficulties were showing themselves *currently*, in her relationship with Harold. To this, Maria replied, "Well, I just seem to bring out the worst in him." She went on to explain how Harold, a 36-year-old faculty member in another department, was a very kind, loving, and sensitive man who, unlike the younger, more macho Carlos, could appreciate and respect a competent woman. Nevertheless, Harold was sometimes sensitive to the point of insecurity: He had some "jealousy issues," which the couple attributed to "traumatic residue" from his ex-wife's affairs some years earlier. Try as she might, Maria had not been able to provide the reassurance Harold seemed to need. In fact, their attempts to discuss the jealousy issue sometimes led to "really bad arguments, like the one last week before I called the clinic"—hence the fear about "bringing out the worst."

Seeking a more behavioral complaint description, the therapist at this point asked Maria to describe what typically happened when she and Harold tried to discuss the jealousy issue, perhaps using the previous week's incident as an example: "How does the issue come up? Who says or does what? What happens then? If we recorded your interaction on video, what would I see?" From questions along this line emerged the outline of a problem-solution loop: When Harold expressed concern about whether Maria found him sexually attractive, she would typically explain (patiently at first) that yes, she did find him attractive, and in fact had never loved a man the way she loved him. Apparently unconvinced, Harold would then ask further questions, either about the details of her past sexual experiences (especially with Carlos) or about men she found sexually attractive now. For her part, Maria responded to this by denying other interests, offering further reassurances that Harold really had nothing to worry about, and expressing her growing frustration with Harold's inability to trust her. Once, in response to persistent questioning, Maria had actually tried to describe her lovemaking with Carlos, calling it "vigorous, at

least on his part," but "unsatisfying for me because I felt used." To Maria's dismay, Harold
questioned her about "vigorous orgasms" in a
later dispute, and the accuse–deny sequence between them had several times escalated to the
point of yelling and name calling. On one such
occasion she had stormed out of the house, and
on another Harold had thrown a book and inadvertently broken a lamp. These "blowups" were
invariably followed by periods of remorse in which
both partners (but especially Maria) would try to
take responsibility for what happened and resolve
not to let it happen again. While allowing that
Harold's fits of jealousy were often "unreasonable," Maria clearly regarded them as anomalous
to his otherwise pleasing personality and felt that
the blowups mainly reflected her inability to meet
his needs. Despite these complications, Maria
confided that she and Harold really did have good
sex—especially when they hadn't tried beforehand
to talk about it—which was all the more reason
to save the relationship.

Toward the end of the first session, the therapist asked what Maria hoped to gain from coming
to the clinic and what she would take as a tangible
sign that the situation with Harold was improving.
She said she most wanted to understand *why* she
was unsuccessful with men, because this might help
her save the relationship with Harold. The therapist did not challenge this, but pressed instead for
a minimum change goal: "What, when it happens,
will let you know that you and Harold are getting
a handle on the jealousy problem? Or that, even
though he might not have proposed marriage, your
relationship is at least heading in the right direction?" Maria said she just didn't want him to be
jealous, and eventually she agreed that not having
arguments about sexual matters, even if Harold
brought such matters up, would be a significant
indication that things were improving. After consulting with the team behind the mirror, the therapist closed the session by suggesting that Maria tell
Harold about at least her first goal (to understand
her contribution to problems in important relationships), and that she ask him whether he might be
willing to help with this later—particularly since he
knew her so well. Perhaps we (the team) could
think of something he could do. (The rationale here
was to open the door for Harold's possible participation in the therapy, yet to do so in a way that
respected Maria's view—and perhaps also his view—
that the problem was *hers* rather than his or even
theirs. In retrospect, it would probably have been
better to ask Maria's permission to call Harold

directly, so that we could better assess his customership and control the message. Later, after the
next session, the therapist in fact did this.)

Maria opened the second session by announcing that her homework assignment had not gone
well. Although Harold had known about the
counseling appointment and felt OK about Maria
getting help, he had not expected (she said) that
so much time would be spent talking about *him*.
Furthermore, as for helping with the therapy, there
was no way that he, a tenured professor at the
university, could be comfortable with the videotaping and observation room setup, or with talking about personal matters to graduate students
and faculty from another department. When asked
why she thought Harold had reacted this way, and
how she had handled it, Maria said she thought
he might have been embarrassed. She had tried to
reassure him that she was really coming to work
on her own problems, not to complain about him,
but this didn't work; rather than risking another
argument, therefore, she decided to quietly apologize and drop the subject. After a phone-in from
the team, the therapist conveyed to Maria the team's
apology for putting her in this awkward position,
and asked permission for us to call Harold and
apologize to him as well. The client was initially
reluctant, but agreed to the call, adding that she
would probably warn Harold what was coming.

The rest of Session 2 was devoted to further
investigation of the problem–solution pattern
identified in Session 1, so as to develop a clearer
picture of what less of the same (the strategic objective) might look like on Maria's side. Although
characteristic "solutions" such as explaining, reassuring, and denying were already in focus, it was
not clear in what situation(s) the escalating interaction sequence most typically occurred. Questions
about this pulled few specific answers: In fact,
Maria found it disconcerting that she couldn't
predict *when* Harold would ask her a "sexual attraction" question, because if she could, she might
prepare for it better. "It can just come out of the
blue, like when he's reflecting on things—even good
things." Another useful piece of information came
from questioning Maria about solutions that did
work for her, at least with other problems. Here
we were particularly interested in how she used
mindfulness meditation, and what this meant to her.
Maria did meditation exercises every morning, and
preferred to do them when Harold was not in the
house so as not to disturb or distract him. She also
said that meditations—and, more generally, the Eastern idea of "yielding"—had helped her cope with

interpersonal stresses, particularly after problems with Harold. When feeling stressed in this way, Maria would try to "yield" by taking a "mini-retreat"—which amounted to a brief period of private meditation, again away from Harold. These mini-retreats were inevitably "healing," at least temporarily, but they were not always possible to arrange. A final line of questions concerned the views and possible solution efforts of people beyond the couple, such as relatives, friends, and colleagues. Here it developed that Maria spoke several times on the phone each week with her mother, whose opinion was that the relationship with Harold was unlikely to succeed, in part because he was from a different cultural and religious background. Maria did not argue with her mother about this, but at the same time stiffened her resolve to succeed in love as well as work. After all, her mother had at first been skeptical about her career plans, too.

The therapist called Harold several days after Session 2 as agreed, and found him symmetrically apologetic about the misunderstandings surrounding Maria's therapy. Harold said that he hoped the counseling could help Maria, who (he felt) was often "too hard on herself," and that maybe if this happened there would be some indirect benefits for the relationship. He hoped the therapist would understand, however, why he did not want to come in himself. Sensing that this was not a matter for negotiation, the therapist said she did understand and that we, too, wished the best for his and Maria's relationship. Although careful not to comment or ask questions about any particulars of the relationship, the therapist did ask Harold whether she might call him again "sometime down the road" to consult, if she and Maria thought that might be helpful. After a brief hesitation, he agreed to this request.

At a staff meeting a few days later, the team reviewed the accumulated information about the case, sharpened its formulation of problem maintenance, and planned the particulars of an intervention for Session 3. When the team focused on the jealousy sequence, it was clear that the main thrust of Maria's solution effort involved *talking* with Harold about his fears and concerns—notably explaining and reasoning with him, offering reassurances, and denying that she was sexually attracted to other men. It was equally clear that less of this solution (the strategic objective that, if accomplished, would suffice to break the cycle) should involve *not* trying to talk Harold out of his concerns, or perhaps better, not talking in the face of accusations at all. The team briefly considered

ways Maria might reverse her usual stance (e.g., by agreeing with Harold and amplifying his concerns), but this seemed provocative and much too risky. Because it is usually easier in such a context for clients to do something than not to do something, the team considered what the therapist could ask Maria to do that would effectively block her usual solution efforts. After some discussion, it was decided that the simple act of meditation, if done at the right time in Harold's presence, could serve this purpose nicely. An advantage was that the behavior of sitting quietly, breathing evenly, and focusing inwardly with her eyes closed was familiar to Maria and was a proven way of coping with stress. On the other hand, because she preferred to meditate alone so as not to distract or disturb him, it could be difficult to persuade her to do this with Harold not only present but actively attempting to engage her in conversation. A final consideration was that the target sequence often came "out of the blue," with no predictable onset. This meant that Maria's strategic meditation would need to occur contingently, and that when to attempt this should be clearly spelled out in the intervention.

As the team pondered how to frame the meditation intervention in a way Maria would accept, several aspects of her preferred views, or "position," seemed especially relevant. First, saving the relationship and being helpful to Harold were high on Maria's list of concerns. Second, she understood that mindfulness meditation and knowing when to yield can help people cope with stressful situations, so perhaps this idea could be extended to include possible future benefits for Harold and the relationship, as well as for her. Third, because Maria believed that self-understanding was the preferred path to personal growth and change, it might be advisable to frame the meditation task as something likely to provoke unforeseen insights, primarily for her but perhaps (eventually) for Harold too. Another aspect of client position the team considered was Maria's resolve not to be constrained by her mother's expectations; however, this did not seem applicable to framing the meditation intervention, and so it was held in reserve for possible use later in the therapy.

Session 3 began with a report on Harold's reactions to the therapist's phone call, which Maria characterized as more thoughtful and considerate than she had expected. Although the couple had had a good week, with no jealousy or sexual attraction disputes, Maria was not optimistic that this state of affairs would continue. The therapist agreed with her assessment, adding that the team had given some thought to Maria's situation and come up with some ideas that might help in her self-analysis. When the client said she'd like to hear about those ideas, the therapist proceeded to frame the intervention: First, she said, it might be helpful if Maria had a way to cope with the jealousy situation on the spot, so it would be less likely to get out of hand. Second, it might be possible to do this in a way that help us understand more about *why* Maria behaved as she did, at least with Harold, which in turn could give clues about how to change. Finally, though the team members weren't sure, what they had in mind might also help Harold with the stress he must be experiencing, and perhaps even help him take stock of what he could do to make the relationship better. (Through all of this, both the therapist and the team behind the mirror carefully watched Maria's nonverbal expressions, particularly her head nods, to see whether she seemed to be accepting the frame. Only the part about Harold's taking stock of his own contributions seemed to evoke skepticism, and the therapist quickly downplayed this as "a pretty unlikely possibility.") Taking a position of mild restraint, the therapist then said that although she knew of several small but specific steps Maria could take to accomplish these things, those steps could be difficult, and she (the therapist) was reluctant to add to Maria's burden. After the client responded to this by affirming her commitment to "doing whatever is necessary," the therapist, with an air of caution, proceeded to lay out the strategic meditation idea and its rationale.

The key to doing the meditation successfully, the therapist explained, would be for Maria to pay close attention to her own reactions. When she was sure she felt like defending herself or reasoning with Harold about sexual matters, she should do the following: (1) look toward the ceiling and politely say, "Excuse me, Harold"; (2) ceremoniously assume a comfortable meditation position on the floor; (3) close her eyes; and (4) begin meditating. If Harold attempted to interrupt this or draw her into conversation, she should simply say, without opening her eyes, "The counselor suggested I do this when I feel stressed. I'll be available again in about 15 minutes." If Harold became upset or tried to roust her from meditation, she would simply remain silent and yield, Gandhi-style, no matter what the provocation. Afterwards, she might do whatever felt natural, either with Harold or without him. The therapist went on to underscore the potential enlightenment value of this exercise, pointing out that the

team was reasonably confident that, should Maria have opportunity to do this a few times, some insights would emerge to shed light either on her habitual difficulties with men, or on what the future might hold for her and Harold. The team did not know what form these insights might take, what they might mean, or how soon they would emerge after a meditation session, but the therapist expressed confidence that she and Maria would know how to handle them when the time came. The session closed with Maria's reassuring the therapist that the meditation experiment would not be too burdensome for her. The client also noted that, in her experience, important awarenesses usually occurred well after a mindfulness meditation—for example, while taking a hike. The therapist was unsure what Maria meant by this, but did not explore it further.

When Maria returned 2 weeks later for Session 4, she reported that there had been no occasions to try the meditation experiment. Although she had considered doing it several times when she was beginning to feel irritated with Harold, these situations were not really related to the jealousy issue, so she held back. Actually, Maria said, knowing what she would do if/when a difficult situation came up had made her feel more confident, and she wondered whether she might have behaved a little differently around Harold because of this. The therapist complimented her on feeling confident, but suggested she "go slow" with behaving differently around Harold, due to uncertainties about how he (and they) might handle it. The therapist also expressed mild chagrin that Harold had not provided Maria with the learning opportunity she had been anticipating. After a period of general discussion about parity in man–woman relationships, the therapist returned to the "missed opportunity" problem and suggested the possibility of delaying the next session until Harold had "misbehaved" to the point of allowing Maria to try the meditation experiment. The client at first seemed puzzled by this, because she thought that talking things out would continue to help her; however, she agreed to call in a month for another appointment, or possibly sooner if she had the fortunate (?) opportunity to meditate in front of Harold.

Roughly a month after Session 4, the therapist received a phone message from Maria announcing: "Big news! Harold proposed!!" And in a session a few days later, she explained what had happened. One evening not long after the last session, Harold had again tried to draw Maria into a discussion of Carlos's sexual prowess, and after only a minute of this, she had invoked the meditation routine. After she began, he had said "What the hell?"; with eyes closed, she repeated the brief explanation about feeling stressed. As best she could tell, Harold had left the room a minute or so later, then left the house. He came back fairly late, after Maria had gone to bed, but the next morning he had prepared pancakes (something he'd not done since early in the courtship) before she finished her shower. At breakfast, after a period of silence, Harold proffered an awkward apology for his insensitivity over the past few months, then asked whether Maria might teach him how to meditate. This was something she had urged him to try a number of times in the past, but then he had shown little interest, and she had thought better of pursuing it further. In any case, Maria and Harold had good sex that evening, and afterwards she instructed him in mindfulness meditation. Much to her delight, they had meditated together every morning since then, except for a few days when Harold went to a meeting out of town. There had been two potential recurrences of the jealousy sequences, but Maria had nipped each of these in the bud—the first by looking at the ceiling and closing her eyes, and the second by playfully saying, "Meditation time." As for "insight and awareness," Maria said that once she and Harold began meditating together, she realized how "enabling" she had been by preventing him from taking a full share of responsibility for the success of their relationship. Again, however, the team was not entirely sure what to make of this realization, so the therapist respectfully validated it without much elaboration.

Finally, when asked how she decided to come back to the clinic, Maria said she had thought about calling to schedule an appointment earlier—at about the time of the first potential jealousy recurrence—but she decided not to risk spoiling her success (and upsetting Harold) by doing that. In fact, she would probably not have called when she did, except that this time Harold suggested it. Therapy terminated at this point, amidst messages that both congratulated Maria (and through her, Harold) on what they had accomplished and cautioned her against thinking the road ahead would be trouble-free. The therapist would be available over the next few months in case she (or they) would want to visit the clinic again, and Maria could count on a routine follow-up call from the clinic in 6–12 months. A few days later the therapist received a personal note from Harold expressing his sincere thanks for "helping Maria come to terms with the stress in her life"—and Harold felt this had helped him, too. In the follow-up contact 9 months later, Maria reported no further recurrences of the jealousy complaint. In addition, she was married and pregnant.

ACKNOWLEDGMENT

This work was partially supported by Grant No. R21-DA13121 from the National Institute on Drug Abuse.

NOTES

1. The term "ironic process" was first used by social psychologist Daniel Wegner (e.g., Wegner, 1994) in connection with his theory of mental control. Shoham and Rohrbaugh (1997) later extended the term to include ironic *interpersonal* processes, such as those highlighted by the Palo Alto group (cf. Rohrbaugh & Shoham, 2001).

2. While Haley and Madanes have sometimes used interventions similar to those practiced by the MRI group, their strategic therapy makes assumptions about relational structure and the adaptive (protective) function of symptoms that the Palo Alto group rejects (Weakland, 1992). Useful descriptions of strategic marital therapy drawing on the Haley–Madanes model can be found in Keim (1999) and in Todd's (1986) chapter in the *Clinical Handbook of Marital Therapy*.

3. A similar concern with avoiding ironic *therapy* processes has influenced the framing of our manualized therapies for couples facing intractable problems with drinking and smoking as "family consultation" (Rohrbaugh et al., 1995, 2001). By connoting collaboration and choice, the term "consultation" arouses less resistance than "treatment" and underscores our assumption that people come to therapy because they are stuck—not sick, dysfunctional, or in need of an emotional overhaul.

4. Bateson (1958) distinguished "complementary" interaction patterns, where participants exchange opposite behavior (e.g., nagging and withdrawal, dominance and submission), from "symmetrical" patterns, where they exchange similar behavior (e.g., mutual blame or avoidance).

5. Most studies indicate that women are on the demand side of demand–withdraw interaction more often than men (Christensen & Heavy, 1993); however, who demands and who withdraws in a conflict may depend more on the situational affordances (e.g., who has power and least wants to change) than on essential differences between the sexes (cf. Klinetob & Smith, 1996).

6. This may have been partly due to the fact that Fisch, Shoham, and the wife shared a cultural familiarity with chicken soup as a credible—and potentially nonverbal—remedy for familial distress.

7. These couple-level results parallel findings from attribute × treatment interaction studies of individual therapy (e.g., Shoham-Salomon, Avner, & Neeman, 1989). In both clinical contexts—one where an individual client resists persistent influence from a therapist, and the other where a male with a drinking problem resists influence from his partner—treatments that exert different levels of direct pressure for change appear to yield different results to the extent that they activate (or avoid) interpersonal ironic processes.

8. In a review of empirically supported couple therapies, Baucom, Shoham, Mueser, Daiuto, and Stickle (1998) concluded that "the findings from this single investigation place systemic couple therapy into the category of possibly efficacious [treatments]" (p. 61). A wider-ranging review of research support for brief problem-focused therapy and the model of ironic processes can be found in Rohrbaugh and Shoham (2001).

9. The therapist, also female, was an advanced graduate student in clinical psychology. She was supervised by MJR, with the help of a consultation team.

REFERENCES

Bateson, G. (1958). *Naven* (2nd ed.). Stanford, CA: Stanford University Press.

Baucom, D. H., Shoham, V., Mueser, K. T., Daiuto, A. D., & Stickle, T. R. (1998). Empirically supported couple and family interventions for marital distress and adult mental health problems. *Journal of Consulting and Clinical Psychology, 65,* 53–88.

Berg, I. K., & Miller, S. D. (1992). *Working with the problem drinker: A solution-focused approach.* New York: Norton.

Bobele, M. (1987). Therapeutic interventions in life-threatening situations. *Journal of Marital and Family Therapy, 13,* 225–240.

Bobele, M. (1988). Reply to "Public policy in life-threatening situations." *Journal of Marital and Family Therapy, 14,* 139–142.

Cade, B., & O'Hanlon, W. H. (1993). *A brief guide to brief therapy.* New York: Norton.

Christensen, A., & Heavey, C. L. (1993). Gender differences in marital conflict: The demand/withdraw interaction pattern. In S. Oskamp & M. Costanzo (Eds.), *Gender issues in contemporary society* (pp. 113–141). Newbury Park, CA: Sage.

Christensen, A., & Shenk, J. L. (1991). Communication, conflict, and psychological distance in nondistressed, clinic, and divorcing couples. *Journal of Consulting and Clinical Psychology, 59,* 458–463.

Coyne, J. C. (1986a). Strategic marital therapy for depression. In N. S. Jacobson & A. S. Gurman (Eds.), *Clinical handbook of marital therapy* (pp. 495–511). New York: Guilford Press.

Coyne, J. C. (1986b). Evoked emotion in marital therapy: Necessary or even useful?. *Journal of Marital and Family Therapy, 12,* 11–14.

Coyne, J. C. (1988). Strategic therapy. In J. Clarkin, G. Haas, & I. Glick (Eds.), *Affective disorders and the family: Assessment and treatment* (pp. 89–113). New York: Guilford Press.

Coyne, J. C., & Smith, D. A. (1991). Couples coping with a myocardial infarction: Contextual perspective on wife's distress. *Journal of Personality and Social Psychology, 61,* 404–412.

de Shazer, S. (1991). *Putting differences to work.* New York: Norton.

de Shazer, S., Berg, I., Lipchik, E., Nunnally, E., Molnar, A., Gingerich, W., & Weiner-Davis, M. (1986). Brief therapy: Focused solution development. *Family Process, 25,* 207–222.

Fisch, R. (1986). The brief treatment of alcoholism. *Journal of Strategic and Systemic Therapies, 5,* 40–49.

Fisch, R. (1990). "To thine own self be true . . .": Ethical issues in strategic therapy. In J. Zeig (Ed.), *Brief therapy: Myths, methods, and metaphors* (pp. 429–436). New York: Brunner/Mazel.

Fisch, R., & Schlanger, K. (1999). *Brief therapy with intimidating cases: Changing the unchangeable.* San Francisco: Jossey-Bass.

Fisch, R., Weakland, J. H., & Segal, L. (1982). *The tactics of change: Doing therapy briefly.* San Francisco: Jossey-Bass.

Fogarty, F. (1976). Marital crisis. In P. J. Guerin (Ed.), *Family therapy: Theory and practice* (pp. 325–334). New York: Gardner Press.

Goldman, A., & Greenberg, L. (1992). Comparison of integrated systemic and emotionally focused approaches to couples therapy. *Journal of Consulting and Clinical Psychology, 60,* 962–969.

Green, S., & Bobele, M. (1988). An interactional approach to marital infidelity. *Journal of Strategic and Systemic Therapies, 7,* 35–47.

Gurman, A. S. (2001). Brief therapy and family/couple therapy: An essential redundancy. *Clinical Psychology: Science and Practice, 8,* 51–65.

Gurman, A. S., Kniskern, D. P., & Pinsof, W. (1986). Research on the process and outcome of marital and family therapy. In S. L. Garfield & A. E. Bergin (Eds.), *Handbook of psychotherapy and behavior change* (pp. 565–624). New York: Wiley.

Haley, J. (1967). *Advanced techniques of hypnosis and therapy: Selected papers of Milton H. Erickson, M.D.* New York: Grune & Stratton.

Haley, J. (1980). *Leaving home.* New York: McGraw-Hill.

Haley, J. (1987). *Problem-solving therapy: New strategies for effective family therapy* (2nd ed.). San Francisco: Jossey-Bass.

Hoebel, F. C. (1976). Brief family–interactional therapy in the management of cardiac-related high-risk behaviors. *Journal of Family Practice, 3,* 613–618.

Keim, J. (1999). Brief strategic marital therapy. In J. M. Donovan (Ed.), *Short-term couple therapy* (pp. 265–290). New York: Guilford Press.

Klinetob, N. A., & Smith, D. A. (1996). Demand–withdraw communication in marital interaction: Test of interspousal contingency and gender role hypotheses. *Journal of Marriage and the Family, 58,* 945–957.

Madanes, C. (1981). *Strategic family therapy*. San Francisco: Jossey-Bass.

Madanes, C. (1991). Strategic family therapy. In A. S. Gurman & D. P. Kniskern (Eds.), *Handbook of family therapy* (Vol. 2, pp. 396–416). New York: Brunner/Mazel.

Miller, G., & de Shazer, S. (2000). Emotions in solution-focused therapy: A re-examination. *Family Process, 39*, 5–23.

Napier, A. Y. (1978). The rejection–intrusion pattern: A central family dynamic. *Journal of Marriage and Family Counseling, 4*, 5–12.

Nichols, M. P., & Schwartz, R. C. (2000). *Family therapy: Concepts and methods*. Boston: Allyn & Bacon.

O'Hanlon, W., & Weiner-Davis, M. (1989). *In search of solutions: A new direction in psychotherapy*. New York: Norton.

Rohrbaugh, M. J., & Shean, G. (1988). Anxiety disorders: An interactional view of agoraphobia. In F. Walsh & C. Anderson (Eds.), *Chronic illness and the family* (pp. 66–85). New York: Brunner/Mazel.

Rohrbaugh, M. J., & Shoham, V. (2001). Brief therapy based on interrupting ironic processes: The Palo Alto model. *Clinical Psychology: Science and Practice, 8*, 66–81.

Rohrbaugh, M. J., Shoham, V., & Schlanger, K. (1992). *In the brief therapy archives: A progress report*. Unpublished manuscript.

Rohrbaugh, M. J., Shoham, V., Spungen, C., & Steinglass, P. (1995). Family systems therapy in practice: A systemic couples therapy for problem drinking. In B. Bongar & L. E. Beutler (Eds.), *Comprehensive textbook of psychotherapy: Theory and practice* (pp. 228–253). New York: Oxford University Press.

Rohrbaugh, M. J., Shoham, V., Trost, S., Muramoto, M., Cate, R., & Leischow, S. (2001). Couple-dynamics of change resistant smoking: Toward a family-consultation model. *Family Process, 40*, 15–31.

Rosenthal, M. K., & Bergman, Z. (1986). A flow-chart presenting the decision-making process of the MRI Brief Therapy Center. *Journal of Strategic and Systemic Therapies, 5*, 1–6.

Shoham, V., & Rohrbaugh, M. J. (1997). Interrupting ironic processes. *Psychological Science, 8*, 151–153.

Shoham, V., Bootzin, R. R., Rohrbaugh, M. J., & Urry, H. (1996). Paradoxical versus relaxation treatment for insomnia: The moderating role of reactance. *Sleep Research, 24*, 365.

Shoham, V., Rohrbaugh, M. J., & Patterson, J. (1995). Problem- and solution-focused couple therapies: The MRI and Milwaukee models. In N. S. Jacobson & A. S. Gurman (Eds.), *Clinical handbook of couple therapy* (pp. 142–163). New York: Guilford Press.

Shoham, V., Rohrbaugh, M. J., Stickle, T. R., & Jacob, T. (1998). Demand–withdraw couple interaction moderates retention in cognitive-behavioral vs. family-systems treatments for alcoholism. *Journal of Family Psychology, 12*, 557–577.

Shoham-Salomon, V., Avner, R., & Neeman, R. (1989). You are changed if you do and changed if you don't:

Mechanisms underlying paradoxical interventions. *Journal of Consulting and Clinical Psychology, 57*, 590–598.

Shoham-Salomon, V., & Jancourt, A. (1985). Differential effectiveness of paradoxical interventions for more versus less stress-prone individuals. *Journal of Counseling Psychology, 32*, 443–447.

Solovey, A., & Duncan, B. L. (1992). Ethics and strategic therapy: A proposed ethical direction. *Journal of Marital and Family Therapy, 18*, 53–61.

Spinks, S. H., & Birchler, G. R. (1982). Behavioral family-system therapy. *Family Process, 21*, 169–185.

Stanton, M. D. (1981). An integrated structural/strategic approach to family therapy. *Journal of Marital and Family Therapy, 7*, 427–440.

Teisman, M. (1979). Jealousy: Systematic, problem-solving therapy with couples. *Family Process, 18*, 151–160.

Todd, T. C. (1986). Structural–strategic marital therapy. In N. S. Jacobson & A. S. Gurman (Eds.), *Clinical handbook of marital therapy* (pp. 71–105). New York: Guilford Press.

Watzlawick, P. (1978). *The language of change*. New York: Basic Books.

Watzlawick, P., Beavin, J., & Jackson, D. D. (1967). *Pragmatics of human communication*. New York: Norton.

Watzlawick, P., & Coyne, J. C. (1980). Depression following stroke: Brief, problem-focused treatment. *Family Process, 19*, 13–18.

Watzlawick, P., & Weakland, J. H. (Eds.). (1978). *The interactional view*. New York: Norton.

Watzlawick, P., Weakland, J. H., & Fisch, R. (1974). *Change: Principles of problem formation and problem resolution*. New York: Norton.

Weakland, J. H. (1988). Weakland on the Woodys–Bobele exchange. *Journal of Marital and Family Therapy, 14*, 205.

Weakland, J. H. (1992). Conversation—But what kind? In S. Gilligan & M. Price (Eds.), *Therapeutic conversations* (pp. 136–145). New York: Norton.

Weakland, J. H., & Fisch, R. (1992). Brief therapy—MRI style. In S. H. Budman, M. F. Hoyt, & S. Friedman (Eds.), *The first session in brief therapy* (pp. 306–323). New York: Guilford Press.

Weakland, J. H., Fisch, R., Watzlawick, P., & Bodin, A. (1974). Brief therapy: Focused problem resolution. *Family Process, 13*, 141–168.

Wegner, D. M. (1994). Ironic processes of mental control. *Psychological Review, 101*, 34–52.

Wendorf, D. J., & Wendorf, R. J. (1985). A systemic view of family therapy ethics. *Family Process, 24*, 443–460.

Wile, D. B. (1981). *Couples therapy: A non-traditional approach*. New York: Wiley.

Woody, J. D., & Woody, R. H. (1988). Public policy in life-threatening situations: A response to Bobele. *Journal of Marital and Family Therapy, 14*, 133–138.

Wylie, M. S. (1990). Brief therapy on the couch. *Family Therapy Networker, 14*, 26–35, 66.

Chapter 2

Cognitive-Behavioral Couple Therapy

DONALD H. BAUCOM
NORMAN EPSTEIN
JASLEAN J. LaTAILLADE

A BRIEF HISTORY

Origins: Behavioral Couple Therapy

Although there are numerous published clinical and research articles devoted to behavioral couple therapy (BCT), only recently have clinicians and researchers noted the importance of examining cognitive variables in theories and treatment of couple distress. Cognitive-behavioral couple therapy (CBCT) claims as one of its precursors BCT, from which treatment strategies focused on changing observable couple and partner behaviors are derived. BCT emerged in the late 1960s with the application of reinforcement principles to clinical problems. Stuart (1969) presented the first published application of behavior exchange principles to couple problems. On the basis of social exchange theory (Thibaut & Kelley, 1959), Stuart hypothesized that successful marriages could be distinguished from unsuccessful marriages by the frequency and range of reciprocal positive reinforcers exchanged by the two partners. As such, distressed relationships were characterized by a scarcity of positive outcomes available for each person in the relationship. Stuart's treatment consisted of obtaining a list of behavioral objectives from each partner, with tokens being exchanged as rewards for targeted desired behaviors. Although his "token economy" has since been replaced with written contracts, communication, and problem-solving skill training, his employment of operant conditioning paradigms was a milestone in the development of BCT and family therapies (Falloon, 1991).

In addition to Stuart, Liberman (1970) utilized a social learning framework (Bandura, 1977; Rotter, 1954) in his work with families. Liberman, employing the imitative learning concepts of Bandura and Walters (1963), added the strategies of role rehearsal and modeling of alternative interpersonal communication patterns to his treatment of dysfunctional family relationships (Falloon, 1991). He also urged that these techniques be employed within the context of a "collaborative therapeutic alliance," accompanied by an extensive behavioral analysis of the presenting problems and family interaction patterns. Furthermore, Liberman advocated the continued use of behavioral analysis throughout the course of therapy, thus allowing the treatment to be modified as needed.

The use of operant conditioning in the modification of children's behavior also had a strong influence on the development of BCT (Patterson, 1974). In training parents to modify their children's behavior, therapists noted the exchange of reinforcers and punishers among adult family members (Holtzworth-Munroe & Jacobson, 1991), and subsequently applied the operant principles used on children's behavior to the treatment of relationship discord. The respective contributions of Patterson and Weiss are seminal in their application of operant principles to couple distress (Patterson & Hops, 1972).

These early writings on couple distress, however, were not comprehensive and specific in terms of clinical technique and application. The integration of disparate principles and the elaboration of clinical skills did not occur until the late 1970s and early 1980s, during which detailed treatment manuals were published (Jacobson & Margolin, 1979; Stuart, 1980), providing both a theoretical understanding of behavioral principles and a guide for the application of specific techniques to couple distress.

Several principles characterize the theoretical and treatment strategies used in BCT. A traditional behavioral model assumes that the behavior of both partners is shaped, strengthened, weakened, and modified by environmental events, particularly those events involving the other partner. These influential events include not only the environmental variables provided by the context of the relationship, but also influential events outside the relationship, which affect the partners' tendency to remain in the relationship as well as their subjective feelings of satisfaction (Jacobson & Margolin, 1979). Thus couple satisfaction is viewed as a function of the ratio of rewards derived to costs incurred from being in the relationship. BCT also assumes that unhappy couples are distressed, in part, because they have not developed or maintained the skills necessary to further closeness in their relationship. These include skills in conflict resolution, as well as skills necessary to make behavior change and facilitate constructive communication. Difficulties with such skills are presumed to result from a "skill deficit" or a "performance deficit"; the latter term implies that the ability to perform the skill is present, despite the dysfunctional interaction patterns exhibited. Heavy emphasis is placed on teaching couples the skills necessary for the performance of relationship roles and functions.

Because each partner is continually providing consequences for the other, and each person has an important controlling influence on the other's behavior, the relationship consists of reciprocal and circular sequences in which each partner's behavior simultaneously affects and influences the other. This dependence of each partner on the reinforcing and punishing behaviors of the other dictates the terms of a functional analysis of the couple's behavior patterns. Use of a functional analysis, in which variables in the environment that maintain the destructive couple or family interaction are identified, is the hallmark of traditional behavioral approaches. As no two couples' learning histories are identical, use of a functional analysis prevents BCT therapists from assuming the existence of universal truths in explaining a particular couple's interaction patterns, and it emphasizes an empirical perspective in examining couples' presenting concerns (LaTaillade & Jacobson, 1995).

From Behavioral to a Cognitive-Behavioral Approach

Across numerous investigations, BCT has consistently been found to be effective (Baucom, Shoham, Mueser, Daiuto, & Stickle, 1998; Hahlweg & Markman, 1988); even so, this approach is not without notable limitations. Results of BCT outcome studies have demonstrated that in many instances, increases in communication skills have not resulted in commensurate improvement in couple adjustment (Halford, Sanders, & Behrens, 1993; Iverson & Baucom, 1990). In addition, comparisons of BCT with other treatment approaches that do not emphasize behavioral skills training have found these interventions to be equally efficacious in alleviating couple distress, indicating that skills training may not be necessary or sufficient for positive treatment outcomes (Baucom, Epstein, & Gordon, 2000; Baucom et al., 1998). Furthermore, clinical research on observable couple behavior noted discrepancies between partners' reports of behavior and between partners' and trained observers' reports of behavior, suggesting a need to examine how partners thought subjectively about their own and their mates' behavior (Fincham, Bradbury, & Scott, 1990).

The combination of these findings indicated that a behavioral skills deficit model was too restrictive in the treatment of couple distress (Epstein & Baucom, 2002), and highlighted the need to attend not only to partners' behavior, but also partners' *interpretations* and *evaluations* of their own and their mates' behavior (Baucom & Epstein, 1990; Fincham et al., 1990). In addition, abundant social-psychological research on attribution theory, as well as the emergence of a science of close relationships within this same area of study, has further contributed to the growing consideration of cognitive factors in marriage (Baucom, Epstein, & Rankin, 1995; Fincham et al., 1990). As cognitive models of individual psychopathology brought attention to the important role of cognitive factors in clinical phenomena (Beck, Rush, Shaw, & Emery, 1979), during the 1980s researchers focused on cognitive variables as a critical element in understanding the relationship between couple behavior and couple distress (Baucom et al., 1995).

CBCT evolved from the gradual expansion of BCT and its treatment strategies to include a focus on cognitive factors in the onset and treatment of couple distress. In CBCT, cognitive, behavioral, and emotional factors are all given attention (Baucom & Epstein, 1990). A major premise of this approach is that partners' dysfunctional emotional and behavioral responses to relationship events are influenced by inappropriate information processing, whereby cognitive appraisals of the events are either distorted or extreme ("You stayed late at the office because you don't really love me. I know you have an annual report due tomorrow and the network went down, but if you wanted to, you'd find a way to be home with me"), or are evaluated according to extreme or unreasonable standards of what a relationship should be ("If you really cared, you'd want to spend all your free time with me. That's what a marriage should be"). Often partners fail to evaluate the appropriateness of their cognitions, and instead trust in the validity of their own subjective, stream-of-consciousness thoughts, or "automatic cognitions," in response to internal or external events in the relationship (Baucom & Epstein, 1990). Consequently, a major task of the CBCT therapist is to help partners become more active observers and evaluators of their own automatic cognitions, as well as their long-standing assumptions and standards regarding their relationship. Cognitive-behavioral approaches assume that once people alter their information processing and cognitions, positive changes in emotions and behaviors will follow (Epstein & Baucom, in press).

Limitations of CBCT

CBCT has established itself as an empirically supported intervention for the treatment of distressed couples (Baucom et al., 1998). However, CBCT has focused on certain phenomena in intimate relationships, while deemphasizing other important aspects. First, cognitive-behavioral approaches to couple relationships have emphasized detailed analyses of discrete, specific relational events and behaviors, or "micro-level" behaviors, without commensurate attention to broader, "macro-level" patterns and core

themes, such as differences in desired closeness and intimacy (Epstein & Baucom, in press). Individual partners and couples demonstrate a tendency to repeat similar behavior patterns over time, and such patterns have different subjective cognitive and emotional experiences for each partner. Moreover, a variety of different behaviors often seem to fit into a similar equivalence class. For instance, Jonathon's routine pattern of coming home and checking through the mail before speaking to Catherine, engaging in little conversation at dinner, and surfing the Internet for hours each night all seemed to fit together to provide a picture of Jonathon as a rather quiet, contemplative person who was not comfortable with intimacy and preferred quietness and solitude. As such patterns repeat and develop over time, partners might organize their experience around broader relationship themes (e.g., intimacy or autonomy). Our inclusion of broader relationship themes is consistent with a similar shift across a variety of theoretical approaches (e.g., emotionally focused therapy—Greenberg & Johnson, 1988; integrative behavioral couple therapy—Jacobson & Christensen, 1996; Insight-oriented couple therapy—Snyder & Wills, 1989). These broader themes can be approached from cognitive, behavioral, and emotional perspectives.

Second, cognitive-behavioral approaches typically focus on a couple's cognitive processing, communication patterns, and the way partners behaviorally respond to each other, while minimizing the influences of personality and other, more stable individual differences between partners on couple functioning (Epstein & Baucom, 2002; Karney & Bradbury, 1995). Traditional behavioral models of relationship distress have tended to characterize maladaptive couple interactions as resulting from normal learning experiences and/or individual skill deficits. Although attending to cognitive distortions and behavioral deficits is important in outlining the topography of relationship distress, current models fail to explain *why* partners behave and interpret events in maladaptive ways. Each partner brings to the relationship not only unique histories and qualities, but also distinct relationship and individual preferences and needs that shape the relationship as a whole, as well as day-to-day couple interactions. Some of these may be normative individual differences, whereas others may stem from individual psychological distress or psychopathology. Research has demonstrated that individual differences among psychologically healthy and well-adjusted partners, as well as individual manifestations of psychopathology, often play a crucial role in relationship satisfaction and functioning (e.g., Christensen & Heavey, 1993; Karney & Bradbury, 1995). As such, increased attention to normative and non-normative differences in partners' individual and relationship needs may facilitate treatment by helping the partners to alter both their cognitions and behavioral and emotional responses to meet their needs more adequately and adaptively, both in and outside of the relationship. In essence, many of the broader themes that seem to be important in contributing to relationship adjustment involve the degree to which the couple is able to respond to each partner's important needs and motivations.

Third, environmental factors also exert a significant impact on all couples, and in many instances external and environmental stressors are critical factors in understanding couples' current functioning (Epstein & Baucom, 2002). The demands of work and children, relationships with extended family members, physical health of both partners, and negative experiences within the larger culture may all constitute significant relationship stressors. Major stressors (such as the loss of a job), as well as minor stressors (such as daily life hassles), can place demands on a couple that tax individual and relationship resources. Although cognitive-behavioral perspectives on marriage have not ignored the role of the environment in relationship functioning, it has typically been given minimal attention.

Fourth, cognitive-behavioral approaches have given primary emphasis to the role of behaviors and cognitions in relationships. Emotions, while not ignored, have been given secondary status, and largely have been viewed as the result of changes in partners' relationship behaviors and cognitions (Epstein & Baucom, 2002). Attending directly to emotional components of a relationship—ranging from an individual's difficulty in experiencing and/or expressing emotions, to partners' difficulty in regulating negative emotions—can increase the range of interventions that the therapist has available to assist the couple.

Fifth, cognitive-behavioral approaches, though historically differentiating between the positive and negative valences of specific behaviors, emotions, and cognitions, have emphasized attending to the negative aspects of these variables (Epstein & Baucom, 2002). As treatment strategies have subsequently focused on alleviating negative thoughts and behaviors, fewer interventions have been designed to highlight and maximize the positive aspects of the couple relationship. In order for couples to derive optimum

fulfillment from their relationships, greater emphasis must be given to the role of positive behavior, cognitions, and emotions (Epstein & Baucom, 2002). It is encouraging to see an increase in basic research on such topics as social support within marriage (Cutrona, 1996; Cutrona, Cohen, & Igram, 1990; Cutrona, Hessling, & Suhr, 1997; Cutrona & Suhr, 1992, 1994; Cutrona, Suhr, & MacFarlane, 1990; Pasch & Bradbury, 1993; Pasch, Bradbury, & Davila, 1997; Pasch, Bradbury, & Sullivan, 1997).

Our expanded model of CBCT includes a balanced perspective and integration of both discrete events and broader relationship themes. In addition, this model takes into account the unique qualities each partner brings to the relationship, as well as the impact of external and environmental factors on couple functioning. Finally, this model recognizes the centrality of emotion in relationship functioning, and balances the roles of positive and negative emotions, cognitions, and behaviors in the quality and treatment of intimate relationships.

THE HEALTHY/WELL-FUNCTIONING VERSUS PATHOLOGICAL/ DYSFUNCTIONAL COUPLE/ MARRIAGE

Traditionally, cognitive-behavioral approaches to understanding couple functioning have focused on the couple as the unit of analysis. However, we believe that a broader contextual perspective is necessary to evaluate whether a relationship is healthy and adaptive. A healthy relationship is most appropriately viewed within the context of the individual partners, the couple, and the couple's environment (with "environment" including all factors and forces outside the two partners). Whereas many cognitive-behavioral theorists and therapists might find such a perspective acceptable, generally the well-being of the individuals and the couple's relations with the environment have been minimized as foci of CBCT.

Consistent with this perspective, a healthy couple relationship is one in which both individuals contribute to the well-being of the relationship as a unit. This means that the partners have formed an effective partnership—reaching decisions and resolving problems effectively, developing a sense of intimacy and caring, communicating constructively, engaging as a couple in a variety of mutually rewarding and engaging activities, and so forth. Maladaptive relationships involve the inverse of these patterns, including poor communication, ineffective problem solving, high levels of negative behavior, and low levels of positive behavior. In fact, cognitive-behavioral conceptions of intimate relationships have emphasized empirically isolating and demonstrating these differences between distressed and nondistressed couples. A review of empirical findings documenting these observations is beyond the scope of this chapter, but is available elsewhere (Epstein & Baucom, 2002). This description of healthy and maladaptive relationships focusing on the couple as a unit coincides with traditional cognitive-behavioral conceptualizations of healthy intimate relationships and marriage.

In addition, a healthy couple relationship is one that contributes to the growth, well-being, and development of the partners, on both a day-to-day and a long-term basis. In terms of day-to-day functioning, the relationship should be responsive to each individual's needs, such as a need to function autonomously, to spend time alone, or to spend time with friends without the partner. In addition, a healthy relationship contributes to an individual's long-term well-being—for example, facilitating appropriate occupational growth and development, improved physical well-being, and so forth. Individual difficulties and distress are also inevitable across the life cycle; when such stresses arise, a healthy relationship provides support to the individual (Cutrona, Suhr, & MacFarlane, 1990; Pasch, Bradbury, & Sullivan, 1997), either instrumentally (e.g., helping with the partner's responsibilities) or emotionally (e.g., listening empathically to the partner's concerns). An unhealthy, maladaptive relationship does not contribute to the growth and development of individual well-being, and can actually be destructive to one or both individuals. Many investigations demonstrate that relationship distress and/or maladaptive interaction patterns can precipitate and exacerbate psychological symptoms and can influence the course of individual recovery and relapse (Butzlaff & Hooley, 1998).

Third, a healthy relationship is one in which the partners relate to their physical environment and social environment in an adaptive manner. The couple is able to make use of environmental supports and resources for the well-being of the couple and each individual. Likewise, a healthy relationship is one that gives back to the broader environment, community, or society—for example, through the couple's involvement in social causes such as protecting the physical environment or contributing to a religious organization. From this perspective, a relationship would be viewed as maladaptive if the couple and partners are happy but interact in a way that is destructive to other individuals or society at large.

An Adaptation Model of Couple Functioning

This broader contextual perspective on relationship functioning has implications for understanding and treating couples. A couple must adapt to an ever-changing set of circumstances involving the individual partners, the couple, and the environment, which can place demands on the couple for change or maintenance of the status quo. The couple's ability to respond to these demands is influenced by individual and couple vulnerabilities, as well as by the resources of both persons, the couple as the unit, and the environment upon which the couple can draw. The couple's responses to these demands can result in enhancement, deterioration, or maintenance of the status quo for the functioning of the couple and each individual. What is perhaps more complicated is that the outcomes for the couple and the individual partners are not always consistent. For example, a couple may adapt in a way that promotes the well-being of one individual, such as moving across the country for one person to further his or her professional opportunities. However, that decision may result in decreased cohesiveness for the couple as a unit. Thus this adaptation model requires that therapists consider ways in which the couple as a unit, the two individuals, and the environment all influence each other and contribute to an adaptive or maladaptive set of outcomes.

Longitudinal Perspectives on Healthy Relationships

A healthy relationship balances the needs of the couple, the individual, and the social and physical environments surrounding the couple. In order to consider a couple fully from this perspective, it is important to understand couple functioning from a longitudinal perspective. As Carter and McGoldrick (1999) have noted, rather predictable changes occur over a family's life cycle based on normative demands. Thus, during courtship, couples often experience strong feelings of love and excitement, with each partner making major efforts to please and impress the other person. As relationships progress, couples often enter a "startup phase" in which they focus considerable energy on establishing themselves in a variety of ways, such as initiating careers, buying a house, and perhaps having children. Many of these tasks require that partners invest energy outside their relationship, and this external focus poses new challenges, such as balancing the demands of jobs with those involved in maintaining intimacy between the partners. Therefore, the partners need to consider the demands created by each phase of their life cycle as they make decisions, interpret each other's behavior, and so forth.

These changes over the course of a relationship can pose difficulty for couples in at least two ways. First, many couples do not appear to recognize that they are entering new phases of the family life cycle that call for new ways of relating. They continue to relate in ways that may have been adaptive in the past, but are no longer functional. For example, when one person is in a demanding educational program, both members of the couple might focus their energies on helping that person succeed, planning according to that individual's schedule, and so forth. However, when that person finishes schooling, if the couple continues to make decisions primarily around that person's needs and wishes, the relationship can become imbalanced.

Second, many couples recognize that they are in a new phase of life and understand the need for change and adaptation, but may not be skilled in adapting to the demands inherent in the new phase. Thus a couple with a new infant may be quite aware of the lack of opportunity for time together as a couple, but may struggle to find ways to maintain a sense of connectedness and intimacy. Consequently, therapists need to help couples recognize the need for adaptive changes—and, when such awareness is present, to help them find reasonable ways to continue to meet important individual and relationship needs within the context of new demands and constraints.

Risk Factors in Relationship Functioning

What do we know about risk factors and couple functioning over time? Karney and Bradbury (1995) reviewed the longitudinal studies of marriage and concluded that two factors appear to predict relationship functioning over time across a wide range of couples. First, couples are at risk if they exhibit poor communication. For example, Markman, Duncan, Storaasli, and Howes (1987) found that relationship distress can be predicted years in

advance from the way partners interact prior to or soon after marriage. Karney and Bradbury (1995) also found that couples are at risk for relationship difficulties if one partner demonstrates a high level of neuroticism or negative affectivity.

Whereas communication and negative affect are important common risk factors for couples, a specific couple may have unique or additional individual, couple, and/or environmental factors that place their relationship at risk. In many instances, relationships involve two relatively healthy, well-adapted individuals. However, this does not ensure that they will have a happy relationship. They may be very different in terms of their needs, personality styles, and so forth. Although each partner may be psychologically healthy, differences between the partners can contribute to relationship distress if the couple interprets the differences negatively or cannot find healthy ways to address them. For example, partners often differ in their needs for closeness and intimacy. The partner who desires greater closeness often initiates more intimate interactions, while the partner who needs less closeness withdraws. Unfortunately, the partners may misattribute the causes of these differences. Thus the pursuing partner may feel unloved by the withdrawing partner, and the withdrawing partner may conclude that the pursuing partner has a desire to control him/her.

In addition, some similarities between the partners can place a relationship at risk. For example, if both partners are fun-loving, playful individuals who are not task-oriented or attentive to detail, this similarity can result in the couple's being disorganized, not paying bills on time, and not making appropriate long-term plans. These similarities and differences do not inevitably lead to relationship discord, but if they are misinterpreted or the couple does not find ways to address them adaptively, the couple is at greater risk.

Beyond these rather normal, expected differences between partners, a couple's relationship can be at risk if one or both people demonstrate significant psychopathology or long-term unresolved issues. These individual sources of distress can pose major stressors for a relationship. For example, if one partner has significant agoraphobia, it can greatly limit the couple's opportunities for social interactions and travel, and can result in an unequal distribution of tasks and responsibilities that is difficult to maintain over the long term.

Couples also are at risk for relationship distress based upon dyadic interactive processes that do or do not occur. Often cognitive-behavioral researchers and therapists have viewed these processes as skill deficits. Some partners may not be effective in communicating and may need to learn skills to express their feelings or solve problems effectively. Although maladaptive interactions can result from skill deficits, in many instances they result when the partners are frustrated that their important needs have not been met. For example, if one partner's desire for intimacy is not being met, over time that individual may become demanding and intrusive. This individual's problematic behavior does not result from an overall skill deficit in communicating, but rather is a maladaptive response to unfulfilled personal needs. A therapist should attempt to understand whether a given behavioral pattern that is prominent when a couple seeks therapy is the core of the relationship difficulties, or whether it results from unsuccessful attempts to address important needs and desires.

We refer to the distress associated with unmet fundamental needs for intimacy, affiliation, autonomy, achievement, and so forth as "primary distress." In contrast, when partners respond in maladaptive ways to their unmet needs and desires (e.g., verbally attacking each other), they can create "secondary distress" (Epstein & Baucom, 2002). This distinction suggests that the therapist must attend to the content of a couple's concerns as well as to how they are interacting when they seek therapy. Helping the couple communicate more effectively can be helpful, but this may not result in the partners' feeling fulfilled in their important needs and desires. Traditionally, CBCT therapists and researchers have minimized the content of couples' concerns and have focused primarily on their interactive processes. However, it is critical to balance a focus on both the process of interacting (e.g., communication) and the major themes and issues (e.g., different needs for intimacy) that serve as the basis for relationship discord.

In addition, a couple whose members otherwise might function adaptively under typical circumstances may respond poorly when major environmental crises occur or when there is a pileup of ongoing environmental demands. Responding to these stressors may involve the partners' interacting differently with their environment or calling upon other outside resources to help them.

Regardless of the relative importance of individual, couple, and environmental factors in disrupting a couple's functioning, what is striking about relationship distress is that it is often self-maintaining. A number of cognitive-behavioral investigators have noted the importance of reciprocity within re-lationships (e.g., Gottman, 1979; Revenstorf, Hahlweg, Schindler, & Vogel, 1984). That is, partners have a tendency to reciprocate or respond to negative behavior with negative behavior; similarly, partners tend to respond to positive behavior from each other with positive behavior. Therefore, regardless of the specific factors that contribute to initial discord and distress, once one or both partners become unhappy in the relationship, a self-perpetuating process tends to maintain the discord. This happens at behavioral, cognitive, and emotional levels. Behaviorally, this can be seen in a specific conversation in which a husband says something negative to his wife, and the wife responds in a negative manner. Cognitively, once the wife starts to perceive her husband in a negative fashion, she is likely to be more attentive to his negative behavior, to make negative attributions for his behavior, and to develop negative predictions or expectancies about how he is likely to behave in the future (Baucom & Epstein, 1990). From an emotional perspective, Weiss (1980) has noted that as partners behave negatively toward each other and come to think about each other in a negative way, each person may develop "sentiment override" or global negative emotions and sentiment toward the other individual. These negative feelings then increase the likelihood of subsequent negative behavior and cognitions. It is important that therapists understand this tendency toward self-maintenance of negative patterns, because therapists need to help couples exit from such patterns that have been established. When partners begin to interact in more positive ways with each other, positive reciprocity can help to maintain and increase relationship adjustment, as one helpful, constructive behavior brings forth reciprocal behavior from the other person.

Gender, Ethnic, and Cultural Factors in Couple Functioning

To this point, we have discussed couples as having two partners, with no distinction about how the two persons experience their relationship as a function of various important characteristics (gender, ethnicity, etc.). A great deal has been written about gender differences, informed in large part from an empirical perspective, as well as informal observation. For example, Christensen and his colleagues (Christensen, 1987, 1988; Christensen & Heavey, 1990, 1993; Christensen & Shenk, 1991; Christensen & Sullaway, 1984) have found that many distressed couples demonstrate a demand–withdraw interaction pattern, in which one partner demands and pushes for interaction and disclosure, while the other partner withdraws and becomes more distancing. Although these roles differ according to the topic being discussed, overall the findings indicate that females are much more likely to be in the demanding role, whereas males are more likely to be in the withdrawing role.

This gender difference in behavioral demand–withdraw patterns is only one gender difference that has been noted. In recent years, we have begun to explore whether males and females differ in information-processing strategies as well. More particularly, we are investigating whether females are more likely to organize information from a relationship perspective ("relationship schematic processing") and whether males are more likely to process and organize information from an individual perspective ("individual schematic processing") (Baucom, 1999; Rankin, Clayton, & Baucom, 1996; Rankin, Baucom, Clayton, & Daiuto, 1995; Rankin-Esquer, Baucom, Clayton, Tomcik, & Mullens, 1999; Rankin-Esquer, Clayton, Baucom, & Mullens, 1997; Sullivan & Baucom, 2000). Our findings to date demonstrate such gender differences, with females being more likely to communicate in ways suggesting that they process and organize information from a relationship perspective, and that they do this in a more sophisticated way than many males do. Similarly, we have found that in response to CBCT, males significantly increase their amount and quality of relationship schematic processing, which correlates positively with their female partners' increases in relationship satisfaction. In essence, these findings seem to suggest that females become happier over the course of therapy as their male partners learn to think and communicate in a more relational manner. Whereas it would be inappropriate to make assumptions about gender differences for a specific couple, understanding that relationship roles, power, and ways of processing information probably differ for females and males as a group should help the therapist be attentive to the role that such differences may play in a couple's level of relationship adjustment.

Differences in relationship functioning exist not only on the basis of gender, but also as a function of different cultures and ethnic backgrounds. Almost all of the empirical information that we have about relationship functioning is based on samples of white, middle-class couples in Western cultures. It is critical that therapists not adapt these models from a given culture as an absolute basis of relationship health. Instead,

the therapist should help a couple differentiate whether a given way of behaving or interacting, along with the values and standards that the couple holds for a committed relationship, is adaptive or maladaptive for that particular couple. The therapist must be cautious in not advocating for his/her personal standards for relationships in an absolute sense. If a couple from a given culture or ethnic group is behaving in a manner that is consistent with the norms of that group, but is contributing to significant relationship discord, then such issues must be addressed. If, however, the partners' standards and values simply differ from those of the therapist but are not central factors in their relationship distress, then the therapist must be careful not to impose his/her own standards on the couple.

THE ASSESSMENT OF COUPLE FUNCTIONING AND DYSFUNCTION

Within a CBCT framework, the primary goals of a clinical assessment are to identify the problems for which a couple has sought assistance; to clarify the cognitive, affective, behavioral, and environmental factors that contribute to the couple's concerns; and to determine the appropriateness of CBCT in addressing these concerns. In doing so, the therapist clarifies both partners' goals for treatment and their respective positions and perspectives regarding the areas of concern. In addition, the therapist also determines each partner's respective emotional investment in, and motivation for continuing with, the relationship. The level of commitment serves as an indication of each partner's willingness to work in treatment toward improving the relationship. Clarification of partners' levels of commitment, and of individual and dyadic goals for treatment, informs the therapist how to structure and guide the assessment process.

Unless a couple enters therapy in a state of acute crisis, the first two or three sessions are devoted to assessment and evaluation (LaTaillade & Jacobson, 1995). The couple is informed during the assessment phase that no commitment has been made by either party to engage in therapy. Rather, the partners are told that the purpose of the initial evaluation is to determine whether couple therapy is the best course of action for them at the present time—and, if this is not the optimal plan, to determine some alternative course of action (e.g., individual therapy for one or both partners to address factors that do not appear to be caused by conditions within the couple relationship).

As the primary focus of the assessment phase is on gathering information to help the therapist understand the relationship, the couple is cautioned not to expect relationship improvement at this time. However, this pretreatment phase often has therapeutic effects. Because the focus is on strengths as well as problems, the questions posed by the therapist often draw partners' attention to the positive aspects of their relationship. Given that distressed couples often enter therapy selectively tracking negative behaviors and events, this refocusing on the positive can increase positive affect and offer couples a sense of hope (Jacobson & Holtzworth-Munroe, 1986).

In conducting a thorough cognitive-behavioral assessment, the therapist attends not only to relationship-specific variables, but to individual and environmental factors as well. In assessing characteristics of individuals that influence or are affected by their current concerns, the therapist attends to partners' respective personality styles; demonstrations of psychopathology or subclinical character traits; individual and communal needs, and the extent to which those are being satisfied; and prior significant relationships, as well as the degree to which earlier relationship concerns continue to affect the present relationship. Dyadic factors assessed by the therapist include macro-level patterns that are a function of the partners' individual characteristics, as well as patterns of couple interaction that have developed over the course of the relationship. Environmental factors include demands experienced by the partners that they have had to adapt and respond to over the course of their relationship, such as nuclear and extended family, work, and broader societal factors (e.g., racial or sexual discrimination).

The initial assessment phase typically comprises several components, and employs multiple strategies for information gathering. These include self-report questionnaires, detailed clinical interviews with both the couple and individual partners, and observational assessment of the couple's interaction patterns. The clinician decides on which of these various components are used, and in what order. Below we provide descriptions of common methods and strategies used in self-report, interview, and observational approaches to assessment, and their use in planning interventions.

Generally, the joint couple interview is a primary method of couple assessment. The initial interviews typically include obtaining a relationship history in order to place current concerns in some meaningful perspective (Baucom & Epstein, 1990). Second, the therapist and partners discuss their current concerns, as well as strengths of the relationship. The partners are also asked to provide a sample of their current communication behavior in one or more relationship areas. In addition, the therapist orients the couple to the process of therapy. Finally, the initial interview provides the therapist's first attempt to establish a balanced and collaborative working relationship with both partners. Given the wealth of information to be obtained, the initial interviews can require 2–3 hours, in one extended session or a few 50- to 60-minute sessions (Baucom & Epstein, 1990). Because a couple may be ambivalent about entering treatment, it is recommended that the evaluation be completed expediently (generally during a 1- or 2-week period), in order to initiate interventions that the partners may view as helpful in dealing with their concerns.

During this initial assessment, several types of behavior are of interest to the therapist. First, the therapist obtains a historical account of the relationship, including a developmental history of the couple's relationship, as well as early relationship and individual behavior patterns that have affected the relationship. Obtaining an individual and relationship history allows the therapist to put the couple's current concerns and patterns into a meaningful context. In most cases, the earlier times in a couple's history are likely to be associated with positive memories and emotions; therefore, taking a relationship history can serve to counterbalance the negativism that partners usually experience when they seek therapy. In inquiring about the couple history, the therapist discusses the circumstances surrounding the partners' first meeting; the qualities that initially attracted them to each other; early relationship events and developmental milestones, such as how the partners decided to commit to one another; individual, dyadic, and environmental circumstances surrounding their decision to commit; the individual partners' prior relationship history; and prior experiences in couple and/individual therapy, if any.

In addition to focusing on historical factors, the therapist also focuses on current relationship concerns, as well as individual, dyadic, and environmental factors that contribute to partners' presenting issues. With regard to dyadic factors, the therapist assesses the overall rate with which meaningful positive and negative exchanges are occurring in the relationship, and the extent to which these exchanges are organized around broader macro-level themes. The therapist will also want to clarify each partner's perspective and position on the presenting concerns. This includes ascertaining partners' perceptions of the problem, attributions for why the problem exists, respective standards for how the relationship should function in that area, and behavioral and emotional responses to the problem (Baucom et al., 1995).

In addition to individual and dyadic factors, the therapist must inquire about environmental factors that contribute to the couple's presenting concerns. As a couple's environment consists of numerous interpersonal layers—such as friends, biological relatives/"kinship" networks, and members of larger social institutions and organizations (e.g., schools, legal agencies, and social service agencies)—the therapist can ask about relationships with individuals at these various levels and identify stressful interactions that occur (Epstein & Baucom, 2002). Because the couple is also embedded within a larger societal context, broader societal influences such as experiences of racial, ethnic, religious, and/or sexual discrimination may affect their presenting concerns. In addition, the therapist makes systematic inquiries about the couple's physical surroundings, including their immediate living conditions and surrounding neighborhood, which may also place significant demands on the relationship (Epstein & Baucom, 2002).

Whereas the discussion of the relationship history is somewhat unstructured in terms of which partner provides answers to which questions, the discussion of current concerns often necessitates more structure and direction on the therapist's part. Usually the therapist discusses each person's concerns with that individual while the partner listens (Baucom & Epstein, 1990). Structuring the conversation between the therapist and each partner, rather than between both partners, decreases the likelihood of escalation and conflict between partners concerning their perceptions and attributions for the source of their concerns. In addition, structuring the conversations in this manner allows each partner an opportunity to express his/her viewpoint in such a manner that the person feels both heard and respected by the therapist. Partners' understanding that their respective feelings and viewpoints will be acknowledged contributes not only to their investment in treatment, but also to their ability to work collaboratively toward making individual positive changes for both themselves and the relationship.

In addition to identifying current concerns, the therapist identifies existing strengths and resources of the relationship and individual partners. As distressed couples are acutely aware of the weaknesses in their relationship, the therapist seeks to balance the discussion of current problems with noting both historical and current relationship strengths. Discussion of positive aspects of the relationship and individual partners can include noting positive aspects in the earlier phases of the relationship, individual resources that may be valued by the other partner, environmental resources available and used by the couple, and the couple's previous attempts to address relationship concerns. Prior efforts, whether successful or not, can be reframed by the therapist as evidence that the couple has some commitment and skills in working together on the relationship (Wood & Jacobson, 1985). Highlighting such strengths can foster hopefulness in the couple for positive outcomes in treatment.

Finally, the therapist will obtain a sample of the couple's communication skills. Observing the couple's interaction allows the therapist to determine whether specific behavioral interventions may be needed. In addition, observing partners' cognitive, emotional, and behavioral responses to certain partner behaviors and/or relationship topics can serve to highlight broader macro-level themes that may be central issues in the relationship. The therapist can ask the couple to engage in many kinds of tasks, including (1) discussing an area of moderate concern in their relationship, to observe how the couple makes decisions; (2) having each partner share thoughts and feelings about themselves or some aspect of the relationship, to assess the partners' expressive and listening skills; or (3) engaging in a task in which partners provide each other with instrumental or expressive support. In assessing a couple's interaction style, the therapist should individualize the interaction task based on information gathered in the assessment regarding current concerns (Epstein & Baucom, 2002).

Although in clinical practice the interview provides much of the basis for assessment, self-report questionnaires can add significantly to and help guide the initial interview. In general, it is recommended that the therapist selectively utilize self-report measures of (1) partners' satisfaction with important relationship areas of their relationship; (2) each partner's individual and communally oriented needs, and the extent to which those needs are being satisfied; (3) the range of

environmental demands experienced by each partner and the relationship; (4) partners' cognitions
and communication patterns; and (5) strengths
that both partners bring to the relationship (Epstein
& Baucom, 2002). Below we briefly describe inventories that address each of these areas of relationship functioning.

Several measures can be employed to assess
an individual's perception of the quality of their
relationship. The Dyadic Adjustment Scale
(Spanier, 1976) and the Marital Satisfaction Inventory (Snyder, 1979; Snyder, Wills, & Keiser,
1981; Snyder & Costin, 1994) produce global ratings of relationship satisfaction, as well as satisfaction in other areas of functioning, such as
parenting, finances, sexual intimacy, leisure time,
and so forth. The Areas of Change Questionnaire
(Weiss, Hops, & Patterson, 1973) asks couples to
indicate which of 34 partner behaviors they would
like to see changed, as well as how much change
is desired and in what direction. Comparison of
the two partners' responses to these inventories can
provide the therapist with information regarding
discrepancies in partners' degrees of satisfaction
and areas of concern.

The Need Fulfillment Inventory (Prager &
Buhrmester, 1998) assesses each partner's ratings
of importance and fulfillment of those needs
that we categorize as individually oriented (e.g.,
autonomy, self-actualization); communal (e.g.,
nurturance, intimacy, sexual fulfillment); and sur-
vival-related (e.g., health, hunger, physical safety)
(Epstein & Baucom, 2002).

The Family Inventory of Life Events and
Changes (McCubbin & Patterson, 1987) lists descriptions of normative and non-normative events,
such as pregnancy and childbearing, changes in
work status, and deaths, that may be current or
prior sources of demands for the couple (Epstein
& Baucom, 2002).

Numerous measures have been developed to
assess relationship cognitions and communication
behavior patterns, such as the Relationship Belief
Inventory (Eidelson & Epstein, 1982), the Inventory
of Specific Relationship Standards (Baucom,
Epstein, Daiuto, & Carels, 1996; Baucom, Epstein,
Rankin, & Burnett, 1996), and the Communication Patterns Questionnaire (Christensen, 1987,
1988). Although these measures are often used
in research, in clinical practice partners' cognitions and behaviors are assessed primarily through
interviews and behavioral observation. Nevertheless, clinicians can administer these measures as
part of a thorough assessment and/or as guide-

lines for clinical interviews (Epstein & Baucom,
2002).

Although the various measures described
above tap into potential concerns and sources of
conflict for the couple, these instruments also can
be used to assess areas of strength within the relationship. For example, the therapist can note areas of relationship satisfaction on which both partners agree, or stressful life events that the couple
handled successfully.

Often it is helpful to have partners individually complete the inventories prior to their initial
interview, in order to afford the clinician an opportunity to review them and generate hypotheses
and identify areas of concern to be explored in the
interview. As such, we inform every couple that
with few exceptions (e.g., individual responses to
questionnaires regarding psychological and physical abuse that may place a partner at increased risk
for assault), partners' responses are not kept confidential from each other and will be shared, as
appropriate, during the couple assessment.

Although the assessment is characterized as
a distinct phase within CBCT, assessment is continuous, occurring throughout the course of treatment. Use of assessment both as a prerequisite to
treatment and as a tool for continued evaluation
is consistent with the social learning tradition on
which CBCT is based (Baucom & Epstein, 1990).
The therapist continues to consider new information that becomes available in his/her therapeutic
work with the couple. Such an ongoing assessment
provides the therapist with opportunities not only
to monitor the couple's progress in targeted treatment areas and changes in relationship satisfaction,
but also to test hypotheses and refine treatment
conceptualizations generated as a result of the initial assessment.

GOAL SETTING

Conceptualizing Relationship Functioning

Typically, following the initial assessment of couple
functioning, the therapist conducts a feedback session with the couple. During this session, the therapist describes what he/she understands to be the
relevant couple, individual, and environmental
factors that are significantly influencing the couple's
relationship. Whereas the therapist is seen as having expertise in the area of relationships, feedback
is not presented in an authoritative manner. Instead, the therapist structures the feedback, providing input and asking for the partners' perspective

on their own relationship. Based on this feedback and on the therapist and couple's evolving shared conceptualization of the factors influencing the relationship, the couple and therapist together establish their long-term treatment goals and the strategies that will be used to achieve these goals.

This explicit goal setting is important for several reasons. When members of a couple are unclear about why they are unhappy, they often feel out of control. If the partners can understand the important factors affecting their relationship, it can provide them with a sense of hope and understanding of how they can take control to improve their relationship. In addition, the therapist is attempting to set a tone and model an interaction style with the couple in which the participants are open and honest, yet speak to each other in a caring and respectful manner. CBCT therapists assume that it is important for partners to take responsibility for their relationship, and that they can do this most effectively if they share a common conceptualization of relationship functioning, long-term goals, and general strategies for achieving those goals. In addition, CBCT strategies typically involve asking a couple to engage in a variety of activities or homework between sessions. Helping the partners understand the reasons for these tasks or assignments and relate them to treatment goals can increase the likelihood that the couple will follow through with the tasks.

Couples and individual partners vary in the degree to which they have a clear understanding of the factors affecting their relationships, have clear goals, and perceive how they can contribute to strategies that are likely to help them achieve their goals. Some individuals are quite psychologically sophisticated and can provide a rich conceptualization of their relationship functioning. Other individuals seem to be more mystified as to how they have reached the current point in the relationship; they only recognize that they are unhappy and not getting along well. Consequently, the therapist adapts the style and level of complexity of his/her feedback to a level that is helpful to both members of each couple.

The therapist is relatively open and straightforward with the couple about his/her understanding of their relationship. At the same time, this is done with tact and timing and with the realization of what both members of the couple are likely to absorb at a given moment. The therapist describes specific behavior and interaction patterns that are contributing to relationship difficulties. Although the therapist does not wish to give false hope, it is important to structure the feedback and set goals in a way that realistically increases the couple's optimism.

Relating Couple Functioning to Goals for Treatment

In providing assessment feedback, it is important for the therapist to understand the couple's goals for coming to therapy. Sometimes these goals are clear from the beginning; at other times they are not. Understanding the couple's goals is important because the therapist often points out how particular factors play roles in the couple's current distress, and how particular interventions can help address those factors and achieve the couple's goals. For example, a couple tells the therapist that both partners are committed to their marriage and want to stay together. Their overall goal is to decrease arguing with each other and to be happier in their relationship over the long term. If this is the case, as the therapist describes the couple's problematic communication patterns, these can be related to their goal of decreasing the number of arguments. The therapist can then proceed by describing specific aspects of communication skills training that will help to achieve that goal. In contrast, another couple may enter therapy with the explicit goal of ending the relationship. The partners may be seeking intervention because they wish to end their relationship in an amiable fashion, in particular out of concern for the children whom they will continue to coparent. With this goal in mind, the therapist is likely to focus on helping the couple to problem-solve in order to establish constructive guidelines for coparenting, with little emphasis on increasing intimacy between the two partners. At other times, the partners are less certain of their own goals; they simply know that they are unhappy and need some assistance. In such instances, one of the therapist's initial tasks becomes helping the partners to develop a shared set of goals.

Addressing Conflicting Goals between Partners

At times, the goals of the partners may seem to conflict. For example, one partner's goal may be to increase the couple's sense of closeness and intimacy. The other partner may be seeking more distance and autonomy in the relationship. Often the therapist will attempt to help reconcile such seeming differences. For example, establishing high levels of intimacy and autonomy need not be mutually exclusive goals in a relationship. In such a circumstance, the therapist can help the couple explore whether there are ways that they can increase a sense of intimacy when the two partners are together and still promote significant opportunities for autonomy—for both people to grow as individuals.

At times, partners have different goals for the relationship that tend to be mutually exclusive. In such instances, the therapist typically points out these discrepancies, with the goal of helping the couple decide how to promote changes to resolve the differences and reach compromises, accept the differences, or decide whether to continue the relationship if each person's goals are significant and of primary importance to him/her.

Addressing Conflicts between the Couple's and Therapist's Goals

On some occasions, the couple and the therapist may have somewhat different goals for the relationship. For example, a couple may have a very dominant–submissive relationship in which the husband makes most of the decisions. In addition, the wife may be quite depressed, seemingly because of her lack of control within the relationship. The two partners may share the goal of helping the wife to feel less depressed, but they may agree that she should be more accepting of the husband's "rightful role as the head of the household." The couple's therapist might want to help them develop a more egalitarian relationship because of the therapist's own value system, or because research generally suggests that egalitarian relationships are more gratifying to couples (Gray-Little, Baucom, & Hamby, 1996; Gray-Little & Burks, 1983). Consequently, in this example the therapist may be concerned about the couple's treatment goal of maintaining the power imbalance, and may view it as incompatible with their goal of reducing the wife's depression. In such instances, the therapist explains to the couple the reasons why he/she believes that their goals are conflicting, or the possible negative implications of pursuing the goal of maintaining their dominant–submissive roles. The therapist and couple then discuss these differences in perspectives, attempting to develop a common set of goals. At times, the therapist may decide that he/she cannot continue to work with a couple because the couple's goals are not attainable, or because the therapist believes that he/she would

be contributing to an unhealthy, maladaptive relationship. This definition of an unhealthy, maladaptive relationship should not be based on an absolute model of relationship health that the therapist endorses, but rather on a functional analysis of the particular couple.

Addressing Primary versus Secondary Distress

As described earlier, we differentiate between "primary distress" and "secondary distress." By "primary distress," we mean the state of unhappiness and discontent that results when important needs, motives, preferences, and desires of one or both partners are not being met in the relationship. When such important needs as a need for a great deal of intimacy or a strong motivation to achieve in one's profession are not met, a partner may behave in ways to alter the relationship or the other person's behavior. At times the change strategies that result from partners' frustrations and anger at not having their needs met result in other maladaptive behavior patterns, which produce secondary distress. Thus the dissatisfied person may become demanding and manipulative in order to meet his/her needs. These interaction patterns then take on a life of their own and become a secondary set of relationship difficulties. Consequently, when the therapist first sees a couple, often the relationship is at its worst. Understandably, the overt negative interaction patterns that typify many distressed couples are most obvious to the therapist. It is important to alter the tone of the relationship by decreasing these destructive interactions while attempting to help the couple behave in more positive, respectful ways. At the same time, if this is the totality of the treatment, then the couple may still be distressed or may relapse in the future. In essence, the therapist may have established goals to address the secondary distress, but may not have dealt with the primary issues of concern to the couple. In fact, we believe that this factor may help to explain the finding in treatment outcome studies that many couples seeking couple therapy improve but are still in the distressed range at the end of treatment, and why some couples receiving strictly skills-based cognitive-behavioral interventions relapse over the years (Jacobson, Schmaling, & Holtzworth-Munroe, 1987). Thus, in addition to establishing goals to deal with the high levels of distress experienced by many couples when they first arrive for therapy, the therapist also needs to help clarify important and fundamental issues of concern to each couple, and to establish goals for addressing those issues as well.

Sequencing Goals for Treatment

Given that there may be multiple goals in working with a given couple, it is important to determine an appropriate sequence for addressing these goals in therapy. Although each couple is likely to have a unique combination of factors influencing the relationship, some general principles apply. First, the partners must feel that the therapist is addressing important issues in their relationship. If they come for a number of sessions and believe that they are not addressing their central areas of concern, their motivation for treatment is likely to decrease. The therapist must be certain to address important issues in a timely manner.

Second, many couples are ill prepared to address their most central concerns when first entering therapy. This is because the partners have developed such hurtful ways of behaving toward each other that discussion of central issues is difficult. In many instances, both partners have become defensive and unwilling to share their areas of vulnerability. In such a case, the therapist needs to help the couple decrease aversive interactions and establish a more positive, safe atmosphere. Only when a high level of negativity is decreased can most couples begin to address their central concerns in an open and respectful manner. This logic is consistent with many CBCT interventions in which treatment proceeds from less fear-inducing or less difficult topics up a hierarchy to more central and difficult issues.

Third, other couples enter therapy rather distant and uninvolved. In such a couple, an early goal might be to help both persons become more open and emotionally expressive, and engage in a variety of activities to increase a sense of closeness so that they can address other issues in their relationship. In essence, the therapist attempts to create a moderate affective tone, with some notable level of positivity and a minimum of negativity.

Fourth, some goals may be difficult or impossible to attain until other goals are achieved. For example, often therapists are confronted with couples presenting with a variety of relationship concerns, along with dissatisfaction in their sexual functioning. In such a couple, one partner may believe that their sexual relationship would improve if the rest of their relationship were more loving

and respectful. The other partner may conclude that if their sex life were better, then the rest of their relationship would be likely to improve. Thus the partners may propose a different order for addressing their concerns. In dealing with such issues, the therapist must understand how both partners think about these issues and propose an appropriate sequence, providing a rationale to the two partners. In the example given above, we often deal with other relationship issues before attempting to address issues related to sexual intimacy. Many individuals find it distasteful and contrary to their value system to have sex with someone when they do not have a loving, caring relationship with that individual. The therapist can convey to the individual who wants to pursue sexual intimacy first that the couple is likely to have a more mutually enjoyable sexual relationship if other areas of concern that detract from closeness are resolved. It is important not to ask a couple to engage in behaviors that violate one or both persons' personal values, and this may influence the sequencing of interventions.

Finally, pragmatic factors help to determine the order in which goals are addressed. For example, the members of a couple may have a large number of ongoing relationship concerns that they wish to discuss in therapy. In addition, they may need to decide whether one person will take a new job in the next 2 weeks. The immediacy and importance of deciding on the job offer may require that this issue be addressed before others. Other behaviors that put an individual or the couple at risk, such as domestic violence and high-risk behaviors such as excessive drinking, typically require immediate attention.

Relating Treatment Goals to Interventions

An integral part of CBCT is to provide a conceptualization of the factors affecting the couple, to develop goals with the couple, and to relate these goals to specific intervention techniques. Thus the therapist describes to the couple his/her recommendations for how they will attempt to achieve these goals, again soliciting input and feedback from both partners. For example, the therapist may discuss how the couple has developed a negative communication pattern in which neither person seems to listen well to what the other is saying, due to frequent interruptions and escalations. In such an instance, one goal may be to help the couple return to a form of listening and understanding each other, much as they described existed earlier in their relationship. The therapist may then relate this goal to specific intervention techniques focusing on their communication.

In selecting and implementing the intervention techniques, it is important for the therapist to differentiate between interventions that help to achieve intermediate goals during the course of therapy, and interventions that the therapist would recommend the couple to maintain over the long term. For example, we often teach couples communication skills for sharing their thoughts and feelings; also, the listener is taught to reflect back the speaker's thoughts and emotions when the speaker has finished talking. As Gottman (1999) notes, nondistressed couples do not routinely use a great deal of reflection in their conversations. Based on this observation, Gottman questions whether it is appropriate or helpful to teach couples to reflect. However, this seems to be based upon a skill deficit model, in which distressed couples are asked to mirror the behaviors of nondistressed couples. Instead, we believe it is important to think about intermediate goals that will be helpful to a particular distressed couple at a given point in therapy. Many distressed couples seem to benefit from reflective listening. This helps to break a destructive communication pattern of interrupting and not listening. We do not anticipate that the members of such a couple will use this structured communication pattern consistently for the rest of their lives. However, it can help to stop or decrease the destructive interaction pattern that has developed. Once the couple has begun communicating in a more respectful manner, these more structured interventions are not needed. Thus the therapist may develop a wide range of structuring strategies that are beneficial to distressed couples in helping them alter ingrained, destructive interaction patterns. As new patterns develop, these more structured interventions can be relaxed. We explain this to couples, noting that ingrained interaction patterns often are difficult to change and that increased structure can facilitate change.

In order to make the above-described guidelines and recommendations concrete, we now provide excerpts from a feedback session early in therapy.

THERAPIST: Janice and Tom, I'm glad to see you both this evening. As we discussed the last time we met, let's spend some time tonight trying to organize what you have told me thus far, and I'll give you some feedback. I know that the two

of you do not see everything exactly the same way, and that is fine. But I want to make sure that we have a general agreement about what is happening in your relationship. So let's try to pull together what you have told me and discuss how we might work together to improve your relationship.

First, I think that you have a lot going for you as a couple. You generally seem to like and respect each other as people, which I think is important. Also, although things are not going well between the two of you right now, you both still seem to value your relationship and are committed to it. That is critical for helping couples get through difficult times like you are experiencing right now. I think it is also important that you have been able to continue to work well together as parents. That is something that both of you value, and although your personal relationship is having some difficulties, you are still working effectively as a team with Annie. What you think? Do these things seem to fit with your experience?

JANICE: I think what you said is accurate, but that is not how I generally experience it from day to day. I do care a great deal about Tom and respect him, and we are good parents. But all of that seems to get lost with the problems we're having.

TOM: I agree. All of those things are true, but when the rest of our relationship is in such a mess, all the bad stuff seems to take center stage.

THERAPIST: Exactly. I don't want to minimize your problems at all, and what you're describing is what often happens to couples. There are a number of problems, and the good aspects of a relationship seem to get lost when things are not going well. We will certainly address the various concerns that you have, but I also want to help make sure that you don't overlook or minimize the good things in your relationship. So one thing I will recommend that we do is try to shift your focus a bit, so that you can enjoy the good things in your relationship as we continue to work on problems. I have some specific things in mind that I'll suggest to you in a few minutes, OK?

TOM: Absolutely. I would welcome the opportunity to start experiencing what is good in our marriage. I try to stay upbeat and positive, but it usually doesn't last long once we start to argue.

THERAPIST: Let's talk for a few minutes about some of the factors that seem to be contributing to your unhappiness. From what you told me, you were doing pretty well as a couple until 3 years ago, when Annie was born. Then things started to get off track. It's not that Annie is the problem, but having children requires couples to make a major shift in their relationship, and that is really hard for a lot of couples. You both mentioned that while you were dating and early in your marriage, you spent a lot of time together as a couple. You both love the outdoors and exercising, and you participated in a lot of community and environmental organizations together. It seems like those kinds of activities both were a lot of fun and helped bring the two of you close together, giving you a sense of real intimacy. Is that right?

JANICE: I know that's right for me. I had never met anyone like Tom, with whom I felt so at ease and so natural. We had a lot of fun together and worked together on things that we believed in. Now it is so different. We do almost nothing together, and we're even too tired to talk. When we try, we just get into arguments.

THERAPIST: Yes. With the birth of a child, you really move into a different phase of life, and I think you have had some problems making that transition. Before Annie's birth, you both worked full-time and had plenty of financial resources. It sounds like the two of you agreed that you wanted Janice to stay home after Annie was born. That means that you've had a real shift in your roles. Tom, you mentioned that you feel much more pressure now as the sole breadwinner. You've been doing some moonlighting to provide for the family and are working hard to get promoted. That means you have less time and energy when you are at home. Janice, your life has changed in major ways as well. You went from a very active professional life to having most of your day with a 3-year-old and occasionally spending time with other mothers and their children.

I think this change in roles has had several effects. First, you simply don't have as much time for each other because you are focusing a lot of time raising Annie, and it sounds like you are great parents to her. Also, when Tom comes home, he is exhausted and just wants to relax. Janice, you have been waiting all day to have a conversation with another adult, and you get really disappointed when Tom turns to the television or goes to work on the computer. Also, it sounds like the nature of your conversations has shifted. Janice, you mentioned that you don't feel that you have very interesting things to contrib-

ute these days. As a lawyer, you used to talk to Tom about your interesting and complicated cases, but now you don't have much to say other than describing your and Annie's activities of the day. Tom, when you get home, it sounds like you're often distracted or exhausted. Is this what you experience?

TOM: [Tom generally agrees with the therapist's comments.]

THERAPIST: I know it will be challenging, but I think this means that we will want to try to accomplish several things within the context of what is realistic. First, we need to find some time for the two of you to be able to talk with each other when neither of you is exhausted. Also, it sounds like your life has become rather restricted, Janice, and you would like to find some ways to get out into the world more as an adult. This might help you to feel that you have more interesting things to contribute in your conversations with Tom, as well as contact with more adults. Would that be helpful to you?

JANICE: I think it would be great. I don't know how to do that, given how our life is arranged, but I don't think I can stay home with Annie around the clock 7 days a week. I feel like I'm starting to wilt as a human being, and I'm not sure it is good for her either as she is getting older. Life feels so unbalanced right now. I need some time for me, and I think you're right. Tom and I need more time for ourselves as a couple.

The therapist and couple continued to discuss individual, couple, and environmental factors that were affecting the relationship. On an individual basis, both Janice and Tom were experiencing a great deal of pressure from the standards that they held for themselves. With the birth of Annie, Tom felt that in order to be a good husband and father, he must provide financial security and a comfortable lifestyle for the family. Janice had always been successful professionally and now felt a great deal of ambivalence. She wanted to be home with Annie, but felt like a failure both personally and as a woman for assuming a traditional female role in the family. Janice and Tom agreed that they were not dealing with these various stressors very well. Janice's typical style for dealing with problems and concerns was to confront them directly and try to resolve them. Tom's more typical response was to withdraw from stressful situations. Over time, they had developed an extreme demand–withdraw pattern in which Janice tried to engage Tom in discussions about their lack of closeness, her frustrations with her new role, and day-to-day problems that arose. Tom routinely attempted to minimize her concerns, sit quietly, or change the subject. As Janice became more frustrated, she began to confide in her mother, who had always expressed concerns about whether Tom was "good husband material." Tom was hurt, embarrassed, and angry that Janice had shared these concerns with her mother. This created more complications for the couple, as Tom wanted to avoid Janice's mother, who visited with Annie several times a week. Janice felt caught in the middle between Tom and her mother, as each complained about the other to Janice. Thus the therapist and couple discussed how their individual differences in dealing with stress, their standards for being good partners and individuals, their interactional difficulties, and the stresses in dealing with their extended family all contributed to their current concerns that developed within the normal developmental progression of becoming new parents. They also broadly discussed the goals that they would have in couple therapy, with brief mention of strategies to accomplish those goals.

STRUCTURE OF THE THERAPY PROCESS

Traditionally, CBCT has been structured within 8–25 weekly sessions for research purposes, with sessions occurring less frequently during the generalization and maintenance phase of treatment. There are no data available on the length of CBCT in applied settings, but the length of treatment probably varies considerably among therapists and for specific couples. Although it is not always possible to predict how long it will take to work with a couple, it is possible to set reasonable goals for treatment, and for the therapist and both partners to assess the amount of progress made as therapy proceeds (Wood & Jacobson, 1985). If it appears that the goals of therapy may not be met in a reasonable time period, it can be useful to reassess with the couple what goals will be reached during the time allotted for treatment, or to negotiate for additional sessions (Wood & Jacobson, 1985).

THE ROLE OF THE THERAPIST

Successful implementation of CBCT hinges on the therapist's ability to be flexible and effective in undertaking multiple roles when working with a couple. The CBCT therapist may adopt the roles of director, teacher, model, scientist, facilitator, and advocate, possibly juggling multiple roles simultaneously while also providing perspective and emotional support to the couple and individual partners as necessary. This balancing of didactic and supportive roles also hinges on the therapist's ability to balance his/her alliances with the two partners (Wood & Jacobson, 1985). Because individuals and couples vary in their needs for structure and support in addressing their concerns, the true challenge for the CBCT therapist lies in his/her ability to adapt treatment to the needs and broader themes of each individual and couple.

The CBCT therapist typically assumes an active and directive role in treatment, particularly in the early stages of therapy. During the assessment phase, the therapist is active in questioning and gathering data to be used for treatment conceptualization and planning. As therapy progresses, the therapist may take on a didactic role—providing clear and cogent rationales for treatment recommendations and homework assignments, modeling skills to be taught in sessions, and coaching the couple as they practice them. The therapist outlines skills, exercises, and homework assignments so that they serve as opportunities to challenge and foster competency and change in the couple's macro-level cognitive and behavioral patterns, without increasing the partners' frustration, demoralization, or reluctance to attempt future assignments (Wood & Jacobson, 1985). A therapist's level of directiveness, however, will vary according to the couple's presenting concerns; their ability to self-monitor their behaviors, emotions, and cognitions; and their preference or need for structure during therapy (Epstein & Baucom, 2002). As the couple makes progress in therapy, the therapist gradually reduces his/her influence in order to foster the couple's competency and confidence in continuing to make positive, global changes in their relationship after treatment has ended.

Assuming a directive role also requires the ability to maintain control of the sessions, with an air of confidence and credibility. In working with distressed couples, the clinician is likely to encounter couples who have difficulty regulating their levels of emotion and negative behavior, and such patterns are likely to manifest themselves during therapy sessions. It is the therapist's responsibility to actively discourage the escalation of such interactions through interrupting inappropriate behaviors, and through establishing and enforcing guidelines for constructive responses. Although partners may initially bristle at such interventions, it is our experience that most couples respond positively to consistency on the therapist's part in maintaining the structure and ground rules of treatment. The therapist must, however, be judicious in his/her directive efforts, such that they motivate a couple to participate actively and collaboratively in treatment, and do not inappropriately impose the therapist's personal agenda on the couple and risk alienating the clients (Epstein & Baucom, 2002).

The therapist is responsible for facilitating the pace of sessions, so that the goals of treatment are met in a timely and reasonable fashion. The therapist is responsible for working with the couple to set the agenda for each session and to ensure that it is followed. Partners in distress often bring multiple concerns into a given session and are likely to become sidetracked. A typical treatment session may include any of the following: review of homework assigned from the previous session; a review and analysis of the positive and negative events that have occurred in the relationship since the last session; work on a specific problem area; acquisition or practice of a particular skill; cognitive restructuring; a review of the session and presentation of a new homework assignment (LaTaillade & Jacobson, 1995). Therefore, the therapist must be able to intervene and maintain control of the session in order to keep the couple on track and address the goals of the session.

In conducting couple therapy, the therapist is a participant in three relationships: one with each individual partner, and one with the couple as a whole. Within each of these relationships, the therapist provides support, empathy, and guidance in facilitating change in broader relationship patterns. However, even the most experienced of couple therapists can have difficulty in simultaneously meeting each of these goals in all three relationships. As such, over the course of treatment, the therapist must balance his/her alliances and interventions with each partner and the couple, so that both partners feel supported and invested in improving the relationship. It is not unusual to shift attention and interventions between partners and the dyad as treatment progresses, particularly if one partner presents with significant individual and psychological distress. Over the course of therapy, such temporary imbalances may be therapeutically beneficial, as long as such imbalances are discussed with the couple and counterbalanced in the long run (Wood & Jacobson, 1985).

Conducting couple therapy involves particular ethical and professional concerns, beyond those involved in clinical work with individual clients (Epstein & Baucom, 2002). Attention to such ethical concerns is critical in building the therapeutic alliance with the couple. As the therapist is working not just with the couple as a unit, but also with two individual partners, the establishment and maintenance of confidentiality become a central issue at the outset of treatment. If an individual's current or prior experience does not appear to exert a significant impact on the couple's relationship or course of treatment, it is recommended that the therapist not press the individual to disclose it to his/her partner (Epstein & Baucom, 2002). When an individual privately discloses to the therapist an experience that is adversely affecting the relationship and may compromise the stated goals of treatment (e.g., ongoing participation in an extramarital affair), the therapist can inform the individual how withholding such information and continuing couple therapy places the therapist in an ethically untenable position. The therapist can then either (1) strategize with the individual ways of disclosing this information to the other partner; or (2) work with the person to find a way to discontinue therapy, if the individual does not want to stop the behavior. Therapists must clearly inform couples about their guidelines for maintaining or breaking confidentiality. For additional guidelines for addressing ethical and professional issues in couple therapy, the reader is directed to Brock (1994), Huber (1994), and Margolin (1982).

COMMONLY USED INTERVENTIONS

CBCT therapists have developed a wide variety of interventions to assist couples. In differentiating among these interventions, it is important to recognize that behaviors, cognitions, and emotions are integrally related. Changes in one domain typically produce changes in the other domains. Thus, if a husband starts to think about his wife differently and understand her behavior in a more benign way, he is likely to have more positive emotional reactions to her and behave toward her in more positive ways as well. Furthermore, an individual's subjective experience is typically a blend of cognitions and emotions that are not clearly differentiated from each other. Therefore, as we discuss interventions focused on behavior, cognitions, and emotions, it is with recognition that these distinctions are made partially for heuristic purposes, and that most interventions affect all these domains of relationship functioning. Specific interventions are often focused on one of these domains, with the explicit intent that other aspects of functioning will be altered simultaneously.

Earlier, we have explained the importance of understanding the roles that individual factors, couple interactive processes, and the environment play in a couple's relationship. Each of these domains can be addressed in terms of the behaviors, cognitions, and emotions focal to that domain. For example, a therapist can focus upon a wife's attributions for why her husband keeps long work hours, her emotional reaction to his behaviors, and her subsequent behavior toward him. Similarly, if a couple needs assistance from the social environment outside their relationship, the therapist can address their standards regarding the appropriateness of seeking outside support, their emotional responses to being helped by others, and the specific actions that they might take to receive assistance. Consequently, any of these interventions for behavioral, cognitive, or emotional factors can be focused on the individual partners, the couple as a dyad, or the couple's interaction with the environment.

Interventions for Modifying Behaviors

CBCT initially focused explicitly on partners' behaviors, with little explicit attention to their cognitions and emotions. The logic behind this approach was that if partners began to behave more positively toward each other, they would think and feel differently toward each other. Hence there has always been a strong emphasis on helping members of couples behave in more constructive ways with each other, and this emphasis continues in our current conceptualization. There are many specific behavioral interventions that the therapist can employ with the couple, but they fall into two categories: guided behavior change and skills-based interventions (Epstein & Baucom, 2002).

Guided Behavior Change

"Guided behavior change" involves interventions that focus on behavior change without a skills component. At times, these interventions have been referred to as "behavior exchange interventions," but this term can be misleading. Typically, these interventions do not involve an explicit exchange of behaviors in a quid pro quo fashion. In fact, it is helpful for the therapist to discuss with

the couple the importance of each person's committing to make constructive behavior changes, regardless of the other person's behavior (Halford, Sanders, & Behrens, 1994). In providing interventions of this type, we might introduce them as follows: "What I want each of you to do is to think about how you would behave if you were being the kind of partner that you truly want to be. What does that mean that you would do and not do? If you behave in this manner, it is likely to have two very positive consequences. First, your partner is likely to be much happier. Second, you are likely to feel better about yourself. One thing that frequently happens when couples become distressed is that they stray from the kinds of behaviors in which they themselves like to engage. So I want you to get back to being the kind of person that you enjoy being in the relationship, that brings out the best in you as an individual." Thus we rarely attempt to establish rule-governed behavior exchanges, as were common in the early days of BCT (Jacobson & Margolin, 1979). Instead, we work together with partners to develop a series of agreements about how they want to make changes in their relationship to meet the needs of both people, help the dyadic relationship function effectively, and interact positively with their environment.

These types of guided behavior changes can be implemented at two levels of specificity and for different reasons. First, a couple and therapist may decide that they need to change the overall emotional tone of the relationship. As Birchler, Weiss, and Vincent (1975) discussed, often members of couples behave more constructively when interacting with strangers than they do with their partners; this is evidenced among happy relationships as well as distressed ones. Consequently, a therapist and couple may decide that it is important to decrease the overall frequency and magnitude of negative behaviors and interactions, and to increase the frequency and magnitude of positive behaviors.

Several interventions have been developed for shifting this overall ratio of positives to negatives. These include "love days" (Weiss et al., 1973) and "caring days" (Stuart, 1980). Although they vary in their specific guidelines and recommendations, these interventions generally involve having each partner decide on enacting a number of positive behaviors to make the other person happier. This might include such small day-to-day efforts as bringing in the newspaper, washing dishes after dinner, making a phone call during the work day to say hello, and so forth. Typically, these types of interventions are used when the therapist and couple conclude that the partners have stopped making much effort to be caring and loving toward each other, have allowed themselves to become preoccupied with other demands, and have treated their relationship as a low priority. In essence, these rather broad-based interventions are intended to help the partners regain a sense of relating in a respectful, caring, thoughtful manner.

Guided behavior change can also be used in a more focal manner. As part of the initial assessment, the therapist and couple typically focus on important issues and themes that serve as the basis of the relationship distress. For example, the couple may be struggling because the wife needs a great deal more autonomy than the relationship currently supports. She may want additional time alone to read, exercise, or take walks. However, the responsibilities of the family along with other responsibilities may make this difficult. In such an instance, guided behavior change may focus on her desire for increased autonomy, and the husband might seek ways during the week to provide her with these opportunities. Rather than attempting to shift the overall balance of positives to negatives, more focal guided behavior change interventions can be designed around important issues and needs that one or both people have noted as central to their well-being.

Skills-Based Interventions

In contrast to guided behavior changes, skills-based interventions typically involve the therapist's providing the couple with instruction in the use of particular behavioral skills, through didactic discussions and/or through other media (e.g., readings, videotapes). The instruction is followed by opportunities for the couple to practice behaving in the new ways. Communication training has typically involved this format. Labeling these as "skill-based interventions" suggests that the partners lack the knowledge or skill to communicate constructively and effectively with each other, although this is often not the case. Many couples report that their communication was open and effective at earlier points in their relationship, but as frustrations have mounted, they now communicate with each other in destructive ways, or they have greatly decreased the amount of communication. Regardless of whether this is a skill deficit or a performance deficit, discussing guidelines for constructive communication can be helpful to couples in provid-

ing the structure they need to interact in constructive ways. We often differentiate between two major goals of communication between partners: couple conversations focusing on sharing thoughts and feelings, and decision-making or problem-solving conversations (Baucom & Epstein, 1990; Epstein & Baucom, 2002).

Guidelines for these two types of communication are provided in Tables 2.1 and 2.2, respectively. These guidelines are presented as recommendations for couples, not as rigid rules. Certain points can be emphasized, and the guidelines can be altered depending on the needs of specific couples. For example, the guidelines for expressiveness emphasize sharing both thoughts and feelings. If the therapist is working with a rather intellectualized couple whose members avoid emotions and address issues on a purely cognitive level, then emphasizing the expression of emotion might become paramount. As Prager (1995) has noted, an important part of intimacy is sharing what is personal and vulnerable in an interaction within which one feels understood. Therefore, if this intellectualizing couple complains about a lack of closeness and connectedness, then an emphasis on sharing emotions is appropriate.

Similarly, during decision-making conversations, we do not routinely ask that all couples brainstorm a variety of alternative solutions before discussing each one. However, if a couple's typical pattern includes each partner's presenting his/her own preferred solution, followed by the couple's arguing over the two proposals to the point of a stalemate, brainstorming may be helpful because it helps the partners avoid their restrictive approach and premature commitment to a particular solution. Likewise, in the decision-making guidelines, some attention is given to implementing the agreed-upon solution. For some couples, reaching a mutually agreed-upon solution is the difficult task. Once they have agreed on a solution, they are effective in carrying it out. Other couples reach solutions more readily, but they rarely implement their agreements. If the latter pattern becomes evident during the course of therapy, the therapist can pay more attention to helping the partners implement their solutions more effectively. In fact, the couple and therapist can problem-solve on how to increase the likelihood that the solution will be implemented; they can talk at length about possible barriers to following through, and ways that both people can be reminded about the agreement during the week.

TABLE 2.1. Guidelines for Couple Discussions

Skills for sharing thoughts and emotions

1. State your views *subjectively*—as your own feelings and thoughts, not as absolute truths. Also, speak for *yourself*—what you think and feel, not what your partner thinks and feels.
2. Express your *emotions* or feelings, not just your *ideas*.
3. When talking about your partner, state your feelings about your partner, not just about an event or a situation.
4. When expressing *negative* emotions or concerns, also include any *positive* feelings you have about the person or situation.
5. Make your statement as *specific* as possible, both in terms of specific emotions and thoughts.
6. Speak in "paragraphs." That is, express one main idea with some elaboration and then allow your partner to respond. Speaking for a long time period without a break makes it hard for your partner to listen.
7. *Express* your feelings and thoughts with *tact* and *timing*, so that your partner can listen to what you are saying without becoming defensive.

Skills for listening to your partner

Ways to respond while your partner is speaking

1. Show that you *understand* your partner's statements and accept his/her right to have those thoughts and feelings. Demonstrate this *acceptance* through your tone of voice, facial expressions, and posture.
2. Try to put yourself *in your partner's place* and look at the situation from his/her perspective, in order to determine how the other person feels and thinks about the issue.

Ways to respond after your partner finishes speaking

3. After your partner finishes speaking, *summarize* and restate your partner's most important feelings, desires, conflicts, and thoughts. This is called a *reflection*.
4. While your are in the listener role, *do not*:
   a. Ask questions, except for clarification.
   b. Express your own viewpoint or opinion.
   c. Interpret or change the meaning of your partner's statements.
   d. Offer solutions or attempt to solve a problem if one exists.
   e. Make judgments or evaluate what your partner has said.

The guidelines for both types of conversations focus primarily on the *process* of communicating, with no particular attention to the *content* of conversations. In addition, it is important for the therapist and couple to develop a joint conceptualization of the primary themes in the couple's areas of concern. These major themes and issues should be taken into account while the couple engages in these conversations. For example, if a lack of intimacy is a major issue for a couple, when the partners have conversations they can emphasize ways of taking some chances to become more vulnerable, such as discussing more personal issues with each other. Alternatively, a couple may be distressed about the distribution of control and power in the relationship, with one person resentful that the more verbal and forceful partner typically dominates the "joint" decisions. Consequently, decision-making conversations may be central to shifting this couple dynamic. The therapist may propose that when the couple discusses possible solutions,

each person put forth a proposed solution before a final decision is made. The therapist may also recommend that before the solution is accepted, both partners clarify whether it contains at least some of each person's preferences, and if not, whether that seems appropriate. Thus the theme of control and power can be addressed explicitly within decision-making conversations.

In essence, during skills training the therapist should be attentive to both the process of communication and the way the couple addresses important themes and issues in their relationship. In earlier approaches to CBCT, therapists commonly restricted their role to being coaches, focusing on the communication process and attending little to the content of what the partners were discussing. We believe that these interventions can be used more effectively if the communication process and the important themes in the couple's relationship are addressed simultaneously. This perspective means that the therapist may not always be a neu-

TABLE 2.2. Guidelines for Decision-Making Conversations

1. *Clearly and specifically state what the issue is.*
   a. Phrase the issue in terms of behaviors that are currently occurring or not occurring or in terms of what needs to be decided.
   b. Break down large, complex problems into several smaller problems, and deal with them one at a time.
   c. Make certain that both people agree on the statement of the problem and are willing to discuss it.

2. *Clarify why the issue is important and what your needs are.*
   a. Clarify why the issue is important to you, and provide your understanding of the issues involved.
   b. Explain what your needs are that you would like to see taken into account in the solution; do not offer specific solutions at this time.

3. *Discuss possible solutions.*
   a. Propose concrete, specific solutions that take both people's needs and preferences into account. Do not focus on solutions that meet only your individual needs.
   b. Focus on solutions for the present and the future. Do not dwell on the past or attempt to attribute blame for past difficulties.
   c. If you tend to focus on a single solution or a limited number of alternatives, consider brainstorming (generating a variety of possible solutions in a creative way).

4. *Decide on a solution that is feasible and agreeable to both of you.*
   a. If you cannot find a solution that pleases both partners, suggest a compromise solution. If a compromise is not possible, agree to follow one person's preferences.
   b. State your solution in clear, specific, behavioral terms.
   c. After agreeing on a solution, have one partner restate the solution.
   d. Do not accept a solution if you do not intend to follow through with it.
   e. Do not accept a solution that will make you angry or resentful.

5. *Select a trial period to implement the solution if the situation will occur more than once.*
   a. Allow for several attempts of the new solution.
   b. Review the solution at the end of the trial period.
   c. Revise the solution if needed, taking into account what you have learned thus far.

tral party when a couple is proposing specific solutions to a problem. If a given solution seems contrary to the couple's overall goals and to the changes that are needed in the relationship, the therapist may point this out and express concern about the solution.

This approach also means that at some point during the couple's decision-making conversation, the therapist may provide educational information that would help to guide the conversation. Thus, if a couple is discussing how the partners might be supportive to each other in addressing work stresses, the therapist may provide information about various types of social support that individuals generally find to be helpful. The partners can then take this information into account and discuss how it applies to their relationship. Similarly, if a couple whose child has challenging behavior problems is discussing parenting issues, the therapist might present didactic "minilectures" or provide the partners with reading materials about parenting strategies, which they can take into ac-

count in making their decisions. We believe that this is an important shift within CBCT, providing a needed balance between addressing interactive processes and attending to the content of a couple's concerns.

Interventions That Address Cognitions

The ways in which people behave toward each other in committed, intimate relationships have great meaning for the participants and a capacity to evoke strong positive and negative emotional responses in each person. For example, individuals often have strong standards for how they believe the two partners should behave toward each other in a variety of domains. If an individual's standards are not met, he/she is likely to become displeased. Similarly, an individual's degree of satisfaction with a partner's behavior can be influenced by the attributions that the person makes about the reasons for the partner's actions. Thus a husband may prepare a nice dinner for his wife, but whether she interprets this as a positive or negative behavior is likely to be influenced by her attribution or explanation for his behavior. If she concludes that he is attempting to be thoughtful and loving, she may experience his dinner preparation as positive. However, if she believes that he wishes to buy a new computer and is attempting to bribe her by preparing dinner, she may feel manipulated and experience the same behavior as negative. In essence, partners' behaviors in intimate relationships carry great meaning, and not considering these cognitive factors can limit the effectiveness of treatment. Elsewhere, we have enumerated some cognitive variables that are important in understanding couples' relationships (Baucom & Epstein, 1990; Epstein & Baucom, 2002):

- *Selective attention*—what each person notices about the partner and the relationship.
- *Attributions*—causal and responsibility explanations for couple events.
- *Expectancies*—predictions of what will occur in the relationship in the future.
- *Assumptions*—what each partner believes people and relationships actually are like.
- *Standards*—what each partner believes people and relationships should be like.

These types of cognitions are important, because they help to shape how each individual experiences the relationship. The therapist does not attempt to have the partners reassess their cognitions simply because they are negative. Instead, the therapist is concerned if one or both partners seem to be processing information in a markedly distorted manner. Thus an individual may selectively attend to instances when a partner is forgetful, paying little attention to other ways in which the partner accomplishes various tasks successfully. Similarly, this same individual might attribute the partner's failure to accomplish particular tasks as due to a lack of respect for the individual's preferences, and as clearly reflecting a lack of love. Understandably, such cognitions are likely to be related to negative emotions such as anger, and under such circumstances the individual is likely to behave negatively toward the partner.

Therefore, at times the focus of therapy will not be on changing behavior, but rather on helping the partners reassess their cognitions about behaviors that are occurring or not occurring, so that these behaviors can be viewed in a more rea-

sonable and balanced fashion. Many different cognitive intervention strategies can be used, some of which are as follows:

- Evaluate experiences and logic supporting a cognition.
- Weigh advantages and disadvantages of a cognition.
- Consider worst and best possible outcomes of situations.
- Provide educational minilectures, readings, and tapes.
- Use inductive "downward arrow" method.
- Identify macro-level patterns from cross-situational responses.
- Identify macro-level patterns in past relationships.
- Increase relationship schematic thinking by pointing out repetitive cycles in couple interaction.

Epstein and Baucom (2002) provide a detailed description of each of these intervention strategies, which can help the couple create a more balanced, reasonable perspective on the individual partners, the relationship, or the environment. In implementing these interventions, the therapist tends to emphasize one of two broad approaches: (1) Socratic questioning and (2) guided discovery.

Socratic Questioning

Cognitive therapy has often been equated with "Socratic questioning," which involves a series of questions to help an individual reevaluate the logic of his/her thinking, understand the underlying issues and concerns that are not at first apparent, and so forth. In work with distressed couples, such interventions can be effective but should be used cautiously. The context for individual therapy is quite different from that of couple therapy. In individual therapy, the individual participates alone and works with a caring, concerned therapist with whom he/she can be open and honest in reevaluating cognitions. In couple therapy, however, the individual's partner is in the room. Often the partner has explicitly blamed the individual for their relationship problems, frequently telling the individual that his/her thinking is distorted. Consequently, if a therapist begins to question one partner's thinking in the presence of the other partner, such efforts may be unsuccessful. With the other person present, an individual is more likely to be defensive and unwilling to acknowledge that his/her thinking has been selective or biased to some degree against the other person. If one individual acknowledges that he/she was thinking in an extreme or distorted way, the other partner may use this against the individual in the future: "Thank goodness you finally admitted it. I've been telling you for years that your thinking is all messed up." Therefore, if the therapist asks a person a series of questions that seem somewhat confrontational in front of a critical or hostile partner, it can arouse the person's defensiveness. These interventions may be more successful with a couple in which the two partners are less hostile and hurtful toward each other.

Guided Discovery

"Guided discovery" involves a wide variety of interventions in which the therapist creates experiences for a couple that lead one or both partners to question their thinking and develop a different perspective on the partner or relationship. For example, if a man notices his partner's withdrawal and interprets it as her not caring about him, the therapist can address this attribution in a variety of ways. First, the therapist can use Socratic questioning and ask the individual to think of a variety of interpretations for his partner's behavior. The therapist can then ask this individual to look for evidence either supporting or refuting each of those possible interpretations. On the other hand, the therapist can structure an interaction in which the man obtains additional information that begins to alter his attributions. For example, the therapist may ask the couple to have a conversation in which the woman shares what she was thinking and feeling at the time when she withdrew. During the conversation, the man may find out that his partner withdrew because she was feeling hurt and cared about him a great deal. Her vulnerability, rather than a lack of caring, might have been the basis of her withdrawal. This new understanding and experience may alter the man's perspective without the therapist's questioning his thinking directly. Similarly, a woman may develop an expectancy or prediction that her partner does not care about her perspective on a variety of issues. If, however, they agree to start having such conversations on a weekly basis and she sees that he is attentive and interested in her perspective when she expresses it, her predictions may change. Thus the therapist in collaboration with the couple may devise a variety of experiences to help the partners experience their relationship differently, either with or without additional behavior change.

Some cognitions involve a set of standards for how a partner should behave in a committed relationship. Standards are not addressed primarily by assessing their logic, because they are not based on logic. Instead, standards for relationships are addressed more appropriately with methods that focus on the advantages and disadvantages of living according to them. Here we provide a detailed discussion of addressing relationship standards as one example of cognitive restructuring with couples. These standards may involve an individual's behavior (e.g., whether an individual should be allowed to curse when upset), the ways the partners interact with each other (e.g., whether it is acceptable to express disagreement with each other openly), or the ways they interact with the environment (e.g., how much time one should devote to an ailing parent). In general, in addressing relationship standards, we proceed through the following steps:

- Clarify each person's existing standards.
- Discuss advantages and disadvantages of existing standards.
- If standards need alteration, help revise to form new acceptable standards.
- Problem-solve on how new standards will be taken into account behaviorally.
- If partners' standards continue to differ, discuss ability to accept differences.

In essence, we discuss how any given standard relevant to the couple usually has some positive and negative consequences. First, it is important to clarify each person's standards in a given domain of the relationship. For example, the partners may differ on their standards for how one spends free time. A husband may conclude that, given that the couple has little free time, he and his wife should spend all of it together. On the other hand, the wife may believe that partners should spend some free time together, but that it is critical to have a significant amount of time away from one's partner as well. Once the partners are able to articulate their standards regarding time together and alone, each is asked to describe the pros and cons of conducting a relationship according to those standards. Thus the husband is asked to describe the good things that would result from spending all or almost all of their time together, as well as potential negative consequences. The wife is invited to add to his perspective. Similarly, the wife is asked to list the pros and cons of spending some free time together and some free time apart, with the husband adding his perspective. Without intervention, partners often become polarized during this phase, with each person emphasizing the positive consequences of his/her perspective, and the other partner noting the negative consequences of the person's point of view. When each person is encouraged to share both the positive and negative consequences of his/her standard, this polarization can be avoided or minimized.

After the partners fully discuss their different standards concerning an aspect of their relationship, they are asked to think of a moderated standard that would be responsive to both partner's perspectives and would be acceptable to each person. Because individuals typically cling strongly to their standards and values, rarely is an individual likely to give up his/her standards totally. Much greater success results from slight alterations in standards that make them less extreme or more similar to the other person's standards. After the couple agrees on a newly evolved standard, they are asked to reach decisions regarding how this new standard would be implemented in their relationship on a daily basis, in terms of concrete behaviors that each person would exhibit.

Interventions Focused on Emotions

Whereas many behavioral and cognitive interventions influence an individual's emotional responding in a relationship, at times more explicit attention needs to be paid to emotional factors in the relationship. In particular, therapists often work with couples in which one or both partners demonstrate either restricted or minimized emotions or excessive emotional responses. Each of these broad domains includes more specific emotional difficulties that individuals experience, with particular interventions that are appropriate.

Restricted or Minimized Emotions

Many partners in committed relationships seem to be uncomfortable with emotions in general or with specific emotions. This discomfort can take a variety of forms. Sometimes it typifies a person's experiences in life in general; at other times it is more focal to the current relationship. In some instances, these difficulties may warrant cognitive or behavioral interventions—for example, if one partner believes that it is extremely rude to express anger and therefore suppresses his/her own ex-

pression of it, and censures the partner for expressing it. In other instances, a person reports experiencing minimal amounts of certain emotions. To a degree, this may reflect the individual's temperament, or it may be the result of being raised in a family or culture in which certain emotions were rarely expressed. Some individuals experience both positive and negative emotions, but their levels of emotional experience are so muted that they do not find their experiences within their relationships very gratifying. Similarly, the partner of such an individual may complain that it is unrewarding to live with someone who has such restricted emotional responses.

In addition, some individuals may have stronger emotional experiences but are somewhat limited in their ability to differentiate among different emotions. They know that they feel very good or very bad, but cannot articulate or differentiate internally the emotions that they are experiencing. The ability to make such differentiations can be helpful to both the individual and his/her partner. For example, if an individual can clarify that he/she is feeling sad, this can often lead both members of the couple to understand that the person experiences a sense of loss, which then can be addressed. More explicit differentiation and expression of emotions may help partners understand and perhaps feel closer to each other.

Likewise, some individuals experience difficulty relating emotions to their internal and external experiences. Thus a wife may know that she is quite angry, but she cannot relate this to what she is thinking or to experiences that occurred in an interaction with her husband. This difficulty can make both persons feel that they have little control over the relationship and are at the mercy of the individual's emotions, which appear to occur in an unpredictable manner rather than in connection with specific thoughts or behaviors.

Finally, some individuals avoid what Greenberg and Safran (1987) refer to as "primary emotions" that are related to important needs and motives. Often individuals avoid the experience or expression of these emotions because they are seen as dangerous or as making the individuals vulnerable. As a result, Greenberg and Safran propose that people cover these primary emotions with "secondary emotions" that seem safer or less vulnerable. Consequently, rather than experiencing fear and anxiety and expressing these to a critical partner, an individual may experience negative feelings such as anger and hostility, which are less threatening and help the individual feel less vulnerable.

The following strategies can help individuals access and heighten emotional experience; these interventions are drawn primarily from the emotionally focused therapy developed by Johnson and Greenberg (Johnson, 1996; Johnson & Greenberg, 1987):

- Normalize emotional experience, both positive and negative.
- Clarify thoughts and then relate these to emotions.
- Use questions, reflections, and interpretations to draw out primary emotions.
- Describe emotions through metaphors and images.
- Discourage an individual's attempts to distract him-/herself from experiencing emotion.
- Encourage acceptance of the individual's experience by the partner.

These interventions are based on several broad principles. First, the therapist tries to create a safe atmosphere; normalizing the experience and expression of both positive and negative emotions can contribute largely to this. In addition, the therapist promotes this safe environment by encouraging the partner to respond to the individual in a caring and supportive manner when the person expresses various emotions. Even so, the individual may attempt to avoid an emotion or escape once the session focuses on emotions. Therefore, the therapist may refocus the individual on an emotional experience and expression if the individual shifts the focus of the session; of course, this must be done with appropriate timing and moderation, in order to avoid overwhelming the individual.

Once a safe environment is created, other strategies can be used to heighten emotional experience. These interventions may include asking an individual to recount a particular incident in detail, ideally evoking the emotional aspect of this experience; encouraging the individual to use metaphors and images to express emotions, if directly labeling emotions is difficult or frightening; and using questions, reflections, and interpretations to draw out primary emotions. Although some trial and error are likely in the process of finding the most effective strategies for each individual, the therapist's goal is to help the individual enrich his/her emotional experience and expres-

sion in a manner that is helpful to both the individual and the couple. A decision to focus on this category of interventions should not be based on a therapist's belief that a "healthy" person should have a rich emotional life as well as a full range of emotional expression; instead, the decision to use such interventions should be based on a careful assessment that this restriction in emotional experience and/or expression is interfering with this particular couple's, or the partners', well-being.

Containing the Experience/Expression of Emotions

At the other end of the continuum, a therapist may be confronted with partners who have difficulty regulating their experience and expression of emotion. Typically, this is of concern to the couple if one or both partners are experiencing and expressing high levels of *negative* emotion or is expressing these emotions in settings that are not appropriate. At the same time, there are couples in which one person's extreme exuberance and frequent expression of strong *positive* emotion can become problematic. At times, one person can feel overwhelmed by being around another individual who is so excited, upbeat, and happy on an ongoing basis. Although this overall positive tone is pleasurable to most individuals, the resulting atmosphere when it is expressed in an extreme fashion may not feel relaxing, and the partner may feel that it is inappropriate to express negative feelings when the other individual is so happy all the time. Even so, clinicians more typically confront couples in which one person seems to have difficulty regulating the experience and expression of negative emotions. A therapist may find such a couple quite demanding, because the couple's life appears to revolve around a series of emotional crises, strong arguments, or extreme behaviors (including partner abuse) that result from extreme negative emotions.

Several strategies seem to be applicable to assisting couples in such circumstances. As noted above, often behavioral and cognitive interventions can be of assistance. For example, if an individual is frequently upset and angry because of the partner's inappropriate behavior, then the therapist will probably focus on behavioral interventions to alter the unacceptable behavior. Similarly, if an individual is frequently upset because that person has extreme standards that few partners could satisfy, then focusing on those standards is appropriate. In addition, there are more focal interventions to address extreme emotional experiences. Several of these are as follows:

- Schedule times for partners to discuss emotions and related thoughts.
- Encourage "healthy compartmentalization."
- Help partners seek alternative means to communicate feelings and elicit support.
- Help partners tolerate distressing feelings.

The first useful strategy listed above is for the couple to schedule times to discuss issues that are upsetting to one or both partners. The goal of this intervention is to restrict or contain the frequency and settings in which strong emotions are expressed. If a couple has not set aside times to address issues, then an individual with poor affect regulation is more likely to express strong feelings whenever they arise. Some people find that they can resist expressing strong negative feelings if they know there is a time set aside to address concerns. This intervention can be helpful in making certain that problems and expression of strong negative affect do not intrude into all aspects of the couple's life. In particular, this can be helpful in ensuring that strong negative expression does not occur at times that are likely to lead to increasing frustration for one or both persons. For example, expressing strong anger when one person is leaving the house to go to work or initiating a conversation with strong negative emotion once the couple has turned off the light to go to sleep likely will result in further upset for both people.

Linehan (1993) has proposed a variety of interventions to assist individuals with poor affect regulation. Although her interventions do not focus on addressing strong affect in an interpersonal context, they are often applicable in such a context. One of these interventions involves teaching individuals to tolerate distressing emotions. Some individuals seem to assume that if they are upset, they should do something immediately to alter their emotional experience, frequently resulting in strong expressions of emotion to their partners. Helping such individuals accept and become comfortable with being upset with their partners or their relationship, without addressing every concern immediately, can be helpful. Similarly, it can be helpful to teach such an individual how to focus on the here and now, the current moment. Many individuals with poor affect regulation allow their upset in one domain of life to intrude or infiltrate many other aspects of their

lives. We explain placing limits on this intrusion to couples as a form of "healthy compartmentalization." That is, it is important to be upset about a given aspect of one's relationship; however, it is also important to restrict that sense of upset to this one issue, and to allow oneself to enjoy other positive and pleasurable aspects of the relationship when they occur.

Finally, it can be helpful to seek alternative ways to communicate feelings and elicit support, perhaps from individuals other than one's partner. For instance, relying on other friends for expressing some of one's concerns, keeping a journal or diary to express one's emotions, or pursuing other alternatives for releasing tension and strong emotion can be productive for the individual. This approach is not intended as an alternative to addressing an individual's concerns with a partner, but rather as a means for moderating the frequency and intensity with which the person's emotions are expressed. Attempting to teach these strategies and skills to an individual in a couple context can be difficult and at times is implausible. Often the other person serves as a strong negative stimulus to the individual who has difficulty regulating emotion. When this is the case, individual therapy for the person who has poor affect regulation may be of assistance, in addition to working jointly with the couple.

A CASE EXAMPLE

With this broad range of intervention strategies in mind, we provide a brief summary of the couple therapy with Janice and Tom, who have been described earlier in this chapter. As noted in the feedback session, the therapist believed that a major factor in their relationship difficulties involved their transition to parenthood and their difficulties in responding to the demands of this new stage of their family life cycle. In particular, with their role overload and frequent arguments, each partner tended not to notice the positive aspects of their relationship or the other person's efforts. Consequently, to counteract this selective attention to negativity, the therapist asked each partner to write down one positive thing that the other person did each day, to compliment or express appreciation to that individual for these actions, and to bring the list to therapy for further discussion.

A significant portion of treatment involved helping Janice and Tom recognize that they were in a new phase of their family life cycle with Annie as a 3-year-old. The therapist taught the partners communication skills, which helped them to share their thoughts and feelings more fully, and to reach decisions or problem-solve. These communication skills were used in important discussions about the couple's standards for what their relationship should be like with a 3-year-old child. As they continued with these discussions, they concluded that they had drifted away from their own value system. Tom acknowledged that that he experienced significant pressure to create a comfortable and secure lifestyle for the family, moonlighting and working extra to earn more money. Whereas security remained important to the couple, they concluded that during this phase of their life they wanted to live a simpler lifestyle and focus on their marriage, each other, and Annie. Janice also concluded that her role had become too restricted as a mother, and that she was in danger of stifling her personal growth and well-being. They agreed that she would return part-time to her law practice; with this increased financial income, Tom would stop moonlighting and spend more time with the family. Tom and Janice also discussed how to spend more time with each other and agreed that it was easier to have lunches together during the day, when they had regular child care, than to arrange evening outings. They also agreed that Tom had spent little time developing his relationship with Annie. Therefore, they agreed that each weekend he would spend one morning or afternoon with Annie, which would also give Janice time to herself.

The stresses of parenthood also highlighted each partner's typical style of dealing with stress; as noted earlier, Janice was a person who liked to address it directly, whereas Tom tended to withdraw. Tom clarified that it was particularly difficult for him to discuss problematic issues when Janice became angry and expressed her feelings loudly. Through intensive effort, Janice learned to express her distress in a more contained way. Tom explained that he feared that when Janice became loud, there would be "explosions," as he had witnessed between his parents while growing up. The therapist emphasized the importance of continuing the conversations so that he could experience his relationship with Janice as different, and noted that discussing difficult issues does not inevitably lead to destructiveness.

Finally, the partners discussed how to address their relationship with Janice's mother and what they could realistically expect. They agreed that it was unproductive for Janice to complain to her mother about Tom, because her disclosures only fueled her mother's negative feelings toward Tom. Janice agreed to discuss her concerns with her female friends, and she would emphasize telling her mother positive things about Tom. When Janice's mother was present, Tom would not withdraw to the computer; instead, he would help Janice with household tasks and spend time with Annie, so that her mother would have the opportunity to see his contributions to the family.

Overall, couple therapy was quite helpful to Janice and Tom. This intervention included an emphasis on cognitive factors (selectively attending to positives in the relationship, standards for this phase of marriage, and expectancies for Tom's relationship with Janice's mother and his fear of "explosions" with Janice); emotional factors (Janice's efforts to contain her anger to a greater degree); and behavioral factors (including numerous discussions and problem-solving interactions resulting in significant behavior change). Therapy for Janice and Tom lasted approximately 6 months, with weekly sessions tapering off over the course of treatment. Two years after the couple terminated treatment, they recontacted their therapist when they were struggling with the birth of their second child. They returned for several booster sessions, which were beneficial to them. The course of this treatment is typical for many distressed couples: They make significant improvement but continue to struggle with some of the inherent difficulties and stresses in life, along with their typical interaction styles. Similarly, it is not unusual for couples to seek additional intervention after therapy has terminated. Rather than viewing such returns as treatment "failures," we encourage couples to use us as consultants in their relationship when needed.

MECHANISMS OF CHANGE

Neither CBCT nor any other theoretical approach to addressing relationship distress has demonstrated strong, consistent findings that isolate the mechanisms of change in couple therapy. More particularly, both Iverson and Baucom (1990) and Halford et al. (1993) unexpectedly found that changes in communication skills during CBCT did not predict couple adjustment at the end of treatment. Furthermore, a review of the treatment outcome literature demonstrates that various theoretical approaches to addressing relationship distress are equally efficacious (Baucom et al., 1998). Combining these sets of findings would suggest that no specific mechanism of change is critical to under-standing relationship functioning for all couples. Instead, different couples may need different types of interventions, and different mechanisms of change may be important. In some couples, the partners may need to understand and experience each other in different ways. Other couples may need significant behavioral change. Some couples may need to focus on the partners' ways of inter-acting with each other. Some couples may need to learn how to provide social support to one part-ner who experiences frequent depression. Other couples may need to learn how to adapt to a highly stressful and external environment. There are prob-ably many different specific interventions and theo-retical perspectives to help couples achieve these varied goals.

Even if we optimize treatment by considering a variety of interventions and theoretical perspec-tives, we must remain cautious about what we can achieve. Even if the partners begin to interact with each other in the ways described above, they may not wish to spend their lives with each other. As couple therapists, we do not know how to create "chemistry" or "sparks" between two partners. We can help partners to create healthy, adaptive ways of interacting with each other, which allow indi-viduals and relationships to reach their potential, whatever that might be.

TREATMENT APPLICABILITY

Most routinely, CBCT has been employed with distressed couples, as described throughout this chapter. In addressing such issues, CBCT has proven to be an efficacious treatment in alleviat-ing relationship distress. CBCT has been demon-strated to be efficacious relative to wait-list control groups (Baucom & Lester, 1986; Baucom, Sayers, & Sher, 1990), and as efficacious as BCT in im-proving couple adjustment and communication (Baucom & Lester, 1986; Baucom et al., 1990; Halford et al., 1993).

CBCT is also applicable to a wide range of specific relationship concerns. A particular class of relationship distress involves couples that have experienced relationship trauma, such as infidel-ity. Traumatic experiences within a relationship can be addressed from a CBCT perspective but require some additional consideration, as described in Part II, Section A of the current volume, and by Gor-don and associates (Gordon & Baucom, 1998,

1999; Gordon, Baucom, & Snyder, 2000). In addition, these same CBCT principles have been adapted to prevent distress and to assist couples in which one partner is experiencing health prob-lems. Although these latter two applications are beyond the scope of this chapter, the results of investigations to date are promising, and excellent descriptions of these applications are provided else-where (Markman & Hahlweg, 1993; Markman, Stanley, & Blumberg, 1994; Schmaling & Sher, 2000). Furthermore, cognitive-behavioral interven-tions have been used when one or both persons experience individual psychopathology along with relationship distress, and these interventions are described in Part II, Section C of this volume. Finally, CBCT can be employed to help a dis-tressed couple whose relationship is complicated by long-standing, unresolved personal issues for one or both partners. We discuss this last applica-tion in more detail below.

Long-Standing, Unresolved Personal Issues

In addition to diagnosable psychopathology, individuals may have had negative relationship experiences in their family of origin or prior ro-mantic relationships that continue to influence patterns in the current relationship. Such unre-solved issues can result in extreme beliefs, emo-tional reactions, and behavioral responses that, while understandable in their prior relationships, do not "fit" the current relationship and lead to inappropriate responses to the current partner. Such an individual develops a set of core beliefs, or schemas, about relationships that leads him/ her to categorize, select, and encode information in a way that supports and maintains extreme beliefs, behaviors, and emotional responses (Epstein & Baucom, 2002).

As with addressing individual psychopathol-ogy, the therapist must decide whether such issues are best addressed in an individual or a conjoint format. Several factors that should be taken into account in deciding about individual versus couple therapy include (1) the severity and pervasiveness of the individual's issues; (2) the individual's level of insight and awareness of his/her issues; and (3) the partner's responses to the individual's disclo-sure and his/her ability to work collaboratively with the individual (Epstein & Baucom, 2002).

Several general principles are important in addressing unresolved personal issues in couple therapy. First, as in individual psychopathology, these previous experiences should be addressed in a way that does not lead to a characterization of the individual as "sick" or pathological. Rather, this exploration should clarify how the individual's response was an adaptive or understandable attempt to cope with a difficult set of prior circumstances. Such an approach may foster empathic understanding from the individual's partner, as well as minimization of defensiveness on the individual's part. Second, exploration of the individual's past may facilitate his/her awareness of how the current relationship is different from the prior relationships, and therefore no longer necessitates use of previous cognitive, emotional, and behavioral responses. Third, the individual and the partner must both be willing to confront these difficult situations and work collaboratively in attempting to create alternate behavioral patterns. As these response patterns are overlearned and well ingrained, much time and effort will be required to unlearn them and develop more adaptive ones. Fourth, it is important for the partners to develop a collaborative perspective toward helping the individual, as change in the couple's micro- and macro-level patterns necessitates concomitant individual changes from both partners. Finally, in many instances, both partners must recognize that they are dealing with an area of vulnerability for the individual. Despite progress and continued efforts, at times the individual is likely to return to former patterns of thinking, feeling, and behaving. The couple should be cautioned to expect the inevitability of such lapses, in order to reduce frustration and discouragement, and to encourage the couple to persist in making positive changes (Epstein & Baucom, 2002).

Across all interventions, the therapist must understand what the individual's long-standing personal issues are, how these issues are exacerbated or maintained within the relationship, how the fulfillment of communal and individual needs is organized around these personal issues, and what changes can be expected in the individual and the relationship as a result of appropriate and effective treatment of both the individual and couple. Through such an understanding, the therapist can decide how to sequence interventions and integrate various individual and relational concerns within conjoint treatment. If the relationship is not highly distressed and the individual's personal issues do not stem from relational difficulties, the therapist may begin by focusing on individual concerns and gradually broaden the focus to the relationship. In instances in which an individual's symptoms are due to relationship distress, frequently therapy can focus on the relationship. However, there is rarely a firm distinction between focusing on the relationship and focusing on the individual (Epstein & Baucom, 2002). The CBCT therapist must be flexible both within and across sessions in his/her ability to shift focus on the individual and the couple, and in his/her ability to shift between types of interventions.

A FINAL CAVEAT

In determining what constitutes a "good outcome" in couple therapy, researchers usually evaluate whether specific couples increase in their levels of relationship adjustment or some other index of their happiness in the relationship. This is certainly a relevant variable, but perhaps it is too narrow. At times, it seems likely that terminating a relationship is a healthy and adaptive outcome for couple therapy. Unfortunately, we have no criteria for establishing this prior to treatment, and for researchers it constitutes post hoc thinking to conclude that divorce is a good outcome after treatment has terminated. Although creating complexities from a research perspective, instances do seem to exist in which the growth and development of one or both individuals is facilitated by ending the current relationship. The treatment outcome literature suggests that only one-third to one-half of couples are in the adjusted range of relationship functioning at the end of CBCT (Jacobson et al., 1984). This may suggest that our interventions are limited; however, continued efforts to improve on this response rate, either by altering an intervention or by attempting to apply different theoretical perspectives, thus far have been unsuccessful. These results probably suggest to some degree that not all partners have the potential to be happy with each other. Initial mate selection is likely to be a critical factor in the potential satisfaction and happiness of the couple. Unfortunately, cognitive-behavioral approaches to relationship functioning have not emphasized this factor. It seems unlikely that any two randomly matched people can join together and be happy for the rest of their lives. From a clinical perspective, therapists must be sensitive to the fact that treatment directed toward preservation of the relationship may be detrimental to the individual partners, and that termination of a relationship may constitute a clinically viable and positive therapeutic outcome.

SUMMARY

In this chapter, we have attempted to demonstrate how CBCT has evolved over the past several decades and how it has continued to develop as new empirical findings emerge and the utility of other theoretical orientations is taken into account. Evolving from an early, almost exclusive focus on behavior change, the model that we currently propose now incorporates an equal emphasis on behaviors, cognitions, and emotions. Furthermore, rather than focusing only on couple interactive processes, the current conceptualization is broader and also includes an emphasis on individual factors (both normal individual differences and psychopathology) and environmental factors. In addition, we recommend that therapists be attentive to broader relationship themes or macro-level patterns that can help to unify many of the specific concerns raised by couples; developmental change must be taken into account, along with gender, ethnic background, and other factors that affect a couple's functioning across the life span. Not all these factors will be of equal importance with a given couple, but being attentive to the myriad of factors that influence a couple's functioning places the CBCT therapist in the best position to assist a wide variety of couples.

REFERENCES

Bandura, A. (1977). *Social learning theory.* Englewood Cliffs, NJ: Prentice-Hall.

Bandura, A., & Walters, P. (1963). *Social learning and personality development.* New York: Holt, Rinehart & Wilson.

Baucom, D. H. (1999, November). *Therapeutic implications of gender differences in cognitive processing in marital relationships.* Paper presented at the 33rd Annual Meeting of the Association for Advancement of Behavior Therapy, Toronto.

Baucom, D. H., & Epstein, N. (1990). *Cognitive-behavioral marital therapy.* New York: Brunner/Mazel.

Baucom, D. H., Epstein, N., Daiuto, A. D., & Carels, R. A. (1996). Cognitions in marriage: The relationship between standards and attributions. *Journal of Family Psychology, 10,* 209–222.

Baucom, D. H., Epstein, N., & Gordon, K. C. (2000). Marital therapy: Theory, practice, and empirical status. In C. R. Snyder & R. E. Ingram (Eds.), *Hand-*

book of psychological change: Psychotherapy processes and practices for the 21st century (pp. 280–308). New York: Wiley.

Baucom, D. H., Epstein, N., & Rankin, L. A. (1995). Cognitive aspects of cognitive-behavioral marital therapy. In N. S. Jacobson & A. S. Gurman (Eds.), *Clinical handbook of couple therapy* (pp. 65–90). New York: Guilford Press.

Baucom, D. H., Epstein, N., Rankin, L. A., & Burnett, C. K. (1996). Assessing relationship standards: The Inventory of Specific Relationship Standards. *Journal of Family Psychology, 10,* 72–88.

Baucom, D. H., & Lester, G. W. (1986). The usefulness of cognitive restructuring as an adjunct to behavioral marital therapy. *Behavior Therapy, 17,* 385–403.

Baucom, D. H., Sayers, S. L., & Sher, T. G. (1990). Supplementing behavioral marital therapy with cognitive restructuring and emotional expressiveness training: An outcome investigation. *Journal of Consulting and Clinical Psychology, 58,* 636–645.

Baucom, D. H., Shoham, V., Mueser, K. T., Daiuto, A. D., & Stickle, T. R. (1998). Empirically supported couples and family therapies for adult problems. *Journal of Consulting and Clinical Psychology, 66,* 53–88.

Beck, A. T., Rush, A. J., Shaw, B. F., & Emery, G. (1979). *Cognitive therapy of depression.* New York: Guilford Press.

Birchler, G. R., Weiss, R. L., & Vincent, J. P. (1975). Multimethod analysis of social reinforcement exchange between maritally distressed and nondistressed spouse and stranger dyads. *Journal of Personality and Social Psychology, 31*(2), 349–360.

Brock, G. W. (Ed.). (1994). *American Association for Marriage and Family Therapy: Ethics casebook.* Washington, DC: American Association for Marriage and Family Therapy.

Butzlaff, R. L., & Hooley, J. M. (1998). Expressed emotion and psychiatric relapse: A meta-analysis. *Archives of General Psychiatry, 55,* 547–552.

Carter, B., & McGoldrick, M. (Eds.). (1999). *The expanded family life cycle: Individual, family, and social perspectives* (3rd ed.). Boston: Allyn & Bacon.

Christensen, A. (1987). Detection of conflict patterns in couples. In K. Hahlweg & M. J. Goldstein (Eds.), *Understanding major mental disorder: The contribution of family interaction research* (pp. 250–265). New York: Family Process.

Christensen, A. (1988). Dysfunctional interaction patterns in couples. In P. Noller & M. A. Fitzpatrick (Eds.), *Monographs in social psychology of language: No. 1. Perspectives on marital interaction* (pp. 31–52). Clevedon, England: Multilingual Matters.

Christensen, A., & Heavey, C. L. (1990). Gender and social structure in the demand/withdraw pattern of marital conflict. *Journal of Personality and Social Psychology, 59*(1), 73–81.

Christensen, A., & Heavey, C. L. (1993). Gender differences in marital conflict: The demand/withdraw interaction pattern. In S. Oskamp & M. Costanzo (Eds.), *Claremont Symposium on Applied Social Psychology: Vol. 6. Gender issues in contemporary society* (pp. 113–141). Newbury Park, CA: Sage.

Christensen, A., & Shenk, J. L. (1991). Communication, conflict, and psychological distance in nondistressed, clinic, and divorcing couples. *Journal of Consulting and Clinical Psychology, 59,* 458–463.

Christensen, A., & Sullaway, M. (1984). *Communication Patterns Questionnaire*. Unpublished manuscript, University of California–Los Angeles.

Cutrona, C. E. (1996). Social support in marriage: A cognitive perspective. In G. R. Pierce, B. R. Sarason, & I. G. Sarason (Eds.), *Handbook of social support and the family* (pp. 173–194). New York: Plenum Press.

Cutrona, C. E., Cohen, B., & Igram, S. (1990). Contextual determinants of the perceived supportiveness of helping behaviors. *Journal of Social and Personal Relationships, 7*, 553–562.

Cutrona, C. E., Hessling, R. M., & Suhr, J. A. (1997). The influence of husband and wife personality on marital social support interactions. *Personal Relations, 4*, 379–393.

Cutrona, C. E., & Suhr, J. A. (1992). Controllability of stressful events and satisfaction with spouse support behaviors. *Communication Research, 19*, 154–174.

Cutrona, C. E., & Suhr, J. A. (1994). Social support communication in the context of marriage: An analysis of couples' supportive interactions. In B. Burleson, T. Albrecht, & I. Sarason (Eds.), *The communication of social support: Messages, interactions, relationships, and community* (pp. 113–125). Newbury, CA: Sage.

Cutrona, C. E., Suhr, J. A., & MacFarlane, R. (1990). Interpersonal transactions and the psychological sense of support. In S. Duck & R. Silver (Eds.), *Personal relationships and social support* (pp. 30–45). London: Sage.

Eidelson, R. J., & Epstein, N. (1982). Cognition and relationship maladjustment: Development of a measure of dysfunctional relationship beliefs. *Journal of Consulting and Clinical Psychology, 50*, 715–720.

Epstein, N., & Baucom, D. H. (2002). *Enhanced cognitive-behavioral therapy for couples: A contextual approach*. Washington, DC: American Psychological Association.

Falloon, I. R. H. (1991). Behavioral family therapy. In A. S. Gurman & D. P. Kniskern (Eds.), *Handbook of family therapy* (Vol. 2, pp. 65–95). New York: Brunner/Mazel.

Fincham, F. D., Bradbury, T. N., & Scott, C. K. (1990). Cognition in marriage. In F. D. Fincham & T. N. Bradbury (Eds.), *The psychology of marriage: Basic issues and applications* (pp. 118–149). New York: Guilford Press.

Gordon, K. C., & Baucom, D. H. (1998). Understanding betrayals in marriage: A synthesized model of forgiveness. *Family Process, 37*, 425–449.

Gordon, K. C., & Baucom, D. H. (1999). A forgiveness-based intervention for addressing extramarital affairs. *Clinical Psychology: Science and Practice, 6*, 382–399.

Gordon, K. C., Baucom, D. H., & Snyder, D. K. (2000). The use of forgiveness in marital therapy. In M. E. McCullough, K. Pargament, & C. Thoresen (Eds.), *Forgiveness: Theory, research, and practice* (pp. 203–227). New York: Guilford Press.

Gottman, J. M. (1979). *Marital interaction: Experimental investigations*. New York: Academic Press.

Gottman, J. M. (1999). *The marriage clinic: A scientifically based marital therapy*. New York: Norton.

Gray-Little, B., Baucom, D. H., & Hamby, S. L. (1996). Marital power, marital adjustment, and therapy outcome. *Journal of Family Psychology, 10*, 292–303.

Gray-Little, B., & Burks, N. (1983). Power and satisfaction in marriage: A review and critique. *Psychological Bulletin, 93*, 513–538.

Greenberg, L. S., & Johnson, S. M. (1988). *Emotionally focused therapy for couples*. New York: Guilford Press.

Greenberg, L. S., & Safran, J. D. (1987). *Emotion in psychotherapy: Affect, cognition, and the process of change*. New York: Guilford Press.

Hahlweg, K., & Markman, H. J. (1988). Effectiveness of behavioral marital therapy: Empirical status of behavioral techniques in preventing and alleviating marital distress. *Journal of Consulting and Clinical Psychology, 56*, 440–447.

Halford, W. K., Sanders, M. R., & Behrens, B. C. (1993). A comparison of the generalization of behavioral marital therapy and enhanced behavioral marital therapy. *Journal of Consulting and Clinical Psychology, 61*(1), 51–60.

Halford, W. K., Sanders, M. R., & Behrens, B. C. (1994). Self-regulation in behavioral couples' therapy. *Behavior Therapy, 25*, 431–452.

Holtzworth-Munroe, A., & Jacobson, N. S. (1991). Behavioral marital therapy. In A. S. Gurman & D. P. Kniskern (Eds.), *Handbook of family therapy* (Vol. 2, pp. 96–133). New York: Brunner/Mazel.

Huber, C. H. (1994). *Ethical, legal and professional issues in the practice of marriage and family therapy* (2nd ed.). New York: Macmillan.

Iverson, A., & Baucom, D. H. (1990). Behavioral marital therapy outcomes: Alternate interpretations of the data. *Behavior Therapy, 21*, 129–138.

Jacobson, N. S., & Christensen, A. (1996). *Integrative couple therapy: Promoting acceptance and change*. New York: Norton.

Jacobson, N. S., Follette, W. C., Revenstorf, D., Baucom, D. H., Hahlweg, K., & Margolin, G. (1984). Variability in outcome and clinical significance of behavioral marital therapy: A reanalysis of outcome data. *Journal of Consulting and Clinical Psychology, 52*, 497–504.

Jacobson, N. S., & Holtzworth-Munroe, A. (1986). Marital therapy: A social learning/cognitive perspective. In N. S. Jacobson & A. S. Gurman (Eds.), *Clinical handbook of marital therapy* (pp. 29–70). New York: Guilford Press.

Jacobson, N. S., & Margolin, G. (1979). *Marital therapy: Strategies based on social learning and behavior exchange principles*. New York: Brunner/Mazel.

Jacobson, N. S., Schmaling, K. B., & Holtzworth-Munroe, A. (1987). Component analysis of behavioral marital therapy: 2-year follow-up and prediction of relapse. *Journal of Marital and Family Therapy, 13*, 187–195.

Johnson, S. M. (1996). *The practice of emotionally focused marital therapy*. New York: Brunner/Mazel.

Johnson, S. M., & Greenberg, L. S. (1987). Emotionally focused marital therapy: An overview. *Psychotherapy, 24*(3S), 552–560.

Karney, B. R., & Bradbury, T. N. (1995). The longitudinal course of marital quality and stability: A review of theory, methods, and research. *Psychological Bulletin, 118*(1), 3–34.

LaTaillade, J. J., & Jacobson, N. S. (1995). Behavioral couple therapy. In M. Elkaim (Ed.), *Therapies familiales: Les principles approaches [Family therapies: The principal approaches]* (pp. 313–347). Paris: Editions du Seuil.

Liberman, R. P. (1970). Behavioral approaches to family and couple therapy. *American Journal of Orthopsychiatry, 40*, 106–118.

Linehan, M. M. (1993). *Cognitive-behavioral treatment of borderline personality disorder*. New York: Guilford Press.

Margolin, G. (1982). Ethical and legal considerations in marital and family therapy. *American Psychologist, 37*(7), 888–801.

Markman, H. J., Duncan, W., Storaasli, R. D., & Howes, P. W. (1987). The prediction and prevention of marital distress: A longitudinal investigation. In K. Hahlweg & M. J. Goldstein (Eds.), *Understanding major mental disorder: The contribution of family interaction research* (pp. 266–289). New York: Family Process.

Markman, H. J., & Hahlweg, K. (1993). The prediction and prevention of marital distress: An international perspective. *Clinical Psychology Review, 13,* 29–43.

Markman, H. J., Stanley, S. M., & Blumberg, S. L. (1994). *Fighting for your marriage: Positive steps for preventing divorce and preserving a lasting love.* San Francisco: Jossey-Bass.

McCubbin, H. I., & Patterson, J. M. (1987). FILE: Family Inventory of Life Events and Changes. In H. I. McCubbin & A. I. Thompson (Eds.), *Family assessment inventories for research and practice* (pp. 81–98). Madison: University of Wisconsin–Madison, Family Stress Coping and Health Project.

Pasch, L. A., & Bradbury, T. N. (1993). *Observation of social support transactions in marriage.* Paper presented at the 27th Annual Meeting of the Association for Advancement of Behavior Therapy, Atlanta, GA.

Pasch, L. A., Bradbury, T. N., & Davila, J. (1997). Gender, negative affectivity, and observed social support behavior in marital interaction. *Personal Relationships, 4,* 361–378.

Pasch, L. A., Bradbury, T. N., & Sullivan, K. T. (1997). Social support in marriage: An analysis of intra-individual and interpersonal components. In G. R. Pierce, B. Lakey, I. G. Sarason, & B. R. Sarason (Eds.), *Sourcebook of theory and research on social support and personality* (pp. 229–256). New York: Plenum Press.

Patterson, G. R. (1974). Interventions for boys with conduct problems: Multiple settings, treatments, and criteria. *Journal of Consulting and Clinical Psychology, 42,* 471–481.

Patterson, G. R., & Hops, H. (1972). Coercion, a game or two: Intervention techniques for marital conflict. In R. E. Ulrich & P. Mounjoy (Eds.), *The experimental analysis of social behavior.* New York: Appleton.

Prager, K. J. (1995). *The psychology of intimacy.* New York: Guilford Press.

Prager, K. J., & Buhrmester, D. (1998). Intimacy and need fulfillment in couple relationships. *Journal of Social and Personal Relationships, 15,* 435–469.

Rankin, L., Clayton, D. C., & Baucom, D. H. (1996, November). *Life Schema Questionnaire: Revision and validation of a self-report measure of relationship versus individual schema.* Paper presented at the 30th Annual Meeting of the Association for Advancement of Behavior Therapy, New York.

Rankin, L. A., Baucom, D. H., Clayton, D. C., & Daiuto, A. D. (1995, November). *Gender differences in the use of relationship schemas versus individual schemas in marriage.* Paper presented at the 29th Annual Meeting of the Association for Advancement of Behavior Therapy, Washington, DC.

Rankin-Esquer, L. A., Baucom, D. H., Clayton, D. C., Tomcik, N., & Mullens, J. A. (1999). Cognitive processing in intimate relationships: Relationship schemas and individual schemas. Manuscript in preparation.

Rankin-Esquer, L. A., Clayton, D. C., Baucom, D. H., & Mullens, J. A. (1997, November). *Individual versus relationships schema use: Replication of a priming procedure in an adult, married population.* Paper presented at the 31st Annual Meeting of the Association for Advancement of Behavior Therapy, Miami, FL.

Revenstorf, D., Hahlweg, K., Schindler, L., & Vogel, B. (1984). Interaction analysis of marital conflict. In K. Hahlweg & N. S. Jacobson (Eds.), *Marital interaction: Analysis and modification* (pp. 159–181). New York: Guilford Press.

Rotter, J. B. (1954). *Social learning and clinical psychology.* Englewood Cliffs, NJ: Prentice-Hall.

Schmaling, K. B., & Sher, T. G. (Eds.). (2000). *The psychology of couples and illness: Theory, research, and practice.* Washington, DC: American Psychological Association.

Snyder, D. K. (1979). Multidimensional assessment of marital satisfaction. *Journal of Marriage and the Family, 41,* 813–823.

Snyder, D. K., & Costin, S. E. (1994). Marital Satisfaction Inventory. In M. E. Maruish (Ed.), *The use of psychological testing for treatment planning and outcome assessment* (pp. 322–351). Hillsdale, NJ: Erlbaum.

Snyder, D. K., & Wills, R. M. (1989). Behavioral versus insight-oriented marital therapy: Effects on individual and interspousal functioning. *Journal of Consulting and Clinical Psychology, 57,* 39–46.

Snyder, D. K., Wills, R. M., & Keiser, T. W. (1981). Empirical validation of the Marital Satisfaction Inventory: An actuarial approach. *Journal of Consulting and Clinical Psychology, 49*(2), 262–268.

Spanier, G. B. (1976). Measuring dyadic adjustment: New scales for assessing the quality of marriage and similar dyads. *Journal of Marriage and the Family, 38,* 15–28.

Stuart, R. B. (1969). Operant interpersonal treatment for marital discord. *Journal of Consulting and Clinical Psychology, 33,* 675–682.

Stuart, R. B. (1980). *Helping couples change: A social learning approach to marital therapy.* New York: Guilford Press.

Sullivan, L. J., & Baucom, D. H. (2000). *Relationship Schematic Processing coding manual.* Unpublished manuscript, University of North Carolina–Chapel Hill.

Thibaut, J. W., & Kelley, H. H. (1959). *The social psychology of groups.* New York: Wiley.

Weiss, R. L. (1980). Strategic behavioral marital therapy: Toward a model for assessment and intervention. In J. P. Vincent (Ed.), *Advances in family intervention, assessment and theory* (Vol. 1, pp. 229–271). Greenwich, CT: JAI Press.

Weiss, R. L., Hops, H., & Patterson, G. R. (1973). A framework for conceptualizing marital conflict, a technology for altering it, some data for evaluating it. In M. Hersen & A. S. Bellack (Eds.), *Behavior change: Methodology, concepts and practice* (pp. 309–342). Champaign, IL: Research Press.

Wood, L. F., & Jacobson, N. S. (1985). Marital distress. In D. H. Barlow (Ed.), *Clinical handbook of psychological disorders.* New York: Guilford Press.

Chapter 3

Object Relations Couple Therapy

JILL SAVEGE SCHARFF
CARL BAGNINI

Object relations couple therapy was developed from psychoanalysis of the object relations school and modified by modern advances in group therapy (D. Scharff & Scharff, 1987). It also has some features in common with the two other major models, behavioral and systems approaches, which were arrived at from quite different theoretical viewpoints (Gurman, 1978). This technical flexibility has been welcomed by Gurman and Jacobson (1986) as a sign of willingness to learn from other models so as to identify the common ground of therapeutic efficacy. Granted that all the major models deal with thoughts, feelings, and behaviors, and with the interactions among the mind, the body, the significant other, and the environment, what distinguishes the object relations approach? It is based on a psychoanalytic view of marriage, derived from a psychoanalytic object relations model of the mind of the individual and from group analytic theory applied to the small group of two; it also employs technique that is generally psychoanalytic in orientation, though not in format. Before we describe object relations couple therapy in depth, we look at some early psychoanalytic applications to understanding and treating families and couples.

Before object relations theory entered the mainstream of American psychoanalysis, psychoanalytic theory had quite an impact on couple therapy through its influence on the early family therapists. Ackerman, Bowen, Cooklin, Lidz, Minuchin, Selvini Palazzoli, Stierlin, Shapiro,

Watzlawick, Wynne, Zilbach, and Zinner were all graduates of analytic training programs. Andolfi, Byng-Hall, and Jackson had analytic training. Framo and Paul were influenced by analytic theory, and Skynner was a group analyst. Working in the 1960s and 1970s with Haley, Bateson, and Weakland (the communications and systems family theorists at the Palo Alto Mental Research Institute), Satir and the Institute's directors Jackson and Riskin (both of whom had analytic training), along with Watzlawick (formerly a Jungian training analyst), integrated psychoanalytic understanding with systems models and preserved a concern for the individual as well as for the family life group. Sullivan's (1953) interpersonal psychiatry offered a relational view that was kept out of the mainstream of psychoanalysis, but it succeeded in influencing Ryckoff (Ryckoff, Day, & Wynne, 1959) and Wynne (1965), who, however, were mainly interested in families rather than couples. According to Bodin (1981), Sullivan's (1953) interpersonal theory of etiology and psychotherapy influenced Jackson, while the Chicago Institute of Psychoanalysis influenced Satir's training at the Chicago School of Social Work and led to her interest in corrective emotional experiences and in the importance of self-concept and self-esteem.

Skynner (1976) applied Freud's (1905) concept of fixation and regression to family functioning. Shapiro and Zinner showed how families that are more in tune with the attitudes of an earlier developmental stage are unable to proceed to the developmental tasks of adolescence (Shapiro, 1979; Zinner & Shapiro, 1972). Although all of these writers addressed the subject of marriage, they tended not to emphasize developmental regression and fixation in couple dynamics. Bowen (1978) noted that spouses tend to operate at a similar "level of differentiation," by which he meant that spouses tend to be at the same distance along the developmental path toward personal integrity, with a capacity for tolerating anxiety, appreciating self and otherness, and taking responsibility for one's own being and destiny (Friedman, 1991). Zilbach (1988), taking off from Erikson (1950), applied a developmental perspective to the family life cycle and described how changes in family needs appropriate to changing developmental stages alter the parents' functioning as a couple; however, marriage was not her primary focus. Though rare, the developmental perspective on marriage can be quite revealing.

Sager and colleagues (Sager, 1976; Sager et al., 1971), who noted that intrapsychic factors determine transactional aspects of a couple relationship, found that conflict dynamics specific to the marriage contract must be interpreted in terms of the spouses' unconscious wishes and aims.

By the late 1950s, partners were seen separately in simultaneous psychotherapy (Thomas, 1956; Dicks, 1957) or together by the same therapist—an approach called "conjoint therapy," a term credited to Jackson by Broderick and Schraeder (1981). Greene (1970) and collaborating cotherapists used individual, concurrent, and conjoint psychoanalytic therapy sessions in a combination which, though flexible, had to adhere to a predictable sequence (Hollender, 1971; Zinner, 1989). Against the mainstream, some object relations and self-psychological analysts persevered to understand the effects of complementary neuroses of the marriage partners on mate selection and in married life. Kohut's (1971, 1977, 1982) self-psychological theory of narcissistic character pathology, and Kernberg's (1975) theory of ego splits and alternating ego states in borderline pathology, have been applied to the couple relationship by Lansky (1986), Kernberg (1991), and Solomon (1989).

OBJECT RELATIONS THEORY APPLIED TO COUPLE THERAPY

Basic Object Relations Terminology and Models

Object relations psychoanalytic theory is the one brand of psychoanalysis that also illuminates fam-

ily dynamics (D. Scharff & Scharff, 1987, 1991; J. S. Scharff, 1989). An individual psychology drawn from study of the relationship between patient and therapist, object relations theory holds that the motivating factor in growth and development of the human infant is the need to be in a relationship with a mothering person, not the discharge of energy from sexual and aggressive, life-and-death instincts. Impulses and driven activity are seen not as primary elemental forces, but as desperate attempts to relate or as breakdown products of failed relationships. According to Sutherland (1980), object relations theory is an amalgam of the work of British Independent group analysts Balint (1968), Fairbairn (1952), Guntrip (1961, 1969), and Winnicott (1951/1958, 1958, 1965, 1971), and of Klein (1948, 1957) and her followers. Of them all, Fairbairn gave the most systematic challenge to Freudian theory. His schema of the endopsychic situation (Fairbairn, 1963) was picked up by Dicks (1967), who applied it to his work with spouses. Bannister and Pincus (1965), Clulow (1985), Dare (1986), Main (1966), Pincus (1960), and Skynner (1976) in Britain, and Framo (1970/1982), Martin (1976), Meissner (1978), Nadelson (1978), D. Scharff and Scharff (1987, 1991), Willi (1984), and Zinner (1976, 1988) in the United States, all acknowledge the influence of Dicks's work on the psychoanalytic model of couple interaction. In his study of unconsummated marriages, Friedman (1962) integrated Dicks's concepts with those of Balint. Bergmann (1987, 1990) applied Dicks's formulation to his study of love. McCormack (1989), who applied Winnicott's concept of the holding environment to the borderline–schizoid marriage, Finkelstein (1987), Slipp (1984), and Stewart, Peters, Marsh, and Peters (1975) all advocated an object relations approach to the theory of couple therapy.

Before we describe Dicks's model of couple dynamics, we need to summarize Fairbairn's (1944/1952, 1954) theory of the individual and then extend it to the relational context (J. S. Scharff & Scharff, 1998). In Fairbairn's view, the infant is not the inchoate conglomerate of drives that Freud described. The infant is born with a whole self through which it regulates affect and executes behaviors that secure the necessary relatedness. Infant research has now corroborated this view of the infant as competent (Schore, 1994; Stern, 1985). The infant is looking for attachment, not discharge. As the infant relates to the mother (or mothering person), attachment develops. Out of the vicissitudes of this experience, psychic structure is built. The experience—even with a reasonably good mother who responds well to her infant's regulatory cycles (Brazelton, 1982; Brazelton & Als, 1979)—is always somewhat disappointing in that needs cannot be met before they cause discomfort, unlike the situation in the womb. When the frustration is intolerable, the infant perceives the mother as rejecting. To cope with the pain, the infant takes in ("introjects") the experience of the mother as a rejecting object, and rejects that image inside the self by "splitting" it off from the image of the ideal mother and pushing it out of consciousness ("repressing" it). This is called the "rejected object." It is further split into its need-exciting and need-rejecting aspects, associated with feelings of longing and rage, respectively. The part of the self that related to this aspect of the mother is also split off from the original whole self and is repressed, along with the relevant unbearable feelings. Now the personality consists of (1) a "central self" attached with feelings of satisfaction and security to an "ideal internal object"; (2) a "craving self" longingly, but unsatisfyingly, attached to an "exciting internal object"; and (3) a "rejecting self" angrily attached to a "rejecting internal object."

Fairbairn's terms for the unconscious parts of self and object were "libidinal ego" and "exciting object," and "antilibidinal ego" and "rejecting object"; however, these terms have been discarded in favor of the "exciting" and "rejecting" parts of the ego and objects, respectively. The exciting part of the ego is sometimes called the "craving self," as suggested by Ogden (1982). Along with the relevant affects, the exciting and rejecting egos and their objects form two repressed, unconsciously operating systems of self called "internal object relationships." Fairbairn's genius was to recognize that the rejecting object relationship system further suppresses the exciting object relationship system. Now we have a view of the personality in which exciting and rejecting subsystems of the central self are in dynamic interaction with each other. Dicks's genius was to see how two personalities in a marriage unite not just at the level of conscious choice, compatibility, and sexual attraction, but also at the unconscious level, where they experience an extraordinary fit of which they are unaware. Glimmers of lost parts of the self are seen in the spouse, and this excites the hope that through marriage unacceptable parts of the self can be expressed vicariously.

Dicks noted that the fit between spouses, their "unconscious complementariness," leads to the formation of a "joint personality" (1967, p. 69). In a healthy marriage, this allows for de-repression of the repressed parts of one's object relations, and

so one can rediscover lost parts of the self in relation to the spouse. In an unhealthy marriage, the fit cements previous repression, because undoing of the defenses would also undo the spouse's similar defensive armature, which the marriage is supposed to consolidate rather than threaten. Now we have a model of two minds united in marriage, their boundaries changing and their internal economies in flux, for better or for worse.

To account for unconscious communication between spouses, Dicks turned to "projective identification" (Klein, 1946) as the crucial bridging concept between the intrapsychic and the interpersonal. Projective identification is a mental process that is used to defend against anxiety during the earliest months of life. Like Freud, Klein remained true to instinct theory. Segal (1964) and Heimann (1973) gave clear accounts of Klein's ideas. Klein thought that the infant has to defend against harm from the aggression of the death instinct by splitting it off from itself and deflecting it by projecting aggressively tinged parts of the self into the maternal object, especially her breast. Boundaries between self and object being unformed, the infant sees those parts of the self as if they were parts of the object. Now the infant fears attack from the breast as an aggressive object. Klein called this stage of personality development the "paranoid–schizoid position." Under the influence of the life instinct, the infant also projects loving parts of itself into the breast and experiences it as a loving object. Aspects of the breast, sorted in primitive fashion into all-good or all-bad, are identified with and taken into the infant through "introjective identification" (Klein, 1946) According to Klein, psychic structure forms through repeated cycles of projective and introjective identification under the opposing influences of the death instinct and the life instinct. Maturation over the course of the first half year of life enables the infant to leave behind primitive splitting between good and bad, and to develop an appreciation of a whole object that is felt to be both good and bad. The infant becomes capable of tolerating ambivalence, recognizing the destructive effect of its aggression, feeling concern for the object, and making reparation for damage done to it. When this is accomplished, the infant has achieved the "depressive position."

At this early age, according to Klein, the infant already has a concept of the parents as a couple involved in mutually gratifying intercourse, perceived as a feeding experience at first and later as a genital relationship from which the child is excluded. This image forms the basis for another aspect of the child's psychic structure—namely, the "internal couple" (J. S. Scharff, 1992). Understanding the functioning of this part of the therapist's personality is particularly important in couple therapy, where it is stirred by interaction with the patient couple. Couple therapy may founder or be avoided by the therapist who cannot face the pain of exclusion by, or frightening fusion with, the couple.

The paranoid–schizoid and depressive positions remain active throughout the life cycle as potential locations along a continuum from pathology to health. Projective identification is retained as a mental process of unconscious communication that functions along a continuum from defense to mature empathy. It is difficult to describe exactly how the process of projective and introjective identification actually takes place. We can become aware of it from its effect upon us as therapists (and ideally also in our domestic life as spouses). It is usually experienced as a feeling that is alien or unexplainable, perhaps a feeling of excitement or of numbness. It can be a sudden idea, a fantasy, a sense of in-touchness, or a fear (such as a fear of going mad). Fantasies can be communicated by tone of voice, gesture, changes in blood flow to the skin, or other overt macro- or micro-level behaviors. But at other times the experience is not detectable with present methods. To some this may sound a bit mystical, but others are willing to accept the occurrence of projective and introjective identification on the basis of their own experience of complexity, ambiguity, and awe in relationships.

Marriage, like infancy, offers a relationship of devotion, commitment, intimacy, and physical-

ity. It fosters regression and offers the partners a durable setting in which to explore the self and the other. Repressed parts of the self seek expression directly in relation to an accepting spouse or indirectly through uninhibited aspects of the spouse. There is a mutual attempt to heal and make reparation to the object refound in the spouse through projective identification, and then to find through introjective identification a new, more integrated self. The dynamic relation between parts of the self described by Fairbairn can now be conceptualized as occurring between the conscious and unconscious subsystems of two personalities united in marriage.

The Steps of Projective and Introjective Identification in Marriage

Figure 3.1 summarizes the mutuality of the processes of projective and introjective identification. They have been described as a series of interlocking steps (D. Scharff & Scharff, 1991; J. S. Scharff, 1992). To describe them more fully, we have to begin at some point along the chain of reciprocity. We start from the wife's original projection.

• *Projection.* The wife expels a part of herself with qualities that are denied (or overvalued) and sees her spouse as if he were imbued with these qualities, whether he is or not. He will certainly be imbued with some of them, accounting for the attraction that his wife felt for him. In other words, the projection may or may not fit. If it does, the spouse

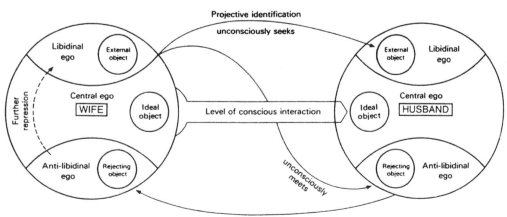

FIGURE 3.1. Projective and introjective identification. Adapted from D. Scharff (1982). Copyright 1982 by David E. Scharff. Adapted by permission of Routledge & Kegan Paul.

has a "valency" (Bion, 1961) for responding to the projection.

• *Projective identification.* The husband may or may not identify with the projection. If he does, he may do so passively (under the influence of his wife's capacity to induce in him a state of mind corresponding to her own, even if it feels foreign to him) or actively (by the force of his valency's compelling him to be identified that way). He tends to identify either with the projected part of the wife's self ("concordant identification") or with the object ("complementary identification") that applies to that part of herself (Racker, 1968). Although the husband inevitably has been chosen because of his psychological valencies and physical (including sexual) characteristics that resonate with parts of the wife's self and object, he also has his own personality and body that are different from those of his wife and her external objects on whom her internal objects are based. *In this gap between the original and the new object lies the healing potential of these bilateral processes.* The husband as a new object transforms his wife's view of herself and her objects through accepting the projection, temporarily identifying with it, modifying it, and returning it in a detoxified form through a mental process of "containment"—analogous to the mother's way of bearing the pain of her infant's distress and misperceptions of her (Bion, 1962). Now, through "introjective identification," the wife takes in this modified version of herself and assimilates her view of herself to it. She grows in her capacity to distinguish self and other. If her husband is not willing or able to offer her the containment that she needs, and instead returns her projections to her either unaltered or exaggerated, growth is blocked.

• *Mutual projective and introjective identificatory processes.* The wife is simultaneously receiving projections from her husband and returning them to him. Together, they are containing and modifying each other's internal versions of self and object. Mutual projective and introjective processes govern mate selection, falling in love, the quality of the sexual relationship, the level of intimacy, and the nature of the marriage in general and its effect on the partners' development as adults (D. Scharff, 1982; D. Scharff & Scharff, 1991). In a mutual process, husband and wife connect according to unconscious complementarity of object relations. Similarly, couple and therapist relate through the reciprocal actions of transference and countertransference.

How is the unconscious complementarity of object relations different from the familiar term "collusion" (Willi, 1982)? We think that "collusion" is another way of describing the same process, at least in those writings where it refers to an unconscious dynamic between a couple. We tend to avoid the term "collusion" because it seems to judge and blame the husband and wife, as if they were intentionally colluding to thwart each other, their families, and the therapist. Nevertheless, mutual projective and introjective identification processes cement the couple in an unconscious collusive attempt to avoid anxiety.

Couple dysfunction occurs when more distress than can be tolerated upsets the balance in the mutual projective identification system. This happens when some of the following conditions apply: (1) Projective and introjective identification processes are not mutually gratifying; (2) containment of the spouse's projections is not possible; (3) cementing of the object relations set happens instead of their modification; (4) unarousing projective identification of the genital zone cannot be modified by sexual experience; and/or (5) aspects of the love object have to be split off and experienced in a less threatening situation, leading to triangulation involving a child, hobby, work, friend, parent, or lover.

The following snapshot, taken from the vignette of a couple that is described later in the chapter, illustrates the way the balance in a couple may shift and lead to breakup.

Michelle and Lenny were drawn to each other by mutual projective and introjective identification processes. She saw in him a solid, loving, thoughtful, and successful man who treated her well and whom her hatefulness could not destroy; he was proud to be her stable base, and in return he enjoyed her vivacity and outrageous disregard of his sensibilities, loving her in spite of herself and treating her like a queen. Lenny treated Michelle as special, the way his mother had treated him, and as her mother had treated her and her brother even more so. Michelle treated Lenny as she had felt treated: He was special to her, as she was to her mother, but not as wonderful as the other person—namely, her brother, corresponding to herself in relation to Lenny as her brother. The problem arose when Lenny could not contain Michelle's projective identification of him as her brother because he was not as exciting, not as aggressive, and not as enviable as the brother. In turn, Michelle could not contain his projective identification of her as his adored self because she was so hateful and destroyed by envy. Michelle longed for Lenny to be more aggressive, but the more she pestered him to be so, the less space she gave to his initiative, and the more she became like a repressed, nagging image of his mother (whom he preferred to think of as adoring). Lenny had helped Michelle with her fear of sex, and so she had been able to modify her unarousing projective identification of the genital zone due to her envy of her brother's genitalia and preferred status, but not sufficiently to reinvest her vagina as a gratifying organ of pleasure and bonding for the couple. No actual triangulation had occurred, but in fantasy Michelle kept herself attached to the hope of a better man who would fulfill all her expectations of virility. She wished to break up, but could not. Against Lenny's wishes, but facing the reality of the destructiveness of their attachment, Lenny decided to break up, because the balance of the projective and introjective identification processes had shifted from the gratifying into the intolerable range, and hope of their modification was lost.

Later in the chapter, we consider the impact of the projective and introjective identificatory system on the therapist's countertransference and how this provides a shared experience from which to understand the couple's dynamics.

THE THEORY OF THERAPEUTIC CHANGE

Object relations couple therapy creates a therapeutic environment in which the couple's pattern of defenses can be displayed, recognized, and analyzed until the underlying anxieties can be named, experienced, and worked through together. In the language of object relations couple therapy, we conceptualize the process as one of improving the couple's capacity for containment of projections. Spouses learn to modify each other's projections, to distinguish them from aspects of the self, and then to take back their projections. The wife is then free to perceive her husband accurately as a separate person whom she chooses to love for himself, rather than for the gratification he has previously afforded to repressed parts of herself. Through this process, reinforced by the joy of more mature loving, the wife finds herself again and becomes both more loving and more lovable. Doing the same work for himself, her husband grows in the same direction. Sometimes, however, their improved capacities for autonomy and mature love will take them in opposite directions. Saving the marriage is not the primary goal. Ideally, *freeing the marriage from the grip of its obligatory projective and introjective identificatory processes is the goal of treatment.* In practice, something short of the ideal may be all that the spouses need to be on their way again. More realistically, the goal of treatment is to enable the projective identificatory cycle to function

at the depressive rather than the paranoid–schizoid end of the continuum more often than before therapy (Ravenscroft, 1991).

This is accomplished through a number of techniques. These are not the familiar techniques of communications-trained or behavioral couple therapists. The techniques of object relations couple therapy comprise a series of attitudes toward the couple and the therapeutic process. Later in the chapter, we look more closely at technique in couple therapy. For now, we show how object relations couple therapists use these techniques in early interviews during the assessment process.

THE DIAGNOSTIC–ASSESSMENT PROCESS

• *Setting the frame.* We set a frame (Langs, 1976; Zinner, 1989) within which to establish a reliable space for work. The frame may be established at the beginning or may emerge according to need as the consultation proceeds. The frame includes the number and length of sessions, the setting of the fee, the therapist's management of the beginnings and ends of sessions, and the establishment of the way of working. Usually about five sessions are needed before we are ready with a formulation and recommendation. This allows for one or two couple sessions, one or more individual sessions for each spouse as indicated, and a couple session where formulations and recommendations about treatment are given. The couple's reactions to the frame and any attempts to bend it are explored in terms of the couple's transference to the therapist's attempts to provide a safe therapeutic space. This exploration is undertaken both to secure the frame against unconscious forces tending to distort it and to discover the nature of the flaws in the couple's holding capacity.

• *Creating psychological space for understanding.* The therapist creates psychological space for understanding (Box, 1981) by containing the couple's anxieties as therapy is begun. As object relations couple therapists, we do this through our way of dealing with the couple relationship rather than the individuals who constitute it, and through the way we listen, allow feelings to be expressed, experience those feelings in relation to ourselves, and interpret our experience. The couple identifies with our containing function and so develops the capacity to create space for understanding.

• *Listening to the unconscious.* We listen in a relaxed way that is both attentive and yet not closely focused. We try to be free of the need to get information and to make sense of things. We listen not to the individuals alone, but to the communication from the couple as a system in relation to us. We listen not only to the conscious communication, but also the unconscious communication. We do this by following the themes emerging from the verbal associations, by noting the meaning of silences, by integrating our observation of nonverbal language with words and silence, and by working with fantasy and dream material. We also attend to the unconscious communication expressed in the physical aspects of sexual functioning. As we listen, we let our senses be impinged on; we hold the experience inside; and then we allow meaning to emerge from within.

• *Following the affect.* We are interested in moments of emotion, because these provide access to the unconscious areas from which the feeling has emerged. These moments bring us a living history of the relationships in the families of origin that is more immediate and useful than a formally obtained social history or genogram. Some psychoanalytic couple therapists, however, such as Dare (1986), recommend the use of the genogram.

• *Transference and countertransference.* Creating the space, listening, and following the affect come together in the "countertransference" (Freud, 1910b)—namely, our feelings about the couple and the individual spouses in response to the couple's "transference" (Freud, 1917), that is, their feelings about us as new editions of figures from their family histories. At times, our countertransference remains unconscious in a way that supports our being in tune with the couple and doing our work. At other times, it obtrudes as a feeling of discomfort, a fantasy, or a dream, and then we can take hold of it and get to work on what it means. How does our feeling correspond to the internal object relations set of the couple?

• *Interpretation of defense.* We point out the couple's recurring pattern of interactions that serve a defensive purpose. Then, speaking from our own emotional experience of joining in unconscious communication with the couple, we interpret the couple's pattern of defenses. Only when we can point out the pattern and the way in which we have been involved in it can we work out what they and we have been defending ourselves against.

• *Confronting basic anxiety.* Lastly, we work with the basic anxieties that have seemed too intolerable to bear in consciousness. When they are named, faced, and adapted to, the couple can proceed to the next developmental phase of the couple's life cycle. During assessment, we are content to identify some aspect of the basic anxiety revealed in the defensive patterns that we have pointed out, without any attempt at thorough exploration.

In general, the diagnostic process is designed as a fair trial of therapy. We are not concerned with getting answers to our questions. We simply create an environment in which issues may be raised—especially the immediate issue of whether or not to invest in therapy. We get an in-depth sample of the couple relationship, while a couple has an opportunity to be in unconscious communication with us and to subject that experience to process and review. Although our intention is to arrive at understanding, our main goal is to facilitate entry into treatment if that is what we recommend. In other words, we do not worry about finding out everything or making magical interpretations or complete formulations. We just want to secure the therapeutic space and give the couple a sample on which to base their decision about commitment to couple therapy.

Some couples come already seeking couple therapy. Others have to be shown that that is the approach most likely to help them, rather than the individual therapy that one of the partners has requested. In that case, an individual problem has to be redefined as a symptom of the relationship. We do not suppose, however, that couple therapy is always best, or that every couple is ready for it. We find it best to start where the spouses are, and to recommend the form of treatment that they will accept and follow through on—including referral for adjunctive medication or behavioral treatment where indicated, or for individual psychoanalysis when that is an appropriate, definitive choice rather than a defense against couple therapy.

SETTING TREATMENT GOALS

Goals are not closely specified, because we find this to be restricting. We do not tailor our approach to the removal of a symptom, because we value the symptom as a beacon that leads us through the layers of defense and anxiety from which it stems. In any case, goals tend to change over time as the couple is freed to experience the potential of their relationship. So we prefer a somewhat open-ended formulation of a couple's aims for treatment. We are content with a general statement of the wish to change behavior, to become more accommodating, to improve communication and understanding, and to function better as a couple. In technical terms, our therapeutic goals are as follows:

- To recognize and rework the couple's mutual projective and introjective identifications.
- To improve the couple's contextual holding capacity, so that the partners can provide for each other's needs for attachment and autonomy, as well as for developmental progression.
- To recover the centered holding relationship that allows for unconscious communication between the spouses, shown in their capacity for empathy, intimacy, and sexuality.
- To promote individuation of the spouses and differentiation of needs, including the need for individual therapy or psychoanalysis.
- To return the couple with confidence to the tasks of the current developmental stage in the couple's life cycle.

TYPICAL STRUCTURE OF THERAPY SESSIONS

The couple therapy session may be of any predetermined length from 45 to 90 minutes, and may occur weekly or twice weekly for as long as necessary, 2 years being the average duration of treatment. Although object relations couple therapy is a long-term method for in-depth work, the same approach can be applied by those at work in managed care situations. In such a limited time frame, we offer as much understanding as we can of the couple's defensive system without feeling under pressure to produce quick changes. We admit the limits of what we can offer, rather than delude ourselves, the families, and their health care planners into thinking that the minimum is all that is necessary, just because it is all that we are authorized to provide.

Family therapists of various orientations share a common goal in seeking to improve technique so that more families can be helped more economically. Fewer sessions can be quite effective in crises and in families with short-term goals. When families see that their presenting symptom is part of a broader dysfunction, some of them make it a financial priority to work for more fundamental change in the family system and in their internal object relations. These are the families for whom short-term, focused methods provide a window of opportunity through which to move on to in-depth family therapy with plenty of time to do the work.

Both in brief therapy and in long-term therapy formats, beginnings and endings of the sessions are important. Anxiety is often most accessible at these times of separation and reunion. The object relations couple therapist is attentive to boundary phenomena because they illuminate the interior of the couple relationship. Other than having a beginning, a middle, and an end, an object relations couple therapy session has no structure imposed upon it, because the therapist does not direct how the couple will use the session. Instead, the therapist follows the couple's lead and comments on how their use of the session reflects their way of dealing with other times, tasks, authorities, and intimate situations.

The main ingredient of the approach is the working space provided by the therapeutic relationship. Training, supervision, peer discussion, and personal therapy ensure that the therapist maximizes the availability of the therapeutic self and calibrates it for use as an effective therapeutic instrument.

THE ROLE OF THE THERAPIST

The working alliance is fostered mainly by the therapist's capacity for tolerating anxiety. The therapist is neither aloof nor gratifying, but is willing to be accommodating, to share knowledge when that will be helpful, and to negotiate a way of working that meets the couple's needs without compromising the therapist's integrity. Some couples may need more support or advice than others (including behavioral sex therapy for some); yet the principle of remaining fundamentally nondirective at the unconscious level still applies. For example, when the couple responds to some parenting advice or resists an assignment in sex therapy, the therapist waits for associations to the spouses' reactions (including any dreams and fantasies) through which to trace the unconscious thread and its relation to the transference. The general attitude is one of not doing too much, so as to let themes emerge in their own form and time. Once the shape of the couple's experience declares itself, then the therapist takes hold of it, interacts, shares the experience, and puts words on it. Reaching into the couple's unconscious life in this way gives the couple the feeling of being understood and held psychologically in the treatment situation. This fosters the working alliance and sustains the couple and the therapist through times when the relationship to the therapist inevitably bears the brunt of the couple's distress.

The therapist aims to become an object that the couple can use—and abuse, if necessary (J. S. Scharff, 1992). She becomes a transitional object that their relationship encompasses and uses, as a child uses a toy or a pet to deflect yet express feelings about self, sibling, or parent. In the quality of their relationship to her, she can discover and reveal to the spouses the defenses and anxieties that confound their relationship. The therapist is not a traditional blank-screen analyst, impassively awaiting the onslaught from the id. The object relations couple therapist is personable yet not seductive, and she remains neutral as to how the couple chooses to use therapy. She will follow rather than lead. She is both supportive and confrontational when communicating to the couple her experience of the use they have made of her. She uses her own presence and her feelings, and yet she is somewhat distant in that she does not allow her mood to dominate the session. She does not share information from her personal life, but she may share a fantasy or a feeling that occurs to her in association to the couple's material. Her therapeutic stance changes little over the course of the therapy, but the way that she interacts with a couple will change as couple and therapist become progressively more able to give up defensive patterns, to tolerate shared anxiety, and to engage in a collaborative relationship.

In the following section on technique, we return to a more detailed examination of the use of the therapist's self. Learning how to use the therapist's self cannot happen by reading alone. The therapist needs to prepare the ground by having therapy himself, as well as supervision, clinical experience, and engagement in group-based affective learning training programs where his internal object relationships can be displayed in interpersonal interaction with fellow students, examined, and understood (J. S. Scharff & Scharff, 2000). Until the therapeutic instrument is finely tuned, the therapist will not be able to allow his internal object relations set to resonate with the couple's.

The most usual error is that of doing too much. The therapist gets anxious about being worthwhile and takes action to dispel the uneasy, helpless feeling. He may end a session early, start late, forget an appointment, make a slip, lose a couple's check, or call one or both spouses by the wrong names. He may speak too much, cut off the flow of communication, or retreat into a withholding silence. He may substitute asking questions for realizing how little he knows or how frustrated he has been by a withholding couple. All of these happenings are to be expected as part of the work of allowing the therapist's self to be affected. Instead of calling them "errors," he can call them "deviations" from which he can recover as soon as he subjects them to process and review.

Another common error is to deviate from the neutral position: Now the therapist is siding with the husband; now she takes the wife's point of view. As object relations couple therapists, we agree that a neutral position is important and that partiality to either spouse is an error. But we disagree about the need to avoid it altogether. Dare (1986) advises scrupulous fairness to spouses and absolute symmetry in the seating arrangements. We share his ideal of fairness as an intention, but we leave room for error. Rather than rigidly guarding against them, we prefer to work with deviations and jealousies that arise and to understand their source in difficulties with triangles in the family of origin.

TECHNIQUE OF COUPLE THERAPY

As object relations couple therapists, we observe the couple relationship primarily through noticing the way the couple deals with us, but we are also interested in how the spouses interact with each other. We are concerned not just with the conscious aspects of their bond, but with the internal object relations operating through mutual projective identification processes in the couple's unconscious (J. S. Scharff, 1992; D. Scharff & Scharff, 1991).

In keeping with this focus, our technique employs nondirective listening for the emergence of unconscious themes, following the affect, analyzing dream and fantasy material and associations offered by both members of the couple, and exploring the family history of each spouse as it relates to the current couple relationship. We point out patterns of interaction that tend to recur, and we look for unconscious forces that drive the repetition. Gradually, we become familiar with the defensive aspects of these repeating cycles. We do this over and over, covering the same ground and making inroads into defended territory, which we find particularly accessible at times when the couple's transference has stirred a countertransference response through which we can appreciate the couple's vulnerability. As their trust builds, we can help the couple figure out and face the nameless anxiety behind the defense. Our help comes in the form of interpretations of resistance, defense, and conflict, conceptualized as operating through unconscious object relation systems that support and subvert the marriage. These interpretations are imparted after being metabolized in the counter-transference. Interpretation may lead to insight that produces change in the unconscious object relations of the couple, or it may lead to increased resistance to the unconscious conflict. Progression and regression succeed each other in cycles as we work through the defensive structures of the marriage to the point where these are no longer interfering with the spouses' capacity for working together as life partners, loving each other, integrating good and bad, and building a relationship of intimacy and sexuality that is free to grow through the developmental life cycle of the marriage.

What does all this mean in practice? Our technique can be explored through its components, as summarized here:

1. Setting the frame
2. Listening to the unconscious
3. Maintaining a neutral position of involved impartiality
4. Creating a psychological space
5. Use of the therapist's self: Negative capability
6. Working with transference and countertransference
7. Interpretation of defense and anxiety about intimacy: The "because clause"
8. Working with fantasy and inner object relations
9. Working with dreams
10. Working through
11. Termination

Setting the Frame

Our first priority is to hold to the frame for therapy that we have established during the assessment interviews (Langs, 1976). This frame offers "a secure and consistent environment in which highly sensitive, private feelings and fantasies can be expressed and explored without the threat of actualizing the feared consequences" (Zinner, 1989, p. 321). The couple tries to bend the frame so that unconscious wishes can be gratified, but their efforts are frustrated by the therapist who holds firm. The ensuing conflict brings into the treatment the issues that have been dividing the marriage.

How is the frame maintained? In our therapy, we do this by being clear about the arrangements and by staying with the agreed-upon treatment format. For instance, the couple is given a firm recommendation for couple therapy, where that is clearly indicated. Spouses who are not ready for

couple therapy and who have not responded to interpretations of their resistance to it will be given a choice of psychoanalytically oriented separate or concurrent marital, family, and individual therapies, with or without necessary or preferred adjunctive treatment or referral for behavioral or communications-based therapy as either an alternative or preliminary treatment. Given a free choice, they can then sometimes move in the direction of our original emphasis on the couple relationship, but if not, their right to begin therapy as they see fit must be respected and accommodated. If they choose to work with us, then, by mutual agreement, we and the couple settle upon the treatment plan. Then the policy of sticking to the plan is explained and discussed: Unless future experience dictates a shift, no change in the arrangements will be undertaken except after thorough discussion and mutual agreement. So the frame is secure, but flexible.

Then we outline other policies, such as fees, vacations, and billing practice. Our billing practice is to bill at the end of the month and to have the couple's check by the 10th of the month. We do this because it helps us to keep in mind the moment when the bill was rendered and to focus on how the couple is dealing with the financial aspects of the commitment. We sell our time not by item of service but by long-term commitment, so we expect the couple to attend as planned. If they have to be absent, we are willing to reschedule within the week; if that is not possible, however, then we hold them responsible for the time. Unlike our work with families, in which we will see a family with a member absent, in couple therapy we do not work unless both members of the couple are present. Suddenly doing individual therapy with one spouse poses a threat to the our therapeutic neutrality and capacity to help the couple. Of course, in keeping with the flexible frame, individual sessions can be scheduled by plan and by mutual agreement, but not as filler for absences from therapy.

At the moment of moving from assessment to treatment, the couple is given the choice of accepting the frame or accepting referral to another therapist whose conditions seem preferable. Here is an example from such a session in which one of us (JSS, the "I" in this vignette) is meeting with a couple we call the Melvilles.

Mr. and Mrs. Melville had both had previous individual therapies and now wanted to work with me in couple therapy for problems in their marriage, the second marriage for each. Mr. Melville had resolved his feelings about his divorce, but for Mrs. Melville her divorce was still a persecutory object (Bagnini, in press). He was a successful organizational consultant who loved his work; enjoyed food, sports, and sex; and felt great about himself, except in his marriage, where he felt unloved. She was a good homemaker, was the mother of three little ones, and ran a small business selling jewelry from her home. She felt exhausted, unaccomplished, and uninterested in sex. Both tended to overspend, and so short-term cash flow problems created financial stress in addition to their couple tension.

I told them my fee and my billing policy. They had no problem agreeing to the amount of my fee and my payment schedule. But charging for missed sessions was another matter. Mr. Melville did not want to be charged because he was a punctual person and because his business travel was out of his control. Mrs. Melville was concerned that her vacation would have to be tied to mine, but since our vacation periods happened to overlap, she was not concerned.

I said, "I see that you react differently to my policy. You, Mr. Melville, feel that since you are a good, responsible person, you do not deserve to be charged, which to you feels like a punishment and a rejection of your worth. You, Mrs. Melville, feel afraid of being trapped in the relationship with me. I assume these feelings also come up between you as you deal with the consequences of the marriage commitment."

Mrs. Melville rushed to concur. She said that she felt so trapped in marriage. She was terrified of feeling financially and emotionally destitute, as she had at the time of her divorce from her first husband. She felt she could lose her self. She thought that her present husband felt punished by her need for space and for her own charge account. Mr. Melville agreed that he felt that way. Unlike her first husband, he insisted on sharing his inheritance with her, even though all her money went directly to her children. He had already recovered financially from his own divorce; he had been generous with his former wife; and he was not worried about risking all in marriage again. He had no idea how frightened she was.

In their transference reactions to the frame, the Melvilles revealed their fundamental problems. His self-worth was tied to his earning capacity rather than to being loved, because the former was more dependable than the latter. His willingness to provide for his wife could not assuage her sense of insecurity, because it emphasized his independence from her and defended against love. How could anyone so apparently confident ever understand her terror of dependency and her fears of annihilation? How could someone so generous be married to someone to whom it meant so little? The answer must lie in their mutual projection of the good, abundant, nourishing, energetic breast into him (as, it turned out, both had experienced their fathers) and the shriveled, nonreplenishing breast, depleted by their neediness, into her (an image that derived from their shared views of their mothers). As the therapist expect-

ing to be paid, I was a replenishing breast to which they had to contribute in partnership—an expectation that threatened them in ways unique to each individual in reflection of the object relations set.

Listening to the Unconscious

At the conscious level, we listen to what the couple is saying—which of the partners is saying what, in what order, and with what affect. We try to listen just as carefully to the silence and to the nonverbal communications in the form of gestures. Yet this careful listening is not as consciously attentive as our description sounds so far. Instead, we experience a drifting state of mind: at one level, interacting, maybe even asking a question and hearing the answer; at another level, not listening for anything in particular. Freud (1912) described this as "evenly-suspended attention" (p. 112), the therapist turning "his own unconscious like a receptive organ toward the transmitting unconscious of the patient" (p. 115). Through affective learning, clinical experience, supervision, peer consultation, ongoing process, and review of our work in sessions, therapy, and self-analysis, we develop an understanding of our own unconscious so that we can separate our own from the patients' material. We tune in our calibrated, unconscious receiving apparatus at the deepest level of communication to the unconscious processes of therapeutic action (J. S. Scharff & Scharff, 2000). Unconscious signals from the couple come through to us as a theme that emerges from the flow of associations and silences, amplified by dream and fantasy, and then resonates in us as countertransference experience from which we can share in and reconstruct the couple's unconscious object relations. When we give the couple our reconstruction in the form of an interpretation, we can check out its validity by evaluating the ensuing associative flow.

Holding the Neutral Position

We maintain a position of neutrality, with no preference for one spouse or the other, for one type of object relationship versus another, for lifestyle choices, or for treatment outcome. Our attention hovers evenly among the intrapsychic dimensions of each spouse, their interpersonal process, and their interaction with us. Although we obviously value marriage as an institution, we do not have a bias about continuation of a couple's marriage or divorce. We are invested in our work with each couple and in the possibility of growth and development, but we do not want to invest in the couple's achievement. We want to hold a position described as one of involved impartiality (Stierlin, 1977). Any deviations from that occur in directions that are quite unique to each couple. From reviewing the specific pull exerted upon us, we learn about the couple's unconscious object relationships.

Creating the Psychological Space

This willingness to work with our experience demonstrates an attitude of valuing process and review. It offers the couple a model for self-examination and personal sharing and creates the psychological space into which the couple can move and there develop its potential for growth. We offer a therapeutic environment in which the couple can experience its relationship in relation to us. Our therapeutic stance derives from our integration of the concepts of "container–contained" (Bion, 1962) and the "holding environment" (Winnicott, 1960). The relationship to the therapist creates a transitional space in which the couple can portray and reflect upon its current way of functioning, learn about and modify its projective identification system, and invent new ways of being. Through clinical experience, training, and supervision, and through intensive personal psychotherapy or psychoanalysis, a therapist develops a "holding capacity"—the capacity to bear the anxiety of the emergence of unconscious material and affect through containment, and to modify it through internal processing of projective identifications. The therapist contributes this capacity to the transitional space that is thereby transformed into an expanded psychological space for understanding. The couple then takes in this space and finds within the couple relationship the capacity to deal with current and future anxiety. Once this happens, the actual therapeutic relationship can be terminated, because the therapeutic function has been internalized.

The Use of the Therapist's Self: Negative Capability

Clearly, the use of the therapist's self is central to our technique. How to use the self can partly be learned from reading, (Jacobs, 1991; J. S. Scharff, 1992), but mostly it is acquired from experience and is nurtured in training and supervision. For fullest use of the self in the clinical setting, therapists need to have had the personal experience of understanding their own family history and object relations in psychoanalysis or intensive psychotherapy, including couple and family therapy, even in the rare instance when this has not been necessary for a satisfactory personal life. This gives the therapist the necessary base of self-knowledge to calibrate the self as a diagnostic and therapeutic instrument. Its continued refinement is a lifelong task, accomplished mainly through process and review in the clinical situation, through discussion with colleagues, and through teaching and writing.

Once the therapist's self is cleared for use as a receiving apparatus and as a space that can be filled with the experience of the couple, the therapist is able to know, without seeking to know actively, about the couple's unconscious. Striving to find out distorts the field of observation. Instead, we recommend a nondirective, unfocused, receptive attitude best described as "negative capability"—a term invented by the poet Keats to describe Shakespeare's capacity as a poet for "being in uncertainties, mysteries, doubts, without any irritable reaching after fact and reason" (Murray, 1955, p. 261). Bion (1970), expanding on Keats's term, urged the therapist to be without memory or desire (i.e., to abandon the need to know and to impose meaning). Negative capability, however, is an ideal state, and we do not advocate irritably reaching for it. Instead, it is a state to sink into, best achieved by not doing too much and allowing understanding to come from inside the therapist's experience. In their anxiety to be understood and cared about, some couples will react with frustration to the therapist's apparent lack of directiveness, activity, and omniscience. As long as their reactions are recognized and intepreted, these couples usually come to value the deeper level of understanding that is promoted by the therapist's inhibition of surface engagement activity. Some couples will not be able to tolerate the initial frustration or the ensuing depth of intimacy offered by the analytic therapist, and will do better with a therapist who relates in a more obviously supportive way and who does not intend to offer an in-depth, growth experience.

Working with Transference and Countertransference

Negative capability fosters our capacity to respond to the couple's transference—namely, their shared feelings about the therapist. The transference gives rise to ideas, feelings, or behavior in the therapist—namely, countertransference. As Heimann (1950) pointed out, "the analyst's counter-transference is an instrument of research into the patient's unconscious" (p. 81). The analyst must value and study the countertranference, because "the emotions roused in him are often nearer to the heart of the matter than his reasoning" (Heimann, 1950, p. 82). This elaboration of countertransference stresses an understanding of the normal countertransference and its deviations (Money-Kyrle, 1956), rather than emphasizing the pathology of the therapist's responses.

In studying our reactions to unconscious material in psychoanalysis, psychotherapy, and couple and family therapy, we have found that our countertransference experiences tend to cluster in relation to two kinds of transferences: the "contextual transference" and the "focused transference" (D. Scharff & Scharff, 1987). "Contextual countertransference" refers to the therapist's reaction to the patient's contextual transference—namely, the patient's response to the therapeutic environment, shown in attitudes about the frame of treatment, unconscious resistance in general, specific conscious feelings, and behavior toward the therapist as an object for providing a holding situation. "Focused countertransference" occurs in response to the focused transference—namely, feelings the patient transfers to the therapist as an object for intimate relating. Usually the contextual transference and countertransference predominate in the opening and closing phases of individual treatment and throughout family therapy. In couple therapy there is often rapid oscillation between the contextual and focused countertransference, as shown in the following vignette of a couple we call Dr. and Mrs. Clark, from an opening session with one of us (JSS, again the "I").

Mrs. Clark, a tall, angular woman with a short, burgundy-colored, spiked hairdo, stormed ahead of her husband, Dr. Clark, a short, round-faced, gentle-looking man. She wore high-style black leather pants and a studded jacket; she threw her jacket on the couch. He meekly laid down his own sheepskin coat and looked expectantly at her through his traditional rimmed glasses, which were, however, unexpectedly bright purple. She was emitting hostility but no words.

I asked whether they were waiting for me to start. He told me that she almost didn't come today. I said, "How come? You, Mrs. Clark, were the one who called me and made the arrangements."

Mrs. Clark explained that she was just mad, today, at him, the big shot, Mr. Doctor God, who (she told me angrily) was indeed no god. Turning back to me, she told me of his berating and belittling her in front of his office staff. Dr. Clark agreed that he had been rude, because he was annoyed by being pestered by her at the office, where she caused upset among the staff. All he wanted was to be in a happy situation with a decent sex life and no ruckus. His friends recommended divorce, but he wanted to work it out for the sake of their four children. Mrs. Clark responded that she didn't feel like being sexual with a man who was so rude about her.

At first I felt ashamed that my sympathies were with the doctor, calm and reasonable and not asking much. But I knew from experience that this was not an opinion. It was just a temporary reaction, not just to her but to them as a couple. For some reason, as this couple crossed the boundary into the therapy space, Mrs. Clark became dominating, interruptive, and crude. But I thought that she was being thrust forward, and that his feelings were hiding behind her anxious and aggressive front.

I said to Dr. Clark, "Is Mrs. Clark the only one who is anxious, or do you have questions, too?" Dr. Clark replied that he was not anxious, but that he did have questions. He wanted to interview me about where I went to school.

This is one question that must always be answered. Without commenting on the denigrating, aggressive tone in his question, I told him my professional background. He was glad to learn that I had graduated from medical school in 1967. He had thought that I was a psychologist (which he would not like) and that I seemed too young. So he felt relieved that I had been practicing as a board-certified psychiatrist for many years. I was temporarily protected from his denigration by the fact of my sharing his medical background—a feature about me that he and his wife overvalued.

I said that I was glad to hear of his concerns, because until now it had appeared as though Mrs. Clark was the one who had all the feelings about therapy's being no use. I told them that I had the impression that she expressed her anxiety by getting angry, but that he expressed his anxiety through her. Now, usefully, he was admitting to it. Both of them, for their own reasons and in their individual ways, were anxious about therapy and about their marriage.

In my countertransference, I experienced a deviation from involved impartiality (Stierlin, 1977). I realized that Mrs. Clark was expressing a focused transference toward me as the doctor (a member of the same profession as her husband), and that this was a cover for the couple's shared contextual transference of distrust in the context of treatment. My task was to address the contextual transference with them, so that as a couple Dr. and Mrs. Clark could modify their reluctance to begin treatment.

In an assessment interview, we do not focus on the details of the individual, focused transferences. Indeed, they may remain subordinate to the shared transference throughout a couple treatment, but more commonly in couple therapy we find ourselves dealing with a rapid oscillation between the two poles of focused and contextual transferences. This example serves, however, to illustrate another idea that is helpful in work with our reactions to focused transferences—namely, Racker's (1968) concept of "concordant transference" and "complementary transference." Racker described his countertransference as a fundamental condition of receiving the patient's projections and tolerating them inside him as projective identifications. His reception of the projections was unconscious, out of his awareness until he subjected his experience to process and review. In Racker's view, countertransference is a fundamental means of understanding the patient's internal world; object relations couple therapists share this view. Racker went further to point out that the therapist might identify with parts either of the patient's self or objects. Identification with the patient's self was called "concordant identification"; identification with the object was called "complementary identification." As couple therapists we can now think of our therapeutic task as the reception and clarification of the couple's projections, followed by analysis of the interpersonal conditions under which these occur.

In the session with the Clarks, Mrs. Clark experienced me (JSS) as a contemptuous and rejecting object, like the object that she projected into her husband. She thus evoked in me an unwelcome state of mind in which I felt contempt for her. My countertransference was one of complementary identification to her object. Dr. Clark experienced me as a denigrated object like the one he projected into his wife, and then switched to seeing me as a part of himself, the wise physician. To him, my countertransference was one of concordant identification with part of his self. I did not experience an identification with his object—perhaps because my identity as a physician protected me from it, but more likely because I was tuning in to an internal process in which Dr. Clark used his ideal object to repress his rejected object, which he split and projected more readily into Mrs. Clark than into me at this stage of the assessment.

Interpreting Defense and Anxiety about Intimacy: The "Because Clause"

The next example comes from the midphase of the couple therapy of a husband and wife we call Aaron and Phyllis (once more, JSS is the "I").

Aaron and Phyllis had had a fulfilling marriage for 10 years—until Aaron's 16-year-old daughter, Susie, came to live with them. Phyllis had raised their shared family without much criticism from Aaron, and without challenge from their very young son and daughter. She felt supported by Aaron in her role as an efficient mother who ran a smooth household. She felt loved by him and by her dependent children. Her self-esteem was good, because she was a much better mother than her mother had been.

But when Susie came to stay, trouble began. Phyllis had firm ideas on what was appropriate for Susie; in contrast, Aaron was extremely permissive. So Phyllis became the target for Susie's animosity. Aaron saw no need for limits and indeed saw no problem between Phyllis and Susie. Phyllis became increasingly angry at Aaron. He bore the situation stoically, only occasionally confronting the problem. Then he would tell Phyllis that she was being small-minded and awful, because she was acting out her jealousy and he felt that this was making her stepchild miserable. She was angry at that attack on her self-esteem and never did recover from it.

They saw a family counselor who verified the 16-year-old's need for limits, supported Phyllis's views, and worked to get Aaron's cooperation. Aaron turned around and in a short time his daughter was behaving well and Phyllis could enjoy her. To this day, Phyllis enjoys visits from her.

This seemed to have been a spectacular therapeutic success. I asked Aaron how he conceptualized the amazing turnabout. He said that once the therapist had made the situation clear to him, he simply told his daughter to do what Phyllis said or she would be out of the house. But Phyllis's anger at Aaron's ignoring her pleas until then was still there. Although she continued to enjoy sex with Aaron, Phyllis "walked out" emotionally for several years, in retribution for the years in which she felt Aaron had "walked out" on her. The family counselor had treated the family symptom and its effect on the couple with a useful prescription that removed the symptom. But she did it so rapidly that the underlying problem in the marriage was not recognized. The use of the focus upon a problem child as a defense against problems of intimacy had not been addressed, and so the issue came up again in their second treatment opportunity.

The force of Aaron's ultimatum about complying or leaving the house suggested to me that he had lived by the same rule himself for the first 10 years of his marriage to Phyllis. Then, however, he began to challenge Phyllis's rule by expressing his alternative way of coping with children—with predictable results. Now the same old problem they had had with Susie was surfacing with their shared older daughter, who was now 15. Because no work had been done on their differences, they had not developed a shared method of child rearing. Now that Aaron was challenging Phyllis, they fought about the right way to do everything, but nowhere so painfully as over the care of their children.

Phyllis went on to give an example—which, however, concerned not the problem daughter, but their 11-year-old son. He had asked to go on a date, and Phyllis had promptly told him that this was inappropriate because he was too young. Aaron had immediately intervened to offer a ride, and Phyllis told me that she had felt undermined. Aaron said that he had spoken up because he felt that she was being unhelpful to their son's social development. I said I could see that either position could be defended; however, the problem was that they had not discussed things so as to arrive at a shared position that met their anxiety about their 11-year-old's burgeoning social independence.

Phyllis was furious at me for a whole day. She thought that I had been unaccommodating and controlling. But to my surprise, and to her credit, she said that she had had to laugh when it struck her that it was not what *I* was doing but what *she* was bringing to the session. She could have made the interpretation herself!

I realized that Phyllis was seeing me in the transference as Aaron saw her, and I was speculating on the origin of this projective identification and admiring her insight, when suddenly Phyllis returned to her argument and pointed out how anyone who could let a child date at the age of 11 could just as well let him cut his arm off. I felt ridiculed for suggesting that they could consider their son's request together. I felt put down, as if I had not a clue about an 11-year-old's social development. I felt I was being small-minded getting into the fight with them about a child, when we knew they had come for help not with child rearing but with their marriage. I thought that dating, meaning independence and intimacy, was equated with severe damage and loss.

Perhaps Phyllis felt that she needed her son close to her and could not yet face being cut off from him. Perhaps Aaron, while wishing to facilitate their son's date, was offering to drive in order to stay close to him too, or possibly to stay close to the issue of intimacy vicariously. I also wondered whether dating signaled sexuality's causing loss, but that was probably not the case, since sexuality was relatively free of conflict for Phyllis and Aaron. So I concluded that the loss referred to sexuality's being cut off from intimacy in the rest of the relationship.

I stuck to my point. I said, "I'm not really talking about whether or not an 11-year-old should date. I'm taking you up on the effect of sticking to alternative positions and not talking about them together."

Here I was confronting their defense of using a child to portray their conflict about intimacy. Aaron agreed that intimacy was a problem, even though sex was not. He said that he felt cramped in every part of his life because he felt that Phyllis was so vulnerable. Phyllis was more concerned with how much they argued. Conflict was killing them and smashing up their marriage, and she was tired of it. She didn't want to leave again, the way she had done to get away from her mother, a dreadful, intrusive person. Phyllis got out by being perfect, an overachiever. Having struggled so hard not to be evil like her mother, Phyllis felt threatened when Aaron said she was small-minded and evil. She didn't want to be anything like the mother that she disliked so much.

Now I understood my countertransference response of feeling small and no-good as reflecting a complementary identification with Phyllis's internal maternal object, and at the same time a concordant identification with Phyllis's most repressed part of her self. Using the explanation that Phyllis had worked out, I was able to make an interpretation integrating her words and my countertransference.

I said to Phyllis, "Now I can see that you retreated from Aaron because you wished to keep your relationship together as the harmonious marriage it used to be, and occasionally still is when you have enjoyable sex. You were trying to protect yourself and him from your becoming as horrible as the angry, intrusive mother spoiling the relationship, or else facing the calamity of having to leave the marriage in order to leave that part of you behind."

This interpretation illustrates the use of the "because clause" (Ezriel, 1952). Ezriel noted that transference contains three aspects: (1) a required relationship that defends against (2) an avoided relationship, both of which are preferable to (3) a calamity. We have found it useful in couple therapy to follow his interpretive model, since it brings the avoided relationship into focus as both anxiety and defense.

Aaron had not yet told me enough about himself to let me complete the picture. It was clear that Phyllis was still using projection and overfunctioning within the marriage to keep herself above being horrible. And Aaron, feeling cramped like the children, was finding her control just as horrible. When he suppressed his angry or critical feelings, as he did most of the time except in irrational fights, he also suppressed his warm, affectionate feelings except when he and Phyllis had sex.

In this example, the sexually exciting object relationship was the required relationship being used to repress the avoided rejecting object constellation. Aaron's conscious suppression felt withholding to Phyllis, who longed for feedback and emotional involvement. Aaron's eventual outbursts against her led her to relentless pursuit for his attention, approval, and affection. The emergence of the avoided relationship unleashed the energy of the exciting object constellation, because it was no longer needed for repression. When Phyllis failed to get what she hoped for from Aaron, she then suppressed her longings and withdrew. Now the rejecting object system was repressing the exciting one. But when this happened, she appeared to Aaron to be pouting, and he withdrew. The cycle continued, their needs for intimacy defended against and frustrated by their mutual projective identifications.

As we read this case account, we can see this pattern, but we would have to wait for more object relations information from Aaron to clarify his contribution. We cannot always achieve the same depth or specificity in interpretation, but the "because clause" is still useful as an intention in which we can ask the couple to join as we move toward understanding.

Working with Fantasy and Inner Object Relations

Instead of taking a genogram in evaluation and telling couples what their relationship to their family of origin is, we prefer to wait for a living history of inner objects to emerge through our attention to object relations' history at affectively charged moments in therapy.

Dr. and Mrs. Clark had been working with me (JSS) for a year, and I now used their first names to refer to them in sessions. I had worked on Arthur's passivity; his inability to earn Rhonda's admiration of him as a successful, ambitious, caring man; and his need to denigrate her by comparison to the nurses at the office. I worked on Rhonda's tirades and her outrageous behavior, which alienated Arthur, his office staff, and his family, and which left her feeling contemptible. Their sex life had improved, because he was less demanding and she was less likely to balk and cause a fight. Their tenacious defensive system (in which she was assigned the blame and was the repository for the rage, greed, ambition, and badness in the couple) had not yet yielded to interpretation, although Rhonda was no longer on such a short fuse. I could see improvement in the diminution in the volume and frequency of her reactions and in the degree of his contempt, but the basic pattern stayed in place until Arthur felt safe enough to tell Rhonda and me the full extent of his sadistic and murderous fantasies against women who had abandoned him. Catharsis played a part in securing some relief for him, but the major therapeutic effect came from work done in the countertransference on the way he was treating the two actual women in the room with him—his wife and me—as he told his fantasies about other women.

As he concluded, Arthur said that he was terrified that people would think that he would act out his fantasies, which he assumed I would understand he had never done and would not do in real sex.

I felt extremely uncomfortable. If I acknowledged that I was familiar with such a fear, I felt I would be siding with him in assuming that his wife was ignorant. His wife was hurt that he thought I would understand, as if she wouldn't. Rhonda felt that neither I nor—she nor he, for that matter—could be sure, because he seemed afraid that it could happen.

I said, "There is no evidence that Arthur will act out the fantasies in their murderous form. But there is evidence that he's scared they'll get out of hand. We also have evidence right here that you do sadistic things to each other in this relationship, not physically, but emotionally."

Rhonda got it immediately. She said that she knew this as well as I did. She was grateful to Arthur for sharing his fantasies, because she felt so relieved that he was taking responsibility instead of blaming her for all that was wrong between them. Arthur maintained that he had always told her about his sadistic fantasies, but Rhonda pointed out that he had never gone into it in detail. She felt that the fantasies were exciting at first, but now she knew that they were out of hand.

I said, "To some extent, the threatening part of the fantasy is arousing to both of you. But by the end of it, Arthur, you are terrified of losing control, and Rhonda, you are frightened for your life."

Rhonda felt that understanding this was a breakthrough.

We are inclined to agree with Rhonda's evaluation. The longer Arthur kept the fantasy to himself, the more it seemed to be the real him—terrified of being found out, hidden inside yet demanding to be heard. Furthermore, the way it got heard was through projection into Rhonda, who identified with it: In her rages and attacks on Arthur, she gave expression to that attacking, chopping-up part of him, for which she had a valency. Meanwhile, he contained for her the greater calamity of the wish for death—a wish and fear that stemmed from early loss of an envied and hated older brother.

Working with Dreams

An important part of the therapeutic process with couples is the analysis of the interpersonal–intrapsychic continuum expressed in dreams. Spouses often report dreams during the course of treatment, and sometimes both spouses have dreams that are found to overlap. Split-off aspects of shared unconscious object relations and linkages within the couple system of mutual projections and multiple unconscious communications are manifested in the couple's dreams. So dreams communicate to the therapist the couple's unconscious object relations, and these can then be made conscious to the couple.

Dreams reveal underlying psychic conflict; repressed affects; shifts from one developmental level to another; attempts to master anxiety and control affective flooding; longings, hurts, or failures in development; transferences to the therapist or the spouse; and the refinding of lost objects.

The reporting of dreams in the company of one's spouse brings to the couple system projective identifications that can become known through the dreamer's interpretations, the spouse's responses, and the therapist's further analysis of the couple intrapsychic–interpersonal narrative. Dreams freeze the action and permit a more dispassionate inquiry into the power of the unconscious. Although the dream is the property of the dreamer, the power of the couple's shared imagination given over to playing with the dream material releases its meaning. Associations to dreams are neither true nor false; hence there is a freedom for the couple to make "mental mudpies," and to feel the relief of meaning emerging from terror and chaos. The next two examples are from work with Midge and Tom, and with Linda and Rob, both couples in ongoing therapy. (The therapist in both cases, and the "I" in these vignettes, was CB.)

Following the Affect in Dream Interpretation

Midge and Tom had been living together for 2 years and trying to work through in couple therapy their aversion to getting married. Four months into the treatment, Tom reported a dream in which he had been driving with Midge to my office. He said that they had driven up and down steep hills, with sharp turns, and he really had to push the car to make it up the hills. Coming downhill was much easier. Near the end of the journey, coming down the last hill, the car began to speed up and Tom found that he couldn't brake fast enough. He said that as he and Midge neared my office, there suddenly appeared a stone wall, and he had to crash into it to stop the car. The car was damaged, but they were OK. I came out to help them out of the car. Once out of the car, Tom saw that there were cliffs below. He concluded that if he and Midge hadn't hit the stone wall, they would have plunged into the ocean.

I approach dreams through the associations of first the dreamer, then the spouse; if I have something to add, I speak last. When I am mentioned in dreams as a particular figure in the life of the spouse or couple, I examine my countertransference to their portrayal of me, so as to figure out what type of object I represent—an ego ideal, a deprecated part of the self, a frightening intrusion, an exciting or elusive object, an Oedipal parent, or a buddy.

Tom said that the dream had disturbed him; he awakened perspiring. He woke Midge up and they cuddled, but they did not discuss what he had experienced. He chose to wait until the session. This was typical of Midge and Tom, who tended to veer away from areas of worry, in favor of the physical comfort they received from each other and valued highly. In the session, however, Tom was eager to continue. He elaborated on the sense of responsibility he felt as the driver: Midge was in his car,

and he was endangering her life. It occurred to him that the frightening ups and downs of the steep hills represented marriage, and that the outside world represented challenge and danger. The car was the real culprit, however, since he could not push it hard enough up the hill, or stop it on the final descent.

Hearing his associations, Midge could not contain herself with excitement. She thought that the dream dramatized Tom's fear of inadequacy. She said that it not only held him back in his work life, where he was overqualified for the job he did; it also interfered with his getting married. Tom responded by saying that he wasn't sure whether he could remain committed to marriage, since his parents had divorced and two of his three brothers were in disastrous marriages.

I said that Tom was in touch with the meaning of the part of the dream where the car then went out of control: It signified to him the return of his terror that he would destroy them both if he married and impregnated Midge. Referring to a recent session in which Tom had chuckled playfully about having children with Midge and being a good father, I added that the part of the dream where the downhill road seemed manageable could represent his openness to marriage after a period of strain and toil in therapy. Tom remembered that in that session Midge had expressed reservations about how she could deal with motherhood, given her background of neglect and deprivation. This comment helped me to see that Tom and Midge had a shared view that marriage would lead to disaster, and yet they had demonstrated a shared willingness to face their fears. They responded by pointing to the stone wall in the dream: They concluded that therapy might have been a good barrier against disaster, but at the same time their fears and doubts had been stonewalling the therapy in case analytic exploration would lead to greater imagined danger.

It was time to examine my countertransference to the dream. I felt like the man who could not prevent the couple from crashing the car. Nor could I remove the threat of the ocean, and their ultimate terror, death. True, I had helped them out of the car, but I could not help it that they had gone on a harrowing journey. Still, they had made it to the session, but at great risk. At that moment, I questioned my adequacy and holding function. Then I realized they were doing better with analyzing the dream than I was. For Tom and Midge, the dream had activated the encapsulated unconscious; far from depressing them, it was enlivening them and their capacity to work together. At first I failed to recognize this accomplishment, because I became overconcerned about analyzing the symbolic meaning of the dream. I neglected to take in fully the cathartic experience of the dreamer in telling the dream, or the alleviation of anxiety that the couple felt because of working with it. No matter how well aspects of a dream may be dissected and analyzed, the full therapeutic potential of the dream cannot be realized until the affect of the dreamer and his spouse during the telling of the dream is appreciated.

I now saw that the dream was enabling Tom and Midge to confront and master their desperate need for safety and their fears of breakdown and catastrophe. Embedded in the dream was their fear of depending on each other and on me. I said that they saw me as one to help them, but they were afraid that it was almost too late and so might lead to the death of the couple. Tom said that he now realized that he had been living with the fantasy that remaining single, even though cohabiting, could ensure independence and therefore a measure of safety for each of them. Working on the dream took Tom and Midge over the wall of their resistance to further work on securing their commitment to remaining a couple.

Discovering the Interpersonal Meaning of a Dream

The wife, Linda, reported that in her dream she was making succotash, otherwise known as lima beans and corn. A friend walked in, and she said to her friend that she must be surprised at what she was making. Linda noticed that she felt tense in the dream. She went on to give me her first association. She said that she liked corn and her husband liked lima beans.

It occurred to me that both vegetables retain their individual forms even after prolonged cooking. The word "succotash" makes it sound as if the beans have softened and become mush. Like the beans, Linda and her husband, Rob, retained their own individual forms, unmodified by the marriage.

Linda went on to say that she and Rob were incompatible in many ways. It seemed to her that her dream referred to her conflict over the marriage, and to her guilt about her wishes to leave Rob. She was further reminded of the powerful guilt feelings she had experienced after her grandmother's death, when she developed a long-standing phobia. She feared that if she left Rob, the guilt would cause the phobia to return. Rob responded that he did not want to be with her if he was just there to prevent a phobia. They went on to talk about the fierce competitiveness between them over the years, which prevented intimate connecting.

I suggested that the failure to combine their two personalities like two vegetables, for a new flavor in marriage, was the couple's major disappointment. They agreed sadly and went on to voice regret at their wasted years.

Working Through

The following vignette comes from late in the midphase of Arthur and Rhonda Clark's couple therapy. (As before, JSS was the therapist.)

Following Arthur's revelation of his sadistic fantasies, the Clarks had a session in which Rhonda talked of her continued sense of gratitude that her husband had shared his fantasies with her. Although she felt unusually tentative about responding to him sexually, she felt close to him and committed to working things out. For the first time, she felt an equal level of commitment from him. Summer was approaching, and she was taking the children to visit her family in Maine for a month as usual. Until now, Rhonda had viewed her annual summer trip as a chance to get away from Arthur's criticizing her and demanding sex of her. For the first time, she felt sad that they would have to spend the summer apart.

The sharing of the fantasy had been a healing experience. The couple could now move beyond a level of functioning characteristic of the paranoid–schizoid position toward the depressive position, in which there is concern for the object and where its loss can be appreciated.

In a session following their vacation, Rhonda reported that she had gotten so much from the last session, it had kept her thinking and working for 4 weeks. Even when Arthur expressed no affection during a phone call to her in Maine, when he did not even say he missed her, she felt hurt but not outraged as before. She realized that in some way he just wasn't there.

I suggested that Arthur had been unaware of feeling angry that Rhonda had left him alone for a few weeks, and had dealt with it by killing her off. Rhonda replied that she had managed not to take it personally. Even though Arthur continued to belittle her, she no longer felt like a little person, and she was glad to have changed.

Arthur's revelation of his murderous fantasies had released Rhonda's capacity for growth, confirming that the silent operation of the unconscious projective identification expressed in the fantasy had been cutting her down and killing off her adult capacities.

As we peel away layers of repression, we experience more resistance. Sometimes it feels as though the further we go, the more we fall behind. The couple is suffering from a defensive system of object relationships that are mutually gratifying in an infantile way inside the couple system. Until more mature forms of gratification are found within the system, it is going to resist efforts at change. "Working through" is the term Freud (1914a) gave to the therapeutic effort to keep working away at this resistance and conflict. Sessions in this phase can feel plodding, laborious, repetitive, and uninspired. Resolution comes piecemeal, until one day the work is almost done.

COMMON OBSTACLES TO SUCCESSFUL TREATMENT

Obstacles to treatment include secrets withheld from spouse or therapist; an ongoing affair that dilutes commitment to the marriage; severe intrapsychic illness in one spouse; financial strain from paying for treatment; severe acting out in the session in the form of violence or nonattendance; and the intrusion of the therapist's personal problems into the therapeutic space, unchecked by training or personal therapy. Unresolved countertransference can lead to premature termination (Dickes & Strauss, 1979).

If we can assume an adequate therapist, then the main obstacle to treatment is a lack of psychological-mindedness in the couple. Despite a therapist's best efforts, the spouses in such a couple do not want to deal in frightening areas of unconscious experience. They will do better with a more focused, short-term, symptom-oriented approach. But it is better to discover this from experience than to assume it from a single diagnostic session. Every couple deserves a chance to work in depth. Some will take to the waters, and others will not.

TREATMENT APPLICABILITY

Indications, Contraindications, and Limitations

Object relations couple therapy is indicated for couples that are interested in understanding and growth. It is not for couples whose thinking style is concrete. The capacity to think psychologically does not correlate with intelligence or social advantage, so object relations couple therapy is not contraindicated in socially disadvantaged couples, many of whom are capable of in-depth work if given the opportunity to choose it. D. Scharff and Scharff (1991) have described its usefulness for developmental crises; grief and mourning (Paul, 1967); communication problems; lack of intimacy, including sexuality (D. Scharff, 1982); unwelcome affairs and secrets (D. Scharff, 1978); remarriage (Wallerstein & Blakeslee, 1989); perversions, homosexuality; unwanted pregnancy or infertility; and apparently individual symptomatology that predates the marriage. It is not good for couples that require support and direction, financial assistance and budgetary planning. Alone, it is not sufficient for couples where one partner has an addiction to alcohol or drugs that requires peer group abstinence support, addiction counseling, or rehabilitation. It cannot produce major character change, although it produces enough change that spouses come to view their characters as modifiable. Although in managed care situations its use has been eschewed as a luxury, the therapist who is constrained to work in a brief format with specific, limited goals will gain more understanding if she applies object relations couple therapy theory to her conceptualization of the problem, even though she cannot work as fully in that way as she might like.

Integration with Other Interventions

Object relations couple therapy integrates well with other formats and methodologies, with which it may be combined sequentially or concurrently. It is fully compatible with individual object relations therapy because of the theory base in common. In object relations couple therapy, the theory is compatible both with individual therapy and with group or family therapy, since the theory refers to endopsychic systems that are expressed in the interpersonal dimension. It is also compatible with structural and strategic family therapy, where the therapist can integrate a structural or strategic approach with an in-depth object relations understanding of defensive patterns (Slipp, 1988).

When a patient in psychoanalysis needs couple therapy, object relations couple therapy is the treatment of choice because of compatibility between the underlying theories. Then the patient will not be told to quit analysis (as happened to a patient in analysis with JSS) in favor of a short-term intervention that, however helpful, will not effect major character change for which analysis has been recommended. Sometimes individual problems cannot be managed with couple therapy alone, but this should not be concluded too early. Individual referral is not resorted to readily because it tends to load the couple problem in the individual arena, but when the couple can correctly recognize and meet individual needs, referral for one of the spouses may be helpful to the treatment process and to the marriage. Object relations couple therapy can then be combined with other treatment for the individual spouse, such as medication, addiction rehabilitation, phobia desensitization programs, or psychoanalysis (Graller, 1981).

When psychoanalysis is required, the couple therapist may become anxious that the greater intensity of individual treatment will devalue the couple therapy. That is not at all inevitable. When it occurs, it does so because one therapist is being idealized while the other is being denigrated, due to a splitting of the transference that will need to be addressed. This risk to couple therapy is more likely to be a major problem if the couple therapist secretly admires psychoanalysis and puts her own work down. It is helpful for the concurrent treatments if both therapists are comfortable communicating with each other, but some analysts will not collaborate because they are dedicated to preserving the boundaries of the psychoanalysis (for what they see as good reasons) and will not betray the patient's confidentiality. To our way of thinking, the greater betrayal lies in not confronting the acting out of split transference.

Object relations couple therapy may be combined with a family session with children, who helpfully speak about things of which the grownups are unaware. Sessions for one spouse with parents and/or siblings may be added, and then the couple can review that spouse's experience and its implications for their marriage (Framo, 1981). A couple may also be treated in a group for couples, either as an adjunct to their private couple therapy or as a primary treatment method (Framo, 1973).

Object relations couple therapy can be combined serially or concurrently with behavioral sex therapy (Levay & Kagle, 1978; Lief, 1989; D. Scharff, 1982; D. Scharff & Scharff, 1991). The sex research of Masters and Johnson (1966, 1970) and Kaplan (1974) vastly improved couple therapists' understanding of sexuality. Kaplan (1974) linked an analytic approach with sex therapy methodology. She showed how blockade in the progression through the behavioral steps requires psychoanalytic interpretation to get over underlying anxieties. She described hypoactive sexual desire (Kaplan, 1977, 1979) as a spectrum of disorders usually relating to psychodynamic issues that require psychoanalysis or psychoanalytic therapy, sometimes in conjunction with medication (Kaplan, 1987).

The object relations couple therapist can apply this knowledge within the usual frame of therapy, or may switch to a specific sex therapy format if qualified to do so. We ourselves may prefer to refer the couple to a colleague temporarily or concurrently, if the strain of holding to the nondirective attitude at the unconscious level during directive behavioral formats is too great, or if the couple needs a therapist who is more experienced and qualified in specific sex therapy or behavioral methods. The object relations couple therapist who works regularly in nonanalytic modes combines them without compromising the integrity of his analytic stance, by recognizing and working with the couple's transference to his directiveness in the nonanalytic role. A systems-oriented or structurally trained couple therapist can integrate the analytic stance into his current way of working by attend-

ing to the impact of his personality and directive behavior on the couple's attitude toward him. The object relations perspective gives more access to the use of the therapist's psyche (Aponte & VanDeusen, 1981) and provides the systems therapist with greater understanding of the system through its patterns that he will find recreated in relation to himself (Van Trommel, 1984, 1985).

An illustration of the link among internal object relations, psychosexual stages of development, and sexual symptomatology is provided in the following vignette from an initial couple therapy evaluation (conducted by JSS, with David Scharff as her cotherapist).

Michelle and Lenny (who have appeared briefly in this chapter's first case vignette) had a hateful attachment. Although diametrically opposite in character and family background, they had been together for 4 years, but Michelle, an outgoing social activist, had been unable to marry quiet, conservative Lenny because he seemed so passive. A nice, attractive man from an upper-class family, successful in business, loyal to her, he had many appealing qualities. He treated her well, he adored her, but she hated his steadfastness. He just could not meet her expectations. Her ideal man would be like her amazingly energetic, confident, and admirable brother. Unlike steady Lenny, Michelle was bubbling with energy. So, why was she still with Lenny? Lenny was a kind, loyal boyfriend, but Michelle criticized him for being boring to her and put him down relentlessly. He seemed immune to criticism and maintained his steady love for her.

Both of us therapists felt uncomfortable with this frustrating relationship, and D. Scharff, who is normally rather energetic, almost fell asleep to avoid the pain of being with Michelle and Lenny. His countertransference response led us to see the underlying sadness in their relationship and to experience the void they would have to face if their destructive bantering were to stop. Lenny's void came from the lack of a father when he was growing up. Michelle's came from her perception of herself as a girl whose brother had more than she did.

Unlike the way she felt about boring old Lenny, Michelle felt special. So why did she hate herself? Her mother felt that her brother was the really special child, and this had given him immense confidence, which Michelle was missing. Michelle explained that, because of this, there was a part of her that constantly found holes in herself.

To an analyst, these words speak of penis envy from the phallic stage of development. Usually we address this issue in the broader terms of envy of the man's world. But in this case, both aspects of Michelle's envy were close to consciousness. And Lenny was not far behind her in the extent of his envy of Michelle's brother. He wished he could be like him.

It turned out that in bed, Lenny was the confident sexual partner who had shown great sensitivity to Michelle's vaginismus. He helped her to tolerate intercourse and find sexual release with him. He found her beautiful, whether she was fat or thin. For Michelle, who hated her body, Lenny's adoration was gratifying, but it was also contemptible because sex was difficult for her. On the other hand, she was grateful for his patience, his sexual restraint, and his comfort with sex. Nevertheless, penetration by a powerful phallus was frightening to her.

I said, "It's sad for you that you can't take sexual pleasure from the penis, because you see it as a source of envied and threatening power." Michelle agreed that she hated it, and added that this was because it seemed like a way of controlling a woman.

Returning to classical Freudian theory for a moment, we could say that as a child, Michelle had thought that boys like her brother did not feel the emptiness and longing that she felt in relation to her rejecting mother; they each had the penis that she was missing, while her vagina felt like an empty hole. In her adulthood, the penis continued to be threatening because it could enter that painful hole. She now felt her childhood hatred of the penis toward the man in her adult sexual relationship. The better Lenny did with her sexually, the more she had to attack him enviously. Lenny, though sexually competent, had some inhibition against being assertive generally and sexually, and used Michelle as a phallic front for himself so that he could avoid castration anxiety.

In contrast, in object relations terms we can say that the couple was using Michelle as a manic defense against emptiness and sadness, and using Lenny as a depository for the schizoid defense against emptiness. Painful longing was projected into Michelle's vagina, for which she had a psychophysiological valency. In therapy, Lenny and Michelle would need to take back these projective identifications of each other and develop a holding capacity for bearing their shared anxieties.

COMMON SIGNIFICANT CLINICAL ISSUES

Working with the Difficult Couple

There are many varieties of difficult couples. Difficulty depends partly on the degree of fixity and severity of a couple's unconscious complementariness and pathology, and partly on the spouses' fit with the object relations set of their therapist. Difficult couples may transfer from previous therapists

in whom they were disappointed. The new therapist may fall into the trap of expecting to be no better than the previous one, or of competing to be much better. Sometimes treatment does go better, usually because of the couple's projection of negative objects into the former therapist. Unless the current therapist can address that issue, the couple will seem better but will not have developed the capacity to integrate good and bad objects. The turning point in treatment of the difficult couple often comes when the therapist is able to experience fully in the countertransference the hopelessness and despair underlying their defense of being difficult (D. Scharff & Scharff, 1991). Sometimes the couple cannot use the assessment process to develop trust in the therapist sufficient for making a commitment to therapy. The disappointment that the therapist feels in failing to make an alliance activates guilt about not being able to repair the damage of the therapist's internal parental couple (J. S. Scharff, 1992).

Managing Resistance and Noncompliance

At worst, a couple may remain too resistant to engage in couple therapy. Nevertheless, one of the spouses may be willing to have individual therapy. It is important to start where the couple is. Change in one partner will effect change in the system, so that couple therapy may be possible later. Before arriving at that conclusion, however, we try as object relations couple therapists to be understanding of the reasons for the resistance. We do not try to seduce the couple into making a commitment or promise symptomatic relief. We do not remove the resistance by paradoxical prescription. We analyze the resistance with the aim of freeing the spouses from the inhibition imposed by their defenses against intervention and giving them control over their decision about treatment.

Sometimes a couple can make the commitment but cannot keep it, when anxieties surface. They may miss appointments, forget or refuse to pay the bill, or substitute one of the partners for the couple. We discuss all these attempts to bend the frame, in the hope that making conscious the unconscious reluctance will help the couple to confront us about the treatment process and our therapeutic style. But we do not agree to work without pay—both because we cannot allow our worth and earning potential to be attacked in that way, and because it produces unconscious guilt in the couple. Our policy is that we do not see a spouse alone to fill a session from which the other spouse is missing. On the other hand, each of us has at times done so when the situation seemed to call for it. Policies differ among object relations couple therapists as they do among therapists of other backgrounds, but the important thing is to establish a policy and a way of working and hold to it as a standard from which to negotiate, experiment, and learn.

Working with the Couple When There Is an Affair

Greene (1970) warned that premature discussion of an affair can disrupt the marriage, and Martin (1976) agreed that the mate should not always be told the secret. D. Scharff (1978) advocated revelation of the secret in every case, but has since modified the rigidity of his view (D. Scharff & Scharff, 1991). Revelation puts the couple and therapist in a position to learn from the affair and to understand the meaning of the secret in developmental terms (Gross, 1951), the significance of the affair (Strean, 1976, 1979), and the attraction of the lover for the spouse. Only when the affair is known can the therapist work with the couple's expression of disappointment, envy, rage, love, and sadness. In the affair (as in a fantasy) lies important information about repressed object relations that cannot be expressed and contained within the marriage. It is worth remembering that the affair is an attempt to maintain the marriage, even while threatening its existence.

Spouses cannot work on their relationship while one of them has another intimate partner at the same time. The integrity of the marriage remains compromised, and the therapy cannot be effective. Nevertheless, our way of working calls for a flexible attunement to the needs of each case. Even though the couple is referred for couple therapy, an individual spouse may not have made the commitment to the therapy or the continuation of the marriage. Revelation of an infidelity is not always immediately possible, or timely. The secret may be kept because the unfaithful spouse finds the affair more gratifying than the marriage and may not have decided that the marriage is worth working on. In this case, a spouse may request individual sessions without telling us why these are needed.

When the spouse reveals a secret affair to the therapist in the individual session, this action may have many meanings. There may be a wish for permission to carry on a duplicitous life, as well as for validation of how horrible the spouse is and how wonderful the lover is. A husband may be uninterested in both marriage and divorce, the preference being to split the maternal image into the dull steady woman by whom to be nurtured and the exciting sexual one with whom to sustain an exciting object experience. That way, no single woman becomes all-powerful and absorbing.

Early sharing of deep ambivalence profoundly tests the therapist's holding capacity. A viable alliance is possible only if the unfaithful spouse is not forced into confessing. Instead, a series of individual sessions provide a thorough exploration of individual development, defenses, anxieties, the meaning of the current plight, and especially the spouse's use of the therapist. During this process, the spouse reviews the choices singly. This individual work may result in ending the marriage and not proceeding with couple therapy, or it may become a prelude to couple treatment. It took 3 months of individual sessions talking about his secret affair before the man in the following example was ready for couple therapy with one of us (CB):

When I saw Marty and his wife together, I was faced with the problem of confidentiality. I would be colluding with Marty's withholding, if I went ahead indefinitely holding his secret. However, if I used a cookie-cutter approach and demanded disclosure too soon, I would be overidentified with presumed hurt of the wife, who was being kept in the dark. I felt guilty and manipulated, as if I were the secret lover. I felt compromised, and resentful, and Marty seemed oblivious to that. This experience brought to mind the missing empathic component of the marriage relationship. I did not want to chase Marty out of therapy before determining whether we could create a working alliance. I also comforted myself with the thought that if a good-faith treatment of the couple was not possible, I could say that and resign.

Often we are best served in working with the individual spouse until the motives for sharing the secret with us can be known. If couple therapy seems viable later on, but the individual spouse chooses to keep the secret from the partner, we cannot be therapeutically effective because we will be constrained by being unable to use what we know. We will not be free to guess at secret interference, and our preferred impartial approach to the couple relationship will be skewed as we are captured by the aims of one partner. It is then better for the couple to find another couple therapist and start afresh.

Marty entered individual therapy feeling highly ambivalent. For 6 months, he had been living a duplicitous existence—in love with another woman, but uncertain about leaving his marriage. The work with him consisted of individual, twice-weekly sessions, lasting for 3 months. During this period Marty explored the realities of his marriage, as well as the exciting relationship with the other woman. She needed him and made him feel very special, particularly in lovemaking. Marty's background included having been seduced by a sister 5 years older than he when he was 12. He also told me that his father had been distant from him during his growing up, while his mother was intimidating and cruel. It seemed clear that his search for excitement and control over women stemmed from his previous experiences: fear of a demanding and unloving mother, a father who left him unprotected, and erotic overstimulation at puberty by the sister. It turned out that Marty's underlying motives for the affair had to do with his reaction to a recent improvement in his wife's appearance. She had lost weight and was going back to school for a teaching degree. Their two young children were also keeping him from leaving impulsively, as he did not want to repeat his father's abandonment. His wife's independent strivings were signaling an anxiety not remembered until now—fears of abandonment by a woman.

The therapy moved from individual to couple therapy at Marty's request. He had used me to examine the consequences of past and present experiences, including betrayals and disloyalties and their symbolic meanings. We also discussed his wished-for future. He was able to recognize how the affair was an attempt to reduce internal conflict, which had been part of his life since preadolescence. As a result of his intensive sessions, he admitted to the affair during the first couple interview. There was tremendous fallout, but the couple worked diligently at the relationship problems. The marital treatment lasted for 2 years.

What was effective in mixing an individual approach with the marital therapy? By not prodding Marty to attempt couple therapy, or to admit the affair to his spouse during the short-term individual therapy, the therapist (CB) remained available to be used by Marty to explore the conscious and unconscious motives for his predicament and to help him understand the sources of his symptomatic behavior. Comprehending the intrapsychic dimensions of infidelity requires patience and time, since splitting good and bad objects is a common feature of infidelity, and is a major defense to be reckoned with. Insisting that Marty give up his objects prematurely would have resulted in flight, and there would have been no hope of therapeutic outcome.

Handling Acute Couple Distress

The prompt offer of a consultation appointment is usually enough to contain acute distress. In more extreme cases, a suicidal or psychotic spouse may require medication or hospitalization, while a violent one will need to be separated from temporarily. When distress is acute, and the therapist has no time to deal with an emergency, it is better to refer the case to someone who has time than to make the couple wait for an appointment. During the delay, a couple problem may be redefined as an individual illness, and the advantage of the healing potential of the crisis in the system is lost. If the therapist does take the referral, a longer appointment time than usual is required to allow enough time for the spouses to express their distress and for the therapist to develop the necessary holding capacity. The therapist needs time to contain the partners' anxiety, offer them a therapeutic relationship on which they can count, and demonstrate the possibility of understanding their overwhelming emotion. Another appointment time within the week is scheduled before the couple leaves the session.

Working with a History of Trauma

Spouses who are overwhelmed by recent trauma will experience it in terms of any previous trauma. They may try to dissociate from it by splitting off their awareness of the traumatic experience and sequestering it in traumatic nuclei inside the marriage (J. S. Scharff & Scharff, 1994). An apparently satisfactory marital relationship may cover these traumatic nuclei or gaps. In those cases, couple therapists may get access to the couple's dissociated material by analyzing their own feelings of discomfort or by examining gaps in the treatment process. When the material inside the nuclei is too toxic to be managed, affect explosions or absences of affect and motivation may bring the couple into treatment. That is how the couple we now describe came to see David Scharff (described more fully in J. S. Scharff & Scharff, 1994).

Tony and Theresa had been happy together in their marriage and now had three children, the eldest adopted from Theresa's first marriage. Tony and Theresa both worked to support the family, and both shared household chores. Suddenly a fulminating infection in Tony's right arm could not be treated medically, and he had to have his shoulder and arm amputated to save his life. An easygoing, cheerful man, Tony bounced right back at first; then depression hit as he realized the enormity of his loss. He refused rehabilitation work and prosthesis fittings. He sat around at home while his wife went out and worked his shift as well as her own. Then, when she came home, he complained about her being away. They were arguing an unusual amount; their eldest child was avoiding the home; the middle child was doing badly in school; and the younger one seemed simply sad.

Telling the therapist about the trauma relieved their stress somewhat, and then it was possible to reveal the trauma base against which their marriage had been organized. Both Tony and Theresa had been physically abused by their parents, and both had taken the role of the child who will get hit to protect the others. When they got married, each promised to respect the other. There would never be any violence in their relationship. When tempers flared, they punched the wall instead. The bricks had absorbed their anger, and in so doing built a wall between them and their feelings. Now Tony had lost his punching arm, and without it he did not know how to express his rage and grief.

The couple therapist noted considerable improvement in Tony and Theresa's capacity to acknowledge anger, but he was puzzled by a new pattern of skipping sessions. Their silences and his own discomfort led him to guess that they were creating a gap to cover over another traumatic nucleus. Perhaps another recent trauma lay beneath the loss of Tony's arm. Since they had already told him about their problems with anger, he asked whether they might be avoiding discussing some other feeling, perhaps in relation to their sexual life. Theresa replied that she had had a hysterectomy some years earlier, and since then had suffered from recurrent vaginal infections. Previously the couple had enjoyed a vigorous sexual life, and now sex had become less frequent. Theresa admitted that she avoided sex because it was painful for her—a secret that she had kept from Tony until that moment.

Prior to the loss of Tony's arm, the couple had lost the use of Theresa's vagina as an accepting, sexually responsive organ. They had thus lost one body part that stood for the control of aggression (Tony's arm) and one that stood for their loving connectedness (Theresa's well-functioning vagina), both of them vital to the maintenance of their commitment to each other. Work with the couple would have to focus on mourning their losses and then finding gratifying ways to express love and anger.

In couples where current sexual interaction is traumatic, compulsively enacted, or phobically avoided, we inquire about earlier sexual experience, including unwanted sexual experience in the family of origin. We help the couple that tends to invoke abusive behavior in one spouse by showing that this is a way of repeating the abuse instead of remembering it. Other couples need to see that their successful efforts to avoid repetition of abuse require a high degree of close control that is less successful for them because it is inhibiting not only to the marital relationship, but also to the next generation. We try to put words to experience. We help the spouses to develop a narrative of the abuse history to share with their family, as an alternative to the reenactment of trauma and the defenses against it.

Termination

The couple has had some rehearsal for termination when ending each time-limited session and facing breaks in treatment due to illness, business commitments, or vacations. We work with a couple's habitual way of dealing with separations in preparation for the final parting. Our criteria for judging when that will be are as follows:

- The couple has internalized the therapeutic space and now has a reasonably secure holding capacity.
- Unconscious projective identifications have been recognized, owned, and taken back by each spouse.
- The spouses' capacity to work together as life partners is restored.
- Relating intimately and sexually is mutually gratifying.
- The couple can envision its future development and can provide a vital holding environment for its family.
- The couple can differentiate among and meet the needs of each partner.
- Alternatively, the couple recognizes the failure of the couple choice and understands the unconscious object relations incompatibility; the partners separate, with some grief work done and with a capacity to continue to mourn the loss of the marriage individually.

These criteria for terminating are really only markers of progress. Couples decide for themselves what their goals are and whether they have been met. Sometimes, they coincide with our idea of completion and sometimes not. We have to let ourselves become redundant and to tolerate being discarded. As we mourn with each couple the loss of the therapy relationship (and in some cases the loss of the marriage), we rework all the earlier losses. The couple relives issues from earlier phases of the treatment, now with greater capacity for recovery from regression. Separating from the therapeutic relationship, we and the couple demonstrate our respective capacities for acknowledging experience, dealing with loss, understanding defensive regressions, and mastering anxiety. As the couple terminates, now able to get on with life and love without us, we take our leave of the spouses and at the same time resolve another piece of our ambivalent attachment to our internal couple. Such a thorough experience of termination seasons us and prepares us to be of use to the next couple.

REFERENCES

Aponte, H. J., & VanDeusen, J. M. (1981). Structural family therapy. In A. S. Gurman & D. P. Kniskern (Eds.), *Handbook of family therapy* (pp. 310–360). New York: Brunner/Mazel.

Bagnini, C. (in press). The persecutory object in divorce. In J. S. Scharff & S. Tsigounis (Eds.), *Detoxifying the persecutory object.* London: Brunner/Routledge.

Balint, M. (1968). *The basic fault: Therapeutic aspects of regression.* London: Tavistock.

Bannister, K., & Pincus, L. (1965). *Shared phantasy in marital problems: Therapy in a four-person relationship.* London: Tavistock.

Bergmann, M. (1987). *The anatomy of loving.* New York: Columbia University Press.

Bergmann, M. (1990, November). *Love and hate in the life of a couple.* Paper presented at the Washington School of Psychiatry Conference on Romantic Love, Washington, DC.

Bion, W. R. (1961). *Experiences in groups.* London: Tavistock.

Bion, W. R. (1962). *Learning from experience.* London: Heinemann.

Bion, W. R. (1970). *Attention and interpretation.* London: Tavistock.

Bodin, A. M. (1981). The interactional view: Family therapy approaches of the Mental Research Institute. In A. S. Gurman & D. P. Kniskern (Eds.), *Handbook of family therapy* (pp. 267–309). New York: Brunner/Mazel.

Bowen, M. (1978). *Family therapy in clinical practice.* New York: Jason Aronson.

Box, S. (1981). Introduction: Space for thinking in families. In S. Box, B. Copley, J. Magagna, & E. Moustaki (Eds.), *Psychotherapy with families* (pp. 1–8). London: Routledge & Kegan Paul.

Brazelton, T. B. (1982). Joint regulation of neonate–parent behavior. In E. Tronick (Ed.), *Social interchange in infancy* (pp. 7–22). Baltimore: University Park Press.

Brazelton, T. B., & Als, H. (1979). Four early stages in the development of mother–infant interaction. *Psychoanalytic Study of the Child, 34,* 349–369.

Broderick, C. B., & Schrader, S. S. (1981). The history of professional marriage and family therapy. In A. S.

Gurman & D. P. Kniskern (Eds.), *Handbook of family therapy* (pp. 5–35). New York: Brunner/Mazel.

Clulow, C. (1985). *Marital therapy: An inside view.* Aberdeen, Scotland: Aberdeen University Press.

Dare, C. (1986). Psychoanalytic marital therapy. In N. S. Jacobson & A. S. Gurman (Eds.), *Clinical handbook of marital therapy* (pp. 13–28). New York: Guilford Press.

Dickes, R., & Strauss, D. (1979). Countertransference as a factor in premature termination of apparently successful cases. *Journal of Sex and Marital Therapy, 5,* 22–27.

Dicks, H. V. (1967). *Marital tensions: Clinical studies towards a psycho-analytic theory of interaction.* London: Routledge & Kegan Paul.

Erikson, E. H. (1950). *Childhood and society.* New York: Norton.

Ezriel, H. (1952). Notes on psychoanalytic group therapy: II. Interpretation and research. *Psychiatry, 15,* 119–126.

Fairbairn, W. R. D. (1952). Endopsychic structure considered in terms of object relationships. In W. R. D. Fairbairn, *Psychoanalytic studies of the personality* (pp. 82–135). London: Routledge & Kegan Paul. (Original work published 1944)

Fairbairn, W. R. D. (1952). *Psychoanalytic studies of the personality.* London: Routledge & Kegan Paul.

Fairbairn, W. R. D. (1954). Observations on the nature of hysterical states. *British Journal of Medical Psychology, 27,* 105–125.

Fairbairn, W. R. D. (1963). Synopsis of an object-relations theory of the personality. *International Journal of Psycho-Analysis, 44,* 224–225.

Finkelstein, L. (1987). Toward an object relations approach in psychoanalytic marital therapy. *Journal of Marital and Family Therapy, 13,* 287–298.

Framo, J. L. (1973). Marriage therapy in a couples' group. *Seminars in Psychiatry, 5,* 207–217.

Framo, J. L. (1981). The integration of marital therapy with sessions with family of origin. In A. S. Gurman & D. P. Kniskern (Eds.), *Handbook of family therapy* (pp. 133–158). New York: Brunner/Mazel.

Framo, J. L. (1982). Symptoms from a family transactional viewpoint. In J. l. Framo (Ed.), *Explorations in marital and family therapy: Selected papers of James L. Framo* (pp. 11–57). New York: Springer. (Original work published 1970)

Freud, S. (1905). Three essays on the theory of sexuality. *Standard Edition, 7,* 125–243.

Freud, S. (1912). Recommendations to physicians practicing psycho-analysis. *Standard Edition, 12,* 111–120.

Freud, S. (1917). Transference. *Standard Edition, 16,* 431–447.

Friedman, E. H. (1991). Bowen theory and therapy. In A. S. Gurman & D. P. Kniskern (Eds.), *Handbook of family therapy* (pp. 134–170). New York: Brunner/Mazel.

Friedman, L. (1962). *Virgin wives: A study of unconsummated marriages.* London: Tavistock.

Graller, J. (1981). Adjunctive marital therapy. *The Annual of Psychoanalysis, 9,* 175–187.

Greene, B. L. (1970). *A clinical approach to marital problems.* Springfield, IL: Charles C Thomas.

Gross, A. (1951). "The secret." *Bulletin of the Menninger Clinic, 15,* 37–44.

Guntrip, H. (1961). *Personality structure and human inter-*

action: *The developing synthesis of psychodynamic theory.* London: Hogarth Press and The Institute of Psycho-Analysis.

Guntrip, H. (1969). *Schizoid phenomena, object relations and the self.* New York: International Universities Press.

Gurman, A. S. (1978). Contemporary marital therapies: A critique and comparative analysis of psychoanalytic, behavioral and system approaches. In T. J. Paolino & B. S. McCrady (Eds.), *Marriage and marital therapy* (pp. 455–566). New York: Brunner/Mazel.

Gurman, A. S., & Jacobson, N. S. (1986). Marital therapy: From technique to theory, back again, and beyond. In N. S. Jacobson & A. S. Gurman (Eds.), *Clinical handbook of marital therapy* (pp. 1–9). New York: Guilford Press.

Heimann, P. (1950). On counter-transference. *International Journal of Psycho-Analysis, 31,* 81–84.

Heimann, P. (1973). Certain functions of introjection and projection in early infancy. In M. Klein, P. Heimann, S. Isaacs, & J. Riviere (Eds.), *Developments in psychoanalysis* (pp. 122–168). London: Hogarth Press and the Institute of Psycho-Analysis.

Hollender, M. H. (1971). Selection of therapy for marital problems. In J. H. Masserman (Ed.), *Current psychiatric therapies* (Vol. 11, pp. 119–128). New York: Grune & Stratton.

Jackson, D. D., & Weakland, J. H. (1961). Conjoint family therapy. *Psychiatry, 24,* 30–45.

Jacobs, T. J. (1991). *The use of the self.* Madison, CT: International Universities Press.

Kaplan, H. S. (1974). *The new sex therapy: Active treatment of sexual dysfunctions.* New York: Brunner/Mazel.

Kaplan, H. S. (1977). Hypoactive sexual desire. *Journal of Sex and Marital Therapy, 3,* 3–9.

Kaplan, H. S. (1979). *Disorders of sexual desire and other new concepts and techniques in sex therapy.* New York: Brunner/Mazel.

Kaplan, H. S. (1987) *Sexual aversion, sexual phobias, and panic disorder.* New York: Brunner/Mazel.

Kernberg, O. F. (1975). *Borderline conditions and pathological narcissism.* New York: Jason Aronson.

Kernberg, O. F. (1991). Aggression and love in the relationship of the couple. *Journal of the American Psychoanalytic Association, 39,* 45–70.

Klein, M. (1946). Notes on some schizoid mechanisms. *International Journal of Psycho-Analysis, 27,* 99–110.

Klein, M. (1948). *Contributions to psycho-analysis, 1921–1945.* London: Hogarth Press.

Klein, M. (1957). *Envy and gratitude.* London: Tavistock.

Kohut, H. (1971). *The analysis of the self.* New York: International Universities Press.

Kohut, H. (1977). *The restoration of the self.* New York: International Universities Press.

Kohut, H. (1982). Introspection, empathy, and the semicircle of mental health. *International Journal of Psycho-Analysis, 63,* 395–407.

Langs, R. (1976). *The therapeutic interaction: Vol. 2. A critical overview and synthesis.* New York: Jason Aronson.

Lansky, M. (1986). Marital therapy for narcissistic disorders. In N. S. Jacobson & A. S. Gurman (Eds.), *Clinical handbook of marital therapy* (pp. 557–574). New York: Guilford Press.

Levay, A. N., & Kagle, A. (1978). Recent advances in sex therapy: Integration with the dynamic therapies. *Psychiatric Quarterly, 50,* 5–16.

Lief, H. F. (1989, October). *Integrating sex therapy with*

couple therapy. Paper presented at the 47th Annual Conference of the American Association for Marriage and Family Therapy, San Francisco.

Main, T. (1966). Mutual projection in a marriage. *Comprehensive Psychiatry, 7,* 432–449.

Martin, P. A. (1976). *A couple therapy manual.* New York: Brunner/Mazel.

Masters, W. H., & Johnson, V. E. (1966). *Human sexual response.* Boston: Little, Brown.

Masters, W. H., & Johnson, V. E. (1970). *Human sexual inadequacy.* Boston: Little, Brown.

McCormack, C. (1989). The borderline–schizoid marriage. *Journal of Marital and Family Therapy, 15,* 299–309.

Meissner, W. W. (1978). The conceptualization of marriage and marital dynamics from a psychoanalytic perpective. In T. J. Paolino & B. S. McCrady (Eds.), *Marriage and marital therapy* (pp. 25–28). New York: Brunner/Mazel.

Money-Kyrle, R. (1956). Normal countertransference and some of its deviations. *International Journal of Psycho-Analysis, 37,* 360–366.

Murray, J. M. (1955). *Keats.* New York: Noonday Press.

Nadelson, C. C. (1978). Marital therapy from a psychoanalytic perspective. In T. J. Paolino & B. S. McCrady (Eds.), *Marriage and marital therapy* (pp. 101–164). New York: Brunner/Mazel.

Ogden, T. H. (1982). *Projective identification and psychotherapeutic technique.* New York: Jason Aronson.

Paul, N. (1967). The role of mourning and empathy in conjoint marital therapy. In G. Zuk & I. Boszormenyi-Nagy (Eds.), *Family therapy and disturbed families* (pp. 186–205). Palo Alto, CA: Science & Behavior Books.

Pincus, L. (Ed.). (1960). *Marriage: Studies in emotional conflict and growth.* London: Methuen.

Racker, H. (1968). *Transference and countertransference.* New York: International Universities Press.

Ravenscroft, K. (1991, March). *Changes in projective identification during treatment.* Paper presented at the Washington School of Psychiatry Object Relations Couple and Family Therapy Training Program Conference, Bethesda, MD.

Ryckoff, I., Day, J., & Wynne, L. (1959). Maintenance of stereotyped roles in the families of schizophrenics. *Archives of General Psychiatry, 1,* 93–98.

Sager, C. J. (1976). *Marriage contracts and couple therapy: Hidden forces in intimate relationships.* New York: Brunner/Mazel.

Sager, C. J., Kaplan, H. S., Gundlach, R. H., Kremer, M., Lenz, R., & Royce, J. R. (1971). The marriage contract. *Family Process, 10,* 311–326.

Scharff, D. E. (1978). Truth and consequences in sex and marital therapy: The revelation of secrets in the therapeutic setting. *Journal of Sex and Marital Therapy, 4,* 35–49.

Scharff, D. E. (1982). *The sexual relationship: An object relations view of sex and the family.* London: Routledge & Kegan Paul. (Re-issued Northvale, NJ: Jason Aronson)

Scharff, D. E., & Scharff, J. S. (1987). *Object relations family therapy.* Northvale, NJ: Jason Aronson.

Scharff, D. E., & Scharff, J. S. (1991). *Object relations couple therapy.* Northvale, NJ: Jason Aronson.

Scharff, J. S. (Ed.). (1989). *Foundations of object relations family therapy.* Northvale, NJ: Jason Aronson.

Scharff, J. S. (1992). *Projective and introjective identification and the use of the therapist's self.* Northvale, NJ: Jason Aronson.

Scharff, J. S., & Scharff, D. E. (1994). *Object relations therapy of physical and sexual trauma.* Northvale, NJ: Jason Aronson.

Scharff, J. S., & Scharff, D. E. (1998). *Object relations individual therapy.* Northvale, NJ: Jason Aronson.

Scharff, J. S., & Scharff, D. E. (Eds.). (2000). *Tuning the therapeutic instrument: The affective learning of psychotherapy.* Northvale, NJ: Jason Aronson.

Schore, A. (1994). *Affect regulation and the origin of the self: The neurobiology of emotional development.* Hillsdale, NJ: Erlbaum.

Segal, H. (1964). *Introduction to the work of Melanie Klein.* London: Heinemann.

Shapiro, R. L. (1979). Family dynamics and object relations theory: An analytic, group-interpretive approach to family therapy. In J. S. Scharff (Ed.), *Foundations of object relations family therapy* (pp. 225–245). Northvale, NJ: Jason Aronson, 1989.

Skynner, A. C. R. (1976). *Systems of family and marital psychotherapy.* New York: Brunner/Mazel.

Slipp, S. (1984). *Object relations: A dynamic bridge between individual and family treatment.* New York: Jason Aronson.

Slipp, S. (1988). *Theory and practice of object relations family therapy.* Northvale, NJ: Jason Aronson.

Solomon, M. (1989). *Narcissism and intimacy.* New York: Norton.

Stern, D. N. (1985). *The interpersonal world of the infant: A view from psychoanalysis and developmental psychology.* New York: Basic Books.

Stewart, R. H., Peters, T. C., Marsh, S., & Peters, M. J. (1975). An object relations approach to psychotherapy with married couples, families and children. *Family Process, 14,* 161–178.

Stierlin, H. (1977). *Psychoanalysis and family therapy.* New York: Jason Aronson.

Strean, H. S. (1976). The extra-marital affair: A psychoanalytic view. *Psychoanalytic Review, 63,* 101–113.

Strean, H. S. (1979). *The extramarital affair.* New York: Free Press.

Sutherland, J. (1980). The British object relations theorists: Balint, Winnicott, Fairbairn, Guntrip. *Journal of the American Psychoanalytic Association, 28,* 829–860.

Sullivan, H. S. (1953). *The interpersonal theory of psychiatry.* New York: Norton.

Thomas, A. (1956). Simultaneous psychotherapy with marital partners. *American Journal of Psychotherapy, 10,* 716–727.

Van Trommel, M. J. (1984). A consultation method addressing the therapist–family system. *Family Process, 23,* 469–480.

Wallerstein, J. S., & Blakeslee, S. (1989). *Second chances.* New York: Ticknor & Fields.

Willi, J. (1982). *Couples in collusion.* Claremont, CA: Hunter House.

Willi, J. (1984). *Dynamics of couples therapy.* New York: Jason Aronson.

Winnicott, D. W. (1958). Transitional objects and transitional phenomena. In D. W. Winnicott, *Collected papers: Through paediatrics to psycho-analysis* (pp. 249–242). London: Tavistock. (Original work published 1951)

Winnicott, D. W. (1958). *Collected papers: Through paediatrics to psycho-analysis.* London: Tavistock.

Winnicott, D. W. (1960). The theory of the parent–infant relationship. *International Journal of Psycho-Analysis, 41,* 585–595.

Winnicott, D. W. (1965). *The maturational processes and the facilitating environment.* London: Hogarth Press.

Winnicott, D. W. (1971). *Playing and reality.* London: Tavistock.

Wynne, L. (1965). Some indications and contraindications for exploratory family therapy. In I. Boszormenyi-Nagy & J. Framo (Eds.), *Intensive family therapy* (pp. 289–322). New York: Harper & Row.

Zilbach, J. (1988). The family life cycle: A framework for understanding children in family therapy. In L. Combrinck-Graham (Ed.), *Children in family contexts* (pp. 46–66). New York: Guilford Press.

Zinner, J. (1976). The implications of projective identification for marital interaction. In H. Grunebaum & J. Christ (Eds.), *Contemporary marriage: Structure, dynamics, and therapy* (pp. 293–308). Boston: Little, Brown.

Zinner, J. (1988, March). *Projective identification is a key to resolving marital conflict.* Paper presented at the Washington School of Psychiatry Psychoanalytic Family and Couple Therapy Conference, Bethesda, MD.

Zinner, J. (1989). The use of concurrent therapies: Therapeutic strategy or reenactment. In J. S. Scharff (Ed.), *Foundations of object relations family therapy* (pp. 321–333). New York: Jason Aronson.

Zinner, J., & Shapiro, R. (1972). Projective identification as a mode of perception and behavior in families of adolescents. *International Journal of Psycho-Analysis, 53,* 523–530.

Chapter 4

Structural–Strategic Marital Therapy

JAMES KEIM
JAY LAPPIN

All clinicians must deal with marriages in some way, because everyone is either married, planning to be married, or avoiding marriage.
—JAY HALEY (1976, p. 161)

No two models are more closely associated with the evolution of family therapy than structural and strategic therapy. In their early years, these two therapy models evolved as synergistic dancers on the newly opened stage of systems therapy. Over the last 30 years, their evolution has paralleled many of the advances and missteps of the family therapy field.

This chapter on structural–strategic therapy (SST) for marital problems attempts to capture the most current range of practice of the Washington school of strategic therapy,[1] founded by Jay Haley and Cloe Madanes, and the structural school, founded by Salvador Minuchin, Braulio Montalvo, and associates.[2] We, as long-time proponents of their respective models,[3] proceed from the following basic viewpoints.

BASIC VIEWPOINTS

Basic Descriptive Assumptions

1. The structural model and the Washington school of strategic therapy are described as existing within a single range of practice rather than as separate models. As employed in this chapter, the term "SST" refers not to a new model of therapy, but rather to this range of practice represented by current structural and Washington school clinical practice. Because SST represents a range of practice rather than a single style, differences are noted without contradicting the single model construct. This definition is similar to that of describing different shades of the color blue; for many purposes, a range of hues may still be best thought of as being different shades of a single color, blue. This approach is informed by the work of Stanton and Todd (Stanton, 1981; Stanton, Todd, & Associates, 1982), Andolfi (1979), and Friesen (1985), as well as by the 1993 conference "The Integration of Structural and Strategic Therapy," held at the National Institutes of Health, and by the works of other major figures in SST.[4]

2. Borrowing from Aponte's and DiCesare's (2000, p. 46) description of structural therapy, we note that SST is "not another insulated, self-contained model of therapy. It has become an approach that contributes a perspective to other models, and can comfortably utilize contributions from them." Both the structural and strategic teaching and supervision traditions have used not only their own constructs, but also those of other models, in order

to conceptualize the treatment of a wide range of range of problems and clients. There is an ongoing, dynamic interchange of ideas with other schools of therapy and research.

3. SST is a skeletal model to which therapists must to some degree bring their own cultural, political, spiritual, and value constructs.

4. SST texts and methods often assume that the clinician has a basic grounding in social, developmental, and abnormal individual and systems theory.

Basic Clinical Assumptions

1. Client report of marital interaction provides an incomplete basis for intervention; observation and participation by the clinician in family interaction over significant issues is needed to inform the therapist's understanding of the family system.

2. The most practical way to help clients resolve marital problems is through active observation of, consideration of, and intervention in the client social system.

3. A social system's sequences, stories, and structures are viewed as both reflecting and maintaining both adaptive and maladaptive problem solving. A change in any one of these areas results in changes in the other two, though such changes do not necessarily result in a change in the presenting problem.

4. There is not a clear boundary between the family's social structure and the individual's cognitive structure and functioning, and the influence flows both ways.

5. Historically and currently, both models are grounded in a core assumption of competence. When problems arise, the couple or family is seen as being "stuck" as opposed to "sick."

6. Although SST practitioners to varying degrees collect information about individual, marital, and family history, the emphasis in information collection and intervention is the current situation.

7. SST is not different from other models of marital/couple therapy in its strong dependence upon the health of the therapeutic relationship. Although possible, a strong relationship between therapist and client should not be achieved merely through validation.[5] A healthy therapeutic relationship should offer a client-inspired balance of validation and initiation of challenges to growth.

Basic Training Assumptions

1. The therapist is expected to train in order to develop a wide range of approaches to the challenges of diplomacy, listening, and intervention in social systems. The widely varied clients, cultures, and presenting problems encountered by the modern therapist require widely varied diplomatic and intervention skills.

2. Ongoing professional interaction is required to support the challenges of clinical growth and to prevent therapists from falling into comfortable procrustean practices and viewpoints. A supportive professional system that encourages a clinician's growth is one requirement of consistent, high-quality clinical practice.

3. Live supervision is emphasized in order to help therapists learn the fine arts of diplomacy, listening, building and maintaining a strong therapeutic relationship, and intervention. The most threatening problems to the therapeutic relationship are often those that the clinician is unaware of, and direct observation through videotape or with the aid of one-way mirrors is a basic aspect of training.

The basic assumptions described above relate to the practice of marital SST therapy and may not necessarily be vital to the competent practice of other models. The authors present this chapter in the spirit and hope of inviting others to join our attempt in furthering the possibilities of those whom we serve.

BACKGROUND OF THE APPROACH

Major Milestones of the 1950s and 1960s

An Unknown Native American

According to an unconfirmed story passed down from Gregory Bateson, the West Coast version of family therapy originated with an unknown Native American. During the 1940s, a Native American veteran was arrested on charges of drunken and disorderly behavior. He went mute in jail and refused to speak to or acknowledge the presence of his jailers. He was thought to be having a catatonic episode and was transferred to the Veterans Administration (VA) hospital. An anthropologist, a certain Dr. X, happened to be visiting that VA hospital some days later and thought that he recognized the detainee as being a member of a tribe he had once studied. The Native American and

Dr. X struck up a conversation, after which the anthropologist went to the head of the hospital. "That man's not crazy," the anthropologist explained. "He is, in the fashion of his tribe, paying you the ultimate disrespect by refusing to acknowledge your presence. He's not schizophrenic; he's just insulting you." The veteran's hospital system was greatly embarrassed by the incident, and, as a consequence, decided to hire two ethnologists as part-time consultants on cultural issues. One of these ethnologists was Gregory Bateson, who was given an office in the VA hospital with the understanding that the space could also be used to pursue a separate, non-VA research project on communication (this included allowing him to store tanks for octopi in the hospital morgue). That non-VA project was to become the Bateson Project (see Haley, 1981), and its location in the VA hospital led to his project's changing its focus from animal communication to schizophrenia, thus catalyzing the West Coast birth of family therapy. According to the story, this same Native American may have inspired the hallucinations of another Bay Area VA hospital employee by the name of Ken Kesey, and thus may have served as part of the model for the character of Chief Bromden in *One Flew over the Cuckoo's Nest* (K. Kesey, personal communication, 2001).

Harry Stack Sullivan

Harry Stack Sullivan was a psychoanalyst and cofounder of the Washington School of Psychiatry. Deeply influenced by the interactionalist social psychologists Charles H. Cooley and George Herbert Mead, Sullivan (1945, 1953) brought their theories into practical use in his interpersonal view of psychiatry. Although Sullivan brought an important, present-tense interpersonal dynamic to his theory, he did not take the next step of actually bringing families into therapy sessions. Many of the major pioneers of family therapy, including Don D. Jackson, Nathan Ackerman, and Salvador Minuchin, would come directly out of Sullivanian psychoanalytic programs.

Don D. Jackson

After 4 years of study with Sullivan and other interpersonal psychiatry leaders at the Washington School of Psychiatry, Jackson moved to California, where he was later tapped by the members of Gregory Bateson's project to advise them on

schizophrenia. Jackson had already published an important paper introducing the concept of "family homeostasis," the tendency of a family system to self-correct in order to *avoid* change (Jackson, 1957). Jackson pioneered critical systems therapy concepts such as "circular questioning," "family rules," "relationship quid pro quo," and (with Haley, Weakland, Bateson, and Fry) the "double bind." Jackson was the first clinician to uncompromisingly maintain a higher-order cybernetic and constructivist position in the actual practice of therapy (Ray, 2001). Jackson and Milton Erickson were the primary psychotherapy supervisors and influences on Jay Haley before the latter joined the Philadelphia Child Guidance Clinic. Jackson's papers and books include several early marital therapy publications, including the book *The Mirages of Marriage* (Lederer & Jackson, 1968). *Mirages* popularized the concept of quid pro quo arrangements, a construct that forms an important basis for SST marital therapy. Jackson died suddenly at the age of 48 in 1968, but his contribution is gaining renewed appreciation in large part due to the work of Wendel Ray, founder of the Don D. Jackson archive.

The Publication of "Towards a Theory of Schizophrenia"

In 1956, the Bateson Project published the single most important paper in the history of family therapy, "Towards a Theory of Schizophrenia" (Bateson, Jackson, Haley, & Weakland, 1956). Minuchin described the importance of this publication thus: "'Towards a Theory of Schizophrenia' was a . . . breakthrough in giving us a language to describe family interaction. Before then, we were stuck trying to use psychodynamic language to describe systems. It was an inspiration" (S. Minuchin, personal communication, 1997). In addition to inspiring existing and future family therapy pioneers, this paper brought a needed boost to the professional respectability to the emerging field of human systems theory and encouraged other family therapy pioneers to publicize their work.

Nathan Ackerman

Nathan Ackerman was a pioneering family therapist who had been trained in a Sullivanian tradition. In contrast to the traditions of the time, Ackerman was willing to cast aside the distant, uninvolved stereotype of the therapist and instead passionately engage the client. This tradition of passionate engagement had a great influence on Minuchin.

Milton Erickson

Milton Erickson was one of the 20th century's most influential therapists. He was a nationally known psychiatrist who was the leading figure in medical hypnosis in the United States and practiced individual, marital, and family therapy in the 1950s. Erickson was interested in therapeutic side of many of the communications issues that the Bateson Project was studying as pathology. For example, Bateson's group was interested in the contribution of the double bind to schizophrenia, while Erickson was interested in how a double bind could help a client get rid of a symptom. Bateson's group studied the pathogenic potential of conflicting messages between levels of communication, and Erickson used contrast between levels of communication for therapeutic purposes.

In contrast to Freud, Erickson believed in the positive potential of the subconscious and held the therapist responsible for catalyzing change. His approaches to problem solving require the therapist to have a large range of competence in direct or indirect, therapist-inspired or client-inspired approaches.[6] Erickson believed that a therapist should have many ways of inspiring change to meet the particular demands of a wide variety of presenting problems and client contexts. Even when seeing individuals, he could take a systemic perspective, and he was particularly adept at changing family relationships by inspiring changes in individual internal dialogues.

From a cultural perspective, Erickson also represented an image of a therapist that was much more compatible with rural and working-class America—a group not socialized yet to accept the European model of the Freudian therapist. He had a multiethnic practice and remained the image of a friendly, small-town doctor ready to dispense typically pragmatic (if sometimes strange) advice. Erickson also understood that rural, Midwestern and Western, working-class Americans were frequently not interested in how their problems developed; rather, they wanted a polite practitioner who fit their image of a healer and who could offer quick and practical relief. Erickson enjoyed the company of Haley and Weakland, who also came from rural, pragmatic backgrounds, and supervised them for years in the practice of psychotherapy. Erickson's influence has been greatly facilitated through the efforts of Jeff Zeig, the Erickson family, and the faculty members of the Milton H. Erickson Foundation, who both train clinicians and apply the model to a diverse clinical population.

The Wiltwyck School for Boys and Families of the Slums

Salvador Minuchin, Braulio Montalvo, Edgar Auerswald, Robert Stuckey, Charles King, Clara Rabinowitz, and Saul Pavin began seeing families of delinquent youths at the Wiltwyck School for Boys in New York. In *Families of the Slums* (Minuchin, Montalvo, Guerney, Rosman, & Schumer, 1967) wrote about their work with poor, minority children and about their studies of both delinquent-producing families and a matched group of nondelinquent controls. As Gerson (1996) noted, Minuchin often it impossible to use individual interview methods in the chaotic and anxiety packed parent–child meetings he was conducting; rather than abandon the family interview, Minuchin's group borrowed and invented the methods required to get results, and this pragmatic creativity created the foundation of the structural approach. Through the use of one-way mirrors, careful study of the unwritten rules governing family life, and the breaking down of larger systems into subsystems, the Wiltwyck families became the first to experience this style of restructuring of the family lifescape (Colapinto, 1982, 1991; Lappin, 1988).[7]

The Mental Research Institute

As the 1950s progressed, the Bateson Project focused progressively more on psychotherapy. As Bateson saw his star protégés Jay Haley and John Weakland fall increasingly under the clinical influence of Don Jackson, the relationship between Bateson and Jackson suffered (J. Weakland, personal communication, 1994). In the early 1960s, Haley and Weakland initiated a slow migration of energy and time over to the Mental Research Institute (MRI) in Palo Alto, California, which had been founded in the late 1950s by Jackson and which had already hired Jules Riskin, Virginia Satir, and other future leaders in systems therapy. In 1962, while Haley was a researcher at MRI, he met and developed a friendship with a visiting psychiatrist by the name of Salvador Minuchin. Cloe Madanes began work at MRI as a researcher for Don Jackson in 1967. In contrast to the Bateson Project's emphasis on research, MRI had a strong focus on psychotherapy in addition to its research activities.

MRI made a crucial contribution to popularizing family therapy among practitioners. During her MRI tenure, Virginia Satir became the first family therapist to master the workshop to the extent that impressive numbers of her audience were actually going out and trying to do family therapy.[8] Satir thus demonstrated how to popularize systems therapy without waiting for it to become popular in university settings and existing professional societies. Thus began family therapy's first success at bypassing the clinical establishment through offering training programs directly to professionals.[9] A strategic therapy training program recently opened at MRI through the inspiration of its current director, Wendel Ray, and of Eileen Bobrow.

You Say You Want a Revolution?

One of the great challenges faced by early family therapists was the tremendous power of the psychoanalytic establishment. It was very entrenched and, with the exception of some smaller institutions such as the Washington School of Psychiatry, was closed to and critical of ideas like family therapy that fell so far outside of its tautology. Intolerance of systems therapy even led on occasion to attempts to professionally discipline family therapists (Nichols & Schwartz, 1998).[10]

Sensitized by their systems orientation, family therapists were loath to accept being silenced. Family therapy gives a voice to family members who are silenced by the constraints of context, and its practice sensitizes clinicians to hierarchical status quos that rob system members of their voices.

The social context of the 1960s further encouraged revolutionary ideas. In the current consumer-based society, such challenges seem normal and necessary, but in the early years of systems therapy, family therapy's direct appeal to therapists and clients was a heretical end run around the establishment. Psychiatry was not being singled out for criticism; all manner of traditions were being questioned. "Medicare was introduced; communes were started; long hair, short skirts, drugs, and strange music were 'in'" (Lappin, 1988, p. 224). Ideas that challenged tradition found enthusiastic allies among the new generations coming out of graduate school. The postmodern genie had been

let out of the bottle, and neither political nor clinical hierarchies could resist its influence.

Milestones in the Development of SST

> I'll play it first and you tell what it is later.
> —MILES DAVIS

The Philadelphia Child Guidance Clinic

Founded in 1925, the Philadelphia Child Guidance Clinic (PCGC) began as a small, traditional neighborhood mental health clinic. In the 1930s, PCGC followed the established practice in which the child was seen by one staff member and the parent(s) (usually just the mother) by another. By the late 1940s, however, the staff became convinced that the father's participation was critical; subsequently, it was rare that a child was seen without both parents' coming in first. Years later, in an unforeseen premonition of the structural approach, PCGC, in relationship with the University of Pennsylvania School of Social Work, adopted the more "here-and-now" methodology of Otto Rank. The "goodness of fit" (Thomas & Chess, 1984) between model and practice grew exponentially from Minuchin's arrival as director in 1965, through his synergistic collaborations with Braulio Montalvo, Jay Haley, Marianne Walters, Bernice Rosman, and the PCGC staff, until his departure in 1981. During those years and until its close in 2000, PCGC furthered its mission of service to poor families, and contributed to the growing evidence of family therapy's effectiveness through its research on the structural model. The model was effectively applied with such diverse symptoms as anorexia nervosa, brittle diabetes (Aponte & Hoffman, 1973; Minuchin et al., 1975; Minuchin, Rosman, & Baker, 1978), substance abuse (Fishman, Stanton, & Rosman, 1982; Stanton et al., 1982; Stanton & Todd, 1992; Szapocznik, 1989; Treadway 1989), divorce (Isaacs, Montalvo, & Abelsohn, 1986), school problems (Aponte, 1976; Eno, 1985), cross-cultural issues (Lappin & Scott, 1982; Lappin, 1983; Lappin, Hardy, & Storm, 1997; Montalvo & Guitierrez, 1983, 1989), and larger systems (Colapinto, 1995; Elizur & Minuchin, 1989; Lappin & VanDeusen, 1994, 1999; Lappin & Steier, 1996–1997; P. Minuchin, Colapinto, & Minuchin, 1998; McCarthy, 1992; VanDeusen & Lappin, 1993; VanDeusen, Lappin, & Morenas, 1992).

In 1969, in what may have seemed yet another snub of established academia, PCGC received a grant to train members of Philadelphia minority groups (who had no formal education or experience as psychotherapists) to become family therapists. The Institute for Family Counseling (IFC) became one of the first training programs to use such innovative methods as one-way mirrors, videotape, and live supervision (Montalvo, 1973). Using the IFC's successful mix of live supervision and didactics, the Family Therapy Training Center (FTTC) was formed in 1974 when PCGC moved to its new facility in West Philadelphia. Adjacent to Children's Hospital of Philadelphia (CHOP) and just down the street from the University of Pennsylvania campus, the FTTC became family therapy's Mecca, training family therapists from all over the world in its year-long clinical externship and summer practica.[11] As PCGC lost energy, structural therapy flourished elsewhere, including the Minuchin Center for the Family in New York City.

The Family Therapy Institute of Washington, D.C.

Jay Haley and Cloe Madanes left PCGC in the mid-1970s and opened up the Family Therapy Institute of Washington, D.C. Haley's *Problem-Solving Therapy* (1976) and Madanes's *Strategic Family Therapy* (1981) were foundational texts of the Washington school of strategic therapy. Between workshops and live supervision training programs, the Institute was one of the most prolific training organizations of the 1970s and 1980s. Many of the Institute's first generations of trainees, such as Michael Fox (1988),[12] Neil Schiff, Marcha Ortiz, Doug Tilly, Stuart Tiegel, Judith Mazza, Richard Belson (1993), George Stone, and others, evolved into supervisors and assumed prominent places in the marital/couple and family field. This first generation of trainees joined Haley and Madanes in training later generations of prominent trainers and authors, including Les Blondino, Eileen Bobrow, Wes Crenshaw (Crenshaw & Cain, 1997), Barbara Peeks Dunn (2001), David Eddy, David Grove (Grove & Haley, 1993), James Keim (1992, 1998, 2000; I. Keim, Lentine, Keim, & Madanes, Evie McClintoch (1998), Skip Meyer, Keiichi Miyata (1995), Neal Newfield (Lemon, Newfield, & Dobbins, 1993), Jerry Price (1996), Randy Fiery, Dennis Schwartz (1993), Richard Spector, Lynn Stachinsky, Jose Szapocznik (1989; Szapocznik & Hervis, 2000),

Joe Tooley, Marilyn Wedge (1996), Richard Whiteside (1998), and Anthony Yeo (1993).[13]

In the late 1970s, the Institute received a contract to train large numbers of state-employed clinicians in family therapy. By the early 1990s, the strategic approach had achieved significant institutional acceptance in the mid-Atlantic region of the United States as these trainees advanced in the coming decade to senior status within their respective organizations.

In the mid-1980s, the Institute received a local government contract that was to last 15 years to treat victims and perpetrators of sexual abuse. Significant innovations in the treatment of sexual abuse resulted from this work (Madanes, 1990; Madanes, Keim, & Smelser, 1995) and became the subject of some of the most widely attended workshops in Institute history.

Jay Haley retired from the Institute in the mid-1990s and currently resides in California, where he remains active in clinical supervision and writing. Although workshop business continued to thrive, the Institute closed its in-house training programs in the late 1990s as key staff members moved to different parts of the country and as the pressures of managed care drove clinicians away from live supervision and into cheaper and less personal workshops. Training is flourishing at programs founded by disciples, including Eileen Bobrow's Strategic Family Therapy Project at MRI, founded with the help of MRI director Wendel Ray.

IMPORTANT CONSTRUCTS

Models of therapy tend to focus on factors that differentiate them from one another, and this emphasis clouds the significance and extent of commonalities that play a significant role in positive clinical outcome (Miller, Duncan, & Hubble, 1997). Some of these generic contributions to good therapy are reviewed later in this chapter. Clinical education requires that a therapist sometimes focus on generic issues and at other times focus on model-specific issues; this chapter is dedicated to a model-specific discussion.

It is worth noting at this juncture that we do not assume that the terms that empower therapists' own thinking and professional communication are empowering to clients as well. There is a kind of self-referential "recursion" around therapists' language, which may make important distinctions for therapists (so that we know what we mean to each other), which has no real meaning for families (Lappin & Steier, 1996–1997). SST assumes until proven otherwise that clients have within their own vocabulary the means to describe the full range of issues central to therapy. Unless a client's choice of terminology is specifically part of the problem that therapy is addressing, the SST therapist uses the client's language whenever possible during interviews. The terms listed below are specifically therapists' terminology.

The Intervention Map

One of the defining qualities of a model of psychotherapy is that it provides a therapist with an "intervention map"—a means of viewing problems and of facilitating change in the context of therapy. SST, like most interactional models, does not attempt a global description of the development of both psyche and psychopathology. Rather, SST pragmatically facilitates change in the context of therapy. And the most practical way of facilitating change is to consider and address the presenting problem's intimate social context. The term "family therapy" is used to describe working with the ongoing, intimate social context of problems, though on occasion this "family" context is a kibbutz community, a group marriage, or other long-term group that has the primary role of socializing, influencing, and caring for its members.

The primary constructs used by SST to consider the presenting problem and its family system are "sequence," "structure," and "stories." As Carlos Sluzki wrote while describing commonalities among certain models,

> Symptomatic/problematic behaviors can be said to be contained and anchored by their own participation in circular, self-perpetuating interactional patterns, by their function as reinforcers and reminders of structural traits, which recursively contribute to maintain them, and by their participation in worldviews that in turn provide the ideology that supports them. (Sluzki, 1983, p. 474)

SST clinicians use the constructs of sequence, structure, and stories to orient themselves in the complexity of family systems and to focus their efforts on inspiring change. "Sequence" is SST's term for a self-perpetuating interactional pattern, also known as a transactional pattern (Minuchin, 1974). The description of sequence simultaneously describes the interaction around the presenting problem and points to what the solution will look like. Change is partially defined in terms of more desirable sequences' replacing "stuck" sequences of interaction. "Structure" refers to the social organization described by sequences, with a special emphasis on the degree of match between role and function that is manifest in the transactions. It describes interactional tendencies not only between members, but also between members and outside systems. Hierarchy, disengagements, enmeshments, boundaries, and coalitions (these are defined below) are means of describing structure. "Stories," which Sluzki describes above as clients' world views, are the client narratives that both reflect and inspire the sequences, structures, and potential for change or inflexibility. The interconnectedness of these concepts is such that a change in any one of these areas results in some degree of change in the others.

Other Important Terms

• *Subsystems.* Groupings of family members that come together to perform various family functions.

• *Hierarchy.* A role- and generation-sensitive description of the organization of a family, especially in regard to the expression of love, authority, and caretaking. It should be noted that the term has different meanings for different intellectual traditions; for example, for some therapists who describe themselves as postmodern, "hierarchy" implies an oppressive, patriarchal arrangement. SST defines "hierarchy" in a neutral manner; although some family hierarchies are oppressive, others are flexible and encourage individual and subsystem growth.

• *Hard and soft hierarchy.* Some SST conceptualizations of "hierarchy" emphasize the importance of a balance between what are termed the "hard" and "soft" sides of hierarchy. The hard side of hierarchy refers to the contribution to the organization of a family made by such activities as protection of others, the setting of rules, and the enforcement of consequences. The soft side of hierarchy refers to the contribution to the organization of a family made by such activities as soothing, expressing empathy and affection, initiating good times, and providing good things. Too often, trainees overemphasize the contribution of rules and consequences to the creation of family structure; this approach to teaching hierarchy helps to emphasize the equal importance of soothing and other overtly loving activities in the creation of family organization.

• *Marital hierarchy.* The perceived balance of influence and contribution between spouses. In other words, each spouse's perceptions of whether each is contributing equivalently and whether each is appropriately open to the other's influence.

• *Boundaries.* The degree of emotional connection, dependence, support, and influence between different subsystems within the family, and between these subsystems and other social systems.

• *Overt role and function.* Overt roles are the self-proclaimed family roles (father, mother, child, etc.). Flexibility of the family is restricted when subsystems perceive significant contrast between the overt role and the actual function of a family member. An example might be a child who is required to take an adult level of responsibility for a younger sibling when such organization is not the cultural norm. In such an example, the child has significant adult functioning; yet the overt role as defined by the child's emotional needs and ability to influence other matters is that of a child.

• *Subsystem overdependence.* A situation in which (1) the fulfillment of interpersonal needs is primarily dependent upon a specific subsystem that is unable to consistently meet these needs over time; and (2) alternative subsystems are not maintained in such a way that they can be easily accessed, should support from the primary system become unavailable.

• *Enmeshment.* A situation in which the intimacy, dependence, and influence between specific subsystems is so intense that it (1) creates an overdependence between certain subsystems to fulfill some emotional needs, while handicapping access to outside systems that are necessary for subsystem growth, individuation, and development; and (2) Reduces the ability of the family subsystems to adapt collaboratively to change.

• *Disengagement.* A situation in which the weak levels of intimacy, dependence, and influence between certain family subsystems (1) prevent subsystems within the family from getting emotional needs met from one another, and creates an overdependence on other subsystems and outside systems to meet these needs; and (2) reduces the ability of the family subsystems to adapt collaboratively to change.

• *Coalition.* A situation in which a minimum of two parties join together to take a position in relation to a third party.

• *Cross-generational coalition.* In the context of marital therapy, a situation in which (1) a spouse tries to change the dynamics of a marriage by actively involving another generation of the family, such as a child or in-law; or (2) a spouse enters a coalition with a member of another generation of the family to deal with responsibilities that were previously the responsibility of the other spouse. Cross-generational coalitions are associated with increased pathology in a system (Haley, 1976), but are not necessarily pathological; in fact, they may at times be highly adaptive. However, this type of coalition and the situations that produce it are associated with great amounts of stress for all in the family system. Furthermore, recognizing cross-generational coalitions is important, because they require greater sensitivity and diplomatic skills on the part of the clinician.

• *Conflict avoidance.* If we conceptualize boundaries between subsystems as a continuum in which one end is characterized by overinvolvement and the other by under involvement, then these concepts appear to be at opposite ends, serving opposite purposes. If, on the other hand, we draw this continuum of boundaries as a circle, the two ends touch. At that meeting point, they serve the same purpose—conflict avoidance. In effect, fighting, or the lack of it, is a collective attempt to remain at level of intimacy that is known and comfortable. To resolve the conflict would result in a change—incurring the loss of the known, albeit unhappy, comfort zone for an unknown, less certain future.[14]

• *Family life cycle.* A means of describing the evolution of family life that is sensitive to major life changes in the constitution, roles, and focus of its members.

• *Marital life cycle.* A description of marital life that is sensitive to the evolution of spouses' problem-solving styles and to the marital challenges posed by changes in role, in focus, and in the constitution of the household.

• *Quid pro quo.* The portion of a couple's relationship that is governed by a set of explicit or implicit two-way agreements (Jackson, 1965). Quid pro quo arrangements of interest to therapists most commonly relate to complimentary aspects of the relationship. Progression through marital life often results in changes that require renegotiation of these contracts. The collaborative restructuring of quid pro quo arrangements to match personal growth and context change is viewed as one of the primary tasks in marital SST.

THE WELL-FUNCTIONING VERSUS DYSFUNCTIONAL MARRIAGE[15]

It is not the strongest of the species that
survive, nor the most intelligent, but the one
most responsive to change.
—CHARLES DARWIN

Happiness is never grand.
—ALDOUS HUXLEY

Character, Couples, Pogo's Conundrum, and Health

In his book *The Tipping Point*, Malcolm Gladwell
(2000) describes the "fundamental attribution error"
as being "the mistake of overestimating the importance of fundamental character traits and underesti-
mating the importance of the situation and context"
(p. 160). He goes on to say, "There is something
in all of us that makes us instinctively want to explain the world around us in terms of people's essential attributes" (p. 161). What we know then as
"character" is not a static set of behaviors, but rather
a collection of "loosely bound" tendencies best predicted by circumstance and context, which bring to
the fore different aspects of self. As Gladwell (2000)
notes, "The reason that most of us seem to have a
consistent character is that most of us are really good
at controlling our environment" (p. 163). The need
for environmental control, and the attendant anxiety that accompanies the perceived loss of self, are
at the heart of a troubled couple's dilemma. Viewing the couple from this perspective, the structural
therapist uses "binocular vision": Two and one come
together, so that "In any couple one person's behavior is yoked to the other's. . . . [The] couple's
actions are not independent but codetermined, subject to reciprocal forces that support or polarize"
(Minuchin & Nichols, 1993, p. 63). Coming to
treatment can mean that this reciprocity has become
skewed so that intimacy begins to feel like the relational equivalent of the toy called "Chinese hand-
cuffs." One finger from each hand slides into opposite ends of a woven tube; when a child attempts
to pull the fingers out, the toy's grip on the fingers
becomes even tighter. The joy of getting out, as every child discovers, is a paradox. If the child pushes
the fingers together, the tube widens, and the child
is released. In situations where spouses need to transform themselves, they are faced with a double
whammy: If they change themselves, they face the
loss of self; on the other hand, if they do not, they
face the loss of each other. Either way, they can feel
stuck. As Pogo, the cartoon character, once said,
"Most people would prefer the certainty of misery
over the misery of uncertainty." How is it then, that
healthy couples seemingly avoid Pogo's conundrum?

In the early works of SST, it was suggested that
certain structures "cause family problems when
adaptive mechanisms are evoked" (Minuchin, 1974,
p. 55). The term "cause" was used to describe a
failure to correct deviance rather than an initiation
of deviance within the system, but some readers,
especially those with backgrounds in models
steeped in issues of causality, did not appreciate
the inadequately clear distinction. Since the mid-
1980s, the language of family organization has been
more clearly related to flexibility and responsiveness during times of stress. As Minuchin noted
in 1993, "When families come to me for help, I
assume they have problems not because there is
something inherently wrong with them but because
they've gotten stuck—stuck with a structure whose
time has passed, and stuck with a story that doesn't
work" (Minuchin & Nichols, 1993, p. 43).

SST's concept of functional versus dysfunctional
marriage now primarily relates to a couple's ability
to be collaboratively and supportively flexible. But
flexibility must be understood in a developmental
and systemic context; the flexibility required by the
demands of dual careers are very different from those
required when a terminally ill spouse enters a hospice. This includes not only an appreciation for developmental stages, but also for the demands and
pressures these place on the interconnection between
the family system and the individual psyche (Jackson, 1965; Schwartz, 1995). There is an emphasis
on avoiding the pathologizing of situations that might
best be thought of as normal but painful transitions
(Haley, 1973; Minuchin, 1974). As Haley wrote,

> Once when I had a family experiment I wished to
> try out on a family, I called a friend whose family
> seemed average and explained that I needed a nor-
> mal family to try out an experiment. When I asked
> if they would come in, they agreed. However, a few
> hours later the wife telephoned and said they would
> not come in. She said they weren't a normal family
> because their daughter was about to go to college and
> everyone was upset and quarreling. I then realized
> that "normal" could only describe a family that was
> not at the moment at a crisis point in their stage of
> family life. (Haley, 1996, p. 74)

Sometimes couples come to a clinician for
help during a life cycle crisis, despite the fact that
they are handling the transition as well as might

be expected. Such couples often (1) have had positive previous therapy experiences; (2) come from backgrounds that view therapy as a "growth" tool, rather than just as a way to address crises; and (3) have the needed money and time to attend therapy. In such cases, intervention is not regarded as "therapy" as much as affirmation that the couples are doing as well as can be expected and encouragement that they should continue with their successful efforts. Such functionality would be characterized by a couple's displaying, both as individuals and as a couple, the following characteristics:

- The couple is not stuck in an argument over whose fault the problem is, and is instead focused on taking action to improve matters (Haley, 1976; Madanes, 1981; Minuchin & Nichols, 1993).
- The couple has an agreed-upon and empowering definition of the problem (Keim et al., 1990).
- There are ongoing, coordinated, and flexible responses to change, including experiments in changing interpersonal routines that aren't working well. This includes the ability "to shift functions and transfer power" within the family (Minuchin & Nichols, 1993, p. 241).
- The marital subsystem's boundaries are strong enough to prevent the improper intrusion of third parties (Minuchin, 1974; Haley, 1976), but permeable enough to allow for good use of resources both inside and outside the family, such that neither spouse is fully dependent upon the other for emotional support.
- The spouses can usually depend upon each other for support, but have access to acceptable alternates should one spouse become unavailable (Minuchin, 1974; Haley, 1976).
- There is a maintenance of (or, if needed, an increase in) self-care, such as participation in social activities outside the home (Keim, 1993, 1999, 2000).
- There is an ongoing sense of balance in contribution to and fulfillment of marital obligation (Jackson, 1965; Lederer & Jackson, 1968).
- Although the couple might need reassurance, they have sufficient optimism, emotional endurance (Gottman, 1994), and physical endurance (Montalvo, Harmon, & Elliot, 1998) to motivate their ongoing adaptation to change.

The therapist's awareness of developmental stages and experience with normal life cycle crisis allows recognition of the adaptive stances described above and prevents the application of a dysfunc-

tional label. Awareness of the marital life cycle can help avoid misidentification of problems, as will be demonstrated in the second case study in this chapter.

Determining the health of functioning also requires an ability to take into account variations associated with age, sexual preference, ethnicity, and varied social, political, and economic contexts (Boyd-Franklin, 1989; Goldner, 1988; Gottman, 1994; Haddock, Schindler Zimmerman, Ziemba, & Current, 2001; Luepnitz, 1988; P. Minuchin, 1985; Minuchin & Nichols, 1993; McGoldrick et al., 1982; Montalvo, et al., 1998; Olson, Sprenkle, & Russell, 1979; Schwartz, 1995; Sue & Sue, 1990; Walsh, 1993; Walters, Carter, Papp, & Silverstein, 1989). The range of presenting problems described in the literature is as broad as that of any model of psychotherapy. Such experience disabuses clinicians of notions of simple and straightforward portraits of normality.

The Maladaptive Couple

> Better to be quarreling than lonesome.
> —IRISH PROVERB

> Marital misery requires quarreling in such a way that nothing is changed and the quarreling must be repeated again and again.
> —JAY HALEY (1996, p. 126)

In contrast with the couple that is coping in as healthy a way as can be expected is the couple that is "stuck" and is not successfully coping with its problems. A couple is "stuck" to the degree that it manifests the following characteristics:

- The spouses energetically disagree as to the nature of the marital problem (Keim et al., 1990) and are focused on who is to blame than on how to improve matters. It appears that what they seek from therapy "is not help but vindication" (Minuchin & Nichols, 1993, p. 63)
- There is an ongoing sense of imbalance in contribution to and fulfillment of marital obligation (Jackson, 1965; Lederer & Jackson, 1968).
- Instead of change being viewed as a negotiation, each spouse wants the other to change as a consequence of being made to feel "wrong." New efforts at improving the situation are thwarted by a fear that such actions would be viewed as an admission that one is responsible for the problems to begin with.

• Instead of experimenting with new approaches to the problem, there is ongoing repetition of what each spouse recognizes as unsuccessful strategies (Jackson, 1965; Haley, 1963; Watzlawick, Weakland, & Fisch, 1974). There is an overwhelming fear on each spouse's part that initiating a new response is likely to be viewed as an admission that one is at fault for the problem, and this fear interferes with experiments in problem solving.

• Having lost confidence in an ability to experiment collaboratively with new solutions, one spouse withdraws and one pursues all the more vigorously, such that one is energetically avoidant while the other is energetically in pursuit (Gottman, 1994).

• Spouses have taken substantial efforts in turning to third parties for help or vindication, and this has made the problem worse, especially if cross-generational coalitions have been formed within the household (Haley, 1976).

• There is substantial neglect of individual and relationship self-care, such as participation in social activities outside the home (Keim, 1993, 1999, 2000).

• Regardless of resources, the spouses lack the optimism and endurance required to motivate their ongoing adaptation to change (Gottman, 1994, Montalvo et al., 1998).

• The needs of at least one spouse are met through coercion of or in secret from the other spouse; this is all the more corrosive to the degree that such interaction is anchored in perceptions of relationship rules, as opposed to evolving out of impulsive or avoidant behavior that is contrary to perceived relationship rules. The "closed door hypothesis" is an example of relationship rules that is associated with coercive and is described later in this chapter.

• Marital roles are so inflexible that adaptation to growth and other change in the marital life cycle and family system is stunted.

Structure and Flexibility

In modern SST, there is an avoidance of describing certain structures as being healthy or unhealthy, and instead a focus on whether the current structure meets the family's current needs for flexibility. To the degree that the structure of a family lacks the flexibility to maintain helpful structures while changing less functional ones, we tend to find the following:

• There is much more repetition of stylized and unsuccessful interpersonal interaction (Minuchin et al., 1967; Haley, 1976; Madanes, 1981; Montalvo et al., 1998). The most severe loss of flexibility is often seen in complimentary behaviors related to family roles (e.g., mothering, fathering, caretaking of a spouse).

• Individual and subsystem emotional range is less flexible, and there is movement toward polarization of emotions in extremes of expression or withdrawal.

• Both the individual and group senses of alternatives become restricted.

• There is reduced individual and group empathy.

• There is an increased polarization in awareness of individual and subsystem needs. There is "numbness" to some needs (Wynne, Ryckoff, Day, & Hirsch, 1958), and hypersensitivity is expressed to other needs.

• Coalitions become more extreme (more enmeshment and disengagement in different subsystems), and family members are much more likely to seek cross-generational coalitions and coalitions with subsystems outside the immediate family.

• The focus of arguments tends to focus more on reestablishing role than on seeking solutions and helping one another.

• Access to social memories (especially to personal and family narratives) that are not consistent with the present mood is impaired.

• The family's ability to discuss difficult topics is reduced, and emotionally charged discussions get out of hand or are diverted to less central topics before the family can negotiate change.

Flexibility and Functioning

A therapist should not define a family structure that limits flexibility as necessarily being maladaptive. Sometimes a structure that creates temporary inflexibility is like a cast on a broken leg—helpful in the short term, but problematic if it doesn't come off when it is no longer needed. Clients tend to come to therapy not when the "cast" is needed, but rather when it is no longer needed and they are having difficulty shedding a previously adaptive structure. The fact that therapists tend to see such structures when they are no longer working can create a myth that such structures were never helpful to begin with.

Marital Violence

The average marriage therapist's caseload includes presenting problems of domestic violence. Although violence is an ongoing treatment issue in many SST publications (Aponte, 1994; Minuchin et al., 1967; Minuchin, 1984; Stanton & Todd, 1979; Madanes, 1990; Madanes et al., 1995), Cloe Madanes's workshops and writings on sexual and physical abuse are some of the best known. Madanes has described in detailed steps an approach that includes making the discussion of abuse explicit in and employing the wider family system in treatment and ongoing prevention of violence (Madanes et al., 1995).

Certain perceptions of family rules appear to be more common in cases of domestic violence. For example, one of us (JK) has noted that "closed-door" perceptions of marital rules appear to be associated with increased risk for violence. Closed-door strategies are coercive strategies for achieving influence that, in the context of a marriage between parties A and B, are informed by the following:

1. Party A wants to influence party B.
2. A believes that B cannot easily escape A (the door for escape by B is perceived by A to be closed; thus the term "closed-door" strategy).
3. A, believing that B cannot easily escape, relies mainly on coercive rather than collaborative strategies to achieve influence.

"Open-door" strategies are those informed by the belief that each party can escape if unhappy with the means by which cooperation is sought. Collaborative approaches to gaining collaboration of a spouse are thus more likely to characterize marital interaction when each spouse perceives the door to escape to be open.

In describing the double bind (Bateson et al., 1956), Bateson's group noted that the acceptance of the perception of difficulty of escape is crucial to the stress of certain interactional patterns. With closed-door strategies, the perception of difficulty of escape is crucial to the volatility associated with domestic violence, but there is a difference; with spouses using closed-door strategies, the moment of greatest risk is when the perception of no escape is challenged rather than accepted. Using the example above of spouses A and B, one of the moments of greatest risk would be when spouse B "goes out the door" and challenges the relationship perception by A that the door to escape is closed. In contrast, volatility associated with the double bind is associated with the acceptance of, rather than the challenge to, the perception of no escape from another's influence (Bateson et al., 1956).

The relationship rules of an abusive spouse or marriage[16] are imbedded in perceptions of the broader family system of past and present, and the SST therapist attempts to alter these perceptions with real interaction with the larger social system (Trepper & Barrett, 1989). SST's approach to changing the use of closed-door strategies and other relationship rules associated with violence might include bringing in the spouses' parents, employers, or other systemic resources or sources of relationship rules.

INTERVENTION

> A crazy man has but one story.
> —OLD YIDDISH PROVERB

> People may live by the stories they tell themselves, but it's the details of their everyday actions that must be changed to create a lasting shift in relationship.
> —SALVADOR MINUCHIN AND MICHAEL P. NICHOLS, (1993, p. 133)

SST intervention is essentially a process whereby the therapist encourages a family's continued problem-solving efforts while inspiring them to go about these in different ways. The process is guided by the three core constructs of structure, sequence, and story—therapeutic threads whose loom is the search for strength. As noted earlier, these core constructs are viewed as being inextricably interrelated; a change in one results in change in the others, although such change may or may not be of clinical significance.

This section on intervention begins by reviewing some basic characteristics and constructs of SST intervention. The stages of a typical first interview, and the steps and stages of typical therapy, are described next. Various categories and aspects of directives and interventions/techniques are then reviewed.

Basic Characteristics

Stanton's (1985) summary of SST still represents the basic characteristics of SST intervention. Quoting from Stanton, we note the following:

1. Treatment is viewed pragmatically, with an eye toward what "works."
2. Emphasis is on the present rather than the past.
3. Repetitive behavioral sequences are to be changed.

4. While the structural approach may not be as symptom-focused as the strategic, both are much more symptom- or problem-oriented than psychodynamic approaches.
5. Process is emphasized much more than content. This includes interventions that are nonverbal and noncognitive, in a sense, "doing away with words." Such interventions derive from viewing the system from a meta level and recognizing that verbalizations, per se, by therapist or family are often not necessary for change.
6. The therapist should be active.
7. Diagnosis is obtained through intervention.
8. Therapeutic contracts are negotiated with clients revolving around the problem and the goals of change.
9. Interpretation is usually employed to "relabel" rather than produce "insight."
10. Behavioral tasks are assigned.
11. Considerable effort may go into "joining" the couple positively and reducing apparent "guilt" or defensiveness. This is more than simply "establishing rapport" as it is often done selectively and with regard to what the therapist deems necessary for system change.
12. Therapy usually cannot progress from the initial dysfunctional stage to a "cure" stage without one or more intermediate stages, which, on the surface, may also appear dysfunctional. For instance, a therapist may have to take sides with a spouse (thereby "unbalancing" the couple in an opposite way from which it entered treatment) in order to restabilize at a point of parity.
13. Therapy tends to be brief and does not exceed 6 months.

(Stanton, 1985, pp. 254–255)

Two Basic Constructs

Clinical Optimism

SST therapists have a defining optimism: Namely, families have untapped strengths and resources that may not be apparent at the onset of therapy (Minuchin & Fishman, 1981). The success of the therapy depends in part upon tapping into this hidden systemic wealth. There are a number of reasons for the expectation of significant strengths that may not be immediately apparent. One of these reasons may be that it is difficult to simultaneously state competence and hire a helper. Another is that the family may lose sight of resources and strengths that have not been recently needed. A third and very significant reason is that tapping into strengths requires flexibility and experimentation beyond the temporarily restricted range of a stressed family. To the degree that there are significant serial stressors on a family (e.g., the ravages of urban poverty), that system tends to become increasingly less flexible and appreciative of its human assets (Aponte, 1994; Colapinto, 1995; Elizur & Minuchin, 1989; Fishman, 1993; Lappin & VanDeusen, 1999; Minuchin et al., 1967). The SST clinician thus begins therapy with an optimism that, despite initial presentations suggesting otherwise, untapped wealth can be found in the family and social system.

Clinical Endurance: Maintaining the Therapeutic Relationship

Couple therapy is not different from problem solving in normal life; the process must be sustainable in the face of repeated failures. The sustainability of the therapeutic relationship in the face of expected failures is referred to as "clinical endurance." Therapist contributions to clinical endurance include taking the following steps:

1. The therapist must create realistic expectations of change, of the amount of effort that will need to be expended, of the likelihood of failure of many experiments in change, and of the amount of time that change commonly takes (pacing of therapy). This is best accomplished in the form of statements of general tendencies, with the express proviso that individual couples often surprise therapists by confounding these estimates.
2. The therapist must also be able to lend clients hope and optimism.
3. Success must be made more vivid than failure. To the degree that individuals and families are stressed, failure becomes significantly more vivid, especially regarding changes in everyday interaction. Interventions that highlight success both inside and outside the sessions help this disparity. Such interventions range from a therapist's taking special care to note and praise change, to strategic homework assignments or "experiments" (Schorr, 1997) that attach such novelty to small changes as to make them extraordinarily vivid.
4. If "Joining is more of an attitude than a technique" (Minuchin & Fishman, 1981, p. 31), then the therapeutic relationship must nurture a context that can sustain itself through inevitable failures in experimentation with change. This requires more than a relationship in which clients trust a therapist's view of themselves. The relationship must be able to withstand the therapist's challenging of roles and behavior. A sign of a strong

therapeutic relationship is that the therapist's mistakes are interpreted as well intended, rather than either as mean-spirited or as proof of the clients' own incompetence.

5. During therapy, clients must maintain normal self-care and relationship care activities. Examples of these might include a couple's nights out without children or an individual's taking a half hour out to relax at the local coffee shop.

6. The therapist is conscious of the level of motivation and endurance of the client, is willing to work to increase the level of each, and is careful not to extend the requirements of therapy beyond this motivation.

7. The therapist is optimistic about the possibility of change and is able to inspire this optimism in clients when desirable.

A Generic First Interview with a Couple

The first interview may be thought of as containing the following overlapping stages (Haley, 1976):

- A social/joining stage
- A problem discussion/diagnostic stage
- An interactional/diagnostic/intervention stage
- A contracting stage
- A homework stage

The Social/Joining Stage

> To deal intelligently with a client, the important thing isn't distance but the ability to feel that I am her.
> —CLOE MADANES (QUOTED IN SIMON, 1991, p. 130)

> The curious paradox is that when I accept myself just as I am, then I can change.
> —CARL ROGERS

This first stage of the first interview establishes and maintains a social context and atmosphere appropriate for therapy. Failure of the therapeutic relationship is one of the most common reasons for failure in therapy. And the clients' perceptions of the helpfulness of therapy are sometimes more dependent upon the quality of the therapeutic relationship than on whether or not the presenting problem is solved.

As is generic in many schools of therapy, the joining process should result in the clients' having confidence that the therapist will provide the necessary structure and support for open and honest communication, and that the therapist will be accepting, understanding, and challenging. The context should provide "appreciative inquiry" (Srivasta & Cooper, 1990) between therapist and couple and between the spouses themselves. The appearance that a therapist is blindly supportive actually works against the therapeutic relationship; the clinician's challenge is how "to impact without being rejected, how to be accepted without losing effectiveness" (Colapinto & Lappin, 1982).

Although sometimes these stages are readily apparent, at other times they blend together in a manner that makes them difficult to appreciate. The goals of joining may be thought of in terms of familiarity, appreciation, competence, and empathy; the acronym is FACE (Keim, 2000).

- "Familiarity" describes the clients' sense that the therapist is developing appropriate familiarity with the problem and its social context.
- "Admiration" describes the clients' awareness that the therapist admires their strengths, courage, and experiences.
- "Competence" refers to the clients' sense that a therapist has the special skills and experience needed to help the clients; clients do not want all-knowing clinicians, but rather ones who know the limits of their own knowledge and allow the clients to educate them.
- "Empathy" describes the clients' sense that the therapist will take the time and energy to truly appreciate the emotional challenges and difficulties they are facing.

The development of FACE begins immediately and continues until the very last interview of the therapy. When FACE is strong enough, a fuller range of client emotions and stories becomes safe to express.

The Problem Stage

In the second stage, the clients as consumers express what they wish to hire the therapist to accomplish. This tends to involve each client's taking turns speaking to the therapist. In this stage, the therapist's stance is usually one of neutrality as special efforts are made to evoke contributions from each client equally.

The manner with which the problem is described provides information on the couple's initial stories, sequences, and structure. The therapist is very observant of who speaks when, how complaints are voiced, and how the conversation proceeds or is interrupted. In this stage, the therapist tries to collect information on the couple's broader social context, including children and other family, work, and other social systems with which the couple may be involved. Like counting the rings on a tree, one way to et a practical, goal-oriented, "at-a-glance" take on the couple's experience is to ask the couple to give a "headline" as to why they are coming to see the therapist. Headlines can range from "My spouse made me" to "My spouse is worried that the marriage is over," and everything in between. The process creates a "shared paradigm" for the therapeutic system and serves as a measure for the progress of treatment.[17]

The Interactional Stage

> Rather than only have a conversation about a problem, he should try at this stage to bring the problem action into the room.
> —JAY HALEY (1976, p. 36)

> Why is it that "a picture is worth a thousand words"? The picture is not talk about something—it is the thing the talk is about.
> —RICHARD HEYMAN (1994, p. 43)

In cardiac medicine, a resting electrocardiogram (EKG) provides significantly less information than a stress EKG, in which the client must stress the heart during monitoring. However, the resting version requires less skill and is easier to give and is consequently more common. If the problem stage is equivalent to a resting EKG, the interactional stage is the interview's stress EKG; it views the couple in action and thus, like the stress EKG, provides significantly more information. This stage is characterized mostly by interaction *between* the clients around the problem. A therapist sometimes allows an enactment to continue and sometimes intervenes to encourage or alter the interaction between the spouses. Problem-specific structure, sequences, and stories may appear that were not visible to the therapist at other times. Special attention is paid to what interferes with and what promotes problem-solving discussion.

The clinician may highlight or modify interactions and, in a manner particular to his/her individual personality and style, challenge roles, power balance, and assumptions. The therapist attempts to influence the spouses' interactions such that they attempt to solve problems in a new manner that is more responsive to each other,

emotively effective, and emotionally diverse. The appearances of "conversation busters," topics or actions that derail problem-solving discussions, are crucial moments. The therapist must work with the spouses to expand their range within the session such that the dialogue can continue.

In this stage, the therapist evokes diagnostically crucial interaction during the session and may begin experimenting with catalyzing new structure, sequences and stories. The challenge is to shift the clients into experimenting with new approaches to problem solving. Even though it may be emotionally stressful for clients to discuss their problem with each other, successful enactments in the context of healthy therapeutic relationships leave clients feeling better understood, more hopeful, better connected to the therapist, and inspired that their relationship can be different. Communication and conflict resolution are learnable skills. But just as with alcoholism, in which the solution is simultaneously simple ("just" stop drinking) and extremely difficult, the anxiety and discouragement of learning new skills—even with their attendant prospect of greater intimacy—can make the security of old, albeit dysfunctional, patterns a respite worth the risk.

The Contracting Stage

> An essential element of the formation of a therapeutic system is the agreement on a therapeutic contract. . . . Like the diagnosis, it evolves as therapy progresses.
> —SALVADOR MINUCHIN (1974, p. 132)

In a sense, contracting begins as soon as the first session starts, and continues as roles are defined and presenting problems are named. But the formal act of contracting does not take place until the couple has the benefit of some degree of fresh perspective from the session. It is thus expected to take place formally toward the end of the session.

The contract should be an honest statement about what the couple truly wants. Participation is increased to the degree that the therapy is addressing that which the clients want most in the world, and the contract should reflect this to the degree possible. The contract should address these questions:

1. What do the clients want from therapy?
2. What is the role of the therapist?
3. What are the roles of the clients?

4. What are the expectations of change and participation?

SST requires an overt and specific contract between the therapist and clients. A dual hierarchy is created by the contract. The therapist is defined as an expert in the sense of having special experience and knowledge in facilitating the change in the presenting problem. Simultaneously, the clients are defined by the contract as being the "boss," and the therapist is the hired help who can also be fired. This balance of simultaneous higher and lower relative positions seems to create a sense of balance that is essential in the helping relationship. Situations that disrupt this balance—compulsory therapy, for example—handicap the clinical relationship unless this imbalance is addressed (Haley, 1996).

A crucial part of the contract is the definition of the problem. The contract sometimes incorporates the intervention of expanding the clients' views of the problem. For example, a foster child who was initially described as being "defiant" may, by the time of the contract, have been relabeled by the therapist and family as having confusion about the nature of authority because of past negative experiences. The definition of the problem that the therapist and couple have developed together is called the "agreed-upon problem," and the goal of this term is to emphasize the joint creation of the focus of therapy. Another way to think about the contract is that when people come to marital treatment, their conceptualization of the problem is at the level of content—"My spouse is the problem." The therapist conceptualizes the problem at a pragmatic, systemic level that emphasizes that investing in solutions should not be dependent upon whose fault the problem is. Assessment thus becomes the task of reconciling these competing world views to arrive somewhere in between, at a shared paradigm (Keim, 1998; Lappin, 1984, 1998–1999). That shared paradigm—neither fully content nor fully systemic, but wholly owned by therapist and clients—is the contract.

Homework Assignments

Homework's goal is to continue experimentation in sequences, structure, and stories outside the therapy session. It is important that the assignment make sense in relation to the change requested by the clients. It is also important for the homework to be assigned with careful consideration of the degree of motivation of the client. Examples and details of homework assignments are given below in the "Directives and Interventions Techniques" section.

The Steps and Stages of Therapy

Nichols and Schwartz (1998) describe structural therapy as containing the following steps, though not necessarily in the order described below.

1. Joining and accommodating (a social process)
2. Working with interaction
3. Diagnosing
4. Highlighting and modifying interactions
5. Boundary making
6. Unbalancing
7. Challenging the family's assumptions (and stories)

To these, we might also add this implied step:

8. Creating the emotional climate that best facilitates honest and open communication

The Washington school of strategic therapy may be described as having similar steps, although there is a greater tendency for the strategic therapists to address them through homework assignments that take place outside the physical presence of the therapist. There has been an increasing emphasis in Washington school training since the late 1980s on moving more of these steps more frequently back into the therapy session, especially with the treatment of violence and abuse. Structural therapists may also use homework assignments to address these steps, but there is a greater tendency to enact these steps in passionate interchange in the session.

The stages of therapy are overlapping. For example, clinicians are constantly redrawing their perceived map of the social system and the agreed-upon problem. But three main stages of therapy stand out, and these are joining/assessment, intervention, and termination. During the joining/assessment stage, interventions may be attempted, but the primary focus of the therapist is on creating a healthy therapeutic relationship and on the therapist's developing a good enough understanding of the problem and its social context. The intervention stage involves a greater focus on experimentation, with changes both inside and outside therapy sessions. When successful, these experiments should lead to clients' discovering and adapting structure, sequences, and stories that work better for them. The termination stage involves the successful withdrawal of the therapist from active involvement in problem solving. This withdrawal must leave the clients feeling competent to handle problems themselves, while leaving the door open to their returning to therapy in the future if necessary.

Directives and Interventions

A "directive" is a communication by the therapist suggesting that a client experience, think, and/or behave differently. An "intervention" or "technique" is a collection of directives given to achieve a clinical goal. SST therapists are expected to be competent in a wide range of directives and interventions/techniques to help clients shift their structure, sequences, and stories. As therapists mature, they continue to experiment with a wide variety of directives and techniques, but most commonly rely on a central set with which they have become most competent.

Milton Erickson noted that there are many types of people and problems, and therapists had better learn an equivalently wide variety of interventions (Haley, 1973). Minuchin (personal communication, 1999) has described this process as similar to that of the healer with a medicine pouch; the healer must collect a wide variety of medicinal herbs, because of the wide variety of problems that people seek relief from. Similarly, the therapist must always be ready to "collect" a new technique that facilitates therapy.

Before we describe a range of directives and techniques, a warning is required. Both structural and strategic approaches are well known for innovative new techniques, and this has created misunderstandings, especially among those whose exposure to the approaches has been limited to 1- or 2-day workshops. SST is not defined by directives and techniques, but rather by a way of conceptualizing problems and change in the context of therapy. The interventions used to achieve change do not define the model. One can use the techniques of Satir and Whitaker to do very mainstream SST therapy, or one can use the techniques developed by Minuchin, Montalvo, Haley, and Madanes to do a therapy that is definitely neither structural nor strategic.

Interventions/techniques must take into account each couple's social and therapeutic context. Specific interventions may be associated with certain presenting problems, but they should not be chosen solely for this reason. In SST, the social context of a problem rather than the presenting

problem itself is the more influential determinant of an intervention. Warm, supportive relations in one family may allow for an intervention that would be inappropriate for the same presenting problem in the context of a family in an angry, unsupportive, disconnected state.

Interventions/techniques must be matched to the therapeutic context. All therapists are challenged by the constantly shifting nature of endurance and motivation. SST emphasizes that a therapist has responsibility to build and maintain endurance and motivation throughout the clinical process.

Types of Interventions

• *Therapist inspired.* A therapist's encouragement of an action or viewpoint that is primarily conceived of by the clinician. *Example:* A therapist states to a couple, "I know an exercise that might help to get the two of you past this impasse. Would you be interested in hearing about it?"

• *Client-inspired.* A therapist's encouragement of an action or viewpoint that is primarily conceived of by the client. *Example:* A therapist states to a couple, "You've just described a wonderful way that you found to overcome this problem a year ago. Why don't you give it a try once again?"

• *Direct.* A therapist's suggestion, in the form of a clearly identifiable direct request rather than by implication or logical extension, that clients take a viewpoint or action. *Example:* A therapist states to a couple, "I would like each of you to do something nice for the other this week."

• *Indirect.* A therapist's suggestion, by implication or logical extension rather than in the form of a clearly identifiable direct request, that clients take a viewpoint or action. *Examples:* A therapist smiles approvingly at a client when that client mentions considering an action that the therapist approves of. A therapist tells a story to a client in which the central character takes action that the therapist hopes that the client will take.

• *Preparatory.* A directive that is not employed to directly solve the presenting problem, but rather with the expectation of creating changes that will prepare the way for the later change of the presenting problem. *Example:* The therapist reframes a problem in such a way that encourages new efforts at problem solving. The new efforts are expected to result in change in the presenting problem, not the reframing itself.

• *Primary.* A directive that is employed with the hope of solving the presenting problem. *Ex-*

ample: A client requests advice on how to solve a problem with his/her partner. The therapist recommends that the client directly discuss the issue with the partner. The hope of the therapist is that the directive to discuss the issue with the partner may result in the solution of the presenting problem.

• Terminal. A directive that is used to help successfully end therapy after the solution of the presenting problem. Example: A therapist asks the clients to write a plan describing how they will approach a reappearance of the problem.

SST consciously employs both therapist- and client-inspired directives, and delivers them through direct and indirect means, and does so in consideration of whether the goal is preparational, primary, or terminal. Some directives tend to be used most often during therapy sessions, and others are more likely to be given as homework to be completed outside the clinician's office. Ethics require that the therapist take full responsibility for the implications of the full range of directives given in therapy.

Therapist-Inspired versus Client-Inspired Directives

There are practical and ethical advantages and disadvantages to both direct and indirect directives. Therapist-inspired directives have the ethical advantage of clarity of influence; when they go wrong, the client blames the therapist. Although some clients will credit themselves for change resulting from therapist-inspired directives, others will tend to give the therapist too much credit unless the therapist works to convince them otherwise. Clients who do not give themselves proper credit for change induced by therapist-inspired directives may respond better to client-inspired directives. The disadvantage of client-inspired directives is the lack of clarity of influence. Clients following a client-inspired directive sometimes forget that they are acting at a therapist's urging and tend to incur higher levels of self-blame when the directive is unsuccessful, thus lessening their confidence in their own acts of self-determination. Both types of directives are part of normal communication, and the proper use of them is a matter of fit with and preference of clients.

Interventions within the Interview

Planned interventions begin after the therapist has sufficiently begun to address the therapeutic endur-

ance issues, with the most important of these being joining, the start of the strong therapeutic relationship. Endurance issues are significant ongoing considerations that require ongoing maintenance.

Interventions are best thought to proceed simultaneously with ongoing diagnosis. However, in the first session the first step is evoking within the interview the family system's stories, sequence, and structure. SST emphasizes the inclusion of the therapist in these equations (Colapinto, 1991; Sullivan, 1953; Haley, 1963, 1976; Lappin, 1988; Minuchin, 1974). The therapist has a strong influence on the choice of information brought forth in an interview.

Structured Techniques

Many SST therapists use a wide variety of structured interventions/techniques, which have ordered and prescribed steps. An example of such a prescribed technique is a negotiation-based intervention for couples described elsewhere (Keim, 1993, 2000).

Structured techniques can be particularly helpful in identifying and negotiating the involvement of third parties in marital troubles. Despite the fact that such a technique is designed so that the couple should not need the intervention of a third party to complete an exercise, the couple will often attempt to triangulate with the therapist in a manner that may be parallel to the involvement of other third parties.

The structured technique is an extension of the skill and knowledge of the therapist. When properly used, structured techniques become a vehicle for a wide range of therapeutic purposes. When improperly used, such techniques are used to offer procrustean solutions that are insensitive to the desires of clients or are attempted without additional consideration of other parties involved in the problem.

Perspective

> If we are always arriving and departing, it is also true that we are eternally anchored. One's destination is never a place but rather a new way of looking at things.
>
> —Henry Miller

In order to understand the desired effect of therapy on clients' perspective, an odd comparison is in order. One reason why couples take vacations is for the chance to look at life from a fresh perspective. Some couples have had the opportunity to take such a vacation and have experienced the fresh perspective that comes from a dramatic change in physical and social context. The therapist attempts to promote a similarly fresh perspective during and as a result of each therapy session. The therapist's interaction in the session creates new sequences, structure, and stories/world views, and these same changes ideally facilitate further experimentation and change outside of the session. The primary goal of homework assignments is to promote this extra-session experimentation and change.

Emotional and Topical Range

People do not come to therapy to fix the calm, collected moments in their lives, and a therapist is misinformed if the therapy fails to move from muted and polite chat to the clients' pains, arguments, and disconnections. Emotional intensity can either facilitate or interrupt a therapy session, and it is the therapist's responsibility to intervene as necessary to keep the therapeutic conversation going. In order to do this, the therapist must be comfortable with the full range of natural, strong emotions connected to important topics. Too often, therapists are conflict-avoidant and will not allow into the session the normal emotional range that is not disruptive to anybody but the therapists. Other therapists provoke strong emotions within the session, with the idea that the venting of emotions alone is therapeutic; this is highly contrary to SST practice. Emotions in SST sessions are a manifestation of the interactions brought into the session, and divorcing these emotions from the interactions that evoke them may at certain times be disorienting and harmful.

In SST, the therapist will frequently bring into a session a part of the couple's emotional repertoire that, although used elsewhere, has not been displayed in therapy. This may be done for diagnostic reasons or as a specifically planned intervention designed to expand the couple's emotional range, so that the partners may better handle the emotional requirements of problem solving. In the latter case, the therapist is not teaching individuals how to have new emotions, but rather how to apply them to the pursuit of their stated goals.

For diagnostic reasons, a couple that almost exclusively occupies the highly emotional range of interaction within an interview will usually evoke a therapist's efforts to expand the range to include examples of how the partners currently or in the past have communicated in calm and respect-

ful ways. A couple that only offers a façade of pseudomutuality (Wynne et al., 1958) in the session may be challenged to display the more emotional and honest style that the clients reported having used with each other elsewhere or in the past.

Structures, sequences, and stories related to problems are often not perceptible when the problems are not occurring. The cognitive states and communication styles of individuals in regular discussion are not necessarily the ones present during difficult, intimate discussions. It is the clinician's responsibility to bring the problem into the office along with the clients.

Expected Conversations

Therapy tends to involve conversations that should be able to take place at home but, for reasons central to the therapy, do not (Keim, 1999; Nichols, 1997). Important conversations that the family expects to have but does not outside of therapy are referred to simply as the "expected conversations." Sometimes a couple will directly tell the therapist what the expected conversations are. Other times, the couple will only indirectly suggest the existence of these expected conversations and leave it up to the therapist to make the topic overt. Simply put, when a couple directly or indirectly brings up an expected conversation, the therapist must highlight it and facilitate its immediate or eventual discussion.

One of the goals of clinical training is to make the therapist a good enough listener that the hints of expected conversations are appreciated. Another goal of training is for therapist to approach expected conversations with emotions that serve to facilitate the couple's discussions rather than shut them down. A conflict-avoidant therapist is all too likely to join into the couple's discomfort over a painful issue, rather than accept the implied or overt invitation to discuss it.

CASE EXAMPLES

For us, choosing case examples was daunting. The range of structural ands strategic cases encompasses startling contrasts in clinical interventions, cultures, sexual preferences, and concepts of marriage. It was tempting to employ for demonstration purposes the therapy of a group marriage (Minuchin, 1984), or the facilitation of a marriage relationship between an actively homosexual man and woman (Haley, 1973), or any number of the published variations in intervention, culture, class, and construction of marriage. But the primary function of these case examples is to clarify the concepts already presented to the reader, and thus two rather unexciting yet revealing cases are described. They contrast in the type of intervention used (a structured vs. an unstructured approach), in the degree of triangulation with third parties (one involved active detriangulation of a third party, the other did not), and in the life stage of the couple (the leaving-home stage vs. the retirement/decline stage).

Case 1: Sandra and Joseph

A couple in their early 50s, Sandra and Joseph, set up an appointment for marital therapy. They had two daughters at home, a 20-year-old who was in college and a 17-year-old high school student. Joseph worked as a corporate bureaucrat, and Sandra described herself as a dance teacher who had chosen to stop working in order to dedicate herself more fully to raising the children. In their first interview, Joseph stated that his primary goal was to get his wife to nag him less. Sandra said that she knew that she nagged and that she had tried unsuccessfully to stop for extended periods. She also added that her primary goal in coming to therapy was to get her husband to communicate more and to follow through on tasks around the house. Joseph admitted that he had a problem with communication and follow-through with chores, but he had been unsuccessful in changing for more than a week at a time. As an example of his failure to follow through, he noted that there was a tremendous backlog of household items that he had agreed to fix.

Sandra and Joseph described their communication as having taken place to a large degree through their older daughter, who now lived at college. The role of communication hub had not been assumed by the younger daughter. For 7 years before going to college, the older daughter had had the job of relaying messages back and forth between her parents. Joseph and Sandra understood that this had not been a healthy way to communicate, but found that they returned to this established pattern when their older daughter returned home for vacations. Joseph and Sandra could thus be viewed as coming to therapy because a previously functional means of interacting had become obsolete. They had tired of their former triangulation with their older daughter, which, at any rate was no longer feasible while she was away at college.

In the context of the family life cycle, this may be viewed as a problem relating to the weaning of parents from children (Haley, 1973).

Joseph and Sandra complained and demonstrated in enactments in the therapist's office the they had great difficulty in talking constructively about how to solve their difficulties. They kept turning to the therapist in hopes that the clinician would say who was correct. In other words, the problem-solving strategy exhibited in the enactments was to triangulate with a third party, rather than to solve the issue by staying within the marital dyad. Significantly, the conversation never moved beyond the discussion "Who is to blame?" to the discussion "What do we do about it?" without very direct intervention by the therapist, who seemed to be offered the role previously taken by the oldest daughter.

Using Don Jackson's concept of quid pro quo, the therapist reframed the problem to the couple as a breakdown in the negotiating process (Jackson, 1965). The therapist defined nagging as an incomplete attempt at negotiation. A "negotiation" was defined as a conversation about an exchange that employs a "this for that" (quid pro quo) trade. For such a negotiation to progress, the therapist explained, one party needs to make a request, and the other party needs to name or agree to a price. But in the case of nagging, one party's request does not result in the other spouse's naming a price. So the initiating party continues to repeat the request, waiting for the other side to name a price.

This reframing allowed Sandra to make requests of her husband without thinking of herself as a nag. The reframing also allowed Joseph to think of his participation in a negotiation as an equal, rather than as a browbeaten husband who was "giving in" to his wife.

The therapist then asked Sandra and Joseph whether they wanted to try a fun exercise that was designed to get a couple back on track with negotiations. The couple asked to give the exercise a try. The therapist then offered a handout describing a very formalized negotiating technique with 14 points (see Figure 4.1). The exercise consists of negotiations using a particular structure. Step 1 of the exercise is to have the spouses read the handout each other and discuss the 14 points. Step 3 is to have the couple experiment with tiny, fun negotiations in the therapists office. Step 3 of the exercise is to have the couple experiment with tiny, fun negotiations at home. Steps 4 and 5 involve employing this exercise to negotiate more emotionally charged subjects in the therapist's office (Step 4) and then at the couple's home (Step 5).

1. Negotiation draws on the reserve of good will that loved ones store for one another. This reserve must be replenished by the couple's having fun together and by the spouses' enjoying each other's company outside the household. Negotiation only works when those involved have had enough fun together. This is why good business negotiators are often big spenders when it comes to entertaining those they plan to do business with.

   [*Therapist's explanation:* Intimate communication involves the directing of intense amounts of attention to one another. Couples' homes are so habitually distracting that often partners are unable to give each other the attention they need. This is especially true if there are children in the house. It is therefore recommended that most couples get out of the house.]

2. Some negotiations take 1 discussion, others 5, and others 200. Have a style that allows negotiations to start, break, and restart easily. If one ends a negotiating session nicely, one can come back to it nicely.

3. Never say "No" during a negotiation unless there is an ethical problem with what is requested. The closest one should come to saying "No" is "I will seriously consider that."

   [*Therapist's explanation:* In our culture, "No" simultaneously denies a request and blocks future discussion. Blocking future discussion is contrary to the spirit of cooperative negotiation. A phrase borrowed from Japanese business negotiating, "I will seriously consider that," is understood to momentarily deny a request while leaving open the possibility of discussing the request again in the future.]

4. Negotiating is only about the present and future. Avoid bringing up the past except as an example of what is being requested.

   [*Therapist's explanation:* This is one of the most important rules in many communication courses. One of the leading causes of failure in negotiation is getting sidetracked. Talking about the past is the best way to avoid completion of a negotiation.]

5. Avoid explanations as to why one wants the package being negotiated. These will only sidetrack conversation.

   [*Therapist's explanation:* Requesting an explanation not only sidetracks the negotiation, but also may be perceived as patronizing.]

6. In negotiation, assume that one knows only what is best for oneself, and not for others.

   [*Therapist explanation:* Assuming that one knows what is best for others sidetracks negotiation. In addition, no matter how well intended, questioning the validity of another's request is usually received as being patronizing.]

7. Each party owes the other a "price" for the request in negotiation, as long as what is being requested is moral.

8. Avoid only doing those activities that both enjoy. Use negotiation to get one's partner to try something new, and be prepared to do the same in return.

9. Each party in a healthy romantic relationship is benevolently trying to change 2% of the other while accepting the other 98%. If one is trying to change much more than 2%, the relationship is characterized by nagging. If one is not trying to change the other at all, the partners grow apart over time and do not feel an adequate amount of intimacy.

   [*Therapist's explanation:* Oddly enough, the perception that one's spouse is interested in changing one is part of the perception of intimacy.]

10. Define time parameters of what is being requested. Be very specific about terms.

    [*Therapist's explanation:* Couples should start by only negotiating for time segments of 1 week at a time and *slowly* build up the amount of time involved in transactions. Also, requests should be described in very behavioral terms, especially early in the therapy. For example, "being more loving" is too general a request, whereas "hugging and cuddling" are appropriately specific requests. Global requests for change must be broken down into simple behaviors.]

11. Hold hands continuously through difficult or emotional negotiations. The physical closeness is a reminder of the love that underlies all discussions.

    [*Therapist's explanation:* This is an especially effective approach for a couple whose arguments quickly spiral out of control even in the therapist's office. Negotiation is not a time for couples to fight, and such unproductive disagreements must be quickly blocked. Therapists know that they should intervene quickly to stop an argument if spouses, in the midst of a disagreement, disengage their hands.]

12. Seal all negotiations with a kiss. Write all negotiations down in a specific place, such as a blank book of the type often sold as a diary.

    [*Therapist explanation:* With emotional negotiations, individuals tend to later confuse the memory of their starting position with the final agreed-upon compromise. Spouses tend to confuse where they started in a negotiation with where they ended. Writing negotiations down addresses this almost inevitable problem.]

13. The negotiation should not end until each partner feels that a "win–win" situation exists, whereby each is happy with the negotiated arrangement.

14. When a couple learns to negotiate explicitly, it is at first more troublesome than helpful. Have patience!

FIGURE 4.1. Negotiation handout (have couple read out loud and discuss before trying).

Some couples can move through two steps in a single week, while others need more time. The therapist emphasizes that this exercise, in its formalized totality, is not meant to be a description of how couples should normally work out problems. This exercise is successful when it allays the spouses' fears that the negotiation will be "win–lose" and leads the couple to playful experimentation with "win–win" discussions instead.

With some amusement, Joseph and Sandra read the 14 steps, and the therapist gave an explanation as to why this type of explicit, "win–win" negotiating would work in the near future to help each change the other. The initial coaching by the therapist of negotiation included frequent shifting of sides as he joined with one spouse and then the other. The couple successfully completed several small negotiations involving fun and household chores during the first interview. Sandra requested that Joseph talk to her for 15 minutes each evening during the week; Joseph agreed to do so in exchange for being able to have 15 minutes of uninterrupted rest upon return from work each evening. Joseph then asked what Sandra wanted in return for "happily" supporting his taking a 3-hour fishing trip that weekend. Sandra agreed to encourage the fishing trip in return for his completing 3 hours of trim painting in the house. The couple negotiated issues related to sex, time spent with children, and other issues. The pair also negotiated "penance" after the husband, on one occasion, did not follow through with his side of the negotiation. After six sessions, Joseph stated that the nagging was no longer a problem and that he was more active with his family and in activities outside of work.

The couple then expressed fear that their older daughter, Sylvia, might try to regain her role as communication hub for the parents. The therapy then progressed to helping the couple deal with other issues related to their change in life cycle. The therapy then was suspended until the older daughter returned for summer vacation and tried to resume the role of intermediary between her parents. Having discussed with the clinician that Sylvia might lovingly try to regain this inappropriate role, the spouses returned to therapy as soon as they realized what was happening.

In order to deal with Sylvia's role confusion, the therapist asked the husband to buy a gift of lingerie for his wife and to give it to her within eyesight of, though not directly in front of, Sylvia. The wife was instructed to give her husband a very sexy kiss. This task caused Joseph and Sandra to laugh as they explained that they were never physically affectionate in front of their children. The therapist explained that romantic affection between parents is one of the best ways to emphasize to a child that he/she is not an equal of the parents. The couple carried out the task, and the older daughter immediately responded to the sight of the lingerie and her parents kissing by asking her father why he hadn't bought her a piece of lingerie as well. As the wife proudly told the therapist, the husband responded by saying, "Because I'm not married to you." The couple reported in a 1-year follow-up that they were more comfortable handling problems with Sylvia after this incident.

Critical to the negotiation intervention described above is that the couple be able to negotiate exchanges that the spouses choose not to consummate. In such situations, one spouse asks another for the price of a change, and though the price is perceived by both parties to be fair, the requesting spouse chooses not to make the quid pro quo exchange. The reason for the failure of the requesting spouse to pursue the exchange is significant: The requesting spouse decides that it is preferable to endure some problems rather than to go through the hassle and price of changing them. This sort of balance in change and acceptance is one of the hallmarks of successful marital therapy (Jacobson & Christensen, 1996). A balance between change and acceptance must be achieved, and there is a parallel need for balance between soothing and pressing for change in the negotiation itself. The negotiation exercise described is typical of many structured techniques in marital therapy, in that it achieves this dual balance between change and acceptance and between soothing and pressing for change.

Case 2: Sarah, Sam, and the Unspoken Contract

In *Family Healing*, Minuchin and Nichols (1993) describe a case involving spouses in their 70s, Sam and Sarah, who were the subject of a consultation with their therapist, Monica, a woman in her 30s. After Sam had retired, Sam had become depressed and Sarah had become resentful of her husband's new demands on her time, energy, and marital role.

Before consulting with Minuchin, the therapist had constructed the problem as being one in which the "relationship was flawed because there was no independence, no autonomy, no fun. . . . Sam and Sarah responded to Monica's challenge of their ways as old people often do to the well-meaning young. They didn't argue; they just walked more slowly" (p. 89). This inspired the frustrated therapist to seek consultation. Minuchin conceptualized the case as being one in which the couple was attempting to weather their transition into retirement and its associated depression and role renegotiation. Sarah and Sam's relationship had been one characterized by dichotomized roles, with Sam having the role of the strong, independent party and Sarah having the role of giving caretaker. "These polarized pairings," the authors wrote, "are as much a product of relationship as of personality. . . . That such contracts don't get spelled out doesn't make them any less powerful. Marriage is a balancing act" (p. 95). There is no pathology connected to such polarization. "Sarah and Sam's rather extreme version of reciprocity had served them well up to now, but old arrangements don't always work in new circumstances" (p. 95). "In their seventies, Sam and Sarah were discovering their differences. . . . I thought that Sam and Sarah were simply in the throes of transition. I was concerned that Monica, defined as the expert in this situation, would see maladjustment where I saw a process of readjustment" (p. 92). Minuchin described the relationship structure thus:

> Every relationship that works must have a formula for stability and a formula for change. Sam and Sarah had achieved stability with an exaggerated form of complementarity—at the expense of autonomy and flexibility. He had subordinated his nature to her, and she had subordinated hers to him. It was the traditional marriage carried to an almost absurd extreme. Their touching mutual dependence was functional when Sam was working, but not anymore.
>
> A successful relationship also requires the ability to adjust to change. Whatever type of balance a couple works out, their relationship will need to be rebalanced at transitional points in the life cycle. Healthy couples need flexibility as well as stability.
>
> Could I give Sarah and Sam a small push in the direction of flexibility? What followed was a playful, friendly struggle. But a struggle nonetheless. (Minuchin & Nichols, 1993, pp. 99–100)

Stepping from behind the mirror into the therapy room, Minuchin made his own interaction with the clients a means of challenging the rigidity of their roles. While joining with them in a teasing manner (old fogies having fun together, he would later note), Minuchin spontaneously offered the wife his silver pen, calling it a magic wand and implying that she should use it to change her husband. Urging the wife to use the magic wand made an important dynamic overt—her effort to change her husband. This was an effort that she had previously been denying, but that became acceptable to admit to, using the playful metaphor of the magic wand. Minuchin would later ask Sam to become incompetent by being sick for 2 days a week; this directive allowed for an additional means of making overt Sam's desire to step out of the rigidity of his role as the caretaker and into the role of the party being cared for, once again making the covert overt.

One of the most characteristic aspects of SST is that the therapist maintains a balance between challenging and soothing the couple, and a similar balance of challenging and soothing interactions is coached or encouraged between spouses. With Sam and Sarah, challenging and soothing sometimes took place simultaneously through gentle teasing; at other times, the soothing and challenging were quite separate and occurred in different parts of the interview. By various means, the therapist thus raised the tension in the interview to the point where spouses responded with new flexibility.

Overcoming the rigidity of the spouses' roles led to an opening up of dialogues. Maladaptive rigidity had squashed heartfelt conversations about relationships, and Minuchin's playful challenging of Sam and Sarah's previously adaptive relationship stances allowed for overt discussion and renegotiation of roles. This movement toward flexibility was characterized by Minuchin's sensitivity to the demands of the couple's late stage in the family life cycle. In making the covert overt, the spouses were able to discuss the statistical likelihood (given their sexes and ages) that Sarah would one day need to care for a dying and dependent Sam and then live on without him. With this discussion came an overt discussion of the need to prepare for the coming change in roles and responsibilities, and such changes could be made in an open and consensual manner.

In a follow-up interview, Sarah and Sam had traded the roles of "stronger" and "weaker" spouse. The basic challenges of their lives had not changed. But, noted Minuchin:

> What did change was that they became a little more tolerant of each other. They continued to complain but no longer with any illusion about changing each other. I helped them see the reciprocity that governed their lives, hoping they would be able both to accept themselves and begin to explore the possibility of change. They settled for acceptance. (Minuchin & Nichols, 1993, p. 102)

CASE COMPARISON

These cases are compared in regard to how each intervention was conceived in terms of clinical optimism, family life cycle, and SST's central triad (sequence, structure, and story).

Clinical Optimism

Spouses are viewed as having tremendous resources that therapy seeks to tap. It required great faith in the human potential for change to expect in Case 2 that a 50-year pattern of dominance and submission could change, and yet our collective clinical experience informs us that humans regularly manage such monumental flexibility. Similarly, the therapist in Case 1 proceeded with the expectation that the charming yet clumsy negotiation exercises would be overshadowed by superior and ongoing efforts by the couple to "make it their own" (B. Montalvo, personal communication, 2000). Almost immediate obsolescence and replacement are the hallmarks of a successful directive.

The starting views of the clients' motivations are also conceived of by an SST therapist as being well intended. From our perspective, one never challenges motive, only method. So, the question is not *whether* someone is being loving, but rather *how*. For example, in Case 1, the triangulation effort of the older daughter was viewed as an attempt to be helpful to the parents. This construction of the case evoked more empathy from the clinician and led to the daughter's being seen as carrying on a job that was no longer necessary, rather than as an individual who was inappropriate and nosy with her parents.

Family Life Cycle

In Case 1, the earlier pattern of communicating through a child was not viewed as necessarily pathological; the problem was viewed as the difficulty of making the transition to a new interaction appropriate for the current stage of family life. In Case 2, the extreme complementarity of the couple was not viewed as pathology, but rather as a once-functioning pattern that was a focus of change because of a change in family life cycle.

Sensitivity to the family life cycle helped Minuchin avoid the consulting therapist's mistake of conceiving of the challenges as those related to a need for the spouses to develop autonomy from each other. Conceptualizing the problem as needing more autonomy and fun was not necessarily wrong but rather inefficient. Such a problem definition might have been appropriate for a younger couple, but was not an appealing basis for therapy for a postretirement couple.

Sequence

The central sequence change in Case 1 was from (1) wife requesting change and husband withdrawing to (2) wife requesting change and husband responding in the context of a quid pro quo arrangement. The central sequence change in Case 2 was from the ineffectual effort to maintain the strong–weak dichotomy of influence. The husband shifted from caretaker to primary recipient of care, and the wife shifted from primary recipient to competent caretaker of not only her husband but also her grandchildren.

The sequence changes in both cases had two important characteristics. First, requests for change were balanced within conversations by soothing, and this was evident in both the therapist's requests of the clients and the clients' requests of each other. Second, the clients' expectations of change were balanced with the need to accept that some aspects of problems are best just endured. This balance of change and acceptance was modeled by the therapist's approach to the clients, as well as by the style of interaction evoked from the clients toward each other.

A characteristic of sequence change is the respectful use of novelty and absurdity to interrupt the sequences that the clients no longer wish to continue. When properly used, absurdity has the effect of encouraging flexibility in deviating from a no-longer-helpful sequence (Haley, 1976). The works of Milton Erickson (Haley, 1973), Carl Whitaker (1975), and other masters of clinical absurdity have offered many vivid and dramatic examples of a method at work in more modest form in many SST interviews.

Absurdity does not offer a new sequence; when successful, it provides clients with a window of opportunity to experiment with change. Only if the clients find preferred sequences during this window of opportunity will change be likely. In Case 1, the extreme limitations of structured exercise combined with both the exercise's affection and the therapist's humor created an air of absurdity that created a window of opportunity for change. Within this window, the couple's success outside the therapist's office in recreating a sense of balance of quid pro quo and the detriangulation of the older daughter actually led the spouses to feel that they had succeeded in dramatic change. In Case 2, a wonderful example of the use of absurdity to interrupt sequences was Minuchin's turning his pen into a magic wand that he urged the wife to use on her husband. Because of Minuchin's success in joining, the wife accepted this absurdity with affection and (within the window of flexibility created) allowed herself to consider that, short of magic, she might just have to learn to accept that some aspects of her husband would not change.

In Case 1, sequence change was mainly achieved through the couple's interaction with the directives (the negotiating exercise) rather than the direct challenge of the therapist. The directives thus served as a medium for the therapist–client interaction. In Case 2, sequence change was achieved mainly through the direct challenges of the therapist; in this second case, interaction resulting from the therapist's directly challenging assumptions and interactions was the primary medium of therapist–client interaction. Sequence change initiated primarily through interaction with a directive is neither superior nor inferior to sequence change initiated through direct challenging of roles and assumptions; the SST therapist must be capable of the full range of such directives and must choose the emphasis of sequence change according to the needs of each individual case.

Structure

Minuchin and Nichols (1993) wrote, "Complementary patterns, such as pursuer–distancer, active–passive, dominant–submissive, exist in most couples. They begin to cause problems when they are exaggerated or fail to shift to accommodate to changing circumstances" (p. 88). Part of the clinician's perception of structure is dependent upon finding the complementary patterns in which roles are manifested. Other parts of the perception of a couple's structure relate to third parties that may be helping and/or complicating transitions and to the organizational changes influenced by changes in individual/family life cycle.

In the case brought to Minuchin for consultation, there did not appear to be any third parties who were handicapping the flexibility of the couple, although the young therapist's initial approach may have come close to just such an impediment. Sam and Sarah were faced with demands in flexibility that are forced upon them by entry into senior years and

by the associated retirement-related, health-related, and emotional challenges. The ability of the couple to adapt to changing circumstances was handicapped by structure that did not allow the role flexibility to experiment with change. Exaggerated roles are commonly (but not always) associated with difficulties in experimenting with change, especially if those exaggerated roles have been stable for a long period of time. The couple in Minuchin's case had been stable in exaggerated roles for some time, and this suggested that greater effort and/or time would be required to create flexibility of the sort that would allow mutual changes in their marital job descriptions.

In the case of Joseph and Sandra, the couple had fallen into complementary patterns that no longer worked because these patterns required the active triangulation of a daughter who had become busy with college. The degree of role exaggeration was not as extreme as in Minuchin's case, but there was much greater involvement of a third party, the daughter. A return by the couple to flexible negotiation of roles required that the daughter's role as communication hub be openly and ritually ended. The overt change was the agreement to negotiate with each other rather than through the daughter, and the ritual change was the gift of the negligee to the wife in a way that drew clear boundaries with the daughter. These two cases demonstrate the central dimensions in SST's use of structure. In Case 2, the therapist's intervention was very much informed by the extremes in complementary roles that the spouses had maintained. In Case 1, bringing the spouses into a more affectionate proximity to each other and detriangulating a member of another generation, the older daughter, were the central changes in structure. The SST must be able to consider each of these dimensions of structure and be empowered by the combination that most efficiently describes marital organization.

Story

> If a therapist must have a theory of personality, then the most helpful one is that of an identity as a mental, abridged anthology of stories, any one of which can be replaced by a story from the total collection. Therapy thus involves editing the abridged edition of perceptions of the present and past. A change in these perceptions is a change in the personality, and a change of shared perceptions is a change in the relationship.
> —I. Keim et al., (1990, p. 247)

Challenging the clients' stories can help overcome the rigidity of marital roles, and this increased flexibility in the marriage can lead to an opening up of dialogues that further allow for the renegotiation of their story that they use to describe their relationship. In Case 2, as noted earlier, maladaptive rigidity had squashed heartfelt conversations about relationships, and Minuchin's humorous challenging of the spouses' previously functional relationship stances permitted overt discussion and renegotiation of roles. By the follow-up interview, Sarah had become the stronger, more empathic spouse, and Sam had become more accepting in the reversal that made him the weaker and more self-focused of the two. What was critical was that the role changes had been made without sacrificing each spouse's feeling of being supported by the other; mutual support was still the perceived state of the relationship.

RESEARCH AND TRAINING ISSUES

Integration of Research

Like their colleagues from other schools of psychotherapy, SST clinicians face a continual challenge in integrating research into their theory and practice. Research has had a particularly important role in understanding the importance of the therapeutic relationship (Miller et al., 1997), the translation of client complaints into the therapist's map, and in defining the balance between change and acceptance (Jacobson & Christensen, 1996). For example, a couple's sense of fairness in the relationship may be enhanced by organizing change in the context of a quid pro quo contract, and this contract may include requests on each spouse's part that the other be more available and kinder. Awareness of research will lead the therapist to focus change efforts not just on "unkind" interaction, but especially on that which is mired in expressions of contempt, criticism, and defensiveness (Gottman, 1994). Awareness of research will also lead the therapist to be particularly concerned that a request for more availability is a sign of avoidance of interaction—a pattern whose dominance in the relationship we know to be particularly corrosive (Gottman, 1994).

Outcome Research

Outcome research on SST in general has focused on a number of issues, including anorexia nervosa

(Minuchin et al., 1978), drug addictions (Stanton & Todd, 1979), and delinquency (Szapocznik & Hervis, 2000). The brief strategic family therapy model described by Szapocznik and Hervis (2000) received an Exemplary II rating from the Office of Juvenile Justice and Delinquency Prevention in collaboration with the Substance Abuse and Mental Health Service's Center for Substance Abuse Prevention. However, there is no parallel research on marital SST in particular.

High-outcome research such as that by Szapocznik and Hervis is, with very few exceptions, the product of university-sponsored grants and study. One of the reasons why SST approaches became popular so quickly is that they bypassed universities and focused on professional rather than graduate training. The regrettable consequence is that there is very little representation of the SST approach in universities, especially in regard to marital therapy research. SST clinicians have unfortunately not been as successful at research, and they have often had difficulty finding outcome researchers interested in collaboration.[18]

Training

One cannot separate the SST concepts of training and practice. These are models that can only be mastered by the therapist's receiving individual feedback from colleagues and clients as to the ability to maintain the therapeutic relationship with the clients and to focus on issues related to positive outcome. The most characteristic facet of the structural and strategic traditions is the seriousness with which they undertake training, especially the use of one-way mirrors. Training takes time and commitment; although techniques can be learned in a short period, the skills of diplomacy and the fine art of listening to clients usually require a year or two of supervision of actual or recorded therapy.

Jay Haley often notes that training a therapist is like training an actor.[19] There are certain skills that both actor and therapist need to be taught, such as how to talk so that others can hear, how to mold one's act to that of others, and how to perceive and communicate the desired emotional range to the audience. Despite the fact that such abilities are called "skills," their integration is measured by the individuality with which they are carried out. To the degree that such skills are imitations of others rather than manifestations of self, they are suspect and create distance or even irritation within the audience or clients.

Other valuable aspects of SST training are (1) an introduction to the oral history of the interactional view and (2) the development of a healthy professional peer group to support the growth of the therapist. An appreciation for the intellectual tradition of systems theory and intervention makes the profession all the more interesting for many clinicians, and the rich oral tradition of stories relating to Bateson, Jackson, Erickson, and others helps the written material come to life. The friendships developed in live supervision programs are often lifelong, and supportive professional context can be as important as any other variable in good-quality clinical practice.

Of particular concern to the future of family therapy was the decline of the family therapy institutes as training center in the 1990s. The live supervision that these programs specialized in became fiscally unmanageable for most therapists and agencies, as managed care destroyed the profit margins that had previously made such training possible. Most institutes that existed in the 1980s closed or sharply curtailed training by the late 1990s. Models of therapy proliferate not so much in relation to the number of therapists trained as they do in relation to the number of supervisors trained, and the loss of independent institutes had an especially devastating effect on the numbers of therapists receiving that advanced level of training.

With the collapse of the institute system, universities have become an even more important source of family therapy training. Since universities traditionally give preference to research over practice in the hiring of tenured faculty, family therapy education and training are often in the hands of faculty members chosen more for their research than for their clinical practice and supervision skills. At many universities, a professor can focus only on research and still be a highly respected, tenured faculty member, but a faculty member who focuses only on clinical work is often a second-class citizen within the department. When more universities equally privilege research and clinical work in their awarding of tenure, the quality of university training will increase substantially.

SST has probably trained more clinicians and more importantly, more supervisors in live supervions than any other family therapy model. There are new and energized generation of therapists who have begun to publish and present at conferences, and one of the most exciting challenges for the future will be the building of new venues for training in the SST approach.

CONCLUSION

East and Central African traders of old often spoke their own regional dialects and at least one contact language, Swahili. Through much of the world, at least three languages are brought to intercultural trade: two regional dialects and a "lingua franca" by which the two parties communicate their thoughts and desires. Therapy is a variation on such intercultural trade, as three views of the problem—the clients', the therapist's, and the jointly created vision through which the two groups interact—are the basis of transactions.

The therapist's own vision is informed by a three-dimensional map defined by the couple's sequences, structures, and stories. Without a sense of all three, the SST clinician may find it difficult to target change. To the degree that intervention takes the form of coaching or encouraging what is already happening, therapy maintains the visions and tones of the existing client situation. To the degree that therapy takes the form of encouraging new flexibility, the clinician challenges the clients' sequences, structures, and stories either directly (by making an explicit request for change) or indirectly (by implication or logical extension), making use of either therapist-inspired or client-inspired ideas. The challenge of the therapy is to maintain a flexible, jointly created vision of the problem, such that problem-solving discussions and efforts can continue until there is some combination of solution and acceptance of various aspects of the problem.

ACKNOWLEDGMENTS

The authors would like to thank their respective families for their patience and support, Allan Gurman for his wise guidance, Braulio Montalvo for his sage advice, and Michael Nichols for his helpful reviews and insights.

NOTES

1. The term "strategic therapy" is generic and has been applied to the work of the Brief Therapy Center at the Mental Research Institute, to the early work of Selvini, Palazzoli, et al., to that of Haley and Madanes, and to other groups as well. To avoid confusion, the model founded by Haley and Madanes is referred to as "the Washington school of strategic therapy." This name was inspired

by the Washington School of Psychiatry, which helped give rise to modern family therapy.

2. Other founders are described in the "Background of the Approach" section.

3. One of us (JK) was the director of training at the Family Therapy Institute of Washington, D.C., under Jay Haley and Cloe Madanes. While at the Philadelphia Child Guidance Clinic, the other author (JL) served as a senior faculty member at the Family Therapy Training Center and as associate director of the Post-Graduate Certificate Program in Family Therapy and Systems Consultation.

4. In November 1993, a meeting entitled "The Integration of Structural and Strategic Therapy" was held at the National Institutes of Health in Bethesda, Maryland. The meeting consisted of case presentation by, and dialogue among Jay Haley, Salvador Minuchin, and Cloe Madanes. JK, the organizer of the event, paraphrased Minuchin when noting that the outcome of the conference demonstrated that differences among the speakers had more to do with their personalities than with theory and practice.

5. The exception to this is coaching clients rather than intervening.

6. A "therapist-inspired" intervention is one that, though inevitably influenced by the client, is primarily inspired by the therapist's experience and creativity. A "client-inspired" intervention is one that, though inevitably influenced by the therapist, is primarily inspired by the client's experience and creativity. The inventor of these terms is unknown to us.

7. In a 1998 interview, Minuchin said that "structure" refers not to therapy, but to an understanding of the family. "I was dealing with family organization and complex systems that were interlocked. For me, the term means flexibility, the possibility of directions. It is about the way that the organization operates in constraining growth in certain directions and not in others" (quoted in Lappin, 1998–1999, p. 11).

8. In a personal communication (1990), Jay Haley told JK: "Before we [meaning other members of MRI] learned to give workshops, we would present and therapists just thought, 'That's interesting.' But when Virginia gave a workshop, people went out and tried practicing family therapy."

9. Approaching therapists directly with workshops as opposed to primarily relying on established clinical institutions may have been inspired by the efforts of Milton Erickson and other hypnotists, who were forced to do most of their training in this manner.

10. Hostility to family therapy was hastened by the sudden death of Don Jackson in 1968; this untimely event deprived the family therapy field of its most respected diplomat to the world of psychiatry and analysis.

11. PCGC's colocation with CHOP began as mutually beneficial, but ultimately succumbed to the resurging dominance and finances of the medical model. By the 1990s, CHOP's finances and biological/medical focus were on the rise, whereas PCGC's community/family focus was waning. Attempting to remain viable, PCGC gradually sold its coveted space to CHOP, which, in exchange for needed cash, required more and more say in PCGC operations. Before long, CHOP took over running PCGC and reinstituted the hierarchy and discipline divisions affiliated with the medical model. In the summer of 2000, PCGC, once the preeminent family therapy clinic in the world, closed its doors for good.

12. During the 1980s. Michael Fox was among the second generation of strategic therapists to introduce a more client-directed approach to clinical work, including the use of medication.

13. This list of prominent strategic clinicians is specific to those trained at the Family Therapy Institute of Washington, D.C., and does not include many prominent figures who trained at earlier times with Haley and/or Madanes at the PCGC or at MRI.

14. Thanks to Jorge Colapinto for illuminating this point.

15. The reader is referred to the work of Beavers (1985), Gottman (1994), Gurman and Kniskern (1978), Jacobson and Addis (1993), Johnson and Greenberg (1988), Renick, Blumber, and Markman (1992), and Wallerstein and Blakeslee (1995) for research-based assessment of healthy and dysfunctional couples.

16. Abuse can involve a situation where either one or both spouses maintain abusive relationship rules. A failure of an abused spouse to avoid ongoing marital violence may involve acceptance of abusive relationship rules, but is more likely to relate to a lack of resources that might allow for escape or for the realistic threat of escape.

17. JL thanks Henry Berger for this wise supervisory heuristic tool.

18. One of us (JK) spent more than a decade at the Family Therapy Institute of Washington, D.C., founded by Jay Haley and Cloe Madanes; during that time, no researchers ever requested collaboration on outcome research. This was despite the Institute's proximity to many top universities in the Washington, D.C., Maryland, Virginia, and Pennsylvania areas. Requests for collaboration with outcome researchers, including those expressed on professional listservs on the Internet, achieved no response. The Institute conducted some of its own research, which was rejected for publication for legitimate reasons; it did not meet modern standards that universities have more competence in designing and achieving.

19. Haley was actually a drama major as an undergraduate at UCLA.

REFERENCES

Allport, G. (1960). The open system in personality theory. In W. Buckley (Ed.), *Modern systems research for the behavioral sciences* (pp. 343–350). Chicago: Aldine.

Andolfi, M. (1979). *Family therapy: An international approach.* New York: Plenum Press.

Aponte, H. J. (1976).The family school interview. *Family Process, 15,* 303–310.

Aponte, H. J. (1992). Training in the person of the therapist in structural family therapy. *Journal of Marital and Family Therapy, 18*(3), 269–281.

Aponte, H. (1994). *Bread and spirit: Therapy with the new poor: Diversity of race, culture, and values.* New York: Norton.

Aponte, H. J., & DiCesare, E. (2000). Structural therapy. In F. Dattilio & L. Bevilacqua (Eds.), *Comparative treatments for relationship dysfunction* (pp. 45–57). New York: Springer.

Aponte, H. J., & Hoffman, L. (1973). The open door: A structural approach to a family with an anorectic child. *Family Process, 12*(1), 1–4.

Aponte, H. J., & VanDeusen, J. M. (1981). Structural family therapy. In A. S. Gurman & D. P. Kniskern (Eds), *Handbook of family therapy* (pp. 310–360). New York: Brunner/Mazel.

Bateson, G. (1972). *Steps toward an ecology of mind.* New York: Ballantine Books.

Bateson, G. (1979). *Mind and nature.* New York: Dutton.

Bateson, G., Jackson, D. D., Haley, J., & Weakland, J. (1956). Towards a theory of schizophrenia. *Behavioral Science, 1,* 251–264.

Beavers, W. R. (1985). *Successful marriage: A family systems approach to couples therapy.* New York: Norton.

Belson, R. (1993). "You wouldn't even say hello" or my three joining principles. *Journal of Systemic Therapies, 4*(12), 66–68.

Blow, A. J., & Sprenkle, D. H. (2001). Common factors across theories of marriage and family therapy: A modified Delphi study. *Family Process, 27*(3), 385–402.

Boyd-Franklin, N. (1989). *Black families in therapy: A multisystems approach.* New York: Guilford Press.

Breunlin, D. C. (Ed.). (1985). *Stages: Patterns of change over time.* Rockville, MD: Aspen.

Carter, E. A., & McGoldrick, M. (1980). *The family life cycle: A framework for family therapy.* New York: Gardner Press.

Cimmarusti, R. A., & Lappin, J. (1985). Beginning family therapy. In D. C. Breunlin (Ed.), *Stages: Patterns of change over time* (pp. 16–25). Rockville, MD: Aspen.

Colapinto, J. (1982). Structural family therapy. In A. M. Horne & Olsen (Eds.), *Family counseling and therapy* (pp. 112–140). Itasca, IL: Peacock.

Colapinto, J. (1991). Structural family therapy. In A. S. Gurman & D. P. Kniskern (Eds.), *Handbook of family therapy* (Vol. 2, pp. 417–443). New York: Brunner/Mazel.

Colapinto, J. (1995). Dilution of family processes in social services: Implications for treatment of neglectful families. *Family Process, 34,* 59–74.

Colapinto, J., & Lappin, J. (1982). *Joining revisited.* Unpublished manuscript.

Crenshaw, W., & Cain, K. (2000). A couple's ordeal of sorrow. In L. L. Hecker, S. A. Deacon, & Associates (2000). *The therapist's notebook: Homework, handouts, and activities for use in psychotherapy* (pp. 228–254). Binghamton, NY: Haworth.

de Shazer, S. (1991). *Putting difference to work.* New York: Norton.

Dattilio, F., & Bevilacqua, L. (Eds.). (2000). *Comparative treatments for relationship dysfunction.* New York: Springer.

Dattilio, F. M. (Ed.). (1998). *Case studies in couple and family therapy: Systemic and cognitive perspectives.* New York: Guilford.

Dicks, H. V. (1967). *Marital tensions.* New York: Basic Books.

Dubos, R. (1978, January). Health and creative adaptation. *Quest,* pp. 74–82.

Dunn, B. (2001). The girl with painful steps. In L. Golden (Ed.), *Case studies in child and adolescent counseling* (pp. 132–145). Columbus, OH: Prentice-Hall.

Elizur, J., & Minuchin, S. (1989). *Institutionalizing madness: Families, therapy, and society.* New York: Basic Books.

Eno, M. M. (1985) Children with school problems: A family therapy perspective. In R. L. Ziffer (Ed.), *Adjunctive techniques in family therapy* (pp. 151–190). Orlando, FL: Grune & Stratton.

Falicov, C. J. (Ed.). (1988). *Family transitions.* New York: Guilford Press.

Ferreira, A. (1963). Family myths and homeostasis. *Archives of General Psychiatry, 9,* 457–463.

Fisch, R.,Weakland, J., & Segal, L. (1982).The tactics of change. San Francisco: Jossey-Bass.

Fishman, H. C. (1993). *Intensive structural therapy.* New York: Basic Books.

Fishman, H. C., Stanton, M. D., & Rosman, B. L. (1982). Treating families of adolescent drug abusers. In M. Stanton, T. C. Todd, & Associates (Eds.), *The family therapy of drug abuse and addiction* (pp. 335–357). New York: Guilford Press.

Fox, M. (1988). Treating families with a member diagnosed as mentally ill. In E. Nunnally, C. Chilman, & F. M. Cox (Eds.), *Families in trouble* (Vol. 4). Newbury Park, CA: Sage.

Friesen, J. (1985). *Structural–strategic marriage and family therapy.* New York: Gardner Press.

Gerson, M. J. (1996). *The embedded self: A psychoanalytic guide to family therapy.* Hillsdale, NJ: The Analytic Press.

Gladwell, M. (2000). *The tipping point: How little things can make a big difference.* Boston: Little, Brown.

Goldner, V. (1988). Generation and gender: Normative and covert hierarchies. *Family Process, 27,* 17–33.

Gottman, J. M. (1994). *What predicts divorce?: The relationship between marital processes and marital outcomes.* Hillsdale, NJ: Erlbaum.

Grove, D., & Haley, J. (1993). *Conversations on therapy.* New York: Norton.

Grunebaum, H. (1988). What if family therapy were a kind of psychotherapy?: A reading of the *Handbook of psychotherapy and behavior change. Journal of Marital and Family Therapy, 14*(2), 195–199.

Gurman, A. S. (Ed.). (1985). *Casebook of marital therapy.* New York: Guilford Press.

Gurman, A. S., & Kniskern, D. P. (1978). Research on marital and family therapy: Progress, perspective, and prospect. In S. L. Garfield & A. E. Bergin (Eds.), *Handbook of psychotherapy and behavior change: An empirical analysis* (2nd ed., pp. 817–901). New York: Wiley.

Gurman, A. S., & Kniskern, D. P. (1981). Family therapy outcome research: Knowns and unknowns. In A. S.

Gurman & D. P. Kniskern (Eds.), *Handbook of family therapy* (pp. 742–775). New York: Brunner/Mazel.

Haddock, S. A., Schindler Zimmerman, T., Ziemba, S. J., & Current, L. R. (2001). Ten adaptive strategies for work and family balance: Advice from successful families. *Journal of Marital and Family Therapy, 27*(4), 445–458.

Haley, J. (1963). *Strategies of psychotherapy.* New York: Harcourt, Brace & World.

Haley, J. (1971). *Changing families.* New York: Grune & Stratton.

Haley, J. (1973). *Uncommon therapy: The psychiatric techniques of Milton H. Erickson.* New York: Norton.

Haley, J. (1976). *Problem-solving therapy.* San Francisco: Jossey-Bass.

Haley, J. (1980). *Leaving home: The therapy of disturbed young people.* New York: McGraw-Hill.

Haley, J. (1981). *Reflections on therapy and other essays.* Chevy Chase, MD: The Family Therapy Institute of Washington, DC.

Haley, J. (1984). *Ordeal therapy.* San Francisco: Jossey-Bass.

Haley, J. (1996). *Learning and teaching therapy.* New York: Guilford Press.

Hare-Mustin, R. T., & Marecek, J. (1988). The meaning of difference: Gender theory, postmodernism and psychology. *American Psychologist, 43,* 455–464.

Heyman, R. (1994). *Why didn't you say that in the first place: How to be understood at work.* San Francisco: Jossey-Bass.

Isaacs, M., Montalvo, B., & Abelsohn, D. (1986). *The difficult divorce: Therapy for children and families.* New York: Basic Books.

Jackson, D. (1957). The question of family homeostasis. *The Psychiatric Quarterly Supplement, 31* (part 1), 79–90.

Jackson, D. D. (1965). Family rules: The marital quid pro quo. *Archives of General Psychiatry, 12,* 589–594.

Jackson, D. D. (Ed.). (1968). *Therapy, communication, and change.* Palo Alto, CA: Science & Behavior Books.

Jacobson, N. S., & Addis, M. E. (1993). Research on couples and couples therapy: What do we know? Where are we going? *Journal of Consulting and Clinical Psychology, 61,* 85–93.

Jacobson, N. S., & Christensen, A. (1996). *Integrative couple therapy.* New York: Norton.

Jacobson, N. S., & Gottman, J. M., (1998). *When men batter women: New insights into ending abusive relationships.* New York: Simon & Schuster.

Johnson, S. M., & Greenberg, L. S. (1988). Relating process to outcome in marital therapy. *Journal of Marital and Family Therapy, 14,* 175–183.

Keim, I., Lentine, G., Keim, J., & Madanes, C. (1990). No more John Wayne: Strategies for changing the past. In C. Madanes (Ed.), *Sex, love, and violence: Strategies for transformation* (pp. 218–247). New York: Norton.

Keim, J. (1992). *The Family Therapy Institute training handbook.* Unpublished manuscript.

Keim, J. (1993). Triangulation and the art of negotiation. *Journal of Systemic Therapies, 12*(4), 76–87.

Keim, J. (1995). Strategic therapy. In M. Elkaim, (Ed.), *Panorama des therapies familiales* (pp. 247–282). Paris: Editions du Seuil.

Keim, J. (1998). Working with oppositional children. In F. Dattilio (Ed.), *Case studies in couple and family therapy* (pp. 132–157). New York: Guilford Press.

Keim, J. (1999). Brief strategic marital therapy. In J. M. Donovan (Ed.), *Short-term couple therapy* (pp. 265–290). New York: Guilford Press.

Keim, J. (2000). Strategic therapy. In F. Dattilio & L. Bevilacqua (Eds.), *Comparative treatments for relationship dysfunction* (pp. 58–78). New York: Springer.

Lappin, J. (1983). On becoming a culturally conscious family therapist. In C. J. Falicov (Ed.), *Cultural perspectives in family therapy* (pp. 122–136). Rockville, MD: Aspen.

Lappin, J. (1984). *The therapeutic weave: A guideline for structural family therapy.* Unpublished manuscript.

Lappin, J. (1988). Family therapy: A structural approach. In R. Dorfman (Ed.), *Paradigms of clinical social work* (pp. 220–252). New York: Brunner/Mazel.

Lappin, J. (1998-1999, Winter–Spring). There and back again: A conversation with Salvador Minuchin. *AFTA Newsletter,* (pp. 10–12).

Lappin, J., Hardy, T. C., & Storm, C. L. (1997). Keeping context in view: The heart of supervision. In T. C. Todd & C. L. Storm (Eds.), *The complete systemic supervisor: Context, philosophy, and pragmatics* (pp. 41–58). Boston: Allyn and Bacon.

Lappin, J., & Scott, S. (1992). Interventions in a single-parent Vietnamese family. In M. McGoldrick, J. K. Pearce, & J. Giordano (Eds.), *Ethnicity and family therapy* (pp. 79–96). New York: Guilford Press.

Lappin, J., & Scott, S. (1992). Interventions in a single-parent Vietnamese family. In M. McGoldrick, J. K. Pearce, & J. Giordano (Eds.), *Ethnicity and family therapy* (pp. 483–491). New York: Guilford.

Lappin, J., & Steier, F. (1996-1997, Winter). Being there—learning how to learn how to talk the talk. *AFTA Newsletter,* pp. 14–18.

Lappin, J., & VanDeusen, J. (1994). Family therapy and the public sector. *British Journal of Family Therapy, 16*(1), 79–96.

Lappin, J., & VanDeusen, J. (1999). Humanizing the impossible case: Engaging the power of a family–larger systems intervention. Commentaries by L. Sharber & E. Imber-Black. In R. Simon, L. Markowitz, C. Barrilleaux, & B. Topping (Eds.), *The art of psychotherapy: Case studies from the Family Therapy Networker.* New York: Wiley.

Lederer, W. J., & Jackson, D. D. (1968). *The mirages of marriage.* New York: Norton.

Lemon, S., Newfield, N., & Dobbins, J. (1993). Culturally sensitive family therapy in Appalachia. *Journal of Systemic Therapies, 4*(12), 66–68.

Lewis, J. M., Beavers, W. R., Gosssett, J. T., & Phillips, V. A. (1976). *No single thread: Psychological health in family systems.* New York: Brunner/Mazel.

Luepnitz, D. A. (1988). *The family interpreted: Feminist theory in clinical practice.* New York: Basic Books.

Mabrey, L. (1995). *An ethnography of family change: The experience of strategic therapy.* Unpublished doctoral dissertation, Texas Woman's University.

Madanes, C. (1981). *Strategic family therapy.* San Francisco: Jossey-Bass.

Madanes, C. (1984). *Behind the one-way mirror.* San Francisco: Jossey-Bass.

Madanes, C. (Ed.). (1990). *Sex, love, and violence: Strategies for transformation.* New York: Norton.

Madanes, C., Keim, J., & Smelser, D. (1995). *The violence of men.* San Francisco: Jossey-Bass.

McCarthy, P. (1992). Steps and strategies at the state level: The Delaware experience. In W. Snyder & T. Ooms

(Eds.), *Empowering families, helping adolescents: Family-centered treatment of adolescents with alcohol, drug abuse, and mental health problems* (pp. 101–109). Washington, DC: U.S. Department of Health and Human Services.

McClintoch, E. (1998). *Room for change: Empowering possibilities for therapists and clients.* Boston: Allyn & Bacon

McGoldrick, M., Pearce, J., & Giordano, J. (Eds.). (1982). *Ethnicity and family therapy.* New York: Guilford.

Miller, S., Duncan, B., & Hubble, M. (1997). *Escape from Babel.* New York: Norton.

Minuchin, P. (1985). Families and individual development: Provocation from the field of family therapy. *Child Development, 56,* 289–302.

Minuchin, P., Colapinto, J., & Minuchin, S. (1998). *Working with families of the poor.* New York: Guilford Press.

Minuchin, S. (1974). *Families and family therapy.* Cambridge, MA: Harvard University Press.

Minuchin, S. (1984). *The family kaleidoscope: Images of violence and healing.* Cambridge, MA: Harvard University Press.

Minuchin, S., Baker, L., Rosman, B. L., Liebman, R., Milman, L., & Todd, T. C. (1975). A conceptual model of psychosomatic illness in children. *Archives of General Psychiatry, 32,* 1031–1038.

Minuchin, S., & Fishman, H. C. (1981). *Family therapy techniques.* Cambridge, MA: Harvard University Press.

Minuchin, S., Lee, W. Y., & Simon, G. M. (1996). *Mastering family therapy: Journeys of growth and transformation.* New York: Wiley.

Minuchin, S., & Montalvo, B. (1967). Techniques for working with disorganized low socioeconomic families. *American Journal of Orthopsychiatry, 37,* 380–387.

Minuchin, S., Montalvo, B., Guerney, B. G., Rosman, B. L., & Schumer, F. (1967). *Families of the slums.* New York: Basic Books.

Minuchin, S., & Nichols, M. P. (1993). *Family healing: Tales of hope and renewal from family therapy.* New York: Free Press.

Minuchin, S., Rosman, B. L., & Baker, L. (1978). *Psychosomatic families: Anorexia nervosa in context.* Cambridge, MA: Harvard University Press.

Miyata, K. (1995) Symbolic therapy: Two cases of refusal to attend school. In S. Lankton, S. Gilligan, & J. K. Zeig (Eds.), *The Ericksonian monograph* (No. 10, pp. 61–68). New York: Brunner/Mazel

Montalvo, B. (1973). Aspects of lie supervision. *Family Process, 12*(4), 343–359.

Montalvo, B. (1981). Family strengths: Obstacles and facilitators. In M. Karpel (Ed.), *Family resources: The hidden partner in family therapy.* New York: Guilford Press.

Montalvo, B. (1985, January–February). On blunder avoidance. *The Family Therapy Networker,* pp. 51–55.

Montalvo, B., & Guitierrez, M. (1983). A perspective for the use of the cultural dimension in family therapy. In C. J. Falicov (Ed.), *Cultural perspectives in family therapy* (pp. 15–32). Rockville, MD. Aspen.

Montalvo, B., & Guitierrez, M. J. (1989). Nine assumptions for work with ethnic minority families. In G. W. Saba, B. M. Karrer, & K. V. Hardy (Eds.), *Minorities and family therapy* (pp. 35–52). Binghamton, NY: Haworth Press.

Montalvo, B., Harmon, D., & Elliot, M. (1998). Family mobilization: Work with angry elderly couples in declining health. *Contemporary Family Therapy, 20*(2), 163–179.

Nichols, M. P. (1997). The art of enactment. *The Family Therapy Networker, 21*(6), 23.

Nichols, M. P., & Fellenberg, S. (2000). The effective use of enactments in family therapy: A discovery-oriented process study, *Journal of Marital and Family Therapy, 26*(2), 143–152.

Nichols, M. P., & Minuchin, S. (1999). Short-term structural family therapy with couples. In J. M. Donovan (Ed.), *Short-term couple therapy* (pp. 124–143). New York: Guilford Press.

Nichols, M. P., & Schwartz, R. C. (1998). *Family therapy: Concepts and methods* (3rd ed.). Needham Heights, MA: Allyn & Bacon.

Nichols, M. P., with Schwartz, R. C. (in press). *The essentials of family therapy.* New York: Guilford Press.

Olson, D. H., Sprenkle, D. H., & Russell, C. S. (1979). Circumplex model of marital and family systems: I. Cohesion and adaptability dimensions, family types, and clinical applications. *Family Process, 18,* 3–28.

Poster, M. (1986). *Critical theory of the family.* New York: Continuum Press.

Price, J. (1996). *Power and compassion: Working with difficult adolescents and abused parents.* New York: Guilford Press.

Ray, W. (2001). *The Don D. Jackson Website* [On line]. Available: http://www.DonJackson.com [January 5th, 2001].

Reiss, D. (1981). *The family's construction of reality.* Cambidge, MA: Harvard University Press.

Renick, M. J., Blumber, S. L., & Markman, H. J. (1992). The Prevention and Relationship Enrichment Program (PREP): An empirically based preventative intervention program for couples. *Family Relations, 41,* 141–147.

Ruesch, J., & Bateson, G. (1951). *Communication.* New York: Norton.

Satir, V. (1967). *Conjoint family therapy.* Palo Alto, CA: Science & Behavior Books.

Schorr, M. (1997). Finding solutions in a roomful of angry people. *Journal of Systemic Therapies, 16*(3), 201–210.

Schwartz, D. (1993). The gamesmanship of betwetting. *Journal of Systemic Therapies, 12*(4), 1–7.

Schwartz, P. (1995). *Love between equals.* New York. Free Press.

Simon, G. M. (1995). A revisionist rendering of structural family therapy. *Journal of Marital and Family Therapy, 21,* 17–26.

Simon, R. (1991). *One on one: Conversations with the shapers of family therapy.* New York: Guilford.

Sluzki, C. (1983). Process, structure and world views: Toward an integrated view of systemic models in family therapy. *Family Process, 22,* 469–476.

Sluzki, C. E. (1981). Process of symptom production and symptom maintenance. *Journal of Marital and Family Therapy, 7,* 273–280.

Srivastva, S., & Cooperrider, D. L. (Eds.). (1990). *Appreciative management and leadership: The power of positive thought and action in organization* (Revised ed.). Euclid, OH: Williams Custom Publishing.

Stanton, M. D. (1981). Strategic approaches to family therapy. In A. S. Gurman & D. P. Kniskern (Eds.), *Handbook of family therapy.* New York: Brunner/Mazel.

Stanton, M. D. (1985). Marital therapy from a structural/strategic viewpoint. In G. P. Scolevar (Ed.), *The handbook of marriage and marital therapy.* Jamaica, NY: Spectrum.

Stanton, M. D., & Todd, T. C. (1979). Structural family therapy with drug addicts. In E. Kaufman & P. Kaufman (Eds.), *The family therapy of drug and alcohol abuse* (pp. 55–70). New York: Gardner Press.

Stanton, M. D., & Todd, T. C. (1992). Structural–strategic family therapy with drug addicts. In E. Kaufman & P. Kaufman (Eds.), *The family therapy of drug addiction and alcohol abuse* (2nd ed., pp. 109–152). Boston: Allyn & Bacon.

Stanton, M. D., Todd, T. C., & Associates (Eds.). (1982). *The family therapy of drug abuse and addiction.* New York: Guilford Press.

Steinberg, F., & Whiteside, R. (1999). *Whispers from the East.* Phoenix, AZ: Zeig, Tucker.

Stone-Fish, L., & Piercy, F. P. (1987). The theory and practice of structural and strategic family therapies: A Delphi study. *Journal of Marital and Family Therapy, 13*(2), 113–125.

Sue, D. W., & Sue, D. (1990). *Counseling the culturally different: Theory and practice* (2nd ed.). New York: Wiley.

Sullivan, H. S. (1945). *Conceptions of modern psychiatry.* New York: Norton.

Sullivan, H. S. (1953). *The interpersonal theory of psychiatry.* New York: Norton.

Szapocznik, J. (1989). *Breakthroughs in family therapy with drug abusing problem youth.* New York: Springer.

Szapocznik, J., & Hervis, O. E. (2000). *Brief strategic family therapy: A revised manual.* Manuscript in preparation.

Thomas, A., & Chess, S. (1984). Genesis and evolution of behavioral disorders: From infancy to early adult life. *American Journal of Psychiatry, 141,* 1–9.

Thomas, V., & Ozechowski, T. J. (2000). A test of the circumplex model of marital and family systems using the clinical rating scale. *Journal of Marital and Family Therapy, 26,* 523–534.

Treadway, D. C. (1989). *Before it's too late: Working with substance abuse in the family.* New York: Norton.

Trepper, T., & Barrett, M. (1989). *Systemic treatment of incest: A Therapeutic handbook.* New York: Brunner/Mazel.

VanDeusen, J., & Lappin, J. (1993). Supervising the system. *AAMFT Committee on Supervision Bulletin.*

VanDeusen, J., Lappin, J., & Morenas, J. (1992). On beyond families: Systemic interventions with organizations. In J. Zamosky (Ed.), *Empowering families: Papers from the Fifth Annual Conference on Family-Based Services* (pp. 3–21). New York: Human Sciences Press.

Wallerstein, J. S., & Blakeslee, S. (1995). *The good marriage: How and why love lasts.* Boston: Houghton Mifflin.

Walsh, F. (Ed.). (1993). *Normal family processes* (2nd ed.). New York: Guilford Press.

Walters, M., Carter, B., Papp, P., & Silverstein, O. (1989). *The invisible web: Gender patterns in family relationships.* New York: Guilford Press.

Watzlawick, P., Beavin, J., & Jackson, D. (1967). *The pragmatics of human communication.* New York: Norton.

Watzlawick, P., Weakland, J., & Fisch, R. (1974). *Change: Principles of problem formation and problem resolution.* New York: Norton.

Wedge, M. (1996). *In the therapist's mirror: Reality in the making.* New York: Norton.

Whitaker, C. A. (1975). Psychotherapy of the absurd: With a special emphasis on psychotherapy of aggression. *Family Process, 14,* 1–16.

Whiteside, R. (1998). *The art of using and losing control.* New York: Brunner/Mazel.

Yeo, A. (1993). *Counseling: A problem-solving approach.* Singapore: Armour.

Chapter 5

Transgenerational Marital Therapy

LAURA ROBERTO-FORMAN

Transgenerational (TG) therapies have been in use since the 1950s, and as a group of methods, their development has reached only its adolescence (Roberto, 1992). This chapter reviews the major TG theories, relevant research, and current techniques in view of what they offer for treatment of couples. Couple therapists of every persuasion use at least some TG tools. In fact, Carl Whitaker once referred to the central tenets of TG theory as "universals." Most therapists probably address family-of-origin issues when treating couples, if only to create a genogram. However, although TG ideas permeate most marital[1] therapy, they are often not given explicit acknowledgment as constituting a school of thought.

There is a significant deficit in the couple literature on TG theory and therapy. A small but growing number of research papers look at the connection between family-of-origin problems (e.g., alcoholism) and later marital issues. This chapter aims to address that deficit, comparing and combining different TG perspectives on couple therapy. I have three major purposes here. First, I hope to show that TG theory and therapy provide a powerful approach to understanding and working with couples in distress, not only for symptom reduction, but for increasing marital resilience and the ability to prevent future symptoms. Second, I continue my previous work of identifying common, bridging concepts among the several schools, to work toward one unitary, powerful TG model. Third, I hope to stimulate interest in TG theory and therapies, in order to increase contributions

to the literature on TG therapies and research in the future.

BACKGROUND OF THE APPROACH

The major schools of TG theory and therapy over the past three decades include natural systems (Bowenian) theory; symbolic–experiential (Whitakerian) theory; contextual (relational ethics) theory; and some aspects of object relations theory (Roberto, 1992; Scharff & Scharff, 1987; Slipp, 1984; Wachtel, 1982). Although several of these schools are currently gaining in popularity (especially contextual and object relations theory), all of them are highly used by marital and family therapists to explain problems and inform treatment of couples. Current object relations theory has become more systemic, striving to address relational problems, even though its interview style focuses on affective, intrapsychic experience. Certain kinds of object relations interventions, such as remembering, eliciting unconscious material, integration of painful memories, and working through in the present, have all been modified for use with couples in conjoint therapy. Since object relations theory works with family-of-origin material to understand marital behavior, some of its tenets are included in the present discussion (see also Scharff & Bagnini, Chapter 3, this volume). Although none of these major theories has been explicitly named "transgenerational," they can be viewed all together as theories that draw on intergenerational (long-term, slow-changing) family processes to explain couple problems.

These theories have been extended to examine specific family and larger-system problems: personal authority in marriage and family (Williamson, 1981, 1982a, 1982b); family-of-origin consults (Framo, 1976); sexual dysfunction (Scharff, 1989; Schnarch, 1997); unconscious marital contracts (Sager, 1976); unresolved loss (Paul, 1967); gender/power conflicts (see, e.g., Goodrich, 1991, and the Women's Project in Family Therapy—Walters, Carter, Papp, & Silverstein, 1988); late-life reconciliation (Hargrave, 1994); and multicultural marriages (McGoldrick, 1989; McGoldrick, Giordano, & Pearce, 1996). A number of authors have specifically sought to apply feminist theory to TG couple therapy (Carter & McGoldrick, 1989; Knudson-Martin, 1994; Roberto, 1992; Walters et al., 1988). Their ideas, as well as my own, have informed and enriched all of the methods presented in this chapter.

I share the hopefulness of Johnson and Lebow (2000), who state in their decade review of couple therapy that "We are, perhaps, beginning to build a generic base for couple intervention that is less constrained by differences in language" (p. 33). However, over the last 30 years, each of the four major theories has been disseminated in different postgraduate training institutes and different publications. Each community of writers has worked in insular ways, at the expense of developing common vocabularies. Each theory is also based historically on large bodies of work by a highly charismatic founder and his trainees: Natural systems theory is based heavily on Murray Bowen's work; symbolic–experiential theory on that of Carl Whitaker; contextual therapy on the work of Ivan Boszormenyi-Nagy; and object relations therapy on the work of David Winnicott. This may explain why very few papers drawing together the commonalities among TG schools have been published (Roberto, 1992, 1998).

Natural Systems Theory

Natural systems (Bowenian) theory was developed in conjunction with research on families with a schizophrenic member. While at the National Institutes of Health from 1954 to 1959, Bowen sought to describe dysfunctional cycles of behavior between parents and their psychotic child (Bowen, 1972/1985). At that time, Bowen was looking for a relational cause for the marked lack

of personal boundaries and ego function in psychotic disorders. He was especially interested in the possible role of family-of-origin enmeshment (and the rebound problem of cutoff) in the eventual emergence of schizophrenia. Bowen subscribed to the diathesis–stress model of psychosis, which holds that illnesses do not necessarily emerge unless a person is stressed and cannot mobilize self-healing tools.

Early clinical research looked only at relational connections between inpatients and their mothers. Later, Bowen began to look at the role of fathers and the quality of parental marriage in very ill clients. Bowen's team observed that in enmeshed relationships, emotional tensions increase to the point where a "triangle," or inclusion of a third person, evolves. He began to look for evidence of fusion and triangulation in families whenever a client experienced frequent relapses. He also predicted that if certain patterns of fusion are present in a marriage or family, modifying these patterns in family therapy will lead to improvement in psychotic symptoms and improved individual resilience ("differentiation").

After 1967, Bowen began to develop and experiment with methods to diffuse enmeshment and increase individual differences and give-and-take in family-of-origin relationships (a direction continued by Williamson in his work on personal authority). He became increasingly interested in the connection between fusion and differentiation, reporting on his own experiences at a national medical conference. This was the first use of self in the history of marital and family therapy, and had a powerful effect on both Bowen (who saw that experiential learning is potent) and those in the audience (who saw a new modality for training in front of their eyes). Through this personal family-of-origin work, Bowen redefined differentiation, which had been viewed as an internal developmental phenomenon, as a function of family tolerance for individual differences and expression. He posited that, once set during rearing, differentiation of self is very difficult to increase later in life.

Bowen began to use assignments and reporting on family-of-origin visits with his own psychiatry residents as a way of teaching his model (Bowen, 1974). He observed that trainees who did family-of-origin assignments seemed to gain more clinical effectiveness than those trainees who did not. He concluded by 1971 that work focused on creating one-on-one, well-delineated relationships with one's own parents effectively raised one's level of differentiation, increasing a therapist's ability to function in marriage, parenting, and therapeutic relationships. Trainees were encouraged to present their own families of origin, and to enter psychotherapy with their spouses to look at how old, unresolved family dilemmas colored their marriages and self-knowledge. Although institutes are no longer encouraged to allow a dual relationship in training, family-of-origin presentations and experiential learning are still highly utilized in advanced therapy externships and supervision.

Like his contemporaries, Bowen used the genogram, an old medical tool for charting family history, but with a twist. He and his trainees mapped symptom bearers in relation to their extended families, and then looked for intense relationships and third-party involvements that might maintain a client's distress. Students such as Fogarty (1978) and Guerin (1976) applied their ideas about triangles to problems of individual despair ("emptiness"), disconnection, and emotional distancing, and began to examine the effect of distancing on marriage. The technique of coaching was developed to allow adult individuals and couples to disengage from family triangles, control distress, and create one-on-one relationships with parents and key family members. Bowen used marital counseling as a way of preventing enmeshment problems between parents and their own young children.

Eventually, the natural systems group at Georgetown University created a "think tank" to generalize these findings on the nature of enmeshment and triangulation in larger systems. Students applied the concepts of poor differentiation, fusion or "undifferentiated ego mass," triangles, and projection (of unresolved issues) to less impaired families, workplace "families," and social groups. This expansion has included relational systems in many types of workplaces; for example, Friedman (1985), an ordained rabbi, created a training model for clergy to apply to church/synagogue relations. The natural systems model works seamlessly with genogram study because it focuses on recursive, repetitive, chronic cycling of symptoms between marital partners and key extended family members.

Symbolic–Experiential Therapy

Carl Whitaker and two colleagues, Malone and Warkentin, also began working with adults hospitalized with psychotic symptoms in the 1940s. Contemporaries of Bowen, Wynne, Bateson, Boszormenyi-Nagy, and Ackerman, they worked in university hospitals and Veterans Administra-

tions facilities. Their emphasis was initially on parental (especially maternal) dysfunction as a contributor to relapse. However, they also consulted at the Oak Ridge atomic research facility during World War II, where they counseled scientists and war veterans who showed severe stress reactions to the classified project. This experience gave the group a sense of how personal disintegration can be a reaction to intolerable breakdowns of societal order—what Whitaker later called "being driven [as opposed to being] crazy" (Whitaker, cited in J. R. Neill and D. P. Kniskern, 1982, p. 36). He later emphasized that one goal of therapy is to allow individuals to believe more in themselves and their potential, and to externalize the forces that lead us to view ourselves as "crazy." Externalization has become a feature of some narrative therapies.

As a faculty member in the Department of Psychiatry at Emory University in the 1950s, Whitaker made the shift from a psychoanalytic, internal-conflict-based model of mental illness to an interactional, systemic model. The symbolic–experiential school of TG therapy thus echoes the same bridging ideas that linked individual symptoms to long-term family dysfunction. Unlike later methods, which are more strategic, problem-focused, and symptom-focused, these TG models were created to provide a relational view of lifetime vulnerability and sudden emotional breakdown. Because he had originally been trained as a child psychiatrist (Neill & Kniskern, 1982; Whitaker & Ryan, 1989), Whitaker continued to feel that nonverbal, affective experiences are an important avenue to self-awareness and resilience. This view distinguished him from his peers, who were viewing the same interactional problems in troubled families, but using analytical, verbally based interventions to treat them (Roberto, 1991, 1992). In addition, intervening with very regressed, trauma-related reactions calls for use of self and the ability to respond personally to frightening affects and perceptions. Therefore, the role of the therapist is unique—neutrality is unhelpful (Roberto, 1992). It is a proximal, emotionally focused, personal therapy rather than an abstract, coaching, educational therapy.

Finally, in what has been called a "third period" of expansion, Malone and Whitaker at Emory University experimented with cotherapy and use of consultation by therapists, as well as with family-of-origin sessions. With colleague Richard Felder, Whitaker, like Bowen, also began to make his residency training groups more systemic, having them do family-of-origin presentations to their training groups. The faculty formed a process group and generated the Sea Island conference of 1955, which was the first family process conference. These ideas have been picked up by other systemic therapies that use observing teams, and by marital therapists who use family-of-origin visits to refocus couples in conflict (Framo, 1976).

After Whitaker went to the University of Wisconsin Psychiatry Department, he and Keith trained residents until the mid-1980s using live and videotaped interviews of extended families to teach marital and family therapy. Symbolic–experiential techniques remain heavily rooted in this collegial context of peer supervision, personal family-of-origin work, and learning use of self in therapy as opposed to an "expert" position. To the other TG models of therapy, it adds heart, warmth, and therapist–client connectivity.

The Contextual Approach

Ivan Boszormenyi-Nagy and colleagues have focused since 1965 on the concept that unresolved multigenerational pressures contribute to later emotional symptoms (Boszormenyi-Nagy & Krasner, 1986). This implicit, invisible network of felt loyalties and the "pull" it exerts constitute another dimension of family functioning—an "ethical" dimension. The contextual model adds a layer of family experience to therapy that is not addressed by the other TG models (Roberto, 1992).

Boszormenyi-Nagy is a contemporary of the other TG founders. In 1957 he served as founder and director of the Department of Family Psychiatry at Eastern Pennsylvania Psychiatric Institute in Philadelphia. Like the workplaces of his peers, it was both a research and a clinical service program, until state funding ended in 1980. Early family observation was again based on intensive care of inpatients with schizophrenia and their families (Boszormenyi-Nagy, 1962, 1965, 1972; Boszormenyi-Nagy & Spark, 1973). The Institute sponsored several of the earliest family therapy conferences in the 1960s, and Boszormenyi-Nagy helped to organize the American Family Therapy Academy in the 1970s.

Contextual theory draws on the ideas of European object relations writers like Fairbairn (1952), and on existentialist, experience-based theories such as Buber's (1958). In the United States, these ideas were developed by Sullivan (1953), Fromm-Reichmann (1950), Searles (1960), and Will (the Chestnut Lodge group, 1958). One of

the central concepts of interest at the time was trustworthiness, especially how a therapist's trustworthiness affects a client's ability to tolerate and manage psychotic symptoms. In the late 1950s and 1960s, Boszormenyi-Nagy made the theoretical shift to systems thinking and began to apply it in his medical setting. It was difficult at first to maintain a focus on relational "ethics" such as loyalty and conflicting loyalties, entitlement in family members, merit and earning of trust, and mutual consideration, in the face of cybernetic theory (Boszormenyi-Nagy & Ulrich, 1981). Contextual theory, which discusses implicit emotional events and types of bonding between people, has a poor "fit" with purely behavioral, problem-focused, cycle-based thinking. It uniquely pursues the "feedforward" of long-term relational quality into the intimate behavior that people show in marriage and parenting two to three generations later. Marital therapy is only now paying attention to the crucial role of these "ethical" stances to marital preservation.

Object Relations Applications

In the history of marital and family theory, the influence of psychoanalytic theory is enormous. This was especially the case in the work of Paul and Framo, whose techniques are reviewed here. Virginia Satir, a TG therapist, was trained in analytic theory, as were Jackson, Wynne, Bowen, Whitaker, Boszormenyi-Nagy, Minuchin, Selvini Palazzoli, and Stierlin—some of the major innovators of current marital and family techniques (Jackson & Lederer, 1968; Minuchin, Montalvo, Guerney, Rosman, & Schumer, 1967; Satir, 1983; Selvini Palazzoli, 1974; Wynne, 1965). In this country, psychoanalytic theory existed mainly as a Freudian theory through the 1950s. In Europe, however, analytic theory was modified from the late 1950s to the 1970s, to become a theory of how self is created in intimate relationships. This was a revolutionary departure from Freud's wish–defense theory of the mind.

Object relations theory is based on a European view of self-in-relation—how a young individual adapts to the family environment that Westerners define as child, mother, and father. Through adaptation to the loved other, one's deeply held wishes, beliefs, and emotional responses arise in the context of family process (Roberto, 1992). Some object relations theorists devoted their lifetime work to how family systems shape the individual's experience of self, although their work has the linear view that a parent shapes a child's experience in a causal direction (Bowlby, 1969, 1973; Fraiberg & Fraiberg, 1980; Mahler, Pine, & Bergman, 1975). Initially, the theory focused mostly on individual behavior and self-concept (Fairbairn, 1952; Klein, 1957; Winnicott, 1965). Fairbairn focused on how internal views of the "ideal object [other]" evolved from interaction between baby and mother, and how painful and disappointing events are taken in ("introjected") and then repressed or buried to preserve this ideal. Klein extended the idea of repression to propose that repressed experiences stay buried in order to avoid emotional pain, but emerge as projections onto important caretakers. Dicks (1963), in an early application to couple work, looked at how projection colors marriage. He posited that although a trusting marriage gives the spouses the opportunity to revisit and come to terms with painful, repressed experiences, frequently the repression–projection cycle is repeated instead.

Object relations theory has been applied in many settings in Europe, the Americas, Australia, and Canada, and has suffused most marital and family therapy theories in use now. Ideas about the place of the unconscious, or unintegrated experience; ego, or self-definition; and internal experiences like introjection, projection, and attribution are actually the bedrock of our Western understanding of psychological development. However, more than other models of marital and family therapy, object relations work is still colored by psychology's androcentric view of development. Feminist-informed and culturally informed applications have been limited up through the last decade.

RESEARCH ON DISTRESSED VERSUS NONDISTRESSED COUPLES

While TG writers and clinicians have been doing "single-subject research" by examining marriages one at a time, researchers from sociology, anthropology, social work and psychology have been surveying couples in the lab. A number of associations have been identified between family-of-origin relationships and courtship/marriage behavior in their sons and daughters. A review of the literature shows that the family of origin has been shown to pass on the following marital patterns: preferred values (VanLear, 1972); patterns of coping with stress in marriage and with children (Juni, 1992); adjustment in and readiness for marriage (Campbell, Masters, & Johnson, 1998; Haws & Mallinckrodt, 1998); age at marriage and/or pregnancy (Manlove, 1997; Thornton, 1991);

illness and resilience patterns (Abrams, 1999; Jankowski, Leitenberg, Henning, & Coffey, 1999; Wallerstein, 1996); and ability to hold a "double vision" of marriage and to resolve conflict (Wallerstein, 1996).

These formative intergenerational patterns provide the structures and patterns of connection that will evolve between their married children and their spouses. Yet, when couples are interviewed to clarify the structure of their marriage and patterns of interaction, the intergenerational template is usually not applied. I discuss this issue as it applies to the most current empirical models of marital dysfunction.

Gottman (1994) and his colleagues have identified seven complex patterns of marital interaction that distinguish satisfied from unsatisfied couples: greater reciprocity of negative affect; lower ratios of positive to negative behaviors; high levels of criticism, defensiveness, contempt, and stonewalling (the "four horsemen"); and negative and lasting attributions about the partner. These researchers have also identified a frequently occurring pattern that they call the "wife demand–husband withdraw" cycle. Gottman and his colleagues have concluded from these differences that positive affect and persuasion work better to preserve stability in marriage, because these skills buffer conflicts and prevent negative attributions and pathologizing of one's partner.

The findings of Gottman and colleagues are extremely germane to TG theory. For example, the researchers point out (Gottman, 1994) that stable marriages function like a "bank account" in which positive contributions compensate for negative feelings during conflict. This finding is a cornerstone of classic contextual theory, and has to do with how much trust builds up between spouses over time. The initial bedrock of trust in a marriage partly also reflects each spouse's history in previous love relationships and the needs and abilities each has brought out of his/her family of origin. But Gottman's research to date does not include concepts from TG theory in looking at his couples' transactions.

Two-generation research studies help to explain the factors that lead to and maintain the skewed interactions of unhappy couples. Goodrow and Lim (1997) described a pattern of high reactivity and defensiveness in an engaged couple, and the relevant behavior patterns transmitted from their respective parents. Larson and Thayne (1998) showed that fusion and triangulation in subjects' families were related to negative opinions and feelings about marriage. Nelson and Wampler (2000) studied 96 couples in counseling, where one or both partners reported childhood abuse (physical or sexual), and showed that the partner who reported abuse functioned especially poorly and that the trauma affected the other partner as well. The authors concluded that "a person may experience secondary trauma issues resulting from identification with the trauma victim" (p. 180). One wonders to what extent the negative attributes discussed by Gottman's team could reflect such mediating family-of-origin problems, and their serious marital consequences.

Interestingly, Gottman and Levenson (1999a, 1999b) state that in their samples, couple interaction is remarkably durable over a 4-year period. These patterns "become part of the fabric of a couple's life and resistant to change" (Lebow, 1999, p. 169). Couples also present with the same issues after a 4-year period in their sample. The nature of these issues, in these couples, has nothing to do with whether a marriage becomes stable and survives. The viability of a marriage thus depends not so much on whether issues are handled, or what issues are handled, as on how partners engage each other. Degree of engagement about these marital issues is crucial. We can speculate that when transactions between spouses are so remarkably stable over time, then it is probable that we are viewing patterns that are "trait" rather than "situational" behaviors (i.e., they reflect underlying perceptions and characteristics of each spouse carried into the marriage).

We may conclude that families of origin pass on preferred values, styles of intimate relating, meanings and beliefs about difference, tolerance and acceptance, fairness, and mutuality, and other intrinsic aspects of family life. Their children then go into marriage with expectations, needs, and dreams colored by these formative experiences. Marriages either develop characteristics of safety, mutual regard, and hope, or are compromised by the past. It seems imperative, given these findings, that couple therapy provide powerful ways to identify and change the modes of attachment by which partners relate to one another. These emotional processes, so deeply ingrained and colored by one's birth family, are beautifully addressed and described by the TG model. In fact, it is the TG model's *pièce de resistance*.

THE HEALTHY PARTNERSHIP

Most TG theories hold that healthy marriages include a love bond. It is certain that the deep psychological bond of love allows couples to form an emotional boundary around the twosome that makes it different from other connections—more intense, focused, and intimate. Although a love bond turns the partner's focus toward one another, the boundary around them must be somewhat permeable for healthy partnership. The loyalty between partners is stronger than the loyalty to family of origin or to other relationships. Falling in love as a basis for marriage is a relatively recent European and American concept. However, the love bond may be of increasing importance in marriage historically. As women and girls are allowed greater access to education and paid work, the economic factors sustaining marriage become less crucial, and marital commitment becomes increasingly choice-based.

Empathy and Mutuality

There is a flow of empathy, understanding, or perspective in a healthy marriage—a shared frame that each partner's behaviors and intentions are meant for the mutual good. It is difficult for partners to build empathy unless each member has an experiential sense of the other's position. Experiential understanding partly comes from dialogues in which each partner confides personal experiences, the meanings he/she derives from the marriage, personal beliefs, and responses to past events that have been formative in and out of the marriage. Empathy is also to some extent a developmental ability, reflecting an internal sense of well-being and the wish to be considerate and generous with others. In dysfunctional families of origin, painful events can destroy an empathic connection and turn members aside into concern for themselves instead ("destructive entitlement").

We do not have a term for the shared emotional "flow" that occurs in satisfied couples. This flow is referred to as "give-and-take" in contextual theory (Boszormenyi-Nagy & Krasner, 1986); as a sense of "we"-ness (Whitaker & Keith, 1981, p. 192) in symbolic–experiential theory; as quid pro quo in behavioral theory; and as reciprocity. We prefer the term "mutuality," which implies that there is a back-and-forth affective quality: ". . . one extends oneself out to the other and is also receptive. . . . There is openness to influence, emotional availability. . . . There is both receptivity and active initiative toward the other" (Jordan, 1991, p. 82). This interconnectedness sustains a couple during times of disagreement, because the partners rely on their fundamental attachment. Trust evolves from the reciprocity: if one goes to the partner, the partner will respond with concern.

Mutuality and a marital quid pro quo involve agreeing to clear rules. Rules are unique to each couple and allow responsibilities and commitments to be carried out as a team. In healthy couples, the agreements and requests are not oriented toward "doing" as much as they are toward "supporting"—trading car repair for housecleaning is not mutuality. It is the sense of agreeing together, of an alliance behind the responsibilities, that is mutuality. Since empathy and consideration are flowing back and forth, there is a sense of being understood and of belonging.

There is a dimension of imagination in healthy couples—they can dream together. In secure marriages, emotional energies are freed up to anticipate the future. The affective bond includes sharing of fantasies, hopes, and expectations. Healthy couples share a connection that transcends today and adds depth—depth that may not be apparent to the casual observer. The partners have a mutual curiosity about each other. It is a good sign when couples come together to marital therapy, because each partner wants to hear more about what the spouse thinks and wants. Likewise, when a spouse does not wonder or ask what the partner is planning or doing about personal concerns and needs, therapists know that ample room is being made for one, or both, to leave the marriage—it has become "pseudomutual," in Carl Whitaker's words. In some ways, the death of hope and imagination is a primary sign of eventual marital dissolution.

Differentiation, Commitment, and Marital Choice

Differentiation is the ability to experience difference—the self in relation to, but separate from, everyone else. Many attempts have been made to conceptualize differentiation, and to define what comprises "enough" or "good" differentiation. Bowen (1966/1985) was foremost among writers trying to define and explain differentiation, not only psychologically, but biologically and sociologically.

Well-functioning couples are able to change their dynamics over time as shifts in family and social network produce "reality stresses of life" (Bowen, 1966/1985, p. 171). The couple's familiar ways of interrelating adapt to the inevitable triangles that form through other commitments, like children, friends, and work (Whitaker & Keith,

1981). However, "outside" relationships and connections are accepted and encouraged between spouses. In order to have resilience, partners have to possess a strong sense of personal identity that is not threatened by change. Without skills at self-observation, spouses revert to emotionally volatile, reactive modes of functioning that do not allow them to tolerate conflict well. Bowen (1966/1985) speculated that "the highest level of differentiation that is possible for a family is the highest level that any family member can attain and maintain against the emotional opposition of the family unit in which he[/she] lives" (p. 175). Capacity for differentiation becomes gradually more and more "set" over generations, with a downward drift into what Bowen termed "undifferentiated ego mass," or family fusion.

Differentiation includes the ability to distinguish one's internal emotions and thoughts, to identify them as separate from those of others, and also to maintain one's own observations and judgment when there is conflict. Differentiation includes a sense of personal goals and direction, self-knowledge, and self-guidance. It allows personal problem solving, self-correction, and change. Recently, writers have responded to newer understandings of female as well as male development, modifying this view of differentiation to acknowledge that self-knowledge always occurs in the context of significant, long-term, intimate relationships—"self-in-relation" rather than "self" (Boszormenyi-Nagy & Ulrich, 1981; Fishbane, 1999; Knudson-Martin, 1994). Differentiation is a prerequisite to a healthy marriage, because when one is emotionally self-sufficient, then "dependency on each other is voluntary" (Framo, 1981, p. 139). Neither partner feels burdened from having to shore up the spouse.

TG models view differentiation as a cornerstone of the ability to enter into long-term commitments and live together. We have only to look at marriages where one or both spouses have poor differentiation to see how even trivial and unimportant disagreements lead into defensiveness, mutual recrimination or blaming, self-aggrandizement, coalitions to bolster one's own position, or discrediting of the partner.

Individual differentiation probably influences the choices adults make in a fiancé or spouse. Whereas other models of marriage do not examine issues of marital choice, TG models provide a framework to understand variations in commitment, marital readiness, and choosing one's partner. The reason for this is that TG models do not view young married persons as individuals, but as members of two families who have been launched (to a lesser or greater degree) and are expected to form their own relationships. As Whitaker commented, humorously, "I do not believe in individuals . . . what we have in marriage is two scapegoats, sent out by their families, to reproduce themselves . . . the only question is, which family will win" (Whitaker, personal communication, 1978)! In a healthy marriage, both partners are able to maintain a caring connection to their families of origin. Even though their loyalty is first to each other, there is room to maintain the bonds that existed before the marriage.

Intimacy and Healthy Attachment

"Attachment" is the metaphor used to explain the supportive properties of committed relationships (Johnson & Lebow, 2000). However, attachment has to develop hand in hand with individual self-awareness. H. Maturana (personal communication, 1986), a research biologist, remarked that from the point of view of environmental biology, love is "the intention to coexist." Attachment and adaptation evolve in the context of two different people who have decided to share their lives. Clinical observation shows that adults who are not differentiated into self-aware individuals have very little ability to share life with a partner.

Marriage requires a significant amount of "accommodation" (Jory, Anderson, & Greer, 1997) or tolerance. Partners must adapt to individual differences and accept each other's limits, in spite of whatever expectations are carried from the past. Accommodation is part of the "relational ethics" of caring and fairness. It involves following through on agreements and rules between partners, instead of questioning one another's needs or vulnerabilities. Accommodation presupposes that partners are able to exercise fairness, and that previous family experiences have not erased or distorted caring. For example, in the concept of the "revolving slate" (Boszormenyi-Nagy & Krasner, 1986), people whose families of origin have harmed or wronged them tend to act entitled or "owed" in destructive ways in their own marriages and families later. If there is not a reasonable amount of accommodation in the marriage, neither partner feels it is safe to disclose personal responses, and there is mistrust.

Marital intimacy also "requires a keen sense of self-identity and self-differentiation. . . . In contrast to distancing, the feelings *inside* a person and *between* people are critically important in developing closeness" (Fogarty, 1978, p. 70; emphasis in original). In order to have closeness, there has to be awareness inside oneself of emotions, responses and ideas that are stirred when with one's partner. Paradoxically, closeness requires that each person have the strength to "bear up" and maintain a sense of personal direction during times of life change.

To a large extent, spouses' capacity for intimate relating also includes a willingness to examine their own internalized beliefs about love, fulfillment, caring, and mutuality (Jory et al., 1997; Schnarch, 1997). This self-examination clarifies their values and expectations regarding closeness, reciprocity, sexual intimacy, and nurturance, so that they can evaluate their marriage and identify desired changes. Self-examination is the direct experience of the inner self, subjectivity, "going deep" into one's core assumptions and expectations of the social world. It is not possible to share this kind of spiritual and emotional subjectivity with a spouse, unless one is willing to explore personal experiences and reflect on them first. When scrutinized, internalized beliefs and memories of love relationships draw heavily on family-of-origin experiences.

Schnarch (1997) points out that intimacy is thus a "two-pronged" process of both examining the self and expressing one's self to the partner. Partners who are capable of self-validation, rather than approval seeking, are better able to contribute to their marriage. This view of intimacy reflects the natural systems concept that chronic anxiety (e.g., approval seeking) is a relational obstacle.

Redefining "Good" Communication

The prevailing view of couple communication is that "good" communication involves active listening, openness, and empathy toward each partner's views. However, in this "open" process, the connection between partners does not necessarily contain "good" communication. There are many forms of problematic communication as well: spilling of anxiety, expressions of self-doubt, unresolved tensions, and projections carried from other relationships.

In contrast, "good" communication is dialogue that has personal accountability and is relevant to the marriage. The concerns must be resolvable; the tension level has to be controlled; the emotions must be contained to some degree; and the spouse must have license to respond. It is a dialogue between two people who are reflecting on an issue from different vantage points in which they each have some understanding and emotional comfort level themselves.

This view of "self-validated" communication creates gender-specific challenges in couple work. Women move toward their partners, trying to clarify their feelings through connection with others (Jordan, Kaplan, Miller, Stiver, & Surrey, 1991). They feel the pressure to "seek relationship and connection," and hide parts of themselves that would appear different (Knudson-Martin & Mahoney, 1999, p. 331). Husbands, pressured by gender "scripts" that "men should protect their independence" (Knudson-Martin & Mahoney, 1999, p. 331), hide parts of themselves that would foster connection. In couple therapy, therapists tend to follow this bias and call on the wife to open the dialogue. It is assumed that this will help the spouse learn to disclose himself. Gender stereotyped behavior—women pursuing while men detach—leads to the burnout (hers) and disengagement (his) that end marriages (Johnson & Lebow, 2000). Ideally, in order for mutual communication to occur, there would have to be more investment of each partner's true (not hidden) self (Scheel et al., 2000). The woman does not aim to be the "sole keeper" of the connection, and can formulate thoughts that are different; the man is willing to risk emotional contact, and can express thoughts that connect.

THE DYSFUNCTIONAL PARTNERSHIP

As I have mentioned elsewhere (Roberto, 1992), "structural" symptoms reflect problems in a couple's emotional "process." Structural symptoms can be marked on a genogram. They are most often boundary problems, in which the marital dyad is distant, "locked" together with or without conflict (fusion), or pseudomutual (an institutional or legal relationship with no bond at all). The marriage may be too open to intrusions from others, or so closed that a spouse is punished for any connection outside. Or it may have triangulated in a third party.

There may be extreme complementarity (the "one-up, one-down" marriage; codependency and addiction; the caretaker marriage); extreme symmetry (two spouses with the same symptoms); or "tilts," where there is an imbalance of power or equity (e.g., the "dollhouse marriage," the parent–child duo). The underlying process problems do not show on

any genogram. These include unworkable types of bonding that produce stress and emotional pain. Process symptoms also include unrealistic or destructive expectations, such as contempt, disrespect and ridicule, narcissism or exploitiveness, idealization and perfectionism, indifference, sexism, or prejudice. Process problems can easily escape discussion in marital therapy, because they are implicit in thought, difficult to verbalize, and painful to admit.

Delegation and Negative Attributions

"Delegation" is the transmission of unresolved family stresses to a child, which are internalized (Boszormenyi-Nagy & Krasner, 1986; Stierlin, 1981). There is a sense of obligation—putting personal wishes second to family needs. As the son or daughter tries to carry out the expectations delegated to him/her, choices become narrower, and the obligations become a heavy burden. Such emotional burdens are usually not examined or articulated, and are likely to find an outlet in marriage instead. Paul (1967) comments on how "losses and associated sense of deprivation lead to deposit of such affects as sorrow . . . guilt . . . bitterness, despair, and regret" (p. 189).

There can be frank exploitation, such as expecting the spouse to take on a sense of obligation also—one kind of "in-law" dilemma. These are the situations in which a husband goes to his parents' home for dinner several times a week, and expects his wife to accept this and remain alone. One can't afford to listen to the wishes and dreams of a partner if one's energies are used up by the family's wishes and dreams. The result is a failure of empathy, loving kindness, and mutuality.

What we cannot abide in ourselves or our loved ones, we suppress and fear. Object relations theory has excelled at describing the dynamics of projection (e.g., Scharff & Scharff, 1987). Object relations writers have looked closely at how the bond with a parent is idealized in childhood, and how painful events then have to be managed in a way that is consistent with that idealization. As a young person splits off negative or disruptive characteristics of the loved ones, these perceptions are suppressed in order to maintain the loving connection (Fairbairn, 1952).

In the phenomenon of projective identification, the partner views his/her spouse (incorrectly) as having certain attitudes or reactions that the partner him-/herself entertains but won't admit.

For example, a husband may take a dim view of his wife's work hours, viewing her as too achievement-oriented, when in fact he is so wrapped up in his work that he relies upon her to get home to the family for him. It is not hard to understand how these frozen, split-off perceptions come to cloud attachments like marriage. Since this is not a conscious or deliberate act, it is not preventable. If a person has been mistreated, the pressures of pushing down his/her reactions find their way into very negative projections onto the spouse. When the spouse protests, the lack of cooperation seems to validate those projections (Roberto, 1992). This is one of the central problems of abusive marriage: The abusive partner may suspect that his spouse does not have his interests at heart (because the parents did not).

In distressed marriages, there is usually "mutual attribution" (Dicks, 1963): Both spouses perceive the other as similar to hurtful significant others from the past. For example, in the narcissistically vulnerable marriage, being considerate to the spouse is experienced as a kind of self-sacrifice. Through understanding the dynamics of suppression and projection, we can recognize Gottman's discovery in the marriage lab of negative attributions as an example of projective behavior. As he and his colleagues have noted, this problem spells the end of marital viability. There can be no trust in a marriage if there is no hope that it will heal hurts or challenges in the past, and if attributions are self-fulfilling prophecies that don't allow healing to take place.

Fusion and Distancing Patterns

Fusion

Natural systems therapists coined the term "fusion," to describe the "glue" that makes some couples too attached. In fused marriages, one partner tends to show greater passivity under stress than the other, and appears dependent on the other to act for both of them, while seeming to give in or adapt. This overadaptive partner tends to lose self-direction and competence, while the underadaptive partner seems to gain it. Over time, the couple merges into a tightly locked unit, with little overt conflict. The underadaptive spouse can be protected from stress for long periods in this way (Roberto, 1992). One or both spouses finally form emotional symptoms, usually the overadaptive spouse (Bowen, 1966/1985, 1972/1985; Kerr, 1981, 1985). The spouse who is gaining functional "self" from the other may

be completely unaware of the pressures on the overadaptive partner. The conflict that drives them into therapy comes when neither spouse will adapt further to the other in the fusion, or when the one who formerly overadapted can't function very well any more.

In the natural systems view of fusion, the "locking" together of partners is a response to chronic anxiety, or "unresolved emotional attachments" to dysfunctional families of origin (Bowen, 1974). Family members are drawn into intense and anxiety-ridden positions with each other. This pull, or "lock," results in a lack of focus on self, and in overfocus on others to one's own detriment. "Family projection process," a related concept, describes how particular children become enmeshed with parents and experience limitations in differentiating a sense of self.

Unconscious Marital Contracts

Psychodynamic theory maintains that when an adult has not addressed important developmental needs before leaving home, they are played out in mate selection. This has been called an "unconscious marital contract" (Sager, 1976). In those areas where people feel incomplete, lack confidence, or cannot accept themselves, they project that need and feel an attraction to others who seem strong in the same areas. For example, a woman who has been raised to believe that she is not competent to make decisions, and who has suppressed her own anger about this, is likely to seek out a spouse who seems more decisive. Of course, she will then notice her anger and frustration when he does (a phenomenon called "projection"), since it is her own decisiveness she wants to experience. However, the attraction is extremely powerful between incomplete or suppressed parts of oneself and the image one forms when another person appears complete in that way. It is very difficult to form a dispassionate perspective on this unconscious "pull" until well into a marriage. If both partners cannot see and admit this "pull" to be aided and completed, and work toward growing stronger individually, a fusion develops.

Fogarty (1978) points out that periods of change also bring a feeling of emptiness and confusion. The tension that accompanies emptiness challenges one's sense of competence, and adults turn to their marriage anticipating support. What people expect from each other creates anticipation or need. When these needs do not match reality, it generates hurt. "It is these crazy expectations that get activated . . . coming from the past, that makes closeness impossible" (Fogarty, 1978, p. 83). Each partner must be able to tolerate disappointments and understand his/her own dissatisfaction. In the process, "one should not expect any more from husband or wife than he would expect from any man or woman outside the family" (Fogarty, 1978, p. 83). These startling remarks on intimacy go against the instinctive sense of intimacy as togetherness.

One extreme form of unconscious contract is the "self-fulfilling prophecy," in which a partner is so greatly distressed by fears or anxieties in the marriage that he/she actually makes them come to pass. For example, a man whose mother left him in childhood may be so riddled with fear that his wife will leave him or be unfaithful that he pushes her away with his doubts and suspicions. Pathological jealousy, pathological guilt, and destructive entitlement (Boszormenyi-Nagy & Krasner, 1986) can each be part of a self-fulfilling prophecy.

Triangles

Fusion is not only expressed in "locking," but also in the reactive conflict and backing away that ensue. In many couples, periods of dependency are temporary and often explosive, leading to backing away. The marriage becomes unstable and shifts back and forth between the two poles of coming together and backing away. Couples react to these extremes by pulling in a third person, who moderates the closeness and distance by being available to one or both partners. This person becomes a "boundary keeper" who stabilizes the shifting marriage (Byng-Hall, 1980, p. 355), much as a goalie in soccer guards a goalpost and keeps the ball (marriage) in play. The spouses then continue their back-and-forth shifting, approaching and then backing away, but without extremes. For example, a wife has an affair; a husband accepts a commuting job for his firm; a wife devotes herself to a volunteer project for their church. When one is bound up in other relationships and emotional systems, it is difficult to focus resources and attention on a marriage relationship. In many couples, emotional triangles can affect the very "intention," as Maturana calls it, to coexist—the desire to share one's life, or to move in that direction.

A child is by far the most common third party. The couple becomes "child-focused" (in structural theory) or creates a "three-way marriage" (in Milan systemic theory). The couple maintains stability for decades of child rearing, with one or both partners

relying on a son or daughter for support. When the son or daughter separates more from the parent(s), often after individual therapy, the parental marriage destabilizes (see, e.g., Braverman's [1981] study). Increased independence, albeit later in life, by that child creates a significant loss for the parents—both the one who "clung" and the one who did not have to "cling" The subsequent emotional distance is not balanced by a strong marriage tie.

Distancing and Cutoff

Chronic fusion can produce a distant marriage. An example is the distancer–pursuer pattern, where one partner tries to speak for or read into the other's concerns, and usually misreads them. An overexpressive spouse pursues an underexpressive spouse. In turn, the underexpressive partner makes decisions, tries to solve problems, and acts without expressing his/her own views or anxieties, leaving the "mind reader" to follow along completely mystified. The more nonexpressive the one partner is, the more verbal and agitated the other becomes; the couple becomes locked tightly together, with one partner as the "rock" and the other as the "emotional wreck."

Significant tension underlies the distancer-pursuer pattern. The tension is related to deeply held beliefs regarding needs for security through being loved; the desire for validation and reassurance from the partner; fears of abandonment, which at times are tested out almost willfully; and bids for accommodation and special consideration. These beliefs and anxieties are internalized TG problems, linked to family-of-origin experiences. Distancers experience themselves as self-sufficient and carry an idealized view of marriage that breaks down under stress. Pursuers, who see themselves as dependent, carry both partners' concern about the marriage and try to "patch up" areas of conflict. It is also possible to have a symmetrical marriage in which each spouse dances toward, then away from, the other.

The extreme of distancing is cutoff. Central characteristics of cutoff include minimization or denial of attachment (as if the relationship had never existed), acting completely self-sufficient, and even physically running away. The cutoff is experienced not as an anxiety reaction, but as a sense of "Things need to end" or "I have to get away from this." The cutting-off partner appears to have great self-determination, strength, and more self-esteem than the partner who is left behind. In reality, it reflects severe deficits in the ability to tolerate conflict, to preserve trust in the face of crisis, and to maintain connection under stress.

Marital Violence as Fusion

Marital violence is probably the premier symptom of marital fusion. Goldner (1998) comments particularly on the "compelling, automatic projection process that has come to possess the [abusively connected] couple" (p. 277). In battered-spouse syndrome, the batterer (usually the husband) retains his sense of control and personal meaning, frightening his wife into agreement; the woman seems to lose any sense of herself apart from trying to contain his violence. Both partners are reluctant even to seek help without the other—a complex situation that forces therapists into interviewing them together, despite the danger in the home. The partner who is overadapting to the more rigid, less differentiated partner ceases to care for herself in the process.

Exploring family histories of abusive spouses has clarified some confusing aspects of violence—for example, why there is TG transmission. The concept of "destructive entitlement," discussed next, describes the exploitive behavior of abusers as a reaction to family-of-origin abuse: If one's parent is not accountable for hurting the family, then why should one be accountable to one's spouse now? Denial and minimization, used to cope with the violent family of origin, leads to lack of accountability in one's own marriage later. Imitation is the purest form of fusion.

In order to unpack any of these underlying issues in the marital fusion, "careful deconstruction of each individual's personal biography is a necessary preamble for the morally crucial discussion of personal responsibility and agency" (Goldner, 1998, p. 277). Jory, using intimate-justice theory, also points out that in order to treat violence, there must be an examination of internalized family experiences. One major clinical intervention involves "exploring experiences with empowerment, disempowerment and the abuses of power in the family of origin" (Jory & Anderson, 1999, p. 350).

Entitlement and Revolving Slates

Any discussion of attributions, projection, and mutual projection leads into discussion of entitlement. "Entitlement" is the experience of having given or contributed to family members, and waiting for acknowledgment and consideration in return (Boszormenyi-Nagy & Spark, 1973; Boszormenyi-Nagy & Ulrich, 1981). "Destructive entitlement" is the experience of being denied acknowledgment or consideration. When a person is not given the caring he/she is entitled to, that unmet need for acknowledgment is carried forward into love relationships and marriage. In a painful and unfair revolving slate, the position of helper and giver is passed on to the spouse. Meanwhile, the negatively entitled partner harbors negative attributions that consideration will be withheld again.

A person caught in a revolving slate of unrequited caring with his/her family of origin plays out the unresolved problem with a spouse. We believe that many repeating marital patterns that are seen on a genogram are the result of the revolving-slate phenomenon. For example, the neglected son of a busy father may expect that his wife and son will compensate him. On the marital genogram, we see a "dotted line" of distancing between husband and his father, and the same "dotted line" between the husband and wife, as well as the husband and son. Whitaker's comment (quoted earlier) that a marriage is really just "two scapegoats, sent out by their families, to reproduce themselves" (1982, p. 368) is a reference to the revolving slate.

Destructive entitlement in marriage is most clearly seen in codependent marriages. Somehow one partner's needs and perceptions are valued as more important, and the other partner's needs and perceptions are buried in the process. If the situation is not rectified, the children in that household are at risk to play out the revolving slate of codependency or negative entitlement. In marital therapy, pointing out that the children are being compromised in this manner can be a powerful motivator for a codependent spouse to begin setting limits and learn not to make so many sacrifices.

Larger-System Problems: Religion, Culture, and Class

Feminist-informed theories of culture and the family have provided powerful larger-system explanations for marital dysfunction. Feminist theory focuses on the ways in which male-centered culture rules how husbands and wives differently approach marital conflict, problem solving, intimacy, managing stress, self-empowerment, sexuality, financial and emotional power distribution, and even defining what constitutes a problem or a marital crisis.

Each TG model in its original form, developed in the 1950s and 1960s, neglected to examine biases of male-centered culture, or "beta bias." Beta bias is the assumption that gender differences are unimportant, making them outside the scope of discussion (Hare-Mustin, 1987). Symbolic-experiential theory does point out the importance of addressing gender inequities in marital therapy, either by moving couples toward egalitarianism, or by acknowledging justice issues for women (e.g., the need for autonomy in family life). Yet there has been little focus on gender inequities in marriage.

For example, feminist theorists would argue that entitlement is gendered—that in marriage, the needs of the husband tend to be valued as more worthy than the wife's (Goodrich, 1991). Slipp (1994) has pointed out that because male children are pushed away from nurturance in their socialization, they carry a certain amount of destructive entitlement into marriage. If, in this transitional society, fathers were to pick up nurturance functions for their sons, there would not be a deficit for their sons to carry into marriage. In the past decade, feminist theory has focused more on larger-system problems, analyzing social and political movements that color the expectations of men and women in marriage.

The implication for marital therapy is that the therapist must take a position about the larger system that refuses to ignore gender inequity, or else the therapist will be in the position of beta bias. As Goldner (1995) puts it, "Given that we are born into a symbolic and material world that is *already* gendered . . . it is impossible to overstate its effects on mind and culture. . . . We cannot 'see through' gender to the person 'inside,' since gender and self have co-evolved throughout the developmental process" (p. 46; emphasis in original). Even if a couple is *not* complaining about inequities in the marriage or the families of origin, the culturally competent marital therapist must address the impact of cultural stereotypes on the couple's functioning.

Therapists must look carefully at what is normative for a family's cultural group when evaluating structural or process symptoms. Marital problems can reflect and even be mediated or have their meaning changed by cultural issues. Culture affects how a family defines its members (McGoldrick, 1989). For example, not every nuclear family is defined as those who live in the home. In many Asian families (e.g., East Indian and Southeast Asian families), the in-laws are central to a couple's loyalties. In a Roman Catholic family, parents, godparents, and the spouses of sons and daugh-

ters may all be seen as part of the nuclear family. In an African American household, neighbors and fellow church members may be part of the marital support system. In a religiously observant family, if there is a relative who is a minister, he/she may be treated as a member of the nuclear family during times of crisis. In a white Eurocentric Protestant family, a couple is usually very split off from other family members when it comes to personal problems and concerns; parents and in-laws are peripheral. *The structure of a family, and the boundary around the couple, are defined by three to four generations of family tradition and ethnicity.*

Emotional process is also cultured. For example, the concepts of entitlement (what is owed to a person by a spouse and family) and destructive entitlement, and attendant problems like the revolving slate, cannot be used in the same way when therapists are looking at families outside Eurocentric culture. For example, the current generation of Korean American young adults has risen to educational and financial advantages through personal sacrifice and hard work by their parents. They carry a tremendous sense of obligation to respond by choosing jobs and marriages that will please their parents.

Political movements can also create legacies that are expressed in marriage. Young couples now are members of the third generation after the American Depression, and it is no accident that many of them are driven by the job market and financial ambition. Some middle-aged adults whose parents were refugees during World War II are seeing their parents sue for international reparation. This historic set of events will create for some people a shift in social identity from "second- or third-generation American" to a more long-term, healing, self-respectful view of family history. We can also expect to see changes in the social class and privilege experienced by families of reparation, who once were the marginalized "greenhorns."

ASSESSMENT OF COUPLES

Procedures for TG assessment of couples are not yet well articulated. Several well-researched tests of family functioning are available; these use a circumplex model that assesses families regarding distribution of power, degree of intimacy and cohesion, degree of autonomy, and other important factors. These tools have been sadly underutilized, reflecting the predominant thinking that couple work is a matter to be confined to the married dyad, instead of viewed as an extension of older family-of-origin problems. Thus, despite the wealth of information about family impact on later adult functioning, couple therapy is cordoned off as if it were a separate modality, and couples are assessed in a vacuum. In contrast, TG therapists "punctuate" the problem cycles observed within a couple by looking at their place in the three-generation grid of their two families during assessment.

It is also important for the therapist to understand what effects will flow outward from changes within a couple to their families of origin. The two families, connected as they are to each spouse in dyads and triangles, will be changed via these connections. In fact, that is one of the tenets of natural systems therapy. The two families will probably experience these shifts as uncomfortable and unfamiliar, and will have their own responses. Poorly differentiated relationships tend to "pull" harder when boundaries are moved, and the pulling will challenge the couple. These responses need to be predicted, considered, and planned for in couple work, by a therapist with a three-generational map of their problems (Roberto, 1992).

Genograms

Assessment usually takes place in the first one to three meetings, with both spouses present. Partners are not seen individually for interviews unless there is potential for danger due to violence. The major tool for identification of couples' problems is the family genogram. Genograms have been adapted in various ways for clinical use. Dynamic markings have been developed to the point that couples' relationship and TG patterns can be easily shown (Friedman, Rohrbough, & Krakauer, 1988; Guerin & Pendagast, 1976; McGoldrick, Gerson, & Shellenberger, 1999, see Figure 5.1).

These markings have use in making certain couple interventions, such as pointing out repeating patterns or complementary relationships. Initially, however, genograms guide the clinician to address problem-maintaining issues in either or both families of origin, and to plan realistically regarding long-term family change. The time line genogram (Friedman, Rohrbaugh, & Krakauer, 1988) plots important family of origin events clearly in their time frames. Genograms have also been adapted to facilitate treatment for specific types of couple problems, such as sexual dysfunction, family illness patterns, spiritual and religious issues, or medical and genetic disorders that could affect

planning of children. They have even been used to provide self-study for medical students and their spouses.

Whereas genogram information is used in other schools of couple therapy to look mainly at family structure, in TG therapy it is used to determine multigenerational patterns. Sometimes patterns of relationship repeat themselves over generations without varying, and the same symptoms are repeated over generations—spousal abuse, poor health, depression, educational failure, multiple divorces or desertions, drug addiction. These can feed forward into marriage problems in the here-and-now—such as distancing, fusion, chronic mistrust, contempt, or triangling in third parties.

Multigenerational patterns can also include patterns of work, religion, or political affiliation. For example, a husband's family may have become progressively more religious, but he may be the exception, or may even have married out of the family faith. It is very common to find people whose parents, grandparents, uncles or aunts, and even in-laws have all been physicians, businessmen, or military officers. Finally, the clinician looks for critical incidents, such as natural disasters or environmental trauma, that have colored a family's relational patterns.

The clinician uses a couple's first one or two sessions to identify key figures in each family of origin, formative and nodal events in each family's past, and the history of the marriage. Dynamic markings are also made to indicate proximity and distance to key family members, the presence of fusion or cutoff that may be affecting the couple's alliance, and any repetitive patterns that are found in more than one generation. For example, a wife in a couple may show a pattern of deferring to her husband instead of participating in important decisions, and in her parents' marriage her mother may also defer to her father and have difficulty with assertiveness.

The partners are asked for their own narratives about their problem, and to describe how each perceives its origin, meaning, and sequence. This technique is not different from other systemic, even ahistorical therapies. TG therapists interview and observe couples with a "wide-angle lens" (Roberto, 1992) to inquire and track three-generational patterns of culture, marital and family structure, and beliefs about marriage. Partners are asked to describe whether, and how, key family members have responded to their problem, in order to clarify whether triangles exist that will need to be addressed. For example, in the classic "mother-in-law"

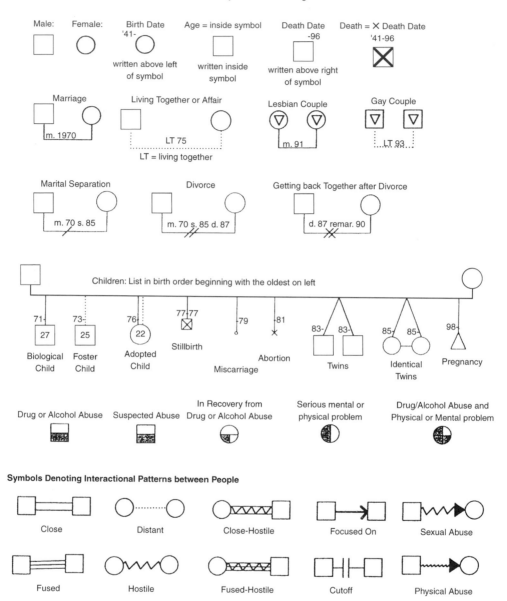

FIGURE 5.1. Standard symbols for genograms. From McGoldrick, Gerson, & Shellenberger (1999). Reprinted by permission.

triangle, a husband maintains distance from his wife, who turns to her mother, who advises her, following which the husband distances more. Of course, assessment is not the same process as therapy, and triangles viewed through the TG lens are not always targeted for change. For example, if the husband and wife become closer through couple work, the mother-in-law may not be as important to the stability of the marriage and may be able to focus less on them. A macro-level view also ensures that a clinician will select workable goals of change with the couple, since he/she will better understand the extended families' existing conflicts and triangles. During therapy, participants will be more aware of potential reactions to marital change in their family members, and considering each family's point of view bolsters self-esteem through "earned merit" (Boszormenyi-Nagy & Krasner, 1986).

Clinicians using genograms for couple assessment must be culturally competent regarding normative family structure. The dynamic markings for genograms as they currently exist are culture-blind, and can imply that some relationships are pathological when in a cultural group they are normative. For example, in Islamic families, the mother, mother-in-law, and other female relatives are important sources of support to the wife in a hierarchical family, religion, and culture still governed by men. Class also intersects with normative life cycle transitions. In poor families, women bear children young; their partners are often not able to provide resources or companionship; and relatives may become central as child care providers. There is more likely to be a history of chronic family stress, violence or desertion due to traumatic effects of poverty, inability to find work, illness and addiction, lack of physical safety, obstacles to education, difficulty planning the birth and spacing of children, and broad lack of access to health services for couples and their children. A couple's genogram must contain information about class, cultural, religious, and historical differences that intersect with the clinical problem, or the clinician runs the risk of pathologizing the partners instead of understanding their needs and the TG meaning of their symptoms.

Assessing Relational Quality: The Clinical Interview

Each partner is interviewed regarding his/her individual views of the presenting problem, as well as the habitual ways each one interacts with the other about the problem. TG therapies do not bypass central complaints. Rather, they use identified problems to expand the field of inquiry *into the "macro-level" context of their long-term connection with each other and with the past* (Roberto, 1991). The object is to begin framing the family-of-origin context immediately, so that the therapist can return to this frame repeatedly while addressing the couple's problem.

A TG therapist participates in classical systemic interviewing in order to identify unique differences in each partner's views. The binocular picture prized by systemic therapists emerges easily in initial assessment. Each spouse has personal meanings that are taken away from events in the marriage, and these personal meanings must be brought into the dialogue. For example, a man may personally feel that he has deliberately tried to depend more on his lover in order to show him trust, whereas his partner believes that he been depending more only as a temporary reaction to stress. The individual meanings that are attached to the couple's experiences will be used as the dynamic core of couple therapy, in order to highlight each partner's emotional needs and family inheritance. Where the differences are causing confusion or conflict, the couple will be helped if possible to frame them in ways that are protective of the marriage.

Timing of symptoms is very important in TG therapies. Once each partner's view of the problems is elicited, the clinician works to construct a hypothesis that accounts for their emergence now. Most marital dysfunctions involve repeated relational impasses, not isolated or short-term stressors. Therefore, a therapist must have a theory about when, and why, those impasses reach runaway proportions. Many long-term TG patterns can combine with life stressors to "blow up" or wither a marriage: unmet expectations that revolve into the marriage; feelings of entitlement or frustrated wishes that interfere with resolving conflicts or produce aggression; difficulty with supportiveness from lack of prior experience; legacies of abuse, maltreatment, or loss that color partners' ability to extend or earn trust.

One of the crucial elements in marital distress is the distribution of power: power to name problems; power to make decisions and solve problems; power to make requests or claims on one's spouse. Currently, there are no dynamic markings that show power relationships explicitly on a genogram, nor have we developed an explicit way of describing power. Assessing the distribution of power in a marriage is as important as assessing its affective and functional qualities. Although some clients maintain that they do not mind an unequal balance of power, it is a developmental challenge for adults to use their influence and ideas to make change. Too often, clients avoid these areas because discussions of power can be "emotional dynamite." It is far easier for someone to claim that he has lost sexual desire because he is depressed, for example, than to challenge his mate and admit that he is dissatisfied. Money and sexual initiatives are good illustrations of how a couple manages power: Are the decisions democratic, unilateral to one spouse, unilateral while seeming to consult the spouse, hidden from the spouse, or avoided by both?

In order to be "emotionally intelligent" (Schwartz & Johnson, 2000), the interview must also include an affective assessment. Affect includes comfort with the quality of the marital connection; degree of trust; positive or negative attributions (projection); presence of alienated or contemptuous feelings (two of Gottman and colleagues' "four horsemen of the apocalypse"); significant reactivity that might connote fusion; anger signifying desire for change (particularly when it is shown by the more accommodating partner); and affects that may be biologically significant (related to mood and physical well-being). Nonverbal behavior gives important contextual information—the words "I'll come if my spouse wants me to" mean one thing when said with concern, and another thing entirely when said in a way that is flat and disengaged.

Partners' affective quality is a key to the relational problems that may underlie their symptoms. Not until recently have marriage therapists understood the importance of a positive affective bond to the survival of a marriage, as Gottman's work has demonstrated. Each school of TG therapy tends to emphasize certain domains of information from the clinical interview. Object relations and symbolic–experiential therapists have written more on assessment of affect. As Wachtel (1982) has noted, "Such a focus enables the therapist to learn more about what the client values than he could disclose consciously" (p. 340). Lacking a well-delineated "DSM-V" of affects and their meanings, a clinician uses his/her own reactions and knowledge base to assess for the presence of negative emotions in the marital couple.

Marital therapies need to explore and demonstrate different types of affective bonding more clearly than in the past. For example, there are vast differences among the kinds of intensity found in a couple fused together by mutual dependency; a couple locked together in sexual obsession; and a couple whose members have established a traumatic bond through mutual abandonment or survival of loss. TG marital therapy gives a unique opportunity to look closely at the pasts of married people, and to get a sense of the needs and wishes that brought them to *this* marriage and *this* commitment.

At the end of the assessment phase, the clinician should have prepared a clear genogram, a description of the presenting problem from each partner's position in the marriage, a theory explaining the differences in the partners' ideas and emotions about the problem, a hypothesis regarding long-term contributing factors in the families of origin, and an idea about what behaviors/attitudes need to be changed. These ideas are fed back to the couple in the goal-setting phase of therapy. The therapist must be able to do the following:

- Articulate central beliefs and mutual values underlying a couple's marital commitment.
- Articulate any differences or conflicts between spouses' closely held beliefs and family legacies.
- Describe the position of each spouse in his/her family of origin regarding important family problems and experiences.
- Predict how these positions will shift if the spouses solve their problem.
- Help each spouse to credit him-/herself for doing couple work and initiating self-change.

SETTING GOALS AND PLANNING THE WORK

TG couple work generally seeks to help spouses achieve greater relational competence; enhance their self-knowledge and self-esteem; increase their confidence that they can solve their own problems; and enhance their ability to support each partner's developmental tasks (Roberto, 1992). The TG therapist recommends a relational therapy, even for problems that appear individual. Even though the public is increasingly informed about the value of spouse-assisted counseling with severe emotional disorders, such as mood and thought disorders, coming with one's partner can be counterintuitive. The client usually struggles with whether to try this approach, because often the serious concerns seem his/hers alone.

Whitaker referred to two great crossroads in family therapy as the "battle for structure" and the "battle for initiative" (Napier & Whitaker, 1978). The term "battle for structure" is a somewhat adversarial way to describe how we enter into the therapeutic alliance and contract for change, but it hints at the uneasiness inherent in conducting the plan. In today's terms, this would be described as a challenge of therapy. Whitaker felt that this battle begins, for the client, even while making the choice whether to include the partner or to request individual therapy.

There are two types of goals. I have made the distinction before between "mediating goals" and "ultimate goals" in systemic work (Roberto, 1991, p. 454). In intermediate-length therapies, unlike brief symptom-focused therapies, the clinician can take the time to evolve a therapeutic system with the spouses that will enhance their own ability to solve problems in the future. This is the "mediating goal" of TG therapy. It includes expanding the presenting problem into a TG frame; activating and allowing "positive anxiety" about change (Whitaker & Ryan, 1989); encouraging a multilateral perspective of problems; creating a boundary around the spouses and their marital work; and creating a shared meaning about the origin and nature of the problem.

In agreeing to work together, a couple in TG therapy also opens the way to understanding formative family-of-origin experiences. This mediating goal may seem irrelevant to mastering the couple's current problem, but it is not. If the clinician can "see" a client's marital behavior in the context of family-of-origin problems, so can the client. For example, a man from an alcoholic family fears he must leave his alcoholic spouse. He may be asked to explore whether he believes that recovery is possible, considering the fact that his own parents never recovered. Couples rarely object to this contextual framing of their current problem.

Like other types of couple therapies, TG therapies hold that ultimate goals of change must be created together among spouses and clinician. Since TG theory is most concerned with the feedforward of long-term family dysfunctions, a couple's ultimate goals are likely to include long-term relational patterns. These can vary widely: greater autonomy for married people; a decrease in fighting and tension; greater and fuller intimacy, including sexual intimacy; support of career, work, and personal development; greater self-esteem and effectiveness in the marital context; commitment; interdependency and nurturance; the decision to bear and nurture children. It has been noted that ultimate goals are sometimes difficult to articulate clearly (Whitaker & Keith, 1981). The spouses may know only that they "aren't getting along," "aren't close any more," or "don't have sex." Discussion of crucial family experiences and legacies helps them to make sense of the painful issues playing out between them.

Problem-focused marriage therapy addresses one unitary problem, or a prioritized list of clearly identified problems. However, this means another course of therapy in the future if there are other problems (Watzlawick, 1984). TG marital therapy aims to go beyond symptoms, including building a couple's "relationship competence." The therapy must strengthen trustworthiness, consideration,

willingness to advocate for oneself, tolerance for differences, mutual respect, nurturance, and empathy. I call this goal "restoration," because it includes the goal of repair—putting back what is out of place or damaged.

ROLE OF THE THERAPIST

The Therapeutic Alliance

A strong, compassionate, "partial" (in contextual therapy terms) alliance is pivotal in this type of couple work. Partiality replaces neutrality. A TG focus opens up the therapy conversation to emotionally laden issues in a way that requires a high degree of trust. Spouses discussing their stories of abandonment, illness, conflict and betrayal, abuse, loss, and stressful family loyalties are looking at a dimension of experience that is far more taxing than problem- or solution-based talk. The therapist is a participant from inside the system, striving to create a safe environment to expand symptoms into their relational context. If "neutrality" means that after a session, no member can tell whose side the therapist is on, then "partiality" means that after a session, each member knows that the therapist is on his/her side. Even systemic neutrality, the position of eliciting views, does not build the partial, concerned alliance necessary.

The strength of the partial alliance provides the "anesthesia for the operation," as Whitaker has commented (personal communication, 1978). It is also true that only if the therapist can offer an affective connection, can the spouses in therapy learn to work on their affective connection. Finally, as Napier (1983) commented, it is a mark of our interest in a humane society that therapists offer kindness and compassion to the clients who entrust them with their marital well-being.

The Clinician's Use of Self

Part of exercising partiality means that the TG therapist has to be personally transparent (Roberto, 1992). Use of self is a method of remaining separate from a couple's relationship while still working from a close position—participant observation. The clinician shares fragments of experience, personal reflections, and teaching stories (Roberto, 1991); these communicate to a couple that it is desirable and healthy to be subjective in their ideas and feelings. As Framo (1981) writes, it is important "that the therapist convey in some form that he[/she] has experienced pain and loss, shame, guilt, and disappointment, as well as the exhilaration and joys of living. . . . It is just as unwise to support the fantasy of the therapist's life as ideal as it is to overburden clients with one's own problems" (p. 147).

Use of self puts the responsibility for change on the couple in therapy, because the therapist is communicating his/her own life experiences outside the therapy hour. These comments use a high degree of disclosure, but they are selected deliberately and thoughtfully. Material shared with a couple must be resolved issues if they are to be useful, so they are not countertransference reactions. Rather, they are well-digested thoughts that mirror or parallel a couple's dilemmas. Finally, the therapist's self-disclosure does not have to be a literal recounting, but can be a metaphorical, abstract, or even dramatic comment.

A Relationship in Stages

A TG therapy unfolds in stages, because it is expanding a couple's framework from the particular (the presenting problems) to the larger system (the families of origin), and from the here-and-now (the recurring conflicts) to a longer-term view (the partners' beliefs and orientations about marriage, themselves, and their own union). The structure moves from high to low; the therapist moves from central position to the periphery; interventions move from directive to nondirective; and use of self increases (Roberto, 1991). This is not as true of Bowenian couples work, but even in natural systems therapy, as clients go home to visit their families and work on diffusing triangles, the stories and feedback probably change a therapist's role with the couple.

In early-stage work, the "battles for structure and initiative" take place as the therapist recommends marital sessions and creates a setting for the couple to commit to relationship focus. During this time, the spouses are encouraged to begin self-study of their marriage; genograms are made; family history is given; and the marriage is examined from each partner's standpoint. The midphase of couple work aims to reorganize the spouses' understanding of key problems in a newly expanded, relational, context. Use of self communicates that the clinician understands the complexity of marital commitment, the difficulty of accepting and changing oneself in a relationship, and the universal struggle to balance intimacy and self-sufficiency. Each partner in the marriage, as he/she responds to the therapist's involvement, becomes more clearly defined.

Late-stage couple work uses less coaching or expert stance. At this point, the partners can observe themselves responding to one another without the therapist's help. They are usually reporting progress in areas of intimacy, disclosure, self-knowledge, and mutuality, and flashpoints as they push themselves and each other toward change. Spouses can create innovative ways of supporting their own and each other's needs and requests—often in ways that the therapist could not have predicted. They are a flexible system that generates its own solutions, and the clinician serves more as a sounding board.

TECHNIQUES WITH COUPLES

Creating a TG Frame

Earlier, genogramming has been explained as an assessment tool. It is also a teaching tool in early therapy (Guerin, 1976). In fact, the genogram can be made as a therapy activity instead of as a personal record by the clinician (Wachtel, 1982). When it is made together, it is a technique of change because it adds to the partners' sense of "where they are each coming from." The mutual self-disclosure and willingness to trust each other with vital information are healing in themselves.

Creating a genogram together with a couple stimulates therapist and clients to think about extended family issues, and contributes to forming connections between events in the marriage and the legacies that came before. Genograms "[enable] family members to learn a 'metaperspective' about their organization and emotionally laden history" (Roberto, 1992, p. 107). Gaining perspective helps to calm intense distress, and clarifies the origin and nature of marital problems. This is especially true if the therapist creates a genogram focused on a couple's presenting problem, such as sexual behavior, religious intolerance, parenting problems, or extreme complementarity. Finally, mapping the marriage in the context of two families also mitigates the profound sense of personal inadequacy or failure that warring spouses have. They are freer to think about, rather than react to, chronic problems. This connection aids partners in reworking their own intimate behavior, as well as working against blaming each other. Therefore, it is one core technique.

Tracking the Presenting Problem

If one asks a TG clinician what problems he/she is tracking during a therapy session, the answer would be the same as it is for other clinicians. A couple is experiencing an escalation of relational tensions, which reflects inadequate solutions to family problems. There are marital symptoms, and cycles around those symptoms, to be understood. The therapist watches which spouse names the problems and which one defers, elicits their individual theories about underlying tensions, and observes how they handle differences in their theories. For example, if their symptom is distance and coldness, the therapist notes what happens when one spouse tries to attract attention. He/she notes which spouse tries to engage the other (or whether both do), and how this is done. Their structural characteristics—distance, fusion, disengagement, or cutoff, conflict, or pseudomutuality—are noted.

Tracking Antecedents

A TG therapist tracks presenting problems with an eye toward antecedent events in the couple's life and the spouses' own lives with their families of origin. It is like watching a "trailing cursor" on a computer mouse: One can see where it is going and where it has come from. Trailing, or tracking antecedents, uses a time frame of two or even three generations.

This trailing inquiry does not replace discussion of how the spouses will help each other with relationship problems. It acknowledges another dimension to their marital experience. Trailing keeps the couple located on the TG map, and so it conveys that the marriage is not occurring in a vacuum. The experience of trailing back from complaints to antecedents makes people feel that they are "getting to the root of things." Each spouse gets a sense that there is an entire family and its history behind a loved one's behavior, and the behavior thus makes more sense. Fighting decreases, and contextual and mutual understanding increases.

Using Family-of-Origin Consults in Therapy

There are few tools so clarifying to the marital therapist as a family-of-origin consult. When a marital partner sits in to witness a meeting between the spouse and the spouse's parents and/or siblings, that clarity is even more powerful. Framo (1976, 1981) has produced a body of work on his experiences in meeting families of couples in counseling. They reflect the orientation that "When . . . adults are able to go back to deal directly with their parents and brothers and sisters about the previously avoided issues that have existed between them, an opportunity exists for reconstructive changes to come about in their marital relationship" (1981, p. 134). It is important to note that organizing a consult does not occur at a couple's request; it is a tool used by the clinician in the midphase of therapy. Clients usually do not connect their ongoing marital problems with larger patterns in their families until much later in therapy, or after therapy.

Family-of-origin meetings can only occur once or twice during most marriage therapies because of distance and cost constraints. They are usually scheduled in 2-hour segments on two consecutive days, although they have also been organized for entire extended families for up to a week (C. A. Whitaker, personal communication, 1979). Meetings are not structured into therapeutic tasks, but organized around making intergenerational connections visible, available for discussion, and amenable to review.

Couples in therapy experience extreme anxiety about bringing parents in, and the idea should be "seeded" for at least a month prior to the meeting. There are many rationales that need to be worked through regarding why the parents (and siblings, if possible) should attend. Experiencing this anxiety in itself, and struggling to come to terms with it, directly assault a client's illusion that the spouse is causing all of his/her distress. One family of origin is brought in at a time. Some TG therapists do not include the spouse in the family meeting (Framo, 1976, 1981), while others believe that observing can greatly aid empathy and understanding in the marriage (Roberto, 1992). When there, the spouse is invited to sit in without any assignment to participate, because unresolved family issues are easily displaced onto a son- or daughter-in-law.

Family consults are arranged by the partner who is preparing for the visit. The invitation can take several forms: an invitation to help move therapy forward by giving the family's viewpoint, or to take the opportunity to discuss important family issues while the married son or daughter has a consultant to provide the forum. The spouses are told that they are the clients in therapy, not their families, and that the families will not be made into clients by the therapist. TG therapists agree on the crucial importance of respecting the generational boundary, and especially of not demoting parents in the eyes of their grown children. While awaiting the visit, the husband or wife in therapy is asked to reflect on personal concerns and issues in the marriage that may be connected to experiences at home. These key experiences will be part of the material for the interviews.

In practice, most clinicians have found that siblings are reluctant to attend—a difficult symptom of resistance. When this occurs, it is most probably because the client in marital therapy has formed an ambivalent relationship with that sibling, or because that sibling is even more distressed by the family than the client is. It is important to expend all means to bring about sibling participation. Later, the bond formed by this visit forms a powerful means of support for the client that may have been absent since his/her childhood; this will create an alliance that takes some pressure off the marriage.

At the consult, the client being visited is asked to describe the problems that brought him/her to marital counseling. Since this is a midphase technique, a client can now explain his/her contribution to the marital problem, whereas at first he/she may have blamed the spouse. The family is encouraged to discuss what they know of the problem and to ask questions of him/her, so that the focus is firmly placed on their child. Every consult is unique in its emotionality, pace of discussion, degree of openness and disclosure, participation, and historical perspective (Framo, 1981). Some families need 2 days just to acknowledge that their son or daughter might be having relationship problems and that family issues might be involved. Others begin with a request for help from a parent that opens the way immediately for a deep and sincere discussion. The meeting can be audiotaped or videotaped; there should be an agreement that all family members will receive a copy of any tape, including absentees.

Although the spouses do not explicitly connect changes in their families of origin to the state of their marriage, consults add to their understanding of the relational problems they have brought into their commitment. There is less other-focusing, more self-observation, more investment in change, and greater self-regard after a consult is held. This is true even though the consult itself can be painful or problematic. Seemingly little movement creates a very different view of self, and of the self-in-relationship.

Creating Personal Authority

"Personal authority" (Williamson, 1981, 1982a, 1982b) is the ability to direct one's own opinions; choose whether to express or not to express oneself; respect one's own judgment; hold a meta-perspective on relationships; take responsibility for decisions; choose whether to be intimate or not with each other person; and treat elders as peers. Williamson's (1981) work on personal authority suggests that many marital impasses are built upon intergenerational intimidation. He believes that by midlife, there is a normative life cycle transition that involves ending the hierarchy with one's parents.

An unrecognized power issue—the investment of lifetime authority in parents—produces a tilt in the family's distribution of power that limits a personal sense of choice. By "intimidation," Williamson refers to a son or daughter's fear of rejection or loss if the parents and their values are challenged too much (Roberto, 1992). Williamson suggests that in middle adulthood the generational hierarchy has to be terminated, leaving in its place an egalitarian, adult–adult relationship. Otherwise, that hierarchy keeps alive old legacies and delegations that continue to produce emotional conflict. It is an enormous challenge to "leave home" in the sense of seeing and relating to parents as peers instead of authority figures (Williamson, 1981). The spouses must give up their expectation of getting approval, and their image of the parents as dispensers of approval.

The technique for accomplishing this is a coaching procedure, in which a client begins to seek more information about the parents as aging individuals and to mourn the end of parental protection (or the lack of it). The client examines his/her lifelong perceptions of the parents, and explains these images and how they arose (Williamson, 1982a). Meetings focus on the relationship with each parent and the changes that need to occur. At this time in therapy, the client works to express him-/herself clearly, and ask important family questions. There is a visit home, in which the client talks with each parent and then with both together about their early life and experiences with love relationships. The client is getting to know the parents as real people.

When the client is no longer suffused with anxiety about family issues, a family-of-origin consult can be held to propose changes and discuss them. I have found that the presence of the spouse in these sessions increases marital understanding a thousandfold, as the spouse gets to view significant issues that he/she may have only heard about before. It may be the first time that a wife's stress-related symptoms, or a husband's ambivalence, are completely clear in the context where they originally formed. It may be the first time that a client finally lets go of overfocusing on his/her mate or blaming the mate for irrational behavior patterns. As Paul (1967) pointed out, facing loss has profound potential to unlock personal resources for solving problems in marriage and personal life.

CURATIVE FACTORS

Family therapy has never been terribly comfortable with emotions. The models that dominated its early development (structural and strategic) were primarily aimed at changing behavior patterns, and through reframing, the cognitions that maintained them. Increasingly, emotion is being viewed as a guide to adaptive behavior and a positive organizing force in human functioning (Damasio, 1994; Johnson & Greenberg, 1994). TG therapies (with the exception of Bowenian techniques) acknowledge the emotions that accompany painful relationships, and use them as motivators for change.

When clients listen to their own subjective responses in a dialogue with each other, reflections, emotions, beliefs, and recollected behavior are integrated together. (Schwartz & Johnson, 2000). Research shows that if emotions carry constructive messages, then adding them to a marital dialogue helps each partner "get the message." Anger can be seen as a demand for change; sadness, as loss; pleasure, as the hope stimulated by a well-resolved disagreement. And as Gottman (1994) and his colleagues have found, conversation that includes personal responses helps to evoke the respectful and accepting reception that couple therapists desire; it increases intimacy.

Gender differences in expression of affect need to be considered. Women may tend to value expression of emotion because it is normally suppressed. When women in families are marginalized in decision making and leadership, they are expected to accept the decisions of others and not to show "negativity" in front of others. Therefore, in trust relationships, women seek to admit the opinions and concerns that they are expected to suppress normally. From this point of view, it is important to encourage this avenue to intimacy for women, and to teach men to respect and value their wives' wish to engage them in honest conversation.

In addition to integrating affect into therapy, TG therapies rely on contextual learning and some experiential learning as curative. The encounter of partners with the clinician, who participates in as well as conducts the sessions, increases their awareness of alternative ways to solve problems. Therapist use of self has unique qualities that model disclosure and self-acceptance rather than justification and defensiveness. The processes of genogram work, as well as family-of-origin visits and consults, widen spouses' perspective on their problems. Like a "connect the dots" puzzle in which the solution requires drawing a single line that goes *outside* the group of dots, a TG perspective allows couples to rework their marital connection in ways that are "outside" their previous problematic repertoires.

NEGATIVE THERAPEUTIC REACTIONS

Freud (1937) first coined the term "negative therapeutic reaction" (p. 243), referring to extremely negative effects after discussing material with a therapist. Couples frequently experience negative effects from meetings that deal with painful subjects. There can be great anxiety related to verbalizing intentions or reactions that have never been voiced in a marriage. Some partners—particularly an overaccomodating spouse, or pursuer, who feels responsible for keeping the marriage smooth—find the process of discussing disagreements intolerable.

Some families feel shamed or embarrassed by the disclosure of marital problems. For example, in a white Protestant couple, discussing sexual problems in front of a clinician is experienced as too intimate—evidence of personal inadequacy. A Jewish couple that prides itself on family accomplishments may feel shame after discussing job problems or destructive behavior such as spouse abuse. A Japanese husband and wife may feel they have "lost face" after voicing complaints about each other or their extended family to an outsider. Cultural competence requires the TG clinician to understand what role he/she, as a community representative, plays in relation to families that are culturally different from his/hers. The therapist will need to practice partiality by asking couples for their consent to discuss specific issues, and for feedback about their comfort level as sessions pass.

Court-mandated marital therapy is complicated by the fact that the therapist is a representative of social control. The therapist in this situation must work hard to hold the boundary between legitimate community concerns (such as the safety of a child) and the legitimate concerns of husband and wife, who are struggling to cope with a marriage in crisis. These couples benefit from use of self and a clear message that the clinician would like to help them learn to strengthen themselves and protect their marriage from intervention from larger agencies.

APPLICABILITY OF TG METHODS

At times, when a couple's cultural legacy is different from the therapist's, it is best to use a consultant or cotherapist with the same heritage. The issue concerns a therapist's ability to understand the meanings, traditions, and history of a couple or family. Whitaker's use of cotherapy partly stemmed from his effort to include a therapist familiar with customs, religious practices, ethnic experiences, and history like that of the family in therapy. The decline in use of cotherapy and treatment teams, related to changes in reimbursement for therapy, has cut off this resource. In the 1990s, practice moved more toward *every* clinician's establishing a personal knowledge base and competence in understanding cultural differences. This awareness has not extended sufficiently to religious differences; marital/family therapy has tended to split off religious discussion to the clergy, who frequently are not comfortable in working with a couple. The TG clinician needs to ascertain carefully whether a couple has cultural or spiritual conflicts that will benefit from a counselor who is indigenous to that community.

It is commonly thought that relational, dynamic therapies require intellectual or academic achievement and self-focus, or insight. Actually, some of the TG theories were created from hospital-based work in large metropolitan areas or mental health catchment areas with a broad mix of cultures, social classes, and religious groups. For example, symbolic–experiential theory was developed at Emory University in Atlanta, Georgia, and at the University of Wisconsin in Madison. The Clinics at the University of Wisconsin, since they are located in the capital of that state, serve families that include rural Swedish-descent Lutheran families; urban families; survivalist families living in remote rural areas; Czech families who migrated to Wisconsin's industrial cities for jobs; married medical students; and poor families of patients with chronic schizophrenia provided for by state health care.

TG therapies have a unique capacity to address gender-based problems common in Western marriage. For men, the opportunity to explore one's relationship with one's parents, especially the father, is often completely new. It is extraordinarily moving to see a husband who has been withdrawn and unresponsive to his wife begin to examine his relationship with his parents and realize that he may be pushing away the first intimate relationship of his adult life. For a woman, whose focus in marriage is maintaining a connection for the husband and children, family-of-origin work gives permission for her to begin reexamining her own needs and wishes.

There are problems inherent in couple therapy with Eastern and Middle Eastern families, as well as many Asian families (e.g., Indian, Pakistani, Southeast Asian, and Chinese). These cultural groups, which ascribe power to parents and previous generations, are extremely averse to any intervention that seems to lay blame on family elders. In some cases, a couple is not viewed as a unit of two at all, on any rung of the family hierarchy. Power here is not even defined by generations of family—but actually at times by the religion, which venerates authority and duty.

There are profound implications in these differences for a couple's awareness of its connection as a dyad. The spouses must be treated in therapy as a segment of their family and their religious community, or therapy will fail. Interactionally based and ahistorical therapies are likely to ask clients to "put the marriage first" or "make a boundary around the marriage." I believe that if properly applied, TG therapy is uniquely relevant for these families, because one's place in one's family is respected and considered.

CASE ILLUSTRATION

Johnna and Carl, a young white couple in their 20s, requested counseling during their third year of marriage. Johnna appeared alone for the first interview, and informed the therapist in tears that she had been fasting and skipping meals for the prior 3 months, losing about 20 pounds. Because she was a petite 5 feet 3 inches, the restriction had left her underweight, and she was haggard, tired, and unwell. When asked why Carl had not accompanied her as planned, she claimed that although she was deeply unhappy in the marriage, she was angry over recent fights and had decided to come alone. She readily agreed to ask him to join her for future sessions, and seemed relieved that the therapist recommended it.

In the second meeting, with Carl present, the couple discussed many stresses that concerned both of them. They had relocated from the Midwest 2 years previously, in order to follow Carl's job in the Marines. The change in orders represented a promotion for Carl, with more duties and frequent evaluations. Johnna had left her job as an operating room nurse, a career for which she had trained and prepared for some time. Johnna saw the relocation as Carl's having "gotten his way" and "forced her to leave nursing." Carl was frustrated and fearful of Johnna's weight loss; he felt that she had withdrawn from him, and that she was not trying to make healthy choices such as making new friends, finding a new job, or planning visits and holidays. The couple reported daily fights, which rapidly reached screaming proportions. Johnna would challenge Carl over his long work hours and career focus. Carl would end up yelling at her to grow up and control herself, stomp out of the apartment in fury, and stay even later at work the next day with his workmates.

A genogram showed that the couple was extremely isolated. Carl's family of origin, including his elder and younger sisters, resided in a distant Midwestern state and was part of a disconnected Lutheran farming family. His father had died suddenly of heart failure while he was in college. He did not maintain much contact with his mother, relatives, or even the sisters, who were married with their own families. Carl viewed the couple's once-yearly visits at Christmas to be sufficient, and did not feel that there were any stresses. In contrast, Johnna was deeply distressed by the lack of communication. She did not feel that her mother-in-law was interested in her, and this made life lonely and dreary during Carl's 6-month deployments with his ship. On the annual Christmas visit, Carl's family seemed upset that he had married at all. There were frequent references to "the man of the family" (Carl), and requests for his advice. Carl stated that he found this position very satisfying, if upsetting to his wife—he had authority, respect, importance, a fine career, and dignity (when he wasn't in a screaming fight with Johnna).

Johnna's family was viewed by the couple as extremely difficult, emotional, disapproving, and troubled. Although her parents and sister lived in a Middle Atlantic state near them, they were currently not speaking to Johnna, because she had married out of their religious sect. Her family members were Jehovah's Witnesses and regarded Carl's Lutheran background as unsatisfactory. The parents had not attended their wedding. They were unhappy over Johnna's decision to "marry out," as well as her choice to go into nursing, which they viewed with disapproval. They had not wanted Johnna to leave her hometown, or to travel the country from base to base among strangers. Although Johnna was hurt and angry at her parents' withdrawal, she missed her family and her church deeply. She secretly feared that if she took another nursing job now, the family would cut her off, and even that her church elders would become offended by her hospital work and excommunicate her. Johnna's sister, who was slightly younger, did not seem available when she called, and Johnna did not feel she had much to say to Sarah. In contrast to Johnna's hurt and anger, Carl's feelings were more equivocal. He viewed her family situation as less dire, stating that his family could be their main support in the future.

Carl assumed that Johnna could have a relationship with his married sisters, and that they did not need her family's goodwill. He admitted that he was confused in some areas, however. For example, when Johnna had fallen ill shortly after the last family Christmas and was hospitalized, he had found himself too nervous to notify her parents. Now the couple fought over that decision constantly. In fact, the couple dated Johnna's loss of appetite, weight loss, and physical decline to that period. Their sexual relationship, which they both described as loving and passionate in the past, had also evaporated.

The couple showed cycles of mutual blame and hurtful accusations, which were escalating into verbal battles. Carl, who was well spoken, seemed to come out ahead and to belittle Johnna. There was a developing pattern of emotional cutoff, which was more ominous, in which the challenges Johnna threw out increasingly failed to "hook" Carl. More and more he left the house for the evening to "cool off," and Johnna retreated into skipping meals and brooding alone. Both spouses were beginning to look on one another with disappointment, and to lose sight of their investment in the marriage. Polarization was setting in, with Johnna playing the emotionally distraught wife and Carl the dissatisfied husband suffering in silence.

The assessment sessions were used to point out these encroaching patterns and to help the spouses set goals together. Johnna and Carl were alarmed at recent events, and named three goals: (1) to get help "talking to, instead of railing at, each other" (in Johnna's words); (2) to begin taking better care of themselves individually (Johnna did not want to lose any more weight); and (3) to try to recapture some of the closeness they had shared early in the marriage.

The TG equivalent of reframing a problem involves expanding the focus of therapy to highlight partners' roles in their larger families, rather than pathologizing the marriage. The therapist first intervened to diffuse this couple's mutual blame, by expanding the focus to illuminate their confusion instead. She pointed out Carl's elevated status in his family, and the fact that he was forced to maintain it with aloofness so that no one knew his real flaws and vulnerabilities. She then suggested to him that Johnna, who lived with him, was exquisitely aware of his aloofness and knew that it was interfering with intimacy. The therapist also pointed out to Johnna how she hid her own opinions and wishes, trying to "fit in," only to reap disapproval and rejection from parents and in-laws.

When spouses are able to voice their desire for change, a working alliance is comparatively easy. The therapist surmised that this husband and wife were becoming fused emotionally (i.e., expecting consensus and sameness) because of their lack of connection with either family. Carl's family had a history of being distant—a pattern typical of its German-descent, rural farming, Lutheran structure. Johnna's family was in a "rebound" state of mutual rejection and distancing because she was different from her parents and sister, and had pushed the limits of their protected world. It is not unusual for members of a fused couple to seek help, to miss past closeness, to experience distress and mood changes, or to have somatic symptoms, as Johnna did. However, the therapist also kept in mind that, given their profound isolation in the community and with their families, drawing each partner out individually in the marital "dance" would not be reassuring or comforting to them. The couple work would have to "hold," or contain, their underlying loneliness and fears of abandonment.

In the plan for treatment for Carl and Johnna, the therapist therefore built in several considerations:

- Each partner "needed" the defensive postures they had taken up in their marriage—Carl's posture of authority, steadiness and knowing all, and Johnna's position of pleading, suffering, and self-denial.
- In order to break up this pattern with cooperation, the therapist would have to help them to understand the benefits of letting go: letting go

of authority and of "knowing all" (Carl) and of self-denial (Johnna).

- Each partner would have to extend any changes to their relationships with their families of origin, in order to ensure long-term gains.
- Although both partners appeared "equal" in their say in the marriage, Carl was being given more authority, due to his gender, their Christian heritage, and his secure job.
- Carl got his ammunition from verbal contests and rejection (not coming home), while Johnna argued quietly and metaphorically, with her body and the threat of illness.
- Any changes made in the marriage would have to respect the fact that Johnna's fundamentalist faith would ultimately color her choices regarding her role as a wife, daughter, and helping professional.

The therapist examined with the couple the three outstanding issues they had named, expanding each one through conversation and family-of-origin discussion. She first addressed their intense fusion by reordering their goals. Taking care of themselves emotionally and physically was to come first, with the awareness that there was little help to be had if one or both partners fell sick in a new neighborhood with no family in a demanding military environment. Second would come help in "talking to, instead of railing at" each other. Using Johnna's formulation for this problem captured their blaming problem in useful, concrete terms, and gave a boost to Johnna's efforts to express herself. It would also create a dialogue that could ideally lead to fuller, clearer views of their individual needs and wishes, without abrupt segues into bitter accusations, pointed fasting episodes (Johnna), or walking out (Carl).

Last would come the more difficult focus on recapturing the closeness they had shared. Increasing deep self-disclosure and self-expression often removes the blocks to intimate understanding that push couples apart. However, in the beginning it is never very clear how spouses define closeness, the degree of intimacy they enjoyed in the past, and the potential remaining after years of conflict and disappointment. Intimacy is partly a function of differentiation (self-awareness), which is easier to address after trust and reliability have been restored. The therapist shared with Johnna and Carl her reordering of these goals, even holding out "more intimacy" as a tantalizing plum that could perhaps be plucked when each partner was fully in control of his/her own feelings and decisions.

The couple was enthusiastic about the plan, and the therapy launched into a discussion of Johnna's descent into self-starvation. Not surprisingly, Johnna immediately tied her illness and weight loss to the stress of traveling to Carl's home state in December, and the lack of support she felt among his family. This was an occasion to begin focusing on Carl's defensive mode (which was activated immediately) and Johnna's attempts to push back by being sick. Carl was invited to consider Johnna's position in his possessive family, and the underlying problems this entailed for him: lack of respect for his marital choice; withholding of support by those who claimed to love him; and a failure to "rally around" after his father's death to truly act like a family. Johnna was urged to look at the burden she was placing on her emotional and physical well-being, the threats to her health and energy, and the fact that it was easier for others (including her own father) to dismiss her as weak or distressed when she wouldn't even feed herself. The bottom line in the therapy was for the spouses to be protecting themselves first, and each other second.

This conversation was to repeat itself many times over the next 4 months, and served to "unpack" or deconstruct their most destructive behaviors (disengagement and starvation) into their symbolic and relational meanings. In my experience, expansion of symptoms into a relational and especially a TG focus captures the intense affects and disaffections that accompany symptoms, and diffuses the intensity of the symptoms. (Sometimes merely the opportunity to "go against" long-term family pressures leads clients to control their own symptoms.)

As Johnna worked on getting more calories into herself and renewing her physical energy, Carl began to take a frank look at whether he himself liked his family's treatment of his wife. Now that this was reframed to Carl as a rejection of his marital choice, he was not satisfied with his mother's and sisters' expectations. He began to acknowledge to Johnna that he was not satisfied, and admitted the ways that pressures around holidays and receiving mail made him tense, unhappy, and on guard. The spouses were now engaged in attending to their own symptoms and understanding their origins—the first goal of the therapy.

The therapist encouraged them to begin discussing the pattern of their fights, especially the presence of accusations ("He got his way," "She's not even trying with my mother"), blaming ("If she would make some friends, she wouldn't feel so upset all the time"), leaving the home ("She's being a shrew, so I'm going to work"), and pointed fasting ("He wasn't going to be home for dinner, so I didn't feel like making it"). The therapist wanted Johnna to know that she was able to "put things in a nutshell" when she allowed herself. She was urged to find ways to voice her opinions instead of giving Carl feedback about himself at this time. A TG piece was added by examining the ways in which Johnna's mother and other women in the family voiced their opinions, at home or in church. Johnna did not have much to go on, since her parents hid their own marital discussions. She was asked to consider how her mother and sister showed her their opinions, however obliquely. She began to see that focusing on Carl, who argued back, did not help her to express her own issues, which centered on rage at her parents; hurt at cutoff from her church friends and sister; and total lack of compatibility with her new, transient, unaffiliated military community. Thus Johnna was moved toward more of a focus on self-in-relation, as opposed to a focus on others, and was asked to consider her worth.

Carl had a problem with overwork, seriousness, and a "wet-blanket" attitude that interfered with personal friendships. His know-all approach prevented his men from liking him more, and his tendency to walk out the door tested Johnna's considerable loyalty. He admitted that he knew that Johnna was frequently left waiting for him—one reason why she kept cutting short any afternoon plans to rush home, only to watch the dinner she prepared get cold. Although he had not acknowledged the unfairness of this, he was readily able to say that if he kept fellow staffers waiting or spoiled a project, his career would have been over. Carl was asked to move toward a position of greater consideration for Johnna, and to make comments to assert himself rather than to wound.

Conversations about use of baiting, taunts, and covert threats (e.g, Carl prepared for a 1-month cruise and did not tell Johnna about it until all the other wives already knew) led into discussions regarding the past. Carl saw that he had been used to a great deal of respect in his family as the only son, and his bond with his father consisted of a kind of mutual approval—two members of some kind of club, the calmer and more practical sex. He had never had to tolerate a close examination of his feelings, motives, or expectations, and did not see Johnna's marital challenges as a good thing. As Carl became willing to discuss his position, the therapist was able to point out the possible advantages of mutual understanding, friendship, and intimacy that might come from giving up the privileged marital "high ground." Johnna had some painful memories of watching her mother silently go along with decisions her father made. For example, in her family, her father's parents received the lion's share of visits and phone calls. Her mother's parents did not live far away, but they were pushed to the side, and her mother did not insist on time with her own family. Johnna saw that some of her angry accusations ("He always gets his way") stemmed from a sense of inequity in the way her own family worked, and sadness at the way that her mother and her sister made themselves accommodating and invisible. As she began to talk more openly about her sadness about her family situation, Carl became much more spontaneously affectionate, caring, and interested.

Each partner was now asked to convey to his/her family some of the ideas he/she was learning about their individual problems, and about what needed to change in order to foster better health. Johnna called her sister and began to rebuild a connection for the first time, checking on how Sarah was doing at home and inviting her to come for a visit. Carl decided to write to his mother and explain how important his marriage to Johnna was in his life, and in his sense of belonging and security when he was deployed so frequently. His task was to explain why this was necessary for his welfare, and only secondarily to ask his mother to show more understanding for himself and his wife. This step in therapy, called "coaching," is primarily a task to test a client's ability to manage stress personally through contact with old family issues.

Sarah did come for a week-long visit during the summer. The two sisters spent time alone for the first time, and Johnna was able to fulfill one of her values—caring for a relative. She took great pride in opening her home to Sarah, and talked to her a little about how her work as a nurse had also given her pride and a feeling of spiritual accomplishment. Although the siblings did not focus on their parents' disapproval of Johnna, Sarah expressed her love, and Johnna began to feel more of a sense of worth. She did not see herself as having dropped off the face of the earth now, and after the visit she began to take an interest in meeting other women at the base and in her neighborhood.

At this point in the therapy, Carl was now home on time most evenings, and there were fewer blowups. Johnna had regained a good amount of weight and was physically well, and the partners

were lovers again. Johnna searched for and found a church they both liked, with a warm minister and an active Sunday school where she began to teach. She also volunteered at the community's free clinic. Fall arrived, and the therapist suggested that the spouses tackle how they would handle the next Christmas holiday. As is often the case, neither spouse seemed eager to discuss it ahead of time—as if avoiding the subject would somehow resolve the stalemated situation.

TG theory holds that families are organized in long-term patterns, with both "horizontal" (life cycle) stressors and "vertical" (cross-generational) stressors. Solving here-and-now interactional problems does not make long-term stressors in family life disappear.[2] Symptom-focused work *can* point the way and teach skills for families to solve similar life crises, but does not create long-term protective effects as family-of-origin work can. It was soon apparent that coaching was important in maintaining the changes that Johnna and Carl had made in their own relationship. When Carl's mother called to ask the couple to stay at her home Christmas week, she stayed on the phone at length to tell Carl that a sister was separating. She asked that Carl intervene, and Carl did just that. He did not fill Johnna in until several days later, and Johnna meanwhile watched a series of urgent phone calls pass back and forth to Carl's home state from the sidelines. This time, Johnna did not feel hurt. She went about her activities and spent time with friends, and told Carl that she would make time for him as well when he showed that he wanted her company. Only 3 days of this were necessary before Carl told his family that he had no more advice for them, and asked them to leave him and Johnna in peace. That Christmas, the mother and sisters were much more inclusive of Johnna than before.

Shortly after the couple finished therapy, Johnna called to say that they were doing well, but that they had come through a difficult time together. Sarah had become engaged to a man that she had met through her part-time job, who was not a Christian. She and her fiancé had been married by a justice of the peace, without informing the parents or Johnna, and sent a note afterward. Johnna had been devastated, and for some weeks she felt shocked and completely left out. She and her sister began talking by phone a great deal after that, and Johnna found herself only now starting to realize how pressured and hesitant they both had felt about revealing themselves. It was the beginning of a real relationship between the sisters. They now had a life together quite separate from their parents, and an alliance to address the thorny problems of religious difference and tolerance between parents and daughters.

NOTES

1. Throughout this chapter, the terms "marital" and "marriage" are used along with "couple" to describe committed partnership. Gay and lesbian couples are included, although they are not allowed legally to marry at the time of this writing.
2. Paul Watzlawick has commented that even in the brief problem-focused model of the Mental Research Institute, "couples must define a clear problem to resolve . . . later, if there is another problem, they can return to therapy to solve that problem" (personal communication, 1984).

REFERENCES

Abrams, M. S. (1999). Intergenerational transmission of trauma: Recent contributions from the literature of family systems approaches to treatment. *American Journal of Psychotherapy, 53*, 225–231.

Boszormenyi-Nagy, I. (1962). The concept of schizophrenia from the point of view of family treatment. *Family Process, 1*, 103–113.

Boszormenyi-Nagy, I. (1965). A theory of relationships: Experience and transaction. In I. Boszormenyi-Nagy & J. L. Framo (Eds.), *Intensive family therapy: Theoretical and practical aspects* (pp. 33–86). New York: Hoeber.

Boszormenyi-Nagy, I. (1972). Loyalty implications of the transference model in psychotherapy. *Archives of General Psychiatry, 27*, 374–380.

Boszormeny-Nagy, I., & Krasner, B. (1986). *Between give and take: A clinical guide to contextual therapy.* New York: Brunner/Mazel.

Boszormenyi-Nagy, I., & Spark, G. (1973). *Invisible loyalties.* Hagerstown, MD: Harper & Row.

Boszormenyi-Nagy, I.,& Ulrich, D. N. (1981). Contextual family therapy. In A. S. Gurman & D. P. Kniskern (Eds.), *Handbook of family therapy* (pp. 159–186). New York: Brunner/Mazel.

Bowen, M. (1974). Toward the differentiation of self in one's own family of origin. In F. Andres & J. Lorio (Eds.), *Georgetown Family Symposia* (Vol. 1). Washington, DC: Georgetown Medical Center.

Bowen, M. (1985). The use of family theory in clinical practice. In M. Bowen, *Family therapy in clinical practice* (3rd ed., pp. 147–181). Northvale, NJ: Jason Aronson. (Original work published 1966)

Bowen, M. (1985). On the differentiation of self. In M. Bowen, *Family therapy in clinical practice* (3rd edition, pp. 467–528). Northvale, NJ: Jason Aronson. (Original work published anonymously, 1972)

Bowlby, J. (1969). *Attachment and loss: Vol. 1. Attachment.* New York: Basic Books.

Bowlby, J. (1973). *Attachment and loss: Vol. 2. Separation: Anxiety and anger.* New York: Basic Books.

Braverman, S. (1981). Family of origin: The view from the parents' side. *Family Process, 20*, 431–437.

Buber, M. (1958). *I and Thou.* (2nd revised edition with postscript by author added. Trans. Smith R. G.). New York: Charles Scribner's Sons.

Byng-Hall, J. J. (1980). The symptom bearer as marital distance regulator: Clinical implications. *Family Process, 19*, 355–365.

Campbell, J. L., Masters, M. A., & Johnson, M. E. (1998). Relationship of parental alcoholism to family-of-origin functioning and current marital satisfaction. *Journal of Addictions and Offender Counseling, 19*, 7–14.

Carter, B., & McGoldrick, M. (Eds.). (1989). *The changing family life cycle: A framework for family therapy* (2nd ed.). Boston: Allyn & Bacon.

Damasio, A. R. (1994). *Descartes' error: Emotion, reason and the human brain.* New York: Putnam.

Dicks, H. V. (1963). Object relations theory and marital status. *British Journal of Medical Psychology, 36*, 125–129.

Fairbairn, W. R. D. (1952). *An object-relations view of the personality.* New York: Basic Books.

Fishbane, M. D. (1999). Honor thy mother and thy father: Intergenerational spirituality and Jewish tradition. In F. Walsh (Ed.), *Spiritual resources in family therapy* (pp. 136–156). New York: Guilford Press.

Fogarty, T. F. (1978). On emptiness and closeness. In E. Pendagast (Ed.), *The best of the family* (pp. 70–90). New Rochelle, NY: Center For Family Learning.

Fraiberg, S. (Ed.), & Fraiberg, L. (Collaborator). (1980). *Clinical studies in infant mental health.* New York: Basic Books.

Framo, J. (1976). Family of origin as a therapeutic resource to couples therapy: You can and should go home again. *Family Process, 15*, 193–210.

Framo, J. (1981). The integration of marital therapy with sessions with family of origin. In A. S. Gurman & D. P. Kniskern (Eds.), *Handbook of family therapy* (pp. 133–158). New York: Brunner/Mazel.

Friedman, E. H. (1985). *Generation to generation: Family process in church and synagogue.* New York: Guilford Press.

Friedman, H., Rohrbaugh, M., & Krakauer, S. (1988). The time-line genogram: Highlighting temporal aspects of family relationships. *Family Process, 27*, 293–303.

Freud, S. (1937). Analysis terminable and interminable. *Standard Edition, 23*, 216–253.

Fromm-Reichmann, F. (1950). *Principles of intensive psychotherapy.* Chicago: University of Chicago Press.

Goldner, V. (1995). Boys will be men: A response to Terry Real's paper. *Journal of Feminist Family Therapy, 7*, 45–48.

Goldner, V. (1998). The treatment of violence and victimization in intimate relationships. *Family Process, 37*, 263–286.

Goodrich, T. J. (Ed.). (1991). *Women and power: Perspectives for family therapy.* New York: W. W. Norton and Company.

Goodrich, T. J., Rampage, C., Ellman, B.,& Halstead, K. (1988). *Feminist family therapy: A casebook.* New York: Norton.

Goodrow, K. K., & Lim, M. (1997). Bowenian theory in application: A case study of a couple intending to marry. *Journal of Family Psychotherapy, 8,* 33–42.

Gottman, J. M. (1994). *What predicts divorce?* Hillsdale, NJ: Erlbaum.

Gottman, J. M., & Levenson, R. W. (1999a). What predicts change in marital interaction over time?: A study of alternative models. *Family Process, 38,* 143–158.

Gottman, J. M., & Levenson, R. W. (1999b). How stable is marital interaction over time? *Family Process, 38,* 159–165.

Guerin, P. J., Jr., & Pendagast, E. G. (1976). Evaluation of family system and genogram. In P. J. Guerin, Jr. (Ed.), *Family therapy: Theory and practice* (pp. 450–464). New York: Gardner Press.

Hare-Mustin, R. T. (1987). The problem of gender in family therapy theory. *Family Process, 26,* 15–33.

Hargrave, T. D. (1994). *Families and forgiveness: Healing wounds in the intergenerational family.* New York: Brunner/Mazel.

Hargrave, T. D., & Anderson, W. T. (1992). *Finishing well: Ageing and reparation in the intergenerational family.* New York: Brunner/Mazel.

Haws, W. A., & Mallinckrodt, B. (1998). Separation–individuation from family of origin and marital adjustment of recently married couples. *American Journal of Family Therapy, 26,* 293–306.

Jackson, D., & Lederer, W. (1968). *The mirages of marriage.* New York: Norton.

Jankowski, M. K., Leitenberg, H., Henning, K., & Coffey, P. (1999). Intergenerational transmission of dating aggression as a function of witnessing only same sex parents vs. opposite sex parents vs. both parents as perpetrators of domestic violence. *Journal of Family Violence, 14,* 267–279.

Johnson, S. M., & Greenberg, L. S. (1994). *The heart of the matter: Perspectives on emotion in marital therapy.* New York: Brunner/Mazel.

Johnson, S. M., & Lebow, J. (2000). The "coming of age" of couple therapy: A decade review. *Journal of Marital and Family Therapy, 26,* 23–38.

Jordan, J. V. (1991). The meaning of mutuality. In J. V. Jordan, A. G. Kaplan, J. B. Miller, I. P. Stiver, & J. L. Surrey (Eds.), *Women's growth in connection: Writings from the Stone Center* (pp. 81–96). New York: Guilford Press.

Jordan, J. V., Kaplan, A. G., Miller, J. B., Stiver, I. P., & Surrey, J. L. (Eds.). (1991). *Women's growth in connection: Writings from the Stone Center.* New York: Guilford Press.

Jory, B., & Anderson, D. (1999). Intimate justice: II. Fostering mutuality, reciprocity, and accomodation in therapy for psychological abuse. *Journal of Marital and Family Therapy, 25,* 349–364.

Jory, B., Anderson, D., & Greer, C. (1997). Intimate justice: Confronting issues of accountability, respect, and freedom in treatment for abuse and violence. *Journal of Marital and Family Therapy, 23,* 399–419.

Juni, S. (1992). Family dyadic patterns in defenses and object relations. *Contemporary Family Therapy: An International Journal, 14,* 259–268.

Kerr, M. E. (1981). Family systems theory and therapy. In A. S. Gurman & D. P. Kniskern (Eds.), *Handbook of family therapy* (pp. 226–264). New York: Brunner/Mazel.

Kerr, M. E. (1985). Obstacles to differentiation of self. In A. S. Gurman (Ed.), *Casebook of marital therapy* (pp. 111–154). New York: Guilford Press.

Klein, M. (1957). *Envy and gratitude.* New York: Basic Books.

Knudson-Martin, C. (1994). The female voice: Applications to Bowen's family systems theory. *Journal of Marital and Family Therapy, 20,* 35–46.

Knudson-Martin, C., & Mahoney, A. R. (1999). Beyond different worlds: A "postgender" approach to relational development. *Family Process, 38,* 325–340.

Larson, J. H., & Thayne, T. R. (1998). Marital attitudes and personal readiness for marriage of young adult children on alcoholics. *Alcoholism Quarterly, 16,* 59–73.

Lebow, J. L. (1999). Building a science of couple relationships: Comments on two articles by Gottman and Levenson. *Family Process, 38,* 167–173.

Mahler, M., Pine, F., & Bergman, A. (1975). *The psychological birth of the human infant: Symbiosis and individuation.* New York: Basic Books.

Manlove, J. (1997). Early motherhood in an intergenerational perspective: The experiences of a British cohort. *Journal of Marriage and the Family, 59,* 263–279.

McGoldrick, M. (1989). Ethnicity and the family life cycle. In B. Carter & M. McGoldrick (Eds.), *The changing family life cycle: A framework for family therapy* (pp. 70–91). Boston: Allyn & Bacon.

McGoldrick, M., & Gerson, R. (1985). *Genograms in family assessment.* New York: Norton.

McGoldrick, M., Gerson, R., & Shellenberger, S. (1999). *Genograms: Assessment and intervention.* New York: Norton.

McGoldrick, M., Giordano, J., & Pearce, J. K. (Eds.). (1996). *Ethnicity and family therapy* (2nd ed.). New York: Guilford Press.

Minuchin, S., Montalvo, B., Guerney, B. G., Rosman, B. L., & Schumer, F. (1967). *Families of the slums: An exploration of their structure and treatment.* New York: Basic Books.

Napier, A. Y. (1983). *Coming of age: Reflections on the journey.* Address presented at the 41st Annual Meeting of the American Association for Marriage and Family Therapy, Washington, DC.

Napier, A. Y., & Whitaker, C. A. (1978). *The family crucible.* New York: Harper & Row.

Neill, J. R., & Kniskern, D. P. (Eds.). (1982). *From psyche to system: The evolving therapy of Carl Whitaker.* New York: Guilford Press.

Nelson, B. S., & Wampler, K. S. (2000). Systemic effects of trauma in clinic couples: An exploratory study of secondary trauma resulting from childhood abuse. *Journal of Marital and Family Therapy, 26,* 171–184.

Paul, N. L. (1967). The role of mourning and empathy in conjoint marital therapy. In G. H. Zuk & I. Boszormenyi-Nagy (Eds.), *Family therapy and disturbed families* (pp. 186–205). Palo Alto, CA: Science & Behavior Books.

Roberto, L. G. (1991). Symbolic–experiential family therapy. In A. S. Gurman & D. P. Kniskern (Eds.), *Handbook of family therapy* (Vol. 2, pp. 444–476). New York: Brunner/Mazel.

Roberto, L. G. (1992). *Transgenerational therapies.* New York: Guilford Press.

Roberto, L. G. (1998). Transgenerational family therapy. In F. M. Dattilio (Eds.), *Case studies in couple and family therapy: Systemic and cognitive perspectives* (pp. 257–277). New York: Guilford Press.

Sager, C. J. (1976). *Marriage contracts and couple therapy.* New York: Brunner/Mazel.

Satir, V. (1983). *Conjoint family therapy* (3rd ed.). Palo Alto, CA: Science & Behavior Books.

Scharff, D. E. (1989). Family therapy and sexual development: An object relations approach. In D. Kantor & B. F. Okun (Eds.), *Intimate environments: Sex, intimacy, and gender in families* (pp. 1–27). New York: Guilford Press.

Scharff, D. E., & Scharff, J. S. (1987). *Object relations family therapy.* Northvale, NJ: Jason Aronson.

Scheel, M. J., Forsythe, N., Kristjansson, S., Pranata, H., Packard, T., & Packard, K. (2000). Marital enrichment: Linking research to practice. *The Family Psychologist, 16,* 6–10.

Schnarch, D. (1997). *Passionate marriage: Love, sex, and intimacy in emotionally committed relationships.* New York: Henry Holt.

Schwartz, R. C., & Johnson, S. M. (2000). Commentary: Does couple and family therapy have emotional intelligence? *Family Process, 39,* 29–33.

Searles, H. F. (1960). *The nonhuman environment in normal development and in schizophrenia.* New York: International Universities Press.

Selvini Palazzoli, M. (1974). *Self-starvation: From the intrapsychic to the transpersonal approach to anorexia nervosa.* London: Human Context Books.

Slipp, S. (1984). *Object relations: A dynamic bridge between individual and family treatment.* New York: Jason Aronson.

Slipp, S. (1994). *Object relations and gender development.* Paper presented at the 16th Annual Meeting of the American Family Therapy Academy, Santa Fe, NM.

Stierlin, H. (1981). *Separating parents and adolescents* (2nd ed.). New York: Jason Aronson.

Sullivan, H. S. (1953). *The interpersonal theory of psychiatry.* New York: Norton.

Thornton, A. (1991). Influence of the marital history of parents on the marital and cohabitational experiences of children. *American Journal of Sociology, 96,* 868–894.

VanLear, C. A. (1992). Marital communication across the generations: Learning and rebellion, continuity and change. *Journal of Social and Personal Relationships, 9,* 103–123.

Wachtel, E. F. (1982). The family psyche over three generations: The genogram revisited. *Journal of Marital and Family Therapy, 8,* 335–343.

Wallerstein, J. S. (1996). The psychological tasks of marriage: II. *American Journal of Orthopsychiatry, 66,* 217–227.

Walters, M., Carter, B., Papp, P., & Silverstein, O. (1988). *The invisible web: Gender patterns in family relationships.* New York: Guilford Press.

Watzlawick, P. (Chair). (1984). *The problems of change, the change of problems.* Invited seminar presented at the Eastern Virginia Family Therapy Institute, Norfolk, VA.

Whitaker, C. A. (1982). Gatherings. In J. R. Neill & D. P. Kniskern (Eds.), *From psyche to system: The evolving therapy of Carl Whitaker* (pp. 365–375). New York: Guilford Press.

Whitaker, C. A. (1982). Three types of craziness. In J. R. Neill & D. P. Kniskern (Eds.), *For psyche to system: The evolving therapy of Carl Whitaker* (pp. 36–37). New York: Guilford Press.

Whitaker, C. A., & Keith, D. V. (1981). Symbolic–experiential family therapy. In A. S. Gurman & D. P. Kniskern (Eds.), *Handbook of family therapy* (pp. 187–224). New York: Brunner/Mazel.

Whitaker, C. A., & Ryan, M. C. (1989). *Midnight musings of a family therapist.* New York: Norton.

Will, O. A. (1958). Psychotherapeutics and the schizophrenic reaction. *Journal of Nervous and Mental Disease, 126,* 109–140.

Williamson, D. (1981). Personal authority via termination of the intergenerational hierarchical boundary: A "new" stage in the family life cycle. *Journal of Marital and Family Therapy, 7,* 441–452.

Williamson, D. (1982a). Personal authority in family experience via termination of the intergenerational hierarchical boundary: Part II. The consultation process and the therapeutic method. *Journal of Marital and Family Therapy, 8,* 23–37.

Williamson, D. (1982b). Personal authority in family experience via termination of the intergenerational hierarchical boundary: Part III. Personal authority defined, and the power of play in the change process. *Journal of Marital and Family Therapy, 8,* 309–323.

Winnicott, D. W. (1965). *The maturational processes and the facilitating environment.* New York: International Universities Press.

Wynne, L. (1965). Some indications and contraindications for exploratory family therapy. In I. Boszormenyi-Nagy & J. Framo (Eds.), *Intensive family therapy: Theoretical and practical aspects* (pp. 289–322). New York: Harper & Row.

Section B

Integrative Approaches

Chapter 6

Affective Reconstruction: A Pluralistic, Developmental Approach

DOUGLAS K. SNYDER
W. JOEL SCHNEIDER

Our pluralistic approach to couple therapy incorporating insight-oriented interventions derives from three assertions. First, an important source of couples' current difficulties frequently consists of previous relationship injuries, which have resulted in sustained interpersonal vulnerabilities and related defensive strategies interfering with emotional intimacy. Moreover, therapeutic approaches that fail to address developmental experiences giving rise to these vulnerabilities and their associated reactivities deprive individuals of a rich resource for understanding both their own and their partners' behaviors—one that could help them to depersonalize the hurtful aspects of their couple interactions and to adopt an empathic stance. However, couples often enter therapy with debilitating crises, deficient relationship skills, or exaggerated defensive postures that preclude their making effective use of an interpretive approach; hence, insight-oriented techniques need to be implemented strategically within a hierarchical, pluralistic model incorporating structural, behavioral, and cognitive interventions earlier in the therapeutic sequence.

In this chapter we emphasize the use of "affective reconstruction"—that is, the interpretation of persistent maladaptive relationship patterns as having their source in previous developmental experiences—within a pluralistic approach building on interventions from alternative theoretical modalities. We begin by describing both the rationale and basic strategies for incorporating multiple theoretical approaches into couple therapy. Because the structural and cognitive-behavioral components of our pluralistic model have been well articulated by others, we focus instead on diverse interpretive approaches to couple therapy and place our own techniques of affective reconstruction within this broader theoretical and historical context. Both the pluralistic model and the approach to affective reconstruction advocated here are contrasted with alternative integrative and interpretive approaches to couple therapy. Initial assessment methods and case formulation, structural considerations, and assumptions underlying the therapist's role as well as the selection and timing of interventions are considered from the perspectives of both affective reconstruction and our broader pluralistic model. A case example illustrates principles of affective reconstruction and one type of couple for which this approach may be particularly useful. The chapter concludes with clinical considerations in practicing competently from a pluralistic perspective.

A PLURALISTIC, DEVELOPMENTAL MODEL

Rationale for Integrative Approaches

The empirical literature provides multiple grounds for challenging the universal efficacy of any one theoretical modality of couple therapy. These include findings regarding (1) the limited effects of any single theoretical approach on couples' long-term response to clinical interventions; (2) the diversity of couples' presenting difficulties across individual, dyadic, and broader systemic domains; and (3) the relation of individual differences to treatment outcome (cf. Lebow, 1997).

Previous reviews affirm that various versions of couple therapy produce moderate, statistically significant, and often clinically significant effects (Baucom, Shoham, Mueser, Daiuto, & Stickle, 1998; Christensen & Heavey, 1999; Lebow & Gurman, 1995; Shadish et al., 1993; Whisman & Snyder, 1997). However, approximately 35% of couples fail to achieve significant gains from treatment. In only 50% of treated couples do both partners show significant improvement in marital satisfaction at termination—a limitation noted by Jacobson and Christensen (1996) as "characteristic of marital therapy outcome research in general" (p. 6). Moreover, long-term follow-up studies of couple therapy show significant deterioration among 30–60% of treated couples following termination (Cookerly, 1980; Jacobson, Schmaling, & Holtzworth-Munroe, 1987; Snyder, Wills, & Grady-Fletcher, 1991a).

What accounts for the limited efficacy of couple therapy? Couple therapists confront a tremendous diversity of presenting issues, couple and family structures, individual dynamics and psychopathology, and psychosocial stressors characterizing couples in distress. Moreover, there exists modest but growing evidence that couple differences in these domains are related to treatment outcome (Snyder, Cozzi, & Mangrum, 2002; Snyder, Mangrum, & Wills, 1993). Because the functional sources of couples' distress vary so dramatically, the critical mediators or mechanisms of change should also be expected to vary—as should the therapeutic strategies intended to facilitate positive change.

The diverse patterns of factors contributing to couples' distress are addressed at varying levels of success by different treatment modalities. Even within the more restricted domain of individual interventions, growing recognition of the unique strengths and limitations of competing theoretical approaches has fueled a burgeoning movement toward psychotherapy integration. For example, advocates of various integrative models of psychotherapy have emphasized the strengths of psychodynamic approaches for identifying enduring problematic interpersonal themes, the benefits of experiential techniques for promoting emotional awareness, gains from cognitive interventions targeting dysfunctional beliefs and attributional processes, and advantages of behavioral strategies for promoting new patterns of behavior (Bongar & Beutler, 1995; Norcross & Goldfried, 1992).

Thus particularly complex or difficult couples may benefit most from a treatment strategy drawing from both conceptual and technical innovations in diverse theoretical models relevant to different components of a couple's struggles. That is, effective treatment is most likely to be rendered when the couple therapist has a solid grounding across diverse theoretical approaches, has acquired a rich repertoire of intervention techniques linked to theory, engages in comprehensive assessment of the couple and family system, and selectively draws on intervention strategies across the theoretical spectrum in a manner consistent with an explicit case formulation (Snyder, 1999a, 1999b).

Eclecticism, Integration, or Pluralism?

In contrast to previous decades, when clinicians often pledged allegiance to a specific theoretical school advocating its own class of therapeutic techniques, a majority of today's clinicians describe themselves as "eclectic" or "integrative"; the latter term is now preferred by a margin of nearly 2:1 (Norcross, Prochaska, & Farber, 1993). Although they are sometimes used interchangeably, there are important differences between eclecticism and integration. Moreover, in distinguishing between the terms, we prefer to add a third construct of "pluralism" and to arrange the constructs hierarchically. Pluralism, eclecticism, and integration are united in their assertion that no single theoretical perspective or therapeutic modality is likely to have optimal efficacy across all applications. Each draws on information or techniques from multiple domains reflecting alternative theories (e.g., object relations, social learning, cognitive, interpersonal, or systemic), epistemologies (e.g., rational, empirical, or experiential), and therapeutic modalities (e.g., individual, couple, family, or community).

"Eclecticism" refers to therapists' willingness to draw on therapeutic principles and techniques from diverse theoretical systems without an overarching or unifying framework. At its simplest level, such eclecticism may reflect a therapist's unsystematic but well-intentioned effort to do what's best for a particular client at a given moment (Beutler, Consoli, & Williams, 1995). While freeing the clinician from the constraints of theoretical myopia, the expedient borrowing of diverse principles or techniques without regard for their potential inconsistency in directing either the relative importance or timing of interventions renders both treatment and client vulnerable to haphazard, disjointed, and contradictory interventions—a limitation noted throughout the literature (e.g., Goldfried & Norcross, 1995; Lebow, 1997; Mahoney, 1991; Norcross, 1985; Patterson, 1997).

By comparison, "integration" entails a commitment to a conceptual synthesis beyond the technical blend of methods. The goal is to create a unified conceptual framework that synthesizes the best elements of two or more approaches of therapy into one (Goldfried & Norcross, 1995; Lebow, 1997). Some integrative approaches are primarily assimilative, in that they explain competing ideas in terms of a preferred theoretical framework. Others are more generative in combining two or more alternative approaches into a novel theoretical structure. However, in his review of integrative approaches to couple and family therapy, Lebow (1997) noted that a frequent shortcoming of integrative approaches is their failure to articulate the specific sequence in which various interventions incorporated from diverse theoretical modalities should be implemented. Moreover, he concluded that "no one integrative therapy has emerged as predominant, nor has there even appeared a serious contender for this distinction" (p. 3).

As an alternative to both eclecticism and integration, we advocate an "informed pluralistic" approach. Pluralism holds that no single theoretical, epistemological, or methodological approach is preeminent, and that there is no one, correct integrative system toward which the field of psychotherapy is evolving. Informed pluralism comprises a contextually based approach toward therapy integration (Safran & Messer, 1997). It is distinct from (1) common-factors approaches, emphasizing active but nonspecific components of therapeutic change processes; and (2) transtheoretical approaches, attempting to translate diverse theoretical models into a single unifying language. Pluralism potentially accommodates more diverse approaches whose basic tenets defy assimilation into a common theoretical framework.

Informed pluralism reflects a systematic conceptual framework distinguished from sloppy thinking or simply "doing what feels right." It is similar to the constructs of "empirical pragmatism" (Goldfried & Norcross, 1995), "systematic treatment selection" (Beutler & Clarkin, 1990), and "prescriptive eclecticism" (Norcross & Beutler, 2000). The last of these is characterized "by drawing on effective methods from across theoretical

camps (eclecticism), by matching those methods to particular cases on the basis of psychological science and clinical wisdom (prescriptionism), and by adhering to an explicit and orderly model of treatment selection" (Norcross & Beutler, 2000, p. 248).

Distinctions among eclecticism, integration, and pluralism at levels of both theory and practice are depicted in Figure 6.1. Similar to Norcross (1985), we regard integration as a subset of eclecticism in that the former draws on both theories and techniques from diverse approaches, but from a smaller universe than eclecticism, because contemporary integrative theories typically synthesize only a small number of theoretical perspectives while leaving many others unaddressed (Lebow, 1997). Although advocates of eclecticism could potentially select from the entire universe of principles and techniques across theoretical modalities, in practice most clinicians adopting an eclectic approach draw on the few theoretical perspectives encountered in their previous training experiences (Norcross & Beutler, 2000). Because a pluralistic approach is less constrained than integrative approaches forced to reconcile competing constructs, it benefits from greater opportunity to accommodate diverse theoretical perspectives. By its systematic inclusion of multiple approaches across the theoretical spectrum, a pluralistic approach also promotes greater attention to diverse constructs and interventions than is paid by the typical eclectic clinician.

Figure 6.1 also distinguishes among eclecticism, integration, and pluralism at the level of intervention versus theory. For example, one could practice eclectically within an integrative conceptual framework by drawing selectively on techniques congruent with that theory and excluding other interventions; we would predict that a clinician adopting this approach might be more effective with particular kinds of clients benefiting from systematic application of that integrative model, but less effective with other clients whose needs or symptomatic complexities fall outside the scope of that theoretical framework. Alternatively, one could practice integratively by synthetically incorporating diverse interventions for a given client, but without an overarching theoretical model guiding treatment selection across clients; we suspect that clinicians adopting this approach might be more effective with specific clients presenting with difficulties less well addressed by existing treatment approaches, but less effective with most clients overall because of the lack of systematic principles directing their selection and

Theory

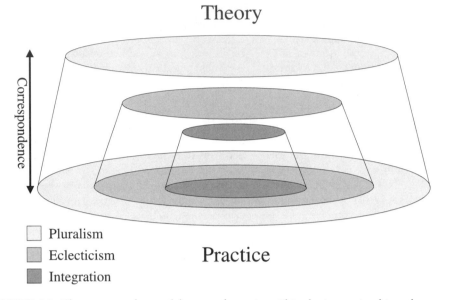

Pluralism

Eclecticism   **Practice**

Integration

FIGURE 6.1. The correspondence of theory and practice within the integration hierarchy.

timing of interventions. In Figure 6.1, the correspondence between theory and practice for any given therapist at any moment is reflected by the vertical distance between the two levels.

A Sequential Model for Organizing Couple Interventions

The pluralistic approach to couple therapy proposed previously by Snyder (1999a, 1999b) and advocated here conceptualizes therapeutic tasks as progressing sequentially along a hierarchy reflecting a couple's overall level of functioning—from the most chaotic relationship rooted in significant behavioral dyscontrol in one or both partners, to the relatively benign but unfulfilled relationship in which conflicts involving such issues as autonomy or trust compromise emotional intimacy. The therapeutic tasks of couple therapy can be conceptualized as comprising six levels of intervention (see Figure 6.2). This model proposes a progression from the most fundamental interventions promoting a collaborative alliance, to more challenging interventions addressing developmental sources of relationship distress. Couples enter treatment at varying levels of functioning and require different initial interventions. Because couple therapy often proceeds in nonlinear fashion, the model depicts flexibility of returning to earlier therapeutic tasks as dictated by individual or relationship difficulties.

The most fundamental step in couple therapy involves developing a collaborative alliance between partners and between each partner and the therapist (Gurman, 1981; Jacobson & Margolin, 1979). The collaborative alliance begins with establishing an atmosphere of therapist competence by engaging in relevant assessment and modeling appropriate communication behaviors. The collaborative alliance also requires establishing an atmosphere of safety by limiting partners' negative exchanges and clarifying policies governing such issues as confidentiality. Finally, the collaborative alliance is strengthened by offering a clear formulation of the couple's difficulties, outlining treatment objectives and basic strategies, and defining all participants' respective roles.

Couples sometimes present with disabling relationship crises that, until resolved, preclude development of relationship skills and progress toward emotional intimacy. Occasionally such crises emerge in otherwise healthy couples who experience unexpected job loss or financial hardship, illness or death of a family member, an unplanned or terminated pregnancy, or similar events. In such crises, therapists can assist couples in developing more adaptive attributions regarding their distress by distinguishing external stressors from relationship characteristics and by actively promoting intermediate solutions (Shoham, Rohrbaugh, & Patterson, 1995; see also Shoham & Rohrbaugh, Chapter 1, this volume). More often, relationship

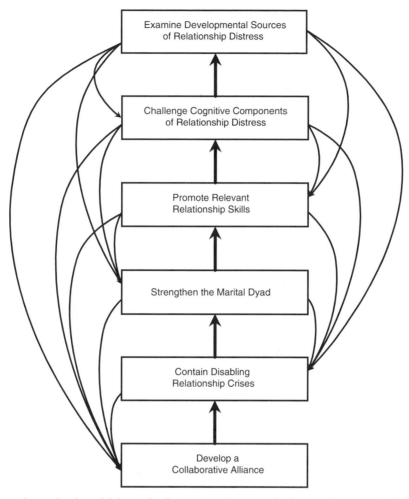

FIGURE 6.2. A hierarchical model for a pluralistic approach to couple therapy. From Snyder (1999b), in *Casebook in Family Therapy*, 1st edition, by D. M. Lawson and F. Prevatt. © 1999. Reprinted with permission of Wadsworth, an imprint of the Wadsworth Group, a division of Thomson Learning.

crises among couples presenting for therapy occur against a backdrop of communication deficits and an impoverished or insecure emotional context. A common crisis involves physical aggression by one or both partners against the other (Holtzworth-Munroe, Beatty, & Anglin, 1995; see also Holtzworth-Munroe, Meehan, Rehman, & Marshall, Chapter 16, this volume). Other crises requiring immediate attention involve major psychopathology and substance use disorders (Halford & Bouma, 1997). Although such crises nearly always contribute to and are frequently exacerbated by relationship difficulties, separate treatment for individual partners or other family members is often warranted—including medical, legal, financial, or other psychosocial interventions.

Couples in distress often describe an erosion of positive exchanges that leaves the relationship more vulnerable to subsequent challenges and conflicts. For such couples, reducing conflict is not sufficient for restoring a healthy relationship; increasing positive interactions is also vital. With only a modicum of direction from a therapist, relatively well-functioning couples can sometimes mobilize dormant communication skills in constructing positive change agreements on their own (Jacobson & Christensen, 1996). However, other couples often require direct therapist interventions aimed at strengthening the relationship and securing a foundation of good will, so that the couples can pursue the more difficult task of developing skills of their own. Strengthening a relationship sometimes requires little more than clearly identifying the dyad as the primary family unit, promoting a hierarchical organization of responsibility and influence within the family system, and establishing appropriate boundaries with respect to the partners' families of origin (Todd, 1986). More often, couples with overwhelming negativity require specific positive exchange agreements negotiated to a large degree by the therapist. That is, at this earlier developmental stage of a couple's therapy, the therapist may need to instigate behavior change directly before assisting the partners to develop behavior exchange and communication skills of their own.

Sustaining a satisfying relationship requires a broad range of skills. Primary among these are communication skills including emotional expressiveness, empathic listening, and conflict resolution (Baucom & Epstein, 1990; Epstein & Baucom, in press). However, the essential skills for a satisfying relationship extend beyond communication. In many domains, effective communication presumes a prerequisite knowledge base—something partners often lack and must be provided with by the therapist or through adjunct resources identified by the therapist. Examples include competence related to parenting (Sanders, Markie-Dadds, & Nicholson, 1997), financial management (Aniol & Snyder, 1997), and negotiating competing demands on time (Thompson, 1997). As with more basic communication skills, the effective couple therapist provides information, assists the couple in developing relevant new skills, and directs the couple to additional sources of information and support outside of therapy.

Common impediments to behavior change are misconceptions and other interpretive errors that individuals may make about both their own and their partners' behavior (Epstein, Baucom, & Daiuto, 1997). Not only do such cognitive mediators contribute to negative affect, but they also result in behavioral strategies that frequently maintain or exacerbate relationship distress. A couple's resistance to interventions aimed directly at strengthening the dyad or promoting relevant relationship skills can often be diminished by examining and restructuring cognitive processes interfering with behavior change efforts. A considerable body of literature has emerged regarding both the nature of cognitive components contributing to relationship distress and strategies for intervention (Baucom & Epstein, 1990; Bradbury & Fincham, 1990; Dattilio & Padesky, 1990).

However, not all psychological processes relevant to couples' interactions lend themselves to traditional cognitive interventions. A primary source of beliefs and expectancies regarding intimate relationships consists of partners' developmental experiences within their families of origin and other prior significant relationships (Gurman, 1992; Snyder, 1999a). Such expectancies operate at multiple levels of awareness and contribute to both affective and behavioral predispositions that may drive interpersonal exchanges in a distorted or exaggerated manner. Of particular importance are previous relationship injuries resulting in sustained interpersonal vulnerabilities and related defensive strategies interfering with emotional intimacy, many of which operate beyond partners' conscious awareness. Consequently, interpretation of maladaptive relationship patterns evolving from developmental processes is an essential component of an informed pluralistic approach to couple therapy.

AFFECTIVE RECONSTRUCTION: INTERPRETING MALADAPTIVE RELATIONSHIP THEMES

Developmental origins of interpersonal themes and their manifestation in a couple's relationship are explored in a process we refer to as "affective reconstruction" (Snyder, 1999a; Snyder & Wills, 1989; Wills, Faitler, & Snyder, 1987)—roughly akin to traditional interpretive strategies promoting insight, but emphasizing interpersonal schemas and relationship dispositions rather than instinctual impulses or drive derivatives. Previous relationships, their affective components, and strategies for emotional gratification and anxiety containment are reconstructed, with a focus on identifying for each partner consistencies in his/her interpersonal conflicts and coping styles across relationships. In addition, ways in which previous coping strategies vital to prior relationships represent distortions or inappropriate solutions for emotional intimacy and satisfaction in the current relationship are articulated.

Theoretical Assumptions

There is not one approach to insight-oriented couple therapy, but many. Theoretical approaches examining affective and developmental components of couples' distress emphasize recurrent maladaptive relationship patterns that derive from early interpersonal experiences either in the partners' families of origin or within other significant emotional relationships (Meissner, 1978; Nadelson &

Paolino, 1978). Diverse approaches to examining maladaptive relationship patterns can be placed on a continuum from traditional psychoanalytic techniques rooted primarily in object relations theory to schema-based interventions derived from more traditional cognitive theory (see Figure 6.3). These approaches vary in the extent to which they emphasize the unconscious nature of individuals' relational patterns, the developmental period during which these maladaptive patterns are acquired, and the extent to which interpersonal anxieties derive from frustration of innate drives. However, these approaches all share the assumption that maladaptive relationship patterns are likely to continue until they are understood in a developmental context. This new understanding and exploration serve to

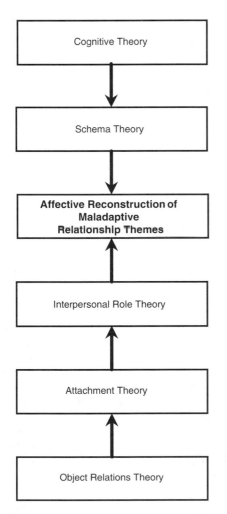

FIGURE 6.3. Theoretical approaches emphasizing affective and developmental components of couples' distress.

reduce the partners' attendant anxiety in their current relationship and permit them to develop alternative, healthier relationship patterns.

Object Relations Theory

Traditional object relations theorists (Fairbairn, 1952; Klein, 1948) argued that the primary drive in infants is to secure attachment to their mothers. From interactions primarily with their mothers they develop internalized images of the self, images of significant others, and sets of transactions connecting these images or objects. From an object relations perspective, maladaptive relationship patterns of adults reflect enduring pathogenic introjects that give rise to inevitable frustration when these are projected onto relationships with significant others (Scharff, 1995; see also Scharff & Bagnini, Chapter 3, this volume). In a distressed relationship, partners' pathogenic introjects interact in an unconscious, complementary manner resulting in repeated disappointments culminating in persistent conflict (Dicks, 1967). Consequently, the goal of psychoanalytically oriented couple therapy is helping partners to modify each other's projections, to distinguish these from objective aspects of their own self, and to assume ownership of their own projections.

Attachment Theory

Evolving from object relations theory, attachment theory (Bowlby, 1969) emphasizes the importance of emotional closeness to others as an innate survival function from which infants develop information-processing capabilities and emotional responses intended to foster secure emotional bonds. From an attachment perspective, difficulties in intimate adult relationships may be viewed as stemming from underlying insecure or anxious models of attachment (Furman & Flanagan, 1997; Hazan & Shaver, 1987). Partners' dominant emotional experiences drive reciprocal feedback loops maintaining such behaviors as excessive clinging or avoidance (Johnson & Whiffen, 1999). The goal of emotionally focused couple therapy (EFT; Johnson & Greenberg, 1995; see also Johnson & Denton, Chapter 8, this volume), reformulated from an attachment theory perspective, is to help partners gain access to their history of attachment experiences stored in schematic memory and to use this information in moving toward more accurate working models of self and partner. Johnson and Greenberg (1995) describe EFT as "one of the few psychodynamic approaches to marital therapy that has been empirically validated" (p. 121).

Interpersonal Role Theory

Interpersonal role theory (Anchin & Kiesler, 1982) regards the persistence of maladaptive interpersonal patterns as resulting from their reinforcement by the responses of significant others. This emphasis involves an important shift from the initial internal object relations giving rise to these patterns to the current interpersonal exchanges perpetuating them. The concept of "role complementarity" derived from interpersonal theory accounts for some of the same phenomena addressed by early object relations theorists, but in a language more closely linked to current events and at a lower level of abstraction. Thus, rather than stressing constructs of projective and introjective identification, interpersonal theory emphasizes the unconscious assignment of specific roles to oneself and others "in which feared and anticipated relational events tend to be elicited and enacted by the individual in his or her interactions with others, who, in turn, will tend to respond in ways complementary to the interpersonal actions of that individual" (Messer & Warren, 1995, p. 120).

The brief psychodynamic models of individual psychotherapy developed by Strupp and colleagues (Strupp & Binder, 1984) and by Luborsky and colleagues (Luborsky, 1984) exhibit a strong linkage to interpersonal role theory. The former use the term "cyclical maladaptive patterns" and the latter "core conflictual relationship themes" to refer to recurrent strategies used to influence relationships in such a way as to minimize expected painful outcomes and maximize desired outcomes in relationships with significant others. Moreover, both approaches emphasize the interpretation of maladaptive relational patterns within the immediacy of the therapist-client exchange as a vehicle for promoting the client's understanding of how these same maladaptive patterns are enacted outside of therapy.

Schema Theory

Schema theory (Horowitz, 1988; Young, 1999) emphasizes relationship schemas extending beyond attachment to the mother (object relations theory) or significant others (attachment theory) to consider more generally how early relationship experiences influence adult intimate relationships. For example, Young (1999) conceptualizes early maladaptive schemas as enduring themes initially developed in childhood that serve as a set of expectancies or "template" for processing one's interactions with the environment. The greater the conflict between the desired and the anticipated or feared interpersonal state, the more rigid and maladaptive the scripted expression of those expectancies is likely to be. Young conceptualizes his work as an extension of cognitive therapy, but his model overlaps considerably with psychodynamic relational models in its (1) emphasis on interpretation of interpersonal exchanges within the therapy session as a vehicle for change; (2) attention to affect during the processing of schema-related events; and (3) emphasis on the childhood origins of maladaptive schemas and the emotional reformulation or reworking of these early experiences.

Affective Reconstruction of Maladaptive Relationship Themes

Drawing on earlier psychodynamic formulations, Snyder and Wills (1989) articulated an insight-oriented approach to couple therapy, emphasizing affective reconstruction of previous relationship injuries resulting in sustained interpersonal vulnerabilities and related defensive strategies interfering with emotional intimacy. In affective reconstruction, as noted earlier, developmental origins of interpersonal themes and their manifestation in a couple's relationship are explored via techniques that somewhat resemble traditional interpretive strategies promoting insight, but that emphasize interpersonal schemas and relationship dispositions rather than instinctual impulses or drive derivatives (Snyder, 1999a). Earlier relationships, their emotional components, and strategies for emotional gratification and anxiety containment are reconstructed, with an emphasis on identifying for both partners commonalities in their interpersonal conflicts and coping styles across relationships. Moreover, ways in which important coping strategies in previous relationships represent distortions or inappropriate solutions for emotional intimacy and satisfaction in the present relationship are delineated.

Affective reconstruction builds on strengths of earlier relational models by capitalizing on features unique to conjoint couple therapy. First, in couple therapy data reflecting current expression of persistent dysfunctional patterns of interpersonal relating are not confined to an individual's interactions with the therapist, but extend more visibly and importantly to *in vivo* observations of the individual and his/her significant other. Thus core conflictual relationship themes having greatest relevance to each partner are more likely to be apparent than in the context of individual therapy. Second, an individual's understanding of maladaptive relationship themes and reformulation of these in less pejorative terms may extend beyond his/her own dynamics to a more benevolent reinterpretation of the partner's more hurtful behaviors. That is, both individuals can be helped to understand that whereas certain relational coping strategies may have been adaptive or even essential in previous relationships, the same interpersonal strategies interfere with emotional intimacy and satisfaction in the present relationship. Finally, in couple therapy the "corrective emotional experience" (Alexander, 1956) of disrupting previous pathogenic interpersonal strategies and promoting more functional relational patterns has an opportunity to emerge not only between the individual and therapist, but between the individual and his/her partner. Thus interpretation of maladaptive interpersonal themes in the context of couple therapy affords unique opportunities for affective reconstruction of these patterns in individuals' primary emotional relationships.

Empirical Support

Although psychodynamic approaches to couple therapy were among the earliest approaches to treating relationship distress, empirical study of their efficacy has been quite limited. Only one study has examined the effectiveness of affective reconstruction as described here. Snyder and Wills (1989) compared behavioral and insight-oriented approaches to couple therapy in a controlled outcome study involving 79 distressed couples. The behavioral condition emphasized communication skills training and behavior exchange techniques; the insight-oriented condition emphasized the interpretation and resolution of conflictual emotional processes related to developmental issues, collusive interactions, and maladaptive relationship patterns. At termination after approximately 20 sessions, couples in both treatment modalities showed statistically and clinically significant gains in relationship satisfaction, compared to a wait-list control group. Treatment effect sizes at termination for behavioral and insight-oriented conditions were 1.01 and 0.96, respectively; treatment gains were substantially maintained at a 6-month follow-up.

However, at 4 years following treatment, 38% of the behaviorally treated couples had experienced divorce, in contrast to only 3% of couples treated in the insight-oriented condition (Snyder et al., 1991a). Based on these findings, Snyder and colleagues suggested an important distinction between *acquisition* of relationship skills through instruction or rehearsal, and interference with *implementation* of these skills on a motivational or affective basis. They argued that individuals' negative views of their partners' behavior "are modified to a greater degree and in a more persistent manner once individuals come to understand and resolve emotional conflicts they bring to the marriage from their own family and relationship histories" (Snyder, Wills, & Grady-Fletcher, 1991b, p. 148).

COMPARISONS WITH ALTERNATIVE APPROACHES

Alternative Psychodynamic and Developmental Approaches

Psychodynamic approaches to couple therapy share the assumption that current interpersonal difficulties evolve at least in part from maladaptive relationship dispositions acquired during earlier developmental struggles and maintained largely on an unconscious level. However, psychodynamic strategies vary considerably in the extent to which they emphasize the genetic interpretation of instinctual strivings and the projection of intrapsychic conflicts, as opposed to the perpetuation of maladaptive interpersonal dispositions as misguided efforts to avoid painful outcomes and to procure relational fulfillment (Barber & Crits-Christoph, 1991; Messer & Warren, 1995).

In its more orthodox application, psychoanalytically oriented couple therapy strives to free the relationship "from the grip of its obligatory projective and introjective identificatory processes" (Scharff, 1995, p. 172). Distressed relationships are viewed as the culmination of frustrated narcissistic needs and an inability to cope with the consequent disillusionment. Thus interpretive strategies emphasize helping partners to modify each other's projections, to distinguish these from objective aspects of their own self, and to assume ownership of their own projections. By contrast, the relational approach to couple therapy advocated here deemphasizes the intrapsychic components of maladaptive patterns rooted in the first years of development, and instead emphasizes the perpetuating aspects of maladaptive interpersonal strategies in the present relationship. A couple's conflicts are viewed as evolving from a self-fulfilling process in which the partners' mutual efforts to minimize or avoid anticipated relationship injuries result in exaggerated or inflexible interpersonal strategies that often elicit and maintain these feared relationship experiences.

In many respects, an emphasis on contemporary relationship dynamics perpetuating each partner's maladaptive relationship dispositions can be discerned in Sager's (1976) formulation of couple "contracts." Working from a psychodynamic perspective, Sager proposed that couples develop an interactional contract incorporating respective conscious and unconscious expectations and needs around such themes as dependence–independence, activity–passivity, closeness–distance, dominance–submission, and autonomy–control. Sager viewed relationship conflicts as resulting from partners' implicit contracts that are internally inconsistent or contradictory. Interventions from this perspective strive to explicate unconscious aspects of partners' implicit relationship expectations and to negotiate interactional contracts that are complementary. Less central to Sager's formulation are the intrapersonal components of maladaptive relationship behaviors that recur across interpersonal relationships, or the need for individuals to gain an understanding and emotional resolution to enduring relational anxiety resulting from previous relationship injuries.

More recently, Wile (1995) has advocated an ego-analytic approach emphasizing pejorative attitudes partners have toward themselves and their resulting difficulty in communicating "leading-edge" feelings because they feel unentitled to them. These unexpressed feelings are viewed as giving rise to more symptomatic relationship behaviors (see also Wile, chapter 10, this volume for a discussion of "collaborative couple therapy" as an extension of his ego-analytic approach.) Wile (1995) argues that developmental interpretations focusing on the inappropriateness of partners' affective responses have the effect of invalidating these responses and maintaining their symptomatic expression. Wile's ego-analytic approach emphasizes the universality of partners' feelings and the hidden appropriateness in the person's seemingly inappropriate behavior. Rather than linking current relationship difficulties to partners' developmental struggles and enduring sensitivities, Wile (1995) encourages partners to own and disclose their primary emotions, to "appeal to each other as resources in dealing with them, and create a joint platform from which to look at them" (p. 118). The approach advocated by Wile offers important strategies for promoting individuals' acceptance of both their own and their partners' primary affect. However, the ego-analytic approach differs critically from the relational model advocated here in its explicit avoidance of interpretive strategies linking current affect to previous relationship experiences and to partners' inadvertent maintenance of maladaptive relationship patterns.

Indeed, the emphasis of Wile's ego-analytic approach on expression of leading-edge emotions and avoidance of developmental interpretations lends this approach striking similarities to EFT described by Greenberg and Johnson (Greenberg & Johnson, 1988; Johnson & Greenberg, 1995; Johnson & Whiffen, 1999) and mentioned earlier. Based on attachment theory, EFT views distressed relationships as "insecure bonds in which essentially healthy attachment needs are unable to be met due to rigid interaction patterns that block emotional engagement" (Johnson & Greenberg, 1995, p. 121). An important assumption of EFT is that understanding of valid attachment needs promotes more empathic responding and less defensive interactions between partners. Similar to the relational model advocated here incorporating interpretive techniques, attachment-based couple interventions strive to "access information that couples have selectively excluded from processing, sustain attention to this new information, and facilitate couples' abilities to incorporate and use this information in moving toward more accurate, integrated working models of self and partner" (Kobak, Ruckdeschel, & Hazan, 1994, pp. 60–61).

The distinction between the interpretive approach proposed here and alternative attachment-based models rests on the extent to which interpretive techniques emphasize previous relationship experiences and the unconscious components of maladaptive relationship patterns. Affective reconstruction emphasizes explication of enduring maladaptive relationship patterns rooted in earlier relationship injuries, with dynamics resulting from these developmental experiences operating largely beyond awareness. Nevertheless, even this distinction is often blurred. For example, in discussing couple therapy from an attachment perspective, Furman and Flanagan (1997) note that when working models from early in development appear implicated in current relationship difficulties, the therapist may help partners "address the unfinished business with parents and in effect rework their models of parents" (p. 197). Interestingly, similar to the hierarchical model advocated here, Furman and Flanagan also describe adopting a sequential approach to couple therapy—beginning with behavioral or other structural approaches, and using resistance to change diagnostically to explore partners' underlying attachment models that may be contributing to relationship difficulties.

Alternative Integrative Approaches

The pluralistic approach to couple therapy proposed here can also be contrasted with several alternative approaches described by their respective proponents as "integrative." Among the first integrative couple therapies to be articulated was Gurman's (1981, 1992; see also Gurman, Chapter 7, this volume) integrative approach drawing on principles of social learning theory, object relations theory, and general systems theory. Gurman emphasizes the critical interrelation of intrapsychic and interpersonal factors in a couple's interactions, and defines the goal of couple therapy as the loosening and broadening of each partner's implicit matrix of assumptions, expectations, and requirements of intimate interpersonal contact. This is accomplished through interpretation, cognitive restructuring, and creation of therapeutic tasks to promote each partner's exposure to those aspects of him-/herself and his/her mate that are blocked from awareness. Although drawing on behavioral interventions to challenge couples' entrenched patterns of negative exchange and to restructure individuals' perceptions of both themselves and their partners, Gurman (1992) has argued that "the most appropriate theoretical foundation for an integrative understanding of marital interaction, dynamics, and change is to be found in psychodynamic thinking, especially in a focused use of certain concepts originating in object relations theory" (p. 453). From this perspective, such behavioral techniques as teaching partners to rely on positive reinforcement for modifying their spouse's behavior may be reconceptualized as "a direct inhibitor of [partners'] proclivities to engage in projective identification" (Gurman, 1980, p. 90).

The pluralistic approach advocated here has much in common with Gurman's model, including attention to enduring maladaptive relationship patterns with early developmental origins. However, there are two important distinctions between the two approaches. Unlike Gurman's more assimilative integrative model, the pluralistic approach advocated here regards behavioral interventions within their original social learning theoretical context, rather than reformulating these from an object relations perspective. Second, although both

Gurman's and our model emphasize the critical role of establishing the therapeutic alliance early in treatment, Gurman appears more likely than we to deploy a psychodynamic formulation of the couple's difficulties from the outset. He suggests that the couple's presenting problems typically contain the clues to identifying partners' interlocking intrapsychic conflicts, "albeit often in disguised or derivative fashion" (Gurman, 1992, p. 434). By contrast, the pluralistic model described here defers examination of enduring maladaptive relationship themes from a psychodynamic perspective until later in the therapeutic sequence, after limited impact of earlier behavioral and cognitive interventions.

Segraves (1982, 1990) has also proposed a combined psychodynamic–behavioral model for addressing both intrapersonal and interpersonal components of chronic relationship discord. Segraves asserts that individuals in distressed relationships are likely to possess internal representational schemas of their partners that are discrepant with objective reality. He attributes distorted schemas to both transference and failure of discriminative learning resulting in limited conceptual dimensions for perceiving and understanding significant others. Similar to a conceptualization from interpersonal role theory (Anchin & Kiesler, 1982), Segraves proposes that individuals reliably elicit behavior from others that confirms their preexisting schemas through a process of stimulus–response chaining. Although conceptualized in part from a psychodynamic perspective, Segraves's strategies for intervening in relationship difficulties are largely cognitive-behavioral (encouraging each partner to observe behaviors of the other that are discrepant with internal schemas for that partner), with less attention to early developmental experiences giving rise to these schemas or to the reconstruction of these experiences on an affective level.

More recently, Jacobson and Christensen (1996; see also Dimidjian, Martell, & Christensen, Chapter 9, this volume) have proposed an integrative approach combining traditional behavioral techniques for promoting change (specifically, communication and behavior exchange skills training) with strategies aimed at promoting acceptance. Acceptance techniques are viewed as essential "when direct efforts to change are blocked by incompatibilities, irreconcilable differences, and unsolvable problems" (p. 11). Jacobson and Christensen describe interventions promoting tolerance and encouraging partners to appreciate differences and to use these to enhance their marriage.

Empathic joining may be facilitated by a partner's "soft disclosure" or by a reformulation from the therapist. Jacobson and Christensen state that acceptance work is sometimes sufficient on its own, and that at other times it facilitates behavior change efforts by promoting a context of collaboration.

In contrast to the interpretive emphasis in affective reconstruction, acceptance interventions in Jacobson and Christensen's model leave largely unaddressed those developmental experiences giving rise to apparent incompatibilities or exaggerated reactivities. Thus an individual is potentially deprived of a rich resource for understanding the partner's behaviors, and thereby for depersonalizing the hurtful aspects of the couple's interactions and adopting an empathic stance. In addition, Jacobson and Christensen advocate beginning couple therapy with acceptance interventions prior to communication and behavior exchange skills training. To the extent that acceptance techniques comprise common interventions promoting a collaborative alliance between partners, this recommendation is consistent with the hierarchical model advocated here, which affirms partners' collaborative alliance as a prerequisite to all subsequent interventions. However, to the extent that individuals' acceptance of their partners' behaviors relies on empathic understanding of those behaviors as coping strategies acquired from previous relationship injuries, the sequential approach advanced here proposes strengthening the relationship and challenging cognitive components of distress more accessible to immediate awareness prior to examining developmental sources of enduring relationship dispositions. Premature exploration of developmental issues may heighten defensiveness and exacerbate rather than ameliorate resistance to change.

The sequencing of interventions prescribed by the pluralistic model presented here mirrors the general progression of interventions characterizing Pinsof's (1994) integrative problem-centered therapy. Pinsof advocates commencing therapy with a focus on the behavioral patterns that prevent a couple from solving its presenting problems. If intervention at that level is not effective, therapy progresses to an exploration of the affective and cognitive components of the maladaptive patterns. Only if interventions at this experiential level fail does Pinsof advocate progressing to a developmental perspective focusing on family-of-origin patterns and specific historical determinants of enduring maladaptive relationship patterns. While similar in their overall sequencing of interventions, our pluralistic model and Pinsof's integrative approach differ in subtle ways. First, the pluralistic model articulated here emphasizes the frequent necessity of attending to immediate relationship crises and distinguishes explicitly between structural interventions for strengthening the dyad and specific skill-building interventions. Our pluralistic model also draws a sharper distinction between cognitive and affective components of relationship distress and associated interventions, regardless of their temporal origins. Finally, although it is consistent with the techniques of affective reconstruction described here, Pinsof's model does not explicitly address unique benefits of conducting developmental interventions in the context of conjoint couple therapy.

HEALTHY VERSUS DYSFUNCTIONAL RELATIONSHIPS: DIFFERENCES OF DEGREE

From the pluralistic perspective advocated here, no couple is immune to potential relationship difficulties, and no couple is without individual and relational resources. The difference between healthy and dysfunctional relationships is one of degree, not kind. What factors promote healthy relationships and resilience to stress? First are those components of individual functioning that promote self- and other-awareness, emotional regulation, and both the capacity and willingness to defer one's own gratification for the sake of another. Although we do not subscribe to the view that relationship dysfunction necessarily implies individual deficits, we do believe that individual deficits necessarily constrain opportunities for relationship health and resilience.

Second, healthy relationships prevail when both partners possess specific knowledge and skills essential to couple and family functioning. These include such communication skills as emotional expressiveness, active listening, and conflict resolution, as well as more specific skills in such domains as the couple's sexual relationship, parenting, management of time and financial resources, and routine household maintenance. Despite research indicating that nondistressed couples often engage in low rates of specific communication behaviors promoted in couple therapy (Gottman, 1999), the skills vital to distressed couples' disruption of intense negativity or recovery from relationship trauma are likely to differ from those processes protecting relatively happy couples from relationship erosion.

Separate from those intrapersonal and interpersonal components distinguishing healthy from dysfunctional relationships are aspects of the extended family, social network, and community that either support or compromise the couple's relationship. Any individual or couple, despite previous high levels of adaptive functioning, can succumb to changes in situational demands (requiring new skills not yet developed) or to atypical stressors (overwhelming usually adequate adaptive resources). Examples include transitions across family life stages, major mental or physical illness, or unexpected tragedies.

In sum, factors differentiating healthy from unhealthy relationships have their sources in individual, couple, and broader systemic functioning; may reflect primarily contemporary or historical influences or their interaction; and tend to vary quantitatively rather than qualitatively (i.e., by degree rather than by kind). Distinguishing among these sources of influence, their relative impact on the couple's relationship, and their implications for intervention requires a comprehensive assessment model reflecting multiple levels and facets from a broad systemic perspective.

ASSESSING COUPLES AND FORMULATING TREATMENT GOALS

A General Model for Assessing Couples

Snyder, Cavell, Heffer, and Mangrum (1995) have proposed a comprehensive model for directing and organizing assessment strategies for couples and families. The model proposes five construct domains: (1) cognitive, (2) affective, (3) behavioral and control, (4) communication and interpersonal, and (5) structural/developmental. Constructs relevant to each of these domains can be assessed at each of the multiple levels comprising the psychosocial system in which the couple or family functions. The model posits five distinct levels of this system: (1) individuals, (2) dyads, (3) the nuclear family, (4) the extended family and related social systems, and (5) the community and cultural systems. Each of the five target domains may be assessed with varying degrees of relevance and specificity across each of the five system levels, via both formal and informal assessment approaches to self-report and observational techniques. The model emphasizes the fluid nature of individual as well as system functioning by linking structural with developmental processes. It also presumes that individual members of a couple or family recursively influence,

and are influenced by, the broader social system. Snyder, Abbott, and Castellani (2002) articulate sample constructs relevant to each domain at each system level.

Initial Goals: Addressing Presenting Issues

The initial clinical interview serves as a means for obtaining important information, informally observing partners' communication patterns, and establishing a collaborative alliance for subsequent interventions. Snyder and Abbott (2001) advocate an extended initial assessment interview lasting about 2 hours in which the following goals are stated at the outset: (1) first getting to know each partner as an individual separate from the couple relationship; (2) understanding the structure and organization of the relationship; (3) learning about current relationship difficulties, their development, and previous efforts to address these; and (4) reaching an informed decision together about whether to proceed with couple therapy and, if so, discussing respective expectations.

The process of promoting an initial therapeutic alliance takes precedence over any specific content. Each member of a couple comes to an initial interview primed to talk about the relationship difficulties and, more often than not, to explain why the other partner is primarily at fault. Beginning the interview with an emphasis on getting to know each individual helps to counteract this tendency. During inquires about the family of origin and previous marriages or similar relationships, inferences can often be drawn regarding patterns of emotional or behavioral enmeshment or disengagement; models of emotional expressiveness and conflict resolution; appropriateness and clarity of boundaries, and standards or expectations regarding authority, autonomy, fidelity, and similar themes.

Although from a pluralistic perspective the therapist may speculate either covertly or explicitly about the potential role of intrapersonal conflicts and their inclusion as eventual treatment goals, more typically initial goals are framed in the context of the couple's presenting complaints. What does each partner identify as the primary contributing factors to their current struggles? How do partners agree or disagree on their definition and understanding of their difficulties? What does each individual believe it would require from him-/herself to promote positive change in the marriage? Although presenting relationship difficulties extend across an infinite range of specific content, Karpel (1994) has identified common themes that can often guide the assessment process. These include (1) repetitive unresolved conflicts, either focusing on one issue or generalized across multiple issues; (2) emotional distance or disaffection related to persistent remoteness, excessive demands, relentless criticism, or physical or emotional abuse; (3) stable but devitalized relationships characterized by an absence of intimacy, passion, or joy; (4) difficulties with third parties, including in-laws, affair partners, or children; and (5) acute crises, including alcohol or other substance abuse, major psychopathology, sudden financial stressors, death of a family member, or similar concerns.

Self-report measures of relationship functioning can also be useful for delineating and prioritizing initial treatment goals addressing areas of conflict and problematic interactional patterns. Among other advantages, such measures are relatively easy to administer, obtain a wealth of information across a broad range of issues germane to treatment, and allow disclosure about events and subjective experiences partners may initially be reluctant to discuss. One such measure is the Marital Satisfaction Inventory—Revised (MSI-R; Snyder, 1997), a 150-item inventory designed to identify both the nature and intensity of relationship distress in distinct areas of interaction. The MSI-R includes two validity scales, one global scale, and ten specific scales assessing relationship satisfaction in such areas as affective and problem-solving communication, aggression, leisure time together, finances, the sexual relationship, role orientation, family of origin, and interactions regarding children. A computerized interpretive report for the MSI-R draws on actuarial validity data to provide descriptive comparisons across different domains both within and between partners (cf., Snyder & Aikman, 1999).

Emergent Goals: Identifying Core Relationship Themes

An essential prerequisite to affective reconstruction of relational themes is a thorough knowledge of each partner's relational history. Critical information includes not only the pattern of relationships within the family of origin, but also relational themes in the family extending to prior generations. Beyond the family, intimate relationships with significant others of both genders from adolescence through the current time offer key information

regarding such issues as perceived acceptance and valuation by others; trust and disappointment; stability of relationships and their resilience to interpersonal injury; levels of attachment and respect for autonomy; and similar relational themes. Some of this information may be gleaned from earlier interventions linked to establishing appropriate boundaries with the family of origin, discussion of the partner's expectancies regarding parenting responsibilities acquired during his/her own childhood and adolescence, or disclosures of traumatic experiences with significant others previous to the current relationship. Alternatively, in anticipating focused work on developmental issues, the therapy may adopt more structured clinical or self-report techniques.

The family genogram (McGoldrick, Gerson, & Shellenberger, 1999) is a graphic means of depicting transgenerational family structures, dynamics, and critical family events potentially influencing family members' interactions with one another. It is constructed from information derived from an extended clinical interview regarding family history, and it both directs the interview content and evolves in response to new information gleaned during the course of therapy. The genogram reflects a family systems perspective positing that relationship patterns in previous generations may provide implicit models for family functioning in the next generation. As such, it provides a subjective, interpretive tool helping the therapist to delineate recurrent relationship themes within partners' extended families of origin as a prelude to interpreting enduring individual relationship patterns.

Developed from his schema-based approach to therapy, Young's Schema Questionnaire (Young & Brown, 1990/1999) is a 205-item measure assessing common maladaptive schemas across four general areas of functioning which involve to varying degrees perceptions of self, others, and relationships. The four general domains and specific schemas within are as follows: (1) Autonomy, with schemas addressing specific issues of dependence, self-subjugation, vulnerability to harm, and fears of losing self-control; (2) Connectedness, with schemas regarding issues of emotional deprivation, abandonment, mistrust, and social isolation; (3) Worthiness, with schemas concerning specific issues of one's own defectiveness, social undesirability, incompetence, guilt, and shame; and (4) Expectations and Limits, including schemas concerning unrelenting standards for self or, conversely, exaggerated sense of entitlement. Young (1999) has provided examples of schema maintenance, avoidance, and compensation for each of these early maladaptive schemas and their relevance to couple therapy (Young & Gluhoski, 1997).

THE STRUCTURE
OF THE THERAPY PROCESS

Participants

From a broad systemic perspective, a pluralistic approach to couple therapy could conceivably target any individual member or combination of members from the broader family or social system. However, when partners presenting for couple therapy define their *relationship* as the focus of treatment—or when our own assessment confirms the centrality of relational difficulties, despite either partner's tendency to focus on shortcomings of the other—our clear preference is to employ conjoint sessions throughout the course of treatment. Nevertheless, although a conjoint format offers unique advantages to promoting partners' shared understanding of each other's developmental contributions to current distress, there may be times when individual therapy provides an important alternative or complement to conjoint sessions. For example, even when a couple has achieved a relatively satisfying relationship, one or both partners may recognize enduring issues of their own that compromise functioning across diverse domains including their relationship, and elect to address these in individual therapy. In such cases, affective reconstruction of maladaptive relationship patterns may produce substantive relationship gains if the individual in therapy has the capacity to initiate positive changes in his/her own behavior and the other partner has the capacity to change as the partner in treatment changes. At the other extreme, individual therapy may prove an important alternative or complement to conjoint sessions for a highly dysfunctional couple whose persistent antagonism precludes the partners' willingness to confront individual issues or initiate unilateral changes that may be essential for collaborative work in couple therapy.

Various treatment formats have been described in the literature, each with its own merits and limitations; these include mixing of individual and conjoint sessions by the same therapist, referral of partners to separate therapists for individual work, using cotherapists for both conjoint and individual sessions, and so on. The use of alternative formats raises both pragmatic and ethical issues, such as managing confidentiality and negotiating competing individual and couple treatment goals (Gottlieb, 1996). Having cotherapists raises particularly interesting possibilities when interpretive techniques are employed, because of the increased potential for transference distortions within the couple therapy as well as the increased opportunity for corrective emotional experiences. However, to date there exists little if any empirical basis for articulating specific criteria for alternative formats within the hierarchical model prescribed here.

Length, Frequency, and Duration of Sessions

With the exception of manualized treatments under scrutiny in controlled studies, the length of treatment for most disorders (individual, couple, or otherwise) typically reflects both the complexity and severity of presenting difficulties. The insight-oriented couple therapy developed by Snyder and Wills (1989) was designed for implementation within 25 weekly conjoint sessions lasting 50 minutes each. In fact, couples receiving this treatment averaged 19 sessions, although roughly 10–15% required fewer than 15 sessions and another 10–15% required twice that many.

Not all couples require each of the treatment components outlined in the pluralistic model proposed here. Individual differences in couples' strengths and concerns often dictate that different components of the model be given greater or less emphasis. For example, some couples require little more than stabilization and crisis resolution to restore a positive relationship; others require extensive assistance in reworking enduring maladaptive relationship patterns established early in their individual development. With relatively higher-functioning couples, we have been able to implement the complete model in as few as 8–10 sessions; with couples exhibiting significant individual as well as relational impairment, successful therapy has required a year or more of intensive intervention.

Ground Rules

There are few ground rules that distinguish affective reconstruction or the pluralistic approach advocated here from other couple therapies. Both partners must agree to the format and proposed schedule of sessions. Both must agree that if physical aggression occurs to any extent in their relationship, strategies for eliminating violence will be the first priority of treatment. Partners must agree in principle to civil behavior in sessions, to allowing the therapist to intervene as necessary to disrupt destructive exchanges, and to a conceptual formulation of the *relationship* as the client.

So long as the treatment is defined as *couple* rather than individual therapy—regardless of any individual sessions that may be held within the couple treatment—an explicit agreement is enforced that any communication occurring unilaterally between either partner and the therapist may be incorporated into conjoint sessions at the discretion of the therapist. Early in the therapy, the therapist reinforces this ground rule by refusing to meet with one individual if his/her partner fails to show for a scheduled conjoint session. Any phone calls or notes from either partner to the therapist between sessions are typically shared in the subsequent conjoint meeting. On the infrequent occasion that one partner unilaterally shares information with the therapist outside conjoint sessions, but insists on this remaining confidential despite the initial explicit agreement otherwise, the therapist may agree to one or two separate sessions with that individual to assist him/her in bringing the information into conjoint therapy; if the individual persists in demanding confidential treatment of that information, the therapist asserts his/her inability to continue as a credible and effective couple therapist and assists in transferring the couple's treatment to an alternative therapist not similarly compromised.

THE ROLES OF THE THERAPIST

In a pluralistic approach, the therapist's roles vary considerably across stages of treatment. Early in therapy, the primary roles include containment of negativity, disruption of destructive exchanges, and repeated encouragement regarding the couple's collective resources for improving the relationship. The therapist remains highly active, lending his/her own expertise and problem-solving abilities to crisis resolution, and directing structural changes in partners' interactions and within the broader family and social system to strengthen the couple's relationship. An active stance continues during skills-building interventions, but emphasis shifts from the therapist's role as problem solver to dual roles as facilitator and educator in assisting the partners to acquire expertise and to implement interventions on their own to resolve conflict and enhance intimacy.

When individual dynamics interfere with the acquisition or implementation of more positive relationship behaviors, the therapist's role shifts to that of "guide" or "auxiliary processor" (Messer & Warren, 1995). Although cognitive components of relationship distress that are reasonably accessible to conscious awareness may be approached from a more psychoeducational stance directed toward both partners, deeper sources of intrapersonal conflict beyond immediate awareness require the therapist to adopt roles more typical of individual psychodynamic therapy. The specific features of these roles become clearer when specific techniques of affective reconstruction are examined.

TECHNIQUES OF AFFECTIVE RECONSTRUCTION

Timing Interpretive Interventions

For interpretation of maladaptive relationship themes to be effective with a couple, the therapist needs to attend carefully to both partners' preparedness to examine their own enduring relational dispositions. Unlike individual therapy, in which clients often accept at least partial responsibility for their own distress, persons entering couple therapy often focus on each other's negative behaviors and resist examining their own contributions to relationship difficulties—particularly those linked to more enduring personality characteristics. Distressed partners often suffer from a long history of exchanging pejorative attributions for each other's behaviors, furthering their initial resistance to clinical interventions emphasizing early maladaptive schemas underlying relationship distress. Consequently, examining developmental sources of relationship distress demands a prerequisite foundation of emotional safety, both partners' trust in the therapeutic process, each partner's ability to respond empathically to feelings of vulnerability exposed by the other, and an introspective stance initially prompted by examining dysfunctional relationship expectancies and attributions residing at a more conscious level.

Linking Relationship Themes to Current Conflict

In affective reconstruction, previous relationships are initially explored without explicit linkage to current relational difficulties, in order to reduce anxiety and resistance during this exploration phase. Often individuals are readily able to formulate connections between prior relationships and current interpersonal struggles; when this occurs, it is typically useful for the therapist to listen empathically, encouraging the individual to remain "intently curious" about his/her own relational history but to refrain from premature interpretations that may be either incorrect, incomplete, or excessively self-critical. Just as important is for the individual's partner to adopt an accepting, empathic tone during the other's developmental exploration, encouraging self-disclosure in a supportive but noninterpretive manner.

Provided with relevant developmental history, the therapist encourages each partner to identify significant relational themes, particularly with respect to previous relationship disappointments and injuries. Gradually, as the partners continue to explore tensions and unsatisfying patterns in their own relationship, they can both be encouraged to examine ways in which exaggerated emotional responses to current situations have at least a partial basis in affective dispositions and related coping styles acquired in the developmental context. Developing a shared formulation of core relationship themes is a critical antecedent to subsequent linkage of these themes to current relationship exchanges. Both individuals can be helped to understand that whereas certain relational coping strategies may have been adaptive or even essential in previous relationships, the same interpersonal strategies interfere with emotional intimacy and satisfaction in the present relationship.

In couple therapy, the therapist's direct access to exchanges between partners affords a unique opportunity for linking enduring relationship themes to current relationship events. Rather than interpreting transferential exchanges between either partner and the therapist, the focus is on partners' own exchanges in the immediate moment. Interpretations emphasize linking each partner's exaggerated affect and maladaptive responses to his/her own relationship history, emphasizing the repetition of relationship patterns and their maintaining factors in the present context. Guidelines for examining cyclical maladaptive patterns in the context of individual therapy (Binder & Strupp, 1991; Luborsky, 1984) readily lend themselves to couple work. How does the immediate conflict between partners relate to core relationship themes explored earlier in the therapy? What are each person's feel-

ings toward the other and his/her desired response? What impact does each wish to have on the other in this moment? How do the partners' perceptions regarding each other's inner experience relate to their attitudes toward themselves? What fantasies does each have regarding the other's possible responses? What kinds of responses from each other would they anticipate being helpful in modifying their core beliefs about each other, themselves, and this relationship?

Specific therapeutic techniques relevant to examining core relationship themes in individual therapy (cf. Luborsky, 1984) apply to affective reconstruction in couple therapy as well. For example, it is essential that the therapist recognize each partner's core relationship themes, that developmental interpretations link relational themes to a current relationship conflict, and that therapy focus on a few select relationship themes until some degree of resolution is achieved and alternative interpersonal strategies are enabled. It is also important that the extent and complexity of interpretations take into account (1) the affective functioning of the individual and his/her ability to make constructive use of the interpretation; (2) the level of insight and how near the individual is to being aware of the content of the proposed interpretation; and (3) the level of relationship functioning and the extent to which developmental interpretations can be incorporated in a mutually supportive manner.

From a psychodynamic perspective, cognitive linkage of relational themes from early development to the current context is frequently insufficient for reconstructing or modifying these interpersonal patterns. The affective component of interpretation is seen in the reconstruction of these critical emotional experiences in the immediate context; new understanding by both partners often promotes more empathic responses toward both themselves and each other, facilitating more satisfactory resolutions to conflict. Often an individual must be encouraged to work through previous relationship injuries, grieving losses and unmet needs, expressing ambivalence or anger toward previous critical others in the safety of the conjoint therapy, and acquiring increased differentiation of prior relationships from the present one. As in individual therapy adopting a relational model, the therapist serves as an auxiliary processor helping to "detoxify, manage, and digest" the partners' relationship themes in a manner that promotes interpersonal growth (Messer & Warren, 1995, p. 141).

Promoting Alternative
Relationship Behaviors

Affective reconstruction makes possible, but does not inevitably lead to, changes in maladaptive relationship patterns. In addition to interpretive strategies, interventions must promote couple interactions that counteract early maladaptive schemas. Thus the couple therapist allows the partners' maladaptive patterns to be enacted within limits, but then assists both partners in examining exaggerated affective components of their present exchange. Partners' exaggerated responses are framed as acquired coping strategies that interfere with higher relationship values. Interpretations of the developmental context underlying the current unsatisfactory exchange help both partners to depersonalize the noxious effects of each other's behavior, to feel less wounded, and consequently to be less reactive in a reciprocally negative manner.

Both individuals are encouraged to be less anxious and less condemning of both their own and each other's affect, and are helped to explore and then express their own affect in less aggressive or antagonistic fashion. Throughout this process, each individual plays a critical therapeutic role by learning to offer a secure context in facilitating the partner's affective self-disclosures in a softened, more vulnerable manner. The couple therapist models empathic understanding for both partners and encourages new patterns of responding that enhance relationship intimacy. That is, by facilitating the nonoccurrence of expected traumatic experiences in the couple's relationship, the therapist helps both individuals to challenge the assumptions and expectations comprising the underlying maladaptive schemas. Thus therapeutic change results from the experiential learning in which both partners encounter relationship outcomes different from those expected or feared. In response, partners' interactions become more adaptive and flexible in matching the objective reality of current conflicts and realizing opportunities for satisfying more of each other's needs.

Although affective reconstruction seeks to promote new relationship schemas facilitating more empathic and supportive interactions, couples sometimes need additional assistance in restructuring long-standing patterns of relating outside of therapy. In the pluralistic hierarchical model for sequencing interventions advocated here, couples already will have been exposed to communication and behavior exchange techniques characterizing traditional behavioral approaches. Consequently, alternative relationship behaviors can often be negotiated more readily after schema-related anxieties and resistance to changing enduring interaction patterns have been understood and at least partially resolved.

MECHANISMS OF
THERAPEUTIC IMPACT

Affective reconstruction strives to bring about critical changes in how partners view themselves, each other, and their relationship. In examining recurrent maladaptive relationship themes, both partners gain increased understanding of their own emotional reactivity and exaggerated patterns of interacting that contribute to their own unhappiness. Increases in the partners' self-understanding can lead to diminished confusion and anxiety about their own subjective relationship experiences. Moreover, insight into developmental influences contributing to current difficulties often facilitates an optimism regarding potential for self-change and restores hope for greater emotional fulfillment in the relationship. Affective reconstruction of maladaptive schemas promotes resolution of persistent dysfunctional relationship patterns through redirected cognitive and behavioral strategies.

When conducted in the context of couple therapy, affective reconstruction offers unique advantages over similar therapeutic strategies conducted with individuals. Specifically, after participating in and observing a partner's work on developmental issues, an individual frequently comes to understand the partner's behaviors in a more accepting or benign manner—attributing damaging exchanges to the culmination of acquired interpersonal dispositions, rather than to explicit motives to be hurtful. This new understanding often facilitates within-session exchanges challenging existing relationship schemas, reducing defensive behaviors, and promoting empathic and mutually supportive interactions.

TREATMENT APPLICABILITY:
SELECTION OF COUPLES

Affective reconstruction of recurrent maladaptive relationship themes is not appropriate for all couples. Some couples enter therapy with relatively healthy relationship schemas but exhibit difficulties resulting from situational stressors or specific relationship skill deficits. Such couples often achieve significant and enduring gains from traditional behavioral strategies emphasizing communication and behavior exchange skills training.

Other couples may be inappropriate candidates for interpretive strategies because of persistent hostility, mistrust, inflexibility, and resistance to change. Unless an atmosphere of safety can be established that extends beyond therapy sessions to a couple's interactions outside of therapy, each individual may be reluctant to disclose the intimate and emotionally difficult material from previous relationships that is essential to the process of affective reconstruction of relationship themes. Ultimately, the capacity of each partner to adopt an empathic stance toward the other's feelings may be as critical as, or more so than, the therapist's own empathic understanding when interpretive techniques are employed in the context of conjoint couple therapy.

As in brief psychodynamic approaches to working with individuals (cf. Luborsky, 1984; Strupp & Binder, 1984), both partners must be open to examining current relational difficulties from a developmental perspective. Both should exhibit some capacity for introspection, be open to examining feelings, and be able to resurrect affective experiences from previous relationships on a conscious level. Each partner also needs to have established a basic level of trust with the therapist, and to experience the exploration of cyclical maladaptive patterns as promoting the individual's own relationship fulfillment. Moreover, both individuals need to exhibit a level of both personal maturity and relationship commitment that enables them to respond to their partner's intimate disclosures with empathy and support, rather than seizing details of previous relationships as new and more potent ammunition in a mutual blaming process.

CASE ILLUSTRATION: RECOVERY FROM AN AFFAIR

The following case illustrates the use of affective reconstruction within a pluralistic approach with a couple struggling to recover from an extramarital affair. One of us (DKS) was the therapist. Although originally conceptualized within the pluralistic model presented here, treatment of this couple parallels the multitheoretical intervention for recovery from an affair developed by Gordon, Baucom, and Snyder (2000), which integrates cognitive-behavioral with insight-oriented perspectives.

Presenting Concerns

Brent and Abby, ages 29 and 26, sought couple therapy after 6 years of marriage following Abby's disclosure of her recent involvement in an extramarital affair. The couple described increasing marital unhappiness over the past 3 years, but reported that their distress had intensified acutely since Abby's disclosure of her affair 2 weeks earlier. At the time of the initial interview, Brent had moved out of the home. Abby acknowledged her ambivalence about continuing her marriage, and confessed reluctance to end her affair or relinquish the emotional gratification it provided. She complained that Brent had been inattentive for a long time to both her and their two sons, ages 3 and 1. Brent acknowledged that he had neglected Abby and their youngsters, and professed his willingness to work with Abby to make whatever changes were necessary. However, he also complained that Abby had a pattern of withdrawing from him in frustration rather than confronting Brent with her feelings; as a result, he probably failed to discern her unhappiness much of the time. Abby responded that she often found it difficult to discuss issues with Brent because of his overbearing manner and his quick temper. She also expressed resentment that Brent was now "using the children" as a compelling reason for his and Abby's need to work things out.

Developmental Background

Abby was adopted as an infant and grew up in South America. Her adoptive mother had died when Abby was 18. Abby described her mother as someone who attended to everyone else's needs at the expense of her own, but never complained. Abby viewed herself as having incorporated many of her mother's strategies for avoiding conflict and pleasing others. For the first 6 months after her mother's death, Abby prepared her father's meals, did his laundry, and offered him emotional support. However, he met and married another woman a year after Abby's mother died. Abby felt wounded by her father's decision, left home to live with relatives in the United States, and didn't speak with her father for 2 years. Her father, an older brother, and her stepmother continued to live in South America. She saw them once a year when she and Brent visited them there, but otherwise only wrote to them every few months. Abby acknowledged her reluctance to let her family members know just how much she missed them, in order not to be disappointed when they didn't reciprocate her feelings.

Brent was the oldest of three children and had grown up in a home centered around academic and professional achievement. His father had a master's degree and managed a highly successful marketing firm, but was frequently gone at night and on weekends. Brent's mother was also a college graduate, but stayed at home to rear the children while Brent's father attended to his business. Brent's younger brother worked as an attorney, and his younger sister had recently completed a graduate degree in engineering. Although Brent's parents lived in a nearby community, he did not speak with or visit them frequently. Brent clearly admired his parents, but acknowledged feeling emotionally distant from them.

Neither Brent nor Abby had completed college—a source of occasional embarrassment for both of them. Abby had completed several courses at a local business college. Brent had attended a nearby university for 2 years, but dropped out of school to pursue a real estate license and open his own business, initially with his parents' financial support. Brent had been quite successful with the business and had repaid loans from his parents. Initially Abby had been fairly involved in the business, but she curtailed her involvement when their first youngster arrived. She acknowledged missing contact with former clients and, prior to her affair, had considered returning part-time to their firm. Brent described his last few years at work as less fulfilling, because the business had achieved stability and no longer challenged him.

Test Findings

Initial MSI-R profiles for Brent and Abby confirmed both partners' overall high level of relationship distress (see Figure 6.4). Although both scored high on a scale assessing global marital distress (GDS), Abby's score reflected more acute ambivalence about her marriage and was typical of wives at higher risk for separation or divorce following couple therapy (Snyder et al., 1993). Both partners reported extensive deficits in problem-solving communication (PSC), with Brent identifying difficulties in conflict resolution as his primary area of relationship concern. By comparison, Abby expressed relatively greater concern than Brent with their lack of emotional intimacy, reflected in her dissatisfaction both with affective communication

(AFC) and with the amount and quality of time spent together (TTO). Consistent with her apprehension regarding Brent's anger expressed in the initial interview, Abby's score for aggression (AGG) affirmed her concerns about his tendency to become argumentative and belligerent during their disagreements.

Despite concerns regarding their difficulty in resolving conflicts and their emotional disaffection, on the MSI-R both partners reported having enjoyed a sexually satisfying relationship (SEX) and a spirit of collaboration in managing their finances (FIN). Although both had initially agreed that Abby would stay at home to care for their youngsters at least during their preschool years, Abby's score for role orientation (ROR) reflected a less conservative perspective than Brent's and her ambivalence about having relinquished work outside the home—feelings unrecognized by Brent. Discussion regarding these differences shed light on the dissatisfaction both partners experienced as parents (DSC) and conflicts with each other over child rearing (CCR). Although she was emotionally close to their two sons, Abby experienced more acutely than Brent their intrusion into her life, and she resented his frequent absence on weekends and his disengagement from child care in the evening during the week. Brent acknowledged modest disappointment that he hadn't yet been able to establish the kind of relationship with his sons he had envisioned, but he particularly resented Abby's criticisms of his parenting efforts and retaliated by withdrawing further.

Differences in the partners' descriptions of their respective families (FAM) were dramatic and consistent with their accounts in the initial interview: Abby reported extensive distress in her family of origin, and Brent acknowledged virtually none in his. The relationship crisis precipitated by Abby's affair and the need to address more immediate issues regarding the couple's interactions precluded further exploration of developmental issues early in treatment. However, indicators from both the initial interview and the MSI-R suggested the importance of subsequent interventions examining the contribution of enduring relationship themes to the erosion of this couple's marriage, culminating in Abby's affair.

Initial Interventions

Developing a collaborative alliance with a couple struggling to recover from an extramarital affair poses a daunting challenge. The "injured" partner

Marital Satisfaction Inventory, Revised (MSI-R)

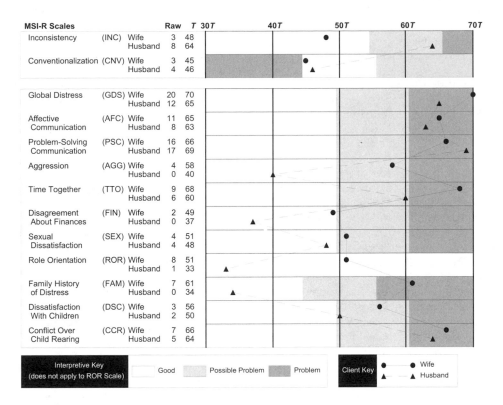

FIGURE 6.4. Initial profiles on the Marital Satisfaction Inventory–Revised (MSI-R) for Brent and Abby. The MSI-R form is from Snyder (1997). Copyright © 1997 by Western Psychological Services. Used by permission of the publisher, Western Psychological Services, 12031 Wilshire Boulevard, Los Angeles, California, 90025 USA. Not to be reprinted in whole or in part for any additional purpose without the expressed, written permission of the publisher. All rights reserved.

typically demands opportunity to express intense feelings of hurt, anger, and anxiety about the future. Concurrently, the "participating" partner frequently alternates among expressions of shame, defensive anger, and the need for the injured partner to recover emotional self-control. Above all, partners need a conceptual framework for understanding the turmoil they're experiencing both individually and as a couple, and reassurance that they can achieve sufficient stability to examine what has occurred and reach an informed decision about how to move forward.

Along these lines, it was important to normalize Brent's hurt and anger and to provide him with an opportunity for conveying these to Abby, while also containing the intensity of their expression. Brent regulated his anger somewhat more effectively when gently confronted by the therapist about his

anger's impact of pushing Abby further away, at the very time that Brent was seeking reassurance of her willingness to move closer. Abby benefited from reassurance by the therapist that no pressure would be exerted to reach an immediate decision about their marriage; on the contrary, they would be discouraged from making long-term decisions until they first understood how their relationship had eroded and could better assess their potential to build a secure and satisfying marriage for both of them. However, the therapist also made clear that so long as Abby continued her involvement (sexually or otherwise) with her affair partner, the resulting turmoil would preclude her and Brent's examining their marriage and reaching decisions collaboratively.

Containing the disabling aspects of an affair crisis requires reestablishing equilibrium and minimizing additional damage (Baucom, Gordon, & Snyder, in press). Equilibrium was promoted for this couple, in part, by Abby's agreement not to be with her affair partner for the ensuing 2 weeks, although she retained the right to talk with him by phone. Because of the intense hurt and anger that persisted between them, Abby and Brent initially concurred that it would be preferable for Brent to continue spending the night at a friend's apartment. However, they brokered an agreement by which they would share dinner at home with the boys, after which Brent would have an hour of play with the youngsters while Abby pursued separate time by herself. Both agreed that if negativity escalated during these times and could not be readily disrupted, Brent would leave the home, and they would wait until the next day to attempt more constructive exchanges.

When the couple returned the following week, Abby disclosed that she had decided to end her relationship with her affair partner and had asked him not to call her any more. She reaffirmed her ambivalence about her marriage, however, stating that although she knew her affair was "wrong," she wasn't yet optimistic that she and Brent could make their own relationship "right." They continued to have arguments during Brent's visits in the evening, particularly at times when he was reminded of Abby's affair and felt uncertain about her decision to end it. Brent's reactivity to his own recollections of Abby's affair was reconceptualized for the couple as a phenomenon similar to posttraumatic stress disorder. This framework helped Brent to assume more responsibility for regulation of these reactions, and helped Abby to respond less defensively.

Over the next 2 weeks, Abby's resolve to end her affair became more evident to Brent, and the intensity of his anxiety and episodic anger diminished. Abby remained apprehensive about restoring a sexual relationship with Brent and worried about his wish to move back home, however. Although hurt by Abby's ambivalence in this regard, Brent agreed to sleep in a separate bedroom and to respect Abby's need for space until they were both comfortable in pursuing greater intimacy. However, in subsequent weeks comfort and intimacy proved elusive. Both Abby and Brent remained emotionally brittle. Neither felt permission to broaden their emotional support through friendships outside the home, but their mutual anxiety, guilt, and hurt prevented them from offering reliable support to each other. An important intervention in strengthening the marriage was directing each partner to pursue separate self-care behaviors, including opportunities for time apart with same-gender friends. As Abby and Brent each developed better means of attending to their own feelings, their comfort with time together gradually increased.

Although the couple's ability to disrupt negative escalations improved, the partners' capacity for intimacy remained compromised. A major source of their emotional distance was Brent's difficulty in conveying the emotional impact of Abby's affair on his sense of security and personal adequacy without lapsing into angry attacks. Even when these were moderated in therapy sessions, Abby's discomfort with conflict led her to retreat, exacerbating Brent's frustration in not feeling understood by her. Two strategies were used to promote the couple's ability to communicate about the affair and associated relationship concerns in a more constructive manner. First, both Abby and particularly Brent benefited from interventions aimed at promoting better skills in sharing and listening to emotions constructively. Interventions included handouts, modeling of more constructive exchanges by the therapist with Abby and Brent separately, guidance and shaping of emotional dialogues between the partners within sessions, and structured exercises for the couple to pursue at home (Snyder, Baucom, & Gordon, in press).

Second, letter writing was used as a means for helping Brent to express his feelings more sensitively in a manner that Abby was more likely to process and respond to empathically. Over the course of several weeks, Brent prepared a letter to Abby describing the impact of her affair, and revised his letter with guidance from the therapist. He then read the letter aloud to her and gave it to her in their next session; interventions at that time emphasized her acknowledging what he had written. Following this session, Abby was assisted in writing her own letter to Brent acknowledging the impact her affair had on him and expressing its impact on her own feelings for Brent and their marriage.

Intermediate Interventions

Once a couple has absorbed the initial blow from an affair, the partners can more constructively examine how the affair came about and evaluate both their motivations and ability to repair its damage to the marriage. Understanding the context for an affair requires examining multiple domains of potential contributing factors and their impact across different phases of the couple's relationship prior to, during, and following the affair's occurrence. This is difficult work. The "participating" partner often perceives little incentive for stirring up additional turmoil, which frequently accompanies this exploration process. The "injured" partner sometimes experiences difficult reminders of his/her hurt and resentment while exploring factors contributing to the affair from their relationship, the "participating" partner, and him-/herself. Sustaining a couple through this process often requires cycling through earlier interventions of resolving intermediate crises, strengthening the relationship, and refining communication and other relevant relationship skills.

Abby and Brent were no exception. Both wanted to understand better how Abby's affair came about; both viewed it as out of character with their relationship history and their mutual value system. And both recognized that unless they more adequately understood how their relationship had become vulnerable to an affair and how to promote its resilience, their marriage remained at risk for eventual dissolution. After about 6 weeks of working toward stabilization and recovering some positive exchanges—including restoration of their sexual relationship—both Abby and Brent expressed their readiness to dig deeper.

Deficits in their communication and quality of time together, addressed during earlier interventions, provided a means of understanding and reducing some important relational sources of vulnerability. Abby and Brent also came to understand how, in the absence of clearer dialogue regarding their respective wishes and expectations for their marriage as well as their individual lives, they each tended to drift toward attributions for the other's behavior that maintained their hurt feelings and escalated their negative exchanges. Each responded positively to interventions encouraging them to challenge both their own and their partner's assumptions and attributions for relationship events. However, as they examined more closely the recurrent hurtful exchanges that began to erode their marriage several years earlier, Abby and Brent each remained confused about the other's reactions. Brent had difficulty understanding why Abby felt as abandoned as she did, and why she found it difficult to discuss these feelings with him. Abby had difficulty understanding why Brent had drawn further away when she thought she had been pleading with him to get closer.

Although their discussions of these experiences rarely contained the same level of intense antagonism as initially in the therapy, they re-

mained difficult and failed to generate emotional resolution for either partner. At this point, helping Abby and Brent to understand both their own and each other's experiences in a broader developmental context seemed critical to further progress.

In a session focusing on Abby's feelings of abandonment by Brent following the birth of their older son, the intensity of these feelings was linked to repeated experiences of loss and broken relationships earlier in her life. A portion of that session is provided here:

DKS: Abby, you've talked previously about sometimes feeling quite alone after Peter was born.

ABBY: That's right.

DKS: I wonder how much Brent understood those feelings at times.

ABBY: Well, he should have understood. I certainly told him.

BRENT: You told me . . .

ABBY: (*Interrupting*) I told him I needed him to help at home, that the baby couldn't carry on a conversation with me. I was tired and needed a break, and it wasn't fair that he had plenty of people to be with all day long. There's no way he couldn't have known . . .

BRENT: What I knew was that you expected me to work all day and then deal with the baby at night . . .

DKS: (*To Brent*) You knew she was upset . . .

BRENT: Of course . . .

DKS: But it didn't make complete sense to you.

BRENT: No, not really. She'd either blow up or stop talking entirely . . .

ABBY: I gave up . . . (*long pause, then starts to weep*)

DKS: It felt hopeless.

ABBY: That's right . . . (*long pause*)

DKS: I need to understand that feeling of hopelessness, where it comes from.

ABBY: It comes from being destined to be alone . . . (*another pause, weeping*)

DKS: Like before . . .

ABBY: That's right.

DKS: It's a familiar feeling for you.

ABBY: Always. My own mother gave me up. My adoptive father never wanted children, but took me and my brother in because my adoptive mother wanted us so bad. And then she goes and dies on me . . . I know it wasn't her fault, but she's all I had.

DKS: Not your father . . .

ABBY: Not really, certainly not after he married Janice.

DKS: Friends?

ABBY: No—I never really understood that. I was different somehow, I don't know. I had one really good friend in high school, but she got involved with a guy and just sort of left me behind.

DKS: And later . . . ?

ABBY: Not really. Aunt Mary let me come here and live with them . . . and I met this kind of crazy guy I got messed up with—Brent knows about him—but that ended too, probably for the better . . . (long pause) Really, after my mom died, probably no one I trusted or felt safe with until Brent . . . (another long pause) I guess that's pretty ironic, huh?

DKS: How so?

ABBY: Trusting him . . . and then betraying him . . .

BRENT: (Gently) Abby . . .

ABBY: I'm so sorry . . . (long pause)

DKS: When did you recognize your own feelings of betrayal?

ABBY: What do you mean?

DKS: Of being left again?

ABBY: I don't know. I know I felt alone. I don't know if I connected that to my mom's death and everything else . . .

DKS: Does that make sense to you as we talk about it now?

ABBY: I don't know. In some ways, I guess. I needed Brent . . .

DKS: Abby, I'm not going to tell you that you didn't have any reasons to feel alone after Peter arrived, and I don't think that Brent's going to tell you that either . . .

BRENT: No, I'm not.

DKS: But I *am* going to suggest to you that perhaps one reason your aloneness hurt so bad at that time was that it reopened some really deep wounds of aloneness that you experienced before you ever met Brent. And I think it was hard for you to understand that, and even harder for Brent.

ABBY: I guess so . . .

DKS: And I think that set you up to lash out or pull back in ways that led to your becoming even more alone.

Abby's willingness to acknowledge sources of hurt and aloneness that were separate from Brent led to a softening of his expressions during the session. Instead of responding defensively, he simply listened, at one point reaching to touch her hand when she wept while recounting the desperate loneliness she felt following her mother's death.

It wasn't clear during this session what impact Abby's disclosures might have on Brent's own understanding of what transpired during their hurtful exchanges years earlier. In the subsequent session, however, it became evident that he had been giving this considerable thought:

BRENT: I've been thinking some more about why I was spending so much time away from home the last couple of years. I mean, it's not like I really had to. I could always find plenty to do, but . . .

ABBY: Even when you weren't at the office, you were often gone—out with your friends or something . . .

BRENT: I'm not going to apologize for having friends, Abby. It's not my fault that you didn't have more friends . . .

ABBY: Well, you didn't exactly give me a whole lot of opportunity to go out.

BRENT: (Silence)

DKS: Brent, I want to understand better what you've been thinking about, what drove you to spend more time away from home than you might otherwise. Abby, for Brent and me to do that, I need you to let me explore this with him for a while today. Would you be willing to listen in while we do that?

ABBY: OK.

DKS: Brent, let's try to understand this better. You said you've been thinking about this. What have you thought about so far?

BRENT: Well, I know for a while in our marriage it seemed to work just fine. She and I were partners, you know? Nobody really expected us to succeed like we did, but we managed it on our own anyway—just the two of us.

DKS: That felt pretty good . . .

BRENT: Yeah. Because we were on the same side, sort of like us against them.

DKS: Who was the "them"?

BRENT: I don't know. Everybody, I guess . . . nobody really . . .

DKS: That's pretty confusing.

BRENT: Yeah, I guess . . .

DKS: You against them . . . What were you trying to win?

BRENT: (Long pause) I don't know. Respect, maybe . . .

DKS: Whose?

BRENT: (Another long pause) I don't know. Mine, maybe. I mean, I know that people respect me. My parents tell me they're proud of me, what I've accomplished.

ABBY: What *we've* accomplished . . .

DKS: Has it always felt that way?

BRENT: Not really. I mean, it still bothers me some times when my high-powered brother and sister start talking, and I get left out.

DKS: You don't feel high-powered?

BRENT: Not really.

DKS: How powerful do you need to feel?

BRENT: I don't know. Not all that powerful . . . I mean, once Abby and I got the business up and running, everything was going really good. I actually *felt* good. Like when I played golf on the weekend with the other guys at the club, I felt like I really *belonged*.

DKS: It was more about belonging than about power?

BRENT: I think so.

DKS: And at home . . . ?

BRENT: I don't know. I mean . . . I know Abby thought I needed to feel powerful at home. Maybe I did in some ways . . .

DKS: I don't think that's why you started spending more time away . . . Talk with me more about that feeling of belonging—especially how much "belonging" you felt at home.

BRENT: Well, it was just different than I thought it would be. I mean, I really wanted to be a good father and husband. And I think mostly I am. I provide well . . .

DKS: How much "belonging" did you feel?

BRENT: (*Long pause*) Well, I know it's stupid, but I guess I was wanting something different with the boys, something better. I guess for *them* to want *me* or something . . .

ABBY: But they do, Brent . . .

BRENT: Well, maybe more now . . .

DKS: It's not stupid to want your sons to want you . . . or to want to belong in your own family . . . not now, and not then . . . (*Long pause*) When the boys seemed disinterested in you, or when Abby was unhappy with you . . . that feeling of not belonging . . . was that familiar?

BRENT: I guess . . .

DKS: And the feelings that go along with not belonging?

BRENT: I don't know . . .

DKS: It hurts . . .

BRENT: Yeah . . .

DKS: Brent, when you get that feeling of not belonging, what's your first impulse?

BRENT: (*Pause*) To get out . . .

DKS: Like you did when you were growing up, and later in college?

BRENT: That's right.

DKS: But it hasn't been working for you . . . and it leads to a vicious cycle. When you leave Abby feels abandoned . . . and then she either pulls back from you or criticizes you for neglecting her and the boys . . . so you feel even less belonging and less inclined to hang around . . . and it escalates from there.

Brent: Yeah, I know . . . it's just that feeling . . . I wish I didn't get that feeling.

DKS: It's a familiar feeling, but I think it's partly a holdover and not a response to what's actually going on in the moment.

BRENT: What do you mean?

DKS: Well, I think growing up, you didn't feel you belonged because either you couldn't meet your parents' expectations or didn't want to.

BRENT: My dad was plenty successful, but that didn't mean he spent any more time with me.

DKS: That's right, and I think that may partly be why you rejected "success" as the criterion for belonging. But what Abby's looking for isn't success—at least not the same kind. I think for her, success as a husband means figuring out how to be more relaxed at home . . . just being available to spend time with . . . realizing that none of us starts out knowing very much about how to be a parent . . . and just hanging in there and learning a day at a time like the rest of us.

ABBY: He's right, Brent. I know that I wasn't very patient with you. I think I got pretty tired and frustrated with the boys myself, and maybe I just found it easier sometimes to direct that toward you. (*Pause*) You know, sometimes I didn't always feel like I belonged either . . . at least not in your life. The boys were all I had . . . Maybe sometimes I was actually glad when they seemed more comfortable with me. But I know that wasn't good.

BRENT: I think we can change that now.

Final Interventions

Abby and Brent continued to work on their marriage and on themselves. In the following months, Brent provided Abby additional support in her pursuing friendships outside the home. He became more patient with the boys, a more playful father, and a better partner with Abby in sharing the frustrations as well as the joys of parenting. Abby worked at communicating more effectively with Brent—expressing her needs proactively, rather than remaining silent and then expressing her disappointment reactively. Despite these gains, Brent's hurt from Abby's affair occasionally resurfaced in the form of angry recriminations when he felt unappreciated by her. Abby's own guilt initially prevented her from challenging this behavior, but eventually she disclosed her growing despair about whether they would ever be able to free themselves from the painful memories of this event in their lives. In the following session, Brent was visibly subdued. He acknowledged sometimes using his recriminations as a way of expressing hurt from events unrelated to Abby's affair, and he recognized this as toxic to their marriage. He expressed a profound wish to move beyond the hurts each of them had experienced in the past, and he pledged to refrain from "dredging up" the affair when feeling hurt in the future.

Toward the end of therapy Brent and Abby exchanged letters expressing their deeper understanding of Abby's affair, how it came about, what its impact had been, their subsequent efforts to strengthen their marriage, and their wish to move on. In his letter to Abby, Brent wrote:

> It's hard for me to say, but I was also at fault for the problems in our relationship that led to your affair. I hope you can forgive me. I also know that we can never move forward if I continue to hang on to my hurt. It will destroy me and our relationship. I am willing to forgive you for your affair so that we can reestablish what was lost in our relationship and also create something better. I forgive you because I love you and because more than anything, I want for us to be happy again. I know we still have some work ahead of us, but I am willing to continue what we have started so far. I am sorry for my part in our problems, and I never again want to come so close to losing you.

Follow-Up

In the following 18 months, the therapist had two unplanned encounters with Brent and Abby in the community. The first occurred 6 months after termination, on a soccer field where Brent was coaching Peter's team of 4-year-olds. Upon seeing the therapist, Brent brought his son to the side of the field and introduced him to "the man who helped Mommy and me last year work out our problems." Brent said that he and Abby were doing well, that she was working two mornings each week at their firm, and that he was enjoying more time with the boys. The second occasion was a year later at a movie theater, where Brent and Abby spotted their therapist. They approached him, smiling; they said

that they had sold their real estate business and were moving to South America for at least 2 years to be near Abby's father while Brent worked as a consultant to an international land development firm. Abby had gotten closer to her father in the past year and had visited him twice. They had corresponded more regularly following her visits, and her father had sent her pictures of her mother holding her as a toddler, which were now among Abby's most prized possessions. The couple acknowledged that they still struggled at times—Brent with his impatience, Abby with her reticence—but they expressed confidence in their future together and gratitude for their work with the therapist in the past.

PURSUING AN INFORMED PLURALISTIC APPROACH

How can couple therapists prepare to practice competently from a pluralistic perspective? For some, the first adapation must be an attitudinal one. Pluralistic practice requires rejecting dogmatism (Mahoney, 1991), resisting factionalism and parochialism (Safran & Messer, 1997), engaging irreducible ambiguity without wallowing in it (Bernstein, 1993), and cultivating "an inclusive and empirical approach in which the valuable contributions of pure-form therapies are collegially acknowledged and their respective strengths collaboratively enlisted" (Goldfried & Norcross, 1995, p. 269). To practice pluralistically requires flexible, synthetic, but critical thinking (Norcross & Halgin, 1997). Similar to clinical interventions helping individuals to integrate repudiated but fundamental aspects of themselves, so too must clinicians embrace the challenge of integrating renounced but valuable or even essential principles and techniques from alternative theoretical perspectives.

The second adaptation critical to pluralistic practice is a behavioral one. Couple therapists must be thoroughly schooled in both the conceptual suppositions and the technical interventions linked to diverse theoretical models of relationship distress and treatment. Equally important is a couple therapist's ability to incorporate these models in a conceptually coherent manner tailored to specific characteristics of individual partners, their relationship, and immediate circumstances of the therapeutic process. Such "deep structure integration" (Norcross & Beutler, 2000, p. 257) may emerge only after formal training in systematic treatment selection and years of clinical experience.

In encouraging couple and family therapists to pursue a personal integrative approach, Lebow (1987) noted that technique offers no substitute for therapeutic skill, and that therapists need to adopt a blend of theory, strategies, and specific interventions with which they are both professionally and personally comfortable. Therapists' vigorous pursuit of both attitudinal and behavioral competence in their own practice may ultimately parallel those same qualities of cognitive flexibility and diverse relationship skills they strive to instill in their clients.

REFERENCES

Alexander, F. (1956). *Psychoanalysis and psychotherapy.* New York: Norton.

Anchin, J. C., & Kiesler, D. J. (Eds.). (1982). *Handbook of interpersonal psychotherapy.* New York: Pergamon Press.

Aniol, J. C., & Snyder, D. K. (1997). Differential assessment of financial and relationship distress: Implications for couples therapy. *Journal of Marital and Family Therapy, 23,* 347–352.

Barber, J. P., & Crits-Christoph, P. (1991). Comparison of the brief dynamic therapies. In P. Crits-Christoph & J. P. Barber (Eds.), *Handbook of short-term dynamic psychotherapy* (pp. 323–352). New York: Basic Books.

Baucom, D. H., & Epstein, N. (1990). *Cognitive-behavioral marital therapy.* New York: Brunner/Mazel.

Baucom, D. H., Gordon, K. C., & Snyder, D. K. (in press). *Treating couples recovering from affairs.* New York: Guilford Press.

Baucom, D. H., Shoham, V., Mueser, K. T., Daiuto, A. D., & Stickle, T. R. (1998). Empirically supported couple and family interventions for marital distress and adult mental health problems. *Journal of Consulting and Clinical Psychology, 66,* 53–88.

Bernstein, R. (1983). *Beyond objectivism and relativism: Science, hermeneutics and praxis.* Philadelphia: University of Pennsylvania Press.

Beutler, L. E., & Clarkin, J. (1990). *Systematic treatment selection: Toward targeted therapeutic interventions.* New York: Brunner/Mazel.

Beutler, L. E., Consoli, A. J., & Williams, R. E. (1995). Integrative and eclectic therapies in practice. In B. Bongar & L. E. Beutler (Eds.), *Comprehensive textbook of psychotherapy: Theory and practice* (pp. 274–292). New York: Oxford University Press.

Binder, J. L., & Strupp, H. H. (1991). The Vanderbilt approach to time-limited dynamic psychotherapy. In P. Crits-Christoph & J. P. Barber (Eds.), *Handbook of short-term dynamic psychotherapy* (pp. 137–165). New York, NY: Basic Books.

Bongar, B., & Beutler, L. E. (Eds.). (1995). *Comprehensive textbook of psychotherapy: Theory and practice.* New York: Oxford University Press.

Bowlby, J. (1969). *Attachment and loss: Vol. 1. Attachment.* New York: Basic Books.

Bradbury, T. N., & Fincham, F. D. (1990). Attributions in marriage: Review and critique. *Psychological Bulletin, 107,* 3–33.

Christensen, A., & Heavey, C. L. (1999). Interventions for couples. *Annual Review of Psychology, 50,* 165–190.

Cookerly, J. R. (1980). Does marital therapy do any lasting good? *Journal of Marital and Family Therapy, 6,* 393–397.

Dattilio, F. M., & Padesky, C. A. (1990). *Cognitive therapy with couples.* Sarasota, FL: Professional Resource Exchange.

Dicks, H. V. (1967). *Marital tensions: Clinical studies towards a psycho-analytic theory of interaction.* London: Routledge & Kegan Paul.

Epstein, N., & Baucom, D. H. (in press). *Treating couples in context: Innovations in cognitive-behavioral therapy.* Washington, DC: American Psychological Association.

Epstein, N., Baucom, D. H., & Daiuto, A. (1997). Cognitive-behavioral couples therapy. In W. K. Halford & H. J. Markman (Eds.), *Clinical handbook of marriage and couples interventions* (pp. 415–449). New York: Wiley.

Fairbairn, W. R. D. (1952). *Psychoanalytic studies of the personality.* London: Routledge & Kegan Paul.

Furman, W., & Flanagan, A. S. (1997). The influence of earlier relationships on marriage: An attachment perspective. In W. K. Halford & H. J. Markman (Eds.), *Clinical handbook of marriage and couples interventions* (pp. 179–202). New York: Wiley.

Goldfried, M. R., & Norcross, J. C. (1995). Integrative and eclectic therapies in historical perspective. In B. Bongar & L. E. Beutler (Eds.), *Comprehensive textbook of psychotherapy: Theory and practice* (pp. 254–273). New York: Oxford University Press.

Gordon, K. C., Baucom, D. H., & Snyder, D. K. (2000). The use of forgiveness in marital therapy. In M. E. McCullough, K. I. Pargament, & C. E. Thoresen (Eds.), *Forgiveness: Theory, research, and practice* (pp. 203–227). New York: Guilford Press.

Gottlieb, M. C. (1996). Some ethical implications of relational diagnoses. In F. W. Kaslow (Ed.), *Handbook of relational diagnosis and dysfunctional family patterns* (pp. 19–34). New York: Wiley.

Gottman, J. M. (1999). *The marriage clinic: A scientifically based marital therapy.* New York: Norton.

Greenberg, L. S., & Johnson, S. M. (1988). *Emotionally focused therapy for couples.* New York: Guilford Press.

Gurman, A. S. (1980). Behavioral marriage therapy in the 1980's: The challenge of integration. *American Journal of Family Therapy, 8,* 86–96.

Gurman, A. S. (1981). Integrative marital therapy: Toward the development of an interpersonal approach. In S. H. Budman (Ed.), *Forms of brief therapy* (pp. 415–457). New York: Guilford Press.

Gurman, A. S. (1992). Integrative marital therapy: A time-sensitive model for working with couples. In S. H. Budman & M. F. Hoyt (Eds.), *The first session in brief therapy* (pp. 186–203). New York: Guilford Press.

Halford, W. K., & Bouma, R. (1997). Individual psychopathology and marital distress. In W. K. Halford & H. J. Markman (Eds.), *Clinical handbook of marriage and couples interventions* (pp. 291–321). New York: Wiley.

Hazan, C., & Shaver, P. R. (1987). Romantic love conceptualized as an attachment process. *Journal of Personality and Social Psychology, 59,* 511–524.

Holtzworth-Munroe, A., Beatty, S. B., & Anglin, K. (1995). The assessment and treatment of marital violence: An introduction for the marital therapist. In N. S.

Jacobson & A. S. Gurman (Eds.), *Clinical handbook of couple therapy* (pp. 317–339). New York: Guilford Press.

Horowitz, M. (1988). *Introduction to psychodynamics: A new synthesis.* New York: Basic Books.

Jacobson, N. S., & Christensen, A. (1996). *Integrative couple therapy: Promoting acceptance and change.* New York: Norton.

Jacobson, N. S., & Margolin, G. (1979). *Marital therapy: Strategies based on social learning and behavior exchange principles.* New York: Brunner/Mazel.

Jacobson, N. S., Schmaling, K. B., & Holtzworth-Munroe, A. (1987). Component analysis of behavioral marital therapy: 2-year follow-up and prediction of relapse. *Journal of Marital and Family Therapy, 13,* 187–195.

Johnson, S. M., & Greenberg, L. S. (1995). The emotionally focused approach to problems in adult attachment. In N. S. Jacobson & A. S. Gurman (Eds.), *Clinical handbook of couple therapy* (pp. 121–141). New York: Guilford Press.

Johnson, S. M., & Whiffen, V. E. (1999). Made to measure: Adapting emotionally focused couples therapy to partners' attachment styles. *Clinical Psychology: Science and Practice, 6,* 366–381.

Karpel, M. A. (1994). *Evaluating couples: A handbook for practitioners.* New York: Norton.

Klein, M. (1948). *Contributions to psycho-analysis, 1921–1945.* London: Hogarth Press.

Kobak, R., Ruckdeschel, K., & Hazan, C. (1994). From symptom to signal: An attachment view of emotion in marital therapy. In S. M. Johnson & L. S. Greenberg (Eds.), *The heart of the matter: Perspectives on emotion in marital therapy* (pp. 46–71). New York: Brunner/Mazel.

Lebow, J. L. (1987). Developing a personal integration in family therapy: Principles for model construction and practice. *Journal of Marital and Family Therapy, 13,* 1–14.

Lebow, J. L. (1997). The integrative revolution in couple and family therapy. *Family Process, 36,* 1–17.

Lebow, J. L., & Gurman, A. S. (1995). Research assessing couple and family therapy. *Annual Review of Psychology, 46,* 27–57.

Luborsky, L. (1984). *Principles of psychoanalytic psychotherapy: A manual for supportive–expressive treatment.* New York, NY: Basic Books.

Mahoney, M. J. (1991). *Human change processes: The scientific foundations of psychotherapy.* New York: Basic Books.

McGoldrick, M., Gerson, R., & Shellenberger, S. (1999). *Genograms: Assessment and intervention* (2nd ed.). New York: Norton.

Meissner, W. W. (1978). The conceptualization of marriage and family dynamics from a psychoanalytic perspective. In T. J. Paolino & B. S. McCrady (Eds.), *Marriage and marital therapy: Psychoanalytic, behavioral, and systems theory perspectives* (pp. 25–88). New York: Brunner/Mazel.

Messer, S. B., & Warren, C. S. (1995). *Models of brief psychodynamic therapy: A comparative approach.* New York: Guilford Press.

Nadelson, C. C., & Paolino, T. J. (1978). Marital therapy from a psychoanalytic perspective. In T. J. Paolino & B. S. McCrady (Eds.), *Marriage and marital therapy: Psychoanalytic, behavioral, and systems theory perspectives* (pp. 89–164). New York: Brunner/Mazel.

Norcross, J. C. (1985). Eclecticism: Definitions, manifestations and practitioners. *International Journal of Eclectic Psychotherapy, 4,* 19–32.

Norcross, J. C., & Beutler, L. E. (2000). A prescriptive eclectic approach to psychotherapy training. *Journal of Psychotherapy Integration, 10,* 247–261.

Norcross, J. C., & Goldfried, M. R. (1992). *Handbook of psychotherapy integration.* New York: Basic Books.

Norcross, J. C., & Halgin, R. P. (1997). Integrative approaches to psychotherapy supervision. In C. E. Watkins (Ed.), *Handbook of psychotherapy supervision* (pp. 203–222). New York: Wiley.

Norcross, J. C., Prochaska, J. O., & Farber, J. A. (1993). Psychologists conducting psychotherapy: New findings and historical comparisons on the psychotherapy division membership. *Psychotherapy, 30,* 692–697.

Patterson, T. (1997). Theoretical unity and technical eclecticism: Pathways to coherence in family therapy. *American Journal of Family Therapy, 25,* 97–109.

Pinsof, W. M. (1994). An overview of integrative problem centered therapy: A synthesis of family and individual psychotherapies. *Journal of Family Therapy, 16,* 103–120.

Safran, J. D., & Messer, S. B. (1997). Psychotherapy integration: A postmodern critique. *Clinical Psychology: Science and Practice, 4,* 140–152.

Sager, C. J. (1976). *Marriage contracts and couple therapy: Hidden forces in intimate relationships.* New York: Brunner/Mazel.

Sanders, M. R., Markie-Dadds, C., & Nicholson, J. M. (1997). Concurrent interventions for marital and children's problems. In W. K. Halford & H. J. Markman (Eds.), *Clinical handbook of marriage and couples interventions* (pp. 509–535). New York: Wiley.

Scharff, J. S. (1995). Psychoanalytic marital therapy. In N. S. Jacobson & A. S. Gurman (Eds.), *Clinical handbook of couple therapy* (pp. 164–193). New York: Guilford Press.

Segraves, R. T. (1982). *Marital therapy: A combined psychodynamic–behavioral approach.* New York: Plenum Press.

Segraves, R. T. (1990). Theoretical orientations in the treatment of marital discord. In F. D. Fincham & T. N. Bradbury (Eds.), *The psychology of marriage: Basic issues and applications* (pp. 281–298). New York: Guilford Press.

Shadish, W. R., Montgomery, L. M., Wilson, P., Wilson, M. R., Bright, I., & Okwumabua, T. (1993). Effects of family and marital psychotherapies: A meta-analysis. *Journal of Consulting and Clinical Psychology, 61,* 992–1002.

Shoham, V., Rohrbaugh, M., & Patterson, J. (1995). Problem- and solution-focused couple therapies: The MRI and Milwaukee models. In N. S. Jacobson & A. S. Gurman (Eds.), *Clinical handbook of couple therapy* (pp. 142–163). New York: Guilford Press.

Snyder, D. K. (1997). *Manual for the Marital Satisfaction Inventory–Revised.* Los Angeles: Western Psychological Services.

Snyder, D. K. (1999a). Affective reconstruction in the context of a pluralistic approach to couple therapy. *Clinical Psychology: Science and Practice, 6,* 348–365.

Snyder, D. K. (1999b). Pragmatic couple therapy: An informed pluralistic approach. In D. M. Lawson & F. F. Prevatt (Eds.), *Casebook in family therapy* (pp. 81–110). Pacific Grove, CA: Brooks/Cole Wadsworth.

Snyder, D. K., & Abbott, B. V. (2002). Couple distress. In M. M. Antony & D. H. Barlow (Eds.), *Handbook of assessment and treatment planning for psychological disorders* (pp. 341–374). New York: Guilford Press.

Snyder, D. K., Abbott, B. V., & Castellani, A. M. (2002). Assessing couples. In J. N. Butcher (Ed.), *Clinical personality assessment: Practical approaches* (2nd ed., pp. 225–242). New York: Oxford University Press.

Snyder, D. K., & Aikman, G. G. (1999). The Marital Satisfaction Inventory—Revised. In M. E. Maruish (Ed.), *Use of psychological testing for treatment planning and outcomes assessment* (2nd ed., pp. 1173–1210). Mahwah, NJ: Erlbaum.

Snyder, D. K., Baucom, D. H., & Gordon, K. C. (in press). *Can this marriage be saved?: How to make the right decisions following an affair.* New York: Guilford Press.

Snyder, D. K., Cavell, T. A., Heffer, R. W., & Mangrum, L. F. (1995). Marital and family assessment: A multifaceted, multilevel approach. In R. H. Mikesell, D. D. Lusterman, & S. H. McDaniel (Eds.), *Integrating family therapy: Handbook of family psychology and systems theory* (pp. 163–182). Washington, DC: American Psychological Association.

Snyder, D. K., Cozzi, J. J., & Mangrum, L. F. (2002). Conceptual issues in assessing couples, and families. In H. A. Liddle, D. A. Santisteban, R. F. Levant, & J. H. Bray (Eds.), *Family psychology: Science-based intervention* (pp. 69–87). Washington, DC: American Psychological Association.

Snyder, D. K., Mangrum, L. F., & Wills, R. M. (1993). Predicting couples' response to marital therapy: A comparison of short- and long-term predictors. *Journal of Consulting and Clinical Psychology, 61,* 61–69.

Snyder, D. K., & Wills, R. M. (1989). Behavioral versus insight-oriented marital therapy: Effects on individual and interspousal functioning. *Journal of Consulting and Clinical Psychology, 57,* 39–46.

Snyder, D. K., Wills, R. M., & Grady-Fletcher, A. (1991a). Long-term effectiveness of behavioral versus insight-oriented marital therapy: A four-year follow-up study. *Journal of Consulting and Clinical Psychology, 59,* 138–141.

Snyder, D. K., Wills, R. M., & Grady-Fletcher, A. (1991b). Risks and challenges of long-term psychotherapy outcome research: Reply to Jacobson. *Journal of Consulting and Clinical Psychology, 59,* 146–149.

Strupp, H. H., & Binder, J. L. (1984). *Psychotherapy in a new key: A guide to time-limited dynamic psychotherapy.* New York: Basic Books.

Thompson, B. M. (1997). Couples and the work–family interface. In W. K. Halford & H. J. Markman (Eds.), *Clinical handbook of marriage and couples interventions* (pp. 273–290). New York: Wiley.

Todd, T. C. (1986). Structural–strategic marital therapy. In N. S. Jacobson & A. S. Gurman (Eds.), *Clinical handbook of marital therapy* (pp. 71–105). New York: Guilford Press.

Whisman, M. A., & Snyder, D. K. (1997). Evaluating and improving the efficacy of conjoint couple therapy. In W. K. Halford & H. J. Markman (Eds.), *Clinical handbook of marriage and couples interventions* (pp. 679–693). New York: Wiley.

Wile, D. B. (1995). The ego-analytic approach to couple therapy. In N. S. Jacobson & A. S. Gurman (Eds.), *Clinical handbook of couple therapy* (pp. 91–120). New York: Guilford Press.

Wills, R. M., Faitler, S. M., & Snyder, D. K. (1987). Distinctiveness of behavioral versus insight-oriented marital therapy: An empirical analysis. *Journal of Consulting and Clinical Psychology, 55,* 685–690.

Young, J. E. (1999). *Cognitive therapy for personality disorders: A schema-focused approach* (3rd ed.). Sarasota, FL: Professional Resource Press.

Young, J. E., & Brown, G. (1999). *Young Schema Questionnaire* (2nd ed.). In J. E. Young, *Cognitive therapy for personality disorders: A schema-focused approach* (3rd ed., pp. 59–69). Sarasota, FL: Professional Resource Press. (Original work published 1990)

Young, J. E., & Gluhoski, V. (1997). A schema-focused perspective on satisfaction in close relationships. In R. J. Sternberg & M. Hojjat (Eds.), *Satisfaction in close relationships* (pp. 356–381). New York: Guilford Press.

Chapter 7

Brief Integrative Marital Therapy: A Depth-Behavioral Approach

ALAN S. GURMAN

Brief Integrative Marital Therapy (BIMT) is a therapeutic approach to the relationship difficulties of married or otherwise committed couples that attends simultaneously and systematically to both interpersonal and intrapersonal factors. Although BIMT was not originally designed to be time-limited, the model's implicit therapeutic values, intervention focus, and usual techniques tend to render it a relatively brief experience. BIMT rests on a foundation of general family systems theory and adult developmental theory (including attachment theory), but it is most pervasively influenced by applied social learning theory—that is, behavior therapy (see Dimidjian, Martell, & Christensen, Chapter 9, this volume)— and object relations theory (see Scharff & Bagnini, Chapter 3, this volume).

BIMT has been developed and refined over the last two decades (Gurman, 1981, 1982a, 1982b, 1982c, 1984, 1985, 1992), and has grown out of a series of works addressing both empirical research in couple and family therapy (Gurman, 1971, 1973a, 1973b; Gurman & Kniskern, 1978a, 1978b, 1978c, 1978d, 1981; Gurman, Kniskern, & Pinsof, 1986) and conceptual considerations (Gurman, 1978, 1980, 1983a, 1990, 2001; Gurman & Knudson, 1978; Gurman, Knudson, & Kniskern, 1978) in the practice of couple therapy. Although developed independently, BIMT is similar in some ways to the integrative models offered by Segraves (1978, 1982), Berman, Lief, and Williams (1981), and more recently by Gilbert and Shmulker (1996) and Snyder (1999; see also Snyder & Schneider, Chapter 6, this volume).

BACKGROUND

The Need for Integrative Approaches to Marital Therapy

It has been reliably established that the most common theoretical orientation among psychotherapists is eclecticism (Bergin & Jensen, 1990; Norcross & Prochaska, 1988). This pattern appears to be true of marital therapists as well (Rait, 1988), despite the intense conceptual divisions that have historically characterized the domain of couple therapy (Gurman & Fraenkel, in press), and that might therefore readily lead clinicians to believe that the merging of models and methods would be not only undesirable but even untenable. Indeed, Lebow (1997) has referred to the integrative "revolution" in couple and family therapy, and has argued that "the move to integration has become so much a part of our work that it largely goes unrecognized" (p. 1).

The rationale for fostering integrative approaches to couple therapy includes both general and specific elements. The general values of such approaches include the understanding of human behavior and the enhancement of treatment flexibility. Choosing to emphasize either intrapsychic or interpersonal forces in intimate relationships while virtually excluding the other domain, as has often happened in marital therapy (Gurman & Fraenkel, in press), can be done only on arbitrary grounds. As Martin (1976) stated over 25 years ago, "Those who prefer to stress either the intrapersonal or the interpersonal aspects alone limit themselves. The separation . . . is an artificial separation that does not occur in the nature of the human being" (p. 8). And Wachtel (1997), a systems-oriented individual therapist, has argued that "Interpersonal and intrapsychic are not really alternatives but rather two poles of a single . . . dialectic process" (p. 338). Like Martin, Wachtel urges that we transcend "the misleading dichotomy between interpersonal and intrapsychic" (p. 338). BIMT thus rests on the assumption that the effective practice of couple therapy requires a broad explanatory base. BIMT further asserts that therapeutic thinking about couples that is genuinely "systemic" is inherently integrative, in that the relationships of human beings (unlike machines or subhuman species) operate not only at multiple levels of organization (Steinglass, 1978), but also at multiple levels of consciousness. BIMT is not "systemic" in the sense of being a "systems purist" approach (Beels & Ferber, 1969); that is, couples and families are not seen as entities with their own reified "unity of purpose" (Bogdan, 1984, p. 19). However, BIMT is most definitely systemic in its "attention to organization, to the relationship between parts, to the concentration on patterned rather than linear relationships, to a consideration of events in the context in which they are occurring rather than an isolation of events from their environmental context" (Steinglass, 1978, p. 304).

The evolution of BIMT and of some other integrative approaches to couple therapy, especially those that incorporate psychodynamic considerations (e.g., Berman et al., 1981; Feldman, 1979, 1985; Pinsof, 1995, 1999; Segraves, 1982), has occurred to a significant degree in reaction to a reified overemphasis in the field of family therapy on the notion of "the family as a system" (Gurman & Fraenkel, in press; Nichols & Schwartz, 1998; Schwartz & Johnson, 2000). By their reinclusion of the psychology of the individual, these integrative approaches have provided practical, intervention-focused support to Ferreira's (quoted by J. Framo, personal communication, 1981) observation that "We had to recognize that the family was a system before we could recognize that it did not always act like a system."

Finally, BIMT asserts that treatment approaches that systematically consider and attempt to produce change on multiple levels of social-psychological experience will facilitate the development of interventions that are more flexible and responsive to differences between patients, and will thus lead to more positive and enduring outcomes. Despite its general effectiveness (Bray & Jouriles, 1995; Gurman & Fraenkel, in press; Lebow & Gurman, 1995), marital therapy has at times been found to yield only moderate rates of improvement, and to show some waning in its effects at longer-term follow-up (Bray & Jouriles, 1995; Jacobson & Addis, 1993; Pinsof, 1999). Such positive yet somewhat limited effects have been found in studies of "singular" methods of therapy, which, not insignificantly, typically emphasize change in certain domains of experience over others, and often to the exclusion of others. For example, behavioral methods emphasize change in overt behavior, whereas more psychodynamic methods emphasize nonobservable intrapsychic change. Interestingly, the couple therapy method that to date has shown the most enduring benefits from treatment has been one that attends to both intrapsychic and interpersonal factors, and to both conscious and unconscious factors in marital satisfaction (Snyder, 1999; Snyder & Wills, 1989; see also Snyder & Schneider, Chapter 6, this volume). Moreover, the behaviorally oriented couple therapy that to date has shown the strongest clinical outcomes is one (Cordova, Jacobson, & Christensen, 1998) that includes treatment elements not contained in more pure-form, "traditional" behavioral couple therapy (cf. Jacobson & Holtzworth-Munroe, 1986), and that balances its attention to both behavior change and affective–cognitive change (see Dimidjian et al., Chapter 9, this volume).

The Nature of Integrative Approaches to Marital Therapy

Integrative approaches to psychotherapy have increased noticeably over the last two decades, and although they are not as common in marital therapy (Gurman & Fraenkel, in press), have shown a greater influence on the field more recently. Couple therapy integrations have brought together structural and strategic approaches (e.g., Stanton, 1980; Todd, 1986), and behavior therapy and systems theory approaches (e.g., Birchler & Spinks, 1980; Smith, 2001; Weiss, 1980); like BIMT, however, have most commonly combined behavioral and psychodynamic approaches (e.g., Bagarozzi & Giddings, 1983; Berman et al., 1981; Feldman, 1979, 1985; Gilbert & Shmulker, 1996; Greenspan & Mannino, 1974; Nichols, 1988; Pinsof, 1995; Sager, 1976, 1981).

It is generally agreed that there are three main types of psychotherapy integration (Messer & Warren, 1995). "Technical eclecticism" calls upon interventions from theoretically diverse methods, and includes "prescriptive matching"—that is, pairing the use of particular techniques with particular symptoms, syndromes or personality (or relationship) types. "Theoretical integration" attempts to combine different theories, as well as the techniques deriving from those theories, and typically identifies one theory that dominates the other(s). Finally, the "common-factors approach" to integration emphasizes therapeutic variables and processes that are presumed to be central to the effective conduct of all types of therapy.

The third type of integration has not yet been offered as the basis for a method of couple therapy (cf. Duncan & Miller's [2000] "conversational" approach to family therapy). Although a significant number of couple therapists probably practice technical eclecticism (Rait, 1988), the great majority of systematic integrations in couple therapy have been of the theoretically integrative type—most often with psychodynamic or object relations theory serving as the conceptual core for understanding marital dynamics, and behavioral techniques being heavily relied upon because of the paucity of techniques that are specific to the practice of psychodynamic marital therapy (Gurman, 1978). This retention of a core or "home" theory, and concurrent incorporation of techniques originating outside the home theory, typify what is generally called "assimilative integration" (Messer, 1992, 2001).

BIMT follows these integrative trends, though perhaps giving more balanced conceptual roles to both behavioral and psychodynamic views than most related models do. BIMT explicitly calls upon both perspectives in both its basic understanding of functional and dysfunctional couple relationships, and in its methods of assessment and intervention. As will be shown, BIMT attempts to integrate the interpersonal with the intrapersonal, and to integrate theoretical perspectives. BIMT aims to integrate people as well as theories and techniques.

A note on the risks of integrative approaches is in order here. Being an integratively oriented couple therapist, whether of the BIMT or other variety, is not without attendant risks and costs. First, while the practice of integrative therapies may

ultimately feel quite rewarding because of the therapist's sense of treating more of the "whole person" than in some single-dimension approaches, integrative approaches are more difficult to learn at first. Thus, for example, in BIMT the therapist needs to be conversant with both social learning ("behavioral") theory (e.g., Bandura, 1969; Kanfer & Phillips, 1970) and object relations theory (e.g., Dicks, 1967; Scharff, 1995). Unfortunately, these historically independent (Gurman & Fraenkel, in press) theories are not commonly taught within the same clinical training institutions. Moreover, such consolidations of disparate-sounding approaches can only be achieved through idiosyncratic personal integration (Gurman, 1990; Lebow, 1987).

In addition, even when the core theories and methods that are integrated within a particular approach have been well learned, there can be a particular "pull" from integratively oriented therapists toward utopian goal setting. Seeing the multileveled ways in which marital relationships play out, for better and perhaps especially for worse, can hypnotize integrative therapists into believing that their job is never quite done. In fact, this "pull" often abates as integrative therapists gain in clinical experience, and come to see that integrative approaches may in fact foster therapeutic brevity by having simultaneous positive impacts on multiple psychological levels.

Finally, the continuing development of integrative and eclectic approaches runs the risk of unintentionally impeding theory development (Liddle, 1982): Ironically, to the extent that integrative movements gain ascendance, less attention and energy may be paid to the refinement and enhancement of the very schools of therapeutic thought from which given integrative approaches draw their core concepts.

BIMT and Therapeutic Brevity

Although BIMT certainly can be practiced within predetermined time limits, this is not a cardinal feature of the approach. Still, BIMT is generally a brief method for two main reasons. First, it adheres very closely to the central values of most brief therapies (Budman & Gurman, 1988), such as clinical parsimony, the use of a developmental perspective, an emphasis on change that occurs outside therapy, and an emphasis on current issues. In addition, BIMT's use of and view of time, its views of the therapist–patient relationship, the nature of its typical treatment focus, and its most common techniques, which together constitute "the four central technical factors of brief therapy" (Gurman, 2001), generally lead to relatively brief courses of treatment. In addition, Donovan (1999) emphasizes as central principles of brief couple therapy the importance of the therapist's technical flexibility, ability to "manage the emotional intensity" (p. 5), and ability to build therapeutic alliances and "arrange an affirming emotional experience" (p. 6). As emphasized elsewhere (Budman & Gurman, 1988), brief therapy is most usefully defined not by the number of therapy sessions, but by the sorts of active ingredients just enumerated. Each of these brevity-inducing factors is considered in what follows.

THE WELL-FUNCTIONING VERSUS DYSFUNCTIONAL MARRIAGE

BIMT accepts as fundamental the assumption that the proclivity of people to form and maintain relational attachments throughout life is probably universal. BIMT agrees with attachment-oriented couple therapies, such as emotionally focused couple therapy (Greenberg & Johnson, 1986, 1988; Johnson & Denton, Chapter 8, this volume; Johnson & Greenberg, 1995), that secure connections to accessible and responsible attachment figures allow for interactional flexibility and open communication, while simultaneously fostering autonomy. Conversely, as Karpel (1994) summarizes the matter, "Difficulties in early attachments can lead to an inability to trust, to unmet and therefore excessive needs for attachment, to internal representations that distort perceptions of the partner, and to unconscious defenses that preclude vulnerability and intimacy" (p. 10). As will be seen, although BIMT focuses very little on early attachment experiences, it certainly respects the power of such experiences in creating conditions for the maintenance of couple conflict.

The Topography of Marital Functioning

In recent years, marital therapists of varying theoretical persuasions have sought a clinically meaningful description of functional vs. dysfunctional intimate relationships that rests on an empirical base (Lebow, 1999). Overwhelmingly, two strands within the scientific study of marital harmony and dysfunction have attracted the attention of marital therapists and clinical theorists: those of cognitive (e.g.,

Baucom, Epstein, & LaTaillade, Chapter 2, this volume; Baucom, Epstein, & Rankin, 1995) and behavioral (e.g., Christensen, Jacobson, & Babcock, 1995; Holtzworth-Munroe & Jacobson, 1991; Jacobson & Holtzworth-Munroe, 1986) investigators, and those of empirically oriented social-psychological investigators, most prominently Gottman (1979, 1993, 1994a, 1994b, 1998, 1999; Gottman, Driver, & Tabares, Chapter 13, this volume). Quite remarkably, the findings emerging from such investigations have been incorporated into the treatment models of marital therapists with orientations ranging from eclectic (Budman, 1999), to cognitive-behavioral (e.g., Epstein & Baucom, 1998) and behavioral (e.g., Holtzworth-Munroe & Jacobson, 1991), to experiential (Johnson & Denton, Chapter 8, this volume), and even transgenerational (Papero, 2000; Roberto-Forman, Chapter 5, this volume).

In like manner, BIMT sees such findings in the aggregate as providing a theoretically and clinically salient description of the typical topography of marital interactional health and dysfunction. Here I present a summary of the pattern of findings from such research that should help to orient the BIMT therapist regarding both the development of a treatment focus and the options available for intervention.

From the combined perspective of assessing marital satisfaction and predicting the longer-term stability of marriages, "unhappy" (dysfunctional, dissatisfied) couples, compared to "happy" (functional, satisfied), show the following characteristics: (1) lower rates of pleasing behavior and higher rates of displeasing behavior; (2) a greater probability of reciprocating negative behavior (as Lederer & Jackson [1968] said, "Nastiness begets nastiness"); and (3) poor communication skills (e.g., expressive skills such as the use of "I" statements, positive requests for behavior change, and receptive skills such as empathizing and reflecting) and problem-solving skills (e.g., clarifying and maintaining a pinpointed focus, avoiding inferences about one's mate, focusing on solutions via brainstorming, and taking responsibility both by focusing on one's own views and by not blaming one's mate for the problem). Poor communication and problem solving are characterized by (3a) "harsh startups" (usually by wives) of problem-focused conversations and poor ability to repair ruptures in the couple exchange (e.g., by the use of humor, shows of affection and interest), marked by a heightened focus on affect rather than problem solving, and accompanied by diffuse physiological arousal (especially in husbands) paired with difficulty in self-soothing. All of this typically culminates in the moment in the rapid escalation of aversive experiences, setting the couple up for a more chronic likelihood of emotional disengagement and withdrawal, via a predictable process of escape/avoidance conditioning. Moreover, (3b) conflictual couples tend to become deadlocked over inherently unresolvable differences, known as "perpetual problems" (e.g., core personality or value differences), but to treat these differences as though they were resolvable, thus addressing them in an inherently inappropriate and ineffective manner.

Furthermore, partners in unhappy couples, in attempting to influence each other, (4) generally use misguided behavior change methods characterized by "pain control" (i.e., providing aversive consequences to undesired behavior, such as criticism, contempt, "stonewalling," and defensiveness) rather than mutual reciprocity. In addition, at a cognitive level, "unhappy" couples (5) show "negative attributional biases" in the form of disregarding both the presence of positive partner behaviors and increases in positive partner behaviors, and see negative partner behavior as reflecting permanent partner characteristics, and positive behavior as reflecting temporary states. Relatedly, negative events have longer-lasting negative effects in unhappy couples, where partners tend to blame each other for couple problems while taking little individual responsibility for them, to make faulty attributions about each other's motivations and intent, and to engage in cognitive distortions such as all-or-nothing thinking, overgeneralization, jumping to conclusions, and catastrophizing/magnification. Finally, in the cognitive realm, "unhappy" couples (6) are more likely than happy couples to have more unrealistic expectations of marriage in general, and of their actual partners in particular.

The Skill Deficit Hypothesis

That a coherent body of research findings such as these should attract the attention of such a diverse range of marital therapists as noted earlier is striking and meaningful. The meaning seems quite clear. That is, this pattern of research findings on marital dysfunction and satisfaction topographically captures the essence of predictable patterns of chronic marital disaffection extremely well—so well, indeed, that clinicians who might disagree with each other on many important matters can agree on what they are treating, topographically at least.

But then the important questions arise: *Why* do dysfunctional couples behave in the particular ways they do? *Why* do such perceptual/attributional patterns emerge? On this matter, behavioral therapists have generally taken a very clear position. These patterns exist because couples who show them have "skill deficits" of various sorts, and, one might say, "cognitive excesses" (i.e., too many cognitive distortions and faulty attributions). Similarly, cognitive-behavioral therapists (e.g., Christensen et al., 1995; Holtzworth-Munroe & Jacobson, 1991) explain that the timing of the emergence of significant couple conflict is often understandable in light of the ever-changing contingencies of adult relationship life that pose new challenges to couples, for which they "lack" appropriate skills. One almost cannot read a publication on behavioral treatment of couple problems without encountering the "skill deficit" hypothesis. This hypothesis logically points to the clinical need for "teaching" and "training" couples in the appropriate "skills."

Several studies (Birchler, Weiss, & Wampler, 1972; Birchler, Weiss, & Vincent, 1975; Birchler & Webb, 1975; Vincent, Weiss, & Birchler, 1975) have found that partners in distressed marriages behave quite differently (more positive and fewer aversive mutual influence attempts) when interacting (i.e., problem-solving) with their partners than when interacting with strangers. Moreover, partners in distressed marriages can change their communication style in a positive direction simply by following an experimenter's instruction to do so (Vincent, Friedman, Nugent, & Messerly, 1979). The central point of such findings in the present context is that the "skill-deficient" partners from unhappy marriages actually can and do exhibit requisite interpersonal skills in another interactional context.

This simple but fundamental observation exemplifies the core distinction within applied social learning theory between problems of acquisition (the person has never learned the behavior in question) and problems of performance (the person shows the requisite behavior in some circumstances, but not under others). Hamburg (1996) refers to the "fundamental and unproven assumption . . . that couples have problems because, in some sense, they don't know how to be married and so must be taught" (p. 57)—in other words, that the kinds of problematic behaviors summarized earlier reflect acquisition problems.

In addition to research findings that cast doubt on the skill deficit hypothesis, it is common—indeed, almost routine—to find clinically that the kinds of "skills" that appear to be in such short supply usually were quite, or at least more, present during early phases of couples' relationships. Do married people "lose" these capacities? Again, clinical experience argues otherwise. It is commonplace to hear that although Susie complains that Bob "shows no feelings, is cold and distant to me, isn't interested in my point of view, and argues about almost everything," Bob consistently displays such apparently "missing" people skills with other people (e.g., coworkers, friends, and children).

It is unfortunate that the skill deficit hypothesis has gained such explanatory ascendance within behavioral marital therapy and even among other therapies, when the undisputed pioneer of the behavioral approach, the late Neil Jacobson, himself acknowledged (but only in passing) that the hypothesis may be a weak one. For example, Jacobson noted that "For many of these skill areas, it is likely that the more appropriate label would be 'performance deficit' rather than 'skill deficit' . . . it may be that . . . the innate abilities are present . . . but the enactments are not occurring under the stimulus control of the partner's presence. The term 'skill' may be a metaphor rather than a term to be taken literally" (Holtzworth-Munroe & Jacobson, 1991, pp. 100–101). And, more recently, Jacobson (Lawrence, Eldridge, Christensen, & Jacobson, 1999) wrote, "Typically, couples know how to communicate effectively, but haven't used these abilities for some time. We elicit the skills they already have" (p. 254).

Moving toward an Alternative Hypothesis

There exists an alternative hypothesis, or perspective, to the skill deficit view. It is possible that the spouse–stranger differences observed in research and related observations from clinical practice may point to the interactional difficulties that certain individuals have in intimate relationships, and to the unfortunate combination of such individual difficulties in chronically distressed couple relationships.

It seems that the dominant skill-focused view of couples in most of behavior therapy has failed to acknowledge the fundamental nonequivalence and noncomparability of intimate versus superficial relationships, which lack a developmental history, privately shared meaning systems, and implicit transactional "rules." Dicks (1967) noted that "The special feature of such apparent hate-relationships in marriage is that they occur within the framework of a compelling sense of belonging. The spouses

are clear in their minds that they would not dream of treating anyone else but each other in this way" (p. 70).

So why do members of unhappy couples not communicate and problem-solve better, please each other more, repair conversational ruptures, stay calm even in the face of discussing differences, and so on? Why do they escalate their conflict, reinforce the very behaviors in each other that they object to so passionately, block out from their awareness the good in their partners and highlight the bad, and attribute the most unkind motivations to each other? Why do they go on, as Dicks said, "treating . . . each other in this way"? What are they really fighting about? Behavioral and social-psychological research on couples has aided us tremendously in describing the topography of marital conflict. But we must turn to other complementary theoretical perspectives to understand the function of the kinds of observable behavior we see so regularly in marital conflict.

The Unconscious Dimension of Marital Interaction

The Marital Quid Pro Quo

A foundational concept relevant here is Jackson's (1965a, 1965b) notion of family "rules"—that is, inferred patterns of redundant interaction that structure the most defining aspects of a relationship. And among family rules, the one of greatest importance in marriage involves the marital "quid pro quo." In contrast to quid pro quo arrangements in, for example, behavior exchange interventions in behavioral couple therapy, quid pro quo exchanges are "not overt, conscious or the tangible result of real bargaining" (Jackson, 1965a, p. 592), and are not point-for-point or "time-bound" (Lederer & Jackson, 1968, p. 272). Rather, the essence of the quid pro quo is an "unconscious effort of both partners to assure themselves that they are equals, that they are peers. It is a technique enabling each to preserve his dignity and self-esteem" (Lederer & Jackson, 1968, p. 179). This view of the quid pro quo is reminiscent of Dicks's (1967) notion of "the foundations of a marriage as a mutual affirmation of the other's identity as a *lovable person*" (p. 36, italics in original). Thus the "quid pro quo pattern becomes another (usually not consciously recognized) set of ground rules" (Lederer & Jackson, 1968, p. 179) that provide "a *metaphorical* statement of the marital relationship bargain; that is, how the couple has agreed to *define themselves* within this relationship" (Jackson, 1965b, p. 12; emphasis added).

As Jackson saw it, the unconscious attribute of quid pro quo exchanges is not the familiar Freudian unconscious or, indeed, the unconscious of any particular theoretical system. It is, one might say, the descriptive unconscious—that is, that which simply is out of awareness. This "descriptive unconscious" is an essential notion in BIMT because it allows, as we shall see, a bridging of an active and strongly behaviorally influenced therapeutic style with an overriding respect for an awareness of factors that influence marital behavior quite outside the realm of direct observation, including conscious self-observation. Even such an influential cognitive-behavioral therapist as Mahoney (1979) has acknowledged that a belief in the existence and influence of unconscious processes does not require an advocacy of any particular dynamic system.

Similarly, Wachtel's (1977, 1993; Wachtel & McKinney, 1992; Wachtel & Wachtel, 1986) concept of "cyclical psychodynamics" combines social learning theory and psychodynamic theory without wholesale acceptance of the metabeliefs of either therapeutic orientation. This approach, like BIMT, emphasizes the repetitive cycles of interaction between people and notes how these cycles reciprocally include both intrapsychic processes and overt behavior—how deep structures and surface structures operate together.

The Contribution of Object Relations Theory

Among the conceptual systems dealing with deeper structures, the one that speaks most directly to couple therapists is object relations theory, which is broadly consistent with Jackson's (1965a, 1965b) notion of the marital quid pro quo. In the BIMT approach, object relations theory provides the specific concepts to explain the mechanisms at work in the quid pro quo. Like Wachtel's (Wachtel & McKinney, 1992) integrative, cyclical psychodynamic approach, BIMT does not incorporate the wider belief system associated with object relations theory (see, e.g., Scharff, 1995; Scharff & Bagnini, Chapter 3, this volume; Dicks, 1967; Skynner, 1976; Meissner, 1978; Willi, 1982). BIMT draws selectively upon object relations concepts that facilitate the development of an integrative treatment approach.

Important Object Relations Concepts in BIMT. BIMT recognizes "the legacies of early attachment" (Karpel, 1994, p. 10), and assumes that early attachment difficulties from "not good enough" parenting play a significant role in the capacity for healthy relating in intimate adult relationships (Bowlby, 1988; Fairbairn, 1963; Klein, 1946; Winnicott, 1960). But BIMT places much more emphasis on the present dyadic reenactment of such unfortunate individual developmental histories—on how, as Bentovim (1979) put it, "interpersonal relationships determine intrapsychic structure and how these structures in the mind come to reactivate such relationships at a later date" (p. 331) and give meaning to interpersonal events.

In this framework, the core source of marital dysfunction is both partners' failure to see themselves and each other as "whole persons" (Dicks, 1967; Stewart, Peters, Marsh, & Peters, 1975). Conflict-laden aspects of oneself, presumably punished or aversively conditioned earlier in life, are repudiated and "split off." These aspects of self are projected onto the mate, who in turn "accepts" the projection (i.e., behaves in accordance with it). The problematic aspect of the unconscious quid pro quo is not only that it is a mutually reinforcing process of projective identifications (similar to what social psychologists call "socially induced affect"—e.g., Cytrynbaum & Ruda, 1999; McIntosh, 1994), but also, and perhaps even more importantly, that there is an implicit agreement or "collusion" not to talk about or challenge the agreement. The collusion is a joint, shared avoidance that involves both intrapsychic and interpersonal defenses against various fears (e.g., merger, attack, abandonment, etc.). Collusion is a bilateral process in which partners seek to maintain a consistent, if maladaptive, sense of self. It represents attempted solutions to individual and dyadic problems. Projective identification and collusion are unconscious forms of communication, in which important information about oneself is exchanged. Scarf (1986), in a manner reminiscent of Jackson's (1965b) quid pro quo, notes that "the exchange of projections is a psychological barter occurring at an unconscious level" (p. 52).

Such collusion is especially problematic in relationships in which each partner's schemas are very rigid, and make it likely that they will see each other, consciously or unconsciously, in terms of past relationships instead of as "real contemporary people" (Raush, Berry, Hertel, & Swain, 1974, p. 25). Such rigidity and associated polarized psychological roles may significantly reduce the capacity of the couple or its individual partners to "adapt to new circumstances" (Raush et al., 1974, p. 25).

Such restrictive schemas are often manifested early in therapy when partners choose causal explanations of their couple problems that put their mates in the villain role—that is, what cognitive-behavioral theories refer to as "negative attributional biases."

Catherall (1992) emphasizes that the major problem with projective identification is not its existence but "the couple's failure—as a system—to manage the disturbing thoughts and feelings that are the substance of projective identifications" (pp. 355–356). To manage such experiences, couples must be able to engage in effective "containing" and "holding." Containing is a self-referential process in which the partner is able to allow painful feelings and thoughts into consciousness, without the need to project them onto the mate. Holding is a dyadic process in which the listener/recipient can identify with the speaker's feelings (i.e., can empathically hear them as belonging to the speaker), whether they are about the speaker or the listener, without experiencing intolerable anxiety (i.e., he/she is able to contain any discomfort associated with the speaker's behavior). If the recipient is unable to identify with the speaker and contain his/her own feelings, he/she is more likely to enact reciprocal, and often rapidly escalating, problematic behavior.

The Functional Value of Marital Conflict and the Functional Value of Skill Deficits. Although these unconscious communication processes may seem malevolent, in fact object relations theory sees them simultaneously as both problematic and positive. In this framework, repetitive, seemingly nonproductive conflict is goal-oriented; it serves to present the awareness of unconscious anxiety stimulated by relationship intimacy. But, in addition to this two-way protective function, collusion is a potentially growthful collaboration—an adaptive effort to resolve individual conflicts through specific, accommodating, intimate relationships.

But cooperation via collusion exacts a high toll. Poor communication and problem-solving behaviors are quite predictable from an observed pattern of paradoxical communication. Moreover, such "unskilled" communication styles are required in order to maintain unconscious collusion. That is, in the BIMT framework, "poor social skills" in intimate relationships more often than not reflect the more basic, unspoken rule of limited intimacy. The unfortunate protective function of "skill deficits" requires that the therapy include explicit attention to the mutually avoidant defensive function of such "deficits" in order to challenge the joint defenses in the very service of which the "deficits" exist.

Thus the "skills deficit hypothesis" is substantially weakened when one recognizes that, as Berman et al. (1981) put it, "marriages are indeed different from other relationships . . . most people do not project the same internal conflict equally on everyone, but only on the person with whom one allows oneself to be intimate" (p. 11).

There is another important functional value of marital conflict as conceived in BIMT. Although attacking aspects of their mates that in part reflect unwanted self-aspects understandably appears negative and destructive to outside observers, such perpetual projections at the same time keep the partners in contact with lost or split-off parts of themselves; in this way, they reflect reparative efforts toward growth (Dicks, 1967; Stewart et al., 1975).

The Emergence of Marital Conflict

J. C. Anchin (personal communication, 1999) has noted that "a *comprehensive* understanding of a given couple's dysfunctionality must . . . capture . . . the determinative psychodynamics of the reflective individuals . . . and . . . the truly fundamental manner in which these problematic individual–intrapsychic and interpersonal–systemic dynamics reciprocally sustain and perpetuate one another" (emphasis in original). Given the centrality in marital satisfaction of self-affirmation and safety, it now becomes clear how marital conflict typically emerges and appears. In large measure, significant conflict—that is, conflict that is both phenomenologically painful and enduring—arises and continues when the "rules" of the relationship that are central to either partner's sense of self or core organizing schema for close relationships are violated. These "rules" can be either explicit and obvious, or implicit and unspoken (cf. Sager, 1976, 1981). When the latter is the case, the conflicted couple is likely to seem quite chaotic and dysregulated, since the partners have no usable cognitive map to allow them to make sense of the pervasive but undeniable tension between them.

People prefer and usually seek to maintain a relatively consistent sense of self, even if the self with which they are familiar is relationally maladaptive. Change, especially change that taps into core aspects of the self, is anxiety-arousing. Such anxiety-arousing violation of central relationship rules can occur in a seemingly endless variety of manifestations, most of which can be subsumed under three headings. The first "violation" of such relationship rules is perhaps the most common source of difficulty, and involves the naturalistic exposure to the reality of the partner beyond the early stage of idealization. Sager (1981) has further differentiated such exposure to the mate's reality by noting that problems may arise when one realizes either that one's partner cannot meet one's needs or that no partner can do so. Sager also emphasizes the commonly found contradictory nature of the needs within partners. The second "violation" of core relationship rules involves changes in one's partner that do not match the real or perceived characteristics of that person that initially contributed to one's romantic attraction (e.g., a partner may seek a good deal more or less closeness than at an earlier point in the relationship). And the third common "violation" involves experiences through which one sees unacceptable aspects of oneself that were previously blocked from awareness, but that are now evoked in the couple's interaction. These various "violations" may stimulate and evoke one or more common intimacy fears, such as fears of merger, exposure, attack, abandonment, or expressing one's own aggression (Feldman, 1979). Although this is not typically the case, all three of these conflict-generating patterns at times are stimulated by externally generated forces.

The relevant relationship "rules" include both conscious and unconscious expectations of, and anxieties about, intimate relating that are brought to the relationship by each partner. The patterned regularities of a marriage do not evolve randomly or only from repeated interactions, but also from a subtle interplay of the implicit relationship rules of each individual (Gurman, 1978; Gurman & Knudson, 1978; Gurman et al., 1978; Sager, 1981). As noted earlier, the BIMT view is not that problems develop because of interpersonal "skill deficits," but that such apparent deficits represent the expression of the fundamental difficulties each partner has in intimate relating and/or a breakdown of the underlying implicit couple "contracts" (Sager, 1976, 1981) about central aspects of the relationship. "Skill deficits" are viewed as manifestations of more fundamental incompatibilities (Hamburg, 2000), or, more accurately, as the emergence into consciousness of these incompatibilities in one or more of the three relationship rule violation pathways described above.

The Maintenance of Marital Conflict: The Synergy of the Interpersonal and the Intrapersonal

When a couple's rule violations occur with such impact (e.g., a single event violates a core symbolic relationship value, such as sexual fidelity) or with such frequency and regularity as to negatively affect the overall tenor of the relationship, each partner attempts to shape the other to stay within, or get within, the limits of behavior allowed by that individual's "rules." The circular problem-maintaining processes that unfold express the inevitable human interconnection among multiple simultaneous levels of experience. These maladaptive circular processes demonstrate that defenses are interactional, and are maintained only via exchanges with one's partner. These defenses operate in order to avoid "seeing" behavior inconsistent with one's internalized image of one's ideal mate and/or with one's requirements for maintaining a consistent view of oneself. The utopian and anxiety-based expectations people bring to marriage are what sensitize them to slight deviations from these relational "rules," which, when they occur, predictably increase the amplitude and frequency of countercontrol maneuvers.

Bagarozzi and Giddings (1983) clearly articulate the pattern of what they call "mutual shaping toward the ideal," or what I have called "implicit behavior modification" (Gurman, 1982c, 1990, 1992). That is, a person unwittingly (and wittingly as well) attempts to reinforce and extinguish behavior in his/her mate that is allowed and disallowed, respectively, according to the person's own conscious and unconscious expectations of a marital partner. The other partner does likewise in response to the behavior of his/her mate that is allowed and disallowed, according to the internal "rules" of how the partner needs to "see" him-/herself. This implicit behavior modification takes several predictable forms, each of which may provide cues to the therapist about useful points at which, and about useful patterns about which, to intervene. Thus in couple relationships, the mutual processes of reinforcement and punishment occur in such a way that (1) each partner reinforces behavior of the other partner that is consistent with his/her own mate ideal; (2) each partner reinforces behavior of the other partner that is consistent with his/her own self-view; (3) each partner (covertly) reinforces his/her own behavior that is consistent with the required self-view; (4) each partner punishes/extinguishes (e.g., via avoidance, denial) behavior in the other partner that is inconsistent with his/her own mate ideal; (5) each partner punishes/extinguishes behavior in the other partner that is inconsistent with his/her own required self-view; and (6) each partner (covertly) punishes/extinguishes his/her own behavior that is inconsistent with his/her own required self-view. In addition, partners in chronically conflicted relationships (7) regularly reinforce the very behaviors in their mates that they complain about.

Since the first six factors operate simultaneously and overlappingly, not as discrete, isolated bits of behavioral events, both partners inevitably contribute to the problem-maintaining cycle. As Goldfried (1995) has pointed out, since the process is circular—that is, reinforcing and punishing contingencies are provided by both partners—it can be triggered by either partner. Moreover, it can be triggered by either publicly observable behavior in either partner, by privately experienced stimuli, or by external "situational" factors. Once begun, the bilateral, interlocking, problematic, implicit behavior modification belongs to no one partner; it belongs to, and in therapy must come to be "owned" by, both partners.

ASSESSMENT AND GOAL SETTING

Because BIMT attends to both individual and relational aspects of couple functioning, it casts a wide net in the opening phase of treatment, in an attempt to identify the most salient factors influencing the couple's appearance in the therapist's office, their core conflictual theme(s), and the obstacles to and potentials for change. BIMT is generally very problem-focused, pragmatic, and oriented toward brevity, and so it may seem inconsistent with this stance that the assessment process is so wide-ranging. The kind of broad initial assessment in BIMT that is discussed here is conducted, ironically, in the service of heightening the focality of treatment, by creating a rich environment of potential clues for the development of a practical, central focus.

General Considerations and Principles

The assessment process in BIMT is almost entirely carried out via traditional clinical interviews. Paper-and-pencil self-report inventories and the like are almost never used. The therapist has the responsibility for creating a clinical formulation that includes "data" not only from patient self-reports and the therapist's direct observations in the interview, but also from the therapist's conceptual understanding of the recursive interplay between the interpersonal and the intrapersonal, and between the conscious and the unconscious forces in couple relationships.

Assessment is almost always done in conjoint interviews, although on occasion, for unavoidable pragmatic reasons such as a clinic's service policies, individual interviews may occur. Since the central theory of change in BIMT requires parallel individual and interactional emphases, the active change-oriented phase of BIMT is almost always carried out conjointly. Early individual sessions, when they occur, are limited to establishing a tentative working alliance with a patient in order to increase the chances of the reluctant partner's eventual appearance.

BIMT views no variables or factors as being inherently more important than others for assessment purposes. In this way BIMT is philosophically aligned with behaviorism, which, as Jacobson (1991) succinctly put it, "treats all behavior as made of the same stuff" (p. 440). The core assessment method in BIMT is the functional-analytic approach of behavior therapists that has been described for both couple (Christensen et al., 1995) and individual (Kanfer & Phillips, 1970) therapy, but with a twist. As traditionally applied, the functional-analytic method usually focuses on rather discrete patient behaviors. In BIMT, the functional approach (see below) is applied both to highly specific couple behaviors and to broader classes of couple behavior; these are roughly equivalent to what Christensen et al. (1995) call "derivative events" (i.e., specific interactions) versus "controlling themes" (i.e., pervasive significant patterns). Unlike this distinction within behavioral couple therapy, the central controlling themes in BIMT regularly also include both the individual and dyadic motivations that are implicit and unconscious to couples, and therefore unrecognized by them as playing pivotal roles in the maintenance of the problems for which they seek help. It is this attribute of BIMT that renders it a "depth-behavioral approach." The functional-analytic approach, which emphasizes case-specific formulation, is seen as the ultimate expression of respect for patients; while certainly incorporating universal principles of behavior maintenance and behavior change, it fundamentally emphasizes the uniqueness of each couple and of each member of the couple. In this very important way, then, the functional-analytic foundation of BIMT is flexible and inherently responsive to differences between couples based on ethnic, racial, class, religious, and gender differences (cf. Hayes & Toarmino, 1995).

Temporally, the BIMT assessment is largely present-oriented, for three reasons. First, because a large proportion of couples come to therapists in crisis, and one or both partners in such a couple are often eager to flee the "enforced togetherness" (Brewster & Montie, 1987) of conjoint therapy, the rapid development of a working therapeutic alliance is essential if the couple is to return to treatment. Conversations in early meetings that focus on the present are usually experienced by patients as more "tuned in" to their perceptions and their pain. Second, present-focused conversations generally allow more useful therapist mappings of the problem-maintaining patterns of the couple via the appearance of real-time enactments (whether prompted by the therapist or not) of recurrent interactional difficulties. Finally, although some history taking is a standard part of the BIMT approach (see below), historically oriented conversations tend to occur in the longer midphase of BIMT. The core assumptions of the change process in BIMT—*that couple therapy can lead to change in both interactional patterns and inner representational models, and that such changes often occur via direct behavior change efforts*—reinforce a decidedly present-time emphasis. Even when historical factors are highlighted during the early assessment phase, this occurs, as Yalom (1975) has said, "not to excavate the past, but to elucidate the present" (p. 28).

Another general characteristic of the assessment phase of BIMT is that there is in fact no sharp distinction between an assessment "phase" and an intervention "phase." Indeed, at least by standards of traditional individual therapy, potentially change-inducing interventions may occur quite early—even in the first session (Gurman, 1992). Naturally, this is more likely to occur when BIMT is practiced by a more experienced therapist. Such a therapist may "construct probes, prescribe tasks, offer interpretive reframings of meanings, pose challenges, and so on" (Gurman, 1992, p. 199) as varied means of assessing central problem-maintaining dynamics, and of testing a couple's capacity for change.

Universal Areas of Assessment

Although the elements of a comprehensive couple assessment are presented here, all these areas do not require equal emphasis. In most cases a few areas will stand out as especially pertinent to the therapist's understanding of the nature and maintenance of the problem(s) at hand, and some will quickly be revealed to be of little or no functional significance. Moreover, whereas in most cases the therapist might need two to four sessions to have a strong sense of understanding the couple in each of these areas,

except with the most severely disengaged, enraged, or disorganized couples, a reasonably experienced couple therapist should be able to form at least tentative impressions in most of these areas (Budman & Gurman, 1988) after one or two sessions.

Presenting Problems, Attempted Solutions, and the Consequences of Change

Axiomatic in all brief therapy and in most couple and family therapy (Gurman, 2001) is that patient-defined "presenting problems" are always to be taken seriously (though not necessarily at face value—see "Goal Setting," below). A functional-analytic understanding of the presenting problem (see "Focal/Functional Assessment," below) is also essential.

It is also imperative that previously attempted but unsuccessful solutions to problems be assessed. Very often, these unfortunate solution efforts reflect not merely poor "problem-solving skills," but also the avoidance of problem resolution for reasons that are not immediately obvious. For example, Papp (1980) has discussed the notion that "successful" problem resolution may carry significant negative ramifications for the functioning of other individuals or relationships within the family system that extends beyond the couple. Change is essential, but the multifarious consequences of ("positive") change must not be overlooked.

Individual and Couple Assets and Strengths

Although couples rarely emphasize their more endearing joint or individual characteristics early in therapy, it is important that the therapist identify such assets and strengths for two reasons. First, these qualities may be called upon directly to foster change. For instance, noting that a couple prizes humor, especially nonsarcastic humor, may cue the therapist to direct the couple to use this joint and individual attribute to defuse conflictual interactions. Second, identifying such characteristics may help foster a working alliance. It may be particularly salient when, for example, a couple's interaction in session is so hostile, or their affect about their relationship is so despairing, that it limits the therapist's motivation to care about the couple jointly or as individuals.

Life Cycle Status and Accomplishment

It is common for couple conflict to arise in the context of developmental impasses of individuals or family systems. At times, directing therapeutic attention to helping a couple get "back on track" is sufficient for resolution of the main problems. Although couple therapists must be familiar with the normal developmental stages of marital and family life, such schemas must not be used prescriptively, as fixed standards of relational health (Gurman, 1983b). Cultural, religious, ethnic, and other variations among couples may significantly change the configuration or sequencing of ordinary developmental challenges. Nevertheless, case formulation-enhancing clues may at times be found as a therapist becomes aware of the couple's developmental history (e.g., locations and relocations; the presence of severe childhood illnesses or developmental delays; earlier marital separations; economic stressors and successes; and the role of work and career in the lives of both partners).

Communication and Problem-Solving Skills

In assessing a couple's communication and problem-solving skills, it is essential to distinguish between problems of acquisition and problems of performance, as noted earlier. Some people have never learned the kinds of interpersonal skills in communication and problem solving that facilitate relationship success. With such couples, the therapist must actively teach such relational skills (through in-session modeling, coaching, etc.) and perhaps also provide bibliotherapy aids, such as *Fighting for Your Marriage* (Markman, Stanley, & Blumberg, 1994). Indirection on the therapist's part cannot draw forth skills that have never been learned adequately. With such couples, communication and problem-solving skills must be acquired.

On the other hand, probably the great majority of couples seen in therapy in fact have learned such skills, but do not show them adequately or often enough in the marriage. Their difficulty is not one of acquisition, but of performance. The therapist's challenge in these two situations is quite different. It is quite a different technical matter to teach unlearned interpersonal skills than to help modify the obstacles to the usage of learned interpersonal skills. Some simple inquiries usually quickly help the therapist sort out whether apparent "skill deficits" for a couple are what they seem. Did the "unskilled" partner (or partners) show such capabilities earlier in the relationship? Does this partner at times (what times?) still intermittently show such capabilities in the marriage? Does this partner show such capabilities in relationships outside the marriage (e.g., is he/she a "good listener" with coworkers, friends, etc.?).

Finally, since BIMT aims to be problem-solving, the therapist may usefully consider the possibility that an apparent interpersonal skill deficit arises largely around a couple's discussion of (or other dealings with) matters that form their central problematic pattern or theme, while infrequently appearing on other topics and issues.

Sexuality and Sexual Functioning

In most couple therapy, sexual dysfunction is not a primary complaint, although dissatisfaction with the sexual dimension of marriage is certainly commonplace among highly and/or chronically conflicted couples. A therapist needs to inquire about this relational domain during the assessment phase, while being sensitive not to push the partners to talk about sexuality beyond their comfort levels. Often one partner is a good deal more comfortable than the other in discussing such matters, and the therapist must guard against the second partner's feeling inadequate in such conversations; this may interfere with the establishment of an adequate therapist–partner alliance, and add tension to an already tenuous partner–partner alliance (see below).

Marital Relationship History

Although BIMT is largely present-centered, there are at least two strategically important reasons to learn about the partners' relationship (with each other) history. First, talking to the partners about their shared evolution may help to build a working therapeutic alliance. Such conversations allow them to "tell their stories" to an unbiased, interested third party, as well as to recount positive aspects of the beginnings of their relationship. Second, such conversations often provide the therapist with clues about why and how the couple's central problems have been maintained over (often a very long) time. They may also suggest salient developmental factors that may have negatively influenced either partner's relationship needs and expectations, or diverted the couple from a normal developmental progression, as alluded to earlier.

Since couple difficulties that are brought to therapists have rarely begun just recently, conversation about the couple's history usually helps to enhance the therapist's understanding of the partners' responses to the central assessment question of all brief therapy: "Why *now* do they seek help?" (Budman & Gurman, 1988).

Specific marital history inquiries might include the following:

1. How and when did the couple meet? The psychosocial context in which the partners met, and the point in their individual lives (development) at which they met, may suggest important hints about the needs each partner hoped to fulfill in establishing this relationship.

2. What attracted the two to each other? Understanding a couple's early connection often sheds light on the partners' current disappointments and dilemmas.

3. How did the couple handle conflict when it first appeared in the relationship? Even a cursory mapping of such interactions after the idealization phase of the couple's relationship often foreshadows present difficulties.

4. Were there any untoward reactions to the couple's dating or marrying from the partners' families of origin, close friends, or other significant persons or institutions (e.g., church)? Are the major presenting problems thematically linked to any such earlier tensions?

5. How has the couple handled nodal events and potential stressors (e.g., deaths, serious illnesses, births of children, shifts in educational/career involvement)?

6. Have there been separations during the relationship (other than those occasioned, e.g., by outside forces, such as military service or work obligations)? How and why did the partners get back together, and did they deal adequately with the issues that lead to the separation?

7. Have there been, and are there now, involvements in extramarital relationships (including nonsexual but emotionally deep involvements)? Are there nonromantic affairs (e.g., with work, friends, family of origin, etc.) suggesting a primary "attachment" to aspects of life other than the partner?

8. Relatedly, what is each partner's commitment to the marriage? Evaluating whether the partners both have a sufficient desire to maintain their relationship, at least for now and the foreseeable future, is essential for adequate treatment planning. Many couple therapies flounder because a distinction has not been made between carrying out marital therapy and conducting separation/divorce therapy (see Glass, Chapter 18, this volume). It takes two to make a marriage, but only one to break a marriage.

In contrast to the BIMT therapist's profound interest in many aspects of the current relationship, there is much less interest in the opening phase of therapy in the histories of each partner's earlier romantic relationships. The same stance is taken with regard to the partners' family-of-origin experiences. At the same time, when either or both partners report a large number of failed and conflict-ridden previous romantic relationships, or significant and recurrent pathological family-of-origin experiences, the therapist looks for patterns that may suggest functionally relevant clues to the present difficulties.

Experience suggests that when the learning legacies from such other relationships and experiences (e.g., separations, abuse, illness, overall disorganization, etc.) make a direct, causal contribution to the difficulties of the current relationship, this is usually revealed and understood as treatment progresses. At those times, such matters are, of course, attended to. As will be discussed below, intrapersonal/"individual" matters are regularly dealt with in BIMT, and functionally relevant residues from past relationships probably constitute the most common content of such conversations.

Readiness to Change; Readiness for Therapy

In addition to BIMT's present focus and interest in the "Why now?" question, it recognizes that marital partners are not necessarily, or perhaps even usually, equally ready to change at the same point in time. The fact that a chronically conflicted couple remains that way through the contributions of both partners does not imply that partners are equally motivated to change (though they may be, or at least see themselves as being, quite receptive to change—i.e., to change in each other!). Such motivation may even wax and wane, with the partners motivationally criss-crossing each other over time.

A partner's low readiness to change may be the result of any of a wide array of factors. Common expressions of this state include a lack of commitment to the marriage, with or without an ongoing affair; a (defensive) belief that marriage should not require "work" to go well, or a desire for a "quick fix" (usually of one's mate); a fear of novelty and self-disclosure; a fear that "open communication" may "make things worse" (e.g., by revealing fundamental and unchangeable differences between the partners that are not acceptable); despair regarding the likelihood of meaningful change, whether due to an individual's pervasive pessimism or to a sense that the couple has "waited too long"; a disbelief in the effectiveness or relevance of psychotherapy; and unspoken anxiety about having to change, which implies a fear that the partner him-/herself has contributed to the couple's central problems, which in turn may be associated (perhaps not unrealistically) with a fear that all the couple's problems will be blamed (by the mate and/or the therapist) on the partner.

Whatever the phenomenology of a partner's level of readiness to change, what is especially salient is the difference between partners' current relative readiness levels. As discussed later in the section of this chapter on the role of the therapist, the therapeutic alliance, as well as the marital (or "partner–partner") alliance, must be managed and kept in awareness at all times. Early imbalances in the alliance between the therapist and each partner, usually expressed through overt side taking or, more often, through unspoken "agreement" that one partner "is" more of the problem than the other, can be deadly for the opening phase of therapy. Psychotherapists are understandably more drawn to patients who are cooperative, easy to engage, and motivated to change. Thus significant partner–partner discrepancies along these lines threaten essential treatment alliances, and thus the therapy itself.

Budman (1999) has drawn particular attention to this motivational factor in couple therapy. Drawing upon Prochaska's (e.g., Prochaska, Norcross, & DiClemente, 1994) influential Stages-of-Change Model, Budman exemplifies and illustrates how combinations of different levels of partner readiness for change are typically manifested early in the process of couple therapy, and what action implications these combinations carry for the therapist. Prochaska's stages include "precontemplation" (where there is little motivation for change—e.g., a partner is in therapy because of the threat of divorce); "contemplation" (where ambivalence dominates—this probably characterizes most couples in therapy); "preparation" (where one is committed to change but has not yet begun to make changes); and "action" (where one has already initiated change and is eager to try new alternatives). Adequate attention to each partner's readiness to change can help to foster viable therapist–partner treatment alliances.

Interestingly, Miles (1980) and Smith and Grunebaum (1976) have pointed out that marital partners may enter and stay in therapy even though their motivation to work toward a more functional marriage is low. Miles emphasizes that these partners may have very strong "alternative" motivations for seeing a therapist (e.g., to justify an already decided-upon separation, to ensure that a partner

has someone to care for him/her after a separation, or to "take the heat off" the less willing partner). Smith and Grunebaum also identify the common partner motivation of "looking for an ally" to help stand up to one's mate. Miles underlines that these alternative motivations (to the ones therapists would prefer to encounter) for being in couple therapy are problematic when they are primary motivations and when the therapist fails to recognize them.

The notion of readiness to change, and hence potential differential readiness to change, may receive more attention in BIMT than in other couple therapy approaches. In addition to the fact that this differential readiness is regularly observed in clinical practice, two other reasons for its importance can be identified. First, there is growing empirical evidence (Prochaska, 1995) that the matching of appropriate interventions to patients' levels of readiness for change is predictive of treatment outcome. Second, acknowledgment of partners' change readiness levels implicitly points to the importance of intrapersonal factors in BIMT—factors that in the most generative phases in the history of couple and family therapy, have been enormously disregarded and, until relatively recently, even impugned (Gurman & Fraenkel, in press).

Focal/Functional Assessment

In addition to these universal or molar areas of assessment, a more fine-grained, molecular assessment of the couple's most salient problem relevant patterns is of course necessary. To this end, BIMT calls upon both an object-relations-based understanding of the couple's core conflictual issues, and a social-learning-theory-oriented assessment of these core issues.

The Role of Functional Analysis

The molecular aspect of BIMT assessment emphasizes what behavior therapists call "functional analysis" or "behavioral analysis." A functional analysis is concerned not with the topography or form of behavior, but with its effects, roughly equivalent to its purposes. Functional analysis, a hallmark of Integrative Behavioral Couple Therapy (see Dimidjian et al., Chapter 9, this volume), is a method of connecting assessment and treatment planning, including technique selection (Hayes, Follette, & Follette, 1995; Hayes & Toarmino, 1995; Haynes & O'Brien, 1990; Karoly, 1975).

The goals of functional analysis are to identify behaviors (or patterns of behavior) of clinical concern, to identify the conditions that maintain these patterns, to select appropriate interventions, and to monitor the progress of treatment (Follette, Naugle, & Linnerooth, 2000).

The function of a behavior (or behavior pattern) is approached by identifying the factors that control, or maintain, the pattern. This typically calls for a verbal description of the behavior (or pattern), including its frequency; the conditions, settings, or contexts in which it occurs; and the consequences of its occurrence. That is, the behavior's antecedents (discriminative stimuli) and consequences (positive or negative reinforcement, punishment) are tracked. When a functional analyst is asked "why" someone does something, he/she provisionally finds the answer in the particular pattern of antecedents and consequences attendant to the behavior. Historical facts or experiences are relevant in a functional analysis to the degree that they establish learned behavior or patterns that continue into the present and are clinically relevant to the problems for which change is sought (as one former colleague put it, "If it doesn't matter now, it doesn't matter").

Typically, couples identify very particular or even singular triggering situations (e.g., a recent argument) as though those situations or events constitute the problem. Although infrequently this is appropriate, it is much more likely that the therapist needs to be cognizant of the recurring pattern that is problematic, the latest (or almost any "chosen") instance of which is probably merely an illustration. The patterns or "themes" (Christensen et al., 1995) are technically referred to as "functional classes" or, more commonly, "response classes." That is, various behaviors are considered to be members of a larger functional class, in that apparently "different" (i.e., topographically dissimilar) behaviors share the same function (purpose, effect). Response classes are not determined by the similarity of the content of particular behaviors or events. The practical implication of thinking in terms of response classes is that because the behaviors that make up the class are functionally equivalent, changing one particularly frequent or salient component of the response class may lead to parallel change in other topographically "different" behaviors within the class, thus fostering generalization (Berns & Jacobson, 2000). Moreover, tracking the function of "different" behaviors may help the therapist identify a functional theme that the couple fails to see, instead seeing each problematic event or interaction as though it were a separate class unto itself.

To facilitate a reasonably coherent experience of therapy, and to have a relatively clear thematic focus, it is essential that the therapist think in terms or such response classes. In most cases, the marital problem will be in a "hot" area—one in which the partners are less likely to respond to change with comfort. Even when a couple's early presentation makes it chaotically appear that there is but an endless "list" of difficulties but no central, unifying theme, there *is* a theme. It is the therapist's responsibility to make thematic sense out of apparent chaos.

Functional Analysis and Private Events

Although behavior therapy is widely known for its emphasis on overt, external, or environmental factors in controlling behavior, internal or covert events (and their antecedents and consequences as well) are legitimate subject matter for a functional analysis (Rimm & Masters, 1974). Private events include thoughts, feelings, and physiological responses (recall Gottman's [1999] finding of problematic diffuse physiological arousal in men in conflicted marriages).

Kanfer and Saslow (1969) set forth a widely influential description of "behavioral diagnosis" (i.e., functional analysis). Their analytic model went beyond the standard A(ntecedents)–B(ehavior)–C(onsequences) assessment model to include variables about the state of the organism, recast as S(timulus)–O(rganism)–R(esponse)–C(onsequences). Consideration of the "O" factor includes, for example, hunger and arousal. It also includes what Kanfer and Saslow call a "motivational analysis."

Now for most behavior therapists, such a motivational analysis would never include anything that smacks of the unconscious. As Jacobson (1991) noted, "the fundamental enemy of a truly behavioristic system is the hypothetical construct, especially one used to describe an internal process" (p. 441). Jacobson argues that such constructs provide "only the illusion of understanding" (p. 441) because they are attributed causal significance. Thus a clinically useful "problem story will describe the emotional reactions that we and our partners experience from the problem without speculating on possible motives in our partners that led to their actions" (Christensen & Jacobson, 2000, p. 150).

Floyd, Haynes, and Kelly (1997) have included among the factors leading to an "invalid functional analysis" (p. 369) the omission of "important causal variables." But note that very often, as Christensen et al. (1995) wrote, "couples cannot articulate what is bothering them" (p. 36). In the view of object relations theory, or any clinical theory that allows for the relevance of motivation that is out of awareness (i.e., unconscious), such difficulty with identifying and describing what is problematic is readily understood as involving denial, repression, and similar defense mechanisms. Although "Many have abandoned the notion of unconscious motives entirely as a useless construct" (Christensen & Jacobson, 2000, p. 147), the BIMT view is that just such unconscious motives may provide useful clues to what is most distressing to a couple. And at the beginning of therapy, it is often only by the use of reasonable therapist inferences and hypotheses about such unspoken, and unspeakable, motives that sense can be made of the underlying pattern of the partners' varied complaints and concerns.

Thus one may say that to identify the central couple collusions, the BIMT therapist must look for the ways in which the S-O-R-C analysis of the marital partners' interactions intersect and mutually affect one another. Marital behavior is as often under the control of self-administered consequences as it is under the control of partner-administered consequences. That is, the relevant contingencies to couple conflict also exist within the partners. The kinds of salient intervening cognitive and emotional cues and events, including those that are either implicit or beyond conscious awareness, are of the sorts referred to in Dollard and Miller's (1950) classic concept of "response-produced cues." These are cues associated with thoughts or experiences that, via previous learning, have become signals (discriminative stimuli) for anxiety or other painful affects or negatively valenced cognitions. When such cues are elicited, there is a natural tendency to avoid them (i.e., to remain unaware of them) As Wachtel (1977) notes, "the clinical observations that present themselves to the clinician often seem most cogently understood in terms of the patient's fear of his own inclinations" (p. 116). This perspective from an integratively oriented clinical theorist was indirectly and ironically supported by the observation of the well-known behavior therapists Kanfer and Phillips (1970) that, "In general . . . little more than hunches based on observed coincidences of target responses and consequences is available for identification of factors maintaining problem behaviors" (p. 516).

Identifying Mutual Projective Identification/Collusion

Within the perspective just presented, it becomes essential in BIMT to help partners modify not only the overt behaviors about which they complain, but also the patterns of reciprocal projective identification around their thematically central concerns. Since the circular process of mutual projective identification, or collusion, is an inferred one (supported, of course, by overt interaction), "it" cannot be observed directly. Nonetheless, there are a number of behavioral patterns that signify its active and pernicious presence. Mutual projective identification is manifested in many forms, usually with several present in the interaction of a particular couple:

- Partners consistently fail to see salient aspects of each other's behavior or personality that are readily perceptible to a third person (e.g., the therapist).
- Partners often fail to see changes in each other that are perceptible to a third party who is familiar with them.
- Partners behave in ways that protect them from behaving in a manner inconsistent with their preferred view of themselves in the relationship.
- Without conscious awareness, partners often reinforce in each other's behavior the very behaviors or characteristics about which they complain.
- Partners largely fail to see, or at least acknowledge, their own contributions to the problems at hand.
- Partners agree that one or the other of them "is" the problem, usually by virtue of that person's purported personality pathology or psychiatric diagnosis.
- Partners argue over whose personality pathology accounts for their problems.
- Partners exaggerate their differences and minimize their similarities, appearing at first blush to be "totally opposite" from each other.

The BIMT therapist tracks, via both partners' reports and his/her own observation of their behavior, the recurring ways in which they punish in each other behavior they claim to value, and reinforce in each other behavior they claim to abhor. How the partners consequate "adherence" to and "violation" of the central rules of their relationship is attended to carefully throughout therapy, since these constitute the primary patterns the therapist seeks to disrupt and replace with new patterns. The BIMT therapist attempts to have a heightened awareness of what Snyder (1999, p. 358), without implying unconscious intent, refers to as the "inadvertent maintenance of maladaptive relationship patterns." This awareness begins in the very first conjoint encounter.

At the outset of therapy, it is less important for the therapist to have a clear sense of the origins of the couple's collusion, historically speaking, though such understanding may become more important later in therapy. The old family systems theory saw that "a system is its own best explanation" applies equally well to early therapy mappings of collusive processes.

Goal Setting

The basic premises in BIMT about clinical change are that (1) since people shape core relationally relevant aspects of each other's personalities, couple therapy can lead to individual change, both behavioral and intrapsychic; and (2) behavior change can lead to change in relationally relevant inner representational models.

BIMT seeks change in both individuals, as well as in their interaction; more accurate self-perception and more accurate perception of one's partner; and resolution of what the partners define as their presenting problem. The form these changes take varies, of course, as defined by the functional analysis. The functional analysis is inherently responsive to individual differences, and thus incorporates whatever factors are deemed relevant, whether their origins or present sources are intrapsychic (cognitive or affective, conscious and unconscious), dyadic, larger family systems, sociocultural (e.g., race, ethnicity, class, gender), or biological/physiological. It is not necessary (or usually appropriate) to attempt to address all identifiable areas of couple discord, or all aspects of spouses' individual conflicts that impinge on the couple relationship. As a well-done functional analysis usually reveals, disharmony is usually determined and characterized by a few major issues.

Just as ultimate treatment goals vary, so do early treatment goals. A couple in crisis may require containment, structuring, and even practical advice at the outset. Only after the crisis has become muted can the partners fully engage in cooperative exploration of their relationship, and of themselves as individuals within that relationship. Even when the immediate stimulus to the couple's crisis is an external event (e.g., job loss, family-of-origin conflict, recovery from illness), the BIMT therapist tries to formulate the working relationship models within each partner, without necessarily voicing these inferences and hypotheses. A different couple (with basically flexible styles of interaction, a more robust degree of self-acceptance, etc.) may face "situational" problems, and can be helped with rather direct, concrete problem-solving guidance. The couple's view of the "presenting problem" must, of course, be taken seriously. Still, even when externally generated problems constitute the couple's initial problem presentation, it is appropriate for the therapist to include in his formulation how the current dilemma or stressor fits within the internal relationship schema of each partner. The great majority of couples seeking therapy, however, present difficulties that are much more complex in both their origins and their maintenance; they thus require a therapist's intervention at multiple levels of experience, using a rather broad array of techniques, as will be discussed below.

THE STRUCTURE OF THERAPY

Who Is Included in Therapy

As already emphasized, in the ideal practice of BIMT all treatment sessions include both couple partners, since it is believed that the core healing components of BIMT lie within that relationship. Consequently, the BIMT therapist is very reluctant to see partners individually, and almost never sees one partner alone for the initial interview. When partners are seen alone, the BIMT therapist maintains particular awareness of any interactions that may carry significant implications for the alliances already established in the three-way conjoint meetings, and is especially attuned to any interactions that may disturb the husband–wife alliance. Relatedly, except in genuine crises or emergencies, partners are never seen alone when one partner fails to appear for a therapy session—whether this failure is due to a marital argument, a lack of interest in continuing therapy, acute illness, unexpected work conflicts, or even bad weather or traffic conditions!

As noted earlier, partners are not separated during the initial assessment phase. During the active intervention phase of therapy, the only time the therapist initiates individual sessions with the partners is when conjoint sessions regularly have become unmanageable to the point of being counterproductive (rather than merely unproductive, as some sessions inevitably are in any course of therapy). This occasion typically involves couples in which both partners have great difficulty self-regulating their anger or dramatic expressions of emotional turmoil, who are not reliably able to be soothed and calmed by the therapist, and/or who persistently engage in mutual blaming, to the virtual exclusion of seeing their own role in the couple's difficulties. Often, a focused short-term series of individual sessions with each partner may allow a more cooperative and less inflammatory ambience to be established when conjoint sessions are resumed.

BIMT can be conducted by either a single therapist or cotherapists, although current patterns in health care delivery, such as managed care programs, will effectively keep the use of cotherapy to a minimum. A cotherapy arrangement is both well suited to the BIMT approach, and not without complications. Because BIMT emphasizes the importance of the therapist's simultaneously understanding the couple on multiple levels and intervening with an appreciation of the possible effects of an action on multiple levels, the presence of a second therapist may enhance such awareness. At the same time, because BIMT therapists regularly intervene at one level of psychological experience with an intent to produce change at another level, cotherapists must be extremely well attuned to each other's thinking; otherwise, a perfectly reasonable intervention by one therapist may lead to confusion or uncertainty in the second therapist, and thus to a disruption of or distraction from the flow and focus of the therapy session.

What Is Included in Therapy

Selection of a Session Focus

Although BIMT values thematic consistency and a clear therapeutic focus (or foci), the therapist does not usually impose a topical agenda on therapy sessions. On the contrary, just as couples are seen as the major healing agents, they are also given the responsibility for deciding what is addressed in therapy. Also, because the BIMT therapist is sensitive to the factors (Gurman, 2001) that bias most couple therapy toward brevity, it is not assumed that a couple will wish to address the same secondary, derivative problem from session to session. Indeed, couples regularly are unaware of how seemingly different problems of the day are connected thematically. It is the therapist's responsibility to foster such understanding. Thus, in BIMT partners are routinely asked at the beginning of the session, "What would you like to focus on today?"

This deceptively simple inquiry implies (1) that the partners are in charge of knowing what matters to them; (2) that all therapy sessions must have a focus, purpose, or goal; and (3) that their needs, sensibilities, and struggles are not static, but shift through time. The therapist also distinguishes between the overtly agreed-upon "negotiated focus" that provides continuity across time, and the "operative focus"—the usually unspoken mediating goals the therapist believes need to be achieved for the couple to reach its negotiated ultimate goals (Gurman, 2001). In BIMT, as in probably all types of couple therapy, couples regularly bring to the session material from the time since their previous meeting. The BIMT therapist is typically quite active in such "troubleshooting" (Jacobson & Holtzworth-Munroe, 1986) conversations, although the form of his/her activity varies.

Not infrequently, some aspects of couple problems become functionally autonomous of their origins. As I pointed out elsewhere (Gurman, 1978), "Regardless of the extent to which marital conflict may have been initially determined by unconscious forces, current interaction not only reinforces shared collusions, but also offers fertile ground for secondary, but very real and salient difficulties that must be treated independently of the historically underlying dynamic struggle" (pp. 456–457). These comments referred to what cognitive-behavioral couple therapists (Baucom et al., Chapter 2, this volume) now refer to as "secondary" (vs. "primary") distress—that is, maladaptive patterns of responding to unfulfilled needs.

Interpersonal versus Intrapersonal Focus

BIMT, like most couple therapies, strongly emphasizes interpersonal couple process issues. At the same time, it is commonplace in couple therapy for "individual" issues to rise intermittently to the fore. These may be centrally and transparently linked to the major couple problem theme, as when an emotionally distancing wife talks about the abuse that took place in her family when she was a child. Or such an "individual" issue may at first seem more tangential to the relational focus, as when one partner expresses anxiety about stresses or conflicts in the workplace. When people are in couple therapy, they know they are in couple therapy. Nothing that is brought up for the therapist to hear about is brought up randomly or without meaning. Almost always this meaning, unclear though it may be at first to the therapist, involves the couple's relationship, the process of the couple therapy, or the like. When partners themselves are not able to see such connections, it falls to the therapist to facilitate such understanding.

There are two common situations in which such "individual" factors arise. The first occurs when one partner has a diagnosable, and probably diagnosed, psychiatric disorder of a largely symptomatic nature (e.g., depression or anxiety). The second situation occurs when an important aspect of one partner's contribution to the couple problem reflects significant psychopathology that is largely of an interpersonal nature (e.g., a personality disorder). In both situations, BIMT focuses on the functional relationships between an individual's symptoms or personality characteristics and central problematic couple themes. BIMT looks upon nomothetic descriptions of psychiatric disorders as a useful source of hypotheses about a given individual, not as a set of "facts." To be of practical use, these hypotheses require verification in the individual case, and once verified must be functionally relevant to the central relational problems (cf. Hayes & Toarmino, 1995). If not, they probably fall outside the purview of BIMT, which insists on maintaining a clear treatment focus.

Some sessions in BIMT may look to an outside observer like individual therapy being done in the presence of a partner. The guiding principle in BIMT is that the implications of such "individual" conversations for the couple's relationship must be made explicit before the end of the session, at the latest. It is especially valuable if this "individual" material can be coherently connected to the central theme(s) of the joint therapy. Not everything that affects the partners' comfort and satisfaction in their relationship is about, or derives from, that relationship. With its simultaneous interpersonal and intrapersonal awareness, BIMT respects the relevance of "individual" issues in the couple's life, but insists that since this is couple therapy, virtually everything that is discussed is considered in a relational light. This is a rather different position from that of many couple therapists, who see such conversations as core clinical errors. Crane (1996), for example, refers bluntly to the "common error" of "trying to do individual therapy with both spouses present" (p. 81). This "mistake" occurs "because the emphasis of therapy *becomes* the interaction of the therapist with each spouse *instead of* the interaction between the partners" (pp. 81–82; emphasis added). The BIMT view is that it is not inherent in the process that the patient–therapist relationship gain such ascendance, but that whether this happens is a function of how the therapist guides the treatment (see Gurman &

Fraenkel, in press, for a historical perspective on this issue). Even more basically, in BIMT there is almost never an emphasis on one domain of psychological experience "instead of" others. To allow this to happen is not to practice integratively and therefore, BIMT argues, not to practice with optimal clinical effectiveness.

The general flow and rhythm of a BIMT session often includes a good deal of conversation between each partner and the therapist, with the other partner "just listening." The other partner is never "just listening," of course, but is processing what is heard, as overtly silent as he/she may be. The BIMT therapist places no priority on having partners talk primarily to each other. This statement may seem at odds with one of BIMT's central theoretical notions involving the centrality of the partner–partner relationship in the couple therapy healing process, but it is not. Since the central mechanism of change in BIMT is seen as the creation of new relational learning experiences for the couple, both inside and outside the sessions, the therapy sessions themselves obviously must allow for conditions where such change is possible. Allowing (and sometimes even directing) partners to speak directly to the therapist helps to foster a listening environment that feels safer to the partners than in everyday life, thus allowing gradual but consistent exposure to the "real" partners. This stance parallels that of therapists oriented toward Bowen's (1978) family systems theory, and for similar reasons involving the reduction of patients' anxiety.

Since, as noted, BIMT assumes that conflicted couples remain locked into painful recurrent dances for perfectly "good" (i.e., potentially understandable) intrapsychic as well as interpersonal reasons, a safe therapeutic environment is essential as the partners encounter each other in new ways. The partners in highly conflicted marriages cannot be expected to trust the safety of the therapeutic situation, and thus each other, unless they experience an adequate sense of order. Direct partner–therapist conversation is an important element in the structuring of such order. Of course, as therapy progresses and trust between the partners increases, the therapist can and should encourage more and more partner–partner conversation. Naturally, most couple therapy sessions include a mixture of partner–partner and partner–therapist conversation. It falls to the therapist to be sensitive to the optimal balance at given points in time.

Naturally, the BIMT therapist wants to maintain a balance between marital partners in the amount of attention paid to such "individual" issues over time, lest an imbalance insidiously shift the healing focus from the partner–partner relationship to the partner–therapist relationship.

Temporal Aspects of Therapy

Length, Spacing, and Number of Sessions

BIMT sessions are typically 50–60 minutes long, though there is no absolute contraindication to scheduling longer sessions when this is arranged in advance. Likewise, the scheduling of sessions is done flexibly and in response to the partners' needs, their availability, and so on. Some couples, not necessarily those in crisis, are wisely seen weekly at first (e.g., when the therapist experiences difficulty in establishing a working alliance, or senses that one or both partners' commitment to staying in therapy may be tenuous). At the other extreme, couples may be seen only monthly if circumstances require that, although such a gap between sessions tends to dilute the central focus and lessen the immediacy of the experience. In practice, sessions are most often held on a biweekly basis, as this period between sessions seems optimal for maintaining an adequate therapeutic focus and, at the same time, allowing enough time to elapse for couples to experiment with change, give adequate consideration to the discussion of the previous session, and so forth. Given BIMT's emphasis on the central healing role of the partner–partner relationship, it follows that meaningfully designed change experiences between sessions are important, and the partners must be allowed adequate space and time to carry their new learning into the natural environment.

Although BIMT, as noted earlier, emphasizes therapeutic brevity primarily through its establishment of a thematic focus, it is not a formally time-limited approach. Helpful and effective courses of therapy have occurred in as few as three or four meetings over just a few weeks, and have also required 100 sessions or more over periods exceeding 2 years. On average, BIMT, like most marital therapies (Doherty & Simmons, 1996; Gurman, 1981, 2001; Gurman & Kniskern, 1978b, 1981), lasts about 12–15 sessions.

It is important to note that couple therapy need not be continuous. In its attempt to be flexibly responsive to developmental changes in a couple's life and to the inevitable waxing and waning of motivation for therapeutic work that is typical of most couples, BIMT often includes discontinuous "courses" of treatment, usually for different lengths of time. Indeed, the rationing of time in therapy in this developmentally sensitive, discontinuous way is a hallmark of much effective brief psychotherapy (Budman & Gurman, 1988; Gurman, 1981, 2001).

Temporal Focus

As noted earlier, BIMT is not a time-limited method, but it does tend to be relatively brief by traditional psychotherapy standards (Gurman, 2001). Although important conversations about the past certainly do occur in virtually all courses of BIMT (e.g., when discussing the historical origins of a patient's fear of closeness, or when exploring changes over time in each partner's expectations of marriage and of one's partner), the temporal focus is decidedly biased toward the present. A common occurrence that should cue the therapist to inquire about historical factors is when a seemingly minor event or seemingly inconsequential behavior elicits very intense or uncomfortable feelings, especially when the recipient partner cannot make sense of the first partner's behavior.

As discussed in the section on assessment, BIMT's central organizing question is "Why now?" BIMT concurs with structural family therapist Aponte's (1992) view that "A therapist targets the residuals of the past in a family's experience of the moment" (p. 326). Wachtel (1993) emphasizes that even when the origins of problematic patterns "can be traced to earlier events . . . those events are no longer what is maintaining the process" (p. 23). Thus, "*whatever* happened in the first few years of life, there is usually an *ongoing* dynamic, involving a transaction between the patient's inner state and the overt events of his life, that is much more germane to understanding how *change* can be brought about" (Wachtel, 1993, p. 21; emphasis in original).

Concurrent Treatments

As noted, a fair amount of "individual therapy" may occur in BIMT; at the same time, BIMT therapists are extremely hesitant to schedule actual individual sessions. Carrying on a parallel true individual therapy with a marital partner who is being seen by the therapist in conjoint couple therapy is never an option in BIMT. Moreover, concurrent individual psychotherapy done by other therapists during the course of BIMT is generally not favored. Unless such therapies are clearly focused on discrete symptoms (e.g., phobias or compulsions), there is a great likelihood that by definition during a time of marital crises or at least intense pain, the couple's relationship will become a prime topic for discussion. Therein lies the risk of either duplicated or (more worrisome) contradictory therapeutic aims and interventions. More broadly, such parallel concurrent individual therapies often dilute a patient's therapeutic energy and focus away from the focused couple therapy, and may weaken rather than strengthen the therapeutic alliance between the marital partners that needs to be sustained for effective work (Gurman, 1978).

On the other hand, concurrent psychopharmacological treatment—for instance, for depression (see Golann, Friedman, & Miller, Chapter 25, this volume) or bipolar disorder (see Miklowitz & George, Chapter 26, this volume)—generally poses few such problems. When the couple therapist is also able to prescribe indicated medications him-/herself, this is preferable to a concurrent treatment arrangement, as it allows immediate three-way processing of the meaning and implications of such prescribing for the couple's relationship. Moreover, such a practice is a concrete expression of the value within BIMT of dealing with couples at multiple levels of experience.

THE ROLE OF THE THERAPIST

The Stance of the Therapist

In BIMT the therapist serves alternately, and at times simultaneously, as teacher/consultant, healer, and provocateur. His/her stance toward the couple and toward each partner varies as a result of what seems to be functionally needed at a given time. At times the therapist is supportive and gentle, at times confronting and insistent. At times he/she is intense and serious, at times playful; at times she/he is empathically centered, at times emotionally somewhat distant. At times the therapist closely structures and directs; at times he/she hovers above the flow of the session, listening for key words, feelings, or themes. The stance is flexibly responsive to the current tone and needs of the couple. On the other hand, the variability of the stance is not whimsical or undisciplined. It is always arrived at with caring consideration for what this couple needs and wants at this time, and in a way that is connected to the partners' central and recurring treatment goals. The therapist's varying stance always rests on a consistent primary foundation of

what is in the best interests of the couple—not what is in his/her personal best interests, or in the best interests of supporting a particular theory of marital dysfunction or marital therapy.

Although the therapist in BIMT is not an expert on how to live life, he/she must be an expert on how to create a therapeutic structure in which the partners can find, create, and implement answers and solutions to their problems. In contrast to some postmodern methods of couple therapy (e.g., Freedman & Combs, 2000; see also Freedman & Combs, Chapter 11, this volume), the BIMT therapist also assumes responsibility for having and using expert professional knowledge about relationships and relationship change, based on clinical or clinically relevant research and theory development. Because, as we shall see in the next section, BIMT calls upon a wide range of therapeutic techniques, the integrative therapist has an absolute responsibility to be familiar with emerging effective treatment methods, especially those that are empirically supported.

The Therapist's Three Central Roles

Beyond this overarching relationship stance with couples, the therapist in BIMT has three very particular roles: inculcating systemic thinking and awareness, teaching and coaching relationship skills, and challenging dysfunctional relationship "rules."

The inculcation of systemic awareness may occur implicitly or explicitly. This style of intervention fundamentally involves enhancing the partners' capacity for doing their own functional analysis. It often involves the modeling of context questions (e.g., "What were you doing, Bob, just before Jill told you how anxious she was feeling?"; "Jill, what was the first thing you saw Bob do after you told him how anxious you were?"). By modeling the basic principles of functional analysis through his/her own questions, reflections, and observations in sessions, the therapist helps the partners become more sensitive to the recurrent circular processes in their relationship that maintain their primary problems, including intrapsychic events and cues. In effect, the BIMT therapist conversationally models and encourages the couple to become curious about the discriminative stimuli that set the occasion for, or become circularly involved in, problematic interaction patterns. Thus they become more adept at being able to solve problems in ways that are meaningful to them. This kind of systemic or functional-analytic sensitivity training directly fosters the development of a more multicausal, "both–and" couple perspective, which may help to counter the common (and always problematic) single-factor, "either–or" style of thinking in which distressed couples regularly engage in their mutual projective dance.

The BIMT therapist's second major role involves the teaching, via modeling and feedback, of facilitative relationship skills, especially those focusing on communication and problem solving. The use of such skill training in BIMT is discussed in detail in the next section.

Finally, in BIMT the therapist plays the all-important role of challenging the couple's maladaptive relationship "rules," especially those that are centrally linked (i.e., functionally related) to the core thematic problem. The therapist must be particularly attuned to the implicit, out-of-awareness rules that govern pertinent and persistent marital patterns. The therapist's role in BIMT in this regard is, in effect, to violate the couple's dysfunctional rules in a safe environment that prevents avoidance of or escape from exposure to new possibilities about one's self and one's partner, and therefore increases the opportunity for new and more satisfying relational learning. Often such a therapeutic "violation" of the couple's rules involves asking the unaskable or saying the unsayable. At times in BIMT, this "violation" may require a therapist to express rather forcefully what one or both partners may be thinking or feeling, but not directly saying, based on a finely nuanced understanding of each partner. In this role, the BIMT therapist attempts to increase the reality of the relationship by, as Bader (1984) called it, "disrupting the couple's symbiosis."

In this third role of eliciting and interpreting unexpressed feelings, the BIMT therapist significantly serves as a model of how the partners can provide effective holding for each other.

The Therapeutic Alliance

All methods of psychotherapy appropriately emphasize the central, change-facilitating role of the therapeutic alliance. In marital therapy, there are in effect three alliances that must be attended to (Gurman, 1981, 1982b): the therapist's alliance with each partner, the therapist's alliance with the couple, and the working alliance between the partners. Although couple therapy is usually brief, so that active change induction needs to be addressed

rather early, a working alliance with the couple must be established to create a safe environment in which change can begin. Thus early therapist interventions must be aimed at both establishing such an alliance and increasing optimism about problem-relevant change. Thus all early change-oriented interventions should also facilitate the patient–therapist alliance, or at least should not interfere with it.

The three targets of early alliance-building usually must be attended to simultaneously, with priority given to the first two areas.

Therapist–Partner Alliances

Therapist–partner alliances require attention in the very first session. Each partner should feel that something of personal value has been achieved, though how this occurs varies from person to person. Some people feel an alliance emerging when they are offered empathy and warmth, while others require insight, beginning directives for behavior change, or reassurance about the viability of their marriage. Consistent with the emphasis on the functional analysis of problems, BIMT requires that the therapist quickly discern what is functionally relevant to each partner, in terms of establishing a therapist–partner alliance that is likely to increase the chances that the partner will continue in therapy. One size, or approach, does not fit everybody, and the therapist must also be prepared to offer different bases for an alliance even within the same couple.

Therapist–Couple Alliance

In addition to learning how to "speak to" each partner of the couple effectively, the therapist must identify early the paired unspoken "language" that simultaneously bonds the partners together and creates the medium for the emergence of the current and continuing conflict. In BIMT, the therapist learns to speak to both partners at once, as it were, even when overtly addressing only one of them. This second alliance area is best established by speaking empathically to the mutually contingent manner in which the partners collude to keep aspects of themselves and of each other out of awareness. In the early phase of therapy, the therapist's aim here is to offer a tentative acknowledgment and attribution of the dominant ways in which the partners' overt struggles reflect the growth-oriented purposiveness of their initial attraction and later commitment.

Partner–Partner Alliance

Such empathically offered interpretation serves not merely to impart insight, but also to strengthen the couple alliance. One common and helpful strategy for fostering the partner–partner alliance is for the therapist, while acknowledging the partners' stylistic differences during conflict, to identify and underscore ways in which the partners show similar relationship strivings. If, however, the therapist forces such a view on the couple without accurately understanding each partner's relationship fears and aims, such an interpretation will appear not only off-target but contrived. Psychodynamically and affectively accurate interpretations along these lines, in contrast, are regularly met by a sense of relieved acceptance.

THERAPEUTIC TECHNIQUES AND THE PROCESS OF THERAPY

The three central therapist roles in BIMT of inculcating systemic awareness, teaching relationship skills, and challenging dysfunctional relationship rules are fulfilled, in large measure, by following three core principles of intervention: the interruption and modification of collusive processes, the linking of individual experience to relational experience, and the creation of therapeutic tasks for the couple. Since BIMT often addresses unconscious experience via rather direct and concrete therapist activity, it is essential that the therapist be equipped to think complexly, yet intervene simply. To this end, BIMT requires of the therapist an attitude of technical flexibility and a concrete mastery of a rather broad range of particular intervention skills.

Interruption and Modification of Collusive Processes

The couple therapist must consistently and persistently track, label, and interrupt the marital collusive process as it occurs in therapy sessions. A therapist who intervenes to change this dysfunctional mutual defensive process implicitly challenges the maladaptive rules of the relationship. Typical ways in which collusion may be seen to operate during therapy sessions have been described in the section on assessment, above.

General Guidelines

The ways in which therapists can interrupt and block collusive processes as they occur in the immediacy of the conjoint sessions are limitless, and probably are constrained in their variety only by the therapist's clinical creativity and technical mastery. A number of therapists (e.g., Greenspan & Mannino, 1974; Segraves, 1982) have endorsed the notion of disrupting collusive processes *in vivo*, but have offered limited guidance as to how this might be accomplished. Some general guidelines can be set forth regarding what it is that the therapist should do (i.e., the therapeutic strategy) as distinct from how to do it (i.e., the therapeutic technique, which is discussed below). In-session interruption and modification of collusive processes are facilitated by doing several things:

1. Encouraging each partner to differentiate between the experiential impact of the other partner's behavior, and the intent attributed to the latter's behavior.
2. Interrupting partner behavior that is aimed at reducing anxiety in the other spouse, especially when that partner is behaving in ways that are historically contrary to the couple's collusive interactional contract.
3. Focusing each partner's attention on concrete evidence in the behavior of the other partner that denies similarly anachronistic perceptions of that partner.
4. Encouraging each partner to acknowledge directly his/her own behavioral changes that are incompatible with the maladaptive ways in which this person has tended to see him-/herself and to be seen by the other partner.

Naturally, as therapy progresses, the therapist will ideally fade out his/her initial responsibility for these types of responses, and increasingly encourage the partners to monitor, interrupt, and shift their own formerly collusive process. Indeed, their increasing capacity to do so is probably a reliable, unobtrusive measure of positive therapeutic change.

Specific Techniques: Blocking Problem-Maintaining Interactions

Here I briefly present some illustrative techniques for interrupting and modifying in-session collusive processes. These methods fall into the first main category of techniques in BIMT, "blocking interventions" (Gurman, 1982a). The aim of blocking techniques is to block, interrupt, or divert couple enactments of habitual unconscious contracts in response to observable in-session behavior. Thus blocking techniques are used reactively and responsively, rather than proactively. Their use and the timing of their use cannot be predicted, anticipated, or planned. They are called upon by the therapist in the natural, emerging flow of the therapeutic conversation. In this sense, blocking interventions are explicitly process-oriented.

Cognitive Restructuring: Unilateral and Bilateral. Techniques derived from cognitive-behavioral therapy, and employed regularly in cognitive marital therapy (e.g., Baucom et al., Chapter 2, this volume), challenge each partner's "automatic thoughts" about and overt reactions to the other partner's behavior, and may usefully be incorporated into BIMT. In BIMT, such automatic thoughts are seen as especially problematic if they center on negative overgeneralizations about the other partner's behavior or character, and particularly if their content implies malevolent purposes or fixed psychological defectiveness. Such attributions, along with selective inattention to (or denial of) who the "whole partner" is, are especially likely to reflect underlying projective elements. In contrast, functionally maladaptive processes regarding general relationship expectations (i.e., those that would pertain to any partner) are somewhat more likely to reflect consciously held values and the direct effects of relationship modeling—for example, by one's parents. As a result of their usually being less evocative of anxiety, they may be clinically addressed by relatively straightforward methods, such as the provision of normative information about relationship functioning or the suggestion of bibliotherapeutic material.

In addition to the use of cognitive techniques that focus on the faulty attributions and selective inattention of individuals, BIMT also urges that therapists develop some deftness at "equalizing the dynamic struggle" (Gurman, 1982a). This strategy calls for the therapist to interpret to the couple rather than to individuals, the salient ways in which their overt differences reflect similar dynamic themes. Such interpretations, which clearly emphasize conscious cognitive understanding, help to increase empathy and to counter defensive projections.

Shifting Affective Gears. Another intervention calls for a refocusing of one partner's negative feelings (e.g., anger) awareness of the undesirable behavior of the other partner to a focus on that partner's internal feelings (e.g., of rejection, sadness, etc.). This shift of affective focus (Gurman, 1982a) is indistinguishable from the refocusing from "hard" to "soft" feelings by emotionally focused couple therapists (Johnson & Denton, Chapter 8, this volume) and integrative behavioral couple therapists (Dimidjian et al., Chapter 9, this volume). The latter therapists call upon this approach as a core strategy in acceptance training, and the former see such affective shifting as central to the development of partners' accessibility and responsiveness.

When the BIMT therapist shifts the focus from "hard" to "soft," and from "outside" to "inside," he/she does so for two reasons. First, at a purely pragmatic level, such a shift interrupts (blocks) recurrent negative interactions, thus allowing opportunities for new behavior to replace old, destructive behavior. At the same time, the utility of such a shift is not its only virtue. The BIMT therapist also actually believes in the psychological truthfulness of the shift itself; that is, the expression of destructive and pain-inducing feelings really is an indirect cover for, or defense against, the direct expression of feelings involving vulnerability.

Note that the "shifting of affective gears" ("high gears" = "hard" emotions, "low" gears = "soft" emotions) also allows the therapist to attach new labels ("high and low gears") to facilitative versus maladaptive expression of feelings in a way that can be seamlessly incorporated into self-control coaching, in a way that parallels the use of "cue-controlled relaxation" in desensitization treatment of anxiety (cf: Gurman, 1970).

Self-Control Coaching: Behavioral Enhancement of Adaptive Containment. The use of self-control strategies—as at times used by behavioral couple therapists (Halford, 1998, 2001; Halford, Sanford, & Behrens, 1994), and other marital therapists (e.g., Arnette, 1997)—is first modeled by and then coached by the therapist, to foster a partner's capacity for containing disturbing internal states. For example, in a moment of escalating argumentation, each partner is coached to say, "Stop!" (or something equivalent) aloud (and eventually silently), and to reflect, also aloud, on what he/she is trying to achieve at that moment. Individual self-control or self-regulation training thus focuses on altering one's response to the partner's undesired behavior, changing one's approach to trying to persuade one's partner to change, and so on.

In addition, bilateral self-regulation coaching is often appropriate and helpful, especially for rapidly escalating, high-intensity, "kitchen-sinking" couples. For example, the therapist may suggest or request an agreement with each partner (1) not to talk about anything, outside the therapy sessions, that is more than a week old and negative, "unless failing to do so would be life-threatening"; (2) not to use obviously provocative language (e.g., "button pushers" such as the "D word" ("divorce"); and (3) to allow either partner unilaterally to terminate an "uncomfortable" couple interchange without further discussion or negotiation, while proposing alternative times to continue the conversation (in or out of the therapy sessions). It is essential that this bilateral couple agreement be seen as a parallel agreement by each partner with the *therapist*, rather than between the partners, thus focusing on each partner's *self-regulation* (containment) as opposed to control of the other partner. Obviously, a solid working alliance with each partner increases the likelihood that the partners will agree to this plan, since it focuses on self-change and thus implicitly acknowledges each partner's own contribution to the problem at hand.

Anticollusive Questioning: Inquiring about and Commenting on Ambivalent Projections. Integrative couple therapists do a good deal of "anticollusive questioning." Anticollusive questioning (1) points to partners' inferred, and hence unspoken, wishes and fears that help to maintain problematic patterns; (2) directs partners' attention to problem-maintaining behavior that is outside their conscious awareness; (3) hints at the "unwitting" (unconscious) ways in which the couple "cooperates" in appearing to be working toward change, yet maintaining the status quo; and (4) identifies self-contradictions between partners' overt behavior and their stated preference and desires. These sorts of questions may be asked in a somewhat rhetorical tone, left only to plant a seed for later questions, and requiring no direct patient response; or they may be asked with the explicit expectation that the partner(s) consider and address the matter, theme, or issue raised by the therapist's question at the time it is presented. As with all blocking techniques, these anticollusive questions are always asked in immediate response to what a partner (or both partners) does or says in the session. Blocking anticollusive questions force attention on the problem-maintaining elements of the couple's relational patterns. In so doing, they invite the partner both to disengage

from relationally destructive behavior at the moment, and to reflect on the unconscious purposes of the broader pattern of which this present behavior is but a therapeutically convenient example. There is no formal limit on the number or types of blocking anticollusive questions that can be asked, but there are several recurrent problematic marital themes for which the following illustrative questions seem often to be appropriate. These questions are typically preceded by a therapist's segue, such as "You know, when you say (or do) that, I wonder . . ."

- ". . . could it be that you fear that you two are really too similar rather than too different?"
- ". . . how do you protect each other from even worse pain?"
- ". . . can you imagine anything negative that might happen if your couple problems just disappeared?" (or "if your partner suddenly started to behave exactly the way you say you wish he/she would?")
- ". . . if, despite your complaining about _____ in your partner right now, might there be times when you actually like or admire _____ ?"
- ". . . even though you often complain about _____ in your partner's behavior, do you ever find that sometimes you do _____ yourself?"
- ". . . are there sometimes moments when your partner is behaving in some way you've really wanted to see more of, and yet you don't 'stroke' him/her for it?"
- ". . . what stops you from accepting what your partner is giving you, especially since it seems to be just what you're asking for?"
- ". . . where did you first learn to be uncomfortable with [whatever the person is repeatedly complaining about in the partner] in yourself?"
- ". . . what do you do to get your partner to behave in ways that, ironically, bother you so much?"
- ". . . when you think of some things you could do differently to help solve the problem, how do you stop yourself from doing these things? What do you say to yourself?"
- ". . . what would it be like if you were married to a person who was virtually identical to yourself psychologically?"
- ". . . how can you help him/her help you to change whatever *you* want to change in yourself?"
- ". . . how do you think you would feel if the two of you were to switch [psychological] roles for a while?"

- "... what can you do to help your partner do less [or more] of what you'd like to be different in your relationship?"

Anticollusive questions such as these cannot be used in a "rote," staged fashion. They must organically and thematically "fit" and be woven into the conversational flow of the session. When appropriately tuned to the affective and substantive context of the session, they appear quite intuitive. When the therapist is well tuned in to the couple's maladaptive "contract" (Sager, 1976, 1981), evocative questions such as these do in fact arise intuitively. When the therapist calls upon an anticollusive question that is well timed, identifies centrally relevant content, and is put forth in the couple's usual expressive style, the recipient usually feels both uncomfortably exposed and deeply understood. This dynamic tension facilitates change. As I have noted elsewhere (Gurman, 1992), "One way to lengthen therapy is to not ask painful or anxiety-arousing questions of patients" (p. 190).

A related, more structured gestalt therapy technique known as "leaning into the accusation" (Sunbury, 1980) can be used in a manner that complements anticollusive questioning. A lists a few of B's most upsetting qualities, especially focused on those related to what A is complaining about in B in the session; A reads one such description aloud, B acknowledges the partial accuracy of the description, and points out ways in which he/she is different from the description as well; and A acknowledges how he/she sometimes behaves in a manner very similar to that about which A has complained about or to B. This process is then reversed. This technique is intended to limit projections and splitting.

Linking Individual Experience and Relational Experience: Insight and the Place of Interpretation

The types of anticollusive blocking actions just described are seen in BIMT as facilitating change by directly modifying each partner's self-experiencing and experiencing of the mate. In general, such therapist-generated experiences in the session should precede, rather than follow, the offering of a cognitive explanation (i.e., interpretations of the underlying dynamic struggles addressed by the therapist's actions). More often than not, prior explanations are actually counterproductive: They may impose so much safe structure that they minimize the level of anxiety or discomfort that the

therapist's actions are designed to expose the partners to in the first place. Thus the potential for experiencing, rather than talking about, new ways of being with oneself and one's partner may be constrained. As Wachtel (1997) notes, "it is not simply awareness that promotes change but awareness that is part of an affective experience" (p. 44).

The BIMT therapist values cognitive awareness as well as behavioral change. In BIMT the development of insight, and the use of interpretation to foster such insight, are seen as but two of many potentially useful therapist interventions. Specifically (and in contrast to its role in traditional "insight-oriented," psychoanalytic therapies), interpretation is one helpful means of fostering therapeutic exposure, which in turn allows for the development of more adaptive and flexible interactions.

In couple therapy, interpretation is intended to expose partners to their hidden feelings (or impulses, etc.) about themselves *and* to their hidden feelings about their mates. Whatever their origins, such feelings are hidden in the present, and so most therapist interpretations in BIMT are present-oriented rather than historically or genetically focused. Even when an interpretation is focused on one partner's experience from an individual historical perspective (e.g., regarding one's family of origin), its implications for the current marital relationship must be identified, or at least struggled with. This is in keeping with the broader principle described earlier—that all "individual" work within the conjoint session must be translated in terms of its marital meaning, ramifications, or consequences. It is also helpful to keep in mind that "not noticing" (Wachtel, 1997, p. 42) what one is doing or feeling parallels not noticing aspects of one's partner that might disconfirm faulty perceptions.

It is probably self-evident that the use of exposure-enhancing therapist interpretations requires a solid therapist–partner alliance as a buffer against anxiety. What cannot be overlooked in the process of couple therapy, however, is that therapist interpretations that expose one partner also require an adequate partner–partner alliance and atmosphere of reasonable empathy and safety, lest a therapist's interpretations be used by the second partner as a weapon against the first partner. For this reason, such individually focused interpretations usually are less common early in therapy than later on.

Thus interpretation has three main purposes in BIMT: first, by naming the previously expressed feeling, to help a person contain the "bad stuff" that would otherwise be projected onto the partner; second, by thus helping a person to accept (by exposure) the projected material as being in him-/ herself, to decrease blame and increase acceptance of the partner; and third, by therapeutically derailing repetitive, redundant interactions from that persisting in the moment, to shift the couple's interaction to allow new relational possibilities (including, prominently, the partners' empathy for each other. "Insight" in BIMT is not sought so much for its "truth" value (although the BIMT therapist rarely offers an interpretation that he/she does not believe) as for its value in shifting couple interactions that are maintained, in part, by existing implicit partner "theories" of what constitutes the couple's dysfunctionality.

Creating Therapeutic Tasks: Instigating Change-Promoting Interaction

Any number of tasks or therapist directives may facilitate the desired change processes in BIMT. There is certainly a place for active and experientially powerful techniques from the Gestalt (e.g., Sunbury, 1980), Structural (e.g., Minuchin & Fishman, 1981), and Strategic (e.g., Stanton, 1980) therapy traditions. Paradoxical techniques such as prescribing symptoms and restraining change (e.g., Papp, 1980), though used sparingly in BIMT, may also foster BIMT goals (Gurman, 1981) for valid psychodynamic reasons (Skynner, 1981). As Skynner (1981) emphasizes,

> All double-binds and other paradoxical communications are attempts to maintain a fantasy world, different from reality, by expressing both fantasy and reality at the same time in a form which conceals the discrepancy between the two, and also by conveying at the same time a "command" to others to collude with the "self-deception" and so preserve the speaker's fantasy world (or the joint fantasy of the marriage or family). Paradoxical therapeutic interventions can then be seen not as "tricks" but as expressions of the most essential truth, which subtly break the rule that fantasy and reality must be kept apart, by relating the two in a disguised, seemingly innocent fashion which expresses only the positive aspects. Once the family or couple accept the bait, they cannot avoid seeing more than appeared to be implied in the original paradoxical intervention. (p. 76; emphasis in original)

Thus a BIMT therapist who positively connotes to a couple the function of a symptom or of an interaction pattern does so with a belief in the actual veracity of what he/she is saying.

Therapeutic tasks refer to the general category of what in BIMT are called "instigative interventions." In contrast to blocking interventions, these interventions typically do not arise out of the immediate natural flow of a therapy session. Rather, in contrast to the more process-oriented blocking interventions, instigative interventions are more goal-oriented and directive; they are "strategic" in Stanton's (1981) sense that "the clinician *initiates* what happens during treatment and *designs* a particular approach for each problem" (p. 361, emphasis added). Thus these interventions are usually more planned by the therapist, even (and often) to the point of being designed outside the therapy sessions. Although the BIMT therapist obviously plans such interventions in a way that is responsive to the treatment needs of each couple as the therapist assesses them, they typically are not set forth in immediate response to the couple's behavior, and are generally experienced as being "brought into" the therapy session. The other major difference from blocking interventions is that blocking interventions are used to interrupt and draw attention to, and increase awareness of, maladaptive couple patterns, whereas instigative interventions are designed to initiate or prompt or model healthier interactions. That is, instigative interventions focus on promoting change in a positive direction.

Out-of-session tasks vary from exploring the consequences of new marital behavior, to reflecting on particular themes identified during therapy sessions, to pinpointing concrete desires for change in one's partner or in oneself. Tasks may be as loosely constructed as asking each member of a couple to "think about how you yourself contribute to the problems that bother you most in your relationship."

BIMT calls upon the active techniques associated with behavioral marital therapy (e.g., Baucom et al., Chapter 2, and Dimidjian et al., Chapter 9, this volume) to facilitate object relations ends. This is not a new phenomenon in couple therapy. Indeed, almost 25 years ago (Gurman, 1978), in a comprehensive comparative analysis of marital therapies, I underscored the fact that "psychoanalytically oriented marriage therapy is largely 'analytic' in the way it organizes the complex material at hand and conceptualizes the nature of marital discord, but is, of necessity, quite pragmatic, if not eclectic, in its selection of actual therapeutic interventions" (p. 466; original emphasis omitted).

In BIMT, most of the most commonly used behavioral methods associated with what Christenson et al. (1995) call "traditional behavioral couple therapy," as distinct from "integrative behavioral couple therapy" (see Dimidjian et al., Chapter 9), are recruited to foster the process of helping couple partners reintegrate denied aspects of themselves and their mates—that is, to work toward the fundamental reintegrative goals of the BIMT approach.

Behavioral Intervention and Therapeutic Couple Exposure

Marital partners in conflict must be exposed to aspects of themselves and their mates that are blocked from awareness. These self-aspects are blocked from awareness because of the anxiety they evoke. As Freud (1909) himself acknowledged almost 100 years ago, people only overcome their anxieties by exposure to that which elicits the anxiety. This exposure can be accomplished in couple therapy in a manner roughly analogous to that used in behavioral treatments for anxiety and phobic disorders, such as systematic desensitization and anxiety management training (Rimm & Masters, 1974). These are specific common technical operations that illustrate the learning theory principle of exposure—or, more specifically, the contact with, and prevention of escape or avoidance from, anxiety-eliciting stimuli. Such exposure concepts have recently been applied quite productively in the short-term individual psychodynamic therapy of McCullough and Andrews (2001). Indeed, McCullough and Andrews assert that "Using active interventions to achieve psychodynamic goals is part of what transforms long-term psychodynamic treatment into short-term psychodynamic treatment" (p. 90).

The use of exposure in couple therapy differs from its usual use in individual behavior therapy in two ways. First, setting up a formal and explicitly negotiated hierarchy of anxiety-eliciting stimuli in couple therapy is practically unmanageable because of the complexity, thematic multidimensionality, and reciprocal interactivity of problematic couple patterns. The second difference from the usual use of exposure treatments in behavior therapy is that the anxiety-eliciting stimuli of clinical concern are events and experiences that occur within the partner/patient, not outside the patient, as in the exposure treatment of, say, a height phobia. Therapeutic couple exposure is more akin to the treatment of agoraphobia, in which the private cognitive and physiological anxiety-eliciting cues constitute the treatment targets (Chambless & Goldstein, 1982). At the same time, therapists need to keep in mind that not all marital avoidant behavior is "irrational" or unwarranted. The partners

in chronically distressed marriages almost always display what behavior therapists would call genuinely "aversive consequences." Marital partners and therapists alike must deal differently with real versus imagined responses to their behavior. Ultimately, for a marital partner to be open to exposing his/her vulnerabilities, there must be good reason for the mate to be seen as "a safe, real person" (Dicks, 1967, p. 43).

Applications of the kinds of principles, strategies, and techniques described above for interrupting and modifying dysfunctional collusive couple behavior in session create opportunities for therapeutic exposure to warded-off aspects of the self and the other. Less obviously, but equally powerfully, commonplace behavioral couple therapy interventions also create such relational learning opportunities. Indeed, it is a practical premise of BIMT that behavioral marital therapy, and Integrative Behavioral Couple Therapy in particular, *is* exposure therapy in large measure. Although various behavioral interventions are used (e.g., behavioral exchange), the traditional defining methods of communication and problem-solving training constitute the foundation and core of BIMT's behavioral techniques. Such techniques can facilitate the process of helping partners reintegrate repudiated aspects of themselves and their mates; that is, they can serve as a means of enabling partners to emerge as whole persons in intimate relationships.

It must be emphasized that in BIMT, rather than quickly attempting to control the dance of projective identification and do away with unpleasant feelings, the therapist often will welcome its real-time enactment in the session. The BIMT therapist may even work to intensify the split-off feelings in the partner in whom they originated, in order to gain access to underlying fears and vulnerabilities, as a step that precedes encouraging the couple to "find a different way to get/say/do what you need or want right now." This intensification process in BIMT is analogous to arranging exposure experiences in the individual behavior therapy exposure treatment of agoraphobia; in these experiences, the patient is required to feel and tolerate, rather than avoid (e.g., by distraction), reasonably high levels of anxiety.

Although BIMT welcomes the recent shift of emphasis in integrative behavioral couple therapy toward acceptance versus behavior change (see, e.g., Dimidjian et al., Chapter 9), the behavioral approach seems to have incorporated only half of the therapeutic formula for inducing change. That is, integrative behavioral couple therapy focuses exclusively on each partner's acceptance of the other partner. In the BIMT framework, both partners must also come to accept in themselves what they have denied in themselves and projected into their mates. Accepting undesired behavior in one's mate is an important step toward acceptance of oneself, but it is not equivalent to doing so.

The Countercollusive Power of Communication and Problem-Solving Intervention

BIMT concurs with Scharff and Bagnini's (Chapter 3) position that the overriding goal of object-relations-oriented couple therapy is to free the couple from the grip of maladaptive and pain-inducing projective processes. BIMT differs substantially from more traditional applications of object relations theory to couple therapy (e.g., Scharff, 1995; Scharff & Bagnini, Chapter 3) regarding the preferred means of reaching such antiprojective ends. Proponents of these more traditional approaches assert that these ends are not reached through "the familiar techniques of communications-trained or behavioral couple therapists" (Scharff & Bagnini, Chapter 3, p. 64). By way of contrast, in BIMT these very interventions are seen as offering some of the most direct available antidotes to unconscious collusion and splitting. Elsewhere, I (Gurman, 1981) have emphasized the common defensive functions of many apparent "skill deficits" for the stability of the troubled couple's relationship. It is not possible to review here in detail the essential elements of communication and problem-solving training, and the reader's familiarity with these methods is assumed (see also Baucom et al., Chapter 2; Jacobson & Margolin, 1979; Jacobson & Holtzworth-Munroe, 1986). At a "meta" level, the use of these techniques requires that the couple partners (1) speak only for themselves, not for each other; (2) assume responsibility for their own thoughts and feelings; (3) systematically track their own affective and cognitive experience; (4) focus on current intrapersonal and interpersonal events; (5) desist from the idealized, defensive stance that each partner should be able to know what the other wants without having to be asked; and (6) attend to their own contributions to displeasing couple patterns.

Thus such traditional behavioral couple therapy techniques collectively discourage collusion and promote relationally healthy integration of the self in several important ways:

1. The techniques emphasize self-differentiation—for instance, even through intermittent en-

couragement by the therapist for partners to state their views and feelings from a time-honored, if a bit overworked, "I" position.

2. The techniques emphasize self-change, and in so doing, counter predictable partner-blaming (projective identification). Inner awareness is promoted in place of outer (and other-) attack.

3. The techniques lower partners' needs to escape and avoid aversive arousal, and thus increase intimate safer engagement.

4. The techniques shift awareness from the unconscious reinforcement of avoidant behavior (in self and partner) to the conscious reinforcement of desired behavior.

5. The empathic emphasis contained in communication skill coaching directly increases partners' acceptance of each other. Moreover, when such empathic relating is focused on a partner's exposing of the vulnerabilities that motivate his/her undesired behavior, the partner's enhanced acceptance includes acceptance of the "bad" or the unchangeable in the mate, plus acceptance of disavowed parts of the self along similar thematic lines. Catherall (1992), from an object relations perspective, has persuasively argued that empathy neutralizes projective identification. Tellingly, Christensen et al. (1995), from a behavioral perspective, have stressed that often when a couple "empathically joins around a problem" (p. 54), the partners more easily accept differences between them; often without further skill-oriented guidance, they more cooperatively engage in new patterns of behavior. Finally, the object relations and behavioral rationales for the central role of enhancing empathic relating in marital therapy were anticipated (Gurman, 1981) in noting that "the therapist's goal . . . is to have spouses learn by experience that unacceptable aspects of themselves and their mates need not be overwhelming. As this aim is being achieved, it often becomes progressively easier for couples to negotiate changes in overt behavior" (p. 446).

6. While improving overt communication, communication "skill-training" techniques also countercollusively decrease each partner's fantasy of who the mate should be, and increase the reality of who the mate actually is. As noted in the earlier discussion of communication and problem-solving "skill deficits," poor communication is more often than not both a symptom of collusion and a maintainer of collusion. Poor communication reflects an implicit rule of limited intimacy through shared avoidance of self-disclosure and self-exposure. Improved communication allows real

differences to be revealed. Private fantasies about the idealized partner may be a natural part of early romantic attraction, but engagement with the real partner is essential for genuine long-term intimacy.

Additional Instigative Interventions for Promoting Change

Other instigative interventions have in common the therapist's planful efforts to stimulate positive change along the lines of the couple's central problematic theme(s). Although instigative intervention other than communication and problem-solving experiences can focus on in-session couple behavior (e.g., directing and encouraging a couple to sustain a conversation about an anxiety-arousing topic), most of these interventions emphasize out-of-session experiences. This aspect of instigative intervention highlights two different but related assumptions of BIMT that are central to brief therapies, and especially to brief marital and family therapies (Gurman, 2001): (1) The central source of healing is within the partner–partner relationship, not the partner–therapist relationship; and (2) effective brief therapy must include change that is reinforced in the couple's natural environment.

Given these guidelines, many therapist interventions may qualify as instigative. For example, encouraging the use of positive reinforcement for change is a deceptively simple technique. This intervention, which calls for the therapist to coach and encourage partners to positively reinforce (via concrete simple acknowledgment, expression of thanks, etc.) the appearance of behavior they have been asking to see more of, by definition is intended to increase each partner's "desired" behavior. In addition, following through on this principle, especially when partners reciprocate, often has the more subtle effect of inhibiting their tendency to engage in projective identification. As discussed earlier, partners in sustained marital conflict often identify behavior that stimulates anxiety about their own impulses, needs, and desires as "unwanted" behavior in their mates. Direct therapist instruction to positively reinforce desired changes in partners' behavior implicitly requires that each partner attend to and acknowledge aspects of the mate that are characteristically minimized or discounted. The couple is put in a "win–win" situation by the therapist's encouragement of reinforcing desired change. If, on the one hand, the partners follows through as suggested, they strengthen valued elements of their relationship. On the other hand, a lack of follow-through, even after it is clear in session that the partners understand the rationale for the therapist's idea, may signify the intensity of their stuck projective process. The therapist can then redirect attention to the unspoken motivations and attributions of each partner that drive them, behaviorally speaking, to continue to emphasize negative perceptions of each other. Such a formulation does not universally explain couples' noncompliance with suggested prosocial behavioral reinforcement approaches, but it provides a conceptual framework that is often very useful in helping a therapist and couple make sense of the partners' anxieties about change. Once thus identified, such anxieties themselves, again following a functional-analytic approach, can then be addressed.

TRANSFERENCE, COUNTERTRANSFERENCE, RESISTANCE, AND THE MECHANISMS OF CHANGE

Transference, Countertransference, and Mechanisms of Change

Unlike the individual therapy setting, in which only one physically real transference pairing (patient–therapist) exists, in marital therapy there exist four transference pairs: husband–wife, wife–husband, husband–therapist, and wife–therapist. In addition, triadic transference may emerge (i.e., husband–wife–therapist). Although partner transferences toward the therapist clearly occur in conjoint therapy, their salience is usually quite attenuated for three main reasons. First, the relative brevity of BIMT inherently caps the impact of most transferential elements of the patient–therapist relationship by countering the sense of fantasied timelessness that often characterizes long-term intensive individual therapy (Budman & Gurman, 1988). Relatedly, BIMT is focused and goal-directed, emphasizing the partners' reality as well as their unspoken fantasies, and the therapist more often than not participates as a real object. A third common characteristic of transference-inducing therapy is the therapist's relative constancy. As shown earlier, the therapist plays many roles in BIMT—from providing and modeling holding functions to provoking warded-off affect, to "coaching" interpersonal social skills, to providing expert information and knowledge about relationships. Although the BIMT therapist certainly provides constant concern, support, and collaborative effort to couples, his/her "job description" includes a describable but widely varying set of action possibilities. Transference reactions in a focused therapy such as BIMT include important information on the partners' feelings, perceptions, misperceptions and attributions of intent, motivation, and loyalties; of course, these must be addressed when they are overt and pose obstacles to the forward movement of the therapy.

At the same time, transference reactions do not typically impede progress in BIMT, as they may be more likely to in longer-term, more uncovering couple therapies based on object relations theory (e.g., Scharff & Bagnini, Chapter 3). In BIMT, the most powerful transferences occur between the marital partners, and it is there that therapeutic attention must be focused. As Skynner (1980) crisply put the central issue, "The unconscious conflicts are already fully developed in the mutual projective system between the couple, and could be better dealt with directly rather than by the indirect methods of 'transference'" (pp. 276–277). Working toward the resolution of a limited number of currently relevant, bilateral marital transference patterns serves well as an overriding orienting aim in BIMT.

This perspective is in line with the contextual family therapy view of Boszormenyi-Nagy and Ulrich (1981), who avoid "substitutive relational contexts" (p. 162) in favor of the "original relational context" (p. 162). This emphasis on treating relationship problems in what social learning theorists call the "natural environment" decreases patients' dependency on the therapist, and promotes generalization of change from the *in vitro* setting of the therapist's office to the *in vivo* setting of everyday life. Thus the classical "corrective emotional experience" is to be found within the couple-as-patient. One of the most corrective of such experiences is learning to discriminate the real current partner from the misperceived, past "inner" partner.

More specifically, BIMT asserts that a rather broad range of therapist interventions, including behavioral interventions, can foster such bilaterally corrective experiences. For example, successful communication and problem-solving experiences (usually not requiring "training") make partners safer and more accessible and responsive (as emphasized in attachment-oriented Emotionally Focused Therapy; see Johnson & Denton, Chapter 8). At the same time, exposing warded-off (and thus indirectly conveyed) feelings to an increasingly nonattacking, empathic partner (as in Integrative

Behavioral Couple Therapy; see Dimidjian et al., Chapter 9) requires the taking back of projections and necessarily leads to a decreased punishing of one's partner for one's own strivings, conflicts, and fears (as emphasized in Object Relations Marital Therapy; see Scharff & Bagnini, Chapter 3). Likewise, the development of relationally relevant insight—for instance, about the childhood or previous adulthood origins of relationship anxieties—facilitates opportunities for bonding (as emphasized in Affective Reconstructive Therapy, formerly known as Insight-Oriented Couple Therapy; see Snyder & Schneider, Chapter 6).

On the other side of the equation, the potential for the therapist's problematic countertransferential reactions to the couple, or to either partner, is heightened in a brief, active, goal-oriented therapy such as BIMT. It is nearly impossible for most couple therapists not to encounter, in their own current or past intimate relationships, the painful issues involved in the relationships of patient couples. Moreover, a therapist's generally high level of activity in BIMT—including actively engaging the couple, and engaging with his/her own thought process, on multiple levels of experience—does not allow a great deal of time and opportunity for in-session self-reflection.

The most common and most dangerous therapist error in BIMT, as in any couple therapy, is nonstrategic side taking—that is, side taking, particularly of a recurrent nature, that is born of the clinician's failure to appreciate the anxiety and pain behind the "negative" behavior of either partner. Although the therapist can and should use his/her own countertransference reactions as important guides to what is most distressing and fearful for the marital partners, again the focus must remain on the partner–partner relationship. The therapist's self-awareness should emphasize an understanding of what it is in the *couple's* relationship that draws side-taking inclinations out of the therapist.

This side-taking error is particularly dangerous very early in therapy, of course. It is at that time that the partners are likely to be most entrenched in their split, rigidly projected negative views of each other, increasing the possibility that the therapist will be unwittingly taken in by one partner whose characteristics or (mis)attributions to the mate strike an uncomfortable chord in the therapist. Such unfortunate (though nearly inevitable) problematic countertransference reactions, if they are not recurrent, can be more easily repaired later in therapy.

Resistance

Because time is generally quite limited in the practice of couple therapy, the BIMT therapist actively intervenes in situations involving change-resistant behavior between a partner (or both partners) and the therapist only when such events or patterns seem clearly to be posing a genuine obstacle to continuing therapeutic progress. Certainly transferences resembling parent–child relationships can develop in couple therapy, but as already noted, they are not especially common in focused, brief couple work.

Just as BIMT views the partner–partner relationship as the source of relational healing, so too does it keep an eye constantly open for resistance to change expressed in that relationship. Haley's (1963) well-known "first law of relationships" is relevant here. Haley wrote that "when one person indicates a change in relationship to another, the other will act upon the first so as to diminish and nullify that change" (pp. 223–224). Haley saw such interpartner resistance to change in terms of power and social influence. In BIMT, by contrast, the bedrock of resistance to change is the "internal pressure generated by the desire to maintain one's own self-esteem and psychic boundaries" (Gurman & Knudson, 1978, p. 127), which in turn is a function of two factors: first, the level of anxiety aroused in the partners as they become aware of (i.e., exposed to) the split-off and projected aspects of themselves; and second, the frequency and intensity of the partners' unwitting reinforcement of each other's efforts to avoid or escape such reintegration (i.e., to avoid change). When one partner no longer fully plays out his/her half of the implicit collusive marital "script," the other partner will commonly work to shape the former to get "back in character." At such moments, the therapist's task is to coach, coax, and support the partner to stick to the revised "script" (i.e., to encourage exposure), while identifying and allaying the other partner's discomfort at the changes and urging the other partner to remain open to the change.

Termination

Aside from problematic terminations—for instance, those ruptures in the therapeutic alliance caused by errors involving therapist neutrality and side taking—the ending of most BIMT work is relatively uneventful and rarely as disequilibrating termination as in long-term individual treatment can be.

Because the primary attachment and transference in BIMT are those between the marital partners, there is little sense of "a wrenching from treatment or a cutting the patient adrift to fend for himself" (Fisch, Weakland, & Segal, 1982, p. 176). Moreover, couples often initiate termination when the central symptoms or problems have been resolved, or at least abated. As Brewster and Montie (1987) have noted, "a family will come in during a crisis and once that is over, its members typically want to back off from the enforced togetherness of the therapeutic session" (p. 34). As much as the therapist may hope to engage with the couple at multiple levels of intervention, there may not be enough time available to do so. As a result, with the anticipation that termination may always be not far away, the BIMT therapist seeks to intervene at multiple levels of experience in an active style that evokes, exposes, and modifies problematic, projectively induced and sustained patterns.

In BIMT, contact with the couple often occurs on a brief, intermittent basis, with couples returning to the therapist about similar or different issues than when they were initially seen. One of the hallmarks of effective and practical brief therapy, including couple therapy, is the development of a therapist–patient (couple) relationship not unlike that of a primary care physician, to whom the patient returns as life demands and changes require (Budman & Gurman, 1988). Thus BIMT does not usually view termination as "final."

Therapy is generally terminated either when the partners have reached their primary goals, or when they find that although they have not fully achieved their aims, they have lost a significant degree of motivation for continuing at this time. Alternatively, of course, one or both partners may call a halt if they see no progress being made, or do not have an adequate alliance with the therapist. The decision to "terminate" is the couple's, although in the interest of directness and efficiency, the BIMT therapist occasionally may also suggest "taking a break" from therapy if he/she believes the couple is not adequately committed to the therapeutic task.

In practical terms, the BIMT therapist again takes advantage of an opportunity to reinforce the central therapeutic messages about relationship change. First, in the belief that one never fully casts off projected aspects of oneself, the therapist may inquire (supportively rather than confrontatively) whether "there is anything problematic about the ways you used to be with your partner that you sometimes feel an urge to return to, even though you mostly don't." This question is not posed "paradoxically," but as an expression of a genuine therapist acceptance of the understandable ambivalence with which people typically engage in meaningful change.

Second, and relatedly, in the "termination session" the BIMT therapist will not only ask the partners to review what changes have occurred, but will also ask (and, if necessary, push) the partners to acknowledge both their own and each other's contributions to the positive changes that have occurred.

APPLICABILITY

Scharff (1995) has taken the position that psychoanalytic couple therapy based on object relations theory is "for couples interested in understanding and growth . . . not for the couple whose thinking style is concrete" (p. 184). Although this may be true of more traditional psychoanalytically oriented couple therapies, which place great emphasis on interpretation and on transference phenomena, it is not true of the variant of object relations couple therapy that is BIMT. BIMT always highlights multileveled formulations of couples' problem maintenance and urges therapists to intervene simply, even while holding moderately complex formulations. Thus a fundamental belief in BIMT is that therapists can use their psychodynamic/object relations understanding of problematic couple relationships without necessarily explicitly "speaking the language of psychodynamics," so to speak. One may practice BIMT without much interpretive activity (e.g., regarding warded-off feelings), with little or no attention to the past (especially the past of the partners as individuals, outside their relationship), and with little or no explicit attention to patient–therapist transference phenomena. To some, this may then sound as if the "psychodynamics" of the treatment have been entirely purged from the therapy experience. But, as has been emphasized here repeatedly, many very direct, practical therapist interventions can go a long way to serve object relations therapy aims. Even with partners whose capacity to empathize is severely limited, whose capacity to contain painful feelings is likewise limited, and who cannot therefore participate well in the newer style of behavioral couple therapy that emphasizes acceptance building (Christensen et al., 1995), old or "traditional" behavioral marital therapy interventions emphasizing behavioral exchange and communication and problem-solving

coaching may still be helpful, albeit to a more limited degree. BIMT would argue that even in such constraining circumstances, BIMT intervention may be able to modify partners' maladaptive inner relationship representations enough to produce a qualitative improvement in the relationship, largely through its feeling safer and more secure to the partners.

Naturally, partners are likely to gain more from therapy if they are able not only to engage with behavioral interventions, but also to (1) respond cooperatively to the therapist's interpretive efforts; (2) "go with the flow" in response to the kinds of "anticollusive" questions the therapist may, seemingly at times "out of the blue," throw into the mix of a particular therapy session; and (3) remain in a good working alliance with the therapist, even when the therapist is unmasking the unspoken, hidden couple interaction by interrupting and blocking problem-maintaining couple interactions. Clearly, the capacity to tolerate such affective arousal and relatively deeper interpretation requires a moderate level of cognitive and affective maturity.

Couples that are typically most responsive to the various levels of intervention included in BIMT can be identified rather straightforwardly, even early in treatment. They are the couples whose members tend, before any therapy experience, to see life interactively and circularly rather than linearly; are somewhat flexible in their ability to entertain new possibilities for both explaining and changing their conflicted situation; are curious about themselves and about relationships generally; and can and do, with or without therapist prompting, acknowledge their own individual contributions to the marital tension. A couple with flexibility in the relationship, ego strength in each partner, and a reasonable capacity for "holding" and "containing" may require only extremely brief and practical problem-solving assistance, usually for difficulties that originate outside the couple's relationship, even if it is consuming the partners' energy and affect.

Thus, although few particular patient or couple characteristics preclude the applicability of BIMT, some do severely limit its role, as with any approach to couple therapy. Such characteristics include most prominently uncontrollable, volatile arguing or otherwise grossly dysregulated behavior in the therapy sessions, or individual psychopathology that simply overwhelms the interaction.

In addition, there is an altogether too common type of couple that appears in therapists' offices and with which multileveled BIMT, or perhaps any method of couple therapy, is difficult. These are the couples whose members are fundamentally incompatible (Hamburg, 2000) in most major spheres of life and probably should not have married in the first place. Such fundamentally incompatible couples typically got together for one or more universally unwise reasons (e.g., "forced marriage" due to a pregnancy, a need to escape a painful family situation, a transitional relationship exit out of another unsatisfying marriage, etc.). As Hamburg argues, such fundamentally incompatible partners may never be able to establish a secure and safe relationship together, because their inherent differences preclude them from feeling mutually validated and valued, and render almost impossible the development of any level of genuine empathy beyond perfunctory and grudging acknowledgment that the two of them have very different feelings and very different views of the world. Some of the behavioral techniques used in BIMT, especially behavior exchange and problem-solving coaching, may allow such partners to tolerate and endure each other, but an outright enhancement of their likelihood of genuine acceptance of each other is not realistic to expect.

BIMT is ideally suited to couples whose members, despite their pain, either intend to remain together or at least are open to the possibility. Severely estranged or separated couples simply do not have enough relational incentive to anaesthetize themselves for a conjoint therapy that not only modifies, but may also expose, hidden vulnerabilities.

CASE ILLUSTRATION

Background

Karl and Sue were referred to me the way many couples are. Sue had been working with a local psychiatrist for about 6 months because of her depression, which Dr. Johnson had been treating with antidepressant medication and supportive, biweekly individual psychotherapy. As her depression improved, and she became more active and took more initiative in general, Sue became less and less tolerant of the long-standing difficulties in her marriage of 14 years. Though Sue was hesitant to "push" Karl into therapy, her psychiatrist repeatedly advised her that an indefinitely long course of individual therapy would probably not lead to an improvement in the marriage, and in fact could potentially threaten it.

Sue called to find out when I might be available to see them, noting that she would have to "check carefully with Karl about his schedule" before actually setting a meeting time. The passage of several weeks until Karl's schedule allowed a meeting was, not surprisingly, symptomatic of the core couple difficulties.

The Presenting Problem and Initial Evaluation

Sue was clearly the initiator of couple therapy. They had seen a "counselor" for a few sessions several years earlier for similar concerns, but that had ended unsatisfyingly for both partners, who felt that the counselor was too "passive and reflective." "I think we need someone to really challenge us," Sue suggested. "Otherwise, we'll just intellectualize ourselves into a dead end." Karl, a university professor deeply involved in genomics research, and Sue, a part-time textile artist and full-time homemaker, had each had long courses of psychoanalytic, insight-oriented individual therapy when they were in college and graduate school at elite east coast universities.

For Sue, the central issue was the emotional distance in the relationship, expressed in Karl's irritability when Sue brought up "emotional topics" (such as their relationship), his apparent loss of sexual interest in her, and in general his absence from the relationship. "I know his work is demanding and stressful," Sue offered, "But he just never seems to *care* that we spend zero time together. It's like he's married to his work." Karl spent "endless" hours in his research laboratory, in addition to his teaching and administrative responsibilities, and Sue was also concerned about the effect on their three children (ages 12, 8, and 3) of having an "absentee father." Indeed, Sue, feeling powerless to influence Karl "just for my own needs," was increasingly drawing the children into their couple struggles—apparently "priming them" and "asking leading questions," as Karl put it, to get them to complain about "missing their father."

These triangulations were no small factor in Sue's recent success at getting Karl to come for therapy. Growing up the eldest son of a struggling Midwestern farm family, Karl knew what it was like "to hardly ever see your father," and as a young man had vowed to himself that he would not "pass on a bad family habit." Moreover, he felt in some degree of competition with Sue over the children, and seemed jealous of her closeness to them. In addition, he was getting concerned about "whether it is appropriate for Sue to still be sleeping with Kyle," their 8-year-old son. "At least he provides me some companionship!" Sue countered.

For his part, Karl felt that Sue "would never be satisfied" by anything he could do. "She's insatiable," he ventured. "She depends on me for too much. I wish she would really get back into her career. She's just wasting all that talent." "I might be able to, if you were ever around to take care of the kids," she retorted. At times when Sue shot back with such sarcasm, Karl would become enraged and threatening, never physically but certainly in his posture and tone of voice, often wagging his finger at Sue in a confronting and critical manner. He had thrown "a couple of things like books near me, but never at me," Sue clarified. Still, she felt in potential danger about interacting with Karl under these sorts of circumstances, and Karl sometimes felt that he might "lose it" in these "outbursts."

Karl and Sue had met in high school, where they were friends, though he had a "crush" on her for "most of the time." They happened to go to college in the same East Coast city, and kept up a "brother–sister relationship." When Sue found herself in a verbally and at times physically abusive relationship with Jim, a graduate student at her university, she would turn to Karl for "emotional support." Being Sue's "protector and confidant" about Jim became a preoccupation for Karl, and a privately highly sexualized one as well. When he finally persuaded Sue to end the relationship with Jim, Karl and Sue spent more and more time together, and soon started what they both considered dating. Sue said that for a long time, she had been "amazed at how much time he could make for me before we were even really a couple, compared to what it's been like most of the time we've been married."

The Course of Therapy

Karl and Sue were seen at approximately biweekly intervals for 13 sessions over a 6-month period, ending when the couple and their children went to the East Coast for the summer ("because of a long-standing, unalterable commitment I made," said Karl) for Karl to complete a research project with a senior colleague at his undergraduate university. Here I provide a sampling of the typical issues that arose over the 13 joint sessions, and how they were addressed both in the therapy sessions and outside the sessions.

Early Sessions: Emphasis on Alliances

Sue was an eager therapy participant; Karl, a reluctant one. Building a working alliance with Sue was quite easy: She spoke the language of therapy, showed at least a moderate amount of flexibility about new ideas or perspectives, and seemed to have more emotional investment in the marriage. Karl, on the other hand, was "married" to his research, and had a strong professional peer group (although he rarely socialized with colleagues off campus) both locally and nationally. Moreover, he was "hell-bent," as Sue put it, "to prove to his family, especially his father, that he was one of the best" in his field. After all, Karl, the eldest child and only son in his family of origin, had effectively betrayed his father by choosing not to carry on the family farming tradition, by moving out of his home state for 10 years ("Why can't you just study agriculture or biology or something at State U.?" his father had implored Karl near the end of his senior year in high school). Karl had never been particularly willing to enter couple therapy until now, with his concerns heightened about his children's psychological welfare.

Sue, the eldest of three children in a family with an alcoholic father and "an incompetent mother," had learned early in life to disregard most of her own needs in deference to taking care of others. She had been an almost straight-A student in high school and had shown remarkable artistic ability. When she followed the urgings of her teachers and school counselors to get out of her rural environment and "expand my horizons," her parents felt abandoned and "tried to use every way of making me feel guilty they could think of to get me to change my decision."

In the first two or three sessions, my central blocking activity focused on eliciting Sue's concerns about Karl's "absenteeism," and trying to draw out of Karl an honest expression of his feelings *and* his thoughts (rationality and practicality were strong values to him) about his "dilemma," as I referred to it, of how to be both an effective scholar and an effective husband and father. I actively acknowledged the inevitable tensions in a life split between a high-powered academic environment and family members desperate for contact with their father/husband, having been there myself a couple of decades earlier. When Sue would interrupt Karl with comments such as "That's just a rationalization; you just don't care about us," I would calm her and invite her to listen to Karl about his "dilemma," "just a bit further." I wanted to draw from him his struggle with *himself* over "trying to live successfully in two worlds," and to see that what mattered was whether *he* wanted to be more engaged at home for his own needs, not merely in response to Sue's frequent "demands."

As Karl's internal struggle emerged in the sessions, Sue softened just enough to occasionally empathize with him over the very real pressures he experienced at work from his senior faculty colleagues, none of whom, he said, seemed to have "much of a life at home"—an assessment that Sue shared. Acknowledging that Karl was in an "academic culture that can be deadly to marriages," I challenged Karl about whether he could be a "leader by example among his department colleagues"—for example, by leaving campus early sometimes to "watch the kids" (while his wife worked in her studio). I used the common sports phrase "leader by example" intentionally, because Sue had earlier mentioned that Karl, a standout basketball player in high school, "was never very vocal on the court, but was a real leader by example." Karl seemed almost intrigued by the idea. He also was relatively comfortable with in the role of "helping Sue out" at this point, as he had been helpful to Sue earlier during her college dating conflict period.

Midphase Sessions: Challenging the Couple's Shared Avoidance of Closeness

After our third session, there was a 3-week hiatus until the next session because of Karl's "previous university commitments." During this time, Karl had rearranged parts of his schedule so that he "could be home more to help with the kids." As I thought might happen, Sue did not immediately glow over Karl's earlier home appearances; in fact, she attacked him for "waiting so long to start to show you care."

Was Sue testing Karl's commitment to change, and/or was she fearing his initial attempts to change? The distance between the partners in a long-term relationship is probably always maintained by each of them in their own way. Sometimes one partner's way is just more obvious.

Both as a supportive move toward Karl and as a move to include Sue as an active change agent herself, and not allow her to be merely a complainant, in the fourth session I raised the question of what it would take to "help her feel OK about helping Kyle give up his mother at bedtime." A concise but precisely worded script was worked out in that session, for Sue and Karl to use together to explain to Kyle why "bedtime things are going to start to be different" (e.g., "Mom and Dad need some more time together"). Protests from Kyle were anticipated and planned for, and a schedule aimed at removing Sue from Kyle's bed altogether over a 1-week period was worked out. Two (weekday) nights a week, Karl was to be present during Kyle's bedtime preparation, and "even be in charge, with Sue sort of in the background" on one occasion. When Kyle settled in, Sue and Karl were to "just hang out together" for about an hour, doing "whatever makes sense to both of you and is comfortable for both of you."

During one of their "hanging-out" times, a most interesting conversation occurred, in which Karl expressed the feeling that he "had too much to do" and asked Sue whether she would consider taking over "managing the everyday family finances" (i.e., their joint checkbook). Karl, raised in a constant state of family economic uncertainty, had until now always insisted on being in charge of his and Sue's finances—fearing that, as he so vividly put it, "The impulsive artist in her might send us all to the poorhouse."

Sue eagerly took on the task, seeing it both as a way of connecting with Karl by implicitly acknowledging his sense of burden, and as a means of moving toward more "balance" (of power, implied but not stated by Sue) in their marriage. Much to Karl's surprise (but not mine), after about 2 weeks of Sue's managing their finances, Karl found that Sue could be "even tighter with money than I am," and that he had "found some freedom to indulge myself [financially] now that I'm not so aware of money every day."

I reflected that it sounded like the "money job" had changed, but not how they dealt with each other. "You just switched roles," I said, "But the dialogue is still the same. The problem with that is, you could end up in the same fights you usually have over money."

Asking the first clearly "anticollusive question" I had felt comfortable expressing until now, I continued, "It seems to me that you are both perfectly competent handling the finances, so who actually takes care of the money doesn't really matter. And, ironically, it seems to me that your values about money aren't particularly different, as it turns out, even though they seemed until recently to be. So this all leaves me wondering—and I realize this is a strange-sounding question—but is there some danger if the two of you *agree* on money things, if you *cooperate* on money things, and see eye-to-eye?"

This question was left with the couple at the end of Session 6 to "take home and think about for the next time we meet."

By dealing as we did with a superficially "simple" and "concrete" issue involving money management, around which there was so much affect, we had unearthed the couple's central, unspoken, and out-of-awareness problem—a jointly shared avoidance of closeness. The central vulnerability theme explored over the next couple of sessions was this: If their differences were not continually focused on, and their similarities were acknowledged, they could become more intimate. For Sue and Karl, this "solution" was, they feared, ironically the problem as well. Both of them had felt unacknowledged in their families of origin; both had felt pressure to suppress their own urges, wishes, and goals for the sake of their families; both of them had felt coerced to "toe the line." For each of them, acknowledging core similarities seemed not comforting and safe, as one might expect, but threatening to their individual senses of self. What had drawn them together to a large degree was the excitement each offered in their apparent differentness (he, the logical, reliable student, the parental protector; she, the expressive, creative, needy artist). But their overt differentness had masked their core similarity.

Still, the most damaging aspect of their situation had not been their differences or their fears of acknowledging their similarities. It was their unwitting, collusive, implicit agreement not to deal with each other openly about these matters.

And as these matters were explored, a clear sense of relief came over Karl and Sue during the sessions. Between Sessions 8 and 9, however, it seemed that the two of them had experienced too much closeness for their comfort. Together, they managed to escalate a seemingly trivial miscommunication of information into a verbally vicious argument that, Sue said, "was as hot as anything in *The War of the Roses*." Sue felt especially endangered by Karl, and he, fortunately, felt especially remorseful about his part of their mutual raging. I seized this opportunity to help coach Karl in a variety of behavioral self-control techniques to be better able to tone down his expression of anger in the future. He was especially sensitive to Sue's acerbic sarcasm. With Sue listening in riveted silence for almost an entire session, I talked to Karl about his high school basketball days as a sports psychologist might do—discussing how he resisted cues from opposing players that could really "get inside your head," how he would fight off the urge to be forced into the kind of "retaliation fouls" that the referees always saw, and so forth. I urged him to "lead by example" once again by developing concrete behavioral alternatives to letting "the other guy [Sue] take your game plan away from you" (a common sports metaphor). Though lacking a sports background, Sue seemed just as drawn to this self-control approach as Karl was; as the session came to a close, she understatedly offered, "I think I could probably use some of those ideas myself."

At our last couple of sessions, calm returned to Sue and Karl. On a few occasions when slights or disagreements might have threatened to escalate, each of them used one or more simple, concrete self-control strategies we had discussed and practiced. Kyle was staying in his bed quite regularly now, and although Karl was still working "70-hour weeks" (according to Sue), he seemed more engaged when present, which he was more often.

When they returned from their summer on the East Coast, Sue phoned to say that they didn't see the need to see me again, at least not at that time. Although a good deal more useful therapeutic work could have occurred with Karl and Sue, our brief work ended at a point at which they seemed to have developed greater (and, for the time being, sufficient) mutual empathy, self-understanding, and interactional responsiveness and flexibility.

REFERENCES

Aponte, H. J. (1992). The black sheep of the family: A structural approach to brief therapy. In S. H. Budman, M. Hoyt, & S. Friedman (Eds.), *The first session in brief therapy* (pp. 324–341). New York: Guilford Press.

Arnette, J. K. (1997). A psychophysiological intervention for marital discord. *Journal of Family Psychotherapy, 8*, 3–15.

Bader, E. (1984, October). *The symbiotic marriage*. Workshop conducted at the annual meeting of the American Association for Marriage and Family Therapy, San Francisco.

Bagarozzi, D. A., & Giddings, C. W. (1983). The role of cognitive constructs and attributional processes in family therapy: Integrating intrapersonal, interpersonal, and systems dynamics. In L. Wolberg & M. Aronson (Eds.), *Group and family therapy 1981* (pp. 207–219). New York: Brunner/Mazel.

Bandura, A. (1969). *Principles of behavior modification*. New York: Wiley.

Baucom, D. H., Epstein, N., & Rankin, L. A. (1995). Cognitive aspects of cognitive-behavioral marital therapy. In N. S. Jacobson & A. S. Gurman (Eds.), *Clinical handbook of couple therapy* (pp. 65–90). New York: Guilford Press.

Beels, C. C., & Ferber, A. (1969). Family therapy: A view. *Family Process, 8*, 280–318.

Berns, S., & Jacobson, N. S. (2000). Marital problems. In M. J. Dougher (Ed.), *Clinical behavior analysis* (pp. 181–206). Reno, NV: Context Press.

Bentovim, A. (1979). Theories of family interaction and techniques of intervention. *Journal of Family Therapy, 1,* 321–345.

Bergin, A. E., & Jensen, J. P. (1990). The meaning of eclecticism: New survey and analysis of components. *Professional Psychology, 21,* 124–130.

Berman, E. B., Lief, H., & Williams, A. M. (1981). A model of marital integration. In G. P. Sholevar (Ed.), *The handbook of marriage and marital therapy* (pp. 3–34). New York: Spectrum.

Birchler, G., & Spinks, S. (1980). A behavioral–systems marital and family therapy: Intervention and clinical application. *American Journal of Family Therapy, 6*–28.

Birchler, G., & Webb, L. (1975, April). *A social learning formulation of discriminating interaction behaviors in happy and unhappy marriages.* Paper presented at the annual meeting of the Southwestern Psychological Association, Houston, TX.

Birchler, G., Weiss, R. L., & Vincent, J. P. (1975). A multidimensional analysis of social reinforcement exchange between maritally distressed and nondistressed spouse and stranger dyads. *Journal of Personality and Social Psychology, 31,* 349–360.

Birchler, G., Weiss, R. L., & Wampler, L. D. (1972, April). *Differential patterns of social distress and level of intimacy.* Paper presented at the annual meeting of the Western Psychological Association, Portland, OR.

Bogdan, J. (1984, March–April). Doctor Pangloss as family therapist. *The Family Therapy Networker,* pp. 19–20.

Boszormenyi-Nagy, I., & Ulrich, D. N. (1981). Contextual family therapy. In A. S. Gurman & D. P. Kniskern (Eds.), *Handbook of family therapy* (pp. 159–225). New York: Brunner/Mazel.

Bowen, M. (1978). *Family therapy in clinical practice.* New York: Jason Aronson.

Bowlby, J. (1988). *A secure base: Parent–child attachment and healthy human development.* New York: Basic Books.

Bray, J. H., & Jouriles, E. N. (1995). Treatment of marital conflict and prevention of divorce. *Journal of Marital and Family Therapy, 21,* 461–473.

Brewster, F., & Montie, K. A. (1987, January–February). Double life: What do family therapists really do in private practice? *The Family Therapy Networker,* 33–35.

Budman, S. H. (1999). Time-effective couple therapy. In J. Donovan (Ed.), *Short-term couple therapy* (pp. 173–197). New York: Guilford Press.

Budman, S. H., & Gurman, A. S. (1988). *Theory and practice of brief therapy.* New York: Guilford Press.

Catherall, D. R. (1992). Working with projective identification in couples. *Family Process, 31,* 355–367.

Chambless, D. C., & Goldstein, A. J. (Eds.). (1982). *Agoraphobia: Multiple perspectives.* New York: Wiley.

Christensen, A., & Jacobson, N. S. (2000). *Reconcilable differences.* New York: Guilford Press.

Christensen, A., Jacobson, N. S., & Babcock, J. C. (1995). Integrative behavioral couple therapy. In N. S. Jacobson & A. S. Gurman (Eds.), *Clinical handbook of couple therapy* (pp. 31–64). New York: Guilford Press.

Cordova, J. V., Jacobson, N. S., & Christenson, A. (1998). Acceptance versus change interventions in behavioral

couple therapy: Impact on couples' in-session communication. *Journal of Marital and Family Therapy, 24,* 437–455.

Crane, D. R. (1996). *Fundamentals of marital therapy.* New York: Brunner/Mazel.

Cytrynbaum, S., & Ruda, V. (1999, June). *The social induction of emotional states: The significance of projective identification in the application of social systems theory to organizational analysis and consultation.* Paper presented at the annual symposium of the International Society for the Psychoanalytic Study of Organizations, Toronto.

Dicks, H. V. (1967). *Marital tensions.* New York: Basic Books.

Doherty, W. J., & Simmons, D. S. (1996). Clinical practice patterns of marriage and family therapists: A national survey of therapists and their clients. *Journal of Marital and Family Therapy, 22,* 9–25.

Dollard, J., & Miller, N. E. (1950). *Personality and psychotherapy.* New York: McGraw-Hill.

Donovan, J. (1999). Short-term couple therapy and the principles of brief treatment. In J. Donovan (Ed.), *Short-term couple therapy* (pp. 1–12). New York: Guilford Press.

Duncan, B. L., & Miller, S. D. (2000). The client's theory of change: Consulting the client in the integrative process. *Journal of Psychotherapy Integration, 10,* 169–187.

Epstein, N. B., & Baucom, D. H. (1998). Cognitive-behavioral couple therapy. In F. M. Dattilio (Ed.), *Case studies in couple and family therapy* (pp. 37–61). New York: Guilford Press.

Fairbairn, W. R. D. (1963). Synopsis of an object-relations theory of personality. *International Journal of Psycho-Analysis, 44,* 224–225.

Feldman, L. B. (1979). Marital conflict and marital intimacy: An integrative psychodynamic–behavioral–systemic model. *Family Process, 18,* 69–78.

Feldman, L. B. (1985). Integrative multi-level therapy: A comprehensive interpersonal and intrapsychic approach. *Journal of Marital and Family Therapy, 11,* 357–372.

Fisch, R., Weakland, J., & Segal, L. (1982). *The tactics of change: Doing therapy briefly.* San Francisco: Jossey-Bass.

Floyd, F. J., Haynes, S. N., & Kelly, S. (1997). Marital assessment: A dynamic functional-analytic approach. In W. K. Halford & H. J. Markman (Eds.), *Clinical handbook of marriage and couples intervention* (pp. 367–377). New York: Wiley.

Follette, W. C., Naugle, A. E., & Linnerooth, P. J. N. (2000). Functional alternatives to traditional assessment and diagnosis. In M. J. Dougher (Ed.), *Clinical behavior analysis* (pp. 99–125). Reno, NV: Context Press.

Freedman, J., & Combs, G. (2000). Narrative therapy with couples. In F. M. Dattilio & L. J. Bevilacqua (Eds.), *Comparative treatments for relationship dysfunction* (pp. 342–361). New York: Springer.

Freud, S. (1909). A phobia in a 5-year-old boy. *Collected Works, 3,* 149–289.

Gilbert, M., & Shmulker, D. (1996). *Brief therapy with couples.* Chichester, England: Wiley.

Goldfried, M. (1995). Towards a common language for case formulation. *Journal of Psychotherapy Integration, 5,* 221–244.

Gottman, J. M. (1979). *Marital interaction: Empirical investigations.* New York: Academic Press.

Gottman, J. M. (1993). A theory of marital dissolution and stability. *Journal of Family Psychology, 7,* 57–75.

Gottman, J. M. (1994a). *What predicts divorce?* Hillsdale, NJ: Erlbaum.

Gottman, J. M. (1994b). *Why marriages succeed or fail.* New York: Simon & Schuster.

Gottman, J. M. (1998). Psychology and the study of marital processes. *Annual Review of Psychology, 49,* 169–197.

Gottman, J. M. (1999). *The marriage clinic: A scientifically based marital therapy.* New York: Norton.

Greenberg, L. S., & Johnson, S. M. (1986). Emotionally focused couples therapy. In N. S. Jacobson & A. S. Gurman (Eds.), *Clinical handbook of marital therapy* (pp. 253–278). New York: Guilford Press.

Greenberg, L. S., & Johnson, S. M. (1988). *Emotionally focused couple therapy.* New York: Guilford Press.

Greenspan, S. I., & Mannino, F. V. (1974). A model for brief intervention with couples based on projective identification. *American Journal of Psychiatry, 131,* 1103–1106.

Gurman, A. S. (1970). A note on the use of "expanded" emotive imagery in desensitization. *Psychotherapy: Theory, Research and Practice, 7,* 226–227.

Gurman, A. S. (1971). Group marital therapy: Clinical and empirical implications for outcome research. *International Journal of Group Psychotherapy, 21,* 174–189.

Gurman, A. S. (1973a). The effects and effectiveness of marital therapy: A review of outcome research. *Family Process, 12,* 145–170.

Gurman, A. S. (1973b). Marital therapy: Emerging trends in research and practice. *Family Process, 12,* 45–54.

Gurman, A. S. (1978). Contemporary marital therapies: A critique and comparative analysis of psychoanalytic, behavioral and systems theory approaches. In T. Paolino & B. McCrady (Eds.), *Marriage and marital therapy* (pp. 445–566). New York: Brunner/Mazel.

Gurman, A. S. (1980). Behavioral marriage therapy in the 1980's: The challenge of integration. *American Journal of Family Therapy, 8,* 86–96.

Gurman, A. S. (1981). Integrative marital therapy: Toward the development of an interpersonal approach. In S. H. Budman (Ed.), *Forms of brief therapy* (pp. 415–462). New York: Guilford Press.

Gurman, A. S. (1982a). Changing collusive patterns in marital therapy. *American Journal of Family Therapy, 10,* 71–73.

Gurman, A. S. (1982b). Creating a therapeutic alliance in marital therapy. *American Journal of Family Therapy, 9,* 84–87.

Gurman, A. S. (1982c). Using paradox in psychodynamic marital therapy. *American Journal of Family Therapy 10,* 72–75.

Gurman, A. S. (1983a). Family therapy research and the "New Epistemology." *Journal of Marital and Family Therapy, 9,* 227–234.

Gurman, A. S. (1983b). The virtues and dangers of a life-cycle perspective in family therapy. *American Journal of Family Therapy, 11,* 67–72.

Gurman, A. S. (1984). Transference and resistance in marital therapy. *American Journal of Family Therapy, 12,* 70–73.

Gurman, A. S. (1985). Tradition and transition: A rural marriage in crisis. In A. S. Gurman (Ed.), *Casebook*

of marital therapy (pp. 303–336). New York: Guilford Press.

Gurman, A. S. (1990). Integrating the life of an integrative family psychologist. In F. Kaslow (Ed.), *Voices in family psychology* (Vol. 2, pp. 250–266). Newbury Park, CA: Sage.

Gurman, A. S. (1992). Integrative marital therapy: A time-sensitive model for working with couples. In S. Budman, M. Hoyt, & S. Friedman (Eds.), *The first session in brief therapy* (pp. 186–203). New York: Guilford Press.

Gurman, A. S. (2001). Brief therapy and family/couple therapy: An essential redundancy. *Clinical Psychology: Science and Practice, 8,* 51–65.

Gurman, A. S., & Fraenkel, P. (in press). The history of couple therapy: A millenial review. *Family Process.*

Gurman, A. S., & Kniskern, D. P. (1978a). Deterioration in marital and family therapy: Empirical, clinical and conceptual issues. *Family Process, 17,* 3–20.

Gurman, A. S., & Kniskern, D. P. (1978b). Research on marital and family therapy: Progress, perspective, and prospect. In S. L. Garfield & A. E. Bergin (Eds.), *Handbook of psychotherapy and behavior change,* (2nd ed., pp. 817–901). New York: Wiley.

Gurman, A. S., & Kniskern, D. P. (1978c). Enriching research on marital enrichment programs. *Journal of Marriage and Family Counseling, 3,* 3–11.

Gurman, A. S., & Kniskern, D. P. (1978d). Behavioral marriage therapy: II. Empirical perspective. *Family Process, 17,* 139–148.

Gurman, A. S., & Kniskern, D. P. (1981). Family therapy outcome research: Knowns and unknowns. In A. S. Gurman & D. P. Kniskern (Eds.), *Handbook of family therapy* (pp. 742–775). New York: Brunner/Mazel.

Gurman, A. S., Kniskern, D. P., & Pinsof, W. M. (1986). Process and outcome research in family and marital therapy. In A. E. Bergin & S. L. Garfield (Eds.), *Handbook of psychotherapy and behavioral change* (3rd ed., pp. 565–624). New York: Wiley.

Gurman, A. S., & Knudson, R. M. (1978). Behavioral marriage therapy: I. A psychodynamic systems analysis and critique. *Family Process, 17,* 121–138.

Gurman, A. S., Knudson, R. M., & Kniskern, D. P. (1978). Behavioral marriage therapy: IV. Take two aspirin and call us in the morning. *Family Process, 17,* 165–180.

Haley, J. (1963). Marriage therapy. *Archives of General Psychiatry, 8,* 213–224.

Halford, W. K. (1998). The ongoing evolution of behavioral couples therapy: Retrospect and prospect. *Clinical Psychology Review, 18,* 613–633.

Halford, W. K. (2001). *Brief therapy for couples.* New York: Guilford Press.

Halford, W. K., Sanders, M. R., & Behrens, B. C. (1994). Self-regulation in behavioral couples therapy. *Behavior Therapy, 25,* 431–452.

Hamburg, S. R. (1996). [Review of Jacobson & Gurman's *Clinical handbook of couple therapy*]. *Child and Family Behavior Therapy, 18,* 55–60.

Hamburg, S. R. (2000). *Will our love last?: A couple's road map.* New York: Scribner.

Hayes, S. C., Follette, W. C., & Follette, V. M. (1995). Behavior therapy: A contextual approach. In A. S. Gurman & S. B. Messer (Eds.), *Essential psychotherapies* (pp. 182–225). New York: Guilford Press.

Hayes, S. C., & Toarmino, D. (1995, February). If behavioral principles are generally applicable, why is it necessary to understand cultural diversity? *The Behavior Therapist*, pp. 21–23.

Haynes, S. N., & O'Brien, W. H. (1990). Functional analysis in behavior therapy. *Clinical Psychology Review*, 10, 649–668.

Holtzworth-Munroe, A., & Jacobson, N. S. (1991). Behavioral marital therapy. In A. S. Gurman & D. P. Kniskern (Eds.), *Handbook of family therapy* (2nd ed., pp. 96–133). New York: Brunner/Mazel.

Jackson, D. D. (1965a). Family rules: The marital quid pro quo. *Archives of General Psychiatry*, 12, 589–594.

Jackson, D. D. (1965b). The study of the family. *Family Process*, 4, 1–20.

Jacobson, N. S. (1991). To be or not to be behavioral. *Journal of Family Psychology*, 4, 436–445.

Jacobson, N. S., & Addis, M. E. (1993). Research on couples and couples therapy: What do we know? Where are we going? *Journal of Consulting and Clinical Psychology*, 61, 85–93.

Jacobson, N. S., & Holtzworth-Munroe, A. (1986). Marital therapy: A social-learning cognitive perspective. In N. S. Jacobson & A. S. Gurman (Eds.), *Clinical handbook of marital therapy* (pp. 29–70). New York: Guilford Press.

Jacobson, N. S., & Margolin, G. (1979). *Marital therapy: Strategies based on social learning and behavior exchange principles*. New York: Brunner/Mazel.

Johnson, S. M. (1999). Emotionally focused couple therapy: Straight to the heart. In J. Donovan (Ed.), *Short-term couple therapy* (pp. 13–42). New York: Guilford Press.

Johnson, S. M., & Greenberg, L. S. (1995). The emotionally focused approach to problems in adult attachment. In N. S. Jacobson & A. S. Gurman (Eds.), *Clinical handbook of couple therapy* (pp. 121–146). New York: Guilford Press.

Kanfer, F. H., & Phillips, J. S. (1970). *Learning foundations of behavior therapy*. New York: Wiley.

Kanfer, F. H., & Saslow, G. (1969). Behavioral diagnosis. In C. M. Franks (Ed.), *Behavior therapy: Appraisal and status* (pp. 417–444). New York: McGraw-Hill.

Karoly, P. (1975). Operant methods. In F. H. Kanfer & H. C. Goldstein (Eds.), *Helping people change* (pp. 195–228). New York: Pergamon Press.

Karpel, M. A. (1994). *Evaluating couples: A handbook for practitioners*. New York: Norton.

Klein, M. (1946). Notes on some schizoid mechanisms. *International Journal of Psycho-Analysis*, 27, 99–110.

Lawrence, E., Eldridge, K., Christensen, A., & Jacobson, N. S. (1999). Integrative couple therapy: The dyadic relationship of acceptance and change. In J. Donovan (Ed.), *Short-term couples therapy* (pp. 226–261). New York: Guilford Press.

Lebow, J. L. (1987). Developing a personal integration in family therapy: Principles for model construction and practice. *Journal of Marital and Family Therapy*, 13, 1–14.

Lebow, J. L. (1997). The integrative revolution in couple and family therapy. *Family Process*, 36, 1–17.

Lebow, J. L. (1999). Building a science of couple relationships: Comments on two articles by Gottman and Levenson. *Family Process*, 38, 167–173.

Lebow, J. L., & Gurman, A. S. (1995). Research assessing couple and family therapy. *Annual Review of Psychology*, 46, 27–57.

Lederer, W., & Jackson, D. (1968). *The mirages of marriage*. New York: Norton.

Liddle, H. A. (1982). On the problems of eclecticism: A call for epistemologic clarification and human-scale theories. *Family Process*, 21, 243–250.

Mahoney, M. (1979). Psychotherapy and the structure of personal revolutions. In M. Mahoney (Ed.), *Psychotherapeutic process* (pp. 157–180). New York: Plenum Press.

Markman, H., Stanley, S., & Blumberg, S. L. (1994). *Fighting for your marriage*. San Francisco: Jossey-Bass.

Martin, P. A. (1976). *A marital therapy manual*. New York: Brunner/Mazel.

McCullough, L., & Andrews, S. (2001). What makes therapy brief? Short-term dynamic psychotherapy for treating affect phobias: An example of assimilative integration. *Clinical Psychology, Science and Practice*, 8, 82–97.

McIntosh, D. N. (1994). Socially induced affect. In D. Druckman & R. Bjork (Eds.), *Learning, remembering, believing* (pp. 251–276). Washington, DC: National Academy Press.

Meissner, W. W. (1978). The conceptualization of marriage and family dynamics from a psychoanalytic perspective. In T. Paolino & B. McCrady (Eds.), *Marriage and marital therapy* (pp. 25–88). New York: Brunner/Mazel.

Messer, S. B. (1992). A critical examination of belief structures in integrative and eclectic psychotherapy. In J. C. Norcross & M. R. Goldfried (Eds.), *Handbook of psychotherapy integration* (pp. 130–165). New York: Basic Books.

Messer, S. B. (Ed.). (2001). Assimilative integration [Special issue]. *Journal of Psychotherapy Integration*, 11, 1–154.

Messer, S. B., & Warren, C. S. (1995). *Models of brief psychodynamic therapy: A comparative approach*. New York: Guilford Press.

Miles, J. E. (1980). Motivation in conjoint therapy. *Journal of Sex and Marital Therapy*, 6, 205–213.

Minuchin, S., & Fishman, H. C. (1981). *Family therapy techniques*. Cambridge, MA: Harvard University Press.

Nichols, M. P., & Schwartz, R. C. (1998). *Family therapy: Concepts and methods* (4th ed.). Boston: Allyn & Bacon.

Nichols, W. C. (1988). *Marital therapy: An integrated approach*. New York: Guilford Press.

Norcross, J. C., & Prochaska, J. O. (1988). A study of eclectic (and integrative) views revisited. *Professional Psychology*, 19, 170–174.

Papero, D. V. (2000). Bowen systems theory. In F. M. Dattilio & L. J. Bevilacqua (Eds.), *Comparative treatments for relationship dysfunction* (pp. 25–44). New York: Springer.

Papp, P. (1980). The Greek chorus and other techniques of family therapy. *Family Process*, 19, 45–57.

Pinsof, W. M. (1995). *Integrative problem-centered therapy*. New York: Basic Books.

Pinsof, W. M. (1999, October). *Building love and transforming conflict in couples therapy*. Workshop presented at the annual meeting of the American Association for Marriage and Family Therapy, Chicago.

Prochaska, J. O. (1995). An eclectic and integrative approach: Transtheoretical therapy. In A. S. Gurman & S. B. Messer (Eds.), *Essential psychotherapies* (pp. 403–440). New York: Guilford Press.

Prochaska, J. O., Norcross, J. C., & Di Clemente, C. C. (1994). *Changing for good*. New York: Morrow.

Rait, D. (1988, January–February). Survey results. *The Family Therapy Networker*, pp. 52–56.

Raush, H. L., Barry, W. A., Hertel, R. K., & Swain, M. A. (1974). *Communication conflict in marriage: Explorations in the theory and study of intimate relationships*. San Francisco: Jossey-Bass.

Rimm, D., & Masters, J. (1974). *Behavior therapy*. New York: Academic Press.

Sager, C. J. (1976). *Marriage contracts and couple therapy*. New York: Brunner/Mazel.

Sager, C. J. (1981). Couples therapy and marriage contracts. In A. S. Gurman & D. P. Kniskern (Eds.), *Handbook of family therapy* (pp. 85–130). New York: Brunner/Mazel.

Scarf, M. (1986, November). Intimate partners: Patterns in love and marriage. *The Atlantic Monthly*, pp. 45–54, 91–93.

Scharff, J. S. (1995). Psychoanalytic marital therapy. In N. S. Jacobson & A. S. Gurman (Eds.), *Clinical handbook of couple therapy* (pp. 164–193). New York: Guilford Press.

Schwartz, R. C., & Johnson, S. M. (2000). Does couple and family therapy have emotional intelligence? *Family Process, 39*, 29–33.

Segraves, R. T. (1978). Conjoint marital therapy: A cognitive behavioral model. *Archives of General Psychiatry, 35*, 450–455.

Segraves, R. T. (1982). *Marital therapy: A combined psychodynamic behavioral approach*. New York: Plenum Press.

Skynner, A. C. R. (1976). *Systems of family and marital psychotherapy*. New York: Brunner/Mazel.

Skynner, A. C. R. (1980). Recent developments in marital therapy. *Journal of Family Therapy, 2*, 271–296.

Skynner, A. C. R. (1981). An open-systems, group analytic approach to family therapy. In A. S. Gurman & D. P. Kniskern (Eds.), *Handbook of family therapy* (pp. 39–84). New York: Brunner/Mazel.

Smith, J. W., & Grunebaum, H. (1976). The therapeutic alliance in marital therapy. In H. Grunebaum & J. Christ (Eds.), *Contemporary marriage: Structure, dynamics and therapy* (pp. 353–370). Boston: Little, Brown.

Smith, R. L. (2001). Integrative couple therapy: Beyond theory and practice. In L. Sperry (Ed.), *Integrative and biopsychosocial therapy* (pp. 43–65). Alexandria, VA: American Counseling Association.

Snyder, D. K. (1999). Affective reconstruction in the context of a pluralistic approach to couple therapy. *Clinical Psychology: Science and Practice, 6*, 348–365.

Snyder, D. K., & Wills, R. M. (1989). Behavioral versus insight-oriented marital therapy: Effects on individual and interspousal functioning. *Journal of Consulting and Clinical Psychology, 57*, 39–46.

Stanton, M. D. (1980). Marital therapy from a structural/strategic viewpoint. In G. Sholevar (Ed.), *The handbook of marriage and marital therapy* (pp. 303–334). New York: Spectrum.

Stanton, M. D. (1981). Strategic approaches to family therapy. In A. S. Gurman & D. P. Kniskern (Eds.), *Handbook of family therapy* (pp. 361–402). New York: Brunner/Mazel.

Steinglass, P. (1978). The conceptualization of marriage from a systems theory perspective. In T. Paolino & B. S. McCrady (Eds.), *Marriage and marital therapy* (pp. 298–365). New York: Brunner/Mazel.

Stewart, R. H., Peters, T. C., Marsh, S., & Peters, M. J. (1975). An object-relations approach to psychotherapy with marital couples, families and children. *Family Process, 14*, 161–178.

Sunbury, J. F. (1980). Working with defensive projections in conjoint marriage counseling. *Family Relations, 29*, 107–110.

Todd, T. C. (1986). Structural–strategic marital therapy. In N. S. Jacobson & A. S. Gurman (Eds.), *Clinical handbook of marital therapy* (pp. 71–105). New York: Guilford Press.

Vincent, J. P., Friedman, L., Nugent, J., & Messerly, L. (1979). Demand characteristics in observations of marital interaction. *Journal of Consulting and Clinical Psychology, 47*, 557–566.

Vincent, J. P., Weiss, R. L., & Birchler, G. (1975). A behavioral analysis of problem-solving in distressed and nondistressed married and stranger dyads. *Behavior Therapy, 6*, 475–487.

Wachtel, E. F., & Wachtel, P. L. (1986). *Family dynamics in individual psychotherapy*. New York: Guilford Press.

Wachtel, P. L. (1977). *Psychoanalysis and behavior therapy: Toward an integration*. New York: Basic Books.

Wachtel, P.L. (1993). *Therapeutic communication: Knowing what to say when*. New York: Guilford Press.

Wachtel, P. L. (1997). *Psychoanalysis, behavior therapy, and the relational world*. Washington, DC: American Psychological Association.

Wachtel, P. L., & McKinney, M. (1992). Cyclical psychodynamics and integrative psychodynamic therapy. In J. C. Norcross & M. R. Goldfried (Eds.), *Handbook of psychotherapy integration* (pp. 335–370). New York: Basic Books.

Weiss, R. L. (1980). Strategic behavioral marital therapy: Toward a model for assessment and intervention. In J. P. Vincent (Ed.), *Advances in family intervention, assessment and theory* (Vol. 1). Greenwich, CT: JAI Press.

Willi, J. (1982). *Couples in collusion*. Claremont, CA: Hunter House.

Winnicott, D. W. (1960). The theory of the parent–infant relationship. *International Journal of Psycho-Analysis, 41*, 585–595.

Yalom, I. D. (1975). *The theory and practice of group therapy* (2nd ed.). New York: Basic Books.

Chapter 8

Emotionally Focused Couple Therapy: Creating Secure Connections

SUSAN M. JOHNSON
WAYNE DENTON

In the last 15 years, research studies have repeatedly demonstrated the effectiveness of emotionally focused couple therapy (EFT) in helping couples repair their distressed relationships. The development of EFT has led the way in fostering the inclusion of a focus on emotion and attachment in the field of couple therapy. The EFT therapist is a process consultant who supports partners in restructuring and expanding their emotional responses to each other. In so doing, they restructure and expand their interactional dance and create a more secure bond. This bond then fosters resilience and flexible coping with existential issues such as life transitions and crises, and promotes recovery from psychological problems such as depression and posttraumatic stress disorder (PTSD).

BACKGROUND OF THE APPROACH

EFT is an integration of an experiential/gestalt approach (e.g., Perls, Hefferline, & Goodman, 1951; Rogers, 1951) with an interactional/family systems approach (e.g., Fisch, Weakland, & Segal, 1982). It is a constructivist approach in that it focuses on the ongoing construction of present experience (particularly experience that is emotionally charged), and a systemic approach in that it also focuses on the construction of patterns of interaction with intimate others. It is as if Carl Rogers and Ludwig von Bertalanffy (1956), the

father of systems theory, sat down to tea to discuss how to help people change their most intimate relationships. Imagine further that during this discussion, the attachment theorist John Bowlby (1969, 1988) came along to help them understand the nature of those relationships more clearly. These three great people then whispered in the ears of two confused but earnest couple therapists who were then working at the University of British Columbia, Leslie Greenberg and Susan Johnson. These therapists had been dismayed to find that dealing with the potent, evolving drama of a couple's session was no easy matter, even for therapists who were experienced in treating individuals and families.

When EFT was taking form in the early 1980s, only behavioral therapists offered clearly delineated interventions for distressed relationships and had data concerning treatment outcome. There was also some literature on how helping members of a couple attain insight into their families of origin might change their responses to each other. However, neither training couples to solve problems and make behavioral exchange contracts nor fostering insight into past relationships seemed to address the potent emotional dramas of couple sessions. After watching numerous tapes of therapy sessions, Johnson and Greenberg began to see patterns in the process of therapy that led to positive changes. They observed both internal changes in how emotions were formulated and regulated, and external changes in interactional sequences. These thera-

221

pists began to map the steps in the change process and to identify the therapeutic interventions that seemed to move this process forward. EFT was born and, even though it was barely out of infancy, began to be empirically tested (Johnson & Greenberg, 1985).

Although the new therapy was a synthesis of systemic and experiential approaches, it was referred to as "emotionally focused" therapy. This was done as an act of defiance and a statement of belief. Although clinicians such as Virginia Satir (1967) were talking about the power of emotion, the prevailing climate in the couple and family therapy field was mistrustful of emotion. It was, as Mahoney (1991) has pointed out, seen as part of the problem and generally avoided in couple sessions. If addressed at all, emotion was regarded as a relatively insignificant tag-on to cognitive and behavioral change for behavioral therapists. Systems theorists did not address emotion, in spite of the fact that there is nothing inherently nonsystemic about recognizing emotion and using it to create change (Johnson, 1998a). The name was therefore an attempt to stress a crucial element that was missing from other interventions, as well as a statement about the value and significance of emotions.

Experiential/Gestalt Influences

The experiential/gestalt perspective has always seen the wisdom in focusing on emotional responses and using them in the process of therapeutic change. In couple therapy, it seemed to Johnson and Greenberg that emotion is the music of a couple's dance. Thus a focus on emotion in therapy seemed most natural. In many ways, EFT shares commonalities with traditional humanistic approaches (Johnson & Boisvert, 2002). EFT follows the basic premises of experiential therapies, including these:

1. The therapeutic alliance is healing in and of itself, and should be as egalitarian as possible.

2. The acceptance and validation of the client's experience is a key element in therapy. In couple therapy, this involves an active commitment to validating each person's experience of the relationship without marginalizing or invalidating the experience of the other. The safety created by such acceptance then allows each client's innate self-healing and growth tendencies to flourish. This safety is fostered by the authenticity and transparency of the therapist.

3. The essence of the experiential perspective is a belief in the ability of human beings to make creative, healthy choices, if given the opportunity. The therapist helps to articulate the moments when choices are made in the relationship drama and supports clients to formulate new responses. This approach is essentially nonpathologizing. It assumes that people find ways to survive and cope in dire circumstances when choices are few, but then later find those ways limiting and inadequate for creating fulfilling relationships and lifestyles. For example, in working with a couple where one partner has been diagnosed as displaying borderline personality disorder, the EFT therapist views this person's intense simultaneous need for closeness and fear of depending on others as an understandable adaptation to negative past relationships that can be revised. As Bowlby (1969) also suggested, all ways of responding to the world can be adaptive; it is only when those ways become rigid and cannot evolve in response to new contexts that problems arise. It is first necessary, however, to accept where each partner has started from, to comprehend the nature of his/her experience, and to understand how each has done his/her best to create a positive relationship.

4. Experiential therapies encourage an examination of how inner and outer realities define each other. That is, the inner construction of experience evokes interactional responses that organize the world in a particular way. These patterns of interaction then, in turn, shape inner experience. The EFT therapist moves between helping partners reorganize their inner world and their interactional dance. Humanistic therapists also encourage the integration of affect, cognition, and behavioral responses. They tend to privilege emotions as sources of information about needs, goals, motivation, and meaning.

5. Experiential approaches take the position that people are formed and transformed by their relationships with others. Feminist writers such as the Stone Center group (Jordan, Kaplan, Miller, Stiver, & Surrey, 1991), and attachment theorists (Mikulincer, 1995), also focus on how identity is constantly formulated in interactions with others. By helping partners change the shape of their relationships, the EFT therapist is also helping them reshape their sense of who they are. Couple therapy then becomes a place where partners may revise their sense of self and so become more able to deal with problems such as depression, generalized anxiety, or PTSD.

6. Experiential approaches attempt to foster new corrective experiences for clients that emerge

as part of personal encounters in the here-and-now of the therapy session. The therapist tracks how clients encounter and make sense of the world, and also helps them to expand that world.

Systemic Influences

The other half of the EFT synthesis is the contribution from family systems theory (Johnson, 1996). In systems theory, the focus is on the interaction (feedback) that occurs between members of the system (e.g., von Bertalanffy, 1956). As applied to families, the assumption is that symptoms/problems are a consequence of what happens in the interaction between people. Arguably, the hallmark of all family systems therapies is that they attempt to interrupt the repetitive cycles of interaction among family members that include problem/symptomatic behavior.

How family systems therapies differ is in *how* they attempt to break these cycles. Thus, for example, the structural family therapist may have clients physically move to help create a boundary (e.g., Minuchin & Fishman, 1981). The strategic family therapist may give a paradoxical directive to bypass resistance in motivating clients to change the cycle of interaction (e.g., Weeks & L'Abate, 1979). Although solution-focused therapists may assert that they have rejected the family systems metaphor in understanding families (e.g., de Shazer, 1991), their techniques can actually be understood as a focus on occasions where the cycle does *not* occur and directing clients (for example) to perform more of these "exceptional" behaviors.

EFT can be understood as falling within this tradition of family systems therapies. Although it draws upon systemic techniques, particularly those of Minuchin's structural/systemic approach with its focus on the enactment of "new" patterns of interaction, the unique contribution of EFT is the use of emotion in breaking destructive cycles of interaction. By helping partners identify, express, and restructure their emotional responses at different points in the interactional cycle, the EFT therapist helps the couple to develop new responses to each other and a different "frame" on the nature of their problems. Clients can then be guided to begin to take new steps in their dance—to interrupt the destructive cycle and initiate more productive cycles.

EFT follows the basic premises of family systems theory, including these:

1. Causality is circular, so that it cannot be said that action A "caused" action B. For example, in the common couple pattern in which one partner demands interaction while the other tries to withdraw, it would not be possible to say whether the "demanding" led to the "withdrawal" or whether the "withdrawal" led to the "demanding."

2. Family systems theory tells us that we must consider behavior in context. This is summed up by the familiar phrase that "the whole is greater than the sum of the parts" (e.g., Watzlawick, Beavin, & Jackson, 1967). That is, to understand the behavior of one partner, it must be considered in the context of the behavior of the other partner.

3. The elements of a system have a predictable and consistent relationship with each other. This is represented by the systems concept of "homeostasis" (Jackson, 1965), and is manifested in couples by the presence of regular, repeating cycles of interaction.

4. All behavior is assumed to have a communicative aspect (e.g., Watzlawick et al., 1967). What is said between partners, as well as the manner in which it is communicated, defines the role of the speaker and the listener. Thus one partner may express, "When you said that, I felt like a child, and like you were trying to be my mother."

5. The task of the family systems therapist is to interrupt these negative cycles of interaction so that a new pattern can occur.

The Experiential–Systemic Synthesis

The experiential and systemic approaches to therapy have important commonalities that make their integration possible. Both focus on present experience rather than historical events. Both view people as fluid entitites, rather than as possessing a rigid core or character that is inevitably resistant to change. The two approaches also bring something to each other. Experiential approaches traditionally focus within the person, to the exclusion of a consideration of external relationships. The systemic therapies, on the other hand, traditionally focus on the interactions between people, to the exclusion of a consideration of the emotional responses and associated meanings that organize such interactions (Johnson & Greenberg, 1994).

To summarize the experiential–systemic synthesis of EFT, there is a focus on the circular cycles of interaction between people, as well as on the emotional experiences of each partner during the different steps of the cycle. The word "emotion" comes from a Latin word meaning "to move." Emotions are identified and expressed as a way to help partners move into new stances in their relationship dance—stances that they then integrate into their senses of self and their definitions of their relationship. This results in a new, more satisfying cycle of interaction that does not include the presenting problem and, moreover, promotes secure bonding.

Contributions of Attachment Theory

Since its initial development, the greatest change in EFT has been the growing influence of attachment on the EFT understanding of the nature of close relationships. Although these relationships have always been seen as bonds in EFT, rather than as bargains to be negotiated in a quid pro quo fashion (Johnson, 1986), the focus on attachment as a theory of adult love has increased in recent years and become more explicit. This is partly because as practitioners we have found this theory of close relationships so useful. It has particularly helped us intervene with depressed and traumatized individuals and their distressed relationships (Whiffen & Johnson, 1998). It is also because both the research on attachment theory and the application of this theory to adults and to clinical intervention have exploded in the last decade and become more directly relevant to the practitioner. This theoretical aspect of EFT is discussed in greater detail below in the section on healthy relationships.

Recent Developments in Practice

As experience with EFT has increased, the therapy has been applied to an increasing range of types of couples and clinical problems. Although clients were always diverse in terms of social class, EFT has recently been applied with couples of more varied ethnic backgrounds (e.g., Chinese and East Indian clients) and to same-sex couples. Originally used in the treatment of relationship distress, EFT has begun to be utilized with clients experiencing other types of dysfunction, such as PTSD and other anxiety disorders (Johnson, 2002), eating disorders, bipolar disorder, and major depression (Johnson, Hunsley, Greenberg, & Schindler, 1999; Johnson, Maddeaux, & Blouin, 1998).

Although outcome studies demonstrate that recovery rates after a brief course of EFT are very encouraging, further investigations into the change process in couples whose relationships improve but still remain in the distressed range are teaching us about the nature of impasses and the factors that block relationship repair. We have recently delineated the concept of "attachment injuries" as traumatic events that damage the bond between partners and, if not resolved, maintain negative cycles and attachment insecurities. These events occur when one partner fails to respond to the other at a moment of urgent need, such as when a miscarriage occurs or a medical diagnosis is given (Johnson, Makinen, & Millikin, 2001). The ongoing study of the change process has been part of the EFT tradition and continues to help refine EFT interventions.

There has also generally been an increasing appreciation within the behavioral sciences of the role emotion plays in individual functioning and health (Salovey, Rothman, Detweiler, & Stewart, 2000; Goleman, 1995). Lack of emotional connection to others and isolation in general have been found to have a negative impact on immune functioning and responses to stress, while supportive relationships have been compellingly linked to physical and emotional resilience. The field of psychotherapy has also moved beyond crass formulations of the role emotion plays in change toward more explicit and refined models (Greenberg & Paivio, 1997; Kennedy-Moore & Watson, 1999). Models of catharsis and expulsion have shifted to models of integration and to viewing emotion as a motivational factor in therapy. Systemic therapists have also begun to include a focus on both the self and emotion in their work (Schwartz & Johnson, 2000). With these developments, along with increasing research evidence supporting efficacy, EFT has become less marginalized and experienced greater respect as an intervention.

Placing EFT in the Context of Contemporary Couple Therapy

Recent developments in the practice, theory, and science of couple therapy are quite compatible with EFT (Johnson & Lebow, 2000), making EFT an attractive approach to working with couples in today's world. Some of these developments include the following:

1. In a climate of managed care, EFT is a relatively brief treatment (Johnson, 1999). Most research studies have utilized 8–12 therapy sessions, although clinical practice with couples

facing additional problems may involve more sessions.

2. EFT is consonant with recent research on the nature of couple distress and satisfaction within the developing science of personal relationships. The findings of Gottman and colleagues (Gottman, 1994; Gottman, Coan, Carrere, & Swanson, 1998) have emphasized the significant role of negative affect in the development of relationship distress, as well as the importance of helping couples find new ways to regulate such affect. Gottman has recommended that therapy, rather than helping couples resolve content issues, should help couples develop soothing interactions and focus on how to create a particular kind of emotional engagement in disagreements. This parallels EFT practice, in that the focus in EFT is on how partners communicate and general patterns that are repeated across a variety of content areas. The process of change in EFT is also very much one of structuring small steps toward safe emotional engagement so that partners can soothe, comfort, and reassure each other.

3. There is an increasing focus in couple therapy on issues of diversity. The experiential roots of EFT promote a therapeutic stance of respect for differences and an openness to learning from clients about what is meaningful for them and how they view intimate relationships. This experiential perspective is consistent with the viewpoint that there are often as many significant differences between individuals within a culture as there are between individuals of different cultures. Every individual or couple thus constitutes a unique culture, and the therapist must learn about and adapt interventions to this unique culture to formulate effective interventions. As in narrative approaches, the EFT therapist's stance is thus "informed not knowing" (Shapiro, 1996).

EFT also assumes, however, that there are also certain universals that tend to cut across differences of culture, race, and class. It assumes that we are all "children of the same mother." In particular, it assumes that key emotional experiences and attachment needs and behaviors are universal. There are convincing similarities in the recognized antecedents, shared meanings, physiological reactions, facial expression of emotions, and actions evoked by emotions (Mesquita & Frijda, 1992). This is particularly true for the eight basic emotions listed by Tomkins (1962): interest/excitement, joy, surprise, distress/anguish, disgust/contempt, anger/rage, shame, and fear/terror. There are, of course, also differences in how central an emotional experience may be to a culture (e.g., shame and guilt seem to be particularly powerful in the Japanese culture). There are also different accepted ways of regulating emotion and display rules in different cultures. However, there is also considerable evidence that attachment needs and responses are universal (van IJzendoorn & Sagi, 1999).

4. EFT has a number of parallels with feminist approaches to couple therapy (Vatcher & Bogo, 2001). Foremost is that both the EFT attachment perspective on relationships and the work of feminist writers such as Jordan et al. (1991) depathologize dependency. This particularly challenges the Western cultural script for men. EFT interventions have been found to be particularly effective for male partners described as inexpressive by their mates (Johnson & Talitman, 1997). This would seem to reflect the emphasis in EFT on supporting both partners to express underlying feelings, especially fears and attachment needs. A feminist-informed therapy should then examine gender-based constraints; work to increase personal agency; and "develop egalitarian relationships characterized by mutuality, reciprocity, intimacy and interdependency" (Haddock, Schindler Zimmerman, & MacPhee, 2000, p. 165).

5. There has been a move toward integration of interventions across models in the last decade (Lebow, 1997). EFT integrates systemic and experiential perspectives and interventions. It is also consonant with narrative approaches in some respects, particularly in Step 2 of the change process, when the therapist "externalizes" the cycle and frames it as the problem in the couple's relationship (Johnson, 1996).

EFT has influenced the evolution of other approaches as well. For example, new versions of behavioral interventions, such as integrative behavioral couple therapy (Koerner & Jacobson, 1994), share with EFT a general focus on both promoting acceptance and compassion and evoking softer emotional responses.

6. Postmodernism has had considerable impact on the field of couple therapy in the last decade. This perspective promotes a collaborative stance wherein therapists discover with their clients how those clients construct their inner and outer realities. This attitude parallels the perspective that Carl Rogers, one of the key founders of humanistic/experiential approaches, offered to individual therapy (Anderson, 1997). The concern is not to pathologize clients, but to honor and validate their realities. This perspective particularly focuses on how reality becomes shaped by lan-

guage, culture, and social interactions (Neimeyer, 1993). In terms of perspective, EFT may be thought of as a postmodern therapy. In terms of specific interventions, EFT therapists help clients deconstruct problems and responses by bringing marginalized aspects of reality into focus, probing for the not yet spoken, and integrating elements of a couple's reality that have gone unstoried. They also help clients create integrated narratives about their cycles, their problems, and the process of change. EFT, on the other hand, does not fit with the more extreme postmodern position that there are no common existential conditions or processes, and reality is arbitary and random—a position that has been questioned in the literature (Martin & Sugarman, 2000). This position suggests that problems generally exist only in language and can therefore be "dis-solved" in language; that it is not possible to delineate patterns in how people deal with problems; and that we do not need models of intervention or theory, but can simply use metaphors as guides to intervention (Hoffman, 1998). In general, in a postmodern world, couple therapy seems to be turning away from impersonal strategic approaches toward a more collaborative approach to change that recognizes clients as actively creating their experience and their world.

7. Last but not least, there is increasing pressure for clinicians to be able to document the effectiveness of their interventions. There is now a sizable body of research on EFT outcomes (Johnson et al., 1999). In brief, results indicate that 70–75% of couples see their relationships as no longer distressed after 10–12 sessions of EFT, and these results appear to be less susceptible to relapse than in other approaches. Interventions with families (Johnson et al., 1998) and with partners struggling with depression have also been positive.

PERSPECTIVE ON RELATIONSHIP HEALTH

A model of a healthy relationship is essential for the couple therapist. It allows the therapist to set goals, target key processes, and chart a destination for a couple's journey. Couple therapy has generally lacked an adequate theory of love and relatedness (Johnson & Lebow, 2000; Roberts, 1992). Healthy relationships were seen as rational negotiated contracts until it became clear that such contracts actually characterized distressed couples (Jacobson, Follette, & Macdonald, 1982). Concepts such as "differentiation," "lack of enmesh-

ment," and "lack of coercion" have also been associated with healthy relationships in other approaches. A healthy relationship, in EFT terms, is a secure attachment bond. Such a bond is characterized by mutual emotional accessibility and responsiveness. This bond creates a safe environment that optimizes partners' ability to regulate their emotions, process information, solve problems, resolve differences, and communicate clearly. In the last 10 years, the research on adult attachment has demonstrated that secure relationships are associated with higher levels of intimacy, trust, and satisfaction (Cassidy & Shaver, 1999; Johnson & Whiffen, 1999).

Bowlby published the first volume of his famous trilogy on attachment in 1969. He believed that seeking and maintaining contact with significant others is a primary motivating principle for human beings that has been "wired in" by evolution. Attachment is an innate survival mechanism. In the first two decades after the publication of Bowlby's first volume, his work was applied mostly to mother–child relationships, despite the fact that his theory was developed as a result of his work with delinquent adolescents and bereaved adults. Furthermore, Bowlby believed that attachment needs run "from the cradle to the grave." He believed in the power of social interactions to organize and define inner and outer realities. Specifically, he believed that a sense of connection with key others offers a safe haven and secure base. Inner and outer worlds then become manageable, allowing individuals to orient themselves toward exploration and learning. Safe attunement and engagement with attachment figures then lead to attunement and engagement with the world and the ability to modulate stress.

More recently, attachment theory has been applied to adult attachment relationships (Bartholomew & Perlman, 1994; Hazan & Shaver, 1987). Adult attachment, compared to attachment between children and caregivers, is more mutual and reciprocal. It is less concrete (e.g., adults need to touch their loved ones less, since they carry them around with them as cognitive representations) and may be sexual in nature. The caregiving and sexual elements of adult relationships were once viewed as separate from attachment. Now, however, they are seen by most theorists as elements of an integrated attachment system. Sexual behavior, for example, connects adult partners, as holding connects mother and child (Hazan & Zeifman, 1994), and adult attachments are formed almost exclusively with sexual partners.

This perspective depathologizes dependency in adults (Bowlby, 1988) and views the ability to be autonomous and connected as two sides of the same coin rather than at two different ends of a continuum. It challenges the North American tradition of rugged individualism and the myth of self-reliance. In Bowlby's view, it is not possible for an infant or an adult to be either too dependent or truly independent. Rather, people may be effectively or ineffectively dependent (Weinfield, Sroufe, Egeland, & Carlson, 1999).

Security in key relationships helps us regulate our emotions, process information effectively and communicate clearly. With adults, as with children, proximity to an attachment figure is an inborn affect regulation device that "tranquilizes the nervous system" (Schore, 1994, p. 244). If distressing affect is aroused by the relationship itself, the secure person has experienced relationship repair and so believes that disruptions are repairable. When people are securely attached, they can openly acknowledge their distress and turn to others for support in a manner that elicits responsiveness. This enhances their ability to deal with stress and uncertainty. It makes them more resilient in crises. It also makes them less likely to become depressed when relationships are not going well (Davila & Bradbury, 1999). The ability to seek comfort from another appears to be a crucial factor in healing after trauma (van der Kolk, Perry, & Herman, 1991).

Security in relationships is associated with a model of others as dependable and trustworthy, and a model of the self as lovable and entitled to care. Such models promote flexible and specific ways of attributing meaning to a partner's behavior (e.g., "He's tired; that's why he's grouchy. It's not that he is trying to hurt me"). They allow people to be curious and open to new evidence, and enable them to deal with ambiguity (Mikulincer, 1997). It may be that secure individuals are better able to articulate their tacit assumptions and see these as relative constructions rather than absolute realities. They are then better able to take a metaperspective and to metacommunicate with their significant others (Kobak & Cole, 1991). Secure individuals tend to be able to consider alternative perspectives, reflect on themselves (Fonagy & Target, 1997), and integrate new information about attachment figures. They can reflect on and discuss relationships (Main, Kaplan, & Cassidy, 1985). In general, insecurity acts to constrict and narrow how cognitions and affect are processed and organized, and so constrains key behavioral responses.

Security involves inner realities, cognitive models, ways of regulating emotion, and patterns of interaction. Each reflects and creates the other. Emotional communication is the bridge between inner and outer realities. Secure partners are more able to engage in coherent, open, and direct communication that promotes responsiveness in their mates. They are able to disclose and respond to their mates' disclosures. Their confidence in their mates' responsiveness fosters empathy and the ability to see things from the mates' point of view. In conflict situations, they tend to respond with balanced assertiveness, to collaborate more, and to use rejection and coercion less (Feeney, Noller, & Callan, 1994; Kobak & Hazan, 1991).

Communication behaviors are context-dependent. It is precisely when stress is high and people are vulnerable that less secure partners have difficulty engaging emotionally and responding to their partners. Attachment theory suggests that incidents in which partners need comfort and reassurance and find their partners unresponsive will be pivotal in the definition of relationships as satisfying or distressed.

PERSPECTIVE ON RELATIONSHIP DISTRESS

EFT looks at distress in relationships through the lens of attachment insecurity and separation distress. When attachment security is threatened, human beings respond in predictable sequences. Typically, anger is the first response. This anger is a protest against the loss of contact with the attachment figure. If such protest does not evoke responsiveness, it can become tinged with despair and coercion, and evolve into a chronic strategy to obtain and maintain the attachment figure's attention. The next step in separation distress consists of clinging and seeking, which then give way to depression and despair. Finally, if all else fails, the relationship is mourned and detachment ensues. Separation from attachment figures can be conceptualized as a traumatic stressor that primes automatic fight, flight, and freeze responses (Johnson, in press). Aggressive responses in relationships have been linked to attachment panic, in which partners regulate their insecurity by becoming controlling and abusive to their mates (Dutton, 1995; Mikulincer, 1998).

The EFT perspective fits well with the recent literature on the nature of relationship distress, specifically with the research of Gottman (1994).

Furthermore, it offers attachment theory as an explanatory framework for the patterns documented in this observational research. First, both recent research and attachment theory suggest that the expression and regulation of emotion are key factors in determining the nature and form of close relationships. Absorbing states of negative affect (where everything leads into this state and nothing leads out) characterize distressed relationships (Gottman, 1979). In EFT we speak of an "alarm being constantly on" in a distressed relationship, and of the "noise" blocking out other cues. Gottman and his colleagues have demonstrated that they are able to predict accurately from partners' facial expressions which couples are on the road to divorce. Emotional disengagement also predicts divorce better than the number or outcome of conflicts. Gottman's research also found that anger is not necessarily bad. This is understandable, if expression of anger helps to resolve attachment issues and evoke responsiveness. From an attachment point of view, any response (except an abusive one) is better than none. This perhaps explains why "stonewalling" has been found to be so corrosive of couple relationships. It is an explicit lack of responsiveness and thus directly threatens attachment security and induces helplessness and rage.

Second, research suggests that rigid interaction patterns such as the familiar demand–withdraw pattern can be poisonous for relationships. Attachment theory would suggest that this is because they maintain attachment insecurity and make safe emotional engagement impossible. Research suggesting that how people fight is more important than what they fight over fits well with the concept that the nonverbal, process level of communication is all-important. What people are fighting about is the nature of the attachment relationship and what that implies about who they are. So Alice criticizes Roger's parenting skills, and Roger ignores her. In the next moment, Alice is criticizing Roger's tone of voice and how it negates her input into the relationship. In another 5 seconds, the couple is fighting about who is " the saint" and who is "the devil." Alice concludes that Roger is incapable of being close and responsive in their relationship.

It is worth noting that the endemic nature of cycles, such as criticize–pursue followed by defend–withdraw, is predictable from attachment theory. There are only a limited number of ways to deal with the frustration of the need for contact with a significant other. One way is to increase attachment behaviors to deal with the anxiety generated by the other's lack of response (and perhaps to appear

critical in the process). The response of the other may then be avoidance of and self-distancing from the perceived criticism. Both Gottman's research and attachment research suggests that this strategy does not prevent emotional flooding and high levels of emotional arousal. Habitual ways of dealing with attachment issues and engaging with attachment figures may be learned in childhood, but they can be revised or confirmed and made more automatic in present relationships.

Third, Gottman points out that the skills taught in many communication training formats are not generally apparent in the interactions of satisfied couples. Attachment research suggests that the ability to "unlatch" from negative cycles will depend on the level of security in the relationship. Such factors as empathy, self-disclosure, and the ability to metacommunicate are associated with security. It is unlikely then that, when flooded by attachment fears, a partner can leap into his/her cortices and follow rules. It may be, however, that more secure couples could use such skills as rituals to deescalate negative cycles. One treatment outcome study (James, 1991) added a skill component to EFT interventions, but this addition did not enhance outcome.

Fourth, both this research and attachment theory stress the importance of "soothing" interactions. Attachment theory suggests that events in which one partner asks for comfort and the other is not able to provide this violate attachment assumptions and disproportionately influence the definition of the relationship (Simpson & Rholes, 1994). In the EFT model, we refer to such events as "attachment injuries" (Johnson et al., 2001). There is evidence that those who generally take the "avoider" position in problem discussions may be relatively social in many situations, but are particularly likely to withdraw when their partners exhibit vulnerability (Simpson, Rholes, & Nelligan, 1992). Attachment theory also suggests that creating soothing interactions at such times may have the power to redefine close relationships. Research on "softenings" (change events in EFT) suggests that this is true.

It is possible to extrapolate specific links between other research on relationships and the nature of attachment relationships. Attachment is being used as a way of understanding the links between depression and marital distress (Anderson, Beach, & Kaslow, 1999), and indeed Bowlby (1980) viewed depression as an inevitable part of separation distress. An explanation of why Gottman's research finds that contempt is so corrosive in couple relationships may be found in the concept that interactions with attachment figures create and maintain a person's model of self. Contemptuous responses may directly convey feedback as to the unworthiness of the self and so create particular anguish and reactivity in distressed partners.

Research on relationship distress, along with contributions from attachment research, thus begins to provide us as couple therapists with an emerging science of relationships. This can help us understand and predict clients' responses to each other and to our interventions. It should also help us depathologize them. For example, viewing a client's behavior as a "disorganized attachment strategy" is more suggestive of how to be helpful than is viewing the client as having "borderline personality disorder." Such a science of relationships should help us formulate goals and target interventions to create lasting change in an efficient manner.

KEY PRINCIPLES

The key principles of EFT, which have been discussed in detail elsewhere (Johnson, 1996; Greenberg & Johnson, 1988), can be summarized as follows:

1. A collaborative alliance offers the members of a couple a secure base from which to explore their relationship. The therapist is best seen as a process consultant to the couple's relationship.

2. Emotion is primary in organizing attachment behaviors and determining how self and other are experienced in intimate relationships. Emotion guides and gives meaning to perception; motivates and cues attachment responses; and, when expressed, communicates to others and organizes their response. The EFT therapist privileges emotional responses and deconstructs reactive, negative emotions (such as anger) by expanding them to include marginalized elements (such as fear and helplessness). The therapist also uses newly formulated and articulated emotions (such as fear and longing or assertive anger) to evoke new steps in the relationship dance. From the EFT perspective, dealing with and expressing emotion can be the best, fastest, and sometimes only solution to a couple's problems. Emotion transforms partners' worlds and their responses rapidly and compellingly, and evokes key responses such as trust and compassion that are difficult to evoke in other ways.

3. The attachment needs and desires of partners are essentially healthy and adaptive. It is the way such needs are enacted in a context of perceived insecurity that creates problems.

4. Problems are maintained by the ways in which interactions are organized and by the dominant emotional experience of each partner in the relationship. Affect and interaction form a reciprocally determining, self-reinforcing feedback loop. The EFT therapist first deescalates negative interactions patterns and the reactive emotions associated with them. The therapist then helps partners shape new cycles of positive interactions, in which positive emotions arise and negative emotions can be regulated in a different way.

5. Change occurs not through insight into the past, catharsis, or negotiation, but through new emotional experience in the present context of attachment-salient interactions.

6. In couple therapy, the actual "client" is the relationship between partners. The attachment perspective on adult love offers a map to the essential elements of such relationships. Problems are viewed in terms of adult insecurity and separation distress. The ultimate goal of therapy is the creation of new cycles of secure bonding that offer an antidote to negative cycles and redefine the nature of the relationship. The three tasks of EFT are thus the following: first, to create a safe, collaborative alliance; second, to access and expand the emotional responses that guide the couple's interactions; and, third, to restructure those interactions in the direction of accessibility and responsiveness.

THE PROCESS OF CHANGE

The process of change in EFT has been organized into nine treatment steps. The first four steps involve assessment and the deescalation of problematic interactional cycles. The middle three steps emphasize the creation of specific change events, where interactional positions shift and new bonding events occur. The last two steps of therapy address the consolidation of change and the integration of these changes into the everyday life of the couple. If partners successfully negotiate these steps, they seem to be able to resolve long-standing conflictual issues as well as to negotiate practical problems. This may be because such issues are no longer steeped in attachment significance.

The therapist leads the couple through these steps in a spiraling fashion, as one step incorporates and leads into the other. In a mildly distressed couple, partners usually work quickly through the steps at a parallel rate. In a more distressed couple, the more passive or withdrawn partner is usually invited to go through the steps slightly ahead of the other. It is easier to create a new dance when both partners are on the floor and engaged. The increased emotional engagement of this partner also then helps the other (often the more critical and active) partner shift to a more trusting stance.

The nine steps of EFT are outlined and discussed below.

Stage One: Cycle Deescalation

Step 1: Identify the relational conflict issues between the partners.

Step 2: Identify the negative interaction cycle where these issues are expressed.

Step 3: Access the unacknowledged emotions underlying the interactional position each partner takes in this cycle.

Step 4: Reframe the problem in terms of the cycle, accompanying underlying emotions, and attachment needs.

The goal, by the end of Step 4, is for the partners to have a metaperspective on their interactions. They are framed as unwittingly creating, but also as being victimized by, the cycle of interaction that characterizes their relationship. Step 4 is the conclusion of the deescalation phase. The therapist and the couple shape an expanded version of the couple's problems that validates each person's reality and encourages partners to stand together against the common enemy of the cycle. The partners begin to see that they are, in part, "creating their own misery." If they accept the reframe, the changes in behavior they need to make may be obvious. For most couples, however, the assumption is that if therapy stops here, the couples will not be able to maintain their progress. A new cycle that promotes attachment security must be initiated.

Stage Two: Changing Interactional Positions

Step 5: Promote each partner's identification with disowned attachment needs and aspects of self. Such attachment needs may include the need for reassurance and comfort. Aspects of self that are not identified with may include a sense of shame or unworthiness.

Step 6: Promote acceptance by each partner of the other partner's experience. As one partner said to another, " I used to be married to a devil, but now . . . I don't know who you are."

Step 7: Facilitate the expression of needs and wants to restructure the interaction based on new understandings, and create bonding events.

The goal, by the end of Step 7, is to have withdrawn partners reengaged in the relationship and actively stating the terms of this reengagement. For example, a partner may state, "I do want to be there for you. I know I zone out. But I can't handle all this criticism. I want us to find another way. I won't stand in front of the tidal wave." The goal is also to have a more blaming partner "soften" and ask for his/her attachment needs to be met from a position of vulnerability. This "softening" has the effect of pulling for responsiveness from the other partner. This latter event has been found to be associated with recovery from relationship distress in EFT (Johnson & Greenberg, 1988). When both partners have completed Step 7, a new form of emotional engagement is possible, and bonding events can occur. These events are usually fostered by the therapist in the session, but also occur at home. Partners are then able to confide and seek comfort from each other, becoming mutually accessible and responsive. Transcripts of softening events are to be found in the literature (e.g., Johnson & Greenberg, 1995).

Stage Three: Consolidation and Integration

Step 8: Facilitate the emergence of new solutions to old problems.

Step 9: Consolidate new positions and cycles of attachment behavior.

The goal of Stage Three is to consolidate new responses and cycles of interaction. This is done, for example, by reviewing the accomplishments of the partners in therapy and helping the partners create a coherent narrative of their journey into and out of distress. The therapist also supports the partners in solving concrete problems that have been destructive to the relationship. As stated previously, this is often relatively easy, since dialogues about these problems are no longer infused with overwhelming negative affect and issues of relationship definition.

OVERVIEW OF INTERVENTIONS

As noted earlier, the therapist has three primary tasks in EFT, and these must be properly timed and completed. The first task, creating an alliance, is considered in a later section.

The second task is to facilitate the identification, expression, and restructuring of emotional responses. The therapist focuses upon the "vulnerable" emotions (e.g., fear or anxiety) that play a central role in the couple's cycle of negative interactions. These emotions are usually those that are most salient in terms of attachment needs and fears. The therapist stays close to the emerging or "leading edge" of the client's experience (Wile, 1995) and uses humanistic/experiential interventions to expand and reorganize that experience. These include reflection, evocative questions (e.g., "What is it like for you when . . . ?"), validation, heightening (with techniques such as repetition and imagery) and empathic interpretation. Such interpretation is always done tentatively and in very small increments. For instance, a therapist may ask whether a husband is not only "uncomfortable," as he has stated, but in fact quite "upset" at his wife's remarks. When the therapist uses the interventions described here, reactive responses such as anger or numbing tend to evolve into more core primary or "vulnerable" emotions such as a sense of grief, shame, or fear.

In the third task, the restructuring of interactions, the therapist begins by tracking the negative cycle that constrains and narrows the partners' responses to each other. The therapist uses structural/systemic techniques (Minuchin & Fishman, 1981), such as reframing and the choreographing of new relationship events. Problems are reframed in terms of cycles and in terms of attachment needs and fears. For instance, the therapist may ask a partner to share specific fears with his/her mate, thus creating a new kind of dialogue that fosters secure attachment. These tasks and interventions are outlined in detail elsewhere, together with transcripts of therapy sessions (Johnson & Greenberg, 1995; Johnson, 1996, 1998b, 1999).

The timing and delivery of the interventions are as important as the interventions themselves. The process of therapy evolves with the couple and the therapist attuning to each other and the therapist matching interventions to each partner's style (Johnson & Whiffen, 1999). Expert EFT therapists, for example, slow down their speech when evoking emotion, use a low evocative voice and incorporate simple images to capture people's felt experience. It is as if they emotionally engage with the clients' experience, reflect it and then invite the client to enter it on the same engaged level. Emotional responses take longer to process, particularly when they are not familiar or are threatening, and are more easily evoked by concrete images than by more abstract statements (Palmer & Johnson, 2002).

THE ASSESSMENT OF COUPLE FUNCTIONING AND DYSFUNCTION

Although a variety of questionnaires have been used in research on EFT (e.g., the Dyadic Adjustment Scale; Spanier, 1976), there are no assessment instruments unique to EFT, and assessment in the clinic takes place through client interviews. After a period of joining, the partners are each asked about what brings them to therapy, and the therapist begins to listen for relational problems experienced by each partner (e.g., "arguments," "poor communication," or "lack of intimacy"). The therapist must be able to identify one or more problems that all three parties (including the therapist) can agree to as goals for therapy. It is not uncommon that the complaints of the partners may initially seem unrelated. In this case, the therapist must find a way in which the complaints are related and "weave" them into a common complaint/goal that both partners will accept as encompassing their own concerns.

The therapist then begins to identify the negative cycle of interaction that typifies the couple's complaint. The therapist may observe the cycle actually being played out in the session, or may begin to "track" the cycle carefully. This is a skill common to most family systems therapies. Briefly, the therapist wants to find out exactly how the cycle begins, who says and does what as the cycle unfolds, and how it concludes. At this point in the assessment, the clients may or may not begin to spontaneously identify the emotions underlying their positions in the cycle. The therapist may facilitate this by beginning to ask questions (e.g., "What was that like for you?"). At this early stage, the emotions expressed will tend to be rather "safe" and superficial.

Although EFT is a present-focused therapy, a small amount of relationship history is obtained during the assessment phase. Clients can be asked about how they met, what attracted them to each other, and at what point the present problems began to manifest themselves. Life transitions and shifts (e.g., birth of children, retirement, immigration) associated with the beginning of the problem are particularly noted, as is cultural heritage. A brief personal history may be elicited with questions such as "Who held and comforted you when you were small?" The answer to such questions gives the therapist a sense as to whether secure attachment is familiar or foreign territory.

The therapist then checks with both partners as to their specific treatment goals by asking what they hope to gain from coming to therapy. The responses to this question will tend to be the inverse of the complaints solicited at the beginning of the assessment. Initially the partners were asked what they were unhappy about, but at this point in the assessment they are asked what they would like their relationship to look like and are helped to specify particular changes they want to make.

The process of therapy usually begins with one or two conjoint sessions, followed by one individual session with each partner. These individual sessions serve to cement the alliance with the therapist; to allow each partner to elaborate on perceptions of the other and of relationship problems; and to enable the therapist to ask sensitive questions about physical and sexual abuse in past attachment relationships and this relationship. If information relevant to the relationship is disclosed that has not been shared with the other partner, the client is supported to reveal this information in the next couple session. The keeping of secrets, particularly secrets about alternative relationships that offer apparent escapes from the trials of repairing the relationship, is presented as undermining the objectives of therapy and the client's goals.

A therapy contract is discussed briefly with the couple. The partners are told that the purpose of therapy will be to shift the negative cycle of interaction so that a new cycle can emerge that fosters a safer and more supportive relationship. Many EFT therapists share an expectation that treatment will be, in all likelihood, concluded in approximately 8–15 weekly sessions. The number of sessions is not set in this manner if one of the partners shows signs of or has a diagnosis of PTSD (Johnson, 2002). In this case, the number of sessions is left open in order to respond to the couple's needs for longer treatment or treatment that is coordinated with the demands of other treatment modalities the client may be involved in.

We attempt to be transparent about the process of change and explain how and why we inter-vene the way we do whenever this seems appropriate. For instance, if a partner wants to renew passion in the relationship, we will break down the process into intermediate goals, suggesting that first the partners will need to deescalate their negative interactions. We encourage partners to view us as consultants, who can and will be corrected, and who will need their active participation to redefine their relationship. We then can admit mistakes and allow clients to teach us about their unique experience in their relationship.

ABSOLUTE AND RELATIVE CONTRAINDICATIONS

In EFT, the therapist asks partners to allow themselves gradually to be open and thus vulnerable to each other. The primary contraindication to the use of EFT is any situation where the therapist believes that such vulnerability is not safe or advisable. The most obvious example would be a couple in which there is ongoing physical abuse. In this case, the abusive partner is referred to a specialized domestic violence treatment program. The couple is offered EFT only after this therapy is completed and the abused partner no longer feels at risk. It is important that the latter is used as the criterion for readiness for couple therapy, rather than the abusive partner's assessment that the abuse is now under control. The goal of treatment, after the assessment, is then to encourage the abusive partner to enter treatment and the abused partner to seek supportive counseling or individual therapy. In general, the field of couple therapy is beginning to address treatment feasibility issues in this area and systematize assessment in a way that all couple therapists can use (Bograd & Mederos, 1999). There may be other, more ambiguous situations where the therapist does not feel it is safe to ask one or both partners to make themselves vulnerable (e.g., certain instances of emotional abuse), or where one partner seems to be intent on harming or demoralizing the other.

Finally, EFT is designed to improve the relationship for partners who wish to stay together and have a better relationship. Some partners need the therapist's help to first clarify their needs and goals before they are ready to work toward this end. These may include situations in which one or both partners admit to being involved in an extramarital affair and are not sure which relationship they wish to maintain, or in which the partners are separated and are not sure whether they want to work towards reconciliation.

PREDICTORS OF SUCCESS

Research on success in EFT (Denton, Burleson, Clark, Rodriguez, & Hobbs, 2000; Johnson & Talitman, 1997) allows us to make some specific predictions as to who will benefit most from EFT, and so to fit clients to treatment. First, the quality of the alliance with the therapist predicts success in EFT. This is to be expected; it is a general finding in research on all forms of psychotherapy that a positive alliance is associated with success. In fact, the quality of the alliance in EFT seems to be a much more powerful and general predictor of treatment success than initial distress level, which has not been found to be an important predictor of long-term success in EFT. This is an unusual finding, because initial distress level is usually by far the best predictor of long-term success in couple therapy (Whisman & Jacobson, 1990). The EFT therapist thus does not have to be discouraged by the couple's initial distress level, but should take note of the partners' commitment to the therapy process and their willingness to connect with the therapist and join in the therapy process. Research indicates that the perceived relevance of the tasks of therapy seems to be the most important aspect of the alliance; it is more central than a positive bond with the therapist or a sense of shared goals. The couple's ability to join with the therapist in a collaborative alliance and to view the tasks of EFT—tasks that focus on such issues as safety, trust, and closeness—as relevant to their goals in couple therapy seems to be crucial. Of course, the therapist's skill in presenting these tasks and in creating an alliance is an element here. These results fit with the conclusion that the quality of the client's participation in therapy is the most important determinant of outcome (Orlinsky, Grawe, & Parks, 1994). Generally, this research suggests that EFT works best when partners still have an emotional investment in their relationship and are able to view their problems in terms of insecure attachment and conflicts around closeness and distance. The first concern of the EFT therapist must be to form and maintain a strong supportive alliance with each partner.

A lack of expressiveness or of emotional awareness has not been found to hamper the EFT change process. In fact, EFT seems to be particularly powerful in helping male partners who are described by their partners as inexpressive. This may be because when such partners are able to discover and express their experience, the results are often compelling, both for them and for their partners. As feminist writers have suggested, it is often positive to challenge typical gender styles and assume that needs are basically the same for both sexes (Knudson-Martin & Mahoney, 1999), particularly in a safe, validating environment. Traditional relationships, in which the man is oriented to independence and is often unexpressive while the woman is oriented to affiliation, seem to be responsive to EFT interventions. Some research results suggest that EFT is also more effective with older men (over 35), who may be more responsive to a focus on intimacy and attachment.

There is evidence that the female partner's initial level of trust—specifically, her faith that her partner still cares for her—is a very strong predictor of treatment success in EFT. Women in Western culture have traditionally taken most of the responsibility for maintaining close bonds in families. If the female partner no longer has faith that her partner cares for her, this may define the bond as nonviable and may stifle the emotional investment necessary for change. This parallels evidence that emotional disengagement, rather than such factors as the inability to resolve disagreements, is predictive of long-term marital unhappiness and instability (Gottman, 1994) and of lack of success in couple therapy in general (Jacobson & Addis, 1993). A low level of this element of trust may be a bad prognostic indicator in any form of couple therapy. The EFT therapist may then help such a couple to clarify their choices and the limits of those choices.

The effects of EFT have been found not to be qualified by age, education, income, length of marriage, interpersonal cognitive complexity, or level of religiosity (Denton et al., 2000). In fact, there is some evidence that clients with lower levels of education and lower levels of cognitive complexity may gain the most from EFT. These findings are significant, as people learning about EFT for the first time sometimes assume that it would be most helpful for highly educated, psychologically minded individuals, since it involves the expression of internal feeling states. Available evidence suggests that EFT may actually be of great benefit for those people who have fewer personal resources in their life to draw upon (e.g., cognitive complexity, finances, and education).

ALLIANCE BUILDING AND ENGAGEMENT IN TREATMENT

From the beginning, the EFT therapist validates each partner's construction of his/her emotional experience and places this experience in the context of the negative interaction cycle. This reflection and validation not only focuses the assessment process on affect and interaction and encourages disclosure; it also immediately begins to forge a strong alliance. A focus on the negative interaction cycle surrounding the problem allows the therapist to frame both partners as victims and to assign responsibility without blame. This aids in creating a secure base and confidence in the process of therapy. The negative interaction cycle in the relationship then becomes the couple's common enemy, and battles about who is "the villain" and who is "the saint" are gradually neutralized.

Assessment and the formation of an alliance are not precursors to or separate from treatment in EFT. They are an integral part of active treatment. By the end of the first session, an EFT therapist usually has a clear sense of the typical problem cycle. The therapist might summarize it from one person's perspective as, for example, "I feel alone and enraged, so I pick at you. You feel you will never please me and become numb and distant. I then intensify my criticisms. You shut down and avoid me for 2 or 3 days, and then we begin again."

Part of the assessment involves actively searching for and validating the strengths of the relationship. For example, a therapist asks a husband what is happening for him as his wife weeps. He states in a wooden voice that he has no empathy. The therapist points out that when she is upset about something other than his behavior, he is very empathic, offering a tissue and asking her about her feelings. As the therapist observes interactions between partners, he/she begins to form tentative hypotheses as to key underlying emotions and definitions of self and other that operate at an implicit level in the couple's interactions. As the therapist actively intervenes with the couple, it is possible to assess how open the partners are and how easy they will be to engage in therapy. From the beginning, the EFT therapist both follows and leads. The therapist is active and directs the partners' disclosures toward attachment-salient interactions, attributions, and emotional responses.

The creation of the alliance in EFT is based on the techniques of humanistic/experiential therapies (Greenberg, Watson, & Lietaer, 1999; Rogers,

1951). The EFT therapist focuses upon empathic attunement, acceptance, and genuineness. Humanistic therapies in general take the stance that the therapist should not hide behind the mask of professionalism, but should attempt to be nondefensive, fully present, and authentic. We assume that the alliance must always be monitored, and that any potential break in this alliance (and there will surely be at least one such break in a course of therapy) must be attended to and repaired before therapy can continue. The alliance is viewed in attachment terms as a secure base that allows for the exploration and reformulation of emotional experience and engagement in potentially threatening interactions. We begin by taking people as they are. We then try, by the leap of imagination that is empathy (Guerney, 1994), to understand the valid and legitimate reasons for partners' manner of relating to each other and exactly how this maintains their relationship distress. We assume that everyone has to deal with difficult life situations where choices are limited, and that the very ways people find to save their lives in these situations (such as blaming themselves or "numbing out") then narrow their responses in other contexts and create problems. We tend to frame patterns of interaction and patterns in the processing of inner experience rather than the person as the problem. This facilitates the building of the alliance. In EFT, therapists are encouraged, if they find themselves becoming frustrated and blaming or categorizing clients, to disclose that they do not understand a particular aspect of the clients' behavior and need the clients' help in connecting with their experience. A therapist takes a deliberate stance of choosing to believe in a client's ability to grow and change, but also allows each client to dictate the goal, pace, and form of this change. So if the therapist suggests that a partner confide in his/her mate rather than the therapist at a particular moment and the partner refuses, the therapist will respect this. However, the therapist will then slice the risk thinner and ask the partner to confide to the mate that it is too difficult to share sensitive material directly with him/her right now. The therapist sets the frame, but the clients paint the picture.

CORE INTERVENTIONS

Once the alliance is established, there are two basic therapeutic tasks in EFT: (1) the exploration and reformulation of emotional experience, and (2) the restructuring of interactions.

Exploring and Reformulating Emotion

The following interventions are used in EFT to address the exploration/reformulation task:

1. Reflecting emotional experience.
   Example: "Could you help me to understand? I think you're saying that you become so anxious, so 'edgy' in these situations that you find yourself wanting to hold on to, to get control over everything, because the feeling of being 'edgy' gets so overwhelming. Is that it? And then you begin to get very critical with your wife. Am I getting it right?"
   Main functions: Focusing the therapy process; building and maintaining the alliance; clarifying emotional responses underlying interactional positions.
2. Validation.
   Example: "You feel so alarmed that you can't even focus. When you're that afraid, you can't even concentrate. Is that it?"
   Main functions: Legitimizing responses and supporting clients to continue to explore how they construct their experience and their interactions; building the alliance.
3. Evocative responding: Expanding by open questions the stimulus, bodily response, associated desires, and meanings or action tendency.
   Examples: "What's happening right now, as you say that?" "What's that like for you?" "So when this occurs, some part of you just wants to run—run and hide?"
   Main functions: Expanding elements of experience to facilitate the re-organization of that experience; formulating unclear or marginalized elements of experience and encouraging exploration and engagement.
4. Heightening: Using repetition, images, metaphors, or enactments.
   Examples: "So could you say that again, directly to her, that you do shut her out?", "It seems like this is so difficult for you, like climbing a cliff, so scary," "Can you turn to him and tell him, 'It's too hard to ask. It's too hard to ask you to take my hand'"?
   Main functions: Highlighting key experiences that organize responses to the partner and new formulations of experience that will reorganize the interaction.
5. Empathic conjecture or interpretation.
   Example: "You don't believe it's possible that anyone could see this part of you and still ac-cept you. Is that right? So you have no choice but to hide?"
   Main functions: Clarifying and formulating new meanings, especially regarding interactional positions and definitions of self.

These interventions are discussed in more detail elsewhere, together with markers or cues as to when specific interventions are used, and descriptions of the process partners engage in as a result of each intervention (Johnson, 1996).

Restructuring Interventions

The following interventions are used in EFT to address the restructuring task:

1. Tracking, reflecting, and replaying interactions.
   Example: "So what just happened here? It seemed like you turned from your anger for a moment and appealed to him. Is that OK? But, Jim, you were paying attention to the anger and stayed behind your barricade, yes?"
   Main functions: Slowing down and clarifying steps in the interactional dance; replaying key interactional sequences.
2. Reframing in the context of the cycle and attachment processes.
   Example: "You freeze because you feel like you're right on the edge of losing her, yes? You freeze because she matters so much to you, not because you don't care."
   Main functions: Shifting the meaning of specific responses and fostering more positive perceptions of the partner.
3. Restructuring and shaping interactions: Enacting present positions, enacting new behaviors based upon new emotional responses, and choreographing specific change events.
   Examples: (a) "Can you tell him, 'I'm going to shut you out. You don't get to devastate me again'"? (b) "This is the first time you've ever mentioned being ashamed. Could you tell him about that shame?" (c) "Can you ask him, please? Can you ask him for what you need right now?"
   Main functions: Clarifying and expanding negative interaction patterns; creating new kinds of dialogue and new interactional steps/positions, which can lead to positive cycles of accessibility and responsiveness.

The EFT therapist also uses particular techniques at impasses in the process of change.

IMPASSES IN THERAPY: INTERVENTIONS

It is quite unusual for the EFT therapist to be unable to help a couple create deescalation or to be unable to foster greater engagement on the part of a withdrawn partner. The most common place for the process of change to become mired down is in Stage Two. This is particularly true when a therapist is attempting to shape positive interactions to foster secure bonding and asks a blaming, critical partner to begin to take new risks with a partner. Often, if the therapist affirms the difficulty of learning to trust and remains hopeful and engaged in the face of any temporary reoccurrence of distress, the couple will continue to move forward.

The therapist may also set up an individual session with each partner to explore the impasse and soothe the fears associated with new levels of emotional engagement. The therapist can also reflect the impasse, painting a vivid picture of the couple's journey and its present status, and inviting the partners to claim their relationship from the negative cycle. This can be part of a general process of heightening and enacting impasses. A partner who can actively articulate his/her stuck position in the relationship dance feels the constraining effect of this position more acutely. For example, sadly stating to one's mate, "I can never let you in. If I do . . ." can begin to challenge this position. The mate also can often then respond in reassuring ways that allow the partner to take small new steps toward trust.

If emotion is very high and interferes with any kind of intervention, the therapist can also offer images and tell archetypal stories that capture the dilemma of the most constrained partner and his/her mate. In the EFT model, these stories are labeled "disquisitions" (Millikin & Johnson, 2000; Johnson, 1996). The partners are then able to look from a distance and explore the story and therefore their own dilemma. This is a "hands-off" intervention that offers the couple a normalizing but clarifying mirror, but does not require a response. Instead, it poses a dilemma that presents the couple with a clear set of choices within a narrative framework that is universal and as unthreatening as possible.

As discussed previously, research into change processes in EFT has examined a particular event that appears to block the renewal of a secure bond. This event we have termed an "attachment injury" (Johnson & Whiffen, 1999). Attachment theorists have pointed out that incidents in which one partner responds or fails to respond at times of urgent need seem to influence the quality of an attachment relationship disproportionately (Simpson & Rholes, 1994). Such incidents either shatter or confirm a partner's assumptions about attachment relationships and the dependability of the mate. Negative attachment-related events, particularly abandonments and betrayals, often cause seemingly irreparable damage to close relationships. Many partners enter therapy not only in general distress, but also with the goal of bringing closure to such events and so restoring lost intimacy and trust. During the therapy process, these events, even if they are long past, often reemerge in an alive and intensely emotional manner—much as a traumatic flashback does—and overwhelm the injured partner. These incidents, usually occurring in the context of life transitions, loss, physical danger, or uncertainty, can be considered "relationship traumas" (Johnson et al., 2001). When the other partner then fails to respond in a reparative, reassuring manner, or when the injured partner cannot accept such reassurance, the injury is compounded. As the partners experience failure in their attempts to move beyond such injuries and repair the bond between them, their despair and alienation deepen. For instance, a husband's withdrawal from his wife when she suffers a miscarriage, as well as his subsequent unwillingness to discuss this incident, becomes a recurring focus of the couple's dialogue and blocks the development of new, more positive interactions

Attachment has been called a "theory of trauma" (Atkinson, 1997), in that it emphasizes the extreme emotional adversity of isolation and separation, particularly at times of increased vulnerability. This theoretical framework offers an explanation of why certain painful events become pivotal in a relationship, as well as an understanding of what the key features of such events will be, how they will affect a particular couple's relationship and how such events can be optimally resolved.

Our present understanding of the process of resolving these injuries is as follows. First, with the therapist's help, the injured partner stays in touch with the injury and begins to articulate its impact and its attachment significance. New emotions frequently emerge at this point. Anger evolves into clear expressions of hurt, helplessness, fear, and shame. The connection of the injury to present negative cycles in the relationship become clear. For example, a partner may say, "I feel so hopeless. I just smack him to show him he can't pretend I'm not here. He can't just wipe out my hurt like that."

Second, the other partner then begins to hear and understand the significance of the injurious event and to understand it in attachment terms as a reflection of his/her importance to the injured partner, rather than as a reflection of his/her personal inadequacies or insensitivity. The mate then acknowledges the injured partner's pain and suffering, and elaborates on how the event evolved for him/her.

Third, the injured partner next tentatively moves toward a more integrated and complete articulation of the injury, and expresses grief at the loss involved in it and fear concerning the specific loss of the attachment bond. This partner allows the other to witness his/her vulnerability. Fourth, the other partner in turn becomes more emotionally engaged; this person acknowledges responsibility for his/her part in the attachment injury and expresses empathy, regret, and/or remorse.

Fifth, the injured partner then risks asking for the comfort and caring from his/her mate that were unavailable at the time of the injurious event.

The mate responds in a caring manner that acts as an antidote to the traumatic experience of the attachment injury. Sixth, the partners are then able to construct together a new narrative of the event. This narrative is ordered and includes, for the injured partner, a clear and acceptable sense of how the other came to respond in such a distressing manner during the event.

Once the attachment injury is resolved, the therapist can more effectively foster the growth of trust, softening events, and the beginning of positive cycles of bonding and connection.

MECHANISMS OF CHANGE

Change in EFT is not seen in terms of the attainment of cognitive insight, problem-solving or negotiation skills, or a process of catharsis or ventilation. The EFT therapist walks with each partner to the leading edge of his/her experience and expands this experience to include marginalized or hardly synthesized elements that then give new meaning to this experience. What was figure may now become ground. Once each partner's experience of relatedness takes on new color and form, they can move their feet in a different way in the interactional dance. For instance, "edginess" and irritation expand into anxiety and anguish. The expression of anguish then brings a whole new dimension into an irritated partner's sense of relatedness and his/her dialogue with the mate. Experience becomes reorganized, and the emotional elements in that experience evoke new responses to the partner. So the irritated partner becomes more connected with his/her fear and aloneness (rather than with contempt for the mate), and then he/she wants to reach for the mate and ask for comfort. Partners encounter and express their own experience in new ways, and this then fosters new encounters—new forms of engagement with the other. Experience is reconstructed, and so is the dance between partners.

The research on the process of change in EFT has been summarized elsewhere (Johnson et al., 1999). In general, couples show more depth of experiencing and more affiliative responses in successful sessions. Although deescalation of the negative cycle and reengagement of the withdrawing partner can be readily observed in EFT sessions, the change event that has been most clearly demonstrated in research is the "softening." A softening involves a vulnerable request by a usually hostile partner for reassurance, comfort, or some other attachment need to be met. When the other, now accessible partner is able to respond to this request, then both partners are mutually responsive and bonding interactions can occur. Examples of these events are given in the literature on EFT (e.g., Johnson & Greenberg, 1995). A brief set of snapshots of one partner's progress through a softening event follows:

"I just get so tense, you know. Then he seems like the enemy."
"I guess maybe—maybe I am panicked. That's why I get so enraged. What else can you do? He's not there. I can't feel that helpless."
"I can't ask for what I need. I have never been able to do that. I would feel pathetic. He wouldn't like it; he'd cut and run. It would be dreadful." (*The partner then invites and reassures.*)
"This is scary. I feel pretty small right now. I would really—well, I think (*to partner*) I need you to hold me. Could you just let me know you care, you see my hurt?"

There are many levels of change in a softening. The ones most easily identified are these:

• An expansion of experience, especially an accessing of attachment fears and of the longing for contact and comfort. Emotions tell us what we need.

- An engagement of the partner in a different way. Fear organizes a less angry more affiliative stance. The partner in the example above puts words to her emotional needs and changes her part of the dance. New emotions prime new responses/actions.
- A new view of the softening partner is offered to his/her mate. The husband in the example above sees his wife in a different light, as afraid rather than dangerous, and is pulled toward her by her expressions of vulnerability.
- A new compelling cycle is initiated. In the example above, she reaches and he comforts. This new connection offers an antidote to negative interactions and redefines the relationship as a secure bond.
- A bonding event occurs in the session. This bond then allows for open communication, flexible problem solving, and resilient coping with everyday issues. The partners resolve issues and problems, and consolidate their ability to manage their life and their relationship (Stage Three of EFT).
- There are shifts in both partners' sense of self. Both can comfort and be comforted. Both are defined as lovable and entitled to care in their interaction, and as able to redefine and repair their relationship.

For a therapist to be able to guide a couple in the direction of such an event and help the partners shape it, this therapist has to be willing to engage emotionally. He/she has to learn to have confidence in the process (the inherent pull of attachment needs and behaviors), and in clients' abilities to reconfigure their emotional realities when they have a secure base in therapy. Even so, not every couple will be able to complete a softening. Some will improve their relationship, reduce the spin of the negative cycle, attain a little more emotional engagement, and decide to stop there. The model suggests that although such improvement is valid and significant, such couples will be more vulnerable to relapse.

TERMINATION

In Stage Three of treatment, the therapist is less directive, and the partners themselves begin the process of consolidating their new interactional positions and finding new solutions to problem-

atic issues in a collaborative way. We emphasize each partner's shifts in position. For example, we frame a more passive and withdrawn husband as now powerful and able to help his wife deal with her attachment fears, while the wife is framed as needing his support. We support constructive patterns of interaction and help the couple put together a narrative capturing the change that has occurred in therapy and the nature of the new relationship. We stress the ways the couple has found to exit from the problem cycle and create closeness and safety. Any relapses are also discussed and normalized. If these negative interactions occur, they are shorter, are less alarming, and are processed differently, so they have less impact on the definition of the relationship. The partners' goals for their future together are also discussed, as are any fears about terminating the sessions. At this point, the partners express more confidence in their relationship and are ready to leave therapy. We offer couples the possibility of future booster sessions, but this is placed in the context of future crises triggered from outside the relationship, rather than any expectation that they will need such sessions to deal with relationship problems per se.

TREATMENT APPLICABILITY

EFT has been used with many different kinds of couples facing many different kinds of issues. It was developed in collaboration with clients in agencies, university clinics, private practice, and a hospital clinic in a major city where partners were struggling with many problems in addition to relationship distress. Many of these hospital clinic couples' relationships were in extreme distress. Some of these partners were in individual therapy as well as couple therapy and some were also on medication to reduce the symptoms of PTSD or other anxiety disorders, bipolar disorder, or chronic physical illness. The EFT therapist will typically link symptoms such as depression to the couple's interactional cycle and attachment security. The therapist focuses on how the emotional realities and negative interactions of the partners create, maintain, or exacerbate such symptoms, and how symptoms in turn create, maintain, or exacerbate these realities and interactions. In general, it seems that placing "individual" problems in their relational context enables a couple to find new perspectives on and ways of dealing with such problems. As one client, Doug, remarked, "I am less edgy now we are more together—but also, if I feel that edginess coming, well, I can go and ask her to touch me, and it makes it more manageable. So I have reduced my meds a bit, and that makes me feel better."

As mentioned previously, EFT is used in clinical practice with couples of diverse ages, classes, backgrounds, and sexual orientations. The traditionality of a couple does not appear to have a negative impact on interventions (Johnson & Talitman, 1997). It seems to us that it is not the beliefs partners hold, but how rigidly such beliefs are adhered to, that can become problematic in therapy. Some beliefs, particularly regarding the pathologizing of dependency needs, are challenged in the course of EFT. Women, for example, may be labeled as "sick," "immature," "crazy," or generally "inappropriate" when they express their attachment needs in vivid ways that their partners do not understand. The ambivalence about closeness that women who have been violated in past relationships express can also be pathologized by frustrated partners. In terms of sensitivity to gender issues, EFT appears to meet the criteria for a gender-sensitive intervention defined by Knudson-Martin and Mahoney (1999): The model focuses on connection and mutuality, and validates both men's and woman's need for a sense of secure connectedness that also promotes autonomy. The ability to share power and to trust, rather than to coercively control the other, is inherent in the creation of a secure adult bond.

EFT is used with gay and lesbian relationships, and although there are special issues to be taken into account, these relationships seem to us to follow the same patterns and reflect the same attachment realities as heterosexual relationships. Special topics (e.g., partners' having differing attitudes to coming out and the realities of HIV) arise and have to be dealt with in sessions, but the process of EFT is essentially the same with these couples. We have not found lesbian partners to be particularly "fused" or gay male partners to be "disengaged," and there is now research suggesting that these stereotypes are inaccurate (Green, Bettinger, & Zacks, 1996). An EFT therapist would tend to see the extreme emotional reactivity that might be labeled as evidence of "fusion" as reflecting attachment insecurity and the negative relationship dance maintaining that insecurity.

What does the research on EFT tell us about how interventions affect couples with different presenting problems? Low sexual desire been found to be difficult to influence significantly in a brief number of sessions (MacPhee, Johnson, & van der Veer, 1995); indeed, this presenting problem seems

to be generally difficult to affect in psychotherapy. However, there is empirical evidence that for other problems that typically go hand in hand with distressed relationships, effects are positive. Depression, the "common cold" of mental health, seems to be significantly influenced by EFT (Dessaulles, 1991; Gordon-Walker, 1994; see later discussion). Marital discord is the most common life stressor that precedes the onset of depression and a 25-fold increased risk rate for depression has been reported for those who are unhappily married (Weissman, 1987). Research also demonstrates that EFT works well with couples experiencing chronic family stress and grief—for example, chronic illness in children (Gordon-Walker, Johnson, Manion, & Clothier, 1997).

Traumatized Partners

EFT has also been used extensively for couples where one partner is suffering from PTSD resulting from physical illness and/or abuse, violent crime, or childhood sexual abuse (Johnson & Williams-Keeler, 1998; Johnson, 2002). EFT appears to be particularly appropriate for traumatized partners, perhaps because it focuses on emotional responses and attachment. PTSD is essentially about the regulation of affective states, and "emotional attachment is the primary protection against feelings of helplessness and meaninglessness" (McFarlane & van der Kolk, 1996, p. 24). As Becker (1973) suggests, "a deep sense of belonging" results in "the taming of terror," and such taming is a primary goal of any therapy for PTSD.

Trauma increases the need for protective attachments, and at the same time undermines the ability to trust and therefore to build such attachments. If the EFT therapist can foster the development of a more secure bond between the partners, this not only improves the couple relationship but also helps partners to deal with the trauma and mitigate its long-term effects. For instance, a husband might say to his wife, "I want you to be able to feel safe in my arms and to come to that safe place when the ghosts come for you. I can help you fight them off." When his wife is able to reach for him, she simultaneously builds her sense of efficacy ("I can learn to trust again"), her bond with her husband ("Here I can ask for comfort") and her ability to deal with trauma ("I can lean on you. You are my ally when the ghosts come for me").

Trauma survivors have typically received some individual therapy before requesting couple therapy and may be referred by their individual therapists, who recognize the need to address relationship issues. Indeed, for someone who has experienced a "violation of human connection" (Herman, 1992), such as sexual or physical abuse in his/her family of origin, the specific impact of such trauma manifests itself in relationship issues; it is in this context that the effects of trauma must be addressed and corrected. When EFT is used with traumatized partners, an educational component on trauma and the effects of trauma on attachment is added to the usual Stage One interventions. This is often crucial, especially for a survivor's partner, who often has no real understanding of what the survivor is dealing with and therefore cannot be expected to respond empathically.

In general with these couples, cycles of defense, distance, and distrust are more extreme, and emotional storms and crises must be expected. The therapist has to pace the therapy carefully, containing emotions a survivor is unable to tolerate. Risks must be sliced thin, and support from the therapist must be consistent and reliable. The endpoint of therapy may be different from that in therapy with nontraumatized partners; for example, some kinds of sexual contact may never become acceptable for a survivor of sexual abuse. For a survivor of either sexual or physical abuse, the other spouse is at once the "source of and solution to terror" (Main & Hesse, 1990, p. 163). Such partners then often swing between extreme needs for closeness and extreme fear of letting anyone close. This ambivalence has to be expected and normalized in therapy. The therapist also has to expect to be tested, and in general has to monitor the alliance on a constant basis, since it is always fragile. The solutions survivors find to the recurring terror that stalks them are often extremely problematic. Such solutions may include substance abuse, dissociation, and violence against self and others. The first stage of therapy may then also include formulating "safety rules" around key stressful moments when trauma cues arise in the relationship (e.g., sexual contact), as well as developing general strategies for dealing with fear and shame. Shame is particularly problematic with survivors; confiding in or showing themselves to valued others is often very difficult for them. A negative model of self as unworthy, unlovable, deserving of abuse, and even toxic is likely to come up, especially in key moments of change (see transcript in Johnson & Williams-Keeler, 1998). The first antidote to such shame may be the validation of a therapist;

however, the most potent antidote is the support and responsiveness of one's primary attachment figure, one's partner. The EFT treatment of survivors and their partners is dealt with extensively elsewhere (Johnson, 2002).

The treatment of disorders such as PTSD or even clinical depression can seem intimidating to a couple therapist who is already dealing with the multilayered complex drama of a distressed relationship. Factors that help the EFT therapist here are, first, the way the client is conceptualized and the alliance is viewed; and, second, the map of close relationships offered by attachment theory. Humanistic theory views clients as active learners who have an intrinsic capacity for growth and self-actualization. The therapist then learns to trust that when clients can be engaged with, in contact with, and fully present to their experience—including the neglected emotions, felt meanings, and tacit knowing inherent in that experience—they can be creative, resourceful, and resilient. The clients' evolving experience becomes a touchstone for the therapist, to which he/she can return when confused or unsure as to the best road to take at a particular moment in therapy. The therapist can also use his/her own feelings as a guide to decode clients' responses and dilemmas.

Depressed Partners

The map offered by attachment theory also facilitates couple therapy with partners dealing with multiple problems as well as relationship distress. Let us take depression as an example. As noted earlier, couple therapy is emerging as a potent intervention for depressed partners who are maritally distressed (Anderson et al., 1999). Couple and family therapy is emerging as the logical treatment of choice in all recent interpersonal approaches to depression (Teichman & Teichman, 1990). Research supports this focus: A partner's support and compassion predict more rapid recovery from depression (McLeod, Kessler, & Landis, 1992), whereas a partner's criticism is related to more frequent relapse (Coiro & Gottesman, 1996).

Attachment theory views depression as an integral part of separation distress that arises after protest and clinging/seeking behaviors have not elicited responsiveness from an attachment figure. Research has found that the more insecure partners see themselves to be and the less close they feel to their mates, the more relationship distress seems to elicit depressive symptoms (Davila & Bradbury, 1999; Beach, Nelson, & O'Leary, 1988). Depressed individuals describe themselves as anxious and fearful in their attachment relationships (Hammen et al., 1995). Attachment theory also suggests that a person's model of self is constantly constructed in interactions with others, so problematic relationships result in a sense of self as unlovable and unworthy. The depression literature has identified the key aspects of depression as follows: (1) unresolved loss and lack of connection with others; and (2) anger directed toward the self in self-criticism, together with a sense of failure and unworthiness, as well as a sense of hopelessness (a sense of the self as having been defeated and disempowered). These aspects of depression—self-criticism and anxious dependency—are often highly intertwined. Many of those who cannot find a way to connect safely with a partner, for example, and are engulfed with loss, also despise themselves for needing others and contemptuously label themselves as weak. In experiential models of treatment for depression, clients are supported to find their voices and use their emotions as a guide to what their goals are, whether it is more secure connectedness with others or a more accepting engagement with themselves (Greenberg, Watson, & Goldman, 1998).

So when an EFT therapist sees a depressed partner who is nagging, seeking reassurance, and trying to control the other's behavior—all behaviors that have been found to characterize depressed partners' interactions with their mates—the therapist will view this as attachment protest. This perspective also predicts that depressive symptoms will arise at times of crisis and transition, such as after the birth of a child, when attachment needs become particularly poignant and partners are not able to support each other to create a safe haven and a secure base (Whiffen & Johnson, 1998). An EFT therapist assumes that even if a partner comes to a relationship with a particular vulnerability to depression or insecurity, new kinds of emotional engagement with his/her emotional experience and with the mate can break old patterns and create new realities and relationships.

How may the process of change in EFT specifically affect a partner's depression? In the first stage of therapy, depressive responses are placed in the context of interactional cycles and unmet attachment needs. The partners then become allies against the negative cycle and the effects of this cycle, including the dark cloud of depression. Legiti-

mizing depressive responses as natural and arising from a sense of deprivation or invalidation in an attachment relationship tends to balance the depressed partner's tendency to feel shameful about the struggle with depression. In the second stage of therapy, the experience of depression evolves into explicit components such as grief and longing, which evokes reaching for the mate, or anger, which evokes an assertion of needs or shame that can be explored and restructured in the session. The process of therapy directly addresses the sense of helplessness that many partners feel by offering them an experience of mastery over their own emotional states and their relationship dance. New positive interactions then offer the depressed partner an antidote to isolation and feedback from an attachment figure as to the lovable and worthy nature of the self.

For instance, when Mary stepped out of her career and had a baby, she was "dismayed" a year later to find her new life "disappointing" and "lonely." Her physician diagnosed her as clinically depressed and referred her for couple therapy. She accused her partner, David, of only caring about his work, while he would state that he did not understand what she wanted from him and he was working for their future. David withdrew more and more, and began sleeping downstairs so as not to wake the baby. Mary became more critical of him and more overwhelmed and depressed. She also felt like a "bad mother" and decided that "David doesn't really care about me. I was a fool to marry him." As therapy evolved, Mary began to formulate her sense of abandonment, and David began to acknowledge his sense of failure and need to "hide" from his wife. After 10 sessions of EFT, this couple no longer scored as distressed on the Dyadic Adjustment Scale. More specifically, Mary's score rose from 80 at the beginning to 102 at the end of therapy. Mary's physician independently reported that she was no longer depressed, and the couple displayed new cycles of emotional engagement and responsiveness. These partners experienced themselves as coping with stress more effectively, and a 1-year follow-up these results remained stable. Since a partner's criticism and lack of supportiveness predict relapse into depression, and secure attachment is a protective factor against stress and depression, we assume that cycles of positive bonding interactions would help prevent a recurrence of Mary's depressive symptoms. If we were to take snapshots of key moments in David's reengagement in the relationship and of Mary's move to a softer position, what would these snapshots look like?

David

"I don't want to run away from you. I just saw your anger, not that you needed me."

"I want to support you and be close, but I need some help here. I need some recognition when I try, like when I look after the baby."

"If you are fierce all the time, it makes it hard for me to hold and support you. I feel like I'm a disappointment. So I hide out and work harder at my job."

"I want to feel like I can take care of you and the baby. I want you to trust me a little and help me learn how to do it."

Mary

"I'm afraid that I will start to count on you, and off you will go again. I was let down in my first marriage, and now in this one too. I'm afraid to hope."

"Maybe I am fierce sometimes. I don't even know that you are hearing me. It's hard for me to admit that I need your support."

"I need to know that I am important to you, and that we can learn to be partners and parents together."

"I want to know that I can lean on you, and that you will put me and the baby first sometimes. I need you to hold me when I get overwhelmed and scared."

Violence in Relationships

Although violence is a contraindication for EFT and for couple therapy in general, couple therapy may be considered if violence and/or emotional abuse is relatively infrequent and mild; if the abused partner is not intimidated and desires couple therapy; and if the perpetrator takes responsibility for the abuse. The therapist will then talk to the couple about a set of safety procedures for them to enact if stress becomes too high in the relationship and increases the risk of abusive responses. The position taken by such authors as Goldner (1999)—namely, that perpetrators must be morally challenged but not reduced to this singular shameful aspect of their behavior, their abusiveness—fits well with the stance taken in EFT. So, for example, a man who has become obsessed with his wife's weight, and frequently becomes contemptuous and controlling, is challenged when he minimizes his wife's outrage and hurt at his behavior. However, he is also listened to and supported when he is able to talk about the desperation and attachment panic that precede his jibes and hostile criticisms. The therapist supports his wife to express her pain and her need to withdraw from him, and facilitates her asserting her limits and insisting on respect from her husband. The husband is encouraged to touch and confide his sense of helplessness, rather than regulating this emotional state by becoming controlling with his wife.

The couple is supported to identify particular cues and events that prime this husband's insecurities and lead him into the initiation of abuse, as well as key responses that prime the beginnings of trust and positive engagement. Rather than being taught to contain his rage per se, such a client is helped to interact from the level of longing and vulnerability. When he can express his sense of helplessness and lack of control in the relationship, he becomes less volatile and safer for his wife to engage with. It is interesting to note that we do not teach assertiveness in EFT, and yet clients like the wife in this couple become more assertive. How do we understand this? First, her emotional reality is accepted, validated, and made vivid and tangible. The therapist helps her tell her husband that she is burned out with "fighting for her life" and that he is becoming "the enemy." Once this wife can organize and articulate her hurt and anger, the action impulse inherent in these emotions, which is to protest and insist on her right to protect herself, naturally arises. She is able to tell him that she will not meet his expectations about her physical appearance, and he is able to piece together how he uses her concern about her appearance as a sign that she cares about his approval and still loves him. This couple illustrates the work of Dutton (1995), which suggests that the abusive behaviors of many abusive partners are directly related to their inability to create a sense of secure attachment and their associated sense of helplessness in their significant relationships.

Having discussed the use of EFT with different kinds of couples and problems, let us now look a little more closely at a typical distressed couple going through the therapy process.

CASE ILLUSTRATION

Brad and Ann told one of us (SMJ) that their 30-year-old relationship was now stuck in "constant bickering." This husband and wife were in their late 50s, and their five children had now all left home. Brad had recently retired from a senior administrative position, but Ann continued to work as a financial analyst. Brad had experienced bouts of depression all through his life, but these were now "well contained" by medication. Both identified considerable anger at each other and a sense of uncertainty as to how important they now were in each other's lives. Ann had begun to take regular trips away from home to visit her adult children and spent long hours working, especially since she had just received a significant promotion. In the first session, Brad tended to speak quietly and to make efforts to be "reasonable," whereas Ann was very quick, very assertive, and at times very sharp with him. They stated that they had begun recently to have strident arguments about their very different perspectives on the history of the relationship. Ann commented that she now understood that this relationship had been "a lie," and that Brad had felt trapped into marriage because she had gotten pregnant. Brad agreed that he had felt trapped at first and had been "resistant" to the level of involvement that Ann wanted, but that he had grown to love his wife very much. He stated that he now felt very desolate about their recent fights, where they would "demean and wound each other" and then not speak to each other for days. He added that he would like to have married someone who was "gentler and more open." Ann responded by becoming very indignant and summing up the history of the relationship as a story of her moving from being "docile" and pursuing Brad for closeness for many years, to finally learning to assert herself and find happiness in her own career.

This couple was typical of many middle-class marriages in which the man's career is winding down just as the woman's career is taking off. Ann stated that she had supported Brad in his long fight with depression (and he agreed with this), but that she had gotten to the point of feeling drained and resentful. Brad experienced that she had withdrawn from him in recent years. She replied that he had not been available to her for most of their marriage, especially when the children were young and she needed his support. This couple were both fervent Catholics, but also fought over points of their religious faith. When Ann also pointed out that Brad had not supported her after a recent minor operation, he replied that this was because she was just too difficult and too angry to take care of. Ann ended the first session by pushing out her chin and stating in a determined voice, "This has to change, or we have to split."

This couple's interactional cycle appeared in the session to be critical attack on Ann's part, fol-lowed by defense and withdrawal on Brad's part. Both would then withdraw for several days until the cycle began again. Ann was also spending less and less time at home, as she and Brad became ever more alienated from each other. They still had occasional moments where they could discuss ideas or enjoy an activity, but they were increasingly spending time apart and had not made love for over a year. Ann agreed with Brad that she was indeed "judgmental" and added that she had very high standards for herself and others. She also noted that he took no responsibility for his passivity and past withdrawal into depression. With some support from the therapist, Brad was able to express his sense of "panic" when he tried to show Ann affection but was "rebuffed again and again." Ann replied that he had always pursued her "just for sex" and that she was not interested. When asked whether she had ever felt supported and taken care of by Brad, she said that he was "too immature" to do that, and anyway, she took care of herself. At such times, Brad would become silent; when the therapist probed, he admitted that he felt upset by Ann's "constant disapproval" and his sense of failure and powerlessness around her.

In his individual session, Brad elaborated on how he felt unsure of his importance to his wife, and how she had turned to her friends in the last few years rather than to him. He felt "dominated" by her but afraid to assert himself, fearing that she would then leave him. He admitted to being surprised when she expressed distress in the first sessions, but he had remained cautious, since he generally did not see her as vulnerable but as "dangerous." In her individual session, Ann admitted that she was "on guard" in the relationship and had "taken over" in the face of Brad's depression. She felt that she had fought in the beginning of the relationship to show she wasn't a "dumb housewife married to the intellectual," and that she saw Brad as "weak" and an "emotional cripple." More sadly, she added, "He can't take care of me." She agreed that she was very angry with him and did not always understand how enraged she felt. She knew she could be "rigid," especially around "broken rules." As the therapist reflected the cycle and noted how it left both of them defeated and alone, and also probed for the emotions underlying the steps in the dance, Brad was able to agree that he did not respond to his wife; instead, he went "still like a stone" because he was so afraid of her judgments. She then became angrier and more contemptuous.

This husband and wife were a highly educated couple from a strict, religious, conservative background. The building of an alliance was not an easy process. They questioned the process, the model, and the way therapy was done; the therapist had to struggle to stay as transparent, genuine, and nondefensive as possible. Respectful curiosity and requests for help in connecting with each partner's experience did gradually create an alliance. They began to see events that had happened in the relationship from each other's point of view, and to admit that both of them were afraid of losing their marriage. They began to spend more time together and to frame the cycle as holding them both hostage. Brad became noticeably more open and began to express his hurts and fears. After six sessions, deescalation seemed to have been achieved.

The process then seemed to move naturally into Brad's becoming more involved and beginning to talk about feeling "discarded" as Ann moved more and more into her career. Brad's friendship with a female cousin who was in a personal crisis and calling on his support also became an issue. Ann did not believe that this relationship was a potential affair, but became enraged when Brad went to spend an hour with this cousin. The most notable rift in the alliance occurred when the therapist tried to modulate Ann's rage by commenting that it was as if Ann wanted Brad to go to confession and admit his "sin" in this matter. She agreed that this would be appropriate, but added that she resented the therapist's light tone. The therapist admitted to being confused about the nature of Brad's offense, and Ann was unable to explain her sense of outrage. Step by step, with the therapist evoking and heightening underlying emotions, Brad moved into a more present and assertive stance. Brad moved toward increased engagement in this series of statements:

"It's hard to be warm to you when you don't give me any respect."
"I can't win here—you are so angry, like you want to tear me apart. It does intimidate me. I'm hurt too. I am not going to plead and plead and spend my life being judged."
"You are right; I wasn't there for you when the kids were small—I got lost in my depression."
"I have been a wimp, but when you get prickly, well, I just freeze—I know I'm a target. I know I will lose. I don't want to be controlled, so I do shut you out."
"I feel like a sinner and you are like Jehovah. If I tell you I'm hurting, you will see me as just weak. So I button up and go off to where it's safe. But I am getting angry now."

"You override me—I have to take a stand. I feel like dirt when you scream at me. I'm tired of being intimidated. I can never pass the test."
"I want to be able to express myself, not withdraw all the time. I won't be constantly tested."
"Just sometimes, here, I see that you are hurt too, not just angry. I want to be there for you. I want to be with you. I want you to respect me."

At this point, just as Ann seemed to be becoming more curious about her partner and less openly hostile, a crisis occurred. Ann walked into the next session and announced the marriage was over. She stated that she now felt that Brad's friendship with his cousin was "morally wrong," and told him, "You are not going to hurt me ever again." A particular event had occurred where Brad had struggled out into a winter snowstorm after a family supper, to help his cousin, who had stumbled on the path, into the house. As Brad tried to reassure his wife that this was polite consideration on his part, she became more and more enraged. He stated that he loved Ann and that his cousin was not important to him. He apologized if he had hurt her by being solicitous of his cousin. Ann replied by saying she felt she was "going crazy" and accusing him of not "seeing my pain at all." The therapist tried to frame her sensitivity to her husband's kindness to his cousin as her hurt at not receiving his attention and support herself, but Ann rejected this and became even more angry, stating that she was "humiliated" and was moving out of her and Brad's bedroom. Just as Brad was reengaging and the opportunity for more mutuality and connection presented itself, Ann withdrew into rage. We were at an impasse.

In the following session, the therapist began to expand Ann's rage with reflection, evocative responding, and heightening. Ann began to speak of how she felt "hysterical" and "off balance," and had begun to avoid Brad altogether by sleeping in the basement. The therapist decided to "unpack"—that is, expand or deconstruct—the incident at the supper. As Ann described again the snowy evening incident, the therapist suddenly heard echoes of the emotions Ann had touched on very briefly in the first sessions, when she had described undergoing her recent operation. As the therapist focused on this, Ann revealed that there had been a moment during this procedure when she had suddenly felt helplessness, realizing that she could die if things went wrong. As the therapist probed for what had happened when she had returned home, Ann shouted in rage that Brad had greeted her with a statement that he was glad she was home, since he could now go to bed. He had then taken his sleeping pill and gone to sleep. He had left the next day for a long trip. The therapist realized that this incident had been an attachment injury for Ann. The incident at the supper was significant in that she watched Brad give caring—caring that she suddenly became aware she had needed but could not ask for on the night of the operation—to someone else. As the therapist linked the emotions of "helplessness" and "lonely abandonment" to both incidents, Ann broke down into sobs and grief. These incidents had become particularly salient when the therapist had begun to frame Brad as accessible and encourage her to consider risking with him in therapy sessions.

Let us look at part of the process that followed.

ANN: I don't think I can do this. It's like I'm in shock. I feel broken—out of control. I am so anxious, I went and got some anxiety pills from my doctor.

SMJ: It's hard for you to touch this place where you feel vulnerable and need Brad—and remember how abandoned and alone you felt. Is that it ? (*She nods.*) You feel broken. [Reflection. Heightening.]

ANN: I guess. I see him trying to be solicitous (*he nods*), but I can't respond.

BRAD: I try to comfort her, but her flashes of anger throw me off balance too. I have never seen her be vulnerable before. I can't quite figure it out.

SMJ: (*To Brad*) It's hard for you to really see her hurt, her fears. You are used to seeing her as so strong and so in control? (*Brad nods emphatically.*) [Validation.]

BRAD: I'd like to comfort her. I'd like to nurture her. (*Therapist gestures to him to tell her this. He does. Ann turns away from him.*) [Shaping interaction with task.]

SMJ: (*Softly*) What is happening, Ann, as Brad says that he'd like to comfort you? [Evocative responding.]

ANN: Fragile. (*Very soft voice, holds herself with her arms.*)

SMJ: When you hear him offer comfort, you feel fragile—broken? It's hard to let him in, to feel that need? You decided never again—after the operation? [Evocative responding. Interpretation.]

ANN: (*Angrily*) Right. It's humiliating.

SMJ: You feel small—somehow ashamed to feel so vulnerable? Am I getting it? You had steeled yourself for years, and then your walls shattered—and he wasn't there. (*Ann nods and cries.*)

BRAD: I am trying. I tried to show you last night that I see how I've let you down in the past and that night after the operation. I never saw you as needing me.

SMJ: What is it like for you to know that Ann needs you and wraps her anger around herself so you won't see how she needs? (Evocative responding. Interpretation)

BRAD: I don't want her to hurt—but to know I am important to her, that's a relief. Makes me feel whole again. I see her differently.

SMJ: Can you tell her, "I see you're hurting. I see how I've hurt you. I want to comfort you. I want to be needed"? [Shaping interaction. Heightening message.]

ANN: (*In an angry voice*) Now you see me—now—do you? After all these years? (*She weeps.*)

BRAD: (*Very softly*) I know. Why should you believe me? I guess I let you down lots, and instead of thinking of my cousin, I should have been thinking of you—taking care of your hurt. I know how much I have hurt you. I guess the party incident was just the last straw.

SMJ: Can you hear him, Ann? Telling you he does see and care about your pain? Is there another voice besides the one that says, "Don't let him in—don't give him a chance to shatter you again"? [Reflection of process. Evocative responding.]

ANN: I feel hopeless. (*She weeps. Her voice goes dead and low.*) I'm invisible if I don't shout. I'd rather be angry—hostile.

SMJ: Can you tell him, "I've felt invisible, so now I dare not hope that you will really want and hold me—and be there when I need you. It's hard to let my guard down and put myself in your hands"? (*She nods.*) "Especially when I touch that night, at the supper—when you leapt up to take care of her"? [Reflection. Validation. Interpretation. Heightening.]

ANN: I'm not ready yet.

This process continued for three more sessions. The therapist framed the partners' responses in terms of attachment needs and fears, and in terms of the cycle of angry protest and defensive withdrawal that kept them apart. Ann began to be less volatile; she started to stand back and reflect on the attachment injury at the party and the long-term patterns in their relationship. She said, "We box each other into narrow corners." She began to talk about the "wound" of watching him offer caring to his cousin, and described how when it was touched, she went into "free fall." Brad stated that he now saw his wife in a different light and felt stronger around her. He said, "We are communicating for the first time in our lives." As the injury of the abandonment after the operation and the party incident began to heal, he became more confident and commented, "I am learning how to lead in the dance." Ann began to express the attachment fears that most partners express when approaching more mutual connectedness at the end of Stage Two in EFT. She talked about how it was hard to "let go of the reins" and to admit that he could hurt her. He reassured and validated her, and asked her to take the risk of leaning on him. This process, having addressed the attachment injury in the relationship, then took on the pattern of a softening event: Ann risked more and spoke of her attachment needs, and Brad stayed available and responsive. They began to hold each other, make love, and be "tender" with each other. The spouses then moved into the third and last stage of therapy, resolving differences about their children and dealing with time management issues related to Ann's career and Brad's retirement needs. They were able to deal with the transition to Brad's retirement in a more cooperative way. The therapist helped them formulate a concise narrative about their relationship, their problems, and how they had repaired their bond. Ann said, "We have fallen in love again—and it feels a bit perilous—but I like it."

At the end of therapy, Ann and Brad reported that they still had "blowups" but were able to end them and reconnect much faster. They also described and demonstrated positive cycles of mutual comfort and reassurance. These cycles define the relationship as a safe haven and a secure base for both partners. As individuals, both Brad and Ann learned new ways to deal with their emotions and had expanded their model of self in the relationship, as well as their view of each other. Ann described herself as less of an "iron lady" and saw Brad as warmer and more open. Brad commented that it had taken him "forever to mature"—to "step out of his depression" and be able to take care of his wife. He told her that he was glad she had stayed with him and worked things out. The repair of this relationship was complicated by alliance issues and by the attachment injury that arose in Stage Two of the process of change. Nevertheless, this process followed the classic pattern of change in EFT and illustrated the research finding that the initial level of distress is less predictive of outcome than the quality of the partners' engagement in the repair process and the female partner's faith that her partner cares about her and her needs and fears.

BECOMING AN EFT THERAPIST

What are some of the challenges that face the novice EFT therapist? We presume that all couple therapists struggle with integrating the individual and the system, the "within" and the "between" dimensions of couple relationships. We also presume that most couple therapists struggle with leading and following their clients. Furthermore, most couple therapists struggle to foster not only new behaviors but also new meaning shifts (Sprenkle, Blow, & Dickey, 1999). However, the EFT therapist assumes that each partner's emotional engagement with inner experience and with the other partner is necessary to render new responses and new perspectives powerful enough to affect the complex drama of marital distress. The novice therapist has to learn to stay focused on and to trust emotion, even when a client does not (Palmer & Johnson, 2002). Our experience has been that clients do not disintegrate or lose control when they access the emotional experience in the safety of the therapy session; however, novice therapists may, in their own anxiety, dampen key emotional experiences or avoid them altogether. We find that novice therapists are reassured by being given techniques such as grounding to enable them to help clients (e.g., trauma survivors) regulate their emotions in therapy, on the rare occasions this becomes necessary (see Johnson & Williams-Keeler, 1998, for an example). In the same way, novice therapists who are distrustful of attachment needs may find themselves subtly criticizing a partner's fragility. The cultural myths about attachment are that "needy" people have to "grow up," and that indulging their neediness will elicit a never-ending list of demands. On the contrary, it seems that when attachment needs and anxieties are denied or invalidated, they become distorted and exaggerated. Supervision or peer support groups that provide such therapists with a safe base can help them explore their own perspectives on emotional experience and attachment needs and desires.

A novice therapist also has to learn not to get lost in pragmatic issues and the content of interactions, but instead to focus on the process of interaction and the way inner experience evolves in that interaction. The therapist has to stay with the client rather than the model, and not try to push partners through steps when they are not ready for them. Sometimes it is when a therapist just stays with a client in his/her inability to move or change that new avenues open up. For example, when one frightened man was able to explicitly formulate his fear of commitment, and the therapist stood beside him in that fear, he was then able to become aware of the small voice telling him that all women would leave him, just as his first love had done on the eve of their wedding. As he grieved for this hurt and registered the helplessness he still felt with any woman who began to matter to him, his partner was able to comfort him. He then began to discover that he could address his fears with his present partner, and they began to subside. This process differed from a previous session, when the novice therapist had pushed the client to make a list of risks he was willing to take and when he would take them, only to find that he became even more withdrawn after this session.

Novice therapists may also have problems at first moving from intrapersonal to interpersonal levels. Therapists can get caught in the vagaries of inner experience and forget to use this experience to foster new steps in the dance. The purpose of expanding emotional experiences in EFT is to shape new interactions. The therapist has then to move into the "Can you tell him/her?" mode on a regular basis. Inexperienced therapists can also become caught in supporting one partner at the expense of the other. It is particularly important, for example, when one partner is moving and taking new risks, to validate the mate's initial mistrust of this, sense of disorientation, and inability to immediately respond to this new risk-taking behavior. When the caveats above are attended to, recent research (Denton et al., 2000) suggests that novice therapists can be effective using this model.

EFT AS A MODEL OF INTERVENTION FOR THE NEW MILLENNIUM

One of the clear strengths of the EFT model in the present social context is that its interventions are clearly delineated, but it still places these interventions in the context of the client's process and responses. It is not an invariant, mechanical set of techniques. It can address general patterns found across many relationships, as well as the unique-

ness of a particular couple's relationship. The need for efficient brief interventions also requires interventions to be on target. It requires that they reach the heart of the process of relationship repair. EFT formulations and interventions are consonant with recent research on the nature of distress and satisfaction in close relationships, and with the ever-expanding research on the nature of adult love and attachment relationships. In the present climate, it is also particularly pertinent that EFT interventions have been empirically validated and found to be effective with a large majority of distressed couples. Results seem to be relatively stable and resistant to relapse. This model appears, then, to be able to reach different kinds of couples in a brief format and to create clinically significant and lasting change.

A recent decade review of the field (Johnson & Lebow, 2000) points out that the utilization of couple interventions has increased enormously in the last decade, and that couple therapy is used more and more as a resource to augment the mental health of individual partners, particularly those who may be suffering from such problems as depression or PTSD. These two individual problems seem to be particularly associated with distress in close relationships (Whisman, 1999). As a client remarked, "Trying to deal with my depression without addressing my unhappy relationship with my wife is like pushing against both sides of the door. I never get anywhere." For individual changes to endure, they must also be supported in the client's natural environment (Gurman, 2001). EFT fits well into the emerging picture of couple therapy as a modality that can address and significantly affect "individual" problems, which are now more and more viewed in their interpersonal context.

EFT also seems to fit with the need for the field of couple therapy to develop conceptual coherence. We need conceptually clear treatment models that are linked not only to theories of close relationships, but also to pragmatic "if this . . . then that" interventions. Research into the process of change in this model offers a map of pivotal steps and change events to guide the couple therapist as he/she crafts specific interventions to help partners move toward achieving a more secure bond. One coherent theme that is emerging in the couple and family therapy field is a renewed respect for, and collaboration with, our clients. We learned and continue to learn how to do EFT from our clients. To echo Bowlby's (1980) words in the final volume of his attachment trilogy, we must therefore thank our clients, who have worked so hard to educate us.

REFERENCES

Anderson, H. (1997). *Conversation, language and possibilities*. New York: Basic Books.

Anderson, P., Beach, S., & Kaslow, N. (1999). Marital discord and depression: The potential of attachment theory to guide integrative clinical intervention. In T. Joiner & J. Coyne (Eds.), *The interactional nature of depression* (pp. 271–297). Washington, DC: American Psychiatric Press.

Atkinson, L. (1997). Attachment and psychopathology: From laboratory to clinic. In L. Atkinson & K. J. Zucker (Eds.), *Attachment and psychopathology* (pp. 3–16). New York: Guilford Press.

Bartholomew, K., & Perlman, D. (Eds.). (1994). *Advances in personal relationships: Vol 5. Attachment processes in adulthood* London: Jessica Kingsley.

Beach, S., Nelson, G. M., & O'Leary, K. (1988). Cognitive and marital factors in depression. *Journal of Psychopathology and Behavioral Assessment, 10,* 93–105.

Becker, E. (1973). *The denial of death*. New York: Free Press.

Bograd, M., & Mederos, F. (1999). Battering and couples therapy: Universal screening and selection of treatment modality. *Journal of Marital and Family Therapy, 25,* 291–312.

Bowlby, J. (1969). *Attachment and loss: Vol. 1. Attachment*. New York: Basic Books.

Bowlby, J. (1980). *Attachment and loss: Vol 3. Loss*. New York: Basic Books.

Bowlby, J. (1988). *A secure base*. New York: Basic Books.

Cassidy, J., & Shaver, P. (Eds.). (1999). *Handbook of attachment: Theory, research, and clinical applications*. New York: Guilford Press.

Coiro, M., & Gottesman, I. (1996). The diathesis and/or stressor role of EE in affective illness. *Clinical Psychology: Science and Practice, 3,* 310–322.

Davila, J., & Bradbury, T. (1999). *Attachment security in the development of depression and relationship distress*. Paper presented at the 33rd Annual Convention of the Association for Advancement of Behavior Therapy, Toronto.

Denton, W. H., Burleson, B. R., Clark, T. E., Rodriguez, C. P., & Hobbs, B. V. (2000). A randomized trial of emotion focused therapy for couples in a training clinic. *Journal of Marital and Family Therapy, 26,* 65–78.

Dessaulles, A. (1991). *The treatment of clinical depression in the context of marital distress*. Unpublished doctoral dissertation, University of Ottawa.

de Shazer, S. (1991). *Putting difference to work*. New York: Norton.

Dutton, D. G. (1995). *The batterer: A psychological profile*. New York: Basic Books.

Feeney, J. A., Noller, P., & Callan, V. J. (1994). Attachment style, communication and satisfaction in the early years of marriage. In K. Bartholomew & D. Perlman (Eds.), *Advances in personal relationships: Vol. 5.*

Attachment processes in adulthood (pp. 269–308). London: Jessica Kingsley.

Fisch, R., Weakland, J. H., & Segal, L. (1982). *The tactics of change: Doing therapy briefly*. San Francisco: Jossey-Bass.

Fonagy, P., & Target, M. (1997). Attachment and reflective function: Their role in self-organization. *Development and Psychopathology, 9,* 679–700.

Goldner, V. (1999). Morality and multiplicity: Perspectives on the treatment of violence in intimate life. *Journal of Marital and Family Therapy, 25,* 325–336.

Goleman, D. (1995). *Emotional intelligence*. New York: Bantam Books.

Gordon-Walker, J. (1994). *A marital intervention program for couples with chronically ill children*. Unpublished doctoral dissertation, University of Ottawa.

Gordon-Walker, J., Johnson, S. M., Manion, I., & Clothier, P. (1997). An emotionally focused marital intervention for couples with chronically ill children. *Journal of Consulting and Clinical Psychology, 64,* 1029–1036.

Gottman, J. M. (1979). *Marital interaction: Experimental investigations*. New York: Academic Press.

Gottman, J. M. (1994). *What predicts divorce?* Hillsdale, NJ: Erlbaum.

Gottman, J. M., Coan, J., Carrere, S., & Swanson, C. (1998). Predicting marital happiness and stability from newlywed interactions. *Journal of Marriage and the Family, 60,* 5–22.

Green, R. J., Bettinger, M., & Zacks, E. (1996). Are lesbian couples fused and gay male couples disengaged? In J. Laird & R. J. Green (Eds.), *Lesbians and gays in couples and families* (pp. 185–230). San Francisco: Jossey-Bass.

Greenberg, L. S., & Johnson, S. M. (1988). *Emotionally focused therapy for couples*. New York: Guilford Press.

Greenberg, L. S., & Paivio, S. (1997). *Working with emotions in psychotherapy*. New York: Guilford Press.

Greenberg, L. S., Watson, J. C., & Goldman, R. (1998). Process experiential therapy of depression. In L. S. Greenberg, J. C. Watson, & G. Lietaer (Eds.), *Handbook of experiential psychotherapy* (pp. 227–248). New York: Guilford Press.

Greenberg, L. S., Watson, J. C., & Lietaer, G. (Eds.). (1998). *Handbook of experiential psychotherapy* New York: Guilford Press.

Guerney, B. (1994). The role of emotion in relationship enhancement marital/family therapy. In S. M. Johnson & L. S. Greenberg (Eds.), *The heart of the matter: Perspectives on emotion in marital therapy* (pp. 124–150). New York: Brunner/Mazel.

Gurman, A. (2001). Brief therapy and family/couple therapy: An essential redundancy. *Clinical Psychology: Science and Practice, 8,* 51–65.

Haddock, S., Schindler Zimmerman, T., & MacPhee, D. (2000). The power equity guide: Attending to gender in family therapy. *Journal of Marital and Family Therapy, 26,* 153–170.

Hammen, C., Burge, D., Daley, S., Davila, J., Paley, B., & Rudolph, K. (1995). Interpersonal attachment cognitions and prediction of symptomatic responses to interpersonal stress. *Journal of Abnormal Psychology, 104,* 436–443.

Hazan, C., & Shaver, P. (1987). Conceptualizing romantic love as an attachment process. *Journal of Personality and Social Psychology, 52,* 511–524.

Hazan, C., & Zeifman, D. (1994). Sex and the psychological tether. In K. Bartholomew & D. Perlman (Eds.), *Advances in personal relationships: Vol. 5. Attachment processes in adulthood* (pp. 151–180). London: Jessica Kingsley.

Herman, J. (1992). *Trauma and recovery.* New York: Basic Books.

Hoffman, L. (1998). Setting aside the model in family therapy. *Journal of Marital and Family Therapy, 24,* 145–156.

Jackson, D. D. (1965). The study of the family. *Family Process, 4,* 1–20.

Jacobson, N. S., & Addis, M. E. (1993). Research on couples therapy: What do we know? Where are we going? *Journal of Consulting and Clinical Psychology, 61,* 85–93.

Jacobson, N. S., Follette, W. C., & Macdonald, D. (1982). Reactivity to positive and negative behavior in distressed and non-distressed married couples. *Journal of Consulting and Clinical Psychology, 50,* 706–714.

James, P. (1991). Effects of a communication component added to an emotionally focused couples therapy. *Journal of Marital and Family Therapy, 17,* 263–276.

Johnson, S. M. (1986). Bonds or bargains: Relationship paradigms and their significance for marital therapy. *Journal of Marital and Family Therapy, 12,* 259–267.

Johnson, S. M. (1996). *The practice of emotionally focused marital therapy: Creating connection.* New York: Brunner/Mazel.

Johnson, S. M. (1998b). Emotionally focused marital therapy: Using the power of emotion. In F. M. Dattilio (Ed.), *Case studies in couple and family therapy* (pp. 450–472). New York: Guilford Press.

Johnson, S. M. (1998a). Listening to the music: Emotion as a natural part of systems theory. *Journal of Systemic Therapies, 17,* 1–17.

Johnson, S. M. (1999). Emotionally focused couple therapy: Straight to the heart. In J. M. Donovan (Ed.), *Short-term couple therapy* (pp. 13–42). New York: Guilford Press.

Johnson, S. M. (in press). An antidote to post-traumatic stress disorder: The creation of secure attachment. In L. S. Atkinson (Ed.), *Attachment and psychopathology* (Vol. 2). Cambridge, England: Cambridge University Press.

Johnson, S. M. (2002). *Emotionally focused couple therapy with trauma survivors: Strengthening attachment bonds.* New York: Guilford Press.

Johnson, S. M., & Boisvert, C. (2002). Humanistic couple and family therapy. In D. Kane (Ed.), *Humanistic psychotherapies* (pp. 309–338). Washington, DC: American Psychological Association.

Johnson, S. M., & Greenberg, L. S. (1985). The differential effects of experiential and problem solving interventions in resolving marital conflict. *Journal of Consulting and Clinical Psychology, 53,* 175–184.

Johnson, S. M., & Greenberg, L. S. (1988). Relating process to outcome in marital therapy. *Journal of Marital and Family Therapy, 14,* 175–183.

Johnson, S. M., & Greenberg, L. S. (Eds.). (1994). *The heart of the matter: Perspectives on emotion in marital therapy.* New York: Brunner/Mazel.

Johnson, S. M., & Greenberg, L. S. (1995). The emotionally focused approach to problems in adult attachment. In N. S. Jacobson & A. S. Gurman (Eds.), *Clinical handbook of couple therapy,* (pp. 121–141). New York: Guilford Press.

Johnson, S. M., Hunsley, J., Greenberg, L., & Schlinder, D. (1999). Emotionally focused couples therapy: Status and challenges. *Journal of Clinical Psychology: Science and Practice, 6,* 67–79.

Johnson, S. M., & Lebow, J. (2000). The "coming of age" of couple therapy: A decade review. *Journal of Marital and Family Therapy, 26,* 23–38.

Johnson, S. M., Maddeaux, C., & Blouin, J. (1998). Emotionally focused family therapy for bulimia: Changing attachment patterns. *Psychotherapy, 35,* 238–247.

Johnson, S. M., Makinen, J., & Millikin, J. (2001). Attachment injuries in couple relationships: A new perspective on impasses in couples therapy. *Journal of Marital and Family Therapy, 27,* 145–155.

Johnson, S. M., & Talitman, E. (1997). Predictors of success in emotionally focused marital therapy. *Journal of Marital and Family Therapy, 23,* 135–152.

Johnson, S. M., & Whiffen, V. (1999). Made to measure: Adapting emotionally focused couple therapy to partners attachment styles. *Clinical Psychology: Science and Practice, 6,* 366–381.

Johnson, S. M., & Williams-Keeler, L. (1998). Creating healing relationships for couples dealing with trauma: The use of emotionally focused marital therapy. *Journal of Marital and Family Therapy, 24,* 227–236.

Jordan, J. V., Kaplan, A. G., Miller, J. B., Stiver, L. P., & Surrey, J. L. (1991). *Women's growth in connection: Writings from the Stone Center.* New York: Guilford Press.

Kennedy-Moore, E., & Watson, J. (1999). *Expressing emotion: Myths, realities, and therapeutic strategies.* New York: Guilford Press.

Kobak, R., & Cole, H. (1991). Attachment and meta-monitoring: Implications for autonomy and psychopathology. In D. Cicchetti & S. Toth (Eds.), *Disorders and dysfunctions of the self* (pp. 267–297). Rochester, NY: University of Rochester Press.

Kobak, R., & Hazan, C. (1991). Attachment in marriage: Effects of security and accuracy of working models. *Journal of Personality and Social Psychology, 60,* 861–869.

Koerner, K., & Jacobson, N. (1994). Emotion and behavioral couple therapy. In S. M. Johnson & L. S. Greenberg (Eds.), *The heart of the matter: Perspectives on emotion in marital therapy* (pp. 207–226). New York: Brunner/Mazel.

Knudson-Martin, C., & Mahoney, A. (1999). Beyond different worlds: A post gender approach to relationship development. *Family Process, 38,* 325–340.

Lebow, J. (1997). The integrative revolution in couple and family therapy. *Family Process, 36,* 1–17.

MacPhee, D. C., Johnson, S. M., & van der Veer, M. C. (1995). Low sexual desire in women: The effects of marital therapy. *Journal of Sex and Marital Therapy, 21,* 159–182.

Mahoney, M. (1991). *Human change processes.* New York: Basic Books.

Main, M., & Hesse, E. (1990). Parents' unresolved traumatic experiences are related to infant disorganized attachment status. In M. Greenberg, D. Cicchetti, & E. M. Cummings (Eds.), *Attachment in the preschool years* (pp. 161–182). Chicago: University of Chicago Press.

Main, M., Kaplan, N., & Cassidy, J. (1985). Security in infancy, childhood and adulthood: A move to the level of representation. In I. Bretherton & E. Waters (Eds.),

Growing points of attachment theory and research. *Monographs of the Society for Research in Child Development*, *50*(1–2, Serial No. 209), 66–104.

Martin, J., & Sugarman, J. (2000). Between modern and postmodern. *American Psychologist*, *55*, 397–406.

McFarlane, A.C., & van der Kolk, B. A. (1996). Trauma and its challenge to society. In B. van der Kolk, A. McFarlane, & L. Weisaeth (Eds.), *Traumatic stress* (pp. 24–46). New York: Guilford Press.

McLeod, J., Kessler, R., & Landis, K. (1992). Speed of recovery from major depressive episodes in a community sample of married men and women. *Journal of Abnormal Psychology*, *101*, 277–286.

Mesquita, B., & Frijda, N. (1992). Cultural variations in emotions: A review. *Psychological Bulletin*, *112*, 179–204.

Mikulincer, M. (1995). Attachment style and the mental representation of self. *Journal of Personality and Social Psychology*, *69*, 1203–1215.

Mikulincer, M. (1997). Adult attachment style and information processing: Individual differences in curiosity and cognitive closure. *Journal of Personality and Social Psychology*, *72*, 1217–1230.

Mikulincer, M. (1998). Adult attachment style and individual differences in functional versus dysfunctional experiences of anger. *Journal of Personality and Social Psychology*, *74*, 513–524.

Millikin, J., & Johnson, S. M. (2000). Telling tales: Disquisitions in emotionally focused therapy. *Journal of Family Psychotherapy*, *11*, 75–79.

Minuchin, S., & Fishman, H. C. (1981). *Family therapy techniques*. Cambridge, MA: Harvard University Press.

Neimeyer, R. (1993). An appraisal of constructivist psychotherapies. *Journal of Consulting and Clinical Psychology*, *61*, 221–234.

Orlinsky, D., Grawe, K., & Parks, B. (1994). Process and outcome in psychotherapy. In A. E. Bergin & S. L. Garfield (Eds.), *Handbook of psychotherapy and behavior change* (4th ed., pp. 270–376). New York: Wiley.

Palmer, G., & Johnson, S. M. (2002). Becoming an emotionally focused couple therapist. *Journal of Couple and Relationship Therapy*, *3*, 1–6.

Perls, F., Hefferline, R., & Goldman, P. (1951). *Gestalt therapy*. New York: Dell.

Roberts, T. W. (1992). Sexual attraction and romantic love: Forgotten variables in marital therapy. *Journal of Marital and Family Therapy*, *18*, 357–364.

Rogers, C. R. (1951). *Client-centered therapy*. Boston: Houghton Mifflin.

Salovey, P., Rothman, A. J., Detweiler, J. B., & Stewart, W. T. (2000). Emotional states and physical health, *American Psychologist*, *55*, 110–1421.

Satir, V. (1967). *Conjoint family therapy*. Palo Alto, CA: Science & Behavior Books.

Schore, A. (1994). *Affect regulation and the organization of self*. Hillsdale, NJ: Erlbaum.

Schwartz, R., & Johnson, S. M. (2000). Does couple and family therapy have emotional intelligence? *Family Process*, *39*, 29–34.

Shapiro, V. (1996). Subjugated knowledge and the working alliance. *In Session: Psychotherapy in Practice*, *1*, 9–22.

Simpson, J. A., & Rholes, W. S. (1994). Stress and secure base relationships in adulthood. In K. Bartholomew & D. Perlman (Eds.), *Advances in personal relationships: Vol. 5. Attachment processes in adulthood* (pp. 181–204). London: Jessica Kingsley.

Simpson, J. A., Rholes, W. S., & Nelligan, J. S. (1992). Support seeking and support giving within couples in an anxiety provoking situation: The role of attachment styles. *Journal of Personality and Social Psychology*, *62*, 434–446.

Spanier, G. B. (1976). Measuring dyadic adjustment: New scales for assessing the quality of marriage and similar dyads. *Journal of Marriage and the Family*, *38*, 15–28.

Sprenkle, D., Blow, A., & Dickey, M. H. (1999). Common factors and other non-technique variables in marriage and family therapy. In M. Hubble, B. Duncan, & C. Miller (Eds.), *The heart and soul of change* (pp. 329–359). Washington, DC: American Psychological Association.

Teichman, Y., & Teichman, M. (1990). Interpersonal views of depression: Review and integration. *Family Psychology*, *3*, 349–367.

Tomkins, S. (1962). *Affect, imagery and consciousness* (2 vols.). New York: Springer.

van der Kolk, B., Perry, C., & Herman, J. (1991). Childhood origins of self-destructive behavior. *American Journal of Psychiatry*, *148*, 1665–1671.

van Ijzendoorn, M. H., & Sagi, A. (1999). Cross-cultural patterns of attachment: Universal and contextual dimensions. In J. Cassidy & P. Shaver (Eds.), *Handbook of attachment: Theory, research, and clinical applications* (pp. 713–734). New York: Guilford Press.

Vatcher, C. A., & Bogo, M. (2001). The feminist/emotionally focused therapy practice model. *Journal of Marital Family Therapy*, *27*, 69–84.

von Bertalanffy, L. (1956). General system theory. *General Systems Yearbook*, *1*, 1–10.

Watzlawick, P., Beavin, J., & Jackson, D. (1967). *Pragmatics of human communication*. New York: Norton.

Weeks, G. R., & L'Abate, L. (1979). A compilation of paradoxical methods. *American Journal of Family Therapy*, *7*, 61–76.

Weinfield, N. S., Sroufe, L. A., Egeland, B., & Carlson, E. A. (1999). The nature of individual differences in infant–caregiver attachment. In J. Cassidy & P. Shaver (Eds.), *Handbook of attachment: Theory, research, and clinical applications* (pp. 68–88). New York: Guilford Press.

Weissman, M. M. (1987). Advances in psychiatric epidemiology: Rates and risks for major depression. *American Journal of Public Health*, *77*, 445–451.

Whiffen, V., & Johnson, S. (1998). An attachment theory framework for the treatment of child bearing depression. *Clinical Psychology: Science and Practice*, *5*, 478–493.

Whisman, M. (1999). Marital dissatisfaction and psychiatric disorders: Results from the National Comorbidity Survey. *Journal of Abnormal Psychology*, *108*, 701–706.

Whisman, M., & Jacobson, N. S. (1990). Power, marital satisfaction and response to marital therapy. *Journal of Family Psychology*, *4*, 202–212.

Wile, D. B. (1995). The ego-analytic approach to couple therapy. In N. S. Jacobson & A. S. Gurman (Eds.), *Clinical handbook of couple therapy* (pp. 91–120). New York: Guilford Press.

Chapter 9

Integrative Behavioral Couple Therapy

SONA DIMIDJIAN
CHRISTOPHER R. MARTELL
ANDREW CHRISTENSEN

Integrative behavioral couple therapy (IBCT), developed by Andrew Christensen and Neil S. Jacobson, has its roots in careful clinical observation and empirical research on the treatment of distressed couples. It is a contextually based behavioral treatment designed to help couples achieve improved satisfaction and adjustment. An innovative treatment, IBCT was first presented in published form in an earlier edition of this *Handbook* (Christensen, Jacobson, & Babcock, 1995). Since then, a detailed treatment manual for therapists has been published (Jacobson & Christensen, 1996), as has a guide for use by couples (Christensen & Jacobson, 2000).

IBCT grew principally from traditional behavioral couple therapy (TBCT), a widely practiced treatment that is perhaps best summarized in the now-classic text *Marital Therapy: Strategies Based on Social Learning and Behavior Exchange Principles* (Jacobson & Margolin, 1979). TBCT is a skill-based, change-oriented treatment, which relies on two primary intervention components: (1) behavior exchange (BE) and (2) communication/problem-solving training (CPT). BE seeks to increase the ratio of positive to negative couple behaviors and is intended to produce rapid decreases in couples' distress. BE, however, is not believed to give rise to long-lasting change, as such interventions do not teach couples the skills that are necessary to address problems in the future. In con-

trast, the second set of interventions prescribed by TBCT, CPT, is designed to teach couples skills that they can use long after treatment has ended. These skills are intended to help couples change fundamental relationship patterns in ways that will protect them from distress for years to come.

Since its early development (e.g., Jacobson & Margolin, 1979), TBCT has become one of the most widely investigated treatments for couple distress. Currently it is unparalleled in its documented success, with over 20 studies attesting to its efficacy (Baucom, Shoham, Mueser, Daiuto, & Stickle, 1998; Christensen & Heavey, 1999; Hahlweg & Markman, 1988; Jacobson & Addis, 1993). In fact, TBCT remains the only couple therapy to date that meets the most stringent criteria for empirically supported treatments—namely, efficacy and specificity (Baucom et al., 1998).

And yet, despite such impressive acclaim, by the mid-1980s Jacobson and colleagues were growing increasingly skeptical of the success of TBCT. They were unsettled by their clinical experience with couples—and by what a careful examination of the empirical data was saying. Jacobson and colleagues had begun to consider not only the statistical significance of the efficacy of TBCT, but the clinical significance as well. In 1984, Jacobson et al. published what was to become a landmark paper in the field of couple therapy. This paper presented a reanalysis of the outcome data on

TBCT and suggested that TBCT was limited in its ability to produce clinically meaningful change. Specifically, Jacobson et al. (1984) reported that about one-half of couples had improved over the course of treatment, but only one-third had moved into the nondistressed range of functioning. Moreover, among those couples that did improve during treatment, one-third experienced a relapse of their distress during the 2-year follow-up period (Jacobson, Schmaling, & Holtzworth-Munroe, 1987). Empirical examinations of the types of couples that benefited most from TBCT were also informative. In particular, it appeared that couples were more likely to respond favorably to TBCT if the partners were less distressed, were younger, were not emotionally disengaged, were not experiencing concurrent individual problems (e.g., depression), and did not have a relationship based on rigidly structured traditional gender roles (Jacobson & Addis, 1993).

These empirical data were consistent with the clinical experiences of Jacobson and Christensen. In their work with couples, they had noticed that TBCT did not appear to be as effective with couples struggling with issues of compromise, collaboration, and accommodation. Christensen and Jacobson began to wonder whether a spirit of compromise was the unifying thread among the characteristics research had found common to couples that responded best to TBCT. Christensen and Jacobson also noticed that certain types of problems did not seem to be well served by the TBCT technology. In particular, problems that represented basic and irreconcilable differences between partners appeared to be less amenable to traditional change strategies. And yet they found that many couples with such intractable problems were still committed to improving their relationships.

Thus, for some couples and some problems, it became increasingly clear that TBCT's emphasis on promoting change seemed to be a poor fit for what the couples needed. In some cases, interventions designed to promote change actually seemed to exacerbate the couples' distress. Christensen and Jacobson began to hypothesize about what was missing from the available treatment technology. For each case, it became clear that the recipe for success was not an increased emphasis on change—but an increased emphasis on acceptance. In their view, acceptance was in effect "the missing link" in TBCT (Jacobson & Christensen, 1996, p. 11).

What is "acceptance," and why is it so important in the resolution of couple distress? First, it is important to note what acceptance is not. Acceptance

is not a grudging resignation about the state of one's relationship. It is not a woeful surrender to a miserable status quo. In contrast, acceptance provides a hopeful alternative for couples faced with problems that are not amenable to typical change strategies. Moreover, acceptance can provide a method by which couples can use problems—once experienced as divisive and damaging—as vehicles for greater intimacy and closeness.

THE HEALTHY VERSUS DISTRESSED COUPLE

IBCT is based on a fundamentally different understanding of relationship distress from that which underlies TBCT and many other therapeutic models. IBCT proposes that over time, even the happiest and healthiest couples will face areas of difference and disagreement, which are assumed to be both normal and inevitable. Distress thus is not caused by such differences, disagreements, or conflicts between partners. In contrast, distress is caused by the ways that some couples respond to these inevitable incompatibilities. In particular, three destructive patterns of response are frequently found among distressed couples: "mutual coercion," "vilification," and "polarization."

In the early phases of a relationship, acceptance and tolerance of difference come easily to many couples. In fact, in many relationships, partners cite each other's differences as the source of their attraction. Lisa, for instance, recalled being enamored of Bruce's outspoken and direct nature, whereas Bruce recalled being impressed with the way that Lisa considered issues carefully before rendering her opinions. Thus, during partners' early days together, these differences are less often experienced as threatening or problematic for the relationship; when such differences do create difficulty, partners often find that their willingness to compromise with each other is high.

Over time, however, some couples experience an erosion in the partner's willingness to accept, tolerate, and compromise around their differences. They no longer look upon each other's styles as sources of attraction, and they begin to exert efforts to change each other. Unfortunately, these efforts are often characterized by negative and coercive behavior (e.g., criticizing, withdrawing, yelling, etc.). As these patterns of mutual coercion become more frequent and common, partners begin to see each other not as different but as deficient. In essence, they begin to vilify each other. Therefore, Lisa was no longer one who carefully considered things; instead, she was "controlling and withholding." Bruce, on the other hand, was defined as "impulsive and insensitive." As vilification increases, each partner feels increasingly justified in his/her efforts to reform the wayward other. As a result, these differences tend to intensify or polarize, and the chasm between the two grows wider and wider. Therefore, through mutual coercion, vilification, and polarization, distress is generated not by the differences between partners, but by partners' attempts to eliminate such differences.

Research has provided substantial support for major components of this model of relationship distress. For example, cross-sectional research comparing distressed with nondistressed couples (e.g., Weiss & Heyman, 1997) and longitudinal research examining the predictors of distress (e.g., Karney & Bradbury, 1995) have documented the role of reciprocal, negative, coercive interaction in relationship distress. Also, research on cognitive factors has repeatedly confirmed the role of negative views of the partner (e.g., negative attributions) in relationship distress (e.g, Noller, Beach, & Osgarby, 1997).

In contrast to distressed couples, happy couples are able to confront their differences with greater acceptance and tolerance. They are not drawn into patterns of coercion, vilification, and polarization. They are able to maintain their positive connection despite (and, at times, maybe even because of) the partners' differences. Perhaps their differences are not as great; perhaps their individual personalities are not as threatened by differences; or perhaps there is greater social support for their union. The research says little about the processes by which couples that are uniformly happy at the beginning travel different trajectories, which lead some to discord and separation and others to stable and fulfilling unions.

THEORY OF THERAPEUTIC CHANGE

As its name indicates, IBCT is a behavioral therapy. In their writings about the approach, Christensen and Jacobson (2000; Jacobson & Christensen, 1996) acknowledge the behavioral roots of their approach. However, they also acknowledge other influences, particularly the work of Daniel Wile (e.g., Wile, 1988). Some may see similarities between Wile's ideas and particular strategies in IBCT. Also, there are similarities between IBCT strategies and strategies in other approaches. For

example, some of our tolerance interventions are similar to techniques in strategic therapy, and our acceptance intervention of empathic joining is similar to client-centered strategies and strategies in emotion-focused therapy. However, what marks IBCT as unique is not only that the strategies are conducted differently and for different purposes in IBCT, but that all the strategies in IBCT come from a behavioral theoretical perspective. We call IBCT an integrative approach because it integrates strategies for change with strategies for acceptance. However, it is also an integrative *behavioral* approach because it integrates a variety of interventions within a coherent behavioral perspective.

Both TBCT and IBCT are distinctly behavioral theories because both view behavior and any changes in that behavior as a function of the context in which the behavior occurs. In a romantic relationship, the primary (although by no means exclusive) context is the partners' behavior. Therefore, each member's behavior is responsive to the context provided by the other's behavior, as well as to other significant features of the context (e.g., the larger family context that includes a critical in-law, an out-of-control child, etc.). The goal of TBCT is to change this context by changing the agents of behavior. For example, if there is dissatisfaction because a husband is too negative or a wife is not affectionate enough, then the goal is to increase the husband's positivity and the wife's affection. BE and CPT are the means by which TBCT achieves those changes. Evidence has supported this theory of change (Jacobson, 1984).

In contrast to TBCT, IBCT focuses as much or more on the recipient of behavior as it does on the agent of behavior. The context can change as a result not only of the agent's altering the frequency or intensity of behavior, but also of the recipient's receiving the behavior differently. In the example above, if the wife is more accepting of her husband's negativity and does not take it so personally, or the husband is more understanding of his wife's lack of affection and is not offended by it, then the context of their relationship and their sentiment about it will also change.

There are two major reasons for the shift in emphasis in IBCT from the agent to the recipient of behavior. First, IBCT believes that in every relationship there are some "unsolvable" problems in which the agent is unwilling or unable to change to the extent that the recipient desires. Improvement in these cases will be mediated by increased acceptance and tolerance. Second, IBCT suggests that, paradoxically, increased acceptance in one partner may at times also mediate increased change. In this way, IBCT suggests that at times, it may be the pressure for change from one partner that contributes to the maintenance of the undesirable partner behavior. Thus, when the pressure to change is eliminated by increased acceptance or tolerance, change may follow. As partners let go of their efforts to change each other, they become less emotionally reactive, and as a result, change becomes more likely.

IBCT not only has a different focus of change from TBCT (the recipient versus the agent of behavior); it also has a different strategy or mechanism of change from TBCT. In TBCT the mechanism of change is through "rule-governed" behavior, whereas in IBCT the primary mechanism of change is through "contingency-shaped" behavior. Skinner's (1966) important distinction between these two mechanisms refers to what controls the behavior in question. In rule-governed behavior, an individual is given a rule to follow and is reinforced for following it or is punished for not following it. Reinforcement depends on the degree to which the behavior parallels the rule. For example, if a member of a couple were to engage in a positive behavior toward his/her partner because the therapist has prescribed the task (i.e., rule) "Do one nice thing for your partner each day," his/her behavior would be shaped by the rule rather than by anything in the natural environment. Rule-governed behavior is often, although not always, reinforced arbitrarily. In other words, the conditions under which the individual will be reinforced (i.e., following the rule) and the reinforcer (e.g., a reciprocal behavior on the part of the partner, therapist praise) are specified in advance. In contrast, contingency-shaped behavior is determined by the natural consequences of doing the behavior. For example, if a partner contacts his/her feelings of tenderness for the other partner and does "one nice thing," the behavior is shaped not by a rule, but by natural contingencies in the couple's environment. In this case, the behavior is reinforced by the experience itself and its consequences (e.g., the partner's genuine surprise and thanks).

In TBCT, change is created through attention to rule-governed behavior, using the strategies of BE and CPT. TBCT is founded on the assumption that the rules prescribed or generated by BE and/or CPT will generate positive behavior, and that this behavior will provide its own reinforcement over time, thereby maintaining the rules. The theory of IBCT, however, challenges these assumptions of TBCT and suggests that enduring

changes are more likely to result from shifts in the natural contingencies operating in couples' lives than from generating rule-governed behaviors. Importantly, rule-governed behavior often "feels" different (i.e., less genuine, less authentic) from contingency-shaped behavior. For instance, a kiss from one's partner upon awakening in the morning, which is generated by a spontaneous feeling of attraction, is often experienced differently from a kiss that is generated by an intervention prescribed during therapy to "express more physical intimacy to each other."

Furthermore, many changes that couples cite as goals for therapy are not easily achieved by a focus on rule-governed behavioral changes. Whereas it may be fairly straightforward to address a partner's desire for more help with housework by negotiating new rules for housecleaning, it is much more difficult to address desired emotional changes with rule-governed behavior. For example, if one partner wants the other to "be more enthusiastic about sex" or to "have more genuine interest in me," it is not clear how therapy could address these issues with negotiation about rules.

Therefore, IBCT focuses on making changes in the natural contingencies that occur during a couple's life. The therapist becomes a part of the context of the couple's interactions within the session, and the interventions used by the therapist create a different experience for the couple than the partners have experienced on their own. For instance, rather than teaching the partners that they should not blame or criticize each other (a rule), the IBCT therapist models noncritical behavior by validating each partner's perspective. Instead of teaching the partners to talk openly about their feelings (another rule), the therapist suggests possible feelings associated with each partner's comments during sessions—particularly so-called "soft" feelings, such as hurt, sadness, and loneliness, as opposed to anger, hostility, and other "harder" emotions. In these and other ways discussed in detail below, the IBCT therapist may work to increase the frequency of positive behavior or improve a couple's communication and problem-solving skills; however, the therapist is consistently seeking to generate these shifts by modifying the context of the couple's life rather than by teaching the partners new rules. Each intervention in IBCT is guided by this emphasis on using the natural contingencies of the couple's life to engage the partners in a new experience that will shift their behavior both in and outside sessions.

Finally, the IBCT theory of change also suggests that the successful practice of IBCT will depend heavily on particular clinical skills and attributes, which are reviewed below (see the discussion of the therapist's role). Because outcome studies to date have employed highly trained and skilled therapists, the role of these qualities in the process or outcome of change has not been independently tested; nevertheless, the theory of IBCT posits that therapist attributes and the couple–therapist relationship are central to the practice of competent IBCT.

Because IBCT has only recently been developed, there is little evidence investigating its theory of change. However, one study has documented that couples treated with TBCT and IBCT demonstrated significant differences in the types of interactional changes observed over the course of treatment (Cordova, Jacobson, & Christensen, 1998). For example, observations of early, middle, and late therapy sessions indicated that couples receiving IBCT expressed more "soft" emotions and more nonblaming descriptions of problems during late stages of therapy than did couples receiving TBCT.

THE ASSESSMENT OF COUPLE FUNCTIONING

A comprehensive and structured assessment process provides the foundation for all future interventions in IBCT. Typically, the assessment phase is structured to involve three or four sessions, which include an initial conjoint meeting with the couple, individual sessions with each partner, and a conjoint feedback session in which the results of the assessment are discussed and a plan for treatment is developed. Optimally, the therapist will also have each partner complete a battery of questionnaires prior to the first conjoint meeting. Self-report questionnaires provide invaluable information for the therapist and can be easily mailed to the couple prior to the first session. The questionnaires we have found to be particularly helpful, and each questionnaire's intended usage, are as follows:

- The Dyadic Adjustment Scale (DAS; Spanier, 1976): A useful global measure of couple satisfaction.
- The Frequency and Acceptability of Partner Behavior (FAPB) Scale (Christensen & Jacobson, 1997): Measures both the frequency of problem behaviors and the degree of dissatisfaction partners feel about such behaviors.
- The Marital Satisfaction Inventory–Revised (MSI-R; Snyder, 1997): Profiles relationship distress in nine general areas for each spouse; also provides a Global Distress score that is a helpful complement to the DAS.
- The Marital Status Inventory (Weiss & Cerreto, 1980): Measures the number of specific steps a partner has taken toward divorce or separation.
- The Conflict Tactics Scale (Straus, 1979): A widely used measure of domestic violence.
- The Spouse Observation Checklist (Weiss, Hops, & Patterson, 1973): Assesses the presence of positive and negative couple behaviors and associated levels of satisfaction.

The foundation of any truly behavioral assessment process is the functional analysis, in which a clinician examines a problematic behavior and finds what stimuli it is a function of. With that information, the clinician can then alter the controlling stimuli and change the problematic behavior. In marriage, the problematic behaviors are negative feelings and evaluations of the relationship that participants often voice to themselves and others (and rate on our measures of relationship satisfaction). Both TBCT and IBCT conduct a functional analysis of this distress, seeking the events that give rise to it. However, assessment in TBCT typically focuses on defining specific, discrete, and observable actions or inactions that partners mention as problematic. For example, one partner may mention that the other watches too much television. In a sense, assessment in TBCT highlights the "topography" of the behaviors that couples cite as problematic; therefore, the therapist learns a great deal about the size and shape of particular behaviors (e.g., how often and for how much time the partner watches television). Unfortunately, as Christensen et al. (1995) suggest, this approach risks eclipsing the "true, important controlling variables in marital interaction" (p. 35) with a focus on variables that are in fact only derivatives of the controlling ones. This risk is particularly salient in couple therapy, given that most couples present with a wide array of seemingly disparate complaints.

In contrast, assessment in IBCT aims to highlight the function as opposed to the topography of behavior. Therefore, the therapist seeks to understand the variables that control dissatisfaction, which are more often broad response classes of behavior (or themes, as we discuss below) than derivative variables. This emphasis on broad classes of controlling variables allows the IBCT therapist to see the common thread in diverse complaints and problems. For instance, Eva may complain that

Dillon spends too much time watching television, but she may also become angry when he goes hiking with friends. In TBCT, these derivative variables would be specified and behaviorally pinpointed as problems for the couple to address. However, in doing the functional analysis and emphasizing broad response classes, the IBCT therapist is able to see the theme of responsibility in Eva's complaints: Actions by Dillon that leave family responsibilities to her are distressing.

A functional analysis in IBCT emphasizes not only the broad class of behaviors by the "agent" that are a source of dissatisfaction for the recipient, but also the reactions of the recipient partner. For example, for Eva these behaviors by Dillon are reminiscent of her past, when she was often left by her working parents to care for her younger siblings, and rouse similar feelings of abandonment and unfairness in her.

How is a functional analysis conducted? Ideally, a therapist conducts a functional analysis by manipulating the conditions that are antecedent or consequent to the behavior and observing the behavioral response to such manipulations. Unfortunately, however, couple therapists do not have experimental control over the conditions that control couples' interactions, so their ability to conduct a functional analysis is limited in a number of ways (Christensen et al., 1995). First, a therapist must rely on a couple's report of behavior and cannot directly observe the conditions surrounding the behavior. Second, people have idiosyncratic learning histories, and diverse stimulus conditions can serve similar functions. For example, Mike may become angry when Ruth gives him the silent treatment, but he may also become angry when Ruth tells him how she feels about his behavior. Thus two different stimulus conditions—Ruth's silence and Ruth's talking—serve the same function of eliciting an angry response in Mike. Third, the therapist cannot directly influence the conditions of the couple's lives. Because of these limitations, the IBCT therapist tries to become aware of the specific problems that maintain a couple's distress, but also emphasizes the broad themes and response classes (hypothesized in the formulation) that are at work in the couple's interactions.

The primary goal of the functional analysis is the development of a case formulation and a resultant treatment plan. In IBCT, the formulation consists of three primary components: the "theme," the "polarization process," and the "mutual trap."

As noted above, the "theme" describes the function of each partner's behavior in regard to conflict areas. The theme is the broad class of behavior that serves as a basic unifying link between apparently disparate areas. In this way, the theme describes the group of behaviors in which each partner engages that serves a similar overriding function in the relationship. Thus, although the IBCT therapist continues to seek behavioral specificity in the assessment process, this aim is balanced by the need to attend to the *linkages* between problem behaviors. For instance, the "closeness–distance" theme is one of the most commonly observed themes among couples seeking treatment. In a couple characterized by this theme, one partner (often the female partner) will seek greater closeness, while the other (often the male partner) will seek greater distance.

Jack and Suzanna, for example, had struggled with the theme of closeness and distance throughout their 26 years of marriage. Jack prided himself on the values of autonomy, independence, and a stalwart approach to life. Suzanna, in contrast, valued open communication, connection, and closeness. Although they argued about many specific issues, ranging from what time Jack returned home from work in the evening to Suzanna's frustration with Jack's stoic response to her recent diagnosis of breast cancer, the function of each of their behaviors was consistent. Whether it was by staying late at work or retreating to his workshop at home, Jack sought greater distance. Whether it was by planning shared outings or tearfully expressing her frustration, Suzanna sought greater closeness. Thus the basic theme of closeness–distance remained consistent and captured the essential *function* of each of their behaviors.

In addition to the closeness–distance theme, some examples of other themes common to couples in therapy include the "control-and-responsibility" theme (in which couples argue about who maintains control and responsibility over particular domains of the relationship), and the "artist–scientist" theme (in which arguments surround one partner's tendency to value spontaneity and adventure and the other's tendency to value predictability and goal attainment). It is, however, important to emphasize that this list is not exhaustive; there are countless themes (and variations on themes) among couples. This discussion is merely intended to provide some examples of frequently observed themes among couples and the ways in which such themes can serve to unify a range of seemingly disparate conflicts.

The "polarization process" refers to the interaction patterns that are initiated when conflict around a theme occurs. Themes typically involve some expression of difference in a couple. Often when partners contend with conflicts about their central theme, they assume that these basic differences are the problem and that eliminating such differences is the necessary solution. Unfortunately, partners' attempts at eliminating these differences often have the unintended effect of strengthening—or polarizing—the differences even more! Thus the polarization process refers to the ways in which partners' efforts to change each other drive them farther apart. As polarization continues, these basic differences become further entrenched and are experienced as intractable and irreconcilable. The "mutual trap" refers to this effect, highlighting the impact of the polarization process on both partners. Both partners feel stuck, discouraged, without hope—in a word, trapped.

A good formulation includes a careful description of the theme, the polarization process, and the mutual trap. However, the success of a formulation is not determined by the presence of these elements alone. The success of the formulation is evaluated primarily according to what has been called the "pragmatic truth criterion" (Pepper, 1942): Namely, does it work? If a formulation "works," it will be a helpful organizing concept for the couple—one that the partners will integrate into their understanding of their relationship, and that will help to diminish blame and criticism and increase their readiness for acceptance and change. In contrast, an unsuccessful formulation will fail to serve as such a central organizing concept; the partners will not feel understood by the presentation of the formulation and will not integrate it into the basic vocabulary of their relationship. Although all formulations will be modified and expanded in an ongoing and iterative fashion throughout the course of treatment, the core of the formulation will be developed during the assessment phase of treatment. Both the structure and the content of the assessment phase have been carefully designed to facilitate the development of the formulation.

Overall, six primary questions are used to guide the assessment phase and to ensure that the therapist gathers information central to the development of the formulation. These are as follows: (1) How distressed is this couple? (2) How committed is this couple to the relationship? (3) What are the issues that divide the partners? (4) Why are these issues such a problem for them? (5) What are the strengths holding them together? (6) What can treatment do to help them?

These questions are explored both during the conjoint interview and in the individual interviews, and the information gathered is then summarized during the feedback session. These components of the assessment phase are discussed in turn below.

The First Conjoint Interview

During the first interview, it is important for the therapist to socialize the couple to the treatment model, establish trust, and instill hope. In order to socialize the couple, the therapist should explain the structure of the therapy, focusing in particular on the distinction between the assessment and treatment phases of the model. It is important to help both partners anticipate the sequence of the upcoming sessions, and to remind them that treatment goals and an overall agreement regarding therapy will be the focus of the feedback session. Carefully explaining the separation of the assessment and treatment phases of IBCT is often helpful when one or both partners have some hesitation about beginning treatment; therefore, the very structure of IBCT helps to honor and respect what is often the very natural ambivalence that partners experience.

The overall goal of the first interview is to achieve a successful balance between focusing on the couple's current presenting problem and focusing on the partners' relationship history. It is important for the therapist to understand what types of problems and conflicts bring the couple into treatment at the present time. Moreover, partners often enter the first session wanting and expecting to talk about their dissatisfactions and disappointments. It is critical for them to leave the first session feeling heard, understood, and supported by the therapist. Therefore, the therapist should ask about the content of the problems as well as basic interaction processes that occur when conflict arises. In addition, the therapist should be alert for precursors of the present problem in the couple's history (e.g., particular stressors the couple experienced in the past).

At the same time, however, it is important for the therapist to balance attention to these areas with a focus on the couple's history. Probing for information about how the couple behaves when things are going well, obtaining a history of initial attractions, and allowing each partner time to talk about times when their relationship was rewarding is critical for the development of the formulation. Unless the couple never had such a time and/or the partners came together for reasons other than love and romance, these strategies allow the therapist to begin setting the stage for a different kind of communication between the partners from the very first interview. Moreover, focusing on these areas helps to minimize the risk of increasing the couple's hopelessness, which may occur if the first session focuses exclusively on the presenting problem.

When discussing the relationship history, the therapist should inquire about the partners' early attraction to each other. Important questions may include these: "How did you meet?" "What was your courtship like?" "What was your relationship like before problems began?" "What initially attracted you to each other?" Often the initial attraction will be a central component of the formulation, as partners find that the qualities that attracted them initially are the very same ones that later cause distress and conflict. To inquire about relationship strengths, the therapist will want to inquire about strengths present in the early phases of the relationship and will want to ask about how things go when they are going well currently. For instance, the therapist may ask, "What were the parts of your relationship that worked well when you were first together?" "What parts of your relationship were you proud of?" "How is the relationship different now during times that you are getting along?" In addition, the therapist will want to focus on possible strengths and hopes for the future. It may be helpful to ask each partner how their relationship would be different if the problems that currently exist were no longer present.

Finally, we often close the initial conjoint meeting by assigning the first part of the IBCT manual for couples, *Reconcilable Differences* (Christensen & Jacobson, 2000). This reading assignment will help to engage the partners in the treatment process and further socialize them to the model. Couples often recognize themselves in the case examples, and the book may help them to consider their problems in light of the formulation proposed by the therapist during the upcoming feedback session. In addition, the couple's success at completing this first assignment will provide important information for the therapist about the partners' level of motivation and commitment to therapy.

Individual Interviews

In IBCT, the therapist meets individually with each partner of the couple. Ideally, the therapist brings each partner in for a full 50-minute session. How-

ever, there are times when financial constraints or limitations of insurance plans make it difficult for a couple to come for two full sessions. Nevertheless, the therapist must stress that at least a split session is important as part of the assessment process. The individual time with each partner is necessary to gather critical information and to begin the process of building a strong alliance with each.

The individual interviews should begin with an explicit discussion of confidentiality. The therapist should explain that his/her confidentiality agreement with the couple differs from such agreements characteristic of individual therapy, in that the therapist has a responsibility to both partners. In general, IBCT therapists explain to couples, "Unless you tell me otherwise, I will assume that any information you share with me is OK to discuss in our conjoint sessions." Given this, an IBCT therapist agrees to maintain the confidentiality of each partner's private communications to the therapist unless the therapist believes that the issue is relevant to the current relationship. In such cases, the therapist will ask the partner in question to resolve the issue (e.g., end an ongoing affair) or disclose the information to the other partner (e.g., tell the partner about the affair). If the partner cannot agree to either of these options, the therapist may suggest a termination of the therapy. Each of these scenarios should be reviewed carefully with partners at the outset of the individual sessions.

During the individual interviews, the therapist will want to gather information about four primary areas: presenting problems and current situation; family-of-origin history; relationship history; and level of commitment. In addition, other special assessment issues, which are discussed in detail in a later section, are covered during the individual interviews.

In regard to presenting problems, therapists may begin by referring to the discussion of presenting problems during the conjoint meeting. The FAPB Scale (Christensen & Jacobson, 1997) also provides a very effective method of assessing the major issues in the relationship from the perspective of each partner. The therapist should assess the interaction patterns that pertain to these major issues and be alert for possible polarization processes and/or traps. In general, the therapist should allow each partner to list his/her complaints and the desired changes.

Discussion of the individual partner's family history should include inquiry about the partner's parents' marriage, the parent–child relationship, and the general family atmosphere. In general, the therapist will want to be alert to possible ways in which these early relationships may serve as a possible model for the couple's current problems. The individual interview also provides an important opportunity for the therapist to review each partner's individual relationship history with previous partners. The therapist will want to be alert to similar patterns or problems that existed in prior relationships, and/or ways in which earlier relationships may serve as a possible model for the current couple's functioning.

Finally, the therapist will want to assess each partner's level of commitment to the relationship. Toward this end, it is important to inquire directly about commitment and to assess each partner's understanding of his/her role in the current problems. Often it is helpful to ask partners, "How do you contribute to the problems in your relationship?" and "What are some of the changes that you need to make for your relationship to improve?" Partners' answers to these questions will help the therapist to determine the degree of collaboration and commitment present in this couple.

Feedback Session

The feedback session serves as the link between the assessment and treatment phase of IBCT. During this session, the therapist will provide a summary of his/her understanding of the formulation and will outline a plan for treatment. The therapist should remind the couple of the focus of this session at the outset: "This meeting is our feedback session, during which I will be providing an overview of my understanding of the problems you are facing and the way in which we will work on these problems. My hope is that this will be a collaborative process and that you will both also provide feedback to me, correcting, confirming, and/or elaborating what I have to say."

In the best feedback sessions, the couple's reactions are solicited throughout the session, and the therapist frequently checks in with the couple to make sure the formulation is meaningful to both partners. If one member of the couple disagrees, the therapist asks for clarification and then incorporates the feedback into the formulation. The therapist should never be defensive about a formulation, keeping in mind the centrality of the pragmatic truth criterion for evaluating the success of the formulation. Although the IBCT therapist wants the couple to buy into the formulation, he/she needs to remain flexible to the couple's understanding of their own

problems and work to present the main points of the formulation using the couple's words and ideas.

The structure of the feedback session follows directly from the six primary assessment questions used to guide the first three sessions. First, the therapist will want to provide feedback about the couple's level of distress. Toward this end, it may be useful to discuss the partners' scores on relevant questionnaires assessing couple satisfaction or adjustment (e.g., the DAS and MSI-R). Second, the therapist should address the issue of commitment. The therapist will again draw from both the completed questionnaires and the individual sessions to discuss commitment. In regard to both distress and commitment, the therapist will need to evaluate whether it is more advantageous to emphasize the couple's relative distress/low commitment in order to highlight the gravity of the couple's problems, or to emphasize their relative satisfaction/high commitment in order to assuage anxieties about their prognosis. Third, the therapist will focus on the issues that divide a couple, or the basic theme. The therapist can refer to the specific items that partners have noted on the FAPB Scale (Christensen & Jacobson, 1997) to present the theme. Fourth, the therapist will provide an overview of why these issues create such problems for the couple, and in so doing, will detail the nature of the couple's polarization process and mutual trap. Fifth, the therapist will integrate a focus on the couple's strengths, often focusing on the basis of the partners' initial attraction to each other. Finally, the feedback session should include a clear discussion of what treatment can do to help the couple. During this part of the session, clear treatment goals and a corresponding plan are outlined, to which both the couple and therapist agree.

Special Assessment Issues

It is important to note that the assessment process may also reveal particular clinical issues deserving of special discussion. As a general rule, there are few contraindications to IBCT; however, evidence of battering, an ongoing and undisclosed extramarital affair, and/or significant individual psychopathology (e.g., one of the partners has a psychotic disorder or is suicidally depressed) may require a referral to another treatment modality. Methods for assessing these areas and making appropriate treatment planning decisions are discussed below.

In general, the individual sessions provide the primary context in which the therapist should probe carefully about the presence of these areas. In regard to domestic violence, partners should be asked directly about the use of physical, sexual, and emotional abuse tactics. It is often helpful to begin an assessment of domestic violence with general questions about how the couple manages conflict (e.g., "Can you describe a typical argument?" "What do you and your partner typically do to express anger or frustration?"). These questions can be followed by questions that assess the consequences of the escalation of conflict (e.g., "Do your arguments ever get out of control?" "Have you or your partner ever become physical during a conflict?"). It is important to use concrete, behaviorally specific terminology at some point during the assessment process (e.g., "Have you or your partner ever hit, shoved, or pushed each other?"), as some partners will not endorse global constructs of "abuse" or "violence" even when specific acts have occurred. It is always important to attend to safety issues, inquiring about the presence of weapons and other relevant risk factors, as well as the possible presence and/or involvement of children during violent episodes. We also strongly recommend the use of self-report questionnaires to assess the presence of violence (e.g., the Conflict Tactics Scale), as research suggests that wives are often more likely to disclose abuse in written, behaviorally specific questionnaires than on general intake questionnaires or during in-person interviews (O'Leary, Vivian, & Malone, 1992). We have couples complete the questionnaires prior to their individual session, so that we can probe for further information about any violence indicated. Finally, it is essential to assess the function of violent tactics, as violence used for the purposes of obtaining or maintaining a position of power and control in a relationship is a particular concern for assessing the appropriateness of couple therapy. Given the complexities of assessing for domestic violence, therapists are also advised to consult more comprehensive sources detailing optimal assessment practices (see, e.g., Bograd & Mederos, 1999; Holtzworth-Munroe, Beatty, & Anglin, 1995; Holtzworth-Munroe, Meehan, Rehman, & Marshall, Chapter 16, this volume). If the assessment of violence reveals the presence of battering, we strongly recommend against couple therapy. "Battering" is defined as the use of violence to control, intimidate, or subjugate another human being (Jacobson & Gottman, 1998); our specific, operational criterion for battering is a history of injury and/or fear of violence by a partner, almost always the woman. Given that couple therapy can

provoke the discussion of volatile topics, couple therapy sessions may increase the risk of battering (Jacobson, Gottman, Gortner, Berns, & Shortt, 1996). Moreover, the conjoint structure of IBCT may communicate to the couple that the responsibility for the violence is shared by both partners. For these reasons, we consider battering to be a clear contraindication for couple therapy. In such cases, we refer the abusive partner to a gender-specific domestic violence treatment program, and the abused partner to a victim service agency that can provide support, safety planning, and legal services if appropriate. If the assessment of violence, however, indicates the presence of low-level aggression in which partners do not report injury or fear, IBCT may be indicated. In these cases, therapists should continue to use great caution and care; as a prerequisite to beginning treatment, therapists should insist upon clearly stipulated "no-violence" contracts, which specify detailed contingencies if violations occur.

The therapist should also directly ask partners during the individual sessions about their involvement in extramarital relationships, including both sexual relationships and significant emotional involvements. In general, IBCT is not conducted with a couple in which a current and ongoing affair is present. In such cases, the therapist will recommend that the involved partner disclose the affair to the other partner and/or terminate the affair. If the involved partner is unwilling to do so, the therapist informs this partner that IBCT is not an appropriate treatment format. For further discussion of affairs, see Jacobson and Christensen (1996). Finally, therapists are advised to inquire directly about the presence of significant psychopathology, including the current or past experience of mood disorders, substance use problems, and other relevant psychological problems. Therapists should employ standard diagnostic assessment practices, inquiring about major symptom criteria and the course of relevant disorders. In addition, current and/or past treatments should be reviewed. In general, IBCT is often appropriate to treat couple issues when individual problems are successfully managed in concurrent individual psychological or pharmacological treatment, or when individual problems are closely tied to the problems in the relationship (e.g., depression as a result of couple discord). If there is evidence that a current episode of a disorder is not well managed by an ancillary treatment, therapists may want to consider postponing couple therapy and making a referral so that an appropriate individual treatment plan can be established.

GOAL SETTING

The major treatment goals in IBCT are to help members of a couple better understand and accept each other as individuals, and to develop a collaborative set whereby each partner is willing to make necessary changes to improve the quality of the relationship. The manner in which this overall goal is achieved differs for each couple, depending on its unique presenting problems and history. Specific goals for treatment are determined collaboratively by the therapist and couple, and are explicitly discussed during the feedback session. In general, treatment goals are guided by the formulation that is developed during the assessment phase. Jacobson and Christensen (1996) believe the formulation to be so important that they describe an overarching goal in IBCT as getting the partners to see their relationship through the lens provided by the formulation. Through reiterating the formulation as it presents itself in their daily struggles and joys, the therapist helps the partners process their interactions throughout the treatment. Using this linchpin of treatment, the therapist can then create an atmosphere where problems are discussed in a fashion that differs from the typical conflict in which the couple has engaged.

Implicit in the goals of understanding, acceptance, and collaboration is the acknowledgment that staying together is not always the right outcome for all couples. It is important for the IBCT therapist to work diligently with partners to improve the quality of their relationship while remaining neutral to the ultimate outcome of their relationship status. This element of IBCT derives both from philosophical and pragmatic bases. Philosophically, IBCT takes no moral position on divorce. In the context of a particular case, IBCT may help a couple consider the benefits and costs of staying together versus separating, for both partners and their children. Pragmatically, a strong emphasis on "saving the relationship" may also have iatrogenic effects. Often a strong emphasis on the importance or value of staying together strengthens the demand from one partner for the other to change. However, the theory of IBCT stipulates that often this very demand is what maintains and exacerbates the couple's distress. For instance, if Belinda believes that she can tolerate Jonathan and stay with him only if he refrains from working excessive overtime and watching ball games on weekends, her desire to stay in the relationship will heighten her sense of needing these changes to happen. However, her demand for change may

spiral into conflict and increase the discord in the relationship, rather than allow Belinda to reach her desired goal—a happier marriage. When partners are allowed to interact with each other without the demand of staying together at all costs, it may be easier for them to begin to understand the motivations and histories behind each other's behaviors and to become more accepting of those behaviors.

THE STRUCTURE OF THERAPY

IBCT is typically provided in an outpatient setting and generally includes one therapist and the couple. Typically, neither other family members nor cotherapists are included, though there is nothing in the theory of IBCT that precludes doing so if such inclusions seem warranted by the needs of a particular case.

Although our empirical investigations of IBCT have used a format of a maximum of 26 weekly sessions lasting 50 minutes each, from a conceptual standpoint the structure and duration of therapy should be individually tailored to the needs of each couple. In general, the 50-minute weekly session format is well suited to many couples, whose members need the continuity and intensity of this structure. However, it is important to note that other couples may elect to have less frequent meetings of the same or a longer duration (e.g., 2-hour sessions), due to the demands of work or family life and/or their need for additional time to practice new behaviors between sessions.

In IBCT, the duration of therapy and the timing of termination should be discussed collaboratively by the therapist and couple. The therapist should review with the couple the original presenting problems and the goals of each partner, and should help the couple to assess the progress made. Because IBCT is based on the premise that differences and disagreements are a natural part of a couple's relationship, neither the therapist nor the couple needs to wait until all problems are resolved prior to deciding to terminate treatment. If the partners are able to discuss issues more calmly, find that they have a better understanding of each other's perspectives, and are less distressed by behaviors that formerly disturbed them, therapy has been successful, and it is appropriate to begin discussing termination. Some couples may prefer to employ a gradual fading procedure or return for booster sessions, while others may not. In fact, there are no hard and fast rules regarding when or how to terminate; as with other aspects of IBCT, we believe that listening carefully to the hopes and feelings of each partner will prove to be the best guide. We have found that on average, couples participate in a total of approximately 15–26 sessions.

The structure of each IBCT session is also more flexible and open than is common in TBCT. In IBCT, the therapist and couple develop an agenda based on what issues or incidents are most salient to the couple. This initial agenda can shift if more salient issues or incidents come to mind for the couple. Acceptance-oriented sessions generally focus on four areas: (1) general discussions of the basic differences between the partners and related patterns of interaction; (2) discussions of upcoming events that may trigger conflict or slip-ups; (3) discussions of recent negative incidents; and (4) discussions of a recent positive interaction between the partners. These discussions, whether they focus on positive, negative, or upcoming incidents, reflect issues germane to the formulation. For example, a couple may discuss an incident in which the wife left on a short business trip, if such partings reflect a problematic theme such as closeness and independence in the relationship; however, the couple will not typically focus on a positive parting (such as a warm kiss goodbye) or a negative parting (such as the husband's losing his way to the airport) if it does not reflect an ongoing relationship theme. In contrast, change-oriented sessions may be more structured and often include more didactically focused training provided by the therapist, as well as in-session role-play exercises and feedback from the therapist.

THE ROLE OF THE THERAPIST

The IBCT therapist functions in different ways, depending on the context of a particular session. Although the IBCT therapist is frequently very active and directive in sessions, the particular form of the therapist's interventions will vary. In this way, being a good IBCT therapist requires comfort with a high degree of flexibility and change. In fact, it has become axiomatic among IBCT therapists that although it is essential to enter each session with a general plan or framework, there is nothing more important than a partner's most recent statement.

There are times, for instance, when the therapist may play the role of teacher or coach during a session, helping a couple to develop or improve skills in communication or problem solving. During these times, the therapist may be more didac-

tic with the couple and may rely on specific and structured rules of engagement and communication techniques (Gottman, Markman, Notarius, & Gonso, 1976). The therapist may, for example, instruct the couple to have a conversation during the session using specific communication guidelines, with the therapist providing feedback on the partners' performance.

Most often, however, the highest priority for the IBCT therapist is maintaining a focus on the couple's formulation. In this sense, being a good and compassionate listener is one of the most important roles of the IBCT therapist. The therapist must be attentive to both verbal and nonverbal communications throughout the sessions and must find ways to skillfully maintain a focus on the couple's central theme, despite the myriad of specific issues and complaints that may arise. To maintain a focus on the formulation, the therapist must also take care to do so in a way that expresses genuine understanding and empathy for each partner. Thus the therapist often acts as a balanced mediator, pointing out to each partner how current problems relate to ongoing themes that cause distress for them both. The therapist as mediator is also a teacher, however. IBCT therapists try to balance change and acceptance techniques. Rather than teaching rules in a didactic fashion (e.g., akin to a classroom teacher's instructing by giving a lecture), the IBCT therapist tries to provide the couple with a different experience in the session (e.g., akin to the same classroom teacher's choosing instead to instruct by taking students on a field trip). In general, the role of the IBCT therapist is to take a nonconfrontational, validating, and compassionate stance in all interactions with the couple (Jacobson & Christensen, 1996).

Another role of the IBCT therapist is to attend to and highlight the *function* of behaviors. Often this will require that the therapist pay close attention to the function of both verbal and nonverbal communications, rather than the content. For instance, Beth and Rick's therapist was able to ascertain that Beth's frequent smiling and laughter during the couple's heated confrontations functioned to express her anxiety about conflict and her fear that Rick wanted a divorce. The therapist's emphasis on the function of Beth's behavior was in marked contrast to the couple's previous arguments over the content of Beth's behavior, which Rick in particular had interpreted as scorn and indifference.

Interestingly, paying attention to the function of behavior frequently requires the IBCT therapist also to play the role of historian with a couple. Consider, for instance, the role played by the therapist of Carol and Derek. Carol complains that her partner, Derek, always goes directly to the sofa and reads the newspaper when he comes home from work. She is angry and frustrated, as she would like to have time to interact with him. Derek, on the other hand, believes that he should have time to himself to unwind when he comes home from a very stressful day at work. The therapist recognizes that each feels isolated and blamed in this interaction; Derek feels accused of being lazy and disengaged, and Carol feels accused of being needy. The therapist has also, however, remained alert during previous interviews to salient historical information. The therapist may know that Derek's father died of a heart attack at the age of 46 and was a "workaholic." She may also know that Carol's family never discussed issues, and that she grew up believing that her parents were not interested in her.

Using this historical context, the therapist suggests that these histories have occasioned the current behaviors and associated feelings. The therapist then solicits information from both Carol and Derek about how they felt during earlier times, and asks whether they feel similarly now. Often this focus will promote softer responses and greater empathy on the part of both partners. Thus Carol, instead of saying, "He never talks to me; he just sits around and reads that damned paper!", may say, "Yeah, when he is reading the paper I feel lonely, very lonely. It seems like that is what home always has felt like, and I didn't want that to happen in my own home when I became an adult. I just want to feel cared about." Derek, instead of saying, "Why can't she give me a break? I work hard all day and I just want some peace and quiet. Talk, talk, talk, is all you want. I'd gladly talk to you, just give me a minute to myself, is that too much to ask?", may say, "You know, I saw Dad dog-tired every single day. He came home late in the evening and would putter around the house on some project or another. He never stopped working, never took time for himself. He gave and gave to everyone, and it killed him. I am so scared that I'll turn into the same thing—that I'll forget that I need time to relax, to be able to stay around for Carol when we are old, to be there for my kids instead of working until I drop dead and leave everyone alone." The therapist, listening carefully, can then point out the theme of loneliness and isolation behind each partner's behaviors. Neither wants to abandon the other or to be abandoned. The therapist—as listener, mediator, and historian—

can redirect the conversation in a fashion that allows the couple to talk about feelings, memories, and fears, which are often obscured by the typical emphasis on accusation and blame.

Finally, a good IBCT therapist will also be skilled at using language in a way that "hits home" (Jacobson & Christensen, 1996). The IBCT therapist uses language with a couple as an important intervention tool, because impactful language is one important way to alter a couple's relationship context. Therapists should be alert to ways in which they can employ metaphors and terms that hold meaning for couples, to increase the power of their interventions and increase the likelihood that couples will integrate the therapeutic ideas into their daily lives.

PRINCIPAL TECHNIQUES

The techniques used in IBCT fall into three categories: acceptance techniques, tolerance techniques, and change techniques. There are two strategies for promoting acceptance: namely, empathic joining and unified detachment. These strategies attempt to provide a couple with a new experience of divisive issues; in essence, these techniques aim to help the partners turn their problems into vehicles for greater intimacy. In contrast, tolerance interventions allow partners to let go of their efforts to change each other, without aspiring to the somewhat loftier goals of empathic joining and unified detachment. Tolerance is promoted through pointing out the positive features of negative behavior, practicing negative behavior in the therapy session, faking negative behavior between sessions, and self-care (Jacobson & Christensen, 1996). Finally, change techniques are used to directly promote changes in partners' behavior and consist largely of BE strategies and CPT interventions (Gottman et al., 1976; Jacobson & Margolin, 1979).

The principal techniques of IBCT are described below, followed by a discussion of how these interventions are sequenced throughout a typical course of therapy.

Acceptance Techniques

Empathic Joining

The primary technique used to foster acceptance is "empathic joining" around a problem. When a couple enters therapy, both partners are typically experiencing a great deal of pain. Unfortunately, when they express their pain, they often do so with accusation and blame, which typically exacerbates their relationship distress. Thus the goal of empathic joining is to allow partners to express their pain in a way that does not include accusation. Jacobson and Christensen (1996) proposed the following formula: "pain plus accusation equals marital discord, pain minus accusation equals acceptance" (p. 104).

Often the therapist will attempt to promote empathic joining by listening to the couple detail particular interactions and then reformulating the problem in light of the theme discussed during the feedback session. For example, a couple experiencing the theme of "the scientist and the artist"—wherein one partner, Madeline, is very analytical in her approach to life, and the other, Stephanie, is creative and free-spirited—may get into arguments over being on time for appointments. The therapist may say something like this:

> "As I see it, this argument between the two of you goes right back to the theme that we have discussed before. The two of you deal with life very differently. (*To Madeline*) You are very analytic, as we have said; you are the scientist. You like to have everything set and orderly. This makes complete sense, given your upbringing and history. I completely understand that you want to be on time when an appointment is scheduled; you get very frustrated otherwise. I also imagine that you feel embarrassed or humiliated to show up late at events. Is that true? (*Madeline nods.*) However, Stephanie (*therapist turns to Stephanie*), you feel very stifled by such orderliness. What is most important to you is that life be comfortable and fluid. You feel very tied down by deadlines and structure. Having a structure makes you feel controlled, like you are a little kid unable to make up her own mind. (*Stephanie says, "Yes, that is exactly right."*) You aren't late in order to annoy Madeline, and, Madeline, you don't push to be on time in order to control Stephanie. You both have very different feelings in this situation. You each feel very vulnerable in these situations in your own ways. Were you aware of this?"

Another empathic joining strategy is to encourage "soft" disclosures rather than "hard" disclosures. Hard disclosures often express feelings of anger or resentment and may place the speaker in a dominant position relative to the listener. IBCT assumes that there is a corresponding soft side to most hard disclosures, usually expressing the hurt and vulnerability behind the anger. In therapy, this is often referred to as getting the partner to talk about the "feeling behind the feeling." Using this metaphor, the therapist communicates to the couple that the public expression is not always the full picture of the private experience of each partner. Encouraging soft disclosures is done not only to soften the speaker, but also to soften the listener.

For instance, one partner may say something such as "You never take time to ask me how my day went. You're just concerned with yourself. Well, I'm sick of it." In this statement, the anger, resentment, and accusation are resoundingly communicated. To encourage soft disclosure, the therapist may ask the partner what other feelings might also exist with the anger. Or, alternatively, the therapist may suggest a feeling by saying, "I imagine that if I were in your situation, I would feel . . ." The partner then is encouraged to disclose the softer feeling. In our example, the partner may say, "I feel like my day doesn't matter to anybody. I spend all of my time taking care of others, and I feel so drained. I feel lonely and unappreciated." The therapist would turn to the other partner, highlights the soft disclosure, and elicits feedback. The therapist may ask, "Were you aware that your partner felt lonely during these times?" Ideally, the listener will begin to soften and may respond with a similar soft disclosure, such as "I never meant to make you feel unloved. You know I love you very much, and am sorry that I often get so wrapped up in my own day that I neglect to check in with you."

Another way of finding the soft disclosures is to allow a safe environment for partners to talk about their vulnerabilities. In fact, it can sometimes be helpful for the therapist to point out mutual vulnerabilities in a couple. For example, Ellen and Craig had frequent arguments about money and child rearing. The therapist was able to help each of them articulate their vulnerabilities in these areas. Both were very responsible people who wanted to be successful in their endeavors. Ellen took primary responsibility for raising the children; therefore, she was very sensitive to doing a good job in this area. When Craig would take the children out for ice cream without first washing their faces or brushing their hair, Ellen would become irate. He considered this an overreaction. However, Craig was very meticulous about money and wanted to be a good provider for the family. When Ellen spent money that Craig did not anticipate, even if it was just a few dollars, it would lead to an argument. In this situation, Ellen thought Craig was the one who overreacted. The therapist pointed out their mutual vulnerability to being less than successful in their respective roles, and the two of them were able to empathize with the reactions that initially seemed irrational and exaggerated.

We should add a warning about the use of soft disclosures. When we speak of "soft" and "hard," we are referring to the function of the speech and not the form or content of the speech. For instance, not all apparently soft statements will actually soften the emotional reaction of a partner. Imagine a couple that experiences distress in response to the wife's depression. If a therapist were to try to get the wife to make a soft disclosure, such as "Sometimes I just feel so sad, like I'm just not good enough," this could lead to an angry response from the husband, who might anticipate such self-deprecating remarks. Although a statement may move the therapist, it may have the opposite effect on a life partner. In this case, the proper "soft" disclosure may actually, in form, look harder. The husband may soften if the wife says something more assertive, such as "What I really want is to have you tell me that you like how my projects turn out at work, and I'd be happy if you would spend just a few minutes looking over the results with me." Here there is an expression of the client's need, without accusation and without the depressive self-debasement.

Therapists must therefore be aware of, and forewarned not to fall into, a trap of accepting a "soft"-seeming statement as the type of disclosure necessary to soften a particular couple. Frequently therapists can be lulled into feeling that they have hit on something good when a speaker begins to cry; however, they must always remember the possibility that what is gold to them may be tin to clients. It is essential that therapists rely on a good functional analysis and the basic formulation to help guide them in selecting the most salient areas to promote soft disclosure.

Unified Detachment

The second principal method for promoting acceptance is "unified detachment." Once referred to as "seeing the problem as an 'it,'" this strategy aims to help partners develop distance from their conflicts by encouraging an intellectual analysis of the problem. Like empathic joining, unified detachment aims to help the partners talk about their problems without accusation and blame; however, unified detachment emphasizes the use of detached and descriptive discussions rather than emotionally laden discussions. Thus, when using unified detachment interventions, the therapist works with the couple to understand the interaction sequences that become triggered and that lead to the couple's sense of frustration and discouragement. The problem is reformulated as a common adversary that the couple must tackle together.

The therapist can promote unified detachment by continually referring the partners back to the major theme in their interactions, their polarization process, and the mutual trap into which they fall. For instance, when Ray and David tried to resolve conflict about Ray's "flirtatiousness" with other men at social gatherings, the discussions quickly deteriorated. Ray accused David of being "jealous, timid, prudish, and overcontrolling." David accused Ray of being "insensitive, rude, slutty, and shameless." The therapist had earlier defined a theme of "closeness–distance" for Ray and David. In essence, Ray was a fiercely independent man who thrived on doing things his own way. He liked time alone and had been raised as an only child. David, however, liked frequent interaction. He had grown up with three siblings, had never lived entirely on his own even in adulthood, and was very attracted to sharing time with others. Although the theme of closeness–distance was not readily apparent in the interaction about flirtatiousness, the therapist was able to make a connection. He described Ray's behavior as being consistent with his independence and need to have time to himself, even when they were in public; and he related David's behavior to his desire for closeness with Ray and a desire for a feeling of belonging. The therapist was then able to help David and Ray recognize that they shared a dilemma that they could seek to resolve together. This took the problem away from being one that involved blame, and allowed them to look at it in a more detached manner.

An IBCT therapist can also promote unified detachment by engaging the partners in an effort to compare and contrast incidents that occur between them. For example, perhaps José was less disturbed by Maria's working last Sunday than he was the previous Sunday, because they had spent such a close time together last Saturday night. If they both see how genuine closeness can allow for unemotional distance, they may be able to better manage their needs for both.

At times, a therapist may also choose to bring in a fourth chair and suggest that the couple imagine the problem sitting in the chair. This visual and experiential cue may help the couple remember to think of their problem as an "it" and as something that is external to their relationship. Often it may also be helpful for the therapist to suggest that the couple designate a chair for the therapist during conflicts that arise between sessions. The partners can be instructed to talk to the imaginary therapist about what they would like to say to each other, rather than actually saying such things to each other. The effectiveness of these techniques may vary widely across couples; if they enable a couple to talk about a problem at a distance, then they are successful.

Tolerance

Like acceptance interventions, tolerance interventions aim to help partners let go of the struggle to change one another. Tolerance interventions are used with problems that the therapist believes have little likelihood of serving as vehicles for greater intimacy for the couple. For these types of problems, the therapist attempts to help the partners build tolerance so that they will become able to interrupt and/or recover from their conflicts more quickly. However, the therapist may also use tolerance interventions for the problems that were the focus of unified detachment and empathic joining. As illustrated below, the tolerance intervention of enacting negative behavior in the session may be an effective and dramatic way of creating unified detachment and empathic joining.

It should be noted, however, that some types of problems are not amenable to acceptance or tolerance interventions. There are some situations that should be neither accepted nor tolerated; the most obvious example is domestic violence or battering. People should not be subject to abuse and danger in their own homes. Other situations that may be intolerable include substance abuse, extrarelational affairs, or compulsive behaviors (gambling, etc.) that may jeopardize the well-being of both members of a couple. Thus tolerance is not promoted as a means of maintaining an intolerable status quo. Partners are not asked to tolerate all of each other's bad choices, but rather are helped to develop tolerance of partner behaviors that are not destructive and are unlikely to change. Four strategies are used to promote tolerance, and these are described and illustrated below.

Pointing Out Positive Aspects of Negative Behavior

Pointing out the positive aspects of problematic behavior can be a useful method of increasing tolerance. A therapist is alert to ways in which one partner's negative behavior may have positive aspects for the other, currently or in the past. Interestingly, the areas of conflict between partners in the present are often the very same areas that attracted them in the past. Alternatively, negative behaviors may serve a useful function in the present by helping partners to balance each other and providing greater equilibrium in some area of the relationship. Highlighting these aspects may help partners see the benefits of the behaviors that otherwise are experienced as so distressing. It is important to note that the therapist relies on an understanding of the function of the behavior, rather than on trying to find the "silver lining" and simply doing a positive reframing of a negative behavior.

The therapist of Madeline and Stephanie, described above, chose to emphasize the positive aspects of negative behavior when addressing their conflicts regarding timeliness. In this case, she emphasized the ways in which Madeline's punctuality and Stephanie's tardiness were expressions of qualities that had once attracted them to one another. The therapist focused on their early courtship, during which Madeline, who was completing her final year of a long, demanding, and highly structured graduate program, was attracted to the sense of fun and spontaneity that Stephanie brought to her life. The therapist also recalled for the couple that Stephanie, who had experienced a chaotic and unpredictable childhood, had also initially appreciated Madeline's structure and discipline. At one time, then, their behaviors had served the function of bringing the couple closer together. Although the partners were currently polarized around the issue of timeliness, the therapist, by focusing on the positive function of each of their behaviors, was able to show them that these classes of "timeliness" behaviors served to create a balance.

As in the case of Stephanie and Madeline, the "positive" aspect of negative behavior frequently will be some function of balancing extreme behaviors. However, IBCT theory does not assume that finding a balance or homeostasis is necessary for therapeutic improvement. For many couples this intervention may be unnecessary, and for many negative behaviors there is no positive function. It is difficult, for example, to see the positive function of slamming kitchen cupboard doors when one partner is annoyed with another.

Another couple, Anna and Eric, differed significantly in their attitudes toward spending money; Anna was more conservative about spending, while

Eric was more liberal. Eric liked to buy new technological gadgets every payday, and he had gotten into the pattern of stopping off at a store on his way home so that Anna wouldn't prevent him from doing so. Anna, however, took money from her paycheck and put it in a savings account to which Eric had no access. Each became irritated by the other's behavior, and this led to many arguments. They had difficulty compromising in this area, because Eric felt that they were living like "paupers" if they didn't spend a little money, and Anna feared that they would squander savings for their future if they spent too casually. Both had legitimate reasons for feeling as they did. The therapist chose to promote tolerance by pointing out the ways in which their behaviors served to balance each other. To do so, she asked both partners what they thought would happen if their way of doing things was the only way the couple managed money. Through this intervention, each partner was able to acknowledge the importance of the other partner's style. The therapist summarized the balancing function of their behaviors by explaining, "If you were both like Anna, you would have very few luxuries and life might seem rather dull, although it would feel stable. If you were both like Eric, you would be a little short-sighted when it comes to handling money and may occasionally have problems paying your bills now. So, even though these differences may continue to irk you both, from my perspective they are necessary to keep you enjoying life in a responsible fashion."

As is the case with all IBCT interventions, the therapist remained nonjudgmental, validating both Eric's and Anna's perspectives. Notice, also, that the therapist did not point out the positive side of the negative behavior and then convey the message "Great, now you are fixed!" In fact, she said, "These differences may continue to irk you." In other words, IBCT therapists are comfortable with the fact that problems may remain long after therapy is over. The hope, however, is that increasing the partners' tolerance of their differences will free them from the traps created by trying to change each other and allow them to live with a greater sense of satisfaction. It also may make them more open to specific compromises and solutions that could ease the problem.

Practicing Negative Behavior in the Therapy Session

The purposes of practicing negative behavior in the session are to desensitize each partner to the other's negative behaviors, as well as to sensitize each of-

fending partner to the impact of his/her behavior on the other. These two objectives apply also to faking the negative behavior at home, which is addressed next. Asking partners to practice negative behavior in session also allows the therapist to closely observe the interaction and may lead to either empathic joining or unified detachment, although this is not always the case.

An illustration is provided by a husband and wife who were polarized around issues of responsibility and control. This couple struggled significantly with a pattern in which the wife would complain frequently, while the husband would purposely do the opposite of what his wife requested when he thought she was nagging him. In the session the therapist asked the wife to complain as much as she could—to really get into complaining. The husband was asked to be obstinate and to disagree with everything the wife said, even if he agreed with her. The first time the therapist tried this exercise, the spouses got into their usual emotional states: The wife got frustrated and felt powerless to influence her husband. The husband felt attacked and simply attacked back by being obstinate. The therapist interrupted the sequence and used empathic joining to connect with the immediate emotional impact the exercise had on them. The next time the therapist tried the exercise, the spouses found it funny. They were unable to get into their usual roles and laughed at what they perceived to be the "silliness" of their pattern. In this way, the exercise helped them achieve some unified detachment from the problem. Thus the exercise to practice negative behavior in the session can result in greater tolerance of the behavior, but it can also provide a vivid occasion for empathic joining and unified detachment.

Faking Negative Behaviors at Home between Sessions

The partners are instructed to engage in the behavior that has been identified as problematic, but only to do so when they do not feel naturally compelled to do so. In other words, they are to do the behavior when they are not emotionally aroused. In the preceding example, the wife was directed to complain at home when she did not feel like complaining, and the husband was asked to be obstinate even though he felt like agreeing. Each partner was to continue with the behavior for only a few minutes and then inform the other that this was a "fake." They were then instructed to take a few minutes and debrief the interaction. Partners should tell each other what they observed during the interaction; in particular, the partner who faked the behavior should explain what he/she observed the impact of the faked behavior to be.

Partners frequently report that they have difficulty actually completing this kind of homework assignment, but that being given the assignment makes them more aware of their behavior. This increased awareness itself serves to decrease the problematic behaviors. Moreover, as partners choose moments during which they will engage in negative behaviors, these behaviors are brought under voluntary control. This experience helps partners to realize that they have choices about how they want to respond to or interact with each other. Finally, as partners are expecting to be "faked out," they tend to react less severely to the negative behaviors that formerly annoyed them. In essence, each partner becomes desensitized to the negative behavior through repeated exposure; as a result, tolerance is promoted. An IBCT therapist very clearly explains to partners what they can expect from this exercise and what the rationale for the intervention is. In particular, the therapist emphasizes that the goals of the intervention are to desensitize the partners to the negative aspects of their interaction, which will help to increase tolerance.

Promoting Tolerance through Self-Care

Since there are many fixed patterns of behavior that individuals will have great difficulty changing, it is often important to help partners learn to engage in self-care. Oftentimes, if partners use self-care to address important personal needs or areas of vulnerability, they will become more tolerant of each other's negative behavior. For instance, Mary's job occasionally required her to stay later than she expects in order to manage crises that arise. On such days, she might arrive at home an hour or two later than she and her partner, Mark, usually arrived home to make dinner together. Mark often became frustrated by Mary's tardiness on these nights; his sense of frustration, combined with feeling hungry while waiting for her, often led him to be irate by the time she got home. It was on these nights that Mary and Mark had some of their most bitter and painful conflicts. Given that the demands of Mary's job seemed unlikely to change in the near future, their therapist worked with Mark to promote self-care during these times. Together, they decided that on such nights, Mark would give Mary a grace period of 30 minutes after their appointed meeting time; if she was late, he would go

out to dinner at his favorite restaurant with a friend or on his own. This intervention helped Mark to satisfy his own needs for a pleasant and relaxing meal. The partners were then able to discuss more calmly and collaboratively their mutual frustration with the demands of Mary's job when she arrived home.

Change Techniques

In addition to the acceptance interventions described above, IBCT incorporates some of the change strategies of TBCT. We describe these strategies only briefly here, since they have been written about extensively (e.g., Jacobson & Margolin, 1979). Then we discuss their integration with the acceptance interventions of IBCT.

Behavior Exchange

The assumption that people are better at changing themselves than at changing others is the underlying principle of BE interventions. When partners commit to changing their own behavior in such a way as to provide pleasure for each other, both will ultimately be more satisfied. Although BE can be implemented in many different ways, a classic BE exercise is to have each member of a couple write a list of behaviors that each believes would bring pleasure to the other. They are asked to do this at home, independently, and only to read the lists in the next therapy session. Each is asked to write specific, observable, and positive behaviors (e.g., "Bring home flowers" or "Massage his shoulders") rather than negative behaviors (e.g., "Stop yelling at her when she forgets to bring in the recycling can"). Once each partner has developed a comprehensive list, the lists are read aloud in the session. Then the other partner rates each item on the list on a 3-point scale, indicating the amount of pleasure he/she would derive from the behavior. Eventually the partners can make requests for additions to the lists. Neither partner is committed to doing any of the specific behaviors on his/her list, although both do commit to doing some of them. The partners can then set aside a day as a "caring day," on which they each agree to do several of the items from their lists. The partners then relate the effects of the caring day to the therapist, who encourages them to continue with additional caring days or daily behavior exchange to increase each partner's reinforcement skills.

Communication/Problem-Solving Training

CPT is a staple of TBCT and has been detailed in many articles and books (Gottman et al., 1976; Jacobson & Margolin, 1979). In general, IBCT employs training in both communication and problem solving, though there is often a greater emphasis on communication training interventions, as active listening and expressive training often overlap more readily with efforts to promote acceptance.

Communication exercises involve teaching couples to level about their feelings with each other, edit out unnecessarily negative comments, and validate each other. Each partner pays particular attention to the role of speaker or listener. The speaker is to use "I" statements; be specific about behaviors; and edit the content of a statement to remove accusation, contempt, overgeneralizations, and the tendency to drag in "everything but the kitchen sink" (Gottman et al., 1976; Gottman, 1994). Specific communication exercises and relevant reading materials are often assigned from *Reconcilable Differences* (Christensen & Jacobson, 2000) and *A Couple's Guide to Communication* (Gottman et al., 1976).

In problem solving, partners are encouraged to take a collaborative approach, be willing to accept their role in problems, clearly define the problem, and then quickly move into considering solutions to the problem. The partners brainstorm solutions, stating as many as possible, without judging or discussing them. Once they have generated a list of possible solutions, the partners use the principles that they learned in communication training (i.e., validating, leveling, and editing) to discuss each possible solution. They finally decide on a solution, and they contract with each other to attempt it, specifying a time limit for trying the solution. After they attempt the solution, they return to discuss and evaluate its success or failure.

When we do CPT in IBCT, we are generally less rule-governed than in TBCT and try to adapt the CPT principles to the idiosyncrasies of a particular couple. For example, we may not insist on the formula of "I feel X when you do Y in situation Z," but instead encourage partners to do more of a particular component that is missing. So, if husband rarely mentions a feeling when he says his complaints to his wife, we may encourage this behavior, even if he says it without the obligatory "I feel" (e.g., "I get really frustrated when you do so and so" would be great). Similarly, if a wife tends to make global characterizations, we may help her specify the particular behaviors that are upsetting. However, we may also respond to her sense that it is not just one or two behaviors but a class of behaviors that are upsetting to her, and that this class of behaviors communicates something to her (e.g., various distancing behaviors communicate a lack of love to her).

Sequencing Guidelines

Because IBCT promotes both acceptance and change in therapy, the therapist moves fluidly between these types of interventions throughout the therapy process. In general, the primary approach is to use the acceptance techniques more than change or tolerance techniques (Jacobson & Christensen, 1996). The overall strategy is to start with empathic joining and unified detachment interventions. When partners appear to be stuck in patterns that are particularly resistant to change, the therapist may consider tolerance interventions. Often acceptance and tolerance interventions may produce as by-products the very changes that partners entered therapy requesting; in these cases, the need for change-oriented techniques may be obviated. With other couples, the acceptance and tolerance work will create the collaborative spirit required for change-oriented work, and therapy will naturally progress toward CPT exercises. In all cases, change techniques can also be interspersed throughout the therapy, though the therapist should be quick to return to acceptance interventions if the emphasis on change appears to exacerbate conflict. IBCT therapists should never try to "force-feed" change strategies to couples at any point in the process of therapy.

Although these sequencing guidelines are recommended for therapists, it is noted that they are only "rules of thumb." In some cases, for instance, couples may enter treatment with a strong collaborative set, and it may be appropriate to begin with change-oriented interventions. In general, the intervention chosen by a therapist at any time is highly dependent on the context in which a certain interaction is occurring, and fixed rules are difficult to delineate.

TREATMENT APPLICABILITY

IBCT has been developed for use with married or cohabiting couples as well as same-gender couples, though outcome investigations to date have focused only on married, heterosexual couples. Although the same basic goals and interventions apply in IBCT with same-gender couples, the therapist must take certain sociocultural differences into account (Martell & Land, in press). Moreover, therapists are cautioned to use discretion before accepting a couple for treatment whose cultural background may be outside the therapist's knowledge and experience; it is essential that IBCT, as a contextually focused treatment, be conducted in a culturally sensitive and specific manner. As noted above, there are few contraindications to IBCT, though we *do not* provide couple treatment in cases of battering and *may not* provide couple treatment if issues of extrarelational affairs or individual psychological problems (e.g., substance abuse) risk undermining the conjoint treatment. In these circumstances, we instead initiate referrals to individual practitioners.

A large-scale empirical investigation of IBCT is currently underway. Preliminary findings from the first study comparing IBCT and TBCT are extremely promising (Jacobson, Christensen, Prince, Cordova, & Eldridge, 2000). In this study, 21 couples were randomly assigned to TBCT or IBCT; results demonstrated that both husbands and wives receiving IBCT reported greater increases in marital satisfaction (as measured by the DAS and the Global Distress score of the MSI-R) than those receiving TBCT at the end of treatment. Moreover, clinical significance criteria further suggested that a greater proportion of couples treated with IBCT (80%) than of couples treated with TBCT (64%) improved or recovered. Although these results must be considered preliminary, given the small sample size, a larger, multisite study is currently being conducted at the University of Washington and the University of California–Los Angeles. This study will be the largest investigation of couple therapy ever conducted and will allow us to provide more definitive answers to questions about the short- and long-term efficacy of IBCT.

CASE ILLUSTRATION

The following case illustration is intended to provide a more detailed example of a typical course of IBCT and some of its primary interventions. First, the information that can be gathered in the initial joint interview is described. Second, the information about each individual that is gathered during the individual interviews is reviewed. Third, presentation of the themes, traps, and polarization process during the feedback session is described. Finally, because IBCT sessions typically focus on debriefing weekly incidents, several of the key in-

cidents that occurred for this couple during therapy are discussed, and examples of empathic joining, unified detachment, and tolerance techniques used with the couple are given.

Information Gathered during the Initial Session

Jennifer and Cole came to therapy because they believed that they were currently as "stuck" as they had been 7 years before. During that earlier time, they had considered divorce, entered couple therapy, and found it very helpful. They had been married for 15 years and had known each other for 19 years. Cole was 53 years old, and Jennifer was 39. They had two small children, a 3-year-old son a 3-month-old daughter. Jennifer had worked as an executive assistant, and Cole was an artist. After the birth of their second child, Jennifer was approaching the time when she would need to return to her former job, and Cole was preparing to be the primary parent at home during the day. Cole's artwork provided less steady employment and income for the family; however, his experience in the past had been that one good commission could provide enough income for the family to live on for a year, even if he only worked for a few months out of the year. Cole did not want to have to give up his career to settle into a full-time job. He needed the flexibility that he currently had in his schedule in order to prepare for exhibitions and to solicit commissions. Therefore, during times when his artwork provided little income, Jennifer took primary financial responsibility for the family. Unfortunately, Jennifer now found that she did not want to return to work; she wanted to be a "stay-at-home mom." When they began therapy, they were locked in conflict regarding this issue.

Cole believed that the issues regarding the division of parenting and employment had been debated and resolved prior to the birth of the second child. He was surprised when Jennifer told him that she wanted to stay at home and not return to work. Jennifer said that she had always wanted to be the primary parent, but that it just was not feasible with their financial situation. Cole and Jennifer agreed that this type of exchange typified their disagreements. They would discuss an issue, and Cole would believe that the issue was resolved; however, then the issue would be mentioned again several months later. Often Jennifer would raise issues that Cole believed were resolved as part of the "kitchen sink" phenomenon (i.e., she would include various unrelated topics in arguments).

Jennifer and Cole had met when Jennifer was in college. Cole frequently exhibited artwork in a restaurant where Jennifer was working part-time as a waitress. Jennifer had been impressed with Cole because he was very handsome and outspoken. Although she didn't think much of his exhibiting his artwork in a restaurant, she knew that he had also had pieces on exhibit in reputable local galleries and that he was successful in his career. She liked the fact that he was older than she was, since she had become disillusioned with the apparent irresponsibility of men her own age. Cole had been married before and had been divorced for 3 years prior to meeting Jennifer. He thought she was one of the most beautiful young women he had ever seen. Jennifer's interest in Cole's artwork, and her guileless approach to life, were very appealing to Cole. He believed Jennifer was someone who would respect and admire him.

The two began dating soon after they met, and she moved into his apartment 3 months later. Although Cole was not interested in getting married again, Jennifer recalled feeling that she knew he was the man she would eventually marry. They lived together for 4 years prior to getting married. Cole remained reluctant about getting married and wanted to be able to have a sense of freedom regarding his career. His first marriage had ended over differences about the area of the country in which he and his wife would live, Cole's irregular income, and the lack of stability inherent in his profession. Jennifer had always planned to be married, however. She had tolerated living together for the first 3½ years, but then began to demand that they legalize their union. Cole did not want to lose her, so he agreed.

Information Gathered in the Individual Interview with Jennifer

Jennifer had been raised by working-class parents in a suburban community. Her parents were very protective of her, and her mother had been demanding and controlling when she was growing up. Her mother would experience very dark moods during which she would harshly criticize Jennifer, and Jennifer would cope with her mother's emotional displays by shutting her out. Although her mother was never abusive, she would demand that Jennifer do chores around the house exactly her way, and Jennifer resented her mother's control

over her. Jennifer had wanted to move away for college, but her mother demanded that she stay at home while she was in school. When she first met Cole, her parents thought he was too old for her. They were particularly unhappy when Jennifer moved in with him so soon after they met. To Jennifer, this was a way out of her mother's house, although she also had fallen deeply in love with Cole.

Jennifer always worried that Cole did not love her. She wanted to please him and usually complied with any of his requests or demands. They agreed on most issues, such as politics and religion, and they shared many values. Cole, however, had not been as interested in parenting as Jennifer was, and she needed to work hard to convince him through the years to have children. In fact, it was the issue of children that had brought them to therapy 7 years before. At this time Jennifer had decided that she wanted to be a mother, and that either Cole must agree to having children or she would need to leave the marriage. Cole thought that Jennifer had not wanted children when she agreed to marry him, and he felt that he had made his own desire not to have any very clear to her.

The two had many arguments, but the arguments never involved physical aggression or violence. Jennifer did not feel intimidated by Cole, although she didn't like it when he became intense and loud. She felt that she could not think fast enough on her feet during those arguments, and that Cole usually got his way as a result. She was also tired of the instability of his career and wanted him to get a regular full-time job so that she could stay home with the new baby. At the same time, Jennifer was very committed to the relationship and was interested in doing what she could to make the marriage work. She denied any extramarital affairs.

Information Gathered from the Individual Interview with Cole

Cole corroborated much of Jennifer's story about the early years of the relationship. He had particularly liked the fact that Jennifer seemed open-minded toward new ideas and nontraditional styles of living. He knew that being an artist required flexibility, and he had already watched one relationship become ruined because of the difficulty of living an artist's life. However, Cole believed that he needed to sacrifice for his art, and that his profession was very important to him. He had agreed to have children with Jennifer, provided that they could work out a way for it not to interfere with his profession. Now that Jennifer wanted to stay home and take care of the new baby, Cole felt resentful. Still, he also felt very committed to Jennifer and stated that he was in the marriage "for the long haul." He too denied any domestic violence or extramarital affairs.

Cole was the elder of two children. His brother had been killed in a car accident when Cole was in his early 20s. Soon afterward his mother had been hospitalized for a major depressive episode, after which Cole reported she was never the same. He had thus felt abandoned by both his brother and his mother during the early years of his career. His father had always been kind but remained emotionally distant. His mother ultimately died by suicide when he was 27, which increased Cole's fears of being left. Cole did not have a history of depression or other psychiatric problems, though he described himself as moody. Prior to the death of his brother and mother, he had believed his family to be very stable. His mother's psychological difficulties had been a shock to him.

The Feedback Session

Cole and Jennifer had completed several questionnaires prior to beginning therapy. The combination of scores on the DAS (Spanier, 1976), the MSI-R (Snyder, 1997), and the FAPB Scale (Christensen & Jacobson, 1997) showed them to be moderately distressed. Jennifer was reporting significantly greater distress on the DAS and the Global Distress scale of the MSI-R than Cole. Areas of concern for the two of them included child rearing, being critical of one another, and finances.

Initially, it appeared that a theme akin to the "artist–scientist" conflict, with one partner being very free-spirited and the other being very analytic, applied to Cole and Jennifer. However, upon reflection, it became clear that this was not the case. Though Cole was clearly the artist, Jennifer was also a dreamer. They simply had different areas of their lives in which they were either more artistic or more analytic. Instead, the theme of "abandonment" as well as the theme of "control and responsibility" seemed most salient for Jennifer and Cole.

They were both vulnerable to the theme of abandonment because each responded to the other in ways reminiscent of their families of origin. When Cole would become critical or animated, Jennifer would become concerned that he was

going to leave her. She had felt unloved by her mother when her mother was critical, and when Cole was critical it made her feel unloved. Cole, on the other hand, feared that Jennifer would leave if she disagreed with him, or if life became too complicated. He would always try to come up with a solution to everything. When she would apparently agree with his solutions, and then tell him months or even years later that she did not agree with him, he would feel that his life was changing in a "flash," just as it had when his brother was killed.

Cole and Jennifer were also polarized around issues of managing finances and taking care of the children because they could not agree on who should be the primary breadwinner. Although Jennifer had been intrigued by Cole's career as a professional artist when they were first together, she had begun to resent it as she experienced the necessary compromises that needed to be made. Cole, who liked the fact that Jennifer had admired and perhaps even idolized him when they were first married, now resented the fact that she did not want to take the primary responsibility for earning money for the family.

They became trapped when they tried to resolve these issues. Cole would try to solve the problem and become more and more adamant about the solutions he generated. As he got more "intense," however, Jennifer would stop talking and simply become silent. Cole would interpret her silence as agreement. The discussions would end, and the couple would not address the issues until Jennifer would bring them up at some point in the future. At this point, Cole would become surprised that an issue he believed to be resolved was again causing distress. He would become more critical of Jennifer, believing that she was "changing on him"; then the pattern would begin again, with Cole taking control and pushing for a solution, and Jennifer becoming silent.

Examples of the Three Primary Techniques

Since the techniques that distinguish IBCT from TBCT are empathic joining around a problem, unified detachment, and tolerance, these are illustrated with examples from Cole and Jennifer's case. Under each technique, the situation and the ways in which the therapist formulated the problem and intervened will be presented. In this case, the structured approaches of CPT and BE were used sparingly. The partners were encouraged at one point to consider doing something nice for each other over a weekend (BE), and they were taught briefly about active listening. Jennifer and Cole benefited from the IBCT approach and were having more meaningful and satisfying conversations at home without formal training. The BE process allowed them to take an alternative approach to feeling distance from each other, and actually to think of things to do that moved them toward each other when there was tension. Although the therapy focused on acceptance or tolerance exercises, the couple made significant behavior changes, but ones that seemed contingency-shaped rather than rule-governed.

Empathic Joining around the Problem

Jennifer's maternity leave was about to end, and she had contacted her boss to discuss returning to work. Cole and Jennifer had a therapy appointment 2 days before her scheduled return. She was very upset about needing to go back to work. Cole was angry with Jennifer for being upset. He, as usual, believed that the issue of Jennifer returning to work had been resolved.

COLE: You know, I just don't understand it. This is always what happens. Jennifer knew she would go to work. We had agreed on this a long time ago.

JENNIFER: I didn't realize it would be so hard to go back. I feel like I have so little time with the baby as it is.

COLE: But that was our agreement—if we had kids, it wouldn't interfere with my art. You know you make more money than I do, and you act as if my staying at home with the kids isn't work as well.

JENNIFER: (*Crying*) This just makes me very angry.

COLE: (*Increasing the volume of his voice*) Well, that makes two of us who are getting angry.

THERAPIST: (*To Cole*) You know, this sounds to me like a situation that is similar to others we have talked about in the past, in which you feel like Jennifer is changing her mind on something midstream.

COLE: Exactly. I thought we had settled this.

THERAPIST: (*To Jennifer*) I suspect that you had settled it, in theory. But I'd imagine now that you find yourself very attached to the baby, and that it is very hard to break away and go back to work.

JENNIFER: It is terribly hard. I feel like I'm only going to see her when she is sleeping, and I want to be able to spend all of my time with her.

COLE: But we agreed . . .

THERAPIST: Hold on a second, Cole. Jennifer, I could be wrong, but it seems like you are not necessarily refusing to go to work, but that you really just need to feel this sadness right now. [The therapist at this point was trying to elicit a softer response from Jennifer, in the hope that this would in turn soften Cole's angry responses.]

JENNIFER: Yes, I know that I need to return to work, but I feel terrible about it. I just want Cole to understand that this is hard for me.

COLE: I know it is hard. It always has been hard.

THERAPIST: (*To Cole*) I want to make sure that you are really hearing what Jennifer is saying. You are getting angry because you think she is changing her mind about returning to work, but in fact she is planning to return to work. She just feels really sad. I'm hearing Jennifer say that she just wants you to sympathize with her sadness. Is that right, Jennifer?

JENNIFER: Yes.

THERAPIST: (*To Cole*) So do you see that this is not about changing plans; it is about feelings associated with the plan the two of you have agreed upon?

COLE: I do see that, but what can I do?

THERAPIST: Now I think that is why you get so angry, because you want to fix this and make Jennifer's feelings go away. To do that, you'd have to take a "straight" job, which would mean sacrificing your art. Jennifer isn't asking you to do that. Isn't that right, Jennifer?

JENNIFER: Well, I'd be glad if Cole did take a regular job, but I know he'd ultimately be unhappy. Plus he couldn't make as much money as I do anyway at this point.

THERAPIST: But you want him to know that this is hard.

JENNIFER: I just want his love and support, and I want him not to make me feel like I need to just return to work and be a trooper.

COLE: I do support you, Jennifer. I don't know what I can do to let you know that.

JENNIFER: Just acknowledge that I am making a sacrifice, and that this sacrifice hurts.

COLE: I know this is a very painful sacrifice for you. I want to make you feel better about it, and I feel impotent to do anything.

JENNIFER: You don't have to do anything. Just be OK about my not being OK about this.

COLE: I can do that.

When using an empathic joining intervention, the therapist does not attempt to encourage the partners to resolve the conflict or to compromise with each other. The task of empathic joining is to help the couple discuss problems in a way that allows both partners to feel that they are being heard. In this example, Cole was feeling accused and guilty. The therapist further explored Cole's feelings later in the session. It was important for Cole first to acknowledge that Jennifer's feelings were valid and that he could feel empathy for her in their situation. Although this did not resolve the problem, it softened the interaction so that they could discuss the problem in a kind and understanding way.

Unified Detachment

Cole had an opportunity to make a financial investment; however, he and Jennifer had become polarized around this issue. Jennifer wanted to pay back debts, and Cole wanted to invest in the hope that he could obtain a good return to help support their children's future. As in many unified detachment interventions, the therapist used empathic joining to help soften the couple around the issue and then pointed out the problem, which was framed as follows: "Cole and Jennifer both want to have a secure future, but disagree about how that is best accomplished." When they were both able to look at the situation as wanting a secure future, they were able to compromise on the investment. Although Cole still made the investment, Jennifer was able to express her concern about their debts and to develop a plan for paying off the debts in a more rapid fashion than they had been doing. Also, Jennifer agreed to become more involved in following the investments, so that she could be aware of what was going on with their money.

Tolerance

One of the primary patterns that distressed Cole and Jennifer involved Cole's raising his voice during arguments and coming across like a salesman rattling off reasons for Jennifer to accept his point of view. Jennifer would consequently "shut down" and become silent. The therapist determined that the couple would probably experience great difficulty in breaking this pattern, since it had existed for so long and it paralleled many of the patterns present in their respective families of origin. Thus the therapist decided that a tolerance exercise could help desensitize them to this pattern and alleviate some of the difficulty it generated. The therapist was therefore not attempting to change the behav-

ior, but was instead helping the couple to build tolerance so that Cole would be less distressed when Jennifer became silent and Jennifer would be less distressed when Cole raised his voice or adamantly argued his point of view.

During a discussion in one session, the therapist suggested that the couple demonstrate this behavior.

THERAPIST: Cole, I want to see you get intense in this session. I'd like you to demonstrate this for me here and now. I want to see how you convince, cajole, and sell your perspective.

COLE: Really? As intense as I can be?

THERAPIST: Yes, I want to actually see what happens between the two of you at home. Can you do that?

COLE: I'll try.

THERAPIST: Jennifer, I'd like you to tell me if you think that Cole is showing it here like you see it at home, OK?

JENNIFER: OK.

COLE: Ready?

THERAPIST: Go ahead.

COLE: I think that we should take money out of our CD and invest it in Harold's venture. I trust Harold, and I wouldn't suggest that we do this if I didn't. (*Cole speaks rapidly and raises his voice.*) I don't understand why you don't want to do that. It makes complete sense to me.

THERAPIST: (*To Jennifer*) is this the way Cole is at home?

JENNIFER: Well, not exactly. He gets more demanding, and more demeaning. Also he just fires his points one after another.

COLE: (*Raising his voice very loudly*) I don't understand how you think I am demanding about this. I think that what I am saying about this investment makes perfect sense. I've looked into other investments. I called about Harold's ideas, and I looked into the reputations of the other investors. I don't demean you; I think things out and I come to you with careful decisions. You seem to think that I'd just toss away our family's security . . .

JENNIFER: (To therapist) Now you're seeing it.

Jennifer was then able to talk about Cole's behavior and her impulse to shut down. She did not shut down in the session, however, and was able to provide feedback to Cole about how his "salesmanship" made her feel. She could identify the exact behaviors that Cole emitted that made her want to withdraw. The beginning of tolerance happened in the session. There was great improvement in her ability to tell Cole when she felt like shutting down and to allow the therapist to help her in the session to remain focused and express the impulse aloud. This is a good example of an in-session tolerance exercise, but it also highlights the fact that acceptance interventions often overlap. This tolerance exercise resulted in empathic joining as well, when Cole was better able to understand the impact his behavior had on Jennifer and when he was able to tell her how he felt when she shut down.

The therapist later suggested the following "faking negative behavior" exercise for them to try at home regarding a related behavior. Cole was troubled by their frequent bickering, because he interpreted bickering as indicative of a bad relationship. They often bickered over issues that Cole thought had been resolved because of the pattern identified earlier: Cole would rattle off his opinions and solutions, and Jennifer would withdraw. He would interpret her resignation as resolution, but when she decided to approach the topic again, Cole would be shocked, thinking that she had shifted positions on him. Jennifer was not as concerned and thought that bickering was a part of relationships, although she found it to be unpleasant when it occurred. They agreed to try a tolerance assignment about bickering. Jennifer was to bring up a topic that she knew had been resolved. She was only to allow this interaction to continue long enough to see Cole's reaction, and then to tell him that this was part of the therapy assignment.

Cole was also given a "fake negative" assignment. Jennifer would get annoyed with Cole when she sought emotional support from him and he would respond with solutions. For example, when she would say, "I am really stressed about work," Cole would immediately say, "Well, maybe you should switch to three-quarter time." His faking behavior was to propose a solution when he knew that Jennifer wanted support, maintain his position for a moment and observe her response, and then debrief the assignment with her.

Cole and Jennifer never actually followed through with their assignments intentionally, but they reported in the following session that their expecting each other to fake the behavior made the behaviors less aversive when they did occur. Moreover, they were able to gain greater awareness of this pattern and were able to identify it more readily when it did occur. The IBCT therapist places less emphasis than a TBCT therapist on requiring couples to complete the homework. Rather, he/she highlights the shifts that occur through the interventions, regardless of the clients' absolute compliance. The therapist maintains a stance of acceptance, and also trusts the shift in context to promote both change and acceptance—even if the couple is complying poorly, but gaining a benefit by becoming more aware of and desensitized to behaviors that had previously caused distress.

Case Summary

Jennifer and Cole completed 26 sessions of IBCT. At the termination of therapy, they both stated that they were better able to understand each other's positions on a number of issues. Cole felt discouraged that they still bickered as much as they did; however, they had developed greater humor about these ongoing patterns, and began to jokingly refer to themselves as the "Bickersons." Treatment did not resolve all of their problems. Jennifer still had to go to work full-time when she didn't want to. Cole, however, recognized the reality of their situation, empathized with Jennifer, and spontaneously took steps to change. He took a part-time job that was outside of his profession to help support the family, and he was then able to devote only a portion of his time to his art. At the end of therapy, however, they felt that they were on the same side and supported each other in areas where they were both vulnerable.

Throughout therapy, there were frequent discussions of familial patterns that were relevant to present feelings. Jennifer's parents had both been very poor in their youth, and they had a very strong work ethic. To them, being in the arts was a luxury. Jennifer realized that she often dismissed Cole's art the same way as her parents would have—namely, as not being legitimate labor. Cole recognized that he was always waiting for Jennifer to suddenly change and do something irrational, although she was in fact an extremely rational and emotionally even person. His expectations were related more to the tragedies that had occurred in his family of origin than to Jennifer's behavior. As they began to understand each other's emotional and behavioral repertoires, they were able to feel less isolated from each other during times of disagreement. Jennifer felt more comfortable expressing her opinions and was less likely to simply choose silence in response to Cole. Cole continued to express himself in a fashion that Jennifer considered intense, but he was more solicitous of her input than he had been prior to therapy.

All three of the IBCT interventions were applicable with Jennifer and Cole. They had become polarized over the major theme of responsibility and control, and around the theme of abandonment. Cole softened in his interactions with Jennifer as the empathic joining techniques were used during therapy. They were able to recognize their problem as an "it" that they could work together toward solving when the therapist made unified detachment interventions. Furthermore, there were areas that were unlikely to change because they involved overlearned, emotion-based, habitual behaviors—such as Cole's rapid-fire intensity when trying to fix problems, and Jennifer's tendency to shut down. Tolerance exercises helped to desensitize them to these interactions, even though they were unlikely to change. Jennifer and Cole also illustrate how IBCT can be useful with couples when traditional behavioral interventions do not work. When the therapist attempted to have them practice "active listening" during one session, they thought that paraphrasing one another felt impersonal and stated emphatically that they were unlikely to do this at home. By using empathic joining and helping them articulate the "feelings behind the feelings," the therapist was able to achieve the same goals without teaching a specific skill set of active listening. Natural contingencies were more powerful in maintaining shifts in this couple's behavior than were artificial reinforcers or rules.

Objective measures showed improvement for Jennifer, who had been significantly more unhappy in the beginning of treatment. On the DAS and the Global Dsistress score of the MSI-R, she made reliable improvements that moved into the nondistressed range. Cole verbally acknowledged that therapy had helped tremendously, but this was not reflected in objective measures, which changed very little for him. Long-term follow-up will allow the final analysis of the benefit of therapy for this couple.

REFERENCES

Baucom, D. H., Shoham, V., Mueser, K. T., Daiuto, A. D., & Stickle, T. R. (1998). Empirically supported couple and family interventions for marital distress and adult mental health problems. *Journal of Consulting and Clinical Psychology, 66*, 53–88.

Bograd, M., & Mederos, F. (1999). Battering and couples therapy: Universal screening and selection of treatment modality. *Journal of Marital and Family Therapy, 25*, 291–312.

Christensen, A., & Heavey, C. L. (1999). Interventions for couples. *Annual Review of Psychology, 50*, 165–190.

Christensen, A., & Jacobson, N. S. (1997). *Frequency and Acceptability of Partner Behaviors Scale.* Unpublished questionnaire, University of California–Los Angeles.

Christensen, A., & Jacobson, N. S. (2000). *Reconcilable differences.* New York: Guilford Press.

Christensen, A., Jacobson, N. S., & Babcock, J. C. (1995). Integrative behavioral couple therapy. In N. S. Jacobson & A. S. Gurman (Eds.), *Clinical handbook of couple therapy* (pp. 31–64). New York: Guilford Press.

Cordova, J. V., Jacobson, N. S., & Christensen, A. (1998). Acceptance versus change interventions in behavioral couples therapy: Impact on couples' in-session communication. *Journal of Marriage and Family Counseling, 24*, 437–455.

Gottman, J. (1994). *Why marriages succeed or fail . . . and how you can make yours last.* New York: Simon & Schuster.

Gottman, J., Markman, H., Notarius, C., & Gonso, J. (1976). *A couple's guide to communication.* Champaign, IL: Research Press.

Hahlweg, K., & Markman, H. J. (1988). The effectiveness of behavioral marital therapy: Empirical status of behavioral techniques in preventing and alleviating marital distress. *Journal of Consulting and Clinical Psychology, 56*, 440–447.

Holtzworth-Munroe, A., Beatty, S. B., & Anglin, K. (1995). The assessment and treatment of marital violence: An introduction for the marital therapist. In N. S. Jacobson & A. Gurman (Eds.), *Clinical handbook of couple therapy* (pp. 317–339). New York: Guilford Press.

Jacobson, N. S. (1984). A component analysis of behavioral marital therapy: The relative effectiveness of behavior exchange and problem solving training. *Journal of Consulting and Clinical Psychology, 52*, 295–305.

Jacobson, N. S., & Addis, M. E. (1993). Research on couples and couple therapy: What do we know? Where are we going? *Journal of Consulting and Clinical Psychology, 61*, 85–93.

Jacobson, N. S., & Christensen, A. (1996). *Integrative couple therapy: Promoting acceptance and change.* New York: Norton.

Jacobson, N. S., Christensen, A., Prince, S. E., Cordova, J., & Eldridge, K. (2000). Integrative behavioral couple therapy: An acceptance-based, promising new treatment for couple discord. *Journal of Consulting and Clinical Psychology, 68*, 351–355.

Jacobson, N. S., Follette, W. C., Revenstorf, D., Baucom, D. H., Hahlweg, K., & Margolin, G. (1984). Variability in outcome and clinical significance of behavioral marital therapy: A reanalysis of outcome data. *Journal of Consulting and Clinical Psychology, 52*, 497–504.

Jacobson, N. S., & Gottman, J. M. (1998). *When men batter women: New insights into ending abusive relationships.* New York: Simon & Schuster.

Jacobson, N. S., Gottman, J. M., Gortner, E., Berns, S., & Shortt, J. W. (1996). Psychological factors in the longitudinal course of battering: When do the couples split up? When does the abuse decrease? *Violence and Victims, 11*, 371–392.

Jacobson, N. S., & Margolin, G. (1979). *Marital therapy: Strategies based on social learning and behavior exchange principles.* New York: Brunner/Mazel.

Jacobson, N. S., Schmaling, K. B., & Holtzworth-Munroe, A. (1987). A component analysis of behavioral marital therapy: Two-year follow-up and prediction of relapse. *Journal of Marital and Family Therapy, 13,* 187–195.

Karney, B. R., & Bradbury, T. N. (1995). The longitudinal course of marital quality and stability: A review of theory, method, and research. *Psychological Bulletin, 118,* 3–34.

Martell, C. R., & Land, T. E. (in press). Cognitive and behavior therapy with same gender couples. In T. M. Patterson (Ed.), *Comprehensive textbook of psychotherapy: Vol. 3. Cognitive, behavioral and functional approaches.* New York: Wiley.

Noller, P., Beach, S., & Osgarby, S. (1997). Cognitive and affective processes in marriage. In W. K. Halford & H. J. Markman (Eds.), *Clinical handbook of marriage and couples intervention* (pp. 43–71). New York: Wiley.

O'Leary, K. D., Vivian, D., & Malone, J. (1992). Assessment of physical aggression against women in marriage: The need for multimodal assessment. *Behavioral Assessment, 14,* 5–14.

Pepper, S. C. (1942). *World hypotheses.* Berkeley: University of California Press.

Skinner, B. F. (1966). An operant analysis of problem solving. In B. Kleinmuntz (Ed.), *Problem solving: Research method teaching* (pp. 225–257). New York: Wiley.

Snyder, D. K. (1997). *Marital Satisfaction Inventory–Revised.* Los Angeles: Western Psychological Services.

Spanier, G. B. (1976). Measuring dyadic adjustment: New scales for assessing the quality of marriage and similar dyads. *Journal of Marriage and the Family, 38,* 15–28.

Straus, M. A. (1979). Measuring intrafamily conflict and violence: The Conflict Tactics Scales. *Journal of Marriage and the Family, 41,* 75–88.

Weiss, R. L., & Cerreto, M. C. (1980). The Marital Status Inventory: Development of a measure of dissolution potential. *American Journal of Family Therapy, 8*(2), 80–85.

Weiss, R. L., & Heyman, R. E. (1997). A clinical-research overview of couples interactions. In W. K. Halford & H. J. Markman (Eds.), *Clinical handbook of marriage and couples intervention* (pp. 13–41). New York: Wiley.

Weiss, R. L., Hops, H., & Patterson, G. R. (1973). A framework for conceptualizing marital conflict, a technology for altering it, some data for evaluating it. In L. A. Hamerlynck, L. C. Handy, & E. J. Mash (Eds.), *Behavior change: Methodology, concepts, and practice* (pp. 309–342). Champaign, IL: Research Press.

Wile, D. B. (1988). *After the honeymoon: How conflict can improve your relationship.* New York: Wiley.

Section C

Postmodern Approaches

Chapter 10

Collaborative Couple Therapy

Collaborative couple therapy (CCT) focuses on the intrinsic difficulty of being in a relationship: the inevitability of slipping repeatedly into withdrawn and adversarial cycles. How partners cope with these cycles determines the quality of life in the relationship and, indeed, whether the relationship lasts. Gottman (1999) can watch newlyweds discuss a disagreement for 3 minutes and predict whether they will stay together. What he is observing is how they relate when in an adversarial cycle.

In CCT, the therapist shows the partners how, by discovering and confiding the "leading-edge" thought or feeling of the moment, they can shift out of their withdrawn or adversarial cycle and into a collaborative one. The goal is to increase their ability to make such a shift themselves.

A defining feature of this approach is an appreciation of how, as therapists, we grapple with the same problems the partners do: being pulled into adversarial states, where we lose the ability to appreciate each partner's point of view, and into withdrawn states, where we lose the ability to engage at all. Partners become dysfunctional, and we, their therapists, do so too. In the course of a session, we keep losing and regaining our ability to do therapy.

CCT is "collaborative" both in the stance the therapist tries to adopt toward the partners and the relationship the therapist tries to establish between them. The term "collaborative therapy" is borrowed from Goolishian and Anderson, who go further than anyone I know in developing a truly collaborative rather than hierarchical relationship with

their clients (Anderson, 1997). The trend in our field is increasingly toward such a client–therapist relationship, as seen in the intersubjectivist, relational, and hermeneutic schools of psychoanalysis and in social constructionism in general. At the forefront of this trend are Duncan and Miller (2000), who view clients as codesigners or even principal designers of their therapy.

EGO ANALYSIS: THE THEORETICAL SOURCE OF THIS APPROACH

CCT emerges out of ego analysis, a form of psychological reasoning developed by Bernard Apfelbaum (Apfelbaum, 2000a, 2000b, 2000c, 2000d; Apfelbaum & Gill, 1989). Ego analysis, although itself emerging out of psychoanalytic thinking, is practically unrecognizable as such. Apfelbaum describes it as "analyzing without psychoanalyzing." He has made what seems on the face of it a simple shift—replacing the id with the superego as the major pathological force—but the result has been the total transformation of the nature of therapy (Wile, 1984, 1985, 1987, 1994). Freud, although laying the groundwork for such a superego-oriented view (Freud, 1923, 1930), placed greater emphasis on the id. He talked about the power of the client's drives, wishes, and fantasies (Freud, 1937). Clients resist change—in part, he said, because of the gratification they get out of their symptomatic reactions. The critical word here is "resist." Therapists who think of their clients as resisting will find themselves to some degree in adversarial relation with them, in reaction to what they see as these clients' adversarial relationship toward them. In a modern-day version of this view, which has been adopted by many nonanalytic as well as analytic therapists, clients are seen as hanging onto their narcissistic and dependent gratifications rather than growing up and accepting the responsibilities of adulthood.

The replacement of the id with the superego as the principal pathological force shifts the client–therapist relationship from one that is intrinsically adversarial (i.e., therapists' seeing themselves as dealing with resistant clients) to one that is intrinsically collaborative. The core of the problem is now seen as punitive superego injunctions—the feeling of unentitlement to what clients are experiencing (their sense of shame or self-blame) that prevents them from getting sufficiently on their own sides to think and talk effectively about it. Therapists become advocates for clients, in order to get the clients on their own sides. Such an approach is particularly characteristic of the following nonpsychoanalytic therapists: Rogers's (1959) client-centered therapy, White and Epston's (1990) narrative therapy, de Shazer's (1985) solution-focused therapy, and Goolishian and Anderson's (Anderson, 1997) collaborative therapy. The heart of the problem, as a superego-based therapist sees it, is not resistance but "loss of voice" (to borrow a term from Hardy, 1998): the inability of clients to speak in their own behalf, or even to know what they think and feel.

Id-based and superego-based approaches are in some ways incompatible. Each approach is seen by proponents of the other approach as countertherapeutic, and in fact as countertransference acting out. Id-based therapists fault superego-based therapists for failing to take a stand against clients' narcissistic demandingness, dependency pulls, self-indulgent strivings, blame of others, and abdication of personal responsibility. They see these therapists as giving in to their clients' anxieties, shrinking from these clients' anger, and lacking therapeutic courage, perhaps as a consequence of a deficiency in their own psychological development.

Superego-based therapists fault id-based therapists for *taking* such stands, rather than recognizing their urge to do so as a countertransference clue. The fact that we feel like exhorting, admonishing, or lecturing clients is a sign that they are doing a poor job of expressing what they are struggling with—that is, of representing themselves—which means that it is our job to help. Our task is to become spokespersons for clients at precisely those moments in which, and for precisely those issues about which, we feel most like reproaching them. CCT applies such thinking to couple therapy. Our task, since there are two partners in front of us rather than just a single client, is to serve as spokespersons for both partners simultaneously.

The approach presented in these pages results essentially from replacing resistance with loss of voice as the core pathological principle.

COMPARISON WITH OTHER APPROACHES

CCT can be thought of as a psychodynamic approach, since you dig out unexpressed fears and wishes. Unlike most psychodynamic approaches, however, you do not view partners as resisting therapy, see their symptoms as serving unconscious purposes, or rely for your therapeutic effect on tracing the problem to the partners' families of origin.

CCT could be thought of as a family systems approach, since you see the partners as caught in a feedback loop. But you see them as caught in a positive (deviation-amplifying) feedback loop, as described by Watzlawick, Weakland, and Fisch (1974), rather than the negative (homeostatic) feedback loop of the classic family systems model. That is, you do not see partners' symptoms as serving the homeostatic purpose of maintaining couple stability. The cycles I talk about—adversarial, withdrawn, and empathic—are, essentially, positive feedback loops; that is, they are self-reinforcing.

CCT could be thought of as a behavioral approach, since you observe how each partner rewards the other in response to feeling rewarded by the other, and also how each punishes the other in response to feeling punished by the other (see Jacobson & Margolin, 1979, pp. 13–17). Unlike behavioral therapists, however, you emphasize solving the moment rather than solving the problem.

CCT could be thought of as a cognitive approach, since you focus on each person's ongoing inner conversation, and you attribute the problem to negative self-talk. Unlike cognitive therapists, however, you rely not on eliminating this negative self-talk, but on creating a compassionate perspective from which partners can appreciate the inevitability of recurrently getting caught in it.

CCT could be thought of as a "Rogerian," client-centered approach, since you provide the facilitative atmosphere that enables partners to connect with themselves and with each other. Unlike Rogers, however, you make speculations about what the partners might be thinking and feeling, dramatize each partner's experience, and speak for them.

CCT could be thought of as a social-constructionist approach, since you adopt a nonpathologizing stance, attribute the problem to negative beliefs that partners have about themselves, enable partners to stand back and look at themselves having the problem, and engage in positive reframing. Unlike some social-constructionists, however, you see the positive reframe as the accurate version rather than as just another arbitrary reality.

CCT adopts the object relations concept of a holding environment. Unlike therapists employing a well-known version of object relations therapy, however, you do not attribute partners' symptomatic behavior to projective identification; instead, you look for hidden ways in which this behavior is an understandable response to the hidden realities in the immediate situation.

CCT shares the communication skills training goal of shifting partners from fighting and withdrawing to talking. In agreement with many communication skills trainers, you do not expect the rules of good communication to deal with couple fighting. You recognize that in a fight these rules go out the window. Unlike communication skills trainers, however, you show how the partners' violations of these rules make sense and how, for example, sometimes nothing but a good "you" statement will do (Wile, 1988).

CCT adopts the psychodrama method of "alter-egoing" along with its underlying assumption, which is that behind each person's symptomatic behavior is an unexpressed heartfelt feeling that you try to bring out.

CCT is similar to Wachtel's (1993) cyclical psychodynamics in its emphasis on entitling people to their experience in the process of suggesting what it is.

CCT is similar to Johnson's (1996) emotionally focused therapy in reframing experience in nonpathologizing terms, facilitating an exchange of heartfelt feelings, and breaking the negative cycles that block attachment. (See also Johnson & Denton, Chapter 8, this volume.)

CCT is similar to Jacobson and Christensen's (1996) integrative behavioral couple therapy in its nonpathologizing stance and goal of getting partners to join around the problem and to adopt a stance of unified detachment from the problem. (See also Christensen & Jacobson, 2000; Dimidjian, Martell, & Christensen, Chapter 9, this volume.)

CCT is similar to Gottman's (Gottman, 1999; Gottman & DeClaire, 2001) "sound marital house" approach in dealing with adversarial and withdrawn cycles by means of repair efforts and bids for contact, building the relationship out of the couple's perpetual problems, and resolving gridlock by bringing out the hidden dream and (as a colleague, Lee Kassan, puts it) the hidden fear. (See also Gottman, Driver, & Tabares, Chapter 13, this volume.)

THE THREE CYCLES

CCT emerges out of the realization that the inner atmosphere of a relationship is continually changing, and that it is possible at any moment to capture an intimacy intrinsic to that moment and to create a collaborative (empathic) cycle. The terms "collaborative cycle" and "empathic cycle" are used interchangeably, since each term highlights an important aspect of the idea.

Creating a Collaborative Cycle: An Illustration

Joe, whom I have been seeing in couple therapy with his wife, Sarah, snaps at her in a session, "You're a workaholic!" His comment begins an adversarial rather than a collaborative cycle. It turns Sarah into an enemy. She says, "Look, I've got this work to do." He says, "You've always 'got this work to do.'" She says, "Don't be such a nag." He says, "I didn't use to be a nag. You've turned me into one." Each person stings in response to feeling stung, which is what generates an adversarial cycle. A crucial factor determining satisfaction in a relationship, Gottman and Silver (1999) say, is the couple's ability to engage in successful repair efforts (i.e., attempts to reduce the tension) in order to keep such cycles from escalating out of control.

Blurting out "You're a workaholic!" provides Joe a certain satisfaction. He would get even more satisfaction, however, were he able to tell Sarah, "I'm ashamed of how lonely I get these evenings when you bring work home." He would be exposing the inner struggle out of which his "You're a workaholic!" has emerged. Let us say that Sarah is moved by Joe's willingness to reveal his tender feelings in this way that is not blaming her. Her heart goes out to him. She says, "Yes, I have let this grant completely take me over; it has made me lonely, too." Joe's confiding would elicit confiding from her, leading to a collaborative cycle. They would be fulfilling the potential for intimacy intrinsic to the moment.

Here, in microcosm, is the theory of couple relationships out of which CCT emerges. When partners cannot confide their leading-edge thought or feeling (which may be because they do not know what it is), they often behave in ways that offend their partners. If you cannot turn your partner into an ally, you get stuck either blurting something out and turning your partner into an enemy (an adversarial cycle), or saying nothing at all about what you are feeling and turning your partner into a stranger (a withdrawn cycle). Each moment in a relationship provides an opportunity for intimacy, but there is a penalty for failure to achieve it: the shift toward an adversarial or withdrawn state. We are continually paying this penalty, since only rarely are we able to come up with the confiding statement.

Fall-Back Measures

This theory of couple relationships leads to an approach to therapy based on recognizing clients' pathological behaviors as fall-back positions (Kohut's [1977] "breakdown products"). When what you would really want to do is closed off to you, you engage in compensatory, second-rate, fall-back measures—Plan B. When your key does not turn in the lock, you first jiggle it around delicately, trying to find the angle that will turn the tumblers. You use finesse. That is Plan A. Plan B (which actually is not so much a plan as it is something you just find yourself doing) is using brute force, breaking the key off in the lock, leaving half of it in your hand.

Plan A for Joe would be to say to Sarah, "I'm ashamed of how lonely I get when you spend evenings doing work from the hospital." Plan B is blurting out, "You're a workaholic!" My task as their therapist is to help Joe come up with this fuller, more satisfying, original version that, because he could not find it, led to his blurted-out accusation. I act as his spokesperson, at times literally so: I may move my chair over next to Joe and start speaking for him, in a method similar to "alter-egoing" in psychodrama. My goal is to interrupt the partners' adversarial cycle (their turning each other into enemies) or their withdrawn cycle (their turning each other into strangers) and to induce a collaborative cycle (their turning each other into allies).

Joe would be triggering a withdrawn cycle—he would be turning Sarah into a stranger—were

he to suppress his feelings about her working evenings and, in an effort to put his best foot forward, say, "So how's your grant writing going?" But there would be a hollowness in his tone. Sarah, taking it to mean that he is not really interested, would lose heart in telling him anything about it and would respond with equal hollowness, "Fine." In this two-sentence exchange, Joe and Sarah would deplete the inner-relationship atmosphere of its emotional oxygen, leaving both a little demoralized. They would be engaging in a withdrawn cycle, in which the polite, restrained, affectless, disengaged, spirit-depleting response of each stimulates the same in the other, much as whispering stimulates whispering.

A *relationship is essentially a shifting among empathic, withdrawn, and adversarial cycles* (Wile, 1999). Partners are either confiding what is on their minds, which means that they are in an empathic (collaborative) cycle, or they are not confiding, which means that they are in a withdrawn cycle, unless there is blaming going on, in which case they are in an adversarial cycle. Every couple spends time in each of these three cycles, although couples differ in the time spent in each and the form each takes. For some couples, being in an adversarial cycle means an out-and-out battle; for others, it may be a simple exchange of looks.

THE THERAPIST'S PROBLEM

Couples repeatedly get caught in adversarial and withdrawn cycles, and I get caught in them too. The problem for me in dealing with Joe's "You're a workaholic!" is that I initially reacted in much the same way that Sarah did. I felt put off by it, which meant that I had been drawn into much the same kind of adversarial relationship with him that she had, although a more reduced version of it. And once in that cycle, I found myself mentally using DSM-IV as a weapon against Joe; I wondered whether he was too narcissistic to be capable of a mature relationship. I found myself wanting to say to him, "Telling Sarah, 'You're a workaholic,' is a 'you' statement. It's name calling. That's not going to get her to listen to you." Were I to say that, I would be criticizing Joe for criticizing Sarah.

In my stance toward partners, I continually shift among adversarial, withdrawn, and empathic modes, just as they do with each other. CCT is possible only when I am in an empathic/collaborative mode myself. When I am in a withdrawn mode, I am tuned out, disengaged, and in no position to do therapy at all. When I am in an adversarial mode, I am so provoked by the client's symptomatic behavior that I forget that it is a fall-back measure; I view it instead as indicating something basic about the person that it is my responsibility as a therapist to do something about. In that mode, I think I would be failing in my duty were I not to confront Joe with his "you" statement and his sense of narcissistic entitlement.

CCT requires recurrently digging myself out of adversarial and withdrawn modes. I tell myself, "Uh-oh! I'm obviously feeling disapproving of Joe—I'm in an adversarial mode—which means that I've temporarily lost the ability to recognize his behavior as a fall-back measure, and I'm just reacting to it." Just realizing that I have forgotten the fall-back principle is all I need to shift back into a collaborative mode, where it again becomes possible to do this kind of therapy. The important question I ask myself that signals my shift back to this mode is this: "What is Joe's inner struggle, out of which his 'You're a workaholic!' emerged, that, were I to help put it into words, might get Sarah, Joe, and me all empathizing with him?" My goal is to create a collaborative spirit and an intimate moment for the three of us.

My feeling of disapproval toward Joe—this obvious impediment in my ability to do therapy with him—has, at the same time, a powerful possible benefit: It puts me in touch with his contribution to the relationship problem of the moment, which is his failure to confide his inner struggle and his engagement instead in a fall-back measure. This measure—attacking Sarah—is what has gotten me feeling disapproving, and it is what has turned Sarah into an enemy. My disapproval is both a hindrance, since it puts me out of position to do therapy, and a useful clue to the relationship problem of the moment. The task is to turn my adversarial stance—my disapproval—from a destructive force into a constructive one.

CCT is based on an appreciation of how, as therapists, we struggle with the same problems the partners do: being pulled into adversarial states, where we lose the ability to appreciate the other person's inner struggle, and into withdrawn states, where we lose the ability to engage at all. As therapists, we struggle with two additional states: anxious states, where the pressure we feel to help couples impairs our ability to do so; and self-critical states, where we lose our therapeutic self-confidence. To dramatize the point—to demonstrate the profound effect that our state of mind has on our therapeutic work—consider how our approach toward a client with a particular diagnosis depends upon the state we have been drawn into at the moment. For example, how I view a person with, say, "narcissistic personality disorder" depends on whether I am in a collaborative, adversarial, withdrawn, anxious, or self-critical state.

When I am in a collaborative (empathic) state, I focus on the narcissistic vulnerabilities, which is what Kohut (1977) did. I view the grandiosity, arrogance, and other symptomatic reactions as fall-back measures, and I try to bring out the inner struggle over loss of self and loss of sense of contact with others that they represent a fall back from.

When I am in an adversarial state, which means I am reacting to the provocative nature of the client's behavior, I focus on this person's grandiose reaction to his/her narcissistic vulnerability—this person's arrogance, claims of narcissistic entitlement, and inability to appreciate what others might feel. I forget that these reactions are fall-back measures, and view them instead as something basic and irreducible about the person that it is my responsibility to confront.

When I am in a withdrawn state, which means I feel stymied, helpless, and passive in the face of the seemingly bedrock nature of the person's pathology, I lose my ability to focus on the person in any kind of useful way at all. I give up for the moment on being able to help him/her. I drift off mentally, daydream about my next vacation, and think of how to redecorate my office.

When I am in an anxious state, which means I feel responsible to help this person but powerless to do so, I go on a desperate mental search of what I have read about narcissistic personality disorder, looking for something to try. I may rush in with fix-it measures. I put pressure on the client to change and, when he/she does not, get frustrated and view the person as refusing to grow up—which means I have shifted to an adversarial state.

When I am in a self-critical state, which means that I take these difficulties in the therapy personally, my attention shifts from the client's defects to mine. I lose my therapeutic self-confidence, imagine that other therapists would be doing a much better job, and think about changing professions. My ability to listen is impaired by the background noise of my negative self-talk and could easily lead to withdrawal, just as my anxious state would lead to an adversarial state.

THE THERAPIST'S SHIFT FROM ADVERSARIAL TO EMPATHIC STANCE

CCT requires taking into account the state of mind the therapist is in. I know I am in a collaborative (empathic) state, which is where I want to be, when I am able to speak from within each partner's experience and appreciate how the reactions of each make sense; they are understandable at least as fallback reactions. When I find myself wanting to tell a wife, "You've been repeating yourself, which is causing your husband to fade out," I know I have slipped into an adversarial state and have lost the ability to appreciate how her reactions make sense. Realizing that I have lost this ability is all I need to regain it. I tell her, "You've been repeating yourself, which is causing your husband to fade out. Of course, the *reason* you're repeating may be that you don't think he has heard it yet—it hasn't gotten through—and it's something important that you want to make sure *does* get through."

When I find myself wanting to tell a husband, "Your wife is doing exactly what you said you wanted, and you're not satisfied with that either," I know I have lost my ability to look at things from his point of view. Again, realizing that I have lost this ability is all I need to regain it. I ask, "Are you *disappointed* that your wife's finally doing what you said you always wanted isn't having more of a positive effect on you?" I offer possible explanations: "Do you feel that it's too little too late? Does having to ask for it take away from the pleasure of getting it? Are you suddenly aware that it's not what you really wanted after all? Does her doing it this one time fill you with longing, and resentment that she hasn't been doing it all along?" Once I consider that his reactions *might* make sense, I often immediately come up with ideas of *how* they might make sense.

When I find myself wanting to tell a husband, "You're trying to control your wife," I know I have forgotten my belief (Wile, 1981) that controlling is typically a reaction to feeling powerless. Remembering this, I am able to tell him, "What a spot you're in! Your effort to convince your wife not to go back to get her master's degree is alienating her, destroying her good will toward you, and imperiling the relationship—not to mention that it's no fun to stand in the way of what this person you care about truly longs for. But you're haunted by the thought that her going back to school is an irretrievable first step toward her leaving you." A moment ago I was seeing him as "controlling"; now I am seeing him as "haunted."

When I find myself wanting to tell a woman that she is being "defensive"—when I use that term to organize my thinking about her—I know I am reacting to her behavior and have slipped into an adversarial state, which means I am out of position to do therapy. I tell myself, "OK, Dan, try to look at things from her point of view." That is all I need to be able to tell her, "I've made several wrong guesses about you today. I wonder if you're feeling that I'm not in tune with you, that I'm unable to appreciate your side of things, and that you're stuck here with two men—your husband and me—who don't understand how a woman feels?" A moment ago I was seeing her as defensive; now I am appreciating her struggle.

As described earlier, CCT results from replacing resistance (and defensiveness) with loss of voice as the core psychodynamic concept. My viewing this client as defensive says more about me—about my frame of mind and the angle at which I am looking at things at the moment—than it does about her. It is my clue that I am out of position to do therapy: I am reacting to her behavior rather than seeing through to the inner struggle. I have stopped too soon in the causal chain. I am thinking, "She's defensive; that's the problem. She's a defensive person." Were I to continue to the next step in the causal chain, I would think, "She is defensive because of the threat she feels—which is what I need to be focusing on."

CCT is born out of the recognition that partners become dysfunctional in the moment, and that as their therapist, I do too. I keep losing the ability to appreciate how their reactions make sense, just as they do with each other. I keep slipping out of a collaborative (empathic) stance toward them and into an adversarial or withdrawn one, just as they do with each other. The realization that I operate according to the same principles as the partners enables me to normalize their behavior, as well as to become more forgiving of my own.

I am in an adversarial state much of the time, as is every other couple therapist. Repeatedly I find myself privately siding with one of the partners—what Bowen (1978) calls "being triangled in"—which means that I am at least to some degree in an adversarial state with the other. And I can change sides quickly. The reason that I am siding against one partner (the "defensive" woman) rather than the other is that she is doing the poorer job of representing herself at the moment. She is not talking about her inner struggle in a way that would move me, win me over, and get me empathizing—which is exactly the problem she is having with her partner. My feeling of disapproval puts me in touch with her part in the relationship problem of the moment, which is this inability to represent herself. The instruction I give myself that shifts me out of my adversarial state and restores my ability to do therapy is this: "My job is to become spokesperson for the partner whom at the moment I find myself siding against."

Being in an adversarial state is not a problem in itself, which is a good thing, since I am repeatedly going to find myself in it. But it is a problem when I do not know I am in it, since I have no choice then but to take my negative reaction as just seeing that person for who he is. If I *know* I am in an adversarial state, I can turn my negative reaction into a therapeutic instrument pointing me to the relationship problem of the moment.

REASSEMBLING THE RELATIONSHIP ON THE NEXT HIGHER LEVEL

Implicit in this theory of relationships is a theory of individual functioning. Recurrently throughout the day, we feel an unease: a longing, ache, worry, disappointment, threat, lonely surge, nagging thought, depressed pang, jealous twinge, wave of regret, 10-minute crisis of confidence, or other such unnerving or disquieting feelings. What we are able to say to our partners and to ourselves about these feelings, rather than just acting on them and becoming symptomatic, determines the quality of life in the relationship. Ideally—and the goal of CCT is to increase our ability to do this—we can turn the feeling that is haunting us into raw material for creating an intimate moment. The wish that many partners have to tell each other about their day is, in part, an effort to confide the stored-up uneases they have experienced.

If you are going to make contact with your partner, it must be in terms of your leading-edge thought or feeling, which is often your unease of the moment. That is what intimacy is: letting your partner in on who you are at the moment, and your partner doing the same with you. If you have an urge to repeat something or to withdraw from your partner, then *that* is who you are at the moment. Confiding (reporting) rather than just acting upon it is how to create an intimate moment.

If the unease you confide to your partner is about your partner, you are in essence taking your partner into your confidence about this difficulty you are having with your partner. You are going

within to discover your inner struggle and then standing back and reporting it. You are creating a second tier in the relationship, an observation post, a metalevel, a joint platform, an observing couple ego. You are solving the immediate problem in the relationship by moving up and reassembling the relationship on the next higher level. You are creating a collaborative cycle by the very fact that you and your partner are talking about the adversarial or withdrawn one the two of you are in.

The wife who repeated herself would be creating such a metalevel were she to say to her husband, "I know I have already said this three times, and this has led you, understandably, to stop listening. But I am about to say it for a fourth time because I don't think I have gotten you to see how important this is to me." The controlling husband would be creating a metalevel were he to say to his wife, "I am so terrified that your going back to school is the first step in your leaving me that I cannot seem to stop acting in this way that is practically *guaranteed* to drive you away."

In making these statements, these people would be recruiting their partners as resources in dealing with this relationship problem of the moment rather than as accomplices in perpetuating it, to use Wachtel's (1991, 1993, 1997) terminology. They would be making their partners part of the solution rather than part of the problem, to apply this familiar phrase to couples, as Johnson has done (Johnson & Williams-Keeler, 1998). But how often are any of us going to be able so eloquently to bring our partners in on what we are struggling with? Not often, which reveals how far out on the fringes of intimacy we all operate. And we pay a price when we cannot: a shift to an adversarial or withdrawn state.

SOLVING THE MOMENT RATHER THAN SOLVING THE PROBLEM

The crucial problem from a CCT point of view is not the one the partners are arguing over, but their inability to recruit each other as resources in dealing with it. To me, that is the real problem—how partners relate to each other about the issue at hand. It is how partners relate about *whatever* is going on that creates the inner atmosphere and quality of life within the relationship.

It is an advantage not to have to solve the couple's problems, since many of these problems are unsolvable (Gottman, 1999; Jacobson & Christensen, 1996; Wile, 1981). Gottman calls them "perpetual problems." Every couple has their own set of perpetual problems that they are going to be wrestling with throughout the relationship. The goal is to build the relationship out of the manner in which they relate to each other about these problems, turning moment-to-moment manifestations of them into moments of intimacy. To the extent that partners are able to recruit each other as resources, they will find themselves automatically coming up with whatever concrete solutions and compromises are possible.

Is such "solving the moment" rather than "solving the problem" possible with partners with character pathology, such as those diagnosed with narcissistic or borderline personality disorder? The challenge with such people, as it is with everyone else, is for the therapist to make the shift from disapproval to empathy—from viewing such people from an adversarial perspective to viewing them from an empathic one. I ask myself, "What is this person experiencing? What is the inner struggle that, were she able to confide it, would get me, the partner, and the person herself all on her side?"

The CCT idea of "inner struggle" is similar to the cognitive therapy idea of "self-talk" and the narrative therapy idea of "self-conversation." All are ways of referring to the ongoing conversation or debate that people hold with themselves. They engage in such inner conversation even if they are unaware of it, just as people dream each night even if they cannot remember doing so. This inner struggle, self-talk, or self-conversation is the plane on which life is experienced. It is the immediate "who I am" that the intimate moment needs to be about.

CCT emerges out of the recognition that at any given moment there is something a partner can say, and a conversation the couple can have, that can reassemble the relationship on a higher level and create a collaborative cycle. Therapists who think in these terms will find themselves automatically trying to come up with this conversation.

Recovery Conversations

It is difficult, when partners are in an adversarial cycle, for them to stand back and talk collaboratively about it. The emphasis in CCT, accordingly, is on increasing the partners' ability to do so afterward—that is, by holding a recovery conversation. The partners get together by talking about having been at odds. They look back at the fight they just had, but now are able to appreciate how each other's reactions made sense. They form an empathic cycle by talking about the adversarial one they have just

been in. They reassemble the relationship on the next higher level.

During the fight, each partner has felt too unheard to listen. In the recovery conversation, since the partners have now shifted out of their adversarial cycle and into an empathic one, each becomes understanding in response to feeling understood; in fact, they often begin making each other's points. A wife may say, "I got so angry—now I realize there was no way for you to see how hurt I was," which is exactly what her husband had been trying so hard during the fight to get her to understand. In response, the husband may say, "Yes, but I should know you well enough by this time to know that," which is what the wife had been struggling so hard during the fight to get *him* to see.

People sometimes say things in fights that they do not mean, but often only in fights are they able to say what they *do* mean. Fights contain information about a relationship. Since the partners are in an adversarial state, the information initially surfaces as an attack. For instance, a husband doesn't say to his wife, "Since I always thought of myself as so independent, I was shocked how much I missed you this weekend." He says, "You'd never think to call me, would you?"—a comment that triggers an adversarial cycle. After the fight, he can make use of the information that came to the surface. He can go to his wife and say, "I guess I really missed you this weekend"—a comment that could easily trigger an empathic cycle. She might say, "That's sweet. I never thought of you as ever missing anybody." He might say, "*I* never thought of me as ever missing anybody, and it makes me a little nervous." Fights provide potential starting points for intimate conversations.

Partners are typically hesitant to talk about their fights afterward in fear of restarting them. A goal in CCT is to improve the partners' abilities to have recovery conversations that do not rekindle the fight, but instead tap the fight for the useful information it has revealed. A recovery conversation can revitalize a relationship so dramatically that the partners may be glad for the fight that occasioned it.

Family-of-Origin Issues

In CCT, the task is to turn the problem of the moment into a way to reach out. But can this focus on the moment deal with problems that go back to the partners' families of origin? Don't you need to contact the early source of the problem—the childhood wound, the problematic early relationships? Don't you need to help partners confront their unresolved feelings toward the important figures in their pasts? The CCT approach of creating an intimate moment can enable partners to deal with unresolved feelings toward these figures in their pasts.

Wachtel (1993, 1997) has elegantly described how a person's family-of-origin-based problems are continually being recreated in the moment; although people may not intend to, they often end up recruiting their partners as accomplices. In CCT, you treat a family-of-origin problem as it is recreated in the couple interaction now, in the moment. What is recreated, in particular, is a kind of automatic incapacity or emotional aphasia that Hardy (1998), in describing the effects of being oppressed, calls a "loss of voice": "an inability to speak on one's behalf, to serve as an advocate for oneself, to exercise agency over one's being."

To return to the earlier example of Joe and Sarah, Joe's father left the family abruptly when Joe was 5, sending his mother into a depression and leaving Joe essentially without either parent. Joe has a family-of-origin-based sensitivity to abandonment. He gets upset when Sarah goes away for a few days, or just mentally abandons him—for example, becoming preoccupied with work from the hospital. The core of his problem, its active ingredient, is the loss of voice: the automatic incapacity that comes over him that prevents him from reaching out to Sarah. We would not think of him as even having a problem were he able to tell her, "Sarah, when you came home this evening with all that work, I felt I was right back there when my father left and my mother immediately disappeared on me too and I got into this kind of lost, hopeless state."

In saying this, Joe would be bringing Sarah in on what he is experiencing. He would be saying, in essence, "Sarah, I've got this problem when you bring work home instead of spending evenings with me. You're doing important work that I want to support. But something gets triggered in me. I get into this kind of lost, hopeless state. However, the wonderful thing is that just telling you about it makes me feel less lost and hopeless. I wish I'd had someone like you to talk with about it when I was a child." Instead of blaming Sarah or asking her to change, Joe is saying that the change has already occurred simply in his being able to tell her this.

This description of what Joe could ideally say makes clear that his problem is his inability to say

it. When he feels a little abandoned by her, he abandons himself, which is the crucial abandonment. He becomes tongue-tied, loses 30 IQ points, gives up, and later blurts out an angry "You love your work better than you do me." Were Joe to react to his moment-to-moment feelings of abandonment in a way that recruits Sarah as a confidant and brings her into his experience, so he is not abandoned (and so he does not abandon himself), that would be the cure.

We would not want to tell him, "Joe, you've got to take responsibility for your fear of abandonment, deal with it on your own, and not burden Sarah with it." We would want to improve his ability to reach out to her. That is the CCT way to take personal responsibility.

Reaching out is the solution because Joe's inability to do so as a child lies at the heart of his problem. What makes childhood trauma so damaging, Layton and Harkaway (1998) say, is that it was uncomforted. The problem is not trauma, but *uncomforted* trauma. The adults in the child's life were nonsupportive presences. In the case of father–daughter incest, the mother was, in addition, a nonprotective presence. Children internalize these nonsupportive and nonprotective adult presences. They become unable to comfort themselves and to reach out to others for comfort. The goal in CCT is to help partners turn themselves and each other into supportive, protective, and comforting presences.

As described earlier, CCT replaces resistance with loss of voice as the key pathological principle. Layton and Harkaway's idea of uncomforted trauma provides a family-of-origin explanation for the development of this loss of voice.

To the extent that Joe becomes able to reach out to Sarah when he feels abandoned, he will be able to transform his family-of-origin special sensitivity into an instrument for detecting undercurrents in the relationship. Just as canaries are sensitive to reduced levels of oxygen—which is why miners take them down in the mines with them, as an early warning system—Joe's early traumatic abandonment sensitizes him to the subtle, everyday ways in which Sarah abandons him. He is the couple's miner's canary for subtle disconnections in their relationship. They are not going to wake up one day, as some couples do, finding themselves in a detached, alienated, devitalized relationship without knowing how they got there. Joe is their protection against that. At the same time, both he and Sarah might wish he were not quite so sensitive.

Everyone has his/her own set of family-of-origin-based special sensitivities. One of Sarah's is her sensitivity to other people's disapproval. She gets upset when those important to her—originally her mother, but now principally Joe—are unhappy with her. At such moments, she disengages. She treats Joe as someone who has to be worked around, rather than someone she really cares about—which then immediately stimulates his family-of-origin-based fear of abandonment.

Sarah and Joe have "interacting sensitivities" (Wile, 1981). Each reacts to having his/her childhood-based special sensitivity stimulated in a way that stimulates that of the other. Sarah reacts to Joe's disapproval by withdrawing; he reacts to her withdrawal by disapproving. The CCT task is to create a compassionate perspective from which partners can empathize with each other about their interacting sensitivities—and about their uncomforted traumas, automatic incapacities, family-of-origin-based vulnerabilities, and moment-to-moment abandonments of each other. Everyone has had traumas that were never comforted. Being in a couple relationship provides the possibility for such comforting. A goal is to turn the relationship into a curative force for solving each partner's family-of-origin problems.

The Key Concept: Entitlement

At the basis of CCT is the idea that confiding your inner struggle is intrinsically empathy-, intimacy-, and collaboration-inducing. Confiding may not be any of these things, however, if what you confide is a feeling such as "I feel lonely," or "I'm feeling abandoned." When Joe confides such feelings to Sarah, he thinks he is making "I" statements, and he is. But here is the problem: "I" statements often have "you" statements hidden in them. And I do not mean just the obvious cases, such as "I feel you are a jerk." I mean even true "I" statements, such as Joe's "I feel lonely," and "I feel abandoned." They can easily be heard as "It's because of you that I'm lonely," and "The reason I feel abandoned is that you abandon me."

Were Joe to confide his inner struggle, however, the effect might be to extirpate the hidden "you" statement. Instead of "I feel lonely," he would say, "I feel ashamed about feeling lonely," which would make clear to Sarah that he is upset with himself rather than with her.

But suppose the person Joe is upset with is Sarah. He is angry at her, which means that he is in an adversarial state. When you are in such a state, you do not want to bring your partner in on your inner struggle; you want to tell your partner off. Your attention is on your outer rather than your inner struggle. Paradoxically, Joe would have more success in his outer struggle (i.e., he would more effectively accomplish his major goal of bringing Sarah around to see his point) were he to bring her in on his inner struggle—for example, by telling her:

JOE: I feel lonely, and I shift back and forth between thinking there's something wrong with me—I'm weak, I should be able to take care of myself—and putting the blame on you, which I'm really into now, big time! I feel you don't care about me at all and that I'm totally alone in this marriage! I'm going be sorry tomorrow about what I'm saying. In fact, I'm going to be sorry any second now, because I'm criticizing you, which is going to leave both of us lonelier and ruin the evening—not to mention that I think I should be supporting you in your work rather than complaining like this.

Joe's telling Sarah, "You're a workaholic!" seems such a pale substitute for this fuller statement. But it is hard to imagine him or anybody else making it. When you are in an adversarial state, which means desperately needing to get your partner to see your point, you lose your most effective means for doing so, which is to confide your inner struggle. All you can do is attack and defend, which is what being in an adversarial state means. You can say angry things like "You're a workaholic!" or "Screw you!", and there's an immediate satisfaction in that. But you're unable to get the deeper satisfaction, or to feel you have the deeper effect on your partner, that comes from bringing your partner in on your inner struggle, as I have just described for Joe.

To be able to make such a statement requires, to begin with, that Joe must admit feeling lonely. But he is too ashamed to do that. He thinks he should be able to take care of himself, adjust to Sarah's work schedule, and help her rather than complain. He sees feeling lonely as an unacceptable personal weakness. He feels *unentitled* to his experience of loneliness.

"Entitlement" is a key concept in Apfelbaum's (2001a) ego analysis. We usually think of entitlement as something bad, as in "outrageous claims of narcissistic entitlement." But Apfelbaum uses the term to refer to something good: to feeling sufficiently free from anxiety and shame about what you are thinking and feeling to be able to accept, claim, inhabit, and embrace this "who you are" at the moment. Kriegman (1983) laments the lack of attention to this more positive meaning of entitlement. To embrace the "who you are" at the moment requires (to say the same thing in various ways) a self-forgiving attitude, a self-generated holding environment, a self-generated unconditional positive regard, a feeling of good will toward yourself, an ability to serve as a comforting and protective presence to yourself, and to feel the same sort of compassion toward yourself that you might feel toward a sympathetic character in a movie, and even (as you might do for such a character) the ability to cry for yourself. It requires being on your own side and imagining that your partner, hearing what you have to say, will also be on your side.

This brings us to the theory of human motivation at the base of CCT. Problems continually arise because people feel unentitled to their experience. They lack the self-compassion—the ability to serve as comforting presences to themselves—to be able to pin down in their own minds what they are thinking and feeling and to confide it to their partners. They experience a loss of voice. This is everybody at least some of the time. Since Joe lacks the self-compassion to be able to pin down and confide to Sarah, "I'm upset with myself for getting so lonely when you spend weekends bringing home work from the hospital," he tries to ignore these feelings and rise above them.

When that does not work, he shifts into action. Since Sarah is unavailable, he calls his friend Alan to suggest a movie. But Alan tells him he is taking his wife out to dinner, which immediately makes Joe envious of Alan for having a wife who is available for dinner. It is at that point that Joe marches in and tells Sarah, "You're a workaholic!"

Confiding versus Avoiding, Fixing, and Blaming

Joe has engaged in a succession of three fall-back measures: avoiding (trying to ignore what he was feeling); fixing (calling a friend in an action-oriented attempt to solve the problem); and blaming. Avoiding, fixing, and blaming constitute the self-alienated version that you are stuck with when you cannot inhabit the experience you are having. That is the theory of motivation at the core of CCT: When you feel unentitled to what you are experiencing and cannot come up with the self-compassionate version, you fall back on the self-alienated version. You engage in the second-rate,

compensatory, fall-back measures of avoiding, fixing, and blaming.

These measures are second-rate but inescapable. Even partners in the best relationships confide in each other only a fraction of the time. We count on avoiding, fixing, and blaming to get us through the day. Some situations are well handled by "avoiding." "Fix-it" efforts often do fix things; had Alan been available to go to a movie with Joe, that might have solved the problem, at least for the moment. Blaming is a blunderbuss way of trying to say something, but it is often the only way to say it. It is the way that important thoughts and feelings can break through to the surface. After the fight, you can address the feeling. You can say to your partner, "You said in our fight that you've been feeling taken for granted lately. Is that true?"

At any moment you can confide, blame, avoid, or fix, and by doing so can turn your partner into an ally, enemy, stranger, or recipient of your fix-it effort. A wife would be confiding, which would turn her husband into an ally, were she to say, "When we're quiet like this, I worry that we're one of those couples that don't talk. Do you worry about that too sometimes?" She would be blaming, which would turn her husband into an enemy, were she to say instead, "Why are you always so quiet?" She would be avoiding, which would turn her husband into a stranger, were she to say nothing about it and just turn on the TV. She would be engaging her husband in a fix-it effort were she to say, "Tell me about your day," or "What do you think about what the President is doing?" in an effort to turn the two of them into a couple that does talk more.

Each moment presents both an opportunity to dig yourself out of the couple problem you may be in and a danger of digging yourself deeper into it. If at that moment you confide, you are promoting an empathic cycle. If you blame, you are promoting an adversarial cycle. If you avoid, you are promoting a withdrawn cycle. If you fix, you could be doing any of these three things.

People are "fixing" while remaining essentially in a withdrawn state if they avoid talking with their partners about the problem and try to solve it in an indirect way. For instance, instead of confiding, "I'm worried that we're not very close," a man may ask, "Do you love me?" His partner's "Yes, I do" may relieve the worry for the moment. In asking for reassurance, the worried man is engaging; that is, it does not look as if he is withdrawn at all. However, since he is not confiding the worry—this "who he is" at the moment—he is in this more important manner disengaged. People are "fixing" in the service of an adversarial cycle when their solution efforts are essentially barbs. If a woman says that she wishes she and her partner would talk more rather than watch so much TV, the partner may say in an abrupt, challenging manner that communicates displeasure with her suggestion and throws the responsibility back on her, "OK, what do you want to talk about?" What everyone wants, of course, is the more durable kind of "fixing" that emerges naturally out of an empathic cycle. When partners are in such a cycle, they find themselves automatically listening to each other, appreciating each other's point of view, and working collaboratively to come up with whatever solutions and compromises are possible. In summary, "fixing" can be, alternatively, an effort to solve the problem without talking about it, a means of expressing anger, or the natural consequence of partners' being in tune with each other.

When Confiding Does Not Create an Intimate Moment

With my help, Joe is able to tell Sarah, "I'm ashamed of how lonely I get when you spend evenings working," which is a confiding statement that could easily elicit an empathic response from her. It does not. That is because Sarah is a person who easily feels that she has done something wrong. The fact that Joe is blaming himself does not register. She hears the "I feel lonely" and immediately assumes that it is her fault. His confiding his inner struggle, which he has done with my help in entitling him to it, has led to an inner struggle in Sarah to which she feels unentitled. *Were* she to feel entitled, she would be able to tell Joe (and this is going to sound strange, because it is hard to imagine anyone talking this way):

SARAH: Joe, I'm having my usual reaction. I'm thinking if you feel lonely, it's got to be my fault. I've done something wrong. I've let you down in some way, even if I don't know exactly how. I'm in this downward spiral, in the grip of something.

Sarah would feel relief were she able to say this (and as her therapist I would try to help her do so). She would be appealing to Joe as a resource and confidant in dealing with the problem she is having with him, just as the moment before, with my help, he has done exactly that with her. She would be exposing her inner struggle, which means that she would no longer feel so alone in it.

Since all of us are repeatedly in the grip of something, we all could profit from talking in such a way. But being in the grip of something almost by definition means being unable to stand back and talk about it. Sarah does not know she is in the grip of something; she just thinks that she has done something wrong and that she is a bad person. Being unable to report that she is in the grip of something, she is stuck engaging in her own version of the same three fall-back reactions that I just described for Joe: avoiding, fixing, and blaming.

She says feebly, "Do we have to talk about this now?" That is avoiding. When Joe says nothing, she fixes. She says, "Well, if that's how you feel, why didn't you tell me sooner?"—a fix-it measure that is really an attack. When Joe still says nothing, she attacks more forthrightly. She says, "Look, I've got to get this work done! I'm doing it for us. Give me a break!"

The CCT View of Unconscious Purposes

Listening to what Sarah says, I go into a therapist version of the same three reactions. I start with an avoiding, demoralized, withdrawn, giving-up reaction in which I tell myself, "I'm not going to be able to help these people." That is followed with a fix-it reaction in which I tell myself, "I'll ask them what initially attracted them to each other in an effort to change the subject to something more positive." That is followed with a blaming reaction in which I tell myself, "Why does Sarah have to act this way?"

Why, indeed? Could she be getting something out of it? Does her symptomatic reaction serve an unconscious purpose? Does she have a hidden agenda? What I see her as getting out of it depends on my particular theory. Were I to have an object relations approach, I might see her as projecting onto Joe her own warded-off neediness. Were I to have a family systems approach, I might see her behavior as an effort to maintain family homeostasis. Were I to have a control/mastery approach, I might see her as provoking a fight in order to avoid the guilt of believing she has a better marriage than her parents. Were I to have a family-of-origin approach, I might view her anger at Joe as anger at her father, or at men in general. Were I to have a strategic therapy approach, I might positively reframe her outburst as an effort to bring passion into the relationship. Were I to have a psychodynamic approach that focuses on defenses, I might see her as getting the blame off herself by putting it onto Joe, proving that he rather than she is the source of their problems.

Sarah *is* getting the blame off herself by getting it onto Joe. That seems clear. She is also accomplishing other purposes: finding a channel for her frustration and punishing Joe for the injury she feels he has done her. From a CCT point of view, however, these are compensatory, second-rate, fallback purposes that she resorts to because what might bring her real satisfaction is cut off to her: bringing Joe into her inner struggle and getting more in touch with it herself.

According to a familiar psychotherapeutic view, people hold onto their symptoms because they get so much out of them. The CCT view is that what they get is a sorry second-best, a consolation prize. The task, rather than confronting partners with what they are getting, is to give them a glimpse of the real satisfaction that they are missing. Were she to come up with a statement that could provide her real satisfaction, Sarah might say:

SARAH: Joe, when you said you felt lonely, I felt it was because of me and that I'm this cold, unloving person and the cause of all our problems—which felt so horrible that I switched it all around and decided, "No, *you're* the source of our problems!"

That is the grand-prize statement that, were Sarah to come out with it, would have made unnecessary the consolation prize of blaming him. She would be standing back and talking with him about her urge to blame him. She would be bringing Joe in on her inner struggle, and bringing herself in on it, too. She would be providing voice to her experience. She would be reassembling the relationship on the next higher level.

Tracking the Shift among Cycles

That is my job: to help Sarah discover the grand-prize statement. Unfortunately, I am unable to do so at the moment, since I have slipped into an adversarial relation with her, which means that I am out of position to do CCT.

Fortunately, realizing that I am out of position is all I need to get back into it. I tell myself, "I know it doesn't look like Sarah's reactions make sense, but if they were to, what would this sense be?" Just the idea that her reactions might make sense, even if I have no notion of how, is all I need to (1) come up with questions that might bring out

this sense; (2) recognize elements when they come along; and (3) make guesses that might enable Sarah to come up with her own more accurate guesses. I suggest to Sarah the following way in which her reaction might make sense:

THERAPIST: Sarah, I thought Joe was criticizing himself. But you seem to feel he was blaming you. You know him better than I do. Could I be wrong and he was blaming you?

Sarah *does* know him better than I do. I certainly could be wrong.

SARAH: I don't know. (*To Joe*) You were blaming me, weren't you?

Sarah's comment is a conciliatory gesture, a softening (Johnson, 1996), a repair effort (Gottman, 1999), a move toward an empathic cycle. Sarah is telling Joe, in essence, "I felt certain you were criticizing, but I could be wrong, so let me ask you." She is admitting that she may have jumped to conclusions—which Joe appreciates.

JOE: Maybe just a little, but mostly I'm upset with myself.

Privately, I congratulate all of us: myself, for asking the question that got this all started; Sarah, for making her repair effort; and Joe, for accepting this effort. Her admitting that she may have jumped to conclusions has led him to admit that she was not entirely wrong. He is automatically rewarding her in response to feeling rewarded by her—which is what people do when they are in an collaborative cycle. Were Sarah and Joe in an adversarial cycle, Joe would automatically punish her in response to feeling punished by her. He would say, "I'm tired of your always thinking that I'm blaming you when I'm not!"

Sarah and Joe are generating a collaborative/empathic force field in which each takes the other's side in response to the other's doing the same (Wile, 1993). They do so automatically, without thinking about it, and with the inevitability of their downward spiral earlier.

SARAH: I shouldn't get so caught up in my work.
JOE: You have to. You're the only one who can handle those grant applications.

To maintain this collaborative force field requires that each partner exonerate the other—that is, talk about only his/her own contribution to the problem (Wile, 1993).

SARAH: But sometimes I go a little overboard.
JOE: (*Blurting out*) You can say that again!

Joe's blurted-out comment threatens the collapse of the collaborative force field. He is no longer exonerating Sarah. He could prevent this collapse by adding, "Oops, I shouldn't have said that." But he does *not* add that. Sarah's "But sometimes I go a little overboard" has thrown *him* overboard. All he can think of now are the people in his past who in one way or another have disappeared on him, leaving him rawly sensitive to the everyday disconnections in his relationship with Sarah. What he needs to be able to say at this point is this:

JOE: I'm stuck on the word "overboard." I'm flooded with feelings about all the people in my life who have gone overboard on me.

He would be taking Sarah into his confidence about being flooded. But he *is* flooded, which means that he is unable to stand back and talk about it. He is stuck as a fall-back measure defending himself.

JOE: Well, you have to admit that you *do* go off the deep end sometimes.
SARAH: (*Snapping back*) No, it's just that you take things too personally sometimes.
JOE: (*Snapping back to that*) Who are you to talk? You take things too personally *all* the time.

A moment ago, Joe and Sarah were generating an empathic force field. Now they are generating an adversarial one. Each stings in response to feeling stung. We can sympathize with them—and with every couple—for how quickly the inner atmosphere of a relationship can deteriorate. We can sympathize with ourselves as couple therapists: We need computer-like mental capacity and god-like omniscience to be able to track these moment-to-moment twists and turns of the relationship.

What do we do? Some therapists trace the problem to each partner's family of origin. When a partner reacts strongly to something, they ask, "Does this remind you of something?" Were I to ask that of Joe, he might describe his early abandonments in a way that might be relieving to him, elicit empathy in Sarah, and regenerate an empathic cycle.

Other therapists engage in communication skills training. Knowing about "I" statements, ac-

tive listening, "always" and "nevers," time outs, appointments to talk later, and listening to one's partner rather than giving advice or trying to fix things may give partners the edge they need to deescalate their fights.

The CCT approach is to follow the twists and turns of the relationship, despite our lack of computer-like mental capacity and god-like omniscience. We believe that whatever success we have in doing so can potentially help. When, earlier in the session, I noticed Sarah's repair effort and Joe's acceptance of it ("You were blaming me, weren't you?" "Maybe just a little"), I asked what each was thinking and feeling that led to these comments. I wanted to provide a compassionate perspective—a joint platform—from which they could look at this particular twist and turn in their interaction.

But suppose I fail to notice this twist and turn, and therefore am unable to ask them about it? That is OK, because I have another chance the very next moment to direct their attention to what is happening then.

THERAPIST: Wow! Suddenly you're shooting live ammunition. Any idea what got that started?

When I am able to track a sequence of twists and turns, I report it to them.

THERAPIST: Here is the conversation I heard in the fight you just had. You can tell me where I'm right and where I'm wrong. For a while, each of you seemed to be taking the other's side. Joe, you said, "I shouldn't give you such a hard time when you work evenings." To which, Sarah, you said, "You've got good reason; I disappear on you." To which, Joe, you said, "You've got good reason to disappear; you have important work to do." To which, Sarah, you said, "Well, I appreciate your being so understanding, but I do go a bit overboard sometimes." To which, Joe, you said, "That's an understatement!" To which, Sarah, you said, in essence—"I was really enjoying our looking at things from each other's point of view, but if you're going to shift gears and take advantage of what I admitted just to rub it in, then I'm going to slash back and point out to you that the *real* problem is that you take things *way* too personally. How do you like that?" To which, Joe, you said, "I *don't* like that. I feel like telling you, 'Who are you to talk? You take things too personally *all* the time'—which, since I know how much you hate it when I say things like that, just shows how upset I am by what you just said."

I end my statement by saying, "That's my version of the exchange you just had. Where did I get it right and where did I get it wrong?"

In my rendition, I am having them announce what they are doing rather than just do it. I am having them say, in essence, "I feel stung by what you just said and I'm about to sting back, and here it is." The effect of such reporting what each partner is doing while doing it is to open up a metalevel in the relationship.

If I am unable sufficiently to track these twists and turns in their relationship to be able to describe it to them in this way, that is OK. I use whatever I am able to track. If I have only a vague sense of what is going on, I can say:

THERAPIST: Things seem to be shifting around here. At times during this session, there seemed a warmth between you. At other times, like right now, you seem to feel totally upset with each other. Do you agree that there were these shifts, and if so, what do you make of them?

What Partners Take Away

My goal is not to get Sarah and Joe to talk to each other the way I talk to them. In order for them to do so, they would have to be in a collaborative state rather than in the adversarial one they are in. My goal, rather, is to provide an X-ray of the moment. Although they will not be able to take such X-rays on their own—they do not have the machine—they have seen the ones I have taken for them. This can make a difference. A person who sees an X-ray of his/her arm will remember from then on that there are bones there. The bones that I want Sarah and Joe to remember are these:

1. There is a conversation that ideally we could have, even though I have no idea what it is, that would turn this grim, "Why do we always have to do this?" fight into an intimate, "I'm glad that we're having this" conversation.

2. My partner has just gotten defensive or angry for no reason, which means that I might have just become blaming or defensive without realizing it.

3. Since we're in a fight, I'm acutely aware of my partner's provocativeness while justifying my own. I'm in danger, therefore, of concluding that my partner shouldn't be having so much trouble seeing past my little bit of anger to the obvious hurt beneath it.

4. Since we're in a fight, each of us feels too unheard to listen and has an irresistible urge to refute what the other has just said. After the fight, I can come back and discover what my partner is trying to say and get my partner to see what I am trying to say.

5. There's a rationality to what my partner is saying, even though I have no way at the moment to see it. My partner's reactions make sense, and mine do also, but the two of us are stuck in something that makes it impossible for us to see this sense.

To the degree that these ideas take hold, the partners will be able, after the fight, to approximate the "I'm glad that we're having this" conversation.

TYPICAL INTERVENTIONS

The following typical interventions give the flavor of the approach. Some are common ones we all use; others may seem surprisingly unfamiliar. I have chosen them because they demonstrate the major tasks of the therapist, which are to:

1. Discover the heartfelt feeling or inner struggle that, because a person could not pin down and confide it, led to the symptomatic response of attacking, avoiding, or fixing.
2. Entitle the person to his/her experience in the process of saying what it is.
3. Demonstrate how each partner's position makes sense (rather than demonstrate how it does not make sense).
4. Serve as each partner's spokesperson, scriptwriter, and advocate.
5. Create a metalevel in the relationship between the partners; that is, turn them into confidants in dealing with their problems with each other.
6. Create a metalevel in the therapist's relationship with the partners; that is, appeal to them as consultants in conducting the therapy.
7. Function as guardian of the conversation.
8. Personify the compassionate perspective.

Each of the following interventions serves several of these purposes, but I categorize it according to the one that it most clearly illustrates. To bring further coherence to this set of disconnected interventions, I am going to organize them around the familiar situation in which the partners are in an adversarial cycle—they are angry at each other—and my task is to create a collaborative cycle.

Purpose 1: Discovering the Heartfelt Feeling or Inner Struggle

When one partner accuses the other, I reshape the accusation to make it more effective in getting the other partner to listen and, even more important, to make it more satisfying to the partner who made it. One way is to dig out the heartfelt feeling that, because the person could not come up with it, led to the accusation.

> "Jack, your telling Tom, 'You're angry,' got him upset because he didn't think he was. But I think what you might really have meant was 'I'm *worried* you're angry. I've been withdrawn lately, and *I'd* be angry if you had disappeared on *me* that way.'"

A second way to reshape a person's accusation to make it more satisfying to him/her is to bring out the inner struggle: the doubts, worries, and reservations the person has about what he/she is saying.

> "Wendy, would it be accurate to add something to what you just said?: 'Bob, I've built up a lot of feeling about this, so I'm probably not saying it in the nicest possible way—which is a shame because it's really important to me that I get you to see.'" Would that be something you would want to add?

After bringing out the inner struggle of the accusing partner (or instead of doing so), I bring out that of the accused partner; that is, I help the partner who has just been accused report what it felt like.

> "Julie, take us on a tour of what passed through your mind as you were listening to Eric just now."

> "Ed, Vicki just said the kind of thing that usually wipes you out. Did it this time?"

I ask about a partner's nonverbal behavior in an effort to dig through to a heartfelt feeling or inner struggle.

> "If you were to put words to that big sigh, what would they be?"

> "Paul, did you notice Maggie shaking her head as you were talking? What do you think that meant?"

> "Sally, you seem poised to say something but you're hesitating, which makes me think that you're thinking of something that you're not sure you want to say, maybe in fear of starting a fight. Am I right? And,

if so, is it your best judgment that it's better not to say it?" [I don't want to press people to say something when they feel it is wiser not to.]

> "Charles, I get the feeling from the way you just moved your hands that you're saying, 'Janet, when you say things like that, I throw up my hands. If that's the way you want to be, well, OK, but leave me out. I've got nothing more to say. I'm stonewalling.'" [I deal with stonewalling by acknowledging for the person that that is what he/she is doing.]

Purpose 2: Entitling the Person to His/Her Experience While Suggesting What It Might Be

I normalize the thought or feeling. That is, I clear away the client's concern over whether he/she *should* be having this feeling, so that the client can look to see whether he/she *is* having it.

> "I wonder, Dora, whether you're feeling _____ . I'm guessing that because that's what I might feel in such a situation."

At times I list a set of possible thoughts or feelings a partner could be having, in which each alternative is an understandable reaction a person might have.

> "Tom, do you think—I'll make it a multiple-choice question—that A, Karen's completely wrong about what she just said, or B, she's at least partly right, or C, she's at least partly right but you don't feel like admitting it because you don't like her tone? Or is it D, something else entirely?"

I suggest by tone and manner that whatever the person is thinking or feeling is undoubtedly understandable, even if it turns out to be something that is not on my list.

> "Judy, when Paul says things like that, does it make you feel hurt, misunderstood, discouraged, hopeless, angry, or what?"

Instead of asking, "Are you angry?" (which Judy could take as an accusation), I offer this smorgasbord of feelings from which she can choose. Since I am listing all these possibilities without advocating any one—I do not have a stake in any of them—she is less likely to be distracted by what she thinks I might want her to say. She can more fully direct her attention to what she feels. She might say, "A little bit of all of those things," or "Mostly hurt and angry," or "I don't know; I'm just kind of confused."

Purpose 3: Demonstrating How Each Partner's Position Actually Makes Sense

I am always on the lookout for the hidden reasonableness in what appears to be a person's unreasonable reaction. Instead of *correcting* a partner—for example, by saying, "Sharon, don't bring up issues from the distant past"—I find the hidden reasonableness in what Sharon is doing.

> "Yes, Alex, you understandably don't like Sharon's bringing up that incident from so long ago; it makes you feel she'll never let you live anything down. And, Sharon, it's understandable that you're bringing it up, since it's the clearest example of what you want Alex to see is still happening in more subtle ways today."

A goal even more important than solving the couple's problem is making the partners understandable to each other. If a partner angrily belabors a point—for instance, if Doris keeps repeating the same angry comment—I make what Doris is doing understandable by saying:

> "Doris, you've been saying this a number of times and in almost those words, which must mean that you don't think Sam and I are getting it."

Purpose 4: Serving as Each Partner's Spokesperson, Scriptwriter, and Advocate

I deal with couple fighting not by encouraging restraint but by serving as spokesperson for both partners and helping them make their points. What keeps the fight going, after all, is their inability to get their points across.

> "Each of you is in the frustrating position of having something important you want to get the other to see and not being able to. Alex, you're trying to get Sharon to see that _____. Sharon, you're trying to get Alex to see that _____ ."

> "Joel, let's see if I can make your point in a way that might convince Ellen. And then, Ellen, I'll try to make your point in a way that might convince him."

> "Phyllis, you say that Mark isn't listening to you. If he were listening, what would he be hearing? And,

Mark, if Phyllis were listening to you, what would *she* be hearing?"

Another way I serve as spokesperson is by amping it up.

> "Beth, you and John value respectfulness and restraint. You don't want to have the kind of angry, take-no-prisoners fights that some couples have. I don't like to have them with my wife, either. But I'm going to make one up for you so we can see what it feels like. You'd say, 'John, you have a helluva nerve! I know you're using your soft tone of voice, but, hello! Listen to what you're saying. And I'm supposed to just sit here and take it!?! Give me a break!'"

I would be serving as Beth's spokesperson by enabling her to make an angry comment without the dangers of doing so, since I am the one doing it, not she. I would be saying, in essence, "Let's find out, Beth, whether you'd enjoy saying such a thing or whether it would make you nervous. And, John, let's find out whether hearing it would be upsetting or the opposite, relieving, since Beth would be bringing out into the open feelings you might have already sensed she had."

When I am speaking for one of the partners, it is possible to serve simultaneously as spokesperson for the other partner—by including in my statement an acknowledgment of what this other partner has been trying to say.

> "Ed, would you like the idea of telling Vicki here, 'Vicki, you're probably making a good point about how _____ , but I can't hear it because I'm still angry about _____ '?"

> "Betsy, I can imagine your saying here, "Ned, you're telling me _____ . So I don't think you're going to like my response, which is that _____ ."

In my role as spokesperson, I operate a tenth of a second ahead of the partners. I bring out what is on the edge of their awareness: what they are about to say; are too caught up in emotion to say; or lack the words, understanding, or presence of mind to say.

> "Bill, I wonder if this is the kind of horrible, going-nowhere, destructive fight that, as you said in the very first session, you feared you'd get into here with David and made you think it might not be such a good idea to come."

My raising this concern—Bill does not have to be the one to do so—frees Bill to focus on other elements in his feelings. Bill may say, "Yes, this is exactly what I feared. But, you know, David and I have to work things out somehow. This might be a place to do it." My getting behind Bill in his fear of how therapy might be damaging enables him to take the other side and to look at how it might be useful. Serving as partners' spokespersons—getting behind each of them in the "who they are" at the moment—frees each of them to be the "who they are" the next moment, as Joe Russo, a colleague, has put it.

Purpose 5: Creating a Metalevel in the Relationship between the Partners

When partners get into a sticky, unresolvable fight, I open up a metalevel from which they can talk about *that*.

"Is this the kind of fight that you've come to therapy to stop?"

"Is this fight frustrating, going nowhere, and you wish I'd interrupted it? Or are you getting something out of it—a chance to say a few things or to hear a few things—and you're glad I didn't interrupt it?" [Partners surprise me at times by saying, "This is good. We never get to argue like this at home," when I expected them to say it was distressing.]

If it looks as if the partners are going to leave the session angry at each other, I open up a metalevel to talk about *that*.

"It looks like you're going to be leaving here tonight angry at each other. What's it going to be like driving home together? And what's it going to be like this evening, and the next couple of days?"

"You left here last time unusually upset with each other. How did each of you cope with it? And how did you eventually work it out—or didn't you?"

I provide a compassionate perspective—a second level—from which partners can look at whatever gridlocked situation they are in.

"Here's the boggle. Alan, it sounds like you need Sally to appreciate that you've made efforts to change before you'll admit that the changes so far haven't been great; Sally, you need Alan to admit that the changes haven't been that great before you'll admit that he's making an effort."

"Our hope, of course, is that you'll be able to solve this difficult problem you're facing, but let's imag-

ine for a moment that you're unable to do so and you were to have ahead of you, say, 40 years or more of struggling with it. Would that be acceptable or unacceptable?"

No matter what problem the partners have—even if it is one that threatens the continuation of the relationship—there is always a way to create a metalevel from which to talk about it.

"Cathy, I get the idea from some of the things you've been saying that you think the relationship is over. Or am I wrong about that?"

"Sue, do you feel devastated by what Ralph just said [about wanting to end the relationship]? Are you in shock?"

"Betsy, from some of the comments you've made, I sense that you're worried that Fred is having an affair, but that you're not sure you really want to ask."

Knowing that I can help each partner get out what he/she needs to say about any issue emboldens me to confront directly such difficult ones.

Purpose 6: Creating a Metalevel in My Relationship with the Partners

I do so not only to model it for them, but even more importantly because it is the best way to conduct any kind of relationship, personal or therapeutic. I bring the partners in on the management of the therapy. A major management problem is how to maintain a minimal sense of order—that is, how to keep the couple's fighting in the office from destroying the therapy. A common way is to establish ground rules or to make traffic control statements, such as "Only one person talks at once," or "Let's keep to one topic." The CCT way is to open up a metalevel and confer with the partners about the problem.

"Is this fight you're having as frustrating and demoralizing as it looks, and should I be trying harder to stop it?"

When partners bring up more topics than can be dealt with, I consult with them about this. Instead of saying, "Let's stick to one topic," I ask:

"You brought up a number of issues in the last 2 minutes. Is one of them more important than the others, and should we focus on that one? Or is it best to do just what you're doing and lay them all out?"

Or I try to find a connection among the topics.

"You've talked about a number of things in the last few minutes. Here's how I think they're connected."

"You started out talking about _____ , but then you shifted to _____ and now to _____ . I know there's a way they're all connected, so let's try to figure it out. Or do you know?"

In opening up a metalevel in my relationship with a couple, I bring the partners in on what I am thinking (i.e., I make myself transparent) and consult with them about what is happening and how to proceed. I say such things as these:

"How do you feel about the way this session is going?"

"How do you understand this sudden shift from playfulness to grimness?"

"Here are the things I was thinking as I was listening to you."

"What you just said makes me think of the various following directions we could go. Which look promising? Or is there an entirely different direction that we should be heading instead?"

"You mentioned at the beginning today that there was this other issue you wanted us to get to. Should we switch to it now, since time is passing, or stick with what we're talking about?"

Since I need to know at any given moment whether the partners are breaking new ground or engaging in a going-nowhere exchange that it is my job to stop, I ask:

"Joel, is there something new in what Ellen just said, or have you heard it before?"

"Rita, is there something intriguing in what Sybil just said, or do you feel, 'Here we go again'?"

Opening up a metalevel with the partners enables me to get their help in maintaining an even-handed attitude toward them.

"Gail, is your point of view getting a fair hearing here?"

"Peter, you mentioned last time that sometimes I don't seem to appreciate your side of things. Is this one of those times?"

Opening up a metalevel with the partners enables me to take their side in dealing with me.

"Louise, you said a few sessions back that I sometimes rush in and speak for you when you'd rather speak for yourself. Should I resist my urge to rush in now?"

"Andrea, as you say, you're getting upset while Cliff is 'being reasonable'—which is getting you even more upset. And here I am, 'being reasonable,' too—for instance, even just in the way I'm talking now. So I wonder whether you feel alone, ganged up on, and that it isn't safe here?"

I use the partners' complaints about me—the problems they are having with me—to build my relationship with them, much as I try to build their relationship out of their problems with each other. Creating a metalevel in my relationship with the partners enables me to help them deal with my authority.

"Bruce, I'm going to make a wild speculation about what you might be feeling. I give myself about a 30% chance of being right."

I am making clear to Bruce that he is the final judge, and that I am offering my speculation for his consideration rather than as something he is supposed to accept (and that I would see as a sign of defensiveness if he does not). Occasionally, I may want to challenge a client or press a point. If so, I open up a metalevel from which to announce (report) that I am doing that.

"I'm going to play devil's advocate and challenge what you just said, so we can explore all the angles."

"I just realized that I've been arguing with you, which means I haven't been listening very well to what you've been trying to tell me. But if I *were* listening to you, I'd realize that what you're trying to tell me is _____ ."

Creating a metalevel from which I announce to clients that I am arguing with them guards against the usual drawbacks of arguing, which are that it can induce defensiveness or passive compliance (i.e., an adversarial or withdrawn reaction). In those few instances—for example, physical abuse—where I take a stand, I create a metalevel from which to talk about doing that.

"Carl, when I said that it's your responsibility never to hit Jane no matter what, rather than that it's her responsibility to avoid saying something that you might take as provocative, did you feel ganged up on—that what I'm saying is unfair, that no one is appreciating your side of things, and that this is a hostile environment?" [I wouldn't say this, or even see the couple, were there any chance that Carl might take it out physically on Jane later.]

Conducting my relationship with the partners on two levels allows me to confront them while maintaining rapport.

Purpose 7: Functioning as Guardian of the Conversation

I try to turn the conversation the partners are having into the one they *could* be having that would fulfill the potential of the relationship in that moment. In my role as executor of this conversation, I spotlight what each partner says. I rescue important things that get lost in the mass of other things, or that go by unnoticed because they were said in passing.

"Glenn, you just said some important things, and here's what I think they are."

"There were a lot of things you just said, Marge. I'm going to list them all, so that we can really look at them and so that, Brad, you get a chance to respond to each."

"There were a lot of things you just said, Cindy, but what struck me in particular was _____ ."

"Fred, you said you weren't sure you were being clear. I'll tell you what I heard and you can say whether this is what you were trying to say. You said _____ ."

"There was something you said in passing a while ago, Rob, that I want us to go back to for a minute, because it was pretty remarkable."

In my role as guardian of the conversation, I help the partners keep the thread of the conversation. I rescue them from tangential arguments, remind them of the subject, and deepen the discussion.

"Ben, you disagree with the particular example that Mike just used, but what do you think of his major point, which as I hear it is that _____ ?"

"What was the week like for each of you struggling with this giant issue of sex? Jerry, what were the shifts you made this week—among, for example, at times taking personally Molly's no longer seeming inter-ested in sex, and at other times seeing it as just something that happens after a baby, and at other times getting frustrated and saying something sarcastic? Molly, what were your shifts—among, for example, at times feeling bad about not feeling more sexual, and at times seeing Jerry as another child with needs you have to deal with? Were there moments when you felt a little sexual, or is that out of the question these days, given your exhaustion caring for the baby or the ill-will you feel coming from Jerry?"

I turn these partners into confidants in dealing with this problem they are having with each other. An important part of the problem is their inability to be such confidants—that is, the lonely, isolated, cut-off manner in which each struggles with the issue in his/her own head. When partners fight, they do not say such things as these:

"OK, you convinced me; I'm glad you told me that; I feel a lot better; that solves the problem."

"That's a good point; I'm not sure how to answer it."

"You might be right—you're pretty convincing—but here are my remaining reservations about it."

"You're more convincing than I want you to be; I'm not ready yet to say you're right."

Instead they say things like these:

"You're a fine one to talk when you are always _____ ."

"What about the time when you _____ ?"

In my role as guardian of the conversation, I introduce these acknowledging statements that the partners leave out. I also draw attention to the momentary reconciliations that the partners overlook.

"Harry just made a number of complaints, Carol, and so you'll want to defend yourself. But did you catch that conciliatory comment at the end? Or was it too little too late, or not as conciliatory as I thought?"

"Jim, Virginia has been trying from the first session to get you to see how she feels lonely in the relationship. From what you just said, it sounds as if you've been feeling that way too, and that Virginia, in a way, has been speaking for both of you."

Hidden among the charges and countercharges in a couple fight are often the makings of an intimate conversation.

"Joan, you're accusing Gus, and you're also saying something important. Let me bring out this important thing you're saying, because I think it's getting lost."

"I was hearing a conversation in the fight you just had, and here's how it sounded: '_____.'"

"You're having a great conversation with important things being said, which you may not realize because of the argument you're also having that's drowning it out. So let me tell you about this great conversation I think you just had."

As part of my effort to bring out this hidden conversation, I help a partner who has just been accused sort through the accusation to find the information (feelings) hidden in it.

"Tony, Janice is accusing you, so you might want to defend yourself. But what do you think about what she just said? Is there some truth to it?"

"Steve, how much of what Amy just said just seems like blaming, and how much seems like an expression of how she feels?"

In my role as guardian of the conversation, I keep track of what the partners say and remind them of it. I serve as "relationship historian," to use Apfelbaum's (personal communication 1970) words.

"Since you haven't mentioned it in a while, I've been wondering what happened to that problem that was so much our focus in the first few sessions? Is it resolved? Has it just gone underground? Did you just give up on our being able to deal with it here?

"Sandy, you said in the beginning of the session today that you wonder whether we've made any progress at all. Was that only because of the horrible week you just had, or is it something you've been feeling generally and that we should really look at?"

"You know, I think you've just come up with an answer to that question we were puzzling over in the beginning of the session. It's what you just said, which is that _____."

In my role as guardian of the conversation, I serve not only as historian, but as troubleshooter and guiding spirit.

Purpose 8: Personifying the Compassionate Perspective

I become an embodiment of the same compassionate perspective that I want to help the partners develop.

"I'm sitting here admiring this great conversation you just had."

"That was very moving, what the two of you just said to each other."

"I'm sitting here moved by what each of you is saying, which may puzzle you, since you're mostly just upset by the other. So let me tell you what I find moving."

"Were you as struck with what you said at the end of last session as I was? I felt it gave us a whole new way to look at things."

THE STRUCTURE OF THERAPY

CCT is an experiment to see whether solving the moment can produce positive change that generalizes to the couple's life outside the therapy. There is no way to know beforehand which couples might profit from such an approach. The best way to determine whether they will is to try. I myself do not preselect couples other than to exclude those in which there is physical abuse that therapy might exacerbate.

Since the principal task, serving as spokesperson for each partner, is rapport building, there is no need for an initial rapport-building stage. Partners immediately enjoy having someone on their side helping them make their points.

Since I immediately start developing each partner's position, partners are immediately exposed to what I am going to do. At the end of the first session, I ask, given what they have seen so far, whether this approach appears promising. I do not ask for a commitment to a set of sessions to give therapy a fair try. As in every other aspect of the approach, I appeal to their judgment rather than ask them to suspend it.

The partners decide when to end the therapy, since they best know when they have reached the point of diminishing returns. There is no absolute point to end the therapy, just as there is none for an athlete to stop being coached. The capacities the partners are developing in therapy—opening up a metalevel, looking for the hidden reasonableness, and so on—can be improved indefinitely.

CCT involves listening to partners in a way that will enable them to listen to themselves and to each other. I try to get behind them in a way that will enable them to get behind themselves and to reach out to each other. I deal with resistance and defensiveness in the same way as I do everything else: by getting behind it and showing how it makes sense. I might say, for example, to a husband who has been dragged in (he does not want to be there):

"OK, Ben, you say that coming in here is humiliating rather than hope-producing, which is what Brenda says it is for her. You feel that people ought to be able to handle their own problems. And you've had bad experience with therapy. Going for counseling with your first wife just made matters worse. You got blamed for the problem, and you're concerned that might happen here, too. You've agreed to come only because it's so important to Brenda. She finally wore you down. You hope that she'll appreciate how hard it is for you, how much it goes against your grain, how uncomfortable you are here. You hope that she'll appreciate your effort to go the extra mile. And you hope that you don't have to come here too long and, ideally, that this will be the only session."

After developing Ben's position in this way, I take Brenda's side in coming up with a response to it. My goal is not to keep the partners together or to save the relationship. It is to get them on the same team, talking about their problems rather than, as they have been doing, arguing over them or, in fear of such argument, avoiding talking about them entirely. I try to get the partners puzzling things out together, which will put them in a position to come up with whatever solutions are possible. I get them commiserating about their problems and about the sadness and sense of loss each would feel were it to come to ending the relationship.

I do not have as a prerequisite for therapy that the partners make a commitment to the relationship, or even that they share the same goals. If one partner wants to fix the relationship and the other wants to end it, I try to create intimate conversations out of that. I work from where the partners are. I raise them onto a metalevel—a joint platform— so they can better see where they are. To help lift them onto this platform, I offer them an audio- or videotape of the session to listen to at home. For many people, listening later proves an effective way to stand back and see what is happening.

COMMON QUESTIONS ASKED ABOUT CCT

What about the Stereotypic Male Who Feels Shame about Confiding His Feelings?

In adopting this approach, which is based on confiding feelings, CCT is open to the criticism that it is accepting the woman's view of relationships. What about the stereotypic men, as well as the many women, who would feel shame rather than relief in confiding their feelings? Jack is such a person. His wife, Alice, comes with him to a therapy session distressed that he will not admit what seems obvious to her: He is jealous of his 3-month-old son, who has replaced him at the center of her attention. Acknowledging that he feels jealous would fill Jack with shame rather than relief. He snaps at Alice, "You're wrong! Why would I be jealous of the baby?"

The CCT task is to come up with the feeling on the edge of Jack's awareness that he would feel relief in getting out into the open. I try to imagine the thoughts and feelings he could be having. I imagine him feeling (1) angry at Alice for accusing him of feeling jealous; (2) worried that she might be right; (3) humiliated at the possibility that she might be right; (4) discouraged about the turn the relationship has taken; (5) dismayed at the loss of good will between them; (6) disappointed that he is not as charmed by the baby as Alice is; (7) distressed at feeling left out of the mother–infant dyad; (8) confused at finding himself shifting between blaming Alice for leaving him out and blaming himself for feeling left out; (9) afraid that he has lost Alice's respect; (10) knowing he's lost much of his own self-respect; (11) alarmed by his wish at times that they had never had the baby; and (12) worried, as a result of all of this, that he is immature.

Jack's "who I am" at the moment is someone caught up in such a cacophony of thoughts and feelings. I try to come up with a statement for him that captures some of this and that he would find relieving. I say to Jack:

"I wonder if you might want to say to Alice something like this: '"Having a baby was supposed to bring us together. Instead, look at what's happened to us! You're accusing me of being jealous, and I'm accusing you of being overinvolved. Things just don't feel good any more."

Jack's whole body relaxes. Alice turns to him and asks, "Is that what you feel?" He nods. They begin to commiserate over what has happened to them since the baby. This approach, which might seem fitted only for the communicative, in-touch-with-her-feelings stereotypic woman, is in fact also well fitted—even especially well fitted—for the noncommunicative, not-in-touch-with-his-feelings stereotypic man. It gives him a voice. For the moment,

Jack is glad that "talking about feelings" was invented, which contrasts with his usual view of such "woman talk."

What about Partners Who Do Not Want to Confide?

CCT is based on the idea that there is always something wanting to be known that, given voice, produces an immediate sense of relief. There is always a way to get behind people in what they are experiencing, speak from within it, and create a moment of intimacy. This definition of the therapeutic task follows naturally from substituting loss of voice for resistance as the core pathological principle. The criterion for the accuracy of an interpretation, Apfelbaum and Gill (1989) have said, is that it produces relief (since it provides the missing voice), which contrasts with the more familiar view that an indication of its accuracy is that it produces anxiety and defensiveness.

But what about partners who do not want a moment of intimacy? Their immediate concern is to establish an area of privacy and separation. If so, that is what the intimate statement needs to be about. For instance, Tony may say to his wife, Rose:

"I know you want something to happen between us tonight, and I just want to fog out in front of the TV. I worry that something's wrong with me that I don't want to get closer. And what really worries me is that I'll lose you if I don't find some better way of showing that I care."

Now *that* is an intimate statement. Tony would feel empowered. It is certainly better than what he would be left to do otherwise—namely, plop down nervously in front of the TV, say nothing, and hope that Rose says nothing.

Everyone knows that "intimacy" is more than just telling your partner, "I love you," "Let's spend more time together," or "I feel lucky to be married to you." It is harder to specify, however, what exactly it is. As I see it, intimacy is bringing your partner in on your leading-edge thought or feeling, whatever it is—even (and particularly) if it is feeling *nonintimate*, and even (and particularly) if it is feeling *angry*. In talking intimately about being angry, Anne may say to her partner, Katie:

"I feel so outraged by what you just said that I'm sitting here in total shock. I can't think of anything to say that will have a tenth of the impact that what you just said is having on me!"

Anne is reporting her anger rather than unloading it, which ironically is more satisfying than unloading it. She is obtaining the relief that comes from confiding her inner struggle. But do people always *want* to confide their inner struggle? What about non-psychological-minded people who are antipsychology, antitherapy, and anticommunication? They believe that problems are better handled if people do not always talk about them. I would help them establish that.

"Jerry, I've got the feeling—you can tell me whether I'm right or wrong—that what you want to tell Liz and me at this point is this: She and I have been talking in circles; none of it seems to the point; and you wish we'd drop it and take seriously what you've been trying to tell us, which is that the problems would take care of themselves if Liz didn't always have to talk about them so much. In fact, you feel that talking just makes things worse."

Jerry would enjoy this particular bit of talking, since I would be making his point. Then I would help Liz make the point she would want to make in response.

"And, Liz, I imagine you might want to say in return—and here I'll be you talking to Jerry—"Jerry, you're right that talking has made things worse. I can see why you wouldn't want to do any more of it. In fact, I'm discouraged about that, too."

Liz is unlikely to say such a thing on her own. When you are in an adversarial cycle, you reflexively refute what your partner says. It does not occur to you to agree unless you can adapt it for adversarial purposes, such as "Yes, you're right about that, which just goes to show: I'm willing to admit things, but you never are!" Liz likes the comment I have made for her, even though she would never think to make it on her own. She immediately recognizes it as both something she feels and something that might get Jerry to listen. I continue to speak for Liz:

"Liz, you might go on to say, 'But, Jerry—and here's the "but"—I don't think our problems *will* take care of themselves. I need to get you to see that, just as you need me to see how destructive talking has been up to now.'"

For a moment, Liz and Jerry would be appreciating how each of their positions make sense and how the two of them are stuck in something. They would be talking collaboratively about their impasse. They would be fulfilling the potential for intimacy intrinsic to the moment. They would be in position to do their best joint thinking about how to deal with this problem.

What about Partners Who Want to End the Relationship?

But what about partners who do not want intimacy? They have given up on intimacy. They want to end the relationship rather than improve it. If so, that is what the intimate statement needs to be about. Helen might say to Barney:

> "We left here last time feeling close, which, to my surprise, I didn't like. It made me realize that what I really want out of coming here is to end our relationship rather than fix it."

Helen is taking Barney into her confidence, which can be useful even if her goal is to end the relationship. Taking your partner into your confidence can be useful in almost any situation—even in the middle of a bitter divorce. Betty might say to Roy:

> "I know it's absolutely essential for our kids that we find some way to get along, at least minimally, so I've been trying hard—and failing monumentally! When you come over to pick up the kids, all I can think of is you and that *woman*, and I go crazy. It's hard to imagine ever getting over that, but what's going to happen to our kids if I don't?"

Even such bitter feelings can be used as raw material for reassembling the relationship on a higher level.

GUIDELINES FOR BECOMING SPOKESPERSON FOR BOTH PARTNERS: A SUMMARY

The problem of how to serve as spokesperson for others is made harder by our pathology-oriented language (as demonstrated by how I found myself using DSM-IV as a weapon against Joe). The terms we use for describing clients—such as "narcissistic," "dependent," "defensive," and "passive–aggressive"—are pejorative. We would not want anyone saying such things about us. They corroborate and legitimate our negative reaction to our clients, and thus make it hard to see that we are having a negative reaction; we think that we are simply seeing these clients for who they are (and that failure to view them in such terms means glossing over their psychopathology).

In a way, we *are* seeing them for who they are. People do behave in narcissistic, dependent, defensive, and passive–aggressive ways. But using such terms to organize our thinking about them means, from a CCT point of view, that we are defining people in terms of their symptomatic behaviors—their fall-back measures—rather than looking for their heartfelt feelings or inner struggles and defining them in terms of those.

When I find myself thinking about clients in these professionally sanctioned pejorative terms, I take it to mean that I am reacting to their symptomatic behavior. I have been drawn into an adversarial state, which means that I am out of position to serve as their spokespersons. I use the following mental guidelines (culled from ideas discussed at various parts in this chapter) to shift me out of this state and back into an empathic one, where I again become capable of serving as their spokesperson.

1. *The inner-struggle principle.* When I find myself focusing on the maladaptive nature of partners' behaviors—thinking of them in terms of their diagnoses and focusing on their deficiencies, immaturities, character defects, and defensive patterns—I remind myself to look for the inner struggle, which immediately shifts me out of my adversarial stance and into an empathic one. Finding myself disapproving of a client because of his/her narcissistic grandiosity, for instance, I focus on the vulnerabilities out of which this grandiosity developed.

2. *The heartfelt principle.* When I find myself put off by the intrinsically offensive nature of a partner's symptomatic behavior—for example, his/her demandingness, explosiveness, sullenness, self-righteousness, bullying, irritability, manipulativeness, or contemptuousness—I remember that there is a heartfelt statement that, because the person could not come up with it, led to this symptomatic behavior. When I hear a husband impatiently tell his wife, "If work is that bad, maybe you should quit your job," I imagine his heartfelt feeling that ideally he could have made instead: "It's hard to hear you tell me about your problems at work because I feel so bad for you, and I feel so powerless to help."

3. *The fall-back principle.* When I am thinking of clients as basically narcissistic, defensive, dependent, and so on, I remind myself that what I am seeing are fall-back reactions—their default positions when things are not going well.

These first three principles form the core of CCT. Putting them together, I look for the inner struggle (Principle 1) and the heartfelt feeling (Principle 2) that, because the partner could not pin down and confide them (they suffer a loss of voice), led as a fall-back measure (Principle 3) to the symptomatic reaction. When a cat cannot find the litter box, it chooses the next best thing. The next four principles help me discover a normality and appropriateness in behavior that seems abnormal and inappropriate.

4. *The normalizing principle* (or the capacity to find yourself in clients, as William Bumberry, a colleague, describes it). When I find myself pathologizing, I normalize and universalize. I ask myself, "What common couple or human issue is this person experiencing in a particularly clear and intense form?" As Apfelbaum (2001b) says, "Our clients are informants about the human condition rather than deviants from idealized norms." I look into the corners of my life in an effort to identify with clients. When I find myself thinking of them in "we–they" terms (i.e., "We are normal and they are abnormal"), I remember times when I have had at least minor versions of the problems they are struggling with.

5. *The hidden-rationality principle.* When I find myself viewing partners' reactions as not making sense, I look for hidden ways in which they do make sense—and in terms of the present situation, not just as carryovers from their families of origin. The person is reacting, although in an exaggerated and distorted way, to something that is actually going on (i.e., to a hidden reality in the present situation).

6. *The miner's canary principle.* When I view partners as infecting their present relationship with leftover issues from their families of origin, I look to see how their family-of-origin-based special sensitivities might be enabling them to detect subtle difficulties in their present relationship. Just as canaries' sensitivity to reduced levels of oxygen can warn miners of danger, so a husband's childhood-based special sensitivity to abandonment can help him detect subtle moment-to-moment disconnections between him and his wife.

7. *The feeling-too-unheard-to-listen principle.* When I feel critical of people for not listening to their partners, I look for the hidden way in which they also feel unlistened to, which is why they cannot listen. I look for the possibility that there is a fight (adversarial cycle) going on, which by definition is a mutually frustrating situation (a self-perpetuating exchange) in which each partner feels too unheard to listen and too misunderstood to be understanding (Wile, 1993).

The final two principles help protect me from my pejorative view of clients as resistant—that is, as hanging onto their symptoms because they are getting so much out of them.

8. *The people-do-not-want-their-symptoms principle.* When I view partners as getting secret (unconscious) benefits from their symptoms—as getting too much out of them to be willing to give them up—I remind myself that primarily people suffer from their symptoms and would *love* to get rid of them. As Apfelbaum (personal communication, 1980) says, "Whatever secondary gain people get from their symptoms is secondary indeed."

9. *The getting-too-little-of-what-they-seem-to-be-getting-too-much-of principle.* When I see people as demanding, greedy, overindulging, self-absorbed, or taking without giving, I look for how, as it often turns out, they may be getting precious little of what they seem to be getting so much of. The following are examples.

a. *Hidden deprivation.* When I see people as too caught up in their immediate pleasure to be able to take other people into account, I look for a hidden deprivation (Wile, 1981). Kohut (1977) describes the self-indulgent, drive-dominated behaviors of clients as "breakdown products" of a failure to develop an adequate sense of self and meaningful connection with others. You come home after a depleting day and eat, drink, or watch more television than you ordinarily would. People who seem self-absorbed and unconcerned for others are, in a hidden way, deprived. Apfelbaum (2001a) offers the example of the neglectful son who does not call his mother. We so quickly think of him as depriving her that we miss how he is also deprived—of having a relationship with his mother in which he would look forward to calling her, get a lot out of it, and miss not getting the chance.

b. *Ineffective dependency.* When I see people as dependent, I realize, as Apfelbaum (1998) says, their problem is ineffective dependency; that is, they are not good at it. They do not inspire a wish in others to comfort, reassure, prize, pamper, attend to, and engage with them, which Johnson (1996) shows to be among the normal attachment wishes everyone has. Were they good at being dependent—were they *effectively* dependent—their partners might feel more inspired to do these things, and even enjoy the opportunity to do so. Recognizing that their partners see them as clingy and burdensome, they feel unloved and unlovable, rejected, unnourished, and in even greater need of reassurance.

c. *Hidden compromise.* When I feel critical of people for being unwilling to compromise, I look for hidden compromises that they have been making all along; that is, they have been compromising themselves away, which makes understandable their hesitancy to make any new ones (Wile, 1981, 1988). In a couple therapy session, I felt critical of a husband when I heard about his unwillingness, on a vacation with his wife, to wait just a few minutes for her to buy some postcards. But then I found out that he had agreed to go on her type of vacation—lying on the beach—when he really wanted to go whitewater rafting. In fact, he did not want to go on a vacation at all, since he had just started a new job, and had gone only because his wife had been looking forward to it so much.

d. *Hidden powerlessness.* When I see people as controlling, I look to see how such behavior might be a reaction to feeling helpless. I help a wife say to her husband, "You always out-argue me—you are better with words—so I get frustrated sometimes, like right now, and just demand that we do it my way."

e. *Hidden unentitlement.* When I see clients as behaving in a narcissistically entitled manner, I look for how this behavior is a reaction to feeling *unentitled.* I help a husband say to his wife, "Since I don't have a very good feeling about myself, it's hard for me to believe that you might actually want to do things for me, so I just build up this big argument about how you owe it to me."

For a therapist with a CCT perspective, being in an empathic state means automatically adopting these principles. But adopting them, even just one of them, is a way to shift out of an adversarial state and into an empathic (collaborative) one. Using these principles is both the means to shift into an empathic stance and a sign of being in it already.

CLOSING SUMMARY

In this approach, you focus on the intrinsic difficulty of being in a relationship—the ease with which partners find themselves in an adversarial or withdrawn cycle without knowing how they got into it, not wanting to be in it, and not knowing how to get out of it. You believe that at every moment there is a conversation that the partners could have in which their hearts would go out to each other. You believe that no matter how irrational a partner's behavior may seem, there is always a way in which it makes sense—in terms of the immediate situation and not just as a carryover from his/her fam-

ily of origin. Believing these things, you find yourself automatically looking for this hidden sense and trying to come up with this conversation.

In this approach, you do the following:

1. Substitute loss of voice for resistance as the key pathological principle.
2. Adopt a nonpathologizing stance.
3. Look for the heartfelt feeling and inner struggle.
4. Create a moment of intimacy.
5. Create the best possible relationship (conversation) you can in that moment.
6. Solve the moment rather than the problem as the way to solve the problem.
7. Adopt the goal of making the partners understandable to each other as even more important than that of solving the problem.
8. Discover the conversation hidden in the fight.
9. Entitle people to their experience in the process of discovering what it is.
10. Recognize symptomatic reactions as fall-back measures.
11. Become spokesperson for both partners simultaneously, taking particular care of the partner who at the moment you find yourself siding against.
12. Serve as guardian of the conversation.
13. Turn your feelings of disapproval toward a partner into a therapeutic instrument pointing you to the relationship problem of the moment.
14. Create a compassionate perspective from which partners can appreciate how their own and their partners' positions make sense.
15. Personify this compassionate perspective.
16. Create an empathic cycle out of the manner in which the partners talk about the adversarial or withdrawn one that they are in.
17. Solve the partners' problems, including their unsolvable ones, by reassembling the relationship on the next higher level.
18. Make this second level (metalevel) in the relationship an increasingly predominant part of the couple's interaction.
19. Conduct your relationship with them on the same two levels—not only to model it for them, but also because it is the best way to conduct any kind of relationship, personal or therapeutic.
20. Conduct recovery conversations that tap the fight for the useful information being revealed about the relationship.
21. Build the relationship out of the partners' unsolvable relationship problems by enabling them to confide the moment-to-moment manifestations of them.

22. Turn the relationship into a curative force for solving both the partners' relationship problems and each partner's personal problems.

The hidden issue is that people often feel alone in their experience. You get on their sides so they do not feel so alone, and you bring out what they feel in a way that might arouse compassion for themselves and empathy in their partners.

REFERENCES

Anderson, H. (1997). *Conversation, language, and possibilities: A postmodern approach to therapy.* New York: Basic Books.

Apfelbaum, B. (1998). *Effective dependency.* Paper presented at the workshop Effective Dependency, Berkeley, CA.

Apfelbaum, B. (2000a). A key to where the bodies are buried in psychoanalysis. In *Bernard Apfelbaum, PhD* [Online]. Available: http://www.bapfelbaumphd.com [2001, January 4].

Apfelbaum, B. (2000b). *Ego analysis: A formal introduction.* In *Bernard Apfelbaum, PhD* [Online]. Available: http://www.bapfelbaumphd.com [2001, January 4].

Apfelbaum, B. (2000c). *Ego analysis vs. id analysis: A brief therapy case.* In *Bernard Apfelbaum, PhD* [Online] Available: http://www.bapfelbaumphd.com [2001, January 4].

Apfelbaum, B. (2000d). *Analyzing, not psychoanalyzing.* In *Bernard Apfelbaum, PhD* [Online]. Available: http://www.bapfelbaumphd.com [2001, February 4].

Apfelbaum, B. (2001a). On entitlement to feelings. In *Bernard Apfelbaum, PhD* [Online]. Available: http://www.bapfelbaumphd.com [2001, January 10].

Apfelbaum, B. (2001b). *Patients as informants about the human condition rather than as deviants from idealized norms.* In *Bernard Apfelaum, PhD* [Online]. Available: http://www.bapfelbaumphd.com [2001, January 15].

Apfelbaum, B., & Gill, M. M. (1989). Ego analysis and the relativity of defense: The technical implications of the structural approach. *Journal of the American Psychoanalytic Association, 37,* 1071–1096.

Bowen, M. (1978). *Family therapy in clinical practice.* New York: Jason Aronson.

Christensen, A., & Jacobson, N. S. (2000). *Reconcilable differences.* New York: Guilford Press.

de Shazer, S. (1985). *Keys to solution in brief therapy.* New York: Norton.

Duncan, B. L., & Miller, S. D. (2000). *The heroic client.* San Francisco: Jossey-Bass.

Freud, S. (1923). The ego and the id. *Standard Edition, 19,* 3–66.

Freud, S. (1930). Civilization and its discontents. *Standard Edition, 21,* 59–145.

Freud, S. (1937). Analysis terminable and interminable. *Standard edition, 23,* 211–253.

Gottman, J. M. (1999). *The marriage clinic: A scientifically based marital therapy.* New York: Norton.

Gottman, J. M., & DeClaire, J. (2001). *The relationship cure: A five-step guide for building better connections with family, friends, and lovers.* New York: Crown.

Gottman, J. M., & Silver, N. (1999). *The seven principles for making marriage work.* New York: Crown.

Hardy, K. (1998). *Overcoming "learned voicelessness."* Paper presented at the Family Therapy Network Annual Symposium, Washington, DC.

Jacobson, N. S., & Christensen, A. (1996). *Integrative couple therapy.* New York: Norton.

Jacobson, N. S., & Margolin, G. (1979). *Marital therapy: Strategies based on social learning and behavior exchange principles.* New York: Brunner/Mazel.

Johnson, S. M. (1996). *The practice of emotionally focused marital therapy: Creating connection.* New York: Brunner/Mazel.

Johnson, S. M., & Williams-Keeler, L. (1998). Creating healing relationships for couples dealing with trauma: The use of emotionally focused marital therapy. *Journal of Marital and Family Therapy, 24,* 25–40.

Kohut, H. (1977). *The restoration of the self.* New York: International Universities Press.

Kriegman, G. (1983). Entitlement attitudes: Psychological and therapeutic implications. *Journal of the American Academy of Psychoanalysis, 11,* 265–281.

Layton, M., & Harkaway, J. E. (1998). *Rethinking borderline diagnosis and treatment.* Paper presented at the Family Therapy Network Annual Symposium, Washington, DC.

Rogers, C. R. (1959). A theory of therapy, personality, and interpersonal relationships, as developed in the client-centered framework. In S. Koch (Ed.), *Psychology: A study of a science* (Vol. 3, pp. 184–256). New York: McGraw-Hill.

Wachtel, P. L. (1991). The role of accomplices in preventing and facilitating change. In R. Curtis & G. Stricker (Eds.), *How people change: Inside and outside therapy* (pp. 21–28). New York: Plenum Press.

Wachtel, P. L. (1993). *Therapeutic communication: Principles and effective practice.* New York: Guilford Press.

Wachtel, P. L. (1997). *Psychoanalysis, behavior therapy, and the relational world.* Washington, DC: American Psychological Association.

Watzlawick, P., Weakland, J., & Fisch, R. (1974). *Change: Principles of problem formation and problem resolution.* New York: Norton.

White, M., & Epston, D. (1990). *Narrative means to therapeutic ends.* New York: Norton.

Wile, D. B. (1981). *Couples therapy: A nontraditional approach.* New York: Wiley.

Wile, D. B. (1984). Kohut, Kernberg, and accusatory interpretations. *Psychotherapy: Theory, Research, Practice, and Training, 21,* 353–364.

Wile, D. B. (1985). Psychotherapy by precedent: Unexamined legacies from pre-1920 psychoanalysis. *Psychotherapy: Theory, Research, Practice, and Training, 22,* 793–802.

Wile, D. B. (1987). An even more offensive theory. In W. Dryden (Ed.), *Key cases in psychotherapy* (pp. 78–102). London: Croom Helm.

Wile, D. B. (1988). *After the honeymoon: How conflict can improve your relationship.* New York: Wiley.

Wile, D. B. (1993). *After the fight: Using your disagreements to build a stronger relationship.* New York: Guilford Press.

Wile, D. B. (1994). An ego-analytic approach to emotion in couples therapy. In S. Johnson & L. S. Greenberg (Eds.), *The heart of the matter: Perspectives on emotion in marital therapy* (pp. 27–45). New York: Brunner/Mazel.

Wile, D. B. (1999). Collaborative couple therapy. In J. Donovan (Ed.), *Short-term couple therapy* (pp. 201–225). New York: Guilford Press.

Chapter 11

Narrative Couple Therapy

JILL H. FREEDMAN
GENE COMBS

BACKGROUND OF THE APPROACH

"Narrative therapy," as we (Freedman & Combs, 1996) use the term, refers to a growing body of practices and ideas (Freeman, Epston, & Lobovits, 1997; Monk, Winslade, Crocket, & Epston, 1997; Morgan, 2000; Zimmerman & Dickerson, 1996) that stem from the work of Michael White and David Epston. White's early published work (e.g., 1986) was based on ideas that stem from the work of Gregory Bateson (1972). David Epston (1989, 1998), who had encountered the narrative metaphor in studying anthropology, and Cheryl White, "who had enthusiasm for this analogy from her readings in feminism" (White & Epston, 1990, p. xvi), encouraged White to use the "story analogy"—the notion that meaning is constituted through the stories we tell and hear concerning our lives. In collaboration with Epston, White (White & Epston, 1990, 1992) found that the story analogy offered a useful direction for their work.

Therapists who began to use the narrative metaphor in White's and Epston's sense experienced quite a large shift in their world view. Instead of trying to solve problems, they became interested in collaborating with people to change their lives through enriching the narratives they and others tell concerning their lives. They began to work to bring forth and develop "thick descriptions" (Geertz, 1978; Ryle, 1971/1990), or rich, meaningful, multistranded stories of those aspects

of people's life narratives that lie outside the influence of problems. It seems that through these alternative stories, people can live out new identities, new possibilities for relationship, and new futures.

This work is more complex than a brief description of the narrative metaphor might suggest. One factor adding to the complexity is that some stories have more staying power than others. In any culture at any given time, certain stories are much more a part of the fabric of day-to-day reality than are others. We are all born into cultural stories, and they shape our perceptions of what is possible. For couples, stories about gender roles and heterosexual dominance, for example, may shape perceptions of what is possible. However, people do not usually think of the stories they are born into as stories. They think of them as "reality." Cultural stories have the power to shape our experience of reality.

An important influence on how narrative therapists work with the stories that circulate in people's cultures has been "poststructuralism," especially as it is expressed in the late work of Michel Foucault (1980, 1985). Foucault was a French intellectual who studied, among other things, the various ways that people in Western society have been categorized as "other." He examined madness (1965), illness (1975), criminality (1977), and sexuality (1985) as concepts around which certain people have been labeled "insane," "sick," "criminal," or "perverted," and described various ways such people have been separated, oppressed, or enrolled in self-policing on the basis of that labeling.

To Foucault, people have power in a society in direct proportion to their ability to participate in the various discourses that shape that society. Although *The American Heritage Dictionary, Third Edition* gives simply "verbal expression in speech or writing" as its first definition of "discourse," scholars like Foucault use the word to refer to the ongoing political/historical/institutional conversations within a society that constitute our notions of what is true and what is possible. Foucault showed how the people whose voices dominated the discussion about what constituted madness, for example, could separate the people *they* saw as mad from "polite society," sequestering them in madhouses where their voices were cut off from the avenues of power.

Foucault argued that there is an inseparable linkage between knowledge and power. Because the discourses of a society determine what knowledge is held to be true, right, or proper in that society, those who control the discourse control knowledge. At the same time, the dominant knowledge of a given milieu determines who will be able to occupy its powerful positions. We see the discourses of power that Foucault studied as historical, cultural metanarratives—stories that have shaped (and been shaped by) the distribution of power in society.

Society is not necessarily benign, fair, or just. As feminist critics (e.g., Avis, 1985; Carter, Papp, Silverstein, & Walters, 1984; Goldner, 1985a, 1985b; Hare-Mustin, 1978; Laird, 1989; Taggart, 1985) of family therapy have reminded us, our cultural institutions constrain us, leading us to see certain possibilities as desirable and blinding us to other possibilities. Laird (1989, p. 430) writes that "sociocultural narratives . . . construct the contextual realms of possibility from which individuals and families can select the ingredients and forms for their own narratives." Some people have readier access to a wider range of sociocultural narratives than others, and some narratives dominate while others are marginalized. Laird (1989, p. 431) reminds of this when she writes of "the politics of storymaking or mythmaking. Clearly there are both obvious and subtle differences in the power individuals and particular interest groups possess to ensure that particular narratives will prevail in family, group, and national life. Not all stories are equal."

Socially constructed narratives have real effects. For example, the myth that "welfare moth-ers" are engaged in a mini-industry in which they get richer and richer as they make more and more babies has had real effects on already underserved women and children. It has provided a rationalization that has allowed those in power to cut funds even further. The story about how women can never be too thin, which gets retold every time one turns on the TV or stands in a supermarket checkout line surrounded by magazine covers displaying anorexia as beauty, has contributed to a real epidemic of self-starvation. The widely circulated stories in which inner-city males are only interested in drugs, sex, and killing each other support the perverse glorification of certain kinds of misogyny and violence. At the same time, they have served as a rationale for giving up on social policies that might offer inner-city males a real chance at a different way of making it in the world.

Foucault was especially interested in how the "truth claims" carried in the "grand abstractions" of reductionist science constitute a discourse that dehumanizes and objectifies many people. He was interested in finding and circulating marginalized discourses—stories that exist, but are not widely circulated or powerfully endorsed—that might undermine the excessive power of the reductionistic scientific discourse. Foucault (1980) wrote of the "amazing efficacy of discontinuous, particular, and local criticism" (p. 80) in bringing about a "return of knowledge" or "an insurrection of subjugated knowledges" (p. 84).

Following Foucault, we believe that even in the most marginalized and disempowered of lives, there is always lived experience that lies outside the dominant stories. White, Epston, and other narrative therapists have developed ways of thinking and working that bring forth the "discontinuous, particular, and local" stories of couples and other social groups, so that people can inhabit and lay claim to the many possibilities for their lives that lie beyond the pale of dominant narratives.

When we use the narrative metaphor and the lens of poststructuralism to orient our work as therapists, we are intensely curious about each new couple we meet. We cherish each couple's stories. We work with the partners in couples in ways that invite them to celebrate their differences and to develop and live out narratives that they prefer around the particularities of their lives. This valuing of the meaning people make of their own experience over the meaning experts make of that experience has been referred to as the "interpretive turn" (Bruner, 1986). It leads us to de-center our meanings and to experience ourselves as interested people—perhaps with an anthropological or biographical or field researcher's bent—who are skilled at asking questions to bring forth the knowledge and experience carried in the stories of the couples we work with. We work to help people notice the influence of restrictive cultural stories in their lives, and to expand and enrich their own life narratives. We strive to find ways to spread the news of triumphs—to circulate success stories in order to keep them alive and growing. We believe that these success stories in turn contribute to keeping our culture growing and flowing in satisfying ways.

THE HEALTHY/WELL-FUNCTIONING VERSUS PATHOLOGICAL/ DYSFUNCTIONAL COUPLE/ MARRIAGE

"Healthy," "well-functioning," "pathological," and "dysfunctional" are not descriptions we generally use. If we are to think in this language, whether couples are "well-functioning" or not has to do with whether the stories they are living and in which they construct their identities are ones that they prefer. We think of relationships as being multistoried. That is, every relationship can be expressed and experienced through a great variety of narratives; many "true" stories can be told about any experience. Therefore, we do not look for health or pathology or quality of functioning in couples. Instead, we look at the stories that are currently shaping a relationship, and seek to facilitate a collaborative re-authoring process in which more suitable stories can be expressed and experienced.

Similarly, we do not consider the partners in a couple to have essential, core identities with fixed, predictable characteristics. Therefore, we do not look for "health" or "pathology" within the members of a couple. Keeping in mind the interpretive turn, we are interested in people's evaluations of what is problematic and preferred, and of how the problems they name affect their lives and relationships. That we are interested in people making their own evaluations does not mean that we think anything goes. We are full participants in the process of therapy, and we inevitably bring our own opinions and hard-won lived experience (and biases) along with us. For example, we are opposed to (among other things) abuse, coercion, and cruelty. When one of these problems appears to have invaded a relationship, we consider it our responsibility to ask questions that invite each partner to

consider the effects of the problem on his/her life, the other partner's life, and their relationship, and to consider the stand he/she wants to take in relation to it.

We seek to create a conversational space in which people can take responsibility for addressing and ameliorating the effects of, for instance, abuse. To us, this means that we must avoid lecturing or imposing rigid rules from a position of moral superiority. Instead, we want to invite people to bring their "best selves" into a consideration of the ways abuse diminishes their relationship, and an exploration of how they might choose ways of living that keep the abuse out of their relationship.

As narrative therapists, one of our principal intentions is to subvert the dominant practice in our society of measuring ourselves, our relationships, and others by standardized norms. For us, two-dimensional normative scales ("healthy–sick," "gifted–impaired," etc.) invite therapists and the couples who consult with them into thin descriptions—pallid, reductionist accounts—of their multistoried lives. These two-dimensional scales pervade contemporary Western culture, and each of them coexists with a prescriptive story about the right or healthy or successful way to live or to have a relationship. And none of us can measure up to the demands of all these norms; we are too fat or too thin, too driven or too passive, too caring or not caring enough. Our relationships are too rigid or too enmeshed, too focused on sex or not sexy enough, too hot or too cold. Even when we do measure up, it is within the dictates of a thin, two-dimensional story.

Rather than looking for pathology or flawed functioning within couples, we seek to examine problematic cultural stories in collaborative and multidimensional ways. We engage in conversations to expose problematic discourses and give couples the opportunity to describe and evaluate the effects of those discourses on their relationship. For example, let us discuss a conversation we had with Ted and Carol. Carol complained that Ted always walked ahead of her, and at malls always led them into the stores he wanted to shop in, not the ones she would prefer. When Carol noticed this pattern, she wondered whether it meant that she was a slow person or that Ted did not care about her and her preferences. Ted thought that all it meant was that he was a fast walker. As we asked questions to explore the cultural stories that shaped their way of walking, it seemed to all of us that gender socialization had supported Ted in unthinkingly setting the pace and Carol in unthinkingly following along, even though it made her feel like a "little girl" or a "puppy dog." Our conversation allowed Carol and Ted to separate themselves from the problem, notice the effects it had on their lives, and consider what they would prefer for their relationship.

We have worked with couples in which corporate values have played the largest role in creating problems, keeping one member of the couple unavailable and inattentive to what was most important both to him-/herself and to the relationship. In the couple we describe later in this chapter, differences in social class contributed to problematic power relations and bred fear and doubt in the relationship. In each instance, the stories about what discourses were negatively influencing their relationship, and about their preferred directions in life, emerged in collaborative conversation with a couple. Our desires in each instance were for the couple to have the last word as to what was preferred, and for the choices to be made within a multidimensional domain, not against a two-dimensional yardstick.

THE ASSESSMENT OF COUPLE FUNCTIONING AND DYSFUNCTION

We think about information as being *generated* rather than "gathered" in therapeutic conversations. In a rather literal way, we believe that we are making ourselves and each other up as we go along. This is a poststructuralist idea. We do not assume that a couple has a particular interactional or relational structure that we can assess. We do not think of people or relationships as having stable, quantifiable identities or "typical" characteristics, so we do not try to discover or gather information about such characteristics. Instead, we think of people's lives as being multistoried, and we believe that each new telling generates new possibilities for interpretation and action.

While we avoid the position of making professional, "expert" assessments, we acknowledge that the role of therapist/interviewer is a powerful one. Each question we ask directs attention to a particular domain and away from many others. We want people to interpret and assess their own experience, but our questions inevitably shape the inquiry. For this reason, we "situate" our questions. That is, we describe where they come from and our intentions in asking them so that people can evaluate our bias and decide how to relate to it. We believe that people are in a better position to interpret, make meaning of, and assess their own experience than outsiders are, even outsiders trained to help.

Since we do not subscribe to normative ideas of what constitutes a healthy couple relationship, we would be at a loss about what criteria to use in assessing couples. Instead of assessment, we are interested in hearing detailed, context-specific narratives. As we ask questions to bring forth their stories, we encourage those with whom we work to evaluate problems and their relationship to problems, as well as evaluating the therapy itself.

We ask questions that invite the partners in a couple to do the following:

- Assess their current situation.
- Name the problems involved.
- Evaluate their relationship to those problems.
- Take a stand in regard to them.
- Tell more satisfying stories of their relationship.
- Assess the usefulness of the alternative stories.

We want to know whether the alternative stories speak to people of a more satisfying identity as a couple. In telling the new stories and reflecting on them, people collaborate with us in an ongoing assessment of their new expressions of themselves and their relationship.

Here are some questions we might ask in inviting people's assessments of their situation and of their therapy experience:

- "What name would you give the problem?"
- "What is it like to have the experience of the problem?"
- "What effect does the problem have on your life?"
- "What effect does the problem have on your relationship with each other?"
- "What has it talked you into about your partner? What impact has that had?"
- "What effect does the problem have on other relationships?"
- "How does the problem alter your relationship with yourself?"
- "Is this what you want for your relationship? Why or why not?"
- "Is this what you want for yourself? Why or why not?"
- "Are we talking about what you want to be talking about?"
- "Is this conversation useful?"
- "How is it useful?"

In telling and living out the many strands of alternative stories, the partners in a couple evaluate many aspects of their lives: their private thoughts, feelings, hopes, and fears; their dyadic interactions; the contributions of each partner's culture of origin to the couple and to the individual partners; their interrelationship with local institutions and traditions; and more.

While we bend over backward to avoid "expert," categorical, reductionist assesment, it would be misleading to imply that we make no assessments of any kind. One kind of assessment that we make has to do with which parts of a couple's story might be shaped by discourses that are invisible to the partners. We ask questions that invite them to unmask the operations of such discourses, and that offer an opportunity to decide where they stand and how they would like their relationship to be in the face of such discourses.

We are particularly interested in bringing forth partners' evaluations of power relations. This often involves asking questions that invite them to consider the effects of discourses of gender, ethnicity, heterosexual dominance, class, corporate culture, patriarchy, age, or other sociocultural factors on their relationship. We might initiate such a conversation with questions similar to those that follow. We try to have thoughtful interactive conversations, with each question being responsive to the last answer. It is difficult to capture that flavor in a series of hypothetical questions. We would not ask these questions in the beginning of a conversation. They would follow a detailed telling of a set of experiences.

- "Martha, you have just said that fear of humiliation keeps you from wanting to go to social events with Brian. You described his failure to introduce you to people he knows and his talking over you when you try to join in. Is that right?"
- "Brian, what is it like to hear your actions being described that way? Does it fit with how you like to think of yourself?"
- "What or who do you think might have introduced you to this way of acting?"
- "Your father and uncles undoubtedly did not make up this way of being. Where do you think they might have learned it?"
- "Martha, I've noticed that all of these examples are of men. Do you think that this is a coincidence?"
- "Do you think it is a way of acting only to women or to children as well?"
- "What should we call this way of acting?"
- "Brian, what do you think it might be like to be a woman or child experiencing discounting?"

- "Is this what you would want women and children to experience from you? Why not? What would you rather have them know about you?"
- "You have already said, Martha, that this discounting keeps you from wanting to socialize with John. Are there other ways it affects your relationship?"
- "Is this what you want for your relationship? What would you prefer?"
- "We've been talking about a strand of our culture in which women and children are invisible or are considered to be property. It is clear, John, that that does not fit with your thinking, although you have gotten pulled into some ways of acting that go with it. Martha, do you think you've been pulled into some of the actions that go with these ideas as well?"
- "What would you name them?"
- "What's that been like for you?"
- "What has it been like for the relationship, do you think? How would you prefer your relationship to be?"

Because we think that "self," "identity," "personhood," and the like are experiences that emerge and are always changing *in relationship*, we do not know exactly who will be answering when we ask a person to draw a distinction or to evaluate the effect of an action. To make this transparent, we might ask, "Is that the problem speaking?" or "Whose values are guiding you in saying that—gay culture's or straight culture's?"

In exposing discourses that support problems, individuals and couples can separate themselves from the ways of being that are supported by those discourses, and can identify and recognize preferred perceptions, attitudes, and actions. Although we do not think of strengths or resources as fixed commodities, and we do not administer questionnaires to inventory them, we are very interested to hear the stories of relationships and events that help people to have a sense of choice, agency, purpose, and accomplishment in their life as a couple.

GOAL SETTING

Our general goal in therapy is to collaborate with people in living out—moment by moment, choice by choice—life stories that they prefer, that are more just, and that make their worlds more satisfying. We are more interested in opening up possibilities than we are in closing them down. This makes us wary of "goal setting" as it is usually defined and practiced. We think that goals, unless they are very tentatively set and rigorously updated, can set single, specific trajectories for people's lives. This can all too easily close down possibilities. The narrative metaphor biases us toward thinking about possibilities that unfold in living out a story, rather than about goals, which are usually set in advance and pursued more or less single-mindedly. Instead of goals, we tend to speak of "projects" or "directions in life."

The process of identifying projects is fluid, shifting as new distinctions are made and as alternative stories unfold. Problems can be thought of as plots and projects as counterplots. Partners in a couple may name joint projects for the relationship, individual projects, or both. For some couples, the collaborative negotiation of shared or complementary directions in life can be a very significant—sometimes even an inspirational—part of the therapy.

THE STRUCTURE
OF THE THERAPY PROCESS

While we take an active role in structuring the therapy, we ask couples to collaborate with us so that the process will fit their circumstances.

Telling and Witnessing

A rhythmic alternation between telling and witnessing characterizes narrative work. We set up a structure early in our work with couples that we come back to over and over again. We ask one member of the couple to tell his/her story while the other listens from a witnessing position. Then we ask the witnesser to reflect on what he/she has heard. Next we switch positions, so that the partner who had been in the witnessing position can tell his/her story.

We initiate this process by making eye contact and speaking primarily with one person at a time, then asking the partner to comment. Sometimes we are more explicit, saying something like this: "What I would like to do is speak with you, Rubin, for a time, with you, Ellen, listening. After a bit I'll turn to you, Ellen, and ask what thoughts you have been having while Rubin has been talking. Then we'll switch and you, Rubin, will be in the listening position while Ellen and I have a conversation. Would that be OK?"

We use the alternation of telling and witnessing in other ways as well. Sometimes a couple describes something and the therapist reflects. Although the two of us most often work separately, many people know us to be partners in marriage and in parenthood as well as in our work. Heterosexual couples in particular sometimes ask us to work with them as a cotherapy team. When we do this, one of us takes the role of interviewer and the other reflects. Sometimes we include an outsider witness group or reflecting team as part of the structure. In that case, the outsider witness group listens while we interview the couple. Then we have a formal break, and the outsider witnesses reflect on what they've heard. In the last part of the interview, the couple responds to the reflections.

At times, particularly as part of training or consultation, reflecting teams are composed of therapists. At other times, in response to our raising the possibility, couples agree to our inviting another couple (whose members have insider experience in dealing with a particular problem) to serve as an outsider witness group. Or couples may invite other people who are important in their lives to join in as an outsider witness group.

Length, Frequency, and Number
of Meetings

We negotiate the time of each next meeting as we go along, one session at a time. At the end of meetings with couples, we ask whether the conversation has been useful. If it has, we ask how. Then we ask whether they would like to meet again, and if so, when.

We ask couples to make these decisions each time, so that they are at least as active as we are in evaluating what schedule would be most useful. Sometimes, as when they are in the middle of intense conversations, couples want to return very soon. More often, because partners have been hearing each other in new ways and making new distinctions, they are interested in allowing some time to find out what difference these new experiences will make in their lives. We listen as they negotiate with each other about how long their explorations will take. Occasionally, because the partners are not sure how much time would be useful, a couple decides to telephone us for the next appointment.

We generally meet with couples for 60 minutes at a time, but have negotiated longer meeting times for future meetings when we all agreed that we wished there was more time to complete a conversation. How long therapy lasts is highly variable and determined by each couple. Some couples come to deal with a single problem, and therapy may consist of two or three meetings. Others become involved in developing very rich, detailed stories of the partners' lives together; their therapy may continue for several years. Most are somewhere in between.

Focusing on New Directions in Life

We wonder whether simply sitting down for a meeting in a therapy office invites people to reimmerse themselves in problematic stories. With this in mind, we structure therapy conversations so as to invite people to continue to explore, describe, and experience directions in life that were unfolding in our previous meetings—new distinctions, positions people have taken about their relationship to problems, and new stories that are developing. Sometimes we read our notes aloud and ask a question such as this: "Can you tell us about new developments that relate to what we were talking about last time?" Sometimes we begin by wondering whether there have been important thoughts or events that connect to our conversation of the time before.

Another way we structure therapy is through thinking about how to keep stories alive and growing between conversations. We use letters, documents, videotapes, and the like to document and circulate alternative stories. For example, after a therapy interview we may write a letter posing questions that invite the partners to develop an alternative story even farther than they had in the interview, or we may send a document noting the stands they have taken in regard to a problem. We think that the reading of such a document between therapy meetings and the conversations that may follow such a reading can contribute to keeping a story alive and growing.

Medication

Our experience is that ideas about medication are so pervasive that the people who come to us for therapy raise the issue before it ever occurs to us. Medications are rarely a focus of couple therapy. If something about one partner's medication or the condition for which it is being prescribed does seem to be problematic for a couple, we address that problem in the same manner that we address other problems—asking each partner to describe the prob-

lem and its effects, identifying "unique outcomes" (those events that stand outside of and would not be predicted by the problem story) concerning the problem, and developing the stories of those unique outcomes.

THE ROLE OF THE THERAPIST

Epston (1999, pp. 141–142) writes,

> I chose to orient myself around the co-research metaphor both because of its beguiling familiarity and because it radically departed from conventional clinical practice. It brought together the very respectable notion of research with the rather odd idea of the co-production of knowledge by sufferers and therapist. . . . This has led, and continually leads, to practices to discover a 'knowing' in such a fashion that all parties to it could make good use of it. Such knowledges are fiercely and unashamedly pragmatic.

We join Epston in thinking of our work as co-research.

In order to engage in co-research, the therapeutic relationship is extremely important. As co-researchers, we have more questions than answers about therapeutic relationships. The following are some questions we (Freedman & Combs, 2000) ask ourselves so that we can adjust our participation in relationships with couples as therapy goes along:

- "Whose voice is being privileged in this relationship? What is the effect of that on the relationship and the work?"
- "Is anyone showing signs of being closed down, not able to fully enter into the work? If so, what power relations/discourses are contributing to the closing down?"
- "What are we doing to foster collaboration? Among whom? What is the effect of that collaboration?"
- "Is this relationship opening up or closing down the experience of agency?"
- "Does this relationship take into account other relevant people, communities, and cultures? Are we considering the effects of the ripples of this relationship?"
- "Am I asking whether and how the work is useful, and tailoring it in line with the response?"

White (2000) describes a therapist's role in this work as de-centered, but influential. We participate not as representatives of professional knowledge, not as authorities on what constitutes a normal or healthy relationship, but as people with skills in facilitating a co-research project.

We ask questions to help expose gaps or contradictions in the problematic stories that bring couples to therapy and to open space for and thickly describe alternatives. We work to keep the conversation focused and relevant. We facilitate people's ongoing evaluation of the process by asking how the conversation is going for them and responding to their answers. At times, we reflect and offer alternative directions for our conversations.

We work to create a collaborative context. We situate our ideas in our own experience and make our intentions transparent. We encourage couples to ask questions about our questions and comments. When therapy goes well (and sometimes even when it does not), we all change. We acknowledge to couples how our work and lives are enriched through meeting with them.

TECHNIQUES OF COUPLE THERAPY

Listening

When we meet people for the first time, we want to understand the meaning of their stories for *them*. This means turning our backs on "expert" filters: not listening for chief complaints; not "gathering" the pertinent-to-us-as-experts bits of diagnostic information interspersed in their stories; not hearing their anecdotes as matrices within which resources are embedded; not listening for surface hints about what the core problem "really" is; and not comparing the selves they portray in their stories to normative standards.

In the beginning, we ask about nonproblematic aspects of the lives of each partner and of their relationship. We are interested in getting to know the members of a couple as people, and in making sure that the problem does not trick us into mistaking them for it. Unless people insist on moving quickly into talking about problems, we spend a while listening to stories about their preferences and pleasures. At some point in this process, people do usually begin to spontaneously tell problem-tinged stories.

As we listen to their stories of the problem, we try to put ourselves in the shoes of the people we work with. We do not assume that we understand the meaning their experience holds for them. We listen and ask. Connecting with people's experience from their perspective orients us to the specific realities that shape, and are shaped by, their personal narratives. This sort of understanding requires that we listen with focused attention, patience, and curiosity while building a relationship of mutual respect and trust.

Deconstructive Listening

When we listen "deconstructively" to people's stories, our listening is guided by the belief that those stories have many possible meanings. The meaning we as listeners make is, more often than not, at least a little different from the meaning that a speaker has intended. We seek to capitalize on this by valuing the gaps we notice in our understanding and asking people to fill in details, or by listening for ambiguities in meaning and then asking people about those ambiguities.

As people tell their stories, we reflect at intervals our sense of what they are saying and ask whether the meaning we are making fits with their intended meaning. Even though our intention is to understand people's realities from something very close to their point of view, their realities inevitably begin to shift, at least a little, as they expand their narrative in response to our retellings and questions. Our very presence makes their world different. Throughout this process, we endeavor to listen with a thoughtfulness about what new constructions are emerging. We wonder aloud whether they are useful or desirable. We strive to co-create a process in which people experience choice rather than "settled certainties" (Bruner, 1986) with regard to the realities that they inhabit.

Deconstructive Questioning

Michael White (1991, p. 27) defines deconstruction actively and politically:

> According to my rather loose definition, deconstruction has to do with procedures that subvert taken-for-granted realities and practices: those so-called "truths" that are split off from the conditions and the context of their production; those disembodied ways of speaking that hide their biases and prejudices; and those familiar practices of self and of relationship that are subjugating of person's lives.

The medical model and other discourses of modern power can lead people to a sense of themselves as "docile bodies" (Foucault, 1977), subject to knowledge and procedures in which they have no active voice. There are subjugating stories of gender, race, class, age, sexual orientation, and religion (to name a few), which are so prevalent and entrenched in our culture that we can get caught up in them without realizing it. We believe it is our responsibility as therapists to cultivate a growing awareness of the dominant (and dominating) stories in our society, and to develop ways of collaboratively examining the effects of those stories when we sense them at work in the lives and relationships of the people who consult with us.

Hare-Mustin (1994, p. 22) has used the metaphor of a "mirrored room" to talk about how the only ideas that can come up in therapy are the ideas that the people involved bring into the therapy room: "The therapy room is like a room lined with mirrors. It reflects back only what is voiced within it. . . . If the therapist and family are unaware of marginalized discourses, such as those associated with members of subordinate gender, race, and class groups, those discourses remain outside the mirrored room." This notion implies that we therapists must continually reflect on the discourses that shape our perceptions of what is possible, both for ourselves and for the people we work with. Such reflection puts us in the position to ask deconstructive questions—questions whose aim is to examine problems in detail and expose discourses that support them.

Externalizing Conversations

White (1987, 1988–1989, 1989; see also Epston, 1993) has introduced the idea that the person is not the problem; the problem is the problem. "Externalization" is a practice supported by the belief that a problem is something operating on or having an impact on or pervading a person's life—something separate and different from the person.

We believe that listening with the belief that problems are separate from people has a powerful deconstructive effect. It biases us to interact differently with people than we would if we saw them as intrinsically problematic. It creates a different receiving context for people's stories—one in which we can work to understand their problems without seeing the people themselves as problematic or pathological. In this kind of context, people's stories almost always become less restrictive.

We can expose dominant discourses by asking externalizing questions about contextual influences on the problem. What "feeds" the problem? What "starves" it? Who benefits from it? In what

settings might the problematic attitude be useful? Which people would proudly advocate for the problem? What groups of people would definitely be opposed to it and its intentions? Questions such as these invite people to consider how the entire context of their lives affects the problem, and vice versa.

As Reiss (1985, p. 257) indicates, a family's construction of reality requires support from outside the family: "Indeed, the family is sustained by, and contributes to, the constructions of the community in which it lives." Many power imbalances in couples are coached and supported by power imbalances in the larger culture—imbalances that are supported by the dominant stories about class, gender, sexual orientation, race, and so on.

As problems are externalized, it becomes established that, rather than *being* the problem, the person or couple has a *relationship* with the problem. Both members of a couple have the opportunity to describe their relationships with problems in a variety of ways. One of the consequences of an externalizing conversation is that it becomes clear that both partners have relationships with the problems they name.

In externalizing conversations, we are particularly interested to hear descriptions of the effects of problems. Asking about the effects of a problem on both members of a couple, their lives, and their relationships can be particularly helpful. It helps keep the identity of the problem separate from either partner. It mobilizes the members of the couple to join together in opposing the effects of the problem. This is particularly helpful in situations in which the problem has kept them apart. People can stop thinking about themselves or their relationships as inherently problematic, and instead can consider their relationships with problems and whether they want to revise them.

Naming the Problem and the Project

When people name a problem, they begin the process of externalization. Naming a problem can also be a way of examining a problem and thinking differently about it. It can be poetic and compelling.

We recently saw a young heterosexual couple. The man described the problem as waking him in the middle of the night with a gun to his head. When we asked him to name the problem (which he had been referring to as "anxiety attacks"), he called it "the thief" because it was trying to steal his sleep. His partner, who had been scornful of the fear and difficulty sleeping until this point, could easily relate to the terror of a burglary in the dark of night. She began to appreciate her partner's bravery in facing it alone. She suggested that he wake her so that she could help.

As we ask people to evaluate their relationship to problems, we often begin to hear what they would prefer. We are especially interested in hearing about preferred directions in life. We listen for words in people's descriptions that might serve as good names for projects. We ask questions inviting them to name projects. These questions can be quite direct. For example, let's say a couple has named "blaming" as a problem. They are recounting an incident in which they could have gotten caught up in blaming, but did not. Julie tells how she finished a major project at work, let Fran know it was finally done, and described a way she would like to celebrate. Fran did not arrange the dinner Julie would have liked that night and did not even come home until late in the evening. In the past, "blaming" would have convinced Julie that Fran did not really care about the relationship. This time Julie was able to escape "blaming," ask Fran what her intention was, and believe Fran's answer. In such an instance, we might ask Julie whether asking about Fran's intention instead of assuming she knew it reflected a preferred direction in life—one that blaming could have kept her from seeing. If Julie agreed, we could ask whether this direction represented a project that the couple was interested in. If they were, we could ask what name they would give the project.

Some problems and projects are shared by partners of a couple. Others are of concern to one partner, but not to the other. Witnessing each other's stories and hearing the problems and projects that shape them may be very important to a couple, even though the partners do not have a shared focus.

As the partners in a couple name problems and projects, we keep track of them. The explicit and direct discussion of projects and their contrast to problems can be a vital part of therapy. Such discussion brings forth and thickens the counterplots to problematic stories. It heightens the meaning that is made of particular experiences. Without an identified counterplot, experiences that lie outside the problem story may go unnoticed or seem trivial. With a counterplot, people can perceive shape and meaning in their nonproblematic experiences. For example, once the partners in a couple have agreed on "listening more with our hopes and less with our fears" as a shared project,

any conversation they have can be plotted into the narrative of how hopes and fears influence their listening. Until such a project is explicitly discussed and agreed upon, conversations may be given many different meanings or no meaning at all.

We keep projects present in the therapy through short names or phrases like "growing intimacy," "having a voice," or "standing against violence." These names often shift as the therapy progresses, and it is a therapist's job to keep up with the couple's changes in language and conceptualization. We seek personal, evocative, and poetic names for problems and projects. Throughout therapy, we ask questions that invite people to shape their perceptions, thoughts, feelings, and actions into stories according to the plots and counterplots they identify as meaningful for their lives.

Unique Outcomes

Our entryway for inviting people to tell and live new stories is through "unique outcomes." A unique outcome, as noted earlier, is any event that would not have been predicted in light of a problem-saturated story. A unique outcome may be a plan, action, feeling, statement, desire, dream, thought, belief, ability, or commitment (Morgan, 2000). Unique outcomes constitute openings that, through questions and reflective discussion, can be developed into new stories.

Sometimes couples offer unique outcomes quite directly. For example, someone describing a problem may say, "It's not always like that," and go on to describe a unique outcome. It is not unusual, as couples become involved in the re-authoring process, for them to save up new unique outcomes to tell their therapist. At other times, unique outcomes are so buried in people's descriptions of their problematic stories that it is important to listen very carefully if we are not to miss them. For example, if one partner says, "Once in a while I get through to him, but usually . . ." and then proceeds to tell a problematic story, if we are listening closely, we can be curious about the "once in a while" part, just as we would be curious about the answers to direct unique-outcome questions.

Sometimes we notice events that, given the problematic story, we would not have predicted: partners who believe they have communication problems eloquently describing the problem, or one partner showing up on time to meet the other for therapy even though the problematic story is one of irresponsibility.

Most often, openings develop "spontaneously" in ways like those we have been describing, as we listen deconstructively and ask couples about the effects of problems on their lives and relationships. If openings do not develop spontaneously, we can inquire more directly about their existence. When we are working with an externalized problem, a straightforward way of looking for openings is to ask about the influence of one or both partners on the life of the problem. That is, we ask questions such as these: "Has there ever been a time when the problem tried to get the upper hand, but you were able to resist its influence?" or "Have you ever been able to escape the problem for even a few minutes?" or "Is the problem *always* with you?" When questions of this sort follow a detailed inquiry into the effects of the problem on the person or couple, people can usually find instances in which they were able to elude the problem's influence. Each such instance is a potential opening onto an alternative life narrative.

Developing Stories from Unique Outcomes

Once we have agreed upon a preferred opening that seems relevant and interesting to one or both partners of a couple, we invite them to develop it into an alternative story. We do not have a formula to follow in this process, but we do keep in mind that stories involve events organized by plot through time in particular contexts, and that they usually include more than one person. A big part of what lets new stories make a difference in people's lives is that, in telling them to other people, a performance of meaning occurs. We work to make the therapy conversation a ritual space in which the performance of meaning can occur. Ideally, people relive the events as they tell them. We can facilitate this by asking questions to develop a story rich in detail and meaning.

White (White & Epston, 1990), following Bruner (1986), speaks of the "dual landscapes" of *action* and *consciousness* (or, in his more recent work, *identity*). He suggests that the stories constituting people's lives unfold in both these landscapes, and that it can be helpful for therapists to inquire about both. Let us look first at the landscape of action.

The landscape of action includes detail in multiple modalities involving the viewpoints of multiple characters in a particular scene or setting. It also includes the action itself. What happened, in what sequence, involving which characters?

Let us take the very simple example of Jack and Lisa at an initial therapy appointment, saying that their relationship has been deteriorating for years and that this is the first time they have sought out therapy. We might wonder whether simply deciding and following through to come to therapy is a unique outcome. The following are some questions we might ask:

- "Who actually made the suggestion that you come to therapy?"
- "What was the look on Jack's face when you suggested it? Did the look change as you talked more?"
- "Jack, what did you think when Lisa first made the suggestion? How did that change for you as you talked?"
- "Were there conversations or interactions between the two of you that prompted you to bring this up, Lisa? Was there something Jack said?"
- "Jack, do you remember that? What were you thinking that got you to say that?"
- "Who would be most pleased that you have taken this step? What would they say about it?"

In the landscape of action, we are interested in constructing an "agentive self" with people. That is, we ask questions with an eye to enhancing those aspects of the emerging story that support "personal agency" (Adams-Westcott, Dafforn, & Sterne, 1993). The very act of re-authoring requires and demonstrates personal agency, and most people experience that in this work. We go a step further in making personal agency apparent by asking, in a variety of ways, how people have accomplished what they have.

In the example above, we might ask the following questions for this purpose:

- "Given the hopelessness you described, Lisa, what did you draw on in deciding to do something in the face of it?"
- "Were you preparing somehow to take this step? What went into that preparation?"
- "Jack, do you think that Lisa knew that you would be willing to come? How did you get past the hopelessness to agree on doing something so foreign?"

We think about the *shape* of a story as it comes forth: What happened before the unique outcome? How smoothly did things unfold? Were there false starts involved? What did this particular episode lead to? In this regard, we are especially interested to know whether there is a "turning point," a place where the story changes for the good. Although "turning point" is not a fitting metaphor for everyone in every situation, when it is, it distinguishes a significant event that we can plot in time. We believe it is useful to focus special attention on this sort of event, bringing forth even more shape and detail, perhaps even treating it as a story within a story.

No matter how vivid a story is in the landscape of action, if it is to have *meaning*, it must also be developed in the landscape of identity. By "the landscape of identity," we refer to that imaginary territory in which people plot the meanings, desires, intentions, beliefs, commitments, motivations, values, and the like that relate to their experience in the landscape of action. In other words, in the landscape of identity, people reflect on the implications of experiences storied in the landscape of action.

In order to explore the landscape of identity, we ask what we (Freedman & Combs, 1993) call "meaning questions." These are questions that invite people to step back from the landscape of action and reflect on the wishes, motivations, values, beliefs, learning, implications, and so forth that lead to and flow from the actions they have recounted. For example, we may ask:

- "What do you think it says about your relationship that you agreed to come together to therapy?"
- "Does it characterize the way the two of you do things to have secret hope in the face of hopelessness?"

In co-authoring stories, we move between the landscape of action and the landscape of identity, weaving the two back and forth again and again.

Time: Developing a "History of the Present" and Extending the Story into the Future

White and Epston (1990, p. 9) write:

> Social scientists became interested in the text analogy following observations that, although a piece of behavior occurs in time in such a way that it no longer exists in the present by the time it is attended to, the meaning that is inscribed into the behavior survives across time. . . . In striving to make sense of life, persons face the task of arranging their experi-

ences of events in sequences across time in such a way as to arrive at a coherent account of themselves and the world around them.

In rendering such accounts, once a preferred event has been identified, we want to link that event to other preferred events across time—so that their meanings survive, and so that the events and their meanings can thicken a person's or couple's narrative in preferred ways. Therefore, once a preferred event is identified and storied, we ask questions that might link it to other past events and develop the story of those events. Here are some examples of questions that might identify such events:

- "When you think back, what events come to mind that you might be building on—that reflect other times when you could have been pulled apart, but that you came together as a couple?"
- "If we were to interview friends who have known you throughout your relationship, who might have predicted that the two of you would have been able to accomplish this? What memories might they share with us that would have led them to predict this?"

We can also ask how the emerging new story influences a person's ideas about the future. As people free more and more of their pasts from the grip of problem-dominated stories, they are able to envision, expect, and plan toward less problematic futures. We might ask:

- "We have just been talking about an accomplishment and several events in the past that paved the way for this accomplishment. If you think of these events as creating a kind of direction in your lives, what do you think will be the next step?"
- "You have learned some things about each other that have changed your view of each other and of the relationship. If you keep this new view in your hearts, how do you think the future might be different?"

Reflecting

Including time and space for reflection in therapy promotes experience of experience, and it is through the experience of reflecting on our experience that we make meaning of it. While the practice of reflection may occur even when we do not formally encourage it, such "natural" reflection does not necessarily focus on the preferred experiences or new narratives that are developing in therapeutic conversations.

In our discussion of "telling and witnessing," we have outlined possible reflecting structures—one partner reflecting on the other's story, the therapist reflecting, and a reflecting team or outsider witness group reflecting. In this section, we describe how we focus reflecting conversations.

Stories need listeners as well as tellers. It is through the interpersonal, societal practice of telling and retelling of stories that they take on enough substance to change people's lives. When we ask one partner to witness the other's story, we hope that he/she will hear it in a new way. We invite reflections so that each partner can give voice to what he/she witnesses. We ask general questions such as the following:

- "What was it like to hear what Brad was saying?"
- "What thoughts were you having while Linda was talking?"

And we ask questions that more directly invite people to respond to unique outcomes and preferred directions that they might have heard in our conversation with their partners. The following are examples:

- "Were you surprised when Raoul described you as taking the time to let others know you care?"
- "What did it mean to you to hear Chantal say how important the relationship is to her?"

We then make space for the original teller to respond to his/her partner's reflections.

Whenever possible, we use reflecting teams made up of therapists (Andersen, 1987), or outsider witness groups (White, 1997) made up of people asked to participate because of some type of insider knowledge to increase the audience for tellings and retellings. For example, if we are working with a couple struggling with infertility, we might ask other couples who have been through infertility struggles to join the group, with the couple's permission. When we have a reflecting team or an outsider witness group, we structure it in a very particular way that includes four parts (Cohen, Combs, DeLaurenti, DeLaurenti, Freedman, Larimer, & Shulman, 1998; White, 1995).

In the first part, the therapist interviews the couple while the outsider witness group observes the interview from behind a one-way mirror (or at a bit of a distance). In the second part, the group switches places with the couple and the therapist. The couple and therapist listen as the group members have a conversation, raising questions and commenting about what they have watched. In the third part, the couple and therapist switch back to their original places, and the couple responds to the reflections as the group observes. In the fourth part, everyone meets together for the purpose of deconstructing the interview or making it transparent. The therapist and outsider witness group members respond to questions anyone has about their questions, purposes, and the directions they pursued in the interview.

In the second part of the interview, if an outsider witness group or a reflecting team with little experience is reflecting, the therapist may ask questions drawing out team members, keeping the focus on what moved team members and on possible preferred directions that emerged during the interview. We ask team members to situate their reflections in their own experience, to acknowledge the trust the members of the couple are showing in opening their lives to the presence of others, and to comment on the difference being part of the conversation makes to their own lives.

Documenting and Circulating New Stories

Because we believe that the new stories that emerge in therapy become transformative as they are enacted outside the therapy room, we are interested in documenting and circulating the new stories (White & Epston, 1990). We take notes in therapy that document new stories as they develop. We often refer back to these notes and read them aloud. When couples take stands or achieve new things or reach turning points, we may create a document or certificate together that formalizes this newly distinguished event in their story. We often make videotapes for their library in which they reflect on how far they have come. We may make tapes or documents about what they have learned that can be used by others facing similar problems (White & Epston, 1990). Through this kind of exchange, couples can band together with others in virtual leagues.

We sometimes write letters between therapy meetings. In these letters, we reflect on unique outcomes and ask questions that we have not asked in the therapy conversation. We hope that this will thicken and extend the knowledge that has begun to emerge there. We sometimes generate formal documents that list important elements of new narratives (Freedman & Combs, 1997). To encourage the circulation of this knowledge, we invite people to share these documents with other people in their lives.

CURATIVE FACTORS IN COUPLE THERAPY/MECHANISMS OF CHANGE

We believe that we all live our lives through stories—the stories we tell and the stories others tell about us. These stories carry the meaning of our lives; they organize the way we experience our relationships, our identities, and the possibilities our lives hold. We think that people's experience of the meaning of their lives and relationships changes through changes in their life narratives. As their narratives change, what they do and what they perceive change as well. We facilitate this process by asking questions to highlight unstoried events, to encourage meaning making around those events, and then to tie the meaning to actions and contexts.

People's life narratives are condensations and abstractions; they contain only a small portion of the events and circumstances of their lives. Of the countless events that occur each day, only a few are storied and given meaning. When couples come to therapy, their accounts of their relationships are generally problematic and limited. This has to do, at least in part, with larger cultural stories or discourses, which support particular sets of stories and meanings and not others.

We approach therapy as an experiential process through which people reclaim, relive, and make meaning of stories that add new substance and possibilities to their lives. Our therapy with couples is also a process in which partners witness each other storying alternative events.

One of us recently had an experience with someone in therapy that illustrates the way lives change when narratives change. Rhonda, a 42-year-old woman, had been sued for malpractice some 15 years previously. Although the suit was settled out of court, there was considerable publicity and scandal. After that lawsuit, Rhonda's experience at first was that she felt devastated. As time passed, she felt numb. Her life was on hold. Although she did not find her relationship with Greg to be satisfying, she stayed in it. She stayed in her job. Life went on, but she did not. She missed the years during which she could have made the choice to have children.

After 13 years, she started therapy and began to reclaim her life. She began to consider her career and whether she would like to interview for other jobs. She ended the relationship with Greg and became involved in what she described as the best relationship of her life—with Jeff.

One day Jeff said, "I can't believe you stayed in that relationship with Greg for so long. Why did you do it?" Rhonda said that she did not know, and they became involved in talking about other things. Two days later, Jeff apologized profusely to Rhonda, saying that he had been really thoughtless in asking that question about Greg. He had somehow forgotten about the whole lawsuit and how it had put her life on hold. Rhonda burst into gales of laughter and told him that she had forgotten too!

She, of course, knew that it had happened, but it was no longer the central story of her life. Other stories had been told, retold, witnessed, documented, and—more importantly—reexperienced. The thicker version of Rhonda's narrative supported new actions and possibilities: a new relationship, new ways of thinking about work, and many smaller changes. The way Rhonda experienced her life had changed through a re-storying of events. Her immersion in the alternative stories supported new relationships and other possibilities.

Another way of describing our ideas about change is to say that in successful therapy new meanings are performed. "Performance of meaning" is a concept that narrative therapists have borrowed from poststructural anthropology, particularly from the work of Barbara Myerhoff (1982, 1986), who gave numerous examples of how, instead of being an innate quality, meaning arises through performance. Unless a story is told and retold (circulated, written down, acted out, sung, etc.), it has no lasting meaning. In the light of this notion, the new strands of story that emerge in response to our questions must be circulated and put into action before they can become meaningful.

When Jeff apologized to Rhonda for his memory lapse, he was performing meaning around the lapse. When Rhonda realized that she too had lost track of those 13 painful years, she added another layer of meaning to Jeff's. Rhonda's retelling of the incident in therapy was a big performance of meaning, and in that performance, her new, joyous relationship with Jeff became appreciably more real and memorable.

We believe that change occurs through the performance of meaning that takes place in waves of telling and retelling such as these.

TREATMENT APPLICABILITY

For us, the most important aspect of narrative therapy is the world view. Narrative practices flow from a narrative/poststructuralist world view. Once we begin to see problems as separate from people and to situate problems in sociocultural discourses, we no longer see people in ways that support making traditional, expert, individual diagnoses. Once we enter into ideas that support collaboration, we no longer experience ourselves as the possessors of expert knowledge about what would be most helpful to people. Instead, we begin to appreciate the insider knowledge that people acquire through struggling with particular problems in particular contexts. The narrative world view leads to a shift in perception. We do not stand outside our work and assess it by scientistic criteria. Instead, we ask people in an ongoing way whether the therapy is helpful and how it is helpful.

If a member of a couple wonders whether medication might be helpful, or requests a formal assessment of a particular problem, we talk about it; if the couple chooses, we make a referral to someone who might collaboratively facilitate a decision about medication, diagnosis, or the like. We do not consider medication or testing a part of narrative therapy, but we support people in exploring whatever kind of approach they think might be helpful.

We have found that the narrative approach has general applicability. Although the length, intensity, and specific outcome of therapy vary from problem to problem and from context to context, the approach is as effective for couples seeking premarital counseling as it is for couples struggling to reclaim their relationship from violence and abuse.

However, our experience is that some couples prefer a different kind of therapy relationship than we offer. Some people are seeking instruction or expert advice. Others are more interested in exploring their histories to "find out" why they are in the situations they find themselves in. We ask people regularly how the therapy is going for them, and we are open to referring and willing to refer couples if they are seeking a different kind of therapy relationship.

At the same time, we have discovered that most couples coming to therapy are not as concerned about how the therapy relationship is structured as they are about whether their relationship improves. Because popular notions of therapy include descriptions such as "getting to the root of the problem," they may initially use words that would seem to indicate a preference for a different kind of therapy relationship. With further conversation, we have found that most couples are simply interested in improving their relationships.

CASE ILLUSTRATION

Since "one of us" (JHF) *was the therapist working with Mark and Victoria, we have written this section primarily in her voice, from her point of view. Throughout the description of the therapy we have also offered commentary in italics to help readers relate the clinical illustration to the first part of this chapter.*

Victoria was referred by a colleague of mine who was her neighbor. On the phone, she told me that she and her husband had been experiencing problems for some time and that they could not work them out on their own.

We usually begin therapy with a new couple by getting to know each member before we get to know the problem. Otherwise, the problem might color our view of them and keep us from seeing possibilities for them outside of the problem. We hope that starting this way helps people feel free to talk about aspects of their relationship and experience that they like, not just those that are problematic.

Since I had spoken with Victoria on the phone, I began the meeting by talking with Mark. He told me that he was 41 years old and that he lived in a small town about an hour and a half away, where he held a job as a supervisor in a manufacturing plant. He had an 18-year-old daughter by a previous marriage, whom he did not see as often as he would like. She seemed to initiate visits only when she wanted money. Mark had been divorced for 13 years and married to Victoria for 8. He enjoyed playing cards, riding a motorcycle, and doing projects around his house.

Victoria told me that she was 40 years old, an artist, and a professor in a fine arts program. She loved going to galleries, seeing films, and traveling. For the last 3 years, because of her work teaching, she had lived in Chicago, separately from Mark, who had to stay in Wisconsin for his work. Before Victoria found her teaching post, the couple had lived together in Wisconsin.

The tone of this early part of the interview was highly interactive. Jill did not listen to what Mark and Victoria said as bits of "information" that she could use to form an assessment. Instead, she was interested in getting to know them as people. She also wanted to present herself as a person, rather than as a representative of professional expertise. She hoped this would contribute to reducing the hierarchy and establishing a collaborative relationship.

After hearing a bit from the couple, I asked whether they would like to ask me any questions.

Jill's intention in asking was to undermine the hierarchy a bit and to create an opportunity for transparency. We want couples to know that we will welcome their questions throughout therapy.

Mark had no questions right then, but Victoria was interested in knowing what I liked to read. We talked a few minutes about books and authors.

We are interested in creating a context in which people's stories can be spoken and heard. In our experience, by the time couples get to therapy, the interweaving stories of their problems tend to follow a well-rehearsed choreography. Blame and defensiveness often overshadow any hopes and constructive intentions either party has for the relationship. We want to facilitate something different from the outset. For that purpose, during much of the therapy (this varies for different couples) we speak to one person at a time, with the other partner in the position of witnessing his/her story. As we have previously described, at particular points we turn to the partner and ask for reflections. Sometimes we explain the structure, saying something like this: "I am going to talk with Mark for a few minutes and ask you to just listen. After we talk for a bit, you'll get a chance to respond to what you've heard. Then we'll switch and I'll talk with you for a while. Will that be OK?" If either partner seems dubious or uncertain about this idea, we will explain that when one person describes an irksome or scary difficulty, the other often feels put on the spot to point out mistakes or counter with a different description. Rather than really listening to the partner's story, the listener composes a rebuttal while the partner is talking. We would like to offer a context where people can really hear their partners, knowing that each person will have an opportunity to tell his/her story and have it heard.

Once we know a bit about each partner, we want to hear and understand the couple's stories of what is problematic. We collaborate with the couple in naming the problem or problems and ask questions to begin deconstructing those problems. We also listen for openings to new, preferred stories.

Jill began discussion of the problem with Mark because of her awareness that women often bear re-

sponsibility for the well-being of relationships. Since Victoria had made the appointment and was most active in the early conversation, Jill wanted to offer Mark the possibility of taking active responsibility for the well-being of the relationship.

I moved into a witnessing structure casually, simply speaking directly to Mark and making eye contact primarily with him while Victoria listened. I asked Mark to tell me about what brought the couple to therapy. He spoke rather hesitantly about "things deteriorating": Victoria was coming home to Wisconsin less, and he was coming to Chicago more; she was always wanting to talk, and he was quiet; she was curious and motivated, and he was trying to be more active and enthusiastic but feeling as if he never quite made it. I wondered what the effects of these differences were. (*"Differences" was the name Jill heard Mark using for what was problematic.*) In our ensuing discussion he created a list of effects: frustration, anger, and defensiveness, which got him to "clam up."

When I asked Victoria what she was thinking while Mark talked (*notice the beginning of the telling-and-reflecting rhythm*), she said that she had been unhappy for a couple of years, but she hadn't realized that he had been too. In response to my questions inviting her evaluation, she said that this was good to realize, because at least they were together in their experience.

Later in the conversation, Victoria said that she felt as if she had been marking time. She declared that she wanted someone to go forward with her to share knowledge and challenge her—somebody who knew things she did not and could open doors for her. She ended by stating, "This relationship has been the safe harbor, but I want a shift to rockier waters."

In Mark's reflections, he said that he could understand how Victoria valued excitement. He said that he valued it too. What was important for him was to share both exciting and quiet times with someone else, and to be with someone who enjoyed the same things he did. When I asked how much of that he already got from this relationship, he said 50–60%. He wondered whether it might help their relationship if, instead of relying on each other, they each found friends to join them in activities that did not interest the other.

Victoria broke into the conversation and wailed, "What can we be intimate about, then?"

As the conversation continued, they tentatively agreed on naming the problems "distance" and "frustration." (*In this instance, Mark and Victoria named shared problems. In other situations, each partner may name a different problem. We do not want people to name shared problems unless that fits their experience.)* Over the remainder of the first interview, and during the second, we mapped the effects of distance and frustration.

For Victoria, although she had not experienced herself as looking for other men, the distance and frustration had contributed to what she called "two and a half relationships" with other men. The half relationship involved frequent meetings and conversations, but was not sexual, as the other two had been. Distance had given her room to see Mark in a different, less favorable light and to have more independent dreams. Seeing him in this new light led her to decide that she did not respect some things about him: He did not have "enough" education, he did not discuss things enough, and reading was a chore for him. Seeing Mark in this way created turmoil for Victoria. She could no longer see the relationship fitting with her larger goals, and she worried that Mark was no longer getting enough from it either.

Mark also agreed that distance and frustration had led Victoria to become involved in other relationships and contributed to their relationship "breaking down." When we unpacked what Mark meant by the relationship "breaking down," we came up with this list:

- Mistrust and anger.
- impatience and sometimes disgust on Victoria's part when they were together.
- Mark's experience of not being able to do anything right.

The effects of distance and frustration were taking a toll on Mark's and Victoria's relationships with themselves. Victoria felt horrible both about the pain she was causing Mark and about how she was not always being honest with herself. Mark found himself more and more involved with self-degradation.

Once we had unpacked some of the effects of distance and frustration, I asked about the partners' evaluation of these effects. I wondered whether they wanted to continue in their current relationship with the effects. I asked questions about each effect, such as "What is it like to be subjected to self-degradation? Is turmoil something that you want for your life? Why or why not?"

Early in this process, Mark suggested that some background information might be helpful. He told me that when he and Victoria married,

they vowed to give each other room to grow and promised to help each other. He had reminded himself of this when Victoria first became interested in another man. For him, the problem was not other relationships per se, but the fact that he felt pushed away while they were going on. Mistrust and anger were problematic, he said, because he would like Victoria and himself to be easy with each other and to be friends again. He could be OK with the amount of time apart if he felt respected, appreciated, cared about, and connected. He did not want disgust and self-degradation to influence his life and relationship. In fact, Mark took a firm stand against disgust and self-degradation, saying that he would like to be together with Victoria, but not if that meant he also had to live with disgust and self-degradation.

When her turn came, Victoria said that the lack of respect she experienced in relation to Mark was not something that she wanted. It created turmoil in her life, and what she wanted instead was to be at peace in the relationship. She did not want peace at any cost. She wanted to step out and be bigger in what she did and what she dreamed. She thought that some of the impatience had to do with not knowing how to step out. As she considered it more, she realized that the impatience did not really serve her well. She thought that there was room to include Mark in her dreams and she realized that impatience stood in the way of that. She said that she would like to talk with Mark about how he might be included in her dreams.

I made note of her wish and of Mark's 50–60% satisfaction. They were potential unique outcomes that I wanted to come back to and ask more about, but first I asked about lack of respect and how it influenced Victoria's experience of Mark. She had mentioned "things about him" (not having a college education, not discussing things as much as she would like, and finding reading a chore) as contributing to the lack of respect. I asked what those things meant to her, and Victoria said, "The first thing that came to mind was that he is not very intelligent, but I know he is intelligent." When I asked how she knew he was intelligent, she described how Mark had advised her in setting up her studio and creating a marketing plan for her work. He did not simply encourage her; he had challenged her in ways that had been quite helpful. She credited him with much of the success she had experienced in the business aspect of her work. She appreciated how intelligently he helped her map out a plan. He did not make assumptions, was very deliberate in setting things in order, and came up with creative ideas.

In the following conversation, Jill asked questions that helped Victoria unmask some of the discourses that tricked her into a problematic view of Mark.

I wondered, given everything she had just said, how Victoria could have been tricked into doubting Mark's intelligence. She thought it odd as well. When I asked who might think that not having a college education, not discussing things, and not enjoying reading indicated a lack of intelligence, she began to wonder about how teaching in a university had influenced her. We talked about different values in the university and in what Victoria called "the everyday world." She said that this discussion really clarified some things for her. When she and Mark first got together, she was not part of the university. She was an artist barely making it in a little town in Wisconsin. And in her situation there, she had not experienced the same feelings about Mark's education and reading habits.

When I turned to him, Mark agreed that things had been different when Victoria lived in Wisconsin. He added that the feelings of disgust seemed to be most apparent after going to the movies. Victoria and her Chicago friends had a way of discussing movies that was not meaningful to Mark. He did not understand why discussing movies seemed so important to Victoria. He now wondered if this discussion thing was part of the university environment. (*Mark was now tracing the feelings of disgust to "the university environment," not to himself or Victoria.*)

Victoria nodded in agreement, but added that she enjoyed the process of critique. Just as she was beginning to declare that she did not want the university dictating her perceptions, Mark interrupted.

"You know I'm going to college," he said. I learned that at Victoria's suggestion, he had decided to pursue labor studies. What Victoria did not know until now was that he was enjoying it. "I like being opened up and seeing new things and meeting new people," he said.

When I asked Victoria what it was like to hear about Mark's experience, she said that she felt better just knowing about it. She also appreciated the way he was standing up for himself. "It is pretty intelligent!" she said.

I asked whether Mark's going to college meant that he, too, would take on university values. Mark said that he preferred to have his own values. Victoria agreed, saying that his approach to school was one she could respect.

In the first two meetings, Jill asked questions that helped Victoria and Mark name and map the effects of some of the problems that were undermining their relationship. Victoria and Mark evaluated the problems and stated their preferences for how to relate to the problems. Jill's questions helped Mark and Victoria expose the role that social class (in the form of "university values") played in shaping the meanings they had made about some of their differences. Several unique outcomes—things that would not be predicted by the problematic story—had come to light, but Jill, Mark, and Victoria had not yet developed a story to support any of these.

At our third meeting, because colleagues were visiting from out of town, we were able to have a reflecting team. When I asked Victoria and Mark, they were open to the experience and also gave permission to make a videotape that they could keep to review later.

After Victoria and Mark had been introduced to the team members, I approached the conversation with curiosity about whether any of the unique outcomes I had previously noted had captured their imaginations. I started the interview by reading my notes aloud, reviewing our conversations, and asking how things had gone since we last met.

Victoria said that she had been thinking about dreams since the last meeting. She had mentioned her dreams the last time and wondered how Mark would fit into them, but what she had realized since our conversation was that she did not know what his dreams were. She wanted to hear his dreams.

Mark was reluctant to talk about his dreams. When I asked questions to unpack his reluctance, he named fear and insecurity as problems, saying they kept him from being able to hold his own in what he called "these kinds of discussions that Victoria always wants to have." As we talked more, he said that he just did not have the dreams of huge accomplishment and artistic achievement that Victoria did. Instead, he looked forward to each weekend, when he would do something like make shelves for the family room. After he described the differences a bit more, I referred back to our conversation about the difference in university values and everyday values. I wondered whether this was another example of that difference. He thought it was. I asked what he thought the difference talked him into. "Insecurity," he said. "Defensiveness."

Just as I was about to ask questions about the effects of fear, insecurity, and defensiveness, Mark told me that things are not always that way. He began to describe an experience he had at fantasy baseball camp. I had never heard of fantasy baseball camp, so I asked him to tell me about it. He explained that fantasy baseball camp was a place where, for a fee, ordinary guys could spend a week playing baseball with major league players in a major league stadium.

Victoria had accompanied Mark for his week in the Big Leagues. She described seeing his skin glow and his eyes shine as he savored playing and trying to accomplish something. They spent the greater part of the hour reliving detailed stories of that time, in which fear and insecurity could have stopped him, but instead he triumphed. For Victoria, remembering these experiences was "fantastic." I asked when else she had appreciated and enjoyed Mark the way she did at fantasy baseball camp. She told me about a camping trip they had gone on with his daughter, early in their relationship. Everything had gone wrong. Victoria found herself burrowing miserably into the tent, shrinking from the rain and mud puddles outside, and wishing she were anywhere but there. Then Mark began dancing and singing in the rain with Emily, his daughter. He kept calling out to Victoria until she joined them. This was now her most treasured memory of camping.

I asked whether it was more important for Mark to stay in touch with this version of himself or for Victoria to be in touch with it. It turned out that it was important for both of them. For Victoria, it meant that she could take Mark to a cocktail party or a movie with her colleagues without worrying that he would have nothing to contribute. It helped her see how he could fit in; it even reminded her of times in the past when he had already fit in. She described two incidents that the "university values" (classism-tinged) perception of Mark had kept her from remembering. For Mark, the "fantasy baseball camp" version of himself meant he could "keep on keeping on" instead of getting bogged down in insecurity.

When we switched places, the team members reflected on different aspects of the conversation. Here I summarize only the comments that Mark and Victoria chose to respond to. One team member noted that Mark said he did not know how to talk about his dreams, yet he brought up fantasy baseball camp. She couldn't imagine a more vivid way to talk about dreams. Another member wondered how someone who only had small dreams was able to make such a grand dream—fantasy baseball camp—come true. A third comment had to do with singing and dancing in the rain. The team member who commented wondered if that event had to do with Mark's not allowing his dreams to get rained out.

Mark and Victoria were moved by the comments of the reflecting team. They came back into the room and told more stories about fantasy baseball camp and how Mark had decided to go there. If "university values" was the problem, I wondered, would "dreams" have something to do with a project they could pursue in the face of that problem? They said it would, and named the project "living our dreams."

Victoria thought back again to the camping experience and realized that Mark had actively coaxed her out of the tent so that she could join in. She thought she had not yet done as much to pave the way for him. Victoria ended by saying that it was more usual for her to be the center of attention. The team had talked about Mark for the most part. She wondered if this was a sign that he was coming forward and growing. "That would certainly have to do with my dream," she said.

In this interview, Mark and Victoria named a project. They began developing an alternative story and a "history of the present." Fortuitously, this new story had a reflecting audience of several people, and it was documented on videotape.

The "fantasy baseball camp" interview seemed to be a turning point in the relationship. Victoria opened the fourth meeting by talking about the "new Mark" who now clearly cared about the relationship. She described him as being more inquisitive and outgoing.

When I turned to Mark, he said that he experienced himself as a better listener. He thought that others around him noticed the change as well. They almost had to have noticed, because he had been speaking his thoughts aloud. He was surprised to discover that sharing his thoughts made him feel better. He said that these changes were possible because he realized he had something to say and to contribute. As we developed the story of this realization, Mark began to wonder whether the reflecting team had helped him reach it. He spoke about how moving it was to feel appreciated by strangers who heard him talking about his life. Through their eyes, he had a greater appreciation of himself. Just realizing that he could make a contribution made him more aware of what went on around him. He now knew that he had abilities to do lots of things.

We have heard this kind of response to a reflect-ing team many times. These responses inspire us to work in teams whenever we can.

After drawing Mark out about the meaning of the new events, I turned to Victoria, who had been witnessing the elaboration of the new story. When I asked her what stood out in my conversa-tion with Mark, she said that she always knew Mark had this in him. While he was speaking, she kept remembering examples of his enthusiasm for doing new things. She thought they had been stuck for a long time on a plateau, but now they were climbing the next mountain.

The usefulness of the reflecting position stands out here. In hearing Mark speak to Jill, Victoria re-viewed the past, remembering other times that fit her view of "the new Mark." As Mark heard Victoria proclaim their progress as a couple, it couldn't help taking on substance. The stories of the new Mark became more real, more solid, and more memorable. Jill now asked some questions with the intention of helping the new stories continue to grow.

Mark said that it would support his reclaimed view of himself to associate with people more, whether Victoria was there or not. He was learn-ing that he was a stronger person, but even for a strong person, being alone can foster insecurity.

I referred back to the beginning of the con-versation and said to Victoria that she had named the changes we were discussing "the new Mark." I did not want to discount Mark's changes, but I did notice that at least some of what she was call-ing "new" had strong roots in the past. I asked whether the new Mark had something to do with "the new Victoria" or "the new relationship."

Victoria nodded and said that she had changed the way she was looking at things, and that doing so made for different possibilities in their rela-tionship. She was now seeing beyond university values.

I wondered if during the times Victoria was in Chicago teaching, surrounded by the academic community, university values might take over again and persuade her that Mark did not fit her dreams. Victoria could see how that might be possible, so she decided to make more of an effort to include Mark in her life in the city—both in terms of invit-ing friends and colleagues to be with them when he was there, and talking more with him about her activities and interests at the university. Part of liv-ing their dreams for Victoria had to do with in-cluding Mark more in her life.

Mark thought he could go along with Victoria's vision, but he warned that it would be important for her to be more part of his life in Wisconsin as well.

Between meetings, during a weekend in Wis-consin, Victoria asked Mark to read a short story she had written. Writing was not her usual me-dium for art, so she thought that she might be more open to Mark's ideas than she would have been with much of her art. He returned the short story to her by fax, 2 days after she left, having corrected the grammar.

Victoria recounted this incident during the fifth therapy meeting. She hadn't talked with Mark about her reaction to his corrections, because it seemed so closely related to what they were work-ing on in therapy that she thought it best to wait. I asked her if her reaction would be different, de-pending on whether it came from university val-ues or from living their dreams. She closed her eyes, took a deep breath, and said that yes, it was differ-ent. I asked her which reaction she preferred. She chose the one that came from including Mark in her dreams. (*Note the change in language from "liv-ing their dreams" to "including Mark more in her dreams." We find that people name their problems and projects fluidly. It is important for therapists to flow along with them.*) If she kept that desire in her heart, the corrections meant that he was interested in what she did and had found a way he could contribute comfortably. I asked if there might have been other times when Mark's response to Victoria's art would have had different meaning if she had focused on her desire to include Mark in her dreams. She told three stories of incidents that now looked differ-ent. One of them had to do with a show of her work. Mark walked through the gallery with her, naming his thoughts about what the models had been for each piece. Victoria now saw that Mark was naming her inspirations and finding connec-tions between their life and her work. University values had created an expectation of a more intel-lectual critique, which had kept her from seeing Mark's loving intentions at the time.

When I asked Mark what it was like to hear what Victoria saw when she followed the desire to include him in her dreams, he said it was a tre-mendous relief. In the past, he had felt tested when she asked him to look at her work or even to talk about a movie. He thought there was a right an-swer that she knew and he did not. This difference put them on unequal footing, as though she was the tester and he the student. The effect of this experience was that he felt cornered. Knowing that he did not know the right answer, his first response was to give no answer; this inevitably led to frustration for Victoria, which in turn increased his feeling of being trapped. I asked him what was different now. He said that if Victoria suspended the university values in favor of including him in her dreams, then there would not be a right answer; anything he said would mean that he was participating in her life.

Victoria agreed and said that she felt hopeful.

Mark said that this turn of events would lessen his fear. He said he already was feeling less frightened at work, and described an incident in which he stood up for himself because he was tired of being pushed around.

For Victoria, the incident at work showed that Mark was trusting his intelligence and his intuition. She saw him showing increased confidence, and she thought as this continued, it would help her know how much he had to contribute. She said that she was proud and happy that Mark was examining his life and taking some stands. She was distressed by the tester–student analogy. I asked whether she could understand where it came from. She could, and was wondering if she had invested more of herself in university values than in art. She preferred art and thought that keeping Mark more present in her art and life would help keep the balance the way she wanted it.

In this interview, power relations and class discourses were exposed in a very down-to-earth and relevant way. The metaphors of unequal footing and the tester–student relationship emerged from the conversation and contributed to the deconstruction of university values. These ideas were not introduced by Jill, but Victoria and Mark had not made these distinctions until Jill asked questions to locate their problems in the discourses of their local cultures. Through this deconstruction, Victoria and Mark were able to see possibilities that they could not see before. These possibilities offered new choices and paved the way for them to re-author their relationship, instead of allowing class differences to write its story.

At the sixth meeting, Mark and Victoria both described important ways that the relationship had moved forward. The two had talked more collaboratively about Victoria's work. They agreed that they had truly exchanged opinions. They had negotiated resolutions to disagreements without anger.

Mark had brought a more positive attitude about himself to this, less influenced by fear and self-degradation. The new attitude allowed him to put his opinions forward strongly, without fear, and to listen nondefensively to Victoria's responses. He also had initiated some of their conversations, which was a new role for him. Victoria had put a whole different attitude and way of listening into practice—one that was more open and not predicated on her assumed greater knowledge in a tester–student relationship. Through reflecting on these interactions, Mark recognized that Victoria was not invested in controlling the relationship. Knowing this, he could participate with lightheartedness. For both of them, these conversations were providing more comfort about talking together. This comfort was not a new thing, but an old way of being that had slipped away from them. Near the end of the sixth meeting, in response to my questions, Victoria and Mark told some stories about past times, early in the relationship, when they had had experienced the kind of comfort that they were now reclaiming.

They agreed that they were hopeful and said that it felt as though they were getting to know each other all over again. For Victoria, the next step would be to connect more emotionally and have more intimacy.

The sixth interview served to thicken Mark and Victoria's story, adding distinctions and events that contributed to an alternative narrative. The stories of past times enriched and revivified the history of the present, and Jill's final questions about next steps invited Victoria to extend the story into the near future.

Mark started the seventh meeting by saying that he was angry about Victoria's other relationships. I said that I was pulled in two different directions. The first was to respond to the anger about the relationships, but I was also intrigued by how Mark had taken the step of initiating a subject for therapy. This was something new, and I wondered whether it was a step away from fear and toward something Mark preferred. I asked Mark which of those two directions he thought was most important to address.

Here Jill was expanding possibilities while leaving the power of choice in Mark's hands.

Mark answered, "I guess both." He went on to explain that although he had known about the relationships while they were occurring, he had not expressed anger about them until the past weekend. Talking about anger, he said, was a step away from fear. It had been important for him to discover that talking—even about anger—helped a lot. He could be mad, express it, and maybe let go of it, and he and Victoria could stay connected.

Victoria agreed, saying that these steps were both good and scary.

I asked whether they wanted to talk more about the relationships, and both Victoria and Mark said they did not. Victoria said that the other relaionships had to do with how disconnected she and Mark were. In this work, they were choosing each other again. Given this choice, there would not be other relationships.

Mark nodded. Their eyes locked.

After a pause, Victoria said that they had been spending their weekends together, but not in isolation. As a couple, they had socialized quite a bit with other people. It seemed that they were joining their lives back together.

In my prelude to the next question, I voiced a thought: "So you are joining your lives back together . . ." Victoria interrupted, "Except in the areas of sexuality and sensuality." She went on to explain that some months before I met them, she had called a halt during sex with Mark because she felt it had no spirituality or intimacy. Mark experienced this as a rejection, and had completely removed himself sexually, believing that this was what Victoria wanted. Now there was no touching at all—no holding hands, no hugging, nothing.

I wondered whether Mark's putting fear aside to voice his anger about the other relationships had something to do with Victoria bringing up their sexual relationship now, or whether it had to do with something else.

Victoria said that it had to do with joining their lives back together.

I asked if that phrase—"joining their lives back together"—was a project they were working on with me.

They both nodded. Victoria said that joining their lives back together was a huge part of living their dreams. Mark agreed.

Victoria said that she was interested in having a sexual relationship with Mark, but also scared, because so much was going well and she did not know whether this would go well.

Although I was interested in finding out about the fear, the hour was nearly over, so I did not ask about it. Instead, I wrote it down with a question mark beside it in my notes.

Mark suggested that he would be most comfortable if they approached sex as an exploration, and said that if they were going to take it on, he wanted ongoing feedback.

We talked about how Victoria had been the one wanting feedback about her work, and I wondered whether they had learned anything in the process of finding a way to talk together about Mark's responses to art that might be helpful here. They agreed that assumptions and thinking there was one right way could mean trouble, and that keeping talking would make them be connected.

I asked Mark if it was important to talk more about the other relationships Victoria had been involved in the next time we met. He said that hearing that she wanted to be sexually involved with him was the important thing.

Although I expected that we would be talking about sex at the eighth meeting, Victoria and Mark talked about talking. After the seventh meeting, Mark had told Victoria how painful her sexual and romantic intimacy with other people had been for him. They told me about some of the details of the conversation. I asked them about its meaning and effects. For Mark, the conversation meant that there was growing honesty between them. For Victoria, it meant that and more. She felt that Mark had opened his experience to her so clearly that she could feel it. She said that she was happy that he had been talking more, but this was a whole different step. Mark said that Victoria had contributed to this different kind of conversation by talking more calmly and with less animosity. She said that what had changed her behavior was that she was really trying to listen to what Mark was saying. She expected this would make it possible to feel Mark's feelings as well as her own the next time she had the possibility of being with another man. But now that she and Mark were talking together, that possibility seemed very remote.

For Mark, Victoria's reaction to their conversation was quite startling. Even as he found himself initiating the conversation about her other lovers, he thought it was a mistake; surely Victoria would either think he was wrong or decide he was whining. Instead, she seemed fascinated. She told him that she just wanted to be in on what he was thinking and feeling. She said that she wanted that in all of their discussions. Mark had thought that new ideas were the only things worth contributing, and he often did not have big, shiny new ideas. He felt the fear evaporate as Victoria reiterated the importance of being included in his thoughts and feelings.

I asked Mark and Victoria about whether they each had experienced friendships in which they had felt free to say what they were thinking and feeling. Both had. Mark told about breakfasts with a roommate he had before meeting Victoria. They would sit at the kitchen table, newspapers propped in front of them, and say whatever came to mind. Mark had often been surprised when Louis referred to things he said and seemed to be affected by them. Reviewing that relationship helped Mark appreciate that he did not have to create something new to say to have something to offer. Victoria told about her best friend, Sally, whom she talked with almost every day in person or on the phone. That relationship reminded her of how precious it could be to share the details of another's life. She recognized how far away that type of sharing is from a university critique.

I wondered if we were talking about intimacy.

An important part of a therapist's job is to ask questions to slow things down, develop detail, and reflect on meaning. In Jill's report, she has omitted many of the careful, detailed questions she asked to bring forth the rich story that Mark and Victoria were telling. I (GC) hope that readers, upon reflection, can appreciate how things might have turned out quite differently without Jill's questions.

Mark and Victoria came to the ninth meeting talking about how good things had felt lately. They agreed that they were "on the same side of the table." They described how they were interacting together more and enjoying it. They told me that Mark had been looking at Victoria with tenderness, and Victoria had been open to that. Victoria said that she thought Mark was opening himself to her as he never had before. Mark thought that he had been just as open before, but this time Victoria was recognizing it. To Mark, that meant that she was trying and that she cared. Mark said that it was easier for him to be open because Victoria had been relaxed, approachable, and receptive. For the first time in a long time, she had told him that she loved him.

There had been more affection, including hugging each other and holding hands in public. For Mark, that meant there was more effort. For Victoria, the hugging and holding hands were outward acknowledgments of the changes under way in their relationship.

They said that the most momentous thing that they had done was make love. They were both glad to have taken that step, and both thought that the most important thing was just that they did it. It signified their renewed commitment and growing love. Victoria reiterated that they had a new con-

nection that she did not want to discount, but she felt that the lovemaking was an old routine. She felt disappointment that she hadn't taken a more active role in changing the routine. She saw that she could have added playfulness and wished that she had. She wanted to be able to communicate about their lovemaking both in and out of bed. I wondered whether anything they had learned about communicating would be helpful. "To say what is in our hearts," she said. Mark agreed.

Once a new story begins to take on life and momentum, therapy conversations tend to be a bit looser. Without prompting, people often talk in more detail about new developments. Problems are mentioned less and less. With Mark and Victoria, Jill was still active in asking questions to draw out detail, complexity, and meaning, but there was more spontaneous talk, and the old problems were not in control of what was being said and felt.

Victoria came into the 10th meeting glowing. A week before, she had awakened in the middle of the night with severe nausea and intestinal cramping. She had called Mark, and he had jumped out of bed and driven to Chicago. A number of things were remarkable about this event, starting with Victoria's making the call. When she woke up uncomfortable and frightened, she immediately called Mark; in the past, she would probably have called Sally. Then they might have called a doctor or gone straight to the emergency room without even letting Mark know. The way Victoria immediately reached for the phone to dial Mark showed what a central position he now had in her life. It spoke clearly of the trust and confidence she felt for him and for their relationship. Upon answering the call, Mark was immediately reassuring and emotionally available. He offered to call a doctor or to help in any other way, all the while dressing for the ride. He never once even mentioned his commitments for the next day.

This incident was clearly meaningful for both Mark and Victoria. Jill chose to ask lots of questions to develop an even thicker, more meaningful experience of the incident for both partners. In reflecting on this choice, we can see that it might have been useful to slow down the conversation and make sure that Jill wasn't being overly influenced by the discourse privileging couples' relationships over other kinds of relationship—especially since Mark had suggested earlier that perhaps he and Victoria should each rely on people outside the relationship for some particular interests and activities. We are not separate from our culture, and we can never be aware of all the discourses that it might be helpful to deconstruct—but that doesn't mean that we shouldn't keep trying.

I reminded the partners that when they first came to see me, they had named the problems they were struggling with "distance" and "frustration." I wondered what this event showed about how far they had come. "This was just the opposite!" Victoria said.

In fact, the incident meant so much to Victoria that she took another step forward emotionally. The following weekend in Wisconsin, with Mark, she went for motorcycle rides, picked apples at an orchard, and went to a birthday bash for a relative at Mark's mother's house. She could participate wholeheartedly in these events because she felt more open and trusting. She wanted to do things so that Mark could have his dreams. Before, she would have brought work with her to Wisconsin and would have spent at least part of the time holed up with it. This time, she found a way to get her work done before going.

Until Victoria described her intentions for the past weekend, Mark had not recognized the significance of the events. He had thought she just had more time. Now that he heard what the weekend had meant for Victoria, he felt less peripheral and more important in her life. For him, feeling this way was like a door opening to their future. Seeing the door made him more willing to plan their future together.

Thinking back again to our first meeting, I reminded them that Mark had said then that he got about 50–60% of what he wanted from the relationship. I wondered what they would each say now. They both said that they were at 80–85%, and named the following as making the difference:

• Their new way of talking.
• Trust.
• Each letting the other in to his/her dreams.
• Touching each other again.

What I probably would have asked if there had been more time at the 10th meeting was what Victoria and Mark could do in relation to the 15–20% of what they wanted that they were not yet getting in the relationship. They seemed to have brought the answer with them to the 11th meeting. They came in clearly focused on the 15–20%. Victoria talked about sadness and anger that had been stirred up by their sexual relationship. Mark talked about frustration and anger. Victoria said

that she wanted Mark to take more authority and responsibility. Mark said that when he did, she backed away. Victoria said that there was just no context for sex. She thought things would go better if he were to stroke her hair and call her beautiful and look into her eyes as they moved into sex. Mark said, "Why don't you just give me a script?"

As mutual blame began to take over the conversation, I asked whether it would be all right if I slowed things down.

Aspects of the old, problematic story were beginning to influence Mark and Victoria again. This is not at all uncommon. Jill became more active in shaping the conversation, moving back into a more deliberate pattern of speaking at length with one partner before asking the other to reflect on what he/she had just heard.

After hearing a bit more of a description of their current problems, I asked whether Mark and Victoria could remember sexual experiences with each other that they felt good about. They could, but were surprised to learn that they remembered different experiences. Mark described experiences in which "things went smoothly," he felt in charge, Victoria seemed receptive and excited throughout, and they both had orgasms. Victoria described experiences in which she felt beautiful and light.

I asked Victoria a bit more about this, and she said that probably the biggest factor for her in how well sex went was how attractive she felt. If she felt fat and sloppy, it put a damper on her participation. When she felt beautiful, which was a struggle, she could really be involved sexually. I wondered if she thought that her ideas about sex had to do with how she was brought up as a girl and a woman. She nodded and said she thought that men did worry about how they looked, but not nearly as much as women, and probably not during sex. I asked where she thought the idea of having to look a certain way came from. "Everywhere," she said. "Films, books, ads even . . ." I asked if the images in films, books, and ads were real, and she said that they were in that they were based on real people. I mentioned that I had once worked with a woman who was a professional model. I asked whether Victoria was interested in what the model had told me about magazine covers and the like. When Victoria said she was, I told her the model had said that the people in ads were a very small percentage of real people who were being photographed at a particular age that would not last. Those people had been freshly made up and positioned in a particular way to create a particular impression. Furthermore, the final image was often airbrushed to "improve" it even more.

Readers may see Jill as imposing her own knowledge here. To us, it is important that Jill asked Victoria whether she wanted to hear her, and it is even more important that Jill is passing along local knowledge from a particular person, not disembodied expert advice.

I wondered what effect the contrived images had on Victoria. "I'm always comparing myself," she said. "Not favorably." I asked if those images talked her into anything about her worth. She said that sexually she did not have much. I wondered if it really fit with her (sexually or any other way) to have her worth depend on matching an image, while leaving the expression of love, passion, creativity, playfulness, and connection out of the picture. She thought, of course, that it was not right. She said that love, passion, creativity, playfulness, and connection were not left out, but dependent on her feeling attractive, which had to do with what Mark said and did.

Then I asked if she thought that a more loving connection could happen between people who were equal or people who were not equal. She thought it would be more likely between equals. If what Mark said and did determined how she felt, I wondered whether they could be on equal ground. She thought not, and found it disturbing that it was set up that way for her. I wondered, given the films, books, and ads that she mentioned, how many women could really *not* be affected by that kind of objectification. The answer "Not many" made sense to Victoria.

I asked Mark what it was like to listen to Victoria's conversation with me. He found it disturbing. He had always thought that Victoria was beautiful and did not know that she had such questions about it. This whole thing felt overwhelming.

This is a clear example of how we work to deconstruct dominant discourses. Jill's many questions opened space for Victoria to notice some of the ways that dominant stories about what constitutes beauty had seduced her and shaped her perceptions and beliefs. The power inequality between men and women around these discourses was also unmasked. Jill soon asked many similar questions to unpack the ways that Mark had been enrolled in patriarchal practices of power without realizing it.

In response to my questions about what he had learned while growing up as a boy and man about his role in a sexual relationship, Mark talked about the idea of conquest. Not having a sexual relationship with his wife for months had been humiliating to him as a man. I told him that I understood that it was common usage to say "my wife," but said that to me, it made Victoria sound more like a possession than a person. He could understand why it felt that way to me. I wondered whether the idea of a partner as a possession fit with conquest. He could see that it did, but hastened to add that of course he knew Victoria was a person. I agreed with him and wondered whether, when it came to sex, the ideas of women as possessions and conquests that still circulate in the world had steered him away from his knowledge that Victoria was a person. He did not know.

We then began talking about what effects the idea that sex is conquest might have on him and on his relationship with Victoria. Mark thought the idea could put a lot of pressure on him to make sex happen. It could influence him to focus on quantity instead of quality. It could keep him from noticing his partner and what the experience was like for her. In some ways it would not matter what she did, as long as she was subservient. I wondered what he thought it would be like to be a woman in this kind of relationship. "Like a prisoner," he said. "Maybe if she were into S and M it would be great, but . . ."

I talked about some of the ways everyday American culture gives men invitations to get caught up in this kind of thinking. Mark agreed that, without realizing it, he could have taken on some aspects of these ideas. He thought that this probably explained why he did not talk more before and during sex.

As she listened to my conversation with Mark, Victoria was able to look beyond the sadness and anger. She said that even though scrutinizing herself for attractiveness often got in the way, she and Mark had at times experienced profound connection and mutuality in sex. She described a particular experience, and on hearing her description Mark agreed it had been wonderful. They both remembered the communication and sense of partnership that were there. They agreed that their memories of this experience were a much better image of an intimate, sexual experience than any glamorized movie scene ever could be. I wondered how Victoria and Mark could keep the glamorized movie scenes out of their sex life. They thought that by paying attention to each other and communicating, they could be in charge of their sex life as partners. They agreed that they wanted to be in charge, instead of having unreal images and unjust ideas rule the sexual aspects of their relationship.

I saw Mark and Victoria three more times. They took the conversation about their sexual relationship very much to heart and felt a tremendous freedom to talk together about their feelings for each other and to try out new things in their ongoing sexual relationship. In the 12th and 13th meetings, they reflected on their unfolding sexual relationship. They told me how they had read poetry to each other in bed. Victoria was absolutely delighted with Mark's willingness to try new things. Mark was learning about himself and Victoria through these experiences. Victoria discovered that once she stopped worrying about how she looked and started noticing Mark, she became a very sexy woman! They both realized that fear had kept them comparing their relationship to an unreal standard. Now that the fear was gone, they both could see different possibilities for their sexual relationship. Victoria discovered that with the fear out of the way, it was easy to accept affection and be open. She wondered if Mark had actually offered more all along than she had known. Mark did not know. He said that although things were quite wonderful, he was struggling to have a voice without being authoritarian. We talked about the moments that he felt most able to do that, and resurrected some of the ideas from the last meeting that helped make that possible.

In the 12th meeting Victoria and Mark made a commitment to step out of what they were now seeing as the self-imposed limitations of their sexual relationship. Outside those bounds, they found laughter, safety, and good feelings, which they reported on at length in the 13th meeting. They agreed to talk with each other about the things they would be comfortable doing, as well as those they would not be comfortable doing. They said they would find ways to "try on" each other's desires.

Nonproblematic narratives were clearly flowing again. Jill continued to ask questions to thicken the new stories as they emerged, and did not have to be as active in structuring the interview. She could sit back and enjoy being part of this joyous conversation.

The 14th and last meeting was a time of looking back over what the couple had learned and accomplished. What stood out for Mark was that he did not have to be a leader, and not having to lead meant he could participate more. He thought he

finally understood what Victoria meant by "sharing dreams." It did not have to do with creating grand plans. It had to do with being open about what was in his heart and mind. Victoria said that the biggest change for her had to do with realizing that she did not need someone who would open doors for her. She and Mark could go through them together.

REFLECTIONS ON THE WORK

In reviewing my notes, I am again grateful to Victoria and Mark for opening their lives to me and, through this writing, to all of us. The work with them did raise a number of dilemmas for me, some unique to their relationship and some common to work with many heterosexual couples. Because we shared both gender and social class, I was likely to understand and privilege Victoria's stories and understandings more then Mark's. Since I am part of the dominant culture, there are many potentially limiting discourses that might have escaped my awareness. Reviewing my notes also reminded me of the power I wield in being given the role of questioner. Although questions are a tremendously valuable tool for collaboration, they still give the questioner power to propose conversational domains. With Mark and Victoria, I asked about the dilemmas of social class difference quite a bit before I asked about gender. I did not plan that sequence, but I am aware that I could have picked up on other strands of conversation that would have led us into considerations of gender or of something else entirely. I was aware that I could have fallen into judgments of either Victoria for engaging in sexual relationships with people other than Mark or of Mark for being caught up in dominant ideas concerning men's sexuality as conquest. We think that either of these sets of judgments would have limited the usefulness of the therapy.

We hope that we have told the story of my work with Mark and Victoria with enough of the right kind of detail to give readers a feel for how we think and act in negotiating this terrain.

REFERENCES

Adams-Westcott, J., Dafforn, T., & Sterne, P. (1993). Escaping victim life stories and co-constructing personal agency. In S. Gilligan & R. Price (Eds.), *Therapeutic conversations* (pp. 258–271). New York: Norton.
Andersen, T. (1987). The reflecting team: Dialogue and metadialogue in clinical work. *Family Process, 26,* 415–428.

Avis, J. M. (1985). The politics of functional family therapy: A feminist critique. *Journal of Marital and Family Therapy, 11,* 127–138.

Bateson, G. (1972). *Steps to an ecology of mind.* New York: Ballantine Books.

Bruner, J. (1986). *Actual minds/possible worlds.* Cambridge, MA: Harvard University Press.

Carter, E., Papp, P., Silverstein, O., & Walters, M. (1984). *Mothers and sons, fathers and daughters* (Monograph Series, Vol. 2, No. 1). Washington, DC: The Women's Project in Family Therapy.

Cohen, S. M., Combs, G., DeLaurenti, B., DeLaurenti, P., Freedman, J., Larimer, D., & Shulman, D. (1998). Minimizing hierarchy in therapeutic relationships: A reflecting team approach. In M. Hoyt (Ed.), *Handbook of constructive therapies: Innovative approaches from leading practitioners* (pp. 276–293). San Francisco: Jossey-Bass.

Epston, D. (1989). *Collected works.* Adelaide, Australia: Dulwich Centre.

Epston, D. (1993). Internalizing discourses versus externalizing discourses. In S. Gilligan & R. Price (Eds.), *Therapeutic conversations* (pp. 161–177). New York: Norton.

Epston, D. (1998). *Catching up with David Epston: A collection of narrative practice-based papers published between 1991 and 1996.* Adelaide, Australia: Dulwich Centre.

Epston, D. (1999). Co-research: The making of an alternative knowledge. In *Narrative therapy and community work: A conference collection* (pp. 137–157). Adelaide, Australia: Dulwich Centre.

Foucault, M. (1965). *Madness and civilization: A history of insanity in the age of reason* (R. Howard, Trans.). New York: Random House.

Foucault, M. (1975). *The birth of the clinic: An archeology of medical perception* (A. M. Sheridan Smith, Trans.). New York: Random House.

Foucault, M. (1977). *Discipline and punish: The birth of the prison* (A. Sheridan, Trans.). New York: Pantheon Books.

Foucault, M. (1980). *Power/knowledge: Selected interviews and other writings, 1972–1977.* (C. Gordon, Ed., C. Gordon, L. Marshall, J. Mepham, & D. K. Soper, Trans.). New York: Pantheon Books.

Foucault, M. (1985). *The history of sexuality: Vol. 2: The use of pleasure* (R. Hurley, Trans.). New York: Pantheon Books.

Freedman, J., & Combs, G. (1993). Invitations to new stories: Using questions to explore alternative possibilities. In S. Gilligan & R. Price (Eds.), *Therapeutic conversations* (pp. 291–303). New York: Norton.

Freedman, J., & Combs, G. (1996). *Narrative therapy: The social construction of preferred realities.* New York: Norton.

Freedman, J., & Combs, G. (1997). Lists. In C. Smith & D. Nylund (Eds.), *Narrative therapies with children and adolescents* (pp. 147–161). New York: Guilford Press.

Freedman, J., & Combs, G. (2000). Therapy relationships that open possibilities for us all. *Dulwich Centre Journal 2000,* Nos. 1–2, 17–20.

Freeman, J., Epston, D., & Lobovits, D. (1997). *Playful approaches to serious problems: Narrative therapy with children and families.* New York: Norton.

Geertz, C. (1978). *The interpretation of cultures.* New York: Basic Books.

Goldner, V. (1985a). Feminism and family therapy. *Family Process, 24,* 31–47.

Goldner, V. (1985b). Warning: Family therapy may be dangerous to your health. *The Family Therapy Networker, 9,* 19–23.

Hare-Mustin, R. (1978). A feminist approach to family therapy. *Family Process, 17,* 181–194.

Hare-Mustin, R. (1994). Discourses in the mirrored room: A postmodern analysis of therapy. *Family Process, 33,* 19–35.

Laird, J. (1989). Women and stories: Restorying women's self-constructions. In M. McGoldrick, C. Anderson, & F. Walsh (Eds.), *Women in families: A framework for family therapy* (pp. 427–450). New York: Norton.

Monk, G., Winslade, J., Crocket, K., & Epston, D. (Eds.). (1997). *Narrative therapy in practice: The archeology of hope.* San Francisco: Jossey-Bass.

Morgan, A. (2000). *What is narrative therapy?: An easy-to-read introduction.* Adelaide, Australia: Dulwich Centre.

Myerhoff, B. (1982). Life history among the elderly: Performance, visibility, and remembering. In J. Ruby (Ed.), *A crack in the mirror: Reflexive perspectives in anthropology.* (pp. 99–117). Philadelphia: University of Pennsylvania Press.

Myerhoff, B. (1986). Life not death in Venice: Its second life. In V. Turner & E. Bruner (Eds.), *The anthropology of experience* (pp. 261–285). Chicago: University of Illinois Press.

Reiss, D. (1985). Commentary: The social construction of reality—The passion within us all. *Family Process, 24,* 254–257.

Ryle, G. (1990). *Collected papers: Critical essays and collected essays 1929–68.* Bristol, England: Thoemmes Press. (Original work published 1971)

Taggart, M. (1985). The feminist critique in epistemological perspective: Questions of context in family therapy. *Journal of Marital and Family Therapy, 11,* 113–126.

White, M. (1986). Negative explanation, restraint and double description: A template for family therapy. *Family Process 25,* 169–184.

White, M. (1987, Spring). Family therapy and schizophrenia: Addressing the "in-the-corner" lifestyle. *Dulwich Centre Newsletter,* pp. 14–21.

White, M. (1988–1989, Summer). The externalizing of the problem and the re-authoring of lives and relationships. *Dulwich Centre Newsletter,* pp. 3–20.

White, M. (1989). *Selected papers.* Adelaide, Australia: Dulwich Centre.

White, M. (1991, Fall). Deconstruction and therapy. *Dulwich Centre Newsletter,* pp. 21–40.

White, M. (1995). Reflecting teamwork as definitional ceremony. In M. White, *Re-authoring lives: Interviews and essays* (pp. 172–198). Adelaide, Australia: Dulwich Centre.

White, M. (1997). *Narratives of therapists' lives.* Adelaide, Australia: Dulwich Centre.

White, M. (2000). *Reflections on narrative practice: Essays and interviews.* Adelaide, Australia: Dulwich Centre.

White, M., & Epston, D. (1990). *Narrative means to therapeutic ends.* New York: Norton.

White, M., & Epston, D. (1992). *Experience, contradiction, narrative, and imagination.* Adelaide, Australia: Dulwich Centre.

Zimmerman, J., & Dickerson, V. (1996). *If problems talked: Narrative therapy in action.* New York: Guilford Press.

Chapter 12

Solution-Focused Couple Therapy

MICHAEL F. HOYT

When you play songs, you can bring back people's memories of when they fell in love. That's where the power is.
—Johnny Mercer (songwriter, quoted in Berendt, 1994, p. 90)

Suppose that one night, while you were asleep, there was a miracle and this problem was solved. How would you know? What would be different?
—Steve de Shazer (1988, p. 10)

Solution-focused therapy is an intervention approach developed by Steve de Shazer (1982, 1985, 1988, 1991a, 1994a) and Insoo Kim Berg (1994a; Berg & Dolan, 2000; Berg & Kelly, 2000; Berg & Miller, 1992; Berg & Reuss, 1997; De Jong & Berg, 1998; Miller & Berg, 1995), with additional valuable explications from a number of contributors (e.g., Bonjean, 1997; Dolan, 1991; George, Iveson, & Ratner, 1999; Lethem, 1994; Miller, 1997; Miller, Hubble, & Duncan, 1996; O'Hanlon & Weiner-Davis, 1989; Tohn & Oshlag, 1995; Walter & Peller, 1992, 2000; Weiner-Davis, 1992). Although there is a theory-based, teachable model with specific techniques—the topic of this chapter—it is important to recognize that the essence of solution-focused therapy is an overarching world view, a way of thinking and being, not a set of clinical operations (see Lipchik, 1994). As the name implies, the focus is on solutions—on what works for clients. It is a "post-structural re-vision" (de Shazer & Berg, 1992; see also de Shazer, 1993a)—a non-normative, constructivist view that emphasizes the use of language in the social construction of reality (see Hoyt, 1994a, 1996a, 1998, 2000; McNamee & Gergen, 1992;

Miller, 1997). It appreciates the power of the subjective and operates with the assumption that clients have the competency and creativity, sometimes with skillful facilitation, to shift perspectives in ways that will open new options for experience and interaction. Solution-focused therapy respects clients' own resources and is directed toward *building solutions* rather than increasing insight into putative maladaptive psychological mechanisms. It is optimistic, collaborative, future-oriented, versatile, user-friendly, and often effective.

BACKGROUND OF THE APPROACH

Solution-focused therapy was developed in the late 1970s and 1980s by Steve de Shazer and his colleagues at the Brief Family Therapy Center (BFTC) in Milwaukee, Wisconsin.[1] de Shazer was influenced by the work of the pioneering Mental Research Institute (MRI) group in Palo Alto, California (Watzlawick, Weakland, & Fisch, 1974; Fisch, Weakland, & Segal, 1982; see Shoham & Rohrbaugh, Chapter 1, this volume), which in turn was influenced by the work of the renowned psychiatrist/ hypnotherapist Milton Erickson—especially Erickson's ideas about strategic intervention and the fuller utilization of clients' submerged competencies.[2] As indicated by the title of their keynote book, *Change: Principles of Problem Formation and Problem Resolution* (Watzlawick et al., 1974), the MRI group focused on how clients create and resolve problems, including how efforts to solve a problem sometimes actually perpetuate the problem. de Shazer and his Milwaukee-based group took a somewhat different view, instead focusing on those times ("exceptions") when the presenting problem was not present, as expressed in the title of their signal counterpaper, "Brief Therapy: Focused Solution Development" (de Shazer et al., 1986). De Jong and Berg (1998, p. 13) describe a watershed moment in their book *Interviewing for Solutions*:

> De Shazer first hit upon the idea that there is not a necessary connection between problem and solution in 1982, when working with a particular family (Hopwood & de Shazer, 1994). As usual, de Shazer and his colleagues asked, "What brings you in?" In response, family members kept interrupting one another until, by the end of the session, they had listed 27 different problems. Since none of the 27 were clearly defined, de Shazer and his colleagues were unable to design an intervention. Still, wishing to encourage the family members to focus on something different from their problems, de Shazer and his colleagues told them to pay careful attention to "what is happening in your lives that you want to continue to have happen." When the family returned, two weeks later, they said that things were going very well and they felt their problems were solved. According to the assumptions of the problem-solving approach, the family should not have improved so dramatically, because the practitioner had not yet been able to isolate and assess the patterns and nature of the problems. Their experience with such cases led de Shazer and his colleagues towards a solution focus in place of a problem focus. They and many others . . . have been continuing to work out the implications of this shift ever since.

The two approaches, BFTC and MRI, are complementary (Weakland & Fisch, 1992); both eschew obfuscating theory in favor of "minimalistic," pragmatic, outcome-oriented approaches. As Shoham, Rohrbaugh, and Patterson (1995, p. 143) explain in their review in the previous edition of the *Clinical Handbook of Couple Therapy*:

> The hallmark of these models is conceptual and technical parsimony. The aim of therapy is simply to resolve the presenting complaint as quickly and efficiently as possible so that clients can get on with life: Goals such as promoting personal growth, working through underlying emotional issues, or teaching couples better problem-solving and communication skills are not emphasized. Both therapies offer minimal theory, focusing narrowly on the presenting complaint and relevant solutions, and both are non-normative in that neither attempts to specify what constitutes a normal or dysfunctional marriage. Both pay close attention not only to what clients *do* but also to how they *view* the problem, themselves, and each other; in fact, both therapies assume that the "reality" of problems and change is constructed more than discovered. Both therapies also attach considerable importance to clients' "customership" for change and to the possibility that therapy itself may play a role in maintaining (rather than resolving) problems. Finally, in contrast to most other treatments for couples, therapists following the MRI and Milwaukee models often see the partners individually, even when the focus of intervention is a complaint about the marriage itself.

The most fundamental difference between problem- and solution-focused therapy concerns the emphasis each gives to the concept of "solution": While the MRI approach aims to interdict existing solutions that maintain the problem and to promote "less of the same," the Milwaukee model seeks to identify exceptions to the problem and develop new solutions that work.

NON-NORMATIVE (IDIOMORPHIC) ASSESSMENT

Solution-focused therapists meet clients where they are (oftentimes beginning a session by asking "What brings you in?" or "What are you hoping to accomplish coming here?") and avoid preconceived notions of what may be healthy/unhealthy or functional/dysfunctional for a particular couple, individual, or family. Although general guidelines can be described, every case is considered unique. The therapist attempts to "keep it simple" by "taking the patient seriously" (de Shazer & Weakland, quoted in Hoyt, 1994b), accepting the clients' version of what is—and isn't—a problem. Primacy is given to clients' experiences, goals, ideas, values, motivations, and world views, which are respectfully accepted as valid and real. Although some discussion of the past allows clients a sense of being heard and acknowledged, and provides an opportunity for exploring clients' ideas about what would be helpful (their theories of change) and a reconnaissance of past successes and exceptions to the problem, the thrust of the solution-focused session is present- to future-oriented.

The therapist needs to have skills to join and work with persons of varying diversities to help them develop solutions that fit *their* frames of reference. The solution-focused approach is client-centered and transcultural in that it truly respects the "local knowledge" (individual, familial, social) of those who seek therapy; "cultural diversity" is honored in that the emphasis is genuinely on learning *from* clients, not just *about* them. The approach tends to be apolitical, however, and sociocultural topics such as ethnicity, class, race, and gender roles are not usually discussed explicitly unless clients make them the focus of conversation.

Initially, the solution-focused approach emerged in an inductive manner, from studying what clients' and therapists did that preceded clients' declaring problems "solved." It was noticed that problems were described as "solved" (or "resolved," "dissolved," or simply "no longer problems") when clients began to engage in new and different perceptions and behaviors vis-à-vis the presenting difficulty (Hoyt & Berg, 1998). This recognition led to de Shazer's "basic rules" of solution-focused therapy:

- If it ain't broke, don't fix it.
- Once you know what works, do more of it.
- If it doesn't work, don't do it again; do something different.

(quoted in Hoyt, 1996b, p. 314)

As previously noted, at times *solutions* may not even seem to have a direct connection to *problems*—development of a solution often involves a reformulation or different construction such that the former position loses its relevance or simply "dissolves." The client couple has "moved on," and what was once a problem is "no longer an issue."

GOAL SETTING

It's the *clients'* therapy (and life). The solution-focused therapist is on the lookout for the *clients'* notions of what would constitute a viable solution or success. As de Shazer (1991a, p. 112) has written:

Early in their conversations, therapists and clients address the question, "How do we know when to stop meeting like this?" Both clinical experience and research indicate that workable goals tend to have the following general characteristics. They are:

1. small rather than large;
2. salient to clients;

3. described in specific, concrete behavioral terms;
4. achievable within the practical contexts of clients' lives;
5. perceived by the clients as involving their "hard work";
6. described as the "start of something" and not as the "end of something";
7. treated as involving new behavior(s) rather than the absence or cessation of existing behavior(s).

Thus goals are depictions of what will be *present*, what will be happening in the clients' lives when the complaint is absent, when the pain that brought them to therapy is absent and they therefore no longer depict life in problematic terms.

de Shazer (1991a, p. 113) goes on to suggest using his well-known future-oriented "Miracle Question" to elicit goals within an interpersonal framework:

Suppose that one night there is a miracle and while you are sleeping the problem that brought you into therapy is solved: How would you know? What would be different? (de Shazer, 1988, p. 5)

What will you notice the next morning that will tell you that there has been a miracle? What will your spouse notice?[3]

How (and where) we look helps determine what we see (Hoyt, 2000). In *Words Were Originally Magic*, de Shazer (1994a, p. 10) elaborates the relevance of this for therapists working with couples:

What we talk about and how we talk about it makes a difference (to the client). Thus reframing a "marital problem" into an "individual problem" or an "individual problem" into a "marital problem" makes a difference both in how we talk about things and where we look for solutions.

"*Goaling*" is an ongoing, dynamic process, open to renegotiation, often more a process of identifying and moving toward possibilities than one of locking in fixed behavioral targets (Walter & Peller, 2000). Partners also may have different ideas, of course, about what constitutes the problem and what would constitute the solution; this provides the opportunity for a "both/and" (not "either/or") negotiation:

HOYT: What about the situation of the so-called "multiproblem family"? . . .

DE SHAZER: . . . We think about them as "multigoal families." . . . First of all, if you ask the miracle question early enough in the session, you oftentimes avoid that difficulty—having all these multiple goals. Sometimes.

HOYT: Who do you ask the miracle question of?

DE SHAZER: Everybody.

HOYT: And if everyone gives a different answer?

DE SHAZER: That's reasonable.

HOYT: Then you have competing goals.

DE SHAZER: That's normal and reasonable. Then you say "Okay, 10 stands for this package—everything you've been talking about, those kinds of things. Whatever it will take for you guys to each individually and collectively to recognize that a miracle has happened, that's 10. Where are we today?" We get different estimates where each of them are. Then we sort of work on getting everybody's number on the scale and ignore, if you will, the fact that their version of 10 is probably different, because it's always going to be different with more than one person. And even with one person, he's going to have more than one goal, and they may conflict with each other anyway. . . . Our studies indicate that most people—most families stop with 7 being good enough, and that 6 months later they will have frequently moved up to 8, but that is almost the outer limit. Very few people make 10. Those that do make 10 usually end up going into the teens as well—"overachievers." (Hoyt, 1996b, pp. 70-71)

Eve Lipchik, a former member of the BFTC group, reminds us of the importance, when working with couples and families, of forming and maintaining a relationship with all the attending members:

When there are two or more people in the room presenting themselves with a problem, I think of myself as having to establish a relationship with each one. . . . Usually they have different views or are in conflict with each other. I often experience myself pulled by clients to accept one view over another. I try to stay connected in a positive way with each person in the room by reminding myself to be curious about how they see things differently and that I must communicate acceptance and understanding to everyone. A technique that helps me stay centered is not to listen to one person talk too long without asking the other for their view of what they heard. Frequent switching and checking between clients is a way of communicating that I am equally interested in what all of them have to say. I have been told by clients after treatment that what they think helped them the most was that I never took sides. They said that while they disagreed bitterly with each other, they trusted their relationship with me, and my acceptance of all views motivated them to give consideration to the perspectives of other family members. (Lipchik, 1997, p. 163; also see Anderson's [1997, pp. 95–96] discussion about "multipartiality," as well as Ziegler and Hiller's [2001, pp. 39–53] discussion about "active neutrality.")

Friedman and Lipchik (1999, p. 325) elaborate and note the utility of using a solution-focused approach:

Differing perceptions between partners requires great sensitivity in acknowledging often strongly held yet divergent points of view while maintaining a working alliance with each member of the couple. In addition, faced with sometimes volatile and emotionally charged communications and affects, the couple therapist must manage high levels of reactivity in ways that offer the couple a path out of its' members' problem-saturated reality. To meet these challenges, the time-effective, solution-focused therapist acts as a facilitator of the therapeutic conversation in ways that open space for the couple to move toward a preferred future. Working from a perspective of competencies and strengths, we take a nonpathologizing approach that respects the clients' goals and utilizes the clients' own resources and "expert knowledges" in reaching these goals (Friedman, 1997; Lipchik, 1993).

THE STRUCTURE OF THE (COUPLE) THERAPY PROCESS

While therapy with a couple may present some particular challenges—such as each member's vying for the therapist's attention and trying to get the therapist on his/her side, or the partners' presenting differing and sometimes seemingly contradictory histories and goals—the basic structure and therapeutic processes of solution-focused intervention are much the same, whoever attends the session.

Is marital therapy somehow different from family therapy? If so, what is the difference? And if there is a difference, does this difference make a difference?

Since our practice and the practice of the Brief Family Therapy Center (BFTC) involve seeing individuals (people who live alone, half a marital pair, or one member of a larger family group), couples (married and unmarried, heterosexual and homosexual pairs), and family groups (two or more people, representing at least two generations or parents without the troublesome child), we found that the distinction between marital therapy and family therapy does not apply. A problem is a problem; the number of people (and their relationship to one another) whom the therapist sees to help solve the problem does not seem a useful distinction. This, of course, presupposes a strong belief in the systemic concept of wholism: If you change one element in a system, or the relationship between that element and another element, the system as a whole will be affected. . . .

The only criterion that seems to make a potential difference is that in "marital therapy" the relationship treated is that between two people of the same generation, whereas in family therapy the relationship of concern is often or usually between people of different generations. But does this affect the nature of the problems encountered or the nature of the solutions or the patterns of intervention–response?

A quick check of case records accumulated over the years at BFTC and some research we have been doing indicated that the nature of problems, the nature of solutions, and the patterns of intervention–response do not differ along the lines implied by this distinction. In fact, the process of therapy seems relatively constant across situations. The kinds of intervention messages used appear over and over, and the patterns of response appear over and over. *Marital therapy, individual therapy,* and *family therapy* do not seem to be separate classes of brief therapy. (de Shazer & Berg, 1985, pp. 97–98)

On initial phone contact, the caller may be invited to bring to the session whoever is involved. "A part is not apart" (de Shazer & Berg, 1985; also see Weiner-Davis, 1995, 1998, 2000), however, and it is recognized that working with only one of the partners present can still have powerful effects upon all concerned. Indeed, de Shazer has suggested:

> As I see it, the idea of bringing more people in is based on the idea that you're stuck because you don't have enough information. That's the premise behind it. My idea, following [linguistic philosopher Ludwig] Wittgenstein, is "The problem is you have too *much* information already, but you just don't know how to organize it." Or, furthermore, from Wittgenstein again, "You're in this situation and you've got what you got and that's all there is. There ain't no more." All you got is a problem of organization. So get people out and talk to just one person at a time, and maybe you can simplify it enough to do something. I haven't invited—I can't remember when last I said, "Bring your husband," or something like that. I can't remember that happening. (quoted in Hoyt, 1996b, pp. 69–70)

Usually there is one therapist, who sits across from the clients. In some clinics and training situations, a team may observe (with the clients' informed consent) and consult from behind a one-way mirror, but in common practice most solution-focused therapists work successfully without this "stimulating but not necessary" (de Shazer, 1985, p. 18) arrangement.[4]

Solution-focused therapy is typically time-unlimited (no preset session maximum), and session appointments are made one at a time—the implica-tion being that one may be enough. A course of therapy generally lasts 1–10 sessions, sometimes longer, and clients can return on an intermittent or as-needed basis (Hoyt, 1995, 2000). Sessions may be scheduled as frequently or infrequently as clients and therapists desire and find convenient and useful—often one to a few weeks apart. A couple wanting another appointment in one week may be complimented for "wanting to get right to it," while a couple wanting to wait a month may be complimented for "wanting time to see some progress" before returning.

In 1991, de Shazer (1991a, pp. 57–58) reported the average number of sessions per case as 4.7; in 1996, he indicated (in Hoyt, 1996b, p. 61) that the average had dropped to 3. Using an approach based on the BFTC model, single-session therapies were demonstrated to be successful in a wide variety of cases (see Talmon, 1990; Rosenbaum, Hoyt, & Talmon, 1990; Hoyt, 1994c). Other research results are reviewed in McKeel (1996) and De Jong and Hopwood (1996).

THE ROLE OF THE THERAPIST

The solution-focused therapist serves essentially as a consultant, interviewing purposefully (Lipchik & de Shazer, 1986; Lipchik, 1987; Weakland, 1993; Weiner-Davis, 1993) to "influence the clients' view of the problem in a manner that leads to solution" (Berg & Miller, 1992, p. 70). The therapist endeavors to help the couple build a solution by asking questions (discussed at length below) and carefully punctuating responses to highlight a positive reality facilitative of clients' goals. Clients usually respond directly to the therapist, as well as talking with each other.

The interview process is designed to assist clients in achieving new perceptions and meanings. It is directive in that it deliberately encourages clients to look at things differently, but it does not supply answers. Rather, it provides a context for clients to focus on "what's right" and other possible ways of being "right," rather than on complaints of "what's wrong." A problem arises and a couple seeks therapy when the partners view their situation in such a way that they do not have access to what is needed to achieve what they consider reasonable satisfaction. By directing clients away from the problem-saturated narrative (story) that has embroiled them, the therapist attempts to create a context for the clients to develop their own, more useful ways of looking and responding.

The solution-focused therapist serves as a skillful facilitator, assisting clients to better utilize their own (perhaps overlooked) strengths and competencies, with a recognition that how clients conceive their situation—the way they "story" their lives—will either empower them or cut them off from existing resources: "Our attention is focused primarily in the here and now, and even more importantly, on the future, since the future provides a blank canvas on which the couple can paint a picture of the pair's wishes and hopes" (Friedman & Lipchik, 1999, pp. 325–326). The solution-focused therapist assumes a posture of "not knowing" (Anderson & Goolishian, 1992; Hoyt & Berg, 1998), allowing the clients to be "experts" instead of telling the clients what is "really" wrong and how to fix it.

The therapist–couple alliance is evolving and dynamic. In his now-classic paper "The Death of Resistance," de Shazer (1984) noted that traditional theories of resistance were tantamount to pitting the therapist against the client in a fight that the therapist had to win in order for the client to be successful. In contradistinction, de Shazer suggested shifting the focus of therapeutic activity to the study of how people *do* change. As de Shazer and Berg (1985, p. 98) explain,

> In our view, the therapist needs to set the stage for the "cooperating" of client and therapist. The therapist needs to assume that the client is also interested in cooperating and, consequently, to build the therapeutic stance on the assumption that changing is inevitable, rather than difficult, as many models built on the concept of resistance assume. Of course, the particular way of cooperating can differ from session to session with the same client (de Shazer, 1982).

From this perspective, clients can be seen as having unique ways of *cooperating with* rather than resisting the therapist in their mutual efforts to bring about desired changes (see Hoyt & Miller, 2000). Although therapists may know that they are helpers—or at least think they are—clients may not be ready for the kind of help the therapist wants to offer. Imposition tends to produce opposition (Hoyt, 2000). Appreciating and working *with* clients' sense of their situation—including their theories, language, motivations, goals, and stages of change (Berg & Miller, 1992; Duncan, Hubble, & Miller, 1997; Duncan et al., 1998)—maintains therapist–client cooperation and vitiates the concept of *resistance*.

Solution-focused therapists (see Berg, 1989) conceptualize three types of therapist–client relationships, which can (and do) alternate within sessions: *customer*, *complainant*, and *visitor*. As Shoham et al. (1995, p. 153, emphasis added) explain,

> Here the distinction between customer, complainant, and visitor-type relationships offers guidelines for therapeutic cooperation or "fit" (de Shazer, 1988; Berg & Miller, 1992). If the relationship involves a *visitor* with whom the therapist cannot define a clear complaint or goal, cooperation involves nothing more than sympathy, politeness, and compliments for whatever the clients are successfully doing (with no tasks or requests for change). In a *complainant* relationship, where clients present a complaint but appear unwilling to take action or want someone else to change, the therapist cooperates by accepting their views, giving compliments, and sometimes prescribing observational tasks (e.g., to notice exceptions to the complaint pattern). Finally, with *customers* who want to do something about a complaint, the principle of fit allows the therapist to be more direct in guiding them toward solutions. . . .

Both de Shazer (1988) and Berg and Miller (1992) emphasize that the customer–complainant–visitor categories represent dynamic, changing attributes of the therapist–client relationship, not static characteristics of the clients themselves. Visitors and complainants can become customers and vice versa. In fact, one of the main reasons to cooperate with clients in this way is to increase possibilities for customership.

As Hoyt and Miller (2000) have noted, therapists may also find it helpful in enhancing therapist–client "fit" and cooperation to recognize where the client-couple may be in terms of *stages of change*. In Prochaska's (1999) *transtheoretical model*, for example, change unfolds over a series of six stages of motivational readiness. Some differential intervention stategies are suggested if one combines Prochaska's transtheoretical model of stages of change with some ideas from solution-focused and strategic therapy (de Shazer, 1985, 1988; Miller et al., 1996), as discussed at length by Miller et al. (1997, pp. 88–104; see especially Hoyt & Miller, 2000):

- *Precontemplation*: Suggest that the client "think about it" and provide information and education.
- *Contemplation*: Encourage thinking; recommend an observation task, in which the client is asked to notice something (such as what happens to make things better or worse); and join with the client's lack of commitment to action with a "Go slow!" directive.
- *Preparation*: Offer treatment options; invite the client to choose from viable alternatives.
- *Action*: Amplify what works—get details of success and reinforce.

- *Maintenance:* Support success; predict setbacks; make contingency plans.
- *Termination:* Wish well; say goodbye; leave an open door for possible return as needed.

As discussed in the next section, the solution-focused therapist uses language and maintains activity in such a way as to keep the couple moving toward solution rather than engaging in extended blame talk and escalating negative affect (see Table 12.1). As I heard Michele Weiner-Davis (2000) succinctly put it, the emphasis is on "What will be happening" rather than on "What isn't happening."

TECHNIQUES OF SOLUTION-FOCUSED COUPLE THERAPY

Although support and encouragement can be given and specific skills can sometimes be taught, the hallmark of solution-focused therapy is the use of questions to invite clients to organize and focus their attention, energy, and understanding in one way rather than another. Questions are asked, and selected responses are explored and elaborated to direct clients toward the realization of their desired outcomes. The therapist functions like a special kind of mirror that can become convex or concave and swivel this way or that. Rather than providing a "flat mirror" that simply "reflects and clarifies," the solution-focused therapist purposely and differentially expands and contracts the reflected

TABLE 12.1. Solution-Building Vocabulary

In	Out	In	Out
Respect	Judge	Forward	Backward
Empower	Fix	Future	Past
Nurture	Control	Collaborate	Manipulate
Facilitate	Treat	Options	Conflicts
Augment	Reduce	Partner	Expert
Invite	Insist	Horizontal	Hierarchical
Appreciate	Diagnose	Possibility	Limitation
Hope	Fear	Growth	Cure
Latent	Missing	Access	Defense
Assets	Defects	Utilize	Resist
Strength	Weakness	Create	Repair
Health	Pathology	Exception	Rule
Not Yet	Never	Difference	Sameness
Expand	Shrink	Solution	Problem

Note. From Hoyt (1994d, p. 4). Copyright 1994 by The Guilford Press. Reprinted by permission.

image, so to speak—opening parts of the story and closing others, making "space" for discourses that support the realization of clients' goals (Hoyt, 2000). As discussed in the following sections, highlighting and amplifying clients' past successes and their agency in bringing about preferred outcomes helps empower couples to construct more self-fulfilling realities.

A Guide for the Perplexed

In his book *Clues: Investigating Solutions in Brief Therapy*, de Shazer (1988, p. 86; see also Walter & Peller, 1992) offers a schematic map or "family tree" of solution-focused interviews, as seen in Figure 12.1.

The Structure of Therapy Sessions

de Shazer and Berg (1997, p. 123) have also outlined the formal characteristics of a "classic" solution-focused brief therapy (here abbreviated as SFBT) session:

Characteristic features of SFBT include:
(1) At some point in the first interview, the therapist will ask the "Miracle Question."
(2) At least once during the first interview and at subsequent ones, the client will be asked to rate something on a scale of "0 > 10" or "1 > 10."
(3) At some point during the interview, the therapist will take a break.
(4) After this intermission, the therapist will give the client some compliments which will sometimes (frequently) be followed by a suggestion or homework task (frequently called an "experiment").

Following this outline, we will first discuss a variety of questions typically asked in solution-focused couple therapy, providing numerous examples. We will then discuss the use of a short break or intermission during the session; and will then consider the postbreak portion of the session, including the use of directives or "homework" assignments.

Sessions, which usually last 50–60 minutes, typically begin with a brief period of *socializing and joining.* As expressed in the title of the book by Ben Furman and Tapani Ahola (1992), *Solution Talk: Hosting Therapeutic Conversations,* the solution-focused therapist attends to creating ("hosting") a comfortable, collaborative therapeutic situation.[5]

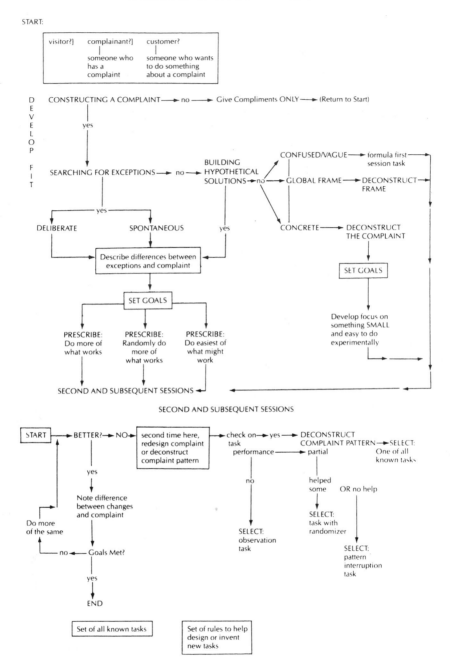

FIGURE 12.1. The central map. From de Shazer (1988, p. 86). Copyright 1987 by Steve de Shazer. Reprinted by permission of W. W. Norton & Co., Inc.

Various types of questions may then be asked. In what follows, a sampler of typical solution-focused therapy questions is provided. Many have been drawn (with some paraphrasings) from Ziegler (2000; see also Ziegler & Hiller, 2001); with additional sources including Berg and de Shazer (1993), Berg and Miller (1992), De Jong and Berg (1998), de Shazer (1985, 1988, 1991a, 1994a), Hoyt and Miller (2000), Miller (1994), O'Hanlon and Weiner-Davis (1989), Walter and Peller (1992, 2000), and Weiner-Davis (1992, 2000).

A Sampler of Solution-Focused Therapy Questions

Before the Session: Eliciting Presession Change

It is useful to recognize that the roots of change exist before the first session. On first contact, usually when there is a phone call requesting an appointment, the solution-focused therapist will make a request that helps direct clients' attention toward *exceptions* to the problem—times the presenting complaint isn't present:

> Between now and next time we meet, I would like you to observe, so that you can describe to me next time, what happens in your [*pick one:* family, life, marriage, relationship] that you want to continue to have happen. (de Shazer, 1985, p. 137; see also de Shazer, 1984; de Shazer & Molnar, 1984)

This "Skeleton Key Question" (a generic "key" that can fit any lock) helps shift perspective; it implies (presupposes) that something positive is happening to be observed and recruits the clients' cooperation. Discussing at the session what was noticed (*Eliciting Presession Change*) can help consolidate and amplify useful new awarenesses (see Adams, Piercy, & Jurich, 1991; Weiner-Davis, de Shazer, & Gingerich, 1987).

Initial In-Session Questions

These are intended to build rapport, make space for partners' views and theories, and establish a team (therapist–couple alliance) framework.

- "What brings you here today?"
- "How can I be helpful to the two of you?"
- "What changes have either of you noticed since you first made the call to set up this appointment?"
- "How do you see the situation—what's your understanding [theory] of what would be helpful?"

- "What needs to happen here so that when you leave you will think, 'It was good that we went to see [the therapist]'?"
- "What can I do that would help you two work better together at getting beyond these troubles and turning your relationship around?"

Goal-Building Questions

Goal-building questions are intended to identify in operational (achievable and observable) terms what the clients desire from therapy.

- *Miracle Question*: "Suppose when you go home tonight and go to sleep a miracle happens and the problems that brought you here are solved. But, because you are asleep, you don't know this miracle has happened. So tomorrow, when you wake up and go through your day you notice things are different between you but you don't know the miracle happened. What will be the first things you notice are different? What will you notice your partner doing differently that will tell you something has changed? What will your partner notice you doing differently?"
- *From general to specific*: "How will the two of you know you have solved the problems that bring you here [or have reached your goals]? How will things be different? What specifically will tell you that you have solved your problem or reached these goals? What will be the first signs [smallest steps] that will tell you that you two are moving in that direction? What else?"
- *Getting specific details—painting the picture*: "What will tell you that you are on track? What else? What will that look like? What else will be different? When you are on track, what will you notice, what will be different to give you the confidence that you two will keep heading in that direction even after we stop meeting?"
- *Ends and means*: "How will it make a difference to you when these changes have happened? How will these changes change the way you feel about your partner and your relationship?"
- *Relationship/outside perception questions*: "When your partner is being more the way you want him/her to be, what will he/she see you doing differently that will tell him/her that his/her changes are having a meaningful effect on you? What will your partner notice different about you when . . . ? How do you suppose this will make a difference to him/her? What will tell him/her that you are on track to solving your marital problems?

What will your children notice is different? Friends? Other family members?"

Exceptions Questions:

These are intended to identify times the presenting problem has not been present. A hallmark of solution-focused therapy, they seek a kernel or "germ" that can be expanded into an alternative view that elevates awareness of clients' abilities to make a positive difference and opens the gateway to a new couple story (one not saturated or dominated by problems). The search is for "symptoms of solutions" (Miller, 1992).

- "When in the past might the problem have happened but didn't [or was less intense or more manageable]?"
- "When have you managed not to . . . . ?"
- "What is different about those times when the problem does not happen?"
- "When [in the recent past] have you experienced some of the things you say make a difference [tell you that you're heading in the right direction]?"
- "When have you noticed that the two of you do better with this problem?"
- "How have you let your partner know when he/she does something that makes a positive difference to you?"

Agency (Efficacy) Questions

These are intended to call attention to clients' self-efficacy—that is, their abilities to make a difference in the desired direction (see Ziegler & Hiller, 2001).

- "How did you do that?"
- "How did you get that to happen?"
- "What was each of you doing differently when you were doing better [or when there wasn't a problem, or when the exception happened]?"
- "How did each of you decide to do that?"
- "What would you say you (your partner) need to do to get that to happen more?"
- "What needs to happen first?"
- "What would your partner say you could do that would encourage him/her to do more of the things you think he/she could do to make a difference? Would you agree, even though it might be hard to do it or go first?"
- "What do you know about [your past, your self, your partner, your situation, other people] that tells you that this could happen for you (that you can make it together)?"

Coping (Endurance) Questions

These are intended to acknowledge the difficulty and painfulness of some situations, while also highlighting the clients' contributions to their resiliency.

- "How have the two of you managed to cope [survive, endure, keep going]?"
- "Given the terrible situation [how bad the arguing, grief, worrying, lack of communication, etc.] has been, how come things aren't worse [how have you managed to avoid it getting even worse]?"
- "What have you been doing to fight off the [arguing, grief, etc.]?"
- "How did you know that would help?"
- "If you hadn't been through this experience personally, would you have ever thought you had the strength to survive?"

Scaling Questions

These are typically asked "to make numbers talk," as Berg and de Shazer (1993) explain:

> Our scales are used to "measure" the client's own perception, to motivate and encourage, and to elucidate the goals and anything else that is important to the individual client. . . . Scaling questions are used to discuss the individual client's perspective, the client's view of others, and the client's impressions of others' view of him or her. (pp. 9–10)

They go on to elaborate:

> Scales allow both therapist and client to use the way language works naturally by agreeing upon terms (i.e., numbers) and a concept (a scale where 10 stands for the goal and zero stands for the absence of progress toward that goal) that is obviously multiple and flexible. Since neither therapist nor client can be absolutely certain what the other means by the use of a particular word or concept, scaling questions allow them to jointly construct a way of talking about things that are hard to describe, including progress toward the client's goal(s). . . . Here the scales give us a way to creatively misunderstand by using numbers to describe the indescribable and yet have some confidence that we, as therapists, are doing the job the client hired us to do. (p. 19)

It is important to recognize that the positive direction and valence of a scale helps shift discourse toward a solution (not problem) focus. For example, asking the members of a couple to rate themselves along the dimensions of how hopeful or motivated they are or how much progress has been made evokes a very different mind set than asking how hopeless or unmotivated or stuck they are. Thinking about where one might be rated along positively worded dimensions *is* much more hopeful, motivating, and likely to stir progress than the latter questions, which are not merely statistical inversions of solutions but entirely different constructions. Once clients give ratings, their responses are respectfully accepted, and the question then shifts to "What will it take to move from a 3 to a 4 [or a 6 to a 7, etc.]?"

- *Hope*: "On a scale from 1 to 10, 1 being absolutely no hope and 10 being complete confidence, what number would you give your current level of hope? What will tell you that your level has gone up one level? What number will be high enough to warrant your working hard to try and change things?"
- *Motivation*: "On a scale from 1 to 10, 1 being no motivation and 10 being a willingness to go to any lengths to solve your problems, what number would you give your current level of motivation? What will cause that level to go up one level?"
- *Progress*: "On a scale of 1 to 10, where 10 is the day after the miracle, and 1 is when this situation was at its worst, where would you say things are today? On a scale from 1 to 10, 1 being when the problems were just before you made the call and 10 being the problems are solved and a thing of the past, what number would you give your current level of progress [where you're at now]? What will tell you that you have moved up one level? What number will tell you that you have made enough progress in solving this problem so that you can consider it solved?"

Self–Other Perception/Meaning Questions

These relationship questions are asked to bring forth and highlight competencies, positive qualities, strengths and successes, and to weave them into the interpersonal context (see Ziegler & Hiller, 2001).

- "What does this say about you as a couple?"
- "What else would you want your partner to know [or have him/her notice] that would tell him how much you [care or love him/her, are working hard, want the relationship to improve, etc.]?"
- "As you continue to see yourselves this way, how do you imagine things continuing to change for the better?"

- "How do you suppose letting your partner know you see these positive changes in him/her will contribute to the two of you turning your relationship around [continuing to make progress]? How does his/her telling you that he/she notices and appreciates how you are changing affect you in your efforts to keep working for positive change?"
- "How will this [does this] make a difference that you want to see continue?"

Timing of Interventions

The purpose of solution-focused therapy is to help clients build a solution they find acceptable. If the client couple is making progress that is adequate and satisfying to both members, it is important to keep in mind the principle "*If It Works, Don't Fix It.*" In these instances, it is helpful to "cheerlead rather than mislead" (Hoyt & Miller, 2000, p. 222). That is, the therapist should elicit details of the clients' success, offer encouragement, highlight their role (instrumentality) in bringing it about—and not push.

If the couple gets stuck (or more likely, *when*—since the clients probably wouldn't be in the therapist's office if they didn't need assistance getting unstuck), the solution-focused therapist earns his/her fee by recognizing how the couple is getting bogged down in "problem talk" and then intervenes appropriately to redirect the clients toward "solution talk." Thus, as discussed above, the therapist needs to discern what type of therapist–client collaborative relationship (customer, complainant, visitor) is active and proceed accordingly. A couple may be stuck because of not having a sense of an achievable goal, or because one or both parties do not feel competent to make a positive difference. Good intentions need to be translated into specific actions. The clients may be ready to proceed as customers, but not know what particular steps to take (or not recognize what steps have worked for them in the past).

The solution-focused therapist intervenes, interrupting "problem talk" before it escalates into demoralizing bickering, cycles of blaming and defending, accusations, and unhappy crescendos. Instead, the therapist reminds the couple of what they want, and asks questions to redirect attention toward their role in achieving solutions past, present and, most important, future. The "Miracle Question" captures clients' imaginations and shifts the tone and flow of the conversation (see Nau & Shilts, 2000). Exceptions, coping, and agency questions evoke resources; relationship questions highlight cooperation and the bond between the partners.

Scaling questions, which can be used at any point during the session, are particularly helpful when complaints (or progress) are vague or nonspecific, as when couples refer to such topics as "communication":

> [A] couple's perception of how well they communicate with each other varies for each of them from time to time. With 10 standing for communicating as well as is possible for a specific couple to communicate, their joint progress and their different perceptions are simply depicted through their ratings. We frequently ask each partner to guess the other's rating, which again simply depicts progress and differences in perception as well as implying that such differences are both normal and expectable. The question is not "Who is right?" but "What does the one giving the higher rating see that the other one does not?" Thus, no matter how vaguely and nonspecifically the clients describe their situation, scales can be used to develop a useful way for therapist and clients to talk together about constructing solutions. (Berg & de Shazer, 1993, pp. 22–23)

Session Break: A Pause to Reflect and Plan

Although many solution-oriented therapists may not take a formal break during a session, in its "pure" or "classic" form a solution-focused therapy session is characterized by the therapist taking a short (typically 5- to 10-minute) break or intermission about 30–45 minutes into the session. The therapist will typically have prepared the clients for this at the beginning of the interview, when he/she indicates the structure of the session and gets the clients' permission to have a team, if available, observe the session. When the time comes ("Let's take a short break so that I can talk with my colleagues"), the clients may be asked to sit in the interview room while the therapist goes next door to consult with a team of observers, or the clients may be asked to take a brief recess in the waiting room while the therapist talks with colleagues. Even if there are no colleagues observing, the therapist can use the break to organize his/her thoughts, to reflect upon what has occurred, and to plan a message (feedback and possible homework task) to be presented to the couple when the session is resumed.

The couple can also be asked to think about what task or postsession activity might be useful for them. Building on the solution-focused idea that it is the client who is "heroic" (Duncan & Miller,

2000) and whose therapeutic contributions should be kept foremost, Sharry, Madden, Darmody, and Miller (2001) describe an interesting variant in which the session break can be used in a more collaborative or client-directed fashion. They suggest this expectation can be established in the way the therapist describes the purpose of the consultation break:

> We're nearing the end of the session and I'd like to take a five-minute break. This is to give you time to think and reflect about what we have discussed; to pick out any important ideas that came up, or to make any decisions or plans. You might also like to think about whether this session has been useful and how you would like us to be further involved, if that would be helpful. While you're thinking, I will consult with my team for their thoughts. We will think together about what you said. When we get back together, I'll be interested to hear what stood out for you today. I'll also share the team's thoughts with you. Together, then, we can put something together that will be helpful. (Sharry et al., 2001, pp. 71–72)

This puts the emphasis clearly on the clients' thinking, reflecting, and planning. Clients are encouraged to participate in the evaluation of the session and the decision about further work. There is no "automatic" assumption that more sessions will be needed or desired, and it is the clients rather than the therapist who have primacy in making decisions about the length of treatment. As Sharry et al. (2001, pp. 74–75) write: "[C]lients as well as the therapist team are encouraged to use the break as an opportunity to reflect on the session, generate their own conclusions and even assign themselves a homework task. . . . it helps clients build on their own strengths and resources, recognizing their central role in any therapeutic change. . . . The responsibility for successful therapy is shared between therapist and client."

Resuming and Concluding the Session: Feedback and Tasks

When the therapist returns or brings the couple back into the room after taking a break, the session resumes. If one endeavors to utilize an especially collaborative or client-directed session break, as Sharry et al. (2001) suggest, it will be important that the therapist "first seeks the views and thought of the clients in evaluating the session and constructing a plan of action" (Sharry et al., 2001, p. 74). The break "punctuates" the session, and clients are usually keen to hear what the therapist has to say after studying the situation and perhaps consulting with other therapists. Hence, while giving primacy to the clients' ideas, the moment also may be ripe for the therapist to introduce a suggestion or a reframing (Erickson & Rossi, 1979; de Shazer, 1985, p. 91). Feedback and "homework" tasks, which flow from the preceding conversation, are designed collaboratively to promote goal attainment by reflecting and reinforcing client competencies and any emerging "solution talk." The therapist works to amplify whatever the clients are doing in the direction they want to go. De Jong and Berg (1998, p. 107) distinguish solution building from problem solving:

> End-of-session feedback in solution building is not the same thing as intervention in the problem-solving approach. In the latter case, the practitioner uses assessment information about the nature and severity of client problems to decide on what actions would best benefit the client. The practitioner then takes those actions or encourages the client to do so. These actions—the interventions—are thought to produce the positive changes for the client. . . .
>
> In solution-building, by contrast, we do not regard session-ending feedback as any more important than any other component of the process. Instead . . . we think that solutions are built by clients through the hard work of applying their strengths in the direction of goals that they value. Clients, not practitioners, are the primary agents of change. In the course of the interview, clients disclose information about themselves and their circumstances; session-ending feedback merely organizes and highlights the aspects of that information that might be useful to clients as they strive to build solutions.

Compliments, a Bridging Statement, and the Task

In classic solution-focused therapy, there are typically three components to what the therapist says after the session break: *compliments*, which acknowledge and validate the clients' point of view, affirming what is important to them, their successes and strengths; a *bridging statement*, which links compliments to the suggestion or directive that is to be offered; and the *task or directive* itself, often involving performance of an "experiment" or "homework."

> [Compliments] are statements from the therapist and/or team about what the client has said that is useful, effective, good, or fun. This helps to promote client–therapist fit and thus cooperation on the task at hand.

> With some frequency, the compliments (in the first session) will include statements about the difficulty of achieving the chosen goal and some statements, based on the exceptions, about the progress toward the goal and the general viability of the goal. In later sessions, the main focus of the compliments will often be on the progress toward the goal. (de Shazer, 1988, pp. 96–97)

The use of compliments, acknowledgment and validation, and a bridging statement near the end of a solution-focused couple therapy session is illustrated in these comments excerpted from a report by Hoyt and Berg (1998, pp. 221–222; see also Berg, 1994b):

> THERAPIST [Insoo Berg]: I really have to tell you that I think your calling to set up this appointment was really good timing. It sounds like you both are very concerned about what's not happening between the two of you, and you want to do something about that. And I am very impressed, Bill, that you responded to Leslie's initiating this meeting and your willingness to take time from your very busy schedule and obviously this relationship is very important to you. . . . And that's why you are here, to do something about this. Both of you really care about this relationship a great deal. But both in a very different way. . . . [She goes on to describe each partner's stated values.] So there's no question in my mind that both of you care about each other in a very different way. And that gets misunderstood. And I think that both of you need both ways. . . . And so I think that you two have a very good start because you're already thinking about right now as well as the future. So the next task for the two of you is to figure out how to fit your concerns together. [Bridging statement] I don't think it's either your way or your way. It's the blending of the two. In order to do that, both of you have to work together to strike this balance. And I really like the way that you want to get started on this. You have lots of ideas of how to get started on that. . . .

In this case, the therapist recognized that each member of the couple was in a complainant position—that is, felt aggrieved but not (yet) instrumental to make a difference. She thus suggested an *observation task*, one designed to shape viewing (and thus affect subsequent interaction) by having each partner notice what the other person was doing that was positive:

> THERAPIST: So what I would like to suggest to you between now and the next time we get together, is for each of you to keep track of what the other person is doing. For you [to the wife] to keep track

of what Bill does, and for you [to the husband] to keep track of what Leslie does to make things a little bit better for the marriage. And it's important for you not to discuss it, but just keep track of them. And when we come back together we will discuss this more, the details of them. But I want you to sort of observe, file it away, and then when we get together we'll talk about it. OK? (Hoyt & Berg, 1998, p. 222; see also Berg, 1994b)

Having each partner notice the positive helped to shift the basis of their interaction from a problem-saturated to a more solution-saturated worldview. Seeing one's partner in a positive light makes one more likely to respond in kind; this may help produce a "virtuous" instead of a "vicious" cycle. Had the partners been in more of a "customer" position, the therapist might have more directly offered them specific suggestions or guidance on how to improve their interaction (as complainants, they would not have felt able to use this information). Had they been in the position of "visitors," disavowing any problem or interest in a remedy, the therapist might have simply paid them courteous compliments and invited them to return (as complainants, however, this would not have resulted in their feeling that their complaints had been acknowledged and taken seriously).

de Shazer (1985, pp. 67–68) provides a decision tree (see Figure 12.2) and some suggestions to therapists for how to respond to clients' responses to tasks in the best way for promoting cooperation (and thus solutions). "Fit" is enhanced by attending to two basic solution-focused principles: "*Once you know what works, do more of it,*" and "*If it doesn't work, don't do it again; do something different.*" de Shazer (1988, pp. 97–99, emphasis in original) also provides some general guidelines for designing tasks:

(1) Note what sort of things the clients do that is good, useful, and effective.
(2) Note *differences* between what happens when any exceptions occur and what happens when the complaint happens. Promote the former.
(3) When possible, extract step-by-step descriptions of any exceptions.
   (a) Find out what is working, and/or
   (b) find out what has worked, and/or
   (c) find out what might work, then
   (d) prescribe the easiest.
   If some aspects of the exception (or of the complaint) are sort of random, then
   (e) include something arbitrary or make allowances for randomness in the task.
(4) When necessary, *extract* step-by-step descriptions of the complaint.

(5) Note *differences* between any hypothetical solutions and the complaint.
(6) Imagine a *solved* version of the problematic situation by:
   (a) making *exceptions* to the rule,
   (b) changing the *location* of the complaint pattern,
   (c) changing who is *involved* in the complaint pattern,
   (d) changing the *order of the steps* involved,
   (e) adding a *new element* or step to the complaint pattern,
   (f) increasing the *duration* of the pattern,
   (g) introducing *arbitrary* starting and stopping,
   (h) increasing the *frequency* of the pattern,
   (i) changing the *modality* of the problematic behavior.
(7) Decide what will fit for the complainant/customer, i.e., which task, based on which variable (a through i) will make sense to the particular client. Which one will the complainant most likely accept? Which one will the customer most likely perform? For instance: If a couple has a joint complaint, give them a joint, cooperative task. If only one member of a couple presents the complaint like a customer, give the "customer" a task that involves doing something and the other person an observation task.

de Shazer (1994a, 1994b; see also his remarks in Hoyt, 1996b, pp. 61–63) also cautions the therapist to keep it simple and not get caught up in overly clever, complicated strategizing, which might have the untoward effects of both disempowering the clients and overburdening the therapist.

Lipchik (1997, p. 170) also describes the importance of attending to cooperative "fit" and maintaining a collaborative set throughout the closing portion of the session:

I believe the summation message has an important function in creating a different reality for clients. I now structure this message to reflect what I believe I understand about the clients' reality ("What I heard you say today is . . ."); my perspective on what I heard ("My response is . . ."), which includes positives, reinforcements of what the clients are doing that they experience as helpful, normalizing statements and sometimes some information; and a suggestion about what they might think about, or do until the next session. I present "the task" as a choice, not an assignment. Then I ask the client(s) for a short response. This gives clients an opportunity to correct anything I reflected on or responded to that they do not agree with before leaving the session. I find this format more fitting a collaborative relationship than my former, more "expert" way of structuring the messages (Compliment: "I am impressed with . . ."; a clue, a task assignment).

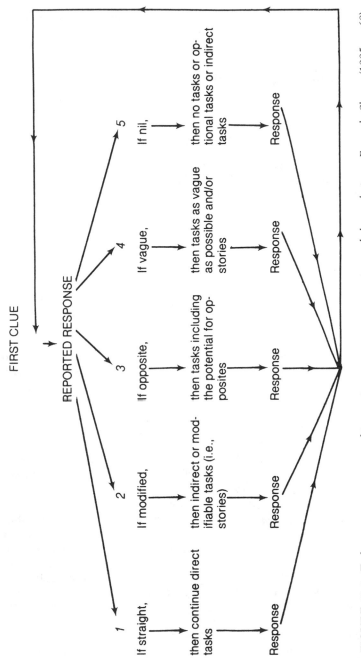

FIGURE 12.2. Task response sequences of interaction to promote cooperation and thus solutions. From de Shazer (1985, p. 68). Copyright 1985 by Steve de Shazer. Reprinted by permission of W. W. Norton & Co., Inc.

349

Common Messages

In their excellent text, *Interviewing for Solutions*, De Jong and Berg (1998, p. 121) provide a number of guidelines for giving feedback, and identify various basic statements—called "common messages"— for recurring situations:

> [W]here you decide to point a client will depend on your assessment of: (1) the type of relationship in which your client stands to your services; (2) the degree to which the client has developed well-formed goals; and (3) the presence or absence of random and deliberate exceptions related to what your client wants.

De Jong and Berg (1998, pp. 120–133, with some paraphrasings here) describe typical common messages for different situations (it is important to remember that compliments and bridging statements would precede these):

Clients in a Visitor Relationship.
• "We are very impressed that you are here today, even though this is not your idea. You certainly had the option of taking the easy way out by not coming. . . . I agree with you that you should be left alone. But you also realize that doing what you are told will help you get these people out of your life, and you will be left alone sooner. Therefore, I would like to meet with you again to figure out further what will be good for you to do. So let's meet next week at the same time."

Clients in a Complainant Relationship.
• *No exceptions and no goal:* "Between now and the next time that we meet, pay attention to what's happening in your life that tells you that this problem can be solved."
• *Exceptions but no goals:* "Between now and the next time we meet, pay attention to those times that are better, so that you can describe them to me in detail. Try to notice what is different about them and how they happen. Who does what to make them happen?"
• *If a client attributes the exceptions entirely to the other person's actions:* "Pay attention for those times when your partner [relationship] is more the way you want. Besides paying attention to what's different about those times, pay attention to—so you can describe it to me next time—what he/she might notice you doing that helps him/her/the two of you to be more _____ . Keep track of those things and come back and tell me what's better."
• *If the clients view the problem as existing outside themselves but are able to identify random*

exceptions: "I agree with you; there clearly seems to be days your partner [relationship] is more _____ and days when he/she/it isn't. So, between now and the next time that we meet, I suggest the following: Each night before you go to bed, predict whether or not tomorrow will be a day when _____ or not. Then, at the end of the day, before you make your prediction for the next day, think about whether or not your prediction came true. Account for any differences between your prediction and the way the day went, and keep track of your observations so that you can come back and tell me about them."

Clients in a Customer Relationship.
• *A clear miracle picture but no exceptions:* "Pick one day over the next week and, without telling anyone, pretend that the miracle has happened. And, as you live that day, pay attention to what's different around your house, so that you can tell me about it when we meet next time."
• *High motivation but no well-formed goals:* "I am very impressed with how hard you have worked on your problem and how clearly you can describe to me the things you have tried so far to make things better. I can understand why you would be discouraged and frustrated right now. . . . Because this is such a stubborn problem, I suggest that, between now and the next time we meet, when the problem happens, you do something different—no matter how strange or weird or off-the-wall what you do might seem. The only important thing is that, whatever you decide to do, you need to do something different."
• *Well-formed goals and deliberate exceptions:* "I am impressed how much you want to make things go better between you and your partner, and that there are already times this is happening [give examples]. I agree that these are the things you have to do to have the kind of relationship that you want. So, between now and when we meet again, I suggest that you continue to do what works. Also, pay attention to what else you might be doing—but haven't noticed yet—that makes things better, and come back and tell me about it."

Other Useful Messages.
• *The overcoming-the-urge task:* "Pay attention for those times when the two of you overcome the urge to [argue, return to the old problem, not look for positives in what the other is saying, etc.]. Pay attention to what's different about those times— especially to what you are doing to overcome the urge.

• *Addressing competing views of the solution* (*without taking sides*): "I am impressed by how much both of you want to improve your relationship. I am also impressed by what different ideas the two of you have about how to do this—I can see that, coming from your different perspectives [backgrounds, families, etc.], you have learned different ways to do things. . . . I [or the team] am [are] split on which way to go: both of you have strong ideas. Therefore, I [we] suggest that each morning, right after you get up, you flip a coin. Heads means that day you improve things the way [Person A] suggests, and the other person goes along; and tails means you improve things the way [Person B] suggests, and the other person goes along. And also—on those days when each of you is not busy being in charge—pay careful attention to what the other does that is useful, and how you help with that, so that you can report it to me [us] when we meet again."

In her best-selling self-help guide, *Divorce-Busting: A Revolutionary and Rapid Program for Staying Together*, Michele Weiner-Davis (1992), another former member of the BFTC group, draws on many solution-focused ideas. Under the heading (pp. 124–125) "Why Focusing on What Works—Works," she provides and discusses four answers:

1. Exceptions Shrink Problems
2. Exceptions Demonstrate that People Are Changeable
3. Exceptions Supply Solutions
4. Focusing on Strengths Strengthens

Weiner-Davis (1992, pp. 127–140) then provides (with extended discussion and numerous practical suggestions for application) the following nine guidelines to help readers "analyze what works in your marriage and give you information you need to get your marriage back on track":

1. Notice What Is Different About the Times the Two of You Are Getting Along
2. If You Are Having Trouble Identifying Current Exceptions, Recall What You and Your Spouse Were Doing Differently in Years Past that Made Your Marriage More Satisfying
3. You Don't Have to Like It, You Just Have to Do It
4. Focus on What's Doable or Possible
5. A Problem that Recurs Doesn't Necessarily Require a New Solution
6. Pay Attention to How Your Conflicts End
7. If There Are No Exceptions, Identify the Best of the Worst

8. Notice What's Different About the Times the Problem Occurs but Something Constructive Comes from It
9. Notice What's Different About the Times the Problem Situation Occurs but Doesn't Bother You

In *Rewriting Love Stories: Brief Marital Therapy*, Patricia Hudson and Bill O'Hanlon (1991; see also O'Hanlon & Hudson, 1994) also highlight many solution-focused/solution-oriented ideas, including the importance of moving from blame to collaboration, changing the clients' way of "viewing" and "doing" their situation, the use of task assignments, the value of humor, and the power of commitments and consequences. More recently, in their *Brief Couples Therapy Homework Planner*, Gary Schultheis, Bill O'Hanlon, and Steffanie O'Hanlon (1999, p. 1) write:

We use homework assignments for many reasons, including that homework:

• Introduces change to the situation
• Encourages a spirit of experimentation
• Encourages clients to take an active part in therapy
• Evokes resources
• Highlights and allows follow-through on something that happened in the session
• Encourages the client to put more attention on an issue
• Encourages the client to take the next step before the next session
• Enhances the client's search for solutions.

They go on (p. 6):

We want to, at the very least, create some sense that the situation is not hopeless. That means we quickly move into making changes. So, in addition to validating, we immediately set about helping the couple make changes in three areas around the problem:
1. What are they paying attention to in the problem situation and how are they interpreting it? (*Changing the Viewing*)
2. How are they typically interacting with one another, including patterns of how each of them act during the problem situation and how they talk with one another or others about the problem? We are searching for repeating patterns and helping couples change those problem patterns. (*Changing the Doing*)
3. What circumstances surround the problem? That is, what are the family backgrounds and patterns, the cultural backgrounds and patterns, the racial backgrounds and gender training and experiences that are contributing to the problem? In what locations do the couple's problems usually happen? (*Changing the Context*)

In each of these change areas, we have two tasks:
1. Recognizing and interrupting typical problem patterns
2. Seeking, highlighting and encouraging solution patterns.

Drawing upon solution-based (as well as other) ideas, they then provide many ready-to-use between-session assignments. When thoughtfully selected, proffered, and explained to couples, such user-friendly "homework" tasks can help couples develop skills for healthier relationships.

Subsequent Sessions

When a couple returns for a second (or subsequent) session, the solution-focused therapist endeavors to co-create a comfortable, cooperative situation; then inquires about progress, seeking detailed descriptions of any movement toward the couple's desired outcome (solution) and the clients' roles in attaining it; and then assists the clients to look forward to how they will take their next pro-solution steps. This process is nicely summarized (with some examples of opening questions) in the acronym E.A.R.S. (Berg, 1994c; De Jong & Berg, 1998):

E (elicit): "What's better?" or "What worked for you two?" or "What happened that you liked?"
A (amplify): "Tell me more," or "Who/what/where/when/how?" or "Walk me through how the two of you did that."
R (reinforce): "Wow!" or "That sounds great!" or "What part did you especially enjoy?"
S (start again): "And what else is better?" or "So, what do you think the next step might be?" or "How can you keep this going?" or "On a scale of 1 to 10 you say your progress [relationship, communication, love life, etc.] is now at a 5—what would a 6 look like?"

Let us return to the marital therapy case (from Hoyt & Berg, 1998) referred to earlier. Consider these excerpts from the therapist's remarks at the beginning of the next session:

THERAPIST [Insoo Berg]: It's been about 2 weeks since you were here the last time. What's been better for the two of you? . . . No kidding! Really! Wow! How'd you manage to do that? . . . No kidding? . . . Wow! That must have been hard. . . . You did, really—without the kids? Some intimate time. . . . You were willing to do that, this time—wonder-

ful! . . . Would you agree, was that fun for you, too? . . . Wow! That must have taken quite a bit of coordination to pull it off, with 4 people's schedules. . . . Huh-huh. . . . That's good! . . . Right! . . . What did Leslie do to make things a little easier for you to do that? . . . Huh-huh . . . Great! . . . Before we get to that, let me ask you: What did Bill do that was helpful? . . . Wow! Yes! It seems like that was very important to you—what does that mean to you?. . . . Is that one of the things he did? Anything else you noticed to make things better? . . . . Huh-huh. . . . What about for you—what did Leslie do to make things better? What else? Say some more about that. . . . Really! . . . How hopeful are you now, on a scale of 1 to 10, that this marriage will make it? A 9? And you? . . . This is a big change, isn't it? What would it take for you to stay on this track? . . . What needs to happen for the two of you to feel you are moving in the right direction? . . . So, how do you solve it—what's the next step for the two of you? (Hoyt & Berg, 1998, p. 222)

If, even after careful inquiry, there has been a lack of discernible progress (including not doing homework that was discussed), *coping questions* ("How did you keep things from getting worse?") may be appropriate. The solution-focused therapist may also recognize "no progress" feedback as an opportunity to repair a possible mismatch. The therapist may have misgauged the clients' stage of readiness or the type of therapist–client relationship pattern (see Hoyt & Miller, 2000). Blaming the client is not useful in building cooperation and solutions. In such instances, questions such as the following may be helpful:

- "What's your idea about what would be useful? What do you think the next step should be?"
- "Are we working on what you want to work on? How is this going for you?"
- "I seem to have missed something you said. What can I do to be more helpful to you now?"

Common Technical Errors and Criticisms

Solution-focused brief therapists focus on solutions. Many traditional therapists, however, are trained and oriented toward problems and pathologies. In addition to highlighting negativities, therapists (solution-focused and otherwise) can engender opposition by trying to take clients to where they don't want to go:

DE SHAZER: Well, if I were to use the word *resistance*—I wouldn't, but if I were—it would translate in my vocabulary as *therapist's error*. That would mean to me that the therapist's wasn't listening, and therefore he told the client to do something the client didn't want to do. That means he wasn't listening during the interview. Most of our stuff is based on the fact of something they told us about, that they did such and such and it worked in some situation, so it's just a matter of transferring that from situation A to situation B. So there's nothing new. Most of our interventions are nothing new for them. . . .

HOYT: I think another advantage, then, to a solution-focused approach is that it doesn't stimulate noncompliance because there's nothing they have to noncomply with. It makes it more user-friendly for both the therapist and for the client. It's less likely to drive clients away.

DE SHAZER: Less likely. What I see sometimes is the amateurs, so to speak—the beginners, who somehow think more is better and, therefore, they give this endless stream of compliments and bore the client silly with them and, therefore, the client stops taking them seriously. That's one thing I see happen with beginners, in particular: There's just too damn many compliments, and that will drive the client away.

HOYT: . . . How do we separate the idea of "influence" from "brainwashing," to call it that? [That w]e're influencing but not imposing our values, manipulating them?

DE SHAZER: There's that line, all right. Clients hire us to influence them; that's why they come. The more you are using their stuff, the less danger you are in of moving into brainwashing. The more you are putting in your stuff, the closer you're getting to brainwashing. That's pretty clear to me. Those are the two ends of it, perhaps. I'm not sure if it is a continuum, but there certainly in a line in between. And, frankly, I see many, many of the psychotherapy models as being closer to brainwashing than to anything else.

HOYT: I think the respectful ethic is that it's truly informed consent. We're identifying what their goals are and helping them meet their goals, rather than imposing our agenda.

DE SHAZER: Right. You know, we have a saying around here [BFTC]—there used to be a sign made by somebody on the team (probably Gale Miller): "If the therapist's goals and the client's goals are different, the therapist is wrong." (Hoyt, 1996b, pp. 63–65)

The approach should not be "model-driven" or "technique-driven" at the expense of the therapist–client relationship (see Lipchik, 1997; Miller & Duncan, 2000). Several commentators (e.g., Efran & Schenker, 1993; O'Hanlon, 1998) have suggested, however, that solution-focused ther-

apy can be applied in a heavy-handed, formulaic manner that results in clients feeling "solution-forced" (Nylund & Corsiglia, 1994) and "rushed to be brief" (Lipchik, 1994), and that solutions may be embraced that serve to perpetuate problem patterns (Fraser, 1998). de Shazer (quoted in Hoyt, 1994b, p. 39) has made his view clear:

> I know what I don't want, and that's for anybody to develop some sort of rigid orthodoxies. I'm afraid of that. I'm always afraid of that. For me, it's a big point of concern. That there's a right way to do this and that. And to see my descriptions—and they've done this to me; I've probably done this to myself—to see my descriptions as prescriptions.

Critics have also suggested that emotion may be downplayed or ignored, and that recurring complaints and important social issues (e.g., oppression of women, domestic violence) will not be recognized unless clients explicitly raise them. When solution-focused therapy is done skillfully, clients do not feel "forced" or "rushed," but assisted to go where they want to go.

> We do not believe solution-focused brief therapy encourages practitioners to force solutions on clients. However, because the approach is usually presented with a heavy emphasis on the idea that solution talk, not problem talk, leads to solutions, it is easy for those learning this approach to prevent clients from talking about their concerns and troubles. We have never heard or read anything in the solution-focused brief therapy literature that suggests clients should be forced to talk only about positive things. Watching de Shazer and Berg on videotapes, we have always noted their respectful attitudes and their skillful ways of "leading from behind." (Ziegler & Hiller, 2001, p. 222)

Emotion is not avoided, but it is also not sought or elicited as a therapeutic "royal road" or as an end in itself (King, 1998; Miller & de Shazer, 1998, 2000; see also Lipchik, 2002). The solution-focused therapist is present as a real, genuinely concerned person, but does not engage in unneeded (by the client) personal self-disclosure. The therapist resists the temptation to be clever or to explore unnecessary topics, although he/she will respond appropriately to situations of obvious abuse, and various solution-focused methods have been described (see Johnson & Goldman, 1996; Lipchik & Kubicki, 1996; Tucker, Stith, Howell, McCollum, & Rosen, 2000; Ziegler & Hiller, 2002) for such situations.

Termination

Solution-focused (couple) therapy stops when the clients are satisfied that their goal or goal(s) have been adequately met or achieved—a situation that can be identified by their response to these questions:

- "How can we know when to stop meeting like this?" (de Shazer, 1991a, p. 120)
- "What needs to be different in your life as a result of coming here for you to say that meeting with me was worthwhile?" or "What number [scaling progress] do you need to be in order not to come and talk with me anymore?" (De Jong & Berg, 1998, pp. 148–149)

In her book *Family-Based Services: A Solution-Focused Approach*, Berg (1994a) elaborates some criteria and methods for ending therapy, including goal achievement, designating a limited number of sessions, no movement in a case, and leaving things open-ended in response to outside restrictions. She writes:

> If you wait until *all* the client's problems are solved, you will never end treatment. . . . What is important to keep in mind is that "empowering" clients means equipping them with the tools to solve their own problems as far as possible. When they can't do it on their own, they need to know when to ask for help and where to go for help. Termination can occur when you are confident that the client will know when and where to go to seek help, and *not* when you are confident that he [she or they] will never have problems. (Berg, 1994a, p. 163)

The solution-focused therapist endeavors to become obsolete and thus to end therapy as soon as possible. The object is to get the client out of therapy and actively and productively involved in living his or her life (Dolan, 1985, p. 29). The approach is characterized more by an attitude than a particular length: "as few sessions as possible, not even one more than is necessary" is the way de Shazer (1991b, p. x) has put it. Hence, the approach is "minimalistic" in two related senses: (1) theoretically elegant, staying close to the clients' goals without introducing unnecessary and potentially distracting topics; and (2) short-term, using the minimum of necessary sessions. When a couple feels ready and able to carry on without therapy— including having some strategies for managing future conflicts (see Carlson, 2000)—it is time for termination. Sometimes termination completes a process; other times a couple has gotten "unstuck"

and back "on track" (Walter & Peller, 1994; Hoyt, 2000), and the partners carry on without the presence of a therapist. de Shazer made a remark at the end of a published conversation that might serve as good advice for therapists considering when to terminate treatment:

> HOYT: How shall we close?
> DE SHAZER: Wittgenstein [1980, p. 77e] has some tremendous advice for all authors: "Anything your reader can do for himself, leave to him." (Hoyt, 1996b, p. 81)

Although "no more than needed" is a guiding desideratum, it is important to make sure that the clients' problems have been "heard" and addressed:

> I have occasionally worked with clients who describe their experience with their past solution-focused professional as he or she having been too positive and not providing opportunity for talking about things that really bothered them. Positive reinforcement alone can initially lead to clients feeling better about their situation and themselves. However, as they begin to feel better and talk more about their complaints, the specific goals may shift, and unless the collaborating professional is aware of this, the collaboration may be ended prematurely. When it appears that goals have been reached, it is important for the collaborating professional to become very curious about how clients have been experiencing the sessions, and what they think has been useful or not useful. "What else would you have wanted me to ask you, or talk about?" could prevent premature termination. (Lipchik, 1997, p. 167)

In keeping with the idea of intermittent or episodic therapy (see Cummings & Sayama, 1995; Hoyt, 1995, 2000), it is also important to leave the door open for possible return. Termination should be structured in such a way that a subsequent decision to pursue more treatment will be seen by clients as an opportunity for further growth, rather than an indicator of failure.

Opening the Lens: Some Useful Ideas and Techniques for Solution-Focused Therapists from Other Models

A number of writers have suggested ways to integrate ideas and methods from seemingly related orientations into the solution-focused approach. However, while psychotherapy integration or the borrowing of techniques from different models is a laudatory endeavor if it better equips the therapist to assist clients, it is not without its perils. Neimeyer (1998, p. 62) warns about the "indiscriminate gallimaufry of deconstructive rules deriving from incompatible metatheories" that might result, for example, if a therapist switched from eliciting, affirming and celebrating a client's emerging self-awareness to suddenly challenging its logical or empirical basis. While one could explore with clients their intentions or even carefully offer another possible way of construing a situation ("Could that be a way he/she tries to show concern?"), solution-focused therapists are wary of the concept of therapist-provided *insight*, since it implies that there is a "right" or "true" psychological reality underlying clients' awareness and elevates the therapist to the role of The Expert able to interpret what is "real" and what is not:

HOYT: What I'm getting from what you're saying is it's best to accept that what the patient is communicating about is accurate. And it's our job to figure out what it's accurate about.

WEAKLAND: That's an interesting way of putting it, rather than converting them.

DE SHAZER: I'm not even sure about the last part . . . just, "it's accurate."

HOYT: It's accurate.

DE SHAZER: Yeah. It's accurate. And that's all there is.

HOYT: But if we're going to be of service to them, not just to take them seriously and listen, what do we add beyond listening?

DE SHAZER: The seriously. Taking them seriously. See, I think a lot of people listen, but they don't take them seriously. (Hoyt, 1994b, p. 30)

Shoham et al. (1995, p. 156; see also Fraser, 1998) note that there would even seem to be core contradictions between MRI problem-focused brief therapy and BFTC solution-focused brief therapy models:

This is no easy task, because despite similarities, there are also many ways in which specific tactics and the general therapeutic stance prescribed by the two models can be quite incompatible (e.g., investigating complaints vs. exceptions to complaints, offering optimism and encouragement vs. pessimism and restraint).

Saggese and Foley (2000, p. 59), however, note that "The SFBT [solution-focused brief therapy] and PFBT [problem-focused brief therapy] models are prime candidates for integration because they share a number of basic assumptions about both the nature and resolution of human problems."

They go on to suggest ways of integrating the different pathways the two models use when seeking to resolve problems.

In practice, most clinicians influenced by solution-focused therapy do borrow from various models (e.g., see Cade & O'Hanlon, 1993; Eron & Lund, 1996; Fish, 1997; Friedman, 1997; Hoyt, 1995, 2000; Jordan & Quinn, 1994; O'Hanlon & Weiner-Davis, 1989; Quick, 1996), and such "technical integration" (Lazarus, 1995) can be consistent with the solution-focused metamessage of *Do What Works*. All therapists, however, more or less think they "do what works" (why else would they do what they do?), so it seems reasonable to establish more specific criteria for what may be consistent with the spirit and intentions of solution-focused intervention. In their thoughtful review, Beyebach and Morejon (1999) refer to Michael Hjerth's (1995) idea that solution-focused therapy can be distinguished along the dimensions of its *philosophy* (or basic premises and assumptions), *use of language*, and *techniques*, and then go on to write:

Provisionally, we would like to describe Solution-Focused Therapy as an approach that includes as its *premises* the beliefs that clients have resources, that change is constant, that in therapy a small change is enough (as long as it is noticed), and that therefore there is no need to understand a problem in order to solve it. The *language* used in Solution-Focused Therapy is usually possibility and future-oriented, with the aim of creating cooperation and putting the client in control of the change process. This language creates a *stance* of cooperation on the part of the therapist, who tries to agree with her clients and is always alert to their use of language and to their changing goals during the process of therapy. This stance includes also an attempt to stay "behind" the clients, to carefully listen to them and to avoid pushing them in the therapist's direction. The therapist does not lecture to the clients or tell them what to do, but tries to help them figure out on their own what course of action to follow. Common, but not necessary *techniques* include goal-talk, exception-talk, and scaling questions, all of which could be described as solution-talk as opposed to problem-talk (de Shazer, 1994[a]). (Beyebach & Morejon, 1999, p. 29; emphasis in original)

In his book *Time-Effective Psychotherapy: Maximizing Outcomes in an Era of Minimized Resources*, Steven Friedman (1997, p. 234; see also Friedman & Lipchik, 1999) draws heavily from solution-focused therapy as he outlines five major processes that define a time-effective, competency-based approach:

1. *Connection:* Listening, affirming, and acknowledging each partner's story while joining with both around a set of mutually agreed-upon goals;
2. *Curiosity:* Opening space for a discussion of multiple perspectives while attending to the couple's resources;
3. *Collaboration:* Working together with both members [of] the couple in the direction of *their* preferred futures. Highlighting successes ("exceptions") and generating hope;
4. *Co-Construction of Solution Ideas:* (a) Introducing novel ideas that emerge from the clinical conversations; (b) defining action steps ("homework");
5. *Closure:* Giving compliments; celebrating and applauding change; offering each partner an opportunity to acknowledge and comment on changes in the other; offering future availability.

If we look through these "lenses," various competency-based, collaborative, and future-oriented ideas and interventions borrowed from strategic, narrative, and systemic frameworks can be integrated into solution-focused work. I cite a few here from my clinical experience as well as from that of Shoham et al. (1995), Beyebach and Morejon (1999), Ziegler and Hiller (2001), and others referenced above.

• *Motivational interviewing* (DiClemente, 1991; Miller & Rollnick, 1991). Clients' goals are clarified and their motivation for change is enhanced when the therapist explores with clients their reactions to their current experience and their reasons for seeking therapy (e.g., "How is what you've been doing working for you?" and "Is that a positive or a negative for you?"). If clients are dissatisfied, sometimes I find it helpful simply to quote the old saying, "If you don't change directions, you'll wind up where you're heading!"[6] Although solution-focused therapists favor solution talk rather than problem talk, hearing some of a couple's woes allows the clients to feel heard and understood. We don't want to get stuck or bogged down, but they're going to tell us anyway, and talking about problems can also be used as a starting point to identifying times the problems are not present.

• *Externalization and relative-influence questioning* (White, 1989; White & Epston, 1990; Zimmerman & Dickerson, 1993; Roth & Epston, 1996; see also de Shazer, 1993b). These well-known narrative therapy methods place the "problem" outside the person/couple and identify both times the problem entraps clients and times they are able to withstand or control the "problem."

Times the couple successfully influences the "problem" may be thought of as "exceptions" (and "coping") within the solution-focused framework, providing a basis for solution development. As Michael White (quoted in Winslade & Monk, 1999, p. 42) notes, these "unique outcomes" (to use the narrative therapy term) or "exceptions" (solution focus) may be nascent and manifest themselves as actions, intentions to act, moments when the effects of the problem don't seem so strong, areas of life that remain unaffected by the problem, special abilities or knowledge about how to overcome the problem, or problem-free responses from others that can be learned from vicariously. As I have suggested elsewhere (Hoyt, 2000, p. 44), seeking a "history of the present recovery" may be more salutary than the conventional psychiatric "history of the present complaint"; rather than (or in addition to) the usual genogram (replete with divorces, suicides, and cutoffs), what useful information might a client and therapist gain from constructing a "solution-focused genogram"?

• *"Go slow" messages and predicting setbacks.* Particularly with couples that have experienced a lot of difficulties and are hesitating to make changes, it may be helpful to compliment them on their taking a cautious approach and to remind them that the course ahead may not be smooth—but that their thoughtful, determined efforts will overall yield progress. Instead of looking at setbacks as failures, a therapist can reframe slips and relapses as reminders that the clients are still improving and need to remain vigilant about their process (see Berg, 1994a, p. 213; Norum, 2000, p. 15). It is also important for therapists, even those who describe themselves as "brief" therapists, to recognize that change is sometimes slow and that patience may be needed to allow couples the time and space to make and consolidate hard-earned gains.

• *Role playing* (especially in-session rehearsals of possible "solution" behavior). Suggesting to one or both members of a couple that they "pretend" or act "as if" a miracle has occurred or the problem is solved allows them a glimpse of a problem-free future. Having them "try it on" makes it more "real" and more likely that they will see themselves differently and thus continue the prosolution enactment. (See Roth & Chasin, 1994, for a good example drawn from narrative couple therapy.)

• *Kindness, humor, faith, and love.* These often assumed or taken-for-granted qualities provide the soil in which various techniques may take root. Solution-focused therapists operate from a deep, abiding belief that people, if treated right, are competent and capable. We are in search of *their* solutions, and I generally (although not always) have found that the harder I listen, the smarter a client gets—often in ways that I would not have expected or imagined. This belief allows solution-focused therapists "to look for the light instead of cursing the darkness," which is sometimes no mean feat when unhappy couples occupy our offices.

• *Evoking a positive his/herstory.* Asking about good times and happy memories helps partners restore a positive sense of themselves, each other, and their relationship. In his self-help book *Why Marriages Succeed or Fail . . . and How You Can Make Yours Last*, couple researcher John Gottman (1994, pp. 224–227) recommends "finding the glory in your marital story" and provides questions to help partners focus on early favorable impressions of each other, identify ways they have overcome problems and made successful transitions, and highlight positive aspects of their marriage.

• *Giving information, education and advice, and building skills.* This is a particularly "slippery slope," since we don't want to interfere with a couple's own solution development. The "prime directive" of solution-focused therapy—that clients' goals and resources be respected—encourages collaboration and purposeful intervention, but does not encourage a "strategic" ploy of using techniques to manipulate or "do" something to the clients, even if it is intended for their own good. However, while respecting clients' capacities and adhering to Erickson's idea (1980, p. 540—see Note 1) that we may not know what's best, I find that particularly when we are in a therapist–couple *customer* relationship, couples often benefit from and appreciate receiving information about ways they may be able to improve their communication, their problem solving, their sex lives, their parenting, and so on. Invitation, not imposition, is paramount ("Would you be interested in . . ." rather than "You ought to . . ."), but not providing new ideas and perspectives when asked and appropriate may unnecessarily constrain clients to working *only* with what they already have. Such a restriction can result in their attempted solution becoming a more-of-the-same repetition of the problem (see Fraser, 1998). There is nothing in the theory or technique of solution-focused therapy that would contravene, say, addressing clients' depression or lack of relationship skills, especially if doing so would be likely to help them toward their therapy goal. Similarly, adjunctive psychopharmacology may sometimes support clients' self-empowerment by relieving suffering and allowing them to better participate

by "restoring restorying" capacities (Hoyt, 2000, p. 74).

Examination of various effective brief therapies, including solution-focused intervention with couples, suggests that they all share certain basic characteristics (Budman, Hoyt, & Friedman, 1992; see also Hoyt, in press):

• Rapid and positive alliance.
• Focus on specific, achievable goals.
• Clear definition of client and therapist responsibilities and activities.
• Emphasis on client strengths and competencies with an expectation of change ("After the miracle . . . when things are better").
• Assistance for the clients to move toward new perceptions and behaviors.
• Here-and-now (and next) orientation.
• Time sensitivity, making the most of each session with the possibility of intermittent return as needed.

THEORETICAL UNDERSTANDINGS (CURATIVE FACTORS/MECHANISMS OF CHANGE)

> Not invisible but unnoticed, Watson. You did not know where to look, and so you missed all that was important.
> —SHERLOCK HOLMES (Arthur Conan Doyle; quoted in Kendrick, 2000, p. 68)

Solution-focused therapy does not conceive of the therapeutic endeavor in terms of "curative factors" (which would imply the medical model of "disease" and "cure") nor in terms of "mechanisms of change" (which would imply an "objectivist" or "cause-and-effect" concept). Rather, solution-focused therapy emphasizes the human, interactional achievement of meaning-making. How we look influences what we see, and what we see influences what we do—around and around. Changes in perception lead to changes in behavior (and vice versa). This happens through language:

> As the client[s] and therapist talk more and more about the solution they want to construct together, they come to believe in the truth or reality of what they are talking about. This is the way language works, naturally. (Berg & de Shazer, 1993, p. 9)

In his book *Becoming Miracle Workers: Language and Meaning in Brief Therapy*, Gale Miller (1997, p. 183) elaborates:

Solution-focused therapists . . . use their questions to construct mutually satisfactory conversations with clients. The questions are not designed to elicit information about worlds outside ongoing therapy conversations, but to elicit information in building new stories about clients' lives. Within solution-focused brief therapy discourse, then, all questions are constructive. They are designed to define goals and to construct solutions that solution-focused therapists assume are already present in clients' lives.

As noted at the beginning of this chapter, solution-focused therapy is a "post-structural revision" (de Shazer & Berg, 1992; see also Riikonen & Smith, 1997); it is an antipathologizing, utilitarian, "postmodern" view that emphasizes the use of language (or "conversation") in the social construction of reality. How we make sense of our worlds—the stories we tell ourselves and each other—does much to determine what we experience, our actions, and our destinies. When clients need a better story, they often come to therapy.

As I have described in *Some Stories Are Better Than Others*:

What makes some stories better than others? Ultimately, of course, the answer must come from each individual freely, lest we impose our own values or beliefs. In general terms, stories involve a plot in which characters have experiences and employ imagination to resolve problems over time. . . . From this perspective, therapy can be understood as the purposeful development of a more functional story; "better" stories are those that bring more of what is desired and less of what is not desired. . . .

Aesthetics, effects, and ethics are all important. We like stories that are well told; that are vivid and eloquent; that involve the generation and resolution of some tension; that see the protagonist[s] emerge successfully, perhaps even triumphantly. A "good" story does more than merely relate "facts"; a "good" story invigorates. (Hoyt, 2000, pp. 19–22)

Some of the implications of "storying" for therapy with couples are elaborated by Phillip Ziegler and Tobey Hiller (2001) in their book *Recreating Partnership: A Solution-Oriented, Collaborative Approach to Couples Therapy* (see also Atwood, 1993, 1997; Sternberg, 1998):

It is a central tenet of our work that all couples live together, interact, and view each other and their relationship through the lenses of certain narratives—narratives that are either relationship supportive or

destructive. These stories, some personal and private, others co-authored and shared by the partners, explain and give meaning to past events, shape each partner's perceptions of ongoing encounters and support their expectations about the future. Whatever their specific content, however long they have been influencing the partners' perceptions and interactions, certain stories, in the case of distressed couples, have woven themselves together into narratives destructive to the relationship—these constructs we call the *bad story* narrative. These *bad stories* have led to an ongoing and regenerating perception and experience of events on the part of the couple that result in an increasing loss of a sense of partnership. The couple no longer views itself as a team through good times and bad, a unit working together for the common good. People in this situation are becoming less and less able to draw upon what we call a couple's shared *good story* narrative. This is a co-authored story running both into the past and into the future which, in distinction to the effects of the *bad story* narrative, keeps good will and feelings of love alive even during times of trouble and struggle. This *good story* is, in general, one in which a couple views itself as uniquely lucky to be together, with a past pleasing to dwell on and a future full of hope and promise. Attention to the function of the *good story/bad story* narratives in couples' lives is very important in the therapeutic endeavor. (emphasis in original)

The solution-focused approach was developed inductively, by noticing what happened that preceded clients declaring their problems solved, and it is a tenet of solution-focused therapy that it is not necessary to know *why* (or even *how*) something works in order to be effective:

For an intervention to successfully *fit*, it is not necessary to have detailed knowledge of the complaint. It is not necessary even to be able to construct with any rigor how the trouble is maintained in order to prompt solution. . . . *any* really different behavior in a problematic situation can be enough to prompt solution and give the client the satisfaction he seeks from therapy. (de Shazer, 1985, p. 7; emphasis in original)

Still, it is interesting to speculate, and a good theory (like a good story) may point the way to something useful. Solution-focused couple therapy endeavors to help partners construct self-fulfilling ("good story") realities (Hoyt & Berg, 1998)—that is, views of themselves, each other, and their relationship that will bring both partners more of what they want. Solution-focused therapists attend to working *with* clients to identify and amplify the clients' goals and their perceptions of their abilities to achieve those goals. Entire stories need not be rewritten ("re-authored"), however, since clients can often "take the ball and run" once they are "unstuck."

Clients in solution-focused therapy are assisted to develop new awarenesses—"insights" not of buried pains and sorrows, but of underappreciated, overlooked, perhaps forgotten hopes, skills, and resources. The focus is on enhancing "*solution sight*":

> This process of solution development can be summed up as helping an unrecognized difference become a difference that makes a difference. (de Shazer, 1988, p. 10)[7]

Clients are conceived as cooperative and competent, and behavior change is seen to flow naturally from changes in the partners' views and viewpoints. Stories and narratives are transformed more easily and clients cooperate (with the therapist and each other) and move forward more readily when they are assisted to develop solutions that embrace their preferred views of self and other (Eron & Lund, 1996; Sluzki, 1998). As Gottman (1994) has noted, marriages are most likely to fail not when there is conflict, but when there is a lack of conflict resolution—specifically, when there is a lack of what he calls *reparative gestures*, or when one (or both) partners frequently ignore the other's attempts to repair whatever hurts have happened when conflicts have occurred. Gottman and Silver (1999, pp. 63–64) also highlight the importance of what they term a *fondness and admiration system*; the therapist needs to help the couple "unearth those positive feelings even more and put them to work to save their marriage." By focusing on solutions and exceptions to the problem, solution-focused therapy emphasizes these repairs and positive elements, and avoids iatrogenesis.[8]

Solution-focused therapy is prospective, not retrospective. There is usually a "future focus," with the therapist drawing attention toward what the clients will be doing differently when they have achieved a desired outcome or solution. Questions are designed to evoke a self-fulfilling map of the future (Lang & McAdam, 1997; Penn, 1985; Tomm, 1987). The language presupposes change ("After the miracle . . ."), the focus being on what *will* be different when the solution is achieved. Indeed, the language is sometimes hypnotic—col-

lapsing time, conflating present with future. As a picture of a positive future develops (or a positive past is reevoked), the partners begin to see themselves differently, and they respond to what they see. They begin living in the solution, not the problem. Once this "virtuous cycle" gets going, the couple is "unstuck" and moving toward where the partners want to go.

TREATMENT APPLICABILITY

There is nothing inherent to solution-focused therapy that would preclude working with any particular problem or group. Indeed, the strong emphasis on identifying and working with clients' own goals, motivations, language, and theories of change makes the approach widely applicable. Solution-focused therapy considers each person, each couple, and each case as unique and potentially cooperative. As Evan George, Chris Iveson and Harvey Ratner (1999, pp. 22–23) write in *Problem to Solution*,

> Like de Shazer, in recent years we have adopted the assumption that *all* clients are motivated for *something*. What we assume is that if, under any circumstances, a client has agreed to speak with us then they are doing so for a good reason, and one connected with our professional role. If we believe otherwise then we are acting on an assumption about the client which is potentially offensive: that they do things without a good reason. Not a good start to what should be a working relationship! (emphasis in original)

Clients who are too psychiatrically impaired to participate in talking therapy would not be expected to do well in solution-focused or any other approach. Clients with so-called "chronic and persistent severe psychiatric illness" may find benefit, however, in that solution-focused therapy works in the here-and-now (and next) toward achievable goals, rather than getting bogged down by long psychiatric histories (see Kreider, 1998; Rowen & O'Hanlon, 1999). Mandated clients—who usually arrive as visitors or complainants—can be productively engaged if a goal can be identified that appeals to the clients. Situations involving severe sociopathy and/or domestic violence may require partners to be seen separately until safety can be assured (see Johnson & Goldman, 1996; Lipchik & Kubicki, 1996; Uken & Sebold, 1996; Ziegler & Hiller, 2002).

CASE ILLUSTRATION[9]

> Hey, Dad—that's good! Instead of letting them
> fight, she's getting them to talk about ways
> they could be happier!
> —ALEXANDER HOYT (then age 7), after watching
> a videotape of Insoo Berg (1994b)
> working with a couple (quoted in
> Hoyt & Berg, 1998, p. 228)

Keeping in mind that a case report is a gloss, a
few brushstrokes that can only suggest (or obscure),
I will attempt to summarize or sketch some of what
characterized the "solution-focused" nature of the
therapy with a particular couple. It is important to
realize, particularly in the spirit of the poststructural,
postmodern perspective informing the work to be
reported, how little (including tone, timing, and
nonverbal communication) can actually be conveyed through a single case presentation. Restraints
of space only allow a few excerpts.

From Session 1

I had not had a chance to call the couple. The
receptionist's intake appointment note gave the
clients' names (Frank and Regina), indicated that
he was 29 and she was 30 years old, and simply
read "Pregnant—not getting along." When I went
to the waiting room, I introduced myself, and we
walked the few steps into my office. Once seated,
I remarked, "Welcome. The purpose of our meeting is briefly to work together to find a solution to
whatever brings you here today. What's up?"

The couple looked at me, then at each other.
Finally, Frank spoke: "Why don't you tell him? It
was your idea to come here."

Regina paused, then launched: "I'm tired of
this crap! Like I told him (*rolling her eyes toward
Frank*), if it doesn't get better, I'm through. I've
raised my 13-year-old daughter by myself, and I can
raise this one, too." She gestured toward her belly.
"I'm almost 4 months pregnant—we had talked
about having a baby, but it wasn't exactly planned.
We've known each other for a couple of years, and
have been been together for around 7 months. At
first it was OK, but now I'm pregnant, and the
last 3 or 4 months it seems like all we do is fight.
I don't need this! Either things are going to get
better, or else! It's Frank's baby and I would never
deny him seeing the child, but if he's not going to
change his attitude and get off his ass and help,
then he can just forget it!"

"Everything's all my fault, huh?"

"I get mad, too, but I'm just tired of all this
fighting. We never seem to have a good time, or
even just get along. And we're barely able to make
ends meet. I was making more money than Frank,
and I'm on disability now [due to a work injury],
and I'm not sure I'll even be able to go back to
work before I'm supposed to go out for maternity
leave. And when he comes home, the first thing
he does when he walks in is ask me when dinner
will be ready! There's no 'How was your day?' or
'I love you,' just 'Where's the food?'"

"It's always about me, isn't it? How about *your*
attitude?" Frank responded.

The bickering continued for a couple of minutes. Finally, I got a word in edgewise: "Wait a
minute! You came here because you want things
to be better, don't you?" They nodded affirmatively.
"That's why you're here. You used to get along,
so you know *how* to—it seems you came here because you want some help figuring out how to get
back to being happy, right?"

"Well, yeah . . ."

"Then let me ask you, each of you—and don't
get into an argument over this—on a scale of 1 to
10, how would you say your relationship is now,
where 1 is 'Horrible—it sucks' and 10 is 'Great—
couldn't be better'?"

"A 2."

"Yeah, like that—a 2."

"OK. That gives us some room to work. Without getting into complaining, what would it take for
you to think things have moved up to a 3, or even
a 4? What will each of you, and the other person,
be doing differently when things are getting better?"

"I don't know."

"I don't know either."

"Oh. OK. Let me ask you this: Suppose tonight, while you're sleeping, a miracle happens . . .
and the problems that brought you here are solved!
But you're sleeping, so you don't know it . . . until you wake up. Tomorrow, when you wake up,
what would be some of the things you'd notice that
would tell you that, 'Hey, things are better?'"

Regina laughed, and then Frank laughed.
They then sat there, looking dumbfounded, then
laughed again together. Regina spoke first: "We'd
be getting along, not hassling."

"Yeah, we'd talk, and she wouldn't get so mad
at me."

Before the window of opportunity closed, I
quickly asked, "You'd be getting along—what will
you be saying and doing? How about you, Regina—
what would you be doing if you and Frank were

getting along? And you, Frank—how would you respond to Regina, and what would you be saying to build on the positive?"

Much of the ensuing discussion expanded this theme. With numerous questions being asked to elicit and elaborate details, Regina and Frank described their initial meeting and courtship, a fun vacation they had taken, and some hopes they shared for raising their child together. When they began to slip back toward arguing, I twice gently interrupted them and redirected the discussion toward their positive stories. With some additional prompting ("When was the last time you got along OK, even for a few minutes?"), they also identified some more recent moments (albeit lately more rare than common) when they had bits of what they desired. Again, numerous questions expanded those "exceptions." They began to see each other more beneficently, slowly shifting figure and ground, moving from problem to solution. Drawing upon both their recall of happier times in the past and their imagination of a positive future, they seemed to be discovering and remembering—and to begin using—important relationship skills they already knew.

As the session drew to a close, I asked whether the meeting had been helpful, and if so, in what ways. They both remarked that it helped to talk about things without arguing, and to keep some perspective and to be reminded about how to get along. I complimented them for making the appointment to come in, connotating it as "an indication of your caring for each other and your both being committed to making a happy home for your child."

I then asked whether they'd like to make another appointment. They accepted for 2 weeks hence. Finally, I offered a homework suggestion: "You've come up with some very good ideas about how to make things better. Between now and when we meet in a couple of weeks—and even after that—please pay attention and notice whatever you do and whatever the other person does to make things better. It may not be perfect, but try to keep track of whatever positives you or your partner do or attempt to do. When we meet, I'll ask you about what you noticed."

From Session 2

It wasn't particularly sunny out, but Frank was wearing sunglasses—and didn't remove them—when he and Regina reentered my office.

I asked them, "Well, how'd the 2 weeks go? What did you notice about things getting better?"

"Ask her" was Frank's reply.

"Things were really good for a couple of days," said Regina. "We were talking and not fighting and were actually having a good time."

"That sounds like a positive—how'd you do that?"

"I was careful about what I said, and Frank was doing better, too. Then we got into an argument."

"What happened?"

"Frank came home late, later than he said he would, and . . ."

"Right. So it's my fault again."

Recognizing that we weren't headed where the clients wanted to go, I intervened: "Oops! I made a mistake. Sorry."

"Huh?"

"Well, you know, if you go to a lot of counselors, they sit there and try to figure out what you're doing wrong, and then they kind of bust you and point out what you should do. Sometimes it helps, but a lot of times people already know what they need to do. I used to do that, but I got tired of it. Now I've got a great job—I sit here and try to help you figure out what you're doing right, and then try to get you to do more of it. I think it works better, and I don't have to spend all day battling and fighting with people who just want to get along and be happier."

Frank removed his sunglasses and put them on the side table. He then spoke: "You know, after we had the fight, Regina called me the next day at work and apologized. I know I was wrong for being late, but it really hurt my feelings the way she yelled at me."

"She called and apologized?"

"Yeah. I really appreciated it, too."

"You called?"

"Yeah, I called him at work the next afternoon. I was still annoyed about his being late, but I knew I had gone too far. I said some things that were out of line. I don't want to be a jerk."

"You really care about Frank and about the relationship, don't you?"

"Yeah. Sometimes it might not seem like it, the way I complain about him, but he's really not such a bad guy."

"You love him."

"Yes."

"What are some of the positives you appreciate about him?"

"He's actually really kind. He puts up with a lot from me. He's also got a good sense of humor, and I know he's trying to make things better."

"How do you know that?"

"I can see how he's trying to be more responsible. And he made me breakfast Sunday morning. And he's been helping out more around the house."

"Frank, did you know Regina was appreciating what you've been doing?"

"Well, kind of, I guess."

"Had she told you?"

"No, not really."

This got us into discussing how they communicated their needs and appreciation to each other. Frank noted, "We could use some help there," and Regina agreed. Frank then acknowledged that "Sometimes my feelings get hurt, and then I withdraw and she gets even madder." I asked their ideas about how to handle tense situations better ("You know yourselves and each other better than I ever could—what do you think would work for the two of you?"). Regina and Frank both suggested alternatives, and I also proffered a few ideas. We discussed back and forth what would make sense that they would be willing to try, and they playfully rehearsed a couple of options.

As the hour again drew toward a close, I complimented them and offered a suggestion: "You've been doing a lot of good work. Things may not go perfectly, of course, so keep track of the things that are happening that you want to continue to happen." I asked when they would like another appointment. They chose 3 weeks, saying that this would allow them time to practice.

From Session 3

The couple reported that Regina had not been able to return to work, and Frank virtually beamed as Regina expressed appreciation for his increased help around the house and for his offering to work extra hours. Frank had also been helping more with Regina's daughter, working with her on a homework assignment and driving her to cheerleading practice. They each rated their relationship as "between a 5 and a 6."

Everything, however, had not been smooth sailing. As they talked about preparing for the baby, they described a tense moment that had erupted into an argument when they were out buying items for the baby's room. Regina had been frustrated, she said, that Frank had not been more enthusiastic about shopping; in turn, Frank described feeling awkward with "baby stuff" and complained about not getting much recognition for having to make endless compromises and adjustments to their new

(and impending) lifestyle as parents. Frank's assistance with Regina's daughter was noted and discussed as an example of his wanting to be helpful. A long discussion then ensued about the changes required by family life, including my sharing a couple of brief stories about ways I had struggled to come to grips with parenting when my son had been born 13 years prior. Even during these "normalizing" self-disclosures, I was very careful to keep the focus (directly and indirectly) on the clients' goals and challenges. I asked Frank and Regina questions ("What are some examples of ways you have compromised successfully?" "How did you make up?" "What did you do differently during those times you coped constructively with your frustration?") that would highlight whatever they were doing in the direction they wanted to go.

To help keep them pointed toward their goal of improved teamwork, at the end of the session I asked them to notice and keep track of whatever either of them did that showed they were working together. I also suggested that they each pick, and invite the other to go on, one fun outing. They agreed to do so, and scheduled another appointment for 3 weeks later.

From Session 4

They reported having had "the best 3 weeks we've had since Regina got pregnant." I mostly listened ("How'd you solve that? Wow!") and asked for details—which they gladly supplied—that further "thickened" the account of their functioning well together. I asked how they would rate their relationship. Regina said "9" and Frank said "10"; they looked at each other and laughed, rather than arguing about the 1-point difference. Alluding to the baby, I commented, "Since you're going to be together for at least the next couple of decades, it's nice to see that you're working on the "Frank *and* Regina Story" rather than the "Frank *or* Regina Story." I again congratulated them on their good "teamwork." We scheduled a follow-up for 3 weeks later. They left smiling and actually holding hands.

From Session 5

Regina complained about feeling tired; Frank was also tired from working overtime, but expressed sympathy and support. They indicated that they had continued to do well and had thought about canceling the session, but felt it would be good to come in to review their progress and talk about what they needed to do to keep it going. We talked at length about what they had learned and accomplished. I complimented them for their commitment and foresight, and also noted, "There's sure to be extra stress ahead with the baby coming." We discussed how to apply what they had achieved as a couple to the challenges of becoming new parents while also raising Regina's daughter. I inquired, "Would it be OK if I ask you both a hard question?"

"Sure—go for it."

"I'm glad that you're doing so well and that you're working as partners, but imagine a time in a few months, after the baby's born, and you're both tired and stressed, and your daughter is being a difficult teenager. How are you going to remember then to work as a team?"

"I'm sure that will happen."

"Yeah."

"So how are you going to deal with it? It could be easy to get back into fighting a lot."

"We'll have to remember why we're together."

"How will you do that?"

"We know we'll have difficulties, but we also know that we can solve our problems."

"Now when we start to have an argument, we stop and remember that we're 'Frank *and* Regina,' and that helps us not get into 'Me *versus* You.' And sometimes we talk about what we've talked about in here—how to use what you called 'solution talk,' how we used to fight, and how we know how to treat each other respectfully, and how to take a time out if we need it, and how to listen to each other, and stuff like that."

Near the end of the session, I asked whether they thought we should make another appointment. "Not now, but we'll be sure to call if we need one."[10] I wished them well and asked whether it would be OK for me to write up their story and put it in a book chapter. "Sure," they said, "but only if you promise to tell people that we did most of the work, not you."

CODA

> When the night has been too lonely and the
>   road has been too long
> And you think that love is only for the lucky
>   and the strong
> Just remember in the winter far beneath the
>   bitter snows
> Lies the seed that with the sun's love, in the
>   spring, becomes the rose.
> —AMANDA MCBROOM (1979, from "The Rose")

Solution-focused therapy is a constructivist, collaborative, postmodern, competency-based, future-oriented approach. The basic premise is deceptively simple: *Increase what works; decrease what doesn't work.* What are the "exceptions" to the problem? What are clients doing differently at those times when they are not anxious or depressed or quarreling? What has worked before? What strengths can the clients apply? What would be a useful solution? How to construct it?

Behind these apparently simple questions is a profound paradigmatic shift: competencies, not dysfunctions, are the focus; the quest is to access latent capacities, not latent conflicts. The orientation is toward the future, with the guiding belief that with skillful facilitation, people usually have within themselves the resources necessary to achieve their goals. Without obviating the idea of a physical universe, solution-focused therapy operates from the radical assumption that clients' experience of psychological problems is part and parcel of their language-based social construction of reality. As I heard my haiku muse whisper (Hoyt, 2000, p. 47),

> Focusing language
> On solutions, not problems
> Miracles happen.

Therapeutic intervention is therefore construed as a process of assisting clients to play better "language games." Although new information and relationship skills training may be provided—if they support the clients' worldviews and movement toward their desired goals—solution-focused therapists primarily endeavor to help clients envision and realize solutions by assiduously calling attention to clients' strengths, resources, past successes, and ways of looking.

As therapists, we are actively involved—whether we realize it or not—in helping clients construe a different way of looking at themselves, their partners, their situations, and their interactions. How we look influences what we see, and what we see influences what we do—and around and around the process goes, recursively. Even if one is unaware of it, one cannot *not* have an epistemology (Bateson, 1972, 1979). We all choose what we use:

Dear Reader,

Suppose tonight, while you're sleeping, a miracle happens! You're asleep, of course, and you don't immediately know it has happened. But tomorrow, while seeing a couple in your office, you begin to notice some things about your clients you haven't noticed or thought much about before. You can still see all the things that your training has allowed you to see, but as you look you begin to see some previously overlooked qualities: perhaps a love or a hope or a dream that somehow manages to survive, maybe some almost-forgotten skill or ability, possibly a quirky interest or sense of humor, something. What might you see? What does the couple see that you don't? What does the couple think would help? What might happen if that could be used therapeutically? What difference might it make?

ACKNOWLEDGMENTS

My appreciation goes to Steve de Shazer and Insoo Kim Berg for their many contributions, including permission to reproduce Figures 12.1 (from de Shazer, 1988) and 12.2 (from de Shazer, 1985), and to quote videotape interview excerpts from Berg (1994b). Additional thanks to the anonymous couple described in the case illustration; to The Guilford Press for permission to use quotations from two published interviews (Hoyt, 1994b, 1996b) with Steve de Shazer, as well as the material in Table 12.1 from Hoyt (1994d) and excerpts from Hoyt and Berg (1998); to W. W. Norton and Company, Inc., for permission to reprint excerpts and Figures 12.1 and 12.2 from de Shazer (1985, 1988, 1991a); to Phillip Ziegler for permission to adapt handout materials from Ziegler (2000); and to Warner Brothers Publications U.S. and Warner-Tamerlane Publishing Corporation for permission to use the excerpt from the Amanda McBroom song "The Rose." I am grateful to Phillip Ziegler, Tobey Hiller, Harvey Ratner, and Alan Gurman for their helpful comments regarding earlier drafts of this chapter. The work contained herein is dedicated to my wife, Jennifer Lillard.

NOTES

1. Although the pressures of managed care for greater efficiency and cost containment (see Hoyt, 1995, 2000, 2001) have contributed to the increased popularity of solution-focused and other time-sensitive approaches, de Shazer (quoted in Short, 1997, p. 18, emphasis in original) has made his position clear: "We are *not* a response to managed care. We've been doing brief therapy for 30 years. We developed this a long time before managed care was even somebody's bad idea."

2. Erickson wrote: "Patients have problems because their conscious programming has too severely limited their capacities. The solution is to help them break through the limitations of their conscious attitudes to free their unconscious potential for problem solving" (Erickson, Rossi, & Rossi, 1976, p. 18); and

"The fullest possible utilization of the functional capacities and abilities and the experiential and acquisitional learnings of the patient . . . should take precedence over the teaching of new ways in living which are developed from the therapist's possibly incomplete understanding of what may be right and serviceable to the individual concerned" (Erickson, 1980, p. 540).

3. In their book *The Miracle Method*, Scott Miller and Insoo Berg (1995, p. 37) recount the origins of the "Miracle Question," which has come to be a signature characteristic of solution-focused therapy:

> A woman called us [in 1984] for an appointment demanding that she be seen that day because it was an emergency. She began sobbing as she told the receptionist how her husband's drinking was out of control and that he had even been violent toward her. As [the client] entered the therapist's office and began to sit down, she said, "My problem is so serious that it would take a *miracle* to solve it!" . . . The therapist simply followed the client's lead, and said, "Well . . . suppose one happened?" Immediately, the client began to describe what she wanted to be different about the situation that was troubling her. As she described what she wanted in more detail, a smile began to creep into her face and the tone of her voice became more hopeful. . . . As she stood to leave the office, she told the therapist that she was feeling "much better." . . . . The following week she returned and reported that she had turned that feeling into some small but significant changes in her life and her marriage.

4. For some group therapy applications, see Metcalf (1998) and Nelson and Kelly (2001).

5. Even if a couple as a unit has not been mandated to treatment by the legal system, one partner may, in effect, be under mandate if he/she has come only under the insistence or threat of the other. With clients who are not there voluntarily, it is especially important to develop goals that appeal to each client (see Friedman, 1993a; Rosenberg, 2000; Tohn & Oshlag, 1996). "What would it take to get your partner off your back?" may not sound very elegant, but for some clients it may be a more engaging and effective starting place than "How would you like to improve your marriage?" or "Let's look at ways you and your partner can enhance your relationship."

6. "More of the same" does not make a change. Even a small pattern deviation can get things moving, as Bill O'Hanlon (1999) suggests in the title of his book, *Do One Thing Different*. In a chapter on "solution-oriented relationships," O'Hanlon (1999, pp. 157–162) discusses "Nine Methods for Resolving Relationship Crises":

   1. Change Your Usual Conflict Patterns or Style
   2. Do a 180: Change Your Usual Pursuer–Distancer Pattern
   3. Catch Your Partner Doing Something Right

4. Unpack Vague, Blaming, and Loaded Words; Instead, Use Action Talk
5. Change Your Complaints into "Action Requests"
6. Make a Specific Plan for Change
7. Focus on How You (Not Your Partner) Can Change, and Take Responsibility for Making That Change
8. Blow Your Partner's Stereotype of You
9. Compassionate Listening

7. Hence the title of de Shazer's (1991a) book: *Putting Difference to Work.*

8. See also Glasser and Glasser (2000, p. 15) regarding the importance of avoiding the "Seven Deadly Habits" of criticizing, blaming, complaining, nagging, threatening, punishing, and bribing. For a more tongue-in-cheek view that uses satire and absurdity to emphasize the value of solution language, see Greenberg and O'Malley's (1983) *How to Avoid Love and Marriage.*

9. Additional case examples of couple therapy based on solution-focused or solution-oriented principles can be found in Berg (1994b), Beyebach and Morejon (1999), de Shazer (1982, 1985, 1991a, 1994a), de Shazer and Berg (1985), Friedman (1992, 1993b, 1996, 1997), Friedman and Lipchik (1999), Gale and Newfield (1992), George et al. (1999), Hoyt and Berg (1998), Hudson and O'Hanlon (1991), Norum (2000), O'Hanlon and Hudson (1994), Johnson and Goldman (1996), Lethem (1994), Lipchik and Kubicki (1996), Nunnally (1993), Quick (1996), Walter and Peller (1988), Weiner-Davis (1992), Ziegler (1998), and Ziegler and Hiller (2001, 2002).

10. As Cummings and Sayama (1995; see also Hoyt, 1995) have written, "brief, intermittent psychotherapy throughout the life cycle" is often precipitated by developmental challenges.

REFERENCES

Adams, J. F., Piercy, F. P., & Jurich, J. A. (1991). Effects of solution-focused therapy's "formula first session task" on compliance and outcome in family therapy. *Journal of Marital and Family Therapy, 17,* 277–290.

Anderson, H. (1997). *Conversation, language and possibilities: A postmodern approach to therapy.* New York: Basic Books.

Anderson, H., & Goolishian, H. A. (1992). The client is the expert: A not-knowing approach to therapy. In S. McNamee & K. J. Gergen (Eds.), *Therapy as social construction* (pp. 25–39). Newbury Park, CA: Sage.

Atwood, J. D. (1993). Social constructionist couple therapy. *The Family Journal: Counseling and Therapy for Couples and Families, 1,* 116–130.

Atwood, J. D. (1997). Social construction theory and therapy. In J. D. Atwood (Ed.), *Challenging family therapy situations: Perspectives in social construction* (pp. 1–40). New York: Springer.

Bateson, G. (1972). *Steps to an ecology of mind.* New York: Ballantine.

Bateson, G. (1979). *Mind and nature: A necessary unity.* New York: Dutton.

Berendt, J. (1994). *Midnight in the garden of good and evil.* New York: Random House.

Berg, I. K. (1989). Of visitors, complainants, and customers. *Family Therapy Networker, 13*(1), 27.

Berg, I. K. (1994a). *Family-based services: A solution-focused approach.* New York: Norton.

Berg, I. K. (1994b). *Irreconcilable differences: A solution-focused approach to marital therapy* [Videotape]. New York: Norton.

Berg, I. K. (1994c). *So what else is better? Solutions for substance abuse* [Videotape] Milwaukee, WI: Brief Family Therapy Center.

Berg, I. K., & de Shazer, S. (1993). Making numbers talk: Language in therapy. In S. Friedman (Ed.), *The new language of change: Constructive collaboration in psychotherapy* (pp. 5–24). New York: Guilford Press.

Berg, I. K., & Dolan, Y. D. (2000). *Tales of solutions: A collection of hope-inspiring stories.* New York: Norton.

Berg, I. K., & Kelly, S. (2000). *Building solutions in child protective services.* New York: Norton.

Berg, I. K., & Miller, S. D. (1992). *Working with the problem drinker: A solution-focused approach.* New York: Norton.

Berg, I. K., & Reuss, N. H. (1997). *Solutions step by step: A substance abuse treatment manual.* New York: Norton.

Beyebach, M., & Morejon, A. R. (1999). Some thoughts on integration in solution-focused therapy. *Journal of Systemic Therapies, 18*(1), 24–42.

Bonjean, M. J. (1997). Solution-focused brief therapy with aging families. In T. D. Hargrave & S. M. Hanna (Eds.), *The aging family: New visions in theory, practice, and reality* (pp. 81–100). New York: Brunner/Mazel.

Budman, S. H., Hoyt, M. F., & Friedman, S. (Eds.). (1992). *The first session in brief therapy.* New York: Guilford Press.

Cade, B., & O'Hanlon, W. H. (1993). *A brief guide to brief therapy.* New York: Norton.

Carlson, J. (2000). How to prevent relapse: Treatment strategies for long-term change. *Family Therapy Networker, 24*(5), 23, 84.

Cummings, N. A., & Sayama, M. (1995). *Focused psychotherapy: A casebook of brief, intermittent psychotherapy throughout the life cycle.* New York: Brunner/Mazel.

De Jong, P., & Berg, I. K. (1998). *Interviewing for solutions.* Pacific Grove, CA: Brooks/Cole.

De Jong, P., & Hopwood, L. E. (1996). Outcome research on treatment conducted at the Brief Family Therapy Center, 1992–1993. In S. D. Miller, M. A. Hubble, & B. L. Duncan (Eds.), *Handbook of solution-focused brief therapy* (pp. 272–298). San Francisco: Jossey-Bass.

de Shazer, S. (1982). *Patterns of brief family therapy.* New York: Guilford Press.

de Shazer, S. (1984). The death of resistance. *Family Process, 23,* 79–93.

de Shazer, S. (1985). *Keys to solution in brief therapy.* New York: Norton.

de Shazer, S. (1988). *Clues: Investigating solutions in brief therapy.* New York: Norton.

de Shazer, S. (1991a). *Putting difference to work.* New York: Norton.

de Shazer, S. (1991b). Foreword. In Y. M. Dolan, *Resolving sexual abuse: Solution-focused therapy and Erickson-*

ian hypnosis for adult survivors (pp. ix–x). New York: Norton.

de Shazer, S. (1993a). Creative misunderstanding: There is no escape from language. In S. G. Gilligan & R. Price (Eds.), Therapeutic conversations (pp. 81–90). New York: Norton.

de Shazer, S. (1993b). Commentary: de Shazer and White: Vive la différence. In S. G. Gilligan & R. Price (Eds.), Therapeutic conversations (pp. 112–120). New York: Norton.

de Shazer, S. (1994a). Words were originally magic. New York: Norton.

de Shazer, S. (1994b). Essential, non-essential: Vive la différence. In J. K. Zeig (Ed.), Ericksonian methods: The essence of the story (pp. 240–253). New York: Brunner/Mazel.

de Shazer, S., & Berg, I. K. (1985). A part is not apart: Working with only one of the partners present. In A. S. Gurman (Ed.), Casebook of marital therapy (pp. 97–110). New York: Guilford Press.

de Shazer, S., & Berg, I. K. (1992). Doing therapy: A post-structural re-vision. Journal of Marital and Family Therapy, 18, 71–81.

de Shazer, S., & Berg, I. K. (1997). "What works?": Remarks on research aspects of solution-focused brief therapy. Journal of Family Therapy, 19, 121–124.

de Shazer, S., Berg, I. K., Lipchik, E., Nunnally, E., Molnar, A., Gingerich, W., & Weiner-Davis, M. (1986). Brief therapy: Focused solution development. Family Process, 25, 207–227.

de Shazer, S., & Molnar, A. (1984). Four useful interventions in brief family therapy. Journal of Marital and Family Therapy, 10(3), 297–304.

Dermer, S. B., Hemesath, C. W., & Russell, C. S. (1998). A feminist critique of solution-focused therapy. American Journal of Family Therapy, 26(3), 239–250.

DiClemente, C. C. (1991). Motivational interviewing and the stages of change. In W. R. Miller & S. Rollnick, Motivational interviewing: Preparing people to change addictive behavior (pp. 191–202). New York: Guilford Press.

Dolan, Y. M. (1985). A path with a heart: Ericksonian utilization with resistant and chronic clients. New York: Brunner/Mazel.

Dolan, Y. M. (1991). Resolving sexual abuse: Solution-focused therapy and Ericksonian hypnosis for adult survivors. New York: Norton.

Duncan, B. L., Hubble, M. A., & Miller, S. D. (1997). Psychotherapy with "impossible" cases: The efficient treatment of therapy veterans. New York: Norton.

Duncan, B. L., Hubble, M. A., Miller, S. D., & Coleman, S. T. (1998). Escaping from the lost world of impossibility: Honoring clients' language, motivation, and theories of change. In M. F. Hoyt (Ed.), The handbook of constructive therapies (pp. 293–313). San Francisco: Jossey-Bass.

Duncan, B. L., & Miller, S. D. (2000). The heroic client: Doing client-directed, outcome-informed therapy. San Francisco: Jossey-Bass.

Efran, J. S., & Schenker, M. D. (1993). A potpourri of solutions: How new and different is solution-focused therapy? The Family Therapy Networker, 17, 71–74.

Erickson, M. H. (1980). Collected papers (Vol. 1). New York: Irvington.

Erickson, M. H., & Rossi, E. L. (1979). Hypnotherapy: An exploratory casebook. New York: Irvington.

Erickson, M. H., Rossi, E. L., & Rossi, S. I. (1976). Hyp-

notic realities: The induction of clinical hypnosis and forms of indirect suggestion. New York: Irvington.

Eron, J. B., & Lund, T. W. (1996). Narrative solutions in brief therapy. New York: Guilford Press.

Fisch, R., Weakland, J. H., & Segal, L. (1982). The tactics of change: Doing therapy briefly. San Francisco: Jossey-Bass.

Fish, J. M. (1997). Paradox for complainants: Strategic thoughts about solution-focused therapy. Journal of Systemic Therapies, 16(5), 266–273.

Fraser, J. S. (1998). Solution-focused therapy—As a problem. In W. Ray & S. de Shazer (Eds.), Evolving brief therapies: Essays in honor of John Weakland (pp. 178–194). Iowa City, IA: Geist & Russell.

Friedman, S. (1992). Constructing solutions (stories) in brief family therapy. In S. H. Budman, M. F. Hoyt, & S. Friedman (Eds.), The first session in brief therapy (pp. 282–305). New York: Guilford Press.

Friedman, S. (1993a). Does the miracle question always create miracles? Journal of Systemic Therapies, 12(1), 71–74.

Friedman, S. (1993b). Possibility therapy with couples: Constructing time-effective solutions. Journal of Family Psychotherapy, 4(4), 35–52.

Friedman, S. (1996). Couples therapy: Changing conversations. In H. Rosen & K. T. Kuehlwein (Eds.), Constructing realities: Meaning-making perspectives for psychotherapists (pp. 413–453). San Francisco: Jossey-Bass.

Friedman, S. (1997). Time-effective psychotherapy: Maximizing outcomes in an era of minimized resources. Boston: Allyn & Bacon.

Friedman, S., & Lipchik, E. (1999). A time-effective, solution-focused approach to couple therapy. In J. M. Donovan (Ed.), Short-term couple therapy (pp. 325–359). New York: Guilford Press.

Furman, B., & Ahola, T. (1992). Solution talk: Hosting therapeutic conversations. New York: Norton.

Gale, J., & Newfield, N. (1992). A conversation analysis of a solution-focused marital therapy session. Journal of Marital and Family Therapy, 18(2), 153–165.

George, E., Iveson, C., & Ratner, H. (1999). Problem to solution: Brief therapy with individuals and families (rev. ed.) London: Brief Therapy Press.

Glasser, W., & Glasser, C. (2000). Getting together and staying together: Solving the mystery of marriage. New York: HarperCollins.

Gottman, J. M. (1994). Why marriages succeed or fail . . . and how you can make yours last. New York: Simon & Schuster.

Gottman, J. M., & Silver, N. (1999). The seven principles for making marriage work. New York: Three Rivers Press/Random House.

Greenberg, D., & O'Malley, S. (1983). How to avoid love and marriage. New York: Freundlich Books/Schribner.

Hjerth, M. (1995, February). New developments in solution-focused therapy. Workshop presented in Salamanca, Spain.

Hopwood, L., & de Shazer, S. (1994). From here to there and who knows where: The continuing evolution of solution-focused brief therapy. In M. Elkaim (Ed.), Thérapies familiales: Les approches principaux (pp. 555–576). Paris: Editions de Seuil.

Hoyt, M. F. (Ed.). (1994a). Constructive therapies. New York: Guilford Press.

Hoyt, M. F. (1994b). On the importance of keeping it simple and taking the patient seriously: A conversation with Steve de Shazer and John Weakland. In M. F. Hoyt (Ed.), *Constructive therapies* (pp. 11–40). New York: Guilford Press. Reprinted in M. F. Hoyt, *Interviews with brief therapy experts* (pp. 1–33). Philadelphia: Brunner/Routledge, 2001.

Hoyt, M. F. (1994c). Single session solutions. In M. F. Hoyt (Ed.), *Constructive therapies* (pp. 140–159). New York: Guilford Press. Reprinted in M. F. Hoyt, *Brief Therapy and Managed Care: Readings for Contemporary Practice* (pp. 141–162). San Francisco: Jossey-Bass, 1995.

Hoyt, M. F. (1994d). Introduction: Competency-based future-oriented therapy. In M. F. Hoyt (Ed.), *Constructive therapies* (pp. 1–10). New York: Guilford Press.

Hoyt, M. F. (1995). *Brief therapy and managed care: Readings for contemporary practice.* San Francisco: Jossey-Bass.

Hoyt, M. F. (Ed.). (1996a). *Constructive therapies* (Vol. 2). New York: Guilford Press.

Hoyt, M. F. (1996b). Solution building and language games: A conversation with Steve de Shazer (and some after words with Insoo Kim Berg). In M. F. Hoyt (Ed.), *Constructive therapies* (Vol. 2, pp. 60–86). New York: Guilford Press. Reprinted in M. F. Hoyt, *Interviews with brief therapy experts* (pp. 158–183). Philadelphia: Brunner/Routledge, 2001.

Hoyt, M. F. (Ed.). (1998). *The handbook of constructive therapies.* San Francisco: Jossey-Bass.

Hoyt, M. F. (2000). *Some stories are better than others: Doing what works in brief therapy and managed care.* Philadelphia: Brunner/Mazel.

Hoyt, M. F. (2001). Getting unstuck: The squeaky wheel— Don't let managed care shortchange your clients. *Family Therapy Networker, 25*(1), 19–20.

Hoyt, M. F. (in press). Brief psychotherapies. In A. S. Gurman & S. B. Messer (Eds.), *Essential psychotherapies: Theory and practice.* New York: Guilford.

Hoyt, M. F., & Berg, I. K. (1998). Solution-focused couple therapy: Helping clients construct self-fulfilling realities. In F. M. Dattilio (Ed.), *Case studies in couple and family therapy* (pp. 203–232). New York: Guilford Press. Reprinted in M. F. Hoyt, *Some stories are better than others* (pp. 143–166). Philadelphia: Brunner/Mazel.

Hoyt, M. F., & Miller, S. D. (2000). Stage-appropriate change-oriented brief therapy strategies. In M. F. Hoyt (Ed.), *Some stories are better than others* (pp. 207–235). Philadelphia: Brunner/Mazel.

Hudson, P., & O'Hanlon, W. H. (1991). *Rewriting love stories: Brief marital therapy.* New York: Norton.

Johnson, C. E., & Goldman, J. (1996). Taking safety home: A solution-focused approach with domestic violence. In M. F. Hoyt (Ed.), *Constructive therapies* (Vol. 2, pp. 184–196). New York: Guilford Press.

Jordan, K., & Quinn, W.H. (1994). Session two outcome of the formula first session task in problem- and solution-focused approaches. *Journal of Family Therapy, 22,* 3–16.

Kendrick, S. (2000, January–February). Zen in the art of Sherlock Holmes. *Utne Reader,* pp. 65–69.

Kerr, L. (2001). An assessment of adaptability to feminist principles of solution-focused brief therapy as practiced by Insoo Kim Berg. *Journal of Systemic Therapies, 20*(3), 7–89.

King, E. (1998). Role of affect and emotional context in solution-focused therapy. *Journal of Systemic Therapies, 17*(2), 51–64.

Kreider, J. W. (1998). Solution-focused ideas for briefer therapy with longer-term clients. In M. F. Hoyt (Ed.), *The handbook of constructive therapies* (pp. 341–357). San Francisco: Jossey-Bass.

Lang, P., & McAdam, E. (1997). Narrative-ating: Future dreams in present living jottings on an honouring theme. *Human Systems: The Journal of Systemic Consultation and Management, 8*(1), 3–12.

Lazarus, A. A. (1995). Different types of eclecticism and integration: Let's be aware of the dangers. *Journal of Psychotherapy Integration, 5,* 27–39.

Lethem, J. (1994). *Moved to tears, moved to action: Solution focused brief therapy with women and children.* London: Brief Therapy Press.

Lipchik, E. (Ed.). (1987). *Interviewing.* Rockville, MD: Aspen.

Lipchik, E. (1993). "Both/and" solutions. In S. Friedman (Ed.), *The new language of change: Constructive collaboration in psychotherapy* (pp. 25–49). New York: Guilford Press.

Lipchik, E. (1994). The rush to be brief. *Family Therapy Networker, 18*(2), 34–39.

Lipchik, E. (1997). My story about solution-focused brief therapist/client relationships. *Journal of Systemic Therapies, 16*(2), 159–172.

Lipchik, E. (2002). *Beyond technique in solution-focused therapy: Working with emotions and the therapeutic relationship.* New York: Guilford.

Lipchik, E., & de Shazer, S. (1986). The purposeful interview. *Journal of Strategic and Systemic Therapies, 5,* 88–89.

Lipchik, E., & Kubicki, A. D. (1996). Solution-focused domestic violence views: Bridges toward a new reality in couples therapy. In S. D. Miller, M. A. Hubble, & B. L. Duncan (Eds.), *Handbook of solution-focused brief therapy* (pp. 65–98). San Francisco: Jossey-Bass.

McBroom, A. (1979). The rose. [Song on B. Midler album, *The rose*]. New York: Atlantic Records/Warner Communications Group.

McKeel, A. J. (1996). A clinician's guide to research on solution-focused brief therapy. In S. D. Miller, M. A. Hubble, & B. L. Duncan (Eds.), *Handbook of solution-focused brief therapy* (pp. 251–271). San Francisco: Jossey-Bass.

McNamee, S., & Gergen, K. J. (Eds.). (1992). *Therapy as social construction.* London: Sage.

Metcalf, L. (1998). *Solution-focused group therapy.* New York: The Free Press.

Miller, G. (1997). *Becoming miracle workers: Language and meaning in brief therapy.* Hawthorne, NY: Aldine de Gruyter.

Miller, G., & de Shazer, S. (1998). Have you heard the latest about . . . ? Solution-focused therapy as a rumor. *Family Process, 37,* 363–378.

Miller, G., & de Shazer, S. (2000). Emotions in solution-focused therapy: A re-examination. *Family Process, 39*(1), 5–23.

Miller, S. D. (1992). The symptoms of solution. *Journal of Strategic and Systemic Therapies, 11,* 1–11.

Miller, S. D. (1994). Some questions (not answers) for the brief treatment of people with drug and alcohol problems. In M. F. Hoyt (Ed.), *Constructive therapies* (pp. 92–110). New York: Guilford Press.

Miller, S. D., & Berg, I. K. (1995). *The miracle method.* New York: Norton.

Miller, S. D., & Duncan, B. L. (2000). Paradigm lost: From

model-driven to client-directed, outcome-informed clinical work. *Journal of Systemic Therapies, 19*(1), 20–34.

Miller, S. D., Duncan, B. L., & Hubble, M. A. (1997). *Escape from Babel: Toward a unifying language for psychotherapy practice.* New York: Norton.

Miller, S. D., Hubble, M. A., & Duncan, B. L. (Eds.). (1996). *Handbook of solution-focused brief therapy.* San Francisco: Jossey-Bass.

Miller, W. R., & Rollnick, S. (1991). *Motivational interviewing: Preparing people to change addictive behavior.* New York: Guilford Press.

Nau, D. S., & Shilts, L. (2000). When to use the miracle question: Clues from a qualitative study of four SFBT practitioners. *Journal of Systemic Therapies, 19*(1), 129–135.

Neimeyer, R. A. (1998). Cognitive therapy and the narrative trend: A bridge too far? *Journal of Cognitive Psychotherapy, 12,* 57–65.

Nelson, T. S., & Kelly, L. (2001). Solution-focused couples group. *Journal of Systemic Therapies, 20*(4), 47–66.

Norum, D. (2000). The family has the solution. *Journal of Systemic Therapies, 19*(1), 3–15.

Nunnally, E. (1993). Solution-focused therapy. In R. A. Wells & V. J. Giannetti (Eds.), *Casebook of the brief psychotherapies* (pp. 271–286). New York: Plenum Press.

Nylund, D., & Corsiglia, V. (1994). Becoming solution-~~focused~~ forced in brief therapy: Remembering something important we already knew. *Journal of Systemic Therapies, 13*(5), 5–12.

O'Hanlon, W. H. (1998). Possibility therapy: An inclusive, collaborative, solution-based model of psychotherapy. In M. F. Hoyt (Ed.), *The handbook of constructive therapies* (pp. 137–158). San Francisco: Jossey-Bass.

O'Hanlon, W. H. (1999). *Do one thing different: And other uncommonly sensible solutions to life's persistent problems.* New York: Morrow.

O'Hanlon, W. H., & Hudson, P. (1994). Coauthoring a love story: Solution-oriented marital therapy. In M. F. Hoyt (Ed.), *Constructive therapies* (pp. 160–188). New York: Guilford Press.

O'Hanlon, W. H., & Weiner-Davis, M. (1989). *In search of solutions: A new direction in psychotherapy.* New York: Norton.

Penn, P. (1985). Feed-forward: Future questions, future maps. *Family Process, 24,* 289–310.

Prochaska, J. O. (1999). How do people change and how can we change to help many more people? In M. A. Hubble, B. L. Duncan, & S. D. Miller (Eds.), *The heart and soul of change: What works in therapy* (pp. 227–255). Washington, DC: American Psychological Association.

Quick, E. K. (1996). *Doing what works in brief therapy: A strategic solution-focused approach.* San Diego, CA: Academic Press.

Riikonen, E., & Smith, G. M. (1997). *Re-imagining therapy: Living conversations and relational knowing.* London: Sage.

Rosenbaum, R., Hoyt, M. F., & Talmon, M. (1990). The challenge of single-session therapies: Creating pivotal moments. In R. A. Wells & V. J. Giannetti (Eds.), *Handbook of the brief psychotherapies* (pp. 165–189). New York: Plenum Press.

Rosenberg, B. (2000). Mandated clients and solution focused therapy: "It's not my miracle." *Journal of Systemic Therapies, 19*(1), 90–99.

Roth, S., & Chasin, R. (1994). Entering one another's worlds of meaning and imagination: Dramatic enactment and narrative couple therapy. In M. F. Hoyt (Ed.), *Constructive therapies* (pp. 189–216). New York: Guilford Press.

Roth, S., & Epston, D. (1996). Consulting the problem about the problematic relationship: An exercise for experiencing a relationship with an externalized problem. In M. F. Hoyt (Ed.), *Constructive therapies* (Vol. 2, pp. 148–162). New York: Guilford Press.

Rowen, T., & O'Hanlon, W. H. (1999). *Solution-oriented therapy for chronic and severe mental illness.* New York: Wiley.

Saggese, M. L., & Foley, F. W. (2000). From problems or solutions to problems and solutions: Integrating the MRI and solution-focused models of brief therapy. *Journal of Systemic Therapies, 19*(1), 59–73.

Schultheis, G. M., O'Hanlon, W. H., & O'Hanlon, S. (1998). *Brief couples therapy homework planner.* New York: Wiley.

Sharry, J., Madden, B., Darmody, M., & Miller, S. D. (2001). Giving our clients the break: Applications of client-directed, outcome-informed clinical work. *Journal of Systemic Therapies, 20*(3), 68–76.

Shoham, V., Rohrbaugh, M., & Patterson, J. (1995). Problem- and solution-focused couple therapies: The MRI and Milwaukee models. In N. S. Jacobson & A. S. Gurman (Eds.), *Clinical handbook of couple therapy* (pp. 142–163). New York: Guilford Press.

Short, D. (1997). Interview: Steve de Shazer and Insoo Kim Berg. *The Milton H. Erickson Foundation Newsletter, 17*(1), 18–20.

Sluzki, C. E. (1998). Strange attractors and the transformation of narratives in family therapy. In M. F. Hoyt (Ed.), *The handbook of constructive therapies* (pp. 159–179). San Francisco: Jossey-Bass.

Sternberg, R. J. (1998). *Love is a story: A new theory of relationships.* New York: Oxford University Press.

Talmon, M. (1990). *Single session therapy: Maximizing the effect of the first (and often only) therapeutic encounter.* San Francisco: Jossey-Bass.

Tohn, S. L., & Oshlag, J. A. (1995). *Crossing the bridge: Integrating solution focused therapy into clinical practice.* Natick, MA: Solutions Press.

Tohn, S. L., & Oshlag, J. A, (1996). Cooperating with the uncooperative. In S. D. Miller, M. A. Hubble, & B. L. Duncan (Eds.), *Handbook of solution-focused brief therapy* (pp. 152–183). San Francisco: Jossey-Bass.

Tomm, K. (1987). Interventive interviewing: I. Strategizing as a fourth guideline for the therapist. *Family Process, 26,* 3–13.

Tucker, N. L., Stith, S. M., Howell, L. W., McCollum, E. E., & Rosen, K. H. (2000). Meta-dialogues in domestic violence-focused couples treatment. *Journal of Systemic Therapies, 19*(4), 56–72.

Uken, A., & Sebold, J. (1996). The Plumas Project: A solution-focused goal-directed domestic violence diversion program. *Journal of Collaborative Therapies, 4,* 10–17.

Walter, J. L., & Peller, J. E. (1988). Going beyond the attempted solution: A couple's meta-solution. *Family Therapy Case Studies, 3*(1), 41–45.

Walter, J. L., & Peller, J. E. (1992). *Becoming solution-focused in brief therapy.* New York: Brunner/Mazel.

Walter, J. L., & Peller, J. E. (1994). "On track" in solution-focused brief therapy. In M. F. Hoyt (Ed.), *Constructive therapies* (pp. 111–125). New York: Guilford Press.

Walter, J. L., & Peller, J. E. (2000). *Recreating brief therapy: Preferences and possibilities.* New York: Norton.

Watzlawick, P., Weakland, J. H., & Fisch, R. (1974). *Change: Principles of problem formation and problem resolution.* New York: Norton.

Weakland, J. H. (1993). Conversation—but what kind? In S. G. Gilligan & R. Price (Eds.), *Therapeutic conversations* (pp. 136–145). New York: Norton.

Weakland, J. H., & Fisch, R. (1992). Brief therapy—MRI style. In S. H. Budman, M. F. Hoyt, & S. Friedman (Eds.), *The first session in brief therapy* (pp. 306–323). New York: Guilford Press.

Weiner-Davis, M. (1992). *Divorce-busting: A revolutionary and rapid program for staying together.* New York: Simon & Schuster/Fireside.

Weiner-Davis, M. (1993). Pro-constructed realities. In S. G. Gilligan & R. Price (Eds.), *Therapeutic conversations* (pp. 149–157). New York: Norton.

Weiner-Davis, M. (1995). *Change your life and everyone in it.* New York: Fireside/Simon & Schuster.

Weiner-Davis, M. (1998). *A woman's guide to changing her man.* New York: Golden Books.

Weiner-Davis, M. (2000, October 12–13). *Putting "marriage" back into marriage therapy: An advanced workshop in solution-based, marriage-saving methods.* Workshop sponsored by the Institute for the Advancement of Human Behavior, San Francisco.

Weiner-Davis, M., de Shazer, S., & Gingerich, W. J. (1987). Using pretreatment change to construct a therapeutic solution: An exploratory study. *Journal of Marital and Family Therapy, 13,* 359–363.

White, M. (1989). The externalizing of the problem and the re-authoring of lives and relationships. In M. White, *Selected papers* (pp. 5–28). Adelaide, Australia: Dulwich Centre.

White, M., & Epston, D. (1990). *Narrative means to therapeutic ends.* New York: Norton.

Winslade, J., & Monk, G. (1999). *Narrative counseling in schools: Powerful and brief.* Thousand Oaks, CA: Corwin Press.

Wittgenstein, L. (1980). *Culture and value* (P. Winch, Trans.). Chicago: University of Chicago Press.

Ziegler, P. B. (1998). Solution-focused therapy for the not-so-brief clinician. *Journal of Collaborative Therapies, 6*(1), 22–25.

Ziegler, P. B. (2000, April 8). *Recreating partnership: A solution-focused, competency-based approach to couples therapy.* Workshop sponsored by John F. Kennedy University, Orinda, CA.

Ziegler, P. B., & Hiller, T. (2001). *Recreating partnership: A solution-oriented, collaborative approach to couples therapy.* New York: Norton.

Ziegler, P. B., & Hiller, T. (2002). Good story/bad story: Collaborating with violent couples. *Psychotherapy Networker, 26*(2), 63–68.

Zimmerman, J. L., & Dickerson, V. C. (1993). Separating couples from restraining patterns and the relationship discourses that support them. *Journal of Marital and Family Therapy, 19*(4), 403–413.

Section D

Psychoeducational and Preventive Approaches

Chapter 13

Building the Sound Marital House: An Empirically Derived Couple Therapy

JOHN M. GOTTMAN
JANICE DRIVER
AMBER TABARES

The interventions described in this chapter represent the products of a new approach to empirically building marital therapy interventions, ranging from inexpensive, psychoeducational workshops to intensive marital therapy in our Seattle Marriage Clinic. What is new is that rather than extrapolating from individual or family therapies, we are trying to build a psychology of marriage by studying how everyday couples go about the tasks of marriage. The approach has arisen from our basic longitudinal research on marriages.

In seven nonintervention studies with 677 couples, this work has investigated (1) the "masters" of marriage, by studying representative samples of stable and relatively happily married couples, varying across the life course (from the newlywed phase through the transition to retirement); (2) the "disasters" of marriage, by doing prediction work attempting to predict marital stability and happiness; and (3) with Neil Jacobson (e.g., Jacobson & Gottman, 1998), a special disorder comorbid with marital distress—various forms of physical violence and battering.

A multimethod approach has characterized this research, sampling from interactive emotional behavior, self-report, and physiology. The self-report data included video recall rating of affect, interviews, and questionnaires. We have also sampled varied contexts of interaction, including discussions of events of the day after a couple was separated for at least 8 hours, a conflict discussion, a positive discussion, and 12 consecutive hours with no instructions in an apartment laboratory. We then followed couples longitudinally, with particular interest in major life transitions, such as the transition to parenthood. When the couples had children, our methods involved following the children's emotional, behavioral, social, and intellectual development. These results were reported in a book titled *Meta-Emotion* (Gottman, Katz, & Hooven, 1996).

The accomplishments of this approach have included the following:

• An ability to predict divorce or marital stability with high accuracy, which has now been replicated across four separate longitudinal studies.
• An ability to predict eventual relationship satisfaction among newlyweds. Our findings on divorce prediction are based on powerful statistical relationships, quite unlike those typically found in the social sciences. In previous research, our laboratories have been able to predict with over 90% accuracy which couples would eventually di-

vorce (Gottman & Levenson, 1992; Buehlman, Gottman, & Katz, 1992), and this prediction has been replicated in two additional longitudinal studies (Gottman, 1994a; Jacobson et al., 1998; Carrère et al., 2000). We have been able to predict the fate of marriages in all three of our domains: interactive behavior, perception, and physiology. Recently, we have moved beyond predicting toward understanding.

• An ability to predict adaptations to the transitions to parenthood and retirement.

• Mathematical modeling of marital interaction, via nonlinear dynamic difference equations. These equations have produced a theory of how relationships work; this modeling integrates the study of affect and power in relationships. This mathematical modeling permits one to fit actual equations to observational data over time. The equations estimate the couple's "emotional inertias," their "influence functions," and the homeostatic set points to which the couple's interaction is drawn. It is then possible to *simulate* what the couple would be like under new conditions, and then to do proximal change experiments to change the couple's interaction. These methods are detailed in several papers (Cook et al., 1995; Gottman, Swanson, & Murray, 1999) and a book (Gottman, Murray, Swanson, Tyson, & Swanson, in press).

The conclusions of this research build on previous research work on marital interventions, yet depart dramatically from the past. The basic new ideas in this therapy are these:

• Earlier work on the resolution of conflict has been misguided.

• Building general positivity in the marriage is essential to ensure lasting change, and that this needs to be based upon improving the couple's friendship.

• Friendship processes, working through sentiment overrides, control the effectiveness and thresholds of the repair of problematic interaction.

More importantly in our view, rather than presenting another checklist of what needs to be changed in dysfunctional marriages, this chapter presents a new *theory* of how marriages either work or fail. We need such a theory. A theory needs to be a recipe; it needs to describe the processes through which marriage work or fail, and the etiology of the failure; and it needs to prescribe a therapy. This one does all that. Much of this theo-

retical understanding has been impelled by the nonlinear dynamic mathematical modeling we have done with the mathematician James Murray and his students. This mathematical modeling unifies affect and power in marriages; it emphasizes the importance of *repair of interaction*; and it provides equations for husband–wife interaction that make it possible to simulate a couple's interaction under imagined conditions, and to test the effects of proximal change experiments.

Recently, in a 14-year prospective longitudinal study, we discovered a bimodal distribution of the time until divorce, with two major points when couples divorce. Gottman and Levenson (2000) constructed a model for divorce prediction for people divorcing either early, in the first 7 years of marriage (average of 5.2 years), or later in the life course (average of 16.4 years). One model, emphasizing the presence of particular types of negative interaction at Time 1 during conflict (the pattern called the "four horsemen of the Apocalypse"—criticism, defensiveness, contempt, and stonewalling), predicted early divorcing. Another model, emphasizing the suppression of affect, involved the general absence of positive affect, but without elevations on the "four horsemen" at Time 1; this model predicted later divorcing. These functional aspects of marriage—namely, avoiding escalating negative conflict, and establishing the presence of positive affect even during conflict—appear to be independent, and both are essential to making a marriage work.

This is also a conclusion that emerges from a selected review of the marital therapy outcome literature. Namely, all intervention studies (which also collected observational data) that have produced lasting results beyond 1 year after treatment have changed three things: (1) They have increased positive interaction outside the conflict context; (2) they have reduced negativity during conflict; and (3) they have increased positivity during conflict. This is true of the Jacobson et al. (1985) study group, which combined behavior exchange and the negotiation of compromise; the Hahlweg Munich marital study (Hahlweg, Schindler, Revenstorf, & Brengelmann, 1984; Boegner & Zielenbach-Coenen, 1984), which replicated Jacobson's intervention; and the Snyder et al. (Snyder, Wills, & Grady, 1991; Snyder et al., 1993) study of insight-oriented marital therapy. With other promising approaches (such as emotionally focused marital therapy; Greenberg & Johnson, 1988) that also appear to produce lasting changes in relationship satisfaction, it is impossible to determine what changed, because no quantitative observational data have been collected.

This hypothesis—that these three things need to change to produce lasting change—must have the status of a hypothesis at this juncture. Nonetheless, the question remains, how does one change a marriage so that it is both generally positive (regardless of context), and during conflict both positive and also not negative? This chapter offers a systematic approach for accomplishing these therapeutic objectives.

WHY IS THERE A NEED FOR A NEW MARITAL THERAPY?

Methodological Issues

Let us briefly reexamine the results of marital intervention studies. We begin with a methodological comment. Marital therapy outcome studies typically use marital satisfaction scores as measures of therapeutic outcome. The rationale is probably that marital therapy should make marriages happier. In our view, this is a big mistake. Scales like the Locke–Wallace and the Spanier Dyadic Adjustment Scale strongly penalize couples for even having disagreements. Yet all the marital therapies are trying to get couples to disagree, but to do so in a different, more constructive way. Hence the scales do not measure the degree to which the objectives of the therapy were accomplished. The objectives of the therapy are generally not clearly stated, nor are the outcome measures systematic assessments of progress toward these objectives.

Meta-analyses (see Bray & Jouriles, 1995, for a summary of these meta-analyses) have suggested that marital therapies are able to create statistically significant short-term effects, compared to no-treatment control groups. We disagree, for the following reasons. The treatment effects may be an artifact of the phenomenon that distressed couples deteriorate so dramatically in no-treatment control groups that almost any experimental effect will appear to be significant (Jacobson & Addis, 1993). Reanalyses of data by Jacobson from his influential behavioral marital studies found that although 55% of the couples made some improvement after treatment, only 35% were in the nondistressed range at the end of therapy. So our current treatment effects may not be that impressive. Furthermore, Jacobson and Addis (1993) noted a pervasive problem for almost all marital therapies that have been systematically evaluated in a long-term

follow-up, which is a ubiquitous relapse effect: A sizable percentage of couples (about 30–50%) who make clinically meaningful initial gains relapse in 2 years. This is the most serious problem confronting our field. In other words, the overall real effectiveness of our *best* behavioral interventions, in terms of producing clinically meaningful outcome after a 2-year follow-up, may only be about 18%.

Another disturbing problem in trying to help couples is that we now know that there is also a pervasive delay effect in marriages. Couples tend to wait to seek help an average of 6 years from the time they detect serious marital difficulties (Buongiorno, 1992).

How to Accomplish the Three Types of Change

Not all therapeutic interventions accomplish all of the three types of changes described above (i.e., increasing positive interaction outside the conflict context, reducing negativity during conflict, and increasing positivity during conflict). For example, a common intervention component designed to increase empathy initially proposed by Guerney (1977; Guerney & Guerney, 1985) uses the active listening model. The active listening model is so prominent that it has become a component of every major school of marital therapy. However, Gottman, Coan, Carrère, and Swanson (1998) reported that newlywed couples whose marriages remained stable did not do anything like active listening during conflict; hence active listening was not a predictor or marital stability or happiness. Furthermore, Schindler, Hahlweg, and Revenstorf (Hahlweg et al., Brengelmann, 1984; Boegner & Zielenbach-Coenen, 1984) found that Guerney's method only decreased negativity (it did not increase positivity during conflict) and that there were substantial decreases in initial gains upon follow-up. So this component of all marital therapies is inadequate by itself to produce lasting change. Research results therefore suggest that both the failure of marriages and their therapy must, in some way, involve both processes.

How are these three therapeutic objectives to be accomplished? This chapter presents a theory that builds on these research findings and shows how to systematically accomplish these three therapeutic objectives in a meaningful way. In our view, the field of marital intervention has desperately needed a theory, one with a strong empirical basis— a grounded theory. Instead, it has based therapeutic interventions on myths that have little or no empirical support. It has gone about the business of designing marital therapies without the guidance of grounded theory.

The theory presented in this chapter, "sound marital house" theory, is parsimonious, but it is an integration of behavior, cognition, and physiology. It represents a new approach to marital conflict and its resolution. It goes well beyond the conflict context into the everyday aspects of marital interaction. It represents a systematic approach toward building a couple's friendship and love.

With respect to conflict, the theory argues that one must deal with the *symbolic* nature of gridlocked marital conflict and with the *creation of meaning* in people's lives. It presents a systematic approach to the creation of shared meaning and culture. Thus the therapy is an existentially based, behavioral, cognitive, affective, and systemic marital therapy (based upon sequential time series and mathematical modeling approaches). The therapy attempts to integrate these major approaches to some extent, and it tries to do this in a practical and systematic manner, with specific exercises and diagnostic and intervention techniques. The goal is the individualization of marital therapy. It is remarkable that after more than 20 years of systematic research with a variety of marital interventions, not one marital treatment exists that is specifically based on any singly measurable dimension of the marriage. The view implicitly promulgated by every marital therapy proposed to date is a "one-size-fits-all" marital therapy. Jacobson and Addis (1993) decried this fact and called for aptitude × treatment intervention research with marriages. The basic research has yet to occur, and so therapists are left with the task of tailoring their interventions to particular couples with no theory to guide them. We suggest that the task of individualization will be assisted by a theory of marriage that guides a standardized and systematic assessment and treatment of marriages, and by the systematic evaluation of treatment effects as progress toward stated objectives. Thus the theory presented in this chapter is designed to make it possible to tailor the marital therapy to the strengths and challenges facing each individual couple seen in therapy. The design of individualized marital therapy is the unique job of the clinician and part of the artistry each clinician brings to therapy. The sound marital house theory will, we hope, make it possible for the clinician to individualize therapy to fit the needs of each couple.

BRINGING MARRIAGE INTO THE SOCIAL PSYCHOLOGY LABORATORY: OUR DATABASE

Our research database includes seven longitudinal studies with a total of 677 couples (see Table 13.1). The longest we have followed couples is 15 years. As noted earlier, the studies range across the life course (from the newlywed stage through the transitions to retirement) and include the study of physically abusive couples conducted with Jacobson (e.g., Jacobson & Gottman, 1998). In the past 6 years, in addition to these studies, we have been conducting intervention research. In this research we are studying the effects of brief interventions on marital interaction. These brief interventions currently include two experiments with approximately 250 couples. In the past 6 years we have been conducting weekend couple workshops (now with approximately 2,000 couples to date). Since we can predict what is going to happen to the marriage based upon marital interaction, we can design *proximal* change experiments whose modest goal is only to improve the second of two conversations a couple has in the lab, so that in the second one the spouses will look more like a couple on a trajectory toward a stable and happy marriage. We are in the midst of a series of brief intervention studies evaluating the effectiveness of eight specific parts of our intervention program. The first study of the series is nearing completion, and the second study is being planned at the time of this writing. In this way we can build up a therapy from effective building blocks, and then study how to maintain gains over time.

These studies have also made it possible to ask questions about why dysfunction occurs—that is, questions about how dysfunction arises, and how it becomes ameliorated over time in some marriages; these questions are especially salient for couples making major life transitions (particularly the transitions to parenthood, midlife, and retirement). Briefly summarizing some of these findings, in our longitudinal study of newlyweds and of middle-aged and older couples we have discovered among stable, happy couples patterns of what we and Greenberg and Johnson (1988) have called "softening" in how conflicts are first presented (mostly by women), physiological soothing, and the acceptance of influence by men. On the other hand, couples who weather these transitions poorly have been characterized by the reverse patterns of harsh startup, physiological arousal, and the rejection of wives' influence by husbands. These patterns ap-

TABLE 13.1. Guide to Gottman and Colleagues' Longitudinal Studies

Begun in year	No. of couples	Sample	Comments and sample references
1. 1980	30	Young couples	Levenson and Gottman (1983, 1985)
2. 1983	79	Varied from newlyweds to old age	Gottman (1994a)
3. 1986	56	Couples with a preschool child (Midwest sample)	Gottman, Katz, and Hooven (1996)
4. 1989	63	Same as 1986 study (Seattle sample)	None
5. 1989	130	Newlyweds (Seattle sample)	Gottman, Coan, Carrère, and Swanson (1998)
6. 1989	156	Middle-aged and 60s couples (San Francisco Bay Area)	Levenson, Carstensen, and Gottman (1994)
7. 1989	160	Four groups: highly abusive, moderately abusive, distressed nonviolent, happily married nonviolent	Jacobson and Gottman (1998)

pear to occur through a "distance and isolation cascade," in which people become flooded by negative affect and then withdraw emotionally from each other, increasingly living their lives in parallel (doing fewer things together) and becoming lonely in the marriage.

In *What Predicts Divorce?* (Gottman, 1994a), Studies 2 and 3 were designed to ask this question: "What is dysfunctional in marriages?" This research was also reported for the general public in the book *Why Marriages Succeed or Fail* (Gottman, 1994b). Study 2 is our longest longitudinal study (15 years). Study 3 was a 10-year study of couples with a preschool child. This study, in addition to being a study of marriage, was a study of parent–child interaction and children's socioemotional development. The books *Meta-Emotion* (Gottman et al., 1996) and *The Heart of Parenting* (Gottman & DeClaire, 1996) came from this study. Study 4 is a replication of Study 3, and we are still analyzing the data from this study. Study 5 involved asking basic questions of what is dysfunctional when newlywed marriages head for divorce and what is functional in those early years of marriage. The first of our reports of this work is the paper by Gottman et al. (1998); Shapiro et al. (2000) is a report of the transition-to-parenthood work with this sample. The newlywed study (Study 5) investigated which interactive processes are "dysfunctional" and which are "functional" in the context of two longitudinal prediction studies. One study was of a sample of 130 newlywed couples that were representative of the major ethnic and racial groups in Seattle. We studied these 130 couples over a 3-year period in cohorts of

approximately 40 couples each; our follow-up has varied from 3 to 6 years. We began studying these couples in the first few months of their marriages. Then we formed three criterion groups based on how their marriages turned out many years later. There were 17 divorced couples, and we picked 20 happily married, stable couples and 20 miserably married (very unhappy) stable couples as comparison groups. Could we use specific models of marital success to predict which criterion group a couple would eventually be in? Now let's look at the models we tested.

In the analyses we conducted, we sought to be able to make two types of predictions: (1) a marital stability prediction, in which we combined the two stable groups (happy and unhappy) and attempted to predict divorce or stability from their Time 1 marital interaction (taken within the first 6 months of marriage) using various process models; and (2) a marital happiness prediction, in which, controlling for stability, we tried to predict a couple's Time 2 marital happiness or unhappiness (from their Time 1 marital interaction taken within the first 6 months of marriage) using various process models. These models were based on the observational data. We tested models of whether anger was a dangerous emotion in marriage (as some have argued—e.g., Hendrix, 1988), or whether the "four horsemen of the Apocalypse" predicted divorce. We examined whether reciprocating negative emotions in kind (e.g., anger by one spouse is met with anger by the partner) predicted divorce. We examined whether accepting influence and sharing power predicted marital stability. We studied the active listening mode. We looked at how the conflict discussion started, the role of positive affect, deescalation, the balance of positive and negative affect, and the role of physiological soothing.

We continued to study these newlyweds as some made the transition to parenthood (50 couples to date). We studied them in their sixth month of pregnancy and built a laboratory to study their interactions with their 3-month-old babies. This laboratory duplicated that of Elizabeth Fivaz-Depeursinge of Lausanne, Switzerland (Fivaz-Depeursinge & Corboz-Warnery, 1999). We are finding that marital conflict transfers to a baby and makes it difficult for the baby to restore physiological calm after being upset or overstimulated. These children are now approximately 7 years old. Approximately 70% of the parents experienced a precipitous drop in marital satisfaction in their babies' first year of life. We are now able to answer the question of what predicts whether a couple will wind up in this 70% group or in the group whose marital satisfaction was maintained. This transition-to-parenthood study will form the basis for a new preventive intervention for expectant couples that will supplement birth preparation training.

WHAT ARE THE CHARACTERISTICS OF "DYSFUNCTIONAL" AND "FUNCTIONAL" MARRIAGES?

The following are seven consistent predictors of divorce and marital unhappiness that are characteristic of marriages when they are attempting to resolve conflict, and hence can be considered "dysfunctional." These can be called "the seven bad habits of unsuccessful marriages." Ailing marriages are characterized by the following:

• More negativity than positivity (the ratio of negativity to positivity in stable marriages is 1:5, whereas in couples headed for divorce it is 0.8:1; this is a huge difference in the affective climate of marriages). The presence of positive affect itself during conflict resolution (and in everyday interaction) is critical. However, this balance theory also implies the unusual point of view that negativity is necessary in marriages (i.e., negativity plays many prosocial functions). Thus marital therapy should not declare war on negativity.

• The "four horsemen of the Apocalypse" (criticism, defensiveness, contempt, and stonewalling) and gender differences in these (female criticism, male stonewalling).

• The failure of repair attempts. That is, the goal of therapy ought not to be to get couples to avoid fights, even ones that are painful and alienating. It should be to help couples process these fights.

• Negative perception in the "subtext" that accompanies interactions—that is, negative sentiment override, negative attributions, recasting the history of the marriage negatively. Another gender difference of importance is that men rehearse distress-maintaining thoughts more than women.

• Flooding (feeling overwhelmed by one's partner's complaints), and the "distance and isolation cascade" (a series of events from flooding through parallel lives to loneliness) that accompanies this flooding.

• Chronic, diffuse physiological arousal and immunosuppression.

• The failure of husbands to accept influence from their wives, manifested in one of two patterns: (1) male emotional disengagement (this eventually becomes mutual emotional disengagement), or (2) male escalation (belligerence, contempt, defensiveness) in response to female low-intensity negative affect (complaining).

The following characterize what is going well when a marriage is stable and satisfying to both spouses—in other words, the marriage is working well:

• Dysfunction does not arise from any of three different marital styles of dealing with conflict: avoidance (the spouses avoid marital conflict and do not try to persuade each other), validation (the spouses listen first and then try to persuade each other), and volatility (the spouses immediately try to persuade each other). Only mismatches in these three styles predict divorce (Gottman, 1994a).

• Only 31% of couples' major continuing disagreements are about resolvable issues. The other 69% are about unresolvable "perpetual problems"—that is, fundamental differences in personalities or basic needs; see below.) Functional problem solving about resolvable issues has the following characteristics:

• It begins with softened startup rather than harsh startup. Softened startup is a gentler way of presenting an issue ("I miss you and need more of you in my day") than harsh startup ("You are so emotionally unavailable to me. What is wrong with you?").

• Accepting influence, rather than batting it back (escalation), occurs.

- Repair attempts are effective.
- Deescalation of negativity is functional, and this is usually the male's role, but only low-conflict negativity gets deescalated.
- Anger is not a dangerous emotion, but the "four horsemen" and belligerence are.
- The most important finding is that *more positive affect* is the only variable that predicts both marital stability and happiness. The positive affect is contingent: It is in the service of conflict deescalation. Only positive affect and deescalation that are in the service of physiological soothing of the male (self-soothing indexed by significantly reduced husband's heart rate after a constructive husband event or a wife's attempt at humor) predict positive outcomes in the marriage.
- As noted above, 69% of the time couples' conflict is about perpetual issues in a marriage that never get resolved. What matters is not solving these problems, but the affect with which they do not get resolved. The goal is to establish a dialogue with a perpetual problem that communicates acceptance of the partner, and even amusement and active coping with the unresolvable problem, rather than the condition of "gridlock."

One of the major limitations of this approach is that checklists are not theories. They do not inform us about process and mechanism.

Implication: Emotional Disengagement as a Major Marital Symptom

Embedded in the second checklist above is a hidden implication that comes as a surprise for many marital therapists: There are many times when therapists see marriages that do not have the "four horsemen," and the marital interaction is *not* characterized by high levels of negativity. The spouses may also be talking about how they have adjusted to things and that everything is really OK. Still, such a marriage can be highly problematic, because the spouses may be in the stages of emotional disengagement and inadvertently arranging their lives so that they are parallel. They can be in the advanced stages of the distance and isolation cascade and still be acting as if everything is OK, because they are trying to adapt to this state of their relationship.

In Gigy and Kelly's (1992) California Divorce Mediation Project, the most common reasons given for divorcing given by close to 80% of all men and women were gradually growing apart and losing a sense of closeness, and not feeling loved and appreciated. Severe and intense fighting were endorsed by only 40% of the couples.

This absence of negativity in marriages can be confusing for student therapists, who can wind up accepting such couples' verbal portrayal that everything is fine, even when there is constrained negative affect and the couples have presented themselves for marital therapy. These couples are often characterized by a sense of nonentitlement to their complaints (Wile, 1993). The problem in these cases is not the content of what they are saying to themselves (i.e., that everything is basically fine) but the emotional disengagement itself. What is very clear in these marital interactions is *the absence of positive affect.* The spouses appear not to be making any emotional connection, and they take almost no humor, affection, or even active interest in each other.

In this type of marriage, we can see a complex of patterns:

1. There is affectlessness; that is, the marriage appears to be emotionally dead. There is no joy, no affection, no humor.
2. The spouses are like ships passing in the night. They are missing each other, not connecting affectively. There is no passion.
3. They do not seem like close friends.
4. There is a lot of tension (facial tension, speech disturbances).
5. They keep saying everything is OK, but, as Wile (1993) has noted, they appear not to feel entitled to their complaints about the marriage. They feel that they should not really complain, or that there is something wrong with them for not being happier.
6. There may be a high level of physiological arousal of one or both spouses during the conflict discussion.
7. There is little attempt on the part of either person to soothe the other.

Intervention with such a couple that tries to induce positive affect will fail. It is likely to lead the spouses to become hostile with each other. Recall that positive affect in the service of deescalation and gentleness in the marital conflict resolution characterizes marriages that wind up stable and happy, but that this positivity cannot be induced. It cannot be the target of therapeutic intervention. The theory that follows will explain how it just happens to be there, as if by magic.

Negative Affect Reciprocity in Marriages Is Not Dysfunctional, or "When is an unpleasant marital pattern really an important symptom?"

There is also a "negative finding" that deserves attention. It is a pattern that did not pan out as a predictor of divorce, and this was surprising. The pattern is usually called "negative affect reciprocity" by researchers. In research, it is assessed by sequential analysis computing the conditional probability that one spouse will be affectively negative after the partner has just been affectively negative. It has been the single most consistent correlate of marital dissatisfaction across laboratories (for a review, see Gottman, 1994a). However, recently (Gottman et al., 1998) we were able to test two forms of negative affect reciprocity. In one form of this pattern, we assessed reciprocity *in kind* (e.g., anger is reciprocated with anger). In the other form of this pattern, we assessed *escalation of negativity* (i.e., milder negative affects, such as anger and sadness, are reciprocated with one of the "four Horsemen"). Using our longitudinal prediction data, we found that the reciprocation of negativity in kind was characteristic of all marriages and did not predict divorce! Only the escalation of negativity predicted divorce. This means that the reciprocation of negative affect is not a symptom that needs to be changed in marriages. It may not be pleasant to observe or be a part of, but it is characteristic of all marriages—stable, happy ones and dissolving ones. It need not be corrected. This is an important point. The fact that an interactive behavior (such as mutual, reciprocated anger) makes a therapist wince and squirm does not mean he/she should intervene clinically. It is normal and natural, albeit unpleasant. This reciprocation of negativity is often given as a justification of the active listening or mirroring intervention (Hendrix, 1988; E. Bader, personal communication, 1997). Our data suggest that this intervention is a response only to the therapist's discomfort. It is not a marital pattern that needs changing.

However, further investigation has revealed that this escalation of negativity is part of a process of *rejecting the partner's influence*. That is, one spouse escalates the partner's complaints as a way to shut the partner down, and it is usually effective. We first observed this pattern in physically violent marriages (Coan, Gottman, Babcock, & Jacobson, 1997). In that case, the rejection of influence was by the male perpetrator of the physical abuse.

We then examined nonviolent newlywed couples to better understand this pattern of rejecting influence from one's partner. We investigated this rejection of influence by the wife and by the husband. We measured it by the sequences of escalation and saw what it predicted in terms of the longitudinal outcome of these newlywed marriages. Wives' rejecting influence from their husbands predicted nothing. However, husbands' rejecting influence from their wives predicted the longitudinal course of the marriage. This was because wives were accepting their husbands' influence at a fairly high level. For husbands, there was huge variability across the sample, and it predicted a lot. This finding makes great sense, given the period of social, political, and historical changes we are living through in the political, economic, and psychological emancipation of women. Further investigation of husbands' accepting influence revealed that the husbands were actively seeking a common ground for agreement. This did not mean compliance; it meant a "give-and-take," with men standing their ground on the things for which they would not yield and yielding on other aspects of the problem. Such characteristics are the ingredients of "give-and-take," of reasonableness, and of compromise. Hence compromise in finding a common ground for "yes" has its roots in the very beginning of a problem discussion, the agenda-building phase (Gottman, 1979).

To use a baseball analogy, these results suggested a hypothesis of a "double-play combination" in what we call "emotionally intelligent" marriages. This combination consists of softened startup by wives, and accepting influence by husbands. Moreover, husbands' emotional responsiveness to and interest in their wives during nonconflict contexts leads to softened startup. This yields a prescription: Emotional responsiveness by men leads to softened startup by women, and if this is coupled with men's accepting women's influence, then the marriage may have repair attempts during conflict that are effective!

Dialogue with Perpetual Problems

We have now studied the stability of marital interaction over a 4-year period (Gottman & Levenson, 1999). We discovered remarkable stability in these interaction patterns, particularly in affect. As we looked at the videotapes in most of the cases, it was as if the couple had changed clothes and hairstyles, and continued talking about the same or analogous issues in precisely the same ways. One thing we had never examined was the content of the interaction. In classifying the discussions of the major areas of continuing disagreement these couples had, we found (as noted earlier) that 69% of the time couples were talking about perpetual problems that they had had in their marriages for many, many years. These were problems that usually had to do with fundamental differences between them—differences in personality or needs that were fundamental to the spouses core definition of self. Only 31% of the discussions involved issues that were solved between Time 1 and Time 2; these were solvable problems. We found that 16% of the perpetual issues involved gridlocked marital conflict on these perpetual problems, while 84% of them were conversations about perpetual problems in which the couple was trying to establish a dialogue with the problem. Thus what we discovered in this study was that, instead of *solving* problems, what seems to be most important is whether spouses can *establish a dialogue* about their perpetual problems.

This exchange needs to feel good for it to be a dialogue. To feel good, the spouses make their peace with the problem to some degree. They may be able to push or pull the problem about somewhat, and change their level of frustration with the problem. They may come to some acceptance of the problem. They seem to be able to simultaneously communicate acceptance of each other and the desire to improve this perpetual problem somewhat. They communicate amusement and affection. However, if they cannot establish such a dialogue, the conflict becomes gridlocked, and gridlocked conflict eventually leads to emotional disengagement.

Hence we suggest that the goal of most therapy centering around perpetual problems ought not to be to facilitate problem solving; it ought to be to help a couple move from a gridlocked conflict with such a problem to a dialogue with the problem. The goal is not to solve the problem. In either case, the problem remains perpetual. For example, in one couple the wife described the husband as a loner who only grudgingly did things with the family. They quoted each other having these arguments. The husband started to quote himself when the wife supplied the quote, saying that he always said, "All right, I'll go." Then the husband added that he said, "OK, sure, anything you say, dear." The wife then added, "We still continue to do that," and the husband then said with a chuckle, "We don't even disagree good, do we?" They had developed a *relationship* with the perpetual problem. They were amused by their own perpetual problem, and did not consider it to be a major issue that caused pain or marital gridlock. They could even laugh at the persistent problem. An issue like this is one that the couple has often been dealing with for many years. The spouses continue to talk about the issue, occasionally making some progress or at least making the situation better for a short time, but then after a while the problem reemerges. In each case the marital discussion is an attempt to establish a dialogue with the problem, which admittedly will never go away or ever be fully resolved. The problem is like a chronic physical condition that one needs to adapt to, but can never cure. The dialogue is the adaptation to this persistent, perpetual problem.

When the problem is perpetual but gridlocked, the spouses have become entrenched in their positions, refusing to engage in any give-and-take (accepting influence); they have been very hurt, and there is mutual vilification. There is very little positive affect in these discussions, and some of the "four horsemen" are present. These findings suggest that spouses and therapists need to change their expectations about solving their fundamental problems in the relationship. We encourage couples to think of these relationship problems as inevitable, much the way we learn to deal with chronic physical ailments as we get older. The chronic back pain, trick knee, tennis elbow, or irritable bowel does not go away, but we learn to live with these unavoidable ailments—to have a dialogue with these problems. We keep trying to make things a little better all the time, but we learn to live with these problems and manage our world so as to minimize them. So it is in all relationships. An example was one couple where ostensibly their major conflict was about money. He wanted to tithe (spend 10% of their income on charity), and she wanted a retirement portfolio for their old age. The spouses could not yield on their positions, because for each of them their positions had embedded life dreams that were very core to their sense of themselves. He had grown up in a family where his mother ran a soup kitchen, and he viewed trying to live a moral life in a selfish world as one of his major life goals. She, on the other hand, has seen her grandmother and mother conflict, and she identified with her grandmother and wanted to have a secure and dignified old age. Both life dreams were reasonable, but they led the spouses to very different ideas on how to use their money. This couple could move from gridlock to dialogue on this issue and find some temporary compromises for being able to honor each other's life dreams.

This is very much like something Wile (1988) wrote in his book *After the Honeymoon*: "Choosing a partner is choosing a set of problems" (p. 12). That is, problems are a part of any relationship, and that a particular person will have some set of problems no matter whom that person marries. The position is also very similar to Christensen and Jacobson's (2000) discussion of fundamental incompatibilities that people need to learn to accept. The major distinction between how we approach helping couples achieve this "dialogue" and the way they approach it is that our methods are fundamentally existential. We believe that most spouses are gridlocked for good reason—because there is a symbolic meaning to their positions. Although they may ostensibly be discussing something like money, there is a hidden agenda, and underneath they are discussing basic philosophical issues (freedom, power, security, love, "my family legacy," "who I am as a person," etc.) There is an unfulfilled *life dream* that needs to be honored in every stubborn, gridlocked conflict.

New Information about Deescalation, Positive Affect, and Physiological Soothing

Why might positive affect and deescalation be related to the relapse effect in marital therapy? The link may lie in spouses' ability to physiologically soothe themselves and each other. The evidence is reported in the Gottman et al. (1998) paper. In many marital therapies, partly through the influence of Murray Bowen's work (for a review, see Papero, 1995), the therapist plays this role of soothing the spouses so that in the analysis of process they will be rationally examining their dysfunctional interaction patterns. The hypothesis here is that if the therapist plays this role instead of the couple, relapse may be the result. That is, we predict a good outcome for the couple to the extent that the spouses are able to soothe themselves and their partners.

There may be gender differences in the importance of this physiological soothing. There is recent empirical evidence from our longitudinal study of newlyweds to support this claim (Gottman et al., 1998). Gottman and Levenson (1988) reviewed evidence for the hypothesis that men and women differ in their responses to negative affect in marriage and other close relationships. They proposed that the research evidence suggests that in the relationship climate of negative affect that pervades unhappy marriages, men withdraw emo-

tionally while women do not. Since their review there has been considerable empirical support for this contention, and it has been called the "female-demand–male-withdraw" pattern by Christensen and his associates (e.g., Christensen, 1987, 1988, 1990; see also Gottman, 1994a, on female criticism and male stonewalling). There is also evidence that young babies do not socially reference their unhappily married fathers, but do continue to socially reference their unhappily married mothers (Dickstein & Parke, 1988). The evidence for this emotional withdrawal of the male in an ailing family has become so widely recognized that it has become the subject of national conferences (e.g., the 1996 National Conference on Men in Families). Writers have presumed that it is related to what has been called "the absent-father syndrome" and the widespread abandonment of children by fathers following divorce (see Griswold, 1993; Parke, 1996; Popenoe, 1996).

Gottman and Levenson (1988) hypothesized that this gender difference is based in part on a biological difference between the sexes. Their hypothesis was that men are in some ways more reactive to stress than women, particularly in the adrenergic parts of the cardiovascular system and in the stress-related endocrine responses that accompany active coping, particularly the catecholamines adrenaline and noradrenaline (Obrist, 1981). There is some evidence to suggest that this difference is found physiologically (autonomic nervous system and endocrine responses) and in emotion-related behaviors (for a review, see Polefrone & Manuck, 1987). Recent evidence suggests that this gender difference may be particularly pronounced in the vigilance–fear–startle system (McCarter & Levenson, 1996), with a greater male adrenergic cardiovascular response to acoustic startle in terms of the reactivity of heart rate and vasoconstrictive responses. McCarter and Levenson (1996) also found that for women, startle was accompanied mostly by feelings of fear, whereas for men it was accompanied by anger and contempt. Not all researchers agree with the universality of this gender difference we claim. It is reversed in fear conditioning research, in our research on violent couples, and in the Glasers' research on the immune system (e.g., Kiecolt-Glaser et al., 1993). The final word is not in. See also Maccoby (1998).

Given the aversive nature of diffuse autonomic arousal, men may attempt to avoid negative affect in close relationships because it is more physiologically punishing for them than for women. Gottman (1994a) reported that men are emotionally flooded by lower levels of negative affective behavior than is the case for females. To evaluate this hypothesis, variables related to either partner's positive affect and to either partner's deescalation of conflict were used as events in interrupted time series analyses of heart rate data collected synchronously with the video time code. The extent to which soothing of either spouse occurred related to these affective events was then assessed and used as a predictor of marital outcome. The Gottman–Levenson hypothesis would be supported only if the only predictors of marital outcomes involved physiological soothing of the male.

The results of these analyses were as follows: The only statistically significant predictions of marital outcome involved the physiological soothing of the male, by either the male or the female. Most of these analyses showed that the husband's self-soothing predicted positive outcomes in the marriage, usually via accompanying positive interaction initiated by the husband. One comparison involved the husband's heart rate being soothed by his wife's humor.

The Etiology of the Demand–Withdraw Pattern

It is critical to learn something about the etiology of dysfunctional patterns of interaction, particularly when it comes to gender differences. This could prevent blaming either gender for marital failures. As noted above, one well-established pattern during conflict resolution is that among distressed couples women are more likely than men to make demands for change, while men are more likely than women to withdraw (e.g., Christensen & Heavey, 1990; Christensen, 1987, 1988, 1990; Cohen & Christensen, 1980). We also found that during conflict resolution women are more likely than men to criticize, while men are more likely than women to stonewall (listener withdrawal). It is well known that women are more likely to start conversations about problems than men are (Ball, Cowan, & Cowan, 1995; Oggins, Veroff, & Leber, 1993). This gender pattern could be taken as blaming women for marital distress, unless it itself has an etiology. In one of our studies, the conflict conversation was preceded by an events-of-the-day discussion after spouses had been apart for at least 8 hours. To index the demand–withdraw pattern, we computed the sum of the differences between men and women based on the criticism and stonewalling during conflict resolution. The results al-

lowed us to build a model for both early and late divorcing in the 14-year longitudinal study. We also found that the female negative startup pattern during conflict did have an etiology, and that it was indeed predicted by the *husband's* affect during the events-of-the-day nonconflict interaction (Gottman & Levenson, 2000).

Other Recent Findings

The Role of Positive Affect

We have seen how important positive affect is in predicting marital outcome. But what is this all about? Don't all marriages and weddings start off equally positive? If so, what is the etiology of the decline in positive affect in newlywed marital interaction? The answer lies in understanding that for only stable, happy couples, the positive affect was used contingently, in the service of the deescalation of conflict, and physiological soothing. In the 14-year follow-up in predicting later divorcing, it was the absence of positive affect and not the presence of negative affect that was predictive. Hence we must conclude that not all marriages start off equally positive either in nonconflict interaction, or in the way positive affect is employed in the deescalation of conflict.

Love Maps and the Fondness and Admiration System

It is well known that over half of all divorces occur in the first 7 years of marriage. Some of this involves a cascade toward divorce that follows the birth of the first child; in our transition-to-parenthood study, 67% of all couples (mainly wives) experienced a precipitous drop in marital satisfaction, while 33% did not. This drop in marital satisfaction is part of a cascade toward divorce. In our study we attempted to discover, in the first few months of marriage, what would predict whether a couple would wind up in the 33% group versus the 67% group. We found these predictors using our Oral History Interview. The first was the amount of "cognitive room" a spouse, particularly a husband, allocated to the marriage and the life of the other spouse; those husbands who essentially had a "map" of their wives' worlds and kept knowing their wives' psychological worlds wound up in the 33% whose marital satisfaction did not drop as they made the transition to parenthood. We called this cognitive room the "love map." The second finding was that the same results held for the "fondness and admiration system." This refers to the dimensions of affection and respect in the marriage, both assessed with our Oral History Interview. The Oral History Interview variables that tapped the same dimensions have also now been found to be predictive of the longitudinal course of marriages in two separate studies we have conducted. But what is the etiology of not making these love maps, or a decline in making them as the marriage proceeds?

The Emotional Bank Account Model: Turning Toward versus Turning Away

The concept of "turning toward" versus "turning away" has its basis in everyday, mundane interactions in our apartment laboratory. The idea is that if partners characteristically turn toward each other rather than away, this is "emotional money in the bank." Here is an example of turning away: W: "Isn't that a beautiful boat?" H: (*No response. He keeps reading the newspaper.*) An example of turning toward is as follows: W: "Isn't that a beautiful boat?" H: (*Putting down the newspaper*) "Yeah, like one of those old schooners." The basis of this idea in research lies in relating the ratio of positivity to negativity in nonconflict discussions and in our apartment lab setting to the way people interact when resolving conflict. In our Study 2 (see Table 13.1), in predicting the wife's ratio in a subsequent conflict conversation from the husband's and wife's ratios in the initial events-of-the-day conversations, multiple $R = .71$, $R^2 = .51$, $F (2, 62) = 31.99$, $p = .0000$. For the husband's conflict ratio, multiple $R = .54$, $R^2 = .29$, $F (2, 62) = 12.46$, $p = .0000$. In other words, the simple ratio of positive to negative affect in mundane everyday conversations sets the stage for the same ratios in conflict conversations, and these ratios in the conflict context predict divorce.

Positive and Negative Sentiment Overrides

Escalating negative affect is a sequential pattern. That is, more intense negative affect by a spouse is more likely than his/her baseline level of affect after the partner has just been mildly negative. To prevent this escalation, it is important that the spouses be able to *repair* the interaction and be able to exit a negative affect cycle once they enter it. It may be the sine qua non of effective marital interaction during conflict. We have been studying these repair processes and have discovered that (1) repair processes occur about once every 3 minutes, on the average; (2) they occur more often when a

couple is less distressed; and (3) the success of the repair attempt cannot be predicted from any parameter of its delivery, context, or timing. Instead, Lorber (n.d.), an honors student in our laboratory, discovered that the success of repair attempts is determined by a concept called "positive sentiment override" (PSO). This concept was first proposed by Weiss (1980), who suggested that reactions during marital interaction may be determined by a global dimension of affection or disaffection rather than by the immediately preceding valence of the stimulus. We have extended Weiss's ideas of PSO and "negative sentiment override" (NSO), and suggest that they have its basis in everyday, mundane, nonconflict interaction. These overrides are determined by insider–outsider coding discrepancies, as follows: In PSO a spouse can say something with negative affect (as judged by observers) and it is received as a neutral message, perhaps with italics, meaning that this is an important issue to the spouse. In NSO, a neutral message (as judged by observers) gets received as if it were negative.

Notarius, Benson, and Sloane (1989) evaluated the validity of this hypothesis in a study in which they employed a sequential stream of behavior and cognitions to operationalize a number of hypotheses linking behavior and cognition. They found that distressed wives were more negative; were more likely to evaluate their husbands' neutral and negative messages as negative (suggesting the operation of NSO); and, given a negative evaluation of their partner's antecedent message, were more likely to offer a negative reply than were all other spouses. Notarius et al. (1989) thus found no evidence for the buffering qualities of PSO. However, Lorber (n.d.) found that the critical element was a *husband's* PSO. It determined the success of repair attempts during conflict resolution. Hawkins (n.d.), also a student in our laboratory, recently discovered that the critical variable in PSO was the wife's perception of her husband's anger. In a marriage that was destined to become happy and stable, the husband did not perceive his wife's anger negatively; he saw it as neutral. He noticed and responded to the anger; he just did not evaluate it as negative using our video recall rating dial. In a marriage headed for unhappiness or divorce, the wife's rating of her husband's anger was negative. It is important to note that this was a categorical and not a small quantitative difference. Wives in these marriages headed for stability and happiness were actually seeing their husbands' anger as neutral, not just as less negative than their counterparts in marriages destined for misery or divorce saw such anger.

The theory described in this chapter suggests that PSO mediates between positive affect in spouses' everyday interaction and their ability to regulate negative affect during the resolution of conflict. It is the basis of successful repair. What determines PSO is positive affect in *nonconflict* interaction. In the theory, this is called the "emotional bank account model," and it suggests that PSO is determined by how much "emotional money in the bank" the couple has. Our data support this linkage in the theory.

Conflict and Its Resolution, Sometimes: A Summary

We have now studied the stability of marital interaction over a 4-year period. We have discovered remarkable stability in these interaction patterns, particularly in affect. As described in detail earlier, in couples' discussions of their major areas of continuing disagreement, 69% of the time couples were talking about what we now call a "perpetual problems." Only 31% of these discussions involved problems that could even be considered as having solutions. In these 31% of the problems, we found a pattern of four skills that predicted the longitudinal course of the marriage in newlyweds: softened startup, accepting influence, repair and deescalation, and compromise. Thus we find that a *two-pronged* approach is necessary for the part of the intervention that deals with conflict resolution: one for problems that have solutions, and one for perpetual problems. We have discovered that what determines the future of a marriage in the problem-solving domain is not whether spouses solve a perpetual problem, but rather the accompanying affect with which they do not solve the perpetual problem. What seems to be important is whether or not spouses can establish a positive affective *dialogue* with their perpetual problems. They communicate amusement and affection while seeking change. However, if they cannot establish such a dialogue, the conflict becomes gridlocked, and gridlocked conflict eventually leads either to high levels of negative affect (particularly criticism, defensiveness, contempt, and stonewalling) or to affectlessness and emotional disengagement.

Repair

We can now estimate the effectiveness of repair and the thresholds of negativity that it reduces, using our mathematical modeling methods. Two recent results are as follows:

1. While negativity (the "four horsemen" and belligerence) during conflict predicts divorce or stability among newlyweds over a 6-year period with 85% accuracy, if we also use data on the effectiveness of repair and the thresholds of negativity, we find that of the high-negativity newlyweds who repair effectively, 83% of them wind up in happy, stable marriages 6 years later. So the knowledge of repair processes (threshold and effectiveness) improves our accuracy of prediction.

2. What is correlated with effective repair? It is PSO, as predicted by our sound marital house theory, and these are very strongly related. PSO is measured by integrating our "affect rating dial" self-report video recall (insider assessment) with objective coding of behavior (outsider coding). We examine, for example, what a husband's mean rating is of his wife's anger. PSO in turn is related to the quality of friendship in the marriage. This is strong support for sound marital house theory. We are now checking these results by directly coding turning toward and turning away in the apartment lab, and directly coding repair in the conflict discussion.

What is related to PSO and NSO? We suggest that it is the quality of the friendship in the marriage, and we specify what we mean by friendship with three processes: (1) love maps, (2) the fondness and admiration system, and (3) turning toward instead of away in response to bids for connection. These processes form the foundation of sound marital house theory (see Figure 13.1), of which we now provide a basic description.

BASIC DESCRIPTION OF SOUND MARITAL HOUSE THEORY

The Foundation: Creating Positive Affect in Nonconflict Contexts—Friendship

We have found that friendship is a major accomplishment that couples in happy, stable marriages have achieved. Unfortunately, it is difficult to create positive affect or to recreate it in a distressed marriage that has lost it. The admonition to be positive, or the setting up of behavioral exchanges, is usually doomed. Vincent et al. (1979), after a neutral no-instruction condition, asked couples to either "fake good" or "fake bad." Although verbal behavior differentiated couples faking from the neutral condition, the positive or negative nonverbal behaviors of couples did not change. To change this dimension of positive affect, the theory says that the therapy has to rebuild the friendship in

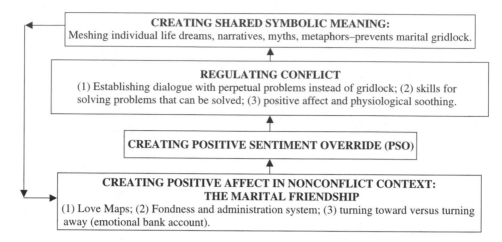

FIGURE 13.1. Sound marital house theory.

the marriage. We have discovered that this is usually not very difficult to do in a short time, but getting it to last is difficult. This first level of sound marital house theory involves creating positive affect in non-conflict contexts. This is all about the marital friendship, which we have found forms the basis for effective resolution of differences.

We have successfully built a "technology" for creating or recreating this part of the marriage. This technology involves three steps. A brief description of each step follows. The first part of friendship is knowing one's partner's inner psychological world, and this means being able to make a "love map." In our workshops, couples do an exercise in which they learn very basic things about one another. In our research program, love maps are assessed from our Oral History Interview using the Oral History Coding system, and are indexed by the amount of "cognitive room" each person has about the marriage, its history, and the other spouse's psychological world. The second part of this level of sound marital house theory is the "fondness and admiration system," which is the antidote for contempt. In our research program, it is also assessed from our Oral History Interview using the Oral History Coding system. The third part of this level of our theory is the concept of "turning toward" versus "turning away" in everyday moments, or what may be called the "emotional bank account" that exists in every marriage. It has been assessed in our research by coding turning toward versus turning away in our apartment laboratory in the newlywed study. We can now also assess these three parts of the marital friendship with questionnaires.

Creating PSO

The first level of sound marital house theory builds the second level, which the theory states is a consequence of the marital friendship's going well. This is Weiss's (1980) idea of PSO. What we have recently found is that PSO determines several critical aspects of the marriage, including (1) the wife's perceiving her husband's anger as neutral, as assessed from our video recall rating dial (discovered by Hawkins, (n.d., in our laboratory); (2) the ability of repair processes to be effective in ending negative affect reciprocity during conflict (discovered by Lorber, (n.d. in our laboratory); and (3) the presence of positive affect in problem-solving discussions, in the service of deescalation and physiological soothing.

Regulating Conflict

What we have found is that the *regulation* of most conflicts, not their resolution, is predictive of longitudinal outcomes in marriages. This is also the process operative in our long-term marriage study with couples in their 40s and 60s. It implies the presence of positive affect within the resolution of conflict, and clinically it usually entails exploring the symbolic meaning of each person's position in the conflict, using our dreams-within-conflict intervention. This level of sound marital house theory consists of three parts. First, we help the couple identify the core issues in the marriage. These are of two types.

- *Type 1.* For all marital problems and especially those that are resolvable, we detail the four parts of effective problem solving. We have discovered, through detailed observational coding and sequential analysis in our newlywed study, that these components of effective conflict resolution (when the problem has a solution) are softened startup, accepting influence, repair and deescalation, and compromise (Gottman et al., in press). Use of positive affect in the service of deescalation is a part of this too. Unfortunately, positive affect during conflict resolution is generally not programmable by intervention. Behavior exchange in the traditional behavioral intervention is one way of attempting to induce positive affect by changing the everyday interactions of the couple. Changing the nature of the couple's friendship is a conceptualization of this process. We have found, clinically, that positive affect during conflict resolution just happens by itself when PSO is in place. Our analyses have shown that the positive affect is in the service of deescalation and physiological soothing.

- *Type 2.* Many conflicts occur because of basic personality and other differences (interests, preferences, needs) between husband and wife that are perpetual in character. For perpetual marital problems, to avoid marital gridlock it is necessary that the spouses do what we call establishing a dialogue with the perpetual problem.

Physiological soothing (of both self and partner) is fundamental to both types of problems. The couple, and not the therapist, needs to be able to do this soothing to minimize relapse after treatment.

Creating Shared Symbolic Meaning

Creating shared symbolic meaning involves meshing individual life dreams, narratives, myths, and metaphors. This meshing of the symbolic meanings the spouses attach to aspects of marriage and family is what prevents marital gridlock. We have found that the basis of a continued positive affective emotional connection involves the perception of the marriage's effectiveness at making personal life dreams and aspirations come true. This aspect of marriage is the basis of unlocking marital gridlock, in which the symbolic values of each person's position must be explored. This leads us to the part of sound marital house theory that concerns the symbolic meanings of many ideas about emotion (our concept of "meta-emotion"), where many ideas

about marriage come from; here we find important dreams, narrative, myths, and metaphors about marriage and family. We assess the ideas that a couple has during our Meanings Interview, which asks about the meaning of family rituals, people's roles, goals, and the meaning of central symbols (e.g., "What does a 'home' mean?" "What is the meaning of family dinnertimes?"). These things are what people tell themselves about emotion and their marriage; it contains a couple's internal thoughts, metaphors, myths, and stories about the marriage. The creation of a marriage and a family involves the active creation of a new culture that has never existed before. Even if the two people come from the same racial, ethnic, and geographic background, the two families they grew up in will be very different, and so their union will always involve the creation of a new world of meaning.

The levels of the sound marital house are interconnected because the narratives, dreams, metaphors, and myths about marriage actually cycle back to the foundation, which is knowing each other (Figure 13.1). We have discovered that affectlessness and emotional disengagement are created in a marriage when the marriage has dealt inadequately with the first level of sound marital house theory, as well as the third, which makes it possible for positive affect during marital conflict resolution to act in the service of deescalation and physiological soothing so that the marital conflict can proceed in a functional manner.

What Are the Potential Contributions of This Theory?

How does this approach alter current thinking about marital therapy? First, it suggests that marital therapy should not be based only on how couples resolve conflict. In fact, it is a theory about intimacy in marriage and its basis. Second, it suggests that the effective resolution of conflict itself is based on the first level of sound marital house theory, which has its roots in everyday marital interaction and thought, and has its effects via PSO. Third, it suggests that when conflicts have a solution, the conflict resolution skills that most therapies are targeting (e.g., through active listening) are the wrong targets, and it proposes four alternative targets. Fourth, it suggests that most marital conflict is about perpetual problems that never get resolved, and that what matters most in such a case is the affect with which the problem does not get resolved. Either the spouses establish a "dialogue" with the perpetual problem and communicate acceptance to each other, or the conflict becomes gridlocked. When it becomes gridlocked, two patterns emerge, depending on the stage of the gridlock. One pattern involves the "four horsemen," and it predicts divorcing early (in the first 7 years of marriage). The other pattern is emotional disengagement and affectlessness, and it predicts later divorcing (about 16 years into the marriage). Fifth, the theory proposes that the resolution of this gridlocked conflict is the same as its etiology, in that it involves the clash in spouses' dreams and in the symbolic meanings of spouses' stands on these issues. This part of the marriage—the metaphors, symbols, narratives, and dreams—constitutes the engine that fuels both intimacy and estrangement. This aspect of people's lives is about *culture*. We do not deal with culture only when we think of how these processes vary with ethnic and racial groupings; rather, the theory says that we are always dealing with the culture that a couple creates when they create a marriage. This culture is their own unique blend of meanings, symbol systems, metaphors, narratives, philosophy, goals, roles, and rituals.

ELABORATING SOUND MARITAL HOUSE THEORY: A HOUSE WITH SEVEN STORIES

The elaborated version of sound marital house theory depicted in Figure 13.2 is the central organizing idea not only in our research, but in our assessment of couples and our interventions. We now discuss this elaborated theory.

These are the seven components of what marital therapy interventions need to target to obtain lasting change in marriages—in other words, the seven stories of the sound marital house.

• The foundation of the house, the "love map," involves the spouses' knowing each other and periodically updating this knowledge.
• The second story of the house is the "fondness and admiration system," which is the antidote for contempt.
• The third story is "turning toward" versus "turning away" in everyday moments, or what we call the "emotional bank account" that exists in every marriage.
• These three stories build the fourth story, which is Weiss's (1980) idea of PSO, or what we call the "positive perspective." This determines a

lot of things, including the presence of positive affect in problem-solving discussions, and the success of repair attempts during conflict resolution.
• The next story consists of two parts of conflict regulation. The therapist helps the couple identify the core issues in the marriage; these are of two types. First, for marital problems that are resolvable, we detail the four parts of effective problem solving. As noted earlier, these are softened startup, repair and deescalation, accepting influence, and compromise. Use of positive affect in the service of deescalation is a part of this too, but it is not programmable—it just happens by itself when the positive perspective is in place. Second, for marital problems that are not resolvable, it is necessary that the couple establish a dialogue with the perpetual problem. The implications of the presence of positive affect are that in assessment, we look for two patterns. Not only do we look for the presence of negativity (e.g., the "four horsemen"), but we also look for the absence of positive affect, even during conflict resolution. Thus many marriages that are at the stage of emotional detachment (farther down the distance and isolation cascade) will be identified in our assessment as problematic marriages.
• What is the basis of a continued positive affective emotional connection? The answer involves the next story of the house: the marriage's effectiveness at making dreams and aspirations come true. This aspect of marriages is the basis of unlocking marital gridlock, in which the symbolic values are explored. This suggests that the basis for moving couples from gridlock to dialogue is having them talk about what we call their "dream with the conflict," by which we mean the symbolic meaning of each person's position. We are suggesting that in gridlock people may ostensibly be discussing an issue such as money, but they are actually also talking about philosophical concepts such as freedom, power, independence, love, and so on. That is, we suggest that people have not compromised on gridlocked issues for good reason. It is not because they are immature, manipulative, or pathological (e.g., narcissistic, borderline), but because they are idealists. They can only compromise if they feel that these fundamental core aspects of their selves will be honored. This is the fundamentally existential/logotherapeutic component (e.g., Frankl, 1997) of the marital therapy.
• The dreams within gridlocked conflict are only the tip of the iceberg. Finally, we have the "attic" of the sound marital house, where the symbolic meanings of many ideas about emotion (our

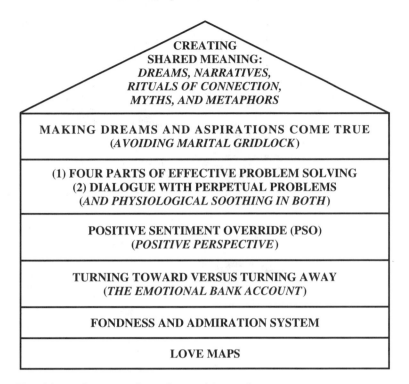

FIGURE 13.2. The elaborated version of sound marital house theory.

concept of "meta-emotion") and the marriage live; in the attic the all-important dreams, narrative, myths, and metaphors about marriage and family find a home. Here lie the narratives about what life means. Here are the informal and formal rituals of connection in a marriage and a family. This is what people tell themselves about emotion and their marriage, and it contains their internal thoughts, metaphors, myths, and stories about the marriage. Here is where the photo albums and the memorabilia live. This is all about culture, and culture is all about what things *mean*. The creation of a marriage and a family is active creation of a new culture that has never existed before. As noted earlier, even if the two people come from similar backgrounds, the families they grew up in will be very different, and so their joining will always entail the creation of a new world of meaning. Every marriage is thus a cross-cultural experience. The marriage's ability to build shared meaning and purpose then feeds back to strengthen and deepen the marital friendship. We use two interviews for our tour of the attic. The first is the Meta-Emotion Interview. In this interview, we determine the history of each person's and the couple's philosophy about the basic emotion (sadness, anger, fear, love,

pride, embarrassment, guilt, and shame). The second is the Meanings Interview. This is an interview about rituals, roles, goals, and symbolic meanings. In this interview we ask the spouses about the meaning of everyday rituals and the meaning of fundamental roles in their families of origin and in their own marriage and family. The interview explores the meanings and history of rituals such as family dinnertimes, reunions at the end of the day, the mornings, playtimes, weekends, time with friends, time with kin, birthdays, holidays, and religious festivals. These include not only rituals within the family, but rituals involving the family with the larger community, the church, charity, helping others in need, the children's school, political parties and political events, and so on. The interview explores the meanings and history of the basic roles of each person: son, daughter, husband, wife, father, mother, worker, provider, protector, nurturer, educator, mentor, friend, religious and philosophical person. Here resides the family's culture. Here we can also search for common ground and discrepancies between spouses, and for discrepancies between their values and the way they actually move through time—that is, their real priorities.

The floors of the sound marital house are interconnected because the narratives, dreams, metaphors, and myths about marriage actually cycle back to the foundation, which is knowing each other.

Now we can comment on part of what creates affectlessness and emotional disengagement in marriages: it is when the marriage has dealt inadequately with the first three levels of the sound marital house, as well as the top two, which make it possible for positive affect during marital conflict resolution to act in the service of deescalation and physiological soothing so that the marital conflict can proceed in a functional manner.

MODIFYING AN UNFORTUNATE HERITAGE IN MARITAL/FAMILY THERAPY

The original general systems theorists of families were inspired by a book written by von Bertalanffy (1968) called *General System Theory*. In this book, von Bertalanffy argued that all systems (biological, organizational, and interactive) are the same and follow some general principles. He had little idea what these principles might be, but he supposed that they would be some mathematical relationship between the parts of the system, a relationship that governed the system's dynamics. He suggested that every system acts to maintain "homeostatic balance," or a stable, steady state. The stability of systems is maintained by feedback mechanisms that bring the system back to its steady state if it is perturbed, much as a thermostat does.

In a marriage, this meant to von Bertalanffy that it would be possible to write down equations that tell us precisely how change in each person over time is affected by the other person. This led to the idea of "circular causality," or the concept that each person's behavior is affected by the other. Instead of labeling one person as pathological, an observer could view each person's pathology as a reaction to the other's. In families, this point of view called attention to *patterns of interactive behavior*, rather than to the personality of individual people.

von Bertalanffy did not know how to write down these equations, nor did the family general systems theorists, so this dream never became a scientific reality. Eventually, this idea of actually creating a mathematical model for families was abandoned. All that remained were the metaphors that von Bertalanffy had suggested.

Unfortunately, as Wile (1993) has pointed out, these metaphors have put therapists into an adversarial position against families:

> Practitioners from all major schools of systems theory start with the assumption that they must find some way of dealing with family homeostasis—that is, the tendency of families to maintain their pathological patterns and resist the therapist's constructive efforts. The major disadvantage of the concept of homeostasis is its assumption of an adversary relationship between therapist and family. Individual family members are viewed as active proponents of the family system, willing victims of this system, or both. Since the aim of systems-oriented therapy is to challenge the family system, a task that requires disrupting the family's homeostatic balance, these therapists often see their goals as directly opposed to those of the family. . . . [There is] the tendency of some to see family members as being duplicitous and manipulative, as using "ploys" (Jackson, 1959) or Eric Berne-type games to get what they want. The systems approach thus appears to lead to a picture of the conjoint therapist struggling gallantly against great odds—against concerted family efforts to maintain homeostatic balance, against family forces sabotaging all attempts to change the family system, and against subtle maneuvers and deceits employed by family members. (pp. 28–29)

Wile goes on to point out that this adversarial position has led to particular approaches to family therapy:

> Thus Ackerman (1966) deliberately charms, ridicules, and bullies family members; Haley (1963b) and Watzlawick, Weakland, and Fisch (1974) strategically manipulate them with paradoxical instructions; Jackson and Weakland (1961) tactically place them in therapeutic double binds; Haley (1977) systematically browbeats certain partners who fail to do the tasks he assigns them; Minuchin and his colleagues (1967) "frontally silence" overbearing wives to "rock the system" and show their passive husbands how to stand up to them; Speck (1965) openly engages in "power struggles" with families; Satir (Haley & Hoffman, 1967) forcefully structures the therapeutic session and undercuts all attempts to challenge her control; and Zuk (1968) intentionally sides with one family member against another, challenges the whole family, and does so in inconsistent patterns in order to shake them up, keep them guessing, and "tip the balance in favor of more productive relating." . . . It is perhaps surprising, considering the dramatic nature of thee methods, that they have been incorporated into the couples and family therapy traditions with so little discussion and debate. . . . An entrant into the field is often taught his general adversary

orientation as if it were the only possible way of doing family and couples therapy. (p. 29)

These adversarial consequences are an unfortunate result of not actually doing the scientific work of writing real equations. This has led to our inheriting an incorrect view of what homeostasis is in family systems. Seven years ago, Gottman began a project with the world-famous mathematician and biologist James Murray to model marital interaction with the kinds of equations von Bertalanffy envisioned, except that they turned out to be nonlinear. These equations reveal that homeostasis in a couple is a dynamic process, in which the couple has its own mechanisms of self-correction and repair when the interaction becomes too destructive. This view of repair provided by the mathematical modeling has an interesting result. It puts the therapist on the side of these mechanisms of repair that are natural in marital interaction, rather than in an adversarial position against "pathological" processes. This research also gathered data from three domains of human experience: behavior, perception, and physiology. These three domains are not independent; rather, they are intricately linked in a relationship we call the "core triad of balance." The idea is that every marriage establishes a steady state, and the "system" of the relationships is repeatedly drawn to this stable steady state. Also, each marital system is capable of repair when this is needed.

To review the classic concept of homeostasis (or stable, steady state) in biological and behavioral systems, consider body weight. By controlling metabolism, the body will act to maintain a particular weight so that the person will either temporarily stop eating or get very hungry and begin eating, regardless of his/her weight. This principle holds true even if the person is anorexic or grossly overweight. When the person tries to change his/her weight away from that stable, steady weight, the body will act to maintain the status quo—a constant internal milieu, a stable homeostasis—even when it is not a healthful one.

Our work has led us to a model positing that every marriage has at least two homeostatic states, a positive and a negative one. Every marriage has the potential of being heaven or hell. In treatment, we seek to increase the attractive force of the positive steady state and to decrease the attractive force of the negative one. A couple may come in with a negative steady state like the attractive force of Jupiter and a positive steady state like the attractive force of Mercury. Our goal in therapy is to reverse this. In other words, the therapist becomes aligned with the couple's desire to make their marriage more characteristically positive than negative.

Marital therapy could be primarily a positive experience. There is really no need to beat clients up about their own dysfunctional behavior. In fact, the entire problem-solving process can be recast as primarily people's basic life dreams in conflict. This is actually usually the case when conflicts become gridlocked and hard for couples to solve on their own. Then the focus during problem solving in marital therapy can be on exploration and understanding, and on using the marital friendship to help make one another's life dreams come true. Much of conflict resolution can be recast in this manner. It can have that self-indulgent quality that is so wonderfully attractive about individual therapy.

In fact, marital therapy can be better than individual therapy. Couples love the Oral History Interview. Spouses love talking about how they met, and telling the dramatic story of how they created a marriage and a family. They love talking about their own past lives and how these have shaped them to have these particular philosophies and attitudes. They enjoy discussing their life search for meaning and the added challenge of finding shared meaning together Much of the resolution of conflict can have this same quality of a journey through the photo album of the mind. It can be a growth experience in which the travel is not lonely, because one's partner is there as well.

Everyone is a philosopher. This is very clear from the writings of Studs Terkel, where people from all walks of life comment on the meaning of work, war, and getting through hard times; it is also seen in the therapy of Viktor Frankl. In her classic book on blue-collar marriage, Komoravsky (1962) described a couple beng interviewed about an important event that had just happened: They had made the last payment on their home. This was especially significant because they were the "runts" of each of their families. Their families thought it amusing that the two "dummies" had found each other, and this family rejection had clearly been a painful part of both their childhoods. But, they said, their children were doing well, in contrast to those of their brothers and sisters, and their marriage was the only one still intact. The two "runts" had banded together and done very well indeed. This shared meaning they created of a crusade to show the world how well they could do—this great strength in union—is a dramatic example of how a couple can develop a strong friendship based on a common shared meaning system. Everyone is an existential philosopher, not just the French. And we believe that therapists are in a great position to help couples in their search to create shared meaning.

Furthermore, the creation of this shared meaning system—this uncovering and blending of dreams— is the way out of the negativity of gridlocked conflict. It is the way to make the whole process one of honoring each person's dreams and developing a system of shared meaning.

GOALS AND PROCESSES OF THE INTERVENTION

There are five goals of this therapy: (1) the couple's movement from gridlock to dialogue on perpetual problems; (2) the couple's ability to process a fight without the therapist in a recovery conversation; (3) the establishment of six social skills: (a) labeling the "four horsemen" and replacing them with their antidotes, (b) softened startup, (c) accepting influence, (d) physiological soothing (of self and other), (e) effective repair and deescalation, and (f) compromise; (4) building friendship as the base for effective repair, including (a) a capacity to process failed bids for connection, (b) changing sentiment overrides, and (c) setting up meaningful rituals of connection; and (5) fading the therapist and setting up relapse prevention and follow-up.

An Overall Structure for the Entire Treatment Plan

The overall structure of the marital therapy is to do the following:

• Create initial, rapid, dramatic change.
• Follow this up with structured change.

Goal 1: Moving from Gridlock to Dialogue

The usual conflict spouses come into therapy with is gridlocked conflict on one or more perpetual issues. They are unable to get over these issues. They have usually had the issues for some time without being able to make any headway. These issues are damaging the marriage and undermining the couple's confidence in the marriage. They feel somewhat desperate. Usually one or both spouses score below 85 on the Locke and Wallace (1959) marital satisfaction scale, and one or score 4 or above on the Weiss and Cerreto (1980) scale of divorce potential. On their first interaction, they are in one of two states: Either the "four horsemen" are present and repair is ineffective; or there are great emotional distance and isolation, with lots of tension, underlying sadness, and no positive affect.

We immediately use the dreams-within-conflict intervention on what seems like the central gridlocked issue. One goal is to create initial and rapid dramatic change. It is important to underscore that the goal is *not* solving the issue, or resolving the conflict; the conflict will probably always be there for the life of the marriage. *The goal is to help the spouses move from gridlock to dialogue on the issue.* What is important is the affect centering around their *not* solving the problem. Accomplishing this goal is a two-step process. The first step is the release of the dreams. For this to happen, both people have to feel understood and supported by the therapist while they talk about the symbolic meaning of each of their positions. The marriage has to feel safe enough for these tender dreams to emerge. The second step in this process is helping the spouses "honor" each other's dreams. We use the word "honor" very deliberately here. Honoring is a hierarchy of the extent to which one spouse can support the partner's dreams. At the lowest level, this honoring can mean interest, respect, and words of encouragement. At the highest level, there is a joining in the partner's dreams and teamwork. But honoring need not be fixed. People may want their own autonomy in their pursuit of a dream, not a joining. That is fine. It can change over time. It is always about respect. The spouses have to arrive at this themselves. Therapists cannot do it for couples, any more than they can clear up their existential questions about God. They can create the conditions for couples to be able to do this themselves, but the couples have to do it. Honoring spouses' dreams is not a therapist's responsibility. Getting them to any level of honoring each other's dreams is the therapist's goal. They may not stay there, and our experience is that as they talk about this issue over time, they will find new ways of honoring each other's dreams.

This whole process will take years. All you are doing is starting them on a new trajectory. They will do the work necessary to move along that path in a way that is consistent with their personalities.

Remember, they will not solve the problem; they will just move off gridlock and on a path toward dialogue with this perpetual problem.

The second step in achieving this first goal requires changing the marital influence patterns on this perpetual issue. This is not difficult to do for a short time, but it is hard to maintain these changes. This may then become the focus of the remainder of the therapy.

Goal 2: Processing a Fight without the Therapist

There is a need for an overview about arguing and fighting. The goal is not to admonish a couple not to fight; our research shows that fighting is natural in all marriages. Almost everyone does the "four horsemen" sometimes. Almost everyone gets critical, attacking, righteously indignant, feels like an innocent victim, gets defensive, reciprocates negativity, wants to aggress or to leave, wants to cut losses and to preserve individual dignity, summarizes self instead of being empathetic, and so on. This is true even in the best of marriages. *The goal is to get the spouses to be able to repair negativity effectively after their interaction about a conflictual issue, without the therapist's help.* This is a far more reasonable goal than having people fight and follow communication rules. The chances are that they will not do this after the therapy. Holtzworth-Munroe and Jacobson (1989) interviewed couples after 2 years of marital therapy and asked them which skills they continued to use. They all commented that they did not use any of the skills in actual marital fights. We believe that it is most useful to learn communication rules so that fights can be processed later. The goal is for the couple to be able to repair *after* the fight. Wile (1993) calls this the "recovery" conversation.

To accomplish this goal, video replay is used to move the couple from what Wile (1993) calls an "adversarial" or "attack–defend" mode to an "admitting" mode. We have two physical areas in the office. Based on a metaphor taken from the sport of boxing, one area is called the "ring," where the spouses talk just to each other (the therapist sits behind a video camera) for 6–10 minutes, and the "corner," where the therapist and couple view the videotape and process it between rounds. After video replay, we use our structured Aftermath of a Fight Questionnaire to guide the spouses in processing the fight and coming up with one thing

that they could do to improve their next conversation on this issue. This processing is first done in the session, with the therapist's help, and then eventually without the therapist's help. The spouses first need to understand the fight. How did they get into this muddle? Why did it not go well? What is the meaning of the issue to them? What are the sources of their gridlock on the issue? In Wile's (1993) terms, "What was the conversation they needed to have, but didn't?" We maintain an emotion focus (Johnson & Greenberg, 1988) on this overview of a fight and on the spouses' movement from what Wile (1993) calls an "adversarial" mode to an "admitting" mode to a "collaborative" mode on this issue. They need not actually do this so much as be able to do a postmortem on the fight. The adversarial mode is one in which, in our terms, the "four horsemen" are present. The admitting mode is one in which they can start seeing their responsibility in the problem and the argument. Videotape playback is useful for moving many couples from an adversarial to an admitting mode. Moving them to an collaborative mode is a greater challenge. It is easier to do after the fight than during it, partly due to diffuse physiological arousal. Soothing is very important in moving spouses to a collaborative mode, as are the lower stories of the sound marital house (those that are related to NSO).

Goal 3: Establishing Six Social Skills

As noted above, we seek to establish six social skills: (a) labeling "four horsemen" and replacing them with their antidotes, (b) softened startup, (c) accepting influence, (d) physiological soothing (of self and other), (e) effective repair and deescalation, and (f) compromise. We begin by labeling destructive patterns, not by ignoring them. We label the "four horsemen" and then build in their antidotes. The antidotes were identified by examining functional marriages. Criticism is complaining by suggesting that there is something defective with the partner's personality; the antidote is complaining by making any statement of the problem that does not criticize. The antidote for defensiveness is accepting responsibility for even a part of the problem. The antidote for contempt is creating a culture of appreciation instead of fault-finding in the marriage; it requires a major transformation of a habit of mind. The antidote for stonewalling (listener withdrawal) is self-soothing, taking productive breaks, and staying connected (not leaving). We work on skills (b) to (f) by selecting from a "library" of interventions and exercises (there are now 47 interventions in the library—see Table 13.2, below). We start by applying these skills to a low-intensity, solvable marital problem—one that does not entail very much conflict. Our methods for testing the effectiveness of these interventions are our proximal change experiments, in which the goal is simply to improve a conversation so it does not look so divorce-prone. These interventions are designed to ease the escalating negativity that characterizes marriages headed for divorce or stable misery.

Goal 4: Building Friendship as the Base for Effective Repair

Our fourth goal is to teach the couple to (a) process failed bids for connection, (b) change sentiment overrides, and (c) set up meaningful rituals of connection.

Horrible fights are not the only burning issues that couples bring into sessions. The other burning issues are failed bids at emotional connection. These result in both spouses' feeling lonely, unaccepted, misunderstood, rejected, unattractive, and unloved. Our apartment lab data show that, in fact, failed bids are the basis of many subsequent fights. These can be bids for interest, attention, excitement, enthusiasm, affection, humor, support, fun, sensuality, sex, and so on; they have been met by the partner's turning away (usually not in a hostile fashion, but with indifference). This feels like a failure of the friendship in the marriage, as if the marriage is "losing its soul." Just as the couple needs to be able to process horrible fights and understand the anatomy of attack and defensiveness, the couple needs to understand the anatomy of bidding and "turning away." The Aftermath of Failed Bids Questionnaire is designed for this purpose. The surprise for us in studying bids and "turning toward" has been that these are the basis not only of closer friendships, but also of romance, passion, and good sex in the marriage. The "emotional bank account" that gets built up through the first three stories of the sound marital house is also the way of making the marriage more emotionally connected and romantic and maintaining it. Bids and "turning toward" may be the way to integrate sex and marital therapy.

To change sentiment overrides, it is necessary, according to the theory, to rebuild love maps and the fondness and admiration system. The mechanism for starting this process quickly is to set up meaningful rituals of connection, both informal and formal. These rituals vary from leave taking and reunion, dinnertime, bedtime, getting sick, dates, celebrations, vacations, and renewals, to more formal rituals like Thanksgiving, Christmas, Passover, Ramadan, and rites of passage. To set these up, we elicit narratives about what these were like in the primary families and how the spouses want them to be in their family.

Goal 5: Fading the Therapist

We recommend 1½-hour sessions, largely because of a very important study done by Boegner and Zielenbach-Coenen (1984). They had three groups. The first group had 14 sessions of therapy, just as the Munich marital study did. A second group offered the same number of hours of therapy, but massed most of them at the beginning of therapy and then faded them out with two structured "vacations" from therapy (a 2-week vacation and a 3-week vacation) near the end of treatment; there was homework during the vacations, and the therapist called to check up during the vacations. There was also a waiting-list control group. These investigators found that the massing-and-fading group produced much larger effects and had significantly lower relapse rates 8 months after termination than the group receiving the standard 14-session treatment condition. This is a remarkable finding.

The Unstated Sixth Goal: Developing a Shared Meaning System

The unstated sixth goal in this therapy is helping the spouses build a meaningful shared system of purpose to deal with any existential vacuum they may have in their lives. This is a serious problem in midlife, but it has also become characteristic of many families today throughout the life course. This is all about building a "culture" in the family that has some meaning. In our work, this begins with family photo albums and uses our Meanings Interview. This part of the therapy is strongly related to doing what may be called "marital logotherapy" (Frankl, 1997). It can be religiously based, but need not be.

The Intervention Library

It is the philosophy of this therapy that a "library" of interventions that have been empirically tested needs to be developed, and that the use of these should be adapted to each case. In the least expensive form of this intervention, the workshop, these consist of a series of exercises couples do to accomplish the goals. In the most expensive form, the therapist uses these interventions and tailors them to each couple.

The beauty of therapy is that in most of the cases the idea for the intervention will emerge from the *process*, particularly the emotional processes going on in the moment. The therapy must seem to be without an agenda to the couple. The spouses bring into the therapy their most pressing issue and latest interaction that was not very successful. These process-based interventions are certainly the most powerful. Furthermore, recall that the ideal situation is for the couple to come up with the intervention. It helps to have a matrix of possible interventions on hand that can be useful. This matrix is in the mind of the therapist. It does not interfere with the couple's ongoing narrative.

There are currently 47 specific interventions in our intervention library. They are organized by the processes of the sound marital house that may be salient in a particular case. These are to be done in the therapeutic office. Many of these interventions are described in detail in Gottman's (1999) *The Marriage Clinic*. Their abbreviated descriptions are given in Table 13.2.

THE DREAM: A "MARRIAGE CLINIC" IN EVERY CITY

Here is our vision. To continually grow and develop, to keep serving the needs of families, and to avoid stagnation and dogmatism, a marriage clinic needs to be a wedding of the research and clinical worlds. To our knowledge, this kind of marriage clinic has never been built before. It needs to be a place where both kinds of knowledge, scientific and clinical, can be honored and can affect one another. Our marriage clinic in Seattle will be designed to provide for research (both basic and applied), education, clinical training, and supervision, as well as service delivery. To accomplish these goals, we need to have accountability of the clinical services. We plan to use a method that has worked effectively in industry, called "evolutionary

operations" (EVOP). In such a factory, an EVOP committee decides on a variant (call it "Brand X") of the standard operating procedure (SOP). Then the two methods of production, SOP and Brand X, are alternated until a sequential statistical test can decide which of the two methods of production is better. If it turns out to be Brand X, then Brand X becomes the new SOP. In our clinic, there will be an ongoing seminar in which cases are discussed, supervision is provided, and also more theoretical discussions are held, with invited speakers and the discussion of new papers. Based on this seminar and its discussions and deliberations, the EVOP committee will then decide on a new Brand X, and the process will continues. The plan is that in our marriage clinic, 10% of all the clinical hours will be research hours. This will not strongly affect the clinic's income, but it will be enough for research. Also, 20% of therapists' time will be for people who cannot afford to pay our standard rates. We will actively seek and encourage population representativeness in both therapist and client populations. Each therapist would then either do SOP or Brand X marital therapy, and treatment adherence would be monitored by taping and blind-coding a random proportion of the sessions. The EVOP committee will consist of both the clinical director, therapists, and staff directly interested in research, including the research director. It is important that everyone feel that they have an investment in both the clinical work and the research. In addition to these functions, our marriage clinic in Seattle could build a network with other such clinics, so that there can be a frank exchange of ideas, including presentations of treatment successes and treatment failures, video teleconferencing supervision, and 2-week clinical sabbaticals in Seattle. A small proportion of the fees generated by our marriage clinic will be used to fund basic and applied research and the development of products for educational uses (for use in therapy, in clinical training, and public education). It is still a dream. Perhaps by writing chapters such as this one, we can help it become a reality.

REFERENCES

Ackerman, N. W. (1966). *Treating the troubled family*. New York: Basic Books.

Ball, F. L. J., Cowan, P., & Cowan, C. P. (1995). Who's got the power? Gender differences in partners' per-

TABLE 13.2. Library of 47 Specific Interventions

Intervention no.	Content	Description
	Friendship, intimacy	
1	Love maps	Introduce concept; love map cards
2	Love maps	Generalization to everyday life
3	Fondness and admiration	Positive Adjective Checklist
4	Fondness and admiration	Thanksgiving exercise
5	Deepening love maps	Injury and healing
6	Deepening love maps	Mission and legacy
7	Deepening love maps	Triumphs and strivings
8	Fondness and admiration	Generalization to everyday life
9	Emotional bank account	Areas of Strength Checklist
10	Emotional bank account	Generalization to everyday life
11	Emotional bank account	Stress-reducing conversation
12	Working as a team	Paper tower exercise
13	Negotiating marital power	Who does what in the marriage
14	Physiological soothing	Soothing one's partner
	Conflict regulation	
15	Softened startup	Problem items and stems
45	Softened startup	The Six-Pack Audiotapes (Male and Female)
45	Editing out negativity	The Six-Pack Audiotapes (Male and Female)
16	Repair and deescalation	Repair Checklist
17	Flooding and self-soothing	Couple break ritual
18	Self-soothing	Five steps of self-soothing
19	Accepting influence	Find common ground
45	Accepting influence	The Six-Pack Audiotapes (Male and Female)
20	Compromise	Steps toward compromise
21	Meta-emotion	Your history w/basic emotion and mismatches
22A	Dreams within conflict A	Acceptance and adaptations already made
22B	Accept one another	Accept what you cannot change
23	Dreams within conflict B	Finding dreams in others' gridlock
24	Part 1, ending gridlock	The dreams emerge
25	Part 2, ending gridlock	Fears of accepting influence
26	Part 3, ending gridlock	Honoring both people's dreams
43	Stuck in attack–defend	Rapoport conflict exercise
44	Stuck in "four horsemen"	Speaking and writing exercise
	Relapse prevention	
27	Reset negativity threshold	Marital poop detector
28	Build rituals of connection	Informal and formal rituals
29	Magic 5 hours a week	Basic emotional connections
30	Culture of pride and praise	Antidote to contempt
31	Decision-making style	Mountain survival
32	Marital mismatches	Confront mismatches
33	Philosophy of marriage	Oral History Interview, dyadic version
34A	Marital mismatches	Decision-making styles
34B	Marital mismatches in influence	Timothy Smith intervention
35	Fondness and admiration	Change cognitions in 7 weeks
36	Team building	Island survival
37	Team building	Shared meanings
38	Team building	Paper tower with straws
39	Marriage contract	17 areas as a contract
40	Building solidarity	Shared values
41	Rituals of connection	Emotional communication
42	One person less committed	Cost–benefit analysis exercise

Note. Interventions are out of numbered order because they were invented out of order.

ception of influence during marital problem-solving discussions. *Family Process, 34,* 303-321.

Boegner, I., & Zielenbach-Coenen, H. (1984). On maintaining change in behavioral marital therapy. In K. Hahlweg & N. S. Jacobson (Eds.), *Marital interaction: Analysis and modification* (pp. 27-35). New York: Guilford Press.

Bray, J. H., & Jouriles, E. N. (1995). Treatment of marital conflict and prevention of divorce. *Journal of Marital and Family Therapy, 21,* 461-473.

Buehlman, K., Gottman, J. M., & Katz, L. (1992). How a couple views their past predicts their future: Predicting divorce from an oral history interview. *Journal of Family Psychology, 5,* 295-318.

Buongiorno, J. (1992). *Wait time until professional treatment in marital therapy.* Unpublished master's thesis, Catholic University.

Carrère, S., Buehlman, K. T., Gottman, J. M., Coan, J. A., & Ruckstuhl, L. (2000). Predicting marital stability and divorce in newlywed couples. *Journal of Family Psychology, 14,* 42-58.

Christensen, A. (1987). Detection of conflict patterns in couples. In K. Hahlweg & M. J. Goldstein (Eds.), *Understanding major mental disorder: The contribution of family interaction research* (pp. 250-265). New York: Family Process Press.

Christensen, A. (1988). Dysfunctional interaction patterns in couples. In P. Noller & M. A. Fitzpatrick (Eds.), *Perspectives on marital interaction* (pp. 31-52). Clevedon, England: Multilingual Matters.

Christensen, A. (1990). Gender and social structure in the demand/withdrawal pattern of marital conflict. *Journal of Personality and Social Psychology, 59,* 73-81.

Christensen, A., & Heavey, C. L. (1990). Gender and social structure in the demand/withdraw pattern of marital conflict. *Journal of Personality and Social Psychology, 59,* 73-82.

Christensen, A., & Jacobson, N. S. (2000). *Reconcilable differences.* New York: Guilford Press.

Coan, J., Gottman, J. M., Babcock, J., & Jacobson, N. S. (1997). Batttering and the male rejection of influence from women. *Aggressive Behavior, 23,* 375-388.

Cohen, R. S., & Christensen, A. (1980). A further examination of demand characteristics in marital interaction. *Journal of Consulting and Clinical Psychology, 48,* 121-123.

Cook, J., Tyson, R., White, J., Rushe, R., Gottman, J., & Murray, J. (1995). Mathematics of marital conflict: Qualitative dynamic mathematical modeling of marital interaction. *Journal of Family Psychology, 9,* 110-130.

Dickstein, S., & Parke, R. D. (1988). Social referencing in infancy: A glance at fathers and marriage. *Child Development, 59,* 506-511.

Fivaz-Depeursinge, E., & Corboz-Warnery, A. (1999). *The primary triangle.* New York: Basic Books.

Frankl, V. E. (1984). *Man's search for meaning* (3rd ed.). New York: Simon & Schuster.

Frankl, V. E. (1986). *The doctor and the soul* (3rd ed.). New York: Vintage Books.

Frankl, V. E. (1988). *The will to meaning.* New York: New American Library.

Frankl, V. E. (1997). *Man's search for ultimate meaning.* New York: Insight Books.

Gigy, L., & Kelly, J. B. (1992). Reasons for divorce: Perspectives of divorcing men and women. *Journal of Divorce and Remarriage, 18,* 169-187.

Gottman, J., Murray, J., Swanson, C., Swanson, F., & Tyson, R. (in press). *The mathematics of marriage.* Cambridge, MA: M.I.T. Press.

Gottman, J., Swanson, C., & Murray, J. (1999). The mathematics of marital conflict: Dynamic mathematical nonlinear modeling of newlywed marital interaction. *Journal of Family Psychology, 13,* 3-19.

Gottman, J. M. (1979). *Marital interaction: Experimental investigations.* New York: Academic Press.

Gottman, J. M. (1994a). *What predicts divorce?* Hillsdale, NJ: Erlbaum.

Gottman, J. M. (1994b). *Why marriages succeed or fail.* New York: Simon & Schuster.

Gottman, J. M. (1999). *The marriage clinic.* New York: Norton.

Gottman, J. M., Coan, J., Carrère, S., & Swanson, C. (1998). Predicting marital happiness and stability from newlywed interactions. *Journal of Marriage and the Family, 60,* 5-22.

Gottman, J. M., & DeClaire, J. (1996). *The heart of parenting.* New York: Simon & Schuster.

Gottman, J. M., Katz, L., & Hooven, C. (1996). *Metaemotion.* Hillsdale, NJ: Erlbaum.

Gottman, J. M., & Levenson, R. W. (1988). The social psychophysiology of marriage. In P. Noller & M. A. Fitzpatrick (Eds.), *Perspectives on marital interaction* (pp. 182-200). Clevedon, England: Multilingual Matters.

Gottman, J. M., & Levenson, R. W. (1992). Marital processes predictive of later dissolution: Behavior, physiology, and health. *Journal of Personality and Social Psychology, 63,* 221-233.

Gottman, J. M., & Levenson, R. W. (1999). Rebound from marital conflict and divorce prediction. *Family Process, 38,* 287-292.

Gottman, J. M., & Levenson, R. W. (2000). The timing of divorce: Predicting when a couple will divorce over a 14-year period. *Journal of Marriage and the Family, 62,* 737-745.

Gottman, J. M., Murray, J., Swanson, C., Swanson, K., & Tyson, R. (in press). *The mathematics of marital conflict.* Cambridge, MA: M.I.T. Press.

Greenberg, L. S., & Johnson, S. M. (1988). *Emotionally focused therapy for couples.* New York: Guilford Press.

Griswold, R. L. (1993). *Fatherhood in America.* New York: Basic Books.

Guerney, B. G. (1977). *Relationship enhancement.* San Francisco: Jossey-Bass.

Guerney, B. G., & Guerney, L. (1985). Marital and family problem prevention and enrichment programs. In L. L'Abate (Ed.), *Handbook of family psychology and therapy* (Vol. 2, pp. 1197-1217). Homewood, IL: Dorsey Press.

Hahlweg, K., & Revenstorf, D. (1982). Treatment of marital distress: Comparing formats and modalities. *Advances in Behavior Research and Therapy, 4,* 57-74.

Hahlweg, K., & Revenstorf, D. (1984). Effects of behavioral marital therapy on couples' communication and problem-solving skills. *Journal of Consulting and Clinical Psychology, 52,* 553-566.

Hahlweg, K., Schindler, K., Revenstorf, D., & Brengelmann, P. (1984). The Munich marital therapy study. In K. Hahlweg & N. S. Jacobson (Eds.), *Marital interaction: Analysis and modification* (pp. 3-26). New York: Guilford Press.

Haley, J. (1963). Marriage therapy. *Archives of General Psychiatry, 8,* 213-234.

Haley, J. (1977). *Problem-solving therapy: New strategies for an effective family therapy.* New York: Basic Books.

Haley, J., & Hoffman, L. (1967). *Techniques of family therapy.* New York: Basic Books.

Hawkins, M. (unpublished). *Sentiment override and marital conflict interaction.* Unpublished manuscript, University of Washington.

Heavey, C. L., Layne, C., & Christensen, A. (1993). Gender and conflict structure in marital interaction: A replication and extension. *Journal of Consulting and Clinical Psychology, 61,* 16–27.

Hendrix, H. (1988). *Getting the love you want.* New York: Henry Holt.

Holtzworth-Munroe, A., & Jacobson, N. S. (1985). Causal attributions of married couples: When do they search for causes? What do they conclude when they do? *Journal of Personality and Social Psychology, 48,* 1398–1412.

Holtzworth-Munroe, A., & Jacobson, N. S. (1989). Relationship between behavioral marital therapy outcome and process variables. *Journal of Consulting and Clinical Psychology, 57,* 658–662.

Jackson, D. D. (1959). Family interaction, family homeostasis, and some implications for conjoint family therapy. In J. H. Masserman (Ed.), *Individual and familial dynamics* (pp. 1–31). New York: Grune & stratton.

Jackson, D. D., & Weakland, J. H. (1961). Conjoint family therapy: Some considerations of therapy, technique, and results. *Psychiatry, 24,* 30–45.

Jacobson, N. S., & Addis, M. E. (1993). Research on couple therapy: What do we know? Where are we going? *Journal of Consulting and Clinical Psychology, 61,* 85–93.

Jacobson, N. S., Follette, V. M., Follette, W. C., Holtzworth-Munroe, A., Katt, J. L., & Scharaling, K. B. (1985). A component analysis of behavioural marital therapy: One-year follow-up. *Behaviour Research and Therapy, 23,* 549–555.

Jacobson, N. S., & Gottman, J. M. (1998). *When men batter women.* New York: Simon & Schuster.

Jacobson, N. S., Gottman, J. M., Gortner, E., & Berns, S. (1998). The longitudinal course of battering: When do the couples split up? When does the abuse decrease? *Violence and Victims, 11,* 371–392.

Jacobson, N. S., Schmaling, K., & Holtzworth-Munroe, A. (1987). Component analysis of behavioral marital therapy: 2-year followup and prediction of relapse. *Journal of Marital and Family Therapy, 13,* 187–195.

Kiecolt-Glaser, J., Malarkey, W. B., Chee, M. A., Newton, T., Cacioppo, J. T., Mao, H. Y., & Glaser, R. (1993). Negative behavior during marital conflict is associated with immunological down-regulation. *Psychosomatic Medicine, 55,* 395–409.

Komoravsky, M. (1962). *Blue collar marriages.* New York: Random House.

Levenson, R. W., Carstensen, L. L., & Gottman, J. M. (1994). The influence of age and gender on affect, physiology, and their interrelations: A study of long-term marriages. *Journal of Personality and Social Psychology, 67,* 56–68.

Levenson, R. W., & Gottman, J. M. (1983). Marital interaction: Physiological linkage and affective exchange. *Journal of Personality and Social Psychology, 45,* 587–597.

Levenson, R. W., & Gottman, J. M. (1985). Physiological and affective predictors of change in relationship satisfaction. *Journal of Personality and Social Psychology, 49,* 85–94.

Locke, H. J., & Wallace, K. M. (1959). Short marital-adjustment and prediction tests: Their reliability and validity. *Marriage and Family Living, 21,* 251–255.

Lorber, M. (n.d.). *Repair during marital conflict.* Unpublished honors thesis, University of Washington.

Maccoby, E. E. (1998). *The two sexes: Growing up apart, coming together.* Cambridge, MA: Harvard University Press.

McCarter, L. M., & Levenson, R. W. (1996). *Sex differences in physiological reactivity to the acoustic startle.* Paper presented at the 32nd annual meeting of the Society for Psychophysiological Research, Vancouver, Canada.

Minuchin, S., Montalvo, B., Guerney, B. G., Rosman, B. L., & Schumer, F. (1967). *Families of the slums.* New York: Basic Books.

Notarius, C. I., Benson, P.R., & Sloane, D. (1989). Exploring the interface between perception and behavior: An analysis of marital interaction in distressed and non-distressed couples. *Behavioral Assessment, 11,* 39–64.

Notarius, C. I., & Markman, H. (1993). *We can work it out: Making sense of marital conflict.* New York: Putnam.

Obrist, P. A. (1981). *Cardiovascular psychophysiology.* New York: Plenum Press.

Oggins, J., Veroff, J., & Leber, D. (1993). Perceptions of marital interaction among Black and White newlyweds. *Journal of Personality and Social Psychology, 65,* 494–511.

Papero, D. V. (1995). Bowen family-systems and marriage. In N. S. Jacobson & A. S. Gurman (Eds.), *Clinical handbook of couple therapy* (pp. 11–30). New York: Guilford.

Parke, R. D. (1996). *Fatherhood.* Cambridge, MA: Harvard University Press.

Polferone, J. M., & Manuck, S. B. (1987). Gender differences in cardiovascular and neuroendocrine response to stressors. In R. C. Barnett, L. Biener, & G. K. Baruch (Eds.), *Gender and stress* (pp. 13–38). New York: The Free Press.

Popenoe, D. (1996). *Life without father.* New York: Free Press.

Shapiro, A. F., Gottman, J. M., & Carrère, S. (2000). The baby and the marriage: Identifying factors that buffer against the decline in marital satisfaction after the first baby arrives. *Journal of Family Psychology, 14,* 59–70.

Snyder, D. K., Mangrum, L. F., & Wills, R. M. (1993). Predicting couples' response to marital therapy: A comparison of short- and long-term predictors. *Journal of Consulting and Clinical Psychology, 61,* 61–69.

Snyder, D. K., & Wills, R. M. (1989). Behavioral versus insight-oriented marital therapy: Effects on individual and interspousal functioning. *Journal of Consulting and Clinical Psychology, 57,* 39–46.

Snyder, D. K., Wills, R. M., & Grady, F. A. (1991). Long-term effectiveness of behavioral versus insight-oriented marital therapy: A four-year follow-up study. *Journal of Consulting and Clinical Psychology, 59,* 138–141.

Speck, R. V. (1965). Some specific therapeutic techniques with schizophrenic families. In A. Friedman (Ed.), *Psychotherapy for the whole family* (pp. 197–205). New York: Springer.

Vincent, J. P., Friedman, L. C., Nugent, J., & Messerly, L. (1979). Demand characteristics in observations of marital interactions. *Journal of Consulting and Clinical Psychology, 47,* 557–566.

von Bertalanffy, L. (1968). *General system theory.* New York: Braziller.

Watzlawick, P., Weakland, J. H., & Fisch, R. (1974). *Change: Principles of problem formation and problem resolution.* New York: Norton.

Weiss, R. L. (1980). Strategic behavioral marital therapy: Toward a model for assessment and intervention. In J. P. Vincent (Ed.), *Advances in family intervention, assessment and theory* (Vol. 1, pp. 229–271). Greenwich, CT: JAI Press.

Weiss, R. L., & Cerreto, M. C. (1980). Development of a measure of dissolution potential. *American Journal of Family Therapy, 8,* 80–85.

Wile, D. B. (1981). *Couples therapy: A nontraditional approach.* New York: Wiley.

Wile, D. B. (1988). *After the honeymoon.* New York: Wiley.

Wile, D. B. (1993). *After the fight.* New York: Guilford Press.

Zuk, G. H. (1968). Family therapy: Formulation of a technique and its theory. *International Journal of Group Psychotherapy, 18,* 42–58.

Chapter 14

Relationship Education and the Prevention of Couple Relationship Problems

W. KIM HALFORD
ELIZABETH N. MOORE

BACKGROUND OF RELATIONSHIP EDUCATION

History of the Movement

In this chapter we review the nature of relationship education, with a focus on skill training approaches. Relationship education developed as an attempt to promote mutually satisfying couple relationships and to prevent relationship breakdown (Hunt, Hof, & DeMaria, 1998). It developed from the work of religious marriage celebrants such as priests, rabbis, and ministers, who offered brief counsel to marrying couples (Hunt et al., 1998). Religious organizations, and in particular the Catholic church, began to offer structured group relationship education programs for marrying couples in the early 1950s (Hunt et al., 1998). By the mid-1950s in the United States (Hunt et al., 1998), Australia (Harris, Simons, Willis, & Barrie, 1992), and other Western countries, secular organizations also began to offer relationship education programs. By the late 1990s, between one-quarter and one-third of marrying couples in the United States, Australia, and Britain were attending some form of relationship education (Halford, 1999; Simons, Harris, & Willis, 1994; Sullivan & Bradbury, 1997).

Major Approaches to Relationship Education

Information and Awareness

Relationship education programs can usefully be seen as falling into three broad categories: information and awareness, inventories, and skills training. Information and awareness approaches emphasize the transmission of information, clarification of expectations, and increasing awareness of key relationship processes that influence relationship outcomes. Some programs include demonstration of relevant relationship skills such as communication, but there generally is not active training in these skills. From the available surveys of marriage and relationship education, it would seem that the majority of couples receiving such education receive this form of it (Harris et al., 1992; *To Have and to Hold*, 1998).

A limitation of the information and awareness programs is that many have been developed locally by practitioners, and the exact content and process of such programs are often not well documented (Halford, 1999). These programs have often grown from the practical experience of delivering marriage and relationship education, and do not draw upon conceptual models or research available in the relevant literature. Their lack of standardization means that they cannot readily be evaluated in scientific research.

Inventory Approaches

Inventory-based programs constitute a second category of marriage and relationship education programs. There are numerous relevant inventories available. The most widely used are PREmarital Personal And Relationship Evaluation (PREPARE) (Olson, Fournier, & Druckman, 1996) and Facilitating Open Couple Communication Understanding and Study (FOCCUS) (Larsen & Holman, 1994; Williams & Jurich, 1995). In these programs each partner completes a self-report inventory that assesses a broad range of dimensions of couple functioning, and the couple is then provided with systematic feedback about the results of this assessment. The use of these inventories varies significantly among educators. Personal reports by educators with substantive experience with these programs indicates that many educators present the results of the feedback and facilitate couples' discussion of their responses to that feedback (Halford, 1999). The goal seems to be to provide awareness and facilitate goal setting for positive change. Other marriage educators report that they use the inventories to diagnose a couple's needs, negotiate with the couple to define particular learning goals that they want to achieve, and may supplement completion of the inventory with various experiential exercises to achieve the negotiated goals. For example, structured exercises have been developed that can be used with PREPARE (Olson, Dyer, & Dyer, 1997). However, the structured exercises still focus largely on promotion of awareness and do not involve specific skill training.

The inventory programs like PREPARE and FOCCUS have the advantage of being clearly structured and hence amenable to scientific evaluation. The constructs assessed in PREPARE and FOCCUS are relevant to the developmental course of couple relationships. In longitudinal studies, both PREPARE (Larson & Olson, 1989; Fowers & Olson, 1986) and FOCCUS (Williams & Jurich, 1995) predict couples' relationship satisfaction and whether they stay together after the first 4–5 years of marriage. However, a presumption underlying inventory approaches is that awareness promotes better couple coping. As Silliman, Stanley, Coffin, Markman, and Jordan (in press) point out, identification of partner differences or relationship weaknesses may be counterproductive unless couples are helped to deal effectively with the differences or issues identified. For example, feedback on divergent expectations may lead to profitable discussion, but couples lacking conflict management skills may be unable to resolve such differences.

Skill Training

The third broad category of relationship education is skill training programs. The essential assumption in this approach is that some people have never learned, or have forgotten, certain crucial relationship skills that promote high-quality intimate relationships. Therefore skill training programs focus on teaching what are assumed to be crucial relationship skills, such as effective communication.

There is some empirical support for the assumption that some people have never learned certain relationship skills, particularly communication skills. It has been argued that modeling of such skills as negative affect regulation and effective communication in the family of origin is central to the development of these skills (Holtzworth-Munroe, 1992; Mihalic & Elliot, 1997; O'Leary, 1988). Consistent with this argument, people exposed to ineffective models of these relationship skills in the family of origin have deficits in communication skills with intimate partners as adults (Halford, Sanders, & Behrens, 2000a).

However, the assumption that couples do not communicate well simply because the partners have never learned crucial communication skills is contradicted by other evidence. Partners in distressed relationship show poor communication toward each other, but do not necessarily show the same deficits in communication when interacting with other people (Vincent, Weiss, & Birchler, 1975). In other words, at least some distressed partners have positive communication within their behavioral repertoires, but sometimes do not exhibit this positive communication when interacting with each other. The failure to utilize available relationship skills may be due to a range of factors, such as high negative affect arousal or some other factor inhibiting the use of skills.

In the context of relationship education, many authors advocating a skill training approach seem to recognize implicitly that skills training alone is insufficient to promote positive couple relationships. Most predominantly, skill training programs include content other than skill training (e.g., development of relationship commitment; Stanley, Blumberg, & Markman, in press), and review family-of-origin experiences as a way of developing helpful relationship expectations (van Widenfelt, Hosman, Schaap, & van der Staak, 1996). In other words, the defining characteristic of skill training programs is an emphasis upon skill training, but few if any such programs focus only on relationship skill training.

There are several examples of skill training relationship education programs, including Guerney and colleagues' (Guerney, 1977, 1987; Guerney & Maxson, 1990) Relationship Enhancement (RE) program; Markman and colleagues' (Markman, Stanley, & Blumberg, 1994; Stanley et al., in press) Prevention and Relationship Enhancement Program (PREP); and the Minnesota Couples Communication Program (MCCP; Miller, Wackman, & Nunally, 1976). In each of these programs, couples receive instruction in the use of key relationship skills, usually involving a mixture of lectures, demonstrations, and audiovisual presentations. Couples also receive opportunities to practice these new skills, and receive feedback from educators about their use of skills. Moreover, most programs involve some structured assignments that partners are asked to undertake between sessions to practice applying skills within their own relationship.

The content of the various programs has a number of common elements. For example, positive communication, conflict management, and positive expressions of affection are included in RE, PREP, and MCCP (Guerney, 1977; Markman et al., 1994; Miller et al., 1976). There are also significant variations. For example, PREP places the most emphasis in content on the prevention of negative conflict, as this is argued to be central to the prevention of relationship problems (Markman et al., 1994). In RE, the development of partner empathy receives very strong emphasis (Guerney, 1977), while this component has less emphasis in PREP. The variation of content in specific skills targeted in relationship education raises the question of what is known about determinants of relationship satisfaction and stability.

INFLUENCES ON RELATIONSHIP OUTCOMES

Relationship satisfaction in couples is almost universally high at the time of marriage, but the typical levels of satisfaction decrease markedly across the first 4–5 years of marriage (Bradbury, Cohan,

& Karney, 1998; Halford, 1999). There is great variability among couples around this average trend, with some couples sustaining high relationship satisfaction, and other couples developing distressed relationships. Between 10% and 15% of couples separate within the first 3–4 years of marriage (McDonald, 1995). Moreover, physical aggression is a substantial problem in early marriage. About one-third of young couples report engaging in physical aggression, most commonly throwing things, pushing, slapping, or shoving (O'Leary, Malone, & Tyree, 1994; Pan, Neidig, & O'Leary, 1994). Even these less severe forms of aggression can lead to injury, and significant physical injury occurs in about 10% of couples (Straus & Gelles, 1986; Straus, Gelles, & Steinmetz, 1980). The occurrence of aggression early in the relationship is a strong predictor of relationship breakdown (Rogge & Bradbury, 1999).

Attempts to enhance relationship satisfaction and stability often focus on the early years of marriage (Halford, 1999). This is logical, given the rapid changes in satisfaction that occur in these early years. If we are to prevent relationship problems through relationship education, then it is important for relationship education to change those variables that influence the trajectory of couple relationships over time. Important information on the influences on relationship outcomes comes from longitudinal studies of the course of relationships. There are over 120 published studies assessing psychological variables and the longitudinal course of couple relationship satisfaction and stability (Karney & Bradbury, 1995). Bradbury (1995) has adapted the stress–vulnerability–coping model to offer a heuristic model by which this comprehensive literature can usefully be summarized. There are also many studies that have examined sociodemographic variables and their relationship to the satisfaction and stability of couple relationships (Glenn, 1998; Larsen & Holman, 1994). Halford (1999) has modified and extended Karney and Bradbury's (1995) model to incorporate these sociodemographic factors. Halford (1999) suggests that four broad classes of variables have an impact upon the trajectory of relationship satisfaction over time: adaptive processes within the couple system, life events impinging upon the couple, enduring individual characteristics of the partners, and contextual variables. "Contextual variables" are the cultural and social circumstances within which couple relationships exist.

Adaptive Couple Processes

"Adaptive processes" are the cognitive, behavioral, and affective processes that occur during couple interaction. Certain deficits in these adaptive processes seem to predispose couples to relationship problems. Specifically, deficits in communication and conflict management behaviors observed in engaged couples predict divorce and relationship dissatisfaction over the first years of marriage (Gottman, Coan, Carrère, & Swanson, 1998; Markman, 1981; Markman & Hahlweg, 1993). Dysfunctional communication in engaged couples also predicts the development of mild- to moderate-severity verbal and physical aggression in the first few years of marriage (Murphy & O'Leary, 1989; O'Leary et al., 1989). Relationship aggression is often established early in the relationship, and usually continues and escalates once established (Murphy & O'Leary, 1989; O'Leary et al., 1989).

It is noteworthy that the communication deficits observed in some engaged couples do not correlate with their reported relationship satisfaction at the time (Markman & Hahlweg, 1993; Sanders, Halford, & Behrens, 1999). It seems that these communication difficulties do not stop couples from forming committed relationships, but the difficulties may predispose couples to develop relationship problems later (Pasch & Bradbury, 1998). In couples that have been married for some time, these same communication difficulties predict deterioration in relationship satisfaction, as well as decreased relationship stability (Gottman, 1993, 1994).

The beliefs and expectations individuals have when entering into relationships and marriage also predict the risk of divorce in the first few years of marriage (Fowers & Olson, 1986; Larson & Olson, 1989). Couples with unrealistic expectations and beliefs in such areas as importance of communication, appropriate methods of conflict resolution, the importance of family and friends, and gender roles have higher rates of erosion in relationship satisfaction than couples not so characterized. Negative attributions, in which partners ascribe blame for relationship problems to stable, negative characteristics of their mates, also predict deterioration in relationship satisfaction (Bradbury & Fincham, 1990a).

Finally, certain patterns of emotional expression are predictive of relationship problems. Partners' showing contempt, disgust, fear or emotional withdrawal during their interaction is predictive of relationship deterioration and taking steps toward separation (Gottman, 1994). Thus certain behavioral, cognitive, and affective characteristics of a couple's adaptive processes predate, and prospectively predict, relationship problems.

Life Events

"Life events" are the developmental transitions, and other acute and chronic circumstances, that impinge upon the couple or individual partners. Relationship problems are often argued to be more likely to develop during periods of high rates of change and stressful events (Karney & Bradbury, 1995). For example, the transition to parenthood is sometimes associated with a decline in couple relationship satisfaction (Cowan & Cowan, 1992). However, many couples report that transition to parenthood enhances relationship satisfaction and commitment. Similarly, partners who successfully support each other through stressful events such as severe illness in one partner often report that the experience brings them closer together (Halford, Scott, & Smythe, 2000). Thus other variables mediate the effect of significant life events upon a relationship, and similar life events may be associated with increased or decreased relationship satisfaction in different couples.

Couple with less robust adaptive processes are believed to be particularly vulnerable to the negative effects of stressful life events (Markman, Halford, & Cordova, 1997). In particular, partners who lack communication skills, or who have inflexible or unrealistic expectations of relationships, find it hard to negotiate the changes required adapting to major life events. For example, couples in which the woman was recently diagnosed with breast or gynecological cancer, and in which the partners have poor communication and ineffective mutual support, show deterioration in their relationships and poor individual coping with the cancer (Halford, Scott, & Smythe, 2000).

Individual Characteristics

"Individual characteristics" are the stable historical, personal, and experiential factors that each partner brings to a relationship (Bradbury, 1995). Most normal personality variations do not seem to contribute much variance to relationship satisfaction (Gottman, 1994; Karney & Bradbury, 1995). Two exceptions are that low ability to regulate negative affect (high neuroticism; Karney & Bradbury, 1997) and insecure attachment (Feeney & Noller, 1996) have consistently been found to predict higher risk for relationship problems.

History of Psychological Disorder

A major risk indicator for relationship distress is past or present history of psychological disorder. Higher rates of relationship problems and divorce have consistently been reported in populations with severe psychiatric disorder in general (Halford, 1995), and in people with depression, alcohol abuse, and some anxiety disorders (especially panic disorder and generalized anxiety disorder) in particular (Emmelkamp, De Haan, & Hoogduin, 1990; Halford, Bouma, Kelly, & Young, 1999; Halford & Osgarby, 1993; O'Farrell & Birchler, 1987; Reich & Thompson, 1985; Ruscher & Gotlib, 1988; Weissman, 1987). Relationship problems and individual problems can exacerbate each other (Halford et al., 1999). In addition, certain personal vulnerabilities may dispose people to both psychological disorders and relationship problems. For example, deficits in interpersonal communication and negative affect regulation are risk factors that predict the onset of both alcohol abuse (Block, Block, & Keyes, 1988), and relationship problems (Markman & Hahlweg, 1993). This common risk factor might be part of the reason for the correlation of marriage and alcohol problems.

Relationship History

Negative family-of-origin experiences also increase the chance of relationship problems. In particular, parental divorce is associated with greater marital problems in the offspring when they become adults (DeGraaf, 1991; Glenn & Kramer, 1987; Glenn & Shelton, 1983; Pope & Mueller, 1976). Parental divorce seems to have a particularly strong impact upon women. Women experiencing parental divorce have a 60% higher divorce rate than women without such a history, whereas men with a history of parental divorce have a 35% higher divorce rate than men without such a history (Glenn & Shelton, 1983). Another well-established risk indicator for couple relationships is violence in the family of origin (e.g., Burgess, Hartman, & McCormack, 1987; Mihalic & Elliot, 1997; Stets & Straus, 1990; Stith & Farley, 1993; Straus et al., 1980; Widom, 1989). Specifically, men who report witnessing violence between their parents

have a substantially higher risk of being violent themselves (Hotaling & Sugarman, 1986; Mihalic & Elliot, 1997; Riggs, O'Leary, & Breslin, 1990; Stets & Straus, 1990; Stith & Farley, 1993; Straus et al., 1980; Widom, 1989).

The mechanism by which exposure to parental divorce or aggression may affect subsequent adult relationships is becoming clearer. Exposure to parental divorce is associated with more negative expectations of marriage (Black & Sprenkle, 1991; Gibardi & Rosen, 1991), and with observable deficits in communication and conflict management in couples prior to marriage (Sanders et al., 1999). Adult offspring of aggressive parents also show deficits in communication and conflict management skills in dating and marital relationships (Halford, Sanders, & Behrens, 2000). Negative expectations and communication deficits may well be learned from the parents' relationship, and subsequently this learned behavior has a negative impact upon the adult relationships of the offspring.

The longer and better partners know each other before marriage, the greater the reported relationship satisfaction after marriage (Birtchnell & Kennard, 1984; Grover, Russel, Schumm, & Paff-Bergen, 1985; Kurdek, 1991, 1993). It has been suggested that shorter dating periods before entering commitment may not allow people to screen out potentially incompatible partners (Grover et al., 1985). Although this may be true, other variables may explain this association. For example, those who choose to marry quickly may differ in attachment style from those who delay marriage. Perhaps the attachment style predicts both rapid marriage and high risk for relationship problems.

Cohabitation before marriage is consistently associated with increased risk of relationship distress and separation (Balakkrishnan, Rao, Lapierre-Adamcyk, & Krotski, 1987; Janus & Janus, 1993; Trussel & Rao, 1987). Choosing to cohabit is associated with a variety of other factors, such as low religiosity, uncertainty about committing to the relationship, and negative perceptions of marriage. Any of these variables might account for the high risk of relationship breakdown in couples whose members cohabited before marriage.

Gender

There are important differences between how men and women function within relationships. For example, women are more likely than men to report dissatisfaction with a lack of emotional closeness in their marriages (Clements & Markman, 1996; Julien, Arellano, & Tugeon, 1997), to be more emotionally expressive when discussing relationship issues (Weiss & Heyman, 1997), to report greater conflict between their work and family roles (Thompson, 1997), and to initiate divorce (Wolcott & Glezer, 1989). There also is evidence that men and women experience intimacy somewhat differently. Women are more likely to experience self-disclosure of feelings as high in intimacy, whereas men are more likely to experience shared activity as intimacy (Markman & Kraft, 1989). Marriage and relationship education programs need to provide information to participants on gender differences, and to assist couples to develop ways to meet the needs of both male and female partners.

Contextual Variables

Cultural Factors

Couple relationships occur within a cultural context that defines how marriage and other couple relationships are supposed to be. Although certain general assumptions are shared across Western cultures, there are also important variations among those cultures. For example, German couples without relationship problems engage in levels of verbal negativity similar to those of Australian distressed couples (Halford, Hahlweg, & Dunne, 1990), suggesting that greater levels of negativity are more acceptable and less dysfunctional in the German cultural context than in Australia. Even within one country, there is great diversity in acceptable relationship behavior. Winkler and Doherty (1983) found that verbal conflict was reported as more common in New York couples whose members were born in Israel than in Anglo couples living in New York. However, verbal conflict was less often associated with physical aggression or relationship distress in the Israeli-born couples than in the Anglo couples. Thus the cultural appropriateness and functional impact of behavior vary considerably even within Western cultures.

It can be important to assess the cultural context within which relationship standards develop and may be reinforced. Partners who differ in their ethnic, racial, or cultural background often differ in their expectations and beliefs about relationships (Jones & Chao, 1997). This diversity in partner assumptions and beliefs can be a source of great strength for a relationship when the partners are able to draw on the wisdom and strengths of different cultural traditions. At the same time, substantial differences in expectations can be a significant source of conflict between the partners (Jones & Chao, 1997), and marriages in which partners have very different cultural backgrounds tend to break down at somewhat higher rates than other marriages (Birtchnell & Kennard, 1984; Kurdek, 1991). The magnitude of effects of ethnic dissimilarity on relationship satisfaction and stability is generally small (White, 1990).

Other Relationships and Roles

Although the partner role is central to most adults in couple relationships, this is not the only relationship or role that the partners have. Other relationships and roles of each partner are part of the context in which couple interaction occurs, and these other relationships and roles can have a positive or negative impact on the couple relationship. For example, work often provides extra stimulation and ideas to enrich the relationship, but work demands can also compete for time with the partner (Thompson, 1997). Friends may provide support and shared activities that complement the relationship, and reduce the chance of excessive dependence upon the spouse. However, friendships can also take away time from the partner. Parenting, sports, hobbies, and community service activities all have the capacity to enrich or erode relationship quality.

There are consistent findings that approval of one's spouse and relationship by friends and extended family are predictive of better relationship satisfaction and stability (Booth & Johnson, 1988; Kurdek, 1991). At the same time, there is evidence that excessive intrusion by family on selection of dating partners and subsequent mate selection may predict relationship problems (Benson, Larson, Wilson, & Demo, 1993).

Implications of Evidence for Relationship Education

One major implication of the existing research on relationship satisfaction and stability is for the targeting of relationship education. As is evident from the preceding overview of research, a broad range of risk variables predicts the trajectory of relationship satisfaction and stability. These variables can usefully be conceptualized as falling into two categories: "static risk indicators" and "dynamic risk factors." Static risk indicators cannot be changed at the time of intervention. For example, age and family-of-origin experiences are static variables that predict risk of relationship problems. In contrast, dynamic risk factors can be changed. For example, relationship expectations and couple communication predict risk of relationship problems and can be changed by relationship education.

Many static risk indicators can be measured relatively easily. For example, parental divorce, age, previous marriages, and the presence of children can be assessed by simple questions. Assessment of these risk indicators can help couples or educators to assess the relative risk level of particular couples for relationship problems, and thus can allow targeting of relationship education for those couples who may benefit most from relationship education.

Dynamic factors, such as couple communication and relationship expectations, are often more time consuming to assess. For example, observed communication is a reliable predictor of relationship distress, but sophisticated audiovisual recording equipment and highly trained raters are required to assess it. However, some dynamic risk factors are reliably associated with certain risk indicators. For example, parental divorce and aggression in the family of origin are associated with negative communication in engaged couples (Halford, Sanders, & Behrens, 2000; Sanders et al., 1999). Thus it is possible to evaluate couples for these easily assessed risk indicators, and to view these risk indicators as markers of likely negative communication. Negative communication can then be targeted in the relationship education, and when communication improves in couples at high risk of relationship problems, this has been shown to help couples sustain relationship satisfaction (Halford, Sanders, & Behrens, in press).

A second major implication of the research on relationship satisfaction and stability is for the timing of relationship education is offered. Traditionally, relationship education has primarily been offered to couples entering committed relationships; it often coincides with marriage (Hunt et al., 1998). Entry to marriage is a good time for relationship education, in that couples often face significant challenges in developing a committed relationship. Many people find that initial overwhelming attraction to their partners moderates, that new relationship roles and routines need to be developed, and that means of negotiating conflict need to evolve (Huston, McHale, & Crouter,

1986; Veroff, Douvan, & Hatchett, 1995). As noted earlier, relationship satisfaction declines in an approximately linear fashion across the first 4–5 years of marriage (Huston et al., 1986; Karney & Bradbury, 1997; Veroff et al., 1995), and about one-third of all divorces occur in the first 5 years of marriage (Clarke, 1995).

In addition to the time of entry to a committed relationship, several other life events and developmental processes that couples experience can be associated with increased risk of relationship problems. For example, the transition to parenthood, relocation, major illness, and unemployment are all associated with increased risk of relationship problems (Belsky & Kelly, 1994; Gagnon, Hersen, Kabacoff, & van Hasselt, 1999; Larsen & Holman, 1994). Relationship education that assists couples to make these challenging life transitions may help them to sustain relationship satisfaction and commitment.

A third major implication of the evidence is that some couples have special needs in relationship education. Couples forming stepfamilies constitute as one important example. There is a particularly high rate of conflict over parenting in stepfamilies (Cissna, Cox, & Bochner, 1990). Negotiating the parenting arrangements in stepfamilies involves special challenges, particularly with respect to the role of stepparents in major decisions about and discipline of children (Visher & Visher, 1991). Effective interventions to promote satisfying stepfamily couple relationships need to address the relationship of stepparents with children, and help partners to negotiate mutually acceptable parenting arrangements (Lawton & Sanders, 1994).

A second example of couples with special needs consists of couples in which a partner has a psychological disorder that affects the relationship, such as alcohol abuse or depression (Halford et al., 1999). In such a couple, helping the partner with the disorder to change his/her behavior is likely to be an important element of promoting a mutually satisfying relationship. For example, encouraging a partner who drinks heavily to moderate the drinking, using a brief intervention consisting of motivational interviewing, goal setting, and coping with high-risk settings, might enhance long-term relationship satisfaction and stability. In addition, educating both partners about the nature of the disorder, and how best to manage the disorder and its effects on the relationship, can be helpful (Halford & Bouma, 1997).

RESEARCH ON
RELATIONSHIP EDUCATION

There are a great many research studies evaluating marriage education and enrichment, and there have been numerous reviews and meta-analyses of that evidence (Bagarozzi & Rauen, 1981; Bradbury & Fincham, 1990b; Christensen & Heavey, 1999; Dyer & Halford, 1998; Giblin, Sprenkle, & Sheehan, 1985; Guerney & Maxson, 1990; Hahlweg & Markman, 1988; Sayers, Kohn, & Heavey, 1998; van Widenfelt, Markman, Guerney, Behrens, & Hosman, 1997). There is a general finding that most couples completing competently run premarriage education programs generally report high satisfaction with these programs (Harris et al., 1992). This high satisfaction is evident across information and awareness programs, inventory-based programs, and skill training programs (Halford, 1999). Although high consumer satisfaction is desirable, this result by itself does not address the effects of relationship education on relationship outcomes.

Only skill-based relationship education has been evaluated in controlled-trial evaluations. Neither awareness- or inventory-based relationship education has been subjected to such evaluations. The conclusions drawn by reviewers of research on the effects of skills-based relationship education on relationship outcomes have diverged quite markedly, even when the same evidence has been examined. For example, Guerney and Maxson (1990), commenting on the meta-analysis of outcome studies undertaken by Giblin et al. (1985), concluded that "there is no doubt that, on the whole, enrichment programs work and the field is an entirely legitimate one" (p. 1133). In contrast, Bradbury and Fincham (1990b) concluded from the results of the same meta-analysis that "prevention programs have not yet been shown to produce lasting changes in relationships" (p. 397).

Given the diversity of conclusions drawn by previous reviewers of the evidence, it is important to analyze very carefully the available evidence on the effects of relationship education. We restrict ourselves to evaluations of relationship education programs that target currently satisfied couples entering committed relationships. There have been reports of the development of relationship education programs for couples during the transition to parenthood, after divorce, and entering step-families. However, there have been only one or two evaluations of such programs in controlled trials,

and none that have evaluated the long-term effects on relationships (Halford, 1999).

In order to evaluate the true status of relationship education, we describe two widely cited meta-analyses of relationship education studies: one by Giblin et al. (1985), and another by Hahlweg and Markman (1988). The Giblin et al. (1985) meta-analysis of 85 relationship education and enhancement programs found an average effect size of 0.44 across all education programs and relationship outcome measures, which corresponds to a small to moderate effect size according to Cohen's (1997) conventions. However, most studies in this meta-analysis lacked any sort of control group, and only a very small number of the studies included any follow-up results. The Hahlweg and Markman (1988) meta-analysis included only seven studies evaluating relationship education, all of which were published studies that included controlled trials. Moreover, they focused their review on programs that included relationship skills training. They found a large mean effect size of 0.79 for education programs relative to controls.

Both the Giblin et al. (1985) and Hahlweg and Markman (1988) meta-analyses found differences in effect sizes as a function of type of measure used to assess change. Observational measures of relationship skills showed substantially larger effect sizes than self-report measures of relationship satisfaction (0.76 vs. 0.35 in Giblin et al., 1985, and 1.51 vs. 0.52 in Hahlweg & Markman, 1988). Furthermore, Giblin et al. (1985) found greater effect sizes for self-report measures classified as assessing relationship skills (0.63) than for measures classified as assessing relationship satisfaction (0.34). Thus, since the mid- to late 1980s it has been well established that relationship education produces large improvements in relationship skills in the short term, and that there are small short-term increases in relationship satisfaction. However, these results still do not address the long-term effects of relationship education on relationship outcomes.

We have been able to locate only eight controlled trials evaluating relationship education programs for currently satisfied couples that include follow-up assessments of 6 months or more. All these programs have targeted engaged, dating, or recently married couples, and have consisted of between four and eight face-to-face group sessions of two to three hours duration. All of these evaluations were of skills-based programs, with almost all of them focusing upon PREP or a variant of PREP.

Across studies there is a consistent finding that, relative to no-intervention or minimal-intervention controls, couples acquire the targeted skills (Avery, Ridley, Leslie, & Milholland, 1980; Markman, Floyd, Stanley & Storaasli, 1988; Miller, Nunnally, & Wackman, 1975; Markman & Hahlweg, 1993; Renick, Blumberg, & Markman, 1992; Wampler & Sprenkle, 1980). Long-term maintenance of acquired skills is less well investigated, but three recent findings show maintenance of acquired skills over a period of some years (Hahlweg, Markman, Thurmair, Engel, & Eckert, 1998; Halford, Sanders, & Behrens, 2001; Markman, Renick, Floyd, Stanley, & Clements, 1993). However, attenuation of training effects was reported to occur over a 5- to 10-year period in the only study to have a follow-up over that period of time (Stanley, Markman, St. Peters, & Leber, 1995).

The long-term effects of relationship education on relationship satisfaction and risk of divorce are not well documented. Short-term increases in satisfaction as a result of relationship education are modest in some studies (Renick et al., 1992; Ridley, Jorgensen, Morgan, & Avery, 1982) and not evident at all in many studies (e.g., Halford, Sanders, & Behrens, 2001; Markman et al., 1988; Markman & Hahlweg, 1993; van Widenfelt et al., 1996). This lack of effect on relationship satisfaction in the short term may be a function of the fact that relationship satisfaction is already high in the targeted populations. In addition, there may be a ceiling effect operating in the measures currently used to measure relationship satisfaction.

The most meaningful index of the efficacy of relationship education is its long-term effects; unfortunately, only four studies have had follow-ups of more than 12 months, and all of these studies have focused on PREP or a variant of PREP. Markman and colleagues have found in two studies that skills-based relationship education was associated with enhanced relationship satisfaction or functioning 2 and 5 years after marriage (Hahlweg et al., 1998; Markman et al., 1993). The Markman et al. (1993) study also found that across the 3-, 4-, and 5-year follow-ups, the intervention couples reported significantly fewer instances of spousal physical violence than control couples. A third study using an almost identical education program did not replicate these results (van Widenfelt et al., 1996). The van Widenfelt et al. study differed from Markman and colleagues' studies in that high-risk couples were targeted. This finding may indicate limitations in developing relationship education programs solely through research at the level of universal populations. Neither the Markman et al. (1993) nor Hahlweg et al. (1998) studies were true, randomized controlled trials. In the case of the Markman et al. (1993) study, couples were randomly assigned to be offered or not offered the relationship education program. Only about one-third of couples offered the program agreed to participate. In the Hahlweg et al. (1998) study, couples could choose whether to undertake the skills-based relationship education program or a standard church-provided program. Thus there is a confound of self-selection into relationship education with access to PREP in both the Markman et al. (1993) and Hahlweg et al. (1998) studies.

The fourth study was a randomized controlled trial of a skills-based relationship education program, with collection of relationship satisfaction and stability data at a 4-year follow-up (Halford, Sanders, & Behrens, 2001). The relationship education program evaluated was Self-PREP, which is similar in content to PREP, but has a self-regulation focus (the self-regulation focus is described in detail later in this chapter). A unique aspect of this study was that couples were stratified into groups at high and low risk for relationship problems on the basis of negative family-of-origin experiences (parental divorce or interparental violence). Couples completing Self-PREP were found to have significantly higher relationship satisfaction at 4-year follow-up than couples in a control condition, but this effect was only evident for couples at high risk of relationship problems. The possibility that relationship education may have differential effects for low- and high-risk couples needs further exploration.

In summary, the effects of skills-based relationship education programs on relationship skills are well established, in that these programs produce increases in skills that are sustained for at least the first few years of a committed relationship. There is some evidence that PREP and its variants prevent the erosion of relationship satisfaction over time, but these effects may be limited to couples at high risk for relationship distress. Given the limitations of the existing small number of studies, replications of the long-term effects of PREP in randomized controlled trials are highly desirable.

There may be positive benefits of relationship education that have not been assessed adequately. Existing evaluations of relationship education have focused primarily on prevention of problems, using marital separation and prevention of erosion of marital satisfaction as the key indices of outcome. The measures of relationship satisfaction used have a heavy emphasis upon problems. For example, the Dyadic Adjustment Scale (DAS; Spanier, 1976) includes a large number of items on conflict. The sensitivity of relationship satisfaction measures to increases in positive aspects of a currently satisfied couple relationship is uncertain, but there may well be ceiling effects (Dyer & Halford, 1998).

ASSESSMENT IN RELATIONSHIP EDUCATION

Descriptions of relationship education programs rarely include assessment of the couples before education, and reports from providers of relationship education suggest that assessment of couples is rarely conducted (Halford, 1999). However, in our experience, relationship education works best when assessment has been done, so that the educator knows the couples and their goals for relationship education. Consequently, before commencing relationship education, we conduct an initial assessment session with each couple. In that session, one aim is to get to know both members of the couple and find out their relationship education goals. A second aim is to screen for factors that contraindicate relationship education for that couple. A third aim is to assess any special needs the couple may have that will require attention during relationship education.

The assessment session typically consists of a conjoint interview, brief individual interviews with each partner, and completion of some self-report inventories. In the conjoint interview, the partners are asked about their relationship history to establish how long they have been together, and they are asked about any particular challenges they face in their relationship and whether there are children in the relationship. The partners are also asked about their goals in attending relationship education. In the individual interviews, we ask about previous relationships, and we ask about any prior history of psychological or psychiatric treatment. We also ask about the occurrence of aggression in the current or previous relationships. Approximately 25% of marrying couples report an episode of violence in their relationship in the previous 12 months (O'Leary et al., 1994; McLaughlin, Leonard, & Senchak, 1992), and the occurrence of aggression early in the relationship predicts relationship breakup in the first few years of marriage (Rogge & Bradbury, 1999). Consequently, it is important to know whether aggression is occurring, and if it is, to assess the risk of injury to each partner, particularly the woman.

In a typical relationship education program we have couples complete a selection of self-report measures prior to commencing relationship education. Spanier's (1976) DAS is part of this initial assessment. The DAS is a 32-item global self-report measure of relationship satisfaction. Scores of 90 or below indicate significant relationship distress. Couples that are experiencing significant relationship distress should not be included in a relationship enhancement and prevention program. For couples that are currently very satisfied in their relationships, it can be distressing to have couples with major distress engage in conflict in the group. Furthermore, distressed couples are better served by attending conjoint therapy rather than group relationship education sessions.

Individuals with severe individual psychological disorder may require specific assistance, and we routinely assess partners for individual problems. For example, the Depression Anxiety Stress Scale (DASS; Lovibond & Lovibond, 1995) is a 21-item self-report measure that provides a useful assessment of depression, anxiety, and stress. Scores for either partner the severe clinical range on any of the subscales of the DASS suggest that work with the couple alone, rather than in a group, is advisable. The Alcohol Use Disorders Test (AUDIT) (Saunders, Aasland, Babor, de la Fuente, & Grant, 1993) is a 10-item screening measure of hazardous and harmful drinking; a score of 8 or more on this scale indicates hazardous drinking levels. Drinking in the harmful range (approximately 40 standard drinks per week for men or 20 for women, or the presence of binge drinking) indicates that work with the drinking partner is advisable before the couple enters a group relationship education program.

THE STRUCTURE OF RELATIONSHIP EDUCATION

The content covered within different skill-based relationship education programs varies somewhat. Given that PREP has the strongest evidence for its efficacy as an approach to relationship education, we have based our approach to relationship education on PREP. The emphasis in our programs is on active training in key skills associated with relationship satisfaction and stability. In addition, we emphasize a self-regulation focus, which encourages each partner to focus on self-directed change. In this chapter, we describe two versions of our relationship education programs. In one version of our program, referred to as Self-PREP, PREP-like skills training is provided in face-to-face groups. Self-PREP has been evaluated in a controlled trial (Halford, Sanders, & Behrens, in press). In a second version, known as Couple Commitment and Relationship Enhancement (Couple CARE), similar content is covered, but it is delivered as a flexible, self-directed learning program. This involves a couple's watching a videotape and undertaking exercises from a guidebook, with the assistance of a telephone-based education service. Couple CARE is currently the subject of a controlled trial evaluation.

The content of both Self-PREP and Couple CARE falls into six units, which are summarized in Table 14.1. The initial session is focused on relationship goal setting. To that end, the members of each couple develop a shared relationship goal statement, which we refer to as their "relationship vision." Development of this vision involves having couples discuss a number of dimensions of expectations about relationships, such as the desired degree of closeness versus autonomy in the

relationship, gender role expectations, expectations about power and control, and expectations about styles of communication. Partners discuss memories of their families of origin, explore and how their families (and subsequent important relationships) may have shaped their relationship expectations. The partners consider the strengths and weaknesses they believe they bring to the current relationship, and develop a shared set of relationship goals. The leader helps couples define specifically and concretely their vision of a good relationship. This then becomes a basis for developing self-change goals that help them move toward their defined relationship vision.

An important element of all skill-based relationship education programs is communication skills training. In our view, what constitutes adaptive communication within a relationship is likely to vary across relationships and across settings (Halford, Gravestock, Lowe, & Scheldt, 1992). Consequently, individuals select goals for enhancing their own communication from an array of

---

TABLE 14.1. Content of Self-PREP and Couple CARE, Six-Session Relationship Education Programs

Module	Details of content
1	*Introduction and goal setting.* Introduction of leader(s) and couple(s); overview of program; rationale for skills training focus of program; identification of key behavioral domains promoting relationship intimacy; review of relationship expectations; development of relationship goals; intimacy enhancement through self-directed goal setting.
2	*Communication.* Review of key communication skills; guided self-evaluation of current communication skills; self-directed selection of communication enhancement goals and practice of implementation of those skills; self-directed goal setting; and definition of homework task to enhance communication.
3	*Intimacy.* Review of communication homework tasks, self-directed further goal selection and definition of further homework task; review of factors promoting intimacy; assessing partner support; expressions of caring; reviewing individual and joint activities; self-directed change plan.
4	*Conflict management.* Review intimacy enhancement tasks; introduction to the concept of the patterns of conflict and effective conflict management; negotiation with partner about relationship rules for managing conflict; self-directed goal setting for effective management of conflict; introduction to the concept of flexible gender roles; couple review of current gender roles; self-directed goal setting for future gender role flexibility.
5	*Sexuality.* Review of communication homework task; review of the role of sexuality in relationship intimacy; couple discussion and goal setting to enhance sexual intimacy; introduction to the concept of partner support; self-directed goal setting to enhance partner support; self-directed definition of homework tasks to implement selected goals in areas of sexuality or partner support.
6	*Managing change.* Review of homework tasks; self-directed selection of any further goals to enhance relationship functioning; introduction of maintenance of relationship functioning; self-directed identification of future life events with possible impact upon relationship; planning to promote relationship adaptation to predictable life events; closure.

available skills, and evaluate their own, rather than their partners', communication. In practice, partners are first asked to have a discussion with each other. After the discussion, each partner is asked to assess his/her own communication during the discussion, using a checklist of potentially helpful communication behaviors set out in the form in Figure 14.1. After completing that form, partners identify for themselves specific communication behaviors that they would like to improve in order to enhance their communication. This does not mean that the leader avoids responsibility for helping the partners determine goals. Rather, the role of the leader is to help both partners to self-evaluate their current communication accurately, and to

develop specific, self-selected goals for enhancing communication.

Conflict management is another important element of relationship education. Once partners have a reasonable level of communication skills, they can then use these skills to better handle difficult conflict. As part of the session on conflict management, there is a discussion of the different settings in which conflict may occur, and of the fact that there are some settings in which it is easier to have a productive discussion than others. Partners are asked to consider the times, places, and circumstances in which they could most productively talk about difficult topics. Couples are also educated about the common maladaptive patterns of couple interaction

---

NAME: _____ DATE: _____

The aim of this form is for you to identify your strengths and weaknesses in communication and to select goals for improvement. Rate each of the skills below using this code:

    0   Very poor use of skill
    1   Unsatisfactory use of skill
    2   Satisfactory use of skill, but room for improvement
    3   Good use of skill
    N/A Not applicable

Skill	0	1	2	3	N/A
Specific descriptors					
Self-disclosure					
Clear expression of positives					
Assertive expression of negatives					
Attending to partner					
Minimal encouragers (e. g., nods, hm-mm)					
Reserving judgment					
Asking questions					
Summarizing content					
Paraphrasing feelings					
Positive suggestions					

Self-identified strengths in communication: _____

Self-identified weaknesses in communication: _____

FIGURE 14.1. Communication skills self-evaluation form.

around conflict, such as the demand–withdraw and mutual avoidance patterns. Partners are led to identify their own usual pattern of interaction around conflict, and then self-select goals that will help them to avoid unhelpful patterns.

In order to enable them to better maintain relationship satisfaction over time, it is important that couples prepare themselves for changes in their relationships produced by major life transitions. The members of each couple fill out an adapted form of the Life Change Event Scale. They are asked to rate the likelihood of various life events' occurring in the next 1–2 years, and the probability that if those events occur, they might have a negative effect on their relationship. They identify the ways in which an event such as birth of a child, loss of a job, or a change of work circumstances might affect the relationship. Partners are then asked to self-select goals that they believe would help them adapt in a relationship-enhancing way to these life transitions. For example, partners in a number of couples have identified that they may have reduced opportunities for having time together as a couple once they have children. They have then set individual goals, such as ensuring that babysitting is available or cultivating activities they can do at home, which will increase their chance of having shared enjoyable activities when they have young children.

In summary, the focus in both Self-PREP and Couple CARE is on developing the relationship metaskills of couples. In common with the original PREP, providing information about influences on relationship satisfaction and active training in key relationship skills are central to these programs. In Self-PREP and Couple CARE, partners are also assisted to set relationship goals, to monitor their individual contributions to the relationship, to set self-change goals, and to implement and evaluate self-change goals for achieving the relationship goals they identify.

APPLICATION OF RELATIONSHIP EDUCATION AND CASE EXAMPLES

The targeting of relationship education to couples can be undertaken in a variety of ways. Three possibilities described in the prevention research area are universal, selective, and indicated targeting. "Universal targeting" refers to any program that targets all members of the population in an effort to promote positive functioning or reduce the overall prevalence of a problem within a defined com-

munity (Muñoz, Mrazek, & Haggerty, 1996). In the context of relationship education, universal targeting applies to all people either entering or in committed relationships. "Selective targeting" focuses on people at high risk for problems; these would include couples currently satisfied with their relationships but at high risk for future difficulties. For example, selective targeting could focus on couples in which one of the partners has experienced parental divorce or violence in the family of origin. These couples have the same initial high relationship satisfaction as other couples, but are at high risk for erosion of relationship satisfaction (Halford, Sanders, & Behrens, 2000; Sanders et al., 1999). "Indicated targeting" refers to early intervention; it focuses on individuals with emerging relationship problems that have not yet developed into severe relationship distress. For example, education may be directed at couples whose members are engaging in relationship aggression, but who are not yet severely distressed, to try to prevent the development of severe problems later.

Most relationship education is offered universally to couples in the early stage of committed relationships (Halford, 1999). As noted earlier, we recommend assessment and referral to conjoint couple therapy rather than relationship education if a couple is currently significantly distressed, or if either partner has an individual psychological disorder. In other words, relationship education is best targeted to currently satisfied couples. Within the population of currently satisfied couples, larger benefits from relationship education have been shown for high-risk than for low-risk couples (Halford Sanders, & Behrens, 2001), and for couples showing early signs of relationship distress than for couples with very high satisfaction (Giblin et al., 1985; Hahlweg & Markman, 1988). However, even low–risk, currently satisfied couples may benefit from relationship education.

The following case illustrations focus on three couples, in each of which the partners reported high relationship satisfaction. The first couple was highly satisfied with the relationship, was at low risk for relationship problems, and would only be included in universal application of relationship education. The second couple was also highly satisfied with the relationship, but was at high risk of subsequent relationship problems, and would be included in a selective application of relationship education. The third couple showed some early signs of relationship problems, though the partners currently reported high relationship satisfaction.

Couple 1: Maggie and Bob

Maggie (aged 26) was a physiotherapist, and Bob (also aged 26) was a builder. A civil marriage celebrant who recommends that all couples attend relationship education referred them to the Couple CARE program. (In Australia, there is a system of accreditation for people who perform civil, nonreligious marriage ceremonies. Civil celebrants perform about 55% of Australian marriages.) Maggie and Bob had met through a cycling club, had been dating for about 2 years, and planned to marry in the next 3 months. At the initial assessment Bob and Maggie both reported being very satisfied in their relationship, and their scores on the DAS (127 and 140, respectively) confirmed this. Both Maggie's and Bob's parents were still married, and both partners reported that both sets of parents were highly supportive of their relationship.

Both partners stated that their relationship education goals were to maintain the loving relationship they currently felt, and to strengthen it against stress. Maggie stated that she particularly wanted to work on her communication, as she felt she did not communicate her thoughts and feelings when an issue arose for her, and this led to "things building up" inside her. Bob stated he wanted to develop skills to help Maggie express herself more clearly, particularly if and when she perceived his actions as being negative.

At the start of the program, the couple displayed good communication and support skills. The partners worked at maintaining positivity in the relationship. For example, they set aside couple time together, and made regular efforts to include new ways of showing caring in the relationship. During the course of the program, Maggie focused on enhancing the communication skills of self-disclosure and of clearly and regularly expressing positives. Both partners committed themselves to ensuring that the household workload was equitable and that they were flexible in regard to their roles. In terms of social support, Bob focused on enhancing his listening skills and emotional support for Maggie and on reducing the number of problem solving he engaged in, unless Maggie specifically asked for it. Both partners identified that finding additional time for positive activities was a goal, and worked to increase the number and variety of activities they shared. They also agreed to regularly put aside time for more sexual intimacy, and to employ someone to take over some of Bob's paperwork in order to free him up for this in the

evenings. In terms of planning to maintain a relationship focus in the future, the couple decided that each month they would review at least one unit of the Couple CARE resources. They also agreed to seek out other resources (e.g., books) that they could use to continue enhancing the relationship.

In spite of having both reported very high relationship satisfaction before undertaking Couple CARE, Bob and Maggie each set numerous goals for change and implemented those changes, especially in the area of skills for building intimacy. At the end of the course, both partners reported being very satisfied with the program (as measured by a consumer satisfaction questionnaire). Bob and Maggie also noted that they had found the unit on communication to be the most helpful, stating that it had provided a broader spectrum of skills for listening and "getting ideas across" to each other. Substantial short gains in satisfaction are not usually reported in highly satisfied couples undergoing relationship education. However, Bob's DAS relationship satisfaction score increased from 127 to 140 across the course of Couple CARE, while Maggie's remained essentially the same (140 before and 139 after Couple CARE).

Couple 2: Carol and Jack

Carol (aged 58) was a receptionist, and Jack (aged 59) was an attorney. They applied for Couple CARE after hearing about the program on a local radio station. They had met through mutual friends, had begun dating about 2 years ago, and had been cohabiting for 17 months. Both Carol and Jack had previously been married and had children with their former spouses, all of whom now were adults now living away from home. Carol's parents had divorced when she was 9 years of age, and she had witnessed substantial interparental violence prior to their breakup. At the initial interview, both Carol and Jack reported being satisfied with their relationship, which was affirmed by their scores on the DAS of 112 and 113, respectively.

On entering the program, both partners noted that their main goal was to ensure they did not "repeat the mistakes" they had made in their previous marriages, and to give their relationship a "sure footing" for the future. Jack noted a desire to enhance the way he communicated, develop more patience, and be more flexible in his dealings with Carol. Carol stated that she wanted to learn to deal effectively with some differences they had—for example, reconciling her "laid-back" way of dealing with day-to-day events with Jack's finer attention to detail. She also said that she would like for Jack to become more relaxed and accepting of her spending time with women from the refuge where she worked on Saturdays.

Communication was a key focus for this couple. Carol set these goals: to express herself more assertively, and to encourage Jack to assert himself by her use of more effective listener skills. Jack set these goals: to enhance his listening skills, and to change his cognitive reactions to Carol's statements that he felt interfered with his listening to her. In particular, he focused on monitoring defensive thoughts in response to criticism, and replacing those thoughts with more helpful thoughts. Both partners also focused on enhancing their couple time together by setting goals to identify places and events they could visit that would bring novelty, affection, and romance to the relationship. They also agreed to bring some new sexual activities into their sexual repertoire and to be more verbally expressive of preferences and enjoyment during sex.

In the course of the program, the couple spent considerable time discussing Carol's desire to spend time at a women's refuge, where she worked as a volunteer. This issue had been a source of substantial conflict for this couple. Jack resented the time Carol spent away from him at the refuge on weekends. Carol felt that Jack was trying to be overcontrolling of her, as well as to restrict her involvement with work she valued highly. Their gradually improving communication skills allowed each to better understand the other's perspective on this issue. As part of the process of discussing the issue, Jack identified a range of activities he could undertake on weekends, and other strategies that allowed him to bolster his enjoyment of weekends without Carol. In turn, this led to a discussion of the desired balance of couple and individual activities within the relationship, which led Carol to resolve to increase her time with Jack by cutting back on some other activities. The couple commented how being able to communicate effectively not only allowed resolution of the immediate issue of the level of Carol's involvement with the refuge, but also opened up discussion of a range of related relationship issues that led to positive relationship changes. The process in which better communication about difficult issues leads couples to explore broader relationship enhancement themes is common in our experience of relationship education.

Another process that helped this couple was mutual encouragement of individual change. For example, once they had learned the process of giving constructive feedback (introduced in the communication unit), each partner used this skill to help the other identify the strengths and weaknesses in their efforts at achieving their self-directed change plans. They also focused on providing reinforcement for these efforts—for example, giving compliments about changes they noticed on a day-to-day basis. Application of these skills appeared to lead to increased positivity in the relationship.

At the end of the program, both partners noted that they had been highly satisfied with the course. They identified the communication and conflict management units as having been the most helpful units. There was some increase in relationship satisfaction for Carol, whose DAS score increased from 112 to 118; Jack's score remained virtually unchanged, going from 113 to 112.

Couple 3: Rose and Antony

Rose (aged 37) was a part-time student, and Antony (aged 41) was a surveyor. They decided to undertake Couple CARE after hearing a radio interview about the program. The couple had met through work 3 years ago, and had been living together for the past 2.5 years. They had twin daughters aged 22 months. It was the second marriage for both partners. Although Rose and Antony reported being satisfied with their relationship at the initial assessment, their scores on the DAS were 105 and 109, respectively; these indicated that they were not in the distressed range, but were not highly satisfied. During the initial assessment, both partners described in individual interviews that they had frequent conflict, particularly around parenting. They each described severe negative escalation of arguing and criticism. Both partners reported three incidents of mutual, low-level violence in the past year (pushing and shoving). Thus, although the couple was not overtly distressed, there were indications of developing relationship problems.

When asked about their hopes and goals for the program, Rose stated that she wanted Antony to improve his communication skills, and to spend more time talking and interacting with her. Rose wanted to cut down on her own interrupting during conversations. Antony noted that he would like to see their level of conflict reduced substantially, and for Rose to have more patience with him, especially when he was disciplining the children. Given the detected violence, we cautioned the couple that Couple CARE might not be the best approach for them, but they were very keen to proceed. We agreed to proceed with Couple CARE, but suggested that a more intensive therapy approach to managing their relationship conflict might be required.

The couple completed the first session of Couple CARE without difficulty. Rose and Antony identified key influences on their relationship expectations, and did not report extreme or conflicting expectations. Both partners completed self-directed change plans that related to communication, with Antony focusing on communicating his thoughts more clearly to Rose, while Rose decided to focus on developing patience by delaying her responses to Antony until she was sure he had finished having his say. The day before the next scheduled telephone education session, Rose telephoned the educator in a distressed state. She noted that while they were completing the unit on communication, their discussion of listening skills had become very heated, with each partner accusing the other of having "lousy" skills. This had culminated in Antony's walking out. The telephone educator debriefed Rose and made a time to call back and speak to both partners about the incident. During the subsequent telephone call, the facilitator reviewed each partner's role in the earlier discussion and helped them identify points at which they could have chosen to use specific listener and speaker skills to keep the discussion on track. Some brief training in the use of conflict management skills was introduced, and each partner was encouraged to move away from blaming verbalizations and focus on his/her own changes rather than on the other's changes. The couple then successfully completed the second unit of Couple CARE.

While undertaking the third unit, Antony called the educator in a distressed state reporting ongoing conflict between him and Rose. The conflict arose both during day-to-day interactions and when they were discussing the Couple CARE program materials. At this point, the couple agreed that it would be helpful to have some face-to-face sessions with a therapist, who would focus on helping them develop more positive communication and manage conflict.

The couple was referred to our university clinic and undertook a series of six couple therapy sessions focused on management of destructive conflict. This work addressed anger management problems that were reported to be long-standing for each partner. Part of this work looked at the underlying cognitions that drove their anger, using the cognitive affect reconstruction procedures described by Halford (2001). The sessions also focused on the prevention of violence by teaching cognitive-behavioral anger management strategies, and the use of time out from discussions when anger was developing.

After the six therapy sessions, the couple resumed the Couple CARE program and completed it successfully. They reported high satisfaction with the program. Couple CARE alone was not successful with this couple; the level of conflict was such that more intensive therapy was required. It is possible that a face-to-face relationship education program such as Self-PREP, rather than the flexible delivery format of Couple CARE, might have better addressed the couple's needs. However, an intensive therapy focus on anger management, violence prevention, and the intensive cognitive affect reconstruction is not provided in any standard relationship education. Relationship education is not a substitute for couple therapy with distressed couples. However, much of the content of relationship education programs can be useful for couples with less severe relationship distress. A combination of some elements of couple therapy and some elements of relationship education was tailored to this couple's needs, and it seemed to be effective.

CONCLUSIONS

There is a substantial history of offering relationship education to couples when they enter committed relationships. Research on the effectiveness of relationship education is slowly accumulating, but more research on the long-term effects of such programs is needed. Also, future research needs to address the needs of couples at stages other than just the transition into the relationship. The available evidence gives cause for some optimism that skills-based relationship education can enhance relationship skills and help maintain relationship satisfaction, though the effects on relationship satisfaction may be limited to couples at high risk of relationship problems.

The targeting of relationship education has largely been universal until now. It is unclear whether this is the optimal approach. As we have tried to illustrate in our first case example, even highly satisfied couples with assessed low risk for future relationship problems can report benefit from skills-based relationship education. However, the data indicating that such couples derive long-term relationship benefits are limited. This may reflect in part a failure to use measures sensitive to improvement in already satisfying relationships, and in part the fact that many couples can develop highly satisfying relationships without professional assistance. Couples whose members are not overtly dissatisfied and show no signs of relationship distress, but are at high risk of future relationship problems, do benefit from skills-based relationship education, which reduces the risk for future relationship problems. Our second case example is intended to illustrate the sort of benefits that may mediate the reduction of risk of future relationship problems in high-risk couples. Finally, there is evidence that indicated relationship education is helpful for couples whose members describe themselves as currently satisfied but show early signs of relationship problems. However, as we have tried to illustrate in the third case example, some "currently satisfied" couples may require couple therapy rather than relationship education.

REFERENCES

Avery, A., Ridley, C., Leslie, L., & Milholland, T. (1980). Relationship enhancement with premarital dyads: A six month follow-up. *American Journal of Family Therapy, 8,* 23–30.

Bagarozzi, D. A., & Rauen, P. I. (1981). Premarital counseling: Appraisal and status. *American Journal of Family Therapy, 9,* 13–27.

Balakkrishnan, R. R., Rao, K. V., Lapierre-Adamcyk, E., & Krotski, K. J. (1987). A hazard model analysis of covariates of marriage dissolution in Canada. *Demography, 24,* 395–406.

Belsky, J., & Kelly, J. (1994). *Transition to parenthood.* New York: Delacorte Press.

Benson, M. J., Larson, J., Wilson, S. M., & Demo, D. H. (1993). Family of origin influences on late adolescent romantic relationships. *Journal of Marriage and the Family, 55,* 663–672.

Birtchnell, J., & Kennard, J. (1984). Early and current factors associated with poor quality marriages. *Social Psychiatry, 19,* 31–40.

Black, L. E., & Sprenkle, D. H. (1991). Gender differences in college students' attitudes toward divorce and their willingness to marry. *Journal of Divorce and Remarriage, 15,* 47–60.

Block, J., Block, J. H., & Keyes, S. (1988). Longitudinally foretelling drug usage in adolescence: Early childhood personality and environmental precursors. *Child Development, 59,* 336–355.

Booth, A., & Johnson, D. (1988). Premarital cohabitation and marital success. *Journal of Family Issues, 9,* 255–272.

Bradbury, T. N. (1995). Assessing the four fundamental domains of marriage. *Family Relations, 44,* 459–468.

Bradbury, T. N., Cohan, C. L., & Karney, B. R. (1998). Optimizing longitudinal research for understanding and preventing marital dysfunction. In T. N. Bradbury (Ed.), *The developmental course of marital dysfunction* (pp. 279–311). New York: Cambridge University Press.

Bradbury, T. N., & Fincham, F. D. (1990a). Attributions in marriage: Review and critique. *Psychological Bulletin, 107,* 3–33.

Bradbury, T. N., & Fincham, F. D. (1990b). Preventing marital dysfunction: Review and analysis. In F. D. Fincham & T. N. Bradbury (Eds.), *The psychology of marriage: Basic issues and applications* (pp. 375–401). New York: Guilford Press.

Burgess, A. W., Hartman, C. R., & McCormack, A. (1987). Abused to abuser: Antecedents of socially deviant behaviors. *American Journal of Psychiatry, 144,* 1431–1436.

Christensen, A., & Heavey, C. L. (1999). Interventions for couples. *Annual Review of Psychology, 50,* 165–190.

Cissna, K. N., Cox, D. E., & Bochner, A. P. (1990). The dialectic of marital and parental relationships within the stepfamily. *Communication Monographs, 57,* 44–61.

Clarke, S. C. (1995). *Advance report of final divorce statistics, 1989 and 1990* (Monthly Vital Statistics Report, Vol. 43, No. 9). Hyattsville, MD: National Center for Health Statistics.

Clements, M., & Markman, H. J. (1996). The transition to parenthood: Is having children hazardous to marriage? In N. Vanzetti & S. Duck (Eds.), *A lifetime of relationships* (pp. 290–309). Pacific Grove, CA: Brooks/Cole.

Cohen, J. (1997). *Statistical power analysis for the behavioral science* (rev. ed.). New York: Academic Press.

Cowan, C. P., & Cowan, P. A. (1992). *When partners become parents.* New York: Basic Books.

DeGraaf, A. (1991). De invloed van echtscheiding van de ouders op demografisch gedrag van de vrouw [The impact of divorced parents on women's demographic behavior]. *Maandststistiek van de Bevolking, 39,* 30–38.

Dyer, C., & Halford, W. K. (1998). Prevention of relationship problems: Retrospect and prospect. *Behaviour Change, 15,* 107–125.

Emmelkamp, P. M. G., De Haan, E., & Hoogduin, C. A. I. (1990). Marital adjustment and obsessive–compulsive disorder. *British Journal of Psychiatry, 156,* 55–60.

Feeney, J., & Noller, P. (1996). *Adult attachment.* Thousand Oaks, CA: Sage.

Fowers, B. J., & Olson, D. H. (1986). Predicting marital success with PREPARE: A predictive validity study. *Journal of Marital and Family Therapy, 12*(4), 403–413.

Gagnon, M. D., Hersen, M., Kabacoff, R. I., & van Hasselt, V. B. (1999). Interpersonal and psychological correlates of marital dissatisfaction in late life: A review. *Clinical Psychology Review, 19,* 359–378.

Gibardi, L., & Rosen, L. A. (1991). Differences between college students from divorced and intact families. *Journal of Divorce and Remarriage, 15,* 175–191.

Giblin, P., Sprenkle, D. H., & Sheehan, R. (1985). Enrichment outcome research: A meta-analysis of premarital, marital and family interventions. *Journal of Marital and Family Therapy, 11,* 257–271.

Glenn, N. D. (1998). The course of marital success and failure in five American 10-year cohorts. *Journal of Marriage and the Family, 60,* 269–282.

Glenn, N. D., & Kramer, K. B. (1987). The marriages and divorces of the children of divorce. *Journal of Marriage and the Family, 49*, 811–825.

Glenn, N. D., & Shelton, B. A. (1983). Pre-adult background variables and divorce: A note of caution about over-reliance on variance. *Journal of Marriage and the Family, 45*, 405–410.

Gottman, J. M. (1993). The role of conflict engagement, escalation, and avoidance in marital interaction: A longitudinal view of five types of couples. *Journal of Consulting and Clinical Psychology, 61*, 6–15.

Gottman, J. M. (1994). *What predicts divorce?: The relationship between marital processes and marital outcomes.* Hillsdale, NJ: Erlbaum.

Gottman, J. M., Coan, J., Carrère, S., & Swanson, C. (1998). Predicting marital happiness and stability from newlywed interactions. *Journal of Marriage and the Family, 60*, 5–22.

Grover, K. J., Russel, C. S., Schumm, W. R., & Paff-Bergen, L. A. (1985). Mate selection processes and marital satisfaction. *Family Relations, 34*, 383–386.

Guerney, B. G. (1977). *Relationship enhancement.* San Francisco: Jossey Bass.

Guerney, B. G. (Ed.). (1987). *Relationship enhancement manual.* Bethseda, MD: Ideal.

Guerney, B. G., Jr., & Maxson, P. (1990). Marital and family enrichment research: A decade review and a look ahead. *Journal of Marriage and the Family, 52*, 1127–1135.

Hahlweg, K., & Markman, H. J. (1988). Effectiveness of behavioral marital therapy: Empirical status of behavioral techniques in preventing and alleviating marital distress. *Journal of Consulting and Clinical Psychology, 56*, 440–447.

Hahlweg, K., Markman, H. J., Thurmair, F., Engel, J., & Eckert, J. (1998). Prevention of marital distress: Results of a German prospective longitudinal study. *Journal of Family Psychology, 12*, 543–556.

Halford, W. K. (1995). Marriage and the prevention of psychiatric disorder. In B. Raphael & G. D. Burrows (Eds.), *Handbook of preventive psychiatry* (pp. 121–138). Amsterdam: Elsevier.

Halford, W. K. (1999). *Australian couples in millenium three: A research and development agenda for marriage and relationship education* (Report to the National Family Strategy Task Force, Australian Department of Family and Community Services). Brisbane: Australian Academic Press.

Halford, W. K. (2001). *Brief couple therapy: Helping partners help themselves.* New York: Guilford Press.

Halford, W. K., & Bouma, R. (1997). Individual psychopathology and marital distress. In W. K. Halford & H. J. Markman (Eds.), *Clinical handbook of marriage and couples intervention* (pp. 291–321). Chichester, England: Wiley.

Halford, W. K., Bouma, R., Kelly, A., & Young, R. (1999). The interaction of individual psychopathology and marital problems: Current findings and clinical implications. *Behavior Modification, 23*, 179–216.

Halford, W. K., Gravestock, F., Lowe, R., & Scheldt, S. (1992). Toward a behavioral ecology of stressful marital interactions. *Behavioral Assessment, 13*, 135–138.

Halford, W. K., Hahlweg, K., & Dunne, M. (1990). The cross-cultural consistency of marital communication associated with marital distress. *Journal of Marriage and the Family, 52*, 109–122.

Halford, W. K., & Osgarby, S. (1993). Alcohol abuse in individuals presenting for marital therapy. *Journal of Family Psychology, 11*, 1–13.

Halford, W. K., Sanders, M. R., & Behrens, B. C. (2000). Repeating the errors of our parents?: Family of origin spouse violence and observed conflict management in engaged couples. *Family Process, 39*, 219–236.

Halford, W. K., Sanders, M. R., & Behrens, B. C. (2001). Can skills training prevent relationship problems in at-risk couples? Four-year effects of a behavioral relationship education program. *Journal of Family Psychology, 15*, 750–768.

Halford, W. K., Scott, J., & Smythe, J. (2000). Couples and cancer. In K. Schmaling & T. Sher (Eds.), *Couples and illness* (pp. 135–170). Washington, DC: American Psychological Association.

Harris, R., Simons, M., Willis, P., & Barrie, A. (1992). *Love, sex and water skiing: The experience of pre-marriage education in Australia.* Adelaide: Center for Human Resource Studies, University of South Australia.

Holtzworth-Munroe, A. (1992). Social skills deficits in maritally violent men: Interpreting the data using a social information processing model. *Clinical Psychology Review, 12*, 605–617.

Hotaling, G., & Sugarman, D. (1986). An analysis of risk markers in husband to wife violence: The current state of knowledge. *Violence and Victims, 1*, 101–124.

Hunt, R., Hof, L., & DeMaria, R. (1998). *Marriage enrichment: Preparation, mentoring, and outreach.* Philadelphia: Brunner/Mazel.

Huston, T. L., McHale, S., & Crouter, A. (1986). When the honeymoon's over: Changes in the marital relationship over the first year. In R. L. Gilmour & S. W. Duck (Eds.), *The emerging field of personal relationships* (pp. 109–132). Hillsdale, NJ: Erlbaum.

Janus, S. S., & Janus, C. C. (1993). *The Janus report on human sexuality.* New York: Riley.

Jones, A. C., & Chao, C. M. (1997). Racial, ethnic and cultural issues in couples therapy. In W. K. Halford & H. J. Markman (Eds.), *Clinical handbook of marriage and couples intervention* (pp. 157–178). Chichester, England: Wiley.

Julien, D., Arellano, C., & Tugeon, L. (1997). Gender issues in heterosexual, gay and lesbian couples. In W. K. Halford & H. J. Markman (Eds.), *Clinical handbook of marriage and couples interventions* (pp. 107–128). Chichester, England: Wiley.

Karney, B. R., & Bradbury, T. N. (1995). The longitudinal course of marital quality and stability: A review of theory, method and research. *Psychological Bulletin, 118*, 3–34.

Karney, B. R., & Bradbury, T. N. (1997). Neuroticism, marital interaction, and the trajectory of marital satisfaction. *Journal of Personality and Social Psychology, 66*, 413–424.

Kurdek, L. A. (1991). Marital stability and changes in marital quality in newlywed couples: A test of the contextual model. *Journal of Social and Personal Relationships, 8*, 27–48.

Kurdek, L. A. (1993). Predicting marital dissolution: A 5-year prospective longitudinal study of newlywed couples. *Journal of Personality and Social Psychology, 64*, 221–242.

Larsen, J. H., & Holman, T. B. (1994). Premarital predictors of marital quality and stability. *Family Relations, 43*(2), 228–237.

Larson, A. S., & Olson, D. H. (1989). Predicting marital satisfaction using PREPARE: A replication study. *Journal of Marital and Family Therapy, 15*(3), 311–322.

Lawton, J. M., & Sanders, M. R. (1994). Designing effective behavioral family interventions for stepfamilies. *Clinical Psychology Review, 14,* 463–496.

Lovibond, P. F., & Lovibond, S. H. (1995). *Manual for the Depression Anxiety Stress Scale.* Sydney: Psychology Foundation of Australia.

Markman, H. J. (1981). The prediction of marital distress: A five-year follow-up. *Journal of Consulting and Clinical Psychology, 49,* 760–762.

Markman, H. J., Floyd, F. J., Stanley, S. M., & Storaasli, R. D. (1988). Prevention of marital distress: A longitudinal investigation. *Journal of Consulting and Clinical Psychology, 56*(2), 210–217.

Markman, H. J., & Hahlweg, K. (1993). The prediction and prevention of marital distress: An international perspective. *Clinical Psychology Review, 13,* 29–43.

Markman, H. J., Halford, W. K., & Cordova, A. D. (1997). A grand tour of future direction in the study and promotion of healthy relationships. In W. K. Halford & H. J. Markman (Eds.), *Clinical handbook of marriage and couples intervention* (pp. 695–716). Chichester, England: Wiley.

Markman, H. J., & Kraft, S. A. (1989). Men and women in marriage: Dealing with gender differences in marital therapy. *The Behavior Therapist, 12,* 51–56.

Markman, H. J., Renick, M. J., Floyd, F., Stanley, S., & Clements, M. (1993). Preventing marital distress through communication and conflict management training: A four and five year follow-up. *Journal of Consulting and Clinical Psychology, 61,* 70–77.

Markman, H. J., Stanley, S. M., & Blumberg, S. L. (1994). *Fighting for your marriage: Positive steps for preventing divorce and preserving a lasting love.* San Francisco: Jossey-Bass.

McDonald, P. (1995). *Families in Australia: A sociodemographic perspective.* Melbourne: Australian Institute of Family Studies.

McLaughlin, I. G., Leonard, K. E., & Senchak, M. (1992). Prevalence and distribution of premarital aggression among couples applying for a marriage license. *Journal of Family Violence, 7,* 309–319.

Mihalic, S. W., & Elliot, D. (1997). A social learning theory model of marital violence. *Journal of Family Violence, 12,* 21–47.

Miller, S., Nunnally, E., & Wackman, D. (1975). Minnesota Couples Communication Program (MCCP): Premarital and marital groups. In D. Olson (Ed.), *Treating relationships* (pp. 21–40). Lake Mills, IA: Graphic.

Miller, S., Wackman, D. B., & Nunnally, E. W. (1976). A communication training program for couples. *Social Casework, 57,* 9–18.

Muñoz, R. F., Mrazek, P. J., & Haggerty, R. J. (1996). Institute of Medicine report on prevention of mental disorders: Summary and commentary. *American Psychologist, 51,* 1116–1122.

Murphy, C. M., & O'Leary, K. A. (1989). Psychological aggression predicts physical aggression in early marriage. *Journal of Consulting and Clinical Psychology, 57,* 579–582.

O'Farrell, T. J., & Birchler, G. R. (1987). Marital relationships of alcoholic, conflicted, and nonconflicted couples. *Journal of Marital and Family Therapy, 13,* 259–274.

O'Leary, K. D. (1988). Physical aggression between spouses: A social learning theory perspective. In V. B. Van Hasselt & R. L. Morrison (Eds.), *Handbook of family violence* (pp. 31–55). New York: Plenum Press.

O'Leary, K. D., Barling, J., Arias, I., Rosenbaum, A., Malone, J., & Tyree, A. (1989). Prevalence and stability of physical aggression between spouses: A longitudinal analysis. *Journal of Consulting and Clinical Psychology, 57,* 263–268.

O'Leary, K. D., Malone, J., & Tyree, A. (1994). Physical aggression in early marriage: Pre-relationship and relationship effects. *Journal of Consulting and Clinical Psychology, 62,* 594–602.

Olson, D. H., Dyer, P., & Dyer, G. (1997). *Growing together: Leaders manual. A group program for couples.* Minneapolis: Life Innovations.

Olson, D. H., Fournier, D. G., & Druckman, J. M. (1996). *PREPARE.* Minneapolis: Life Innovations.

Pan, H. S., Neidig, P. H., & O'Leary, K. D. (1994). Predicting mild and severe husband-to-wife physical aggression. *Journal of Consulting and Clinical Psychology, 62,* 985–981.

Pasch, L. A., & Bradbury, T. N. (1998). Social support, conflict, and the development of marital dysfunction. *Journal of Consulting and Clinical Psychology, 66,* 219–230.

Pope, H., & Mueller, C. W. (1976). The intergenerational transmission of marital instability: Comparisons by race and sex. *Journal of Social Issues, 32,* 49–66.

Reich, J., & Thompson, W. D. (1985). Marital status of schizophrenic and alcoholic patients. *Journal of Nervous and Mental Disease, 173,* 499–502.

Renick, M. J., Blumberg, S., & Markman, H. J. (1992). The Prevention and Relationship Enhancement Program (PREP): An empirically-based preventive intervention program for couples. *Family Relations, 41,* 141–14.

Ridley, C. A., Jorgensen, S. R., Morgan, A. C., & Avery, A. W. (1982). Relationship enhancement with premarital couples: An assessment of effects on relationship quality. *American Journal of Family Therapy, 10*(3), 41–48.

Riggs, D. S., O'Leary, D. K., & Breslin, F. C. (1990). Multiple correlates of physical aggression in dating couples. *Journal of Interpersonal Violence, 5,* 61–73.

Rogge, R. D., & Bradbury, T. N. (1999). Till violence does us part: The differing roles of communication and aggression in predicting adverse marital outcomes. *Journal of Consulting and Clinical Psychology, 67,* 340–351.

Ruscher, S. M., & Gotlib, I. H. (1988). Marital interaction patterns of couples with and without a depressed partner. *Behavior Therapy, 19,* 455–470.

Sanders, M. R., Halford, W. K., & Behrens, B. C. (1999). Parental divorce and premarital couple communication. *Journal of Family Psychology, 13,* 60–74.

Saunders, J. B., Aasland, O. G., Babor, T. F., de la Fuente, J. R., & Grant, M. (1993). Development of the Alcohol Use Disorders Identification Test (AUDIT): WHO collaborative project on early detection of persons with harmful alcohol consumption—II. *Addiction, 88,* 791–804.

Sayers, S. L., Kohn, C. S., & Heavey, C. (1998). Prevention of marital dysfunction: Behavioral approaches and beyond. *Clinical Psychology Review, 18,* 713–744.

Silliman, B., Stanley, S. M., Coffin, W., Markman, H. J., & Jordan, P. L. (in press). Preventive interventions for couples. In H. Liddle, D. Santisteban, R. Levant, & J. Bray (Eds.), *Family psychology intervention science.* Washington, DC: American Psychological Association.

Simons, M., Harris, R., & Willis, P. (1994). *Pathways to marriage: Learning for married life in Australia.* Adelaide: Centre for Research in Education and Work, University of South Australia.

Spanier, G. B. (1976). Measuring dyadic adjustment: New scales for assessing the quality of marriage and similar dyads. *Journal of Marriage and the Family, 38,* 15-28.

Stanley, S. M., Blumberg, S. L., & Markman, H. J. (in press). Helping couples fight for their marriages: The PREP approach. In R. Berger & M. Hannah (Eds.), *Handbook of preventive approaches in couple therapy.* New York: Brunner/Mazel.

Stanley, S. M., Markman, H. J., St. Peters, M., & Leber, B. D. (1995). Strengthening marriages and preventing divorce: New directions in prevention research. *Family Relations, 44,* 392-401.

Stets, J. E., & Straus, M. A. (1990). The marriage license as a hitting license: A comparison of dating, cohabiting and married couples. In M. A. Straus & R. J. Gelles (Eds.), *Physical violence in American families: Risk factors and adaptation to violence in 8,145 families* (pp. 131-164). New Brunswick, NJ: Transaction.

Stith, S. M., & Farley, S. C. (1993). A predictive model of male spousal violence. *Journal of Family Violence, 8,* 183-201.

Straus, M. A., & Gelles, R. (1986). Societal change and change in family violence from 1975 to 1985 as revealed by two national surveys. *Journal of Marriage and the Family, 48,* 465-479.

Straus, M. A., Gelles, R., & Steinmetz, S. K. (1980). *Behind closed doors: Violence in the American family.* New York: Doubleday.

Sullivan, K. T., & Bradbury, T. N. (1997). Are premarital prevention programs reaching couples at risk for marital dysfunction? *Journal of Consulting and Clinical Psychology, 65,* 24-30.

Thompson, B. M. (1997). Couples and the work–family interface. In W. K. Halford & H. J. Markman (Eds.), *Clinical handbook of marriage and couples intervention* (pp. 273-290). Chichester, England: Wiley.

To have and to hold: Strategies to strengthen marriage and relationships. (1998). Canberra: House of Representatives Standing Committee on Legal and Constitutional Affairs.

Trussel, J., & Rao, K. U. (1987). Premarital cohabitation and marital stability: A reassessment of the Canadian evidence. *Journal of Marriage and the Family, 51,* 535-544.

van Widenfelt, B., Hosman, C., Schaap, C., & van der Staak, C. (1996). The prevention of relationship distress for couples at risk: A controlled evaluation with nine-month and two-year follow-ups. *Family Relations, 45*(2), 156-165.

van Widenfelt, B., Markman, H. J., Guerney, B., Behrens, B. C., & Hosman, C. (1997). Prevention of relationship problems. In W. K. Halford & H. J. Markman (Eds.), *Clinical handbook of marriage and couples intervention* (pp. 651-677). Chichester, England: Wiley.

Veroff, J., Douvan, E., & Hatchett, S. J. (1995). *Marital instability: A social and behavioral study of the early years.* Westport, CT: Praeger.

Vincent, J. P., Weiss, R. L., & Birchler, G. R. (1975). A behavioral analysis of problem solving in distressed and nondistressed married and stranger dyads. *Behavior Therapy, 6,* 475-487.

Visher, E. B., & Visher, J. S. (1991). Therapy with stepfamily couples. *Psychiatric Annals, 21,* 462-465.

Wampler, K. S., & Sprenkle, D. (1980). The Minnesota Couple Communication Program: A follow-up study. *Journal of Marriage and the Family, 42,* 577-585.

Weiss, R. L., & Heyman, R. E. (1997). A clinical-research overview of couples interactions. In W. K. Halford & H. J. Markman (Eds.), *Clinical handbook of marriage and couples intervention* (pp. 13-41). Chichester, England: Wiley.

Weissman, M. M. (1987). Advances in psychiatric epidemiology: Rates and risk for major depression. *American Journal of Public Health, 77,* 445-451.

White, L. K. (1990). Determinants of divorce: A review of research in the eighties. *Journal of Marriage and the Family, 52,* 904-912.

Widom, C. S. (1989). Does violence beget violence?: A critical examination of the literature. *Psychological Bulletin, 106,* 3-28.

Williams, L., & Jurich, J. (1995). Predicting marital success after five years: Assessing the predictive validity of FOCCUS. *Journal of Marital and Family Therapy, 21,* 141-153.

Winkler, I., & Doherty, W. J. (1983). Communication style and marital satisfaction in Israeli and American couples. *Family Process, 22,* 229-237.

Wolcott, I., & Glezer, H. (1989). *Marriage counselling in Australia: An evaluation.* Melbourne: Australian Institute of Family Studies.

Chapter 15

The CARE Program: A Preventive Approach to Marital Intervention

RONALD D. ROGGE
REBECCA M. COBB
MATTHEW JOHNSON
ERIKA LAWRENCE
THOMAS N. BRADBURY

BACKGROUND OF THE APPROACH

The Compassionate and Accepting Relationships through Empathy (CARE) program seeks to enhance marriages and improve marital outcomes by encouraging and promoting development of the nurturing, compassionate behaviors that couples already naturally possess to some degree. The core focus of CARE is on empathy, and the program strives to teach couples a set of skills to handle external and internal challenges to their marriages in more constructive and compassionate ways. "Empathy," defined as "an affective state that stems from the apprehension of another's emotional state or condition, and that is congruent with it" (Eisenberg & Miller, 1987, p. 91), is viewed as a fundamentally important ingredient for satisfying, enduring marriage. Although empathy is not a novel component in marital interventions, prior approaches have primarily focused on increasing empathy in the context of conflict management and problem-solving behavior. The CARE program seeks to extend the scope of these programs by teaching couples skills to enhance empathy in multiple domains of relationship functioning.

Specifically, CARE teaches empathy-based skills to enhance spouses' friendships with their partners and to promote constructive healing when feelings have been hurt in addition to teaching empathy-based communication skills. These domains were chosen to reduce the frequency and severity of conflict by strengthening the positive aspects of marriages; to facilitate the resolution of conflict when it does occur; and to restore intimacy following a breach of empathy from miscommunication or hostile conflict. Thus the CARE program seeks to promote greater levels of empathy in three main areas: social support, conflict management, and forgiveness.

Social Support

As couples contend with the ordinary daily stresses of life, empathy is reflected in "social support," which Cutrona (1996) defines as responsiveness to another's needs involving acts that communicate caring; that validate the partner's worth, feelings, or actions; and that help the partner cope with life's problems. A focus on social support follows from our observation that couples value this aspect of their relationships, and from recent findings suggesting the importance of prosocial behaviors in marital outcomes. For example, Pasch and Bradbury (1997) demonstrated that social support behaviors displayed by newlyweds predicted 2-year marital outcomes even after the contribution of observed problem-solving behavior was controlled for. This finding suggests that handling relationship conflicts and providing social support represent different domains of skills, and that the ability to provide effective support is important for the long-term viability of relationships. Consequently, CARE teaches couples a set of skills, based upon the suggestions of Cutrona (1996) and Sullivan, Pasch, Eldridge, and Bradbury (1998), that help partners handle the daily stresses of life as a team, supporting each other instead of letting those stresses erode their relationship.

Conflict Management

When conflict arises between partners, empathy is manifested as "acceptance," which can be defined as the capacity to experience some offensive, unacceptable, or blameworthy action by the partner as understandable and tolerable, if not necessarily desirable, or even as something worthy of appreciation (see Christensen, Jacobson, & Babcock, 1995, and Dimidjian, Martell, & Christensen, Chapter 9, this volume). This emphasis arises from an expanding body of longitudinal literature supporting the importance of skillful problem-solving behavior (see Fincham & Beach, 1999, for a review) and beneficent interpretation of a partner's behavior (Bradbury & Fincham, 1990) as indicators of interpersonal health and relationship stability. Drawing on the acceptance approach of integrative behavioral couple therapy (IBCT) developed by Christensen et al. (1995), and on the Relationship Enhancement (RE) approach (Guerney, 1977; Guerney, Brock, & Coufal, 1986), CARE teaches partners skills that increase their ability to approach conflict with empathy by shifting their focus toward understanding and accepting each other instead of trying to change or attack each other.

Forgiveness

Finally, when feelings are hurt and trust is betrayed, empathy is reflected in "forgiveness," which is de-

fined here as "the set of motivational changes whereby one becomes (a) decreasingly motivated to retaliate against an offending relationship partner, (b) decreasingly motivated to maintain estrangement from the offender, and (c) increasingly motivated by conciliation and goodwill for the offender, despite the offender's hurtful actions" (McCullough, Worthington, & Rachal, 1997, p. 322). Despite its increasing use as a core construct in clinical treatments, forgiveness has only recently begun to receive empirical validation (see Gordon & Baucom, 1998, and Gordon, Baucom, & Snyder, 2000, for reviews). CARE operationalizes forgiveness in a set of skills based on an intervention by McCullough (1997), which challenges partners to work as a team to repair their relationship and which rebuilds trust by having partners focus on understanding each other through acceptance and empathy instead of attacking or punishing each other following a transgression.

Origins of the CARE Program

The CARE program was developed in the context of a growing trend to expand the scope of marital interventions beyond conflict resolution skills. Intuitively, it seems clear that people typically do not marry because they have found someone with whom they argue well. Although the ability to resolve disagreements with an intimate partner can be rewarding, the presence of positive features and exchanges (e.g., a supportive friendship, affection, and companionship) is probably more important than the management of differences early in a relationship. In addition, most newlywed couples will probably spend more time discussing day-to-day concerns and frustrations than dealing with marital conflict. At a conceptual level, effective conflict resolution skills alone do not ensure satisfying relationships (see Karney & Bradbury, 1995), for marital satisfaction involves more than just the absence of discord and hostile conflict. Thus, although it is plausible to expect that conflict resolution skills can moderate the impact of conflict on a relationship, they cannot ensure that the members of a couple will continue to enjoy each other's company and maintain an intimate bond. In contrast, the regular enactment of support in intimate relationships has great potential to sustain these positive aspects of relationships by serving as a buffer for external stressors and strengthening couples' friendships in the process. Indeed, it might be argued that marriages deteriorate in part because the prosocial factors that bring couples together (e.g., the promise of caring, compassion, and understanding) decline naturally, in actuality or in their salience, and that failing to adapt to these declines proves detrimental to the well-being of the dyad.

In addition to the potential importance of social support, forgiveness represents a salient domain for improving empathy in interpersonal relationships. Even with high levels of social support and strong conflict resolution skills, partners will occasionally hurt each other's feelings. Such interpersonal transgressions—even when they are inadvertent and unintentional—represent a significant threat to a couple's empathic bond, because it is exceedingly more difficult for an offended spouse to set aside his/her own feelings and focus on those of the partner. Consequently, to strengthen and promote empathic interaction, we believe that it may be necessary to teach couples skills that repair their intimate bonds and that restore empathy when they have been threatened or damaged. Following these arguments, CARE was designed to expand the scope of marital interventions by teaching partners to appreciate the value of understanding each other's feelings and motivations; to recognize opportunities for empathic interaction; and to enact behaviors that will foster empathy in the areas of social support, conflict resolution, and forgiveness.

From a historical perspective, the CARE program contains a number of elements common to previous marital interventions, as well as a number of significant departures. Here it is necessary to discuss CARE in the context of the Prevention and Relationship Enhancement Program (PREP; Markman, Renick, Floyd, Stanley, & Clements, 1993). PREP represents the most thoroughly researched workshop for developing marriages, and it holds promise for strengthening relationships over several years of marriage; most similar programs have either not been studied systematically or have been studied over a very short follow-up interval. Although PREP has evolved and expanded since its inception more than 20 years ago, its central focus remains on the "speaker–listener technique," a communication device that imposes a formal structure on couples' discussions to slow the pace of discussions and prevent them from escalating into hostile conflict. In a series of 14 lectures, 8 exercises, and several homework assignments, couples are taught to use the speaker–listener technique with additional behavioral skills

(e.g., problem solving, XYZ statements, uncovering hidden issues) to manage conflict effectively in their relationships. CARE adopts the empirical philosophy of PREP as well as its psychoeducational approach, and it uses a series of structured lectures, homework assignments, and exercises to teach couples a set of specific behavioral skills.

CARE is similar to PREP in that it seeks to provide couples with skills that will help them to minimize or prevent hostile and attacking interactions. However, CARE takes a markedly different approach toward attaining these goals, in that partners are taught how to approach discussions with greater empathy and compassion for each other. Rather than using the speaker–listener technique to contain and manage negative interaction, CARE is designed to prevent hostile conflict by shifting the emotional tone of the discussion toward empathy and understanding. CARE also differs from PREP in that CARE skills are applied to the domains of social support and forgiveness, in addition to conflict resolution; five of the nine primary CARE exercises are devoted to developing empathy-based skills in these domains. PREP now includes lectures on developing better friendships and on forgiveness, but compared to CARE these lectures constitute a smaller portion of the workshop, contain no associated skills or exercises, and are presented to couples more in the form of general advice. These differences follow from the differing conceptual origins of the two programs, and the superiority of one approach over the other—if any such difference exists—remains an empirical question.

CARE also bears a strong resemblance to the RE program developed by Guerney (1977). RE is a psychoeducational program offered in a group format in which couples are taught four basic sets of skills: the "expressive mode," the "empathic responder mode," "effective mode switching," and the "facilitator mode." Compared to PREP, RE is less structured and more affective in its approach to conflict resolution. In the empathic responder mode, partners are instructed to go beyond paraphrasing and to communicate an empathic understanding of each other's perspective; the amplification technique used in CARE (described below) is quite similar. However, in contrast to CARE, RE focuses primarily on conflict resolution and does not formally extend the practice of this skill into the domains of social support and forgiveness. In addition, RE retains a structured set of rules for switching between empathic listening and expressing modes (i.e., the mode-switching skills) that is more comparable to the structure provided in the

PREP program than to that taught in CARE. Thus CARE focuses heavily on prosocial skills and is designed to enable couples develop those skills in three key interpersonal domains.

THE WELL-FUNCTIONING VERSUS DYSFUNCTIONAL COUPLE

Prevention Approach to Dysfunction

CARE aims to educate couples about central psychological principles of relationships, to provide them with an environment in which to develop skills relevant to those principles, and in turn to prevent marital distress. Consistent with these aims, CARE was developed specifically for couples who are functioning well in their relationship and, at least at the time of intervention, enjoy high levels of satisfaction. In fact, in an ongoing experimental study of CARE (described below), couples are excluded from the sample if they are maritally distressed. The preventive focus is adopted in view of evidence that (1) marital therapy often comes too late (or not at all) to help couples (e.g., see Veroff, Kulka, & Douvan, 1976, p. 190); (2) many couples do seek some form of premarital or early marital counseling (Sullivan & Bradbury, 1997); and (3) a high proportion of divorces occur in the first 5 years of marriage (National Center for Health Statistics, 1990). The demographics of divorce suggest that the seeds for marital dysfunction are often sown in the early stages of marriage, and this in turn provides a window of opportunity to help couples achieve strong, enduring unions. Supporting this view, researchers have recently been able to utilize data taken near the time of marriage to classify marital outcomes over the early years of marriage with 70–90% accuracy (see Rogge & Bradbury, 1999a, for a review). CARE targets couples in these early years of marriage and endeavors to teach them a basic set of skills to navigate more effectively the challenges they are likely to face, so that their marital outcomes are enhanced. From this perspective, couples deficient in basic relationship skills are expected to be at higher risk for subsequent marital dysfunction than those couples possessing these skills.

Model of Marital Dysfunction

CARE focuses on a set of skills designed to build empathy in dealing with stressors that impinge upon and arise within an intimate relationship. This approach assumes that all couples must deal with such stressors as a natural part of life, albeit to varying degrees, and CARE begins by normalizing these stressors for couples. Using the metaphor of a rocky road, CARE casts internal stressors (such as conflict, disagreements, and unresolved hurt feelings) and external stressors (such as work stress, bad moods, and long commutes) as the rough spots or bumps in the road of life. Empathy—or, more specifically, the set of empathy-focused skills taught in CARE—is then introduced as a means to cushion those rough spots and make the journey more comfortable and enjoyable. Thus stressors can be viewed as opportunities for partners either to grow closer together as they develop deepening levels of empathy to ease their journey together, or to grow apart if they allow hostility and conflict to erode their empathy. As already mentioned, these skills fall roughly into three primary domains: support skills to manage external stressors and maintain a healthy friendship; conflict skills to manage internal conflict constructively; and forgiveness skills to mend hurt feelings and get the relationship back on track.

In line with most skill-based approaches, CARE adopts a social learning perspective on the development of relationship dysfunction. Building on the stress–adaptation model proposed by Karney and Bradbury (1995), CARE views stressors as potentiators that moderate the relationship between poor coping skills and marital dysfunction. Thus the mere absence of strong coping skills or high levels of stress does not lead automatically to marital dysfunction. However, when stressors arise, they serve as catalysts for diminished support and negative patterns of conflict in couples that lack effective coping skills, thereby exposing the destructive nature of these skill deficits. As described by the social learning model, over time a couple's ineffective attempts to cope with internal and external challenges tend to grow more aversive, particularly as the outcomes continue to be dissatisfying, and this leads to persisting frustration and perhaps escalating conflict. After repeated failures to successfully manage internal and external stressors, partners may begin to disengage from the relationship and to provide and receive less empathy as the hurt and distance between them build. In contrast, for partners with strong coping skills, internal and external stressors serve as opportunities to gain a deeper understanding of each other, strengthening their empathy and helping them grow together instead of apart.

ASSESSMENT OF COUPLE FUNCTIONING AND TREATMENT EFFICACY

Because CARE targets relatively high-functioning couples, formal assessment does not play an integral part in treatment. CARE is offered in a group format in which all couples receive the same instruction and participate in the same exercises, regardless of their individual levels of functioning. However, exercises are done privately, at which time couples are asked to discuss areas of disagreement within their relationships and other forms of stress and tension. Couples therefore are free to tailor the CARE program to their own specific needs by choosing the topics to be addressed in the exercises. This process occurs in collaboration with a trained staff member (referred to as their "coach") at the beginning of the exercises, but is not part of a formal assessment process.

In the ongoing 3-year pilot study of the CARE program at UCLA, couples have undergone an extensive assessment prior to treatment, for the purposes of assessing couples' level of risk for marital dysfunction and evaluating treatment efficacy. Couples in the study have been assigned randomly to receive either the CARE program or the PREP program (Markman et al., 1993) either with or without a 4-hour module covering empathy-based forgiveness skills, thus creating a 2 × 2 factorial design. The study will also examine the efficacy of the workshops in high- and low-risk couples separately, using stratified random assignment to allow risk for subsequent marital discord to be analyzed as an independent factor. PREP is used as a comparison condition because it is the most widely tested program in this domain, but also because its emphasis on conflict resolution skills provides a theoretical contrast with the focus on empathy in CARE. The following criteria have been used to screen potential participants: (1) The marriage is the first for both partners; (2) both spouses are between 18 and 45 years old; (3) couples have been married less than 6 months or are engaged with a date set within the next year; (4) both spouses are willing to participate; and (5) couples fail to exhibit clinically significant levels of marital discord.

GOAL SETTING

The overarching treatment goal in CARE is to train couples in the use of empathy-based skills when dealing with various sources of tension in their relationships. This goal is stated expressly to couples in the first lecture of the program and remains the same for all couples regardless of differences among them. To facilitate this goal, couples are given individual instruction in the use of the CARE skills during the exercises presented in each lecture, to ensure that they are exposed to and work to enact all of the skills presented. A basic assumption of CARE is that couples must enact and practice the skills presented in the workshop, instead of merely being told that they are important, in order to benefit from the experience. Couples are also given homework assignments between sessions to encourage practice at home.

It is important to note that the resolution of specific relationship problems is not a goal of the CARE program. Couples are asked to discuss relationship problems in the course of the exercises, but the main goal of the exercises is to practice the CARE skills, not to resolve these problems. In fact, the time allotted to the exercises is often insufficient for couples to completely resolve issues. When partners find themselves in the middle of a discussion at the end of an exercise, they are encouraged to continue the discussion at home using the same CARE skills as part of their homework that week. In this way, couples are empowered to resolve their problems themselves, using their coach as more of a collaborator or resource than a therapist.

STRUCTURE OF THE THERAPY PROCESS

Overall Structure

CARE workshops follow a psychoeducational format and are delivered to small groups of about four to six couples. The workshops take place over 4 days; the first day is a weekend session that lasts about 5 hours, and the remaining lectures are spread over three weeknights of 3 hours each. Thus workshops last a total of 14 hours and are completed in less than a month. Couples participating in our study also complete a fourth 3-hour weeknight where they receive the Stop Anger and Violence Escalation (SAVE; Neidig, 1989) program, an intervention designed specifically to prevent physical and verbal aggression in marriage. This module has been implemented in view of evidence that about half of all newlyweds engage in some form of physical aggression, and that this is detrimental to their relationships (e.g., Lawrence & Bradbury, 2001; Rogge & Bradbury, 1999b).

CARE consists of three modules: social support, conflict management, and forgiveness. The core concepts of each of the three modules are described in a series of 16 lectures presented by leaders with some degree of formal clinical training (psychologists, counselors, clergy, etc.), who have undergone approximately 40 hours of training in CARE. Lectures generally take about 15–40 minutes and include some group discussion, role plays, and discussion of actual couples' discussions to illustrate core concepts. The focus in each module is on identifying common problems that couples face and on teaching prosocial skills to handle those problems.

Exercises

In addition to the lecture portion of the workshop, each couple is given an opportunity to practice CARE skills in a private setting under the guidance of a coach in a series of 11 exercises coordinated with the lectures. Coaches need not be professionally trained mental health care providers, but they require a minimum of 40 hours of training in basic clinical skills and in the CARE skills specifically, in addition to ongoing clinical supervision. Ideally, the same coach works with one couple for the duration of the workshop. The exercises last from 30 to 50 minutes, and the primary goal is for partners to practice using the various CARE skills in their discussions with each other. The coach's role is primarily to serve as a guide in the couple's discussions, to keep the couple on task, and to help the partners use CARE skills effectively. In most of the discussions, partners are asked to choose a topic that is either a conflict in their relationship (conflict module), a personal issue that they would like help with (social support module), or a time when feelings were hurt within the relationship (forgiveness module); however, as mentioned above, the main goal of the exercises is to practice the CARE skills, not to resolve the issues under discussion.

Homework Assignments

Couples are assigned two to three brief homework exercises at the end of each workshop session, in order to practice the CARE skills outside the workshops. Homework generally consists of 10- to 20-minute discussions that may be seen as extensions of the exercises in the workshops. At the beginning of each subsequent workshop session, partners are given about 10 minutes to discuss the homework with their coach. Coaches are instructed to address any difficulties that couples might have engaging the CARE skills at home, to encourage them to complete homework assignments, and to correct any misunderstandings about the CARE skills.

THE ROLE OF THE THERAPIST

In the format of the CARE workshops, the therapist functions essentially as a teacher. CARE is based on a skill acquisition model; couples are told that they can learn some basic skills that will help them maintain satisfying relationships over time. The therapist, or leader, of the workshops explains common difficulties or stressors that couples encounter in marriage, normalizes the presence of such difficulties, and helps couples develop a proactive empathy-based perspective on managing those stressors as a team. Instead of seeing problems as threats to their relationships, couples are encouraged to see them as opportunities to grow closer through understanding and empathic discussions that promote intimacy. To achieve this understanding, spouses are taught new skills that help them develop tolerance and understanding for each other's perspective.

Whereas the leaders function as teachers and provide couples with information about the CARE skills, the coaches function as consultants and provide practical help and immediate feedback to partners as they learn to use the skills in their discussions with each other. Each exercise focuses on a specific new skill, but also incorporates CARE skills taught in previous lectures. During the discussions, partners are encouraged by the coach to talk to each other, while the coach provides highly specific feedback about their use of the skills. Partners are discouraged from engaging the coach in a discussion about their relationship and from coaching each other in the use of CARE skills.

While observing the couple's discussions, the coach attends to the verbal content of the interaction, nonverbal behaviors, and interaction process. The coach takes an active role in working with the couple and frequently interrupts the couple's discussion to correct partners' use of the skills and to note any behavior that threatens the discussion. For example, if one spouse responds to the other by rolling his/her eyes or making sarcastic comments, the coach will interrupt and highlight this behavior in a nonattacking manner and will offer specific suggestions about how to improve the discussion using CARE skills. In addition to commenting on the potentially maladaptive tactics couples use, coaches routinely provide couples with positive feedback and reinforcement when CARE skills are used effectively.

Throughout the workshop, coaches have many opportunities to interact with couples informally on breaks and more formally during the practice sessions. This interaction offers coaches an opportunity to develop a strong working relationship with couples, and to build the rapport and trust necessary for couples to feel comfortable discussing intimate relationship issues in the exercises. However, coaches are trained also to maintain a professional relationship with the couples they coach, to help ensure that the coaches remain in control of the exercise during the practice sessions. Consequently, coaches are discouraged from disclosing personal information with their couples. Coaches are instructed to use only abstract and generalized self-disclosure in order to normalize couples' problems or concerns, rather than specific and personal self-disclosures that might threaten the coaches' ability to function effectively as consultants and might introduce nonspecific effects into the treatment paradigm. Thus, for example, if a couple asks (when struggling with a specific skill such as amplification), "So did you get your husband/wife to do this, too?" a coach might typically respond as follows: "Don't worry; most people find amplification difficult at first, especially when you have strong feelings of your own. But I can assure you that it really does get easier with practice."

TECHNIQUES OF THE CARE PROGRAM

Building Empathy through a Language of Acceptance

The main focus of CARE is to teach partners ways to introduce empathy and compassion into their interactions in each of three areas: when one partner has a personal problem for which he/she is seeking consolation and support, when they have a relationship conflict, and when one partner has been hurt by the other. The core skill used to promote greater levels of empathy in all three domains is "amplification." In a manner similar to the empathic skill outlined in RE therapy (Guerney et al., 1986), amplification involves a spouse's setting aside his/her own point of view as much as possible and actively taking up the other partner's position and arguing it for him/her emphatically. This requires the spouse to extend beyond simple paraphrasing, filling in "soft" feelings (e.g., sadness, hurt, loneliness) that the partner might not have mentioned, and validating those feelings for the partner. The spouse is asked to "play detective" and explain for the partner not only *what* the partner felt, but also *why* it makes sense that the partner might have felt that way.

The use of amplification shifts the discussion away from blaming and attacking, and toward a dialogue focused on mutual understanding and emotional acceptance similar to that described in IBCT (Christensen et al., 1995; Dimidjian et al., Chapter 9, this volume). By amplifying each other, spouses are no longer trying to change or blame each other, but instead are working to understand and accept each other. In addition, the use of amplification in discussions (and the environment of emotional acceptance it elicits) serves as a powerful form of validation, reducing spouses' defensive barriers, and creating a safe environment for them to disclose and be emotionally intimate with each other. By using amplification in their discussions, spouses develop greater levels of understanding for each other, and they strengthen their bond of intimacy.

Drawing once again from IBCT, couples are also taught the distinction between hard feelings (e.g., anger, resentment) and the soft feelings that often lie underneath them (e.g., sadness, hurt, fear, disappointment, loneliness). Couples are taught that although hard disclosures are easier to make because they assert control and mask vulnerability, they often come across as attacking and tend to elicit hard disclosures and defensiveness in response. Couples are encouraged instead to identify and focus on their soft feelings, as these tend to elicit compassion and greater vulnerability from both sides in a discussion. The use of amplification with a primary focus on the soft feelings involved is called the "language of acceptance," after the equivalent IBCT technique. Given the central nature of this empathic skill, all of the CARE exercises incorporate the language of acceptance as an integral part of the tasks, in much the same way that the speaker–listener technique is common to all PREP exercises (Floyd, Markman, Kelly, Blumberg, & Stanley, 1995).

Social Support

The social support module begins with a lecture describing the importance of social support in intimate relationships. External stressors to relationships are normalized and reframed as opportunities for couples to grow closer together if handled with compassion and empathy. The main skills introduced in this module are (1) listening like a friend, (2) managing moods, and (3) random acts of kindness and affection.

Listening like a Friend

The skill of "listening like a friend" helps people to focus on providing effective support when a friend (or spouse) is seeking help with a personal problem. This skill is essentially the language of acceptance applied to problems outside the relationship. Specifically, couples are taught the basic skill of amplification, and a few ground rules for providing support are established: (1) "Keep the focus on your partner until he/she feels understood" (using amplification), (2) "Focus on understanding your partner's feelings and emotional experience," (3) "Avoid providing advice unless asked," and (4) "Avoid evaluating your partner." Basically, spouses are encouraged to use the language of acceptance and are discouraged from doing anything that might abort the discussion (e.g., offering unsolicited advice, judging, playing devil's advocate). Although spouses often struggle with this skill at first—as they are more accustomed to offering solutions immediately when they see each other in distress—spouses who use the skill successfully come to realize the mutual benefit of simply listening and offering emotional support. In the CARE workshops, couples are taught to use the language of acceptance first as a tool for providing emotional support before it is introduced as a tool for managing conflict. This makes the skill easier for couples to master, because spouses are less likely to have strong feelings about problems external to their relationship—making it easier to set aside their own point of view and effectively amplify each other's perspective.

Managing Moods

The component of "managing moods" challenges couples to take a proactive approach to managing external stress and the bad moods that they can create. After stress and bad moods are normalized, and the negative effects they can have on relationships are examined, partners are asked to shift their perspectives and view external stressors as an opportunity to build empathy by tackling them together as a team. Following a number of the suggestions offfered by Sullivan et al. (1998), couples are taught that one kind act—even something as simple as a cup of coffee or a hug—can go a long way toward dissolving a bad mood and reducing stress. Using a detailed questionnaire to guide them, spouses explore sources of external stress; triggers for bad moods; the effects that bad moods have on their thoughts, feelings, and behavior toward each other; triggers for trivial conflict with each other; and the coping strategies that they find most helpful in managing bad moods. After each partner has examined his/her own behavior, the partners then discuss managing bad moods together and generate a plan for protecting their relationship through reciprocal support. Spouses are encouraged to manage their own moods actively when they catch themselves slipping into negative moods, and to extend themselves and provide support to their partners if they notice them slipping into bad moods as well. In addition, partners are urged to provide support that suits each other's needs and wants, rather than simply providing the form of support they themselves would prefer.

Random Acts of Kindness and Affection

The "random acts of kindness and affection" component extends the proactive emphasis one step further by encouraging partners to build kind and affectionate acts toward each other into their daily routines, rather than waiting until one partner is in need of social support. Spouses brainstorm an array of simple affectionate acts that they can perform on a daily basis to let each other know how much they care. The spouses are challenged to come up with a wide range of gestures to choose from, extending beyond the traditional flowers and candy—a phone call from work, a Post-it Note in a briefcase, filling the car with gas, doing each other's least favorite chore one day, a scavenger hunt through the house, a back rub, or any other act that they would appreciate. Here we are careful not to suggest specific actions or times when they might be implemented, so as to minimize the receiving partner's tendency to discount the prosocial intention underlying the act.

Conflict Management

The conflict management module of CARE draws upon RE (Guerney et al., 1986) and IBCT (Christensen et al., 1995) to yield a set of empathy-based skills that enable couples to handle problems in their relationships in a more compassionate manner. The main skills introduced in this module are (1) language of acceptance, (2) reformulation, (3) detaching from problems, (4) time outs, and (5) practicing relapse.

Language of Acceptance

The first component applies the language of acceptance to the management of problems and disagreements within a marriage. By shifting the focus of the problem discussion toward understanding each other instead of trying to change or blame each other, this core skill helps partners achieve "empathic joining around the problem" as described in IBCT (Christensen et al., 1995). In striving to understand each other, partners create an environment of acceptance where they can approach the problem together as a team instead of attacking each other as enemies. As mentioned above, relationship conflict presents a more challenging context for spouses to amplify each other, because they tend to have strong personal feelings about the issue being discussed, which are difficult to set aside even temporarily. Consequently, partners are encouraged to pick low-conflict topics for the exercise.

Reformulation

Drawing upon the IBCT technique bearing the same name, the "reformulation" component of the conflict management module encourages spouses to build acceptance and tolerance of each other's behaviors by exploring the origins of those behaviors and reformulating their understanding of each other's actions. Partners first mutually select a communication pattern that creates conflict in their relationship—for example, a demand–withdraw pattern. Next, they separately complete a brief questionnaire that helps them think about the origins of their behaviors and how behavior patterns that cause conflict in their current relationship were adaptive coping mechanisms in previous relationships with romantic partners and their families of origin. Spouses then use the insights generated by the questionnaires to explain the origins of their own behavior patterns to each other, emphasizing the pain that both partners experience during hostile conflict and the efforts (however unsuccessful) they each make to help resolve the situation. As this discussion is completed using the language of acceptance, each spouse hears his/her own side of the struggle validated by the other in an amplification, which allows the couple to join empathically

around the divisive pattern of conflict (Christensen et al., 1995). Thus, by using the language of acceptance to reformulate their understanding of each other's behavior, the partners forge an environment of emotional acceptance, once again shifting the focus from trying to attack or change each other to trying to understand and accept each other. This approach should make it easier for spouses to tolerate and cope constructively with each other's behavior, and it should bring about the desired change in their own behavior by replacing the demand for change with acceptance from their partners.

Detaching from Problems

Drawing upon the IBCT technique of emotional acceptance through detachment from the problem, the third skill helps couples distance themselves, or to detach, from destructive patterns of conflict. This interaction allows couples to discuss the process of those communication patterns without experiencing the intense emotions associated with them. Partners join together as a team in an intellectual discussion in which they trace the behavioral exchange and the associated thoughts and feelings that occur when they have a bad fight—analyzing the process that occurs, rather than the content. To help the partners distance themselves from their emotions, they are encouraged to speak of their pattern in the third person, as if they were discussing a problem between two close friends. Partners are also encouraged to give the destructive pattern its own identity—labeling it, using a metaphor to capture the dynamic it creates, and even using humor to underscore the futility of the pattern. In fact, couples are encouraged to view their destructive conflict patterns as if they were bullies that had been terrorizing their relationships. With this exercise, the couples are asked to join forces against these destructive patterns and regain control of their relationships. Without falling into the intense negative emotions, partners are able to see more clearly both sides of a pattern, thereby fostering greater compassion and understanding. This allows the partners to join together and forge emotional acceptance even with some of their most divisive issues.

Time Outs

Regardless of how well couples master the CARE skills, for most couples there will still be times when their conflicts become heated and argumentative.

Couples are taught to use "time outs" when this happens, following three main steps. First, couples are taught to recognize their own early warning signs of hostile conflict. For most couples, this entails identifying when each partner's own heated emotions get in the way of listening to and understanding the other. This strategy helps the partners learn to call time outs before their conflict becomes so heated that it does damage to the relationship. Second, partners are instructed on how to effectively call a time out, by sharing responsibility and avoiding blame, expressing the importance of protecting their relationship, and using a soft disclosure if possible. This method of calling time outs helps to ensure that the act of calling a time out itself does not become another form of attack, inadvertently intensifying the argument instead of diffusing it. Finally, partners are given a few basic rules for using time outs effectively: (1) "Take a break for as long as necessary to calm down," (2) "Set a time to come back to the discussion," and (3) "Actively use the time to cool your own emotions" (e.g., by calling a friend, exercising, reading, etc.).

Practicing Relapse

Finally, couples are given training to prepare for relapse into old patterns of communication and to practice recovery from relapse. Partners are instructed to begin a discussion about a relationship conflict without using CARE skills, allowing themselves to revert to relatively counterproductive patterns of conflict; after a few minutes and before the conflict becomes too heated, they are instructed to attempt to shift back into the use of the CARE skills. After the exercise, the partners engage in a group discussion with the leader about the process of relapse and recovery, the factors that made it difficult for them to recover, and the differences in their conversation when they are and are not using the CARE skills. Partners are encouraged to anticipate when relapse might be more likely and to discuss together how they might avoid it, or to catch lapses quickly.

Forgiveness

In the forgiveness module, the primary goal is to help couples understand forgiveness as a process in a marriage that involves rebuilding trust and repairing empathy in the relationship when it has been damaged by the hurtful actions of one partner. The forgiveness skills include (1) language of

acceptance, (2) effective apologies, and (3) monitoring assumptions.

Language of Acceptance

In the first skill of this module, couples apply the language of acceptance to a new domain of discussions: hurt feelings. In the lecture preceding the exercise, hurt feelings in relationships are normalized by emphasizing that even partners in the strongest marriages will occasionally hurt each other's feelings. Each couple is then asked to discuss an instance when one or both partners' feelings were hurt, using the language of acceptance, with the goal of building emotional acceptance through mutual understanding. Thus both partners are expected to amplify each other's feelings and experiences during the discussion.

Effective Apologies

An important part of the forgiveness process is a constructive apology. In addition to learning to use amplification and discussion of soft feelings in situations where feelings have been hurt, couples are presented with the elements that make a sincere apology: demonstrating concern for and an understanding of the hurt partner's feelings, demonstrating honest regret for hurtful actions, and changing hurtful behavior (McCullough, 1997). Often spouses report difficulty in making effective apologies because they do not see their hurtful actions as "wrong." Consequently, couples are presented with a model for understanding various dimensions of regret, including a form called "other-oriented" regret, in which a spouse can feel regret for the other partner's becoming upset even if the spouse's actions were unintentional, unavoidable, or misinterpreted. After the components of an effective apology are discussed, couples are given further instruction on the timing of apologies. More specifically, a partner is encouraged to apologize only after there has been enough discussion to ensure that both partners feel completely understood. This approach helps to prevent premature and superficial apologies from stifling the discussion and leaving the feelings unresolved.

Monitoring Assumptions

In the final part of the forgiveness module, spouses are taught to monitor the interpretations and assumptions that they make about each other's behaviors. They are first instructed in the effects that negative interpretations can play in marital outcomes. Subsequently, spouses are asked to think of a time that they made negative assumptions about each other, to consider the role that the assumptions played in their emotions and their reactions to each other, and then to discuss those situations with each other. Furthermore, spouses are encouraged to identify negative attributions and to challenge those attributions by "checking them out" with each other, or looking on their own for contrary evidence.

Common Forms of Resistance

Several types of problems can arise during the practice sessions across the three modules. One common problem arises when couples deny having any problems to discuss. These seemingly "perfect" couples state that everything is "great" in their relationships and they "really don't argue about anything." Of course, some young low-risk couples do have very few problems, but in our experience these couples tend to be very cooperative about rapidly identifying suitable discussion topics. Other couples do have difficulties, but are reluctant to raise them at a time when their relationships are strong and satisfying. These couples tend to use this stance of perfection as a means of actively resisting the exercise, and they require additional assistance from their coaches to select discussion topics. When this occurs, coaches work with these couples to identify a topic for discussion, reassuring the couples that it is normal to have disagreements at least sometimes and reminding them that this is only to practice the skills. Thus, the content of what a couple discusses is less important than actually using the practice time to try out the skills with a coach present. Coaches may ask couples about typical conflicts or about their most recent disagreement, even if that disagreement was resolved. If all else fails, coaches are provided with a list of 20 common problems that couples report, and they then ask the couples to choose a topic from the list to discuss. This form of resistance tends to become less of a problem as the workshop progresses and the couples become more comfortable engaging the skills.

A second common difficulty occurs when partners attempt to engage their coach in a discussion of their relationship instead of practicing CARE skills. The partners may employ this strategy as a means of avoiding emotionally arousing discussions with each other, or out of a genuine desire to elicit feedback from the coach. The coach is instructed to gently redirect the spouses to speak to each other, and if necessary will remind them that this is a time for them to practice talking to each other, not to the coach. Ultimately, the coach will refuse to participate in such a discussion, using silence and gentle suggestions to guide them back to the task at hand.

A third issue that arises in the practice sessions is that spouses may have difficulty identifying their emotions. More specifically, they may have difficulty identifying the "soft" emotions that underlie the "hard" feelings. Again, it is the coach's role to guide each spouse in identifying the emotions, often by asking the other partner to amplify and perhaps assist the spouse in understanding his/her own feelings. If after several prompts spouses are unable to identify their emotions, the coach will provide a list of 40 "hard" and "soft" emotions, which allows the spouses to choose from the list. Because helping spouses to develop their own emotional vocabulary is important in CARE, coaches are discouraged from simply suggesting what they believe to be the correct emotion; this latter strategy is used in those rare instances when all else has failed.

Finally, amplification can be a difficult skill for a couple to master, because it requires the spouses to set aside their own feelings, take each other's perspective, and discuss each other's feelings fluently. Some spouses struggle with this skill, due to a lack of experience in any one of these tasks. However, even spouses who show considerable skill at amplifying each other's position can run into difficulty when discussions become heated or touch upon sensitive topics. At these times, it becomes much more difficult to put aside one's own feelings and perspective, and concentrate on amplifying and understanding a partner's view. When a spouse is having particular difficulty in amplification, the coach will work with him/her until at least one satisfactory amplification is generated in the practice session. If after repeated attempts the spouse is unable to do so, the coach will model the skill as a last resort. Difficulty with amplifying can also arise when partners feel they are not being given a chance to present their own sides; thus the coach must be sensitive and not focus on the partners' amplification to the exclusion of letting them talk about their own perspectives on the situation. Often one spouse will emerge as more capable of using CARE skills; we have found that it is helpful to capitalize on this strength by having that person amplify first during the exercises, to firmly establish an emotionally accepting environment for his/her partner.

CURATIVE FACTORS/MECHANISMS OF CHANGE

Change through Skill Acquisition

The CARE program seeks to instruct couples in basic relationship skills to prevent serious marital discord from developing in the first place. Consequently, the primary goal of CARE is not to cure couples, but to help them refine and master basic prosocial skills that will protect and strengthen their relationships over time. The mechanism of change underlying this approach lies in the stress–adaptation model of relationships described above. All couples must deal with disagreements, pressures, and stresses both internal and external to their marriages. Enhancing the prosocial skills that couples use to deal with these stresses is expected to benefit their relationships by enabling them to handle them in an accepting and compassionate manner rather than a hostile and divisive manner. Thus, with the use of the empathy-based skills taught in CARE, partners can use stressors as opportunities to grow closer together rather than further apart, thereby preventing destructive patterns of interaction and building greater levels of intimacy. From this perspective, CARE encourages spouses to engage the skills being taught and to work as a team to tackle problems together.

Influence of Therapists on Change

The therapists offering CARE workshops have limited individual influence on this process of change, due to the highly structured, skill-based, psychoeducational approach of the program. To ensure competent administration of the workshops, the leaders must instruct couples effectively in the prosocial skills of CARE. Although this requires that the leaders possess good communication and teaching skills, with engaging and interactive lecturing styles, extensive clinical skills are not a prerequisite. Furthermore, to ensure consistent presentations across leaders, the CARE leaders' manual (Rogge & Bradbury, 2000) details the specific points to be made in each lecture, including the examples and analogies used to illustrate various concepts. Thus the leaders of CARE workshops affect the process of change primarily in their ability to teach couples the CARE skills. In contrast, the coaches for the CARE workshops interact more directly with the couples as they practice the skills in the 11 exercises built into the workshops. The primary goal of a coach is to provide constructive and immediate feedback to a couple as partners practice the prosocial skills. To work effectively with a couple, a coach must develop a minimum level of rapport with the couple to create a relaxed and safe environment. In addition, coaches must possess basic clinical skills and extensive training in the CARE skills in order to provide useful feedback. Coaches are required to observe a CARE workshop and then undergo approximately 40–50 hours of additional training; this includes regular group supervision with the current workshop staff, role-play practice in both using and coaching the CARE skills, and a written qualifying examination. A CARE coach develops a collaborative relationship with his/ her couple, and serves as an expert on the skills being practiced, while insisting that the partners serve as experts on any problem being discussed. Consequently, the quality of coaches does not lie in their ability to intuit and reflect upon deeper dynamics, but in their ability to provide useful feedback on the skills being practiced in each exercise. In short, the leaders and coaches of CARE workshops influence the mechanisms of change through their abilities to instruct couples in the prosocial skills and facilitate their practice of those skills.

Influence of Nonspecific Factors on Change

Nonspecific effects, such as the rapport developed among the couples and the workshop staff, can also have an indirect impact on the process of change. The modular format of the CARE program allows for flexibility in how it can be offered to couples. As noted earlier, CARE is currently being offered in a four-session format, including one weekend day followed by three weekly sessions held on weeknights. This format was chosen to provide an opportunity for distributed practice, but it has the unfortunate side effect of creating opportunities for attrition: Couples often find it difficult to clear their schedules for so many different sessions, particularly when confronted with the prospect of an extended commute through rush-hour traffic after a long day of work. Anecdotally, we have found that building rapport between the couples and the CARE staff is the most effective means of reducing attrition. When couples are engaged in conversation during breaks, and particularly during the lunch provided on the first weekend day, they become more involved in the treatment and miss fewer sessions. Nonspecific factors of this kind are a consideration in all psychoeducational treatment programs, of course, but we were surprised at first that such a small change in behavior during a 30-minute lunch could have such a dramatic impact on the couples' engagement in treatment.

TREATMENT APPLICABILITY

Stage of Marriage

CARE is currently being tested with engaged and newlywed couples to determine its efficacy at preventing discord and divorce during the early stages of marriage when so many marriages fail. Despite this focus, the skills in CARE enhance prosocial behaviors that would benefit couples at any stage of marriage. Thus, although CARE will need to be validated in a sample of established marriages, no differential predictions are made about its efficacy with couples at different stages of marriage.

Level of Functioning

The group format of the lectures and the coaching format of the exercises require couples to tolerate discussions of individual and relationship problems and the feelings surrounding those problems. Couples therefore must possess a minimum degree of relationship functioning to be able to participate constructively in the CARE workshops. If a couple's relationship has grown distressed to the point of requiring marital therapy, the psychoeducational format of the CARE workshops is unlikely to provide the structure and attention necessary to ensure a safe environment for the partners to improve their relationship. Thus couples exhibiting significant levels of marital discord would be better served by some form of marital therapy.

Efficacy with Couples at Risk for Marital Discord

A basic premise of CARE is that it should prevent adverse marital outcomes, particularly for couples for whom such an outcome is a real possibility. As mentioned above, couples in the outcome study of CARE have been stratified on risk for marital dysfunction prior to being randomly assigned to treatment, to permit us to examine directly the effect of risk on treatment response. In a sample of 96 newlywed couples from Germany, Rogge, Bradbury, Hahlweg, Engl, and Thurmaier (2002) demonstrated that couples at risk for marital dys-

function (couples high in negative communication and hostile tendencies) showed the poorest response to a German version of the PREP program. This finding underscores the strong need to develop early marital interventions that will prove effective even for difficult couples.

CASE ILLUSTRATION

Mark, aged 27, and Mary, aged 25, came to CARE 3 months before their wedding. Both felt that they had a strong relationship and were happy with how things were going in general. However, with the pressures of planning and financing the upcoming wedding, they had a handful of arguments that did not end well. Although the arguments were not serious enough to change their plans for marriage, the arguments left them both a little unsettled and unsure of how to prevent such blowups in the future. After learning about CARE, Mark and Mary decided to enroll in a workshop to learn how to handle problems more effectively and keep their relationship strong.

Mark worked as a general contractor, and Mary operated a catering truck. Mary had moved in with Mark a year earlier, after dating for 3 years. They found it "pretty easy" to get along with each other, but they also had their differences, and occasionally those differences led to conflict. The following is an example of a discussion that Mark and Mary had during the apologies exercise in the forgiveness module of CARE. Although the example includes instruction on effective apologies, it also serves as an excellent example of more basic CARE skills, such as the language of acceptance, and the active coaching involved in the CARE exercises.

MARK: It made me mad when you threw out those 33's I'd been saving. Those were some of the first records I ever owned. I can't believe that you just threw them out.

MARY: I told you, I didn't know they were so important to you. I'm sorry.

COACH: Mary, it is normal to want to apologize right away, but let's hold off on apologizing until you both feel understood.

MARK: All you had to do was ask me, and I would have told you they were important. It still makes me mad that you just threw them out. I can't believe you did that!

COACH: Mark, that was a good start, but you only mentioned hard feelings. What are some of the softer feelings underneath?

MARK: Well, I guess it hurt my feelings. I mean, those records meant a lot to me. They were 33's of all of the bands that I loved as a kid. I was planning to use them to decorate a wall of the rec room . . . but what really hurt my feelings was that you didn't even ask. I can understand that they might have irritated you when you found them because they were in your way, but it seems like you just threw them out without thinking about my feelings.

COACH: Much better.

MARY: Honey, you're a pack rat. I didn't mean to throw out something that was important to you, but it's hard to know what is and what isn't important.

MARK: That's why I'd like you to ask me before throwing my stuff out.

MARY: Well, you're not usually home when I'm cleaning, and when you are home, I'd rather spend time with you than sorting through the stuff in the basement. That's why I developed the 2-month rule. If I find something that I think you need a little help letting go of, I move it to the garage, and if you haven't noticed it missing in 2 months, I throw it away. I didn't think you would miss a box of old records, especially since we don't even have a turntable any more.

COACH: I think Mark has made his side of the story very clear. Mary, how about trying to amplify what Mark has said?

Now that Mark had presented his perspective, the coach seized this opportunity to help Mary amplify Mark's thoughts and feelings. This would require Mary to set aside her own viewpoint temporarily and actively argue Mark's point for him. Many spouses have difficulty with this skill initially, particularly if they have strong feelings of their own that they must set aside. The coach devoted the next few minutes of the exercise to helping Mary develop a strong amplification, giving her as much feedback and guidance as she needed to apply the skill successfully. This particular exercise occurs near the beginning of the workshop, and couples usually require more guidance at this point. However, as the workshop progresses, the coaches strive to interrupt less frequently as the couples begin to master the skills on their own.

MARY: OK, you said that it hurt your feelings that I threw those old records out, because they were important to you and I didn't ask you first.

COACH: That was a good start, but remember, when you amplify, you want to really argue Mark's point

for him—even filling in some of the feelings that he didn't mention. How about starting with *why* the records were important to him?

MARY: (*After a few more attempts*) Those records were really important to you. They were some of the first records you ever bought, and you were saving them because they carried memories from your childhood that you didn't want to lose. In fact, they meant so much to you that you wanted to mount a bunch of them on the wall of the family room so that you could enjoy them every day. Now that we live so far from your family, things from your childhood that remind you of your brothers and sisters are probably even more important to you than they were before. So, when you found out that I'd thrown the records away without asking, it made you really mad. You couldn't understand how I could do something like that.

MARK: Yes.

COACH: Excellent job, really nice. You mentioned Mark's hard feelings. Explain his softer feelings now.

MARY: Well, when you discovered that I'd thrown them out, you felt hurt and sad.

COACH: Good paraphrase, now amplify: *Why* do you think he felt hurt and sad?

MARY: OK, you felt sad because you'd lost something so important to you—something you could never get back. And you felt hurt because I didn't think to ask you about the records.

COACH: Much better, but *why* do you think your not asking hurt Mark's feelings so much?

MARY: When I just threw the records away without asking, it probably seemed like your feelings just weren't important to me at all—like they didn't matter or didn't factor into my thinking. It might have even made you feel like *you* weren't important to me.

MARK: Yes! Yes! I've waited so long to hear you say that! That's exactly how I felt. I mean, I know that I'm important to you and I know that you do care about my feelings, but when I found out that you threw the records away, it made me doubt those things, and that hurt a lot.

MARY: I do care about you, and I care about your feelings, and I didn't mean to hurt you like that.

Mary thus successfully amplified Mark's point of view. In contrast to active listening techniques that require paraphrases for each new point, amplifications do not require such regular and sustained application throughout a discussion. Conversations are allowed to progress normally (with a focus on soft disclosures), and amplifications occur once a spouse has a relatively clear understanding of his/her partner's point of view. If a spouse does an excellent job of amplifying his/her partner the first time, then another amplification of that same partner might not be necessary in that discussion. Consequently, the explicit goal in most CARE exercises is for each spouse to generate an effective amplification of their partner's perspective at least once during the discussion. As the conversation between Mark and Mary progressed, Mary's own point of view came out. After she had explained the basics of her experience, the coach guided Mark as he developed the following amplification.

MARK: (*After a number of attempts*) Well, I'm a pack rat and you're an organizer, so my piles of stuff that lie all around the house tend to drive you crazy. It was easier when we weren't living together, because you had your own space and you didn't have to look at my clutter every day. But when you moved in with me, it really started to irritate you, because you felt surrounded and overwhelmed by the clutter. You started cleaning and organizing my place so that it could feel like home to you too, so that we could have a home together. . . . You never meant to throw away something so important to me and felt horrible about it afterwards, but when I got so upset and angry about it, you probably felt like an outcast in your own home.

MARY: Yes, those 2 days you refused to talk to me were horrible. Part of me wanted to make it up to you, but part of me felt hurt and betrayed by the way you were acting.

MARK: You maybe even felt like I was telling you that you didn't belong in my house and weren't allowed to make it your home. I know that you felt really bad about throwing out the records, but you probably felt worse because of the mean way that I acted afterwards.

COACH: Excellent job, Mark. Both of you did very well amplifying for each other. It sounds like both of you are feeling more understood at this point. Mary, why don't you try apologizing to Mark now?

MARY: (*After a few attempts*) Mark, I'm sorry that I threw those records out. I understand now that they were a piece of your childhood that meant a lot to you and that you wanted to hold on to. As a result, it hurt a lot to lose them, and even more because it seemed like I didn't care about you or your feelings when I threw them away without asking first. But I do love you, and your feelings are important to me. I never meant to hurt you like that, and I'm sorry that I did. My 2-month rule is obviously not a good rule. In the future, I will check with you before I throw anything of yours out, to make sure that I don't make this same mistake again.

Here Mary included the three essential components of an effective apology: (1) showing that she understood and cared about Mark's feelings (using an amplification), (2) showing honest regret for what happened, and (3) changing her behavior to avoid the similar problems in the future. Later, in the same exercise, Mark apologized to Mary for his actions following the loss of the records.

Although Mark and Mary had discussed this event previously, by using the language of acceptance (focusing on the soft feelings and amplifying each other's perspectives) they were able to come together and resolve the issue, putting their hurt feelings behind them in the face of the newfound empathy and understanding they had achieved. In subsequent exercises, it became easier for Mark and Mary to amplify each other, and this allowed the coach to take a less active role. Coaches are encouraged to interrupt as little as possible during the exercises, offering feedback and guidance only when necessary to maintain a safe environment and facilitate skill acquisition.

CONCLUSION

CARE is a psychoeducational program for couples that seeks to strengthen relationships and prevent adverse marital outcomes by encouraging and promoting the use of prosocial, empathy-based skills that couples already possess to varying degrees. CARE focuses on fostering skills to help partners: (1) cope with external stresses and pressures as a team, providing support and maintaining the friendship that initially brought them together; (2) manage conflict arising within the marriage in a compassionate and accepting manner; and (3) repair their relationship via mutual acceptance and understanding after they have been damaged by the hurtful actions of one partner. CARE is currently under investigation and has not yet been empirically validated. It represents an attempt to integrate an array of current marital research findings and elements from other intervention programs, and the systematic application of such knowledge to the process of strengthening developing relationships and preventing marital discord and divorce.

ACKNOWLEDGMENTS

Development of the CARE program and preparation of this chapter were supported by the John Templeton Foundation. Preparation of this chapter was also supported by grants from the National Science Foundation (to Ronald D. Rogge), the National Institutes of Health (to Erika Lawrence and Thomas N. Bradbury), and the Social Sciences and Humanities Research Council of Canada (to Rebecca M. Cobb).

REFERENCES

Bradbury, T. N., & Fincham, F. D. (1990). Attributions in marriage: Review and critique. *Psychological Bulletin, 107,* 3–33.

Christensen, A., Jacobson, N. S., & Babcock, J. C. (1995). Integrative behavioral couple therapy. In N. S. Jacobson & A. S. Gurman (Eds.), *Clinical handbook of couple therapy* (pp. 31–64). New York: Guilford Press.

Cutrona, C. E. (1996). *Social support in couples.* Thousand Oaks, CA: Sage.

Eisenberg, N., & Miller, P. A. (1987). The relation of empathy to prosocial and related behaviors. *Psychological Bulletin, 101,* 91–119.

Fincham, F. D., & Beach, S. R. (1999). Conflict in marriage: Implications for working with couples. *Annual Review of Psychology, 50,* 47–77.

Floyd, F. J., Markman, H. J., Kelly, S., Blumberg, S., & Stanley, S. (1995). Preventive intervention and relationship enhancement. In N. S. Jacobson & A. S. Gurman (Eds.), *Clinical handbook of couple therapy* (pp. 212–226). New York: Guilford Press.

Gordon, K. C., & Baucom, D. H. (1998). Understanding betrayals in marriage: A synthesized model of forgiveness. *Family Process, 37,* 425–449.

Gordon, K. C., Baucom, D. H., & Snyder, D. K. (2000). The use of forgiveness in marital therapy. In M. E. McCullough, K. I. Pargament, & C. E. Thorensen (Eds.). *Forgiveness: Theory, research, and practice* (pp. 203–227). New York: Guilford Press.

Guerney, B. (1977). *Relationship enhancement.* San Francisco: Jossey-Bass.

Guerney, B., Brock, G., & Coufal, J. (1986). Integrating marital therapy and enrichment: The relationship enhancement approach. In N. S. Jacobson & A. S. Gurman (Eds.), *Clinical handbook of marital therapy* (pp. 151–172). New York: Guilford Press.

Karney, B. R., & Bradbury, T. N. (1995). The longitudinal course of marital quality and stability: A review of theory, method, and research. *Psychological Bulletin, 118,* 3–34.

Lawrence, E., & Bradbury, T. N. (2001). Physical aggression and marital dysfunction: A longitudinal analysis. *Journal of Family Psychology, 15,* 135–154.

Markman, H. J., Renick, M. J., Floyd, F. J., Stanley, S. M., & Clements, M. (1993). Preventing marital distress through communication and conflict management training: A 4- and 5-year follow-up. *Journal of Consulting and Clinical Psychology, 61,* 70–77.

McCullough, M. E. (1997). Marital forgiveness: Theoretical foundations and an approach to prevention. *Marriage and Family: A Christian Journal, 1,* 77–93.

McCullough, M. E., Worthington, E. L., Jr., & Rachal, K. C. (1997). Interpersonal forgiving in close relationships. *Journal of Personality and Social Psychology, 73,* 321–336.

National Center for Health Statistics. (1990). *Advance report of final marriage statistics* (Monthly Vital Statistics Report, Vol. 38, Suppl.). Hyattsville, MD: Author.

Neidig, P. H. (1989). *Stop anger and violence escalation (SAVE).* Stony Brook, NY: Behavioral Science Associates.

Pasch, L. A., & Bradbury, T. N. (1997). Social support, conflict, and the development of marital dysfunction. *Journal of Consulting and Clinical Psychology, 66,* 219–230.

Rogge, R. D., & Bradbury, T. N. (1999a). Recent advances in the prediction of marital outcomes. In R. Berger & M. T. Hannah (Eds.), *Preventive approaches in couples therapy* (pp. 331–360). Philadelphia: Brunner/Mazel.

Rogge, R. D., & Bradbury, T. N. (1999b). Till violence does us part: The differing roles of communication and aggression in predicting adverse marital outcomes. *Journal of Consulting and Clinical Psychology, 67,* 340–351.

Rogge, R. D., & Bradbury, T. N. (2000). *Care leaders' manual.* Unpublished document.

Rogge, R. D., Bradbury, T. N., Hahlweg, K., Engl, J., & Thurmaier, F. (2002). *Prediction of response to a premarital intervention.* Manuscript in preparation.

Sullivan, K. T., & Bradbury, T. N. (1997). Are premarital prevention programs reaching couples at risk for marital dysfunction? *Journal of Consulting and Clinical Psychology, 65,* 24–30.

Sullivan, K. T., Pasch, L. A., Eldridge, K. A., & Bradbury, T. N. (1998). Social support in marriage: Translating research into practical applications for clinicians. *The Family Journal: Counseling and Therapy for Couples and Families, 6,* 263–271.

Veroff, J., Kulka, R. A., & Douvan, E. (1976). *Mental health in America.* New York: Basic Books.

Part II

APPLICATIONS TO SPECIAL POPULATIONS AND PROBLEMS

Section A

Violence, Trauma, Infidelity, and Divorce

Chapter 16

Intimate Partner Violence: An Introduction for Couple Therapists

AMY HOLTZWORTH-MUNROE
JEFFREY C. MEEHAN
UZMA REHMAN
AMY D. MARSHALL

AN INTRODUCTION TO THE PROBLEM

Differing Types of Couple Violence

Researchers and clinicians increasingly acknowledge that couple violence is a heterogeneous phenomenon, and that different types of violence may be conceptually and etiologically distinct. A consensus is growing that couple aggression can be differentiated into at least two types. One type of aggression has been called "severe physical aggression" (O'Leary, 1993) or "patriarchal terrorism" (Johnson, 1995), and is probably what most people imagine when they think of battering. It is usually studied among samples of battering men entering domestic violence treatment programs or samples of battered women seeking help at shelters (Straus, 1999). This type of violence is believed to be characterized by severe male violence, with less severe female violence or severe female violence perpetrated primarily for self-defense. It is also characterized by a high risk of female injury and a high degree of female fear of the male. This severe aggression is believed to function to control and dominate the woman. The second type of aggression has been called "mild physical aggression"

(O'Leary, 1993) or "common couple violence" (Johnson, 1995). It is often studied among newly-wed, community, or (sometimes) couple therapy samples (Straus, 1999). It is characterized by more bidirectional violence (i.e., both partners engage in physical aggression) that is mild to moderate in severity and frequency. It is believed to be less likely to cause fear in or to endanger the woman, and is less likely to be used to control her.

Clinical experience suggests that the second type of physical aggression will be seen more often than the first among couples seeking marital therapy. Unfortunately, the research literature on couple violence often does not distinguish between these two types of violence. Thus, when possible, we point out which of the reviewed research findings are of most relevance to couple therapists.

Also, as discussed later, our conjoint therapy recommendations are geared toward couples experiencing mild physical aggression (i.e., the second type of aggression), because we believe (along with others) that conjoint treatment may be inappropriate for couples experiencing severe male violence. Yet, even while recommending couple therapy for mild physical aggression, we would caution that it is inappropriate to discount the potential of any

441

physical aggression—even mild aggression—to have negative and injurious consequences. At this point in time, almost no data are available that would enable therapists to predict which couples experiencing low levels of aggression will escalate to increasingly severe and dangerous levels of violence, and which couples will either maintain a low level of violence or even cease their aggression. Thus, in our opinion, the occurrence of any physical aggression in a relationship is a serious problem, deserving attention in therapy. Before discussing our treatment recommendations, we wish to briefly introduce couple therapists to the current research findings regarding couple violence, so that they will be well informed about the problem to be addressed.

Prevalence of Couple Violence

Survey data gathered from nationally representative samples suggest that each year, one out of every eight husbands engages in physical aggression against his wife, and up to 2 million women are severely assaulted by their male partners; lifetime estimates suggest that 30% of couples experience physical aggression at least once in their marriage (Straus & Gelles, 1990). Demonstrating that aggression often begins early in a relationship, two studies of couples planning marriage each found that one-third of the men had used physical aggression against their fiancées in the previous year (Leonard & Senchak, 1996; O'Leary et al., 1989). Husband physical aggression is even more prevalent among couples seeking marital therapy; in such samples, over 50% of the husbands have engaged in physical aggression against their wives in the past year (Holtzworth-Munroe et al., 1992; O'Leary, Vivian, & Malone, 1992).

Women also engage in physical aggression in their intimate relationships; indeed, a recent meta-analysis found that, particularly among community and young dating samples, women engage in slightly more physical aggression than men (Archer, 2000). Among marital therapy clinic samples, as much as 86% of partner aggression is reciprocal, with both partners engaging in primarily low levels of physical aggression (Cascardi, Langhinrichsen, & Vivian, 1992). As discussed below, we believe that it is important for couple therapists to help both partners end their use of aggression; however, we also view male violence as a more serious problem than female violence, because it results in more negative consequences, including more injury (e.g., Archer, 2000) and psychological distress.

Stability of Violence

Findings from longitudinal studies suggest that once violence has occurred in a relationship, it may continue, particularly if the initial violence is severe or frequent. Two research groups have examined stability of physical aggression among newlywed samples. First, in a study of over 200 couples, O'Leary et al. (1989) found that the conditional probability of physically aggressing against one's partner at 30 months, given that an individual had engaged in physical aggression against the partner at premarriage and at 18 months after marriage, was .72 for women and .59 for men. Quigley and Leonard (1996) found that among husbands who had engaged in physical aggression in the first year of marriage, 76% engaged in further violence in the second or third years of marriage. The best predictor of continued husband violence was the initial severity of violence, with the risk of continued violence increasing to 86% among the most severely violent men.

In studies of nationally representative samples, Feld and Straus (1989) examined male violence over 1 year. Among men who had committed three severe assaults in the year prior to the initial assessment, 67% continued their violence in the following year. In a national family violence survey of approximately 800 couples, Aldarondo (1996) found that from the first to the second year of the study, 39% of violent men continued their violence, and from the second to the third year, 44% continued their violence. Unfortunately, 37% of the husbands who had discontinued violence at the first follow-up resumed violent acts by the second follow-up assessment.

Aldarondo and Kaufman Kantor (1997) evaluated predictors of female assault persistence among a national survey sample. Compared to men who ceased their violence, persistent offenders were more likely to be unemployed, to have a lower family income, and to engage in more frequent and severe fights with their spouses. Aldorondo and Sugarman (1996) also identified risk markers for the continuation of wife assault over a 3-year period. Men who were younger, who used high levels of verbal aggression, and whose relationships were characterized by high levels of conflict were more likely to engage in, and continue violence against, their female partners.

As is evident from the O'Leary et al. (1989) findings cited above, a substantial number of women also continue their physical aggression against their partners. To our knowledge, however, there has been no systematic investigation of predictors of reassault by women.

Differing Consequences of Male and Female Violence

Although the rates of female physical aggression are comparable to those of male physical aggression, research indicates that male violence has more severe physical and psychological consequences for women than vice versa (see review in Holtzworth-Munroe, Smutzler, & Bates, 1997). Given the greater size and strength of men, they are more likely to physically injure their partners (Archer, 2000; Browne, 1993). For example, in a study of couples presenting for marital therapy, Cascardi et al. (1992) found while most violence between husbands and wives was reciprocal, wives were more likely to sustain severe injuries as a result of such violence. In addition, assessments conducted in a military domestic violence treatment program showed that fear of one's partner was rated significantly higher by women than by men (Cantos, Neidig, & O'Leary, 1993). In another study, when couples were asked to rate the impact of marital violence, husbands typically rated the impact of wife aggression as less negative than wives rated the impact of husband aggression (Cascardi & Vivian, 1995).

Psychological Impact of Male Violence on Women and Children

Male violence is associated with serious psychological effects for both battered women and their children. Relative to comparison samples, battered women are at particular risk for symptoms of post-traumatic stress disorder and depression (see review in Holtzworth-Munroe, Smutzler, & Sandin, 1997). Although most of this research has examined women experiencing severe male violence, some researchers have studied the consequences of male violence among women seeking couple therapy. The results of these studies suggest that, relative to women in nonaggressive relationships, women in aggressive relationships were still more likely to report clinical levels of depressive symptomatology (Cascardi et al., 1992). In addition, in a study of newlyweds, Quigley and Leonard (1996) found that wives who experienced husband physical aggression over the first 3 years of marriage reported higher levels of depressive symptomatol-

ogy than women whose husbands were consistently nonviolent or who desisted from their violence during this same time period.

Empirical evidence also indicates that children from homes with couple violence are at risk for behavior problems, emotional distress, and impaired social and academic functioning (for reviews, see Holtzworth-Munroe, Jouriles, Smutzler, & Norwood, 1998; Margolin, 1998). Research on marital conflict suggests that more intense and frequent conflicts (e.g., violent fights) have more negative consequences for children. Although no empirical data examining the effectiveness of interventions to help children of battered women have yet been published, two research groups (i.e., E. Jouriles and colleagues at the University of Houston; C. Sullivan and colleagues at Michigan State University) are currently conducting such research.

Effects of Marital Violence on Relationship Functioning

Studies of newlywed samples have demonstrated that the presence of physical aggression in early marriage is a longitudinal predictor of later relationship problems. O'Leary et al. (1989) found that individuals who were married to stably aggressive spouses (i.e., aggressive at more than one point in time) were less satisfied with their marriages than individuals married to stably nonaggressive spouses. In addition, in the O'Leary et al. (1989) sample, Heyman, O'Leary, and Jouriles (1995) found that husbands' premarital aggression longitudinally predicted both wives' steps toward divorce and lower marital adjustment. Similarly, Quigley and Leonard (1996) found that the presence of stable husband-to-wife physical aggression in the first 3 years of marriage was associated with declines in the wife's marital satisfaction. Among a different sample of newlyweds, Rogge and Bradbury (1999) found that whereas negative marital communication (i.e., not the presence of violence) predicted later marital dissatisfaction, the presence of interspousal physical aggression predicted relationship dissolution (i.e., separation and divorce).

The Related Problem of Psychological Aggression

Increasingly, researchers also are examining male-to-female psychological aggression as an important correlate and predictor of physical abuse (e.g., see a special issue of *Violence and Victims*, edited by O'Leary & Maiuro, 1999, on the topic). Initial studies, unfortunately, indicate that behaviors labeled "psychological aggression" (e.g., swearing, name calling) commonly occur among all couples, with prevalence rates of 89–97% among couples seeking marital therapy and 67–87% among engaged couples (Barling, O'Leary, Jouriles, Vivian, & MacEwan, 1987). Of course, the widespread nature of these behaviors raises the question of whether such behavior can be labeled "abusive" or whether such behaviors only become abusive when they reach a certain level of severity and frequency (e.g., a couple we saw in which the husband called the wife a whore and spit at her; when the husband calls the wife names on a daily basis, not just during heated conflicts). Alternatively, it is possible that such behaviors become abusive in the context of a physically violent relationship, as it is assumed that such actions carry an additional threat when they have previously preceded violence.

It is known that psychological aggression is a correlate of physical aggression, even among less severely violent samples. For example, Cascardi, O'Leary, Lawrence, and Schlee (1995) reported that, relative to nonabused women (maritally discordant or satisfied), women who had experienced husband violence and were seeking marital therapy reported their husbands to be significantly more coercive and psychologically aggressive. Existing data also show that psychological abuse has damaging consequences for battered women. For example, in a study by Follingstad, Rutledge, Berg, Hause, and Polek (1990), 72% of a sample of more severely battered women reported that emotional abuse had a more negative impact on them than physical abuse. Finally, the available data suggest that psychological aggression may predict physical aggression, as Murphy and O'Leary (1989) found that husbands' use of psychological aggression at 18 months after marriage significantly predicted physical aggression 30 months after marriage.

The Need to Increase Therapist Awareness of the Problem

Given the prevalence of couple violence, it is likely that all couple therapists, at some point, will treat a violent couple even if they do not specialize in the treatment of relationship violence. Unfortunately, however, many therapists have never received formal training regarding the problem and may not be well prepared to address this issue.

Two studies, conducted by Harway, Hansen, and Cervantes (1997), demonstrate reason for such concern. In the first, over 350 family and couple therapists were presented with a description of one of two actual cases involving family violence (in real life, one case ended in the husband killing the wife) and asked therapists what they would do with these cases. The results indicated that 40% of the respondents did not acknowledge family violence as a problem, and 55% did not suggest any intervention for the violence. It was unclear whether the therapists' responses were due to an inability to identify indicators of violence or to suggest appropriate interventions even when they considered violence to be a problem. To address this issue, Harway et al. (1997) asked over 400 American Psychological Association members to read a case in which family violence was implicated (i.e., the case stated that the husband murdered his wife). Respondents were asked how they would have intervened in this case. The results showed that 50% of the responding therapists did not generate appropriate interventions. These data strongly demonstrate the need for greater awareness among clinicians regarding how to assess for, and treat, cases of couple violence. We hope that the present chapter will provide part of that training.

THEORIES OF MALE VIOLENCE

It is important to briefly review some prominent theories of male violence, in order to provide basic information on the problem and suggest possible interventions. Theories of male violence are often divided into three groups, based upon their level of analysis: those focusing on the intrapersonal, interpersonal, or sociocultural causes of violence. Although most recent theories include two or more levels of analysis, we present theories based upon their primary component. We have chosen to focus primarily on theories suggesting the potential usefulness of couple therapy and/or cognitive-behavioral approaches in treating couple violence.

Intrapersonal Theories

Intrapersonal theories of male violence assume that characteristics of the individual increase one's risk of engaging in physical aggression. We briefly review two such theories.

Bandura (1973) has outlined a social learning theory of aggression, which has often been applied to male violence (e.g., Dutton, 1995; O'Leary, 1988). Bandura argues that aggressive behavior is acquired through learning, including observational learning (e.g., one's family or subculture), symbolic modeling (e.g., television violence), or direct experience. He also hypothesizes that aggression is activated through learning, as particular stimuli gain aggression eliciting functions through an association with differential consequences. The aggression elicitors most typically discussed in the couple violence literature include aversive treatment (e.g., threats, emotional withdrawal), anticipation of positive consequences (e.g., relief from tension), and factors unique to the subjective perspective of the aggressor (e.g., unfounded jealousy). Focusing on factors that maintain aggression, Bandura has noted that sources of reinforcement may include direct external reinforcement (e.g., tangible rewards, social and status rewards), observational reinforcement (i.e., observing the rewards and punishments of others' aggressive actions), and self-reinforcement (i.e., regulation of actions through self-produced rewards and punishments). As behavior is regulated by its consequences, this theory also allows that aggression may be punished by aversive consequences or extinguished by reward withdrawal. Using this theory, therapists would do well to regard couple violence as a learned behavior, and to examine and change the stimuli eliciting aggression and the balance of positive to negative consequences received for aggression.

Another intrapersonal theory that lends itself well to the interventions introduced below is the social information-processing model (see Holtzworth-Munroe, 2000). Social information processing involves three stages. In the first stage, decoding, one must perceive and interpret the relevant social stimuli in any situation. Misconstrual of social stimuli may occur due to interference of such factors as distraction, inattention, unrealistic expectations, faulty attributions, anger, or alcohol use. In the second stage, response generation and selection, one must consider possible behavioral responses and choose a response. In the third stage, enactment, one must carry out the chosen response and monitor it to see whether it has the expected impact. This monitoring will then be used to adjust future behavior. Each of these steps must be successfully completed in order for one to respond competently in a social interaction. Incompetent responses may escalate a conflictual situation, increasing the risk of violence. As reviewed below, relative to nonviolent men, violent men evidence skill deficits at each of these three stages (Holtzworth-Munroe, 2000), suggesting that a focus on social

and conflict resolution skills is an appropriate target for interventions with violent men.

Interpersonal Theories

Interpersonal theories of male violence focus on the interaction patterns between partners. For example, family systems theory and studies of the communication patterns of violent couples concentrate primarily upon the interactions between partners. In family systems theory, the couple relationship is a system defined by repetitive patterns in the interactions of spouses. As events occur, it is hypothesized that the couple relationship system works to maintain a state of homeostasis or balance (Day, 1995). Thus the theory assumes that couple violence is a product of all the interdependent parts of a relationship. Each reaction is considered to be a precipitant in a continuous causal chain of interactions that work to maintain homeostasis. Couple violence is, therefore, viewed as a product of dysfunctional interactions in which both partners contribute to an escalation of tension. Numerous system characteristics of battering relationships have been hypothesized (e.g., inflexible family rules, tight boundaries between the relationship and the outside world), but the communication patterns of violent relationships have been the subject of the most empirical research.

Feminist critics maintain that family systems theory both ignores the existence of unequal power in couple relationships and implies that the woman is responsible for the violence (e.g., Bograd, 1984). As reviewed below, however, studies of couple communication processes demonstrate that, relative to nonviolent couples, couples experiencing male violence are characterized by high levels of negative escalation, hostility, and demand–withdraw communication. Such data suggest the potential usefulness of communication and problem-solving training to break these negative patterns of communication.

Sociocultural Theories

The broadest level of theoretical analysis is that of sociocultural theories, which maintain that couple violence exists because violent and patriarchal societies allow, and even encourage, the use of violence as a means of dominating women (e.g., Dobash & Dobash, 1979). Feminist theories suggest that violence against women is caused by a patriarchal social organization in which men possess greater power and privilege, as well as a concomitant ideology that legitimizes this organization. Contributing to male dominance are men's economic advantage, adherence to traditional gender roles, and the accepted use of violence to settle disputes. Male violence is assumed to be supported by society through such factors as peer support, lack of police response to domestic violence, and minimal criminal sentences for domestic violence offenders.

As reviewed in Gelles and Straus (1979) and Bersani and Chen (1988), other sociocultural theories of violence have been proposed. For example, it has been suggested that the uneven distribution of violence in society is a function of differential cultural norms concerning violence and related issues (e.g., values regarding masculinity, the worth of life, and the meaning of honor). Others suggest that when resources (e.g., status, income) are lacking, violence may be used as a resource to maintain dominance or may be due to the frustration associated with few opportunities for achievement, power, or prestige. Other sociological theories assume that people will commit crimes, including violence, if social controls do not restrain them.

Although theories at this level of analysis may have few direct implications for therapy with violent couples, they can be useful in the therapist's conceptualization of male violence. For example, the therapist may wish to view violence in the context of the gendered power difference found in most couples (see Vivian & Heyman, 1996, for an example) or may wish to consider the subcultures in which couples live and the stressors they confront in their lives.

RESEARCH ON MARITALLY VIOLENT MEN

It is also important to briefly review available data on the correlates of male violence. Such information may help familiarize therapists with risk factors for violence and help them to consider relevant issues in their conceptualization of cases involving physical aggression. Data on the correlates of violence may be useful in planning assessment and interventions, as it is hoped that modifying the correlates of violence will change the problem itself.

Background Correlates of Male Violence

The factors reviewed here generally cannot be a direct target of intervention. Nonetheless, it is im-

portant to understand these risk factors to increase the chances of identifying couples experiencing male violence, and to consider intervention modifications that might be necessary when working with such couples.

• *Age.* Similar to most antisocial behaviors, younger couples are found across many studies to be at significantly higher risk for experiencing male violence than are middle-aged and older couples. In particular, couples under the age of 30 have the highest risk of intimate aggression (e.g., Pan, Neidig, & O'Leary, 1994).

• *Socioeconomic status (SES).* Men from lower-SES classes (McLaughlin, Leonard, & Senchak, 1992; Straus & Geles, 1990) and with low incomes (e.g., Pan et al., 1994) tend to have higher rates of intimate aggression than others. In addition, unemployment (e.g., Kaufman Kantor, Jasinski, & Aldarondo, 1994; Magdol et al., 1997) and lower educational attainment (McLaughlin et al., 1992; Magdol et al., 1997) have been associated with a heightened risk for male violence.

• *Race and ethnicity.* Some studies have demonstrated higher rates of intimate aggression among black and Hispanic couples than among white couples. The available data, however, suggest that the link between race and violence may be explained by the fact that minority group couples are often at a social disadvantage compared to white couples. For example, racial differences may disappear when income and urbanicity (i.e., risk factors for violence) are statistically controlled (for a review, see Holtzworth-Munroe, Smutzler, & Bates, 1997).

• *Marital status.* Cohabiting couples have consistently been shown to have higher rates of intimate violence than married (McLaughlin et al., 1992) and dating (Magdol, Moffitt, Caspi, & Silva, 1998a) couples. Relative to dating couples, cohabiting couples may have more at stake in their relationships and thus may be more willing to tolerate aggression. Relative to married couples, cohabiting couples' lack of commitment and related jealousy may explain these findings, or cohabiting couples may have higher rates of violence because they are younger.

• *Childhood influences.* A recent study following children from birth until adulthood (Magdol, Moffitt, Caspi, & Silva, 1998b) suggested that childhood predictors of later engagement in partner violence mirror concurrent correlates of adult intimate violence. For instance, children from lower-SES backgrounds were at risk for perpetrating intimate aggression in young adulthood. In addition, poor parent–child attachment in adolescence predicted later aggression. The most powerful predictors of later male-to-female aggression were lower educational attainment and conduct problems or juvenile delinquency in childhood and adolescence.

Much empirical attention has been devoted to comparing violent and nonviolent men's retrospective reports of experiences of violence in their families of origin. The findings are fairly consistent across studies: For men, exposure to violence in the home as a child is a correlate of later adult engagement in intimate aggression (e.g., Sugarman & Hotaling, 1989).

• *Head injury and neuropsychological deficits.* Men who aggress toward their partners are more likely than nonviolent men to have suffered a head injury (e.g., Rosenbaum et al., 1994). Similarly, initial data suggest a link between neuropsychological deficits and perpetration of male violence (Cohen, Rosenbaum, Kane, Warnken, & Benjamin, 1999). In particular, it has been suggested that deficits reflecting problems in areas such as the frontal lobes interfere with impulse control and planning, and thus increase the risk of violence.

Correlates of Male Violence That May be Amenable to Treatment

The review above alerts therapists to clients at particular risk for male violence and to relevant issues in therapy (e.g., modifying assignments for a client with neuropsychological deficits or low educational attainment). It is also important, however, to review correlates of violence that may be directly modifiable.

• *Social skills.* Based on an application of a social information-processing model to the study of male aggression, we have conducted a series of studies demonstrating that, relative to nonviolent men, violent men display social skills deficits in problematic couple situations (see review in Holtzworth-Munroe, 2000). Violent men are more likely than nonviolent men to attribute hostile intentions to their partners' negative actions; such attributions may help a man to justify his own aggression, as it may be perceived as retaliation against a hostile partner. Regarding response generation and selection skills, when presented with hypothetical conflict situations, violent men provide less competent and more aggressive responses

than nonviolent men. In addition, when asked what would be the "best" thing to do in these situations, violent men still provide less competent responses, suggesting that either they do not know or do not care. As a final example of their skill deficits, when asked to enact a competent response to a hypothetical couple conflict situation, violent men's enactments were rated as less competent than those of nonviolent men, suggesting that something in their behavior undermined their ability to enact a competent response.

• *Power.* Consistent with feminist theories, some researchers have posited that men become violent when they feel entitled to or desire power in their relationships, and that they use violence to maintain their power (e.g., Dutton & Strachan, 1987; Straus, 1990). Others have argued that men become violent when they desire power but perceive themselves to be powerless (e.g., Dutton & Strachan, 1987; Prince & Arias, 1994). In addition, consistent with this notion, other researchers have found that violent men report lower levels of perceived control than nonviolent men and reportedly resort to violence when they feel out of control (Stets, 1988), and that both husbands and wives in violent marriages feel more coercively controlled by their partners than do nonviolent spouses (Ehrensaft, Langhinrichsen-Rohling, Heyman, O'Leary, & Lawrence, 1999).

• *Social support.* In one large study, the availability of social support resources was inversely related to the probability of intimate aggression in men, while social involvement (i.e., the number of groups to which one belongs) and religiosity were not related to aggression (e.g., Magdol et al., 1997). It is important to note, however, that not all friends are equal: Data suggest that association with peers who support the use of aggression (e.g., Smith, 1991) or who are involved in delinquent behavior (e.g., Holtzworth-Munroe, Meehan, Herron, Rehman, & Stuart, 2000) may be risk factors for male violence.

• *Stressful life events.* Stressful life events, as conceptualized separately from sociodemographic stressors (e.g., poverty) and martial stress (e.g., conflict and distress), have been inconsistently linked to intimate aggression. For instance, work-related stress and negative life events have correlated with male aggression in some studies (e.g., Margolin, John, & Foo, 1998; Neff, Holman, & Schulter, 1995), whereas others have failed to find such a link (e.g., Pan et al., 1994). It may be that stressful events are more problematic for susceptible individuals; for instance, Seltzer and Kalmuss

(1988) found that husbands who were exposed to family violence as children were much more likely to be violent during periods of stress than those who did not have a family history of violence.

• *Anger and hostility.* Although there are methodological problems in much of this research, some consistent findings emerge (see review in Eckhardt, Barbour, & Stuart, 1997). First, men's self-reported general anger and hostility often correlate with intimate aggression, although there are exceptions. Perhaps more important is anger and hostility directed at a partner (i.e., partner-specific anger), which is positively related to increasing severity of male-to-female violence. As reviewed below, group differences in hostile behavior are also found in observational studies of couple interactions, with violent couples displaying more hostility than nonviolent couples.

• *Attitudes.* Attitudes supportive of the use of violence and approval of the use of force against women are positively correlated with the abuse of female partners (see review in Sugarman & Frankel, 1996). However, as these studies are cross-sectional, they do not allow us to disentangle whether positive attitudes toward violence precede or follow the use of aggression. Interestingly, conventional sex role beliefs and attitudes toward egalitarianism in relationships have not emerged as strong predictors of intimate aggression (see review in Sugarman & Frankel, 1996). In contrast, however, there is increasing evidence that hostile and adversarial attitudes toward women are related to male violence (e.g., Holtzworth-Munroe et al., 2000).

• *Jealousy and attachment.* Some theories suggest that men who are highly dependent upon and/or anxiously attached to their female partners are jealous and hypervigilant to any threats to their relationships, using violence in a rage when they fear the loss of their partners (Dutton & Golant, 1995). Consistent with such notions, in some studies violent men have scored higher on measures of jealousy than nonviolent men (e.g., Dutton, van Ginkel, & Landolt, 1996; Holtzworth-Munroe, Stuart, & Hutchinson, 1997), although there are exceptions (e.g., Murphy, Meyer, & O'Leary, 1994). Compared to nonviolent men, violent men also are more dependent on their partners and more likely to score high on measures of fearful and preoccupied attachment (e.g., Dutton, Saunders, Starzomski, & Bartholomew, 1994; Holtzworth-Munroe, Stuart, & Hutchinson, 1997; Murphy et al., 1994).

• *Alcohol use.* Violent men are more likely than nonviolent men to have drinking problems and to engage in binge drinking (e.g., Kaufman Kantor & Straus, 1987; Pan et al., 1994; Magdol et al., 1997). In addition, alcohol intoxication is a common factor in many incidents of intimate aggression (Kaufman Kantor & Straus, 1987). Prospectively, husbands' premarital alcohol use predicts future husband-to-wife aggression in newlywed samples (Heyman et al., 1995; Leonard & Senchak, 1993, 1996). In addition, illegal drug use is associated with severe male-to-female violence (Holtzworth-Munroe et al., 2000; Magdol et al., 1997; Pan et al., 1994). Ingestion of alcohol has been shown to increase husbands' negativity toward their wives in a subsequent marital interaction, suggesting that alcohol may increase verbal aggression, which then increases the risk for physical aggression (Leonard & Roberts, 1998).

• *Psychopathology.* Antisocial personality disorder is more common in violent than in nonviolent men (e.g., Magdol et al., 1997), and borderline personality disorder scores are elevated in men who perpetrate male-to-female violence (e.g., Dutton & Golant, 1995). In addition to Axis II disorders, studies have shown that violent men are more likely than nonviolent men to report symptoms of depression (e.g., Pan et al., 1994) and other psychological problems (e.g., anxiety, bipolar, and psychotic disorders; Magdol et al., 1997).

Subtypes of Familially Violent Men

Up to this point, we have highlighted general differences between familially violent and nonviolent men; however, recent research has made it clear that samples of violent men are heterogeneous, varying along theoretically important dimensions. Based on a review of previous batterer typologies, Holtzworth-Munroe and Stuart (1994) suggested that batterer subtypes can be identified using three descriptive dimensions: (1) severity/frequency of male violence; (2) generality of male violence (i.e., familial only or extrafamilial also); and (3) the man's psychopathology or personality disorders. Using these dimensions, Holtzworth-Munroe and Stuart proposed that three subtypes of batterers can be identified. First, "family-only" batterers would engage in the least intimate violence, exhibit the least violence outside the home, and evidence little or no psychopathology. Second, "dysphoric/borderline" batterers would engage in moderate to severe abuse, but their violence would be primarily confined to their female partners; this group would be psychologically distressed and the most likely to evidence borderline personality characteristics. Finally, "generally violent/antisocial" batterers would engage in the highest levels of familial violence and extrafamilial violence, and evidence characteristics of antisocial personality disorder.

Holtzworth-Munroe and Stuart (1994) then integrated intrapersonal models of aggression into a developmental model of these differing types of violent husbands. Based on this model, we predicted that family-only men should evidence the lowest levels of risk factors for violence. The violence of family-only men was proposed to result from a combination of stress (personal and/or couple) and low-level risk factors (e.g., lack of relationship skills), such that on some occasions, during escalating marital conflicts, these men engage in physical aggression. Following such incidents, however, their low levels of psychopathology, combined with their relatively positive attitudes toward women and negative attitudes toward violence, lead to remorse and help prevent their aggression from escalating. In contrast, dysphoric/borderline batterers were hypothesized to come from a background involving parental abuse and rejection. As a result, these men have difficulty forming stable, trusting attachments with intimate partners. Instead, they are highly dependent upon, yet fearful of losing, their partners, and very jealous. Dutton and Golant (1995) suggest that when these men are frustrated, their borderline personality organization, anger, and insecure attachment lead to violence against their adult attachment figures (i.e., their partners). Finally, generally violent/antisocial batterers were predicted to resemble other antisocial, aggressive groups, with high levels of many risk factors (e.g., impulsive, lack social skills), and their intimate violence was conceptualized as one part of their general use of aggression and engagement in antisocial behavior.

More recent batterer typologies have provided indirect support for this typology (e.g., Hamberger, Lohr, Bonge, & Tolin, 1996; Waltz, Babcock, Jacobson, & Gottman, 2000). In addition, in our own study of physically aggressive men recruited from the community, we found the three predicted subtypes, along with one additional subgroup (Holtzworth-Munroe et al., 2000). The predicted subgroups generally differed as hypothesized. The fourth, unpredicted cluster was labeled the "low-level antisocial" group, given their moderate scores on measures of antisociality, marital violence, and general violence.

Although researchers have not yet studied the question of how different subtypes of battering men

fare in conjoint couple therapy, we have hypothesized that family-only men may be the only group for whom conjoint treatment is appropriate. Family-only men are the least violent and have the fewest risk factors for violence, but, importantly, the risk factors that do characterize them (e.g., social skills deficits) may be amenable to conjoint therapy. Indeed, in the Holtzworth-Munroe et al. (2000) study, the family-only group did not differ significantly from a comparison group of nonviolent but maritally distressed men on any measure except that of marital violence, suggesting that family-only men resemble nonviolent/distressed men (who are often the target of conjoint therapy).

RESEARCH ON DYADIC-LEVEL VARIABLES

The research reviewed above has focused on individual correlates of male violence. In this section, we briefly review two dyadic-level correlates that may be amenable to conjoint therapy: couple distress and couple communication.

Couple Distress

Couples experiencing male violence typically have lower levels of relationship satisfaction than nonviolent couples, although they may not experience significantly less satisfaction that nonviolent distressed couples (see Holtzworth-Munroe, Smutzler, & Bates, 1997, for a review). The relationship between couple distress and aggression is not well understood. It was originally assumed that couple dissatisfaction leads to conflict, and ultimately to aggression (O'Leary, 1996). In contrast to these ideas, recent longitudinal studies of newlyweds suggest, as reviewed above, that the temporal ordering may be different—that male physical aggression in an otherwise satisfying relationship leads to a decline in wives' marital satisfaction (e.g., Heyman et al., 1995; Quigley & Leonard, 1996) or to relationship dissolution (Rogge & Bradbury, 1999).

Couple Communication

Researchers have compared the interaction behavior of violent and nonviolent couples. Across studies, the findings are consistent. During discussions of couple problems, compared to nonviolent men, violent men display more negative behaviors, including defensiveness and overtly hostile behavior (e.g., Margolin, Burman, & John, 1989). Even compared to men in nonviolent but maritally distressed couples, men in violent/distressed couples display more hostile and provocative forms of anger (e.g., contempt, belligerence, blame; Holtzworth-Munroe, Smutzler, & Stuart, 1998; Jacobson et al., 1994). These behaviors continue over the course of the discussion, as violent/distressed couples demonstrate more negative reciprocity, and this pattern lasts longer for them than for nonviolent couples (e.g., Burman, Margolin, & John, 1993; Cordova, Jacobson, Gottman, Rushe, & Cox, 1993). In addition, violent couples escalate their negativity; for example, violent/distressed men react to low-level negative female affect with escalated negativity (Coan, Gottman, Babcock, & Jacobson, 1997). Moreover, violent couples engage in both more demanding and withdrawing behavior (e.g., Berns, Jacobson, & Gottman, 1999), particularly male-demand–female-withdraw communication (e.g., Holtzworth-Munroe, Smutzler, & Stuart, 1998), than nonviolent couples. These high levels of negativity may also characterize other types of couple discussions, as one study of discussions of wives' personal (i.e., not relationship) problems found that, relative to nonviolent men, violent husbands displayed more contempt/disgust, anger/frustration, tension/anxiety, and belligerent/domineering behavior, as well as less social support, less positive behavior, and less acceptance of their wives' problem definitions (Holtzworth-Munroe, Stuart, Sandin, Smutzler, & McLaughlin, 1997).

Data from longitudinal studies have shown that premarital communication negativity may predict marital dissatisfaction (Rogge & Bradbury, 1999), but it does not appear to predict husband violence (Smith, Vivian, & O'Leary, 1991). In contrast, in a longitudinal study of husbands who were already moderately to severely violent, men who displayed more negativity (i.e., belligerence, contempt, defensiveness, domineering) in a marital problem discussion were less likely than others in the sample to decrease their level of violence over time (Jacobson, Gottman, Gortner, Berns, & Shortt, 1996).

ASSESSMENT

Assessment of Physical Aggression

As discussed above, over half of couples seeking couple therapy have experienced male physical aggression in the past year. However, therapists may easily fail to detect the presence of physical aggression, as couples often do not spontaneously report it as a presenting problem. O'Leary et al. (1992) found that only 6% of wives reported violence on an intake form. Yet, during individual interviews with direct questioning about violence, 44% of these wives reported the occurrence of husband violence. This figure increased to 53% when the wives were asked to complete a behavior checklist questionnaire, the Conflict Tactics Scales (CTS; Straus, 1979). Similarly, Ehrensaft and Vivian (1996) found that about half of spouses reporting mild husband physical aggression on the CTS failed to mention this aggression during an interview, and approximately one-quarter of spouses reporting severe husband physical aggression on the CTS had not mentioned this violence during an interview. Ehrensaft and Vivian (1996) asked couples seeking marital therapy why they did not report violence at intake. The most common reasons given were that the violence was not considered a problem, that the violence was unstable or infrequent, or that the couple perceived the violence to be a secondary problem that would resolve once primary relationship problems were addressed.

These data clearly indicate that to increase the likelihood of detecting male violence, a structured instrument such as the CTS should be routinely administered to all couples seeking therapy. We recommend administering the CTS to both partners, asking them to complete it individually and in privacy from each other. The CTS assesses the frequency of occurrence of psychological and physical aggression in the past year. As partners often provide incongruent reports regarding the occurrence of specific violent behaviors, either partner's report of violence should be accepted as valid and further assessed.

Although the CTS is the most widely used self-report measure of couple violence, it has a number of shortcomings. It assesses only a limited set of violent behaviors and only violence occurring during conflicts; yet male violence can occur in other situations (e.g., a man comes home angry about work and turns his anger onto his partner). Another important limitation is that the CTS does not assess the context of violence (e.g., the events leading to violence, the sequence of events during a violent incident, the aggressor's intentions, the partner's responses, and consequences of the violence); such variables may be important in understanding the role violence plays in a relationship. The CTS was recently revised, creating the Revised Conflict Tactics Scales (CTS2; Straus, Hamby,

Boney-McCoy, & Sugarman, 1996). Both the Psychological and Aggression scales were expanded, and two new scales were added (i.e., Sexual Coercion and Physical Injury). The CTS2 still does not assess the context of the violence, however.

To do this, we recommend conducting separate interviews with each partner, so that both partners—particularly frightened woman—may be more honest regarding such issues as the behaviors leading to violence, the sequence of violent actions once begun (e.g., established patterns of interaction), the severity of violence and resulting injuries, actions following the violence (e.g., possible reinforcers or punishers for violence), the involvement of third parties (e.g., police), and potential danger to others (e.g., children). This assessment should also address issues that may help to determine whether conjoint treatment is appropriate for a couple. For example, the therapist should assess the level of the woman's fear for her safety, as well as each partner's motivation to enter conjoint treatment and to remain in the relationship. In addition, therapists should try to ascertain each partner's willingness to acknowledge that the physical aggression is a problem and to take responsibility for his/her own violent actions; related to this, previous attempts to deal with the aggression should be assessed.

If severe or frequent violence is reported, the potential lethality of the situation should be assessed immediately. Such assessments should gather information regarding the presence of guns or other weapons in the home, recent escalations in violence, direct and indirect threats of lethality, level of the woman's fear, and whether substance use is associated with the violence. If the therapist determines that the likelihood of continued violence and/or lethality is present, he/she should immediately, and individually, discuss safety planning and resource mobilization with both partners. The discussion with the man should focus on the seriousness of the problem, developing a series of emergency steps that he can take to prevent his use of violence (e.g., time outs, calling the therapist or a crisis line), and emphasizing the need for safety planning on the part of his partner. Discussion with the woman should include developing a detailed and individualized plan for situations in which she may fear for her safety. Such discussions should cover practical issues such as how she can get herself and her children out of the home; a safe place where she can go (e.g., a relative's or friend's home, a shelter); and how she can get quick access to items such as car keys, money, and impor-

tant documents. The woman should also be informed of appropriate local resources, including shelters and social service agencies, as well as legal options available to her in the area.

Assessing Other Relevant Issues

Although the CTS provides a fairly limited assessment of psychological abuse, psychological abuse often accompanies physical abuse and is a predictor of violence. Thus, therapists may prefer to administer more comprehensive measures of psychological abuse (e.g., the Psychological Maltreatment of Women Inventory; Tolman, 1999). For the woman, the psychological consequences of the violence, particularly posttraumatic stress disorder and depressive symptoms, should be assessed. Similarly, both partners should be asked about the effects of their conflicts on children in the home and about any problems the children may be experiencing. Given the research findings and the need to identify targets for intervention, therapists may wish to assess correlates of male violence, including a man's level of anger and hostility, jealousy and dependency on his partner, and attitudes toward women and violence. Substance abuse, and other psychopathology, should be assessed. Therapists should also assess men's communication skills, perhaps through observation of marital interactions. Therapists may find it helpful to screen for subtypes of violent men, although it should be noted that further research is needed to determine the actual extent to which therapists benefit from applying typology research to practice (Langhinrichsen-Rohling, Huss, & Ramsey, 2000). If therapists choose to screen for the Holtzworth-Munroe and Stuart (1994) typology, they should assess the severity of male violence, generality of violence, and psychopathology/personality disorders. Using the CTS2, an interview regarding violence outside the home, and the Millon Clinical Multiaxial Inventory (Millon, 1983), therapists can compare a man's scores on these measures to the mean scores for each subtype in the Holtzworth-Munroe et al. (2000) paper.

DECIDING WHETHER OR NOT CONJOINT THERAPY IS APPROPRIATE

After completing a thorough assessment and dealing with any necessary safety planning, therapists must decide whether to proceed with conjoint therapy or refer the individual partners to gender-specific treatment (GST; i.e., men's and women's groups). GST is the treatment format most commonly used for the treatment of domestic violence, with men being seen in batterer treatment programs (described below). Indeed, many state standards for batterer treatment programs of men who have been court-ordered to receive treatment recommend that batterers be treated in groups of men and indicate that conjoint treatment of couples is inappropriate. For example, Section 4.5 of the Massachusetts state standards states, "Any form of couples or conjoint counseling or marriage enhancement weekends or groups are inappropriate initially . . . couples counseling shall not be considered a component of batterer treatment" (*Massachusetts Guidelines and Standards*, 1994, p. 13). Such guidelines have been developed, in part, because the use of a conjoint treatment format with male-violent couples is considered controversial.

Potential Disadvantages and Advantages of Conjoint Treatment

Indeed, the conjoint format has potential disadvantages. There is concern that seeing both partners in therapy and focusing on such issues as a couple's communication patterns may imply that the man's violence is caused by both partners, rather than being the man's sole responsibility. An additional concern is that the woman may not feel comfortable expressing herself in the man's presence (e.g., she may not be able to be fully honest about such issues as the level of violence she experiences, her level of fear, or her desire to end the relationship), as she may fear further violence from her partner if she is honest about such issues. Also, there is concern that the process of discussing difficult relationship problems could increase male anger and conflict, such that the therapy itself would increase the risk of male violence (for further discussion of such issues, see O'Leary, Heyman, & Neidig, 1999, and Bograd, 1984).

In contrast, the conjoint treatment format also has potential advantages. One is the ability to obtain a more accurate picture of the violence (i.e., the partners' reports may differ significantly). In addition, in conjoint treatment, therapists can ensure that both partners understand the therapist's conceptualization of violence and of how techniques should be implemented. In our experience, some interventions go more smoothly when both partners are present to hear the rationale and procedures for them (e.g., both partners understand what an appropriate vs. an inappropriate time out involves), and a man may be less likely to use therapy to further abuse his partner when the woman has also heard what the therapist says (e.g., in batterers' treatment, some men go home and tell their partners such things as "My therapist told me that it's your fault I'm violent"). Conjoint therapy also allows couples to postpone volatile discussions until the therapy sessions, thus helping them to avoid escalating arguments at home until they are better trained to discuss such problems.

There are also theoretical rationales for using conjoint treatment. First, given that physical violence often occurs in the context of an argument between partners (O'Leary et al., 1999), direct intervention to decrease negative communication in conjoint treatment may decrease violence by changing the interactional patterns that precede it. Second, most couples presenting for relationship therapy have experienced bidirectional violence, and self-defense accounts for fewer than 20% of these cases (Cascardi & Vivian, 1995), suggesting that both partners may benefit from learning to control their use of physical aggression. Moreover, although male violence often can have severe physical and psychological effects, many women seeking couple therapy are not experiencing that level of violence, nor are they fearful of participating in treatment with their partners (O'Leary et al., 1999). Indeed, in many cases, these women are seeking conjoint therapy and wish to remain in their relationships.

Guidelines for Deciding Whether or Not Conjoint Treatment is Appropriate

Unfortunately, no available research provides empirically based rules for deciding whether or not conjoint treatment is appropriate. However, three studies have examined the efficacy of couples' therapy with violent couples (all are reviewed in more detail below), and an examination of the subject exclusion criteria used in these studies may provide ideas for guidelines. Similarly, examination of the additional steps these researchers took to protect women's safety may give therapists ideas for procedures to follow when working with aggressive couples.

Harris, Savage, Jones, and Brooke (1988) compared conjoint treatment to GST and a waitlist control. For a couple to be eligible for the study, the woman had to indicate, during an individual interview, that she wanted to remain in the relationship and that she did not feel endangered by her partner's knowledge that she had discussed his violence with a counselor. In addition, the man had to exhibit no psychotic symptoms, serious brain injury, psychopathic disturbance, or substance abuse that was not being treated concurrently. Intake workers helped the women construct individualized safety plans and provided them with information about community resources for battered women.

O'Leary et al. (1999) compared group couples' therapy to GST. They used extensive screening criteria to protect the safety of the wives in these married couples, including a couple in the study only if the wife did not report sustaining injuries that required medical attention; the wife reported, during a private interview, feeling comfortable being assigned to conjoint treatment; the wife was not afraid of living with her husband; the husband did not meet criteria for alcohol dependence; and neither spouse reported psychotic symptoms or met criteria for psychopathology severe enough to interfere with participation. In addition, the man had to admit the perpetration of at least one act of physical aggression.

Brannen and Rubin (1996) also compared group conjoint therapy to GST. In contrast to the other two studies, Brannen and Rubin did not exclude couples based on the severity of husband violence or alcohol abuse; they offered couple therapy to a more severely violent sample (i.e., the men were court-ordered to receive treatment). However, precautions were taken to ensure the wives' safety. For instance, a separate orientation was provided for the wives, during which they were provided a 24-hour emergency phone number, as well as phone numbers for law enforcement officials and shelters. In addition, husbands and wives completed weekly reports concerning the use of psychological and physical abuse or threats. If any indication of a threatening situation existed, follow-up calls and additional help were provided for the wife.

Based on their clinical and research experience, others also have written about possible guidelines for determining when conjoint therapy is inappropriate for violent couples (e.g., Holtzworth-Munroe, Beatty, & Anglin, 1995; O'Leary, 1996). Most authors agree that severity of violence and danger to the woman are important factors; they concur that conjoint treatment is only appropriate if levels of aggression are low to moderate and if

the woman is not perceived to be in danger of imminent physical harm. Related to this, the woman must not fear the man, must feel comfortable in therapy with him, and must not feel so intimidated or dominated by him that she cannot be honest in therapy. In addition, both partners must be interested in staying in the relationship. A conjoint format is most suitable for partners who believe that physical aggression is a problem and are willing to work toward a nonviolent relationship; it is inappropriate if one partner does not acknowledge the existence or problematic nature of the violence or is not willing to take steps to reduce it (e.g., removing weapons from the home, seeking drug/alcohol treatment, temporarily separating).

ALTERNATIVES TO CONJOINT THERAPY

If it is determined that conjoint therapy is inappropriate, then both partners should be provided with referrals to other sources of help. We explain such referrals by telling the partners that we are very concerned about the level of violence they have experienced, and that the level of violence occurring is too severe to begin conjoint treatment (e.g., concerns about safety and the possible escalation of violence if difficult issues were to be addressed in therapy). We also clearly convey our belief that each partner is responsible for his/her own behavior (i.e., the battered partner did not "provoke" the violence) and thus must take steps to end it. We usually offer to reevaluate the appropriateness of conjoint therapy once they each have sought appropriate help elsewhere (see the referral suggestions below) and after the man has completed a domestic violence treatment program.

Referrals for Battered Women

For women, referrals to support groups for battered women and advocacy services may be important, as a battered woman often is not able to begin considering her long-term options or dealing with the trauma of the violence she has experienced (i.e., more traditional psychotherapy) until she has obtained adequate support and resources (e.g., housing, legal protection, and child care). Indeed, a recent study demonstrated that such advocacy can significantly reduce a woman's likelihood of being subjected to future abuse. Sullivan and Bybee (1999) tested a 10-week intervention program in which undergraduate students assisted battered women leaving a shelter to develop individualized safety plans and obtain needed community resources (e.g., education, legal assistance, employment, housing, child care, transportation, financial assistance, health care). Over a 2-year follow-up period, women who received the advocacy experienced less violence in their intimate relationships, fewer depressive symptoms, and more social support, and were more effective in obtaining resources themselves, than women who had not received advocacy services. Once such issues are addressed, a woman in a violent relationship may wish to address other issues (e.g., trauma symptoms, long-term planning) in more traditional therapy (e.g., see Dutton, 1996).

Referrals for Battering Men

If a couple does not appear to be an appropriate candidate for conjoint treatment, therapists should refer the man to (GST). Referring the man to GST gives both partners the clear message that the man is responsible for his violence and for learning to become nonviolent. It also is often a test of a man's willingness to change, providing his partner with additional information about the level of his willingness to work to become nonviolent. For example, in some cases, after a thorough assessment and the chance to discuss violence, women have chosen to leave their violent partners upon seeing that the men do not follow our recommendation to seek GST.

Many communities offer batterer treatment programs, usually including a mixture of men referred by the legal system or other therapists and self-referred men. There are numerous examples of GST in the literature (e.g., Malloy, McCloskey, & Monford, 1999; Dutton & Golant, 1995); thus, we only provide a brief description here.

These programs vary widely in length, from 6 to 52 weeks. A group format is most commonly used in GST. The hope is that some men may be more willing to listen to their peers then to therapists, and that men at more advanced stages of change may provide positive examples, confrontation, and support for other men. In addition, group therapy may help men to avoid feelings of isolation. It is also cost-effective. Male and female cotherapists are generally preferred, to model a respectful male–female relationship and provide differing perspectives on important issues. Many states have adopted standards regarding such issues as program length and format, so local guidelines should be considered when making therapy referrals.

GST for violent men typically involves a combination of feminist theory and cognitive-behavioral techniques. GST material taken from the feminist perspective includes examination of the role of aggression and other forms of abusive behavior in maintaining a male's control of his partner, sex roles, and patriarchal power. From the cognitive-behavioral perspective, psychoeducational techniques are used, including anger management, time outs, and communication skills training.

The effectiveness of GST for male violence has not been clearly established. In a pessimistic review of studies evaluating the effectiveness of court-ordered treatment of male violence, Rosenfeld (1992) concluded that, overall, men who are arrested and ordered to treatment appear to recidivate at rates equivalent to men who are arrested and not sent to treatment. In contrast, Davis and Taylor (1999) concluded that recent, more methodologically rigorous studies (i.e., quasi-experiments or true experiments with random assignment to treatment vs. control groups) suggest that treatment is significantly more effective than no treatment in reducing violence. However, not all of the studies they reviewed are so convincing. For example, in the largest study to date (i.e., over 800 men in the U.S. Navy), Dunford (2000) assessed the relative effectiveness of (1) a cognitive-behavioral gender-specific batterer treatment program for violent husbands; (2) a group in which the same type of treatment was offered, but wives were also invited to participate (note that most did not); (3) a rigorous monitoring condition (i.e., the men were told that monthly checks for further violence would be conducted and, if further violence occurred, their commanding officer would be notified and further steps would be taken); and (4) a control group that involved safety planning with the wife. The GST men's groups did not lead to lower recidivism rates at a 1-year follow-up than any of the other groups, raising questions about the necessity of extensive intervention programs. On a positive note, however, across all four treatment conditions, approximately two-thirds of the men ended their physical aggression.

We would conclude that the effectiveness of batterer treatment programs has not yet been definitively established. Nonetheless, we currently still recommend referral of a violent man (who is judged to be an inappropriate candidate for conjoint treatment) to such a program, given a lack of any empirically demonstrated effective alternatives and our hope that referring the man to a program designed for this problem and staffed by experienced therapists may be effective.

CONJOINT TREATMENT PROCEDURES

Setting of Goals and Therapy Contracts

Before conjoint treatment begins with a couple experiencing male violence, the couple needs to be made aware of the therapist's expectations and goals for treatment. Specifically, the partners should be clearly informed that cessation of male violence is one of the primary goals of treatment. Despite our careful assessment of aggression during intake procedures, many couples still are surprised by our concern regarding their aggression and wish to dismiss it as excessive.

Thus, as part of an effort to motivate couples to change, we usually review a series of reasons for our concern. We note that while the current level of aggression may be low, any level of physical aggression always carries with it a risk of injury, and we give examples of relevant cases (e.g., a man pushed his partner with no intent to hurt her, but as the floor was wet that day, she slipped and hit her head on the kitchen counter, suffering a concussion). We also explain that although the research data demonstrate that some couples cease their aggression or maintain low levels of aggression, research also demonstrates that many couples escalate their levels of aggression—and, unfortunately, the current data do not allow us to predict which couples are at risk for continuing or escalating aggression. Thus, to be conservative, we must assume that every aggressive couple we work with is at risk for escalating violence. Similarly, if, during the assessment, we have discovered that this couple has risk factors for violence (e.g., psychological aggression, excessive substance use, violence in the family of origin, etc.), we present these as factors that make us concerned that the aggression may escalate, explaining the relevant research. To further motivate a couple to work on aggression, we discuss any possible negative consequences of the aggression that has occurred. For example, often the partners are concerned about their children's awareness of their fights and wish to model better conflict resolution for their children. Finally, we explain that without a direct focus on ending the aggression, there is a risk that the therapy itself may escalate the aggression, as the couple will be asked

to discuss difficult topics likely to engender anger and frustration. Indeed, the assessment sometimes reveals that one way the couple is avoiding aggression is to avoid the discussion of sensitive topics, but now the therapist is going to ask the couple to address these issues. Thus we must ensure that aggression will not occur in the course of such discussions.

Related to this concern, we then explain that treatment will focus first on helping the partners to control their behavior when angry. Once anger management skills are learned, they will be in a safer position to engage in problem solving regarding their major presenting problems. We find that following such a discussion, most couples are willing (though some are still reluctant) to agree to a treatment plan that will initially focus on anger management and controlling aggression.

In many cases, both partners have used physical aggression. Thus we acknowledge that both partners must take responsibility for their own aggression and any consequences of it. We discuss our belief that violence is a learned behavior and a choice, and, accordingly, that both partners must take responsibility for stopping their physical aggression. In most cases, however, we also emphasize that because male violence carries greater risk (e.g., physical injury, negative psychological effects), it will be a particular target of treatment.

If it has not already been done, it is important to consider safety plans with both partners. In a couple accepted for conjoint therapy (i.e., less severe violence), detailed planning may not be necessary. There still, however, should be a conversation with the woman about her safety (e.g., safe places to go if a fight is escalating, information about relevant local resources). In addition, both partners should be asked to consider steps they could take to prevent their further perpetration of physical aggression (e.g., discussing heated issues only in public or in therapy sessions) and to lessen the danger of any injury (e.g., removing guns from the home).

Both partners should be asked to make a "no-violence" contract, either written or oral, with the therapist. In doing so, the couple should agree to report any incidents of physical aggression to the therapist. To remove the burden on (or danger to) partners in bringing up such events, the therapist should explain that he/she will regularly ask about the occurrence of any physical aggression. The therapist should explain that further occurrences of aggression will lead to a reexamination of the level of danger, the reasons the treatment plan is not working, and the appropriateness of the treatment plan. In some cases, continuing or worsening violence will be grounds for termination of conjoint treatment and referral of the partners to GST specializing in relationship violence. This message is an important motivator, demonstrating to both members of the couple how concerned the therapist is about their aggression.

We use a cognitive-behavioral approach to conjoint treatment. Thus the therapist next explains to the couple that therapy involves a "two-pronged" approach, in that the remaining bulk of the therapy time will be dedicated to two modules: (1) anger recognition and management, and (2) communication and problem-solving skills. These sections parallel, to a large extent, the treatment protocols for other existing conjoint treatment programs for male violence and relationship aggression (e.g., Geffner, Mantooth, Franks, & Rao, 1989; Heyman & Neidig, 1997).

Anger Management

Because intimate aggression frequently occurs during an argument, as part of an escalation of angry feelings, the first set of skills introduced in conjoint treatment for physical aggression usually involves anger management. We explain to couples that the term "anger management" is a misnomer, as anger is a natural emotion; we are actually trying to help partners manage their behavior (i.e., aggression or abuse) when they are angry. In most cases, given the lower levels of aggression among the couples we accept into conjoint therapy, we find that one to three full therapy sessions devoted to anger management, followed by attention to these skills in subsequent therapy sessions, provides adequate coverage of anger management. Our procedures are borrowed from previous programs for anger management (e.g., Novaco, 1975), batterer treatment (e.g., Hamberger & Hastings, 1988; Saunders, 1989), and conjoint therapy for relationship aggression (e.g., Heyman & Neidig, 1997).

Recognition of Anger

To manage and control their anger adequately, partners must first be able to identify anger. Thus the therapist should solicit examples from each partner regarding how they experience anger, helping them to identify the physical, cognitive, and behavioral cues that accompany their anger. Physical cues include physiological changes (e.g., flush-ing, tenseness, rapid heart beat, sweating). Cognitive cues are best described as "hot thoughts" or "anger-up statements"; they can be broken into categories such as labeling (e.g., "She's so stupid"), hostile attributions (e.g., "She did that just to spite me"), catastrophizing (e.g., "Now my whole life is ruined"), and "should" statements (e.g., "She should have known better than to do that"). Behavioral cues consist of the ways in which anger is expressed, through facial expression, verbalizations, and motor behavior (e.g., tapping fingers, slamming doors, violence). It is important to point out to clients how anger (which is a feeling) differs from aggression (which is a response to having this feeling).

Next, the therapist asks each partner to construct a personalized anger continuum from the least to most extreme anger they experience, using a line marked from 1 to 10. To facilitate an appreciation for the different intensities of anger, the therapist helps the clients to label key anchor points along the line (e.g., "frustrated" vs. "angry" vs. "furious" vs. "no longer in control of behavior and in danger of using aggression"). The therapist should guide the discussion so that physical, cognitive, and behavioral signs of anger are listed for each of these key points along the continuum.

Anger logs are introduced as an important ongoing homework assignment. On their anger logs, partners report the details of one or more episodes during the week when they felt angry. They record the situation; the intensity of the anger (on the 1–10 scale); and the physical, cognitive, and behavioral anger cues experienced. Partners are instructed to keep these anger logs and, across situations and weeks, to look for patterns in their anger (e.g., when and with whom they are angry, how they know they are angry); perhaps helping them to identify high-risk situations for arguments and aggression (e.g., a couple discovered, after completing anger logs for several weeks, that their major fights always occurred when the husband was running late in preparation to go out as a couple).

Time Outs

The first skill taught for managing anger is taking a time out to avoid engaging in aggression during conflicts. We find that some couples have a difficult time accepting time outs, as this procedure (i.e., leaving a fight) runs counter to many common cultural beliefs (e.g., that one should never walk away from a fight, that it is better to hash out an issue until some insight or resolution is reached).

In such cases, it is important that the therapist help the couple to weigh the risk of continued aggression against the temporary suspension of the discussion of a heated issue. In other cases, a couple may have avoided discussing issues for years, and there is a danger that time outs can be used to continue such a pattern. In either situation, it is important for both partners to understand that a time out does not permanently end discussion of the problem; they will be asked to discuss the issues calmly after the time out, or, if this is impossible, to bring the issue to therapy for eventual discussion. We also have found that many couples initially respond negatively to the term "time out," having heard it applied to the discipline of children. In contrast, we introduce the procedure by using analogies to the time outs taken during sporting events (e.g., as a chance for players to regroup and collect themselves before making a costly mistake that could lose the game).

Time outs have several components. First, a partner must recognize his/her anger and take responsibility both for acknowledging the anger and for taking a time out. In addition, this person needs to inform the other partner of these facts, saying, "I am beginning to feel angry, and I need to take a time out." Each part of that statement is discussed in detail (e.g., using an "I" statement to take responsibility for one's feelings, acknowledging the anger without blaming the other partner, calmly announcing a time out rather than just leaving the discussion, etc.). We have implemented a rule that neither partner can tell the other when to take a time out, as this quickly becomes another weapon of abuse (e.g., "You need to take a time out"). However, given that some women report that they fear their partners' anger but the men are not taking time outs, we have implemented another version of time out, in which either partner can take a time out for any negative feeling that is likely to make further discussion of an issue unproductive (e.g., "I am beginning to feel frightened and need to take a time out").

The time-out statement also includes another important component—notifying the partner of when one will return. This is necessary to prevent abuse of time outs (e.g., one man left home for 3 days and nights during a "time out"!). With men in batterer treatment programs, we find that 1–3 hours is usually necessary for the men to calm down. With couples in therapy, we have found that partners often need less time (e.g., 15–90 minutes). Thus, we usually ask partners to try a 30-minute period initially, to see if this is too long or too short.

The full time-out statement becomes, "I am beginning to feel angry, and I need to take a half-hour time out."

After announcing the time out, the partner is to leave the area where the argument was occurring. Ideally, he/she should leave the house or apartment, as we have found that this person may get angrier while listening to the other partner in another room (e.g., "How can she be calmly watching TV after what she just said to me?"). In some situations (e.g., a woman taking a time out late at night), this rule needs to be modified. Couples should be asked to consider how they would take time outs in various problematic situations (e.g., a fight in the car or in public).

During a time out, partners are encouraged to engage in techniques aimed at decreasing anger. Meditation and relaxation techniques can be used, as can physical exercise. Also helpful is teaching couples "cool thoughts" or "anger-down statements" that can be used to deescalate angry thoughts. Activities to be avoided during a time out include things that may further escalate the anger and/or be dangerous in an angry state, such as alcohol and drug use, aggressive exercising (e.g., chopping wood), driving, and ruminating about the argument.

At the end of the specified time, the person taking the time out must either return or contact the other partner and take another time out (e.g., "I am still angry and need to take another half-hour time out"). After the time out is over, the partners should continue discussing the problem. The couple is encouraged to take another time out if needed or to suggest another time (including therapy) in which to continue discussing the problem.

The act of taking a time out can be awkward for many couples, and it is helpful to have them practice taking time outs in session and at home. Using time-out logs, clients should write down incidents in which they used a time out, including the argument that led to the time out, how the time out was implemented, and what happened after the time out. Therapist debriefing of these incidents often can pinpoint problems in the use of time outs, as well as problem areas in the relationship that may be amenable to problem solving.

We also have found it useful to ask partners to take a time out during therapy sessions in which they are becoming angry (i.e., *in vivo* training). In such cases, usually the therapist suggests that they take a time out (a short one). One partner makes the time-out statement and leaves the room. The therapist also should leave the room and go to a neutral place, so as not to get drawn into an alliance with the partner left in the therapy room. Both the partner and the therapist should return at the agreed-upon time. At that point, the therapist can help review the time out from both partners' perspectives. What steps did the partner taking the time out use to calm down? How did the partner who didn't take the time out feel (e.g., abandoned, angry that the conversation was cut short)? Such discussions often help to elucidate potential problems with time out, allowing the couple and therapist to brainstorm methods for handling such issues.

Other Anger Management Skills

Although many methods of managing anger are covered in the time-out procedure, it is often necessary to develop these methods further. Such discussions should focus on learning methods to manage the three components of anger discussed during anger recognition: physical (e.g., relaxation, slow breathing, exercise), cognitive (e.g., self-statements), and behavioral (e.g., communication skills to be taught). Once these skills are taught, the weekly anger logs should be modified to include an additional section regarding what steps each partner took to manage each of the three components of anger. Anger logs and time-out logs can be combined and should be monitored for many weeks, and, in some cases, for the entire course of therapy.

Communication and Problem-Solving Skills

Once couples are managing their anger more appropriately and have not engaged in further aggression, it is appropriate to begin communication and problem-solving skills training. The couple is often eager to do so, as attention to their presenting problems may have been delayed for the few weeks of anger management training. At this point, we generally use techniques derived from behavioral couple therapy (e.g., Jacobson & Margolin, 1979). Given that such methods are well outlined in various publications, we present them only briefly here.

We introduce this topic by asking the couple to discuss reasons why good communication is important for a couple (e.g., avoid misunderstandings, build intimacy) and the fact that there are good and bad times to communicate. Times and places where it is difficult to concentrate and where there are distractions and interruptions are poor occasions to talk (e.g., in front of the television, while tending to a child, or while fatigued). The thera-

pist should acknowledge that problems do sometimes arise at times when good communication is not possible. In such instances, until they are more skilled, the partners may wish to choose not to tackle the problem at that time, but rather to set a specific future time when the problem can be discussed (i.e., it is not sufficient for the partners simply to decide that they will "talk about it some time in the future"). Once ground rules for good times to communicate have been established, the next stage is to practice the skills involved in the two parts of communication: listening and speaking.

Nonverbal Listening

Regarding listening, a further breakdown into nonverbal and verbal listening is useful for practicing skills. It is helpful to ask clients to identify nonverbal cues indicating that they either are or are not being listened to (e.g., cues indicative of a good listener include making eye contact, turning toward the speaker, leaning forward, and nodding at appropriate points in the speaker's narrative). This point can also be made by having therapists model first poor, and then good, nonverbal listening with each client, and asking for their thoughts and feelings during each. Partners should then practice good nonverbal listening with each other.

Verbal Listening and Paraphrasing

The distinction between good and bad verbal listening is somewhat subtle, and it is often helpful for the therapist to model poor verbal listening to stories from the clients (e.g., frequent interruptions for tangential or distracting comments and questions, mind reading, sentence finishing, and incorrect paraphrasing). There is no one model for good verbal listening, but paraphrasing is a good place to start. It should be emphasized to clients that paraphrasing is not a part of normal communication and is not to be used in all conversations; rather, it is useful in conversations in which it is important to be heard accurately by one's partner (e.g., discussion of topics that could lead to arguments). Paraphrasing feels unnatural, but the unnatural structure of paraphrasing is what prevents escalation of conflicts, by slowing down the discussions and preventing misunderstandings.

Paraphrasing involves careful listening (i.e., the speaker should not be preparing what to say in response to the speaker) and saying what one heard back to the speaker. Initially, repeating what was said word for word reduces the possibility of misinterpretations. Then the listener should check for accuracy. If the paraphrasing was accurate, the conversation can go on; if not, the speaker can correct what was said, and the listener should paraphrase this correction. Sometimes the listener will feel overwhelmed by the amount of information given by the speaker; in these cases, the listener should be trained to request a break, and to paraphrase what has been said up to that point.

Expressing Feelings

Although speaking involves a large number of skills, we initially focus on the skill of expressing feelings. One important point is to distinguish between thoughts and feelings (i.e., one-word descriptors). For instance, "I feel you should take out the garbage" is a thought, not a feeling. Another point is that a person's feelings are his/her own responsibility. Therefore, statements that begin with "You made me feel" or "It made me feel" are unsuitable; instead, "I" statements should be used. To help clients label their feelings, the therapist supplies a list of feeling words to be used as a guide. This list can also help clients replace the use of vague feeling words (e.g., "good," "bad," or, among violent couples, the ubiquitous "angry") with more precise, informative, or "softer" emotions (e.g., "disappointed," "rejected"). Therapists may want to discuss how men tend to have more difficulty than women with this exercise, as women usually are more explicitly socialized to pay attention to and express their feelings. For some men, anger is one of the few emotions they feel comfortable sharing; such men should be helped to generate other feeling words. Assigning feeling logs for homework, where clients identify feelings and their intensity over the course of a week, may be a useful exercise.

After completing these exercises in the sessions, homework might include one partner's telling a story (e.g., an incident at work) to the other, using the appropriate feeling words for the situation. The listener then paraphrases the story, making sure to correctly identify the feelings expressed. Partners then switch roles. We generally ask that these stories not involve negative feelings about the relationship or partner, as it is often too difficult to practice new listening skills while being criticized.

Problem Solving

Clients should be informed that the problem-solving structure will seem artificial and stilted,

and we know that it does not resemble the naturalistic problem discussions of happily married or otherwise committed couples. Although we do not know how to make couples experiencing relationship problems interact like happy couples (in part due to the large variety in communication styles across happily married couples), we do know, from many observational studies, the mistakes that distressed couples make when discussing problems. The problem-solving format is designed to eliminate these destructive behaviors; as a result, it can prevent the escalation of discussions into arguments and can keep couples on task to solve problems.

Clients should be informed that a collaborative approach to problem solving is critical (e.g., being willing to accept responsibility for one's own contributions to the problem and for changing behavior). Part of this collaboration involves being able to overlook the short-term costs in a problem-solving solution for the long-term gains of an improved relationship. In addition, problems should be thought of as mutual problems, not just a problem for one partner or the other. The problem-solving format is divided into two parts: a problem definition stage and a problem solution stage.

Problem Definition. The problem definition component builds on the skills already introduced. The general format is as follows: Person A says, "I like it when you _____, but when you _____, I feel _____." Person B paraphrases A and checks for accuracy, and then accepts responsibility for some aspect of the problem. Person A paraphrases the new information in B's statement and checks for accuracy; then A accepts responsibility for some aspect of the problem. Person B paraphrases the new information in A's last statement and checks for accuracy.

The positive statement at the beginning puts the problem in context by reminding both partners of some positive aspect of their relationship. It also makes complaints easier for the listener to hear, as it reduces the possibility that the listener will become defensive.

The complaint should be as specific as possible, preferably focusing on explicit behaviors. In this way, it will be easier for the partner to make changes and for the results of these changes to be clearly visible to both partners. Derogatory labels (e.g., "You are insensitive"), overgeneralizing and exaggerating (e.g., "You are always doing this"), mind reading (e.g., "You did that on purpose"), and defining the other's feelings (e.g., "You are overly sensitive") are to be avoided. Examples of problem behaviors can be given, but "kitchen-sinking," or bringing up every instance of transgression, is to be avoided, for it often can escalate the discussion into an argument.

The complainer should use the appropriate feeling words in the problem definition, as the partner may be unaware of the complainer's feelings about the situation. When softer feeling words are used, feeling statements can generate sympathy in partners.

Perhaps the most difficult portion of the problem definition format is the acceptance of responsibility by both partners. This is especially true for the complainer, who often has not considered his/her role in the problem. Still, these acceptances of responsibility enhance a couple's collaborative efforts. Admission of responsibility should be as truthful as possible, but should not include possible solutions to the problem. For example, "I admit I do that, and I'll stop it" would be inappropriate, as it will cut off any discussion of other possible solutions; if the problem were that easily solved, it would have been solved already!

Problem Solution.   Once a problem definition has been generated and understood by both partners, the couple can move to the problem solution phase, which is divided into brainstorming, solution evaluation, contract development, and troubleshooting. In brainstorming, both partners list as many possible solutions to the problem they can. Given a tendency for members of violent couples to blame each other, we have established a rule that the first proposed solution offered by each partner must involve something that he/she can personally do to change the problem. After an extensive list of possible solutions has been generated, the couple should go back and evaluate each of the solutions one at a time, discussing the advantages or "pros" and then the disadvantages or "cons." After listing the pros and cons of a solution, the couple should decide whether to eliminate it, keep it, modify it, or "hold" it until other solutions have been considered.

Once all possible solutions have been evaluated, the remaining ideas should be combined into a contract. The contract should be as specific as possible (who will be doing what and when) and can include ways in which partners can remind each other of the contract (e.g., reminder notes on the refrigerator). Contracts should also include a time when the couple will review the contract, evaluate how well the problem solution has worked, and make changes or adjustments as necessary. This step is useful, as one partner often resists agreeing to a solution unless it is guaranteed that the solutions can be changed if they are not working.

The last phase of problem solutions is troubleshooting, which entails thinking about potential problems that might arise when implementing the contract. For instance, if a contract were about who was to make dinner on a given night, the therapist initially, and later the partners, should ask questions such as "What would happen if one of you is sick or out of town?" Couples should write ideas for how to handle potential problems into the contract.

Using Problem Solving.   Once partners have acquired the problem-solving skills and applied them to minor and then moderate-sized problems in their relationship, the bulk of therapy sessions involves applying these methods to their major presenting problems.

Other Therapeutic Interventions

At this point in therapy, other interventions or methods may be considered to address additional problems. For example, we find that many aggressive couples benefit from some sessions of parent training, so that they can learn to discipline their children in nonaggressive ways. In addition, many couples need a more direct focus on restoring positives to their relationship, using behavior exchange methods (e.g., Jacobson & Margolin, 1979), exercises such as "caring days" (e.g., Stuart, 1980) or simply planning "dates" together. Furthermore, some couples may need more specific help with sexual problems.

On a regular basis (e.g., every four to five sessions), the therapist and couple jointly review the progress the couple has made on presenting problems and new problems identified during the course of therapy. They then adjust the therapy plan to make sure that all of these problems are addressed before termination. Once violence has been eliminated, the major issues have been addressed, and the skills taught are being successfully applied, the therapist moves to less frequent meetings (e.g., every other week and then once per month)—serving as a consultant to the partners in managing their problems on their own, and helping them to anticipate upcoming stressors or major life changes.

RESEARCH ON THE EFFECTIVENESS OF CONJOINT THERAPY

To our knowledge, only three research teams have published studies examining the effectiveness of conjoint therapy with couples experiencing male violence. All compared conjoint treatment to GST.

Conjoint Treatment versus GST

Harris et al. (1988) recruited couples that had experienced male violence and were requesting therapy at a family service agency. Couples were assigned to either couple counseling that explicitly addressed violence as the primary relationship problem, or a treatment combining GST and couple groups. At follow-up, only 28 (of the original sample of over 70) women were interviewed. Considering that such attrition poses severe limitations on interpretation of the data, we nonetheless note that the two treatment conditions were equally effective in reducing the men's physical violence (based on woman's reports).

Brannen and Rubin (1996) randomly assigned couples in which violent men were referred to treatment by the court system, and had indicated a desire to remain in their relationships, to either a couple group treatment (addressing husband violence as a primary problem) or GST (a men's group for batterers and a group for battered women). Six-month follow-up data showed no significant differences between the two groups in levels of recidivism; in both therapy conditions, just over 90% of the subjects reported that they were violence-free. These researchers also found that couple treatment did not seem to increase the risk of abuse for women, as only two of the six instances of physical and emotional abuse that occurred during therapy were among couples assigned to the conjoint treatment.

O'Leary et al. (1999) recruited couples that responded to a newspaper ad offering free therapy to couples experiencing low levels of physical aggression. It is not clear how generalizable their findings are to couples seeking relationship therapy, since such couples usually do not report violence as a presenting problem. A total of 75 couples were randomly assigned either to couple therapy focusing on husband violence or to GST. Unfortunately, only 37 couples completed treatment. Although both treatment approaches resulted in statistically significant changes in men's violence and psychological abuse, neither appears to have been particu-

larly effective (i.e., over 70% of the men engaged in physical aggression during the follow-up period); there were no differences across the two treatment conditions in rates of physical aggression. In addition, no differences were found across the two treatments in husbands' psychological aggression, wives' depressive symptomatology, or wives' marital adjustment; husbands' marital adjustment was higher at follow-up for husbands in the conjoint therapy condition. Women in the conjoint treatment did not report fear of their husbands during therapy and did not report that therapy discussions led to physical aggression.

Thus, across these studies, no difference in outcome favored either GST or conjoint therapy. As all of the studies involved couples whose members were interested in remaining together and willing to enter conjoint therapy, these samples may resemble couples likely to be seen by couple therapists. However, the couples in these studies were seeking help for male violence, but most couples seeking relationship therapy do not report male violence as a presenting problem. In addition, in all of the studies a specialized couple treatment, addressing male violence directly, was used; in two of the studies (Brannen & Rubin, 1996; O'Leary et al., 1999), a group format was used for the couple therapy. Thus there currently exist no empirically supported conjoint treatments of male violence based on standard couple therapies, as such tests have not yet been conducted.

Predicting Dropout from Treatment and Therapy Outcome in Conjoint Treatment

Brown, O'Leary, and Feldbau (1997) examined predictors of dropout from the O'Leary et al. (1997) study. Across the two treatment conditions, compared to couples who remained in treatment, those who dropped out were significantly more likely to report severe husband-to-wife psychological aggression and mild wife-to-husband psychological aggression. When couples were asked why they dropped out, the most frequently cited reasons were treatment-related issues, such as "Treatment needed to focus on individual needs." Using the same sample, Heyman, Brown, Feldbau-Kohn, and O'Leary (1999) examined couples' communication during marital interactions before treatment began to predict treatment response and dropout. Treatment completion was predicted by low levels of husbands' hostility following wives' self-disclosures and husbands' distress-maintaining attributions; yet couples engaging in these patterns also had poor treatment outcome. Such husbands were described as being active in therapy, but using the therapy to blame their wives. Wives' nonhostile responses to husbands' self-disclosures were associated with increased treatment dropout; it was hypothesized that this pattern represented wives' resignation to their husbands' domineering style. Low levels of husbands' reciprocity of wives' hostility was the strongest predictor of positive treatment outcome. These initial findings require replication, to help therapists identify predictors of treatment completion and success among aggressive couples.

CONCLUSION

Physical aggression is a common problem among couples seeking relationship therapy. Indeed, most therapists, once they begin to screen for violence, will find that over half the couples seeking help report the occurrence of male aggression in the past year. Familiarity with theories of male violence and research on the correlates of such aggression will help therapists assess potentially important aspects of the problem and better understand the potential causes and consequences of violence for each aggressive couple they treat. Assessments sensitive to such issues will help therapists decide whether or not conjoint treatment is appropriate for a given couple. Current data suggest that conjoint therapy with a direct and specific focus on eliminating male violence may be as effective as the more widely utilized GST, although existing data are mixed regarding the effectiveness of such interventions. In general, we suggest a cautious and informed approach, focusing on anger management and communication skills, to help couples end the violence in their relationships.

REFERENCES

Aldarondo, E. (1996). Cessation and persistence of wife assault: A longitudinal analysis. *American Journal of Orthopsychiatry, 66*, 141–151.

Aldarondo, E., & Kaufman Kantor, G. (1997). Social predictors of wife assault cessation. In G. Kaufman Kantor & J. L. Jasinski (Eds.), *Out of darkness: Contemporary perspectives on family violence* (pp. 183–193). Thousand Oaks, CA: Sage.

Aldarondo, E., & Sugarman, D. B. (1996). Risk marker analysis of the cessation and persistence of wife as-

sault. *Journal of Consulting and Clinical Psychology, 64*, 1010–1019.

Archer, J. (2000). Sex differences in aggression between heterosexual partners: A meta-analytic review. *Psychological Bulletin, 126*, 651–680.

Bandura, A. (1973). *Aggression: A social learning analysis.* Englewood Cliffs, NJ: Prentice-Hall.

Barling, J., O'Leary, K. D., Jouriles, E. N., Vivian, D., & MacEwen, K. E. (1987). Factor similarity of the Conflict Tactics Scales across samples, spouses and sites. *Journal of Family Violence, 2*, 37–53.

Berns, S. B., Jacobson, N. S., & Gottman, J. M. (1999). Demand–withdraw interaction in couples with a violent husband. *Journal of Consulting and Clinical Psychology, 67*, 666–674.

Bersani, C. A., & Chen, H. T. (1988). Sociological perspectives in family violence. In V. B. Van Hasselt, R. L. Morrison, A. S. Bellack, & M. Hersen (Eds.), *Handbook of family violence* (pp. 57–86). New York: Plenum Press.

Bograd, M. (1984). Family systems approaches to wife battering: A feminist critique. *American Journal of Orthopsychiatry, 54*, 558–568.

Brannen, S. J., & Rubin, A. (1996). Comparing the effectiveness of gender-specific and couples groups in a court-mandated spouse abuse treatment program. *Research on Social Work Practice, 6*, 405–424.

Brown, P. D., O'Leary, K. D., & Feldbau, S. R. (1997). Dropout in a treatment program for self-referring wife abusing men. *Journal of Family Violence, 12*, 365–387.

Browne, A. (1993). Violence against women by male partners: Prevalence, outcomes, and policy implications. *American Psychologist, 48*, 1077–1087.

Burman, B., Margolin, G., & John R. S. (1993). America's angriest home videos: Behavioral contingencies observed in home reenactments of marital conflict. *Journal of Consulting and Clinical Psychology, 61*, 28–39.

Cantos, A. L., Neidig, P. H., & O'Leary, K. D. (1993). Men's and women's attributions of blame for domestic violence. *Journal of Family Violence, 8*, 289–303.

Cascardi, M., Langhinrichsen, J., & Vivian, D. (1992). Marital aggression: Impact, injury, and health correlates for husbands and wives. *Archives of Internal Medicine, 152*, 1178–1184.

Cascardi, M., O'Leary, K. D., Lawrence, E. E., & Schlee, K. A. (1995). Characteristics of women physically abused by their spouses and who seek treatment regarding marital conflict. *Journal of Consulting and Clinical Psychology, 63*, 616–623.

Cascardi, M., & Vivian, D. (1995). Context for specific episodes of marital violence: Gender and severity of violence differences. *Journal of Family Violence, 10*, 265–293.

Coan, J., Gottman, J. M., Babcock, J., & Jacobson, N. (1997). Battering and the male rejection of influence from women. *Aggressive Behavior, 23*, 375–388.

Cohen, R. A., Rosenbaum, A., Kane, R. L., Warnken, W. J., & Benjamin, S. (1999). Neuropsychological correlates of domestic violence. *Violence and Victims, 14*, 397–411.

Cordova, J. V., Jacobson, N. S., Gottman, J. M., Rushe, R., & Cox, G. (1993). Negative reciprocity and communication in couples with a violent husband. *Journal of Abnormal Psychology, 102*, 559–564.

Davis, R. C., & Taylor, B. G. (1999). Does batterer treatment reduce violence? A synthesis of the literature.

In L. Feder (Ed.), *Women and domestic violence* (pp. 69–93). Binghamton, NY: Haworth Press.

Day, R. D. (1995). Family-systems theory. In R. D. Day, K. R. Gilbert, B. H. Settles, & W. R. Burr (Eds.), *Research and theory in family science* (pp. 91–101). Pacific Grove, CA: Brooks/Cole.

Dobash, R. E., & Dobash, R. P. (1979). *Violence against wives.* New York: Free Press.

Dunford, F. W. (2000). The San Diego Navy experiment: An assessment of interventions for men who assault their wives. *Journal of Consulting and Clinical Psychology, 68,* 468–476.

Dutton, D. G. (1995). *The domestic assault of women: Psychological and criminal justice perspectives.* Vancouver: University of British Columbia Press.

Dutton, D. G., & Golant, S. K. (1995). *The batterer: A psychological profile.* New York: Basic Books.

Dutton, D. G., Saunders, K., Starzomski, A., & Bartholomew, K. (1994). Intimacy–anger and insecure attachment as precursors of abuse in intimate relationships. *Journal of Applied Social Psychology, 24,* 1367–1386.

Dutton, D. G., & Strachan, C. E. (1987). Motivational needs for power and spouse-specific assertiveness in assaultive and nonassaultive men. *Violence and Victims, 2,* 145–156.

Dutton, D. G., van Ginkel, C., & Landolt, M. A. (1996). Jealousy, intimate abusiveness, and intrusiveness. *Journal of Family Violence, 11,* 411–423.

Dutton, M. A. (1996). Working with battered women. *In Session: Psychotherapy in Practice, 2,* 63–80.

Eckhardt, C. I., Barbour, K. A., & Stuart, G. L. (1997). Anger and hostility in maritally violent men: Conceptual distinctions, measurement issues, and literature review. *Clinical Psychology Review, 17,* 333–358.

Ehrensaft, M. K., Langhinrichsen-Rohling, J., Heyman, R. E., O'Leary, K. D., & Lawrence, E. (1999). Feelings controlled in marriage: A phenomenon specific to physically aggressive couples? *Journal of Family Psychology, 13,* 20–32.

Ehrensaft, M. K., & Vivian, D. (1996). Spouses' reasons for not reporting existing physical aggression as a marital problem. *Journal of Family Psychology, 10,* 443–453.

Feld, S. L., & Straus, M. A. (1989). Escalation and desistance of wife assault in marriage. *Criminology, 27,* 141–161.

Follingstad, D. R., Rutledge, L. L., Berg, B. J., Hause, E. S., & Polek, D. S. (1990). The role of emotional abuse in physically abusive relationships. *Journal of Family Violence, 5,* 107–120.

Geffner, R., Mantooth, C., Franks, D., & Rao, L. (1989). A psychoeducational conjoint therapy approach to reducing family violence. In P. L. Caesar & L. K. Hamberger (Eds.), *Therapeutic interventions with batterers: Theory and practice* (pp. 103–133). New York: Springer.

Gelles, R. J., & Straus, M. A. (1979). Determinants of violence in the family: Toward a theoretical integration. In W. R. Burr, R. Hill, F. I. Nye, & I. L. Keiss (Eds.), *Contemporary theories about the family* (Vol. 1, pp. 549–581). New York: Free Press.

Hamberger, L. K., & Hastings, J. E. (1988). Skills training for treatment of spouse abusers: An outcome study. *Journal of Family Violence, 3,* 121–130.

Hamberger, L. K., Lohr, J. M., Bonge, D., & Tolin, D. F. (1996). A large sample empirical typology of male

spouse abusers and its relationship to dimensions of abuse. *Violence and Victims, 11,* 277–292.

Harris, R., Savage, S., Jones, T., & Brooke, W. (1988). A comparison of treatments for abusive men and their partners within a family-service agency. *Canadian Journal of Community Mental Health, 7,* 147–155.

Harway, M., Hansen, M., & Cervantes, N. N. (1997). Therapist awareness of appropriate intervention in treatment of domestic violence: A review. *Journal of Aggression, Maltreatment, and Trauma, 1,* 27–40.

Heyman, R. E., Brown, P. D., Feldbau-Kohn, S. R., & O'Leary, K. D. (1999). Couples' communication behaviors as predictors of dropout and treatment response in wife abuse treatment programs. *Behavior Therapy, 30,* 165–189.

Heyman, R. E., & Neidig, P. H. (1997). Physical aggression couples treatment. In W. K. Alford & H. J. Markman (Eds.), *Clinical handbook of marriage and couples interventions* (pp. 589–617). Chichester, England: Wiley.

Heyman, R. E., O'Leary, K. D., & Jouriles, E. N. (1995). Alcohol and aggressive personality styles: Potentiators of serious physical aggression against wives? *Journal of Family Psychology, 9,* 44–57.

Holtzworth-Munroe, A. (2000). Social information processing skills deficits in maritally violent men: Summary of a research program. In J. P. Vincent & E. N. Jouriles (Eds.), *Domestic violence: Guidelines for research-informed practice* (pp. 13–36). London: Jessica Kingsley.

Holtzworth-Munroe, A., Beatty, S. B., & Anglin, K. (1995). The assessment and treatment of marital violence: An introduction for the marital therapist. In N. S. Jacobson & A. S. Gurman (Eds.), *Clinical handbook of couple therapy* (pp. 317–339). New York: Guilford Press.

Holtzworth-Munroe, A., Jouriles, E., Smutzler, N., & Norwood, W. D. (1998). Victims of domestic violence. In A. S. Bellack & M. Hersen (Eds.), *Comprehensive clinical psychology* (Vol. 9, pp. 325–339). Oxford: Pergamon Press.

Holtzworth-Munroe, A., Meehan, J. C., Herron, K., Rehman, U., & Stuart, G. L. (2000). Testing the Holtzworth-Munroe and Stuart batterer typology. *Journal of Consulting and Clinical Psychology, 68,* 1000–1019.

Holtzworth-Munroe, A., Smutzler, N., & Bates, L. (1997). A brief review of the research on husband violence: Part III. Sociodemographic factors, relationship factors, and differing consequences of husband and wife violence. *Aggression and Violent Behavior, 2,* 285–307.

Holtzworth-Munroe, A., Smutzler, N., & Sandin, E. (1997). A brief review of the research on husband violence: Part II. The psychological effects of husband violence on battered women and their children. *Aggression and Violent Behavior, 2,* 179–213.

Holtzworth-Munroe, A., Smutzler, N., & Stuart, G. L. (1998). Demand and withdraw communication among couples experiencing husband violence. *Journal of Consulting and Clinical Psychology, 66,* 731–743.

Holtzworth-Munroe, A., & Stuart, G. L. (1994). Typologies of male batterers: Three subtypes and the differences among them. *Psychological Bulletin, 116,* 476–497.

Holtzworth-Munroe, A., Stuart, G. L., & Hutchinson, G. (1997). Violent versus nonviolent husbands: Differences in attachment patterns, dependency, and jealousy. *Journal of Family Psychology, 11,* 314–331.

Holtzworth-Munroe, A., Stuart, G. L., Sandin, E., Smutzler, N., & McLaughlin, W. (1997). Comparing the social support behaviors of violent and nonviolent husbands during discussions of wife personal problems. *Personal Relationships, 4,* 395–412.

Holtzworth-Munroe, A., Waltz, J., Jacobson, N. S., Monaco, V., Fehrenbach, P. A., & Gottman, J. M. (1992). Recruiting nonviolent men as control subjects for research on marital violence: How easily can it be done? *Violence and Victims, 7,* 79–88.

Jacobson, N. S., Gottman, J. M., Gortner, E., Berns, S., & Shortt, J. W. (1996). Psychological factors in the longitudinal course of battering: When do the couples split up? When does the abuse decrease? *Violence and Victims, 11,* 371–392.

Jacobson, N. S., Gottman, J. M., Waltz, J., Rushe, R., Babcock, J., & Holtzworth-Munroe, A. (1994). Affect, verbal content, and psychophysiology in the arguments of couples with a violent husband. *Journal of Consulting and Clinical Psychology, 62,* 982–988.

Jacobson, N. S., & Margolin, G. (1979). *Marital therapy: Strategies based on social learning and behavior exchange principles.* New York: Brunner/Mazel.

Johnson, M. P. (1995). Patriarchal terrorism and common couple violence: Two forms of violence against women. *Journal of Marriage and the Family, 57,* 283–294.

Kaufman Kantor, G. K., Jasinski, J. L., & Aldarondo, E. (1994). Sociocultural status and incidence of marital violence in Hispanic families. *Violence and Victims, 9,* 207–222.

Kaufman Kantor, G., & Straus, M. A. (1987). The "drunken bum" theory of wife beating. *Social Problems, 34,* 213–230.

Langhinrichsen-Rohling, J., Huss, M. T., & Ramsey, S. (2000). The clinical utility of batterer typologies. *Journal of Family Violence, 15,* 37–53.

Leonard, K. E., & Roberts, L. J. (1998). The effects of alcohol on the marital interactions of aggressive and nonaggressive husbands and their wives. *Journal of Abnormal Psychology, 107,* 602–615.

Leonard, K. E., & Senchak, M. (1993). Alcohol and premarital aggression among newlywed couples. *Journal of Studies on Alcohol, 11,* 96–108.

Leonard, K. E., & Senchak, M. (1996). Prospective prediction of husband marital aggression within newlywed couples. *Journal of Abnormal Behavior, 105,* 369–380.

Magdol, L., Moffitt, T. E., Caspi, A., Newman, D. L., Fagan, J., & Silva, P. A. (1997). Gender differences in rates of partner violence in a birth cohort of 21-year-olds: Bridging the gap between clinical and epidemiological approaches. *Journal of Consulting and Clinical Psychology, 65,* 68–78.

Magdol, L., Moffitt, T. E., Caspi, A., & Silva, P. A. (1998a). Hitting without a license: Testing explanations for differences in partner abuse between young adult daters and cohabitators. *Journal of Marriage and the Family, 60,* 41–55.

Magdol, L., Moffitt, T. E., Caspi, A., & Silva, P. A. (1998b). Developmental antecedents of partner abuse: A prospective-longitudinal study. *Journal of Abnormal Psychology, 107,* 375–389.

Malloy, K. A., McCloskey, K. A., & Monford, T. M. (1999). A group treatment program for male batterers. In L. VandeCreek & T. L. Jackson (Eds.), *Innovations in clinical practice: A source book* (Vol. 17, pp. 377–395). Sarasota, FL: Professional Resource Exchange.

Margolin, G. (1998). Effects of domestic violence on children. In P. K. Trickett & C. J. Schellenbach (Eds.), *Violence against children in the family and the community* (pp. 57–101). Washington, DC: American Psychological Association.

Margolin, G., Burman, B., & John, R. S. (1989). Home observations of married couples reenacting naturalistic conflicts. *Behavioral Assessment, 11,* 101–118.

Margolin, G., John, R. S., & Foo, L. (1998). Interactive and unique risk factors for husbands' emotional and physical abuse of their wives. *Journal of Family Violence, 13,* 315–344.

Massachusetts guidelines and standards for certification of batterers' treatment programs (1994, May). Boston: Commonwealth of Massachusetts.

McLaughlin, I. G., Leonard, K. E., & Senchak, M. (1992). Prevalence and distribution of premarital aggression among couples applying for a marriage license. *Journal of Family Violence, 7,* 309–319.

Millon, T. (1983). *Millon Clinical Multiaxial Inventory manual.* Minneapolis, MN: Interpretive Scoring Systems.

Murphy, C. M., Meyer, S., & O'Leary, K. D. (1994). Dependency characteristics of partner assaultive men. *Journal of Abnormal Psychology, 103,* 729–735.

Murphy, C. M., & O'Leary, K. D. (1989). Psychological aggression predicts physical aggression in early marriage. *Journal of Consulting and Clinical Psychology, 57,* 579–582.

Neff, J. A., Holman, B., & Schulter, T. D. (1995). Spousal violence among Anglos, blacks, and Mexican Americans: The role of demographic variables, psychosocial predictors, and alcohol consumption. *Journal of Family Violence, 10,* 1–21.

Novaco, R. W. (1975). *Anger control: The development and evaluation of an experimental treatment.* Lexington, MA: Lexington Books.

O'Leary, K. D. (1988). Physical aggression between spouses: A social learning theory perspective. In V. B. Van Hasselt, R. L. Morrison, A. S. Bellack, & M. Hersen (Eds.). *Handbook of family violence* (pp. 31–55). New York: Plenum Press.

O'Leary, K. D. (1993). Through a psychological lens: Personality traits, personality disorders, and levels of violence. In R. J. Gelles & D. R. Ioseke (Eds.), *Current controversies in family violence* (pp. 7–29). Newbury Park, CA: Sage.

O'Leary, K. D. (1996). Physical aggression in intimate relationships can be treated within a marital context under certain circumstances. *Journal of Interpersonal Violence, 11,* 450–452.

O'Leary, K. D., Barling, J., Arias, I., Rosenbaum, A., Malone, J., & Tyree, A. (1989). Prevalence and stability of marital aggression between spouses: A longitudinal analysis. *Journal of Consulting and Clinical Psychology, 57,* 263–268.

O'Leary, K. D., Heyman, R. E., & Neidig, P. H. (1999). Treatment of wife abuse: A comparison of gender-specific and couples approaches. *Behavior Therapy, 30,* 475–505.

O'Leary, K. D., & Maiuro, R. D. (Eds.). (1999). Psychological abuse in domestically violent relationships [Special Issue]. *Violence and Victims, 14* (1).

O'Leary, K. D., Vivian, D., & Malone, J. (1992). Assessment of physical aggression against women in marriage: The need for multimodal assessment. *Behavioral Assessment, 14,* 5–14.

Pan, H., Neidig, P., & O'Leary, K. D. (1994). Predicting mild and severe husband-to-wife physical aggression. *Journal of Consulting and Clinical Psychology, 62,* 975–981.

Prince, J. E., & Arias, I. (1994). The role of perceived control and the desirability of control among abusive and nonabusive husbands. *American Journal of Family Therapy, 22,* 126–134.

Quigley, B. M., & Leonard, K. E. (1996). Desistance of husband aggression in the early years of marriage. *Violence and Victims, 11,* 355–370.

Rogge, R. D., & Bradbury, T. N. (1999). Till violence does us part: The differing roles of communication and aggression in predicting adverse marital outcomes. *Journal of Consulting and Clinical Psychology, 67,* 340–351.

Rosenbaum, A., Hoge, S. K., Adelman, S. A., Warnken, W. J., Fletcher, K. E., & Kane, R. L. (1994). Head injury in partner-abusive men. *Journal of Consulting and Clinical Psychology, 62,* 1187–1193.

Rosenfeld, B. D. (1992). Court-ordered treatment of spouse abuse. *Clinical Psychology Review, 12,* 205–226.

Saunders, D. G. (1989). Cognitive and behavioral interventions with men who batter: Application and outcome. In P. L. Caesar & L. K. Hamberger (Eds.), *Treating men who batter: Theory, practice and programs* (pp. 77–98). New York: Springer.

Seltzer, J. A., & Kalmuss, D. (1988). Socialization and stress explanations for spouse abuse. *Social Forces, 67,* 473–491.

Smith, M. D. (1991). Male peer support of wife abuse: An exploratory study. *Journal of Interpersonal Violence, 6,* 512–519.

Smith, D. A., Vivian, D., & O'Leary, K. D. (1991). The misnomer proposition: A critical reappraisal of the longitudinal status of "negativity" in marital communication. *Behavioral Assessment, 13,* 7–24.

Stets, J. E. (1988). *Domestic violence and control.* New York: Springer-Verlag.

Straus, M. A. (1979). Measuring intrafamily conflict and violence: The Conflict Tactics (CT) Scales. *Journal of Marriage and the Family, 41,* 75–88.

Straus, M. A. (1990). Social stress and marital violence in a national sample of American families. In M. A. Straus & R. J. Gelles (Eds.), *Physical violence in American families* (pp. 181–189). New Brunswick, NJ: Transaction.

Straus, M. A. (1999). The controversy over domestic violence by women: A methodological, theoretical, and sociology of science analysis. In X. B. Arriaga & S. Oskamp (Eds.), *Violence in intimate relationships* (pp. 17–44). Thousand Oaks, CA: Sage.

Straus, M. A., & Gelles, R. J. (Eds.). (1990). *Physical violence in American families: Risk factors and adaptations to violence in 8, 145 families.* New Brunswick, NJ: Transaction.

Straus, M. A., Hamby, S. L., Boney-McCoy, S., & Sugarman, D. B. (1996). The Revised Conflict Tactics Scales (CTS2): Development and preliminary psychometric data. *Journal of Family Issues, 17,* 283–316.

Stuart, R. B. (1980). *Helping couples change: A social learning approach to marital therapy.* New York: Guilford Press.

Sugarman, D. B., & Frankel, S. L. (1996). Patriarchal ideology and wife-assault: A meta-analytic review. *Journal of Family Violence, 11,* 13–40.

Sugarman, D. B., & Hotaling, G. T. (1989). Violent men in intimate relationships: An analysis of risk markers. *Journal of Applied Social Psychology, 19,* 1034–1048.

Sullivan, C. M., & Bybee, D. I. (1999). Reducing violence using community-based advocacy for women with abusive partners. *Journal of Consulting and Clinical Psychology, 67,* 43–53.

Tolman, R. M. (1999). The validation of the Psychological Maltreatment of Women Inventory. *Violence and Victims, 14,* 25–37.

Vivian, D., & Heyman, R. E. (1996). Is there a place for conjoint treatment for couple violence? *In Session: Psychotherapy in Practice, 2,* 25–48.

Waltz, J., Babcock, J. C., Jacobson, N. S., & Gottman, J. M. (2000). Testing a typology of batterers. *Journal of Consulting and Clinical Psychology, 68,* 658–669.

Chapter 17

Couple Therapy When a Partner Has a History of Child Sexual Abuse

JILL S. COMPTON
VICTORIA M. FOLLETTE

There has been an increase in awareness about the effects of traumatic life events in recent years, both in society at large and in the helping professions. Clinical and empirical pursuits have expanded our understanding of the correlates of trauma and have supported it as a risk factor for developing a wide range of disruptions in functioning (Browne & Finkelhor, 1986; Polusny & Follette, 1995). Both the immediate and long-term aftermaths of trauma are characterized by emotional, cognitive, behavioral, and interpersonal difficulties. With such widespread impact, it is not surprising that the clinical presentation associated with a history of trauma varies tremendously from person to person. Despite the type of traumatic stress experienced (e.g., sexual abuse, physical assault, other crime, military combat, natural disaster, etc.), some individuals demonstrate remarkable resilience, and report few or circumscribed difficulties (Liem, James, O'Toole, & Boudewyn, 1997; Valentine & Feinauer, 1993). For others, the associated level of individual and interpersonal dysfunction ranges from moderate problems to chronic and severe psychological disorders, including posttraumatic stress disorder (PTSD; Widom, 1999), major depression (Weiss, Longhurst, & Mazure, 1999), and personality disorders (Johnson, Cohen, Brown, Smailes, & Berstein, 1999). Thus the breadth and degree of psychological outcomes associated with

trauma prohibit an exhaustive account of all possible clinical scenarios. Instead, the purpose of the current chapter is to provide a template to assist clinicians with conceptualization and treatment when trauma is a factor in the course of couple therapy.

This chapter addresses couple functioning among women with a sexual trauma history, primarily child sexual abuse (CSA). CSA was chosen because it is identified more frequently than other trauma as a relevant issue in clinical cases, and because couples often regard it as a significant factor in the etiology and maintenance of relationship distress. Although CSA is similar to other forms of interpersonal violence in some ways, it also has unique characteristics. CSA often takes place in a close interpersonal relationship that has a number of similarities to traditional couple relationships. Especially in the case of incest, CSA is likely to be associated with emotional and sexual intimacy that develops gradually over time, sometimes spanning months or even years. Thus the context in which CSA occurs may predispose victims to experience emotional distress and confusion in subsequent adult relationships (Feinauer, 1989).

It is generally accepted that about one-third of women in the United States experience some form of sexual trauma before 18 years of age (Briere, 1992). These experiences include CSA, date and stranger rape, harassment, and other forms of victimization. Although these numbers are extremely high, they are even more staggering when clinical samples are considered. Estimates indicate that about half of women pursuing psychotherapy have histories of sexual trauma (Briere & Zaidi, 1989). By comparison, national estimates show that approximately 10% of men report CSA (Finkelhor, Hotaling, Lewis, & Smith, 1990). Thus the majority of research regarding the impact of CSA has been based on work with women. Though findings pertaining to the the long-term differences between genders are mixed (e.g., Ketring & Feinauer, 1999), clinicians should be aware that current guidelines are based on women and should be generalized to men with caution. In addition, although CSA trauma is highlighted in this chapter, it is important to note that the clinical strategies described here may be largely applicable to other populations of trauma survivors. Traumatic experiences differ in many important topographical ways, and survivors also have many different outcomes associated with these experiences. However, the long-term problems associated with couples' issues when there is either sexual or nonsexual traumatic events are often more similar than they are different (Compton & Follette, 1998).

The goal of this chapter is to review the literature concerning CSA trauma and couple functioning, and to provide guidelines to effectively treat couples for whom CSA trauma is a significant factor. The empirical and clinical evidence for couple interventions among trauma survivors are reviewed. The challenges commonly experienced by clinicians when treating trauma issues are discussed, and clinical guidelines for assessment, treatment goals, and potential outcomes are outlined. Finally, a contextual/behavioral couple therapy approach is proposed as a viable strategy for the treatment of both individual symptoms and relationship distress associated with a history of CSA.

CSA TRAUMA AND COUPLE RELATIONSHIPS

Psychology has long conceptualized traumatic life events in intrapersonal terms, despite evidence supporting a number of interpersonal outcomes. The literature is replete with studies that document associations between CSA and the development of individual psychopathology and problems in living. However, this literature is still in an early phase of development, and the influence of family environment, physical abuse, and more proximal stressors on adult outcomes are not fully understood. Nevertheless, when compared to nonabused women, CSA samples are at greater risk for many negative internal experiences, including depression, anxiety, intrusive memories, rage, and shame (Browne & Finkelhor, 1986; Polusny & Follette, 1995). Women who report a history of CSA also engage in self-harming behaviors, including binge eating, substance misuse, suicide attempts, and self-mutilation (e.g., Briere & Runtz, 1993). Of course, individual problems of this kind are likely to pose a serious strain on couple relationships. Studies investigating the interaction between individual disorders such as depression, anxiety, and substance use problems on the one hand, and couple functioning on the other (e.g., Biglan et al., 1985; Jacobson, Holtzworth-Munroe, & Schmaling, 1989), find that individual dysfunction has a negative influence on social and intimate functioning, and conversely that distressed couple relationships negatively influence individual health and well-being.

Although empirical study of the interpersonal correlates of sexual trauma has been limited, clinical patterns have emerged that provide evidence of a similar interaction between individual and couple distress. Trauma survivors commonly experience severe disruptions in social adjustment and couple relationships (Briere, 1992; Buttenheim & Levendosky, 1994; Follette, 1991; Follette & Pistorello, 1995; Johnson, 1989; Serafin, 1996). CSA has been associated with increased fear and distrust of others (Briere & Runtz, 1991), and with difficulties in assertiveness and effective communication (Van Buskirk & Cole, 1983). Women with a history of CSA may have general deficits in relating to others, including both a subjective ambivalence and objective skill deficits in forming close relationships (Briere, 1992). Difficulties of this kind make the process of initiating and maintaining close relationships both frightening and chaotic. In fact, interpersonal turbulence in the wake of sexual trauma characterizes not only couple relationships (Finkelhor et. al., 1989; Herman, 1981), but also relationships with family members, friends, and children (e.g., Briere, 1992; Gold, 1986).

Intimacy and Emotional Expression

Probably the single most important effect of CSA on long-term couple functioning is that it is associated with significant disruptions in the development of intimacy. Research indicates that emotional closeness and intimate communication are associated with both relationship satisfaction and individual well-being (Brown & Harris, 1978; Jacobson, Waldron, & Moore, 1989). Longitudinal research shows that low emotional engagement between partners and patterns of withdrawing during couple interactions predict less long-term relationship satisfaction and poorer response to couple interventions (Gottman & Krokoff, 1989; Hahlweg, Revenstorf, & Schindler, 1984). Although it is common for partners to report conflict over the level of closeness desired in their relationships (Christensen, 1988), discrepancies in this area are a core issue for couples affected by CSA (Pistorello & Follette, 1998).

Research findings suggest that a history of CSA may be related to a unique pattern of relationship difficulties, regardless of whether comparisons are made to community or clinical samples. When compared to other couples in the community, women with a history of CSA and their partners experience less relationship satisfaction, but do not engage in the critical, sarcastic, and defensive behaviors commonly associated with relationship distress. Alternatively, when compared to other couples in therapy, couples affected by CSA experience similar or greater relationship satisfaction and have lower potential for divorce (Compton & Follette, 2000; Gelster & Feinauer, 1989). Despite this presentation, these couples do not engage in positive relationship behaviors that typically characterize well-functioning and more satisfied couples (Compton, 1999). Rather, they show a pattern of decreased emotional expressiveness, less mutual engagement, and more difficulties with emotional communication and feeling connected (Compton, 1999). Research with women who have been raped shows a similar pattern of emotional withdrawal in couple relationships, including difficulties with feeling understood and problems with commitment, emotional support, and communication (Miller, Williams, & Bernstein, 1982).

Emotional expression is necessary both to establish and to maintain intimacy in couple relationships. The finding that women with a history of CSA and their partners experience inhibited emotional expression is consistent with both clinical observations (e.g., Follette, 1991, 1994; Follette & Pistorello, 1995; Maltz & Holman, 1987; Serafin, 1996) and cognitive-behavioral models. Linehan (1993), for example, attributes the development of problems in emotional relating not only to the trauma experience itself, but also to the concurrent invalidation that is experienced. More specifically, perpetrators of CSA are often in roles that include an expectation of care and trust (e.g., father figures).

Yet, by definition, they violate trust by engaging in abusive behavior. In the process, a child's private feelings, thoughts, and wishes are invalidated by being ignored, contorted, or simply devalued by the perpetrator and often by the family system (Alexander & Lupfer, 1987). In fact, a child may experience more devastating effects in later life when the relationship with the perpetrator is characterized by a stronger emotional bond and expectation of trust (Feinauer, 1989). The invalidation and violation of trust associated with CSA may lead to feelings of ambivalence about intimate relationships, and to the development of strategies to avoid emotional experiencing more generally (Briere, 1992).

Experiential Avoidance and Emotional Numbing

Among those who suffer adverse reactions to CSA, it is common to observe a wide range of emotional and behavioral difficulties, and there has been some speculation about the function of symptoms associated with this trauma. Many problem behaviors associated with CSA have been conceptualized as efforts to traverse extremely difficult emotional reactions and thoughts by avoiding the intensity and emotional impact of these experiences (Briere, 1992; Follette, 1994). Although this general concept has been explicated from a number of theoretical perspectives, we use a contextual/behavioral paradigm and have defined this construct as "experiential avoidance."

Experiential avoidance is thought to be a two-part process involving both an unwillingness to experience painful thoughts, feelings, and memories (associated with CSA or other unpleasant experiences), and behavioral attempts to minimize, numb, or eliminate the experience of these internal events (Follette, 1994; Hayes, 1994). For example, substance misuse, dissociation, or self-mutilation may function similarly to reduce emotional states such as anger or shame that are perceived to be intolerable by distracting a person's attention away from the feelings (through getting high, spacing out, or focusing on physical sensations).

Although experiential avoidance provides some degree of immediate relief from excruciating affective states, long-term functioning appears to be poor among individuals who rely primarily on this coping strategy (Hayes, 1994; Leitenberg, Greenwald, & Cado, 1992). Over time, individuals engage more frequently in deliberate efforts to avoid internal and external stimuli associated with immediate suffering, while losing opportunities to develop skills and confidence to confront difficult internal events. Moreover, when efforts at avoidance are no longer effective at reducing distress associated with the traumatic experience, there may be a global numbing of emotional responsiveness, including widespread detachment from others and restricted affect (Foa, Riggs, & Gershuny, 1995). Experiential avoidance and emotional numbing have a tremendous impact on individual well-being, and are likely to have grave implications for couple functioning as well.

Couple researchers strive to identify commonly occurring patterns of behaviors that develop between partners, and several patterns have been discussed in the literature (Gottman, 1979; Sullaway & Christensen, 1983). Mutual constructive communication (positive reciprocity), for instance, has been associated with couple satisfaction. Alternatively, mutual distancing interactions and engage–distance (or demand–withdraw) patterns have been associated with couple distress (e.g., Gottman & Levenson, 1986; Margolin & Wampold, 1981). Interaction patterns of this type are related to individual psychopathology and to predictions about long-term couple functioning (Gottman & Krokoff, 1989).

There is evidence that the experiential avoidance and emotional numbing common among survivors of CSA may translate into problematic interaction patterns with their partners. Male partners of women with CSA histories have been found to engage in frequent avoidance behavior during couple interactions, and are particularly likely to do so in response to avoidance behavior by their female partners (i.e., mutual avoidance; Compton, 1999). This finding suggests that women with a history of CSA may set the tone for avoidance in their couple relationships, and may develop interaction patterns with partners who reinforce their avoidance through reciprocal avoidance. This pattern is likely to establish or maintain a context of invalidation in which emotional expression and personal disclosure is viewed as unacceptable (Linehan, 1996). In the absence of mutual acceptance and validation, partners are unlikely to experience sufficient emotional closeness and intimacy. Furthermore, relationships that are deficient in emotional closeness are also likely to exacerbate individual difficulties and distress (Gottman & Krokoff, 1989; Greenberg & Johnson, 1988), thereby continuing a cycle of emotional withdrawal and invalidation.

Domestic Violence and Sexual Revictimization

Many women with CSA histories experience a cycle of recurrent trauma in which abuse and other maltreatment in early childhood are associated with further trauma over time, including more frequent sexual, physical, and emotional abuse in adulthood (Liem & Boudewyn, 1999). About 65% of battered women presenting for services at domestic violence shelters report a CSA history (Follette, Polusny, Bechtle, & Naugle, 1996), and survivors of CSA may be twice as likely to experience sexual assault in adulthood. Although the experience of CSA trauma appears to correlate with greater vulnerability to subsequent domestic violence and sexual victimization in relationships (Briere & Runtz, 1988; Wyatt, Guthrie, & Notgrass, 1992; Wind & Silvern, 1992), the causal variables involved in this phenomenon have not been adequately addressed. Some researchers have proposed that women with CSA histories often lack the skills needed to discriminate dangerous individuals and situations from those that are safe (Naugle, Follette, & Follette, 1995). Whatever the cause, this revictimization is of significant consequence to these women. Repeated abuse and multiple traumatic experiences are associated with increased levels of individual distress and poor long-term functioning (Feinauer, 1989; Follette et al., 1996).

Sexual Relating

The majority of research investigating the interpersonal correlates of CSA has focused on long-term sexual functioning. Results indicate that CSA is correlated with a wide range of sexual difficulties, including decreased sexual satisfaction; intrusive thoughts, memories, and flashbacks during sexual activity; and increased sexual dysfunction and anxiety (Briere & Runtz, 1988, 1991; Courtois, 1988; Maltz & Holman, 1987). A commonly reported clinical problem for women with a history of CSA is decreased sexual desire. Conversely, others experience a compulsive need for sexual contact and a tendency to engage in multiple, short-term sexual relationships (Briere, 1992; Browne & Finkelhor, 1986; Courtois, 1988).

Given the variety and extensive nature of sexual difficulties correlated with CSA, sexual problems are common among couples affected by CSA. Communication about sexual issues may be especially problematic for this population. For example, these couples appear to approach the topic of sexuality with more caution than they approach other topics (Compton, 1999), and many women with CSA histories find it difficult to communicate their sexual and contraceptive needs to their partners (Wyatt & Lyons-Rowe, 1990).

Gender Roles and Distribution of Power

The distribution of power and responsibilities between partners is considered to be fundamental in couple relationships (Christensen, Jacobson, & Babcock, 1995) and may be problematic for couples when trauma is an issue. There is some evidence that women with a history of CSA experience both higher needs for power and greater fears of power than nonabused women (Liem, O'Toole, & James, 1992). Their couple relationships are often characterized by traditional gender roles and family ideologies that regard men as the head of household (Serafin & Follette, 1996; Van Buskirk & Cole, 1983). However, it is possible for survivors to obtain power in their relationships through indirect means, without having to challenge traditional beliefs and roles outwardly.

Two common interaction patterns observed during therapy with couples affected by CSA may result in an increased perception of relationship power for trauma survivors. First, women with CSA histories obtain power by limiting the development of emotional closeness in the relationship. For example, when there are discrepancies in intimacy needs between partners, the partner who desires less emotional engagement typically controls how intimate the relationship will become. By limiting closeness in this way, survivors of CSA may be able to ensure a more favorable distribution of power without addressing the issue directly. This covert strategy is not only consistent with ambivalent feelings regarding power, but also serves to maintain the pervasive avoidance and detachment commonly observed in the aftermath of trauma.

The second interaction pattern associated with shifting the distribution of power for survivors of trauma is also problematic. Some women with a history of CSA report being seen as "patients" in their relationships. They may experience individual difficulties and dysregulation that are readily apparent to their partners, and are frequently viewed as disabilities or impairments. In such cases, trauma survivors may be treated as though they are fragile. Their partners may take charge of day-to-day responsibilities within the home, to shield the survivors from further stress and exhaustion. Although the patient role inherently includes a significant degree of control over the behavior of others, it inhibits recovery from the trauma and is overly restrictive. Furthermore, when responsibilities are distributed in such an obvious and uneven way, dissatisfaction and resentment between partners are likely to result.

ASSESSMENT OF COUPLE FUNCTIONING

The assessment and treatment procedures outlined in this chapter originate in social learning and behavioral theory, and have been adapted for use with couples affected by CSA. From this perspective, the aim of case conceptualization is to understand the primary controlling variables in couple interactions, rather than to solve the unlimited number of problems derived from these variables (Christensen et al., 1995). This approach is consistent with traditional behavioral assessment procedures that emphasize functional relationships rather than topographical assessment (see Dimidjian, Martell, & Christensen, Chapter 9, this volume). In a functional analysis, the context of behavior is examined to identify important relationships between events that set the occasion for the problem behavior or maintain the behavior of interest.

For simplicity's sake, couple problems are often discussed as difficulties that originate either within the individual or at the level of interaction patterns between partners. Although this may provide a useful way to communicate relationship problems, it does not capture the natural evolution of couple difficulties. Rather than being two independent and distinct levels of analysis, intrapersonal and interpersonal functioning influence and are influenced by each other. For example, many studies have investigated couple functioning when individual problems such as depression, anxiety, and substance use disorders are present (e.g., Biglan et al., 1985; Jacobson et al., 1989); as noted earlier, these studies show that individual distress influences social and intimate functioning, and conversely that the quality and type of relationships established by couples influence individual health and well-being. Therefore, assessment related to both individual and couple functioning is addressed.

The goal of assessment is to understand conflict between partners in terms of response classes, that is behaviors that are topographically different but serve a similar function in the relationship

(Koerner, Prince, & Jacobson, 1994). The focus is on recurring themes in the relationship, rather than on each specific complaint or instance of the problem. For example, a survivor of CSA may go to bed early, start an argument, get drunk, or even threaten suicide to avoid sexual intimacy with her partner. At face value, these behaviors seem to be important treatment targets and appear different in kind and intensity from each other. However, to the extent that these behaviors result in a lack of sexual intimacy, they share a common function (avoidance of sex).

The therapist's task is to identify when problem behaviors are likely to occur in the relationship and how they are maintained over time. Assessment includes an understanding of each partner's history (including experiences with trauma, prior relationships, family of origin, etc.) and of the interaction patterns that occur between partners. Antecedents and consequences of behavior are examined in a chain-like fashion, as each partner's behavior provides the context for the other's behavior. Over time this procedure helps to clarify how partners influence each other, as well as how variables outside the relationship affect the couple. Although assessment procedures are separated here into individual and relationship factors for ease of discussion, there is typically a great deal of overlap between these domains.

Assessment of Individual Functioning

Trauma

Despite increased awareness about the long-term problems associated with trauma in some individuals, traumatic experiences are frequently overlooked during assessment for couple therapy. Given that there is increasing evidence that CSA and other traumas have much of their impact on interpersonal functioning, it is advisable to include routine questions about trauma history during initial interviews and questionnaires. Clinicians are likely to find many survivors of CSA reluctant to discuss their trauma experiences during initial sessions. Many women report feeling uncomfortable discussing these issues in the presence of a new therapist, and others have difficulties discussing these issues in the presence of their partners. Often there are intense feelings of shame, guilt, and stigma associated with the abuse, and these feelings interfere with open communication about these events and their impact. Some individuals and couples attempt to avoid, minimize, or evade discussion of the role

of CSA in their relationships, while others have trouble identifying other relationship issues. It is often helpful to meet with partners for individual interviews to assess a variety of concerns; such interviews provide a context for assessing issues that might be difficult to discuss in the presence of the partner. Questions should be asked in a direct and supportive manner, with some attention paid to specifics of the abuse in order to assess the possible need for individual therapy.

When a traumatic event has been experienced, it is important to assess whether and in what ways this event (or set of events) has affected the individual. Given that problems and symptoms associated with CSA vary tremendously in kind and degree, it is wise to refrain from assumptions about how a particular individual has been affected. It is important to understand the CSA in the broader context of the client's life, and assessment should span pretrauma functioning, characteristics of the trauma, immediate responses, subsequent adjustment, treatments, and current functioning. Because so many factors affect response to childhood sexual trauma, couple therapists may find it useful to familiarize themselves with this literature (e.g., Briere, 1992).

Despite the potential value of this information to successful treatment, many survivors are hesitant to be forthright about this information. The development of a trusting and safe environment is paramount in work with trauma survivors, and this may be more difficult to establish in couple therapy, because relationships with both one's therapist and one's partner must be strong. Thus assessment may be an ongoing process in which sensitive information is gathered over time in the context of developing therapeutic and couple relationships.

Although our approach does not emphasize syndromal classification, a strong interest in individual symptoms and syndromes continues in mental health disciplines. The primary diagnosis associated with any trauma exposure is PTSD. If desired, structured diagnostic interviews are available for the assessment of PTSD, including the Clinician-Administered PTSD Scale—Form 1 (Blake et al., 1990) and the Anxiety Disorders Interview Schedule (Blanchard, Gerardi, Kolb, & Barlow, 1996). Moreover, the Trauma Symptom Inventory (TSI; Briere, 1995) is an efficient, 100-item, self-report questionnaire that provides information that is often useful during couple therapy. The TSI is designed to measure posttrauma symptoms, including individual and interpersonal difficulties commonly associated with psychological trauma. An overall score is obtained, and there are 10 clinical subscales: Anxious Arousal, Depression, Anger/Irritability, Intrusive Experiences, Defensive Avoidance, Dissociation, Sexual Concerns, Dysfunctional Sexual Behavior, Impaired Self-Reference, and Tension Reduction Behavior.

Depression and Suicidality

Empirical evidence supports links between CSA and increased rates of major depression, suicidal ideation, and suicide attempts (Polusny & Follette, 1995). Depression is also commonly associated with couple distress and relationship problems (Coyne, 1976; Nelson & Beach, 1990), and couple interventions are often effective for treating individual depressive symptoms (e.g., Jacobson et al., 1989). Thus routine assessment of depressive symptoms is indicated in all work with couples, regardless of their trauma status.

A detailed history of suicidal ideation, threats, and attempts is a part of any good clinical interview, regardless of trauma status. However, an accumulating literature shows that CSA and childhood physical, and emotional abuse are associated with the development of personality disorders, particularly borderline and antisocial personality disorders, among men (Raczek, 1992) and women (Herman, Perry, & van der Kolk, 1989). Individuals with these diagnoses often experience chronic depression and suicidal ideation. They frequently make suicide threats and attempts, engage in other self-injurious behavior (e.g., cutting, burning, and banging), and require repeated psychiatric hospital admissions. When one is treating couples with serious behavior problems, it is important to assess whether relationship variables are among the precipitating circumstances for these behaviors, as well as to clarify what consequences follow these behaviors (both desired and undesired). Behaviors of this kind often serve to decrease emotional pain, to communicate, to get one's needs met, or to avoid demands in couple relationships. In these cases, couple interventions may be more effective if suicidal (or parasuicidal) behaviors are addressed in individual therapy (e.g., dialectical behavior therapy; Linehan, 1993).

Substance Misuse

Like depression, substance misuse occurs at higher rates among survivors of CSA (Briere, 1988; Ruzek, Polusny, & Abueg, 1998) and may also be a common problem for their partners (Compton & Follette, 2000). Substance use screening should take place early in treatment, and relationship patterns associated with drug and alcohol use should be identified. Substance misuse often inhibits open communication and the development of intimacy between partners, and may be a convenient way to maintain a comfortable level of emotional distance. Moreover, many women with CSA histories report that drugs and alcohol have become necessary in order for them to be willing to engage in sexual activity with their partners. Although severe substance use disorders may necessitate individual detoxification and treatment, research suggests that couple interventions are both desirable and effective when substance use is an issue (Jacobson et al., 1989; McCrady & Epstein, 1995; see also Epstein & McCrady, Chapter 23, this volume).

Medical Problems and Somatization

Many women report that physical force, violent assault, or bodily injury was associated with their CSA. It is not uncommon for abused children to experience forceful anal and vaginal penetration by adult men, or for some perpetrators to involve unusual objects in their sexual practices. Moreover, many women are threatened with knives or held at gunpoint, and cuts and bruises often result. For some survivors, medical recovery may be a significant issue, and they may never fully return to their pretrauma level of health or physical functioning. In addition to physical injury directly associated with sexual trauma, many survivors experience their health less favorably and use medical services at higher rates than controls (e.g., Koss, Koss, & Woodruff, 1991). Medical problems including pelvic and gynecological pain have been associated with CSA, particularly when the abuse was severe or violent (Briere & Runtz, 1988; Pribor & Dinwiddie, 1992; Walker et al., 1988).

Individual Historical Factors

Many historical variables influence expectations for couple relationships, and discrepancies between partners can be the source of conflict. It is often useful to assess experiences with parents; observations of parental relationships and gender roles in the family; and the characteristics of relationships with previous partners, friends, and children, in order to gain an understanding of the quality and type of intimate relationships experienced. When trauma is an important factor, significant relationships with others may have been delayed, disrupted, or avoided altogether. It is important to explore interpersonal skills, as the ability to communicate effectively (Jacobson & Holtzworth-Munroe, 1986) and to be emotionally available (Greenberg & Johnson, 1988) have been identified as necessary for success in couple interventions. Thus assessment should outline interpersonal functioning before, during, and following trauma when this information is available. Analysis of historical relationships may provide a useful context for explaining and challenging rigid gender roles or dysfunctional tolerance for being treated in abusive ways.

Individual Strengths

Although the proceeding discussion has outlined various problem areas that may be particularly important for couples affected by trauma, it is important to note that various individual strengths are often associated with having experienced difficult and challenging events, and that these may affect couple work in positive ways. Recent findings suggest that some survivors of CSA perceive that they have benefited from their traumatic experiences by being better able to protect themselves and their children, having an increased knowledge of CSA, and being made stronger by their experiences (McMillen, Zuravin, & Rideout, 1995). Many survivors of trauma report that their compassion and caring for others have been enhanced through their own misfortunes. In addition, given the challenges and struggles associated with traumatic life events, many survivors have a willingness to admit individual weaknesses and to seek support or treatment when it is appropriate to do so.

Assessment of Relationship Factors

Areas of Conflict and Relationship Satisfaction

Although intrapersonal factors provide useful contextual information about current couple functioning, it is also essential to understand how the couple interacts and functions as a unit. At the onset of treatment, it is useful to gain an understanding of how the partners describe their current situation and problems. Some problems commonly experienced by couples affected by CSA are diffuse and difficult to identify, such as emotional distancing and withdrawal. Other couples may present in response to domestic violence,

violations of trust, stressful life events, or problems in sexual adjustment.

A quick self-report measure such as the Dyadic Adjustment Scale (DAS; Spanier, 1976) provides quantitative data about level of global relationship distress, areas of agreement and conflict, discrepancies between individual descriptions of relationship problems, and commitment to the relationship in general. In addition to the DAS, the Areas of Change Questionnaire (Margolin, Talovic, & Weinstein, 1983) may be an efficient means of understanding the amount and type of change partners hope for treatment to target in their relationship. It is also useful for the therapist to take notice of areas within the relationship that are not problematic, functioning well, or even providing pleasure for the couple.

Safety and Conflict Style

Violence is a problem for about 50% of couples seeking conjoint therapy, and couple therapists are encouraged to routinely assess the occurrence and extent of these issues (Holtzworth-Munroe, Beatty, & Anglin, 1995; see also Holtzworth-Munroe, Meehan, Rehman, & Marshall, Chapter 16, this volume). Physical, emotional, and sexual abuse may occur even more frequently among couples affected by trauma. However, it is frequently not identified as a presenting problem when couples request therapy. Thus it is absolutely essential that current and historical violence be assessed directly with this population, and that partners be given an opportunity to discuss these issues in private.

Violence is always considered a primary presenting problem and must be addressed before additional treatment can proceed. There is controversy regarding the best modality of therapy when violence is a problem in the relationship, and therapists are strongly cautioned to consider whether conjoint couple or individual treatments are more suitable.

It is not uncommon for couples to minimize the level of violence in their relationships and the impact this violence has on partners as individuals. Many couples report that rage reactions alternate with periods of remorse, and this expression of regret may make it more difficult for partners to address issues of violence and risk "rocking the boat." For couples affected by CSA, family violence histories are common and may provide a context in which this behavior appears to be normative. Therapists should be aware of this tendency and should avoid behavior that functions to collude with the couple to avoid dealing with violence issues in treatment. Domestic violence itself has been associated with PTSD symptoms among battered women (Houskamp & Foy, 1991), and should be conceptualized as a form of trauma in its own right.

Intimacy, Emotional Expression, and Interaction Patterns

Interpersonal trauma is certainly associated with disruptions in the development of trust and intimacy, and long-term couple relationships are clearly affected by these issues. Couple assessments should include analyses of emotional expression and levels of closeness between partners, including obtaining an understanding of how these variables have evolved during the course of the couple's relationship. Levels of closeness and distance characterizing couple relationships are core relationship issues, and commonly lead to conflict and discontent when discrepancies exist between partners (Christensen et al., 1995).

Two brief assessment measures may provide useful information about couple interaction patterns. The Closeness and Independence Questionnaire (updated from the Relationship Issues Questionnaire; Sullaway & Christensen, 1983) provides data about the desire for more or less closeness or independence in the couple relationship. The Communication Patterns Questionnaire (Christensen, 1988) provides each partner's perceptions of constructive and destructive communication patterns characteristic of the relationship, including negotiating, blaming, demanding, withdrawing, and avoiding during conflict.

One common interaction pattern identified from questionnaire and interview data has been labeled "demand–withdraw" or "engage–distance" (Fruzzetti & Serafin, 1995) and is associated with differences in desired levels of intimacy between partners. In this scenario, one partner's requests or demands for increased closeness and emotional sharing are met by the other partner's desire to withdraw and distance from the relationship. This pattern has been associated with decreased relationship satisfaction and poor long-term relationship success (Christensen, 1988), and may be particularly common among therapy-seeking couples when trauma is a factor.

Research suggests that there is a strong correlation between traumatic life events and disruptions in the ability to be emotionally available (e.g., Miller et al., 1982), and trauma survivors may seek partners with similar difficulties or expectations.

Thus partners may initially be attracted by a mutual desire to limit closeness and emotional expression in the relationship. Mutual disengagement of this sort has been associated with poor relationship adjustment over time (Gottman & Krokoff, 1989), and partners may eventually seek treatment precisely because this interaction pattern is not tenable. Unfortunately, it is likely that one partner may desire change in this area while the other desires to continue maintaining a comfortable distance, establishing a demand–withdraw or engage–distance interaction pattern. Alternatively, a partner may sacrifice his/her own needs for closeness and intimacy as an initial method of caring for a trauma survivor, who is unable to be emotionally present in the relationship (Rabin & Nardi, 1991). Over time, the partner may become increasingly unhappy in the relationship and begin to place increasingly higher demands on the partner, resulting in the demand–withdraw or engage–distance interaction pattern.

Sexual Functioning

Finally, sexual issues are among the most difficult areas for couples to discuss openly during the assessment phase of couple therapy. Sexual functioning is traditionally thought of as a private domain, and is even more difficult to discuss when it is the source of long-standing difficulties, as it may be for couples affected by trauma. However, it is important to gain knowledge about sexual functioning and satisfaction from both partners' perspectives, even when the trauma under consideration is not of a sexual nature. Sexual functioning goes hand in hand with intimacy more generally, and may be affected directly (e.g., flashbacks of a rape experience) or indirectly (e.g., difficulties with trust) by a traumatic experience. One clinically relevant assessment device for sexual functioning is the Sexual History Form (LoPiccolo & Friedman, 1988), which provides an expedient and less intrusive alternative to interviewing. Partners respond privately to questions addressing levels of sexual satisfaction and desire, the frequency and duration of sex, and symptoms of sexual dysfunction.

Sexual activity requires a degree of vulnerability and openness. Moreover, some survivors of trauma may experience increased levels of self-loathing or disgust during sexual interactions. Questions may arise about whether their partners could truly love them if they knew the whole story (e.g., a survivor of CSA experienced physical pleasure during the abuse, a combat veteran raped several women in Vietnam), and dissociation or avoidance may be used to cope with these feelings. Like other areas of importance, sexual functioning before, during, and after the trauma should be assessed.

Functional assessment is an ongoing process in a behavioral treatment approach. As the therapy progresses, partners may feel able to express areas of concern more openly, and the therapist may gain new information that clarifies the couple's issues. As noted previously, the therapist must balance a number of issues simultaneously. The unit of analysis may shift at times between the individual and couple, and although individual issues related to the trauma must be considered, the therapist must avoid inadvertent collusion with the nontraumatized spouse in subtly blaming the survivor for all of the couple's issues. In addition, the therapist will move between current and historical issues during the course of treatment, with the goal of understanding how events in the past function in the present. Finally, though therapy is aimed at ameliorating current problems, strengths of both the couple and each partner must be recognized.

THERAPY GOALS

Pretreatment: Safety and Commitment

Prior to engaging in the thorough individual and couple assessment procedures described above, the therapist must first establish whether individuals are safe enough to proceed. For this reason, we recommend that each couple be considered to be in the pretreatment stage until the potential for suicide, homicide, violence, child abuse or neglect, or any other issue of direct safety has been assessed and resolved. When safety issues are imminent, the issue should become the single and primary focus of treatment until it is resolved. Individual or group interventions are frequently necessary to address suicidal intent, parenting skills, or severe substance misuse. Of course, proper reporting actions must be taken when safety issues overlap with legal and ethical obligations. Couple therapists may consider referring one or both partners to community agencies to address individual issues. However, at times the therapist may work with partners individually or utilize conjoint couple sessions to resolve safety issues prior to beginning couple therapy.

When safety issues have been resolved, the focus of pretreatment shifts to the second priority in pretreatment: commitment to the relationship and the process of couple therapy. Thus a second central goal is always to obtain a unilateral commitment from each partner (i.e., independent of the other's ability to commit) to engage actively in couple therapy for some proscribed amount of time (e.g., 12 weeks, 6 months, etc.). Much as in other treatment strategies (Fruzzetti & Serafin, 1996; Linehan, 1993), a clear commitment to treatment is obtained by acknowledging the benefits and difficulties of the upcoming work, and highlighting any obstacles that may affect either partner's ability or willingness to remain committed over time. It is essential that the couple make commitments to maintain a safe and open therapeutic environment, and to be willing to address individual issues in the service of enhancing their relationship and individual functioning. Of course, the ability to make commitments of this nature varies over time, and therapists are encouraged to accept successive approximations of committed behavior, especially any commitment to addressing those factors and issues that make it difficult to commit to treatment.

It is also important to discuss any obstacles that make it difficult for partners to be committed to working on their relationship during the time period identified. Examples include reluctance to be vulnerable, fear of getting hurt, having "one foot out the door," an ongoing affair, a wish not to burden the partner by disclosing information about the trauma, and anything else that might be a problem for a particular couple. It is important to impress upon the couple that during this phase of treatment they are merely being asked to consider what might hinder their ability to engage treatment in a committed way. They are not being asked to discuss these issues. It is important to establish a positive working relationship with the couple and a thorough assessment before engaging in treatment.

The Therapist's Role in Goal Setting

Treatment goals differ between partners and from couple to couple. It is important to discuss the goals of treatment explicitly with each couple to maximize the likelihood that therapy will serve their needs. It is not uncommon for couples with a CSA history to be satisfied with a relationship free of egregious conflict, even if the relationship appears to lack a level of closeness that would be desired by other couples. Although the therapist would be wise to bring this observation to the couple's attention, it is equally important to accept their relationship goals as reasonable. This may require that the therapist set aside his/her values. At the same time, it is the therapist's right and responsibility to confront relationship patterns that are destructive and/or harmful. This is particularly the case when there is violence, even low-level violence that the couple may minimize.

STRUCTURE OF THERAPY

Selection of Couples for Treatment

Although relationship difficulties are among the most frequent problems identified by survivors of trauma, many survivors present for individual or group therapy rather than couple modalities. It is not uncommon, for instance, for survivors to request individual or group interventions despite their intention to address relationship difficulties in treatment (Pistorello & Follette, 1998). Although interpersonal difficulties may be more apparent when survivors present for therapy with their partners, a routine and thorough assessment should be completed at the onset of therapy to identify which treatment modalities best suit the current needs of the survivor and/or couple.

Although the therapist may recommend couple treatment, some clients with a trauma history are not amenable to that and pursue individual therapy (e.g., the survivors report that their partners are reluctant or refuse to participate in couple treatment). The non-treatment-seeking partner may also not be particularly supportive of the other partner's treatment and may even be uncomfortable with the therapy. In these cases, it is important to ascertain whether the relationship issues will be the primary focus of treatment, or merely one among several areas to be addressed. If relationship change is the survivor's primary goal, it is important to inform the survivor that progress made in individual therapy may not generalize to their couple relationship (Follette, Alexander, & Follette, 1991), and may even have iatrogenic affects on the couple relationship (Brody & Farber, 1989).

Other survivors present for individual rather than couple therapy because they have not yet disclosed their trauma histories to their partners. Although this type of secret may have a severe impact on levels of intimacy in their relationships, survivors should seriously explore their individual expectations and hesitancies related to disclosing this information prior to making the choice to disclose. Furthermore, in this situation it is frequently useful to provide partners with educational materials about CSA and the impact this trauma may have on significant other relationships.

Collaboration with Concurrent Therapists

Generally, clients with a trauma history pursue individual treatment prior to presenting with their partners, or hope to alternate between individual and couple sessions. Many survivors report a need for an appropriate forum to sort out unpleasant and vivid details of the trauma (abuse histories, rape experiences, war atrocities, etc.) that their partners may find overwhelming. Although some clinicians report success alternating between roles as an individual and a couple therapist (Johnson, 1989), when intensive couple work is indicated it may be more appropriate to refer the couple to another therapist. However, it is essential that the couple therapist and individual therapist have a good working relationship. Though this caveat seems obvious, we have found that such situations easily lead to triangulation, even for therapists who have reasonable working relationships. Thus we suggest a two-way release of information, with the therapists consulting at regular intervals regarding treatment goals and current difficulties. Not only does this approach facilitate the therapy, it also provides a model for collaborative relationships that involve open communication and respect. Many of our clients report a great deal of dysfunction in their family of origin, including but not limited to the sexual abuse that may have occurred. Thus, the modeling provided by the therapists can be particularly salient to this population. Finally, survivors may present for individual therapy to address relationship difficulties so severe that it may not be advisable to include their partner in treatment initially.

Length of Therapy

Because of the many ways that this population presents for treatment, it is difficult to specify the length of therapy. The vast majority of trauma survivors that we treat will have had at least one year of individual therapy before entering couples work. Frequently, individual work will involve exposure therapy (Meadows & Foa, 1998) and some aspect of dialectical behavior therapy (Linehan, 1993). Intensive work of this type also includes values clarification within an acceptance and commitment therapy format (Hayes, 1994; Hayes, Strosahl, & Wilson, 1999). In the context of working on values, the majority of our clients identify the desire for healthy intimate relationships, and the progression into couple therapy often emerges from this foundation. Couple therapy generally lasts 6 months to a year, with weekly sessions. On the one hand, we prefer briefer treatment models; on the other, in our experience of working with this population, the difficulties are often sufficiently severe and long-standing to warrant this longer-term intervention. The therapist develops a treatment plan that is reviewed periodically (e.g., every 12 sessions) to evaluate progress and to contract for additional sessions of therapy.

ROLE OF THE THERAPIST

The therapist serves as a consultant, teacher, and coach to the couple. The therapist's primary role at any given time is determined by a number of factors. As noted earlier, case conceptualization via a functional analysis of the couple's problems is essential for effective treatment. However, the conceptualization is not a static one, but rather evolves over time as the therapist gains more information about the couple and as the couple changes over the course of treatment. The therapist initially works with the couple to identify areas of effective and ineffective working in the couple's relationship. Frequently, the therapist may identify skill deficits that will impede successful working in later, more difficult parts of the therapy. Thus the therapist's first role is often one that is frequently observed in behavioral therapies, which is serving as a teacher. There are a number of requisite skills for successful couple interactions, such as the ability to label and regulate intense emotions. In early phases of treatment, the therapist teaches these skills through instruction and modeling. Over the course of treatment, the therapist becomes more of a coach, reminding partners of skills and helping them to use those skills when they are under stress and may show a tendency to retreat to old patterns of communication.

Our perspective on the therapeutic alliance is strongly influenced by work with a behavioral foundation as described by Linehan (1993) and Kohlenberg and Tsai (1991). Although they have discussed this issue primarily in the context of individual therapy, we find it equally relevant (although at times more difficult to implement) in couple work. The beginning of a strong alliance is based in acceptance and validation of the couple as individuals. Balancing this need for acceptance without invalidating either of the partners can be a complex task. Careful conceptualization of the couple's presenting problems involves the opportunity to validate each individual, acknowledging that current relationship problems are understand-

able in the context of recent and more distant historical factors. Though we recognize the importance of these experiences, it is important that the therapist remain balanced in interpreting the roles of both partners in the maintenance of current problems. At times, we have seen couples where the partner with a trauma history is subtly blamed for the couple's current problems. We have referred to this problem as "benevolent blame," in that this may occur in a very sympathetic and understanding manner. However, it is essential that the therapist be alert to this issue and not inadvertently collude with the partner who has not been victimized in helping to fix the "broken" partner, sometimes referred to as the "identified patient." Therefore, the therapist's integrative conceptualization represents yet another dialectic in the treatment, in which the vulnerabilities related to a trauma history are recognized without being overly emphasized.

It is essential that the therapist be able to structure an environment that will evoke what Kohlenberg and Tsai (1991) have described as "clinically relevant behaviors." Clinically relevant behaviors are those behaviors occurring in session that are of therapeutic relevance. Fortunately, there is no better medium for producing those behaviors than couple therapy sessions. Although a couple may initially try to present in a socially desirable manner, having both partners present results in discriminative and eliciting functions that override those tendencies to remain on their "best behavior." Early in treatment, the therapist helps the couple to identify client problems that occur in session. As treatment progresses, the therapist identifies improvements occurring in session and helps the partners observe and describe their own behavior. Frequently in couple work, especially where there is a significant trauma history, sessions will involve intense affect associated with the discussion of the painful details of the trauma. Not only must the therapist be able to tolerate these experiences; he/she must also assist the nontraumatized partner in dealing with this experience. Although it is not essential, or even appropriate, for couple sessions to involve detailed descriptions of the trauma (as would occur in exposure therapy), some recounting of the experience can serve to promote acceptance of the traumatized partner and enhance intimacy.

TREATMENT STRATEGIES

After a couple has completed pretreatment, and assessment procedures have been used to identify areas of conflict, relationship themes, controlling variables, and areas of strength, the couple is ready to move into the treatment phase of therapy. Therapy has two primary goals: (1) to facilitate acceptance and change strategies within the dyad, and (2) to resolve relationship conflicts by facilitating individual change. Change and acceptance strategies are interwoven into treatment rather than occurring in a sequential manner, and should be emphasized more or less depending on the needs of the individual couple.

Change Strategies

Behavior exchange (BE) strategies have been a mainstay in behavioral couple therapy (Jacobson & Christensen, 1996; Jacobson & Holtzworth-Munroe, 1986; Dimidjian et al., Chapter 9, this volume) and are particularly useful in work with couples affected by trauma. BE strategies require partners to focus on individual behaviors that may contribute to relationship distress, and are used to increase the amount of positive reinforcement in the relationship. Although various techniques can be used, the essence of BE is to ask each partner to generate a list of behaviors he/she would be willing to engage in that would be likely to function as reinforcers for the other partner, and therefore increase the partner's day-to-day relationship satisfaction. Eventually, individuals are directed to engage in many of these behaviors and asked to notice when their partners are also engaging in behaviors expected to be reinforcing to them.

Trust is a primary difficulty for many couples coping with past traumas, and BE strategies are useful for encouraging partners to take small risks that facilitate and build trust over time. Since the phase of treatment involving BE strategies is generally characterized by minimal conflict, it is a useful time for encouraging a couple to work as a collaborative team rather than as the "survivor" and the "partner." It is important to note that partners who have been severely disengaged for the duration of their relationship may have difficulty identifying behaviors that will be reinforcing for each other. Thus the therapist can predict that this may be a difficult task that often takes time and skillful communication.

Although BE homework may continue throughout the therapy process, communication and problem-solving training should be added soon after basic trust and a collaborative set have been established. It is likely that the majority of couples in which one or both partners have a trauma history will have significant skill deficits in these areas, as many survivors are not able to identify or negotiate their individual needs and limits. Couples are taught to use receptive and expressive communication skills, including learning and practicing basic listening skills (showing attention and interest), using "I" statements, paraphrasing, making constructive requests, and other skills facilitating intimate interaction (Jacobson & Holtzworth-Munroe, 1986). Given that many individuals have experienced traumatic life events within their family environments, they often have significant histories of invalidation in which their private experience (e.g., needs, thoughts, feelings, selves) were minimized, ridiculed, disregarded, or rejected. Therefore, it may be necessary to teach such skills as mindfulness, distress tolerance, emotion regulation, and interpersonal effectiveness (Linehan, 1993), and to practice recognizing and engaging in validation within the relationship (Fruzzetti, 1996).

In work with survivors and their partners, it is particularly important to introduce topics of conflict in a gradual manner, with increasingly difficult issues being addressed as the corresponding individual skills are developing or established. Since many survivors and their partners have worked hard for years to avoid contacting internal experiences that are uncomfortable and painful, they are likely to use avoidance strategies when overwhelmed in treatment (e.g., when topics of conflict are introduced too quickly). It is important to monitor behaviors that might indicate experiential avoidance, including dissociation during session, substance misuse, binge eating, abrupt topic changes, or any other behavior that may be serving the function of avoidance. At times this could include interacting around issues that may appear important, but are really not critical for the couple to resolve. When avoidance behaviors are noticed, it is important to engage in a collaborative and objective analysis of the triggers for the problematic response, as well as the function that the behavior serves. The emphasis during the functional analysis should be on "understanding" rather than "blaming" the partner or couple for the behavior. It should be communicated that even the least skillful behavior is an understandable one, given a person's learning history and/or the current characteristics of the relationship or session.

The reciprocal nature of communication should always be emphasized; therapy should explore how each partner's communication and level of emotional availability affects the other. Videotaping couple interactions may help to isolate interaction patterns, and it may be a useful tool for communicating about interaction patterns during couple sessions (Fruzzetti & Serafin, 1995). While viewing the taped interaction, it is important for the therapist to alternate inquiries from partner to partner. It may be useful to identify particular moments in the interactions, and to ask questions that challenge individuals to view their behavior in the context of the relationship. Inquiries might include asking partners (1) to observe and describe their private experience; (2) to observe and describe their perception of each other's private experience; (3) to notice under what circumstances own (or each other's) behavior is engaged, distant, or aversive; (4) to identify what their goals were and/or what they needed from each other; and (5) to identify alternative behaviors that might have been more effective in meeting their goals or getting their needs met. It is useful for the therapist to express how he/she might have felt in the same conversation, to point out validating and invalidating responses, to notice positive behaviors (listening, not being defensive, being emotionally available), and to guide examination of the context and consequences for partner behaviors.

Acceptance Strategies

In conjunction with the change strategies of BE and communication and problem solving, several other strategies should be used to facilitate acceptance and communication of acceptance for issues in the relationship that cannot be changed. Jacobson and Christensen (1996) identify several strategies for facilitating acceptance during couple interventions: (1) empathic joining around the problem, (2) turning the problem into an "it," (3) tolerance building, and (4) self-care. In the following discussion, these strategies are each reviewed, and their utility for treating trauma couple populations is explored.

The strategy of empathic joining around the problem attempts to facilitate acceptance by encouraging each partner's experience of the other's pain, without blame or accusation. The focus of treatment shifts from the content areas typically associated with recurrent conflicts, to the theme or overarching source of those conflicts. The theme is discussed in terms of common differences between partners (e.g., wanting more closeness and time together vs. wanting more independence), and each partner's perspective is validated as legitimate. Care is taken to attribute relationship distress to the

problematic (e.g., blaming, negatively evaluating, etc.) reactions to their differences, rather than to the differences themselves. Thus the therapist encourages the couple to identify, understand, and accept the partners' differences as individuals, while changing the problematic ways each partner has tried to resolve these differences.

During this process, the therapist also promotes acceptance by helping the couple to work collaboratively toward viewing the problem as an externalized "it," rather than as something one partner does to the other. This strategy may facilitate an understanding of the other's experience and perspective by creating a level of emotional distance from the problem. In work with couples whose relationships are characterized by emotional distance and experiential avoidance, it is important to notice whether this strategy is merely one way of minimizing an important relationship issue that is difficult to discuss. It is important to distinguish between emotional distance *from* the problem (which facilitates understanding and closeness to the other) and emotional distance that merely *adds to* the problem.

The strategy of promoting acceptance through tolerance building seeks to extinguish negative behavior patterns between partners by prescribing that the partners engage in negative behavior when they would not typically do so. Through assignments that "ritualize" negative behaviors, it is hoped that partners will begin to understand both their own and each other's roles and vulnerabilities during conflict. When one is using this technique with couples affected by trauma, it is important to distinguish between learning to tolerate negative behavior better (not the goal) and learning when and why both partners react in the ways they typically do during conflict. In other words, by engaging in problem behavior patterns out of context, partners learn to identify the bodily sensations, feelings, and reactions that are often associated with their negative couple interactions. Another form of acceptance is recognition of the fact that partners influence each other, and that seemingly automatic responses are actually a series of complex interactions that can be explored and understood.

Promoting acceptance through self-care is a strategy designed to help partners to identify individual needs not being met in the relationship, and to use newly acquired skills to consider other avenues for getting those needs met. This strategy is particularly complicated when working with couples affected by trauma, as many survivors are unable to identify their needs or to ask their partner to meet them. Thus this strategy should be introduced toward the end of treatment, with a goal of problem-solving how a particular need will be met within or outside of the relationship.

Sexual Issues

Sexual issues are often targets for treatment in work with trauma survivors, whether or not the traumatic experience was sexual in nature. Although a subset of couples may present for therapy specifically to address sexual problems, many will not report sexual problems without prompting, and the range of sexual problems will vary across couples and forms of trauma. Problems with sexual relating are among the most troublesome effects of trauma on significant others. It is common for an intimate partner to experience feelings of inadequacy and rejection because of a survivor's dislike and reluctance for sexual intimacy or compulsive quest for sexual attention (Graber, 1991; Maltz & Holman, 1987). Partners of trauma survivors frequently complain of feeling sexually unfulfilled. Sexual problems such as difficulties achieving or maintaining an erection, decreased sexual desire, and impotence are common clinical complaints among male sexual partners of trauma survivors, and many cognitive-behavioral sex therapy techniques may be helpful (Gold, Letourneau, & O'Donohue, 1995; Graber, 1991; LoPiccolo & LoPiccolo, 1978; Maltz & Holman, 1987).

It is important to note that sexual problems are typically intertwined with issues of intimacy and emotional expressiveness, and treatment should address each level of functioning. In some cases, low sexual desire on the part of the survivor may develop as a way of avoiding intolerable levels of closeness in the relationship. This phenomenon has been observed in other couples with sexual difficulties where the partners report discrepant needs for closeness in their relationships (LoPiccolo & Friedman, 1988). In such a couple, low sexual desire tends to be perceived by the sexually functional partner as rejection, and often results in withdrawing behaviors. This pattern may function to decrease closeness in survivor relationships, maintaining a level of intimacy acceptable to the survivor.

As with other painful topics, a couple in which one member has a trauma histoy may avoid communication about sexual issues, and open discussions about each partner's fears, feelings, desires, and difficulties is often quite therapeutic. However, problem solving about sexual matters is a difficult topic for a couple to engage in even when the rela-

tionship is going fairly well, and should only be introduced with a trauma survivor when communication skills are well established. It is important to discuss avoidance of sex, flashbacks, nightmares, and dissociation during sexual activity, and each partner's sexual preferences and dislikes. Efforts should be aimed at understanding activities, settings, smells, and other aspects of the sexual context that trigger emotional withdrawal or other sexual problems. Finally, a distinction should be made between simply engaging in sexual activity and being emotionally present during sexual activity, as this difference clearly affects the quality of the sexual relationship.

At times in working with any couple, the therapist may note that one partner seems unable to empathize with the other's perspective because the partner's own emotional pain is so intense. For example, a female partner with a history of CSA may still be in the process of working through that trauma and may not be able to identify with the sadness of her partner, which is associated with years of feeling distanced from the relationship. Validation is essential to acceptance-based couple therapy. However, a client whose history involves a very invalidating family environment will be working to develop and strengthen a sense of self in individual therapy. In the earlier phases of treatment, validation of the partner may be threatening, in that the client feels that "if I validate my partner, I will lose my perspective and myself." Thus part of the couple therapy involves learning both to have one's own position and to see that empathizing with another person's position does not lead to an obliteration of self.

COMMON TREATMENT OBSTACLES AND POSSIBLE SOLUTIONS

In addition to the common obstacles of experiential avoidance and domestic violence, two other salient issues situations can affect treatment of couples affected by trauma: a dual-trauma couple, and a couple in which the nontraumatized partner blames relationship problems on the survivor.

The Dual-Trauma Couple

A dual-trauma couple, or a couple with two trauma survivors, is one special circumstance that complicates couple therapy. Whereas a couple with one trauma survivor often relies on the stability of one partner or the other, partners in a dual-trauma couple may find it difficult to support each other in times of stress (Balcom, 1996). Moreover, as one partner struggles to cope with his/her trauma and make sense of the related experiences, this process may trigger painful memories for the other partner. Thus reciprocal reexperiencing and repeated crises may severely disrupt the development of closeness, trust, and emotional connection within the relationship. In fact, a pattern of mutual withdrawal and disengagement is often expected, and partners in many dual-trauma couples choose each other precisely because neither of them wants to be challenged in ways that require emotional vulnerability. It will be important to identify dual-trauma issues at the onset of treatment, and to inquire routinely about each partner's individual functioning. It may be necessary to refer partners for individual therapy concurrent with their couple interventions if they find it difficult to remain regulated.

Blaming the Survivor

In recent years, couple interventions have become increasingly used for the treatment of many individual psychological problems. Unlike disorders such as depression and agoraphobia, PTSD is not theorized to be caused by couple distress. There is always an identifiable traumatic event (or multiple events) that survivors and their partners can point to and assign blame. Thus, although many survivors seek conjoint couple therapy with their partners, it is common for the nontraumatized partners to view their role in therapy as merely facilitating individual growth on the part of the survivors. Although often well-meaning, a partner who views a survivor as the identified patient in couple therapy may attribute primary responsibility for relationship difficulties to the survivor or to the trauma history (Follette, 1991). This pattern of "benevolent blame" may perpetuate feelings of shame and stigmatization already experienced by many survivors, and can maintain or even exacerbate PTSD symptoms.

It is important that partners routinely be reminded that a relationship is not a solitary activity, and that their problems are mutually determined and mutually resolved. This notion of "mutual responsibility" should be addressed directly throughout treatment, both verbally and behaviorally. Alternating the emphasis of treatment from one partner to the other, and from historical issues to current relationship problems, may facilitate increasingly collaborative interactions among couples (Follette &

Pistorello, 1995). Moreover, this strategy may help the therapist by ensuring a position of neutrality during couple therapy.

MECHANISMS OF CHANGE

As indicated throughout this chapter, therapy constantly involves balancing a number of factors, some of which seem to be inconsistent on the surface. For example, although we believe an emphasis on current problems is of most value in couple treatment, an analysis of historical factors is critical in understanding the origins of some of those problems. Thus we are always examining distal and more proximal antecedents to problems, as well as factors that are maintaining those problems currently. In that we see all behavior as contextual and interactive in nature, system change will involve change at both an intra- and an interpersonal level.

As Linehan (1993) has described for dialectical behavior therapy, the therapist serves as a teacher, coach, and support person at various phases of treatment. Often each member of the couple has a number of skill deficits that require specific didactic training. However, later in the therapy the therapist steps back to the position of coach, gently shaping the use of skills. The therapist must be fearless in supporting both partners in the exploration of problems that will be extremely painful to all three of them. Discussing trauma and its wake is never easy. The therapist can model strength and acceptance for both the survivor and her partner. The therapist's willingness to explore these topics can be much more powerful than any "words of advice."

Using this treatment paradigm necessitates that the therapist be able to understand and use dialectics in his/her own life. We believe that the ability to work with a model embracing such seeming opposites as acceptance and change is not simply a treatment approach, but rather a world view that is somewhat different from what we traditionally observe in Western culture. The therapy is often long-term and demanding, and in our experience the consultation and support of a supervision team are invaluable in keeping the therapy moving forward in a positive manner.

EVALUATION OF TREATMENT EFFECTIVENESS

Like all treatments, couple therapy with trauma survivors should be evaluated on an ongoing basis to test hypotheses about controlling variables; inform treatment planning; and ultimately provide information about when to continue, modify, or terminate treatment. Many of the assessment measures discussed throughout this chapter are brief and sensitive to short-term changes. Thus it is both economical and reasonable to have couples complete repeated measures throughout treatment at regular intervals.

When using videotaped assessments of couple interactions, therapists have records of interaction patterns over time and can refer back to previous sessions to rate change in the couples' relationships. Feedback regarding areas that have changed or remained the same can be given to couples by showing them previous videotapes, and this may be a powerful intervention in its own right. Finally, it is important to discuss each couple's satisfaction with the process of therapy, the rate of change, and the impact it has had on both individuals and on relationship distress. Treatment often seems to make things worse before making it better. For couples exploring the effects of trauma on their relationships for the first time, the therapeutic process is likely to bring problems and difficulties to the forefront that had been overlooked or avoided in the past. One way of minimizing anxiety or premature termination of treatment is to predict that change may take more time than a couple expects, and that it is common to experience the relationship as worse off at times during the process. It may be useful to describe therapy as being like a glass of water with sand at the bottom. Treatment begins by observing and discussing issues that have been dormant (or festering) in the sand; this results in mixing the sand and water together and making the relationship seem more "cloudy" than it did before treatment. The goal of therapy is to become aware of what is in the sand, to change what can be changed, and finally to guide the sand to settle and clear in ways that facilitate individual and relationship satisfaction.

CASE ILLUSTRATION

Elizabeth responded to an advertisement for a research program evaluating group psychotherapy for women who had been sexually abused by a father or father figure. She had not previously disclosed her abuse history to anyone outside her family. After the initial evaluation, she reported that she did not feel ready to address her abuse issues in a group format; in fact, she was questioning whether

to pursue therapy at all. Elizabeth was extremely sad during her interactions with the project evaluator and reported that while she felt that the abuse she suffered at the hands of her stepfather had haunted her throughout her life, she doubted that anything could be gained by working on the issues. In addition, although both her mother and stepfather were deceased, she still felt very fearful about revealing the abuse. She was not able to describe her fears precisely, but she had a general sense that something "terrible" would happen if she disclosed her history. In addition to the sexual abuse (which had lasted for many years), she had suffered physical abuse, neglect of health problems, and emotional abuse, and had witnessed serious physical abuse of her mother. The family environment had been extremely chaotic, and there was constant invalidation of both her experience of physical events and her emotional reactions to those events. Elizabeth had internalized many of her family's messages, learning to see herself as a fundamentally bad person who deserved nothing but pain and suffering. After several consultations with the project coordinator, Elizabeth agreed to enter individual therapy.

The therapist was a graduate student working in a training clinic, and the client was seen in intensive individual therapy for over a year. After many sessions were spent developing rapport and trust with the client, the therapist went on to address the client's problems via a number of behavioral techniques. The primary treatment approach was based on the tenets of Hayes's (1999) acceptance and commitment therapy and Linehan's (1993) dialectical behavior therapy. Initial treatment goals involved stopping therapy-interfering behaviors, which included skipping or canceling sessions. Issues related to suicidal ideation and parasuicidal behavior were also a focus of treatment, both early on and later in therapy when new stresses would emerge. Later therapy tasks included teaching the client emotion regulation, problem solving, and communication skills. When Elizabeth was more able to regulate her emotions, basic exposure work was done regarding her abuse history, which was much more extensive than the client had initially reported.

While the therapist continued sessions that involved exposure therapy, current life stressors were also discussed. It became clear that there were a number of issues in the client's marriage, and that these were actually exacerbated as she continued to improve in her individual treatment. To some degree, the relationship had been predicated on a mutual understanding that there would be little emotional intimacy; rather, it would be based primarily on the instrumental tasks of being a couple. The husband, Alex, had no idea about his wife's abuse, and in fact knew very little about her general thoughts and feelings on a day-to-day basis. Although this arrangement had been mutually agreeable at one time, as Elizabeth improved she not only wanted more from her marriage but also became dissatisfied with other aspects of the relationship, such as Alex's dominance in many aspects of decision making and the quality of their sexual relationship.

Because of the long-term and intense therapeutic relationship with the individual therapist, the couple was referred to a family therapist in the community. However, a number of tasks needed to be accomplished before the referral. First, the client requested that the individual therapist meet with the couple so that Elizabeth could tell Alex about her abuse history. Alex had only recently become aware that his wife was in treatment, and he had expressed concerns that maybe she was magnifying her problems. Several sessions were spent helping Elizabeth to decide what she wanted to say to her husband and exploring possible responses he might have. Although she was extremely afraid and ashamed, she was able to disclose her history to Alex. The therapist did not say much, but rather served as a source of quiet support, with minimal coaching of Elizabeth. However, Alex was clearly unprepared, both intellectually and emotionally, for the content of the session. He had not suspected the abuse and was somewhat overwhelmed by the disclosure. The therapist was able to coach him in some basic communication skills, such as conveying support to his wife and validating her feelings of sadness and anger. He remained somewhat unclear about the need for couple therapy, but he did agree to an assessment session with the family therapist.

Although the individual therapist obtained a release, the couple therapist preferred doing the intake before learning more from the individual therapist. After the initial session, which involved a fairly standard assessment of the couple's strengths and weaknesses, the two therapists spoke about the individual therapy and the trauma history. Individual and couple therapy progressed concurrently over the next year. This fairly long-term course of treatment was necessitated by a number of difficulties that arose, including a significant exacerbation of Elizabeth's symptoms.

Early therapy sessions integrated BE, but to a lesser extent than we would generally do. Rather, the couple was so disengaged that the primary emphasis of treatment was on communication, especially around emotions. Neither partner had a strong repertoire of noticing and labeling a range of feelings. Of course, this had been a focus of treatment in Elizabeth's individual therapy; however, in the presence of her husband, Elizabeth became confused and unsure of herself. This pointed to the necessity of couple therapy, in that while Elizabeth was able to use some emotion-related skills in individual sessions, those skills had not yet generalized to her relationship. The couple had been married over 10 years, and the process of helping the spouses to open up to each other was a very painful one, given their long history of feeling alienated from each other. As each withdrew, not only were opportunities for support missed, but also new wounds were inflicted on both of them.

Over the initial 6 months of treatment, two issues were critical. First, Alex began to recognize and accept his own role in creating their unhappy marriage. Although he had not suffered any particular abuse in his family of origin, the family had been very emotionally avoidant and had tended to have very traditional role expectations for men. Thus he was a good provider and helpful around the house, but was not good at eliciting or sharing thoughts and feelings of a more intimate nature. When difficulties arose, he thought it best to work hard and wait out the bad times. Conflict was to be avoided, and the husband was seen as the ultimate head of the household, so many sessions were spent exploring the historical roots of both partners' current behaviors. This was done less in the service of insight than as a vehicle to acceptance and emotional intimacy. The second issue was one that occurred outside the therapy: The therapists kept in close contact about progress in both therapies. This was done partly for informational reasons, but it was also important that they work collaboratively and not second-guess each other. As noted earlier, it is easy for different therapists to become triangulated into the problems of a couple affected by trauma. This triangulation does not serve any part of the group well and can often lead to premature termination.

Therapy moved into problem solving around core issues, with an emphasis on the partners' acceptance of each other and themselves. Alex came to recognize and appreciate his wife's strength and abilities, and was able to see the value in a relationship that was more balanced in terms of power and responsibility. There were many issues to address, including contact with Elizabeth's family, parenting, and Elizabeth's desire to return to work. While all of this progressed with slowly but steadily, everyone knew that the spouses still had to face dealing with their sexual relationship.

As initial phases of sex therapy were explored, Elizabeth destabilized and reported more problems with self-injury and medication abuse. Her flashbacks and night terrors increased. This was distressing not only to her but to Alex, who could not understand her emotional withdrawal after all the work they had done. Individual work intensified, with sessions being conducted twice a week. The couple therapy continued at a slow rate, with more and more exposure and sexual interaction. Gradually the spouses were able to resume sexual relations, with clear communication so that Elizabeth could let Alex know if she became frightened or disoriented. Alex's willingness to work through this process with her led to enhanced feelings of intimacy between them.

Final phases of treatment included a focus on generalization and maintenance of their treatment gains. Predictably, there were some setbacks during this period, and the therapist used these experiences to support the couple in working through these problems more autonomously. Therapy was faded over a period of 2 months, with more time between sessions and less active involvement by the therapist. When therapy ended, both Alex and Elizabeth recognized that they would always face a number of difficulties, based both on past vulnerabilities and new stresses. However, they also were now deeply committed to each other, with a sense of having worked through and survived a very painful set of experiences. Couple therapy ended on a positive note, and Elizabeth gradually terminated her individual therapy.

This case demonstrated some of the most fundamental aspects of our treatment approach. We believe that it is essential to understand the unique strengths and vulnerabilities that a survivor of CSA brings to treatment. Rather than deliver a packaged treatment, we conduct ongoing analyses of the client's issues and treat problems accordingly, working in a contextual/behavioral framework. Our clients frequently report couple problems, and when dyadic treatment is indicated, we work to balance two sets of issues. First, there must be an interaction between current problems and an understanding of some of the historical factors associated with those problems. Second, although the survivor's issues are considered, she should not be stigmatized in the relationship; rather, both members of the couple need to understand

their own roles in the development and maintenance of their problems. We believe that a therapy emphasizing acceptance (of both the self and the other) and change in valued directions can enhance the lives of both members of the couple.

REFERENCES

Alexander, P. C., & Lupfer, S. L. (1987). Family characteristics and long-term consequences associated with sexual abuse. *Archives of Sexual Behavior, 16*(3), 235–245.

Balcom, D. (1996). The interpersonal dynamics and treatment of dual trauma couples. *Journal of Marital and Family Therapy, 22*, 431–442.

Blake, D. D., Weathers, F. W., Nagy, L. M., Kaloupek, D. G., Klauminzer, G., Charney, & Keane, T. M. (1990). A clinician rating scale for assessing current and lifetime PTSD: The CAPS-1. *The Behavior Therapist, 13*, 187–188.

Blanchard, E. B., Gerardi, R. J., Kolb, L. C., & Barlow, D. H. (1996). The utility of the Anxiety Disorders Interview Schedule (ADIS) in the diagnosis of posttraumatic stress disorder (PTSD) in Vietnam veterans. *Behaviour Research and Therapy, 24*, 577–580.

Biglan, A., Hops, H., Sherman, L., Friedman, L. S., Arthur, J., & Osteen, V. (1985). Problem solving interactions of depressed women and their husbands. *Behavior Therapy, 16*, 431–451.

Briere, J. (1988). The long-term clinical correlates of childhood sexual victimization. *Annals of the New York Academy of Sciences, 528*, 327–334.

Briere, J. (1992). *Child abuse trauma: Theory and treatment of the lasting effects.* Newbury Park, CA: Sage.

Briere, J. (1995). *Trauma Symptom Inventory.* Odessa, FL: Psychological Assessment Resources.

Briere, J., & Runtz, M. (1988). Symptomatology associated with childhood sexual victimization in a nonclinical adult sample. *Child Abuse and Neglect, 12*, 51–59.

Briere, J., & Runtz, M. (1991). The long-term effects of sexual abuse: A review and synthesis. In J. Briere (Eds.), *Treating victims of child sexual abuse* (pp. 3–13). San Francisco: Jossey-Bass.

Briere, J., & Runtz, M. (1993). Childhood sexual abuse: Long-term sequelae and implications for psychological assessment. *Journal of Interpersonal Violence, 8*, 312–330.

Briere, J., & Zaidi, L. Y. (1989). Sexual abuse histories and sequelae in female psychiatric emergency room patients. *American Journal of Psychiatry, 146*, 1602–1606.

Brody, E. M., & Farber, B. A. (1989). Effects of psychotherapy on significant others. *Professional Psychology: Research and Practice, 20*, 116–122.

Brown, G. W., & Harris, T. O. (1978). *Social origins of depression: A study of psychiatric disorder in women.* New York: Free Press.

Browne, A., & Finkelhor, D. (1986). The impact of child sexual abuse: A review of the research. *Psychological Bulletin, 99*, 66–77.

Buttenheim, M., & Levendosky, A. (1994). Couples treatment for incest survivors. *Psychotherapy, 31*, 407–414.

Christensen, A. (1988). Dysfunctional interaction patterns in couples. In P. Noller & M. A. Fitzpatrick (Eds.), *Perspectives on marital interaction* (pp. 31–35). Clevedon, England: Multilingual Matters.

Christensen, A., Jacobson, N. S., & Babcock, J. C. (1995). Integrative behavioral couple therapy. In N. S. Jacobson & A. S. Gurman (Eds.), *Clinical handbook of couple therapy* (pp. 31–63). New York: Guilford Press.

Compton, J. S. (1999). *Childhood trauma, individual distress, and couple functioning: Using observational coding to examine intimacy process and affective expression.* Unpublished doctoral dissertation, University of Nevada–Reno.

Compton, J. S., & Follette, V. M. (1998). Couples surviving trauma: Issues and interventions. In V. M. Follette, J. I. Ruzek, & F. R. Abeug (Eds.), *Cognitive-behavioral therapies for trauma* (pp. 321–352). New York: Guilford Press.

Compton, J. S., & Follette, V. M. (2000). *Interpersonal correlates of sexual trauma: Couple functioning in a clinical sample.* Unpublished manuscript.

Courtois, C. C. (1988). *Healing the incest wound: Adult survivors in therapy.* New York: Norton.

Coyne, J. C. (1976). Toward an interactional description of depression. *Psychiatry, 39*, 28–40.

Feinauer, L. L. (1989). Comparison of long-term effects of child abuse by type of abuse and by relationship of the offender to the victim. *American Journal of Family Therapy, 17*, 48–56.

Finkelhor, D., Hotaling, G. T., Lewis, I. A., & Smith, C. (1990). Sexual abuse and its relationship to later sexual satisfaction, marital status, religion, and attitudes. *Journal of Interpersonal Violence, 4*, 379–399.

Foa, E. B., Riggs, D. S., & Gershuny, B. S. (1995). Arousal, numbing, and intrusion: Symptom structure of PTSD following assault. *American Journal of Psychiatry, 152*, 116–120.

Follette, V. M. (1991). Marital therapy for sexual abuse survivors. In J. Briere (Ed.), *Treating victims of child sexual abuse* (pp. 61–71). San Francisco: Jossey-Bass.

Follette, V. M. (1994). Survivors of child sexual abuse: Treatment using a contextual analysis. In S. C. Hayes, N. S. Jacobson, V. M. Follette, & M. J. Dougher (Eds.), *Acceptance and change: Content and context in psychotherapy* (pp. 255–268). Reno, NV: Context Press.

Follette, V. M., Alexander, P. C., & Follette, W. F. (1991). Individual predictors of outcome in group treatment for incest survivors. *Journal of Consulting and Clinical Psychology, 59*, 150–155.

Follette, V. M., & Pistorello, J. (1995). Couples therapy: When one partner has been sexually abused. In C. Classen (Eds.), *Treating women molested in childhood* (pp. 129–162). San Francisco: Jossey-Bass.

Follette, V. M., Polusny, M. M., Bechtle, A. E., & Naugle, A. E. (1996). Cumulative trauma effects: The impact of child sexual abuse, adult sexual assault, and spouse abuse. *Journal of Traumatic Stress, 9*, 15–25.

Fruzzetti, A. E. (1996). Causes and consequences: Individual distress in the context of couple interactions. *Journal of Consulting and Clinical Psychology, 64*, 1192–1201.

Fruzzetti, A. E., & Serafin, J. M. (1995). *A functional approach to observing couple intimacy and distancing processes.* Paper presented at the World Congress of Behavioural and Cognitive Therapies, Copenhagen.

Fruzzetti, A. E., & Serafin, J. M. (1996). *Integrated individual, couples, and family DBT program at the University of Nevada.* Poster presented at the First Annual Convention of the International Society for the Implementation and Training of Dialectical Behavior Therapy, New York.

Gelster, K. P., & Feinauer, L. L. (1989). Divorce potential and marital stability of adult women sexually abused as children compared to adult women not sexually abused as children. *Journal of Sex and Marital Therapy, 14*, 269–277.

Gold, S. R. (1986). Long-term effects of sexual victimization in childhood: An attributional approach. *Journal of Consulting and Clinical Psychology, 54*, 471–475.

Gold, S. R., Letourneau, E. J., & O'Donohue, W. (1995). Sexual interaction skills. In W. O'Donohue & L. Krasner (Eds.), *Handbook of psychological skills training* (pp. 229–246). Needham Heights, MA: Allyn & Bacon.

Gottman, J. M. (1979). *Marital interaction: Experimental investigations.* New York: Academic Press.

Gottman, J. M., & Krokoff, L. J. (1989). Marital interaction and satisfaction: A longitudinal view. *Journal of Consulting and Clinical Psychology, 57*, 47–52.

Gottman, J. M., & Levenson, R. W. (1986). Assessing the role of emotion in marriage. *Behavioral Assessment, 8*, 31–48.

Graber, K. (1991). *Ghosts in the bedroom: A guide for partners of incest survivors.* Deerfield Beach, FL: Health Communications.

Greenberg, L. S., & Johnson, S. M. (1988). *Emotionally focused therapy for couples.* New York: Guilford Press.

Hahlweg, K., Revenstorf, D., & Schindler, L. (1984). Effects of behavioral marital therapy on couples' communication and problem-solving skills. *Journal of Consulting and Clinical Psychology, 52*, 553–566.

Hayes, S. C. (1994). Content, context, and the types of psychological acceptance. In S. C. Hayes, N. S. Jacobson, V. M. Follette, & M. J. Dougher (Eds.), *Acceptance and change: Content and context in psychotherapy* (pp. 13–32). Reno, NV: Context Press.

Hayes, S. C., Strosahl, K. D., & Wilson, K. G. (1999). *Acceptance and commitment therapy.* New York: Guilford Press.

Herman, J. L. (1981). *Father–daughter incest.* Cambridge, MA: Harvard University Press.

Herman, J. L., Perry, J. C., & van der Kolk, B. A. (1989). Childhood trauma in borderline personality disorder. *American Journal of Psychiatry, 146*, 490–495.

Holtzworth-Munroe, A., Beatty, S. B., & Anglin, K. (1995). The assessment and treatment of marital violence: An introduction for the marital therapist. In N. S. Jacobson & A. S. Gurman (Eds.), *Clinical handbook of couple therapy* (pp. 317–339). New York: Guilford Press.

Houskamp, B. M., & Foy, D. W. (1991). The assessment of posttraumatic stress disorder in battered women. *Journal of Interpersonal Violence, 6*, 367–375.

Jacobson, N. S., & Christensen, A. (1996). *Integrative couple therapy: Promoting acceptance and change.* New York: Norton.

Jacobson, N. S., & Holtzworth-Munroe, A. (1986). Marital therapy: A social learning–cognitive perspective. In N. S. Jacobson & A. S. Gurman (Eds.), *Clinical handbook of marital therapy* (pp. 29–70). New York: Guilford Press.

Jacobson, N. S., Holtzworth-Munroe, A., & Schmaling, K. B. (1989). Marital therapy and spouse involvement in the treatment of depression, agoraphobia, and alcoholism. *Journal of Consulting and Clinical Psychology, 57*, 5–10.

Jacobson, N. S., Waldron, H., & Moore, D. (1980). Toward a behavioral profile of marital distress. *Journal of Consulting and Clinical Psychology, 48*, 696–703.

Johnson, J. G., Cohen, P., Brown, J., Smailes, E. M., & Berstein, D. P. (1999). Childhood maltreatment increases risk for personality disorders during early adulthood. *Archives of General Psychiatry, 56*, 600–606.

Johnson, S. M. (1989). Integrating marital and individual therapy for incest survivors: A case study. *Psychotherapy, 26*, 96–103.

Ketring, S. A., & Feinauer, L. L. (1999). Perpetrator-victim relationship: Long-term effects of sexual abuse for men and women. *American Journal of Family Therapy, 27*, 109–120.

Koerner, K., Prince, S., & Jacobson, N. S. (1994). Enhancing the treatment and prevention of depression in women: The role of integrative behavioral couple therapy. *Behavior Therapy, 25*, 373–390.

Kohlenberg, R. J., & Tsai, M. (1991). *Functional analytic psychotherapy.* New York: Plenum Press.

Koss, M. P., Koss, P. G., & Woodruff, W. J. (1991). Deleterious effects of criminal victimization on women's health and medical utilization. *Archives of Internal Medicine, 151*, 342–347.

Leitenberg, H., Greenwald, E., & Cado, S. (1992). A retrospective study of long-term methods of coping with having been sexually abused during childhood. *Child Abuse and Neglect, 16*, 399–407.

Liem, J. H., & Boudeweyn, A. C. (1999). Contextualizing the effects of childhood sexual abuse on adult self- and social functioning: An attachment theory perspective. *Child Abuse and Neglect, 23*, 1141–1157.

Liem, J. H., James, J. B., O'Toole, J. G., & Boudeweyn, A. C. (1997). Assessing resilience in adults with histories of childhood sexual abuse. *American Journal of Orthopsychiatry, 67*, 594–606.

Liem, J. H., O'Toole, J. G., & James, J. B. (1992). The need for power in women who were sexually abused as children: An exploratory study. *Psychology of Women Quarterly, 16*, 467–480.

Linehan, M. M. (1993). *Cognitive-behavioral treatment of borderline personality disorder.* New York: Guilford Press.

Linehan, M. M. (1996). Validation and psychotherapy. In A. Bohart & L. S. Greenberg (Eds.), *Empathy and psychotherapy: New directions in theory, research, and practice* (pp. 1–22). Washington, DC: American Psychological Association.

LoPiccolo, J., & LoPiccolo, L. (1978). *Handbook of sex therapy.* New York: Plenum Press.

LoPiccolo, J., & Friedman, J. M. (1988). Broad-spectrum treatment of low sexual desire: Integration of cognitive, behavioral and systemic therapy. In S. R. Leiblum & R. C. Rosen (Eds.), *Sexual desire disorders* (pp. 107–144). New York: Guilford Press.

Maltz, W., & Holman, B. (1987). *Incest and sexuality.* Lexington, MA: Lexington Books.

Margolin, G., Talovic, S., & Weinstein, C. D. (1983). Areas of Change Questionnaire: A practical approach to marital assessment. *Journal of Consulting and Clinical Psychology, 51*, 920–931.

Margolin, G., & Wampold, B. E. (1981). Sequential analysis of conflict and accord in distressed and nondistressed marital partners. *Journal of Consulting and Clinical Psychology, 49*, 554–567.

McCrady, B. S., & Epstein, E. E. (1995). Marital therapy in the treatment of alcohol problems. In N. S. Jacobson & A. S. Gurman (Eds.), *Clinical handbook of couple therapy* (pp. 369–393). New York: Guilford Press.

McMillen, C., Zuravin, S., & Rideout, G. (1995). Perceived benefit from child sexual abuse. *Journal of Consulting and Clinical Psychology, 63*, 1037–1043.

Meadows, E. A., & Foa, E. B. (1998). Intrusion, arousal, and avoidance: Sexual trauma survivors. In V. M. Follette, J. I. Ruzek, & F. R. Abeug (Eds.), *Cognitive-behavioral therapies for trauma* (pp. 100–123). New York: Guilford Press.

Miller, W. R., Williams, M., & Bernstein, M. H. (1982). The effects of rape on marital and sexual adjustment. *American Journal of Family Therapy, 10*, 51–58.

Naugle, A. E., Follette, W. C., & Follette, V. M. (1995). *Toward prevention of revictimization: A functional analytic model.* Paper presented at the annual meeting of the Association for Advancement of Behavior Therapy, Washington, DC.

Nelson, G. M., & Beach, S. R. (1990). Sequential interaction in depression: Effects of depressive behavior on spousal aggression. *Behavior Therapy, 21*, 167–182.

Pistorello, J., & Follette, V. M. (1998). Childhood sexual abuse and couples' relationships: Female survivors' reports in therapy groups. *Journal of Marriage and Family Therapy, 24*(4), 473–485.

Polusny, M. A., & Follette, V. M. (1995). Long-term correlates of child sexual abuse: Theory and review of the empirical literature. *Applied and Preventative Psychology, 4*, 143–166.

Pribor, E. F., & Dinwiddie, S. H. (1992). Psychiatric correlates of incest in childhood. *American Journal of Psychiatry, 150*, 1507–1511.

Raczek, S. W. (1992). Childhood abuse and personality disorders. *Journal of Personality Disorders, 6*, 109–116.

Rabin, C., & Nardi, C. (1991). Treating post traumatic stress disorder couples: A psychoeducational approach. *Community Mental Health Journal, 27*, 209–224.

Ruzek, J. F., Polusny, M. A., & Abueg, F. R. (1998). Assessment and treatment of concurrent PTSD and substance abuse. In V. M. Follette, J. I. Ruzek, & F. R. Abeug (Eds.), *Cognitive-behavioral therapies for trauma* (pp. 226–255). New York: Guilford Press.

Serafin, J. M. (1996). Disrupted relationships and couple therapy: Treating female survivors of child sexual abuse and their partners. *PTSD Clinical Quarterly, 6*, 42–45.

Serafin, J. M., & Follette, V. M. (1996). *Female survivors of sexual trauma and their partners: Issues in couple functioning.* Paper presented at the annual meeting of the International Society for Traumatic Stress Studies, San Francisco.

Spanier, G. B. (1976). Measuring dyadic adjustment: New scales for assessing the quality of marriage and similar dyads. *Journal of Marriage and the Family, 38*, 15–28.

Sullaway, M., & Christensen, A. (1983). Assessment of dysfunctional interaction patterns in couples. *Journal of Marriage and the Family, 45*, 653–660.

Valentine, L., & Feinauer, L. L. (1993). Resilience factors associated with female survivors of child sexual abuse. *American Journal of Family Therapy, 21*, 216–224.

Van Buskirk, S. S., & Cole, C. F. (1983). Characteristics of eight women seeking therapy for the effects of incest. *Psychotherapy: Theory, Research, and Practice, 20*(4), 503–514.

Walker, E., Katon, W. J., Harrop-Griffiths, J., Holm, L., Russo, J., & Hickok, L. R. (1988). Relationship of chronic pelvic pain to psychiatric diagnoses and childhood sexual abuse. *American Journal of Psychiatry, 145,* 75–80.

Weiss, E., Longhurst, J. G., & Mazure, C. M. (1999). Childhood sexual abuse as a risk factor for depression in women: Psychosocial and neurobiological correlates. *American Journal of Psychiatry, 156,* 816–828.

Widom, C. S. (1999). Posttraumatic stress disorder in abused and neglected children grown up. *American Journal of Psychiatry, 156,* 1223–1229.

Wind, T. W., & Silvern, L. (1992). Type and extent of child abuse as predictors of adult functioning. *Journal of Family Violence, 7,* 261–281.

Wyatt, G. E., Guthrie, D., & Notgrass, C. M. (1992). Differential effects of women's child sexual abuse and subsequent sexual revictimization. *Journal of Consulting and Clinical Psychology, 60,* 167–173.

Wyatt, G. E., & Lyons-Rowe, S. (1990). African American women's sexual satisfaction as a dimension of their sex roles. *Sex Roles, 22,* 509–524.

Chapter 18

Couple Therapy after the Trauma of Infidelity

SHIRLEY P. GLASS

According to a survey of marital therapists and family psychologists by Whisman, Dixon, and Johnson (1997), affairs are the third most difficult problem to treat and the second most damaging problem that couples encounter. Disclosure of infidelity is a frequent catalyst for couple therapy, whereas ambivalence about resolving a secret affair more often leads to individual therapy. Approximately 30% of couples initiate marital therapy because of a crisis of infidelity (Glass & Wright, 1988; Greene, Lee, & Lustig, 1974; Whisman et al., 1997), and an additional 30% disclose infidelity during the course of treatment (Humphrey, 1983). Among 316 clinically referred married couples, 23% of the wives and 45% of the husbands were unfaithful; 57% of all the couples had an extramarital involvement by one or both spouses (Glass, in preparation).

National opinion surveys report conservative findings that approximately 15% of women and 25% of men engage in extramarital sex (Laumann, Gagnon, Michael, & Michaels, 1994; Wiederman, 1997). Other studies report that 25% of women and 50% of men have experienced extramarital sex (Glass & Wright, 1977, 1985; Hunt, 1974; Kinsey, Pomeroy, & Martin, 1953; Yablonsky, 1979). More women are becoming involved in extramarital relationships because of increased premarital sexual experience and increased opportunity. Since women have entered what were formerly male-dominated professions, the workplace

relationship has become the most common context for extramarital affairs.

The literature on extramarital involvement has failed to provide a coherent conceptual framework or consistent treatment approach, despite the prevalence of extramarital involvement. There is a dearth of clinical research and articles even in marital and family therapy journals, and only a handful of books have been written on treatment of infidelity (Brown, 1991; Glass, 2000; Harvey, 1995; Moultrop, 1990; Strean, 1980), whereas self-help books on surviving infidelity have proliferated (Lusterman, 1998; Pittman, 1989; Spring, 1996; Subotnik & Harris, 1999; Weil, 1993). Furthermore, my survey of 365 therapists at nine different professional conferences found that only 11% had read any books or journal articles about infidelity (Glass, in preparation).

Clinical approaches have reflected the dominant theoretical orientation or social trends of a particular era. Psychoanalytic approaches toward infidelity, which prevailed from the 1930s through the 1960s, concentrated on individual psychopathology and obsessional neuroses (e.g., Levine, 1938; Neubeck & Schletzer, 1962). The only edited book on nonconsensual extramarital sex was published in 1969 by Neubeck. The extramarital literature during the 1970s was influenced by the sexual liberation movement and focused on consensual extramarital sex and "swinging" (Smith & Smith, 1974). Integrative approaches for treating infidelity in the

1990s (Glass & Wright, 1997; Gordon & Baucom, 1999) incorporate psychodynamic (Strean, 2000), systemic (Brown, 1991; Moultrop, 1990), and cognitive-behavioral (Spring, 1996) techniques.

Clinicians regard "infidelity" as a secret sexual, romantic, or emotional involvement that violates the commitment to an exclusive relationship. However, population studies have utilized the more restrictive criteria of extramarital sexual intercourse. "Extramarital involvement" is defined herein as encompassing a wide range of behaviors including sexual intimacies without intercourse and extramarital emotional involvement. Classification schemes are distinguished by either systemic emphasis on marital aspects, such as conflict avoidance (Brown, 1991); individualistic emphasis on personal aspects, such as "temporary insanity" (Pittman, 1989); or emphasis on type of extramarital involvement, such as one-night stands or prolonged love affairs (Subotnik & Harris, 1999). My own classification scheme defines three types of involvement by levels of sexual and emotional involvement: (1) "Primarily sexual" involvement is any sexual intimacy (from kissing to sexual intercourse) that occurs without a meaningful emotional involvement; (2) "primarily emotional" involvement is a moderate to deep emotional attachment with negligible physical intimacy; and (3) "combined-type" involvement is extramarital intercourse accompanied by a deep emotional attachment (Glass & Wright, 1985; Thompson, 1984a).

Extramarital emotional involvement differs from platonic friendship because it entails (1) emotional intimacy, (2) secrecy, and (3) sexual chemistry (Glass & Wright, 1997). Internet affairs are a prototype for extramarital emotional involvement: (1) Emotional intimacy is greater than in the marriage; (2) e-mail correspondence and private chat room discussions are kept secret; and (3) sexually arousing fantasies and titillating conversations are shared. The marital disruption caused by Internet infidelity (Schneider, 2000; Shaw, 1997) exemplifies how emotionally intense a relationship can become without actual physical contact.

Clinical assumptions about extramarital involvement vary according to gender, personal experience, and theoretical orientation. There is lack of consensus among "infidelity experts" about the role of gender, how to handle secret affairs, how much disclosure is appropriate, and whether to monitor the involved partner for further signs of betrayal (Nelson, 2000). My treatment approach is based on both empirical research and clinical experience. Tom Wright and I have conducted research on gender differences in extramarital attitudes, types of extramarital involvement, and behaviors and marital satisfaction in two nonclinical samples (Glass & Wright, 1977, 1985, 1992). I have also analyzed data from 316 clinical couples treated throughout a 15-year period (Glass, in preparation).

This chapter presents an interpersonal trauma model for treating infidelity, which is an extension of the individual trauma recovery literature. Disclosure of infidelity evokes a traumatic reaction in the betrayed partner, because of the basic assumptions about the committed relationship that are shattered. Janoff-Bulman (1992) has described shattered assumptions about safety within the world in traumatized victims of violent crimes and natural disasters. The betrayal of infidelity creates a parallel loss of innocence in a relationship that was considered loving and safe. Deception and lying shatter the interpersonal assumptions of honesty and trustworthiness.

PATTERNS OF AND ATTITUDES TOWARD INFIDELITY

Clinicians regard individual and relational pathology as explanations for extramarital involvement, but they seldom consider the influence of attitudes and social context. Although studies have found that marital satisfaction is lower in involved individuals (especially women in combined-type affairs), many involved individuals describe their marriages as happy (especially men in primarily sexual affairs). In a nonclinical sample, 56% of the men and 34% of the women who had extramarital intercourse reported that their marriages were happy (Glass & Wright, 1985).

Many clinicians perceive that infidelity signifies an unhappy marriage (Brown, 1991; Harvey, 1995), and some even subscribe to the "prevention myth"—namely, that meeting a partner's needs can "affair-proof" a marriage (Harley, 1986; Staheli, 1998). In my therapist survey, women were less likely than men to agree that "extramarital involvement occurs in happy marriages and is not necessarily a symptom of a distressed relationship" (47% vs. 61%). Few of the clinicians I surveyed agreed with Myers and Leggitt's (1972) observation that infidelity not only occurs in happy marriages but can be relationship-enhancing.

Relationship distress in couples being treated for infidelity may have been precipitated by the disclosure. Separated and divorced individuals in one study believed that marital problems caused their own affairs but were the result of their partners' affairs (Spanier & Margolis, 1983). Dysfunctional interactions (such as conflict avoidance, power struggles, and fear of intimacy) have been associated with extramarital involvement, but these patterns may be just as prevalent among couples who have remained faithful.

Women's affairs are predicted more by unmet relationship needs, and men's affairs are predicted more by individualistic attitudes. Women justify their extramarital relationships most often for love, next most often for emotional intimacy, and least often for sex (Glass & Wright, 1992). One of the most robust gender differences in a meta-analysis by Oliver and Hyde (1993) was men's belief in casual sex. Therefore, it is not surprising that men endorse sexual justifications more than do women.

Clinicians and researchers observe different phenomena. Clinicians witness the devastation caused by the disclosure of infidelity, but they are not familiar with numerous relationships where secret infidelity has a negligible impact. Divorce is less likely when extramarital involvement is undisclosed (Glass, in preparation; Lawson, 1988). Systems-oriented therapists assert that betrayed partners are codependent and collude by denying the existence of an infidelity (Edell, 1995; Weiner & DiMele, 1998). However, affairs are rarely detected when the involved partner is a skilled liar or compartmentalizes the extramarital involvement and remains unchanged at home (Glass & Wright, 1997; Hunt, 1974; Lawson, 1988; Lusterman, 1998). Stiff, Kim, and Ramesh (1992) found that a truth bias in intimate relationships influences individuals to perceive their partners as honest and truthful. Thus suspiciousness is apt to be allayed by persuasive denials or explanations from a loving partner.

Men's sexual liaisons are often undetected and do not come to the attention of therapists until some catastrophic event surfaces (e.g., a sexually transmitted disease or a cell phone bill). However, involved men in conjoint marital therapy are more likely to be struggling with the deep emotional attachment and threat of a combined-type involvement. Extramarital intercourse with minimal emotional involvement was reported by 44% of men in my nonclinical samples, compared with 26% in my clinical sample (Glass, in preparation).

Women engaging in extramarital intercourse are more likely than men to be in love with their extramarital partners (Glass & Wright, 1985). Women are also more likely to engage in combined-type affairs that are associated with marital dissatisfaction and divorce. These women are seen more often in individual therapy than in conjoint therapy, because they have already detached emotionally from their marriages. In conjoint therapy, they may appear resistant to working on their marriages and unwilling to discuss their affairs.

Men and women have different codes regarding extramarital involvement. The male code is more permissive about sexual involvement, and the female code is more permissive about emotional involvement. A related finding is that husbands are more jealous of wives' sexual involvement, and wives are more jealous of husbands' emotional involvement (Buss, 1994; Francis, 1977). Therefore, men are more likely to deny emotional involvement, and women are more likely to deny sexual involvement.

Although therapists observe emotional disturbance and personality disorders in unfaithful partners, contrasting views are offered of extramarital involvement as "healthy adultery" (Ellis, 1969) or as personal growth (Myers & Leggitt, 1972; Thompson, 1984b). Extramarital sex has been associated with increased depression among involved individuals in couple therapy (Beach, Jouriles, & O'Leary, 1985). Studies focusing on nonrelational extramarital sex have found evidence for entitlement and interpersonal exploitativeness (Hurlbert, Apt, Gasar, Wilson, & Murphy, 1994), and sexual narcissism (Wryobeck & Wiederman, 1999). Low conscientiousness, high narcissism, and impulsiveness were linked to susceptibility for infidelity during the first year of marriage (Buss & Shackelford, 1997).

Promiscuous extramarital sexuality can represent either entitlement or addiction (Glass, 2000). Addiction to sex, love, or romance is characterized by a compulsive drive toward excitement that temporarily relieves feelings of emptiness or anxiety. A history of child or adolescent sexual abuse is often observed in individuals with sexual addiction. Love and romance addicts seek the passion and idealization of new relationships. In contrast, entitlement is noncompulsive. The person who feels entitled to extramarital sex takes advantage of opportunities for it but is not driven to seek opportunities. Individuals with avoidant attachment styles are more likely to pursue one-night stands and sex without love than are individuals with a secure attachment style (Hazan, Zeifman, & Middleton, 1994).

A strong normative influence for both men and women is the perception of peers engaging in extramarital relationships (Atwater, 1982; Buunk, 1980; Thompson, 1984a), independent of marital dissatisfaction (Prins, Buunk, & VanYperen,

1993). Attitudes and values derived from the sociocultural context are more predictive of male extramarital involvement (Glass & Wright, 1992). Cross-cultural studies have found that a double standard exists in which extramarital sex is condoned in men and condemned in women (Penn, Hernandez, & Bermudez, 1997).

ASSESSMENT

Assessing the meaning and the impact of an extramarital involvement begins at intake on the telephone and continues throughout treatment. It is important to determine whether the couple is in crisis because the infidelity was just discovered, or whether infidelity is an unresolved chronic issue. The identity of the caller can indicate the relative commitment of the partners; that is, the involved spouse who calls in a frantic attempt to save the marriage after the disclosure will be more receptive to treatment than one who is dragged in by the betrayed partner. Callers who request individual therapy instead of couple therapy are often ambivalent about their commitment to their marriages and they do not want to discuss their extramarital relationships in front of their spouses.

The level of chaos and despair should be assessed before a therapist agrees to see a couple. A therapist whose schedule is already crowded should consider referring the couple to a colleague, because crisis phone calls and emergency sessions can be the norm at the beginning. The most important questions to ask are whether the affair is over and whether the affair partner is still on the scene. Ascertaining how and when the disclosure occurred gives a sense of both the immediacy of the situation and the extent of the deception.

Each partner is mailed self-report questionnaires prior to the first session to obtain information that is not easily obtained in conjoint sessions (Glass & Wright, 1988). Incomplete forms may indicate lack of commitment or concerns about confidentiality. Items and scales are included that measure satisfaction with love, sex, and emotional intimacy (Glass, 1998a); commitment (Spanier, 1976); caring (Stuart, 1983); overall marital adjustment (Locke & Wallace, 1959); equity in the marriage and the affair (Wright & Glass, 1988); extramarital justification attitudes; and extramarital sexual and emotional involvement (Glass & Wright, 1992). Resources that improve the prognosis are a recent history of loving feelings and satisfying sex, as well as a strong commitment to work on the relationship.

Depression and anxiety inventories are also important assessment tools, because adjustment disorders with anxiety, depression, or mixed emotional features are frequently present. Suicidal ideation is common in both spouses, and homicidal fantasies of revenge by the betrayed spouse toward the affair partner may also need to be monitored. An absence of self-reported symptoms may indicate a numbing response rather than a stable mood. Assessing posttraumatic symptoms in the betrayed partner is reassuring to both partners, because it gives a framework for the intensity and craziness they are experiencing. Although the actual symptoms may meet the criteria for posttraumatic stress disorder (PTSD), a formal DSM-IV diagnosis of PTSD (American Psychiatric Association, 1994) can only be made when a stressor is life-threatening.

Confidentiality is maintained regarding the responses to the questionnaires. However, conjoint therapy is not undertaken unless extramarital involvement that is unknown to the noninvolved partner is either terminated or revealed. Therefore, the partners are seen separately when the forms indicate a secret affair, and the involved partner is advised that couple therapy cannot proceed unless he/she either ends the affair or discloses it to the naive partner. Agreement to suspend the affair is monitored by individual sessions, particularly when there are indications that the secret affair has not stopped. Signs of continuing infidelity are resistance to caring behaviors and negative attributions about the marital partner that appear to be frozen and unyielding. In order to avoid creating a hidden agenda that could be harmful, the involved partner who refuses to "stop *or* share" is advised to state at the end of the intake session that he/she not comfortable with conjoint therapy and does not want to return.

The meaning of the infidelity will be a continuing issue with many levels of inquiry throughout the therapy. The initial information identifies "who," "what," "where," and "when"; interpretations about "why" are discouraged at this early stage. The therapist assists in the betrayed partner's need to learn the degree of sexual and emotional involvement. However, the involved partner is likely to minimize the frequency of encounters, as well as the duration and depth of the relationship. Recovery of trust is impaired by staggered disclosure of significant facts, such as how many partners there have been and when the extramarital involvement began (Schneider, Corley, & Irons, 1998). Therefore, the therapist should encourage honesty about the extent of extramarital involvement from the beginning, although discussion of explicit details should be deferred until a later stage of treatment.

Previous infidelities that were unsuspected do not need to be revealed unless the presenting problem is extramarital involvement. On the other hand, infidelity which represents a repetitive pattern of behavior must be explored through sexual and social histories to differentiate addiction from culturally sanctioned infidelity. When the presenting problem is cybersex or online infidelity, the possibility of Internet addiction should also be considered.

The individual, relational, and contextual influences that created the vulnerability for infidelity are assessed throughout the course of treatment, with a particular emphasis during the middle stage. The marital relationship is assessed through the lens of the entire marital lifeline (from courtship to the present) and through direct observation of interactional patterns. The couple's current distress may be either an exacerbation of preexisting problems or a reaction to extramarital involvement, so that assessing the recent history clarifies the nature of the couple's relationship before and during the affair. The involved partner may rewrite marital history with a negative slant in order to justify his/her actions, whereas the betrayed partner may appear to idealize the marital relationship. These black-and-white views will be transformed as the spouses work through the aftermath of the disclosure.

Situational events in the preceding 2-year period should be explored. Professional achievement and material success can change the balance of power and equity in a marriage. Serious illnesses, personal losses, or work difficulties can incite a need to escape stressful and depressing reminders. Individual styles of coping with life-altering events can cause spouses to feel more separate and more open to support from others.

Resources in the couple are not only important to assess, but important to present as positive feedback. Discussing the courtship history in the initial phase of treatment can reestablish a positive bond of shared memories. Partners who are able to enumerate caring behaviors (Stuart, 1983) on the intake forms have a reservoir of good will that is missing in partners who are unable to list any caring behaviors.

By the end of the first session, the conjoint therapy should be openly labeled as "marital," "reconciliation," "separation," or "ambivalence" therapy. "Marital" therapy is for couples who are living together and are committed to reconstructing their relationship, and "reconciliation" therapy

is for separated couples whose stated goal is to reestablish their marriage. "Separation" therapy is for couples who want to obtain closure about the breakdown of their relationship either before or after they separate. "Ambivalence" therapy is for a couple where one or both partners cannot decide whether they want to stay or leave.

The therapist and the betrayed partner may believe that the goal is to rebuild the marriage, whereas the involved partner's hidden agenda for therapy may be to separate after proving that the relationship cannot work and providing the rejected spouse with a support system. Once the therapist and couple clarify that one partner wants separation therapy, the other partner may refuse to participate in any further treatment. Confidentiality in ambivalence and separation therapies must be clarified, because the boundaries and goals will be different than in marital and reconciliation therapies.

GOAL SETTING

Almost every couple entering therapy has some doubts about whether the relationship can survive infidelity, so a common goal is to decide whether to stay married or separate. Since the commitment to work on the relationship varies greatly, resolving ambivalence can be either a short-term or long-term goal. Some individuals know after one or two sessions that they do not want to stay married. Betrayed partners may decide to terminate their marriages if they do not hear any remorse. Some involved partners appear to resolve their ambivalence when they suddenly wake up from a prolonged trance state and spontaneously declare their intent to end their affairs and rebuild their marriages. Others require many months of individual and conjoint sessions to "get off the fence."

An immediate goal is to provide safety within the therapy for both spouses to discuss issues and express feelings while rage and despair are contained. For couples who are rebuilding, creating safety in the marriage is impossible until the extramarital relationship has stopped. Understanding the meaning of the infidelity is another goal—regardless of whether the contract is for reconciliation therapy or separation therapy. Committing to conjoint therapy is not equivalent to a commitment to remain in the relationship. For separating couples, a sense of closure allows them to part with less hostility and fewer unresolved issues so they can co-parent with a united front.

Creating good will and hope is another early goal. Couples are advised that they have to "make some deposits in their relationship account," because the hard work of talking about the extramarital involvement will be painful. Encouraging caring behaviors is done throughout the therapy, but it is particularly useful at the beginning when the relationship account is depleted. Hope is also created through a description of the treatment process and reassurances about how many couples end up with stronger, more intimate relationships than before.

The long-term goals of recovering from the trauma and rebuilding trust are accomplished throughout treatment—especially by discussing the story of the extramarital involvement. Initially, the involved partner is reluctant to share the story, and the betrayed partner is relentless and accusatory. Therefore, the therapist's goal is to develop a process for compassionate communication.

THE STRUCTURE OF THE THERAPY PROCESS

Couples who initiate therapy immediately after the disclosure of infidelity are usually in crisis and may require sessions twice a week until affect is stabilized and safety is established. Urgent phone calls are received as information about the extramarital involvement is uncovered. The number of total sessions is greater when the unfaithful partner is the husband, because unfaithful wives are more likely to end therapy and leave their marriages (Glass, in preparation).

Although it is preferable to share as much information as possible in conjoint sessions, individual sessions provide support that members of a fractured couple are unable to give each other in the early stage. The betrayed partner cannot bear to witness the grief of the involved partner over the loss of the affair partner. The involved partner cannot bear the rage and wounded looks of the betrayed partner. Individual sessions validate feelings and provide private coaching on how to repair the relationship. Individual sessions should not be used to obtain secret information that cannot be shared in conjoint sessions, unless confidentiality has been provided for individuals in ambivalence or separation therapy.

Cotherapy is an extremely useful approach to avoid replicating the destructive coalitions of an extramarital triangle. Cotherapy allows each partner to create an alliance with a therapist who supports that partner during sessions with the other spouse and that spouse's therapist. I have offered a cotherapy team approach for 20 years, and many couples have deliberately chosen this treatment model to offset potential gender bias. My cotherapist and I make it clear that we will have no secrets from each other when doing marital or reconciliation therapy, because we do not want to do "collusion therapy" (Glass & Wright, 1997). In ambivalence or separation therapy, confidentiality is negotiated. However, we often suspend conjoint sessions during a period when we have constructed a wall of confidentiality between us.

We each treat couples alone when cotherapy is not feasible because of cost, scheduling, or other constraints. Many therapists find it more stressful to work alone with these severely distressed couples, and proceed at a slower pace because they cannot be as confrontational without another therapist to provide balance. Therapists working alone must be even more aware of their clinical biases, in order to maintain objectivity and provide an evenhanded approach.

In this approach, individual psychotherapy with outside therapists is discouraged, and exploration of individual issues in conjoint sessions to provide insight and intimacy within the couple is preferred. Unfortunate experiences often occur in which ambivalence therapy conducted by individual therapists undermines the goals of couple therapy. An individual therapist treating the unfaithful partner may be "the extramarital therapist" who hears about the extramarital involvement while the marital therapist is denied similar access to ongoing information about the infidelity. Moreover, the betrayed partner may receive messages in individual therapy that are at odds with the goals of marital therapy (e.g., "Anyone who remains with a philandering partner must be weak and codependent"). A working model requires continual collaboration between treating therapists with complete sharing of clinical information. Furthermore, boundaries must be clarified, so that the individual therapist addresses individual issues such as an underlying depression or family-of-origin issues.

Weekly and biweekly sessions are often necessary during the first months of resolving ambivalence and coping with posttraumatic symptoms. The period of exploration that follows may stretch out over many months and even years. New crises and setbacks may require additional sessions along the way. Maintenance and booster sessions are scheduled over longer intervals after recovery and healing are completed. Anniversary events associated with the infidelity will trigger flashbacks, and couples need support to deal with the long-term reminders. Although couples say they will return to therapy if they begin to slide back into unhealthy patterns, the reality is that they seldom return unless a crisis occurs. Therefore, it is often advisable to continue treatment for at least 2 years, in order to address lapses and manage situational stressors while relationship bonds remain intact.

THE ROLE OF THE THERAPIST

Therapists need to assume an active role when dealing with the explosive aftermath of infidelity. In the early stage of treatment, the major source of emotional support will come from the therapist, because both partners are usually too depleted and self-focused to provide empathic concern for each other's distress. A working alliance is fostered by validating the intensity of feelings while assisting them to express their feelings with some constraint and semblance of consideration and respect. Spouses who talk to each other through the therapist are encouraged to communicate directly through guided "speaker–listener" activities (Notarius & Markman, 1993), although expressions of rage continue to be filtered through the therapist. The role of the therapist as healer is gradually transferred back to the rebuilding couple, whereas the therapist continues as the primary healer for a longer period in an ambivalent or separating couple.

The therapeutic alliance is enhanced when the spouses perceive the therapist as a purveyor of knowledge and realistic expectations. Since progress is marked with recurring crises and setbacks, the therapist predicts what the pathway to recovery will look like and guides couples back on that pathway when they get off course. Providing normative education and cognitive restructuring is also essential to correct faulty perceptions and inappropriate attributions. The therapist educates the couple about "assumed similarity" errors (i.e., the spouses' projections of their own motives onto each other). The aspiration to restore the relationship that existed before the infidelity is unrealistic because of the loss of innocence and fractured trust. However, the therapist can align with the couple in using this crisis to create a stronger and more intimate relationship.

One significant marker of progress is achieved when the couple productively handles difficult issues and discusses details about the extramarital involvement outside of therapy. It can take months of therapist modeling and coaching before an empathic process occurs at home. It is noteworthy when a betrayed wife says that her husband disclosed some very explicit information she sought that was too personal to discuss in therapy. The end of treatment is near when intimacies are more easily shared within the couple's private relationship than within the couple therapy.

It is inappropriate for the therapist to disclose information about any personal experience with infidelity that he/she may have had. However, therapists can share less intimate stories that teach coping strategies, illustrate relationship skills, or serve as examples of gender differences. Metaphors and case examples that create hope are valuable tools, but should be utilized without any identifying information that would compromise or threaten confidentiality.

Therapists dealing with the trauma of infidelity must withstand intense expressions of rage and despair. The obsessive rumination, hypervigilance, and intrusive thoughts of the betrayed partner should be accepted as posttraumatic reactions, rather than perceived as pathological or annoying. The slow journey to recovery is usually stormy and tedious, so brief therapy is not the norm; therefore, patience is a therapeutic necessity. On the other hand, tolerance for ambivalence and continuing deception at the beginning of treatment should not continue indefinitely. The therapist needs to guard against working harder than the couple to save the marriage. At some point in the treatment, the therapist should confront lack of progress and possible covert acceptance of a stable triangle.

Clinical assumptions about extramarital involvement have a profound impact. Unfortunately, the clinical literature tends to perpetuate clinical biases, so therapists should acquaint themselves with research findings. Preexisting relationship problems should be addressed without blaming the betrayed partner for the involved partner's decision to have an extramarital relationship. It is not uncommon for a therapist to blame the injured partner for the extramarital involvement; indeed, Weil (1993) has asserted that if deceived partners don't drive unfaithful partners to adultery, "they usually give him/her permission to go there—and even carfare" (p. 87).

Countertransference resulting from unresolved trust issues can result in identification, projection, and reaction formations. For example, a male therapist with extramarital sexual experience may support a husband's stance that his wife is overreacting to a "meaningless" one-night stand; in contrast, a female therapist who has been betrayed may project her own unresolved anger onto an unfaithful husband. Kaslow (1993) observed contrasting reactions, such as vicarious excitement, emasculation, and censure, by supervisees toward the "adulterer." Silverstein (1998) differentiates between "objective" countertransference, which is a common response toward infidelity, and "subjective" countertransference, which is an idiosyncratic response.

Therapist neutrality may be not only impossible, but undesirable. Personal values and experiences regarding extramarital involvement are deeply felt and cannot be ignored. Therefore, therapists need to be aware of clinical assumptions derived from gender roles, personal experience, and theoretical orientation in order to maintain a balanced perspective and be open to each couple's unique story. An appropriate stance to take with a couple is that it is usually the therapist's task to help the spouses rebuild the marriage, but that the therapist will help them separate if that is the desired or inevitable outcome.

TECHNIQUES OF COUPLE THERAPY FOR EXTRAMARITAL TRAUMA

The treatment model presented herein is an integrative trauma-based model for reconstructing marriages after the disclosure of infidelity. The initial stage of extramarital trauma recovery creates safety and hope, validates and manages traumatic symptoms of emotional hyperarousal, and fosters interpersonal caring. The middle stage focuses on the story of the affair, which is essential for the cognitive stage of trauma recovery. The final stage of healing is to master the meaning of the infidelity within the context of the individuals, the marriage, and the sociocultural influences. Establishing safety is the central task of the first stage of recovery in Herman's (1992) individual trauma model.

The magnitude of the traumatic reaction depends on the extent of shattered assumptions, the level of deception, and preexisting psychological vulnerabilities in the betrayed partner. Even spouses in "open" marriages are traumatized when explicit restrictions regarding secrecy or emotional involvement are violated. Although Lusterman (1992) connects posttraumatic stress reactions with "protracted infidelity," a one-night stand can be extremely traumatic if the unfaithful partner was formerly perceived as a morally righteous individual.

Establishing Safety and Hope

Herman (1992) believes that in addition to the therapist's avoidance of traumatic material, a common treatment error is premature engagement in exploratory work without establishing safety and obtaining a sufficient therapeutic alliance. Safety and stability are enhanced by getting a verbal contract for a specific number of conjoint sessions. The couple feels more secure when the commitment to therapy and the marriage does not hang on each spouse's hour-by-hour mood swings. It is preferable to get an initial commitment for 12 sessions, but 6 weeks may be more feasible when there is marked ambivalence and a fragile commitment.

Safety and trust are predicated on whether the involved partner is willing to "stop AND share." To "stop" means that all verbal and physical intimacy with the affair partner is terminated. To "share" means to volunteer any ongoing or unavoidable encounters with the affair partner. Information that is obtained by interrogation or detective work erodes trust. An extramarital triangle builds "walls" of secrecy and lying in the marriage and "windows" of emotional intimacy in the affair. These "walls and windows" must be reversed, to place the betrayed spouse on the inside and the affair partner on the outside (Glass & Wright, 1997). Continuing contact at the workplace requires delineating firm boundaries. Continuing deception deepens the traumatization and prolongs the period of healing. Recovery does not begin until the extramarital relationship is no longer a threat.

Knowledge builds safety and structure by creating realistic expectations about setbacks and marking the guideposts for recovery. Traumatic reactions are validated by introducing the symptom list of PTSD (American Psychiatric Association, 1994) and exploring the shattered assumptions. Information about the normality of flashbacks, obsessive rumination, and hypervigilance is reassuring to both spouses. Recommending mass market books (e.g., Lusterman, 1998; Pittman, 1989; Spring, 1996; Subotnik & Harris, 1999) and distributing articles about infidelity (e.g., Glass, 1998b) provides information and enhances hope about surviving infidelity.

Fostering Caring and Good Will

Promoting positivity and giving feedback about relationship resources can combat hopelessness.

Discussing their courtship recapitulates earlier bonding through shared memories, while at the same time the therapist simultaneously assesses what perceptions and expectations formed the core of their relationship. Solution-oriented questions (Weiner-Davis, 1992) in the first or second session direct them to recount examples of each of the partners' productive interactions in the past and present. The "miracle question" focuses them on a future together: "If you woke up tomorrow morning and a miracle had occurred, what would your relationship look like?"

Fostering caring behaviors combats inevitable comparisons between the mutual admiration in the affair and the mutual disillusionment in the marriage. The positive mirroring in the affair is like a vanity mirror that illuminates with a rosy glow, whereas the tarnished image in the marriage is like a makeup mirror that magnifies flaws. Caring behaviors foster positive mirroring and opportunities for reciprocal appreciation. Caring assignments make both partners responsible for change.

"Caring checkups" are used as early as the first or second session to shift affect after an emotionally charged session. Each partner is asked, "What caring did you receive during the past week?" Stuart's (1983) Caring Behaviors form is used to elicit discussions about what pleases each partner about the other, what each desires more of, and what each believes the other desires. Individual sessions can be used to suggest "bull's-eye" caring without creating expectations for change in conjoint sessions that are resisted by passive–aggressive partners.

Resistance to demonstrating caring or expressing appreciation can connote ambivalence or a hidden agenda to prove the marriage cannot succeed. Partners who are too depleted or disenchanted to respond to the idea of "caring" can be encouraged to work on "consideration" and "respect." Partners who are hostile and angry can be advised to "treat each other as nicely this week as you would treat a stranger."

Sometimes openly ambivalent partners deliberately restrain spontaneous feelings of affection, to guard against communicating greater devotion than they feel. In order to capitalize on these fleeting affectionate feelings, the therapist clarifies that any display of affection should be interpreted only as a momentary expression of good will. Another example of resistance is waiting for loving feelings before they are willing to act in loving ways. Since behavior can precede feelings, they are directed to act "as if" they already feel the way they want to feel. Only through investing time and energy into

the marital relationship will they reexperience their bond. The allure and intensity of an affair are magnified by the investment of time, energy, and caring.

It can actually be empowering for the therapist to be in the dark, so that resistance that indicates continuing extramarital involvement can be confronted in conjoint sessions. Secret information that is obtained in individual sessions creates the risk of colluding in the deception of the betrayed partner. Signs of resistance and deception that are addressed by the therapist in conjoint sessions can loosen a "stuck" marital system.

Relapses in the form of distancing or conflict are common after a particularly pleasurable or loving interaction. Intimacy is associated with increased vulnerability. The involved partner may suddenly experience the sensation of being unfaithful to the affair partner. Emotional or sexual intimacy may trigger a flashback in the betrayed partner to the time of innocent bliss before the infidelity was disclosed. Predicting these setbacks diminishes their impact, and processing the fear of intimacy alleviates the confusion and despair.

Managing Affect and Posttraumatic Symptoms

The therapist validates intense feelings, elicits the underlying meaning of those feelings, and contains destructive impulses. Spouses are advised to deal with painful issues during therapy, while they concentrate at home on rebuilding through positive interactions. They are encouraged to table issues that threaten to get out of control and save them for therapy. Although individual sessions provide an outlet for emotions that cannot be tolerated by distressed partners, the long-term goal is for them to share these feelings with each other. The involved partner grieves over the loss of the affair partner and wonders whether the marriage can ever provide the joy of the affair. The betrayed partner typically grieves for the loss of innocence and trust, rages at the deception, and engages in self-blame.

During the emotional stage of recovery, it may be necessary to alternate between individual and conjoint sessions. A cotherapist makes this aspect of treatment more manageable. Moreover, cotherapy allows for breaking a conjoint session into two individual sessions when intense affect in the conjoint session needs to be contained. Spouses are encouraged to leave stormy messages on the therapists' answering machines rather than storming at each other. Violence and relentless tirades are not acceptable, so the couple is instructed in "time out" and other anger management procedures (Bach & Wyden, 1970; Notarius & Markman, 1993). Suicidal and homicidal ideation in both partners must be monitored until formal assessments indicate that emotions have stabilized. The therapists must do whatever is necessary (including hospitalization) so that suicidal threats are not used as emotional blackmail. Severe anxiety or depressive symptoms, particularly prolonged loss of appetite and sleep disturbance, suggest that medication may be necessary.

Crisis telephone calls are often received when additional material about the affair is unearthed or the affair partner intrudes with hang-up calls or surprise visits at their front door. Intrusions by the affair partner may eventually require changing the home phone number or getting a restraining order. The involved partner is usually unwilling to take these actions in the early stage because of split loyalties. Efforts to protect the affair partner at the expense of the marriage are perceived as part of the ongoing assessment by the therapist. A united front to deal with these intrusions is the goal.

Obsessive rumination by the betrayed spouse about the affair represents the cognitive stage of recovery. Eventually, all of the questions must be answered to the satisfaction of the betrayed partner, because the reality is usually no worse than the betrayed partner's imaginings. Midnight interrogations are common but not necessarily healing. The betrayed partner is directed to write down all of his/her questions and bring them to therapy. These questions are placed in their file for the middle stage of treatment, when the story of the affair will be discussed in greater detail. Complex questions about the meaning of the infidelity should be reserved for this middle stage, after caring, commitment, and a process of compassionate communication have been established. The traumatized individual's need to recapitulate and go over the minute details over and over can test the therapist's patience (Everstine & Everstine, 1993), as well that of the involved partner. Obsessing is likely to continue until the full story has been told.

The betrayed partner's waking and sleeping periods are disturbed by intrusive thoughts and dreams about the lies, the moment of disclosure, and sexual images of the affair. The troubled spouse is instructed to schedule structured worry times every day to obsess, to record thoughts and feelings in a journal, and to temporarily bury the mental tapes and give him-herself a vacation from obsessing. Imagery rehearsals provide practice in "switching the tape to another channel." Eye movement desensitization and reprocessing (EMDR) may alleviate traumatic images in the betrayed partner (Shapiro, 1995).

Flashbacks may be cued by anniversary events, songs about "cheating," and TV talk shows. The couple is warned that flashbacks occur for a prolonged period, which can extend into years. The intensity of a flashback may cause spouses to feel they are "back to square one," so they are reassured to hear that improvement is marked first by a decrease in flashback frequency, then by a shorter duration, and last by a reduced intensity. Improving communication skills is an essential component of flashback training (Glass & Wright, 1997). The betrayed partner practices expressing pain without attacking, and the involved partner practices empathic listening. Compassionate communication leads to a healing process.

Hypervigilance is characterized by suspiciousness, jealousy, and searching for clues of further betrayal. Hypervigilance associated with loss of safety typically lessens as security and trust increase. Although the instincts of the betrayed spouse are often accurate signals of further deception, panic reactions are also set off by harmless activities that provided a cover for infidelity. For example, a betrayed husband was anxious when his wife went to the health club that had served as an excuse to meet her lover. The inquisitions after she returned from the gym were eroding their relationship, so he was instructed to "be a detective—not an inquisitor," and she was told that it could be trust-building for him to check her assertion out. When he made a surprise visit to the gym, finding her on the treadmill was a great relief. Sometimes a couple is advised to establish a fund to hire a detective at the will of the betrayed partner; this strategy is necessary only when the deception has been overwhelming. A reasonable period of safety should eliminate the necessity for this type of surveillance.

Telling the Story of the Affair

Recalling the story of the traumatic event is an essential stage of recovery. Betrayed partners have trouble accepting stories that differ from what they either know or believe to be true. Sometimes a betrayed partner's story is a projection about infidelity based on gender or personal experience. "Assumed similarity" errors occur when a betrayed wife cannot believe that her husband did not love the affair partner, or a betrayed husband cannot believe that his wife did not have sexual intercourse with the affair partner. The final story must be a co-construction of both partners, and it must account for all of the secrets, the unanswered questions, and the contrasting interpretations and attributions.

Disclosure content is used to develop a co-constructive process. The early stage of truth seeking is an adversarial process, like that of a district attorney and a criminal. Truth seeking gradually shifts to a neutral process of information seeking, such as that between a journalist and an interviewee. An empathic process in the final stage has mutual understanding as the goal, rather than explicit facts and details.

It is preferable to delay the detailed story of the affair until the relationship has stabilized. However, a sketch of the affair must be shared early in treatment, because the betrayed partner's agitation can only be relieved by hearing basic information about the infidelity. In cases of sexual addiction staggered disclosure about the extent of extramarital involvement, results in a poorer recovery and lower trust building (Schneider et al., 1998). Nevertheless, disclosure of explicit sexual details that evoke painful images should be delayed; the desire to hear them sometimes recedes when the relationship becomes more secure.

During the truth-seeking stage, the therapist takes an active role and asks some basic questions about the infidelity. The betrayed partner is directed not to interrupt, interpret, or contradict while the therapist elicits information with a calm, nonjudgmental approach. The betrayed partner is offered index cards to record his/her comments while pretending to sit behind a one-way mirror. The involved partner may stonewall, respond tersely, or divert the conversation to other topics. Encouraging openness in the involved partner is balanced with encouraging inhibition in the betrayed partner.

The couple should be warned during the information-seeking stage that earlier lies are likely to be unearthed as the truth is revealed. Discussing the details satiates the obsession of the betrayed partner, demystifies the romantic idealization of the involved partner, and hinders further infidelity by exposing the modus operandi. The therapist controls negative fallout by doing the "dirty work" first, conducting the exploration second, and restoring calm in the final third of the session (Herman, 1992).

The betrayed partner will often focus on where the involved spouse and the affair partner went, what gifts were exchanged, whether they planned for a future together, and the extent of emotional and sexual intimacy. The involved partner (and often the therapist) is usually opposed to discussing these details, so the betrayed partner needs to express appreciation and reinforce the idea that hearing the truth is painful but healing.

The therapist initiates discussions directed toward the meaning of the infidelity. The cognitions that reflect values and vulnerabilities are explored by asking how the involved partner gave him-/herself permission to cross various thresholds into infidelity. Contrasting attributions through the eyes of each spouse about the affair partner (as "saint" vs. "sinner") must be integrated into a realistic portrayal. Extramarital relationships offer an opportunity to experience new roles, so the involved partner is asked, "What did you like about yourself in the affair that can be brought back to the marriage?"

Understanding the Vulnerabilities

Mastery of meaning is enhanced by understanding the context that created vulnerabilities for an extramarital involvement. Therapists need to explore in depth the multidimensional predictors associated with marital, individual, and sociocultural influences. Unfortunately, many therapists tend to look for explanations that reflect a particular theoretical orientation. Recognizing multiple determinants and strengthening all of the areas of vulnerability are essential elements for diminishing relapse potential. Transgenerational patterns of infidelity, occupational and social norms, and cultural double standards must all be accounted for (Glass, 2000).

Psychodynamically oriented clinicians may focus on individual pathology but overlook personal attitudes and values. Individual aspects include personality disorders such as narcissism, mood disorders such as depression, and psychosexual disorders in which there is splitting of sex and affection. Other individual vulnerabilities include developmental and existential issues, personal crises, and attachment style. Compulsive needs for excitement, romantic love, or admiration create powerful incentives for extramarital involvement, because the romantic projections and positive mirroring provide an escape from depression and feelings of emptiness. In multiple involvements, the current episode must be addressed as a pattern of behavior to be disclosed and understood.

Systemically oriented therapists, who perceive infidelity as a symptom of relationship dysfunction, may minimize the role of individual issues and contextual influences. Although marital dissatisfaction contributes to extramarital involvement, personal and moral values act as deterrents in couples that remain unhappy but faithful. The therapist must explore the marital problems that have created vulnerability without justifying the decision to engage in an extramarital relationship.

Dysfunctional patterns of pursuing–distancing, nagging–procrastinating, or blaming–placating must be addressed. Child-centered couples need to become more couple-centered by setting aside "date nights" or other private time. Since there is greater reciprocity in an affair than in a marriage (Glass & Wright, 1988, 1997), an overbenefited spouse is guided to invest more in the marriage, and an underbenefited spouse is guided to diminish acts of overfunctioning.

Mastery of Meaning and Successful Termination

The mastery stage of empowerment establishes the meaning of the affair and incorporates the lessons learned into a stronger marriage. The spouses recognize vulnerabilities and share responsibility for enhancing their relationship. Their communication process is characterized by mutual empathy and understanding. They have restructured the "walls and windows" to erect a united front with children, in-laws, and any others who could threaten the primacy of their relationship. The positive growth and new roles that were experienced in the affair are integrated into the marital relationship. They have clarified and shared values regarding commitment and monogamy. Couples are encouraged to develops rituals of forgiveness and recommitment as a final step in the process of healing and recovery.

Failure to Heal

Delayed healing results from unresolved issues such as unanswered questions, uncertain loyalty, or individualistic issues. A betrayed partner who remains suspicious and anxious may be tuned in to cues of ongoing deception or ambivalence in the involved partner. Pathological jealousy is diagnosed within the context of premorbid suspiciousness and possessiveness. An involved partner who remains unwilling to disclose details about the extramarital involvement may be devoted to the affair partner or hiding a pattern of extramarital sex. Further-more, unfinished business must be completed (e.g., getting rid of gifts, or burning love letters after sharing the contents). A common request is for the involved partner to write a final letter to the affair partner, which makes it clear that the decision to stay in the marriage is based on love—not duty.

On the other hand, a betrayed partner who holds on to pain and suffering despite having gone through all of the essential stages of recovery may be mired in a state of "accusatory suffering" (Seagull & Seagull, 1991). The traumatized individual who fails to heal may fear that letting go of his/her misery would diminish the significance of the betrayal and exonerate the perpetrator from blame. Exploring the childhood history of the unremittingly wounded partner may reveal infidelities by parental figures or sexual molestations by trusted adults. The therapist takes an active role and asks, "What else will it take for you to heal? How many 'glass mountains' must your partner climb before you can forgive?" Medication can be a useful adjunct when failure to heal is associated with depressive and obsessional disorders.

Clinical Errors

Therapy for extramarital trauma feels like walking a clinical tightrope, because most clinical errors result from a failure to maintain balance. Expressing affect must be balanced with containing affect. Understanding the shattered assumptions of the betrayed partner must be balanced by understanding the dreams and disillusionments of the unfaithful partner. Discussing the explicit details of the affair cannot be done too early or too late. The gender differences described in the research literature on extramarital involvement must be accounted for, but the uniqueness of each individual may contradict traditional gender roles. Therapists should not assume that the marriage is at fault, but they also should not accept statements saying that there are no problems in the marriage which could have caused an extramarital involvement without further assessment.

Perhaps the most serious clinical error is giving up on a couple too soon. Couples that have had fewer than 10 sessions appear to be more likely to separate (Glass, in press). It takes many months and even years for the healing process to be completed. A bad termination is often a premature termination. After a few sessions, the involved partner has seen the error of his/her ways, has confessed the transgressions, and is ready to stop therapy. The betrayed partner colludes with this "flight into health." However, this process of denial and superficiality possibly characterizes the interactional style of this couple. Bad terminations also occur when one of the partners refuses to continue the therapeutic process without resolving the unfinished business of the other. The worst type of termination occurs when ambivalence is unresolved, and the extramarital triangle continues as a source of pain and mistrust.

CLINICAL CONTROVERSIES AND MECHANISMS OF CHANGE

Change is not a linear progression, but a series of steps forward and backward on an upward slope. Each setback generates insight about dysfunctional patterns and lays the groundwork for subsequent therapeutic interventions. For example, a particularly intense "interrogator–criminal" interaction during the truth-seeking stage may reflect a preexisting pattern of pursuer–distancer. The therapist has an opportunity to interrupt destructive processes as they occur and to channel the partners' energy into more productive interactions. Skills are shaped as the need presents itself for flashback training, empathic listening, or "bull's-eye" caring.

Staying together is not necessarily a sign of successful treatment, nor is separation necessarily a sign of failure. After optimizing their relationship potential, couples may realize that they do not have shared values. A philandering spouse whose sexual addiction is ego-dystonic may be more capable of monogamy than an individual whose sense of entitlement is ego-syntonic. Successful treatment develops insight about the individual, relational, and contextual elements that created the vulnerability for extramarital involvement. A successful outcome is less likely for individuals who are unable to empathize with their partners' pain. Although attitudes and behaviors can change, character defects are unlikely to change.

Predictors of separation at the time of termination from therapy have been identified as follows (Glass, in preparation): (1) There is a failure to end extramarital involvement; (2) there is combined-type involvement, with a deep emotional attachment and extramarital intercourse; (3) both partners are involved in extramarital relationships; (4) involved women are less than 31 years old; (5) Men in long-term marriages whose extramarital involvements were characterized as more emotional than

sexual; (6) there is low commitment to the marriage at the onset of therapy.

This trauma-based model for treating infidelity is consistent with the treatment approaches of Lusterman (1992, 1998) and Gordon and Baucom (1999). Common aspects in trauma-based treatment models are establishing safety, telling the story, and understanding the meaning of the infidelity. Distinctive features of this interpersonal trauma model are that it targets posttraumatic symptoms, fosters caring, manages resistance, resolves ambivalence, and uses disclosure content to transform the interactions from an adversarial process to mutual understanding. Furthermore, research findings on equity in the marriage and the affair suggest clinical approaches to increase reciprocity in the marriage. Gender differences and "assumed similarity" errors are also addressed as a unique aspect of this treatment model.

There is a lack of clinical consensus about how to handle secrets, how much detail should be disclosed, and whether to monitor signs of further infidelity. Refusing to conduct conjoint sessions is a prevailing stance if one partner is engaged in a current extramarital involvement that remains secret. A minority view is presented by therapists who assert that such an individual's presenting problem of extramarital involvement must be respected and kept confidential, because mandating conditions for treatment is coercive (Humphrey, 1982; Kaslow, 1993; Moultrop, 1990). Humphrey (1982) reports successful outcomes in cases where he maintains secrets in individual and conjoint sessions while working to resolve ambivalence.

Although studies report that sharing information about the infidelity is associated with a better recovery (Schneider et al., 1998) and with increased trust and intimacy (Vaughan, 1999), infidelity experts in Nelson's (2000) survey were sharply divided about how much detail should be revealed. In my therapist survey, 41% agreed with this statement: "A spouse's desire to know details of the partner's extramarital involvement should be discouraged by the therapist." In contrast, 57% of 1,083 betrayed spouses in an online survey reported that couple counseling was "mostly frustrating," because it dealt with general marital problems instead of focusing directly on the affair (Vaughan, 1999). Discussing the affair is also beneficial to the involved partner who is trying to detach from the affair partner. One study found that maintaining secrecy made unfaithful partners more likely to experience arousing thoughts about their affair partners and less likely to develop intimacy in their committed relationships (Layton-Tholl, 1998). I advocate sharing whatever details a betrayed partner needs for healing at the appropriate time in a safe setting.

Monitoring an unfaithful partner for further signs of deception and betrayal is an unpopular treatment approach. Infidelity experts in Nelson's (2000) survey were largely opposed to spousal monitoring. Only 17.5% of the therapists in my survey agreed with this statement: "The betrayed spouse who becomes hypervigiliant and suspicious about the whereabouts of the marital partner after an affair ends should be supported by the therapist in their attempt to track down clues to further acts of infidelity." However, when a partner who has been loving and trustworthy for many years becomes dishonest and deceptive, the only reality that can be trusted is actual evidence that the extramarital involvement is over. DiBlasio (2000) supports monitoring and the idea of a private detective escrow fund (Glass & Wright, 1997) in his decision-based forgiveness treatment of infidelity. Addiction counselors are opposed to monitoring out of concern for codependent behaviors. A relationship that continues to require lie detectors and detectives is unhealthy and not likely to recover.

TREATMENT APPLICABILITY

The interpersonal trauma recovery model is particularly relevant for couples who want to rebuild their marriage after the disclosure of infidelity. This approach is also appropriate for spouses who want to make an informed decision about whether to continue their marriage by clarifying whether they have compatible values regarding extramarital involvement. Since honest communication is fundamental to this approach, an involved partner can resolve ambivalence in couple therapy if he/she is willing to be open about the continuing attachment to the affair partner.

This approach is not appropriate when the infidelity is suspected by the noninvolved partner but denied by the involved partner. Spouses with a history of violence or pathological jealousy cannot easily manage the level of openness that this approach entails. Infidelity associated with substance abuse or dependence cannot be addressed until the involved individual is in recovery for the substance use disorder. Sexual addiction does not preclude successful treatment if the involved individual acknowledges the compulsive sexuality and empathizes with the partner's pain.

Treatment should be time-limited for difficult couples that are resistant to change. Treatment is onerous but not impossible in a couple whose members appear to have no emotional or physical bonds. However, an ongoing assessment should be made and termination of therapy recommended if neither partner budges from a frozen, blaming position after several months. The involved partner who rigidly resists disclosing information about the infidelity may soften this position as treatment progresses, but an absolute refusal to discuss the extramarital involvement or the identity of the affair partner(s) usually leads to a recommendation to terminate conjoint treatment.

Outside resources are often utilized when the level of distress in either partner is extreme or chronic. Psychiatric referrals to evaluate the need for medication, and collaboration with other treating physicians, can be advantageous. Inpatient psychiatric hospitalization may be indicated for suicidal or homicidal ideation that does not respond to psychotherapy or medication. Self-help groups available through the Internet are useful adjuncts; these include Codependents Anonymous (CODA), Sex and Love Addicts Anonymous (SLAA), and the Beyond Affairs Network (BAN). In situations where rage gets out of control, referrals to women's shelters or the legal system may be necessary. A cautionary note is that individual therapy by an outside therapist may be counterproductive without open collaboration.

Sound clinical judgment is essential to this approach, particularly since clinical issues can overlap with ethical issues. For example, the clinical goal of truthfulness should never be accomplished by the therapist's revealing secret information that violates the privilege of confidentiality. On the other hand, the principle of "doing no harm" is relevant in the case of the suspicious spouse for whom the denial of infidelity is crazy-making. This apparent conflict of interest necessitates clarifying the nature of confidentiality at the outset of treatment and obtaining informed consent. Individuals can be told that secrets pertaining to relationship issues will not be kept. The negative impact is that the involved individual may choose to keep the therapist in the dark, as well as the betrayed partner. Duty to warn in cases where unprotected sex occurred is an unresolved legal/ethical issue.

Other ethical issues arise over conflicts of interest between divergent goals; for example, one partner is desperate to save the marriage, and the other partner is determined to leave. The therapist who feels more sympathetic toward one spouse than the other must guard against triangulating. The couple therapist who agrees to secretly see a still-married individual with his/her affair partner is not only being unethical, but may be committing an illegal act in states that prosecute outside parties for alienation of affection.

There is very little clinical research on the efficacy of treatment approaches to extramarital involvement. Separation data provide one outcome criterion of the interpersonal trauma model, and 38% of couples with extramarital involvements were separated at the time therapy was terminated in one sample (Glass, in preparation). Studies on treatment of sexual addiction in married individuals offer the most comprehensive analyses about the benefits of disclosure, the impact of cybersex on the family, relapse statistics, and components of recovery (Schneider, 2000; Schneider et al., 1998; Schneider, Irons, & Corley, 1999). Gordon, Baucom, and Snyder (2000) have evaluated stages of forgiveness in their integrative approach and found that individuals had more negative assumptions about themselves in the initial stage of the treatment process than individuals in the final stage. These researchers have also obtained evidence for posttraumatic symptoms in betrayed partners. Infidelity experts in Nelson's (2000) survey achieved a consensus that treatment of an affair can be used to create a stronger marriage, when this is what both partners choose.

CASE ILLUSTRATION

Background

Gary and Marie initiated couple therapy 6 weeks after Marie discovered his infidelity while the two of them were on vacation. Marie had become suspicious about his numerous phone calls, so she listened to his voice mail while he was in the shower. She thought she was going to die when she heard his secretary saying, "I miss you, sweetheart." She then badgered Gary until he finally admitted having had sex with Tina. They returned home immediately, because Marie was too distraught to continue their trip. Gary resisted Marie's pleas to let Tina go, because he regarded her as too valuable to his business. Marie was hysterical every morning when he left for work. Tina finally left 3 months later, upset by Gary's decision to end their affair. Marie's recovery was prolonged because

of this extended period of continuing contact and the fact that Tina left on her own initiative.

Individual and conjoint sessions were held during a 16-month period, with frequent crisis phone calls for the first year. Neither Gary nor Marie had had prior psychotherapy. They described their marriage as very happy and loving prior to the infidelity, and their treatment goal was to restore their life together.

During their marriage, Marie and Gary had assumed the traditional roles of homemaker and provider. They had close ties to their extended families, children and grandchildren, ethnic neighborhood, and religious community. Marie was shy and placating, and Gary was outgoing and short-tempered. She said that she had tolerated his anger and domineering ways because she admired him so much. Although he treated her well, she felt that he didn't listen to her opinions with respect. He regarded her as a wonderful wife and had no complaints. Following the disclosure, they experienced a "honeymoon" period of sexual activity.

Assessment

Marie and Gary each exhibited hyperarousal marked by severe anxiety reactions. Marie was referred to a psychiatrist at the first session and received an antidepressant for major depressive disorder marked by anhedonia and medication for sleep disturbance. Both of them were treated for hypertension throughout the course of therapy. Their commitment was high, and neither of them indicated relationship problems except for the explosive aftermath of the infidelity. Her posttraumatic symptoms were still severe when she was assessed 10 months later.

Managing Posttraumatic Symptoms

Marie's catastrophic reaction was associated with the magnitude of her shattered assumptions and the protracted period of deception. She regarded Gary's infidelity as worse than a death. She had believed that Gary had strong moral values, and he had never lied to her before. She recalled his telling her she would be the only person in his life until he died, "even if a Playmate of the Year was attracted to him." She had always trusted him when he worked late, but she felt like a fool for accepting his excuses for being late when he was spending time with Tina.

During sex, Marie had intrusive images of Gary making love to Tina in his office. Flashbacks were triggered by nudity on TV, love songs, and gossip about cheating neighbors. She exhibited constriction by avoiding situations that reminded her of his affair. She was unable to attend social and family gatherings or to engage in routine activities such as grocery shopping.

Gary dreaded coming home to her mood swings. He cried over her pain, but felt he couldn't take it any more. He cursed back at her when she began ranting about his betrayal. We practiced anger management techniques, and they learned to use time outs for escalating anger. Her medication was increased, and he also began taking an antidepressant.

Gary was frustrated and mentally exhausted by Marie's flashbacks. He complained that almost anything served as a reminder of his affair. We discussed the involuntary nature of her flashbacks, and they received "flashback training" (Glass & Wright, 1997). At first she'd screech, "I can't even watch TV any more because of you and that slut," and he'd yell back, "Get over it already. How long are you going to punish me?" He gradually learned how to comfort her during flashbacks. It took months of flashback training before they shifted to the more constructive process illustrated by the following exchange. Marie said, "I just saw a TV show that upset me, and I am having a really hard time." Gary responded, "I am so sorry that you are having such a hard time. If it will help, I'll come home and stay with you for a while."

EMDR was used for Marie's traumatic images, but the decrease in her SUDS level (subjective units of distress) could not be sustained. Relaxation exercises and imaging a safe place reduced her anxiety for short periods. We also created a written narrative to relieve her need to talk about his betrayal over and over again. A family session with their son and daughter-in-law explained Marie's changed behavior, and she experienced the session as validating because they understood the basis for her traumatic reaction. Although she began to sleep better and started driving again, she still had crying jags a year into treatment.

Establishing Safety

Establishing safety was impossible while Marie was being retraumatized every day that Tina continued to work for Gary. Marie was devastated to hear that Gary had confided in Tina about what a hard time he was having at home with his wife since the disclosure. Marie was enraged to learn from another employee that Tina called Gary several times after she left to discuss business details. We discussed what it means to "stop *and* share," and Gary was advised that he had missed a golden opportunity to rebuild trust by failing to share Tina's calls with Marie.

Developing Compassionate Communication

Gary's "worst thing" consisted of Marie's unpredictable accusations (he called them "zingers") about what he had done. Her "worst thing" was when he reacted to her distress with "It didn't mean anything. It was just a little sex." Sometimes he comforted her when she cried, but at other times he made fun of her. When he complained that buying her gifts did no good, she stated, "If you were more understanding, we wouldn't even have to come to therapy."

Active listening skills to foster mutual empathy took months of directed practice. Their conflicts formed the content for communication skill training through "Take Two" role plays, in which they revisited the scene while the therapist directed a more constructive process. A year later she said, "I don't attack him any more. I just tell him how I feel." She reported that he listened better, didn't leave the room when she was upset, and acknowledged her hurts. She became more understanding about his vulnerabilities and fears.

Fostering Caring

We focused on caring behaviors at the second session, in order to alleviate some of the tension and negativity. Gary had very few requests for change, except that he wanted Marie to return to the way she was before, when she had been such a loving partner. Marie tried not to say mean things, forced herself to act normal at family gatherings, and made his favorite foods. He held her at night and brought her cups of soothing tea. He spent more time with her, taking her to movies and out to eat. He also helped her for the first time with household tasks such as grocery shopping and making beds. They exchanged hugs and kisses when they weren't fighting.

Understanding Vulnerabilities

Gary related that sex with Tina resulted from his fears of aging and declining sexuality. He had been avoiding sexual intercourse with Marie for the year preceding his infidelity because of erectile dysfunction. Tina's attention was flattering because she was much younger, and he felt as if he had visited the "fountain of youth." Furthermore, his excitement temporarily overcame his impotence. He had had many casual sex partners before marriage, and he didn't believe that occasional sex with Tina was really an extramarital affair. He viewed Marie and Tina to be as different as night and day; specifically, Tina was "loose," whereas Marie was a "good woman." This Madonna–whore complex allowed him to compartmentalize sex with Tina while remaining committed to Marie.

Co-Constructing the Story of the Affair

One of the greatest obstacles to recovery was their dispute about the meaning of Gary's extramarital sex. Marie went ballistic when he said he was always committed to her, and he was only "having a little fun." Gary finally understood that his "little fling" was devastating to Marie because he had made love to another woman for 2 years. He finally agreed with her that he had committed adultery, but he would not agree that he had had an "affair," because he had never been in love with Tina.

Marie couldn't heal until Gary validated her feelings of rejection and stopped denying behaviors that had hurt her. He finally saw Marie's perspective when we did role plays and role reversals. He said, "It hurts me now to realize that everything you have been saying about me betraying you is true." Marie recalled suspicious events, and Gary was truthful about the times and ways he had deceived her. Although she trusted he would never betray her again, she still continued to obsess about his extramarital relationship with Tina.

Rebuilding the Marriage

We explored their courtship history and the history of their marriage. Gary had no unresolved concerns because Marie had been so devoted and loving to him, but he did wish she were more sociable. In contrast, she had suppressed her resentment and hurt about his unilateral decisions and his loyalty to family members and friends who had been unkind to her. His affair had stirred up thoughts of other relationship triangles where "he puts other people ahead of me." The time he made for Tina also evoked bitter memories of being home alone throughout their marriage while he worked nights and weekends.

As Marie became more assertive about expressing her needs, Gary became fearful of losing his macho image. Although they were guided toward greater reciprocity, it was also important to support and maintain his position as head of the family. Nevertheless, he received pleasure from pleasing her and spending time with her, and he became more considerate and respectful of her. When Marie began to take the role of initiating sex, he reported with a smile on his face that "Marie seduced me last night, and I loved it."

Course of Treatment

Progress was extremely erratic. Good times and displays of affection were interspersed with episodes of rage and mutual threats to leave. Recovery was a struggle because Marie's anguish and Gary's aversive reactions persisted for so long. At one point, we discussed the possibility of hospitalizing Marie; at another point, she called a divorce attorney for a consultation. Their strongest resources were their years of devotion to each other and their religious convictions about the permanence of marriage. After 1 year, she stated that she had finally survived for an entire day without crying.

This case portrays standard elements in treating infidelity, such as traumatic reactions in the betrayed partner and minimizing by the unfaithful partner. However, Marie and Gary were especially challenging because of their excessive reactivity. It is not uncommon for betrayed partners to have invested more in the marriage than they have received. Gary's infidelity unleashed a torrent of inequities that Marie had silently endured throughout the marriage.

Gary had virtually no relationship complaints to explain his infidelity, but he had a short fuse for Marie's obsessive ruminations in the aftermath. His frustration and inexperience as a nurturer were additional hurdles to overcome. Assuming the unfamiliar role of healer is often hard for the involved partner because of the guilt aroused by the betrayed partner's pain. Gary's cavalier attitude toward extramarital sex and Marie's catastrophic reaction are consistent with research findings about gender differences in attitudes toward casual sex.

It was critical to establish safety in the therapy, because there was so little safety in the marriage. Both spouses relied on their therapist for understanding and support through crisis phone calls and individual sessions. Conjoint sessions were used to resolve and recover from the preceding week's events, to foster caring, and to coach both spouses in compassionate communication. When therapy finally shifted out of a crisis mode, we explored their individual childhood histories and addressed unresolved issues in the marriage. We also discussed the prevailing double standard toward extramarital involvement within their culture. Gary admitted that he would have divorced Marie if she had been unfaithful to him.

They developed a united front to deal with their adult children and in-laws. She began to assert herself more with friends and other family members. She controlled her "zingers," and he didn't holler as much. They talked softly to each other and felt calmer. When they took another vacation 1 year after the disclosure, she didn't have any flashbacks while they were away. At his class reunion, she forced herself to socialize despite her discomfort. After 14 months of therapy, she said that she had forgiven him, although it still devastated her that they could never regain what they had lost. They terminated treatment 2 months later in fair condition.

In a follow-up with Marie 2 years after termination, she reported that she had resumed some of her former activities, such as doing needlepoint and having people over to the house. Gary was much more considerate and caring, and she was more assertive and outgoing. However, her flashbacks and crying could still be triggered easily, and she still reminded him of his betrayal. He had consulted a physician about his erectile dysfunction, and she was still under the care of a psychiatrist.

Treatment was only able to achieve partial recovery and incomplete healing, because Marie could not let go of her pain. Her childhood history left her especially vulnerable to broken trust. Although she regretted that things would never be the same again, Gary's betrayal had caused a shift in their roles that was empowering to her. Furthermore, she probably feared that moving on would deny her suffering and minimize the consequences of his betrayal.

REFERENCES

American Psychiatric Association. (1994). *Diagnostic and statistical manual of mental disorders* (4th ed.). Washington, DC: Author.

Atwater, L. (1982). *The extramarital connection: Sex, intimacy and identity.* New York: Irvington.

Bach, G. R., & Wyden, P. (1970). *The intimate enemy: How to fight fair in love and marriage.* New York: Avon Books.

Beach, S. R., Jouriles, E. N., & O'Leary, K. D. (1985). Extramarital sex: Impact on depression and commitment in couples seeking marital therapy. *Journal of Sex and Marital Therapy, 11,* 99–108.

Brown, E. M. (1991). *Patterns of infidelity and their treatment.* New York: Brunner/Mazel.

Buss, D. (1994). *The evolution of desire: Strategies of human mating.* New York: Basic Books.

Buss, D., & Shackelford, T. K. (1997). Susceptibility to infidelity in the first year of marriage. *Journal of Research in Personality, 31,* 193–221.

Buunk, B. P. (1980). Extramarital sex in the Netherlands: Motivation in social and marital context. *Alternative Lifestyles, 3,* 11–39.

DiBlasio, F. A. (2000). Decision-based forgiveness treatment in cases of marital infidelity. *Psychotherapy, 37,* 149–158.

Edell, R. (1995). *How to save your marriage from an affair: Seven steps to rebuilding a broken trust.* New York: Kensington.

Ellis, A. (1969). Healthy and disturbed reasons for having extramarital relations. In G. Neubeck (Ed.), *Extramarital relations* (pp. 153–161). Englewood Cliffs, NJ: Prentice-Hall.

Everstine, D. S., & Everstine, L. (1993). *The trauma response: Treatment for emotional injury.* New York: Norton.

Francis, J. L. (1977). Toward the management of heterosexual jealousy. *Journal of Marriage and Family Counseling, 3,* 61–69.

Glass, S. P. (1998a). Aspects of Marital Satisfaction Questionnaire, Justifications for Extramarital Involvement Questionnaire, and Emotional Affair Questionnaire. In V. Rutter & P. Schwartz (Eds.), *The love test* (pp. 56–60, 132–136, 137–139). New York: Perigee.

Glass, S. P. (1998b, August). Shattered vows. *Psychology Today,* pp. 34–42, 68–70, 72, 74–76, 78–79.

Glass, S. P. (2000, January). *Infidelity* (Clinical Update No. 1052). Washington, DC: American Association for Marriage and Family Therapy.

Glass, S. P. (in preparation). *The trauma of infidelity: Research and treatment.* New York: Norton.

Glass, S. P. (in press). *Not just friends: Protecting your relationship from infidelity and healing the trauma of betrayal.* NY: Free Press.

Glass, S. P., & Wright, T. L. (1977). The relationship of extramarital sex, length of marriage, and sex differences on marital satisfaction and romanticism: Athanasiou's data reanalyzed. *Journal of Marriage and the Family, 39,* 691–703.

Glass, S. P., & Wright, T. L. (1985). Sex differences in type of extramarital involvement and marital dissatisfaction. *Sex Roles, 12,* 1101–1119.

Glass, S. P., & Wright, T. L. (1988). Clinical implications of research on extramarital involvement. In R. A.

Brown & J. R. Field (Eds.), *Treatment of sexual problems in individual and couples therapy* (pp. 301–346). New York: PMA.

Glass, S. P., & Wright, T. L. (1992). Justifications for extramarital involvement: the association between attitudes, behavior, and gender. *Journal of Sex Research, 29,* 1–27.

Glass, S. P., & Wright, T. L. (1997). Reconstructing marriages after the trauma of infidelity. In W. K. Halford & H. J. Markman (Eds.), *Clinical Handbook of marriage and couples interventions* (pp. 471–507). New York: Wiley.

Gordon, K. C., & Baucom, D. H. (1999). A multitheoretical intervention for promoting recovery from extramarital affairs. *Clinical Psychology: Science and Practice, 6,* 382–399.

Gordon, K. C., Baucom, D. H., & Snyder, D. K. (2000). The use of forgiveness in marital therapy. In M. E. McCullough, K. Pargament, & C. Thoresen (Eds.), *Frontiers of forgiveness* (pp. 203–227). NY: Guilford Press.

Greene, B. L., Lee, R. R., & Lustig, N. (1974, September). Conscious and unconscious factors in marital infidelity. *Medical Aspects of Human Sexuality,* pp. 87–91, 97–98, 104–105.

Harley, W. F. (1986). *His needs, her needs: Building an affair-proof marriage.* Old Tappan, NJ: Fleming H. Powell.

Harvey, D. R. (1995). *Surviving betrayal: Counseling an adulterous marriage.* Grand Rapids, MI: Baker Books.

Hazan, C., Zeifman, D., & Middleton, K. (1994). *Adult romantic attachment, affection, and sex.* Paper presented at the Seventh International Conference on Personal Relationships, Groningen, The Netherlands.

Herman, J. L. (1992). *Trauma and recovery.* New York: Basic Books.

Humphrey, F. G. (1982). Extramarital affairs: Clinical approaches in marital therapy. *Psychiatric Clinics of North America, 5,* 581–593.

Humphrey, F. G. (1983). *Extramarital relationships: Therapy issues for marriage and family therapists.* Paper presented at the annual meeting of the American Association for Marriage and Family Therapy, Washington, DC.

Hunt, M. (1974). Postmarital and extramarital sex. In *Sexual behavior in the 70's* (pp. 235–291). Chicago: Playboy Press.

Hurlbert, D. F., Apt, C., Gasar, S., Wilson, N. E., & Murphy, Y. (1994). Sexual narcissism: A validation study. *Journal of Sex and Marital Therapy, 20,* 24–34.

Janoff-Bulman, R. (1992). *Shattered assumptions: Towards a new psychology of trauma.* New York: Free Press.

Kaslow, F. (1993). Attractions and affairs: Fabulous and fatal. *Journal of Family Psychotherapy, 4,* 1–34.

Kinsey, A. C., Pomeroy, W. B., & Martin, C. E. (1953). *Sexual behavior in the human female.* Philadelphia: Saunders.

Laumann, E. O., Gagnon, J. H., Michael, R. T., & Michaels, S. (1994). *The social organization of sexuality: Sexual practices in the United States.* Chicago: University of Chicago Press.

Lawson, A. (1988). *Adultery: An analysis of love and betrayal.* New York: Basic Books.

Layton-Tholl, D. (1998). *Extramarital affairs: The link between thought suppression and level of arousal.* Unpublished doctoral dissertation, Miami Institute of Psychology of the Caribbean Center for Advanced Studies.

Levine, M. (1938). Notes on the psychopathology of suspicions of marital infidelity. *Cleveland Journal of Medicine, 19.*

Locke, H. J., & Wallace, K. M. (1959). Short marital adjustment and prediction tests: Their reliability and validity. *Marriage and Family Living, 21,* 251–255.

Lusterman, D. (1992). *The Broderick affair.* Workshop presented at the annual meeting of the American Association of Marriage and Family Therapy, Miami, FL.

Lusterman, D. (1998). *Infidelity: A survival guide.* Oakland, CA: New Harbinger.

Moultrop, D. J. (1990). *Husbands, wives, and lovers: The emotional system of the extramarital affair.* New York: Guilford Press.

Myers, L., & Leggitt, H. (1972). A new kind of adultery. *Sexual Behavior, 2,* 52–62.

Nelson, T. S. (2000). *Internet infidelity: A modified Delphi study.* Unpublished doctoral dissertation, Purdue University.

Neubeck, G. (Ed.). (1969). *Extramarital relations.* Englewood Cliffs, NJ: Prentice-Hall.

Neubeck, G., & Schletzer, V. M. (1962). A study of extramarital relationships. *Marriage and Family Living, 24,* 279–281.

Notarius, C., & Markman, M. (1993). *We can work it out: Making sense of marital conflict.* New York: Putnam.

Oliver, M. B., & Hyde, J. S. (1993). Gender differences in sexuality: A meta-analysis. *Psychological Bulletin, 114,* 29–51.

Penn, C. D., Hernandez, S. L., & Bermudez, J. M. (1997). Using a cross-cultural perspective to understand infidelity in couples therapy. *American Journal of Family Therapy, 25,* 169–185.

Pittman, F. (1989). *Private lies: Infidelity and the betrayal of intimacy.* New York: Norton.

Prins, K. S., Buunk, B. P., & VanYperen, N. W. (1993). Equity, normative disapproval and extramarital relationships. *Journal of Social and Personal Relationships, 10,* 39–53.

Schneider, J. P. (2000). Effects of cybersex addiction on the family: Results of a survey. *Sexual Addiction and Compulsivity, 2,* 12–33.

Schneider, J. P., Corley, M. D., & Irons, R. R. (1998). Surviving disclosure of infidelity: Results of an international survey of 164 recovering sex addicts and partners. *Sexual Addiction and Compulsivity, 5,* 189–217.

Schneider, J. P., Irons, R. R., & Corley, M. D. (1999). Disclosure of extramarital sexual activities by sexually exploitative professionals and other persons with addictive or compulsive sexual disorders. *Journal of Sex Education and Therapy, 24,* 277–287.

Seagull, E. G., & Seagull, A. A. (1991). Healing the wound that must not heal: Psychotherapy with survivors of domestic violence. *Psychotherapy: Theory/Research/Practice/Training, 28,* 16–20.

Shapiro, F. (1995). *Eye movement desensitization and reprocessing: Basic principles, protocols, and procedures.* New York: Guilford Press.

Shaw, J. (1997). Treatment rationale for Internet infidelity. *Journal of Sex Education and Therapy, 22,* 29–34.

Silverstein, J. L. (1998). Countertransference in marital therapy for infidelity. *Journal of Sex and Marital Therapy, 24,* 293–302.

Smith, J. R., & Smith, L. G. (1974) *Beyond monogamy.* Baltimore: Johns Hopkins University Press.

Spanier, G. B. (1976). Measuring dyadic adjustment: New scales for assessing the quality of marriage and similar dyads. *Journal of Marriage and the Family, 38,* 15–28.

Spanier, G. B., & Margolis, R. (1983). Marital separation and extramarital sexual behavior. *Journal of Sex Research, 19,* 23–48.

Spring, J. A. (1996). *After the affair: Healing the pain and rebuilding trust when a partner has been unfaithful.* New York: HarperCollins.

Staheli, L. (1998). *Affair-proof your marriage: Understanding, preventing and surviving affairs.* New York: HarperCollins.

Stiff, J. B., Kim, H. J., & Ramesh, C. N. (1992). Truth biases and aroused suspicion in relational deception. *Communication Research, 19,* 326–345.

Strean, J. S. (2000). *The extramarital affair.* New York: Jason Aronson Publishers.

Stuart, R. B. (1983). *Couples pre-counseling inventory.* Champaign, IL: Research Press.

Subotnik, R., & Harris, G. (1999). *Surviving infidelity: Making decisions, recovering from the pain.* Holbrook, MA: Bob Adams Press.

Thompson, A. P. (1984a). Emotional and sexual components of extramarital relations. *Journal of Marriage and the Family, 46,* 35–42.

Thompson, A. P. (1984b). Extramarital sexual crisis: Common themes and therapy implications. *Journal of Sex and Marital Therapy, 10,* 239–254.

Vaughan, P. (1999). *Partial results of survey on extramarital affairs* [Online]. Available: http://www.dearpeggy.com/results.html [11/10/1999].

Weil, B. E. (1993). *Adultery: The forgivable sin.* New York: Birch Lane Press.

Weiner, M. B., & DiMele, A. (1998). *Repairing your marriage after his affair: A woman's guide to hope and healing.* Rocklin, CA: Prima.

Weiner-Davis, M. (1992). *Divorce busting.* New York: Simon & Schuster.

Whisman, M. A., Dixon, A. E., & Johnson, B. (1997). Therapists' perspectives of couple problems and treatment issues in couple therapy. *Journal of Family Psychology, 11,* 361–366.

Wiederman, M. W. (1997). Extramarital sex: Prevalence and correlates in a national survey. *Journal of Sex Research, 34,* 167–174.

Wright, T. L., & Glass, S. P. (1988). Relationship Equity Questionnaires (p. 331). In R. A. Brown & J. R. Fields (Eds.), *Treatment of sexual problems in individual and couples therapy.* New York: PMA Publishing.

Wryobeck, J. M., & Wiederman, M. W. (1999). Sexual narcissism: Measurement and correlates among college men. *Journal of Sex and Marital Therapy, 25,* 321–331.

Yablonsky, L. (1979). *The extra-sex factor.* New York: Times Books.

Chapter 19

Addressing Separation and Divorce during and after Couple Therapy

ROBERT E. EMERY
DAVID A. SBARRA

Whether therapists like it or not, divorce is a stated or unstated issue in most couple therapy cases. This is true if for no other reason than that divorce and alternative family forms are a part of contemporary family life. Families have evolved across the course of history, but marriage and family life went through a sudden and dramatic upheaval in the second half of the 20th century. Contemporary policy makers are busily inventing new forms of more restrictive marriage—most notably "covenant marriage," in which couples agree to go through premarital counseling, profess their value of marriage, and commit to a more stringent set of divorce rules (e.g., a 2-year separation for a no-fault divorce instead of only 1 year). At the same time, American couples have been voting with their feet for new, less restrictive family options. As the millennium ended, young people in the United States delayed marriage until their late 20s; about half of young couples cohabited prior to marriage; more than 40% of marriages ended in divorce; and over a quarter of all children were born outside of marriage (Cherlin, 1992; Emery, 1999; Hernandez, 1992).

The United States has the dubious distinction of being the world leader in divorce, but similar changes in family life have occurred throughout the industrialized world in the latter part of the 20th century (Burns & Scott, 1994; Pryor & Rodgers, in press). In fact, many European countries, particularly the Scandinavian countries, have experienced much higher rates of cohabitation and nonmarital childbearing than the United States. One difference, however, is that almost all children born outside of marriage in Europe are born into two-parent cohabiting unions, as opposed to only between 25% and 50% of children born outside of marriage in the United States (Bumpass & Raley, 1995; Burns & Scott, 1994; McLanahan & Garfinkel, 2000). Thus separation and divorce, as well as alternative family forms including gay and lesbian domestic partnerships, pose potential issues in couple therapy—if for no other reason than their high prevalence.

Of course, divorce and separation are also aspects of couple therapy because of the unhappiness that brings couples into treatment. Clearly, this unhappiness comes in many forms. Sometimes the problems that cause couples to consider separation are chronic, as in the case of long-standing emotional disengagement, persistent conflict, or ongoing episodes of violence. Other times the possibility of separation is sudden—for example, following the discovery of an affair. Sometimes the desire for a separation is kept hidden in couple therapy; other times it is made all too explicit. Sometimes the mention of a separation is a genuine statement of one partner's intentions; other times it is a sign of his/her ambivalence, or even a test of the other partner's commitment to the relationship.

There is one commonality, however, in most cases where separation is a serious possibility in couple therapy: The desire to separate is not mutual. Typically, while one partner is contemplating the end of the relationship, the other is hoping for it to continue. In dealing with the possibility of separation in couple therapy, it is essential to recognize this basic imbalance in the partners' commitment, emotions, and ultimately in their grief. In fact, differences between the "leaver" and the "left" continue to form a central dynamic in the partners' relationship during and long after separation and divorce (Emery, 1994).

In this chapter, we focus both on issues of separation and divorce in couple therapy (in the first major section of the chapter) and on research-based information and interventions available to couples following separation (in the remainder of the chapter). Unlike the corresponding chapters in earlier editions of this *Handbook* (Rice & Rice, 1986; Walsh, Jacob, & Simons, 1995), our chapter does *not* focus in detail on either "separation therapy" (emotionally preparing a couple for an impending separation) or "divorce therapy" (helping the former spouses to emotionally reintegrate their relationship after divorce). Rather, we instead cover a variety of specific issues about separation and divorce that couple therapists can expect to encounter both prior to and after a decision to separate is made, as well as conceptual issues related to how couple therapists can best address issues of separation and divorce in therapy.

Most of our research and clinical experience has emphasized divorce—particularly divorce mediation, in which a third party helps couples to negotiate separation and divorce agreements in as cooperative a manner as is possible (Emery, 1994). In this chapter, however, we do not limit ourselves to the period of time following separation, for one practical and one theoretical reason.

Practically, our goal is to outline the major issues related to separation and divorce for therapists who work primarily as couple therapists. Couple therapists obviously must address the issue of separation if it is a common, if perhaps unstated, part of treatment. Even if their overriding goal is to save marriages, moreover, couple therapists need to know how best to help their clients when couple therapy ends with a separation, as it often does.

Theoretically, this chapter includes divorce issues both in couple therapy and following separation because divorce is a process, not an event. In fact, most of the same family processes that affect the well-being of children in marriage also affect their well-being following separation and divorce.

Ironically, however, the same is not necessarily true for parents/partners. This is so because the needs of children and the needs of adults do not overlap perfectly, either in marriage or in divorce. Because marital conflict, separation, and divorce involve a process of family transition, one overriding theme of this chapter is that a couple's decision to separate should lead to a transition in psychological— and legal—interventions with the family, and not to the end of the former approach and the beginning of the latter one.

CONSIDERING SEPARATION OR DIVORCE IN COUPLE THERAPY

The possibility of separation and divorce is an issue that must be considered and raised from the beginning of couple therapy. From the outset of treatment, the therapist needs to know whether both members of the couple are committed to staying together, whether they hope to improve the relationship but would seriously consider ending it, or whether the individuals have differing goals and commitments in the relationship. In this section, we consider four essential issues related to separation and divorce in couple therapy: (1) the therapist's own beliefs about marriage and divorce; (2) staying together "for the children's sake"; (3) hidden agendas, in which separation is the real goal for one or both members of the dyad in couple therapy; and (4) two traditional grounds for a "fault" divorce—infidelity and violence—as they relate to the possibility of separation and divorce in couple therapy.

The Therapist's Beliefs about Separation and Divorce

As a starting point, all therapists must examine their own issues in regard to separation and divorce in order to deal with these topics fairly and effectively in couple treatment. All therapists bring all sorts of their "own issues" to therapy, of course, but few topics can involve such strong personal beliefs and emotions or hold the potential for having such a significant effect on clients. Among the issues that each therapist must consider are the following:

• What are the therapist's religious beliefs? In particular, many religions discourage divorce, and some directly prohibit it.

• What are the therapist's personal beliefs not only about marriage and divorce, but also about such "hot topics" as appropriate gender roles, what constitutes intimate violence, or affairs?

• How does the therapist's family history, both in the family of origin and in the current family, affect his/her views? The effects of a personal or parental divorce may be more salient, but the subtle influences of various experiences with a happy or an unhappy marriage also need to be considered.

• How does the therapist define success in couple therapy? Is helping the partners stay together the therapist's goal in couple therapy, or is the goal to increase the individuals' happiness even if this means ending a bad relationship?

• What is the therapist's goal when the partners have conflicting positions about staying together?

• How does the therapist view separation or divorce when children are involved?

• Who is the client? According to the therapist's conceptual and/or personal view, is the client each partner? The couple? The children? The entire family?

As with other personal issues, the therapist's goal in relation to probing his/her personal beliefs about marriage, separation, and divorce is to increase awareness, not achieve resolution. Couple therapists need to recognize their own "family values" and the ways their belief systems affect their couple therapy. Still, there is no one "right" set of beliefs for a couple therapist. In fact, we believe that couple therapy can and should be offered by therapists who hold a full range of personal views. However, perhaps more than with any other issue, couple therapists need to be clear about their biases both with themselves and with their clients. There are many ways in which therapists can address the topic. For example, some therapists may want to be explicit that their goal is always to keep couples together. Other therapists may want to acknowledge their therapeutic emphasis on each partner's happiness, even if this means ending an unhappy relationship. A discussion of the therapist's goals early in therapy makes the therapist's agenda clear; it allows a couple to choose whether or not to continue with this therapist; and it raises a central issue for the couple at the outset of treatment.

Our own practice is, during the first conjoint session, to inform a new couple that our overriding goal in couple therapy is to improve communication and increase mutual understanding. We also inform the couple that our hope is that treatment will help the partners to have a better and enduring relationship, but we reiterate that our goal is to improve communication and understanding, not necessarily to "save" the relationship at all costs. Not only is this position consistent with our personal beliefs and an important objective for successful couple treatment; it is also a goal that can be maintained if we discover that one partner does not want to save the relationship. In coming to conjoint therapy, one member of a couple often has a hidden agenda concerning the possibility of separation and divorce—an issue we discuss in detail shortly. This motivation perhaps is more common in our own practice than for other couple therapists, because most clients who come to us are aware of our expertise in divorce mediation as well as in couple work. Thus we have adopted the goals of increasing communication and understanding, because these goals anticipate the possibility of one partner's desire for a separation; they are consistent with our personal beliefs; and, most importantly, they are essential goals for the effective treatment of partners who stay together.

"Should We Stay Together for the Children's Sake?"

Another issue that therapists need to examine personally and professionally is one that commonly is a central concern for parents who are considering separation: "Should we stay together for the sake of the children?" The phrasing of the question may be trite, but the emotional, philosophical, and empirical issues it raises are deep and profound.

Accepting Responsibility

Our first response to this question, both in couple therapy and in theory, is that ultimately no one should stay together for the children's sake. But our position should not be misinterpreted. We agree that it is likely that many children would be better off if their parents stayed together in unhappy but relatively conflict-free marriages—a position that is increasingly supported by empirical evidence (discussed shortly) (Amato & Booth, 1997). We also take the position that parents should put their children's needs ahead of their own desires in weighing decisions about whether or not to remain in a marriage.

Our objection to "for the children's sake" is a more subtle one. We hold that parents/partners need to accept responsibility for their own decisions about whether or not to stay in a marriage. This responsibility should not be placed on the shoulders of children or on the principle of the children's well-being. In claiming the role as martyr, parents who assert that they stayed together (or got divorced) "for the children's sake" fail to accept that the decision is *theirs*, not the children's. In so doing, they transfer responsibility and guilt, perhaps inadvertently, onto the shoulders of their children.

In taking our position against "for the children's sake," we are concerned both about children and about the dynamics of the partners' relationship. With respect to the children, our rationale is based on a straightforward philosophy: Adults, not children, should assume responsibility for major decisions about their family life. As an example of adults who seemingly have shirked this responsibility, numerous young people have told us that one or both of their parents informed them of an impending separation shortly after the youths' graduation from high school or college. The parents also told these young people that they had only been staying together for their sake. Learning about the separation was hard enough for these young adults, but worse was the guilt they felt over having been responsible for years of their parents' unhappiness.

These parents may have been doing the right thing in staying together for their children. In our view, however, these parents clearly made a mistake in failing to "own" their decision. The children may have been the deciding factor in the parents' choice to remain in their marriage, but the decision nevertheless belonged to the *parents*. Like everyone, parents/partners need to accept that their choices have consequences—good and bad. Because decisions about separation (or staying in an unhappy marriage) can carry a huge weight of responsibility, many partners/parents end up shifting the burden for the choice onto their children (or onto each other).

Our position about accepting parental responsibility is not idiosyncratic, but an outgrowth of a more general view of the appropriate hierarchical structure of family relationships and the adverse consequences of "parentification" of children (Emery, 1992; Tuer, 1995). Another example of an inversion of the family hierarchy in the divorce context is when parents ask children with whom they want to live following a separation. This question is tantamount to asking children to choose between their parents, and we view it in the same way. The needs of children should be of paramount importance in parental decision making. However, parents, not children, need to accept the responsibility for making the incredibly difficult decisions about what residential arrangements will be in their children's best interests following separation and/or divorce.

Ending the "Hot Potato" Game

With respect to the couple's own relationship, the emphasis on accepting personal responsibility can also be a step toward ending the game of "hot potato" that is often played by separating couples. The "hot potato" consists of fault and blame for the demise of the relationship, and one or both partners often attempt to toss this responsibility to the other partner. Many people have a difficult time accepting the burden of this decision. When only one person wants the separation, he/she may justify the decision with a litany of complaints about the other partner, or may insist that the breakup is for the children's sake—that is, the children will do better, not worse, following a separation. Such assertions may in fact be accurate. Nevertheless, our position is that the person who wants to leave must take responsibility for that decision, even if his/her reasons are fully legitimate. Vehement debates about who is "at fault" are eliminated when one partner accepts responsibility for the decision to separate.

Although our position is strong, we do not take the notion of responsibility lightly. A person has to muster considerable courage in order to embrace ownership of the decision to end a relationship. As clinicians, we acknowledge the need for courage, especially when the choice is unpopular or is difficult to justify. It is an important step, however, because acceptance of responsibility reduces ambiguity—and therefore ambivalence—in the couple's relationship. In the long run, the greater clarity and lessor ambivalence can help both members of the dyad to move forward as individuals.

Research Evidence

Notwithstanding issues of accepting responsibility, the question of whether or not to stay together is an incredibly important and difficult one. Partners/parents often turn to couple therapists for information and advice about how children cope with divorce or with family life when the marriage is unhappy. Fortunately, a large body of research can be used to educate parents about possible consequences of their decisions—although no research, or no therapist, can provide definitive answers in an individual case.

As a general summary, the following facts can be gleaned from research on children's family experiences and psychological adjustment following separation and divorce (for a review, see Emery, 1999):

- Separation and divorce create a number of stressors for children and for parents, ranging from economic hardship to distant or troubled parent–child relationships to increased (rather than lessened) family conflict.
- Most children struggle emotionally with a parental separation for a period of a year or more, depending upon their personality, age, and family circumstances.
- Separation/divorce is associated with a significantly increased risk (often a doubling of the risk) for a variety of emotional and behavioral problems among children.
- However, the most common long-term outcome for children from single-parent, separated, or divorced families is *resilience*, not risk. That is, the majority of children from divorced families do *not* have emotional, behavioral, academic, or mental health problems.
- Resilience carries some costs. The majority of children from divorced families do not have psychological problems, but many resilient children nevertheless report painful memories, troublesome feelings, and ongoing concerns about their families.
- Parents have a strong influence on whether children are at risk or resilient following separation/divorce. In fact, the major predictors of children's adjustment to divorce are much the same as for their adjustment in a married family: a good relationship with one parent, preferably with both; being kept out of the middle of parental conflicts; and economic stability.
- Still, it is true that, on average, children fare better in a happy two-parent family than in a separated, divorced, or single-parent family. In fact, on average it is easier to foster good parent–child relationships, to keep kids out of the middle, and to maintain economic stability in a two-parent family.
- At the same time, there are cases where a separation is an escape from major family problems, such as violence or chronic conflict. In such circumstances, children as well as parents will fare better, not worse, following a separation.

- Finally, in deciding whether or not children will fare better, worse, or merely differently following a separation and divorce, parents (and therapists) should carefully note that children have a lower threshold for what constitutes a "good enough" marriage than do parents. Many children are unaware of or unconcerned about their parents' marital happiness, but these same children can be stunned by a separation and end up in the middle of new, postseparation parental conflicts.

This last point requires some elaboration now, whereas the other summary points are discussed in more detail later in the chapter. The increased acceptance of separation and divorce has been justified in law, in society, and in innumerable individual cases, based on the empirically supported assumption that children have fewer psychological problems when they live in a happy separated, divorced, or single-parent family than when they live in a conflict-ridden two-parent family (Amato & Keith, 1991; Emery, 1982, 1999). For several reasons, however, this does *not* mean that children will be better off if their parents separate rather than remain in a unhappy marriage.

Perhaps the most important empirical reason for questioning this conclusion comes from a recent line of research. In an intriguing, longitudinal study, Amato, Loomis, and Booth (1995) found that young adults were *better* adjusted psychologically following a divorce if their parents' marriage was characterized as high-conflict. However, their psychological adjustment was *worse* following a divorce if the marriage had been low-conflict. The first finding is consistent with the rationale for allowing divorce, and it is predictable from the literature demonstrating the adverse effects of parental conflict on children (Cummings & Davies, 1994; Emery, 1982; Grych & Fincham, 1990). However, the latter finding is more surprising and potentially very important. The evidence suggests that a marriage may be "good enough" from the perspective of children's well-being, even though it is not "good enough" in terms of the happiness of (one of) the parents. To offer an obvious example, sexual satisfaction is likely to be important to the partners' marital happiness, but to the children their parents' sexuality is unimportant (and unthinkable). More generally, children whose parents have succeeded in protecting them from unhappiness and conflict in the marriage may be shocked by a separation, and they may find their parents' separation to be a struggle, not a relief.

Importantly, the interaction between level of marital conflict and adjustment following separation/divorce has been at least partially replicated in two subsequent and independent investigations (Jekielek, 1998; Morrison & Coiro, 1999). There are also other reasons why more parents should consider staying together for the children's sake. One reason comes from studies of child custody disputes demonstrating that conflict actually may increase, not decrease, following marital separation. The parental disputes may come to focus more squarely on children, who form one of the few remaining ties between former partners (Buchanan, Maccoby, & Dornbusch, 1996; Emery, Matthews, & Kitzmann, 1994; Johnston, 1994). A second reason is that other family stressors that affect children's well-being—most notably economic security—are clearly a function of living in a two-parent household, not of parental conflict (Duncan & Hoffman, 1985). Third, although most children are resilient, separation and divorce nevertheless are linked to distressing feelings among even resilient children. Such feelings do not impair the young people's functioning, but they are painful nevertheless (Laumann-Billings & Emery, 2000). In summary, research indicates that interparental conflict is detrimental to children's psychological functioning. However, it also indicates that conflict in many unhappy marriages may be successfully hidden from children; that divorce does not always resolve conflict; and that other stressors clearly created by divorce (e.g., financial hardship) are also important to children's well-being.

What implications does this research evidence hold for the individual case? Education is one straightforward implication. For example, parents can be informed about the recent, more nuanced research evidence. Such information is likely to be more accurate and detailed than the often subjective and overly simplified advice that parents are likely to obtain from friends and family, as well as from the popular media and self-help resources. More direct implications of the research are less obvious, however. For example, there is no clear research-based cutoff for determining how much marital conflict is "too much" for children; nor is there research indicating which parents are likely to have a "good divorce" (Ahrons, 1995). One conclusion that parents should *not* reach is that they should fight more in their marriage if they want the children to adjust more easily to separation. Rather, parents who are considering a separation, despite their success in protecting the children from their conflicts, would be wise to inform the children about the marital problems—as a means both of being honest and of preparing the children for the possibility of separation. An ideal outcome in this circumstance would be for the parents to resolve their problems successfully. If so, this would teach the children who have been warned about the serious marital problems that, despite important difficulties, resolution is possible.

Hidden Agendas

All parents worry about their children's adjustment to separation, but many individuals have decided, often privately, to separate before coming for couple therapy. These people may begin couple treatment with any number of hidden agendas with respect to separation and divorce. One maneuver is for one partner, perhaps both, to be able to say "I tried" either to themselves, to each other, or to their social world. This motivation may be stated openly and explicitly, particularly in cases where both partners are uncertain about the future of the relationship. In other cases, however, this motivation becomes clear (if it does at all) only after one partner's willingness to change is questioned in therapy, or perhaps after therapy has failed.

Another hidden agenda is when one partner uses couple therapy as a vehicle for revealing that he/she wants a separation or divorce. In our experience, such a revelation rarely comes in the first session, but it typically occurs within the first several sessions. In some of these cases, the reason for the rapid announcement is that the partner's ambivalence was resolved early in therapy. In other cases, however, the partner planned to leave from the outset. The reason for the delay may be to create the appearance of trying; it may be a lack of courage or a sincere desire not to hurt the other partner; or the person who wants to leave simply may not know how to tell the other partner that he/she wants the relationship to end.

A closely related hidden agenda is when one partner uses couple therapy as a means not only of announcing the end of the relationship, but also of ensuring that the partner who is left has some social support—in this case, the therapist. In some such circumstances, the partner who is left may indeed have serious and long-standing emotional problems that need treatment, and these psychological problems likely helped to precipitate the separation. Examples of these problems include chronic depression or substance misuse. In other cases, the maneuver is more of an attempt to make sure that the left partner will be "OK" after the separation. Both the partner who is left and the therapist can feel duped and used in this circumstance.

A fourth and final tactic we have observed is that one member of the couple wants to end the relationship and uses couple therapy as a means to begin negotiating an amicable separation agreement. The plan is to end the relationship on a friendly, cooperative note, and to begin the divorce negotiations in the same manner. As with other hidden agendas, the partner who wants to leave the relationship may have good intentions or selfish ones, but the unstated goal of couple therapy is obviously very different from the stated one.

When we first encountered hidden agendas in couple therapy, we were left feeling infuriated and used, regardless of the intentions behind the maneuvers. Keeping couples together is our hope if not our explicit goal, and these hidden agendas left us feeling cheated and defeated. After many such experiences, we are more prepared for—and, to a degree, more accepting of—such maneuvers. We now view our task as couple therapists as being aware of the various possible hidden agendas from the outset of couple therapy; assessing for them directly early in treatment; and being prepared to follow alternative courses, including facilitating divorce and separation.

Assessing Marital Commitment and Plans of Separation

We use some straightforward and some more subtle ways of assessing when one member of the dyad has a hidden agenda regarding separation—and, conversely, when one member of the dyad threatens but is unlikely to follow through with separation. The simplest assessment is to ask each partner individually about his/her commitment to the relationship. In the first or second session, we routinely see each partner individually, and a central goal of this meeting is to assess this partner's commitment to the relationship. Ordinarily, the individual meeting is a brief, 10-minute interview that takes place as a part of a conjoint session. Seeing each partner individually immediately after interviewing them together often allows us to inquire further about some aspect of the observed interaction—for example, "You didn't respond when your husband said he was 100% committed to your marriage. Why?" Also, the conjoint meeting is often emotionally arousing, especially if there was open conflict, and the strong emotions facilitate disclosure during the individual meeting.

Typically, we start the individual meeting with a general opening, such as "Tell me what I should know to be helpful to you, but maybe is too hard to say in front of your husband/wife." We are always amazed at how frank people can be in response to this question. A client may immediately disclose hidden agendas, ranging from being captivated with an affair to having videotapes of the spouse in an affair. Of course, many people have also disclosed more mundane information (e.g., details of their own or their partners' mental state, their characteristic patterns of relating, or some key aspect of family history). In still other cases, it is helpful and gratifying simply to hear each partner clearly articulate a strong commitment to the relationship, even when interviewed in private.

If indirect or general questions do not lead into a discussion of the individual's commitment to the relationship, we ask directly about this issue. Depending upon the circumstances, we may probe directly about affairs, or perhaps we may be mildly confrontational about hidden agendas—for example, "You don't seem very engaged in treatment. Do you want to be here, or is this really your husband's/wife's idea?" In all cases, we guarantee confidentiality for any information disclosed privately, and we rarely have difficulty maintaining the confidence. (Of course, we also tell clients that we are extending confidentiality to their partners as well, so they will know that we may learn of a secret before they do.) Although we offer confidentiality, we often strongly encourage individuals to be honest and direct with their partners about their secrets or plans. Finally, we may take the common position that we will discontinue therapy (without disclosure of the reasons for discontinuation) unless circumstances change—for example, until a partner ends an affair. (We discuss affairs shortly.) We take this position in order to avoid being triangulated in a couple's relationship by becoming party to a serious, manipulative deception.

Nevertheless, there are cases where we decide to continue therapy despite the uncomfortable knowledge of a secret. For example, we may continue couple therapy when one person has disclosed an affair to us and the partner is strongly suspicious, but the affair has not yet been acknowledged openly. We recognize that many therapists are uncomfortable holding such secrets, and protect themselves from being put in the middle by not seeing the partners alone. This "don't ask, don't tell" strategy can protect a therapist, but we believe it deprives the therapist of an opportunity to learn important but not inflammatory information (e.g., each person's directly stated insights about the partner or him-/herself). Moreover, we believe that addressing hidden agendas in a straightforward way may benefit therapy, even when it proceeds with our sharing secret knowledge. For example, the fact that we know a secret (and the client with the secret knows that we know) may limit ongoing deception and encourage honesty in conjoint therapy.

Assessing the Seriousness of Threats of Separation

It is also very important to assess the seriousness of a plan to separate. Many people consider separation, but do not really plan to follow through. Others threaten their partners with separation, but the threat is idle and ultimately may be designed to test the partners' emotional investment in the relationship. One useful way to conceptualize the assessment of the seriousness of a separation threat is to draw an analogy with the assessment of suicide risk. Like more serious plans of suicide, more serious plans to separate are specific, fully developed, involve past and present steps toward separation, and often are accompanied with something of a sense of relief. Like suicidal ideation, an impending separation is probably less likely following a vague, emotional statement that "I just want out!" Conversely, the likelihood of separation is likely to be quite high following a more calm, detailed statement, such as "I've been saving money in a secret bank account; I've been searching the want ads for apartments; and I made an appointment to see a lawyer next week."

The emotional tone of a statement about separation during a conjoint session can also be informative about the seriousness of a plan to separate. In contrast to Sullivan's (1953) continuum of intimacy in which hate and love form opposite poles, we believe that love and hate are not far apart, and instead conceptualize indifference as the polar opposite of love (Emery, 1992, 1994). Thus we are likely to view a sudden, angry, and emotional cry of "I want a divorce!" during a couple session as perhaps being a test of the other partner's emotional investment. The partner is supposed to beg for forgiveness or at least get angry in return. In contrast, we view a dispassionate, planful, and perhaps guilt-ridden statement of "I want a divorce" as more serious.

Such observations help to guide our hypotheses, but not they do not provide evidence for final decisions about a separation threat. Like suicide

threats, we take all statements about separation seriously and continue to monitor them during the course of treatment.

Grounds for Divorce: Infidelity and Violence

A fourth and final issue that we consider regarding separation/divorce in couple therapy is a situation in which one partner has committed an egregious harm—in particular, has had an affair or become violent—but nevertheless expresses regret and wants the relationship to continue. The offended partner may believe that ending the relationship is the only acceptable option in the face of such an offense, but emotionally he/she may feel ambivalent about this decision (as well as devastated, shocked, hurt, angry, and frightened about the incident).

We certainly do not condone affairs, violence, or other any other action that is seriously hurtful and potentially devastating to a partner, a marriage, and a family. We do believe, however, that (1) both affairs and episodes of violence are relatively common in intimate relationships; (2) the harm created by them is not inevitably irreparable; and (3) contrary to a legalistic view of marriage ("Our contract is over because you broke it"), ending the relationship is not the *only* reasonable response to such offenses.

Adultery and cruelty (and desertion) have been long-standing legal grounds for obtaining a fault-based divorce (Eekelaar, 1991); thus there is no doubt that such harmful actions are clearly legitimate, socially sanctioned reasons for ending a marriage. This does not mean, however, that it is either right or easy for the offended partner to end a marriage under these circumstances. Even if ending the relationship offers relief from the pain of an affair or from the threat of violence, moreover, the separation may bring about other adverse consequences for the injured party (e.g., economic hardship, social isolation, harm to or lost contact with the children). Furthermore, the injured party often *wants* the relationship to continue, and it may be possible to repair much of the damage to the relationship even after such a devastating experience.

As noted at the beginning of the chapter, affairs and violence are "hot-button" issues for therapists as well as their clients, and we recognize that others may legitimately hold positions vehemently different from our own. Nevertheless, we think it is important to raise these difficult and controversial issues, and to offer a few of our perspectives on them (for more details, see Glass, Chapter 18, and Holtzworth-Munroe, Meehan, Rehman, & Marshall, Chapter 16, this volume). Affairs and episodes of violence are common problems in intimate relationships, and couple therapists need to be prepared to deal with them.

Infidelity

In a major survey of sex in America, Michael, Gagnon, Laumann, and Kolata (1994) found that 80% of women and 65–85% of men reported that, while they were married, they had no partners other than their spouses. This level of sexual faithfulness is very similar to recent reports of findings from the Kinsey interviews, based on a more thorough use of the complete and cleaned data set of over 6,000 participants: 65% of men and 81% of women did not have sexual intercourse with partners other than their spouses during their first marriage (Gebhard & Johnson, 1998).

Although these numbers are fairly consistent and similar to estimates in other surveys (National Opinion Research Center, 1991), they may underestimate the prevalence of infidelity. The validity of reports of sexual behavior has been widely questioned generally; more specifically, the respondents in the Michaels et al. (1994) survey were questioned about affairs during a time while their partners were (literally) in the house (Gottman, 1999). It would not be surprising if a person would not admit to having an affair while his/her spouse was in the next room. In any case, survey data indicate that nearly a quarter of women and over a third of men report having extramarital intercourse, and there are good reasons to believe that this is a low estimate. Clearly, affairs are prevalent.

Given these population base rates, it is hardly surprisingly that infidelity is a common problem among couples in therapy. One report indicated that roughly 25% of couples initiating therapy present with the issue of extramarital sex, and an additional 30% or more disclose an affair during the course of therapy (Glass & Wright, 1997). A recent survey of practicing couple therapists found extramarital affairs to be the second most damaging problem couples face and the third most damaging problem to treat among a list of 29 problems and issues commonly encounter in marital/couple therapy (Whisman, Dixon, & Johnson, 1997). The complications created by affairs were trumped only by a lack of loving feelings and communication

problems, according to the therapists' perceptions.

Not surprisingly, affairs are also common complaints among divorcing couples. South and Lloyd (1995) reported that in at least one-third of divorce cases, one or both spouses had been involved with another person prior to marital disruption. Janus and Janus (1993) found that 40% of divorced women and 44% of divorced men reported having extramarital sexual contact.

Obviously, affairs often cause serious marital problems. Unless there is sincere expression of remorse, a low risk for recurrence, and an unencumbered desire for reconciliation on the part of the offended party, our couple work with affairs typically occurs in the context of separation and divorce. In this case, our focus commonly is on mediating very painful and practical topics, such as establishing limited contact between the couple's children and the "new" partner, at least for an extended period of time.

We also believe, however, that infidelity can sometimes be a consequence of relationship troubles. Although we are aware of no empirical data on the issue, we agree with other couple therapists that partners may be particularly vulnerable to affairs when they feel lonely, bored, unloved, or conflicted in a relationship (Gigy & Kelly, 1992; Gottman, 1999). In such circumstances, we believe that it may be possible to use the crisis of an affair to begin to explore and (ideally) improve the relationship. In so doing, we hold to our goals of improving communication and increasing understanding, not saving marriages at all costs. If nothing else, the exploration of an affair in couple therapy may help to alleviate some of a couple's conflicts after separation. Complicated legal disputes in divorce can often be traced to the emotional dynamics in the former partners' intimate relationship, as unresolved feelings about an affair (or other issues) are enacted in a legal battle (Emery, 1994).

Separation and divorce are the focus of this chapter, and our most basic point is straightforward: We do not believe that an affair must automatically lead to a divorce, and there is a role for couple therapy even if dissolution is the eventual outcome. With respect to the successful resolution of the crisis of an affair and the eventual improvement of a troubled marriage, space allows us only to note that various experts have developed approaches to helping couples negotiate the crisis (e.g., Glass & Wright, 1997; Gordon & Baucom, 1999; Pittman & Wagers, 1995). A central goal in all intervention strategies is to reestablish trust. Forgiveness is another goal (Gordon & Baucom, 1999), and one that we believe has been too long neglected in psychology.

Violence

Violence is another egregious offense that often occurs in intimate relationships. As many as a third of married couples report episodes of throwing objects, grabbing, or pushing each other, and about 4% of couples in random samples of the general population report more serious incidents of choking, beating up, or kicking a partner (O'Leary et al., 1989; Straus & Gelles, 1990). Although only a small percentage of couples in therapy spontaneously report physical aggression to be a major problem in their relationships (see Hotlzworth-Monroe, Smutzler, Bates, & Sandin, 1997), research suggests that violence is widespread among couples in treatment. In one study, about half of couples seeking marital therapy in different regions of the country reported incidents of male physical aggression (Holtzworth-Monroe et al., 1992). In another investigation of a university marital clinic, 44% of wives and 46% of husbands reported episodes of physical aggression (O'Leary, Vivian, & Malone, 1992).

Episodes of violence may offer sufficient personal, as well as legal, grounds for separation and divorce. As with affairs, however, our view is that a permanent separation is not the only acceptable response to an episode of violence—provided that it is not severe or part of a chronic pattern. We agree with Holtzworth-Munroe et al.'s (1997) assertion that conjoint treatment is contraindicated when (1) the woman is in grave danger, (2) the man refuses to take steps to reduce the violence, and (3) the woman is afraid to participate in conjoint treatment. However, couple treatment may be warranted when the battering partner expresses regret, and when treatment begins with a contract to end all physically aggressive behavior. Some evidence does indicate that couple treatment can be successful with partners who have been violent (Brown & O'Leary, 1997). In such cases, O'Leary (1996) indicates that couple treatment should focus on helping such partners eliminate psychological and physical violence, accept responsibility for the escalation of angry interchanges, recognize and control angry thoughts, communicate more effectively, and understand that each partner has the right to be treated with respect.

Acceptance versus Change

Jacobson and Christensen (1996) have highlighted that the dichotomy between acceptance and change poses a basic dilemma for couple and for couple therapists. We conceptualize the very difficult issues of infidelity and violence within the context of this dilemma. For some couples, and for some couple therapists, an affair or an episode of violence provides an automatic answer to the acceptance versus change question: The action is simply unacceptable, and therefore the only option is change in the form of ending the relationship.

We also believe, however, that acceptance, and ultimately forgiveness, of even an egregious wrong are sometimes possible, and thus can be important goals in couple therapy. In closing, we want to be clear that we are *not* advocating acceptance of an ongoing affair or of an ongoing threat of violence. Although we help couples to deal with issues created and/or revealed by an affair, we generally hold to the position that couple therapy cannot proceed if one partner continues to remain involved in an affair, as noted earlier in this chapter. Similarly, we will not proceed with couple therapy, and urge a separation, if the threat of violence is ongoing. However, by suggesting that some couples can recover from these harms, we are suggesting that affairs and violent acts are not unitary phenomena, and that some individuals legitimately want to continue an intimate relationship despite the pain such an act has caused them.

HEALTHY VERSUS DYSFUNCTIONAL DIVORCE: RENEGOTIATING FAMILY RELATIONSHIPS

Many clients and therapists believe that the reasons for couple therapy end with a decision to separate. If a couple has children, however, we assert that the family intervention needs to be transformed, not ended. Family relationships do not end with separation and divorce; instead, these relationships must be renegotiated (Emery, 1994). This includes the relationship between former partners who remain parents. In fact, the coparenting relationship is critical to family functioning after separation and divorce, and consequently to the well-being of children. At precisely the moment that a husband and wife decide they can no longer live together as intimate partners, they need to begin to find new ways of relating as coparents. Couple therapists can help families to prepare for and begin the process of renegotiation. This is why we have considered at length the issues of separation and divorce in couple therapy, when we could have easily devoted the entire chapter to research and intervention following separation and divorce.

There are clearly better and worse ways for family members to renegotiate their relationships in separation and divorce—both immediately and in the long run. A couple therapist can be enormously important in helping clients to recognize that the children's perspective on separation differs from their own; in referring clients to mediators, divorce therapists, and lawyers; and perhaps in continuing to work with the couple or family. In the remainder of this chapter, we review the major issues and alternatives for parents and for therapists following the decision to separate. Our discussion throughout assumes that a couple has children. If no children are involved, we are content to follow songwriter Paul Simon's advice that there are "50 Ways to Leave Your Lover.

Telling One's Partner

Sometimes one partner will tell a couple therapist of his/her desire and intention to separate, and then ask this impossibly difficult question: "How am I going to tell my mate?" If the individual is resolved to make this choice, our first piece of advice is to "own" the decision, as we have discussed earlier in the chapter. Each member of the couple may bear half of the responsibility for the problems in the marriage, but the decision to separate is one-sided (even if it is fully understandable or justifiable). The client who wants to separate should not—and ultimately cannot—place blame on the partner for the choice. In the end, both the couple and the individuals will benefit if the leaving partner accepts rather than shirks this responsibility.

Our second piece of advice is that the leaving partner should expect to feel ambivalent about the decision, but nevertheless should act with certainty (or not act until he/she is certain enough). Even a person who is eager to "move on" commonly feels much ambivalence about ending a marriage, for reasons ranging from his/her own sense of failure to fears about losing the children to continued emotional attachment to the former partner. Thus ambivalence is "normal," and it is often appropriate to share some of these conflicted feelings with the partner. However, we emphasize the importance of *acting* with certainty despite *feel-*

ing uncertain, because the partner who is left is likely to experience much more fragile and intense grief than the leaving partner. In general, grieving is greatly complicated when a loss is potentially revocable versus irrevocable (e.g., divorce vs. the death of a spouse), and to the extent that the leaving partner behaves consistently, he/she is helping the mate to begin to resolve the loss by making the end clear. In contrast, to the extent that the partner who leaves shows ambivalence (through frequent contact, affection, or sexual reunitings), he/she prolongs the other partner's grief by encouraging hope. Ultimately, our rationale for working toward behavioral consistency in the midst of emotional turmoil is that although affective upheaval may be acceptable to parents, it creates chaos for children. Thus more clear and well-defined separations may ultimately help both adults and especially children who are struggling to come to terms with their parents' parting (Emery, 1994).

Because of differences in the grief, a third piece of advice to the leaver is to be patient. Typically, the leaver has been mourning the end of the relationship for a long time, perhaps years; by contrast, even if he/she was aware of the problems, the left party experiences a much more recent and unwanted loss. The left party needs and deserves as much time as the leaver has had to come to terms with the end of the marriage. Because of this, and because the leaver is getting what he/she wants, the burden falls on the leaver to be patient rather than on the left party to adjust quickly.

Finally, a fourth piece of advice is for the leaver to be honest and direct about the reasons for leaving the relationship. Being honest can be extremely difficult, of course, and it is often uncertain how much detail should be conveyed. One example from our experience is a husband who was involved in an affair. He admitted to his suspicious wife that he had "fallen in love" with someone else, but he did not confirm the actual physical affair in order not to hurt her further (or not to jeopardize his legal case; "fault" continues to play a role in legal negotiations and in some legal statutes, even now that every U.S. state allows "no-fault" divorce). In this case, which we expand upon later in the chapter, the wife was not surprised (her own lawyer had hired a private detective and had videotapes of her husband and his lover). Still, she was relieved by her husband's direct admission of at least part of the truth, and his (reluctant) willingness also to admit to their teenage children that the reason for the end of the marriage was that he had fallen in love with someone else.

Telling the Children

Telling the children of an impending separation is incredibly difficult for parents and, of course, for children. Children are likely to remember this pivotal moment throughout their lives, and how parents manage the difficult circumstance may set the tone for coparenting after divorce, which is critically important.

We encourage parents, if at all possible, to tell the children together, but also to be available separately afterward in case a child has questions that are better asked and answered alone. We also advise parents to keep the discussion brief, and to be sure to include practical matters, such as where the children will live after the separation and how they will see each of the parents. Children also deserve a direct and honest explanation about the reason for the separation, and it is essential that parents agree on an acceptable public explanation for the children (including, if necessary, an agreement to disagree politely).

The reasons for the end of a marriage are complex, of course, but parents must reduce the complexity to a brief explanation that is simultaneously direct, honest, and acceptable to both parents and to the children. In crafting the explanation prior to meeting with the children, a useful analogy for parents is to think of explanations about the reasons for separation that are akin to answers to their children's questions about sex. That is, like responses to children's queries about sex, explanations about the reasons for the separation should be developmentally appropriate, focused on the children's rather than the parents' needs, brief, direct, and honest—but not overly detailed or personalized.

Finally, although we encourage parents to put aside their own issues in presenting a united front when telling their children of the separation (and hence forth), we also encourage parents to show some of their emotions. Although a show of strong anger is inappropriate (if often difficult to control), tears and other sad feelings are appropriate to share with the children. After all, the parents' separation *is* incredibly sad for parents and for children. At the same time, parents should allow the children to have their own unique reactions to learning of the separation, including disbelief, sadness, anger, fear, relief, or no apparent reaction. Just as the leaver and the left grieve differently, children's experience of a separation does not necessarily match the feelings of either parent. In short, we are suggesting that the family hierarchy should be preserved even during this incredibly difficult time. Children's needs come first, and although parents can appropriately share some of their very difficult feelings, this should be done while conveying the overriding sense that the parents can take care of themselves; the children need not take care of them.

Conflicting Feelings and Perspectives

Parents, children, and therapists should expect family members to have conflicting feelings about and perspectives on a separation. For the partner who wants to end the relationship, the actual separation often brings about relief, and a separation can also be a relief for children from a high-conflict family. For many adults and more children, however, the separation is a time of crisis. The partner who wants the relationship to continue is often shocked, devastated, and emotionally volatile. Even the relief felt by the partner who wants to end the relationship can be strongly tinged with sadness, ambivalence, and guilt. Depending upon their age and the family circumstances, moreover, children may be predominantly confused, angered, embarrassed, or depressed about their parents' separation.

Separation and divorce invariably lead to a period of turmoil that can last for several years (Hetherington, Bridges, & Insabella, 1998). Even if the separation leads to a relief from family conflict, children still must cope with each parent's emotional trials, the interparental conflict that may focus more intently on them, and perhaps other major changes in family life (including relocation, switching schools, and economic hardships). In the long term, the adjustment of parents and children depends in large part upon how the divorce is managed. Children fare better when they maintain a good relationship with at least one, and preferably both, of their parents; when they are kept out of the middle of parental conflicts; and when there are fewer disruptions in their lives, including disruptions due to economic factors (Emery, 1999).

In terms of couple therapy, this means therapists can tell parents that they can and inevitably will continue to help to shape their children's psychological well-being after a separation. This seemingly simple message can be incredibly powerful. For parents who feel like failures, the message may help them to feel empowered and hopeful about their children and the future. For parents who are engrossed in their own emotions (ranging from depression to blind rage to returning to adolescent behavior), the message may help them to appreciate and respect that their children's perspective on separation differs from their own.

As noted, the idea that children will not necessarily react in the same manner as adults can be extremely important. Parents need to be sensitive to children's unique, developmentally appropriate needs, and they also need to be careful not to project their own emotions and wishes onto the children. A parent who is devastated by a separation may, for example, erroneously assume that the children feel the same way; or a parent who wants the relationship to end may be overeager to "fix" the children, perhaps to the extent that the children are not allowed even to grieve. Another important and related message is that although the psychological adjustment of children and that of adults are generally linked with the same stressors, there are differences. Two differences of particular importance are these: (1) Parents understandably are hurt and angry about the end of the relationship, but children need to be protected from parental anger and conflict; and (2) the parents' desire for limited contact with each other is understandable, but the children form an enduring link between the two former partners who remain parents. Thus parents need to separate the hurt and anger that naturally feel in their role as former lovers in order to keep children out of the middle, as the former partners preserve and transform their role as parents (Emery, 1994).

Research on the Consequences of Divorce for Children

As briefly summarized earlier in the chapter, there is a large and complicated body of research on the consequences of divorce for children, and it touches many areas of family functioning and child well-being (Emery, 1999). Nevertheless, the empirical literature is quite consistent with the clinical advice offered on working with separated parents. In addition to guiding the goals of the separation process, therapists may want to educate parents about research on the consequences of divorce for children. We organize our discussion in the following sections around six main conclusions. First, divorce causes much stress for children, ranging from loss of contact with one parent to economic hardship. Second, divorce increases the risk for psychological difficulties among children, often doubling the risk. Third, despite the increased risk, most children from divorced families function as

well as children from married families; that is, they are resilient in coping with the multiple stressors caused by divorce. Fourth, resilience is not invulnerability. Despite their competent functioning, children from divorced families report a number of painful feelings, unhappy memories, and ongoing distress. Fifth, there are substantial individual differences in children's adjustment to divorce, and postdivorce family functioning in large part explains whether children are at risk or resilient following separation and divorce (Emery & Forehand, 1994; Emery, 1999). Sixth, even among families that adjust well to separation and divorce, children and families typically experience a difficult period of disruption lasting 1–2 years or more following a separation. Elsewhere, we have expanded in detail on these conclusions and the research behind them (Emery, 1999).

Divorce Stressors

Divorce causes a number of important, and often intense and prolonged, stressors for children. The process of separation, or of learning to alternate between households, is extremely difficult for most children, especially when they are attached to both parents (Emery, 1999). Moreover, contact with the nonresidential parent (typically the father) can be uncertain and erratic, and it is often infrequent and diminishes over time (Emery, Laumann-Billings, Sbarra, Waldron, & Dillon, 2001; Seltzer, 1991). In addition, the quality of children's relationships with *both* parents commonly declines following divorce, at least for a time (Hetherington et al., 1998). Furthermore, conflict may not end with a separation; it may escalate and focus more directly on the children (Emery et al., 1994). Parents also may become depressed or otherwise preoccupied with their own feelings during a divorce, another potential source of stress for children (Wallerstein & Kelly, 1980). Finally, divorce inevitably has a negative financial impact on a family; for children, this may lead to changes in residence, schools, and peer groups, or to increased and perhaps lower-quality child care (Duncan & Hoffman, 1985).

Divorce as a Risk Factor

Divorce is associated with an increased risk for a number of psychological problems among children. In studies of nationally representative samples, divorce is associated with a doubling of the risk of seeing a mental health professional (Zill, Morrison, & Coiro, 1993), dropping out of school, and teen childbearing (McLanahan & Sandefur, 1994). In studies of convenience or clinical samples, divorce is also linked with an increased risk (but generally not as much as a doubling of the risk) for a number of psychological problems among children, including conduct problems (Amato & Keith, 1991), symptoms of depression (Conger & Chao, 1996), and subsequent divorce when they become adults (Bumpass, Martin, & Sweet, 1991). Furthermore, the family processes associated with divorce (e.g., interparental conflict) are known to be related to an increased risk for child behavior problems across two-parent, divorced, and never-married families (Emery, 1999).

Resilience

Despite the increased risk, however, resilience is the normative psychological outcome of divorce for children—at least as indexed by standard measures of psychological, educational, and behavioral problems. A meta-analysis of 92 studies comparing children from married and divorced families found an average effect size of only 0.14 standard deviation units (this effect size is equivalent to 2–3 IQ points) across all child outcomes (Amato & Keith, 1991). Similarly, national studies documenting the risks associated with divorce also find that the great majority of children from divorced families are not "at risk," even though divorce is associated with the doubling of the risk for certain serious outcomes, such as dropping out of school (McLanahan & Sandefur, 1994; Zill et al., 1993). Furthermore, existing studies of risk must be tempered, because evidence demonstrates that many of the psychological problems found among children predate divorce in time and thus cannot be consequences of divorce (e.g., Cherlin et al., 1991). In a similar vein, parental and socioeconomic characteristics that predate both marriage and childbearing account for many of the psychological troubles found among children after divorce (Emery, Kitzmann, & Waldron, 1999).

Distress

Children confront a number of stressors as a result of their parents' separation, but the majority of children are resilient nevertheless. Still, even successful coping can carry some of the costs. Children's subclinical distress in grappling with divorce—their "pain"—is as important to recognize as their resilience. Recent empirical evidence documents, for example, that resilient young adult children from divorced families report such subtle

concerns as wishing they had grown up in married families, believing that their childhoods were cut short, worrying about events where both mothers and fathers will be present (e.g., weddings), and doubting their fathers' love (Laumann-Billings & Emery, 2000).

The distinction between distress and disorder (or symptoms or disturbances in life functioning) suggests a more nuanced approach to understanding the emotional consequences of divorce for young people. In fact, an appreciation of the subtleties may both increase sensitivity to young people and help to reconcile some controversies in research. In regard to clinical issues, our experience is that although children, adolescents, and young adults from divorced families appreciate our focus on their strengths, they also appreciate our recognition of their struggles—their distress. Resilience is not the same as invulnerability, and there are some inner costs of successful coping with divorce or any other major life stressor. After all, the term "resilience" has been applied to children's successful coping with stressors ranging from poverty to warfare, but no one expects such traumas to leave no psychological residue. In regard to research, the distinction between distress and disorder may explain some of the vehement, ongoing controversies about the effects of divorce on children. Clinicians often highlight the dramatic and lasting pain reported by young people whose parents have divorced (e.g., Wallerstein, Lewis, & Blakeslee, 2000), whereas researchers emphasize the overwhelming evidence documenting generally competent life functioning (e.g., Amato & Keith, 1991). We suggest that both approaches may be accurate and inaccurate (Laumann-Billings & Emery, 2000). Clinicians may see the trees (the details of an individual's distress) but miss the forest (the overall competent functioning of a child or young person from a divorced family). Researchers may suffer from the opposite problem of documenting generally "normal" functioning on the usual measures of psychological maladjustment, but overlooking the subtleties of inner experiences that can be difficult to measure objectively.

Individual Differences

In an extensive overview of research on children and divorce, Emery (1999) concluded that there are large individual differences in children's adjustment to divorce, and that these can be predicted from a few key aspects of postdivorce family life. In order of their importance for the absence of psychological problems among children, these factors are (1) a good relationship with the residential parent, usually the mother; (2) lower levels of parental conflict and less exposure of children to, or involvement of children in, inevitable disputes; (3) the family's financial stability; and (4) children's relationship with the nonresidential parent, typically the father. As a rule, we believe that therapists should encourage all of these family processes in order to facilitate children's adjustment to separation and divorce. However, they are listed in order of importance, because there may be times when one goal must be given priority over another. For example, the ordering indicates that in the presence of high levels of conflict that is not contained around the children, children will fare better if they have less contact with one parent. Although this is not the preferred circumstance, less contact will mean that children will also be less exposed to/involved in the parental disputes.

Process of Adaptation

As a final point, we wish to underscore that children and families commonly experience a lengthy period of difficulty during the first years following a separation. Longitudinal research documents that children's adjustment to, and acceptance of, separation and divorce improves over the 2 years following separation (Hetherington, 1993). Although contact with the nonresidential parent often diminishes over time, residential parent–child relationships improve; conflict between parents can lessen; and the divorced family typically finds new stability among its members, both economically and in relating to the larger community. Fortunately, the trite saying carries considerable truth for divorced families: Time heals.

Research on the Consequences of Divorce for Adults

Although the psychological consequences of divorce for children are of paramount importance, it would be a clinical and empirical mistake to overlook the fact that separation and divorce can be emotionally damaging to parents as well. Empirical evidence documents that separation and divorce are linked with multiple problems in the psychological well-being of the parents/partners. Indeed, the extant literature suggests that almost all spheres of adult functioning are disturbed—at least temporarily—by the dissolution of marriage.

Divorcing men and women commonly report elevated levels of depression, anxiety, and antisocial behavior (Gotlib & McCabe, 1990; Lorenz, Simons, & Chao, 1996; Simons & Johnson, 1996). Increased rates of illness, morbidity, and suicide are especially notable for divorced men (Burman & Margolin, 1992; Hu & Goldman, 1990). Although many of the consequences of divorce can be viewed as a result of a decline in marital quality (cf. Fincham, Beach, Harold, & Osborne, 1997; Gotlib, Lewinsohn, & Seeley, 1998), longitudinal evidence indicates that a number of the psychological correlates are specific to marital dissolution (Bruce, 1998). For example, in their 4-year panel study of 1,106 adults, Menaghan and Lieberman (1986) found that individuals who subsequently divorced were not significantly more depressed at the first time point than those who would remain married. However, 4 years later, the newly divorced had become significantly more depressed.

Two issues deserve special note with respect to adults' psychological adjustment to their own divorce. First, there is a pervasive—and largely unsupported—assumption that there are substantial gender differences in adjustment to separation and divorce. The mistaken view is that men benefit from marriage regardless of its quality, while women are better off being separated and divorced than remaining in an unhappy relationship (Glenn, 1997). Although the relationship between marital satisfaction and certain psychological problems may be stronger for women than for men, separation and divorce cause short-term distress, are associated with an increased risk for psychological difficulties, and create a number of practical hardships (e.g., economic problems and troubled parent–child relationships) for both men *and* women. Second, children's adjustment to separation and divorce is linked, in part, with parents' adjustment (Wallerstein & Kelly, 1980). Thus one contribution that parents can make to children's well-being is to take care of themselves emotionally.

INTERVENTION ALTERNATIVES WITH DIVORCING FAMILIES

Many interventions are available for divorcing families, and it is important for the couple therapist to be aware of these alternatives. Various treatments may be offered during or shortly after the initial separation, whereas others take place long after a divorce. Some efforts involve only one family member, but others include many or all family members in different configurations. Finally, some interventions address legal as well as psychological aspects of separation, divorce, and child rearing. Unfortunately, there is one point of common ground among these diverse approaches to intervention: Surprisingly few have been studied empirically and systematically.

Space allows us to include only a limited overview of the array of different interventions available to separating and divorced family members. The overview is divided into three sections, based on the targets of intervention: the coparenting relationship, individual parents and parenting, or the individual child. Although we note examples of a range of possible treatments, we highlight interventions with the coparenting relationship (the focus of this chapter) and treatments that have at least some research support. We should note at the outset that methodologically adequate research on coparenting interventions is limited to divorce mediation; that controlled trials of therapy for postdivorce parenting are limited to group therapy; and that systematic research on treatments for individual children is limited exclusively to school-based interventions (Emery et al., 1999).

Coparenting: A Brief Focus on Divorce Mediation

Difficulties in children's coping with and eventual adjustment to divorce can often be traced to conflict in coparenting (Emery, 1999); thus this relationship is a frequent target of intervention. Coparenting problems frequently become a focus in postseparation couple or family therapy, but unfortunately there are no empirical evaluations of family therapy for postseparation coparenting problems. This is surprising and disappointing, since divorce is so prevalent, since it is associated with an increased risk for children's and adults' psychological problems, and since family treatment appropriately conceptualizes the postdivorce family as a family nevertheless.

Parent Education

Work in a very different vein suggests some more specific goals for and potential benefits of interventions designed to improve postseparation coparenting. Parenting and coparenting education is being offered by various groups; in fact, attendance at these educational programs for parents seeking a divorce is increasingly being mandated by state legislation or local court rulings throughout the United States. These education programs can vary widely, but a common format is for mental health professionals to offer a few hours of lecture with some discussion to relatively large groups of divorcing parents. The lectures may focus on a number of related topics designed to highlight children's experience of divorce, including the consequences of divorce for children, the need to limit interparental conflict, and the importance of the involvement of both parents in children's lives after divorce.

Studies of parent education programs are generally limited to evaluation research, and several reports indicate high levels of parent satisfaction (e.g., Buehler, Betz, Ryan, Legg, & Totter, 1992). Studies using a no-treatment comparison group are also encouraging; their findings suggest that divorce education may produce lower levels of parental conflict, raise levels of parental cooperation, and lower relitigation rates (Arbuthnot & Gordon, 1996; Arbuthnot, Kramer, & Gordon, 1997; Kramer, Arbuthnot, Gordon, Rousis, & Hoza, 1998). The lack of random assignment and high rates of participant attrition raise a number of important uncertainties about the findings of these early studies of a new concept, but the efforts represent a needed step in the right direction. The only study using random assignment to alternative treatments (Kramer et al., 1998) produced no consistent pattern of results and suffered from high attrition rates. Still, the goals of parent education programs are laudable ones; if nothing else, these efforts may help to prepare and to encourage parents to pursue more intensive coparenting interventions such as divorce mediation.

Divorce Mediation

Clearly, the majority of research on interventions with coparenting has focused on divorce mediation—including our own work, which includes randomized trials of the mediation versus the litigation of child custody disputes (Emery et al., 1999). Mediation is intended primarily to be a technique for resolving legal disputes, but the process can also be viewed as a preventive intervention that may improve the coparenting relationship and thereby affect children's well-being following divorce (Emery & Wyer, 1987a). Mediation offers parents a forum for dispute settlement at a time when communication is extremely difficult, and the attempt to cooperate in coparenting can both facilitate short-term dispute settlement and promote continued parental cooperation. Mediation may take place in courts, social service agencies, or private practices, and it typically involves a limited number of sessions ranging from 1 to 15 or perhaps 20 hours. Most mediation, and most research on mediation, has focused on structured, short-term intervention offered in a court setting.

We have developed a detailed treatment manual for our own empirically supported method of divorce mediation (Emery, 1994). Ours is a short-term, problem-solving approach, in which the mediator recognizes and directly and indirectly addresses ambiguities in the boundaries of the postseparation family relationships, particularly the former partners' relationship. In our model, the mediator also clearly recognizes each partner's grief, as well as conflicts in the partners' experience of grief. The mediator may directly intervene briefly with these emotional issues, in addition to working on negotiating the details of a separation and divorce agreement.

In an initial study and in a replication using our model, families randomly assigned to mediation versus litigation were much more likely to resolve their disputes outside of court; they reached agreements more quickly; and, as a whole, they were more satisfied with their various experiences in mediation versus litigation (Emery & Wyer, 1987b; Emery, Matthews, & Wyer, 1991). Compliance with child support payments also was higher 2 years following mediation than litigation, and higher levels of parent satisfaction were maintained over time, and recent evidence has revealed that 12 years after an average of 6 hours of mediation, nonresidential parents stayed more involved in their children's lives, while conflict was lower and coparenting involvement was significantly and substantially greater, for parents who mediated versus litigated (Emery et al., 1991, 2001).

Our findings are broadly consistent with other research on mediation, as is our general failure to detect any differences in the mental health outcomes of children or parents following mediation or litigation (Benjamin & Irving, 1995; Kelly, Gigy, & Hausman, 1988; Kelly, 1989; Pearson & Thoennes, 1984). One important direction for intervention and research is to increase the duration of mediation, particularly by including intermittent contact following dispute settlement or even ongoing supervision/arbitration. Johnston and Roseby (1997) found that "therapeutic mediation," which included rather extensive assessment, individual counseling, and some group therapy, produced considerable agreement among families who had repeatedly litigated divorce disputes. Coming full circle, this again suggests the potential benefits

of family treatment, and it highlights the need for research on family therapy as well as mediation with separated and divorced families.

For the couple therapist, research on mediation underscores the point we have emphasized earlier: A couple's decision to separate signals the need to transform couple or family intervention, not the time to end it. For a number of reasons, it may often be impossible for the same therapist to move from working as a couple therapist to becoming a divorce mediator and therapist. For example, one of the partners may view the therapist as having failed in couple therapy. Regardless of such circumstances, however, couples therapists can educate separating parents about mediation, make appropriate referrals, and help separating people to distinguish their understandably hurt and angry feelings as former partners from their ongoing roles as parents.

Parent and Parenting Interventions: A Brief Focus on Group Therapy

Most parent-focused interventions in separation and divorce, and all research evaluations, involve group therapy with individual parents from different families. Parenting groups generally have three goals: (1) improving the parents' psychological adjustment; (2) improving parenting; and (3) improving family relationships. In practice, most emphasize adult adjustment, with less emphasis on parenting skills and family relationship issues. Many groups have a "single-parent" and self-help focus (Cantor & Drake, 1983; Lee, Picard, & Blain, 1994). Such parent-based intervention programs are commonly used by the community and are even court-mandated in some areas.

A handful of controlled studies have been conducted on the efficacy of various groups for separated and divorced parents (Forgatch & DeGarmo, 1998; Hodges & Bloom, 1986; Wolchik et al., 1993). In general, research on parenting interventions indicates high levels of satisfaction, and some (sometimes temporary) improvements in parent adjustment and parenting, but small or no direct effects on children's adjustment. Still, the research highlights the importance of positive postdivorce parenting for children's well-being; as in the research on mediation, the available evidence offers much justification for more research—and for therapists to recommend such programs to their clients. Separated and divorced parents often do report feeling alone, isolated, and overwhelmed, and the social support offered by parenting groups is welcome.

Child-Focused Treatments: A Brief Focus on School-Based Divorce Interventions

Children from divorced families are overrepresented in the mental health treatment population, but there are no systematic data on the treatment these children typically receive. Many are likely to be in individual psychotherapy or play therapy (Hodges, 1991); surprisingly, however, there have been no systematic attempts to evaluate the efficacy of such treatments. In fact, the only research on child-focused intervention in divorce is on school-based treatment groups. A group format is relatively inexpensive, and it offers children contact with others who have had similar experiences (Grych & Fincham, 1992; Pedro-Carroll, 1997; Stolberg & Cullen, 1983). Supportive peer groups may help to lessen feelings of isolation and loneliness; foster feelings of support and trust; and offer opportunities to clarify divorce-related misconceptions, such as feelings of responsibility or blame for the parents' breakup (Pedro-Carroll, 1997).

Two research groups have systematically studied school-based groups for children whose parents are separated and divorced, and these investigators find empirical support for the intervention in terms of improving children's concerns and their behavior in school (e.g., Pedro-Carroll & Alpert-Gillis, 1997; Stolberg & Mahler, 1994). However, in a review of child- and parent-focused interventions, Lee et al. (1994) noted that child interventions generally produced modest results, as measured by an average effect size of 0.27 standard deviation units. It also appears that child-focused interventions may be more successful in alleviating children's distress (e.g., altering their beliefs about divorce) than in eliminating disturbances (e.g., conduct problems in school) (Emery et al., 1999). In short, school-based groups appear to be a helpful but limited intervention for children in coping with parental divorce. As noted throughout this chapter, this perhaps should not be surprising, given the strong influence of parenting and coparenting on children's adjustment to separation and divorce.

CASE ILLUSTRATION

As we have noted throughout this chapter, there are many issues and possible interventions for couple therapists to recognize about divorce during couple therapy, while a couple is in the midst of a separation, and following separation and divorce. We have chosen the following case, in part, because it illustrates the overriding theme of this chapter—the need to conceptualize divorce as a process that begins while the couple is still married and continues long after the legal action is concluded.

From Couple Therapy to Mediation

Ron and Linda were a white couple in their middle 40s with three boys, aged 20, 17, and 14. They came for couple therapy at Ron's initiation. Ron had sent an e-mail requesting an appointment, but also noted that mediation might be necessary if couple therapy failed.

When interviewed together during the first appointment, Ron and Linda were polite to each other despite obvious underlying tensions. They agreed that there had been long-standing problems in the marriage, including Ron's lack of involvement with the boys (until the last year or two, when he had become quite involved), a lack of affection or a satisfying sex life, and a great emotional distance between the two of them. Linda, a deeply religious person, adamantly maintained that she was committed to the marriage despite the long-standing problems and her strong suspicion that Ron was having an affair. Ron denied having an affair, although he admitted to having a special friendship with this woman. He said that as a close and caring friend, she met his emotional needs, which Linda ignored. Ron insisted that he too was committed to making the marriage work, although he said that he was discouraged to the point where the unthinkable—a separation—was something he had considered.

When interviewed briefly alone during the first session, Ron continued to deny the affair, but admitted to being more pessimistic about the marriage than he had been with Linda. He noted that he had contacted a lawyer just to learn about legal issues in divorce; in fact, the lawyer had made the referral to couple therapy and possibly mediation. Despite this, Ron continued to insist that he wanted the marriage to work. Linda also maintained her unwavering commitment to the marriage when interviewed alone, but she admitted that she too had been to a lawyer in order to protect herself. She did not trust Ron as a husband, father, or financial provider. (Linda worked part-time, but

Ron made far more money than Linda—and she believed he made even more money as a self-employed businessman than he told her about.) Linda also offered this bombshell observation: Not only did she suspect that Ron was having an affair, but her lawyer had hired a private detective who had a videotape of Ron entering a hotel room with this woman. She did not want to tell Ron of the tape, however—in part because she still had hopes for her marriage, and in part because she hoped that Ron would be honest with her.

Although the complex circumstances obviously presented concerns for the therapist as well as the couple, the decision was made to continue with couple therapy. Ron and Linda had never seen a therapist individually or together, and seeking help was a major step for them. They also had few friends and no family members in the area to offer them support. Furthermore, the likely consequences of a legal battle seemed to be worse than the land mines presented by couple treatment. The spouses were told that the goal of couple therapy would be to improve communication and increase emotional understanding, in the hope that this would help them with their marriage. If treatment ended in separation, however, the therapy might be helpful for their mutual understanding—and they still would need to communicate because of the boys.

The couple met for four additional conjoint sessions, which also included individual caucuses. Much of the focus was on the affair, as Ron continued to deny it, and Linda did not reveal the videotape. At the therapist's direction, the discussions moved from accusation and denial to include some exploration of the hurt and damage that even a platonic "special friendship" might cause, as well as to some of the problems in the marriage that might have led Ron to meet his needs elsewhere. Individually and together, Ron and Linda were encouraged to be honest with each other, but they refused to do so until the fifth session. At this time Ron admitted to the therapist (and, with coaching, to Linda) that he wanted a separation, and though he still steadfastly denied having an affair, he was able to tell Linda at the therapist's urging that he had "fallen in love" with this woman.

Linda was emotionally disengaged from the marriage, if morally committed to it, and she was in fact greatly relieved by Ron's admission. She did not press him to admit to a sexual relationship, but instead was relieved to hear him admit to part of the truth. She also insisted that—in the eyes of her sons and in the eyes of God—Ron must accept responsibility for leaving the marriage. Even though she was the injured party, she was willing to forgive him and continue to work on the marriage, but he was not.

Couple therapy did not end with Ron's admission; instead, treatment was transformed to focus on the psychological and eventually the legal details of the separation. The therapist offered to make a referral to a new psychologist or mediator, but both Ron and Linda asked to continue with him, since the therapist/mediator knew them and they were comfortable with him. In the next several appointments, Ron agreed to admit to the boys that he had indeed fallen in love with someone else, and that although he believed that various problems in the marriage justified his decision, it was his decision to leave the marriage. Linda accepted this explanation, and also wanted the boys to know that she was still willing to work things out. Before talking with the boys, the parents worked out a temporary arrangement with the therapist/mediator. For the next several months, Ron would move into an apartment near the family home, see the boys on a regular and frequent basis, and continue to pay all expenses for both residences. Both Ron and Linda consulted with their lawyers about this plan. Although each lawyer raised informative concerns about various things that potentially could go wrong without an ironclad legal agreement, Ron and Linda decided that they could address these concerns themselves.

As the therapist suggested, the parents told the boys together about the separation and the reasons for it. (The boys had been well aware of problems in the marriage.) The parents also discussed their plan to separate in several weeks, indicated where Ron would be living, and how they wanted the boys to spend time with them each (taking into account the teenagers' own busy schedules). According to the parents, the boys reacted as well as possible and in their own ways. The oldest took things in stride, as his focus was on college, which Ron said he would continue to pay for. The middle child, who was closer to Ron, was angry at both of his parents—his mother for being difficult, and his father for not working on the marriage. The youngest said little, but he later went to his mother to make sure she was all right. As had been discussed in therapy, Linda shared some of her feelings, but reassured her son and helped him to consider some of his own emotional reactions.

Postseparation Mediation and Family Therapy

Over the course of the following 8 months, the couple negotiated a detailed separation/divorce agreement with the help of the therapist/mediator, and eventually signed it after careful legal review. (Meetings took place at irregular intervals as needed, not weekly.) The agreement addressed both financial issues and matters of child rearing, with both parents being generous in their respective domains of family power and expertise. Ron was generous financially, and Linda was generous in supporting Ron's relationship with the boys.

During the year and a half after the separation, the parents also brought the two youngest boys to the same psychologist for a few therapy sessions at various times to work on their respective issues of anger and caretaking. The boys were not interested in ongoing therapy, but they seemed to appreciate knowing that there was someone available to help them. The meetings also gave them a forum for dealing with their parents either alone or together.

None of this was easy to accomplish for the parents, the boys, or the therapist. Linda was hurt despite her emotional disengagement from Ron, and she also felt like a failure as a wife, mother, and Christian. Ron was guilt-ridden and anxious, and eventually hurt, angry, and confused when his "new" relationship failed. (He had engaged in painful negotiations with Linda and eventually with the boys, in mediation and outside it, about how the boys would be introduced to this woman. During this time, Linda never revealed the existence of the videotape.) Ron was so distraught that he sought therapy for himself, and asked to be treated by the same therapist. The therapist/mediator referred him elsewhere, however, to avoid a conflict of interest and to remain available to the whole family. Finally, the boys continued to be variously sad, disappointed, hurt, and angry about their parents' divorce. The youngest vowed that he would never put his own children through a divorce, and the middle boy continued to harbor anger toward each of his parents. However, the boys also noted that their worst fears had not come true. Their parents were not "at war" like the divorced parents of some other kids they knew; they were seeing both of their parents frequently and getting along reasonably well with each of them; and, most importantly, their lives were pretty "normal." They were doing as well as ever in school and in their own relationships, and seemed reasonably happy despite the pain of their parents' divorce. The divorce certainly was not the best outcome for them, but fortunately it was not devastating.

REFERENCES

Ahrons, C. (1995). *The good divorce: Keeping your family together when your marriage comes apart.* New York: HarperCollins.

Amato, P. R., & Booth, A. (1997). *A generation at risk: Growing up in an era of family upheaval.* Cambridge, MA: Harvard University Press.

Amato, P. R., Loomis, L. S., & Booth, A. (1995). Parental divorce, marital conflict, and offspring well-being during early adulthood. *Social Forces, 73,* 895–915.

Amato, P. R., & Keith, B. (1991). Parental divorce and the well-being of children: A meta-analysis. *Psychological Bulletin, 110,* 26–46.

Arbuthnot, J., & Gordon, D. A. (1996). Does mandatory divorce education for parents work?: A six-month outcome evaluation. *Family and Conciliation Courts Review, 34,* 60–81.

Arbuthnot, J., Kramer, K. M., & Gordon, D. A. (1997). Patterns of relitigation following divorce education. *Family and Conciliation Courts Review, 35,* 269–279.

Benjamin, M., & Irving, H. H. (1995). Research in family mediation: Review and implications. *Mediation Quarterly, 13,* 53–82.

Bloom, B. L., Asher, S. J., & White, S. W. (1978). Marital disruption as a stressor: A review and analysis. *Psychological Bulletin, 8,* 767–801.

Brown, P. D., & O'Leary, K. D. (1997). Wife abuse in intact couples: A review of couples treatment programs. In O. K. Kantor & J. L. Jasinski (Eds.), *Out of darkness: Contemporary perspectives on family violence* (pp. 194–207). Thousand Oaks, CA: Sage.

Bruce, M. L. (1998). Divorce and psychopathology. In B. P. Dohrenwend (Ed.), *Adversity, stress, and psychopathology* (pp. 219–232). New York: Oxford University Press.

Buchanan, C. M., Maccoby, E. E., & Dornbusch, S. M. (1996). *Adolescents after divorce.* Cambridge, MA: Harvard University Press.

Buehler, C., Betz, P., Ryan, C. M., Legg, B. H., & Trotter, B. B. (1992). Description and evaluation of the orientation for divorcing parents: Implications for postdivorce prevention programs. *Family Relations, 41,* 154–162.

Bumpass, L. L., Martin, T. C., & Sweet, J. A. (1991). The impact of family background and early marital factors on marital disruption. *Journal of Family Issues, 12,* 22–42.

Bumpass, L. L., & Raley, R. K. (1995). Redefining single-parent families: Cohabitation and the changing family reality. *Demography, 32,* 97–109.

Burman, B., & Margolin, G. (1992). Analysis of the relationship between marital relationships and health problems: An interactional perspective. *Psychological Bulletin, 112,* 39–63.

Burns, A., & Scott, C. (1994). *Mother-headed families and why they have increased.* Hillsdale, NJ: Erlbaum.

Cantor, D., & Drake, C. (1983). *Divorced parents and their children: A guide for mental health practitioners.* New York: Springer.

Cherlin, A. J. (1992). *Marriage, divorce, remarriage* (2nd ed.). Cambridge, MA: Harvard University Press.

Cherlin, A. J., Furstenberg, F. F., Chase-Lansdale, P. L., Kiernan, K. E., Robins, P. K., Morrison, D. R., & Teitler, J. O. (1991). Longitudinal studies of effects of divorce on children in Great Britain and the United States. *Science, 252,* 1386–1389.

Conger, R. D., & Chao, W. (1996). Adolescent depressed mood. In R. L. Simons (Ed.), *Understanding differences between divorced and intact families* (pp. 157–175). Thousand Oaks, CA: Sage.

Cummings, E. M., & Davies, P. (1994). *Children and marital conflict.* New York: Guilford Press.

Duncan, G. J., & Hoffman, S. D. (1985). Economic consequences of marital instability. In M. David & T. Smeeding (Eds.), *Horizontal equity, uncertainty and well-being* (pp. 427–469). Chicago: University of Chicago Press.

Eekelaar, J. (1991). *Regulating divorce.* New York: Oxford University Press.

Emery, R. E. (1982). Interparental conflict and the children of discord and divorce. *Psychological Bulletin, 92,* 310–330.

Emery, R. E. (1992). Family conflict and its developmental implications: A conceptual analysis of deep meanings and systemic processes. In C. U. Shantz & W. W. Hartup (Eds.), *Conflict in child and adolescent development* (pp. 270–297). Cambridge, England: Cambridge University Press.

Emery, R. E. (1994). *Renegotiating family relationships: Divorce, child custody, and mediation.* New York: Guilford Press.

Emery, R. E. (1999). *Marriage, divorce, and children's adjustment* (2nd ed). Thousand Oaks, CA: Sage.

Emery, R. E., & Forehand, R. (1994). Parental divorce and children's well-being: A focus on resilience. In R. J. Haggerty, L. Sherrod, N. Garmezy, & M. Rutter (Eds.), *Risk and resilience in children* (pp. 64–99). Cambridge, England: Cambridge University Press.

Emery, R. E., Kitzmann, K. M., & Waldron, M. (1999). Psychological interventions for separated and divorced families. In E. M. Hetherington (Ed.), *Coping with divorce, single parenting, and remarriage* (pp. 323–343). Mahwah, NJ: Erlbaum.

Emery, R. E., Laumann-Billings, L., Waldron, M., Sbarra, D. A., & Dillon, P. (2001). Twelve-year follow-up of mediated and litigated child custody disputes. *Journal of Consulting and Clinical Psychology, 63,* 323–332.

Emery, R. E., Matthews, S., & Kitzmann, K. (1994). Child custody mediation and litigation: Parents' satisfaction and functioning a year after settlement. *Journal of Consulting and Clinical Psychology, 62,* 124–129.

Emery, R. E., Matthews, S., & Wyer, M. M. (1991). Child custody mediation and litigation: Further evidence on the differing views of mothers and fathers. *Journal of Consulting and Clinical Psychology, 59,* 410–418.

Emery, R. E., & Wyer, M. M. (1987a). Divorce mediation. *American Psychologist, 42,* 472–480.

Emery, R. E., & Wyer, M. M. (1987b). Child custody mediation and litigation: An experimental evaluation of the experience of parents. *Journal of Consulting and Clinical Psychology, 55,* 179–186.

Fincham, F. D., Beach, S. R. H., Harold, G. T., &

Osborne, L. N. (1997). Marital satisfaction and depression: Different causal relationships for men and women? *Psychological Science, 8,* 351–357.

Forgatch, M. S., & DeGarmo, D. S. (1998). *Promoting boys' academic outcomes: An effective parent training program for divorcing mothers.* Unpublished manuscript, Oregon Social Learning Center, Eugene, OR.

Gebhard, P. H., & Johnson, A. B. (1998). *The Kinsey data: Marginal tabulations of the 1938–1963 interviews conducted by the Institute for Sex Research.* Bloomington: Indiana University Press.

Gigy, L., & Kelly, J. B. (1992). Reasons for divorce: Perspectives of divorcing men and divorcing women. *Journal of Divorce and Remarriage, 18,* 169–187.

Glass, S., & Wright, T. (1997). Reconstructing marriages after the trauma of infidelity. In W. K. Halford & H. J. Markman (Eds.), *Clinical handbook of marriage and couples interventions* (pp. 471–507). Chichester, England: Wiley.

Glenn, N. (1997). A textbook assault on marriage. *Responsive Community, 7,* 56–66.

Gordon, K. C., & Baucom, D. H. (1999). A multitheoretical intervention for promoting recovery from extramarital affairs. *Clinical Psychology: Science and Practice, 6,* 382–399.

Gotlib, I., Lewinsohn, P. M., & Seeley, J. R. (1998). Consequences of depression during adolescence: Marital status and marital functioning in early adulthood. *Journal of Abnormal Psychology, 107,* 686–690.

Gotlib, I., & McCabe, S. B. (1990). Marriage and psychopathology. In F. D. Fincham & T. N. Bradbury (Eds.), *The psychology of marriage* (pp. 226–257). New York: Guilford Press.

Gottman, J. M. (1999). *The marriage clinic: A scientifically-based marital therapy.* New York: Norton.

Grych, J. H., & Fincham, F. D. (1990). Marital conflict and children's adjustment: A cognitive-contextual framework. *Psychological Bulletin, 108,* 267–290.

Grych, J. H., & Fincham, F. D. (1992). Intervention for children of divorce: Toward greater integration of research and action. *Psychological Bulletin, 111,* 434–454.

Hernandez, D. J. (1992). *When households continue, discontinue, and form* (Current Population Reports, U.S. Bureau of the Census, Series P-23, No. 179). Washington, DC: U.S. Government Printing Office.

Hetherington, E. M. (1993). An overview of the Virginia Longitudinal Study of Divorce and Remarriage with a focus on early adolescence. *Journal of Family Psychology, 7,* 39–56.

Hetherington, E. M., Bridges, M., & Insabella, G. M. (1998). What matters? What does not?: Five perspectives on the association between marital transitions and children's adjustment. *American Psychologist, 53,* 167–184.

Hodges, W. (1991). *Interventions for children of divorce: Custody, access, and psychotherapy.* New York: Wiley.

Hodges, W., & Bloom, B. (1986). Peventive intervention program for newly separated adults: One year later. *Journal of Preventive Psychiatry, 3*(1), 35–49.

Holtzworth-Munroe, A., Smutzler, N., Bates, L., & Sandin, E. (1997). Husband violence: Basic facts and clinical implications. In W. K. Halford & H. J. Markman (Eds.), *Clinical handbook of marriage and couples interventions* (pp. 129–151). Chichester, England: Wiley.

Holtzworth-Munroe, A., Waltz, J., Jacobson, N., Monaco,

V., Fehrenbach, P. A., & Gottman, J. M. (1992). Recruiting non-violent men as control subjects for research on marital violence: How easily can it be done? *Violence and Victims, 7,* 79–88.

Hu, Y. R., & Goldman, N. (1990). Mortality differentials by marital status—An international comparison. *Demography, 27,* 233–250.

Jacobson, N. S., & Christensen, A. (1996). *Integrative couple therapy: Promoting acceptance and change.* New York: Norton.

Janus, S. S., & Janus, C. L. (1993). *The Janus report on sexual behavior.* New York: Wiley.

Jekielek, S. M. (1998). Parental conflict, marital disruption and children's emotional well-being. *Social Forces, 76,* 905–936.

Johnston, J. R. (1994). High conflict divorces. *The Future of Children, 4,* 165–182.

Johnston, J. R., & Roseby, V. (1997). *In the name of the child: A developmental approach to understanding and helping children of conflicted and violent divorce.* New York: Free Press.

Kelly, J. B. (1989). Mediated and adversarial divorce: Respondents' perceptions of their processes and outcomes. *Mediation Quarterly, 24,* 71–88.

Kelly, J. B., Gigy, L., & Hausman, S. (1988). Mediated and adversarial divorce: Initial findings from a longitudinal study. In J. Folberg & A. Milne (Eds.), *Divorce mediation: Theory and practices* (pp. 453–474). New York: Guilford Press.

Kramer, K. M., Arbuthnot, J., Gordon, D. A., Rousis, N. J., & Hoza, J. (1998). Effects of skill-based versus information-based divorce education programs on domestic violence and parental communication. *Family and Conciliation Courts Review, 36,* 9–31.

Laumann-Billings, L. L., & Emery, R. E. (2000). Young adults painful feelings about parental divorce. *Journal of Family Psychology, 14,* 681–687.

Lee, C. M., Picard, M., & Blain, M. D. (1994). A methodological and substantive review of intervention outcome studies for families undergoing divorce. *Journal of Family Psychology, 8,* 3–15.

Lorenz, F. O., Simons, R. L., & Chao, W. (1996). Family structure and mother depression. In R. L. Simons & Associates (Eds.), *Understanding differences between divorced and intact families* (pp. 65–77). Thousand Oaks, CA: Sage.

McLanahan, S., & Garfinkel, I. (2000). *The Fragile Families and Child Well-Being Study: Questions, design, and a few preliminary results.* Unpublished manuscript, Center for Research on Child Well-Being, Princeton University.

McLanahan, S., & Sandefur, G. (1994). *Growing up with a single parent: What hurts, what helps.* Cambridge, MA: Harvard University Press.

Menaghan, E. G., & Lieberman, M. A. (1986). Changes in depression following divorce: A panel study. *Journal of Marriage and the Family, 48,* 319–328.

Michael, R., Gagnon, J. H., Laumann, E. O., & Kolata, G. (1994). *Sex in America: A definitive survey.* Boston: Little, Brown.

Morrison, D. R., & Coiro, M. J. (1999). Parental conflict and marital disruption: Do children benefit when high-conflict marriages are dissolved? *Journal of Marriage and the Family, 61,* 626–637.

National Opinion Research Center. (1991). *General social survey.* Chicago: University of Chicago Press.

O'Leary, K. D. (1996). Physical aggression in intimate relationships can be treated within a marital context under certain circumstances. *Journal of Interpersonal Violence, 11,* 450–452.

O'Leary, K. D., Barling, J., Arias, I., Rosenbaum, A., Malone, J., & Tyree, A. (1989). Prevalence and stability of physical aggression between spouses: A longitudinal analysis. *Journal of Consulting and Clinical Psychology, 57,* 263–268.

O'Leary, K. D., Vivian, D., & Malone, J. (1992). Assessment of physical aggression against women in marriage: The need for multimodal assessment. *Behavioral Assessment, 14,* 5–14.

Pearson, J., & Thoennes, N., (1984). *Final report of the Divorce Mediation Research Project.* (Available from the authors, 1720 Emerson St., Denver, CO 80218)

Pedro-Carroll, J. (1997). The Children of Divorce Intervention Program: Fostering resilient outcomes for school-aged children. In G. Albee & T. P. Gullotta (Eds.), *Primary prevention works: Vol. 6. Issues in children's and families' lives* (pp. 213–238). London: Sage.

Pedro-Carroll, J., & Alpert-Gillis, L. (1997). Preventative interventions for children of divorce: A developmental model for 5 and 6 year-old children. *Journal of Primary Prevention, 18,* 5–23.

Pittman, F. S., III, & Wagers, T. P. (1995). Crises of infidelity. In N. S. Jacobson & A. S. Gurman (Eds.), *Clinical handbook of couple therapy* (pp. 295–316). New York: Guilford Press.

Pryor, J., & Rodgers, B. (2001). *Children in changing families: Life after separation.* Oxford: Blackwell.

Rice, D. G., & Rice, J. K. (1986). Separation and divorce therapy. In N. S. Jacobson & A. S. Gurman (Eds.), *Clinical handbook of marital therapy* (pp. 279–299). New York: Guilford Press.

Seltzer, J. A. (1991). Relationships between fathers and children who live apart: The father's role after separation. *Journal of Marriage and the Family, 53,* 79–101.

Simons, R. L., & Johnson, C. (1996). Mothers' parenting. In R. L. Simons (Ed.), *Understanding differences between divorced and intact families* (pp. 81–94). Thousand Oaks, CA: Sage.

South, S., & Lloyd, K. M. (1995). Spousal alternatives and marital dissolution. *American Sociological Review, 60,* 21–35.

Stolberg, A., & Cullen, P. (1983). Preventative interventions for families of divorce: The Divorce Adjustment Project. In L. A. Kurdek (Ed.), *New directions in child development: Vol. 19. Children and divorce* (pp. 71–81). San Francisco: Jossey-Bass.

Stolberg, A., & Mahler, J. (1994). Enhancing treatment gains in a school-based intervention for children of divorce through skill training, parental involvement, and transfer procedures. *Journal of Consulting and Clinical Psychology, 62,* 147–156.

Straus, M. A., & Gelles, R. J. (1990). How violent are American families?: Estimates from the national family violence resurvey and other studies. In M. A. Strauss & R. J. Gelles (Eds.), *Physical violence in American families: Risk factors and adaptations to violence in 8,145 families* (pp. 95–112). New Brunswick, NJ: Transaction.

Sullivan, H. S. (1953). *The interpersonal theory of psychiatry.* New York: Norton.

Tuer, M. (1995). *Mother–daughter relations in divorced families: Parentification and internalizing and relationship problems.* Unpublished doctoral dissertation, University of Virginia.

Wallerstein, J. S., & Kelly, J. B. (1980). *Surviving the breakup: How children actually cope with divorce.* New York: Basic Books.

Wallerstein, J. S., Blakeslee, S., & Julia, L. M. (2000). *The unexpected legacy of divorce.* New York: Hyperion.

Walsh, F., Jacob, L., & Simons, V. (1995). Facilitating healthy divorce processes: Therapy and mediation approaches. In N. S. Jacobson & A. S. Gurman (Eds.), *Clinical handbook of marital therapy* (pp. 340–365). New York: Guilford Press.

Whisman, M. A., Dixon, A. E., & Johnson, B. (1997). Therapists' perceptions of couple problems and treatment issues. *Journal of Family Psychology, 11,* 361–366.

Wolchik, S. A., West, S. G., Westover, S., Sandler, I. N., Martin, A., Lustig, J., Tein, J., & Fisher, J. (1993). The Children of Divorce parenting intervention: Outcome evaluation of an empirically based program. *American Journal of Community Psychology, 21,* 293–331.

Zill, N., Morrison, D. R., & Coiro, M. J. (1993). Long-term effects of parental divorce on parent–child relationships, adjustment, and achievement in young adulthood. *Journal of Family Psychology, 7,* 91–103.

Section B

Gender, Sexual Orientation, Race, and Culture

Chapter 20

Working with Gender in Couple Therapy

In the 7 years since the publication of the previous edition of this volume, so much has changed with regard to the place of gender in the field of family and couple therapy as to warrant an entirely new chapter, rather than a revision or update. Whereas the chapter on gender in the previous edition included a fairly extensive description of the feminist critique of family and couple therapy, it no longer seems necessary to articulate the critique. The field has accepted that gender matters, and is now focused on precisely how gender enters into the formulation of a problem and into its solution. Recent scholarship addresses the specific ways that gender informs the experience of two people in an intimate relationship, and how that experience influences the problems couples bring to therapy.

A decade ago, it seemed possible that there might emerge a feminist model of couple therapy. It has now become clear that gender is a template that can (and should) be used both in the assessment and in the intervention process, regardless of a therapist's theoretical orientation. The current chapter is an attempt to synthesize the developments in how gender is understood by couple therapists, and to demonstrate one method of applying feminist principles in a case of couple therapy.

THE DEVELOPMENT OF GENDER IN COUPLE THERAPY

Feminist Critique of Family and Couple Therapy

The acceptance of gender as a major organizing construct in couple therapy has followed the same process that resulted in gender's becoming a major category of social reality in society as a whole: critique, advocacy, resistance, and reformation. Beginning in the late 1970s (a decade after the current women's movement began), a small number of family therapists began to offer critiques of family/couple therapy theory and practice that addressed how, by ignoring gender as a meaningful construct, the field was perpetuating some of the same inequities that feminists were challenging in every aspect of public and private life (Caust, Libow, & Raskin, 1981; Goldner, 1985b; Hare-Mustin, 1978; James & McIntyre, 1983). By the early 1980s, these feminist critiques were appearing as workshops on the programs of major national conferences, and some senior women in the field organized the Women's Project in Family Therapy (Walters, Carter, Papp, & Silverstein, 1988). During the mid-1980s, two important invitational conferences were held in Connecticut (known as the Stonehenge Conferences, after the inn where they

533

took place). These conferences brought together a diverse group of 60 or so women therapists who had begun to think, write, teach, and practice about how gender influenced their clients' behavior, they way they construed their clients' problems, and the very practice of family and couple therapy.

The feminist critique of family and couple therapy was well articulated and widely known by practitioners by the mid-1980s. It included analysis of relatively universal systemic concepts, such as complementarity and neutrality, as well as critiques of specific models of family and couple therapy (Avis, 1985; Jacobson, 1983; Margolin, Fernandez, Talovic & Onorato, 1983). It also included a broader inquiry into the homeostatic, politically conservative nature of family therapy in general and couple therapy in particular (Goldner, 1985a; Hare-Mustin, 1978).

Like all social revolutions, the transformation that feminists were advocating for the field was not universally applauded. From the beginning of the critique, there was resistance; this took the form of assertions that applying feminist principles to the practice of couple therapy was itself a form of sexism, and further that it was a violation of the ideal of therapeutic neutrality. Carefully and persistently, feminists challenged the premise that therapeutic neutrality is possible, making the case that neutrality is implicitly supportive of the status quo, which in a sexist society means that neutrality is an inherently prosexist position (Hare-Mustin, 1980). A number of authors drew attention to the issue of wife battering as an example of a situation in which therapeutic neutrality can be particularly devastating, leaving a battered woman to draw the conclusion that she is as responsible for her victimization as her partner (Almeida, 1993; Bograd, 1984; Goldner, Penn, Sheinberg, & Walker, 1990). Slowly the *Zeitgeist* of the field began to change; by the late 1980s, family and couple therapists were generally accepting of Goldner's (1988) claim that gender ought to be considered as salient as generation in therapists' thinking.

Advocacy of Feminist Therapy

In the past decade, writings about gender and family/couple therapy have shifted away from critique and toward the specification of exactly how gender influences the ways men and women experience their problems, interact with each other, and conceptualize their appropriate roles within their relationships to each other (e.g., Knudson-Martin

& Mahoney, 1998; Larson, Hammond, & Harper, 1998). What began as a critique evolved into an exploration of how feminist principles could be applied to the theories and practices of family and couple therapy. This has proven to be a more complex and arduous process than the critique. Feminists could easily agree that women are disadvantaged by the structure of heterosexual marriage, and that traditional marital therapy has done little to address that disadvantage. Specifying how to redress gender inequities in marriage and other committed relationships has proven to be a thornier problem, about which there is still no universal agreement.

Resistance to Feminism

As an intellectual project in family and couple therapy, feminist revisionism in the past decade has lost the momentum described by Sprenkle (1990) in his review of family therapy in the 1980s. Several factors have contributed to this. A number of early voices have left the field, retired, or moved on to other projects (e.g., Betty Carter and Olga Silverstein). Practitioners who were never comfortable with close scrutiny of gender as a therapeutic variable have been eager to define the problem as solved. Therapists, as well as clients, have been willing to accept the tiniest token of change (e.g., a husband talks to a wife for a few minutes a day; a wife opens her own checking account) as an adequate response to gender inequities in marriage. Gender has been subsumed under the larger umbrella of diversity. The economics of the field have pushed practitioners in the direction of concrete, behavioral solutions to only those problems that can easily be described on a symptom checklist. Finally, family/couple therapy has not been immune from the backlash against feminism that Susan Faludi (1991) has documented in other domains of society.

"Genderism" versus Feminism

Current discourse in family therapy has largely replaced feminism with a less politically charged interest in gender effects. As a consequence of this transformation, participation has expanded from a small group composed almost entirely of female feminists to include both men and women—many of whom would not characterize themselves as "feminist," but are nonetheless interested in the ways that gender influences how clients construe their problems and enact solutions to those problems. The broadening base of therapists interested in gender issues has had multiple effects. On the one hand, it has legitimized gender as a clinical issue. It would be difficult in the year 2002 to find a therapist willing to assert that gender has *no* impact in psychotherapy. On the other hand, the broader acceptance of gender as a legitimate variable in therapy has considerably diluted the original focus of the critique—namely, that heterosexual relationships (especially legalized marriages) are relationships in which power counts heavily, and in which power is most often distributed unevenly, in a way that favors husbands over wives. Many of the practitioners who currently write about gender prefer to identify themselves as "nonsexist" or "gender-sensitive" rather than "feminist." In general terms, these labels seem to indicate a belief that gender has *some* consequence in male–female relationships, but also an unwillingness to view such relationships as having significant power dimensions. Consequently, gender issues in couple therapy, though more widely accepted as relevant, have often been removed from the political context in which feminists placed them.

Men's Issues

In the beginning, there was hope among feminist family therapists that their male colleagues would join in the press for fundamental change in the tenets of the field. That hope quickly evaporated in the face of indifference or open resistance to the ideas feminists were promulgating. With a very few exceptions (e.g., Jacobson, 1983; Taggart, 1985), men did not write from a profeminist position or attend feminist presentations at conferences. Nonetheless, gender has become increasingly relevant in the lives of many men in the past two decades. While many women flocked to feminism, some men became interested in the study of maleness, and particularly focused on reclaiming aspects of maleness that had been diluted or lost in postindustrial society (Bly, 1990; Keen, 1991; Pasick, 1992).

Just as feminism in family and couple therapy has been embedded within a larger and broader social movement, so also the men's movement in such therapy has existed in the context of a larger men's movement. The differences between these movements are noteworthy. Whereas feminism has been a *political* movement, advocating fundamental change in every aspect of male–female relations, the men's movement has been largely focused on

personal growth for men. Within family/couple therapy, the men's movement has taken the form of groups of men working on recognizing the personal costs of fitting themselves into culturally acceptable definitions of maleness, and making healing connections to other men. With few exceptions (Pasick, 1992), questions of gender politics and male–female relations have not figured into the project. Thus the work of the two movements is not parallel and not characterized by any attempt at coordination.

THE FEMINIST PRACTICE OF COUPLE THERAPY

How to *do* feminist therapy is much less well understood or articulated than is the critique of traditional family and couple therapy. It is one thing to be sensitive to the differences of power and privilege between partners in intimate relationships, but quite another to know how to redress such inequities without alienating the more privileged or powerful partner. Although there is no monolithic feminist method of couple therapy, all feminist-informed approaches carefully attend to the ways in which power differences are manifested in the couple relationship. This task is not easily accomplished, because the overarching myth about adult couple relationships in this culture is that each participant is an equal partner, and that distinctions of role and function reflect either the personal preferences or complementary competencies of each person, rather than a difference in status.

Analyzing power in an adult couple's relationship draws attention to how agreements are established in the relationship—to distinctions between collaboration and consent versus coercion and control. Some tasks in a couple's life can be accomplished under the condition of unequal power, whereas others are rendered impossible. Many instrumental tasks of family life, such as paying bills, providing meals, and even raising children, can be handled under a model in which one partner is the policy-making executive, while the other implements those policies. Other couple functions, however, may be precluded by an imbalance of power between partners. Intimacy, for example, requires that each partner feel empowered to co-create the meaning of the intimate moment (Weingarten, 1991). One person in the dyad cannot define a moment as intimate without the agreement of the other. Thus equality is a precondition for intimacy (Larson et al., 1998).

In regard to power, a distinction feminists use is the difference between "power *over*" and "power *to*" (Goodrich, 1991). The former refers to coercive power—people's ability to make others bend to their will because they have the means to make the others do so. In its more benign form, this is the power exercised by good parents on behalf of their children. In its darker form, it is exemplified by the oppression of a dictator who forces people into action against their judgment or will. It is power exercised by someone of higher status over someone of lower status. In contrast, power *to* is more akin to personal authority—the ability to perform and produce, and the freedom to do so. Feminists have particularly focused on heterosexual relationships as places where men have exercised power *over* women, while simultaneously denying that they are doing so.

The question of male power in couple relationships has been made more confusing by the fact that men often do not feel powerful, even as they assert power over their partners. Men who batter their partners, for example, often describe themselves as feeling powerless and frustrated, even as they are being violent and abusive. Furthermore, the fact that men may wield power over their partners in their intimate relationships is not to deny that others wield power over men in different domains of their lives; that is, other, higher-status people control and dictate to them.

Women, it must be noted, have also gone to great lengths not to notice the role of submission in their marriages or not to face up to their own ambivalence about exercising power. Fearing success, equating helplessness with femininity, and making submission erotic (Benjamin, 1988) are just a few of the ways that women deny and avoid directly expressing their desire for power. Women are often as reluctant to claim power for themselves as men are to give it up.

Finally, spouses or partners often collude in the creation of a relationship story that claims equality between the sexes, suppressing or ignoring data that do not support this ideal (Knudson-Martin & Mahoney, 1998). Both men and women *want* to believe that they are neither oppressive nor oppressed, and will construct all sorts of "evidence" to support the claim of equality. For example, a man and a woman may say that they share the responsibility of maintaining their home. However, a detailed deconstruction of that assertion may reveal that she takes care of the inside and he takes care of everything outside—a distribution in which the overwhelming majority of the regular mainte-nance is *her* responsibility. Or, by way of demonstrating what a good and responsible father her spouse is, a wife may say that her husband will "babysit the children" whenever she needs him to—not noticing that the very use of the term "babysit" conveys that the children are not his responsibility, but rather something he does on occasion and as a volunteer. *Whatever else is on the agenda in couple therapy, a feminist approach looks carefully at the distribution of power and works toward balancing it.*

This task depends, first of all, on establishing a strong alliance with each partner (see below). Male clients must believe that the therapist is challenging sexist ideology, not maleness per se, and must see the connection between this challenge and attaining the goals of therapy. Interactions, both large and small, must be unpacked of their assumptions about who is entitled, who is required, and on what basis tasks and roles get assigned. Dominant narratives (the accepted stories about what is real) must be identified, and suppressed narratives (the stories about alternate views of reality) must be revealed.

The feminist therapeutic conversation must mirror the goals of feminism. It must be critical of the status quo; respectful of each person's dignity; and sensitive to the often subtle ways that gender ideology constrains thought, feeling, and action—inhibiting both men and women from knowing and expressing their full human potential.

Alliance Issues

No matter what mental model of change the therapist has, the sine qua non of successful therapy lies in a strong alliance between client and therapist. Decades of psychotherapy research have repeatedly shown that clients report more improvement when they regard their therapist as genuine, caring, and empathic, no matter what the therapist's theoretical orientation. Alliance issues are notoriously tricky in work with a couple, as each partner may feel concern that the therapist is more interested in what the other partner has to say, or believes that the other partner's positions are more valid. Working with a couple thus requires that the therapist pay exquisite attention to balancing concern, care, and validation between the partners.

Practicing as a feminist makes the task of alliance building even more challenging, as the very premise of feminism—namely, that men as a group have been privileged over women—may draw the therapist into challenging the male partner or working directly to change the power balance of the couple to favor the woman more and the man less. Such interventions, although they may be necessary to solve the problem, put an undeniable burden on the alliance that must be attended to by the therapist. Most feminist therapists who work with heterosexual couples address this dilemma by attending overtly to the costs that privilege have exacted from men, and by attending to the ways in which men have been injured or hindered by patriarchy.

The translation of a political reality like gender into a clinical conversation about a relationship dilemma requires care and subtlety. The fact that *some* men exploit women is not sufficient to explain the experience of any particular male client. Neither is the notion that women are disempowered by the institution of marriage sufficient to explain how a particular female client perceives and uses power within her marriage. Feminist couple therapy attends to the details and daily practices that determine how privilege and responsibility are allocated and enacted within the relationship.

Therapists who are interested in exploring the gender beliefs of their clients must also be interested in and attuned to their personal beliefs about gender, and be able to bring these beliefs into therapeutic conversations in a way that is not shaming, aggressive, naïve, or polemical. A sense of humor helps, as does the ability to separate the evils of patriarchy from the behavior of a particular male client. It is useful to bear in mind (and sometimes to share with clients) that male–female relationships have changed more in the past three decades than in the previous 300,000 years. All of us are in the midst of this great cultural transformation, and the fact that we experience stress, confusion, and conflict about what constitutes gender and how it should be enacted is a normal (albeit uncomfortable) consequence of that transformation.

Therapeutic Approach

In addition to feminist theory, the approach to therapy described here has been most influenced by two methods. The first of these is a model that has been developed by my colleagues at the Family Institute (FI) at Northwestern University over the past 15 years (Breunlin, Schwartz, & Mac Kune-Karrer, 1992; Goodrich, Rampage, Ellman, & Halstead, 1988; Pinsof, 1995). Within this model, the change process starts with the present, here-and-now issues, and addresses those issues at the

most overt and behavioral level. Only if working at this level does not provide relief does the therapist move toward the more intrapsychic and historical.

Although meaningful change can occur at the behavioral, cognitive, or affective level, human beings tend to have more direct control over their behavior than their beliefs and feelings; hence the FI model begins by attempting to influence behavior. Sometimes changes in behavior promotes changes in beliefs and feelings as well. If a change in behavior or action does not lead to resolution of the problem, the therapist must move the inquiry into the domain or belief or meaning, exploring how the ways in which the clients think about the problem and its solution may actually be getting in the way or resolution. If an exploration of meaning does not lead to a shift in the problem, the therapist will need to focus more directly on the feelings of the clients, and examine how those feelings hold the problem in place. Obviously, in the course of a single session the therapist may address all three domains of experience, attempting to understand how each is influencing the others.

Just as the therapist starts with the behavioral and moves inward (psychologically) only if it proves necessary, likewise the therapist begins with the present and only moves to the historical if it is essential in order to solve the problem. For example, if the presenting problem is sexual dissatisfaction, modification of each partner's behavior might be sufficient to achieve resolution. On the other hand, if the problem is held in place by beliefs and feelings resulting from one partner's past sexual abuse, then successful resolution of the problem may very well require a detailed exploration of the historical bases of that partner's beliefs and feelings about sex.

The central activity of therapy within the FI model consists of identifying and removing the constraints that are preventing clients from living their lives the way they would like to be doing. Some problems that clients bring to therapy have few, relatively simple constraints, and will therefore be fairly easy to resolve. An example of such a problem might be a couple in conflict over managing a young child's refusal to go to sleep without a parent's presence. If this is a relatively isolated conflict within a relationship where the partners are generally able to agree on parenting issues, and there is no physiological reason for the child's difficulty, a single session of therapy may be sufficient to develop a successful intervention strategy. On the other end of the spectrum, the very same presenting problem may exist within a complicated web of constraints that includes intrapsychic and family-of-origin issues, biological or developmental conditions, cultural differences, and gender conflict. In general, the more complicated the web of constraints surrounding a problem, the more difficult it will be to resolve.

The FI model uses various lenses, or "metaframeworks," to guide the therapist in discovering what is constraining the system. Gender is one of these lenses. In the process of assessment, the therapist will consider a variety of metaframeworks (which also include such categories as culture, organization, internal process, and development). In working with heterosexual couples, gender will always be considered. This is not to say that gender issues *always* constitute the heart of relational problems between men and women; rather, gender is so commonly at least part of the constraint that not to consider it would be equivalent to ignoring the impact of recent immigration on the cultural identity of a family.

A second clinical influence on the present approach has been the narrative therapy method developed by Michael White (1995) and others (Freedman & Combs, 1996; White & Epston, 1990; Zimmerman & Dickerson, 1994; see also Freedman & Combs, Chapter 11, this volume). The narrative approach is grounded in postmodern epistemology, which assumes that human beings construct their social realities through interactions with other people and social institutions. Furthermore, these realities are largely constituted through language. Thus narrative therapists believe, in a very real sense, that we cannot "know" what we cannot "name."

Our experience of self is carried by the story or narrative we believe about that self. Each of us lives our story. Some stories easily support change, growth, optimism, and problem solving. Other stories turn in on themselves and always seem to lead to the same unsatisfying outcome. The narrative therapist attempts to draw out hidden or unexamined elements of each client's story, and to open up space for new aspects of the story to be known to the client, in the hope that this space will allow new, more satisfying storylines, plots, and outcomes to emerge.

The narrative approach is particularly useful as a tool to explore gender, because it has as one of its goals the drawing out of suppressed or marginalized discourses—aspects of the story that are unavailable to clients because they violate the "rules" of what society accepts as true, real, or even

possible. Few clients who come for couple therapy tell the story of their troubles in terms of gender politics. In part, this is because the cultural story of gender in contemporary North American society is that men and women are equal partners; that gender-based marital/couple inequities are relics of the past; and that all differences in the power and privilege of heterosexual partners must therefore stem from some other source than gender politics. This dominant narrative obscures how gender-determined power differences can shape a couple's life and thus make those differences difficult to "see," much less to challenge. Using a narrative approach, a feminist therapist can draw out elements of clients' stories that are colored by gender inequities, and look for exceptions to the story—"unique outcomes" that demonstrate possible directions for change. (For a more complete discussion of these concepts, see Freedman & Combs, 1996, Ch. 3.)

CASE ILLUSTRATION

The following case illustrates how gender beliefs and practices can severely constrain a couple's functioning, and how using a feminist analysis of the relationship can help identify ways to lift those constraints.

Background

Debbie and John had been married for about a decade when they entered couple therapy. Within a few minutes of beginning our first session, several pieces of information were revealed that strongly suggested the presence of a power imbalance in the relationship. First, John was 15 years older than Debbie; second, he came from a solidly upper-middle-class family, whereas her father had been a mail carrier; third, he was a named partner in a very successful law practice, while she had left paid employment as a legal secretary at the time of their marriage. Their presenting problems were fairly mundane: John felt unappreciated by Debbie; she was often angry with him; and their sexual contact had been deteriorating in both frequency and satisfaction for several years.

This was John's second marriage and Debbie's first. He had two sons from his first marriage—one in his third year of college, the other recently graduated and working in another city. One of the chronic disagreements between Debbie and

John was whether to try to conceive a child. John was reluctant, but had never taken a definite position on the matter; Debbie had felt too overwhelmed in the first few years of the marriage to consider the possibility, but had been pressing John to try for the past 3 years. John was 49 and Debbie was 34 at the time therapy began.

Another nagging and unresolved issue in the marriage concerned the prenuptial agreement John had insisted upon before the wedding. After an engagement of 6 months, and with just 4 weeks left before the wedding, John asked Debbie to accompany him to a meeting with his family attorney, to discuss "wills and estate planning." When she arrived at the meeting, Debbie was surprised and dismayed to be presented with a prenuptial agreement stipulating that she held no claims against any of John's considerable wealth or property, and that in the event of a divorce she would be entitled only to her personal property and maintenance (amounting to less than 10% of John's annual salary, with a small increment depending on the length of the marriage). Debbie was offended and hurt, and tried to dissuade John from pursuing the matter, but he was adamant that the document must be signed before the wedding could take place. He explained that the agreement was more for his children's protection than his own, and that although he loved Debbie and fully expected to be married to her for the rest of their lives, he felt he needed to prepare for every contingency. Debbie took the agreement to an independent attorney, who advised against signing it, saying that it was very punitive. By that time, however, the wedding was only 3 weeks away; rather than risk a postponement, she decided to sign it and hope for the best.

Although he readily acknowledged that he had handled the prenuptial agreement poorly, John was truly perplexed about why money was a sticking point in the marriage, since "Debbie has a credit card with no ceiling on it, and total control of the checkbook. She buys anything she wants. *She* pays the bills. When she tells me she's short of money in the account, I make a deposit. So what's the problem?" In fact, Debbie herself had some difficulty articulating the problem. She felt that she was living a life of extraordinary privilege, and that it was only possible because of John's success and generosity. At the same time, her interpretation of the facts was that it *was* all John's money, and that she had no legitimate authority to determine how it got spent.

Useful conversations about their problems were hindered by some mismatches in their communication styles. John was a sober, almost stern man who prided himself on his rationality and his ability to stay calm in emotionally intense situations. Debbie was generally cheerful and affable, but could quickly become very distressed and angry with John when she felt he was being critical or withholding. As Debbie became more upset, John would appear to become more stoic and withdrawn. She interpreted his behavior as uncaring; he interpreted hers as immature and irrational.

The couple's sexual relationship had initially been extremely positive for both partners. John, in particular, felt that being with Debbie had been very fulfilling, especially in contrast to his first wife, who had never seemed very interested. But over the last several years of this marriage, John felt that Debbie had become much less interested, and that she had sex with him mostly to keep him from getting angry with her. Debbie agreed that she had gradually felt less interested in sex, but didn't want to acknowledge that it had anything to do with John. She supposed it was just what happened to people after they'd been married for a while.

Assessment

The first step of assessment involves recognizing the relational assets that a couple brings to the therapy process. In this case, there were several obvious assets. First, John and Debbie still cared deeply about each other and did not want to give up on their marriage. Second, although neither spouse could get a useful grip on his/her own contribution to the problem, they were each willing to concede, in principle, that there must be some shared culpability for the decline of the marriage. Third, they shared a very positive narrative about the history of the relationship, including a passionate romance and a very satisfying sex life.

The next important question to ask is this: "What is getting in the way of their having the kind of life they want?" The assumption behind this question is that people come to therapy when they are stuck, and that the purpose of therapy is to break through the impasse, allowing the clients to move forward into whatever life they wish to create for themselves. The complexity of the task for the therapist is not in prescribing how life should be, but rather in deciphering the constraints that prevent the clients from achieving their goals. Usually, at least some of these constraints are not apparent to the clients. Furthermore, most problems addressed by therapists are multiply constrained, requiring patient inquiry and careful observation of clients' interactions, beliefs, and feelings.

For Debbie and John, the goal was to have a highly intimate marriage. To them, intimacy meant both having a full sexual relationship and feeling emotionally close. They realized that the decline of their sexual life and their difficulty resolving some of the chronic major disagreements between them must somehow be related, and they were looking to therapy to help them sort out this relationship.

Analysis

Looking at Debbie and John's marriage through the lens of gender revealed marked differences in the roles they played and the rules under which they operated. For example, although Debbie literally kept the family checkbook, she would never think of making a major purchase without consulting John. In contrast, after winning a particularly large case 2 years earlier, John had impulsively treated himself to a new sports car, driving it home and surprising Debbie with it. Although she told the story of the sports car to illustrate how different they were about spending money, and how unfair the difference seemed to her, Debbie immediately felt the need to add that John was extremely generous and would often give her an expensive piece of jewelry "just because."

Without a feminist analysis, it would be easy to see the financial arrangements of this marriage as simply enviable. First of all, there was more than enough wealth that no real need would ever have to go unattended; second, John's delegating of the checkbook to Debbie gave her apparent control over a considerable amount of money; and, third, John was clearly a generous person, who took pleasure in giving material things to people he loved.

A feminist analysis would go beyond the overt practices of money handling (and similar practical matters) in the marriage to look at the underlying assumptions and rules. Such an analysis would need to include these factors: Debbie's control of the checkbook was at John's pleasure; *he* was the one who funded the account, and who could decide at any time not to continue doing so. The fact that their spending habits were so different might not be coincidental. The paradigm for money in this marriage was established in the prenuptial agreement, which stipulated that the money belonged to John. Debbie was keenly aware

that her access to wealth was due to John's largesse, and she chose not to test the limits of that generosity by making any large purchases without John's agreement. Nevertheless, Debbie's experience of the money as John's and not hers both informed her spending choices and supported her experience of inequality in the marriage. In the domain of finances, John clearly had both *personal authority* (of which he was both aware and proud) and *power over* Debbie (which he denied). This marriage demonstrates the "golden rule" that "whoever has the gold makes the rules" (Carter & Peters, 1996).

Gender also seemed relevant in understanding the difficulties John and Debbie were having sexually. Each reported that their sexual attraction to the other had been very powerful at the beginning of their relationship. John was separated from his first wife and in the process of divorcing her when a casual chat with Debbie at an office function turned into an entire evening engrossed in deep conversation with each other. Within weeks they became lovers, spending much of their weekends in bed. They both reported this as an idyllic period, full of experimentation and highly satisfying.

Two months into the relationship, John's wife pressed for reconciliation. Reluctantly, but with the support of his therapist and the urging of his sons, John agreed to attempt repairing the marriage. Debbie was overtly supportive, but also devastated; she was already in love with John, and felt wounded and abandoned. They agreed to have no contact outside the office. Debbie sank into depression and began her own therapy. Although she had had previous relationships, John was the first man she ever felt in love with.

Three months into the reconciliation, John realized that he was not able to reengage himself emotionally in his marriage, and left again—this time permanently. He immediately contacted Debbie, who was initially reluctant to risk further disappointment, and so refused his calls. Debbie's withdrawal only seemed to increase John's pursuit, and after several weeks she gave in to his request that they spend some time together to "sort things out." Shortly thereafter they moved in together, and 5 months later (1 week after John's divorce was final), they became engaged.

Although Debbie initially denied any lingering effect from the early difficulties that the relationship had faced, she described her interest in sex as never again reaching the same level she had experienced in those first 2 months with John. Apparently John's attempt to reconcile with his first wife had created some fundamental insecurity in Debbie, from which she had never recovered.

Another area of difference between spouses that is clarified by a feminist lens has to do with the decoding of their communication patterns. In recent years, both feminist and nonfeminist writers have addressed gender-related communication styles. Some of these writings make sweeping generalizations about the vast chasm that separates men and women in conversation, claiming that men *only* want to talk about problems to be solved, while women *only* want to discuss feelings (Gray, 1992). Such writing is distinctly unhelpful from a feminist perspective—both because it overstates the differences between men and women, and because it posits those differences as enduring gender-determined traits, rather than socially constructed roles and habits.

More helpful work has focused on empirically specifying what men and women actually do differently in conversation, under what conditions, and with what outcomes. Such research has revealed, for example, that a wife is more likely than a husband to initiate discussion of a marital problem; once he is engaged in the discussion, however, her effort goes into maintaining his attention rather than pursuing her own points (Ball, Cowan, & Cowan, 1995). In a related finding of interest to feminists, husbands are sensitive to and repelled by their wives' criticism, and will withdraw from conflict if such criticism comes up during the earliest part of a disagreement (Gottman, 1994). In some cases (e.g., Knudson-Martin & Mahoney, 1996), these findings are placed in the context of a feminist analysis, and thus will address the power dimensions of husband withdrawal as a conflict tactic. Nonfeminist researchers will simply report the differences without addressing their meaning within the politics of marriage (Gottman, 1994).

In the case of John and Debbie, their patterns of communications certainly fell within the customary gender roles. John was rational and stoic; even while discussing a conflict that occurred between sessions, he exuded a calm that seemed to indicate how little he was touched by the fray. In sharp contrast, Debbie could easily become either tearful or furious in the retelling of some troubling episode that had occurred the previous week, and associate it to a string of similar episodes stretching back over a number of years. On any measure of expressed emotion, Debbie would probably outscore John by a factor of three.

Since the enterprise of psychotherapy is primarily conversational, and since conversation is facilitated by following rules that make it possible to speak, be heard, reach understanding, and plan future actions, it is biased toward exactly the kind of style demonstrated by John. Indeed, therapists (whether male or female) tend to feel more similar to clients like John, and to be more challenged by a style like Debbie's, which tends to be dramatic, spontaneous, nonlinear, and intuitive. John's style may seem overly rational, but such a client is not disruptive, hard to follow, or overtly uncooperative. Thus many therapists will regard this type of client as the easier of the two.

For a feminist therapist, one question to consider would be this: "Why was Debbie's style so dissimilar from John's?" Rather than resorting to explanations about innate gender differences, a feminist might be drawn to consider whether Debbie expressed herself in such dramatic ways exactly because she felt that her position was weaker than John's, and her points less likely to be taken seriously. Rather than tell Debbie to do what John did (i.e., tell her to be more like him), one feminist approach would be to work on getting John to be more responsive to Debbie's need for validation of her position. This would involve his listening to her so well and so responsively that she would not need to escalate the intensity of her communication to try to get his attention. At the same time, it would be useful to help Debbie work on what Gottman (1994) calls a "soft startup" to a discussion of difference, since research has shown that men's withdrawal during conflict is frequently triggered in reaction to women's rapid emotional escalation at the front end of an argument.

Therapy

Over the course of the first few sessions of therapy, we clarified the major issues John and Debbie wanted to address: money, sex, whether to have a baby, and managing conflict more successfully. I began introducing the idea of constraints, and asked them to hypothesize with me about the various factors that might be constraining their relationship. John suggested that he would be less reluctant about the idea of a baby if he felt their sexual relationship wasn't already so shaky. Not surprisingly, Debbie thought that their sexual relationship would be improved if she didn't feel so resentful of John, both for his reluctance to have a baby and what she described as his control over her life in general.

Merely acting on the decision to come to therapy led to a noticeable decrease in the tension within the marriage. It was therefore possible to use the early sessions of therapy to build rapport and strengthen the therapeutic alliance. We spent some time discussing how different their lives were from each other, and how each spouse felt that the other had little appreciation for the tensions and difficulties his/her own particular role created.

John lived a very structured, highly routinized life. He arose very early each day, exercised for an hour before getting ready to go to the office, spent 10 to 12 hours at work, returned home between 7:30 and 8:00 P.M. each evening, had dinner with Debbie, read or watched television for a short while, and usually fell asleep before 10:30. In contrast, Debbie's life was both more varied and less predictable. She normally awoke at about the time John left for the office, and spent her day attending to the management of their home, social life, extended family relationships, personal finances, and charitable commitments. Debbie's plans were often modified as the day went along, depending on what John needed her to do, whether she needed to wait at home for repair people, or whether some elderly family member needed attending to.

Each partner envied the other's life. John felt that Debbie had tremendous freedom to do what she wanted, while Debbie felt that John had order, predictability, and the ability to designate to others (associate attorneys, his secretary, Debbie herself) those tasks he did not care to do. John longed for more time to pursue his own interests (particularly fly fishing and photography). Debbie wished she felt more control over her life, as well as a greater sense of accomplishment.

Early in therapy, I had the opportunity to draw their attention to the methods they used to try to influence each other. Debbie began a session complaining that John took her completely for granted. She cited an example from earlier that week, when he had called her from the office to ask that she quickly arrange a dinner party for an associate who was leaving the firm. Debbie's experience was that John had not asked her, but instructed her; that he was completely disrespectful of what was already on her agenda; and that he treated her as if she were his employee, not his spouse.

As usual, John's response to Debbie's accusations was calm and rational, although he was clearly irritated. He reminded Debbie that she was far more skilled as a social organizer than he, that she was the one who knew the caterer, that he was very busily occupied running a business, and that

it was reasonable to expect her to contribute to their lives together. But, he added, if the dinner party was too much for her to handle, they could have the event at a restaurant. At this point in the conversation, Debbie became tearful and dejected. She told John that maybe this was just hopeless, that he should find someone better suited to this marriage than she could ever be, and that there must be something seriously wrong with her that she was so overwhelmed with ordinary life.

This interchange exemplified two gendered dimensions of the marriage. First, John's request of Debbie felt to her like an instruction rather than a request for cooperation; it was a demonstration (to her) of his greater power and authority in the marriage. As such, it created in her an urge to resist—to rebalance the power in the relationship. Unfortunately (and this was the second gendered dimension demonstrated in this interaction), the method of resistance that Debbie used was both ineffectual and self-depreciating. Faced with John's overt rationality, Debbie became exceedingly emotional and extreme in her response. Instead of challenging John effectively for imposing an agenda on her, she became despairing—partly blaming herself for having such difficulty getting things done, and partly blaming John for putting her in a position of being reminded about this "defect." For his part, on hearing his wife express such strong feeling about a problem, he proceeded to "solve" it by offering to stage the party at a restaurant.

Intervention

I used this incident to begin a conversation about how aspects of their gender arrangements were constraining the marriage. First, I asked John and Debbie to join me in attempting to see the problem in all its complexity—in examining it from a number of angles, to get the fullest possible description of it before we attempted to solve it. With some support and coaching from me, they were able to untangle several aspects of the problem. First, John approached Debbie in a way that conveyed both his discouragement that he would succeed in getting her cooperation, and also his irritation at the unfairness he felt in having to "beg" for her help. Debbie acknowledged that she felt reluctant to simply cooperate with John's request, because she took his discouragement and irritation as entitlement and intimidation. She affirmed that she did indeed feel that it was fair of John to ask for her support and assistance, and that the task at hand was well within her competence. She just didn't want to be taken for granted or ordered about.

Once we elaborated the various meanings and misinterpretations of the problem, it became easier to solve. However, the problem of getting cooperation was embedded in a larger issue in the marriage: the imbalance of power that stretched all the way back to the beginning of the relationship, and that was formalized in the prenuptial agreement. My hypothesis was that Debbie resisted John's influence in part because she constantly felt the need to assert herself and her own autonomy, so as not to be completely dominated by John. But Debbie herself was not clear about her motivations. At some moments, she spoke as if she believed she was simply not competent to be John's partner in life; at other times, her anger in denying John seemed strongly to suggest that she was protesting what she regarded as the unfairness of their marital arrangement. However, any time that Debbie came close to challenging John on the basic arrangement of the marriage, he effectively silenced her by reminding her that (1) she had agreed to the arrangement long ago; and (2) she lacked for nothing, and had access to almost anything she wanted.

By this time in the therapy, I was convinced both that the prenuptial agreement was a legitimate problem in its own right, and that it also was symbolic of the overall inequality in the marriage. I asked John whether he would be willing to discuss the possible consequences, good and bad, of modifying the agreement. His response was understandably defensive. How could he consider increasing his vulnerability while the marriage was in such precarious condition? If he and Debbie were in a better place as a couple, he could see that it might make sense to modify the agreement, in order to make her feel less disadvantaged; as things stood, however, it made no sense to him. Like most people with power, John both underestimated its significance and was reluctant to yield it.

Given just this much support for her position, Debbie was able to challenge John more effectively than she had ever been able to do on her own. She admitted to John that some of her resistance to his ideas and agendas probably stemmed from her anger at him over the inequities in their marriage. Some of these inequities—such as their ages, family backgrounds, and educational differences—could not be changed. Others—such as like the way money was handled, whether they had a child, and

the quality of their collaboration as a couple—were decisions they could make and remake to fit their goals.

At this point, I invited Debbie to think out loud about what might constitute a meaningful change in the prenuptial agreement and how she imagined it might change her relationship to John. Debbie immediately made two concrete suggestions: first, that John should put some of the assets accumulated during their marriage in her name; and, second, that from this time on, all assets (including property that might be purchased during their marriage) should be jointly held in both of their names. John's immediate reply was to argue that what Debbie wanted was impractical for a variety of reasons having to do with tax implications. Rather than continue an argument on terms with which Debbie could not engage, I instead suggested to John that he assume for the sake of discussion that his accountants could solve any technical problems that might arise from a transfer of assets, and instead discuss with Debbie how it would change the climate of their marriage to accomplish such a shift.

Being deflected from his usual argument with Debbie created space for John to express some of his underlying concerns. Reluctantly, he acknowledged that openly granting Debbie direct entitlement to the wealth he generated made him feel fearful that she had married him for his money, rather than because she truly loved him for himself. Second (and paradoxically), John admitted his fear that if Debbie had money in her own right, she would leave him. John's feelings did not surprise Debbie; rather, they confirmed what she had always suspected. In part, she was indignant that John would attribute such mercenary motivations to her, but another part of her was relieved to have the issue made explicit.

I encouraged Debbie to relate to the part of John that was afraid of losing control—afraid even of losing *her* if she didn't need him for his money—and asked her to share with John her version of their story together if money were not the main theme. Debbie's version of their story emphasized respect, caring, and mutuality. She created a vision of the relationship in which she cast John and herself as equal and loving partners, in contrast to the subordinate and often resentful role she currently believed she played.

I asked Debbie and John to go home and continue thinking about the story they wanted to have about their relationship and what changes in their lives would be necessary to enact that story. When they returned the next week, John reported having been very moved by the previous session. He told Debbie that he had never realized how he used money to handle his fear of abandonment. For the first time, he expressed a clear understanding of the difference between paying the bills and really having control. He proposed a postnuptial agreement that would give Debbie assets in her own name, a regular income, and shared ownership of their two homes and several autos.

Within a couple of months, all the changes John had proposed to Debbie were legally formalized. John embraced the idea that he would never have to wonder again whether Debbie stayed with him because she wanted to or because she needed to. It actually took Debbie longer to incorporate her new status into her self-perception. It was hard for her to think of herself as independent and self-sufficient. Removing the constraint of their financial arrangement revealed other, more internal constraints that kept Debbie from feeling herself to be John's equal.

Changing the Self

The first of these internal constraints had to do with Debbie's fundamental theory about male–female relationships, which turned out to be very traditional, equating male caretaking and providing with love. If John no longer needed to take care of her, what would be the basis of the relationship? Furthermore, if John's financial withholding was no longer the barrier to her having the kind of life she wanted, what would she need to change in order to create that life?

While Debbie grappled with these questions, John too faced some internal obstacles to further change, such as his preference for being in charge, his certainty that his preferred way was almost always the "right" way, and his discomfort with exposing his own emotional vulnerabilities.

The marital therapy ceased to focus on their struggle to get each other to change, and instead became centered on the personal growth each partner needed to achieve in order to be capable of participating in the kind of marriage both said they wanted. For Debbie, this required developing a larger life in which her marriage was an important, but not the exclusive, element. With my encouragement, Debbie became involved in her church's very active choir group, where she quickly became a soloist. She also joined a women's investment club, to become more educated about financial matters, and was asked to sit on the board of a charitable foundation that she and John had contributed to over the years. As Debbie carved out a life for herself apart from her identity as John's wife, she gained self-confidence, was less dependent on John's approval, and became less resentful of the requests he made of her.

John's work at this stage of therapy was more inward, and in some ways more difficult. Whereas each step Debbie took into the world received support and validation from the various people and organizations she made connections with, John's efforts to shift his role in his marriage was done in private, almost secretively. John was convinced that his male friends and colleagues would think he'd lost his mind if he told them he was modifying his prenuptial agreement with Debbie, and would see it as a sign of weakness. Likewise, he was certain that they would be uncomfortable in any discussion linking money, power, and intimacy. So all the changes John made—modifying the prenuptial agreement, accepting greater influence from Debbie, and becoming more aware of his feelings and more expressive of them—took place with no other support or feedback than that which he received from her.

Fortunately, the changes that John made in the ways he related to Debbie were very meaningful to her, and were received with great enthusiasm. The marital climate began softening and became warmer and more affectionate. As Debbie's sense of personal authority grew, she was able to see her husband as having his own vulnerabilities, which increased her empathy and compassion for him. Over time, this also seemed to lead to a renewal of Debbie's sexual interest in John.

Ending Therapy

Although the question of whether to have a baby was still unanswered, Debbie and John felt that they had received what they wanted out of the therapy, and terminated after about 2 years of work. Compared to their initial presentation, they left therapy a warmer, more intimate, less distressed couple. The power imbalance between them had been lessened to the point where it no longer constrained their marriage. Their occasional disagreements were far less disruptive than they had been at the start of treatment, and their general level of understanding and acceptance of each other's needs and feelings had increased significantly.

REFERENCES

Almeida, R. (1993). Unexamined assumptions and service delivery systems: Feminist theory and racial exclusions. *Journal of Feminist Family Therapy, 5*, 3–23.

Avis, J. M. (1985). The politics of functional family therapy: A feminist critique. *Journal of Marital and Family Therapy, 11*, 127–138.

Ball, F., Cowan, P., & Cowan, C. (1995). Who's got the power?: Gender differences in partners' perceptions of influence during marital problem-solving discussions. *Family Process, 34*, 303–321.

Benjamin, J. (1988). *The bonds of love: Psychoanalysis, feminism and the problem of domination.* New York: Pantheon.

Bly, R. (1990). *Iron John.* Reading, MA: Addison-Wesley.

Bograd, M. (1984). Family systems approaches to wife battering: A feminist critique. *American Journal of Orthopsychiatry, 54*, 558–568.

Breunlin, D., Schwartz, R., & Mac Kune-Karrer, B. (1992). *Metaframeworks: Transcending the models of family therapy.* San Francisco: Jossey-Bass.

Carter, B., & Peters, J. (1996). *Love, honor and negotiate.* New York: Simon & Schuster.

Caust, B., Libow, J., & Raskin, P. (1981). Challenges and promises of training women as family systems therapists. *Family Process, 20*, 439–447.

Faludi, S. (1991). *Backlash: The undeclared war against American women.* New York: Crown.

Freedman, J., & Combs, G. (1996). *Narrative therapy: The social construction of preferred realities.* New York: Norton.

Goldner, V. (1985a). Feminism and family therapy. *Family Process, 24*, 31–47.

Goldner, V. (1985b). Warning: Family therapy may be dangerous to your health. *The Family Therapy Networker, 9*, 19–23.

Goldner, V. (1988). Generation and gender: Normative and covert hierarchies. *Family Process, 27*, 17–31.

Goldner, V., Penn, P., Sheinberg, M., & Walker, G. (1990). Love and violence: Gender paradoxes in volatile attachments. *Family Process, 29*, 343–364.

Goodrich, T. J. (1991). *Women and power: Perspectives for family therapy.* New York: Norton.

Goodrich, T. J., Rampage, C., Ellman, B., & Halstead, K. (1988). *Feminist family therapy: A casebook.* New York: Norton.

Gottman, J. (1994). *Why marriages succeed or fail.* New York: Simon & Schuster.

Gray, J. (1992). *Men are from Mars, women are from Venus.* New York: Harper-Collins.

Hare-Mustin, R. (1978). A feminist approach to family therapy. *Family Process, 17*, 181–194.

Hare-Mustin, R. (1980). Family therapy may be dangerous to your health. *Professional Psychology, 11*, 935–938.

Jacobson, N. (1983). Beyond empiricism: The politics of marital therapy. *American Journal of Family Therapy, 1*, 11–24.

James, K., & McIntyre, D. (1983). The reproduction of families: The social role of family therapy? *Journal of Marital and Family Therapy, 9*, 119–129.

Keen, S. (1991). *Fire in the belly.* New York: Bantam.

Knudson-Martin, C., & Mahoney, A. (1996). Gender dilemmas and myth in the construction of marital bargains: Issues for marital therapy. *Family Process, 35*, 137–153.

Knudson-Martin, C., & Mahoney, A. (1998). Language and processes in the construction of equality in new marriages. *Family Relations, 47*, 81–91.

Larson, J., Hammond, C., & Harper, J. (1998). Perceived equity and intimacy in marriage. *Journal of Marital and Family Therapy, 24*, 487–506.

Margolin, G., Fernandez, V., Talovic, S., & Onorato, R. (1983). Sex role considerations and behavioral marital therapy: Equal does not mean identical. *Journal of Marital and Family Therapy, 9*, 131–145.

Pasick, R. (1992). *Awakening from the deep sleep: A powerful guide for courageous men.* New York: HarperCollins.

Pinsof, W. (1995). *Integrative problem-centered therapy.* New York: Basic Books.

Sprenkle, D. (1990). Continuity and change. *Journal of Marital and Family Therapy, 16*, 337–340.

Taggart, M. (1985). The feminist critique in epistemological perspective: Questions of context in family therapy. *Journal of Marital and Family Therapy, 11*, 113–126.

Walters, M., Carter, B., Papp, P., & Silverstein, O. (1988). *The invisible web: Gender patterns in family relationships.* New York: Guilford Press.

Weingarten, K. (1991). The discourses of intimacy: Adding a social constructionist and feminist view. *Family Process, 30*, 285–305.

White, M. (1995). *Re-authoring lives: Interviews and essays.* Adelaide, South Australia: Dulwich Centre.

White, M., & Epston, D. (1990). *Narrative means to therapeutic ends.* New York: Norton.

Zimmerman, J., & Dickerson, V. (1994). Using a narrative metaphor: Implications for theory and clinical practice. *Family Process, 33*, 233–246.

Chapter 21

Gay and Lesbian Couples in Therapy: Homophobia, Relational Ambiguity, and Social Support

ROBERT-JAY GREEN
VALORY MITCHELL

Imagine that you are invited to write a chapter on the topic of "therapy with heterosexual couples" for the newest *Clinical Handbook of Couple Therapy*. Where to begin? At the very least, this invitation requires you to make broad generalizations about the population of heterosexual couples in North America, if not the world. This is no small challenge.

A request for such a chapter also implies that other chapters in the *handbook* will not deal sufficiently with heterosexual couples in therapy. It is *your* job alone to explain how general theories of couple therapy need to be altered to fit the characteristics of heterosexual couples:

- Are certain kinds of clinical problems more frequently found among heterosexual couples in therapy?
- Does the status "legally married" (which is unique to heterosexual couples) increase or diminish their relationship problems?
- What different goals are required in work with heterosexual couples?
- What strategies would you suggest for building an effective therapist–client relationship when a couple is heterosexual?

- Taking into account a couple's heterosexuality, what change-oriented techniques are especially suitable in therapy?
- How might a couple's heterosexuality require special adaptations in the way particular approaches to couple therapy are practiced (e.g., cognitive-behavioral, structural–strategic, emotion-focused, psychodynamic, integrative, etc.)?
- Given that so many married couples enter therapy in a crisis following the discovery of a spouse's affair, how can therapists help couples cope with this aspect of the heterosexual lifestyle?

As these questions illustrate, it is extremely difficult to make generalized statements about heterosexual couples in therapy. Answers to such questions are elusive, and the risk of stereotyping is high. Heterosexual couples are not generally viewed as a homogeneous cultural group based on their sexual orientation. Ordinarily, experts writing on the topic of couple therapy do not consider how heterosexual couples might stand out from the lesbian/gay crowd. Rather, being in the majority, heterosexual couples blend in; their curious ways go unnoticed, apparently not needing further dissection because they are so common.

Just as our field has no book about White families in therapy, but excellent books about African American families in therapy (Boyd-Franklin, 1989), Latino families in therapy (Falicov, 1998), and Asian American families in therapy (Lee, 1997), we are not likely any time soon to see a book with the title *Heterosexual Families in Therapy*. However, heterosexual couples are no less a subculturally bound, norm-driven, singular group than are same-sex couples (who are just as diverse in all the sociodemographic and psychiatric ways imaginable).

The reason we are engaging you in the "thought experiment" above is our belief that to think clearly about "therapy with gay and lesbian couples," one must at least tacitly understand that coupled heterosexuality is also a distinct social status (or social role), with expectations, norms, and sanctions affecting a particular population of couples in this society. One must grasp that coupled heterosexuality has certain built-in advantages and stresses, just as does coupled homosexuality. Most importantly, one has to comprehend the myriad ways heterosexual relationships are shaped by historical traditions, given legal legitimization, and offered widespread social supports, rendering them simultaneously more secure but also more constrained than lesbian/gay relationships.

FOCUS OF THIS CHAPTER

Most of the literature on couple therapy presumes a heterosexual status among couples seeking treatment. Over a 20-year period, only 0.006% of articles in the major family therapy journals focused on lesbian/gay issues (Clark & Serovich, 1997; Laird, 1993, 1996). The consequence is that many couple therapists are uncertain about how to conceptualize and intervene actively in the problems of lesbian and gay couples. Recent surveys have shown that nearly half of all members of the American Association for Marriage and Family Therapy report that they do *not* feel competent treating lesbians or gay men in therapy (Doherty & Simmons, 1996).

Nevertheless, a very large majority of such therapists (72%) state that at least one out of every ten cases in their practices involve lesbians or gay men (S. K. Green & Bobele, 1994). The data from these and other surveys imply that large numbers of mental health professionals are treating same-sex couples without feeling adequately prepared. It is inevitable under these circumstances that some of their lesbian and gay clients will suffer the consequences (Garnets, Hancock, Cochran, Godchilds, & Peplau, 1991).

We are not implying that one needs a whole new theory of therapy in order to work effectively with same-sex couples. Homosexuality and heterosexuality are not opposites. Distressed couples, regardless of sexual orientation, often present similar kinds of problems. However, lesbian/gay couples face some special challenges, which, if not mastered by the partners on their own, may become problems.

In our view, these special challenges include (1) coping with homophobia in families of origin and the larger society; (2) resolving relational ambiguity in the areas of commitment, boundaries, and gender-linked behaviors; and (3) developing adequate social supports (a so-called "family of choice"). Well-functioning lesbian and gay couples handle these tasks on their own. Our prior research (Green, Bettinger, & Zacks, 1996) and the many studies by Kurdek (1995) and Peplau (1991) on community samples of lesbian, gay, and heterosexual couples show that as a group, same-sex couples are generally functioning as well as heterosexual couples. In fact, lesbian couples actually seem to be functioning the best in terms of overall relationship quality.

Many same-sex couples that have mastered these lesbian/gay-specific tasks may seek therapy for problems identical to the problems of heterosexual couples. We want to emphasize at the outset that our purpose in this chapter is to focus only on same-sex couples *in distress* (a minority of such couples), and then only on special problems arising from the unique challenges or stresses of being lesbian or gay couples. We do not cover the many problems lesbian/gay couples may present that are identical to those of heterosexual couples in therapy.

In this context, the therapist's first task is to assess whether and to what extent the couple's problems are connected to these special challenges of being lesbian/gay, as opposed to other generic processes (such as basic attachment issues, communication patterns, or conflict negotiation strategies). If, after exploration, a couple's problems seem unrelated to the special issues of being lesbian/gay, the major models of couple therapy and sex therapy can be used essentially intact.

However, many same-sex couples explicitly enter therapy to deal with lesbian/gay issues, such as conflicts over how to deal with prejudice in one or both partner's families of origin. Other couples come in with common psychiatric symptoms (such as depression in one partner), which seem to be compounded by homophobia in their families or at work, ambiguity in a partner's commitment, or lack of social support from friends. In each instance, therapists working with same-sex couples face the twin dangers of either ignoring or exaggerating the importance of lesbian/gay factors. Only a case formulation based on careful, continual assessment of these special areas and other couple dynamics can guide treatment effectively for a given couple.

Because other chapters in this *Handbook* present generic models of couple therapy that can be used with same-sex couples whose problems are not lesbian/gay-specific, we limit our focus below to how therapists can help same-sex partners (1) deal with homophobia; (2) make their couple commitments and relationship roles less ambiguous; and (3) build a more closely knit network of social support. For each of these issues, we describe problem-specific dynamics and related therapeutic techniques. We then discuss how therapists (especially heterosexual therapists) can prepare themselves personally and professionally for this kind of work.

HOMOPHOBIA AND THE CULTURAL CONTEXT

When we ask ourselves what distinguishes lesbian and gay couples from heterosexual couples as a group, the most salient characteristic is that regardless of their enormous sociocultural diversity, all same-sex couples are vulnerable to similar kinds of prejudice, discrimination, and marginalization by persons and institutions outside their relationships. In this section we review this aspect of lesbian/gay people's lives—first defining this prejudice, then looking at its effects on couple relationships, and finally considering how therapists can help couples resist being undermined by homophobia.

Prejudice and Discrimination

Several terms have been coined to describe the specific types of prejudice, discrimination, and related stresses faced by lesbians and gay men. "Homophobia" has been defined as a person's irrational fear and hatred of homosexuality and of lesbian/gay people. Homophobic attitudes are correlated with conservative social attitudes generally, and with gender role traditionalism and fundamentalist religious beliefs in particular (Herek, 1994, 1998). Males tend to be more homophobic than females. Studies reveal that heterosexuals—

including couple and family therapists—who have more direct contact with lesbians and gay men as friends, family members, and/or clients express more accepting attitudes about homosexuality (S. K. Green & Bobele, 1994; Herek, 1994).

"Internalized homophobia" occurs when lesbian and gay persons (who also have acquired society's antihomosexual attitudes) direct those negative attitudes toward themselves. Internalized homophobia is associated with lesbian/gay persons' devaluation of self (lowered self-esteem), higher rates of concealing sexual orientation, greater depression in response to homophobic prejudice, suicidality, increased HIV risk-taking behaviors, and mental health and substance use problems (Malyon, 1982; Meyer & Dean, 1998; Shidlo, 1994).

It is axiomatic that all openly lesbian and gay people, including members of couples, have had to counter and unlearn internalized homophobia to some extent in order to achieve a measure of self-acceptance and to form same-sex relationships. However, in many couples, one or both partners may continue to suffer from internalized homophobia, which frequently contributes to the demise of couple relationships in direct or indirect ways. In the context of couple therapy, an important aspect of internalized homophobia is that some lesbian and gay clients nihilistically believe the cultural stereotype that enduring love relationships between same-sex partners are wrong or impossible to achieve. Then they unconsciously sabotage their relationships in a kind of self-fulfilling prophecy, often giving up too quickly and pessimistically, rather than trying to work through the inevitable impasses in any long-term relationship. Therapists can help such clients to challenge negative stereotypes about lesbian and gay relationships and to achieve a greater degree of freedom to commit to same-sex couplehood.

"Heterocentrism" (sometimes referred to as "heterosexism") consists of assumptions and processes embedded in mainstream society and its institutions, implying that human beings are naturally heterosexual and that heterosexual lifestyles are the normal standard against which those of lesbians and gays should be compared in order to be understood and evaluated (Herek, 1998). Heterocentric attitudes lead to the unwitting or intentional marginalization and exclusion of lesbian and gay people, rendering them unequal in terms of access to social opportunities, benefits, and civil rights protections. In the mental health fields, heterocentrism occurs when theories or research based on heterosexuals are automatically assumed to apply to gays, lesbians, and bisexuals, or the assumption that heterosexuality is a better psychological adjustment even though the research evidence does not support that conclusion (Gonsiorek, 1991).

Effects of Prejudice on Lesbian/Gay Couples

The combination of these external and internalized sources of prejudice create "minority stress" for all lesbian and gay people at various points in their lives (DiPlacido, 1998). This kind of stress typically reaches a crescendo in adolescence, when the individual begins self-identifying as lesbian, gay, or bisexual but still has not disclosed these feelings to others (Savin-Williams, 1996). However, most lesbian and gay people continue to experience some degree of prejudice and fear of discrimination throughout their adult lives, depending on their life circumstances (Bepko & Johnson, 2000).

A couple's sexual orientation affects that couple's relationship to almost all other entities in society—family, work, school, medical care, insurance, the legal system, housing, religious institutions, government, and so on. The very right of same-sex persons to associate with each other in a sociosexual relationship has been against the law in most states in the past and is still against the law (the so-called "sodomy" statutes) in some states, such as Georgia. Same-sex couples are vulnerable to discrimination and harm if they are "out" and visible, or they live with fear of discovery if they conceal their relationships. Discrimination and fear of discovery may undermine the couple's relationship if the partners do not have internal ways of countering the social stigma of homosexuality, as well as having a social support system to buffer that stress.

Lesbian and gay relationships are not supported by tradition, rarely sanctified by mainstream religions, and not generally protected by law in the United States. Even in those states that have abolished their sodomy statutes, the civil rights of lesbian and gay couples are challenged almost every year by court cases, ballot initiatives, legislative proposals, and regulatory revisions at all levels of government (Hartman, 1996). In most jurisdictions, it still is entirely legal for lesbian and gay people to be summarily fired from their jobs without cause or discriminated against in hiring decisions and in housing, simply because they are homosexual.

Although there are pockets of increasing political support for same-sex couples, and although the U.S. Bureau of the Census has begun counting households headed by same-sex partners, the overall message from the mainstream of American politics to lesbian and gay couples is something like this: "We don't want you to exist, so we simply decline to acknowledge or support your relationships in the way we support heterosexual relationships." In this way, much of heterosexism is presumptive and exclusionary rather than overtly aggressive, and it contributes to a feeling of marginality and invisibility for lesbian and gay couples.

In this context, to engage in a committed couple relationship becomes both a personal and a political act for lesbian and gay people, who are still literally outlaws in some states. No matter how mundane their everyday suburban lives, Rozzie and Harriet's couplehood is at variance with the dominant social and political status quo. They are caught in a cultural vortex of conflicting attitudes—support from some quarters, neglect from most, overt hostility from some. In most circumstances in the United States and around the world, they still risk being gawked at if they hold hands in public. In some circumstances, they will be verbally or physically attacked for such public displays of everyday couplehood.

Their vulnerability to these external dangers renders lesbian and gay couples vigilant for discrimination, especially in unfamiliar surroundings, and it increases their stress. If each partner in a couple has reached a high level of self-acceptance about being lesbian or gay, this external stress is manageable, unless of course it involves physical violence. However, to the extent that partners are still dealing with internalized homophobia themselves, their relationship can be threatened even by subtle forms of prejudice and discrimination and the vigilance necessary to protect against these.

For example, realistic fears about holding hands and being affectionate in certain public contexts can stimulate a partner's internalized homophobia, leaving him/her feeling defective, ashamed, bad, unworthy, sick, sinful, depressed, and so on. Or in certain work environments, the necessity to self-monitor statements and actions may leave a partner feeling stressed and believing that his/her gayness is causing this problem, rather than locating the problem's cause in society's ignorance. When partners' internalized homophobia is triggered in these ways, it sometimes translates into couple difficulties, including (1) inexplicable arguments (e.g., one partner's frustration is displaced onto the other, or self-hatred turns into criticism of the other partner); (2) sexual desire or performance difficulties (caused by inhibition or guilt); and (3) depression and withdrawal (one or both partners feel unworthy, or feel ambivalent about committing to a lesbian or gay relationship). For couples in which these dynamics seem to be operating, the stated goals of couple therapy (agreed upon collaboratively with the clients) should include a reduction in the partners' internalized homophobia.

Interventions for Countering Homophobia

In a sense, all of the techniques discussed in this chapter can serve to counter clients' internalized homophobia and help them cope with external discrimination. However, we present some very specific strategies below. In this aspect of our work, we make use of feminist, profeminist, gay-affirmative, multicultural, and narrative family systems therapy principles.

The two central ideas in applying feminist and profeminist theories of therapy to same-sex couples are the notions of cultural "resistance" and "subversion," implicit in the early feminist therapy and "radical therapy" movements of the late 1960s and 1970s (Radical Therapist Collective, 1971). Most recently, these notions have been well articulated by Brown (1994):

> . . . In feminist theory, resistance means the refusal to merge with dominant cultural norms and to attend to one's own voice and integrity. . . . Each act of feminist therapy . . . must have as an implicit goal the uncovering of the presence of the patriarchy as a source of distress so that this influence of the dominant can be named, undermined, resisted, and subverted. . . . awareness and transformation mean teaching of resistance, learning the ways in which each of us is damaged by our witting or unwitting participation in dominant norms or by the ways in which such norms have been thrust upon us. (p. 25)

In terms of applying these concepts of resistance and subversion to the treatment of lesbian and gay couples, we start with the basic awareness that by loving someone of the same sex, lesbians and gay men are violating the most basic gender norms of the society. We then collaborate with our clients in an exploration of all the oppressive social influences in their lives—influences that pressure them not to engage in same-sex love and to regard their capacity for same-sex love as bad, sinful, disturbed,

inferior, and so on. This includes a careful, detailed reconstruction of all the various messages they got about homosexuality (in their families, in school, in their neighborhood, in their religious institutions, through the media, and more generally from members of their specific racial/ethnic group) as they were growing up.

We particularly examine with clients the internalization of traditional gender norms, as well as the overt prejudice and discrimination they continue to face from their current social environments (family, neighbors, coworkers) and from the "impersonal" institutions of society (the media, government, insurance companies, employment settings, health care institutions, etc.). Most importantly, we counter these oppressive messages, neutralizing society's condemnation of same-sex love in terms of our viewing it as a normal human variation, not reinforcing (in subtle or unsubtle ways) its pejorative framing by the larger society (Mitchell, 1988). We thus function as celebrants, ordainers, and witnesses of constructive lesbian and gay relationships, giving them our enthusiastic approval and support.

This approach is roughly equivalent to what has become known as "gay-affirmative therapy." As Malyon (1982) wrote in first describing this approach,

> Gay-affirmative psychotherapy is not an independent system of psychotherapy. Rather, it represents a special range of psychological knowledge which challenges the traditional view that homosexual desire and fixed homosexual orientations are pathological. . . . This approach regards homophobia, as opposed to homosexuality, as a major pathological variable in the development of certain symptomatic conditions. (pp. 68–69)

Thus gay-affirmative therapy involves actively challenging society's negative attitudes toward homosexuality that are contributing to the problems of a lesbian or gay couple. This approach entails helping the couple to dispute, deconstruct, and subvert society's prejudicial views, rather than continuing to internalize or be limited by them. In a sense, the work is similar to what narrative therapists have described as "externalizing the problem" (in this case, viewing homophobia rather than one's sexual orientation as the problem) (White & Epston, 1990), and what cognitive therapists have sometimes called "disputation" of irrational beliefs.

In some couple therapy cases, partners are at markedly different levels of accepting their sexual orientations. Individual therapy may be warranted for the partner who suffers from a great deal more internalized homophobia than the other, especially if he/she seems ashamed to explore these aspects of self in the presence of the partner. However, if both partners are at roughly the same stage on this dimension, it is most helpful to see them together in conjoint sessions, because each then benefits by self-exploration in the other's presence.

In addition to this work of deconstructing internalized homophobia in the sessions, we frequently encourage clients to engage in various forms of participation in lesbian/gay community organizations, including political activism if it fits their sensibilities (i.e., the cultural "subversion" aspect of liberationist therapies). For example, one client (who had played a musical instrument in her high school band) was encouraged to join the San Francisco Lesbian/Gay Freedom Band, which marches in the local Pride Parade and performs in other venues throughout the city. Another client, because of his skills in advertising research, was encouraged to become active in the local chapter of the Gay and Lesbian Alliance Against Defamation, which monitors media representations of lesbian and gay people. Acts such as these constitute an important way in which lesbian and gay clients who suffer from internalized homophobia can stand up (in unison with others) for their right to exist, meet others who can model high levels of self-esteem and empowerment, and contribute to the reduction of homophobia in the larger society. We view these acts of gay community participation as a form of subversion of the status quo and legitimization of the self, implicitly naming society's homophobia (rather than the self) as the problem that needs to be eliminated.

In concluding this section, we should add that feminist and gay-affirmative principles of treatment are being increasingly incorporated into another orientation to psychotherapy, sometimes called "multicultural family systems therapy" (see especially Boyd-Franklin, 1989; Falicov, 1998; McGoldrick, 1998; Pinderhughes, 1989). As one of us has written elsewhere on the topic of "race and the field of family therapy":

> In this new era, we will need to distinguish clearly between matters of minority group *differentness* and matters of minority group *oppression*. . . . Our focus on different cultural patterns *within* groups often obscures our understanding of the oppressive relations *between* groups. Cultural, racial, and sexual orientation differences are *not* problems in and of themselves. Prejudice, discrimination, and other forms of aggressive intercultural conflict based on

these differences *are* problems. (Green, 1998a, pp. 99–100; emphasis in original).

Similarly, Olkin (1999) has developed a minority group model for treatment of people with disabilities, and an approach she refers to as "disability-affirmative therapy":

> We reframe "I can't climb stairs" to "why isn't there a ramp?". . . . This is the crux of the minority model, this shift in focus from personal, individual, and problem in isolation, to group, environment, attitudes, discrimination—from individual pathology to social oppression. (p. 28)

A multicultural family systems approach can still incorporate the more traditional ways of looking at the variability in mental health functioning of individuals, couples, and families within a specific minority group. For example, although all same-sex couples encounter a certain amount of prejudice and discrimination, some of them face a lot more of it than others, and some couples cope with it much more effectively than others.

In particular, when confronted with similar levels of external prejudice, same-sex couples with more internalized homophobia will tend to cope less successfully. Depending on the kind of discrimination same-sex partners face, coping successfully may require (1) working actively for change in the couple's current social environment; (2) changing to a different social environment (literally relocating geographically or quitting a job to escape an intransigent or dangerously homophobic situation); (3) reattributing distress to different factors (e.g., attributing it to external prejudice and ignorance rather than to personal inadequacy); or (4) recognizing that some discriminatory situations cannot be changed, and then focusing on other life areas.

RELATIONAL AMBIGUITY

In contrast to heterosexual couples, there are no "givens" in same-sex relationships—no preordained expectations, mutual obligations, or contracts, and few visible models of lesbian and gay couplehood to follow (partly because prior generations remained closeted). Lacking historical traditions or a religious or legal framework for same-sex couplehood, the partners in each same-sex couple have both the freedom and the necessity of developing their own definition of a suitable couple commitment and of their boundaries vis-à-vis the outside world.

This is not to say that same-sex partners do not bring to their relationship many of the "lessons" about couplehood acquired in their families of origin and from observing many heterosexual marriages during their lifetimes (Laird, 1996). However, there is no certainty about the extent to which the customs and assumptions of heterosexual marriages may apply to their own lesbian/gay relationship. Same-sex partners must therefore devote much more time and energy to "negotiations" in order to figure out exactly what it means that they are a couple, especially in the beginning stages of their relationship. Much of this negotiation takes place implicitly through the "permitting" of behavior patterns that neither party challenges. However, some of the negotiations occur explicitly through conversations about the meaning of their commitment and about their mutual obligations.

Without normative traditions and mainstream pressures that unconsciously shape their intimate relationship patterns, lesbians and gay men are freer to invent their own relational configurations, depending more on their individual needs and whatever opportunities arise than on fixed traditions of couplehood. Although many same-sex couples have the skills to create a mutually satisfying and clear structure for their relationships, couples in which the rules and boundaries remain extremely vague, changeable, or contested over time are likely to become distressed and require help.

Boundary and Commitment Ambiguity

A key concept in couple and family systems theory has been the notion of "boundaries" of subsystems, especially interpersonal boundaries between individuals, generational boundaries between the partners and their families of origin, and boundaries between the couple and the social network surrounding it. Minuchin (1974) defined family boundaries as "the rules defining who participates and how" (p. 53). It is just as important to consider who or what is excluded from participation in a subsystem as to consider who or what is included.

Also basic to the notion of boundaries is the way a relationship is defined by the participants. Is it a best friendship, a social acquaintanceship, a romantic involvement, a lifelong primary commitment, a temporary dating relationship, a mainly sexual encounter, a commercial exchange, a temporary separation, a mentoring arrangement, an ongoing affair secondary to a primary relationship, or a former-lovers-now-friends bond? With lesbian and gay couples in therapy, we frequently observe a lack of clarity in how they define their couplehood to themselves and to others. We believe this is partly because lesbian and gay couples (in contrast to legally married heterosexual couples) lack a socially endorsed, legally framed, normative template for how couplehood should be. Overall, partners do not know what they can expect from a same-sex relationship because there is no prescribed kind of couplehood for them and no prevailing way of being a same-sex couple.

We find Boss's concept of "boundary ambiguity" very relevant here: "a state in which family members are uncertain in their perception about who is in or out of the family and who is performing what roles and tasks within the family system" (Boss & Greenberg, 1984, p. 536).[1] Boss's own research (see Boss, 1999) has focused primarily on situations of "ambiguous loss" (e.g., families of patients with Alzheimer's disease, families of men who were missing in action after combat during war, and families following divorce or a death in the family). Her studies have demonstrated convincingly that family members' perceptions of ambiguous loss are associated with signs of family stress and with dysfunction (e.g., depression) (Boss, Caron, Horbal, & Mortimer, 1990).

We extend the concept of boundary ambiguity to situations that might best be labeled "ambiguous commitment," where one or both partners' intentions or degree of joining in the relationship remain in doubt. Ambiguous commitment is prevalent in lesbian and gay couples in therapy, partly because the partners' decisions to be together are not usually preceded by an extended courtship or engagement phase, demarcated by a commitment ceremony, governed by statutes for legal marriage, approved by the partners' respective families of origin, or (in most cases) solidified by becoming coparents to children.

Relationships that we are characterizing here by the phrase "ambiguous commitment" are closest to having what Boss et al. (1990) describe as "physical presence" but "psychological absence." The partners are physically in the relationship (physically present), but the extent and exact nature of their psychological commitment to the relationship are unclear.

In addition, terminations of lesbian and gay couple relationships are sometimes characterized by ambiguous loss, partly because of the absence of formal divorce proceedings to demarcate the ending clearly. This is not to say that most relationships between lesbian or gay ex-lovers are ambiguous and dysfunctional, or that divorce proceedings are necessarily preferable to informal separations. In fact, one of the most distinctive features of lesbian and gay relationships is that close and constructive friendships between gay or lesbian ex-partners are common (perhaps normative), even when no children are involved to keep them connected as coparents (Becker, 1988). This stands in sharp contrast to relationships between formerly married heterosexual spouses, who usually sever all ties unless children are involved.

However, the absence of a legal ritual formalizing divorce may increase the likelihood that boundary ambiguity will occur and last longer during transitions out of some lesbian and gay couple relationships. In Boss et al.'s (1990) terms, these relationships are closest to having "physical absence" but "psychological presence." The partners are out of the relationship (e.g., they may no longer be living together or defining themselves publicly as a couple), but the extent and nature of their ongoing commitment to the relationship are still in doubt. Sometimes, with a lesbian or gay couple in therapy, one partner's ongoing connection with an ex-partner seems to interfere with the new couple relationship or with the new partner's sense of primacy over the former partner.

What is strikingly different for same-sex couples is that almost all of the usual expectations that heterosexuals bring to marriage (monogamy, pooled finances, caring for each other through serious illness, moving together for each other's career advancement, providing and caring for each other's families in old age, mutual inheritance, health care power-of-attorney rights in the event of a partner's mental or physical incapacity) do not necessarily apply to same-sex couple relationships unless they are discussed and explicitly agreed to by the partners. Typically, same-sex couples do not clarify these expectations before moving in together, and discrepancies in their visions of the relationship only become apparent when expectations are suddenly breached, which can be shocking and very hurtful to the partners.

For example, it may not be clear whether or when same-sex partners' commitment includes the traditional marriage vow "in sickness and in health." For a married couple, the wedding ceremony officially signals this transition in level of commitment and stated intent. But since a lesbian/gay couple is unable to have a legal wedding, what marks it for the partners? Is it when they start seeing each other every day? Is it when they move in

together? Three years later? Ten years later? When does Partner A know that Partner B has the intent to stay in the relationship "in sickness and in health, till death do us part"?

This issue could be discussed by the partners at any time, but typically such issues do not get explicitly raised until the couple comes face to face with a serious illness or disability, such as HIV or breast cancer. The same, of course, is true for unmarried cohabiting heterosexual couples, but they have the option of getting legally married to clarify their commitment. In fact, most cohabiting heterosexual couples eventually either separate or get married, suggesting that they are implicitly viewing cohabitation as a trial run before making a lifelong commitment.

Although heterosexual spouses sometimes abandon each other during medical crises despite the marriage vow, spouses are more likely to have the expectation of caregiving during illness, because it is built into the template for marriage and is expected of married people by their parents, neighbors, coworkers, physicians, children, and others. By comparison, at what point does society expect lesbian and gay partners to stay with and take care each other during sickness, injury, or disability? Many lesbian and gay partners remain unclear as to what it will mean pragmatically in the future that they are "committed" to each other. Is moving in together a lifelong commitment in the same way a marriage is supposed to be?

The same kind of ambiguity may permeate other basic parameters of a same-sex couple's relationship. Does being a "couple" mean that the partners will be monogamous? Does it mean that they will share each other's financial obligations from the time they live together? Or will they pool financial resources completely, partially, or not at all? When they move in together as a couple, will each partner authorize the other to have health care power of attorney to make decisions in a medical emergency? Will each name the other as the executor of and a beneficiary in his/her will? Or are these privileges going to remain with the partners' families of origin indefinitely, or until the partners reach some greater (but unspecified) level of emotional commitment?

Ambiguity about Monogamy for Gay Male Couples

Contrary to stereotypes, the majority of both lesbians and gay men at any given time prefer, and are involved in, ongoing couple relationships (Peplau, 1991). However, unique norms in the gay male community sometimes work against committed couples. Most observers agree that these norms favor singlehood and sexual experiences without emotional/romantic involvement (Johnson & Keren, 1996). They do not favor long-term couple commitments.

In general, men tend to be more oriented than women toward a recreational and visual (as opposed to romantic or emotional) approach to sex, and they tend to be less monogamous. The presence of two men in a couple relationship therefore doubles the likelihood that at least one member of the couple will engage in sex outside the primary relationship, and that the overall rates of this behavior for gay male couples will be much higher than for lesbian couples or for heterosexual couples. Moreover, a gay male couple's monogamy usually is not protected by other gay men, who assume that anyone they are attracted to (coupled or single) is fair game for recreational sexual activity (called "tricking" in gay vernacular).

Fitting with this ethos, a large percentage of long-term gay male couples have sexually open (non-monogamous) relationships by agreement; that is, the partners have sex with outsiders purely for pleasure, without emotional involvement (Blumstein & Schwartz, 1983; McWhirter & Mattison, 1984). The attitude of these gay male couples toward monogamy is quite different than in the heterosexual world, where sex outside marriage tends to be viewed as a form of betrayal, lack of love, immaturity, hostility, immorality, inability to commit, or a "triangulation" to deal with unresolved marital problems. In open gay male relationships, sex with others is typically viewed as just a pleasurable experience—a kind of pastime, nothing more.

Several studies have shown that long-term open relationships among gay male couples are generally functioning as well as monogamous ones in terms of overall relationship satisfaction, stability, and other qualities (Blasband & Peplau, 1985; Blumstein & Schwartz, 1983; Kurdek, 1988b). However, sexual openness at the beginning of a relationship seems to increase the risk of dissolution (Blumstein & Schwartz, 1983), especially if there are even moderate dissatisfactions in the relationship and if the parameters or agreements about the extrarelational sex are unclear (who, what, when, where, how often, etc.).

After a gay male relationship is firmly established, however, it appears that the couple can more easily sustain sexual openness, provided that the rules limiting emotional involvements with outsiders are very clear, mutually agreed upon, and followed (Blumstein & Schwartz, 1983; McWhirter & Mattison, 1984). Thus, for couples who choose nonmonogamy, it typically is not sex with outsiders per se that becomes problematic, but rather any ambiguity in their agreements about it (including secrecy, lying, unclarity about the parameters, or inconsistent adherence to the parameters—all of which can trigger feelings of insecurity about the primary commitment).

On the other hand, a large number of gay men have more traditional monogamous relationships and view any extrarelational sex as a betrayal of commitment, an impediment to intimacy, and so on. In a recent study, 70% of gay male partners reported being in monogamous relationships (Campbell, 2000), but earlier studies (prior to the discovery of HIV) reported rates of monogamy as low as 18% (Blumstein & Schwartz, 1983). Still other male couples change their monogamy agreements over the years, or alternate between periods of sexual openness and periods of monogamy.

Most important is the fact that each of these kinds of sexual arrangements is very visible, talked about frequently, and considered acceptable within the gay male community; this gives couples greater permission to discover an approach that fits for them as individuals. However, the sense that "anything goes" also increases ambiguity (and sometimes instability) as each new gay couple finds or fumbles its way toward a relatively permanent agreement about whether to be monogamous or to have an open relationship. Almost every male couple must deal repeatedly with the question of monogamy, because their agreements in this regard will be tested by many opportunities for, and the easy availability of, casual sex with others in the gay community.

Ambiguity Related to Same-Gender Couple Composition

Being composed of two women or two men, a same-sex couple cannot rely on traditional male–female (instrumental–expressive) role divisions to structure their overall interactional patterns. Most same-sex couples go though a long period of trial and error before settling on "who does what" in their relationship (Carrington, 1999). Such couples obviously cannot fall back on the usual gender-linked division of tasks in such areas as financial decision making, relationship maintenance (talking about feelings and problems), earning money, doing housework, preparing meals, taking the lead in sex, arranging their social life, or taking care of children and elderly relatives if applicable. The fact that both partners are the same sex holds the possibility of greater equality if neither is attached to traditional gender roles, but it also increases the ambiguity about who is supposed to do what in the relationship and in the management of the household (Mitchell, 1996).

Furthermore, to the degree that both partners were socialized into and still adhere rigidly to traditional gendered behavior for their sex, they may develop more conflicts or certain deficiencies in their relationship (Roth, 1989). In general, women are socialized for more caring, connection, and cooperation, whereas men are socialized for more independence, competition, and dominance (Green, 1998b; Miller, 1976). Although the majority of lesbians and gay men at least partially defy gender role prescriptions (Green et al., 1996), a minority of lesbians and gay men still conform to traditional gender roles in all respects except for their sexuality. Such strict gender conformity produces predictable problems in this particular subset of same-sex couples: (1) Both women try to please the other too much and neglect to communicate their own needs (i.e., the so-called problem of "fusion" in the lesbian relationship) (Krestan & Bepko, 1980); (2) neither man will relocate for the other's job offer; (3) both men want to be the leader in sex; (4) neither woman feels comfortable initiating sex; (5) the man who has a lower-status job than his male partner acts competitively in other areas of the relationship; (6) the woman who earns more money than her female partner feels guilty and disempowers herself in other areas; or (7) a very traditionally gendered man is domineering toward his less traditional male partner, who feels overly dependent on the relationship and depressed. In other words, these problems arise not because the relationship is composed of two women or two men, but rather because some pairs of women or men rigidly cling to narrow, traditional gender roles, which creates conflict or deficits in their relationships.

In sharp contradiction to cultural stereotypes perpetuated by such popular films as *Le Cage aux Folles* (more recently remade as *The Birdcage* in the United States), only a small minority of lesbian or gay couples nowadays divvy up the relationship roles in such a way that one partner plays the traditional "husband" role while the other plays the traditional "wife" role. In fact, even in the early 1970s, only about 7% of lesbian and gay couples organized their relationship roles that way (Bell &

Weinberg, 1978). As one of us wrote with colleagues previously,

> the general public still seems quite convinced of, and scandalized by, what it imagines is the widespread playing of artificial "butch/femme" roles by partners in same-sex relationships. Yet this same public remains largely unconscious . . . about its own problematic conformity to the socially constructed "butch/ femme" roles in heterosexual relationships. (Green et al., 1996, p. 218)

The ideal for most lesbian and gay couples consists of equality of power, and sharing of the instrumental and emotional tasks usually associated with the male or female role (Carrington, 1999).

To achieve this kind of compatibility without fixed complementarity requires a great deal of gender flexibility from both partners. The division of labor has to become a more conscious, deliberative process than it is for heterosexual couples. This is not to say that contemporary heterosexual couples never struggle with such issues, but rather that a majority of them still devolve (sometimes despite their egalitarian aspirations) toward traditional gender-linked roles in the areas of housework, child care, care of elderly relatives, cooking, and so on (Hochschild, 1989). Lesbian and gay couples cannot rely on these gender-linked divisions.

Interventions for Relational Ambiguity

We are not advocating any à priori, formulaic solutions for resolving these ambiguities. Nor do we believe that the outcomes should look like heterosexual marriages, in which many of these uncertainties are settled by law and tradition. In general, however, a couple tends to function best when there are clear agreements about the partners' commitment and boundaries, and when the couple's relationship is given higher priority than any other relationships (in terms of emotional involvement, caregiving, honesty, time, and influence over major decisions). From the therapy standpoint, regardless of the presenting problems, we believe that asking certain kinds of questions and arriving at clear answers can be helpful to many same-sex couples:

1. "How do you define being a 'couple' [or what does it mean to you that you are a 'couple']?"
2. "What has been your history as a couple?"
3. "How did your becoming a couple affect your relationships with other family members, friends,

the lesbian/gay community, and the straight community?"

4. "What are the rules in your relationship regarding monogamy versus sex outside the relationship? What are the rules in terms of safer sex practices with each other and/or with others [being very explicit in terms of exact sexual practices to prevent HIV transmission]?"

5. "What are your agreements with each other about monthly finances, current or future debts, pooling versus separation of financial resources, ownership of joint property, and other financial planning matters?"

6. "Who does what tasks in the relationship, and the household, and how is this division or sharing of tasks decided? Are you satisfied with the current division or sharing of these tasks?"

7. "What do you see as your obligations to each other in terms of caring for each other in illness, injury, or disability?"

8. "Are you viewing this as a lifetime commitment? If so, have you prepared legal health care power-of-attorney documents and wills to protect each other's interests in case of serious illness or death?"

Clarifying the extent and nature of partners' emotional commitments to each other is central to the work we do with a couple in the early stages of a relationship. Sometimes this clarification involves resolving partners' conflicts of allegiance between the couple relationship and other family members, friends, or ex-partners. At other times, it involves spelling out what promises and reassurances each partner is willing to give the other (caregiving, time, monogamy, or other guarantees) that might increase the partners' sense of security, durability, and potential longevity of the relationship.

If it is in keeping with their sensibilities, partners can be encouraged to have a commitment ceremony and a formal exchange of vows covering some of these issues. A book we recommend for this purpose is *The Essential Guide to Lesbian and Gay Weddings* (Ayers & Brown, 1999). For partners who view their relationship as entailing a lifetime commitment, we strongly encourage drawing up appropriate legal documents (especially health care power of attorney and wills/trusts). The book *A Legal Guide for Lesbian and Gay Couples* (Hayden, Clifford, & Hertz, 2001) is an excellent resource for this purpose.

If one or both partners' gender conformity is creating problems in a same-sex couple, a therapist can help by reviewing the clients' original gender role socialization experiences and by challenging limitations associated with current gender role behavior, much as the therapist might do with heterosexual partners in relationships. If ambiguity or dissension exists about who does what in the relationship, then the therapeutic work includes making sure that these emotional and instrumental tasks are clarified and distributed equitably, as well as challenging any polarization of roles or dominance–submission patterns that will be destructive to the relationship over the long run. If ambiguity exists in the monogamy agreement, this also should be spelled out, based on full exploration of the partners' underlying emotions and motivations. If they choose an open relationship, the specific behavioral rules for sex outside the relationship should be delineated and agreed upon in great detail (in terms of who, what, when, where, how often, with how much communication about each encounter, and with what limitations).

In dealing with relational ambiguity of the kinds described above, we often find homework assignments or in-session exercises that involve negotiating and sometimes putting relationship contracts or "relationship vows" in writing useful for a couple. Such vows (in addition to the legal contracts mentioned above) require that the partners address specific issues and come up with specific behavioral agreements for the future. Any intervention that helps the partners clarify expectations and agreements in contested areas or areas that have never been discussed (such as finances or monogamy) will help reduce relational ambiguity. This in turn will increase partners' feelings of secure attachment and belief in the permanence of their union, anchoring their relationship in tangible definitions of what it means that they are a couple.

SOCIAL SUPPORT

Well-functioning lesbian and gay couples are able to develop and maintain cohesive systems of social support. Distressed same-sex couples in therapy, by contrast, tend to be more isolated and to have smaller and less interconnected sources of support. In such a case, therapeutic goals should include helping the partners build a support system that is both closely knit and supportive of their being a couple.

Usually same-sex couples get more of their social support from their friends, whereas heterosexual couples rely more on support from their families of origin. In part, this is because many lesbian and gay couples receive only qualified acceptance of their relationships from their families. To varying degrees, these couples must turn elsewhere to achieve a sense of belonging to an intimate, ongoing group. Below, we discuss families of origin as a source of emotional support and then turn to nonfamily sources.

Families of Origin

It is impossible to understand the psychological issues for lesbian and gay couples unless one first has a sense of what it is like to grow up lesbian or gay and to be a couple in a heterocentric world. Lesbian and gay people occupy an existential position during childhood unlike any other group in our society. Except in rare instances, lesbian girls and gay boys grow up in families in which they are the only ones of their kind—the only lesbian or gay family members. This has profound implications throughout the lifespan of almost every lesbian or gay person.

In most other minority groups (e.g., racial, ethnic, or religious minority groups), children and parents typically share the same minority status. These children are able to observe their parents dealing with and discussing minor or major acts of discrimination in everyday life. Many minority group parents and their communities intentionally teach children how to mentally counter society's negative views and maintain a sense of connection and pride in their heritage, through participation in customs, rituals, and cultural or religious organizations. In these ways, parents and children build a strong identification with one another as members of the same minority group. They are on the same side against the potential prejudice and discrimination in society, and parents take a protective stance toward their children in this respect.

This is not so for lesbian and gay children. Their parents do not share the same minority group status, do not face the same discrimination, cannot recount the history of the lesbian/gay minority group, and would not be able to prepare their children to cope with homophobia even if they were aware of their children's sexual orientation. In contrast to the parents of other minority children, parents of lesbian/gay children frequently do not side with their children against the oppressive forces in society, and in fact sometimes become the children's main oppressors. At worst, some lesbian/gay children and adolescents are truly "living with the enemy," risking verbal abuse, physical abuse, and/or ejection from the home if their sexual orientation becomes known (Savin-Williams, 1994).

Parents who suspect that their children may be lesbian or gay because of the child's gender nonconformity (Bailey & Zucker, 1995) may react by withdrawing from their children or engaging in aggressive attempts to make the children's behavior more gender-typical (Bell, Weinberg, & Hammersmith, 1981). Parental withdrawal or attempts to reform markedly effeminate male children or markedly masculine female children sometimes begins at a very early age, contributing to basic attachment disorders (insecure attachment, or preoccupied attachment styles), which may have negative consequences in adulthood for the couple relationships of these children (Byng-Hall, 1995).

Even in the best of circumstances, heterosexual parents typically lack exposure to gay life and have no personal experience of being lesbian or gay themselves. It thus remains very difficult for even the most accepting heterosexual parents to concretely imagine and identify with the experience of being a lesbian or gay person in this society, in comparison to the ways they are able to identify with their heterosexual children's life experience. For this level of understanding and mutual identification, lesbian and gay people almost always have to turn to one another rather than to heterosexual family members.

A child's revelation of homosexuality and the family's adaptation to the news tend to be filtered through the family members' usual coping mechanisms, as well as their specific attitudes about gender and sexuality (Laird, 1996). The family that was mostly distant and conflict-avoidant before the disclosure is likely to remain so afterward. Parents who were intrusive and critical before the disclosure are not likely to become suddenly more respectful of boundaries and individuality in response to this disclosure.

About 25% of lesbian/gay adults in the United States report *not* being out to their mothers, and almost 50% report *not* being out to their fathers (Savin-Williams, 2001). After the disclosure of sexual orientation, only about 10–15% of parents reject their lesbian or gay children over the long run; about 70–75% show varying degrees of acceptance; and the remaining 10–15% are fully accepting and reach a high degree of comfort (Savin-Williams, 2001). Most families react very negatively at first, but become more tolerant or accepting over time (Crosbie-Burnett, Foster, Murray, & Bowen, 1996; Savin-Williams, 1996, 2001).

We have been concerned that there seems to be a normative ideology among many couple and family therapists that it is always good (i.e., mentally healthy) for lesbian and gay clients to come out to their families of origin, without regard for the sociocultural context (Chan, 1989, 1995; Green, 2000b; LaSala, 2000; Liu & Chan, 1996). In some family therapy circles (particularly Bowenian), the decision to keep a major secret like this from one's family is almost inconceivable, because coming out to the family of origin is viewed as an essential sign of differentiation of self. However, this maintenance of the secret may have nothing to do with being a "differentiated" or "mentally healthy" person. Staying closeted in the family may have more to do with not needing the family's approval and not wanting to be hassled and burdened with the family's irrational upset. Or it may have to do with a person's basic physical safety and economic survival in the family and community.

Being lesbian/gay and coming out to one's heterosexual family members almost always carries some risk of being "disowned" and losing one's ties to biological kin (Weston, 1991). The quintessential lesbian/gay experience of deciding whether to come out to parents leaves lesbian/gay people very aware that continuation of family-of-origin relations is entirely voluntary on the part of parents and their adult children. Although, as described above, most parents do not actually reject their children after disclosure, the *possibility* of being completely cut off or marginalized by their families is one that most lesbian/gay persons contemplate seriously:

> Of course, heterosexuals can also be disowned. But when straight people encounter rejection by relatives, that rejection arises on a case-by-case basis, generally in response to something done rather than something fundamental to their sense of self. Self-identified lesbians and gay men, in contrast, experience rejection as an ever-present possibility structured by claiming a stigmatized sexual identity. (Weston, 1991, p. 74)

Because of these possible risks of disclosure, a therapist should not assume that keeping such a secret from parents is inevitably going to be deleterious to a client's mental health or couple relationships. For example, a 2-year longitudinal study of 48 lesbian couples found that outness to family-of-origin members was unrelated to lesbian couples' satisfaction at the start of the study, the couples' staying together during the 2-year follow-up period, or level of satisfaction among couples that stayed together (Green et al., 1996).

In our experience, family-of-origin support is important to couple functioning in some but not all cases. For those offspring who decide to come out to their families, acceptance is certainly easier to manage than rejection. However, this does not mean that the act of disclosure automatically leads to greater family support or to better couple functioning, especially for lesbians/gays who are the most reluctant or unwilling to disclose to their families, based on what they believe are realistic appraisals of their family members' attitudes toward homosexuality. In fact, coming out to family members may lead to less support from the family, or to poorer functioning of the couple, or to no change in couple functioning at all.

The psychological consequences of being out to family members and of the family's acceptance versus rejection depends on the centrality of the family as a source of social support and the availability of nonfamily resources (Green, 2000b). Lesbian and gay people who have little contact with their families of origin, whose self-esteem and decision making are not dependent on family members' approval, and who receive substantial social support from friends or other sources may not be adversely affected by remaining closeted in their families or by receiving rejection from their families following disclosure. The most difficult situation is that in which a lesbian/gay individual or couple is closely involved with the family, has few or no other sources of social support, is psychologically vulnerable to family disapproval, and either remains closeted or receives rejection from the family after coming out.

Ordinarily, after a lesbian/gay adult has been out to the family for some time and is in a couple relationship, parents are at least cordial toward the partner and frequently accept him/her into their homes on holidays and other occasions. However, there may be crucial ways in which the lesbian/gay person's sexual orientation sets this couple relationship apart in the family. For example, despite inclusion in most or all family-of-origin events, parents may still treat the lesbian/gay offspring's partner as a sort of temporary "friend of the family" rather than as a bona fide family member, the way a son-in-law or a daughter-in-law is treated (Weinstein, 1996).

In addition to seeking family support, the couple sometimes has to protect its functioning from the intrusion of family members who are unsupportive and who seek to undermine the couple's integrity and cohesiveness. A recent study (LaSala, in press) showed that gay sons benefited by setting firm boundaries in relation to family members who were unsupportive of their couple relationships. Basically, this involved either insisting that their gay partnerships be acknowledged and treated with respect by family members, or distancing themselves from their families if this level of family acknowledgment was not forthcoming. However, lesbian couple relationships seemed to benefit more from lesbian daughters' playing a mediating, nurturing role between their families and their partners—not distancing from the families or the partners, but continuing to work at a reconciliation based on the family members' acceptance of the partners. In both situations, however, the lesbian/gay offspring had to affirm the legitimacy of and commitment to their same-sex partnerships, even in the face of family disapproval, or their couple relationships were adversely affected.

Families of Choice

In a seminal ethnographic study, *Families We Choose: Lesbians, Gays, Kinship*, Weston (1991) highlighted a crucial existential difference in the life experiences of lesbian and gay people as compared to heterosexuals. Because of their heightened awareness of the volitional nature of adult kinship ties, lesbians/gays become more psychologically open than heterosexuals to broadening the notion of "family" so that it can encompass nonbiological relations ("families of choice").

Lesbian and gay persons' greater openness to nonkinship sources of social support seems to lessen their dependence on family-of-origin connections during adulthood. In contrast to most heterosexuals, for example, lesbian/gay adults are continually exposed to peers who have experienced varying degrees of rejection and exclusion from their families of origin but still are functioning well. This exposure underscores the fact that parental emotional support during adulthood may not be as crucial as the heterosexual cultural ideal implies. Furthermore, the social support that may be lacking from one's kin can often be found outside the family.

Support from friendship networks seems exceptionally important for the well-being of lesbian and gay people, and therapists should pay at least as much attention to families of choice as to families of origin in assessing social support for these couples. For example, studies in the United States have found consistently that social support from families of origin is unrelated to the mental health of lesbians/gay individuals in couple relationships, but social support from friends is related to these individuals' mental health and better relationship functioning (Campbell, 2000; Kurdek, 1988a; Kurdek & Schmitt, 1986, 1987; Roper, 1997; Smith & Brown, 1997).

In a large-scale national survey (Bryant & Demian, 1994), the sources of social support reported by partners in lesbian and gay male couples were as follows (from most to least support): lesbian/gay friends; various lesbian/gay organizations and groups; heterosexual friends; coworkers; siblings; boss; mother; other relatives; father; and mainstream church. In this listing, it is remarkable that coworkers were ranked higher as a source of support than any family members, and that parents were ranked lower than bosses. If heterosexuals were to be asked this same question, they would typically rank family members much higher. It seems that well-functioning lesbian and gay male couples are making up for the lower amounts of social support they receive from family members by getting such support from friends.

As a result of this difference, well-functioning lesbian and gay couples typically form very close friendships (Nardi, 1999; Weston, 1991). In the optimal situation, these collections of friends have what is called "high density"—meaning that not only is a couple friends with a number of individuals, but these individuals are also friends with one another. When a friendship network has many close interconnections that last over time, it begins to take on a family-like quality; hence the term "family of choice." For same-sex couples, especially those with less family-of-origin connection and support, the social density dimension of their friendship networks is extremely important. We believe that all couples benefit by being embedded in an ongoing social matrix if that set of relationships is nurturing and reciprocal.

Interventions to Increase Social Support

When assessing a couple's social support, most family therapists in the past have focused almost exclusively on the partners' family-of-origin relations and have neglected to take friendships as seriously. We believe that this is a grave oversight when working with lesbian and gay people, because both family and nonfamily sources of support can be relevant, and sometimes the friendship sources are more significant. In the following sections, we discuss issues in the assessment and treatment of couples for whom more social support from family and friendship sources might help alleviate their distress and sustain their relationships in the future.

The Social Network: Assessing Combined Family and Nonfamily Sources of Support

In evaluating a same-sex couple's overall social support from both family and nonfamily sources, it frequently helps to do a sociogram as well as a family genogram to map out the people in the couple's social network. Because the formats for drawing genograms are well known (McGoldrick, Gerson, & Shellenberger, 1999), we focus here only on a format for doing a sociogram with lesbian/gay couples.[2]

A simplified sociogram can be drawn as five concentric circles. These circles can be labeled from innermost to outermost as follows (and the names of the couple's relevant network members can then be written in the appropriate concentric rings):

- *The couple* (the innermost circle).
- *Very close/supportive ties* (including usually two to six closest people, such as best friends or closest family members).
- *Close/supportive ties* (including other close friends or family members).
- *Instrumental ties/acquaintances* (which typically include ongoing work associates who are not close friends, ongoing acquaintances with whom the partners might get together a few times a year, or perhaps family members with whom the partners do not have very close ties).
- *Others* (the outermost circle—a miscellaneous category that might include the couple's attorney, neighbors who are not friends, members of organizations the couple is connected to, family members from whom the couple is very disengaged, etc.).

After the names of relevant network members are written in the appropriate rings based on the partners' input, lines can then be drawn depicting which network members are also connected to each other (solid lines indicating close/supportive connections, dotted lines indicating loose connections). All the rings together make up the couple's social network. The people in the innermost two or three rings constitute what we would call the couple's emotionally supportive relationships. However, these people only constitute a social support "system" or "family of choice" if they are also close to and supportive of one another (solid lines between them).

When the sociogram and genogram are completed, further assessment of the couple's support system should be based on the criteria listed below, which are adapted from the field of network therapy (Kliman & Trimble, 1983):

1. *Size and composition of the support system* (number and types of people in the couple's support system, such as friends, family members, coworkers, neighbors).
2. *Frequency and lengths of contacts.*
3. *Modes of contact* (in person, by phone, mail, e-mail).
4. *Types of activities or rituals* (recreation, meals, holidays, transition celebrations, etc.; see Imber-Black, Roberts, & Whiting, 1988, for examples).
5. *Multiplexity of ties* (the extent to which relationships have more than one role dimension, such as friends who are also coworkers, coworkers who are also cousins, neighbors who are also in the same religious congregation). Multiplex ties tend to be more enduring than uniplex ones, which have only one role dimension.
6. *Types of support* (emotional support, material/financial assistance, or practical support such as child care, moving, cooking, health-related assistance, pet care).
7. *Quality of support* (satisfaction with support received).
8. *Reciprocity of support* (either bilateral, where both persons give and receive support, or unilateral, where one gives and the other receives)
9. *Density of ties* (the extent to which members of the support system know and provide support to one another, including the extent to which close subgroups within the support system have overlapping memberships—"cross-ties". Subgroups could include, for example, a family-of-origin subgroup, a heterosexual coworkers subgroup, and a lesbian/gay friends subgroup. Single ties—relationships with individuals who are not connected emotionally to others in the support system—tend to be less enduring than multiple ties.)
10. *Structural stability of the support system* (changing vs. stable membership over time due to geographical moves, emotional cutoffs, illness/disability, deaths, divorces/separations, addition of new members, and any patterns in termination of ties).

In general, lesbian and gay couples tend to have less interconnected social networks than heterosexual couples do. Their lesbian/gay friends and their heterosexual family members and friends may meet only rarely, if at all. Even their lesbian/gay friends may hardly know one another, because these friendships usually have to be found outside of everyday mainstream situations such as work settings, schools, or churches, where many heterosexuals meet their friends and where these friends already would know one another. The tendency toward social segregation of the straight and gay worlds generally—and between the straight and gay segments of an individual's social network (Oswald, 2001)—usually requires same-sex couples to expend more deliberate effort to create an integrated social support system that has family-like qualities. The ideal would be to integrate family members, lesbian/gay friends, and heterosexual friends into a cohesive support system.

Support from Families of Origin: Assessment and Intervention

In assessing family-of-origin support, we are interested in three distinct issues: family members' general support for the clients as individuals; family members' support specifically related to the clients' being lesbian/gay individuals; and family members' support for the same-sex couple as a unit. Toward these ends, the following kinds of questions have proven useful:

1. "When did you first become aware that you might be lesbian or gay?"
2. "How do you think this 'differentness' may have affected your relationships with family members as you were growing up?"
3. "If you have *not* come out to certain family members, what factors led to this decision? Are there any ways that your remaining closeted with your family is affecting your couple relationship positively or negatively?"
4. "If you have come out to certain family members, describe the process, including what preceded, happened during, and has followed the disclosure up to the present time."
5. "If you have introduced your partner to your family of origin members, how have they treated your partner up until now? How have you responded to their treatment of your partner and of the two of you as a couple?"

Although a full discussion of family-of-origin interventions related to coming out and getting family support is beyond the scope of this chapter (see Beeler & DiProva, 1999; LaSala, 2000; Herdt

& Koff, 2000; and Savin-Williams, 1996), the first step in any such effort involves helping the lesbian or gay partners work through any residual internalized homophobia (as described earlier). When adult children can accept their own sexual orientation and partner choice, dealing with their families is emotionally much easier; clients can then cope with familial homophobia more dispassionately, planfully, assertively, and with fewer setbacks to the couple's functioning.

Disapproving family members quickly sense any internalized homophobia and often will exacerbate a lesbian/gay person's self-doubts with critical comments and attempts to diminish the importance of the couple relationship. An offspring with internalized homophobia will sometimes collude with this process, not bringing the partner home on visits and rarely mentioning the partner in the family member's presence. Typically, when the lesbian/gay person reaches a high level of self-acceptance and can calmly manifest that level in the family's presence, the family will either adapt to and become more accepting of the individual's sexual orientation and choice of partner, or the lesbian/gay person will make family relationships less salient, sometimes decreasing the amount of contact.

Therapeutic interventions in family-of-origin relations can include (1) Bowen-type coaching assignments, in which the client takes steps toward differentiation of self in the family of origin without the therapist present (Iasenza, Collucci, & Rothberg, 1996; McGoldrick & Carter, 2001); (2) conjoint family therapy sessions with all family-of-origin members together in the therapist's office (Framo, 1992); or (3) a combination of both methods. We caution against doing any coaching assignments or conjoint sessions with family-of-origin members until a lesbian/gay person has reached a reasonably sustainable level of self-acceptance. After that point, the client's talking directly with family members about the self and partner issues will be much more successful, regardless of whether the therapist is present during those encounters.

Interventions to Build Families of Choice

In working on social support, a therapist should encourage a couple to take a very proactive, deliberate stance toward the goal of developing an ongoing social support system consisting of about 8–12 individuals (Berger & Mallon, 1993). This goal should be discussed with the couple explicitly, and some of the research findings on the importance of friendship support for the psychological well-being of lesbian/gay individuals and couples should be shared. Many same-sex couples in therapy spontaneously report feeling isolated and wishing they had more and closer friendships, especially with other same-sex couples, and they immediately grasp the importance of developing a stronger support system. Defining some of the traits of a strong social support system for them (size, accessibility, frequency, quality, multiplexity, reciprocity, density, stability) in laypersons' terms is itself very helpful in orienting the couple to the task at hand.

Surprisingly, many clients seem to believe that this kind of interconnectedness ought to happen naturally, magically, on its own, and without any deliberate effort on their parts. A few feel that if they have to work at creating such a support system so intentionally, then perhaps they are defective compared to other people. Therapists can normalize both the need for this kind of support as well as the necessity for being proactive, especially for clients who are geographically or emotionally distant from their families of origin.

In our experience, the term "families of choice" resonates somewhat more strongly with lesbian couples than with gay male couples. However, some couples (particularly male couples) may find this family metaphor and language hyperbolic, or they may have negative reactions to the idea of being part of anything called "a family." With this latter group of couples, we use the phrase "social support system" or sometimes "sense of community," because these phrases connote both the warm/nurturing and the reciprocal/interconnected (density) aspects of the goal we are discussing. We also convey that a social support system or a family of choice can include supportive family-of-origin members as well as friends.

A couple has to take two basic steps in building a personal support system: first, developing or maintaining a reciprocally supportive relationship with each individual who would be a member of the couple's support system; and, second, "knitting" these individuals together into an integrated system of support (the density factor). The first step is already familiar to all therapists, who have much experience helping clients develop new friendships and deepen existing ones. The couple's relationships with the individuals in the support system must be reasonably close before the second step of creating cross-ties among those individuals can be accomplished.

If the couple's existing number of friendships is small, the perennial questions of where to meet people and how to move the friendships forward will arise. Other than work settings, ideal venues for meeting potential new friends in urban environments are lesbian/gay social, recreational, religious, charitable, self-help, educational, artistic, musical, or political organizations. In our experience, the best strategy is for partners to become very active in one well-established organization, attend its events very regularly in order to become familiar faces, and take on positions of leadership or active committee involvement that require repeated interaction with the same people frequently and over months or years. In smaller or rural communities with fewer lesbian/gay organizations, the local gay bar may still be the best venue for starting friendships. Many such bars are the focal point for lesbian/gay social life in their locales—regularly celebrating patrons' birthdays, life transitions, and holidays; raising funds for people in special need; and so on.

The great advantage of meeting new people through existing lesbian/gay organizations is that those organizations already will have some degree of interpersonal density or "groupness" to them, so that a couple may be able to become an integral (rather than peripheral) part of an already existing social support system. Therapists who work with lesbian/gay couples should familiarize themselves with lesbian/gay organizations in their communities, or at least know where to suggest that clients find such information.

Alternatively nowadays, some couples are advertising for friendships online ("Lesbian couple seeks similar for friendship, shared child care, recreation, travel . . .") and having success with that method. Obviously, if the 8–12 individual relationships are accrued at different times from different settings, more effort has to go into weaving these disparate relationships into a more cohesive unit. The only way to increase the density of a fragmented support system is for the couple to actively and persistently take the lead in physically bringing together the disconnected individuals or subgroups.

One route is for the members of a couple to take charge of arranging repeated social events and invite all members of their support system to attend these events. We have seen some extroverted client couples have great success becoming the "social directors" of their support systems—arranging group tickets for movies, plays, concerts, and picnics; setting up hikes, picnics, boat rides, ski trips, vacation rentals, or group volunteer efforts in the community; and so on. A more intimate approach is for the partners to invite everyone to their home for holiday events, brunches, Sunday dinners, movie nights, or the like. A long-term lesbian or gay couple's relationship and home can become powerful anchoring points for close friends and family members on the holidays or for regular weekly or monthly get-togethers (Johnson & Keren, 1996).

In our experience, what is most remarkable as therapy progresses is that partners who can sustain this effort find that other members of their support system "spontaneously" start to develop autonomous dyadic friendships, getting together on their own. Ultimately, these members will start organizing ways for the larger support system to get together, along with some of their other individual friends. The two key ingredients for reaching this goal are simply for the couple to maintain the closeness of the individual relationships and then to bring these individuals together as frequently as possible in pleasant circumstances. Given that structure, the emotional interconnections among other members of the support system tend to happen spontaneously, starting at about 6 months into the effort.

In our experience, it takes about a year to knit a disconnected collection of about 8–12 individual relationships into the beginnings of a functional social support system with a sustainable life of its own beyond the original couple's involvement. After that, it requires progressively less effort to keep the system going, but a support system (like a garden) always needs to be tended periodically or it will start to go downhill. New people must continually be introduced, as some members will inevitably withdraw because of other interests and demands, or because of geographical relocations or deaths.

In the ways described above, couple therapists should view friendship sources of social support as being at least as important as family-of-origin support for lesbian/gay persons' mental health and their couple functioning. Many aspects of therapy with a same-sex couple—taking a history; mapping the relevant people in the couple's life; formulating the problem; setting goals; deciding whom to include in sessions; and referrals to adjunctive therapeutic, educational, and support services—should reflect this expanded social network focus.

THERAPIST ISSUES

The Importance of Personal Comfort

We could say this a thousand times in a thousand ways and still not have emphasized it enough: *The single most important prerequisite for helping same-sex couples is the therapist's personal comfort with love and sexuality between two women or two men.* Therapists who are not comfortable with such love and sexuality may actually increase lesbian and gay clients' minority stress and exacerbate their problems unintentionally.

This statement does not mean a misguided blind approval of everything a lesbian or gay person does, or avoidance of dealing directly with destructive patterns of behavior by lesbian or gay couples. It does not mean superficial acceptance or patronizing overprotectiveness with clients. It requires familiarity with lesbian and gay culture; the ability to empathically identify with (but still remain sufficiently objective about) the behavior of lesbian and gay clients; and genuine personal ease ("comfort in your bones") when dealing with lesbian/gay partners' emotions for each other. It also requires an ability to ask and talk about homosexual sex in explicit terms with couples who are having sexual difficulties.

We believe that with sufficient good will, motivation, and openness to learning and feedback, most therapists (regardless of sexual orientation) can achieve this level of preparedness for therapy with lesbian and gay couples. The American Psychological Association (2000) has recently published a superb set of treatment guidelines for all mental health professionals working with lesbian, gay, and bisexual clients, and this article is an excellent starting point for those who wish to learn more.

In the field of couple and family therapy, many important ideas about lesbian and gay matters can be found in the review by Laird (1993), the books by Greenan and Tunnell (2002) and by Laird and Green (1996), and a recent journal section (Green, 2000a). In the latter two publications, there are excellent articles about straight therapists working with lesbian/gay clients (Bernstein, 2000; Siegel & Walker, 1996) and about strategies of couple therapy (Bepko & Johnson, 2000; Johnson & Keren, 1996).

Although such readings are vital, there is ample evidence that heterocentric stereotypes persist among mental health professionals, even after they presumably know (or should know) the basic information about lesbian and gay issues (Garnets et al., 1991; Johnson, Brems, & Alford-Keating, 1995). Didactic information is not sufficient to override unconscious prejudice that has been acquired over a lifetime. Working effectively with lesbian and gay clients involves more than just good intentions, significant reading, and the perfunctory kinds of preparation that are common now in our field. Affective and attitudinal learning is at least as important.

As a rule of thumb, we would suggest that therapists who personally would not feel comfortable seeing a competent lesbian or gay therapist for their own relationship problems may not be ready to work with lesbian or gay couples themselves. If therapists are employed in small communities or settings, or on managed care panels where they are essentially the only possible clinicians for such couples, we recommend seeking expert consultation on every lesbian or gay couple's case until the therapists can answer affirmatively to our rule-of-thumb criterion. If therapists do not live in areas with an expert consultant for these kinds of cases, we advise arranging confidential, long-distance telephone consultations. We would be happy to provide suggestions of appropriate consultants for this purpose.

Guarding against Heterocentric Bias: Countertransference

If heterocentric biases were fully conscious, therapists could counteract them through rational self-monitoring. Unfortunately, we all—therapists included—tend "not to know what we don't know." Hence some therapists believe they are sufficiently knowledgeable about lesbian/gay issues without having immersed themselves in the clinical and research literature (Green, 1996) and without having received sustained supervision from lesbian/gay-knowledgeable colleagues. Even lesbian and gay therapists are not immune to heterocentric assumptions or homophobic reactions, as those of us who are lesbian or gay know from years of shedding our own internalized homophobia bit by bit. The main advantage lesbian and gay therapists have is extensive exposure to ordinary, nondistressed lesbian/gay persons and relationships, which helps disconfirm prejudicial stereotypes promulgated in the larger society.

The field of family therapy is just beginning to build culturally attuned treatment models for working with lesbian and gay couples and families (D'Augelli & Patterson, 1995; Greenan & Tunnell, 2002; Laird & Green, 1996). On a personal level, the first step is to acknowledge that heterocentric assumptions are inevitable for all members of our society, including couple therapists. The goal is to make these assumptions conscious and examine them in light of existing psychological knowledge and professional ethics. Below we discuss a few additional steps that therapists can take.

Examining Unconscious Biases and Assumptions

How do therapists personally view lesbian and gay people's lives, and do their views fit with recent research findings? What are the emotional cues of bias in this area? In general, the signs of bias among professionals tend to be subtle—consisting of inchoate feelings of discomfort, ambivalence, pessimism, anxiety, or "reactive" eagerness to please and appear "expert" when working with lesbian/gay clients. The antidotes to acting out such bias are for a therapist to become comfortable with "not knowing," retain a willingness to learn from clients, take a collaborative stance, and make space for discussion of cultural discrepancies and misunderstandings between him-/herself and the clients. The optimal attitude is one of nondefensive humility about the true limits of one's training, personal experience, and expert knowledge, while still retaining one's overall professional integrity and realistic confidence.

Personal Immersion in Lesbian/Gay Culture: Becoming "Bicultural"

The research on homophobia and the clinical literature on heterosexual therapists working with lesbian/gay clients both point to the positive effects of more social contact to reduce prejudice (Bernstein, 2000; S. K. Green & Bobele, 1994; Siegel & Walker, 1996). Heterosexuals (including therapists) who have more interaction with lesbians/gays as personal friends, colleagues, family members, and clients report significantly less heterosexist attitudes. High levels of immersion in lesbian/gay culture involve therapists' taking concrete actions to work against heterosexism in their own families, friendships, professional settings, and communities. On the political level, couple therapists can contribute by participating in local chapters of Parents, Families, and Friends of Lesbians and Gays (PFLAG; see PFLAG's Web site, http://www.pflag.org). It is important to keep in mind that although unbiased psychotherapy and psychological research have made positive contributions, the gay civil rights movement has made the single greatest contribution to the psychological well-being of lesbian and gay couples. For lesbians and gay men, the political is very personal, and working toward the elimination of homophobia in therapists' own social networks and community institutions is good preparation for doing therapy with lesbian and gay couples.

Getting Case Consultations from Experts in Lesbian/Gay-Affirmative Therapy

Starting with the assumption that we all have unconscious biases about homosexuality, it becomes imperative for therapists to seek training and consultation for working with lesbians and gays as clients. Few practicing couple therapists have had as much as a semester-long course on lesbian/gay issues or have been supervised by an expert on lesbian/gay therapy. Clinicians should seek expert consultation early in treatment if they are not knowledgeable about lesbian/gay couple therapy, and especially if progress with such a couple is slower than seems desirable.

Sharing Power in Sessions

In work with lesbian/gay populations, it is important to continually acknowledge and respect mutual expertise, including sharing the power to interpret. A couple therapist should be willing to discuss in laypersons' terminology all assessment results, treatment goals, and therapeutic plans in a collaborative manner with clients, soliciting the partners' active input. The key is for the therapist to guard against making unwarranted assumptions and to check out his/her perceptions about lesbian/gay issues with the clients themselves. If the therapist believes that the therapeutic goals for a given couple should include resolving internalized homophobia, reducing relational ambiguity, and building a family of choice, these objectives should be discussed in laypersons' terms with the partners. Their understanding and shared commitment to these stated goals should be achieved before proceeding further.

CONCLUSION

As a caveat to everything that appears above, we wish to emphasize that our generalizations about same-sex couples do not apply uniformly to all lesbian or gay couples. In particular, because of limitations of space, we have not been able to cover specialized therapeutic issues for lesbian and gay couples of color, interracial same-sex couples, couples in which one or both members are bisexual, or couples in which one or both members are transgendered (for these topics, see especially Burke, 1996; Fox, 1996; Greene & Boyd-Franklin, 1996; Liu & Chan, 1996; and Morales, 1996). Readers should also keep in mind that this chapter focuses only on lesbian/gay couples whose members are distressed and need professional help with particular kinds of problems.

However, couples in therapy do not represent the majority of same-sex couples, who are reasonably satisfied with their relationships and are not distressed. In the past, the mental health fields have shown a tendency to blur the distinction between well-functioning and distressed lesbian/gay couples, and to assume that all same-sex couples are like the dysfunctional couples described in the clinical literature. For example, the notions of "fusion" in lesbian couples and "disengagement" in gay male couples—which came from clinical work with distressed couples (Krestan & Bepko, 1980)—became a kind of legend about all lesbian and gay couples. However, research with community, nonclinical samples has since clarified that lesbian couples in general are extremely cohesive but not fused, and that gay male couples are actually more cohesive than heterosexual married couples, not more disengaged (Green et al., 1996; Mitchell, 1988). In this light, we wish to emphasize once again that although all same-sex couples face special challenges in terms of overcoming prejudice, dealing with greater relational ambiguity, and creating cohesive support systems, most lesbian and gay couples are able to manage these tasks successfully without professional help and are functioning well.

To the extent that we have offered generalizations about same-sex couples in therapy, we also wish to underscore that such statements are valuable only insofar as they serve as initial hypotheses in a new case—ideas to be tested and either retained or discarded, depending on one's observations in that particular case. Our descriptions of dysfunctional same-sex couples in this chapter should be taken as statements of "possible characteristics" rather than "universal truths" about lesbian and gay couples in therapy. The particulars of real clients in treatment should always supersede abstract generalizations about categories of clients. Otherwise, therapy with lesbian and gay couples would become little more than the imposition of yet another set of stereotypes about them.

ACKNOWLEDGMENTS

We are grateful to Joan Laird, Holden H. Lee, Richard A. Rodriguez, and Karen Franklin for comments on earlier drafts of this chapter and for discussions of the conceptual material.

NOTES

1. RJG is indebted to Romana F. Oswald, PhD, University of Illinois at Urbana-Champaign, for the general suggestion that Boss's concept of boundary ambiguity might have utility for understanding the couple and family relationships of lesbians and gay men.
2. We are indebted to Karen Franklin, PhD, Clinical and Training Director, Alternative Family Institute, San Francisco, for her input in developing this format for sociograms.

REFERENCES

American Psychological Association. (2000). Guidelines for psychotherapy with lesbian, gay, and bisexual clients. *American Psychologist, 55,* 1440–1451.

Ayers, T., & Brown, P. (1999). *The essential guide to lesbian and gay weddings.* Los Angeles: Alyson.

Bailey, J. M., & Zucker, K. J. (1995). Childhood sex-typed behavior and sexual orientation: A conceptual analysis and quantitative review. *Developmental Psychology, 31,* 43–55.

Becker, C. (1988). *Unbroken ties: Lesbian ex-lovers.* Los Angeles: Alyson.

Beeler, J., & DiProva, V. (1999). Family adjustment following disclosure of homosexuality by a member: Themes discerned in narrative accounts. *Journal of Marital and Family Therapy, 25,* 443–459.

Bell, A. P., & Weinberg, M. (1978). *Homosexualities: A study of diversity among men and women.* New York: Simon & Schuster.

Bell, A. P., Weinberg, M. S., & Hammersmith, S. K. (1981). *Sexual preference: Its development in men and women.* Bloomington: Indiana University Press.

Bepko, C., & Johnson, T. (2000). Gay and lesbian couples in therapy: Perspectives for the contemporary family therapist. *Journal of Marital and Family Therapy, 26,* 409–419.

Berger, R. M., & Mallon, D. (1993). Social support networks of gay men. *Journal of Sociology and Social Welfare, 20,* 155–174.

Bernstein, A. C. (2000). Straight therapists working with lesbians and gays in family therapy. *Journal of Marital and Family Therapy, 26,* 443–454.

Blasband, D., & Peplau, L. A. (1985). Sexual exclusivity versus openness in gay couples. *Archives of Sexual Behavior, 14,* 395–412.

Blumstein, P., & Schwartz, P. (1983). *American couples: Money, work and sex.* New York: Morrow.

Boss, P. (1999). *Ambiguous loss: Learning to live with unresolved grief.* Cambridge, MA: Harvard University Press.

Boss, P., Caron, W., Horbal, J., Mortimer, J. (1990). Predictors of depression in caregivers of dementia patients: Boundary ambiguity and mastery. *Family Process, 29,* 245–254.

Boss, P., & Greenberg, J. (1984). Family boundary ambiguity: A new variable in family stress theory. *Family Process, 23,* 535–546.

Boyd-Franklin, N. (1989). *Black families in therapy: A multisystems approach.* New York: Guilford Press.

Brown, L. S. (1994). *Subversive dialogues: Theory in feminist therapy.* New York: Basic Books.

Bryant, A. S., & Demian (1994). Relationship characteristics of American gay and lesbian couples: Findings from a national survey. In L. A. Kurdek (Ed.), *Social services for gay and lesbian couples* (pp. 101–117). Binghamton, NY: Harrington Park Press.

Burke, P. (1996). *Gender shock: Exploding the myths of male and female.* New York: Doubleday.

Byng-Hall, J. (1995). Creating a secure family base: Some implications of attachment theory for family therapy. *Family Process, 34,* 45–58.

Campbell, K. M. (2000). *Relationship characteristics, social support, masculine ideologies and psychological functioning of gay men in couples.* Unpublished doctoral dissertation, California School of Professional Psychology, Alliant International University, San Francisco, CA.

Carrington, C. (1999). *No place like home: Relationships and family life among lesbians and gay men.* Chicago: University of Chicago Press.

Chan, C. S. (1989). Issues of identity development among Asian-American lesbians and gay men. *Journal of Counseling and Development, 68,* 16–20.

Chan, C. S. (1995). Issues of sexual identity in an ethnic minority: The case of Chinese American lesbians, gay men, and bisexual people. In A. D'Augelli & C. Patterson (Eds.), *Lesbian, gay, and bisexual identities over the lifespan* (pp. 87–101). New York: Oxford University Press.

Clark, W. M., & Serovich, J. M. (1997). Twenty years and still in the dark?: Content analysis of articles pertaining to gay, lesbian, and bisexual issues in marriage and family therapy journals. *Journal of Marital and Family Therapy, 23,* 239–253.

Crosbie-Burnett, M., Foster, T. L., Murray, C. I., & Bowen, G. L. (1996). Gays' and lesbians' families of origin: A social-cognitive–behavioral model of adjustment. *Family Relations, 45,* 397–403.

D'Augelli, A. R., & Patterson, C. J. (Eds.). (1995). *Lesbian, gay, and bisexual identities over the lifespan: Psychological perspectives.* New York: Oxford University Press.

DiPlacido, J. (1998). Minority stress among lesbians, gay men and bisexuals. In G. M. Herek (Ed.), *Stigma and sexual orientation: Understanding prejudice against lesbians, gay men, and bisexuals* (pp. 138–159). Thousand Oaks, CA: Sage.

Doherty, W. J., & Simmons, D. S. (1996). Clinical practice patterns of marriage and family therapists: A national survey of therapists and their clients. *Journal of Marital and Family Therapy, 22,* 9–25.

Falicov, C. J. (1998). *Latino families in therapy: A guide to multicultural practice.* New York: Guilford Press.

Fox, R. (1996). Bisexuality in perspective: A review of theory and research. In B. Firestein (Ed.), *Bisexuality: The psychology and politics of an invisible minority* (pp. 3–50). Thousand Oaks, CA: Sage.

Framo, J. L. (1992). *Family-of-origin therapy: An intergenerational approach.* New York: Brunner/Mazel.

Garnets, L., Hancock, K. A., Cochran, S. D., Godchilds, J., & Peplau, L. A. (1991). Issues in psychotherapy with lesbians and gay men: A survey of psychologists. *American Psychologist, 46,* 964–972.

Gonsiorek, J. C. (1991). The empirical basis for the demise of the illness model of homosexuality. In J. C. Gonsiorek & J. D. Weinrich (Eds.), *Homosexuality: Research implications for public policy* (pp. 115–136). Thousand Oaks, CA: Sage.

Green, R.-J. (1996). Why ask, why tell?: Teaching and learning about lesbians and gays in family therapy. *Family Process, 35,* 389–400.

Green, R.-J. (1998a). Race and the field of family therapy. In M. McGoldrick (Ed.), *Re-visioning family therapy: Race, culture, and gender in clinical practice* (pp. 93–110). New York: Guilford Press.

Green, R.-J. (1998b). Traditional norms of the male role. *Journal of Feminist Family Therapy, 10,* 81–83.

Green, R.-J. (Ed.). (2000a). Gay, lesbian, and bisexual issues in family therapy [Special section]. *Journal of Marital and Family Therapy, 26,* 407–468.

Green, R.-J. (2000b). Lesbians, gay men, and their parents: A critique of LaSala and the prevailing clinical "wisdom." *Family Process, 39,* 257–266.

Green, R.-J., Bettinger, M., & Zacks, E. (1996). Are lesbian couples fused and gay male couples disengaged?: Questioning gender straightjackets. In J. Laird & R.-J. Green (Eds.), *Lesbians and gays in couples and families: A handbook for therapists* (pp. 185–230). San Francisco: Jossey-Bass.

Green, S. K., & Bobele, M. (1994). Family therapists' response to AIDS: An examination of attitudes, knowledge, and contact. *Journal of Marital and Family Therapy, 20,* 349–367.

Greenan, D., & Tunnell, G. (2002). *Couple therapy with gay men.* New York: Guilford Press.

Greene, B., & Boyd-Franklin, N. (1996). African American lesbians: Issues in couples therapy. In J. Laird & R.-J. Green (Eds.), *Lesbians and gays in couples and families: A handbook for therapists* (pp. 251–271). San Francisco: Jossey-Bass.

Hartman, A. (1996). Social policy as a context for lesbian and gay families: The political is personal. In J. Laird & R.-J. Green (Eds.), *Lesbians and gays in couples and families: A handbook for therapists* (pp. 69–85). San Francisco: Jossey-Bass.

Hayden, C., Clifford, R. L., & Hertz, F. (2001). *A legal guide for lesbian and gay couples.* Berkeley, CA: Nolo Press.

Herdt, G., & Koff, B. (2000). *Something to tell you: The road families travel when a child is gay.* New York: Columbia University Press.

Herek, G. (1994). Assessing heterosexuals' attitudes toward lesbians and gay men: A review of empirical research with the ATLG Scale. In B. Greene & G. Herek (Eds.), *Lesbian and gay psychology: Theory, research, and clinical applications* (pp. 206–228). Thousand Oaks, CA: Sage.

Herek, G. M. (Ed.). (1998). *Stigma and sexual orientation: Understanding prejudice against lesbians, gay men, and bisexuals.* Thousand Oaks, CA: Sage.

Hochschild, A. (1989). *The second shift: Working parents and the revolution at home.* New York: Viking.

Iasenza, S., Colucci, P. L., & Rothberg, B. (1996). Coming out and the mother–daughter bond: Two case examples. In J. Laird & R.-J. Green (Eds.), *Lesbians and gays in couples and families: A handbook for therapists* (pp. 123–136). San Francisco: Jossey-Bass.

Imber-Black, E., Roberts, J., & Whiting, R. (Eds.). (1988). *Rituals in families and family therapy.* New York: Norton.

Johnson, M. E., Brems, C., & Alford-Keating, P. (1995). Parental sexual orientation and therapists' perceptions of family functioning. *Journal of Gay and Lesbian Psychotherapy, 2*(3), 1–15.

Johnson, T. W., & Keren, M. S. (1996). Boundary creation and maintenance in male couples. In J. Laird & R.-J. Green (Eds.), *Lesbians and gays in couples and families: A handbook for therapists* (pp. 231–250). San Francisco: Jossey-Bass.

Kliman, J., & Trimble, D.W. (1983). Network therapy. In B. Wolman & G. Stricker (Eds.), *Handbook of family and marital therapy* (pp. 277–314). New York: Plenum Press.

Krestan, J.-A., & Bepko, C. S. (1980). The problem of fusion in the lesbian relationship. *Family Process, 19,* 277–289.

Kurdek, L. A. (1988a). Perceived social support in gays and lesbians in cohabiting relationships. *Journal of Personality and Social Psychology, 54,* 504–509.

Kurdek, L. A. (1988b). Relationship quality of gay and lesbian cohabiting couples. *Journal of Homosexuality, 15,* 93–118.

Kurdek, L. A. (1995). Lesbian and gay couples. In A. R. D'Augelli & C. J. Patterson (Eds.), *Lesbian, gay, and bisexual identities over the lifespan: Psychological perspectives* (pp. 243–261). New York: Oxford University Press.

Kurdek, L. A., & Schmitt, J. P. (1986). Relationship quality of partners in heterosexual married, heterosexual cohabiting, and gay and lesbian relationships. *Journal of Personality and Social Psychology, 51,* 711–720.

Kurdek, L. A., & Schmitt, J. P. (1987). Perceived emotional support from family and friends in members of homosexual, married, and heterosexual cohabiting couples. *Journal of Homosexuality, 14,* 57–68.

Laird, J. (1993). Lesbian and gay families. In F. Walsh (Ed.), *Normal family processes* (2nd ed., pp. 282–328). New York: Guilford Press.

Laird, J. (1996). Invisible ties: Lesbians and their families of origin. In J. Laird & R.-J. Green (Eds.), *Lesbians and gays in couples and families: A handbook for therapists* (pp. 89–122). San Francisco: Jossey-Bass.

Laird, J., & Green, R.-J. (Eds.). (1996). *Lesbians and gays in couples and families: A handbook for therapists.* San Francisco: Jossey-Bass.

LaSala, M. (2000). Lesbians, gay men, and their parents: Family therapy for the coming out crisis. *Family Process, 39,* 67–81.

LaSala, M. (in press). Walls and bridges: How coupled gay men and lesbians manage their intergenerational relationships. *Journal of Marital and Family Therapy.*

Lee, E. (Ed.). (1997). *Working with Asian Americans: A guide for clinicians.* New York: Guilford Press.

Liu, P., & Chan, C. (1996). Lesbian, gay, and bisexual Asian Americans and their families. In J. Laird & R.-J. Green (Eds.), *Lesbians and gays in couples and families: A handbook for therapists* (pp. 137–152). San Francisco: Jossey-Bass.

Malyon, A. K. (1982). Psychotherapeutic implications of internalized homophobia in gay men. In J. Gonsiorek (Ed.), *Homosexuality and psychotherapy: A practitioner's handbook of affirmative models* (pp. 59–69). New York: Haworth Press.

McGoldrick, M. (Ed.). (1998). *Re-visioning family therapy: Race, culture, and gender in clinical practice.* New York: Guilford Press.

McGoldrick, M., & Carter, B. (2001). Advances in coaching: Family therapy with one person. *Journal of Marital and Family Therapy, 27,* 281–300.

McGoldrick, M., Gerson, R., & Shellenberger, S. (1999). *Genograms: Assessment and intervention* (2nd ed.). New York: Norton.

McWhirter, D. P., & Mattison, A. M. (1984). *The male couple: How relationships develop.* Englewood Cliffs, NJ: Prentice-Hall.

Meyer, I. H., & Dean, L. (1998). Internalized homophobia, intimacy, and sexual behavior among gay and bisexual men. In G. M. Herek (Ed.), *Stigma and sexual orientation: Understanding prejudice against lesbians, gay men, and bisexuals* (pp. 160–186). Thousand Oaks, CA: Sage.

Miller, J. B. (1976). *Toward a new psychology of women.* Boston: Beacon Press.

Minuchin, S. (1974). *Families and family therapy.* Cambridge, MA: Harvard University Press.

Mitchell, V. (1988). Using Kohut's self-psychology in work with lesbian couples. *Women and Therapy, 8,* 157–166.

Mitchell, V. (1996). Two moms: Contribution of the planned lesbian family to the deconstruction of gendered parenting. In J. Laird & R.-J. Green (Eds.), *Lesbians and gays in couples and families: A handbook for therapists* (pp. 343–357). San Francisco: Jossey-Bass.

Morales, E. (1996). Gender roles among Latino gay/bisexual men: Implications for family and couples relationships. In J. Laird & R.-J. Green (Eds.), *Lesbians and gays in couples and families: A handbook for therapists* (pp. 272–297). San Francisco: Jossey-Bass.

Nardi, P. (1999). *Gay men's friendships: Invincible communities.* Chicago: University of Chicago Press.

Olkin, R. (1999). *What psychotherapists should know about disability.* New York: Guilford Press.

Oswald, R. (2001, August). *Ritual as the site of family integration and disjunction.* Paper presented at the meeting of the American Psychological Association, San Francisco.

Peplau, L. A. (1991). Lesbian and gay relationships. In J. C. Gonsiorek & J. D. Weinrich (Eds.), *Homosexuality: Research implications for public policy* (pp. 177–196). Newbury Park, CA: Sage.

Pinderhughes, E. (1989). *Understanding race, ethnicity, and power: The key to efficacy in clinical practice.* New York: Free Press.

Radical Therapist Collective. (1971). *The radical therapist* (J. Agel, Ed.). New York: Ballantine Books.

Roper, K. (1997). *Lesbian couple dynamics and individuals' psychological adjustment.* Unpublished doctoral dissertation, California School of Professional Psychology, Alliant International University, San Francisco, CA.

Roth, S. (1989). Psychotherapy with lesbian couples: Individual issues, female socialization, and the social context. In M. McGoldrick, C. M. Anderson, & F. Walsh (Eds.), *Women in families: A framework for family therapy* (pp. 286–307). New York: Norton.

Savin-Williams, R. C. (1994). Verbal and physical abuse as stressors in the lives of lesbian, gay male, and bisexual youths: Associations with school problems, running away, substance abuse, prostitution, and suicide. *Journal of Consulting and Clinical Psychology, 62,* 261–269.

Savin-Williams, R. C. (1996). Self-labeling and disclosure among gay, lesbian, and bisexual youths. In J. Laird & R.-J. Green (Eds.), *Lesbians and gays in couples and families: A handbook for therapists* (pp. 153–182). San Francisco: Jossey-Bass.

Savin-Williams, R. C. (2001). *Mom, dad. I'm gay: How families negotiate coming out.* Washington, DC: American Psychological Association.

Shidlo, A. (1994). Internalized homophobia: Conceptual and empirical issues in measurement. In B. Greene & G. Herek (Eds.), *Lesbian and gay psychology: Theory, research, and clinical applications* (pp. 176–205). Thousand Oaks, CA: Sage.

Siegel, S., & Walker, G. (1996). Connections: Conversation between a gay therapist and a straight therapist. In J. Laird & R.-J. Green (Eds.), *Lesbians and gays in couples and families: A handbook for therapists* (pp. 28–68). San Francisco: Jossey-Bass.

Smith, R. B., & Brown, R. A. (1997). The impact of social support on gay male couples. *Journal of Homosexuality, 33,* 39–61.

Weinstein, D. L. (1996). No place in the family album. *Journal of Feminist Family Therapy, 8,* 63–67.

Weston, K. (1991). *Families we choose: Lesbians, gays, kinship.* New York: Columbia University Press.

White, M., & Epston, D. (1990). *Narrative means to therapeutic ends.* New York: Norton.

Chapter 22

Couple Therapy Using a Multicultural Perspective

KENNETH V. HARDY
TRACEY A. LASZLOFFY

A multicultural perspective (MCP) is a world view, an epistemological stance. It involves not only how we view the world, but, more importantly, how we place ourselves in the world. It endeavors to promote understanding of "other," but also understanding of "self" and, especially, "self in relation to other." It is not a set of codified techniques or strategies that a therapist uses with "this family" or "that family," but rather a philosophical stance that significantly informs how one sees the world both inside and outside therapy.

BASIC ASSUMPTIONS

An MCP is shaped by several key assumptions, which are explicated below.

Culture Is a Broad-Based, Multidimensional Concept

The MCP is predicated on the assumption that culture is a complex, fluid, dialectical concept. It cannot be reduced to a singular dimension, such as gender, ethnicity, or race. Although each of these dimensions is often used interchangeably with the term "culture," none in isolation captures the complexity of the concept. Culture is a broad-based

concept comprising a host of interrelated dimensions that include, but are not limited to, race, religion, ethnicity, age, gender, or sexual orientation (Hardy & Laszloffy, 1995b). It is the intricate interaction between and among these dimensions, as well as how each informs the others, that ultimately shapes how an individual defines oneself. These dimensions also have a profound impact on the relationship(s) that one person develops with another.

When culture is considered within the context of an MCP, one inevitably has to question popularized notions that it refers only to "people of color," "ethnic minorities," or other marginalized groups. Culture, as we conceptualize it here, pertains to "everyone." The failure or inability to adequately identify one's cultural heritage, background, or identity does not negate the existence of culture and its pervasive influence on attitudes and behaviors. In this regard, we often liken culture to parentage. For example, in the case of an adoptive child, it would be imprudent to assume that lack of knowledge of one's birth parents is tantamount to "not having birth parents," or that these parents have had no impact on the child's life because they are unknown and uninvolved. Lack of knowledge does not nullify the fact that all children have birth parents, and that these parents in some form or fashion shape who the children become, even in situations where the influence is not readily identifiable. Culture, like parentage, is a powerful organizing principle in human lives, regardless of circumstances.

Conceptualizing culture very broadly is important, because this challenges the belief that it is a fixed and static process. This is significant from our perspective, because it encourages a more complex view of the concept. When culture is conceived in the manner we are suggesting here, it illuminates how a person can simultaneously occupy two seemingly divergent roles, such as privileged and subjugated. For example, an African American male simultaneously occupies the privileged role of being a male and the subjugated role of being a racial minority.

Our view of culture also helps to explain the critical differences that may exist among members of the "same" cultural group. For example, we would expect to find compelling similarities (and differences) among a group of Irish Catholics who share ethnicity and religion, but who are from divergent regions of the country and class backgrounds. Having the ability to appreciate how phenomena can be simultaneously the same and different is integral to an MCP, and is one of the major tenets associated with it.

Segregated Thinking Limits Our View

Western culture promotes segregated thinking, which involves a rigid, "either–or" approach to life that obscures the connections uniting all things. Segregated thinking involves taking the complexity of life and reducing it to simplistic, dichotomous categories that are treated as if they represent oppositional and unrelated aspects of an entity. For example, segregated thinking underpins the notion that there are two, and only two genders that are mutually distinct and inherently oppositional. Segregated thinking makes it difficult to acknowledge that those who belong to the respective groups of "male" and "female" have similar and shared qualities. Moreover, because segregated thinking involves polarization and rigid dichotomies, it also prevents the possibility of recognizing that more than two genders can exist.

An MCP specifically emphasizes how segregated thinking often results in artificial divisions with respect to the following: individuals, families, and culture; sameness and difference; past, present, and future; and oppressor and oppressed.

A core dimension of an MCP involves challenging segregated thinking and emphasizing the ways in experiences are interconnected. From this perspective, therapists encourage clients to resist "either–or" conclusions about reality by advocating a "both–and" approach to their lives (Hardy, 1995, 1997b). Therapists using an MCP encourage clients to recognize and embrace all the parts of their identities and their experiences, including seeing the connections among individual, family, and cultural contexts; finding ways of recognizing and simultaneously embracing similarities and differences; recognizing the links among past, present, and future; and seeing the ways in which we are all both oppressors and oppressed.

When therapists operate according to an MCP, they emphasize the ways in which life often involves contradictions, conflict, and complexity. Although most of us have been conditioned to deny the complexity of reality and engage in the denial that accompanies either–or thinking, therapists using an MCP encourage clients to embrace the contradictions, conflict, and complexity of reality. They encourage clients to assume a both–and stance.

For example, when Patti and Sandy came to therapy, one of the issues that surfaced was the fact that Patti, who was biracial (her mother was European American, her father African American), had rejected the part of herself that was black. As Sandy said, "Patti uses her light complexion to deny her blackness and tries to pass as white. I think she's actually convinced herself of it." Patti had been unable to find a way to embrace the complexity of her identity, choosing to acknowledge only her whiteness while denying her blackness. She was unable to embrace the complexity of her identity—to hold the fact that she was both white *and* black, and she was neither white *nor* black.

Embracing both–and thinking is critical, because it allows us to begin to appreciate the ways in which all matter is potentially connected. Although we speak of it here as a "way of thinking," it is really an orientation toward the world. Thus both–and thinking is not merely a cognitive exercise. Instead, it is a paradigmatic shift in one's most basic orientation toward the world. When this feat is accomplished, one begins to "see" and appreciate more acutely how sameness and difference, for example, can coexist; how the seemingly rigid lines of demarcation that exist among past, present, and future become obscured at best, if not completely obliterated; and how aspects of both "batterer" and "victim" can reside within the skin of the same individual. Embracing both–and thinking not only invites us to think about the ways in which these phenomena may be connected; it also encourages us to respond in ways that place these interconnections at the forefront of what we *do*. In other words, from the point of view of an MCP, it is simply not enough for a therapist to understand or believe that "batterer" and "victim" aspects may coexist within the same individual, if he/she is unable to authentically "hold" (embrace) both in treatment.

Context Is Significant and Reality Is Relative

As human beings, our lives are embedded in contexts that may be varied, interlocking, overlapping, and seemingly discrete. "Context" refers to the sense of embeddedness we all have that helps define the nature of our existence. It is the various milieus, perspectives, and experiences that we all have that help define the nature of our existence. It is context that actually gives meaning to communication (Watzlawick, Beavin, & Jackson, 1967). One could advance the argument that communication that occurs void of context (to the degree that such is possible) is virtually impossible to decipher and thus is either noninterpretable or overinterpretable. The absence of context removes any and all possible parameters or markers that otherwise might help to give meaning to or punctuate a given message (Watzlawick, 1984). There is a virtually inextricable relationship between context and reality, in that context shapes our reality and it defines and punctuates the meanings we attach to our lives. For example, when someone gives an interview to a reporter and the reporter picks certain pieces to emphasize within the subsequent article, it is not uncommon for the interviewee to say, "My remarks were taken out of context." The interviewee in this example is referring to the way his/her remarks were removed from the broader text in which they were embedded, which changes their meaning.

An MCP, as is common with many systemically based approaches to psychotherapy, places a high premium on the significance of context. Like many other family therapy approaches, it recognizes the salience of the familial context as a major meaning-making marker of one's subjective experience, and it emphasizes the dimensions of culture as major contextual variables to be con-

sidered as well. Thus an MCP posits that each of us has multiple selves that are embedded in and defined by multiple contexts.

As an illustration, consider our client Marissa, who is a 38-year-old, female, Vietnamese, Catholic, first-generation, middle-class, "American" cardiologist. The contexts in which her life is embedded are quite varied and serve as a powerful meaning maker for her. Hence the presenting problem that brings her to therapy cannot be exorcised from the various dimensions of culture that help to define how she perceives her "problem," the solutions she attempts, the thoughts and feelings that underpin her suffering and pursuit of therapy, and so on. An MCP would suggest that to really know and understand the complexity of Marissa's suffering, it would be beneficial to know something about her context. Yet to accomplish the latter, it would be essential for us to know something about how the various dimensions of culture are delicately interwoven to create and inform the complexity of her condition. This same knowledge, more often than not, may also provide a powerful pathway to helping Marissa understand and potentially transform her difficulties.

An MCP assumes that two integral aspects of context must be attended to: historical and contemporary. This is a critical dynamic that often needs to be examined if not deconstructed in human relationships, whether between individuals or groups; however, not everyone acknowledges the significance of both of these. Some individuals and groups have very different orientations with respect to historical and contemporary contexts. Many people of color, for example, have a strong orientation toward the relationship between the historical and contemporary contexts. It is difficult to discuss one of these temporal spheres without devoting simultaneous, acute attention to examining the other. This is very much reflected in the way many African Americans find it difficult to discuss present-day injustices without making references to the historical injustices of slavery. Moreover, many Jewish families have a similar focus on the ties between the historical and contemporary contexts. This may in part be why many Jewish families raise their children with the injunction "Never forget what happened." For these families, the ties that bind past and present are inextricable.

On the other hand, there are some groups whose mantra is "You live your life where you look; if you look in the past you live in the past, and if you look forward you move forward." This represents another, very different way of emphasizing the significance of historical and contemporary contexts. Hence, if one is interacting across ethnic and racial groups, differences of this nature can contribute to communication impasses based on different perceptions of the relationship among past, present, and future.

Another significant aspect of context is its profound impact on one's perceptions of reality, which refers to that which one "knows" to be true (Bateson, 1979). An MCP, in concert with many of the nascent postmodern theories, believes that reality is subjective; it is derived from many and varied experiences. This is why we believe that context is significant and reality is relative. In fact, one of the major assumptions of an MCP is that different contexts often render different realities. What we see or fail to see is heavily influenced by our "unique" subjective experiences and circumstances. We believe that when context is variable, reality too must be considered variable. In our view, the variation in context and its impact on the construction of reality are what underpin most conflicts in human relationships. The generalized belief in the "rightness" and "purity" of one's context and reality often supports a lack of openmindedness to the possible (co)existence of other "legitimate truths." Being mindful of other possible truths—another way of seeing or doing something—facilitates negotiation, compromise, and resolution. On the other hand, incessant and "irreconcilable" conflicts, acts of domination–subjugation, and acts involving polarization–withdrawal are all the offspring of fixed and rigid notions about context and reality. Since intimate couple relationships constitute fertile ground for the expression and exposure of clashes in contexts and reality, our work with distressed couples devotes considerable attention to these issues.

All Therapy Is Cross-Cultural

The notions (perhaps biases) that we have regarding culture, complexity, context, and reality provide a useful foundation for the next assumption of an MCP—that all therapy is essentially a cross-cultural experience. Our view of "cross-cultural" therapy is based on the assumption that cultural differences exist between clients and therapists. Given our definition of culture, it is virtually impossible for any two human beings to share exactly the same cultural identity. For example, even two people with the same racial, ethnic, and religious identities may differ in class and gender. Due to the broad nature of culture, it is our assertion that all human

relationships are characterized by both sameness and difference. The differences form the basis for the "cross-cultural" nature of our interactions. Therapy, especially couple work, involves a series of complex dynamics and relationships simultaneously involving similarities and differences, most of which are rooted in culture. The process of attempting to identify and understand the similarities and differences that exist between and among others and ourselves is the essence of cross-cultural work and a defining characteristic of an MCP.

In all relationships, each of us is always working across and through boundaries that make it impossible for any of us to fully know and understand another's context and experiences. Each of us is always learning about ourselves and each other; therefore, all therapy must be approached from a stance of "knowing less" and "being curious" (Anderson & Goolishian, 1992). Such a stance can help the therapist attend to the ways in which all relationships are shaped by differences. It also can be a welcome reminder that an integral part of healthy relationship development involves learning about differences (as well as similarities) and finding ways to live with and accept them. Yet, having said all this, we recognize that some differences make more of a difference than others. One of the reasons the terms "culture" and "cross-cultural" are often used as synonyms for "ethnicity" and "race" is the underlying recognition that differences across these boundaries are especially potent. Thus, while we believe all therapy is cross-cultural, we also recognize that ethnic differences in general and racial differences in particular have unique potency and volatility in our society, and therefore warrant special consideration within an MCP.

Therapists Should Engage in a Constant Process of Self-Exploration

One of the best ways for therapists to develop an appreciation for the cross-cultural nature of human experience is to begin with an intensive examination of themselves. We recommend that therapists begin by exploring the richness of their own identities and of the multiple factors that shape who they are. This process will help them to identify the dimensions of sameness and difference that exist within any therapeutic relationship.

A core therapeutic assumption of an MCP is that therapists' knowledge and use of self is critical to the process of therapy (Falicov, 1995). Accordingly, we believe it is essential for therapists to have some baseline knowledge regarding the self with regard to the dimensions of culture. Our use of the term "knowledge" refers to more than simply having the ability to name one's religion, for example, it refers to a process that culminates in contemplating the meaning associated with one's identity. It means that therapists have devoted critical attention to understanding how their values, beliefs, and so forth have been influenced by who they are and how they think of themselves, particularly within the context of culture.

This process of introspection and critical self-reflection is vital to the development of an MCP, because it assists therapists in seeing themselves in more complex ways. In so doing, therapists are better equipped to see their clients in more complex ways. The type of shift in thinking that we anticipate is one in which a therapist begins to think of the self not just as "a therapist," but also as someone who is for example, white, male, Irish, Catholic, and so on. A shift of this kind is essentially what is needed in order to see clients in more complex ways. Once this occurs, it becomes easier to appreciate the ways in which therapy is often a rich cross-cultural experience. It becomes possible for a male, Irish, Catholic therapist to recognize that even though the members of the couple he is treating are also Irish, they are Protestant. The similarities and differences that define the therapeutic relationship are worthy of notation and possibly negotiation.

THEORETICAL ROOTS

An MCP is an integrative approach that involves extrapolations from several family therapy models. It draws heavily from a number of contemporary postmodern theories (e.g., social constructionism, narrative therapy) inasmuch as these focus on how reality is a constructed phenomenon, how people's lives are shaped by dominant and subjugated stories, and how issues of social justice shape family life (Hare-Mustin, 1978; Hoffman, 1990; White & Epston, 1990). Just as the shift from psyche to system within the mental health field generated an epistemological revolution, it can be argued that the emergence of the postmodern theories within family therapy signaled a similar revolution. When the field of family therapy was born nearly 50 years ago, it presented a radical challenge to traditional psychotherapy through its emphasis on looking at the family context rather than examining individuals in

isolation. Within the last two decades, family therapists have been similarly challenged by postmodern theories to expand our notions of context in a way that locates some part of human suffering within the broader sociocultural context (Laird, 1998).

Postmodern theories have significantly shaped an MCP, which strongly emphasizes the power that the social context plays in shaping human experience. Like postmodern theories, an MCP assumes that reality is subjective and socially constructed, and that language and the stories evolving through language are fundamental shapers of reality. And yet the constructed nature of reality does not preclude the existence of social inequity and injustice (Goldner, 1985; Hare-Mustin, 1987). Hence an MCP, like postmodern theories, devotes substantial attention to examining the ways in which social experience is organized around power differentials that afford some individuals and groups great privilege while oppressing others.

An MCP also shares certain foundational assumptions with several traditional family therapy theories. For example, experiential therapy (Satir & Baldwin, 1983) and Emotionally Focused Therapy (Greenberg & Johnson, 1988) shape an MCP through an emphasis upon the salience of affect in human experience. Where the MCP departs from these other theories is through its emphasis upon the ways in which cultural issues greatly inform the norms governing how affect should be expressed.

An MCP, like intergenerational theories (e.g., those of Bowen, Boszormenyi-Nagy, and Framo), focuses on the role historical context plays in human experience in general and family life specifically (Boszormenyi-Nagy & Spark, 1984; Bowen, 1978; Framo, 1981). However, with the exception of Boszormenyi-Nagy's contextual theory, traditional intergenerational family therapy theories tend to take a narrow view of the historical context. They focus almost exclusively on the interior of the family, with little to no attention devoted to examining how the intergenerational transmission of social and cultural experiences shapes family patterns and dynamics.

From the communications theories (e.g., that of the Palo Alto Mental Research Institute), an MCP borrows the notion that all behavior is communication, and that since one cannot not behave, one cannot not communicate (Watzlawick et al., 1967). Operating from this premise, an MCP emphasizes attending to the relevance of all behavior that is viewed as a form of communication. Where an MCP departs slightly from the Mental Research Institute's model is through its attention to the ways in which the social context shapes the meaning that is associated with certain types of behavior/communication. Hence an MCP focuses heavily on the importance of understanding that role that cultural contexts play in shaping the meaning of communication.

Finally, an MCP is influenced by those theories that punctuate the role of the therapist in shaping the process of therapy. Psychodynamic and object relations theories have contributed to this aspect of an MCP through their attention to such processes as transference and countertransference, which acknowledge the relationship that exists between client and therapist and the ways each influences the other (Dicks, 1967; Scharff & Scharff, 1987). However, whereas the psychodynamic and object relations traditions assume that objectivity is possible and advance notions of the detached, external observer/therapist, an MCP has more in common with postmodern theories, which challenge the notion of the distant observer/therapist. Like postmodern theories, an MCP operates according to the assumption that the therapist is a part of the system and brings to the therapy process all of his/her values, biases, and experiences, which interact with the client's. Hence the therapist is as much a part of the therapy as the client; for this reason, attention must be devoted to understanding the ways in which the identity and experiences of the therapist shape the therapy process.

HEALTHY/WELL-FUNCTIONING COUPLES VERSUS UNHEALTHY/ DYSFUNCTIONAL COUPLES

The Basis of Health and Dysfunction

Health is rooted in the capacity to balance seemingly oppositional, contradictory forces, feelings, and experiences. For instance, members of a healthy couple find ways to balance the forces of separation and connection; they are able to embrace their similarities and their differences; and they can acknowledge and integrate both the pleasures and the pains they experience together as a couple. An MCP focuses specifically on how partners are able to achieve health through balancing their similarities and their differences, and through balancing power.

Balancing Similarities and Differences

Dominant, mainstream American culture teaches most of us to believe that differences are threaten-

ing and lead to disconnection. To a great extent, the hatred and violence in our world are based upon the perception and the repudiation of differences. Hence, within an MCP, a couple's ability to balance the partner's similarities and differences is especially critical. When partners can accept their differences in a genuinely respectful way, this creates an essential basis for bonding and intimacy.

According to an MCP, the members of a healthy couple can openly discuss their differences along a variety of parameters. In such a couple, each partner is able to accept the differences that exist between them; in fact, both partners are comfortable with their differences. Within an MCP, differences are a point of connection and not division. Both partners are able to be who they are, to embrace all of the parts of their respective identities, and to assert these parts with each other. Even in instances when one partner dislikes some aspect of the other person, this does not result in distancing, denial, or domination. Rather, both partners openly express these feelings, and they bond around their openness, honesty, and the integrity each brings to the relationship through their willingness to be true to how they each think and feel, and who they are as human beings.

Dysfunction arises when one or both partners believe that they have to disavow valued parts of themselves to appease each other or to ensure the survival of the relationship. When a couple cannot accept differences, the result is usually some combination of disconnection, disavowal, and domination. For instance, Partner A may try to intimidate Partner B into disavowing some part of the self that is unpleasant to A. Partner B may acquiesce, resulting in disavowal of this part of self, which ultimately undermines connection and fosters disconnection. Or B may "push back," and the ensuing conflict escalates in a way that results in hostility, contempt, and dysfunction.

Much of what we are describing as the basis for health or dysfunction is rooted in the Bowenian notion of differentiation. And yet, where we part from traditional Bowenian theory via an MCP is through our systematic and persistent focus on helping couples learn to negotiate and embrace differences that are specifically linked to broader dimensions of culture. Whereas Bowen and other transgenerational theorists devoted minimal attention to considering the role that sociocultural issues play in couple and family functioning, an MCP places these issues at the center. The conversations about differences that we encourage between partners almost always have roots in broader dimensions of culture that need to be acknowledged and directly addressed. For example, consider a couple where Partner A is very comfortable with the expression of strong affect and is openly expressive, and Partner B prefers a much more low-key, restrained form of expression. Using an MCP, we would encourage the partners to "hold onto" their respective positions and ways of being. The change that we would encourage would be with respect to helping each partner learn to accept the other's preferred way of being. But, most importantly, we would attempt to understand each of their respective ways in terms of the dimensions of culture. We might consider the roles that the families of origin play in their respective approaches to emotional expression, and we would also want to consider the possible influences of ethnicity or gender as well.

Balancing Power

In a healthy couple relationship, power is evenly distributed between partners. Although one partner may yield greater power in one aspect of the relationship or at a particular moment in time, a healthy couple relationship as a whole is characterized by a balance in the distribution of power and its associated privileges. However, it is all too common within many couple relationships for the dynamics of power to become organized in such a way that one partner has greater power than the other. This rigid asymmetry is one whereby Partner A consistently has power over Partner B, and A assumes the role of "the privileged" while B assumes the role of "the subjugated." The privileged partner possesses more power and derives various overt and covert benefits from having it. The subjugated partner has less power and is more vulnerable to exploitation, violation, and degradation within the relationship. Rigid asymmetry is most likely to develop in a couple relationship when both partners are unable to simultaneously embrace and balance their privileged/oppressor and subjugated/oppressed parts. In reality, all people carry pieces of both within themselves; unfortunately, however, many people learn to connect with only the dominating or subjugated part of themselves, and generally fail to recognize the other part. Hence they magnify and distort only one of these parts, while denying the other. For a couple to achieve health with regard to the distribution of power, both partners must have access to the privileged/oppressor and subjugated/

oppressed parts of themselves. When the partners develop both–and relationship with these parts, it becomes easier to develop an equitable distribution of power in the relationship, and to acknowledge and struggle openly with any inequalities that may emerge.

Many complex factors shape how power becomes divided in a couple relationship. It may be related to each partner's unique personality as shaped by specific family-of-origin factors, as well as the intricate interaction of cultural factors. The role that various dimensions of culture (e.g., gender, race, ethnicity, class, religion) played in each partner's family of origin, and the ways each partner is informed by these dimensions as an adult, also strongly influence how the couple ultimately negotiates power. Moreover, the distribution of power in a relationship may be affected by something as simple as "the principle of less interest," whereby the partner with less interest in the relationship has more power because he/she has less emotional/psychological investment in the relationship.

In some instances it could be argued that a couple might decide to distribute power unequally in their relationship, and that if this is the partners' choice, then is it not an imposition to challenge their arrangement? This issue becomes all the more loaded when cultural variables are taken into account. For example, some cultural groups specifically mandate that husbands exert absolute power over their wives. We recognize the complexity of this issue, but we remain firm in our conviction that health requires a balancing and sharing of power. If each partner willingly chooses this arrangement and is able to freely integrate this differential possession of and access to power into the relationship without compromising its quality or integrity, we would make no effort to challenge their agreement.

In cases where power is rigidly asymmetrical, the very nature of such an arrangement defies the possibility that the subjugated partner has had any voice in choosing this. Hence the arrangement cannot represent a couple's choice, because as long as one partner remains subjugated, that person has no true choice. Rigidly asymmetrical power arrangements can only be *chosen* by a couple when they constitute mock asymmetries. In other words, both partners may begin from a place of equality, and use their comparable power to choose an arrangement that appears to skew the distribution of power rigidly. But the mere fact that each initially has enough power to make this choice indicates an underlying equality in the distribution of power.

Moreover, along with the power to choose a certain arrangement comes a corresponding power to un-choose it. Hence, in the case of mock asymmetries, the subjugated partner can step outside of the frame of his/her powerlessness and choose to "stop the game," hence overtly (re)claiming his/her power.

In any case, it is our contention that health requires equal access to power. Health demands that both partners have the freedom to choose the type of arrangement they want in the relationship, and that each has equal opportunity to reap the benefits that come along with access to power.

ASSESSMENT OF COUPLE FUNCTIONALITY–DYSFUNCTIONALITY AND GOAL SETTING

Questions for Assessing Health–Dysfunction

There are no formal assessment tools associated with an MCP. However, we consider several basic questions integral to conducting an informal assessment of couple health–dysfunction.

1. *How do the partners make meaning in their lives?* An MCP considers notions of health and dysfunction as subjective concepts. Everyone has a unique way of making meaning in the world. These ways are shaped by a vast array of factors, ranging from highly idiosyncratic issues to more broad-based, culturally specific considerations. Therefore, before we can assess a couple's overall health–dysfunction, we begin by trying to understand how both partners make meaning in their lives, and what *they* regard as the basis of health and dysfunction. Toward this end, we devote considerable attention to listening carefully to a couple's language, and we try to hear and understand the partners' recurring themes and the dominant and subjugated stories that shape their lives. At this stage in the therapy, our goal is to enhance our understanding, not to challenge. Therefore, even if we encounter a meaning-making system that raises concerns from our point of view, we refrain from challenging it at this initial stage of therapy because we first want to understand. Gradually we begin to develop an understanding of how a couple makes meaning.

2. *Where are areas of incongruence between the couple's stated beliefs and the partners' actual practices (or behavior)?* For example, a couple may be conceptually committed to principles of equality,

but the ways in which the partners actually relate to each other may not reflect this ideological commitment. From within the MCP, we attend closely to areas of congruence and incongruence between what the partners say they believe in and value, and what their actual actions (or inactions) may imply.

3. *How does the couple negotiate differences?* A critical dimension of assessing a couple's relative health–dysfunction from within an MCP involves examining how partners respond to differences. As we have discussed in the previous section, health or dysfunction is related in part to how partners negotiate differences. Therefore, to assess a couple's overall health–dysfunction, one of the first things we look for is how the partners deal with their differences. Specifically, we are looking to see whether differences are openly acknowledged and how the partners talk about and negotiate their differences. When couples respond to differences through either domination/subjugation or disconnection/withdrawal, we regard this a sign of dysfunction.

Partners negotiating their differences through domination/subjugation experience a discomfort with difference. When one partner uses force or the threat of force to crush the other's spirit, this is often the basis of dysfunction. In other words, dysfunction occurs when intimate relationship dynamics are akin to a "hostile takeover" whereby one person persistently tries to subjugate or bend the other to his/her will. When one partner denigrates the other's sense of self, this is a tactic of domination motivated by a lack of acceptance of difference. The denigration stems from a discomfort with and lack of acceptance of some part of the other partner that is viewed as different and therefore unacceptable. We are much more likely to observe violence and abuse among couples where the response to difference is largely one of domination.

Another unhealthy response to difference is one that culminates in disconnection/withdrawal. In this case, there is an absence of constructive engagement; instead, such couples rely upon tactics of withdrawal and distancing. Affairs are much more common among couples who respond to difference through disconnection. With both domination/subjugation and disconnection/withdrawal, there is an underlying hostility that is associated with the perception of differences. The hostility does not have to be overt, but if it is, this is a further indication of dysfunction.

In contrast to the tactics of domination/subjugation and disconnection/withdrawal, it is possible for couples to respond to their differences in healthy ways. We regard it as a sign of health when we observe partners who express intense conflict over differences and yet are able to find "win–win "solutions that allow each to maintain his/her position without assaulting or denigrating the other's.

We also look for any indicators that triangulation is used as a way of gaining an edge in a relationship where partners are not comfortable with their differences. For example, consider an interfaith relationship where one or both partners attempt to triangulate a child into their religious differences, including denigrating the other partner's religion and trying to persuade the child to accept one's own religion while rejecting and disavowing the other. This is not only hurtful to the child, but also indicates that the couple has failed to come to terms with the religious differences in a constructive and respectful manner.

4. *What are the culturally based pride–shame issues prevalent in the relationship, and how are these negotiated?* To assess cultural pride–shame issues, it is first necessary to gain some understanding of how each partner defines his/her culture of origin. Our use of the term "culture of origin" reflects our work with the cultural genogram process (Hardy & Laszloffy, 1995b), where we define this concept as "the group or groups from which a person has descended and from which [the person derives] a sense of peoplehood" (p. 229). During the early stages of therapy, we routinely ask both partners how they define their cultures of origin. Following this, we begin to explore the unique cultural pride–shame issues commonly associated with each of the groups that constitutes each partner's culture of origin.

5. *What are the "invisible wounds of oppression," and how do they shape the couple dynamics?* We focus upon several "invisible wounds of oppression" as part of an MCP. These are listed below, with descriptions of the types of markers that indicate their presence.

a. *Silence/learned voicelessness.* The primary indicator of this wound is a pervasive difficulty in defining one's experience for oneself. The difficulty in self-assertion is accompanied by perpetually having others defining one's experiences, as well as an inability to advocate on one's own behalf.

b. *Psychological homelessness.* This is an insatiable yearning for "home" as a place of comfort, security, rootedness, and familiarity. Other indicators are a generalized feeling that one does not belong anywhere; a feeling of being estranged from other people; a sense of being lost, isolated, and alienated; and the lack of any sense of community with others (Hardy, 1997a).

c. *Rage.* Rage is an intense, persistent, all-consuming sense of anger—a feeling of relentless fury and frustration that is associated with a perceived injustice, an overwhelming sense of pain, and loss (Hardy & Laszloffy, 1995a).

d. *Self-hate/internalized oppression.* This is a wound that is often the culmination of internalized dominant messages about one's lack of worth. Expressions of self-hate/internalized oppression can be channeled at the literal self or the symbolic self. Substance use disorders, eating disorders, severe depression, suicide attempts, and self-mutilation are examples of self-hate directed at the literal self. In contrast, hostility and violence toward others who are symbolic representations of the hated parts of self (e.g., a woman's aggressiveness toward other women) are examples of self-hate directed at the symbolic self. It also is useful to identify self-hate/internalized oppression by attending to disparaging comments and remarks that a person might make about members of a group in which he/she has membership. For example, a poor mother on welfare may describe other women in a similar position as lazy and deserving of what they get (or don't get).

e. *Orientation toward survival.* This typical and predictable response to oppression is often characterized by an unrelenting preoccupation with survival in the most literal sense. Efforts to survive become all-consuming and take precedence over all other aspects of everyday living. The Orientation toward survival is usually evident when all of a person's actions and behaviors are focused on preparing for the worst—in other words, when a person lives his/her entire life expecting suffering and is therefore singularly focused on a "mission" to meet real and imagined disasters with the ferocity of a warrior. While the person is in this mode, it is impossible for him/her to rest, relax, or to expose vulnerabilities that are essential for developing and nurturing intimacy.

6. *What are the cultural legacies and loyalties that each partner brings to the relationship, and how do these inform their couple dynamics?* Consistent with the tenets of the transgenerational theories, we believe in the intergenerational transmission of legacies and loyalties. However, while most transgenerational theories focus on family-of-origin ties, within an MCP we also consider the influence of culture of origin. Specifically, we are interested in how cultural legacies and loyalties have uniquely shaped each partner's family across generations.

Hence we attempt to identify what specific cultural legacies have been passed down through the generations, and how these have created and nurtured loyalties that influence the lives of each partner in a couple relationship.

Maya and José Lopez, a Mexican American couple, were the children of immigrant parents. Their parents had come to the United States in search of better opportunities for their families. Each partner had vivid memories of how hard his/her parents worked, of the devaluation they endured within a society that negatively defined Mexican American people, and deprived them of fair consideration, equal opportunity, and basic respect. Both partners remembered the many days and nights their parents labored ceaselessly for low wages and no benefits within a devaluing social context. And yet, despite the hardships they endured, their parents never complained. They often shared their belief that there was no shame in working hard, and that they endured the trials of life in the United States because they were devoted to paving the path for their children to have better lives. As adults, both Maya and José were deeply influenced by the cultural legacies and loyalties they had inherited from their parents. They believed strongly that they needed to work hard in their own lives, because this was what they had learned from their parents. They also felt the need to be successful as a way of legitimizing the sacrifices their parents had made for them. Though all four of their parents had died, Maya and José were still organized by an intense sense of loyalty to their parents and the legacy that they had inherited.

During one session, José made a revealing statement that nicely captured the essence of the cultural legacies and loyalties he was driven by, as both a child and an adult: "I remember these Anglo kids at school saying ugly things about Mexicans, like we are all lazy and dirty and just come to this country to take advantage of the system here. That's crazy. We work harder here than most rich white people do, because we have to survive. There are no easy rides for most Mexican people living in the U.S., or even in Mexico, for that matter. But we don't let it beat us down, because it's in our blood to face adversity with courage. The native blood that flows through our veins is the blood of people who always worked hard to survive and never relied on others to lighten our loads." His comment revealed his sense of cultural and familial relatedness to those who came before him, as well as his powerful allegiance to his ancestors and the legacy they had passed on to him.

Level of Assessment

Assessment using an MCP focuses on both intrapsychic and interactional processes. However, the greatest emphasis is placed upon interactional processes, at both the micro/interpersonal level and the macro/sociocultural level. An MCP is heavily systemic and places great significance on relational dynamics. Even when the therapist attends to intrapsychic factors, these are always connected to interactional dynamics. For example, a client may present with an intrapsychic profile revealing a person who is highly suspicious, guarded, and untrusting. Such a person may appear defensive, distant, and even hostile in nature. But from within an MCP, the therapist quickly moves to understand the experiences this person has had in life that shaped the sense of guardedness and suspicion. The therapist looks closely at key attachment relationships (e.g., with parents) where violations and betrayals may have occurred. But the therapist considers broader sociocultural factors as well. For example, if the client is a member of a socially devalued group, the therapist explores how experiences with discrimination and oppression may have fostered a sense of mistrust and guardedness within the client.

Relationship between Assessment and Treatment

Although assessment plays an especially important role in the early stages of therapy, it is important to emphasize that there is a recursive relationship between assessment and treatment. The more information the therapist gathers, the more this guides treatment; and the deeper the therapist moves into the treatment process, the more information he/she gathers, which further shapes how treatment is approached.

Goal Setting

An MCP is shaped by several overarching therapeutic goals. These goals apply to all types of couples and are not specific to certain types of couple configurations or presenting problems. The therapeutic goals associated with an MCP are as follows:

1. To develop an understanding of the specific ways in which clients view the world (and their corresponding values and beliefs).
2. To challenge segregated thinking by promoting a fuller understanding of the ways in which all aspects of existence are interconnected. This

includes encouraging awareness of the ways in which experiences at the individual, family, and cultural levels are all related; in which each partner is simultaneously same and different; in which past, present, and future are related; in which both partners have cultural pride–shame issues that shape their lives and their relationship; and in which both partners have parts of the oppressor and the oppressed within themselves, and these parts shape their relationship with each other.

3. To respectfully challenge beliefs and dynamics that support domination and oppression.

4. To identify and heal the invisible wounds of oppression. This involves challenging structures of domination that inevitably lead to the infliction of invisible wounds.

5. To rehabilitate each partner's image of the other. This consists of helping each partner see the humanness, vulnerability, and goodness in the other person.

6. To work actively to achieve justice. This involves "righting past wrongs" and ensuring that appropriate steps have been taken to remedy injustices that have occurred in relationships.

7. To promote intimacy. This involves the ability to balance separation and connection, and to achieve closeness through embracing differences, emotional intensity, and constructive conflict.

Ways in Which Therapists Negotiate Goals with Clients

When guided by an MCP, rarely if ever does a therapist list goals for clients and provide an overt, mechanistic description of these goals. Rather, therapists are guided by the goals in a broad way and follow whatever unique dynamics and content issues the clients present with as a way of ultimately adhering to the goals. An MCP is an open, flexible guide that allows therapists to maneuver in diverse and loosely structured ways. In other words, there are no hard and fast rules about how therapists should structure the therapy to achieve the goals. Once again, an MCP is a world view, a way of thinking. Therefore, any therapist who embraces an MCP will find ways to work in accordance with its overarching goals, and will not have to follow a narrowly defined map for doing so. Consistent with the focus on multiple realities, we believe it is possible for therapists to develop an infinite number of ways to work therapeutically while ultimately advancing the goals of an MCP.

With respect to what therapists convey to clients, we do expect that therapists working from an MCP will inevitably communicate possible goals to clients. We support this because we believe in the transparency of therapists. It is consistent with an MCP for therapists to disclose their personal beliefs, assumptions, and understandings about the goals for treatment.

THE STRUCTURE OF THE THERAPY PROCESS

Length and Frequency of Sessions

The therapy process may vary in length and frequency. An MCP does not specify a certain number, length, or spacing of sessions. This perspective does challenge traditional notions of the 50-minute hour that occurs on a weekly basis (Hardy, 2001); we see these as arbitrary social constructions and do not believe that there is any connection relevance between these constructions and high-quality care. Hence we give ourselves maximum permission to follow the energy of a therapy session, and take as much or as little time as seems needed to see the session through. Moreover, we consider the timing of sessions on a case-by-case basis, with some clients clearly requiring more frequent sessions than others. Such determinations are based on a therapist's subjective perceptions and professional experiences, as well as on clients' needs.

Decisions about Whom to Include

In a couple case we always begin with the couple, and from there, an MCP encourages expanding the therapy to include all others who are connected to the presenting problem. There are no rules that dictate who should be included. However we do frequently assume that the couple is connected to a vast relational network, and that the more people we include in the therapy, the greater our capacity to deal with relational complexity (which advances a key component of an MCP).

The Role of Psychotropic Medications

An MCP does not deny that in some cases, the problems that plague couples may be related to an underlying physiological disorder requiring medical intervention. In such cases, psychotropic medications may indeed be a necessary component of medical treatment. However, this perspective places far greater emphasis upon relational dynamics as the basis for the problems that most couples present with; hence treatment within an MCP relies very little on psychotropic medications as a basic component of treatment. On purely ideological grounds, we are wary about psychotropic medications, because we believe they are part of a broader cultural mind set that in some instances is antithetical to healing. The widespread reliance on drug therapies in the field of mental health is grounded in the politics of pathology and profit, whereby therapists, physicians, and pharmacological companies are economically rewarded each time an individual is labeled with a mental illness that requires drug intervention.

On philosophical grounds, we object to the ease with which many therapists resort to drugs as a form of therapy. Such actions belie the spirit of an MCP, which involves taking time to understand the anatomy of suffering that underpins clients' presenting problems, and taking more time to gradually work through and heal the complex emotions and relational patterns that paralyze growth and undermine functional ways of being. And yet, having said all of this, let us reiterate that we are not emphatically denouncing the need for or the benefits of psychotropic medications. There are instances where we believe such a course of action is useful and even necessary, particularly in conjunction with more relationally based therapies.

How we determine those few instances where we really believe psychotropic medications may be necessary is tricky. In general, we assume that drug therapies are rarely necessary. We begin to entertain the possibility of drug therapies after we have spent time with a client and begin to sense that we cannot make an inroad and move forward because certain disturbed cognitive, emotional, and behavior patterns seem unaltered by the course of therapy. Medication also may be considered when clients are convinced that they are both indicated and integral to their healing.

One, Two, or a Team of Therapists?

There is nothing in an MCP that dictates the number of therapists who may be involved with a given case. However, consistent with the emphasis upon multiple realities and the socially constructed nature of "truth," we believe that therapy generally benefits from the presence of a cotherapy team and/or the inclusion of a reflecting team.

THE ROLE OF THE THERAPIST

The Role of the Therapist–Couple Alliance

A therapist collaborates with clients to bring about desired change. Therapist and clients are cocreators in the therapy process. They work as a team. Each person brings expertise to the process, and all contribute to the progress of therapy. The therapist has a general expertise about relationship dynamics and the process of therapy, while clients have specific expertise about their lives and their contexts. Both are necessary for positive change to occur; therefore, both therapists and clients must work together as a team.

However, an MCP distinguishes between collaboration and equality. Although therapists using an MCP tend to collaborate with clients, they also recognize the ways in which they possess socially reinforced and institutionally buttressed power in the therapy relationship that clients do not have. Because of the politics of power and the broader context within which therapy occurs, the expertise that therapists bring to the therapy process is generally regarded as more valid and more valuable than the specific expertise that clients bring. The social forces that privilege the therapist's knowledge and expertise greatly fortify this position of power. This being the case, we believe that the therapist using an MCP has a responsibility to (1) be aware of his/her power; (2) use his/her power to empower clients (i.e., to act as a "broker of permission," which is tantamount to using power to help clients gain their voices—see below); and (3) recognize and challenge any of his/her behaviors that may result in a misuse/abuse of power.

Essential Roles of the Therapist

According to an MCP, the therapist assumes several roles or functions within the process of therapy. Some of these are as follows:

1. *Broker of permission.* Therapists must often grant clients permission to "speak the unspeakable." In their role as brokers of permission, therapists help clients find the safety and comfort necessary to risk saying things that they have been unable to say. In particular, therapists act as bro-

kers of permission with respect to politically sensitive, volatile topics, such as those involving issues of race and sexual orientation. Most clients (and therapists) find it especially difficult to discuss issues such as these openly and directly; therefore, it is incumbent upon a therapist to set the stage in a way that invites these types of difficult dialogues. This role is largely defined by what the therapist does, rather than what is said.

2. *Healer.* Therapists must also assume the role of healers. They find ways to soothe the pain that haunts their clients. This involves first finding ways to support clients in "giving voice" to their stories of pain, and then providing the salve of acknowledgment and validation that cuts the sting of the clients' wounds. Another aspect of the role of healer involves creating pathways for repairing strained relationships.

3. *Agent for social change.* This role refers to the fact that a therapist operating from within an MCP is attuned to the politics of domination of oppression and understands how structured social inequalities shape all of our lives, including the process of therapy. Moreover, such a therapist is committed to challenging any and all instances of injustice and inequality. Because of the belief that all life is interconnected, therapists using an MCP realize that what happens outside therapy greatly informs what happens within therapy, and vice versa. Therapists also recognize that what occurs in the psychosocial interior of couples and families is shaped by and shapes broader sociocultural dynamics as well. Therefore, therapists operating from an MCP use their power to challenge acts of domination and oppression in all aspects of life, both within and outside therapy. In this regard, such therapists are agents for social change; they recognize that relational justice (and injustice) does not exist within a vacuum.

Therapist Activity

Therapists have the freedom to vary in how much they actively direct and control sessions versus how much they step back and encourage clients to take a more active role in their change processes. More important than how active or restrained a therapist is in the sessions are some of the issues described above (i.e., to how much the therapist understands the nature of his/her power and how he/she uses this power to heal and transform). We believe that to some extent, therapist activity is determined by the stage of therapy. In general, it is more common for a therapist to direct therapy in its initial stage by inviting clients to share of themselves, so that the therapist can discern how they see the world and observe how they relate. By the later parts of the initial stage of therapy and throughout the middle stage, we envision the therapist as assuming a more actively directive role. It is during this phase that the therapist is working to reshape problematic patterns of thinking and behavior by teaching and encouraging the acquisition of new skills. The therapist also works assiduously to help clients nondestructively express and work through intense emotions. In the later stages of therapy, therapists assume a far less active role in directing the sessions, because by now clients should have acquired the types of skills and ways of being that enable them to guide and direct themselves in the most beneficial ways.

Facilitating Couple Conversations

A therapist working within an MCP encourages clients to talk directly to each other. Convincing clients to engage actively in an ongoing intense, intimate, and nondestructive conversation can be one of the most daunting challenges associated with intensive couple therapy. Relationship distress is often exacerbated and magnified when partners avoid direct conversation, or engage in direct conversations that involve tactics of domination and aggression. Therapy from an MCP has as a key goal helping clients to learn how to talk with each other directly and in constructive ways. The less conversation is channeled through the therapist, the more likely it is that clients will learn these skills.

Key Clinical Skills
and Therapist Attributes

These attributes and clinical skills are essential for therapists who use an MCP:

1. *Self-awareness.* This ties into a basic assumption of an MCP, which is that therapists need to know themselves first and foremost. The more therapists understand about themselves, the better able they will be to understand others, because ultimately perceptions of "other" reflect aspects of self. Although therapists can never know all there is to know about themselves, it is critical for them

to remain open, and willing to interrogate themselves, especially with regard to their beliefs, biases, feelings, perceptions, and reactions.

2. *Capacity to tolerate intensity.* An MCP posits that constructive engagement in relationships is difficult to achieve without emotional intensity. It is our belief that the process of change often precipitates tension, conflict, and generalized discomfort. We accept this as a necessary part of the process of healing and transformation. For this reason, we believe that having the ability to encourage and tolerate discomfort is a critical attribute for a therapist. The therapist's ability and willingness to tolerate intensity may be manifested by any of the following: being open to moving toward conflict; encouraging difficult dialogues; inviting clients to deal directly with their differences; and/or enduring the strong affect that often arises when people are hurting or disagree.

3. *Ability to both validate and challenge.* Validation is an integral component of therapy based on an MCP. Thus it is imperative for therapists to have the ability to identify the redeemable aspects of all human behavior, no matter how seemingly egregious it might otherwise appear. At the same time, therapists also need to have the ability to see where problems reside, and they must have the fortitude to name and confront the weaknesses that also challenge people's lives. The capacity to both validate and challenge (in affirming ways) is an essential characteristic of therapists who effectively use an MCP.

4. *Capacity to hold two seemingly contradictory ideas simultaneously.* Therapists who can both validate and challenge are in fact demonstrating the ability to balance opposites. The aptitude to simultaneously see the strengths and weakness of a person or situation, to recognize the pleasure and pain in a condition, to see both similarities and differences, and to understand both the privileged and subjugated parts of a person is essential for MCP therapists. Challenging segregated thinking is a core aspect of using this approach effectively, and therapists must be able to do this through their capacity to simultaneously hold seemingly contradictory concepts.

5. *Understanding of the dynamics of power and oppression and commitment to thinking in terms of context and relationships.* This involves a specific knowledge of how power organizes human relationships and how it shapes interactions at both the micro and macro levels. Therapists using an MCP must be well versed in the politics of domination and oppression. They must understand how racism, sexism, classism, homophobia/heterosexism, and all other -isms operate, shape intimate relationships, and are inextricably linked.

STRATEGIES AND TECHNIQUES OF COUPLE THERAPY

The strategies and techniques of couple therapy within an MCP correspond to the various goals associated with this approach. We reiterate each goal described earlier and follow with a description of the strategies and techniques associated with each.

The first goal we have listed above is to develop an understanding of the specific ways in which clients view the world (and their corresponding values and beliefs). The strategies and techniques we use to accomplish this goal are these:

1. *Paying close attention to language.* Language constructs reality. Therefore, to grasp another's view of reality, it is essential to pay close attention to how that person uses language. For example, in a first session with a heterosexual couple, the 52-year-old male partner's frequent references to his 27-year-old female partner as a "girl" revealed a key aspect of his perception of her in relation to himself.

2. *Exploring the multiple dimensions of clients' selves.* In our efforts to understand how clients view the world, we strive to understand their views from a variety of complex perspectives. We focus upon gathering information about clients that is both broad and specific. For example, in addition to asking standard family-of-origin questions about clients' parents and siblings, and the quality of these relationships while the clients were growing up and at present, we also ask about how clients define themselves ethnically, racially, religiously, and sexually. We ask questions designed to assess the class status the clients grew up in, as well as the class status they presently occupy. All of these various dimensions of culture profoundly shape how clients view the world. For example, in our work with a couple who came to therapy for sexual problems (she wanted more and he wanted less sex), our initial conversation eventually turned to a discussion of their early social class experiences. This discussion revealed how their early class experiences had shaped their general views about life and their goals as a couple. Despite the fact that both grew up extremely poor, they had divergent perceptions of reality as adults. The husband wanted to devote himself to social activism, and

cared little about making lots of money and living "the good life." The wife wanted them to nurture high-powered careers, earn lots of money, and live among the privileged classes. As an adult, his class background had shaped him to believe that life is difficult and that the hedonistic trappings of pleasure should be resisted in favor of embracing hardship and struggle. The wife's early class experiences had shaped her to believe that it was terrible living without pleasure and that she should devote herself to the pursuit of accumulating an abundance of wealth and pleasure. Because we were open to exploring the broader aspects of their identities, we were able to acquire these critical pieces of information about how each viewed the world, and why.

Our second goal is to challenge segregated thinking by promoting a fuller understanding of the ways in which all aspects of existence are interconnected. This includes helping partners embrace the parts of their experiences that are most challenging, threatening, and uncomfortable for themselves and each other to accept. To accomplish this goal, we do the following:

1. *Changing what we look for.* Most therapists included, are socialized to think in either–or terms. Therefore, we become singularly focused on either seeing only the positives or only the negatives. It is much more difficult to recognize both the positive and negative aspects of our experience. To begin to challenge either–or thinking, we begin with a shift in the lens we use to view the world.

2. *Expanding the definition of the problem.* When clients present their views of reality to us, it is never our goal to have them change their views, although we often strive to expand their definitions of their problems. It is typical for clients to define their problems in narrow, linear ways, which tend to simplify the complexity of experience. Because we believe in complexity and believe it is possible for seemingly contradictory things to coexist simultaneously, we seek to broaden and expand how problems are defined. In so doing, we pose a challenge to segregated thinking. For example, a classic complaint we observe is one partner's blaming the other for being withdrawn and neglectful, while the other partner blames the initial blamer for being intrusive and demanding. Their definitions are linear and based on either–or thinking. Neither is willing to accept any role in their mutual difficulties. In our efforts to challenge segregated thinking, we begin by accepting each of their definitions of the problem, which in and of itself is already

an expansion of how the problem is being defined. Essentially we say, "You are both right in your views." In so doing, we don't take anything away from either, but already we are proposing something broader, more expansive. We are suggesting that both views can be correct, which challenges segregated thinking.

3. *Using the VCR approach.* An essential tool we utilize heavily within an MCP is the VCR approach. "VCR" stands for the following: "V" is for validation, "C" is for challenging/confronting, and "R" is for request.

Beginning with the "V," we always validate first. Regardless of the issue presented, whatever a client's character may be, we always find something in every person and every situation to validate. At this point, it is helpful to draw a distinction between "validation" and "agreement." It is possible to validate an issue without agreeing with it. "Validation" is synonymous with "understanding," while "agreement" is synonymous with "condoning." The two are very different. However, a word of caution is necessary at this point: It is difficult to validate something with which we disagree. When confronted with such a dilemma, it becomes enticing to immediately challenge or confront. When this occurs, it almost always quickly undermines our ultimate goal—introducing a different viewpoint that will be considered seriously. It is helpful to bear in mind that validation is only the first step, and that when it is used effectively and generously, it facilitates efforts to challenge and confront. This raises another question: How much is enough validation? There is no simple formula for answering this question. Ultimately, the person being validated determines when enough is enough; hence this will vary considerably with each person and each situation. Sometimes a few phrases of validation are all that is required, while in other instances one may have to validate for weeks before presenting a corresponding challenge. The mechanism for determining when enough is enough is intuitive and draws heavily upon a therapist's attention to the subtleties of human communication.

After we have sufficiently validated a person or a position, we move on to the "C," which is challenging or confronting. Yet even here, we challenge and confront in ways that are carefully designed to preserve a person's dignity. We never want to resort to an attack, assault, or disparagement of a person or position. Rather, we routinely take whatever the validating part of our message was, and use it as a springboard for presenting our challenge. Thus the "challenging/confronting" message is always the other side of the validating message. Through this process, a client is actually being encouraged to consider how one behavior pattern, for example, can have two different sides.

We end with the "R," which entails making a request that presents the person with a concrete way of responding to our challenge. We find that it is unhelpful to challenge without offering some corresponding suggestion for what a client might do differently.

The VCR approach challenges segregated thinking, because it emphasizes the strengths and weaknesses of any given position. It allows us to recognize the positive dimensions of a particular situation, while simultaneously presenting an associated challenge to the downside of that same situation.

4. *Identifying and exploring seemingly contradictory dimensions of experience.* Often we challenge segregated thinking directly—by simply inviting clients to identify and explore, and ultimately embrace, seemingly opposite aspects of reality. There are various ways in which we can accomplish this.

a. *Examining cultural pride–shame issues.* We believe that all of us carry both pride and shame issues related to our cultural identities, and that these heavily influence our lives and our relationships, whether we realize it or not. Since we approach issues of identity in a complex, multilayered way, we frequently enlist clients in explorations of different dimensions of their cultural identities; these explorations invariably include a consideration of the parts of these identities that are a source of pride and shame. Segregated thinking often seduces people into overfocusing on only the pride or shame aspects of their identities, and more often than not the pride aspects prevail. As a critical aspect of challenging segregated thinking, we strongly encourage clients to name and embrace both pride and shame issues. To aid in our excavation of cultural pride–shame issues, we often use the cultural genogram, which is an expanded version of the standard genogram that many therapists use in their work with clients. We refer the reader to our discussion of the cultural genogram (Hardy & Laszloffy, 1995b) for a more detailed discussion of this tool.

b. *Examining similarities and differences.* As we emphasize throughout this chapter, all partners have both similarities and differences. Often, as an extension of segregated thinking, partners become overly focused on either their similarities or their differences. In our efforts to promote both/and thinking, we purposefully guide clients in a naming of their similarities and differences and we hold both of these "out there" as a way of challenging segregated thinking. Sometimes we even write two columns on the blackboard and have clients list similarities and differences in each as a way of graphically highlighting both/and.

c. *Examining the oppressor and oppressed within.* Another common manifestation of segregated thinking involves the dichotomization of "oppressor" and "oppressed," or "victim" and "perpetrator." Therapists are as guilty of this schism as are clients. For example, we frequently meet therapists who tell us they will work only with abused partners, for instance, and refuse to work with abusing partners. This, in a sense, epitomizes either–or thinking, since it is rare that someone is ever exclusively one or the other. Even when one of these aspects of self is more dominant than the other, all people possess aspects of both to some degree. In therapy, we work with clients to draw out and highlight how each partner possesses both aspects of self; this poses a powerful challenge to segregated thinking.

Our third goal is to respectfully challenge beliefs and dynamics that support domination and oppression. We do this as follows:

1. *Deconstructing the needs and the beliefs that underpin the tactics of domination.* Those who resort to tactics of domination often do so in response to underlying unhealed trauma wounds and/or vulnerabilities. For example, in the case of a person who secretly feels powerless and insecure, the reliance on tactics of domination may serve as a reaction formation. In other words, this person is so overwhelmed by feeling vulnerable that he/she compensates by projecting an air of exaggerated power that results in treating others in a degrading and disempowering way. A person also may resort to tactics of domination as an expression of an underlying belief system about how the world works. For example, many men are domineering because they have internalized social messages that teach them to believe that a successful man is all-powerful and never vulnerable. To begin challenging domination and oppression within couple relationships, we attempt to engage clients in conversations that are designed to expose the needs and beliefs underlying oppressive behavior.

2. *Examining costs and benefits.* This consists of identifying what both partners and the couple as a whole gain and lose when couple dynamics are organized around domination and oppression. The value of this exercise is that is makes explicit issues of power and inequality within a relation-

ship. It also challenges segregated thinking by acknowledging that domination and oppression within relationships have both positives and negatives. The pervasiveness of either–or thinking often makes recognition of the gains *and* losses associated with the unequal exercise of power in a relationship difficult to appreciate.

3. *Using the VCR approach.* As therapists begin to understand what resides beneath oppressive dynamics in couple relationships, the VCR approach provides a useful tool for communicating with clients in ways that will ultimately challenge their reliance on the old tactics. Using this approach, therapists can validate the needs that often underpin a client's dominating ways, while simultaneously challenging their actual behaviors and the consequences of these behaviors. The VCR also allows therapists to provide clients with a clear, concrete directive or suggestion for how they can both address the needs underpinning domination and oppression, while challenging specific oppressive and dominating beliefs and behaviors.

Our fourth goal is to identify and heal the invisible wounds of oppression. This involves challenging structures of domination that inevitably lead to the infliction of invisible wounds. We go about this in several ways:

1. *Healing silence/learned voicelessness.* The best "medicine" for the pain associated with silence and learned voicelessness involves gaining access to one's voice. Therapists can assist clients toward that end by conducting "voice lessons" with clients. This involves creating enough safety so that the act of speaking becomes less threatening. At this point, therapists should focus solely on helping clients to "speak" and not to worry about the specifics of what or how something is said. As clients develop enough courage to speak, therapists should directly recognize and celebrate this speaking or coming to voice. Initially, clients rarely say it "right," but at this point the emphasis is upon just trying to get them to "say it," whatever "it" may be. Therapists can also encourage a client's voice by bringing in an "audience" to bear witness. The presence of an audience honors and legitimizes a person's speaking, which is vital. Those who have been silenced suffer from a complete lack of validation for the use of their voices. They believe that their voices lack worth. Hence, after the initial voice lesson, inviting in an affirming audience "to hear" and "to honor" the person is an excellent way of healing the wound of silence/learned voicelessness. It is

also critical during this phase of treatment for the observing partner to be assisted in sharpening his/her listening skills, and to receive coaching regarding how to deliver effective feedback. The major challenge regarding this task involves helping the couple to genuinely appreciate the interlocking nature of the couple dynamics around power, silence, and personal authority.

2. *Healing psychological homelessness.* Healing psychological homelessness begins with an examination of the specific forces that have disrupted clients' sense of "home." It is imperative for therapists to spend time with clients exploring the various forces and factors that have contributed to their sense of dislocation. On one hand, therapists encourage clients to "be" with the emotions that psychological homelessness creates—pain, alienation, loneliness, and confusion. On the other hand, therapists actively challenge psychological homelessness by helping clients discover how they are connected to others and the world around them. This involves focusing clients on the multiple dimensions of their identities by probing their connection–disconnection to their families of origin, friends, and intimate partners, as informed by race, ethnicity, religion, sexual identity, class, and gender.

3. *Rechanneling rage.* Because we believe that rage is a natural response to pain and injustice, it is never our intention to work toward the elimination of rage. Rather, we strive to rechannel it. We begin by encouraging clients to identify their rage and explore the underlying roots of it. We also support clients in expressing their rage directly, although always nonviolently. Other related emotions (e.g., grief, pain, fear, and shame) may also be explored; we draw attention to how these are often tied to rage. Finally, we invite clients to consider ways that they can harness their rage and make it work for, rather than against, them.

4. *Healing self-hate.* Self-hate, regardless of how it is manifested, is usually the result of internalized negative messages. As a process, it is usually so subtle and insidious that those who ingest and harbor it do so without the slightest awareness. A major step toward healing self-hatred involves uncovering the anatomy of it. In the most tedious and painstaking way, it involves examining and reexamining the vast array of behaviors, messages, and life experiences that have helped shape the current view of self. Once adequately identified and deconstructed, the extant internalized messages have to be supplanted with those that support the emerging sense of self. The therapist must be vigilant in ensuring that each

partner continues to explore the ways in which this seemingly individually focused problem is rooted and supported within the context of the couple relationship.

Our fifth goal is to rehabilitate each partner's image of the other. This consists of helping each partner see the humanness, vulnerability, and goodness in the other person. We do this in these ways:

1. *Spending some time early on with each partner individually.* When both partners are in the therapy room initially, the dominant stories of each make it hard for the subjugated stories to surface. The partners routinely interrupt each other and make it hard for the stories within the stories to emerge. We work around this by breaking down the client system into two to three individual sessions as a way of learning more about each partner individually. We use the individual sessions to talk in a more concentrated way about each partner's individual psychology and human complexity. Following this, we bring the partners back together, beginning with a disclosure about how each partner has done something with or for the other that will support the rehabilitation of their images in each other's eyes. Through this, we act as ambassadors for the relationship, taking back bits and pieces to each partner that influence new information designed to rehabilitate the image of the other.

2. *Identifying the vulnerabilities that reside beneath the surface.* The partners' images of each other are in need of rehabilitation when they see each other in simplistic, unidimensional, totalizing ways. When one person sees the other as all-powerful or all-weak, or when the partners fail to see each other's humanity, image rehabilitation is needed. One way of achieving this is by directly targeting the essence of each partner's humanity—his/her vulnerabilities. Recognizing these vulnerabilities makes it possible, for instance, to see that a domineering, abusive partner has a fearful, wounded part of self that he/she is defending against through aggression. The recognition of such vulnerabilities promotes the partner's humanization. This helps the partners to see each other as individuals with obvious irrefutable flaws, but also as people with diverse experiences, emotions, and thoughts, who have suffered and who are doing the best they can to survive under a given set of circumstances. Ultimately, the recognition of vulnerabilities should dramatically punctuate the pain and suffering that

resides within each partner, as a way of challenging each partner to see the other more holistically and perhaps humanistically.

Our sixth goal is to work actively to achieve justice. This involves "righting past wrongs" and ensuring that appropriate steps have been taken to remedy injustices that have occurred in relationships. The following techniques and strategies are used to achieve this goal:

1. *The AVAF model.* To achieve relational justice, we have developed a simple four-step model ("AVAF") that consists of the following:

- A: *Acknowledgment,* which involves an openness to the possibility that an injustice occurred.
- V: *Validation,* which involves recognizing and legitimizing both that the injustice occurred and the impact that it has had. It consists of recognizing directly the pain that the injustice has caused, and extending some gesture or marker that legitimizes the injured party's related thoughts or feelings.
- A: *Apology,* which involves owning one's responsibility in the occurrence of the injustice.
- F: *Forgiveness,* which involves a request for clemency or reprieve. The cycle is complete if and when the injured party accepts the apology and grants forgiveness. Until this occurs, the offending party continues to validate and assume responsibility.

Although the AVAF model is simple in its design, its actual execution is far more complicated. It takes a lot of time for a couple to advance through the four steps fully and completely. Often the partners move forward and then regress. Here the therapist plays a critical role in helping to keep the partners on track, and constantly guiding and redirecting them through the lengthy and painful process of healing relational injustices.

2. *Tasks of the privileged.* In addition to using the AVAF model to help guide couples in their work to heal relational injustices, it is critical for therapists to help clients engage in a healing process that recognizes and responds to the realities of power—or, more specifically, the unequal distribution of power. In situations where the infliction of a relational injustice corresponds with a rigidly asymmetrical distribution of power, the process of remedying and healing must be organized in a way that recognizes specific but different tasks that must

be fulfilled by the offending (privileged) partner and the injured (subjugated) partner. We refer to these as the "tasks of the privileged" and the "tasks of the subjugated." The specific actions associated with the tasks of the privileged are as follows:

a. *Distinguishing between intent and consequence.* The privileged partner must recognize the distinction between intentions and consequences. It is entirely possible for pure intentions to render impure consequences. In most situations where an infraction in a relationship has occurred, the offender attempts to clarify his/her intentions, as in "I didn't mean to do that" or "I only did that because . . ." It may well be that the offender's explanation is true and valid, but from the point of view of the subjugated, what matter most are the consequences. For example, consider a relationship where a husband has an affair and the wife is emotionally devastated upon discovering it. If the husband responds to her devastation by explaining why he did it, and stating that it was never his intention to hurt her, he ignores the fact that what is most salient for his wife is the consequence of his behavior. In this case, the consequence is the profound sense of hurt and violation that she feels. This is not to suggest that his intentions are irrelevant. It does make a difference if he never intended to hurt her, but ultimately, she is hurt. The consequence of his actions, which have left the wife feeling deeply betrayed and wounded (at least initially), are most critical. Consequently, the husband, as the privileged person in this scenario, must first respond to his wife by dealing with the consequences of his actions and not his intentions.

b. *Having "heart."* It is critical for the privileged to "have heart," which, paradoxically, involves developing a "thick skin." Whenever a violation has occurred in a relationship, the victim of the violation will inevitably experience anger, rage, and grief. It is incumbent upon the offending partner to have enough inner strength and fortitude to endure the anger and hurt of the subjugated. If one makes an initial gesture toward the subjugated and this gesture is rebuffed, the privileged person must have enough heart (i.e., courage and ego strength) to endure the rebuffing and to "hang in there."

c. *Being cautious of "language designed to negate."* The privileged partner must be wary of resorting to sophisticated language that is designed to negate. There are many ways that the privileged participate in conversations that are subtly designed to negate the experiences of the subjugated. For example, among an interfaith couple where one

partner was Jewish and the other Protestant, the Jewish partner explained, "As a Jew, I feel targeted in society." The other partner responded by saying, "Well, lots of people feel targeted." Here the partner's response subtly negated what was being initially communicated. It is this type of soft negation that severely undermines the healing of strained relationships. Moreover, negation precludes acknowledgment and validation, because negation is invalidation.

d. *Resisting mistaken notions of equality.* The privileged partner must resist mistaken notions about equality that involve obscuring the role power plays in relationships. It is all too common for those with power to be oblivious to it and the benefits associated with it. Moreover, because their power tends to be invisible to them, the privileged also have a tendency to engage in the equalization of suffering. They tend to assume equality even in the midst of massive inequality.

John and Lori came to therapy because of marital difficulties. John was a high-powered attorney who worked for a major law firm, and Lori was a stay-at-home mom who cared for their three children. Lori expressed many questions about her physical attractiveness and the pain she felt about the loss of her youth. At one point she became frustrated and began to scream and cry about how unattractive and undesirable she felt. John responded by lashing back, saying, "I bought you an entire home gym. Why don't you use it if you are so worried about your weight? You know it's not easy for anyone to get older, Lori. Do you think I'm happy about being 45 years old? But I deal with it. Why can't you?" Lori was debilitated by John's aggressive retort. What John failed to realize was the inequality between them in terms of gender and power. As a man with a prestigious career and vast economic resources, he wielded far greater power in the relationship than Lori, a middle-aged woman with a high school diploma. By virtue of gender and class dynamics, the two were unequally positioned in society and in the relationship. It was true that John may also have struggled with his aging process, but as a man—especially one with a successful career—his physical attractiveness did not control his definition of self-worth in the way it did for Lori. In society and in their relationship, Lori had less power than John; as a result, her suffering was magnified by this skew, which John was remiss in appreciating.

3. *Tasks of the subjugated.* The privileged partner is not the only one with tasks to fulfill. The tasks of the subjugated are as follows:

a. *Resisting internalized oppression.* Anyone who has been subjugated struggles with messages and stories about him-/herself that are devaluing. It is all too common for subjugated parties to internalize some pieces of the messages and stories that defile them. As long as the subjugated internalize disparaging messages about themselves, healing cannot occur. Until the subjugated challenge their own acceptance of notions of inferiority, they will never be able to receive apologies from the privileged. They will never be able to receive love and healing.

b. *Overcoming "addictions."* There are two major "addictions" the subjugated must overcome. The first of these is educating the privileged about their suffering. Those in subjugated positions often find the task of conversing with the privileged to be an emotional challenge of monumental proportions. Although constructive dialogue is essential to the process of healing, it is often difficult to execute effectively. If such a dialogue is to progress, it is crucial for the privileged to adhere to the aforementioned tasks, and for the subjugated to enter the conversation free of any intention or effort to "educate" or convince the privileged. Subjugated partners are best served in these situations when the impetus for their participation in the dialogue is connected to their healing process. In other words, the dialogue becomes an opportunity to break their oppression-related silence—to become the authors of their own stories. In this regard, the interaction has little to do with correcting, educating, or convincing the other; instead, it is about the actualization of self.

The second, and all-too-common, "addiction" among the subjugated involves taking care of the privileged. This consists of denying one's own suffering and humanity to protect the privileged from discomfort. It is virtually impossible to acknowledge the pain of the subjugated without implicating the privileged, who are the direct beneficiaries of this pain. Hence conversations that acknowledge the suffering of the subjugated invariably create some distress for the privileged. Unfortunately, the subjugated are often compelled to protect the privileged from having to face up to the consequences of their privilege. For example, it is typical for the subjugated to minimize their suffering and/or to deny their pain altogether.

Our seventh goal, *the promotion of intimacy*, has the greatest overlap with traditional methods of couple therapy. Therapeutic strategies toward this end within an MCP approach draw liberally and eclectically from behavioral, psychodynamic, transgenerational, experiential, and narrative methods, as discussed in detail elsewhere in this volume.

CURATIVE FACTORS/MECHANISMS OF CHANGE

The Role of Insight and Interpretations

The mechanisms that lead to change within an MCP involve a combination of insight-oriented and action-oriented processes. With respect to insight-oriented processes, therapists strive to help clients recognize and understand the patterns, dynamics, and processes that underpin their problems. In accordance with the both–and orientation of an MCP, therapists promote a combination of historical and present-focused insight, as well as insight that is rooted in intrapsychic and interactional dynamics.

For example, Karen and Solena came to therapy to work out their "communication problems." Karen was a Jewish female of European descent, and Solena was a biracial female of Puerto Rican and African American parentage. During the second session, Karen complained that she was frustrated with Solena's insistence on wearing fur coats and her apparent indifference to the suffering of animals. Solena said she was frustrated with Karen for treating animals as if they were more important than she, Solena, was. During the therapy process, we encouraged historical and present-focused insight, as well as insight that was connected to psychological, familial, and sociocultural processes.

First we punctuated the role that each of the women's historical experiences played in their respective positions on fur coats. In Karen's case, she grew up surrounded by animals in a family that emphasized the importance of recognizing and attending to the feelings and sensibilities of animals. Solena, who grew up without pets, was raised to view animals as dirty creatures and as inferior to humans. Moreover, Karen grew up in an upper-middle-class family, where she was not subjected to the wounds of socioeconomic deprivation. Solena, on the other hand, grew up in a poor family, where she constantly yearned for the material privileges that always seemed beyond her reach. She felt the constant sting of social devaluation associated with not having access to the social prestige associated with material wealth. Despite achieving great economic success in adulthood, she continued to be haunted by these early childhood experiences, which was why she so desired the fur coats that symbolized social status and respect. By uncovering the role that both partners' early life experiences played in their positions on fur coats, we were encouraging historical insight. Moreover, we focused on the interaction between familial and sociocultural experiences in shaping each woman's position.

Second, we utilized interactional insight by identifying and making explicit "here-and-now" dynamics that were occurring during the therapy. In our work with Karen and Solena, we observed that whenever Karen would express her distress regarding Solena's fur coats, she did so in a castigating way that seemed to alienate Solena, who responded by withdrawing emotionally. We used interactional insight by pointing this pattern out during the therapy.

In addition to stimulating insight, therapists using an MCP should also encourage interpretations, both their own and the clients'. The combination of insight and interpretation is a primary mechanism for promoting change with an MCP. Utilizing insight and interpretation opens up the possibility for developing new ways of approaching old problems. Hence, with her newly acquired insight, Karen could better understand that Solena's fur coats were representative of her experiences with devaluation and her need to feel respected and successful. This insight helped Karen understand how counterproductive her condemnations were with Solena: She was only irritating the very wounds that drove Solena to desire the fur coats in the first place. Karen was also able to have compassion for Solena because she saw that Solena, like the animals, was a victim of societal oppression. As Karen's view of Solena changed, so did her behaviors. She began to treat her partner with greater respectfulness, patience, and kindness. Karen also was able to see how her identification with the animals was related to her own experiences with suffering as a Jew, where she often felt targeted and trapped.

For Solena, insight helped her gain greater compassion for her pain and some realization of what resided beneath her need for the fur coats. With this enhanced sense of self-awareness, Solena's need for the fur coats was diminished, because she came to realize that all the fur coats in the world could not soothe the pain carried within her. She also was able to make a connection with Karen around their shared suffering as members of persecuted groups, which enabled Solena to move closer to Karen. As Solena started to deal directly with the pain that resided beneath her desire for fur coats, eventually she found that she no longer craved them. In fact, she came to appreciate the relationship between her pain and suffering and that of the animals whose fur she was wearing.

The Role of Skill Development

An MCP also incorporates action-oriented processes that entail skill acquisition as a mechanism for change. There are two ways that therapists can encourage clients to learn and apply new skills in their lives. The first is indirectly through modeling: Therapists teach clients new skills by utilizing them within the therapy. The second way that therapists can promote skill development is through the use of more structured didactic experiences: Therapists explicitly identify various types of skills and guide clients in how to integrate these into their relationships. As the partners interact throughout

the course of treatment, acute attention is devoted to their efforts to adopt the new skills. During these phases of the treatment process, the therapist typically assumes the role of coach, gently but firmly guiding the couple to simultaneously rid itself of destructive ways of being and replace them with new skills. Ideally, therapists using an MCP should use some combination of modeling and direct instruction to help clients develop new skills. For example, in the case of the VCR approach, therapists must initially introduce this communication technique didactically and instruct clients in how to use it successfully. Following this initial instruction, therapists should encourage clients to use the VCR approach during the course of their natural communication. Moreover, therapists should model the application of the approach in the ways that they interact with clients. Hence therapists should use the VCR approach to inform their communication with clients, and in particular to inform the ways in which they provide clients with feedback and further direction on how they themselves can use the approach in their communications with each other.

Therapist Factors

Self-of-the-therapist work is an integral component to providing couple therapy within an MCP. The degree to which therapists can assume a stance of nondefensiveness, openness, and an awareness of and interest in learning more about themselves is critical. Because an MCP assumes that reality is relative, therapists are not viewed as objective, neutral directors of the therapy process, but rather as subjective, active participants. Accordingly, this approach assumes that therapists' identities shape and inform what they see and don't see, and the actions and inactions they exercise. The more therapists understand themselves and their biases, beliefs, and experiences, the less likely they will be to inadvertently impede clients' healing and growth because of their own perceptual limitations and emotional reactivity.

Although other approaches to couple therapy emphasize the importance of therapist self-awareness, the MCP is unique in its strong emphasis upon the multiple dimensions of self. In other words, all aspects of the self shape and inform how therapists approach therapy. Therefore, effective therapists have a complex understanding of how the various dimensions of their selves influence their work.

A tool that we have tailored to explore the intersection between family-of-origin issues and culture-of-origin issues (in terms of race, ethnicity, gender, class, sexual orientation, religion, etc.) is the cultural genogram process (Hardy & Laszloffy, 1995b). Using this tool, therapists are guided in an exploration of how their family-of-origin and culture-of-origin issues shape who they are as human beings and as therapists. Consider, for example, one dimension of culture, sexual orientation. Within an MCP, therapists who have not thought critically about their own sexual identity and what this means will inevitably have blind spots that interfere with their ability to implement an MCP effectively. Hence it is important for all therapists to spend some time exploring their own sexual orientation, including what they learned about sexual orientation growing up in their families, and what their beliefs, biases, and experiences are related to their sexual orientation. Without this type of self-examination, it is questionable how well therapists can help clients (of any sexual orientation) negotiate sexual and relationship issues.

The exploration and awareness of self is a lifelong process, and we do not believe that any therapist reaches a plateau where he/she "has arrived." There is always more one can explore and learn about oneself. What is most essential is possessing the willingness and openness to engage in continual self-exploration. Therapists who use an MCP most effectively are those who are committed to knowing more about themselves, and specifically who are committed to exploring their selves in terms of many different levels and dimensions of identity.

Techniques versus the Client–Therapist Relationship

Although an MCP has a set of techniques that play an important role in the successful utilization of this approach, ultimately techniques are regarded as secondary to the client–therapist relationship. This approach assumes that the therapist is the channel for the change process. The education and supervision of family therapists trained to provide couple therapy from an MCP places a heavy emphasis on self-of-the-therapist work. This approach to training is designed to enhance the therapist's awareness and sensitivity to the myriad of issues that might impede the delivery of effective couple therapy. An MCP is predicated on the premise that a therapist who is self-aware, who is transparent, and who has some mastery of the effective use of self has the attributes necessary to establish a good client–therapist relationship. In our view, the development of an authentic client–therapist relationship is of greater salience than is the implementation and execution of specific techniques—that is, of course, unless the use of a specific technique is instrumental in helping to solidify the client–therapist relationship. For example, the VCR approach is often used very liberally in the initial phases of treatment, because it contributes to the creation of a therapeutic milieu where clients genuinely feel understood, respected, and validated.

Factors That Limit Success within an MCP

It should be fairly obvious at this stage that one of the greatest impediments to effectively utilizing an MCP is segregated thinking. When therapists find it difficult to resist either–or thinking—that is, they consistently divide the world into binary categories and rigidly favor one set of categories, as opposed to embracing multiple, contrasting categories—segregated thinking prevails. At its core, an MCP challenges segregated thinking through its focus on recognizing and simultaneously balancing diverse perspectives. We take it as a given that most clients will probably employ segregated thinking, since this is the dominant approach in our society. For this reason, therapists must be especially cued into a both–and orientation, so they can work to help clients achieve this as well in their lives.

Another factor that limits success with an MCP is therapists' failure to recognize their personal biases. We operate from an assumption that all of us have biases; the issue is not *if*, but *what*. In other words, the problem is not having particular biases, but rather failing to recognize what these are and how they shape how we relate to others. Ultimately, what we see and don't see, how we interpret various phenomena, and our conclusions about reality are all reflections of who we are as human beings, the things we believe, and the experiences we have had. Within the context of therapy, we believe it is necessary for therapists to understand the factors that shape their standards for judging the world around them. The failure to do so can often result in overgeneralizations, cultural blind spots, and premature clinical judgments and unwarranted conclusions.

Another great challenge to effectively using an MCP involves resisting tactics of domination. Most of us receive systematic socialization in the art of employing tactics of domination; it is the nature of the world in which we live. Particularly when we feel threatened or unsafe, many of us resort to some form of domination almost impulsively. When we, as therapists, use domination as a strategy in our work with clients, it greatly undermines a basic premise of an MCP. One of the things that makes this issue especially tricky is the fact that some tactics of domination are subtle and may be hard to detect. For example, using language that softly devalues or degrades is a covert way in which domination can be manifested.

Finding ways to openly acknowledge, deal with, and eventually embrace differences is another critical aspect of an MCP. Yet, many of us are extremely uncomfortable when we are confronted with differences. We find numerous ways to deny differences, to emphasize similarities, or to avoid situations where differences are blatant. When therapists cannot tolerate the intensity that arises from dealing with differences directly, it makes it extremely difficult to effectively implement an MCP.

The capacity to identify redeemable qualities in others and to validate is essential to an MCP. This important task, as discussed elsewhere in this chapter, is as central to the process of therapy as is the capacity to challenge and tolerate the intensity associated with challenging. Hence the inability of therapists to validate as well as challenge can be another major deterrent to the effective employment of an MCP.

TREATMENT APPLICABILITY

Appropriateness of an MCP with Different Types of Couples/Situations

Initially an MCP was developed to work with racial minority and other marginalized clients. However, over the course of its evolution, it has been applied effectively with a much wider range of couples. This represents a shift in our thinking that has led us to conceptualize culture more broadly and to challenge our tendency toward segregated thinking.

However, the appropriateness and utility of an MCP are drawn into question in any situation in which one or both partners manifest severe cognitive or emotional impairment due to either chronic substance abuse or a severe mental illness. The cognitive and emotional impairments associated with addictions and/or severe mental disturbances make it virtually impossible for therapists to connect with clients in a meaningful way and to engage in constructive therapeutic work. In situations such as these, we refer clients to treatment for their addictions and/or underlying mental disturbances as a precondition for couple therapy using an MCP.

Also, in situations where there are chronic, irreconcilable differences involving the clients' goals for therapy, or in cases involving an explosively violent couple, conjoint therapy with an MCP is best deferred in favor of individual sessions. We are more likely in such instances to start with individual sessions, and if it appears possible to bring the couple together in a relatively constructive manner, we may do so at a later date.

Ethical Considerations

A common criticism of an MCP is that it places too much emphasis upon issues of diversity and the various dimensions of culture. There are some who believe that it is entirely possible to address human suffering without considering the broader sociocultural context; in fact, some of these critics allege that focusing too much attention on sociocultural issues detracts from the "real" issues clients bring to therapy. An MCP is considered by some to be "too political" and "too global." In some instances we have been challenged for confusing good therapy with sociopolitical activism, and for imposing our political agenda on clients.

Our position is that such criticism reflects the dangers of segregated thinking. We believe that an MCP does reflect a strong commitment to sociopolitical activism, but this is entirely consistent with good, ethical therapy from our point of view. Because we believe all matters are interconnected, we believe that what happens in the broader society affects the immediate experiences of individuals, couples, and families. We believe that the "global" and the "local" are interrelated. Therefore, we believe that it is ethically indicated to address micro- and macro-level issues within therapy. With respect to political activity, we believe that all therapy is politically motivated. Therapists who choose to not address macro-level issues, and issues of culture and diversity, are as politically motivated as those of us who do address them. There is no neutral ground in our way of viewing the world. Hence, in our politically motivated efforts to challenge segregated thinking, it is internally consistent with the basic tenets of an MCP for therapists to address the relationship between micro- and macro-level issues, and to approach human suffering from an assumption that all matters are interconnected. We see such things as entirely consistent with "good therapy practices."

Another aspect of an MCP that raises various ethical questions involves our positions on issues of oppression and domination on one hand, and our position of the relativity of reality on the other. Because we respect the relativity of reality, we recognize that it is problematic to define certain types of actions and behaviors as oppressive and abusive. No matter how much something may appear oppressive to us, it may have a very different meaning to others, given their context. And yet an MCP, while advocating a respect for relativism on one hand, also takes a strong position against tactics of domination and oppression on the other. We believe that therapists have an ethical mandate to challenge expressions of violence, domination, and oppression whenever and wherever they may exist. The way we attempt to bridge the contradiction between our two respective positions is through recognizing that it is possible to respect a position that differs from our own, while also presenting a challenge to that position.

Often challenge is confused with disrespect. Many of us have the mistaken notion that if we express a concern about or take issue with something, inherent in the challenge is some violation of another's right to his/her position. The key for us involves how we express our difference of opinion with someone else. If the expression of our opinion involves the denigration of another point of view, or if we advance our views in a way that is condescending and self-righteous, then we ourselves are guilty of engaging in the very tactics of domination that we seek to resist. So once again we find ourselves employing the VCR approach, because in its simplicity, it offers everything we deem necessary to engage in difficult dialogues in a healthy way. The VCR approach allows us to demonstrate a respect for another's position on a matter, while also allowing us to present our own view. Essentially, we are employing both–and thinking by attempting to create enough space for the coexistence of two contrasting views. Although we never deny the passion with which we believe in our views, never at any point does this passion result in a need to destroy or defile differing points of view.

Our efforts to simultaneously hold a respect for different realities with our commitment to challenging domination and oppression do get tricky at times. For example, in a couple where one partner is actively violent toward the other, the abused partner, by virtue or his/her subjugated status, may find it difficult to assert his/her anger about the violence. Out of fear of retaliation, or as a function of his/her own internalized oppression, the abused partner may be unable to advance a position that challenges the other aggressiveness. The abused client may even deny altogether that violence is a problem, which places the therapist in the difficult position of having to probe for something that is in direct contradiction to what the clients are overtly asserting. Although situations like these are complicated, we maintain that by using the VCR approach, it is possible for therapists to challenge any and all acts of domination and violence, while still demonstrating a respectfulness toward differing opinions advanced by clients.

For example, Rudy and Donna came to therapy because Rudy was "pissed off" with Donna's inefficiency around the house and her failure to "be a more pleasing wife." Rudy was extremely authoritarian, critical of his wife, aggressive in his presentation, and unwilling to consider his contribution to any of the "problems" in the relationship. Donna was meek and quiet. She appeared afraid of her husband. She expressed a desire to please him and said, "I know I am not good at making him happy, and I want to learn how I can be a better wife." This was a classic case of "the abuser and the abused." Both partners advanced the story that Donna was the problem, and that the solution involved helping her become more pleasing as wife. Never once did we challenge their essential view of the problem; rather, we attempted to expand the definition of the problem. Of course, we initially devoted a lot of energy to joining with the couple, and especially to making Rudy, as the power broker in the relationship, feel safe and comfortable. As we gained his trust, we gradually began to introduce concepts that were designed to challenge the partners' view, while at the same time respecting their definition of the problem. For example, we made the point that it is often difficult for people to do their best in a situation when they feel afraid or criticized. As a general rule, Rudy was able to agree to this. We also made the point that Rudy was a very strong, powerful man, and that sometimes he seemed oblivious to the vast power he possessed. Because Rudy was invested in seeing himself this way, he did not resist our characterization.

Once Rudy agreed to this description of himself, we moved on to pointing out that his strength and power (a view of himself that was pleasing to him) might also have been contributing to the problems in the relationship. We asserted that it was possible that his strength and power were so intimidating that they had the effect of scaring others who were less powerful, like Donna, and even us. We used ourselves in this way to support Donna and normalize her fear. We said that we sometimes felt intimidated by Rudy, even though we believed intellectually that he would never actually hurt us. Ultimately we wanted him to recognize the role that his style of relating had in the relationship, and how he may have inadvertently been undermining his own interests in ways he was unaware of. This allowed us to respect the clients' self-defined agenda for the therapy in a way that also permitted us to respectfully challenge the tactics of domination that we observed.

Assessing Outcome

Determinations about outcome with an MCP reflect our assumptions about the subjectivity of reality and the co-constructed nature of truth. Hence we do not utilize standardized instruments for evaluating efficacy. Within an MCP, efficacy is defined between therapists and clients, with clients exercising the ultimate authority over whether or not the therapy has worked for them.

Routinely, we conduct interviews with therapists and clients at some point around the fourth session and following termination. Interviews are conducted by someone who is not associated with the therapy process, and they utilize open-ended questions that are designed to gather as much rich, narrative data as possible regarding therapists' and clients' perceptions of the therapy process.

CONCLUSION

This chapter has provided a description of the philosophical underpinnings of couple therapy utilizing an MCP. It has been emphasized that an MCP is not based on a set of techniques or skills that can be easily codified and applied in isolation. Instead, it represents an epistemological stance that takes into account the pervasive role that notions of reality, context, and culture play in our lives as therapists and clients, and in the work we do together.

REFERENCES

Anderson, H., & Goolishian, H. (1992). The client is the expert: A not-knowing approach to therapy. In S. McNamee & K. Gergen (Eds.), *Therapy as social construction* (pp. 26–39). Newbury Park, CA: Sage.

Bateson, G. (1979). *Mind and nature: A necessary unity.* New York: Dutton.

Boszormenyi-Nagy, I., & Sparks, G. (1973). *Invisible loyalties: Reciprocity in intergenerational family therapy.* New York: Harper & Row.

Bowen, M. (1978). *Family therapy in clinical practice.* New York: Jason Aronson.

Dicks, H. V. (1967). *Marital tensions: Clinical studies toward a psychological theory of interaction.* New York: Basic Books.

Falicov, C. J. (1995). Training to think culturally: A multidimensional comparative framework. *Family Process, 34,* 373–388.

Framo, J. (1981). The integration of marital therapy with sessions with family of origin. In A. Gurman & D. Kniskern (Eds.), *Handbook of family therapy* (pp. 133–158). New York: Brunner/Mazel.

Goldner, V. (1985). Feminism and family therapy. *Family Process, 24,* 31–47.

Greenberg, L. S., & Johnson, S. M. (1988). *Emotion-focused marital therapy.* New York: Brunner/Mazel.

Hardy, K. V. (1995, November–December). Embracing both/and. *The Family Therapy Networker,* pp. 42–57.

Hardy, K. V. (1997a, January). Not quite home: The psychological effects of oppression. *In the Family,* pp. 7–8, 26.

Hardy, K. V. (1997b, April) Steps toward becoming culturally competent. *Family Therapy News,* pp. 13–19.

Hardy, K. V. (2001). Healing the world in 50-minute intervals: A response to family therapy saves the planet. *Journal of Marital and Family Therapy, 27*(1), 19–22.

Hardy, K. V., & Laszloffy, T. A. (1995a). Therapy with African Americans and the phenomenon of rage. *In Session: Psychotherapy in Practice, 1*(4), 57–70.

Hardy, K. V., & Laszloffy, T. A. (1995b). The cultural genogram: A key to training culturally competent family therapists. *Journal of Marital and Family Therapy, 21*(3), 227–237.

Hare-Mustin, R. T. (1978). A feminist approach top family therapy. *Family Process, 17,* 181–194.

Hare-Mustin, R. T. (1987). The problem of gender in family therapy theory. *Family Process, 26,* 15–28.

Hoffman, L. (1990). Constructing realities: The art of lenses. *Family Process, 29,* 1–12.

Laird, J. (1998). Theorizing culture: Narrative ideas and practice principles. In M. McGoldrick (Ed.), *Re-visioning family therapy: Race, culture, and gender in clinical practice* (pp. 20–30). New York: Guilford Press.

Satir, V., & Baldwin, M. (1983). *Satir step by step: A guide to creating change in families.* Palo Alto, CA: Science & Behavior Books.

Scharff, D. E., & Scharff, J. S. (1987). *Object relations family therapy.* Northvale, NJ: Jason Aronson.

Watzlawick, P. (1984). *The invented reality: How do we know what we believe we know?* New York: Norton.

Watzlawick, P., Beavin, J. H., & Jackson, D. D. (1967). *The pragmatics of human communication.* New York: Norton

White, M., & Epston, D. (1990). *Narrative means to therapeutic ends.* New York: Norton.

Section C

Selected Psychiatric Disorders and Medical Illness

Chapter 23

Couple Therapy in the Treatment of Alcohol Problems

ELIZABETH E. EPSTEIN
BARBARA S. McCRADY

That alcoholism and marital/couple problems are interwoven is a fact well known to mental health professionals and addiction specialists. Less well understood are the factors that maintain alcoholic relationships, and the ways change can be effected that is good both for people with drinking problems and for their relationships. Scientific efforts to understand the interrelationships between drinking and marriage have been reported since the early 1900s, and treatment models that address both drinking and marital/couple functioning have been developed and tested for almost 60 years. In this chapter we present our current research-based model for conceptualizing and treating individuals with alcoholism and their partners, and address clinical techniques and issues in the implementation of our treatment model.

Drinking and the marital/couple relationship are often so closely bound that clinicians have referred to the "alcoholic marriage" (e.g., Paolino & McCrady, 1977). Early theoretical models suggested that women married alcoholic men as a defense against neurotic conflicts with control or dependency. These models suggested that these wives needed their partners to continue to drink to avoid more serious decompensation themselves (e.g., Lewis, 1937; Whalen, 1953). These early psychodynamic models firmly placed responsibility for an individual's continued drinking in the hands of the disturbed spouse. Sociological perspectives, predominant in the 1950s and 1960s, viewed the spouse as responding to the chronic stress introduced by living with an alcoholic partner (e.g., Jackson, 1954), placing responsibility for the family's problems with the alcoholic individual rather than the spouse. Family systems models, which first came to prominence in the 1970s and 1980s, emphasized the homeostatic balance between drinking and family functioning, hypothesizing that drinking stabilized the family system and allowed for the expression of certain facets of family relationships that could not be expressed during sober periods (e.g., Steinglass, Bennett, Wolin, & Reiss, 1987).

Contemporary models of alcoholism and couple relationships are based on social learning theory and family systems models, and draw from empirical literatures on interactional behavior, the connections between individual psychopathology and interactional behavior, and the broader literature on social support. Alcohol behavioral couple therapy (ABCT) includes elements of behavioral self-control training and skills training to facilitate abstinence, better coping by the nonalcoholic partner with drinking-related situations, and communication techniques drawn from behavioral couple therapy (BCT) to improve relationship functioning. ABCT treatments developed by different investigators vary in their degree of emphasis on these domains (McCrady & Epstein, 1995; O'Farrell, 1993).

Research suggests that ABCT results in significant reductions in alcohol consumption and improvements in couple functioning (McKay, Longabaugh, Beattie, Maisto, & Noel, 1993; McCrady, Epstein, & Hirsch, 1999; McCrady, Noel, Abrams, Stout, Nelson, & Hay, 1986; McCrady, Noel, Stout, Abrams, & Nelson, 1991; McCrady, Stout, Noel, Abrams, & Nelson, 1991; O'Farrell, Choquette, & Cutter, 1998; O'Farrell, Choquette, Cutter, Brown, & McCourt, 1993; O'Farrell, Cutter, & Floyd, 1985). Clinical researchers continue to develop and study new applications of the basic ABCT treatment model (Beutler et al., 1993; Epstein & McCrady, 1998; McCrady, Epstein, & Hirsch, 1996; O'Farrell et al., 1993). Recently, ABCT has been adapted to treat other drug use disorders (Fals-Stewart, Birchler, & O'Farrell, 1996). However, almost all of the work done over the past 25 years on BCT and substance use disorders has focused on alcohol; thus this chapter focuses primarily on alcohol problems.

THE HEALTHY/WELL-FUNCTIONING VERSUS PATHOLOGICAL/DYSFUNCTIONAL MARRIAGE

Definitions and Diagnosis of Alcohol Problems

Before we consider the relationships between couple functioning and drinking problems, it is important to consider the nature of drinking problems themselves (Epstein, 2001). Alcohol and drug use disorders, as specified in the *Diagnostic and Statistical Manual of Mental Disorders*, fourth edition (DSM-IV; American Psychiatric Association, 1994), fall into two major categories: substance abuse and substance dependence. The term "substance" refers to alcohol or 10 other classes of drugs. Substance abuse is diagnosed if the individual's substance use results in failure to fulfill major role obligations at work, school, or home; occurs repeatedly in situations where use is physically hazardous; creates recurrent legal problems; or is continued despite recurrent substance-related interpersonal or social problems. The substance dependence diagnosis is based on the individual's meeting at least three of seven criteria involving physical tolerance; physical withdrawal symptoms; loss of control over consumption of the substance; unsuccessful attempts to cut down; excessive time spent obtaining, using, or recovering from use of the substance; substitution of substance use for other important social, occupational, or recreational activities; and continued use of the substance de-

spite knowledge of a recurring substance-related physical or psychological problem.

Because most of the research done thus far on ABCT has not used the formal diagnostic approach, the terms "alcohol and drug use problems," "alcoholism," "alcohol (substance) abuse and dependence," and "substance misuse" are used interchangeably in this chapter, except where stated specifically. Similarly, the adjective "alcoholic" is used here to refer to individuals with a diagnosis of either alcohol abuse or dependence.

In contrast to the formal psychiatric diagnosis of alcohol dependence, behavioral researchers and clinicians have suggested that alcohol problems are part of a continuum of drinking that ranges from abstinence to nonproblem use to different types of problem use. From this perspective, problems may be exhibited in a variety of forms—some of which are consistent with a formal diagnosis, and some of which are milder or more intermittent. Babor, Kranzler, and Lauerman (1989) have suggested that persons with drinking problems be classified as "vulnerable," "hazardous," or "harmful" drinkers. Vulnerable drinkers are those whose current drinking does not create any harm to themselves or others, but are at particularly high risk for developing alcohol problems. Hazardous drinkers are those whose current drinking creates current or potential hazards in their lives or the lives of others. Harmful drinkers have begun to experience serious negative consequences of their alcohol use, or their pattern of use has become stereotypic and repetitive.

The alcohol problems perspective exemplified by Babor et al. (1989) and other behavioral researchers stands in contrast to the psychiatric diagnostic approach of the DSM-IV. The alcohol problems perspective does not exclude the possibility of an underlying syndrome or disease state, but does not assume its existence, as does the psychiatric diagnostic approach. Our treatment model is based on an alcohol problems perspective; we work with the specific behaviors presented by each couple. However, our model can be used with clients who hold a disease perspective on their alcohol problem if they can accept that changing behavior is necessary to control the disease.

Couple Distress and Substance Use Disorders

Extensive research has demonstrated that substance use behaviors affect the quality and nature of a couple's relationship, and that the relationship similarly affects the substance use. Thus, from a systemic perspective, the two domains of function (substance use and the relationship) are interconnected. Alcoholic couples report substantial levels of marital dissatisfaction and marital problems. Alcoholic husbands are similar to husbands in other conflicted marriages in avoiding responsibility for problems in their relationships (O'Farrell & Birchler, 1987). Results from clinical and nonclinical samples reveal a close relationship between heavy drinking and relationship violence. Alcoholic couples have high rates of relationship violence, regardless of the gender of the alcoholic partner (Rotunda, 1995), and communication patterns of maritally aggressive alcoholic couples are characterized by high rates of aversive–defensive behaviors and negative reciprocity (Murphy & O'Farrell, 1997). Similar data from nonclinical samples suggest a relationship between heavier alcohol consumption and marital violence (Leonard & Senchak, 1993). Women with alcohol problems and marital distress expect alcohol to increase conflict engagement in the relationship, and such expectations are correlated with high rates of verbal and physical aggression (Kelly & Halford, 1994). Sexual dysfunction and dissatisfaction are also common in alcoholic relationships. Alcoholic men and their partners have less sexual satisfaction, less frequent intercourse, and more disagreements about sex than nonconflicted couples (O'Farrell, Choquette, & Birchler, 1991). In general, their sexual problems are similar to those of couples with other types of marital conflict, but impotence is a more common problem with alcoholic men (O'Farrell, Choquette, Cutter, & Birchler, 1997). In women, the frequency of sexual relationships has been found to decrease as the severity of women's alcohol problems increases (Noel, McCrady, Stout, & Fisher-Nelson, 1991). No such relationship has been found for alcoholic men and their partners. Married women with drinking problems report that they drink to continue to function in their relationships, to be more assertive, and to deal with sexual "demands" from their partners (Lammers, Schippers, & van der Staak, 1995).

There is substantial evidence that the spouses and children of alcoholic men experience psychological distress, health problems, and behavioral problems. Wives of actively drinking alcoholic husbands have elevated levels of depression, anxiety and psychosomatic complaints, and utilize more medical resources (Moos, Finney, & Gamble, 1982;

Moos & Moos, 1984). Children growing up with an alcoholic parent experience a variety of psychological, behavioral, and school problems (Moos & Moos, 1984) and are at increased risk for developing drinking problems themselves (Bierut et al., 1998). Even in samples of older problem drinkers, spouses have poorer health and social functioning and use more cognitive avoidance strategies than spouses of older, nonproblem drinkers (Brennan, Moos, & Kelly, 1994). The interrelationships among individual psychopathology, marital problems, and drinking vary, depending on the drinking individual's consumption pattern. Some data suggest that heavier drinking is inversely correlated with individual and marital distress for wives of men who are steady drinkers (Jacob, Dunn, & Leonard, 1983). For men who drink outside their homes, however, drinking reliably predicts decreases in marital satisfaction (Dunn, Jacob, Hummon, & Seilhamer, 1987).

Alcohol consumption and communication are also linked closely. Hersen, Miller, and Eisler (1973) reported that wives of alcoholic men looked at their husbands more when discussing an alcohol-related than a non-alcohol-related topic. Alcoholic husbands become more negative toward their wives when drinking (Jacob & Krahn, 1988), and surprisingly the husbands' problem solving increases when drinking (Jacob & Leonard, 1988). Research suggests that there may be differences in the interrelationships between drinking and communication, depending on the usual pattern of drinking. For example, women whose husbands drink in an episodic style tend to use less negative communication behaviors when their husbands drink, whereas women whose husbands' drinking is steadier tend to increase their negativity when the husbands are drinking (Jacob & Leonard, 1988).

The relationships between relationship functioning and drinking outcomes are complex. In late life, problem drinkers, whose drinking problems remit tend to have had less spousal support for their drinking (Schutte, Brennan, & Moos, 1994), and greater spouse stress is associated with poorer outcomes (Brennan, Moos, & Mertens, 1994). Support for abstinence from the spouse or other members of an alcoholic's social support system appears to interact with the degree to which the individual is socially invested in that support system in predicting outcome, so that those who are highly invested in their social network and receive good support from that network after treatment will have better outcomes (e.g., Longabaugh, Beattie, Noel, Stout, & Malloy, 1993). Finally, there is evidence that alcoholic individuals perceive marital problems to be significant precipitants of relapses after treatment, but that marital and family problems also serve as important stimuli for trying to resume abstinence after a relapse (Maisto, McKay, & O'Farrell, 1995).

Theoretical Model of Alcohol Problems and Couple Functioning

Our theoretical model integrates research findings about alcohol and couple relationships, and draws from sociological, family systems, and behavioral perspectives. We conceptualize many behaviors of the partner of an alcoholic individual as attempts to cope with a difficult situation, but we also emphasize the reciprocal interactions between the partner and the alcoholic behavior in determining repetitive and dysfunctional interaction patterns. Generally we use a social learning framework, which assumes that drinking can be treated best by examining current factors maintaining the drinking, rather than historical factors. Factors maintaining the drinking can be nondyadic and/or rooted in the interpersonal relationship. The model assumes that (1) external antecedents to drinking have a lawful relationship to drinking, through repeated pairings with positive or negative reinforcement or through the anticipation of reinforcement; (2) cognitions and affective states mediate the relationship between external antecedents and drinking behavior; (3) expectancies about the reinforcing value of alcohol play an important role in determining subsequent drinking behavior; and (4) drinking is maintained by its consequences, and these consequences may be at a physiological, individual psychological, or interpersonal level.

A variety of individual, familial, and other interpersonal factors may be associated with drinking (Lowman, Allen, Stout, & The Relapse Research Group, 1996). At the individual level, environmental antecedents may be associated with specific drinking situations, particular times of the day, or the mere sight or smell of alcohol. Organismic variables may include craving for alcohol; withdrawal symptoms; negative affects, such as anger, anxiety, or depression; negative self-evaluations or irrational beliefs; or positive expectancies about the effects of alcohol in particular situations. Individual reinforcers may include decreased craving or withdrawal symptoms; decreases in negative affect or increases in positive affect; decreased negative self-evaluations; or being able to forget problems.

Various antecedents to drinking also occur at the familial level. Alcohol use is integral to many families, and may be a usual part of family celebrations or daily rituals. Family members may engage in a variety of attempts to influence the drinking member's behavior, such as nagging him/her to stop drinking, or attempting to control the drinking through control of the finances or the liquor supply. Families in which alcohol problems are present have often evolved poor patterns of communication and problem solving, and have developed a variety of marital, sexual, financial, and child-rearing problems over time. All of these can serve as antecedents to further drinking. The drinking individual may have a range of reactions to these familial antecedents, experiencing negative affect, low self-efficacy for coping with problems, or retaliatory thoughts (e.g., "She's not going to control me").

Positive consequences of drinking may also come from the family. For example, families often engage in caretaking of the drinking member—cleaning up after him/her, covering for him/her at work, or being particularly gentle and nonconfrontational during drinking episodes. Although these behaviors can be understood as normal reactions when a family member is sick or in a bad mood, such behavior in alcoholic families may serve to reinforce drinking. A number of investigators have observed positive changes in marital interactions associated with drinking, suggesting that drinking may be reinforced by its positive marital consequences (e.g., Billings, Kessler, Gomberg, & Weiner, 1979; Frankenstein, Hay, & Nathan, 1985).

Families provide a number of negative consequences for drinking as well. These include withdrawal and avoidance of the drinking member; negative verbal comments about the drinking (either during or after a drinking episode); and, in some families, physical violence directed at the drinking member. These negative consequences, instead of suppressing the drinking, usually have two undesired effects. First, the drinking member begins to avoid the family when drinking or tries to hide the drinking. This hiding often leads to a pattern of couple interactions characterized by the drinking individual's avoidance and lying, and the nondrinking partner's hypervigilance. Second, negative consequences from family members may serve as cues to further drinking, thus maintaining a complex circular interaction between the drinking and family interactions.

Other interpersonal antecedents to drinking also occur. These may revolve around social pressures to drink; work-related drinking situations; friendships in which alcohol consumption plays a major role; or interpersonal conflicts with work associates, friends, or acquaintances. The alcoholic individual may react to interpersonal antecedents to drinking with craving, positive expectancies for alcohol use, social discomfort, or negative self-evaluations for not drinking. Positive interpersonal consequences of drinking may include decreased social anxiety or increased social comfort or assertiveness.

In summary, our model assumes that the drinking behavior of a person with alcoholism or problem drinking is embedded in a complex network of factors relating to the individual's physiology and psychology, the family, and other social networks. In each component of the network, there is a reciprocal relationship between the drinking and the functioning of network; the individual's behavior influences the social network and is influenced by it.

Nondyadic Factors Contributing to Etiology and Maintenance of Alcohol Problems

Several important nondyadic factors contribute to the etiology and maintenance of alcohol problems. First, there is fairly strong evidence for the familial transmission of more severe forms of drinking problems (Bierut et al., 1998). Persons with an alcoholic parent are at increased risk for developing alcoholism (particularly males with a male alcoholic parent), even among those not raised by their biological parents.

A second important individual factor in conceptualizing alcohol problems is the comorbidity of alcoholism with other psychiatric disorders. Research has shown that a high percentage of alcoholic individuals suffer from other psychiatric problems, which are concurrent with, antecedent to, or resulting from their alcohol problem (Rosenthal & Westreich, 1999). The most common comorbid Axis I disorders, aside from other substance abuse/dependence, are depression and anxiety disorders. The most common Axis II disorder found to be comorbid with alcoholism in males is antisocial personality disorder (ASPD). Some research has shown that ASPD affects alcoholic couples (Epstein, McCrady, & Hirsch, 1997; Ichiyama, Zucker, Fitzgerald, & Bingham, 1996).

Third, individual differences in race/ethnicity, age, and gender have implications for development of and response to ABCT (Castro, Proescholdbell,

Abeita, & Rodriguez, 1999; Gomberg, 1999; Sanjuan & Langenbucher, 1999). Rates of alcohol abuse and dependence vary in different groups, as do barriers to utilization of treatment. Little is known about variability in couple relationships depending on individual differences. Some research with alcoholic women suggests that their partners are more likely also to have alcohol or drug problems, that women are more likely to drink in response to relationship discord, and that male partners are relatively uninvolved and unresponsive to the women's drinking (McCrady & Epstein, 1999).

A fourth important set of nondyadic factors affecting the etiology and maintenance of drinking revolves around the family-of-origin interactions of both the drinking individual and his/her partner. Bennett and Wolin (1990) have reported a strong association between continuing interactions between offspring and their alcoholic parents, and the probability of developing alcoholism in the offspring. For example, if an adult male who grew up in an alcoholic family continues to have contact with his family, he is more likely to develop drinking problems himself. In additionally, if there is alcoholism in his female partner's family, and the couple continues to have contact with her family, his risk of developing alcoholism is also significantly increased.

Treatment for persons with alcohol problems thus occurs within a complex network of psychological, sociocultural, familial, and interpersonal contexts and problems. The ABCT model takes this complexity into account.

THE STRUCTURE OF THERAPY

Theory of Therapeutic Change: Curative Factors and Mechanisms of Change

Our model for conceptualizing drinking problems necessitates our intervening at multiple levels—with the drinking individual, his/her partner, the relationship as a unit, the family, and the other social systems in which the individual is involved. Implicit in the model is the need for detailed assessment to determine the primary factors contributing to the maintenance of the drinking, the skills and deficits of both the individual and the couple, and the sources of motivation to change. At the individual level, the treatment helps the client assess individual psychological problems associated with drinking; potential and actual reinforcers for continued drinking and for decreased drinking or abstinence; negative consequences of drinking and abstinence; and beliefs and expectations about alcohol use and its consequences. Assessment of the relative strength of incentives for continuing to drink or changing drinking provides an incentive framework for the rest of the therapy. A number of other strategies (described below) are also used to enhance motivation to change. Teaching individual coping skills to deal with alcohol-related situations is a second important individual intervention. These skills include self-management planning, stimulus control, drink refusal, and self-monitoring of drinking and drinking impulses. Teaching behavioral and cognitive coping skills to handle psychological and interpersonal antecedents to drinking, individually tailored to the types of situations that are the most common antecedents to drinking ("high-risk situations"), is a third type of individually focused intervention. These skills include, for example, assertiveness, cognitive restructuring, relaxation, lifestyle balance, and recreational activities. Finally, we believe that providing clients with a model for conceptualizing drinking problems and ways to change is an important part of the therapy for both partners.

A second set of interventions flowing logically from our model revolves around the coping behaviors of the partner. The partner's own motivation for entering and continuing in treatment, and the partner's perceptions of the positive and negative consequences of changes in drinking and in the couple relationship, are important factors contributing to the partner's willingness to engage in new behaviors and be an active participant in the therapy. The model also suggests that the partner learn a variety of coping skills to deal with drinking and abstinence. An individualized assessment of the partner's behaviors that may either cue drinking or maintain it is essential. Partner coping skills may include learning new ways to discuss drinking and drinking situations, learning new responses to the drinking and alcohol-related behavior, or individual skills to enhance the partner's own individual functioning.

The third component of treatment is a focus on the interactions between the partners, around both alcohol and other issues. Alcohol-focused couple interventions use alcohol-related topics as a vehicle to introduce communication and problem-solving skills. Such topics as how the couple can manage in a situation where alcohol is present, whether or not to keep alcohol in the house, how the partner can assist the drinking individual in dealing with impulses to drink, or what the couple will tell family and friends about the alcoholic individual's treatment are all relevant topics that the couple must face in the process of dealing with the drinking. By using such topics as vehicles for discussion, the couple learns basic communication skills. In addition, the model suggests that many alcoholic couples need to learn general communication and problem-solving skills to decrease conflicts that may cue drinking and to increase the rate of positive exchanges. When appropriate, the treatment also incorporates general reciprocity enhancement interventions to increase the overall reward value of the relationship.

The fourth set of interventions focuses on other social systems in which the drinking individual and his/her partner are currently or potentially involved. Clients are helped to identify interpersonal situations and persons who are associated with heavy drinking; they are also helped to identify potential social situations that, would be supportive of abstinence or decreased drinking. Social skills such as refusing drinks or general assertiveness may be taught. In addition, some clients are encouraged to become involved with Alcoholics Anonymous (AA) or other self-help programs, such as Self-Management and Recovery Training (SMART) Recovery. Self-help groups provide a strong social support network for abstinence, opportunities to meet abstinent individuals, and a set of time-structuring activities that are incompatible with drinking.

Finally, the model includes techniques to increase generalization to the natural environment and maintenance of new behaviors. Homework assignments, teaching clients how to anticipate high-risk situations, and planned follow-up treatment sessions are all designed to contribute to maintenance of change.

Hypothesized Active Ingredients in the Treatment

Four major factors are hypothesized to contribute to therapeutic change. First, the intensive assessment of drinking and its consequences, feedback from the nonalcoholic partner, and the increased knowledge about drinking problems should facilitate motivation to engage in new behaviors that support change. Second, the treatment is designed to enhance self-efficacy by introducing a series of small, successful changes in the behavior of each partner, thus increasing each partner's self-efficacy for engaging in more difficult behavior change. Third, the treatment is designed to increase positive reinforcers for abstinence in general, and to increase the overall reinforcement value of the relationship as a way to provide a strong incentive to maintain changed drinking behavior. Fourth, learning new cognitive and behavioral coping skills provides couples with an expanded behavioral repertoire for coping with high-risk situations.

Overall Strategy and Techniques for Bringing about Change

To implement the therapeutic model, we provide conjoint therapy throughout the treatment. Partners are seen together, to educate both partners about the nature of drinking problems and the model of change; to decrease the avoidance, lying, and hypervigilance that may characterize the relationship; to improve communication and problem-solving skills; and to use the differing perspectives of each partner to increase the information available to the therapist. Under certain circumstances, separate individual sessions are an appropriate part of an overall conjoint treatment approach. An individual assessment is always used to assess for domestic violence, and individual sessions are appropriate when there are continued concerns about domestic violence, when one or both partners are involved in extramarital affairs, or when the volatility or level of hostility of the couple's relationship dramatically interferes with the therapist's ability to work directly on the drinking.

Therapy typically follows a sequence in which alcohol is the primary focus of the early treatment sessions, and the relationship increasingly becomes a target for attention as therapy progresses. By focusing on alcohol at the beginning of treatment, the therapist allies with both partners, who are presenting with drinking as their major concern. If the alcoholic client is successful in changing his/her drinking, the partner may be more amenable to examining and changing his/her own behavior. Discussing alcohol-related topics that affect the couple as a unit, encouraging simple shared activities, and teaching the partner to provide reinforcement for the positive changes in drinking behavior are the earliest interventions directed at the couple as a unit, and provide a medium for the introduction of communication and problem-solving skills. As treatment progresses, the therapist focuses more explicitly on the couple relationship as a whole.

A list of commonly used treatment techniques in ABCT is included in Table 23.1.

Diagnostic/Assessment Procedures

The primary goals of assessment are to evaluate the immediate needs of the couple; to assess the extent and severity of the drinking problem, in order to determine the appropriate level of care; to identify antecedents to drinking, consequences maintaining the drinking, cognitive and affective aspects of the drinking, and positive and negative aspects of the partner's drinking-related behavior; and to assess strengths and weaknesses in the couple's relationship.

A number of different assessment strategies are used to complete a comprehensive evaluation that can be used for treatment planning. Intensive interviews; self-report questionnaires; observation of interactional behavior; use of physiological measures, such as blood alcohol levels, tests of liver functioning, and urine screens for drug use; and self-recording cards all may contribute to the assessment.

Structure of the Therapeutic Protocol

Therapy is conducted as conjoint sessions, typically 90 minutes in length, with a single therapist working with the couple. For our research, we see couples for 20 weekly sessions over 6 months, but this arrangement can be tailored to individual situations in the clinical setting. Sessions begin with the use of a hand-held Breathalyzer to assess whether or not the person with problem drinking has any alcohol in his/her system.

The therapy session typically proceeds with a review of self-recording cards (described below) and a discussion of other homework. The balance of the session revolves around specific topics introduced by the therapist, as well as work on therapeutic issues introduced by the couple. Even if the focus of a particular session is on individual behavior change (such as self-management skills to avoid drinking situations), both partners are actively engaged in the treatment, and the therapist encourages the couple to interact, providing guidance and coaching on specific communication skills during these interactions. Treatment is active and goal-directed, and sessions include active problem solving and behavioral rehearsal of new skills.

Time is left at the end of each session to review high-risk situations that are likely to come up during the subsequent week. We use a worksheet for this, writing down the possible high-risk situations and a plan to deal with each one without

TABLE 23.1. Sample Outline of Treatment Techniques (20-Session Therapy)

Session	Individual intervention	Partner intervention	Couple intervention
1	a. Feedback b. Self-recording	a. Motivation enhancement b. Self-recording	
2	c. Functional analysis d. Dealing with urges		
3	e. Motivation enhancement f. Functional analysis	c. Functional analysis	
4	g. High-risk hierarchy	d. Functional analysis	a. Discussion of alcohol in the house
5	h. Self-management planning i. Contingency management: Self-reinforcement	e. Partner reinforcement	
6	j. Contingency management: Rehearsing negative consequences of drinking	f. Partner decreasing attention to drinking	b. Shared fun activity
7	k. Dealing with alcohol-related thoughts	g. Partner decreasing protection for drinking	c. Shared fun activity
8	l. Drink refusal training	h. Partner role in drinking situations	d. Shared fun activity with behavior change
9	m. Assertiveness	i. Partner assertiveness	e. "Love" day
10	n. Problem solving		f. Communication I
11	o. Cognitive restructuring p. Thought stopping		g. Communication II
12	q. Cognitive restructuring		h. Communication training
13	r. Seemingly irrelevant decisions		i. Leveling and editing
14	s. Review of all coping skills		j. Acceptance/change k. Negotiating/problem solving
15	t. Identifying signs of relapse	j. Identifying signs of relapse	l. Problem solving m. Building tolerance
16	u. Managing signs of relapse	k. Managing signs of relapse	n. Problem solving o. Building tolerance
17	v. Handling relapse	l. Handling relapse	p. Increasing self-care
18	w. Relapse road map	m. Relapse road map	q. Increasing self-care
19	x. Maintenance planning	n. Maintenance planning	r. Relapse contract
20	y. Review and congratulations	o. Review and congratulations	s. Signing relapse contract

drinking. Also at the end of the session, homework for the week is assigned and written down.

Motivational Enhancement

A continuing focus throughout the therapy is the client's and partner's level of motivation for change. Traditional alcohol treatment models viewed motivation as a trait, and viewed alcoholics as ready to change only when they had "hit bottom." In contrast, contemporary models recognize that cli-

ents vary along a continuum in the degree to which they recognize their drinking as problematic, and in their personal readiness to change (Prochaska, DiClemente, & Norcross, 1992). Motivational models suggest that individuals initiate change when the perceived costs of the behavior outweigh the perceived benefits, and when they can anticipate some benefits from behavior change (Cunningham, Sobell, Sobell, & Gaskin, 1994).

Contemporary models view motivation as a state that can be influenced by therapeutic behaviors and the client's life experiences (Yahne &

Miller, 1999). Therapeutic approaches designed to enhance motivation are associated with less client resistance to treatment and with more positive drinking outcomes (Miller, Benefield, & Tonigan, 1993); these approaches appear to be particularly effective with clients who enter treatment very angry and hostile (Project MATCH Research Group, 1997). Recognition of the degree of readiness to change; use of specific motivational enhancement techniques; and use of "motivational interviewing" (Miller & Rollnick, 1991) and a nonconfrontational therapeutic style are new parts of the ABCT approach.

Goal Setting

Traditional approaches to alcoholism treatment view abstinence as the only appropriate drinking goal, because they regard alcoholism as a progressive disease that can only be arrested with abstinence. The alcohol problems perspective, which makes no a priori assumptions about an underlying disease, provides a more flexible approach to client goal setting. Some behavioral clinicians have examined alternatives to abstinence and have developed a number of strategies to teach clients how to drink moderately. Harm reduction approaches (e.g., MacCoun, 1998) suggest the use of moderate drinking goals to help reduce potential harm from heavy drinking among clients not motivated for abstinence. Although moderate drinking is better accepted as a goal for certain individuals with alcohol abuse (rather than dependence), moderation training and harm reduction approaches more generally continue to be controversial.

Our treatment emphasizes abstinence as the preferable drinking goal for treatment, for several reasons. First, most of our clients have experienced serious medical, social, legal, or occupational consequences of their drinking. The potential for problems if they continue to drink in an uncontrolled manner is substantial. Second, we believe that many clients overvalue alcohol, underestimate the seriousness of the consequences of their drinking, and/or overestimate the negative aspects of abstinence. With such a client, we believe that part of the therapist's responsibility is to help the client make a more realistic appraisal of the positive and negative consequences of drinking and abstinence. Third, a couple often enters treatment at the specific request of the nonalcoholic partner, who may not agree to a goal of moderation. Finally, if we want clients who have limited social support systems to use AA as a resource, then abstinence is a necessary goal.

Thus we ask clients to agree to an initial goal of abstinence. For clients with medical sequelae of drinking, or severe and chronic drinking problems, we stress the importance of continued abstinence. For other clients, we may define abstinence as a provisional goal that allows them to be the most "clear-headed" during treatment, and gives them the opportunity to evaluate the experience of abstinence. Most clients agree to abstinence, given the provisional rather than absolute nature of the goal.

In addition to drinking goals, there are several other major goals for the treatment. These goals include the development of coping skills to deal with alcohol-related situations (for both partners); development of positive reinforcers for abstinence or changed drinking; enhancement of relationship functioning; development of general coping skills; development of effective communication and problem-solving skills; and development of strategies to maintain therapeutic gains and deal with relapses. Other couple-specific goals may also be identified.

Termination

Termination raises an interesting problem in the context of alcoholism treatment, in light of the fact that many treatment professionals in this field view alcoholism as a relapsing disorder or habit that requires continued treatment. Thus, defining therapy either as time-limited, or as lengthy but eventually ending, may well be altered in the treatment of alcoholism as research begins to document the benefits of continued periodic contact between the alcoholic client and the therapist after a block of more intense treatment (e.g., O'Farrell et al., 1998).

Currently, the conjoint model of treatment for alcoholism is a time-limited approach, with the option of "booster" or maintenance sessions continuing for as long as the involved parties see fit. The case described later in this chapter spanned twenty 90-minute sessions. Depending on the case, the number of sessions needed to cover assessment and the alcohol-related and couple skills can range from 15 to perhaps even 30 or more. Two major criteria should be used to assess when it is time to terminate a successful course of treatment:

1. *Resolution of the alcohol use.* Has the alcoholic individual been abstinent long enough to feel

comfortable with changes made in his/her life to support sobriety or decreased drinking? Have the cravings and urges for alcohol become manageable? Have other pleasurable activities been substituted for positive consequences that the alcoholic formerly derived? Are social supports in place that support abstinence?

2. *Improved couple relationship.* Do both the alcoholic client and his/her partner report greater satisfaction with the relationship? In sessions, is there evidence of increased good will toward each other? Is there evidence of better communication and more effective problem solving? Have both partners adjusted to the changes in their relationship that resulted when the alcohol was eliminated?

If these criteria are met, and the therapist feels comfortable that he/she has introduced at least most of the skills that would be potentially helpful to the couple, the process of terminating the intensive weekly portion of the therapy can begin. One way to ease termination and to help the couple continue to discuss issues regularly is to introduce the concept of "couple meetings," and have the couple practice these meetings in sessions and as homework between sessions toward the end of therapy.

In the cognitive-behavioral conjoint model, termination need not be a particularly jarring event for the clients, because of several factors built into the model:

1. The therapist–patient relationship is not the core component of treatment, as it is in more psychoanalytic approaches.
2. The focus of the therapy is on teaching the client and his/her partner skills that ideally, by the end of treatment, come naturally and will remain in both clients' behavior and couple repertoire; thus the couple should feel a decreasing need for continued weekly sessions.
3. The relapse prevention model recommends the use of occasional or regular maintenance sessions on a long-term basis, if necessary.
4. The partners should have learned in the course of treatment to use each other as a resource and as a support system, so that dependence on the therapist to fulfill such a function should have waned as the treatment progressed.
5. At the last session, a relapse contract should be drawn up and signed by both partners, stating explicitly the conditions under which they should seek treatment again or call the therapist for help.

THE ROLE OF THE THERAPIST

Establishing and Fostering a Working Alliance

As with any form of therapy, the therapist's relationship to the couple and the therapeutic stance assumed by the therapist are important. Empathy, active listening, instillation of hope, and establishing a sense that the therapist and couple are working toward mutually agreed-upon goals are essential (Miller, 1985). However, in therapy with alcoholic individuals and their partners, such a stance is sometimes difficult to attain or sustain. By treating a client with a drinking problem along with a partner who wants that client to stop or decrease drinking, the therapist is allied de facto with the nonalcoholic partner. Because of the inherent imbalance in the treatment relationship, the therapist must make particular efforts to ally with the drinker. Developing such an alliance may be difficult for the therapist, both because of the individual's behavior during treatment, and because of the history of drinking-related behaviors that the therapist may find repugnant or upsetting. The client also may lie about or minimize drinking during treatment. To further complicate the therapist's task, the nonalcoholic partner may attempt to enhance his/her alliance with the therapist by echoing the therapist's comments, expressing anger at the alcoholic client's behavior, and being confrontational—or, alternatively, being submissive and allowing the alcoholic partner to be verbally aggressive or dominant.

To handle the difficulties of the inherently imbalanced nature of the therapeutic situation, the therapist uses several techniques. First, the therapist must be able to separate the alcoholic *person* from the person's *actions* in regard to alcohol. The therapist must find aspects of the client as a person that are likable, and begin to form a connection around these characteristics. Second, the therapist needs to validate the perceptions and information provided by each partner. Empathizing with how difficult the alcoholic client finds honesty after having tried to hide his/her drinking from everyone, while also empathizing with the partner's frustration with deceit, communicates that the therapist is concerned with both of their experiences and sees both partners' experiences as valid and worthy of discussion. Third, the therapist must always ally with the goals of the therapy as agreed upon by the couple. Before a formal treatment contract has been developed, the therapist assumes that the implicit therapeutic goals are change in drinking behavior and diminution of problems that have arisen from the drinking. Thus, if the alcoholic partner appears to be lying or minimizing, the therapist can emphasize that lying has probably been adaptive in the past, but that part of therapy will involve learning how to be honest as a way to support change. Or if the nonalcoholic partner is confrontational and hostile, the therapist can reframe anger as an understandable problem that the partner must learn to deal with differently as the alcoholic client changes.

In addition to managing the potentially imbalanced therapeutic relationship, the therapist uses a variety of other techniques to foster a working alliance with the couple. First, the therapist may predict for the couple that new information will emerge during the course of therapy, and these discoveries can be normalized as a positive part of the change process. Such a prediction is intended to reduce hostile confrontations and accusations in the therapy sessions. Second, the therapist defines him-/herself as an expert consultant who has particular knowledge about alcohol, alcohol problems, and ways to change drinking and couple problems, and uses this knowledge to educate the couple. Taking the stance of teacher and consultant (a familiar stance for behavior therapists), the therapist becomes a teacher rather than a person who will judge the rightness or wrongness of either partner's position. To support his/her stance as teacher, the therapist explains that each partner will have to learn a variety of new skills in therapy. Taking a neutral, teaching approach decreases both partners' sense that they are being judged as flawed or pathological.

The therapist also forms an alliance with the couple by making the therapist's expectations for the couple's behavior clear: coming to scheduled sessions on time, calling if unable to attend, paying the bill for therapy, coming in sober, and completing assigned homework. The therapist also makes his/her own commitment to the therapy clear, by being at sessions on time, being reasonably available by telephone, providing coverage when away, and providing treatments with the best empirical support for their effectiveness. Being clear about expectations for therapy behavior emphasizes the therapist's commitment to therapy as a serious process.

Finally, it is important to the treatment to provide encouragement to the couple. Interrupting an alcohol habit and/or physical dependence is quite difficult; there may be several slips or even relapses during treatment; and it is sometimes difficult for the clients and the therapist to remain optimistic about the outcome of treatment. Therapy

sessions can be quite painful for both partners. The therapist needs to be aware of this and to highlight the "bigger picture" to help the clients feel more optimistic at the end of the session. The slow, difficult process of learning to deal with cravings, rearranging one's lifestyle and daily habits, adjusting to a sober relationship, and facing painful issues without the help of alcohol can be overwhelming at times but can be normalized by the therapist. Just as eating right and exercising seem to be the slow but only way to permanent weight loss, therapy is difficult but necessary. It is often enormously helpful to empathize with the clients' occasional feelings of despair and frustration, while at the same time imparting positive expectancies, a sense of normality regarding the struggle, and (most of all) hope.

Use of the Therapist–Client Relationship to Foster Change

Our model of therapy does not view the therapist–client relationship as a central agent of change in any specific or technical sense. Thus we do not foster transference or interpret transferential reactions. However, the therapist's positive relationship with the couple can be used to reinforce positive behavior change. Also, if the therapist has established a good working alliance with the couple, he/she can use that relationship as a vehicle for feedback and confrontation if either partner is being noncompliant. The therapist may also use self-disclosure at times as a way to validate some of the clients' difficult or embarrassing experiences of the clients, or as a way to model active coping with life problems.

As described above, the therapist takes the role of teacher or expert consultant. Working with couples with drinking problems requires the ability to be flexible and to respond to the unexpected. The therapist may be supportive, empathic, and encouraging in one session, and limit-setting and confrontational in the next. In general, the therapist is fairly active and directive, within an overall framework that is client-centered and respectful of the clients' concerns, struggles, and ultimate goals.

Changes in the Therapist's Role during Therapy

As therapy progresses, the therapist may become less directive, fostering the clients' ability to direct their own behavior in the session and to select issues that they see as most important to discuss. The therapist may also use more self-disclosure as therapy progresses. The focus of the therapist gradually shifts from teaching new skills in the therapy session to emphasizing generalization to the natural environment, with the therapist prompting the use of skills learned in the sessions, rather than teaching clients new skills.

Common Therapist Errors

There are several common errors that therapists make in working with alcoholic individuals and their partners. First, therapists may underestimate the complexity of the clients' psychological problems, as well as the importance of the social agencies with which they are involved. The importance of assessing and appropriately treating co-occurring disorders cannot be emphasized enough. If other health care professionals are involved with treatment, it is essential that the clinician confer with these other professionals. If clients are involved with other systems, such as the legal system or child welfare, clinician contact (with appropriate consent) with these agencies is also important to the overall planning and execution of the therapy.

A second common therapeutic error may be one of two different responses to a client's use of other psychoactive drugs: Either the therapist makes an excessively authoritarian pronouncement to the client of the necessity for abstaining from all drugs, or he/she focuses narrowly on the presenting substance of abuse without considering the larger drug use context. Careful assessment of the client's use of other drugs; consideration of the degree to which that use is impairing or potentially impairing the client's functioning; and understanding the functional relationship between alcohol and other drug use are important first steps. Attention to motivational issues related to other drug use then helps the therapist to determine the degree to which the use of other drugs will be a focus of treatment.

A third common error is that therapists may overestimate clients' motivation to change and underestimate their ambivalent feelings about change. We assume that every couple enters treatment with mixed feelings about change. Alcohol is familiar to the couple and has provided many positive experiences in the past, and not drinking requires a new set of unfamiliar skills and experiences. The therapist who ignores this fundamental ambivalence will have difficulty in the therapy. Conversely, clinicians may at times spend too much time on motivational enhancement, not realizing that some of the clients' difficulties in achieving change may be related to skills deficits rather than low motivation.

A fourth common error made by therapists is overestimating the skill level of these couples. Many alcoholic individuals have good verbal skills that cover significant cognitive deficits (resulting from long-term heavy alcohol intake) in abstraction and problem solving (Parsons, Butters, & Nathan, 1987). A therapist may not observe these deficits in the course of a therapy session, and may assume that a client can apply concepts to situations outside the therapy without detailed discussion, explanation, and planning. The more concrete, detailed, and specific the therapist can be, the easier the therapy will be for the drinking individual.

A fifth common therapeutic error occurs when the therapist underestimates the degree of anger or other "lethal" pathology in the couple. In some couples with drinking problems, the partners appear superficially to be committed to each other, but at the same time have a wealth of anger based on years of disappointment, hurt, and vicious interactions. Some such partners begin therapy with a rather positive stance, but after several sessions the degree of the negative feeling between them becomes much more apparent.

A sixth common error occurs when the therapist allows the couple to avoid homework or avoid discussing or dealing with alcohol-related issues. Some couples are highly compliant with homework assignments, but others do not complete assignments, forget the assignments completely, or attempt to avoid discussing them in the treatment session. Since such a pattern of avoidance and lack of follow-through on commitments has often been characteristic of a couple's relationship, allowing the partners to engage in the same behavior in therapy undermines the therapist's credibility, and cheats the couple out of the opportunity to have a different learning experience in therapy.

Finally, as discussed at the beginning of this section on the role of the therapist, a common technical error occurs when the therapist allies with the nonalcoholic partner against the noncompliant alcoholic client. Although this is easy to do, such an alliance probably assures that the therapy will not come to a successful conclusion.

TREATMENT APPLICABILITY AND COMMON OBSTACLES TO TREATMENT

Resistance and Noncompliance

In ABCT, resistance comes in many forms, some more blatant than others. Resistance can be characterized as a conscious or unconscious unwillingness on either partner's part to comply with the components or goals of treatment. In general, the alcoholic individual's resistance stems from ambivalence about giving up drinking and all the positive consequences associated with it. The nonalcoholic partner may be ambivalent about change in the family or couple system that will occur as the alcoholic partner stops drinking. A nonalcoholic partner often assumes more responsibility over time to "keep the family going" as the alcohol interferes more with the drinking individual's abilities to meet family obligations. When the individual first stops drinking, the partner often hesitates to relinquish control of family decisions and caretaking duties— because of either uncertainty that the abstinence will continue and the drinker will be effective and reliable, or perhaps unwillingness to relinquish a level of autonomy that may in fact be very positive in some ways. Both partners may be ambivalent about changing their relationship, because they are used to the current relationship, regardless of how unsatisfying it may be. In a conjoint model of alcoholism treatment, the therapist must be aware of potential resistance not only from the alcoholic individual about sobriety, but also from both partners about relationship change.

Resistance in its more subtle form is minimization of the alcohol problem, often called "denial" in traditional alcoholism treatment. It is not atypical during the initial assessment session to hear some variation of the following: "I don't think I have a drinking problem. My wife said she'd leave me if I didn't come here. So I'm here. But I think it's her problem—she freaks out if the word 'beer' is even mentioned." In response to quantity–frequency questions, this man may reply, "Well, I don't drink every day. I never miss work because of drinking. I drink on weekends [Friday, Saturday, Sunday]. Usually I drink between 6 and 12 [12-ounce] beers a night," or "I only drink two six-packs a day." He may also minimize the negative consequences he has suffered. It is not uncommon for the wife to respond to the husband's minimization with anger and an intense intolerance, even disgust, for any drinking by her husband. Often

the wife's intense reaction further polarizes the couple.

Reduction of minimization usually happens gradually, and the therapist must be aware that confronting an alcoholic client too forcefully can result in treatment dropout. As noted, the act of reporting one's drinking history and negative consequences often facilitates awareness. The therapist can help by gently "lending perspective" with his/her expertise, as in this example:

> "It sounds like, compared to what your brothers and your friends at the bar drink, you don't drink much. But I must tell you that, compared to a wide range of patients I have seen, and based on the severity of the negative consequences you have suffered, I see your drinking as a problem for you. Most people don't drink two six-packs every night after work. Most people come home after work and think about what's for dinner, or what's on TV that night, or what they need to repair around the house, or whether they will go out with their wife to the mall—not how many cold beers there are left in the refrigerator, and how many they can drink before an argument starts between them and their wives. The major reasons I see your alcohol as a problem, though, are that you've have two DWIs in the past 2 years, and alcohol is really affecting the quality of your marriage."

Feedback about the severity of a drinking problem must be imparted in a respectful, didactic manner. The therapist must remain aware of the alcoholic client's ambivalence and convey understanding of the difficulty involved in giving up drinking. The therapist's empathy in the context of limit setting can serve as a role model for the nonalcoholic partner, who also needs to be made aware that becoming sober is a very difficult task.

Resistance of the nonalcoholic partner can manifest itself in various ways. He/she may come in every session with a "couple crisis" that must be dealt with in lieu of focusing on the drinking, or may make comments such as "You can try all you want—he'll give you lip service but he won't follow through. He'll never stop drinking," or otherwise may sabotage the alcoholic client's efforts to change.

Resistance can take the more blatant form of noncompliance with treatment. The most obvious type of noncompliance is unwillingness to attend treatment. Typically, it is the female partner (alcoholic or nonalcoholic) who calls to make a first appointment, and in many cases her next task is to convince the male partner that he needs to attend. Many canceled appointments have been explained similarly: "He won't come. He says he doesn't have a problem," or, "He won't come. He says it's my problem." In these cases, we encourage the woman to have the man call us directly so that we can do a short assessment over the phone, give him some feedback, and describe the program in the hope that he will be less fearful of a treatment session. If the resistant man is the partner with the alcohol problem, we offer the nonalcoholic woman four or five individual sessions to work on strategies for getting her partner into treatment. This approach is somewhat similar to "unilateral marital therapy" for alcoholism (Thomas & Santa, 1982) or the CRAFT model (Miller, Meyers, & Tonigan, 1999), in which the partner of a treatment-refusing alcoholic individual comes to therapy alone and learns skills such as reinforcing sober behavior, ignoring drinking behavior, and not protecting the alcoholic person from negative consequences of drinking (see McCrady, 2001). If the male partner of a female with a drinking problem refuses, we also may see her individually. Other types of noncompliance include refusal to complete homework assignments, frequent cancellations or "no-shows" for therapy sessions, refusal to stop drinking, and dropping out of treatment.

Acute Couple Distress

It is difficult and sometimes irrelevant to proceed calmly through completing a functional analysis and teaching self-management skills when partners are very angry with each other in session. If the couple distress is at a lower level, it is usually best to explain that the first few sessions will be devoted to helping the alcoholic individual become sober, and then couple issues will be dealt with in more detail.

But if the partners are screaming, threatening, or not speaking to each other in session, the couple issues are acute and need to be addressed. The therapist may try several techniques to "bring down the temperature," including very basic communication skills training (e.g., stressing that each partner must let the other finish before speaking, or modeling respectful communication); helping the couple define and refocus on common goals related to the drinking; or setting limits about in-session behavior. The therapist also may consider separate therapy for each partner as an alternative to conjoint therapy if the couple is not able to work together at all to deal with the drinking problem.

As long as the alcoholic individual is sober and not going through withdrawal (which can cause irritability, and in which case the argument can be framed as a direct negative consequence of drinking), negative couple behaviors in session should be managed according to standard cognitive-behavioral couple techniques (e.g., Baucom & Epstein, 1990).

Acute couple distress can be manifested in session as excessive bickering, nasty comments, negative nonverbal behavior, and/or references to separation or divorce. In these cases, the couple problems are too pressing to be deferred until treatment of alcohol problems is underway. The therapist can choose to spend the first half of the session exploring couple issues and then make an explicit shift to the alcohol problem. This approach should be announced beforehand:

> "You two are so mad at each other today, you won't be able to hear what I have to say about alcohol. But I think it's important that we discuss the alcohol problem, and I have some very important skills to introduce to you today. So let's spend the first half of the session—say, 45 minutes—on discussing what's bothering you both, and then we'll switch to talk about alcohol for the second half."

Similarly, if either partner reports physical violence at home, this must be the first topic addressed. The therapist must first determine whether conjoint therapy is appropriate—an assessment that should be conducted privately with each partner. If the alcoholic individual is motivated to stop drinking, the violence has occurred only during drinking episodes, and the nonabusive partner is not concerned about retribution for topics discussed in conjoint therapy, then couple therapy can be considered. If the violence occurs separate from the drinking, or the drinking partner is not motivated to stop, or the nonabusive partner expresses concerns about personal safety, conjoint therapy is contraindicated.

Even if the therapist and couple decide to proceed with couple therapy, a basic safety plan should be developed for the abused partner, and an agreement should be made to remove weapons from the home. A cognitive-behavioral treatment model of domestic violence (see Holtzworth-Munroe, Beatty, & Anglin, 1995, and Holtzworth-Munroe, Meehan, Rehman, & Marshall, Chapter 16, this volume) can be used, taking into account that in most cases, intoxication will be a primary "high-risk" situation for the violence. Often domestic violence can be framed as an intense negative consequence for the alcoholic man who abuses his partner when intoxicated. He typically feels very guilty afterward, and finds his loss of control repugnant. Unfortunately, domestic violence is often the negative consequence that finally brings the couple in for treatment.

Multiple-Drug Use

Figures on comorbid drug abuse in alcoholic populations hover around 50% for males (Ross, Glaser, & Stiasny, 1988; Hesselbrock, Meyer, & Keener, 1985) and 40% for females (Gomberg, 1999). Thus clients who come for conjoint therapy of alcoholism must be evaluated carefully for other drug abuse. Polydrug use can complicate the therapy model in several ways:

1. Abstinence from alcohol may result in clients' seeking new drugs to cope, leading to increases in their use of other drugs. New problems relating to the other drugs may then be created, such as excessive money spent on cocaine.

2. It may be difficult to link negative consequences specifically to either alcohol or other drugs.

3. Different measures may need to be taken to wean the client off different drugs. For example, outpatient detoxification may suffice for the alcohol problem, but the client may require hospitalization to withdraw from benzodiazepines.

4. Using other drugs may create "high-risk situations" for alcohol use.

5. A client does not experience and adjust to a "drug-free lifestyle" if abstinent from alcohol but using other drugs. There remains a place in his/her daily lifestyle for substance use, which could result more readily in a relapse to alcohol use.

6. Couple issues are complicated by polydrug use. For example, a nonalcoholic wife may object to alcohol, but not to her husband's smoking two or three joints every day. In fact, she may join her husband in smoking pot or using cocaine occasionally. It becomes difficult for the therapist and the spouse to set limits when the limits of what is acceptable and what is not are unclear.

For the aforementioned reasons, it is typically better to address all drugs of abuse, not just the ones either partner dislikes. Strategies for dealing with polydrug use vary, depending on the nature of each substance and its negative consequences. For instance, the client can keep a separate self-recording card for each substance and monitor urges separately. In some cases, it may be prudent to treat the more disruptive substance problem first, and then address other substances. For instance, one client reported that he had urges to use cocaine only after drinking a certain number of beers. After achieving abstinence from alcohol, he still used cocaine, and in fact began to use it more often. Attention was turned to control of his cocaine problem, separate from his alcohol use. In general, the conjoint model can be modified to handle polydrug use. This requires, however, that the therapist be knowledgeable about effects, dosages, withdrawal symptoms, and treatment of a wide range of substances.

The ABCT model does not translate seamlessly into treatments for current drug-dependent populations, and thus must be modified to deal with characteristics of primary drug-dependent samples. These drug-dependent samples generally have more severe problems in multiple life areas (legal, occupational, financial, etc.), polysubstance abuse, comorbid psychiatric disorders, and poor education (Moras, 1993).

Other factors must be considered that may require modification of the ABCT model's theoretical and clinical aspects when the model is applied to drug abuse. For instance, the social context of illicit drug acquisition and use is different from that of alcohol, which is a legal substance and easily available in liquor stores and bars. Thus the potential negative consequences of drug use for an individual's family may be even more serious than those of alcoholism. Partners and children are put at much higher risk by a person's involvement in the illegal activities necessary to obtain and use drugs, including loss of employment, danger in dealing with other drug users and dealers, higher risk for AIDS, and incarceration. This may result in even more secretive behavior by the individual using drugs, more damage to the couple relationship and to the trust of the nonusing partner, and less willingness of the nonusing partner to tolerate involvement with the partner who uses drugs. The couple's lifestyle may be affected more drastically by cessation of drug use than of alcohol misuse, if the person using drugs has been either spending a great deal of money to obtain drugs or earning money by dealing drugs. Discriminative stimuli for drug use may be more distinctive and salient than for alcohol use, including drug paraphernalia (cocaine vials, syringes, etc.). Since certain drugs have a higher reinforcement value than alcohol, high-salience reinforcers for abstinence must be considered.

Clinically, the nonusing partner may play a smaller role in drug refusal, and may be less involved in general in the system of antecedents and consequences of drug use. The nonusing partner may also be more angry and fearful, and less committed to the relationship, than a partner of an alcoholic individual. Couple relationships in drug abuse may be different from those in alcoholism, in terms of stability, commitment, and behavioral and verbal interaction.

Other Comorbid Psychopathology

As noted, research has shown that high percentages of alcoholic individuals have other psychiatric problems that either are concurrent with, antecedent to, or resulting from their alcohol problems. Rates of psychopathology among persons with alcoholism are much greater than in the general population, and thus have several implications for treatment. In the context of the conjoint model, this means that assessment should include screening for other Axis I and Axis II disorders. Diagnosing depression, anxiety disorders, and ASPD can be problematic in an alcoholic patient, because several of the symptoms and consequences of alcohol misuse mimic those of other disorders, and vice versa. For instance, withdrawal from heavy alcohol use can result in anxiety, irritability, sleeplessness, and/or depression—all of which are symptoms of other disorders. The therapist should be careful to assess the primary or secondary nature of the comorbid psychopathology before deciding whether separate treatment is necessary. Just as couple issues emerge when the "smoke screen" of alcohol and its withdrawal symptoms begins to lift, so may the true nature of depressive or anxious symptoms. Of course, if depression is extremely severe at any point during treatment, the client should be treated or referred for treatment for the depression through psychotherapy, medication, and/or hospitalization. In severe cases, the depression may preclude further work on alcohol-related and couple issues, which can resume after the depression is treated. If the depression does not warrant such immediate action, it should nonetheless be monitored closely. If the alcoholic client stays depressed for several weeks after becoming abstinent, if the depression worsens, or if the client reports a history of depression that is antecedent to alcohol abuse or occurred during a long period of abstinence, depression should at the very least be assessed as a separate disorder. Likewise, anxiety symptoms that do not abate or that get worse with treatment of alcohol problems indicate

that the patient may have a comorbid anxiety disorder and may have been "self-medicating" the anxiety with alcohol.

Axis II disorders in general, and ASPD in particular, have been shown to negatively affect the course of alcoholism and response to treatment (Rounsaville, Dolinsky, Babor, & Meyer, 1987; Yates, Petty, & Brown, 1988). Since a hallmark of ASPD is a history of unstable relationships, it is unlikely that many persons in their 20s with ASPD will seek couple treatment for alcoholism; most people with ASPD in that age range are not married or are not invested enough in their relationships to attempt to solve couple problems. It is more common for an older person with ASPD (past age 35) to come to treatment with a partner (often, for a man, his second or third wife) for treatment. It is, however, quite complicated and difficult to treat even older clients with ASPD. Often their relationships are still markedly unstable. They are more likely to have severe polydrug abuse and/or gambling problems, and couple issues centering around trust are intensified. Although some studies have reported better outcomes for clients with ASPD than for those without it (Longabaugh et al., 1994), most research suggests that clients with ASPD are less likely to remain in treatment, demonstrate tolerance for the negative affect that is usually involved in therapy, or have a positive outcome. Patient–treatment matching research provides mixed data about treatment approaches for ASPD. Earlier research suggested that a skills training approach might be best suited for a population with ASPD and alcoholism (Kadden, Cooney, Getter, & Litt, 1989), but a later multisite study did not support these earlier findings (Project MATCH Research Group, 1998). Specific patient–treatment matching research related to conjoint treatment suggests that individuals with ASPD may respond better to individual than to relationship-focused treatment (Longabaugh et al., 1994). It may also be that external coercion or other "external" measures, such as the use of disulfiram (Antabuse), are more effective for these patients. More research is necessary to determine whether this is indeed so.

When Both Partners Have a Drinking Problem

The conjoint model can be modified to allow treatment of both partners. Such treatment, however, may necessitate a longer therapy program than described previously, because cognitive-behavioral skills will have to be covered for both partners' drinking patterns. The partners will almost certainly benefit from sharing and watching each other go through the learning experience; from learning the additional couple skills of reinforcing sobriety, eliminating partner-related triggers, and so on, and from the couple skills training aspects of the therapy. Also, other issues may need to be addressed. These may include possible differences in level of motivation for sobriety; the development of support systems for abstinence outside the couple relationship; subsequent differences in the partners' level of support for each other; and difficulty in both giving support to and receiving it from a partner while trying to curb one's own abusive drinking or drug use.

Alternately, a couple may present with one partner identified as having the alcohol problem, but the therapist may conclude after assessment that both partners have an alcohol problem. In fact, many couples tend to drink together; alcoholic women presenting for treatment are especially likely to have partners who drink heavily. In our clinic, due to the research aspects, we assess both partners in a couple but treat only the "identified patient." If we determine that the other partner has a drinking problem, we attempt to refer this partner for his/her own drinking-related treatment. Many such individuals who participate in our program prefer not to seek treatment themselves, but may cut down or stop drinking during the course of their partners' alcohol treatment. Some change their own drinking behavior in support of their partners in treatment. Others learn a great deal about drinking, strategies to stop, and even their own drinking patterns in the course of attending treatment with the "identified patients."

LIMITATIONS AND CONTRAINDICATIONS

Limitations

ABCT was developed as an outpatient treatment model, and has been used successfully as a stand-alone treatment. However, sometimes the alcoholic client (or the other partner) requires a higher level of care, and ABCT should be either suspended if the client is not improving, or presented as an aftercare option after more intensive treatment. For instance, if an alcoholic client simply is not having success in stopping or substantially decreasing drinking by perhaps the fifth session, it may be

wise to consider more intensive treatment. If either partner presents with a worsening depression or increased use of other drugs, it may be advisable to refer him/her to a psychiatric unit, a residential or intensive outpatient substance abuse treatment program, or (if need be) a dual-diagnosis treatment program.

A different kind of limitation of ABCT involves the complicated nature of the cases seen and the need to focus on so many levels of treatment. The limitation here is not insurmountable, but it requires the therapist to set treatment priorities and try systematically to address each set of treatment issues. Such a couple often presents with severe relationship discord—enough to keep any therapist quite busy for many sessions—yet the conjoint therapist must handle the additional, not insignificant, problem of alcoholism.

Several factors can render what seems an overwhelmingly complicated case manageable:

1. The therapist should use good diagnostic tools at the start, so that he/she is more knowledgeable about and prepared for potential complications.

2. The therapist should have at his/her disposal an excellent referral network. This should include local detoxification centers and rehabilitation programs; physicians who have expertise in the addictions and can supervise an outpatient detoxification or a course of Antabuse or naltrexone therapy; and therapists and psychiatrists with special expertise in the addictions, who are available to handle referrals for individual therapy or medication consultations.

3. The therapist needs to know when to make use of the referral network. That is, he/she needs to be aware of the limitations of the conjoint model, and to know when to supplement the treatment with other interventions.

4. The therapist should have a good support network of colleagues with whom to consult and from whom to obtain support in dealing with these complicated couples.

Indications and Contraindications

ABCT is most appropriate for clients who have a stable relationship in which the nonalcoholic partner is willing to be involved in treatment and can function in a supportive manner in the early phases of treatment. Additional factors suggested as positive indicators for conjoint therapy are these: (1) clients who have a high school education or better, are employed, and are still living together; and (2) clients whose drinking problems are serious and of longer duration (O'Farrell & Fals-Stewart, 1999). Couples that have experienced severe domestic violence, couples where there is a court-issued restraining order, couples with severe individual psychopathology, and couples in which one partner's commitment to the relationship is highly ambivalent are less appropriate for couple therapy (O'Farrell & Fals-Stewart, 1999). Preliminary research also suggests that couples with very severe relationship problems may be noncompliant with conjoint treatment, and may drink more frequently or intensively during treatment (McCrady & Epstein, 2000).

CASE ILLUSTRATION

The case described here is a fictional composite of several patients who were part of a treatment research program, in which the assessment and treatment are manual-based and standardized across clients. In other treatment settings where research is not involved, the therapist is freer to pick and choose among assessment tools, order of administration of therapy interventions and so on. Thus the reader is encouraged to view this case study as a "generic treatment plan" that a therapist can modify and individualize for each couple as necessary.

Identifying Information and Presenting Problem

Heidi, aged 38, and Bob, aged 42, had been married for 9 years and had dated for 2 years prior. It was Heidi's first marriage and Bob's second. Bob had been married previously from ages 24 to 30, and had a 13-year-old son, Shawn, who visited Bob and Heidi every other weekend and came over one evening a week for dinner. Heidi and Bob had two daughters, Bridget, aged 7, and Toby, aged 3. Heidi had a bachelor's degree and had worked as a research assistant in a medical school setting for several years. Bridget was born when Heidi was 31; at that time, Heidi left her job to be a full-time homemaker. Bob had a degree in chemistry and worked full-time as a sales representative for a large pharmaceutical company. For his job, Bob traveled frequently (approximately two times per month for 2 to 3 days each time). Bridget was in second grade, leaving home at 8:30 A.M. and returning home at 4:00. Toby had started preschool at age 2 and was currently attending 5 days per week from 10:00 to 3:00.

Heidi had seen an ad for our program in a local newspaper and had called a year earlier to inquire about the program, but she decided at that time not to participate. When she called a year later, she said she felt ready to try our program. In the interim, she had tried to stop drinking on her own by attending a few AA meetings. She did cut back on her drinking and even stopped completely for 1 month, but then relapsed back to her old daily drinking pattern. She was finding it difficult to stop again, though she had been able to cut down on the quantity she drank each day over the past month. Heidi said that she hadn't asked Bob whether he would come to treatment with her (a requirement of participating in our program) when she first saw the ad, because she assumed he was too busy with his work and wouldn't have time or interest. Over the year, however, as her drinking decreased and then worsened again, Bob sought advice from a psychiatrist he knew professionally, and then attended three Al-Anon meetings. Bob began to express his concern and anger to Heidi, and when she told him about the women's couple program, he readily agreed to attend with her. Heidi maintained that their relationship "had its ups and downs," but that she loved her husband and "would do what it took to stay together." Bob was more ambivalent; he expressed love for Heidi and a desire to keep the family together, but became tearful during the intake interview while talking about his anger and frustration over the past year, his worry about his children, and his concern for Heidi. He said that her drinking had gotten steadily worse over the past 7 years; it wasn't until the past 2 years that he'd fully realized how much and how often she drank, and how it was affecting the kids. He also said that the past year had clarified a lot for him, as he saw Heidi struggle to stop drinking, the improved functioning of the entire household during the month she stopped, and her return to drinking. Heidi sat in stunned silence during much of the time Bob spoke during the intake interview; she was unaware that Bob had noticed so much or worried so about her drinking and the situation at home. The two had not talked about the drinking much, except for several angry interchanges at the height of Heidi's drinking career.

Assessment

Heidi and Bob underwent an extensive (4-hour) evaluation, which is a routine part of our research/ treatment program. The assessment focused on diagnosis, history, and severity of the alcohol problem; alcohol consumption over the prior 90 days; negative consequences of alcohol use over the past 6 months; and spouse coping. Marital functioning was assessed in terms of marital satisfaction, communication, power balance in the relationship, satisfaction with the sexual relationship, and conflict resolution. General psychosocial functioning was also assessed, as was Heidi's degree of social support for abstinence and drinking. Her family history of alcohol problems was assessed, as well as Heidi's intentions to change drinking behavior and motivation to stop drinking. The information was obtained during two clinical interviews that Heidi and Bob attended together; both semistructured interview protocols and self-report questionnaires were used.

At the start of the first meeting, as would be the case before every meeting thereafter, the clinician (EEE) administered a Breathalyzer test to Heidi to ascertain that her blood alcohol level was below 0.05 mg%. While preparing to administer the test, the therapist asked Heidi whether she was familiar with the test, and went on to explain the rationale behind its administration. Heidi and Bob were told that clinicians in our program routinely administer the breath test to ensure that a client is sober, because intoxication makes it difficult to think clearly and benefit fully from the evaluation and therapy sessions. The therapist informed Heidi that any session at which she arrived with an elevated blood alcohol level would need to be rescheduled. The Breathalyzer test, when explained in this respectful and positive light, serves both to educate clients and to model clear, reasonable limit setting. Rather than being insulted by the breath test procedure, most clients seem to appreciate it if it is explained fully and administered consistently. For clients who have a drug problem as well, we use on-site test cups to test for the presence of five different drug classes—morphine (opiates), tetrahydrocannabinol (THC, cannabis), cocaine, amphetamines, and phencyclidine (PCP)—as well as urine sticks to test for benzodiazepines and barbiturates. Results are apparent within 4 minutes, so a positive test can be treated as a clinical issue or used as part of clinical intervention such as behavioral contracting, there in the session.

Heidi's blood alcohol level was 0 at her initial interview, so the therapist began to evaluate the presenting problem by asking first Heidi and then Bob what led them to seek treatment at this time, how they each perceived the drinking problem, how the problem affected them, and whether there were any other personal problems that concerned them. The therapist also inquired about Heidi's family history for alcoholism (her mother and brother both had drinking problems), and then asked some general questions about frequency, quantity, and types of alcohol currently used by Heidi. Heidi said that she drank heavily in college and in her early 20s, but then cut back and drank socially for years. She did not drink during her first pregnancy. After her first child was born, Heidi suffered postpartum depression for 7 months and was treated with imipramine. During this period Heidi got into the habit of drinking a glass or two of wine in the evening after the baby was put to bed, before Bob came home from work. When Bob came home, he and Heidi would sit together and have a glass of wine two or three evenings a week. Heidi's psychiatrist had suggested that Heidi retain a standing babysitter for Saturday nights in order to get out at least once a week, since Heidi spent most of her time during the week at home with the baby. Thus on Saturday nights Heidi and Bob would typically go out to dinner and then a club, and Heidi would consume about three vodka martinis and one after-dinner drink. This drinking pattern persisted for 4 years, with a break during Heidi's second pregnancy, during which she drank only an occasional glass of wine. After Toby was born, Heidi again suffered postpartum depression, but this time she sought treatment earlier and the depression lifted after only 4 months. However, Heidi's drinking increased during these 4 months, and it had remained at this elevated level until recently. At about the time Toby was born, Bob received a promotion at work, resulting in even longer hours and more travel. The new position as a pharmaceutical marketing consultant also required that Bob entertain potential clients quite often; this took him out of the house at least one night a week. Bob had to plan and attend events involving buffets with open bars, trips to concerts and plays in a liquor-stocked limousine, and so on. Heidi was expected to accompany Bob on many of these occasions, primarily on weekends. As a "drug rep's wife," Heidi felt obligated to help her husband entertain his clients.

After the first assessment session, the therapist already had a good sense of Heidi's drinking pattern and alcohol consumption, as well as a general idea of her triggers (to use later in a functional analysis of her drinking). Heidi had, for the first time, talked in front of Bob about how much she had been drinking; to her surprise, Bob was reacting in a much more supportive way than she had anticipated.

The two initial clinical interviews with any couple are quite comprehensive, as we assess presenting problem, family history, motivation for changing behavior, lifetime and recent alcohol and drug use and diagnoses, other psychopathology, mental status, and marital functioning including domestic violence. From the interview and the Michigan Alcoholism Screening Test (Selzer, 1971), the therapist learned that Heidi had a relatively severe alcohol problem, as determined by the number of negative consequences she had experienced in her lifetime as a result of alcohol use: blackouts, Bob's complaints about her drinking, inability to stop drinking, feeling bad about drinking, and not feeling that she was a "normal drinker." According to the Substance Use Disorders Module of the Structured Clinical Interview for DSM-IV (SCID; Spitzer, Williams, Gibbon, & First, 1996), Heidi met DSM-IV criteria for alcohol dependence with physiological dependence. She met criteria for symptoms of loss of control over alcohol, withdrawal, tolerance, spending substantial time drinking or being intoxicated, repeated efforts to cut down, and not fulfilling obligations. Age of onset was determined to be 21, when Heidi graduated from college and drank almost daily with her friends at night for a 2-year period. Her alcohol dependence then was in sustained partial remission until age 32, after the birth of her first child. Heidi's first independent drink was at age 15, at a high school party at her friend's house. At that time Heidi drank beer, and reported "feeling no pain" until she "fell asleep."

As part of the assessment for our research/treatment study, we also assess the impact of the partner's drinking habits on the "identified patient." According to the SCID, Bob also qualified for a diagnosis of alcohol dependence with physiological dependence. Bob's drinking was not daily, but was quite frequent and typically occurred in contexts of entertaining clients or drinking wine with Heidi. He did sometimes experience loss of control over drinking, tolerance, and substantial time being intoxicated. This interview was administered to Bob in a straightforward and matter-of-fact way, with the explanation that clinicians in our program routinely ask these questions of the partner. Feedback regarding his diagnosis was not given, since he was not the "identified patient." The therapist noted that his drinking probably had an important influence on Heidi's own drinking pattern, and that dealing with spouse-related triggers for Heidi's drinking would be a necessary part of the treatment. The therapist also planned to incorporate motivational interviewing as the therapy progressed, to help Bob change his own drinking behavior or at least seek treatment himself.

At the initial interview, each partner completed the Modified Conflict Tactics Scale (Pan, Neidig, & O'Leary, 1994), and the therapist spent some time individually with each partner to query about any history of violence in the home, whether it was secondary to substance abuse, and whether each partner felt safe in couple therapy. If individual therapy was indicated because moderate to severe physical violence occurred even in the absence of intoxication, or because either partner felt unsafe in couple therapy, the couple would have been referred appropriately. In Heidi's case, there was no history of moderate or severe physical violence in the home. In the last 12 months, however, Heidi had thrown objects in the house when intoxicated, and once she had tried to push Bob out of the way as she was attempting to leave the house when intoxicated.

We assess other life problems by directly asking the clients whether they have concerns about other areas of life functioning. The clinician can also draw from a wide variety of structured measures to assess life problems separate from drinking or drug use, including simple problem checklists and formal interviews.

After establishing that Heidi had had no extended period of abstinence during the preceding 3-month period, it was fairly easy to estimate Heidi's alcohol intake, both from the clinical interview and from the Timeline Followback Interview (TLFB; Sobell, Maisto, Sobell, Cooper, & Saunders, 1980). She drank approximately five standard drinks 6 days a week, and nine standard drinks on Saturday nights, by her self-report. It was estimated that Heidi had accompanied Bob to three company events over the past 3 months (a concert and two open-bar cocktail receptions), and had consumed approximately nine standard drinks on those nights.

Bob was seen separately from Heidi, to obtain his account of her drinking and his description of his own drinking as well (using the TLFB). Bob thought that on one or two weekdays Heidi began drinking earlier in the day than she had reported, perhaps 4:00 P.M., and on these days drank a mixed drink or two in addition to the wine she typically had. Bob's reasons for this belief were Heidi's passing out on the couch and her "extra-slurred voice" on the phone. Bob also told the clinician that he was embarrassed to report this, but that he had been finding empty pint bottles of vodka hidden in garbage bags in the basement, and in the cabinet under the sink. At one point he found himself sifting through the garbage can in the kitchen and found an empty whiskey sour mix. The information obtained in this interview would be important for later use for a motivational intervention, and also in developing a functional analysis of Heidi's drinking behavior. Heidi was surprised to realize, during the course of the interview, how consistent and predictable her drinking pattern really was.

In addition to assessment of the alcohol problem, the therapist began to evaluate the marital relationship. From the initial interview, the therapist developed a sense of how Heidi's drinking affected the relationship, and also began to develop ideas about Bob's contribution to the drinking problem. Moreover, the therapist was able to observe the couple interact during the interview and began to formulate hypotheses about the quality of the marital relationship. It is important in any assessment to establish which couple problems seem directly related to the alcohol problem, and which are likely to persist after abstinence is attained.

Heidi and Bob completed self-report questionnaires designed to assess marital satisfaction and content areas in which they wanted behavior change from each other, including the Dyadic Adjustment Scale (Spanier, 1976), and the Areas of Change Questionnaire (Margolin, Talovic, & Weinstein, 1983). The therapist noticed that both Bob and Heidi indicated that they agreed more often than not on major marital issues; that they were "moderately happy" (Bob) and "happy" (Heidi) with their relationship; and that they wanted very much for their relationship to succeed. However, the therapist identified several areas in which one partner wanted behavior change from the other. These areas had to do with engagement in the relationship and communication, and pointed to a need in therapy to enhance interactive behavior and reduce conflict in the relationship.

From these two extended evaluation sessions, the therapist knew a great deal about Heidi and Bob even before therapy began. She had information about Heidi's drinking history and the parameters of her current problem; the initial information about alcohol's effects on her marriage; data on Bob's perception of, and his contribution to, the drinking problem; and information regarding the status of Heidi and Bob's marital satisfaction and commitment. The therapist could proceed to the first therapy session, using these data as the groundwork for further analyzing Heidi's drinking behavior and for teaching both spouses how to change destructive habits contributing to her alcohol intake. In addition, the therapeutic process had already begun—with Heidi's self-disclosure; Bob's relief at their seeking help together and the opportunity to model the therapist's calm, reasonable limit setting; and the development of rapport between the couple and the therapist.

Assessing the Need for Detoxification and Determining Level of Care

Based on the intake information, the therapist determined that ABCT would be appropriate for Heidi and Bob, but that Heidi was at risk for serious withdrawal symptoms if she stopped drinking suddenly, and would be a good candidate for detoxification before beginning outpatient treatment. When she had tried to stop drinking in the past year, she had experienced some minor withdrawal symptoms (including shaking, irritability, nausea, and sweating) for the first 4 days following cessation of drinking, as well as difficulty sleeping for the entire month she was abstinent. She reported no history of major withdrawal symptoms, such as hallucinations and seizures. Since she was a daily drinker of fairly high quantities and because she had experienced withdrawal symptoms in the past, the therapist recommended that she undergo some form of detoxification before beginning ABCT. Options available to her were reviewed, including a 2- to 5-day inpatient stay, or an outpatient detoxification. The therapist did not insist on an inpatient stay, because Heidi had no history of major withdrawal symptoms, no medical problems and no family history of seizures or stroke.

Heidi was resistant to any form of detoxification, saying that she could get through it herself. She was unwilling to go to an inpatient facility away from her children, and she said she didn't want to be medicated, or to see another doctor and tell him/her the whole story again. The therapist then advised her not to stop drinking "cold turkey," but instead to cut down on her drinking gradually. She was told to start measuring her drinks and drink one standard drink less every 2–3 days. Heidi was instructed to write in her calendar book what she was to drink each day. They planned to review Heidi's progress at the first therapy session and plan for her quit date. Or, her therapist said, Heidi could simply wait until the first therapy session to devise an abstinence plan, but she should not stop drinking suddenly before that. Heidi said she would try to cut down gradually by herself.

Therapy Sessions 1–4: Motivational Techniques, Analysis of the Drinking Pattern, and Attaining Abstinence

The first four therapy sessions focused on continuing to develop rapport, enhancing motivation to change, functional analysis of the drinking pattern, and early sobriety strategies such as developing an abstinence plan, stimulus control, and learning to deal with cravings (see McCrady, 2001, for a more detailed review of early session strategies).

In Heidi's case, she was in the "action stage" on the continuum of readiness for change (Prochaska et al., 1992; Yahne & Miller, 1999). This meant that she was highly motivated to change her drinking behavior and was aware of several negative consequences of her drinking. Thus, since Heidi presented as determined to become and remain abstinent but needed to learn the skills, the therapist did not need to use too much time for motivational enhancement techniques. However, two important motivational interventions were done. First, her therapist summarized information obtained in the first two evaluation sessions, highlighting the drinking pattern observed thus far, as well as the positive and negative consequences of Heidi's drinking on several areas of her life. The therapist also was careful to summarize her understanding of the effect of Heidi's drinking on her marriage and family, in order to reinforce and maintain Heidi's strong motivation for abstinence.

Toward the end of the first session, the therapist introduced self-monitoring to the couple. Heidi was instructed to monitor on a daily basis the frequency and intensity of her urges to drink, the number of drinks consumed, and her daily marital satisfaction. Bob kept records of his daily estimate of Heidi's alcohol consumption and intensity of her urges, along with his daily marital satisfaction. Bob proved to be remarkably accurate in his estimations of Heidi's urges, which underscored the potential for him to be a supportive "coach" to help Heidi fight the urges. Heidi was surprised at how tuned in Bob was to her urges, and felt gratified that perhaps he had paid more attention to her than she understood all along.

Thus the first session, covering an introduction and rationale for couple treatment, motivational enhancement, and abstinence plan, was completed. Over the following three sessions, some basic early sobriety strategies were covered, as well as more motivational enhancement techniques. The abstinence plan was enforced and modified each week, based on Heidi's success with it.

In the second session, the therapist continued to maintain some focus on motivation by having Heidi complete a decisional balance sheet to examine positive and negative consequences of abstinence versus continued drinking. On her Decisional Matrix (Marlatt & Gordon, 1985; McCrady, 2001), Heidi listed (1) positive consequences of drinking (relaxing by herself after devoting all day to the kids, socializing with Bob, "feeling young again," enjoying the taste of wine, socializing more easily with Bob's clients, and the initial feeling of euphoria); (2) negative consequences of drinking (letting herself down, arguing with Bob, needing to lie to Bob, hating the feeling of loss of control over the drinking, health consequences, not being a good mother, possibly losing the kids, Division of Youth and Family Services [DYFS] involvement if things got worse); (3) positive consequences of quitting drinking (feeling proud of herself, feeling closer to Bob, being a better mother, the kids' being better off, no fear of losing her family, long-term health benefits); and (4) negative consequences of quitting drinking (difficulty relaxing, no more feeling high, feeling shy at social gatherings, effort needed to fight cravings, no more happy drinking time with Bob). It was important for Heidi to identify positive aspects of her drinking, so that she could begin to think about alternative ways to attain the positive things alcohol did for her. For Heidi, the negative consequences of drinking were much more damaging and dangerous than the short-term positive consequences.

Functional analysis began with an assignment for Heidi and Bob separately to fill out the Drinking Patterns Questionnaire (Zitter & McCrady, 1979). This was used in the second session to help identify all the triggers and "high-risk situations" (Marlatt & Gordon, 1985) to which Heidi responded by drinking. Further information about drinking triggers came from her daily cards on which she recorded drinks and urges to drink. The therapist explained a "drinking chain" (the stimulus–organism–response–consequences or S-O-R-C analysis of drinking) as a learned sequence of events. (See Figure 23.1 for an S-O-R-C analysis of three drinking-related situations for Heidi.) In session Heidi made a list of all of her triggers, broken down into categories: environmental, interpersonal, physiological, emotional, and cognitive. She then ranked them in a "high-risk hierarchy" as most to least difficult to deal with on a scale of 100 to 1.

Analysis of Heidi's drinking pattern revealed four major high-risk situations:

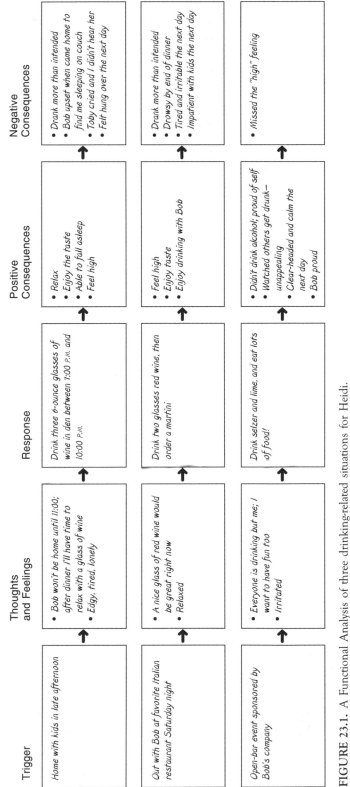

Trigger

Thoughts and Feelings

Response

Positive Consequences

Negative Consequences

Home with kids in late afternoon

- Bob won't be home until 11:00; after dinner I'll have time to relax with a glass of wine
- Edgy, tired, lonely

Drink three 6-ounce glasses of wine in den between 7:00 P.M. and 10:00 P.M.

- Relax
- Enjoy the taste
- Able to fall asleep
- Feel high

- Drank more than intended
- Bob upset when came home to find me sleeping on couch
- Toby cried and I didn't hear her
- Felt hung over the next day

Out with Bob at favorite Italian restaurant Saturday night

- A nice glass of red wine would be great right now
- Relaxed

Drink two glasses red wine, then order a martini

- Feel high
- Enjoy taste
- Enjoy drinking with Bob

- Drank more than intended
- Drowsy by end of dinner
- Tired and irritable the next day
- Impatient with kids the next day

Open-bar event sponsored by Bob's company

- Everyone is drinking but me; I want to have fun too
- Irritated

Drink seltzer and lime, and eat lots of food!

- Didn't drink alcohol; proud of self
- Watched others get drunk—unappealing
- Clear-headed and calm the next day
- Bob proud

- Missed the "high" feeling

FIGURE 23.1. A Functional Analysis of three drinking-related situations for Heidi.

1. *Home alone with the girls in the late afternoon and evening.* Heidi would usually wait until they went to sleep and then sit with a glass of wine in her den. Or she would have a glass of wine or a mixed drink while cooking dinner, as the girls played or watched TV.

2. *At night after Bob got home from work.* Heidi would sit with him during dinner and have a glass of wine while he ate, and then they would each have a glass in the den.

3. *At restaurants with Bob on Saturday nights.*

4. *At Bob's work-related events on weekends, when Heidi would help him host his clients.* Here were temptations such as open-bar buffets, limousine rides to concerts with unlimited beverage service, and so forth, as noted earlier.

Three of the four major triggers listed were spouse-related triggers. When these were reviewed more specifically, the therapist reiterated the notion that Heidi was personally responsible for her drinking and that Bob was not to blame for her drinking. Another, subtler spouse-related trigger was Bob's silence regarding his feelings about Heidi's drinking. He admitted in therapy that he was usually at a loss when it came to Heidi's drinking. Up until the last 2 years he didn't think too much about it, and then he began to see that she was often different when she drank. He said that some nights by the time he got home, she was irritable and talkative—more likely to complain about the late hour or about how lonely she had been that day. Over the past year, he said, she was even a bit obnoxious sometimes at the company events; she would talk loudly to clients or laugh too much. Once she almost fell asleep at the dinner table; that week Bob went to an Al-Anon meeting during his lunch break. He tried to talk to her about her drinking a few times, but she would fly off the handle and start screaming at him, so he stopped bringing it up. Thus he had a strong reaction to the fact that three of four of Heidi's high-risk situations were related to him.

Given that Heidi had attended AA in the past and Bob had gone to Al-Anon, the therapist also brought up AA and Al-Anon attendance. Discussion of Heidi's attitude toward AA revealed that she preferred to use the skills training approach offered at our clinic, because she had tried AA in the past and had found it helpful but not sufficient. As a rather shy person, Heidi felt uncomfortable in the group and found it difficult to open up there. The therapist encouraged her to reconsider AA, and suggested that she and Bob go to a meeting together, perhaps a couple meeting. The therapist thought

that Heidi might benefit from the availability of the meetings, from contact with a sponsor with whom she could discuss her urges, and especially from a "sober network" of friends to see or talk to during the day. The therapist also reinforced the value of Al-Anon for Bob, since attending a few meetings in the past year had helped him view Heidi's drinking more objectively. Bob and Heidi had both felt out of place at meetings and were hesitant to try again. The therapist did not insist, but did from time to time in subsequent sessions bring up the possible value of AA and Al-Anon.

By the fifth session, Heidi had carried out her abstinence plan. After the second session, she followed a plan that she would drink just two drinks per day all week; at the third session, she decided to go down to one glass of wine a day for 3 days and then stop drinking altogether. She came to the fourth session triumphantly reporting that she had skipped the 3 days of one drink and just stopped drinking the day after the last session. She said it was harder to keep room in her life for that one drink than it was just to stop. She reported that she was still having strong urges to drink every day in the late afternoon, but that they seemed to be getting less frequent, except on the nights when Bob was traveling. The couple hadn't gone out alone or to a work-related function on Saturday nights, so Heidi had not had to deal with these two particularly high-risk situations. One weekend night Bob went to a company function alone; on two Saturdays they canceled the babysitter and took the kids to an amusement park; and on one Saturday they stayed home, had Heidi's sister and brother-in-law over for a barbecue, and didn't serve any alcohol. Heidi told her sister what was happening in treatment, and that helped her stay sober. She reported having some withdrawal symptoms during the first couple of weeks, such as irritability, some nausea, some shakiness the first few days, and depression. In fact, at the third session Heidi was quite irritable and had difficulty speaking to Bob without snapping at him. The therapist reframed her behavior as reflecting withdrawal symptoms and assured them that it would pass in a week or two. After the third session Heidi began complaining of insomnia, which heightened her urges to have a couple of glasses of wine to fall asleep. She mentioned the idea of asking her family physician for sleeping pills. The therapist reiterated that since alcohol disrupts the sleep–wake cycle, insomnia is a common and very burdensome withdrawal symptom. Upon cessation of drinking, the sleep–wake cycle can remain disrupted for weeks and even months. The therapist assured Heidi that in most cases patients report suddenly being able to sleep fine after about 3 weeks of insomnia, and that this was one of the hardest parts of getting sober, but encouraged her to "stick it out" and it would get better.

On the positive side, Heidi reported that she and Bob were talking much more than usual, and that she was beginning to talk to him about alcohol outside the therapy sessions. After the fourth session, Heidi drank on two nights when Bob was away on a trip. But she recorded it on her cards and talked about it at the fifth session, saying that she managed to throw away the wine after two glasses, and that in fact the wine made her feel a bit sick.

Therapy Sessions 5–9: Developing Self-Management Plans and Enhancing the Marital Relationship

By now the clients and therapist felt that they understood Heidi's drinking pattern, her high-risk situations, her triggers, and Bob's role. Thus Sessions 5 through 9 were devoted to developing and practicing stimulus control procedures, so that Heidi would have a self-management plan to help her respond without alcohol to her trigger situations. Though she had stopped drinking, she was continuing to experience cravings, as was expected. She was assured that over time the frequency and intensity of the cravings would decrease, but that the initial abstinence was a difficult period to get through. Also, Heidi and Bob began to rearrange consequences to increase the salience of negative consequences of drinking and the positive consequences of abstinence. One positive consequence was a better marital relationship, which also was given more attention during these sessions. Another positive consequence for Heidi was that Bridget and Toby were much better behaved and seemed happier. She attributed this change to her better mood during the day and increased ability to deal with them patiently, since she no longer suffered hangovers and intense cravings during the day.

Heidi decided to deal with her "highest-risk" situation—drinking wine and/or mixed drinks in the late afternoon/evening—by changing and avoiding aspects of this situation, and by identifying antecedent emotional triggers. First, she and Bob decided to give away all the wine they had in their wine cellar, despite its worth. Bob said that he didn't need to drink, especially in front of Heidi,

and he wanted to make it easier for her. He did want to keep a few bottles of hard liquor around for company, and the couple decided to buy a locked cabinet for that; Bob hid the key. Heidi realized that her daily activities revolved exclusively around her daughters and her household, with no time for herself. She got the girls ready for school, then drove Toby to preschool, went grocery shopping, cleaned up the house, did the laundry, walked the dog, picked up Toby from preschool, and then spent two afternoons driving Bridget to and from her dancing and religion classes. In addition, Toby had a gymnastics class one afternoon a week, and a piano teacher came to the house one afternoon for Bridget. By the time dinner rolled around, Heidi felt frazzled, lonely, and resentful, and just wanted some quiet time sitting by herself with a glass of wine. Thus, to deal with this high-risk situation, changes were made to Heidi's entire daily schedule to reduce the intensity of the antecedent emotional triggers.

First, Heidi decided to join a gym, where she went after taking Toby to preschool. She used to enjoy aerobics and swimming, and felt that she might have fun there and meet people while getting in shape. She also asked Bob whether they could afford to hire a local high school girl twice a week to come over, help tidy the house, and look after the girls so Heidi could relax a bit before starting dinner. Bob muttered that the cost of the wine they used to consume each week had been more than a mother's helper. It was springtime, so Heidi decided to join a pool club for the summer, instead of sending the girls to camp. This way, they could all go to the pool club together, and the mother's helper could go with them 2 days a week as well. Heidi also suggested that maybe in the fall Toby could go to preschool for extended hours, so that she could pursue a part-time job. She realized how much she missed working outside of the home, mingling during the day with others who had similar interests, and having activities other than child rearing and homemaking to think about. Bob initially disagreed, but then agreed to "take it slow" and to reconsider that option as they neared the end of the summer. In the late afternoon, Heidi began making it a point to have "tea time" with the girls, sitting down for 15 minutes together and having a drink (for Heidi, either herbal tea, decaffeinated coffee, soda, or club soda with a lime in it). This became an enjoyable fixture in their daily schedule; it was difficult for Heidi to slow down, interrupt, or put off cooking for that time, but she found that sitting down with the girls for "tea" really helped her relax and take the edge off wanting a glass of wine. During dinner preparation, Heidi made sure to keep handy a glass of club soda with lime or an iced tea to sip. She also decided to order out twice a week, and to use the time formerly spent cooking on playing with the girls outside, watching TV, or reading together.

After dinner, Heidi did the dishes, gave the girls a bath, and watched a movie with them or took a ride to the mall. After they went to bed, Heidi avoided the den for a while, sitting on the deck with an iced tea and a novel. A few weeks later, she was able to relax in the den with a rented movie or just watch TV with an herbal tea. On nights when Shawn came over, Heidi and he sat with his homework or played Scrabble together. When Bob got home she would sit with him and eat dessert, which she'd saved from dinner. Bob didn't drink wine with dinner any more, and after dinner the two would go up and rest in their bedroom rather than the den, watching TV or reading. Bob was also making an effort to get home earlier at least twice a week, so that he could eat dinner with the family more often. He also called home often during dinnertime when he had to work late, to check in with Heidi and give her verbal reinforcement for not drinking.

To make negative consequences of drinking more salient, Heidi carried a 3" x 5" card on which she had listed negative consequences of drinking, and sometimes spent a moment before dinner reading the list. At these times Heidi sometimes practiced the relaxation and imagery techniques that she learned in therapy. After taking a minute to relax, she would close her eyes and imagine in as vivid detail as possible the course of events if she drank: passing out, leaving Toby unattended to walk out of the house, the police arriving, the DYFS coming to take Toby and Bridget away, living alone without her family, and so on.

Heidi also began to call Bob at work one to two times per day (something she had been hesitant to do for fear of bothering him). Bob said that he liked it when she called; it was a welcome break from his harried day, and he felt that her calling him to tell him what was going on was far better than letting her resentment and loneliness build to the point of strong cravings for alcohol. Heidi even learned to tell Bob when she had cravings for alcohol, and Bob learned to respond supportively in these conversations and not to confuse her wish to drink with the act of drinking. He might suggest an alternative: "Sounds like the kids have been difficult today. Why don't you skip their bath?

I think I can come home by 6:00 today—why don't we all go out for ice cream after I eat? Then I can give them a bath and you can relax."

Heidi considered Bob's responses in these situations to be "too good to be true." It was difficult for her to talk to him about drinking, and to "bother" him at work. The therapist gave copious verbal reinforcement to both partners for their efforts in supporting each other, and for Heidi's getting accustomed to trusting Bob to respond supportively. Bob saw his efforts rewarded with a sober wife when he arrived home, no worry about his kids' safety, and more pleasant evening time upon arrival home from work. Heidi found that changing her daily schedule, allowing for more "Heidi time" (as she called it), and calling Bob during the day were all helpful in reducing the intensity of her urges. Before, she had been lonely and resentful during the day; now she was talking about her feelings to Bob and looking forward to spending the evening with him.

The therapist built on the initial deepening of supportiveness and intimacy by assigning "marital enhancement" homework: Bob was to give Heidi at least four compliments each week as "verbal rewards" for abstinence. Heidi was to return the favor by saying at least four nice things to Bob during the week. Over the weeks, other homework was introduced to stimulate interchange of positive feelings and good will toward each another. For instance, their weekly "date" was discussed, and both partners listed ideas they had for spending time together without alcohol (including a burger and a movie, dinner and a walk along the boardwalk, season tickets to classical music concerts, and more socializing with other couples they wanted to renew relationships with). By the ninth session, Bob surprised Heidi with a special outing on her birthday: He hired a limousine to take the family into the nearby big city for dinner at a fancy Chinese restaurant (Heidi generally didn't have urges to drink at Chinese restaurants), and gave her a pair of sapphire earrings. He and Heidi both commented on how much both of them had been focused on drinking as their primary leisure-time activity, and how good it felt to be doing other things with their time. Bob didn't see himself as having an alcohol problem, but he did say that in cutting back on his own drinking in the service of helping Heidi, he felt much better physically and was more alert at work.

The fourth high-risk situation—work-related events with open bars—continued to prove difficult for Heidi. At these functions, Bob was busy entertaining clients, so he couldn't give too much attention to Heidi. In the past she hadn't minded, since she drank enough to feel comfortable on her own. Without the help of alcohol, and with the temptation of an open bar, Heidi was nervous about resuming her attendance at these events. A self-management plan was drafted for this difficult situation. At the next event, Heidi would skip the open-bar prelude to a concert, and would meet Bob as the concert began. At an event planned for later in the month, Heidi and Bob decided that she would situate herself in an area far from the bar, and get herself a plate of food instead. Bob would bring her seltzers from the bar. She made sure to bring her cell phone, and the two agreed in advance that if Heidi were having strong cravings, they would call a taxi for her to go home. At home she would take a warm bath with some new bath salts she had bought and was saving for a special occasion. Bob insisted during the session that this solution was fine with him, that he wouldn't be embarrassed, and that her sobriety was more important to him that what some of his clients might think. Again, Heidi was surprised and grateful at the extent of his supportive response. Heidi and Bob agreed that they would discuss each upcoming event in advance, and that Heidi retained the right to decide not to attend if she felt that the temptation would be too great. Bob understood that she felt bad about this and would try to make the effort to attend, and he had no problem enlisting the help of two young, eager sales representatives in his department to help host these events with him. Or, Heidi decided, she could occasionally bring one of her close girlfriends who didn't drink and was single, and who knew the situation. Her friend was delighted to attend these functions, and Heidi found her presence very helpful in reducing social anxiety and enjoying the evening without drinking alcohol.

Therapy Sessions 10–15: Additional Self-Control Skills and Communication Skills Training

By the 10th session, Heidi had been sober for 5 weeks. Her urges were 50% less frequent, and their average intensity was a 2 (on a scale from 1 to 7), as opposed to 6 during the first 2 weeks of treatment. During Sessions 10–15, Heidi practiced the self-management plans already in place, and continued to develop new plans for other high-risk situations. In addition, the therapist introduced several other skills (including drink refusal and

Bob's role in drink refusal) related directly to Heidi's drinking, as well as skills more indirectly related to Heidi's urges to drink (such as general assertiveness, problem solving, and cognitive restructuring). Also during this phase in therapy, cognitive-behavioral couple therapy was introduced more explicitly, focused primarily on improving communication skills and continuing marital enhancement work.

Drink refusal training focused on the work-related events described above, where there was a fair amount of peer pressure to drink alcohol. Heidi's self-management plans were helpful, but they didn't prevent Bob's colleagues and clients she knew from offering her drinks and pressuring her to join them in their revelry. In fact, Heidi came to the 11th session reporting that she had drunk that weekend for the first time in 6 weeks. She and Bob had gone to a steakhouse with two other couples. One of the couples suggested that they wait in the bar for their table. Bob ordered an expensive bottle of wine for the table, caught up in the business of hosting these couples. Heidi felt a strong craving for a glass of wine, and found herself thinking that she could relax, enjoy the taste, and socialize more enjoyably if she just had one glass. At that point Bob ordered a round of iced tea for everyone, and asked for a lime in Heidi's. This was a code they had come up with for situations like this, and Heidi was grateful for Bob's sensitivity and understanding that she wanted a drink. She was able to stand up, explain that she preferred to wait outside, and enjoy the cool evening. One of the clients' wives went with her, and the two stood outside enjoying a pleasant conversation. Then a waiter appeared with two glasses of wine, sent by the woman's husband. At this point, Heidi's resolve broke down and she began sipping her glass. By the end of the evening, Heidi had consumed four glasses of red wine. Since her tolerance was low, she felt quite intoxicated, and by the end of the evening she was slurring her words and getting drowsy at the table. She felt ill the next day, and was thoroughly ashamed of herself for not being able to avoid drinking after doing so well.

This situation was discussed in Session 11 in the context of several skills, including self-management plans, drink refusal skills, seemingly irrelevant decisions, and challenging irrational thoughts. The therapist reframed the event as a slip that Heidi and Bob could learn from. Drink refusal training was covered in some detail, including role playing in the session, as well as completing a homework assignment to write a list of situations where an assertive response would be called for. Heidi decided that she would be comfortable telling people who knew her as a "drinker" that she simply wasn't drinking any more.

Since Heidi and Bob had a strong, loving foundation for their marriage, it was relatively easy to help them relearn to support each other and communicate better. Both had rated their relationship in the 3's and 4's (on a 1–7 scale) when they came to treatment; by the 12th session they were both consistently rating their marriage 5–7 on a 7-point scale. However, several topics were listed as problem areas: (1) Heidi's reluctance to be assertive with Bob and tell him when she was feeling lonely or resentful of his intense devotion to his work; (2) Bob's concern for Heidi's relationship with his son, Shawn, who stayed with the family every Wednesday and every other weekend; (3) Heidi's desire to go back to work and feel less lonely, and (4) Heidi's resentment of Bob's close relationship with his family, particularly his mother. In addition, Bob thought that Heidi didn't keep the house clean enough, and Heidi in turn believed that Bob could help around the house a bit more. In terms of communication process, the therapist noted several problems. First, Heidi was more emotional and verbal than Bob, who didn't always say what he was thinking in response to Heidi's comments. Heidi would then interpret Bob's silence as disregarding or negating her feelings, and would get very angry with him, whereupon Bob would withdraw and talk even less. Second, the spouses didn't always allow each other to finish a sentence before jumping in with a comment. Better listening skills were needed. Third, Both Bob and Heidi had difficulty bringing up a topic that was potentially conflictual, which resulted in a gradual lessening of intimacy as resentment built.

In session and for between-session homework, Bob practiced verbally responding to Heidi's comments—first with validation of her position, followed by his reaction to what she said. Heidi learned to be more assertive with him, asking for validation and feedback if he wasn't forthcoming. Each spouse tried hard to listen better, wait for the other to finish, and then repeat back what he/she thought the other said. Both thought that the ideas of "leveling and editing" (e.g., Gottman, Notarius, Gonso, & Markman, 1976) were particularly helpful in bringing up a bothersome topic, as well as paying close attention to good communication skills

in responding. Of course, Heidi and Bob still argued occasionally, but they felt that their communication had improved in both frequency and quality over the past weeks. Especially important was the fact that alcohol was a frequently discussed topic. This helped Heidi deal well with her urges to drink, while strengthening Bob's trust in her sobriety.

In addition to marital enhancement techniques such as "fun days" and "love days," the therapist introduced the notions of acceptance (tolerance), and self-care as part of the marital therapy work (Christensen, Jacobson, & Babcock, 1995; Hayes et al., 1996; Strosahl, 1996; Wilson & Hayes, 1996). In Heidi and Bob's case, the acceptance discussion revolved around her increased tolerance of Bob's devotion to his job, and his to Heidi's emotionality (see McCrady, 2001). Heidi's increased recognition of the benefits his employment imparted to her and the children was important to her acceptance of his focus on his work. Bob began to see Heidi's emotional reactions as part of her passionate personality, which had attracted him to her in the first place. He also accepted her alcoholism as a condition to which she was vulnerable because of her family history, and not entirely under her control, though he insisted that she was responsible for not drinking.

In terms of self-care, the therapist spent substantial time with the couple discussing and helping them to discuss the problem of loneliness that Heidi faced. This was not only a trigger for her to drink; it was also an issue of basic lifestyle satisfaction. After Toby was born, Heidi and Bob had moved to a new town 2 hours away. It was closer to Bob's job, and was also close to where his ex-wife had moved with his son. Heidi had agreed that it was best that they were near his son, but she had not met new friends and missed her home-town and her family and friends there. This was discussed in the context of a problem-solving exercise, and both Bob and Heidi had many ideas for remedying the situation. Heidi had been so busy drinking, it seemed, that she had never given herself a chance to engage in activities where she might meet people. Her self-care activities, as discussed above, included joining a gym and hiring a mother's helper/housecleaner. Heidi also decided during the course of treatment that she would like to look for a part-time job in September, when Toby would be in school for more hours. This way she would get out of the house and meet people, feel more independent, and be less resentful of Bob's rich occupational life.

Therapy Sessions 16–20: Consolidating Skills, Relapse Prevention, and Maintenance Planning

In the final sessions, the therapist and couple reviewed and continued to practice skills learned thus far. Heidi was becoming more comfortable with her sobriety, and both she and Bob were beginning to settle into a new, sober lifestyle. The last few sessions focused on establishing "marital meetings," identifying signs of possible relapse, handling relapses, developing a relapse contract, and finally scheduling booster sessions.

Toward the end of the 6-month treatment protocol, the therapist and couple directly addressed the possibility of relapse and developed both preventive and responsive strategies related to relapse. Heidi and Bob were told that use of alcohol after treatment is not uncommon, and treatment addressed this possibility. They made a list of signs of an impending relapse, including behavioral, cognitive, interpersonal, and affective signs. After they developed this list, they developed a set of possible responses, should these signs arise. Most important was for the couple to recognize that these were warning signs that should trigger action, rather than inaction and fatalistic cognitions about the inevitability of relapse.

Heidi's list of warning signs for relapse included (1) catching herself thinking that she "could have just one," (2) feeling lonely and depressed for more than 2 days in a row, (3) telling Bob that she felt OK in a drink-related social situation when she really didn't, and (4) being on vacation. Her strategies for dealing with a drinking slip were (1) throwing away the rest of the liquor; (2) leaving the drinking situation as soon as possible; (3) telling Bob as soon as possible, and enlisting his help in not drinking more; (4) giving herself a delay before drinking anything more; (5) reviewing the abstinence violation effect; and (6) reviewing the relapse contract.

In order to facilitate identification and handling of relapses, the couple decided on the following "relapse contract" (Marlatt & Gordon, 1985):

1. Heidi needs to be as honest as possible and inform Bob of any drinking or strong urges to drink.
2. If Heidi drinks at all, she will do a functional analysis of the drinking with Bob to try to figure out what happened; she will also call the therapist to discuss it.

3. Heidi and Bob will discuss the necessity of returning to treatment if Heidi has a drink once a week for 2 weeks in a row, or after 2 weeks of frequent moderate to strong urges.

Heidi and Bob were given the option of returning for "booster sessions" every month, then every 2 months, and so on. They liked that idea, and also agreed to have weekly "marital meetings" on their own at a restaurant in lieu of their appointment at the clinic. In therapy, they role-played establishing an effective agenda and using good communication skills. They decided that they would use these meetings to clear the air of any conflict or negative feelings about each other that had come up during the week; to discuss any family topics that needed attention that week; to anticipate high-risk situations that might be coming up in the week ahead, and to problem-solve how Heidi could deal with them and how Bob could help Heidi with them; and to discuss the frequency and intensity of Heidi's urges to drink that week.

By the end of 20 sessions, Heidi had tapered her drinking down to zero over the first 5 weeks, had been abstinent for 5 weeks, had had one slip, and then had remained abstinent again for 9 weeks. Both Heidi and Bob noticed improvements in several areas of their lives, including their relationship, Heidi's caring for the children, Bob's performance at work, and Heidi's enjoyment of her daily activities. Heidi no longer felt the burden of keeping "drinking secrets" from Bob, and they spent more time together enjoying each other's company. Heidi also felt free of guilt and self-doubt that she would be able to control her drinking. She was aware that she would probably continue to have urges to drink, but felt that the more her lifestyle was alcohol-free and satisfying, the less she would think about drinking.

ACKNOWLEDGMENTS

Preparation of this chapter was supported in part by National Institute on Alcohol Abuse and Alcoholism Grants No. AA 07070 and No. DA 10835.

REFERENCES

American Psychiatric Association. (1994). *Diagnostic and statistical manual of mental disorders* (4th ed.). Washington, DC: Author.

Babor, T. F., Kranzler, H. R., & Lauerman, R. J. (1989). Early detection of harmful alcohol consumption: Comparison of clinical, laboratory, and self-report screening procedures. *Addictive Behaviors, 14,* 139–157.

Baucom, D. H., & Epstein, N. (1990). *Cognitive-behavioral marital therapy.* New York: Brunner/Mazel.

Bennett, L. A., & Wolin, S. J. (1990). Family culture andalcoholism transmission. In R. L. Collins, K. E. Leonard, & J. S. Searles (Eds.), *Alcohol and the family. Research and clinical perspectives* (pp. 194–219). New York: Guilford Press.

Beutler L. E., McCray Patterson, K., Jacob, T., Shoham, V., Yost, E., & Rohrbaugh, M. (1993). Matching treatment to alcoholism subtypes. *Psychotherapy, 30,* 463–472.

Bierut, L. J., Dinwiddie, S. H., Begleiter, H., Crowe, R. R., Hesselbrock, V., Nurnberger, J. I., Jr., Porjesz, B., Schuckit, M. A., & Reich, T. (1998). Familial transmission of substance dependence: Alcohol, marijuana, cocaine, and habitual smoking. A report from the Collaborative Study on the Genetics of Alcoholism. *Archives of General Psychiatry, 55,* 982–988.

Billings, A. S., Kessler, M., Gomberg, C. A., & Weiner, S. (1979). Marital conflict resolution of alcoholic and nonalcoholic couples during drinking and nondrinking sessions. *Journal of Studies on Alcohol, 40,* 183–195.

Brennan, P., Moos, R. H., & Mertens, J. R. (1994). Personal and environmental risk factors as predictors of alcohol use, depression, and treatment-seeking: A longitudinal analysis of late-life problem drinkers. *Journal of Substance Abuse, 6*(2), 191–208.

Brennan, P. L., Moos, R. H., & Kelly, K. M. (1994). Spouses of late-life problem drinkers: Functioning, coping responses, and family contexts. *Journal of Family Psychology, 8*(4), 447–457.

Beutler, L. E., McCray Patterson, K., Jacob, T., Shoham, V., Yost, E., & Rohrbaugh, M. (1993). Matching treatment to alcoholism subtypes. *Psychotherapy, 30,* 460–472.

Castro, F. G., Proescholdbell, R. J., Abeita, L., & Rodriguez, D. (1999). Ethnic and cultural minority groups. In B. S. McCrady & E. E. Epstein (Eds.), *Addictions: A comprehensive guidebook* (pp. 499–526). New York: Oxford University Press.

Christensen, A., Jacobson, N. S., & Babcock, J. C. (1995). Integrative behavioral couple therapy. In A. S. Gurman & N. Jacobson (Eds.), *Clinical Handbook of Couple Therapy,* (2nd ed., pp. 31–64). New York: Guilford Publications.

Cunningham, J. A., Sobell, L. C., Sobell, M. B., & Gaskin, J. (1994). Alcohol and drug abusers' reasons for seeking treatment. *Addictive Behaviors, 19,* 691–696.

Dunn, N. J., Jacob, T., Hummon, N., & Seilhamer, R. A. (1987). Marital stability in alcoholic-spouse relationships as a function of drinking pattern and location. *Journal of Abnormal Psychology, 96,* 99–107.

Epstein, E. E. (2001). Classifcation of alcohol-related problems and dependence. In N. Heather, T. J. Peters, & T. Stockwell (Eds.), *Handbook of alcohol dependence and related problems* (pp. 47–70). London: John Wiley.

Epstein, E. E., & McCrady, B. S. (1998). Alcohol behavioral couples therapy: Current status and innovations. *Clinical Psychology Review, 18,* 689–711.

Epstein, E. E., McCrady, B. S., & Hirsch, L. S. (1997). Marital functioning among early versus late alcoholic couples. *Alcoholism: Clinical and Experimental Research, 21,* 547–556.

Fals-Stewart, W., Birchler, G. R., & O'Farrell, T. J. (1996). Behavioral couples therapy for male substance-abusing patients: Effects on relationship adjustment and drug-using behavior. *Journal of Consulting and Clinical Psychology, 64,* 959–972.

Fingarette, H. (1988). *Heavy drinking: The myth of alcoholism as a disease.* Berkeley: University of California Press.

Folstein, M. F., Folstein, S. E., & McHugh, P. R. (1975). "Mini-Mental State": A practical method for grading the cognitive state of patients for the clinician. *Journal of Psychiatric Research, 12,* 189–198.

Frankenstein, W., Hay, W. M., & Nathan, P. E. (1985). Effects of intoxication on alcoholics' marital communication and problem solving. *Journal of Studies on Alcohol, 46,* 1–6.

Gomberg, E. S. L. (1999). Women. In B. S. McCrady & E. E. Epstein (Eds.), *Addictions: A comprehensive guidebook* (pp. 457–541). New York: Oxford University Press.

Gottman, J., Notarius, C., Gonso, J., & Markman, H. (1976). *A couple's guide to communication.* Champaign, IL: Research Press.

Hayes, S., Bergan, J., Strosahl, K., Wilson, K., Polusny, M., Nagle, A., McCurry, S., Parker, L., & Hart, P. (1996, November). *Measuring psychological acceptance: The Experiential Avoidance Scale.* Paper presented at the Association for Advancement of Behavior Therapy Convention, New York.

Hersen, M., Miller, P., & Eisler, R. (1973). Interactions between alcoholics and their wives; a descriptive analysis of verbal and nonverbal behavior. *Quarterly Journal of Studies on Alcohol, 34,* 516–520.

Hesselbrock, M., Meyer, R., & Keener, J. J. (1985). Psychopathology in hospitalized alcoholics. *Archives of General Psychiatry, 42,* 1050–1055.

Holtzworth-Munroe, A., Beatty, S. B., & Anglin, K. (1995). The assessment and treatment of marital violence: An introduction for the marital therapist. In N. S. Jacobson & A. Gurman (Eds.), *Clinical handbook of couple therapy* (pp. 317–339). New York: Guilford Press.

Ichiyama, M. A., Zucker, R. A., Fitzgerald, H. E., & Bingham, C. R. (1996). Articulating subtype differences in self and relational experience among alcoholic men using structural analysis of social behavior. *Journal of Consulting and Clinical Psychology, 64,* 1245–1254.

Jackson, J. K. (1954). The adjustment of the family to the crisis of alcoholism. *Quarterly Journal of Studies on Alcohol, 15,* 562–586.

Jacob, T., Dunn, N. J., & Leonard, K. (1983). Patterns of alcohol abuse and family stability. *Alcoholism: Clinical and Experimental Research, 7,* 382–385.

Jacob, T., & Krahn, G. L. (1988). Marital interactions of alcoholic couples: Comparison with depressed and nondistressed couples. *Journal of Consulting and Clinical Psychology, 56,* 73–79.

Jacobson, N., & Margolin, G. (1979). *Marital therapy: Strategies based on social learning and behavior exchange principles.* New York: Brunner/Mazel.

Kadden, R. M., Cooney, N. L., Getter, H., & Litt, M. D. (1989). Matching alcoholics to coping skills or interactional therapies: Posttreatment results. *Journal of Consulting and Clinical Psychology, 57,* 698–704.

Kelly, A. B., & Halford, W. K. (1994, November). *Problem drinking women's expectancies about the effects of alcohol on their marital relationships*. Presented at the Annual Meeting of the Association for Advancement of Behavior Therapy, San Diego, CA.

Lammers, S. M. M., Schippers, G. M., & van der Staak, C. P. F. (1995). Submission and rebellion: Excessive drinking of women in problematic heterosexual partner relationships. *International Journal of the Addictions, 30*, 901–917.

Leonard, K. E., & Senchak, M. (1993). Alcohol and premarital aggression among newlywed couples. *Journal of Studies on Alcohol, 11*, 96–108.

Lewis, M. L. (1937). Alcoholism and family casework. *Social Casework, 35*, 8–14.

Longabaugh, R., Beattie, M., Noel, N., Stout, R., & Malloy, P. (1993). The effect of social investment on treatment outcome. *Journal of Studies on Alcohol, 54*, 465–478.

Longabaugh, R., Rubin, A., Malloy, P., Beattie, M., Clifford, P. R., & Noel, N. (1994). Drinking outcomes of alcohol abusers diagnosed as antisocial personality disorder. *Alcoholism: Clinical and Experimental Research, 18*, 778–785.

Lowman, C., Allen, J., Stout, R. L., & The Relapse Research Group. (1996). Replication and extension of Marlatt's taxonomy of relapse precipitants: Overview of procedures and results. *Addiction, 91*(Suppl.), S51–S71.

MacCoun, R. J. (1998). Toward a psychology of harm reduction. *American Psychologist, 53*, 1199–1208.

Maisto, S. A., McKay, J. R., & O'Farrell, T. J. (1995). Relapse precipitants and behavioral marital therapy. *Addictive Behaviors, 20*, 383–393.

Margolin, G., Talovic, S., & Weinstein, C. D. (1983). Areas of Change Questionnaire: A practical approach to marital assessment. *Journal of Consulting and Clinical Psychology, 51*, 920–931.

Marlatt, G. A., & Gordon, J. R. (1985). *Relapse prevention*. New York: Guilford Press.

McCrady, B. S. (2001). Alcohol use disorders. In D. H. Barlow (Ed.), *Clinical handbook of psychological disorders* (3rd ed., pp. 376–433). New York: Guilford Press.

McCrady, B. S., & Epstein, E. E. (1995). Marital therapy in the treatment of alcohol problems. In A. S. Gurman & N. Jacobson (Eds.), *Clinical handbook of couple therapy* (pp. 369–393). New York: Guilford Press.

McCrady, B. S., & Epstein, E. E. (1999, November). *Alcohol-dependent women in treatment: The women, their partners, their relationships*. Paper presented at the annual meeting of the Association for Advancement of Behavior Therapy, Toronto.

McCrady, B. S., & Epstein, E. E. (2000, June). *Are bad marriages bad for conjoint alcohol treatment?* Paper presented at the annual meeting of the Research Society on Alcoholism, Denver, CO.

McCrady, B. S., Epstein, E. E., & Hirsch, L. S. (1996). Issues in the implementation of a randomized clinical trial that includes Alcoholics Anonymous: Studying AA-related behaviors during treatment. *Journal of Studies on Alcohol, 57*(6), 604–612.

McCrady, B. S., Epstein, E. E., & Hirsch, L. S. (1999). Maintaining change after conjoint behavioral alcohol treatment for men: Outcomes at 6 months. *Addiction, 94*, 1381–1396.

McCrady, B. S., Noel, N. E., Abrams, D. B., Stout, R. L., Nelson, H. F., & Hay, W. M. (1986). Comparative effectiveness of three types of spouse involvement in outpatient behavioral alcoholism treatment. *Journal of Studies on Alcohol, 47*, 459–467.

McCrady, B. S., Noel, N. E., Stout, R. L., Abrams, D. B., & Nelson, H. F. (1991). Comparative effectiveness of three types of spouse-involved behavioral alcoholism treatment: Outcome 18 months after treatment. *British Journal of Addictions, 86*, 1415–1424.

McCrady, B. S., Stout, R., Noel, N., Abrams, D., & Nelson, H. F. (1991). Effectiveness of three types of spouse-involved behavioral alcoholism treatment. *British Journal of Addiction, 86*, 1415–1424.

McKay, J. R., Longabaugh, R., Beattie, M. C., Maisto, S. A., & Noel, N. E. (1993). Does adding conjoint therapy to individually focused alcoholism treatment lead to better family functioning? *Journal of Substance Abuse, 5*, 45–59.

Miller, W. R. (1985). Motivation for treatment: A review with special emphasis on alcoholism. *Psychological Bulletin, 98*, 84–107.

Miller, W. R., Benefield, R. G., & Tonigan, J. S. (1993). Enhancing motivation for change in problem drinking: A controlled comparison of two therapist styles. *Journal of Consulting and Clinical Psychology, 61*, 455–461.

Miller, W. R., Meyers, R. J., & Tonigan, J. S. (1999). Engaging the unmotivated in treatment for alcohol problems: A comparison of three strategies for intervention through family members. *Journal of Consulting and Clinical Psychology, 67*, 688–697.

Miller, W. R., & Rollnick, S. (1991). *Motivational interviewing: Preparing people to change addictive behavior*. New York: Guilford Press.

Moos, R. H., Finney, J. W., & Gamble, W. (1982). The process of recovery from alcoholism: II. Comparing spouses of alcoholic patients and matched community controls. *Journal of Studies on Alcohol, 43*, 888–909.

Moos, R. H., & Moos, B. S. (1984). The process of recovery from alcoholism: III. Comparing functioning of families of alcoholics and matched control families. *Journal of Studies on Alcohol, 45*, 111–118.

Moras, K. (1993). Substance abuse research: Outcome measurement conundrums. In L. S. Onken, J. D. Blaine, & J. J. Boren (Eds.), *Behavioral treatments for drug abuse and dependence* (NIDA Research Monograph 137, pp. 217–248). Rockville, MD: National Institute on Drug Abuse.

Murphy, C. M., & O'Farrell, T. J. (1997). Couple communication patterns of maritally aggressive and nonaggressive male alcoholics. *Journal of Studies on Alcohol, 58*(1), 83–90.

Noel, N. E., McCrady, B. S., Stout, R. L., & Nelson, H. F. (1991). Gender differences in marital functioning of male and female alcoholics. *Family Dynamics of Addiction Quarterly, 1*, 31–38.

O'Farrell, T. J. (1993a). A Behavioral Marital Therapy Couples Group Program for alcoholics and their spouses. In T. J. O'Farrell (Ed.), *Treating alcohol problems: Marital and family interventions*. New York: The Guilford Press.

O'Farrell, T. J., & Birchler, G. R. (1987). Marital relationships of alcoholic, conflicted, and nonconflicted couples. *Journal of Marital and Family Therapy, 13*, 259–274.

O'Farrell, T. J., Choquette, K. A., & Birchler, G. R. (1991). Sexual satisfaction and dissatisfaction in the marital relationships of male alcoholics seeking marital therapy. *Journal of Studies on Alcohol, 52*, 441–447.

O'Farrell, T. J., Choquette, K. A., & Cutter, H. S. G. (1998). Couples relapse prevention sessions after behavioral marital therapy for male alcoholics: Outcomes during the three years after starting treatment. *Journal of Studies on Alcohol, 59,* 357–370.

O'Farrell, T. J., Choquette, K. A., Cutter, H. S. G., & Birchler, G. R. (1997). Sexual satisfaction and dysfunction in marriages of male alcoholics: Comparison with nonalcoholic maritally conflicted and nonconflicted couples. *Journal of Studies on Alcohol, 58*(1), 91–99.

O'Farrell, T. J., Choquette, K. A., Cutter, H. S. G., Brown, E. D., & McCourt, W. F. (1993). Behavioral marital therapy with and without additional couples relapse prevention sessions for alcoholics and their wives. *Journal of Studies on Alcohol, 54,* 652–666.

O'Farrell, T. J., Cutter, H. S. G., & Floyd, F. (1985). Evaluating behavioral marital therapy for male alcoholics: Effects on marital adjustment and communication from before to after therapy. *Behavior Therapy, 16,* 147–167.

O'Farrell, T. J., & Fals-Stewart, W. (1999). Treatment models and methods: Family models. In B. S. McCrady & E. E. Epstein (Eds.), *Addictions: A comprehensive guidebook* (pp. 287–305). New York: Oxford University Press.

Pan, H. S., Neidig, P. H., & O'Leary, K. D. (1994). Male–female and aggressor–victim differences in the factor structure of the Modified Conflict Tactics Scale. *Journal of Interpersonal Violence, 9,* 366–382.

Paolino, T. J., Jr., & McCrady, B. S. (1977). *The alcoholic marriage: Alternative perspectives.* New York: Grune & Stratton.

Parsons, O. A., Butters, N., & Nathan, P. E. (Eds.). (1987). *Neuropsychology of alcoholism: Implications for diagnosis and treatment.* New York: Guilford Press.

Prochaska, J. O., DiClemente, C. C., & Norcross, J. C. (1992). In search of how people change: Applications to addictive behaviors. *American Psychologist, 47,* 1102–1114.

Project MATCH Research Group. (1997). Project MATCH secondary a priori hypotheses. *Addiction, 92,* 1671–1698.

Project MATCH Research Group. (1998). Matching alcoholism treatments to client heterogeneity: Project MATCH three-year drinking outcomes. *Alcoholism: Clinical and Experimental Research, 22,* 1300–1311.

Rosenthal, R. N., & Westreich, L. (1999). Treatment of persons with dual diagnoses of substance use disorder and other psychological problems. In B. S. McCrady & E. E. Epstein (Eds.), *Addictions: A comprehensive guidebook* (pp. 439–476). New York: Oxford University Press.

Ross, H. E., Glaser, F. B., & Stiasny, S. (1988). Sex differences in the prevalence of psychiatric disorders in patients with alcohol and drug problems. *British Journal of Addiction, 83,* 1179–1192.

Rotunda, R. J. (1995, November). *Domestic violence among couples with an alcoholic or depressed partner compared to nondistressed couples on the Conflict Tactics Scale.* Presented at the Annual Meeting of the Association for Advancement of Behavior Therapy, Washington, DC.

Rounsaville, B. J., Dolinsky, Z. S., Babor, T. F., & Meyer, R. E. (1987). Psychopathology as a predictor of treatment outcome in alcoholics. *Archives of General Psychiatry, 44,* 505–513.

Sanjuan, P. M., & Langenbucher, J. W. (1999). Age-limited populations: Youth, adolescents, and older adults. In B. S. McCrady & E. E. Epstein (Eds.), *Addictions: A comprehensive guidebook* (pp. 477–498). New York: Oxford University Press.

Schutte, K. K., Brennan, P. L., & Moos, R. H. (1994). Remission of late-life drinking problems: A 4-year follow-up. *Alcoholism: Clinical and Experimental Research, 18,* 835–844.

Selzer, M. L. (1971). The Michigan Alcoholism Screening Test: The quest for a new diagnostic instrument. *American Journal of Psychiatry, 127,* 1653–1658.

Skinner, H., & Allen, B. A. (1982). Alcohol dependence syndrome: Measurement and validation. *Journal of Abnormal Psychology, 91,* 199–209.

Sobell, M. B., Maisto, S. A., Sobell, L. C., Cooper, T., & Saunders, B. (1980). Developing a prototype for evaluating alcohol treatment effectiveness. In L. C. Sobell, M. B. Sobell, & E. Ward (Eds.), *Evaluating alcohol alcohol treatment effectiveness: Recent advances.* New York: Pergamon Press.

Sobell, M. B., Maisto, S. A., Sobell, L. C., Cooper, T., & Saunders, B. (1980). Developing a prototype for evaluating alcohol treatment effectiveness. In L. C. Sobell, M. B. Sobell, & E. Ward (Eds.), *Evaluating alcohol and drug abuse treatment effectiveness: Recent advances.* New York: Pergamon Press.

Spanier, G. (1976). Measuring dyadic adjustment: New scales for assessing the quality of marriage and similar dyads. *Journal of Marriage and the Family, 38,* 15–28.

Spitzer, R. L., Williams, J. B. W., Gibbon, M., & First, M. B. (1996). *Structured Clinical Interview for DSM-IV–Patient Edition (with Psychotic Screen–Version 1.0).* Washington, DC: American Psychiatric Press.

Steinglass, P., Bennett, L. A., Wolin, S. J., & Reiss, D. (1987). *The alcoholic family.* New York: Basic Books.

Strosahl, K. (1996, November). *Acceptance commitment therapy: Examining basic mechanisms and clinical effectiveness.* Paper presented at the Association for Advancement of Behavior Therapy Convention, New York.

Thomas, E. J., & Santa, C. A. (1982). Unilateral family therapy for alcohol abuse: A working conception. *American Journal of Family Therapy, 10,* 49–60.

Whalen, T. (1953). Wives of alcoholics: Four types observed in a family service agency. *Quarterly Journal of Studies on Alcohol, 14,* 632–641.

Wilson, K. G., & Hayes, S. C. (1996, November). *The role of acceptance in substance abuse.* Paper presented at the Association for Advancement of Behavior Therapy Convention, New York.

Yahne, C. E., & Miller, W. R. (1999). Enhancing motivation for treatment and change. In B. S. McCrady & E. E. Epstein (Eds.), *Addictions: A comprehensive guidebook* (pp. 235–249). New York: Oxford University Press.

Yates, W. R., Petty, F., & Brown, K. (1988). Alcoholism in males with antisocial personality disorder. *International Journal of the Addictions, 23,* 999–1010.

Zitter, R. E., & McCrady, B. S. (1979). *The Drinking Patterns Questionnaire.* Unpublished manuscript.

Chapter 24

Sexuality, Sexual Dysfunction, and Couple Therapy

BARRY W. McCARTHY

Masters and Johnson (1970) were the founders of couple sex therapy. Their model of 2-week intensive therapy by a male–female cotherapy team is almost extinct, but two of their concepts form the essence of contemporary sex therapy. First, sexual dysfunction is best conceptualized, assessed, and treated as a couple issue. Second, sexual comfort, skill, and functioning can be learned. Sexual exercises are the preferred modality for helping couples develop a comfortable, functional sexual style. Sexual exercises (McCarthy & McCarthy, 2002; Wincze & Barlow, 1996) have been greatly expanded from the original sensate focus exercises to include exercises involving bridges to sexual desire, nondemand pleasuring, and erotic scenarios, as well as exercises for specific male and female sexual dysfunctions.

Although the culture (especially the mass media), is saturated and obsessed with sexual scandals and jokes, the reality is that rates of sexual dysfunction, dissatisfaction, and trauma continue to be high (Laumann, Gagnon, Michael, & Michaels, 1994). There has been significant growth in theoretical and clinical knowledge in the sexuality field, although the research base remains weak. A classification of sexual dysfunctions and disorders is included in the DSM-IV (American Psychiatric Association, 1994).

MODELS OF SEXUAL FUNCTION AND DYSFUNCTION

Sexual dysfunctions are classified utilizing the triphasic model proposed by Kaplan (1974)—disorders of desire, arousal, and orgasm. The most common clinical complaints involve desire disorders, a category that was not considered in the original Masters and Johnson model. In the 1970s, primary sexual dysfunction predominated (i.e., a person has never been functional). An example is primary early ejaculation, in which the man has always ejaculated prematurely. In the past 30 years, secondary dysfunctions have increased (i.e., a person has been functional, but is now dysfunctional). For example, the woman has been orgasmic during partner sex, but now is nonorgasmic.

Traditional causes of sexual dysfunction were lack of information, repressive attitudes, high anxiety, lack of sexual skill, and rigid sexual roles. Sexuality is a multicausal, multidimensional phenomenon with biological, psychological, relational, and cultural components (Rosen & Leiblum, 1995). Rates of dysfunction and dissatisfaction remain high, but their causes and types have significantly changed. With the growth of sexuality courses and self-help books, lack of knowledge has been alleviated. Unfortunately, it has been replaced by unrealistic expectations and performance demands. The importance of sexuality for couple and life satisfaction is overemphasized, resulting in confusion, dissatisfaction, and performance anxiety. The cultural milieu has gone from one extreme (repression, rigidity, lack of information, and noncommunication) to the other (sexual overload, confusion, intimidation about one's body and sexual performance, and conflicting models of sexual meaning and expression). There have been significant cultural shifts in the frequency of premarital sex, increases in sexually transmitted diseases (STDs), the beginning of the HIV/AIDS epidemic, an increase in the divorce rate, and heightened sensitivity to sexual trauma (especially child sexual abuse). Those kinds of changes have led to a counterreaction from religious and conservative groups, especially the "family values" movement.

With the introduction of Viagra in 1998 (Goldstein et al., 1998), a paradigm shift occurred in the conceptualization of male sexuality. Tiefer (1986) warned against the "medicalization of male sexuality," but this perspective is gaining momentum not only in the treatment of erectile dysfunction, but of early ejaculation. The movement to medicalize female sexuality (Rosen, Philips, Gendrano, & Ferguson, 1999) is now growing. What does this mean for couple sex therapy?

The traditional marital/couple therapy approach was to view sexual dysfunction as symptomatic of an unresolved relationship problem (e.g., poor communication, power imbalances, struggles with emotional intimacy, family-of-origin conflicts). The focus was on individual and couple dynamics, with the assumption that once these were dealt with, sexual issues would take care of themselves or be resolved with minimal intervention. There is little empirical support for this position, especially when the dysfunction is anxiety-based or there are skill deficits.

The couple therapy field has not given sufficient attention to sexuality and sexual dysfunction. Few training programs in the field have courses, practica, or internships in which sex therapy is an integral component. Couple theory, research, and practice emphasize sexual trauma, not sexual dysfunction or sex therapy. Some writers have advocated the integration of couple and sex therapy (Weeks & Hof, 1987; Schnarch, 1991).

Couple sex therapy is best understood as a subspecialty field. The clinician—whether trained as a psychologist, social worker, psychiatrist, couple therapist, pastoral counselor, or psychiatric nurse—

must possess skills in individual therapy; couple therapy; the assessment of individual, couple, and sexual factors; and the ability to develop and implement a sexual intervention. Sex therapy involves comprehensive assessment and treatment components, and attention to a wide range of physiological, psychological, relational, cultural, and sexual factors. Of central importance is the clinician's comfort with prescribing, processing, and individualizing sexual exercises.

Unfortunately, the sex therapy field is not growing. Among young clinicians it is shrinking, especially in comparison to couple therapy. Few clinicians choose sex therapy as their primary professional identity. There are a number of reasons for this change: National sexuality organizations are struggling in terms of membership and resources; there is no licensing for sex therapists; few insurance companies reimburse for sex therapy; there are few graduate sex therapy programs; and there are few granting agencies or financial resources for sex research (with the exception of drug companies). In addition, the controversy surrounding sexual trauma, especially recovered memories of sexual abuse, has made the field suspect and less scientifically and professionally respected.

The number of couples with sexual dysfunction or dissatisfaction has not decreased; if anything, it has increased. Of special concern is the nonsexual relationship. When the criterion of being sexual fewer than 10 times a year is used, approximately 20% of married couples and 30% of nonmarried couples who have been together at least 2 years have nonsexual relationships (Michael, Gagnon, Laumann, & Kolata, 1994).

A perspective couples often find motivating is that when sexuality goes well it is a positive, integral component of a relationship, but not a major factor. A clinical adage is that sexuality contributes 15–20% to a marriage, serving as a shared pleasure, a means to reinforce intimacy, and a tension reducer to deal with the stresses of life and marriage. Sexuality energizes the marital bond and facilitates special couple feelings. When sexuality is dysfunctional or nonexistent, it plays an inordinately powerful role, perhaps 50–75%, draining the marriage of vitality and intimacy (McCarthy, 1997a). Paradoxically, bad sex plays a more powerful negative role than good sex plays a positive role in marriage. The most commonly cited reasons couples separate in the first 2 years of marriage are a sexual conflict/fertility problem (e.g., unwanted pregnancy or infertility), an extramarital affair, or a sexual dysfunction (especially inhibited sexual desire).

ASSESSMENT IN COUPLE SEX THERAPY

There are a number of paper-and-pencil measures of sexual function and dysfunction (Derogatis, 1975; LoPiccolo & Steger, 1974; Rust & Golombok, 1986). In addition, there are specific measures for desire, erectile dysfunction, and pain (Davis, Yarber, Bauserman, Schree, & Davis, 1998). These instruments are used primarily for research purposes and have yet to show high levels of clinical utility.

History Taking

The prime assessment technique in couple sex therapy is the semistructured sexual history (Leiblum & Rosen, 1989). The protocol is a conjoint initial session that enables the therapist to assess the couple's motivation and appropriateness for sex therapy; to explore the sexual problem in the context of the relationship; to understand past attempts at resolving the problem and coexisting problems; to explore medical problems (including side effects of medications); to decide whether there is a need to consult a urologist, gynecologist, psychiatrist, or endocrinologist; and to answer questions about the process of sex therapy. Sexual histories are conducted individually in order to obtain a clear, uncensored review of each partner's sexual development, as well as his/her attitudes toward, feelings about, and experiences with the partner. At the beginning of the session, the client is told, "I want to know as much as possible about both the strengths and problems in your sexual development and in this relationship. I ask you to be as frank and honest as possible. At the end, I will ask whether there are sensitive or secret areas you do not want shared with your partner. I will respect that and not share information without your permission, but I need to understand sensitive or secretive issues if I'm going to be helpful."

The history taking follows a semistructured chronological format, moving from general, less anxiety-provoking material to sensitive and anxiety-provoking issues. Open-ended questions are utilized. The clinician is supportive and nonjudgmental; he/she follows up and probes to elicit attitudes, experiences, feelings, and values.

The beginning question is "How did you learn about sex and sexuality?" This question allows exploration of formal education, religious background, parents as sex educators and as marital and sexual models, as well as sexual experiences with siblings, neighborhood children, friends, and others. Social and sexual experiences as a child are addressed, including self-exploration/masturbation, comfort with body and gender, and sexual experimentation. Age at and reaction to first orgasmic experience (by oneself or with others) is explored.

The format of the questions facilitates disclosure. Yes–no questions are not used. Open-ended questions with the expectation of "yes" are utilized (e.g., "How and when did you begin self-exploration/masturbation—what were your feelings and reactions?"). This format is used to explore sexual experiences with members of the same sex and extramarital affairs (e.g., "People often have sexual feelings, fantasies, and experiences with someone of the same sex—what have your experiences been?"). If the person has not masturbated, had same-sex experiences, or had extramarital affairs, it is easy to say "no."

A particularly important issue to explore is sexual trauma. Once it has been established how old the client was when he/she left home, the therapist asks, "As you review your childhood and adolescence, what was your most negative, confusing, guilt-inducing, or traumatic experience?" Toward the end of the history taking, the therapist asks about the most negative or traumatic sexual experience in the client's life. Although the therapist has spent 1–1½ hours reviewing the entire sexual history, as many as 25% of clients disclose significant new information. The therapist should explore cognitions and feelings about the traumatic incident, both at the time and in retrospect. Especially crucial is whether traumatized clients see themselves as survivors or as victims (McCarthy & McCarthy, 1993).

An increasingly relevant assessment topic is that of past or current medical evaluations, interventions, and medications. Sexuality involves physiological as well as psychological and relational factors. Ideally, the nonmedical therapist will have a consultative relationship with a sexual medicine subspecialist. Often one or both members of a couple have consulted a family practitioner, internist, gynecologist, urologist, psychiatrist, or endocrinologist. It is important to be aware of both partners' health and disease status, especially side effects of medications. There is a large literature on sexual side effects of antidepressant medications and strategies to reduce side effects (Balon, 1999; Segraves, 1998b). Other psychiatric drugs, antihypertensive medications, and a number of other medications have been implicated in sexual dysfunction (Segraves, 1988). With the introduction of Viagra in 1998, the use of sexual pharmacology for the treatment of male dysfunction has immensely increased. The potential benefits and pitfalls of medical interventions are discussed below.

Feedback Session: The Core Sex Therapy Intervention

The couple feedback session is a powerful method for promoting understanding, increasing motivation, and setting the stage for change. It is scheduled as a double session, with a threefold focus: (1) establishing a new understanding of the problem, with positive expectations of change as the couple functions as an intimate team; (2) outlining a change strategy involving individual, couple, and sexual components; and (3) assigning the first set of exercises (either nondemand pleasuring or sexual desire enhancement), with a specific plan for their implementation.

The clinician gives feedback about the partners' sexual development, noting the strengths and vulnerabilities of each person, as well as those of the couple as a unit. The fundamental concepts of each person's being responsible for his/her sexuality and of the couple's working as an intimate team are made personal and concrete.

The feedback session focuses and motivates the couple. It sets the stage for thinking of therapy as an integrated assessment–intervention program. Reactions to exercises, both positive and negative, provide crucial diagnostic information. For example, if nongenital pleasuring builds comfort with sensual touching, taking turns initiating, openness to the giver–recipient format, and utilizing feedback, but the process falls apart with the addition of genital pleasuring, the clinician becomes aware of one type of vulnerability (trap). If another couple does well as long as the woman is the initiator of the exercise and recipient of pleasure, but cannot function when the man is the recipient or because he is too passive to initiate, the clinician explores a different type of vulnerability for this couple. Sexual exercises have both a diagnostic and an intervention function. Exercises provide feedback to address anxieties and inhibitions. Processing exercises allows the clinician and couple to individualize and refine subsequent exercises. Anxieties and vulnerabilities are addressed, with a focus on increasing sexual awareness, comfort, and skill.

Many couples find the metaphor of building a sexual house helpful. The foundation of the house consists of trust, intimacy, awareness, and comfort. With nongenital and genital pleasuring, and the addition of erotic scenarios and techniques, the couple can build on this foundation (i.e., develop a functional, satisfying sexual style).

THE PROCESS OF SEX THERAPY

The sex therapy format begins with weekly sessions, with the couple engaging in two to four homework assignments between sessions. These tasks include reading, discussion, watching psychoeducational videotapes involving pleasuring, eroticism, or a specific dysfunction. The major interventions are behavioral sexual exercises. The exercises follow a semistructured format (McCarthy & McCarthy, 2002), which is modified and individualized as the couple progresses. This format continues with exercises for the specific dysfunction. Exercises are refined and individualized as a result of the couple's experiences and their feedback to the therapist.

A core theme of sex therapy, in contrast to general couple therapy, is the focus on sexual attitudes, behavior, and feelings. Unlike other problems (e.g., dealing with conflict, parenting, money), the therapist never directly observes the behavior; the partners never do anything sexual in the therapist's office or in front of the therapist. Moreover, the code of ethics of the American Association of Sex Educators, Counselors, and Therapists (1993) specifically prohibits sexual interaction between a therapist and client.

Assigning, processing, and designing sexual exercises is a core skill in sex therapy. Marital/couple therapists are usually more comfortable exploring feelings, family-of-origin dynamics, attitudes and values, and the context of couple intimacy than focusing on sexual behavior, with attendant feelings of anxiety, aversion, or eroticism. The primary goal of sex therapy is to establish a comfortable, functional couple sexual style, meaning that each person is capable of experiencing desire, arousal, orgasm, and emotional satisfaction. Unless the clinician is willing and able to structure therapy so that sexual problems are confronted directly, and anxieties, inhibitions, and/or skill deficits are dealt with, the goal of a functional sexual style will probably not be achieved.

Therapy sessions are structured, especially at the beginning. The first agenda item is to discuss experiences and exercises of the previous week; the therapist should emphasize detailed processing, rather than asking whether the behavior occurred and providing an overall evaluation. The discussion involves a fine-grained analysis of initiation patterns, comfort levels, receptivity and responsivity to specific pleasuring techniques, interfering anxieties or inhibitions, and subjective and objective feelings of arousal. The therapist's own anxieties may center around fear of appearing invasive or voyeuristic, eliciting erotic feelings or fantasies in the clients (or him-/herself), and crossing ethical or legal boundaries. Although these reactions do occur in therapy, there is no evidence that they are more likely to occur in sex therapy. Because of the therapist's heightened awareness of such matters, they may actually be less likely. In processing sexual exercises, the clinician uses his/her best clinical judgment in eliciting a clear picture of progress and difficulties, so that therapy is maximally effective. Therapist issues of boundaries, personal discomfort, or values are best dealt with in supervision with an experienced sex therapist.

Discussion of the following week's homework and exercises should not be left for the last 5 minutes, but should be integrated throughout the session, especially in processing exercises. Individualizing exercises promotes sexual comfort, receptivity to sensual and erotic touching, and sexual skill and responsivity.

This pattern reinforces the one–two combination of personal responsibility for sexuality and being an intimate team. Each person is responsible for his/her desire, arousal, and orgasm; it is not the other partner's role to give him/her an orgasm. Sexuality is an interpersonal process. Ideally, the partners view each other as sexual friends, and one's arousal facilitates the other's arousal.

The sex therapist is active, especially in the early stages of therapy, and serves as permission giver, sex educator, and advocate for intimate sexuality. As therapy progresses, structure and therapist activity decrease. The partners take increasing responsibility for processing experiences and feelings, creating their own agenda, moving to individualized and freeform sexual exercises, exploring personal and relational anxieties and vulnerabilities, and acknowledging strengths and valued characteristics. Therapy becomes less sexually focused and more intimacy-focused. The meanings of intimacy and sexuality are discussed, along with creating positive, realistic expectations. The couple and therapist collaborate in designing a relapse prevention program to maintain and generalize sexual gains.

The two worst mistakes therapists make are diverting the sexual focus and prematurely terminating treatment when sex becomes functional. The therapist and couple may collude in avoidance because sexuality can be a sensitive and anxiety-provoking area, especially talking about erotic scenarios and techniques. Permission giving, information, and sexual suggestions are helpful. However, dealing with specific inhibitions or avoidance—for instance, a man's fear of the "wax-and-wane" erection exercise (i.e., specifically allowing the erection to subside and then resuming erotic stimulation to arousal and erection), or a woman's intimidation by the exercise to guide the partner's hand and mouth to increase eroticism—is therapeutically challenging. It is essential that the therapist stay with the therapeutic strategy and process exercises. Doing so requires maintaining focus without being invasive or voyeuristic. The line between facilitating sexual awareness/comfort and making the sexual situation clinical and self-conscious requires that the therapist be sensitive and skillful. Many clinicians and most clients would rather talk about nonsexual issues, such as conflicts with families of origin or the meaning of intimacy, than stay focused on sexual dysfunction. It requires clinical skill and judgment to decide when to stay sexually focused and when to switch the focus to nonsexual issues.

Learning to be sexually functional is easier than integrating sexual expression into the couple's life. Most important is maintaining gains and preventing relapse. Researchers (e.g., Jacobson & Addis, 1993) have reported high levels of relapse among couples, and there is every reason to believe that this applies to sexual dysfunction as well.

Stopping therapy at the first sexually functional experience is not only premature, but can also be iatrogenic. Even among sexually functional couples, there are occasional problems of dysfunction and dissatisfaction (Frank, Anderson, & Rubinstein, 1978). By its nature, couple sexuality involves variability in both function and satisfaction. The unrealistic expectation that each experience must include equal desire, arousal, orgasm, and satisfaction for each partner sets a performance demand that will inevitably lead to relapse.

An integral component of high-quality, comprehensive sex therapy is a relapse prevention program, which is discussed below (McCarthy, 1993). The keys to maintaining therapeutic gains are positive, realistic (nonperfectionistic) expectations. Partners who accept a variable, flexible sexual style, and who realize it is normal to have occasional dysfunctional, unsatisfying, or mediocre experiences, will be inoculated against sexual problems associated with aging and the aging of the relationship.

COMMON SEXUAL DYSFUNCTIONS

Sexual dysfunction is more common among women than men. The most common female dysfunctions are (1) inhibited sexual desire, (2) nonorgasmic response during partner sex, (3) painful intercourse (dyspareunia), (4) female arousal dysfunction, (5) primary nonorgasmic response, and (6) vaginismus. The most common male sexual dysfunctions are (1) early ejaculation, (2) erectile dysfunction, (3) inhibited sexual desire, and (4) ejaculatory inhibition.

The definition of sexual function is the ability to experience *desire* (positive anticipation and feel deserving of sexual pleasure), *arousal* (receptivity and responsivity to erotic touch resulting in lubrication for the woman and erection for the man), *orgasm* (a voluntary response which is a natural culmination of high arousal), and *satisfaction* (feeling emotionally and sexually fulfilled and bonded). As noted earlier, "primary sexual dysfunction" means that the problem has always existed (e.g., primary ejaculatory inhibition means that the man has never experienced intravaginal ejaculation), whereas "secondary dysfunction" means that the person was once functional, but is now dysfunctional (e.g., secondary inhibited sexual desire means that a person at one time anticipated and felt deserving of sexual pleasure, but now has lost desire).

Sexual dysfunction often involves more than one problem and may be comorbid with a partner's dysfunction. The most common example of partner comorbidity is the male with secondary erectile dysfunction and inhibited desire, and the female with primary inhibited desire and secondary arousal and orgasmic dysfunction. Dysfunction is usually not total, but is predominant. For example, the woman with painful intercourse may have occasional comfortable experiences, or the male with ejaculatory inhibition may ejaculate intravaginally 30% of the time.

Female Sexual Dysfunctions

Inhibited Sexual Desire

In the previous edition of this *Handbook*, Heiman, Epps, and Ellis (1995) described the literature on inhibited sexual desire. Although there have been a number of books, chapters, and articles on this topic (e.g., Kaplan, 1995; Leiblum & Rosen, 1988; LoPiccolo & Friedman, 1988), assessment and intervention remain at an early stage of technical development.

It is often assumed that if the woman has an orgasm, everything is functional. However, a fine-grained analysis reveals that some women, once involved sexually, become aroused and orgasmic, but with low desire. The core components of desire are positive anticipation and a sense of deserving pleasure. Anticipation involves a number of factors—openness to touch, the presence of romantic or erotic fantasies, a desire for orgasm, and responsiveness to the partner's desire. Contextual factors, such as an inviting milieu, a weekend away without children, or a romantic or fun night out, can also influence anticipation. The organizing concept is to have "his," "her," and "our" "bridges to sexual desire" (McCarthy, 1995). The initial romantic love/passionate sex desire found in premarital and extramarital sex does not maintain desire in ongoing relationships.

Schnarch (1991) has challenged common therapy concepts and intervention regarding desire dysfunction. He emphasizes the crucial role of individuation and autonomy in maintaining sexual desire. Schnarch has also challenged the use of sexual exercises, believing that they promote an other-centered need for sexual validation, which subverts desire. Lobitz and Lobitz (1996) acknowledge the value of Schnarch's emphasis on autonomy, but take this to the critical next step of being open to the partner's sexual feelings and preferences and integrating these into the couple's sexual style. With integrated sexuality, each person's desire and arousal plays off the other's. The major aphrodisiac is an involved, aroused partner. Sexual exercises used in a mechanistic manner can be self-defeating; however, if they are used in a manner that confronts avoidance and inhibitions, and that facilitates involving both partner's in the sexual process, they can be invaluable in revitalizing sexual desire.

Our culture idealizes spontaneous, nonverbal, intense sexual scenarios (the movie model). Such idealization creates unrealistic performance demands and expectations. Not surprisingly, marital sex is rarely shown in movies—only premarital sex or extramarital affairs. Another unrealistic theme in such media is that both people are very turned on before touching. These scenarios make good entertainment, but are poisonous for marital sex.

One in three women complain of inhibited sexual desire (Laumann, Rosen, & Paik, 1999); half of such complaints are of primary inhibition and half of secondary inhibition. With primary inhibited desire, the woman does not experience sexuality as a positive, integral part of her personhood. Primary desire problems can be caused by a number of factors—antisexual family learnings, poor body image, lack of experience with self-exploration/masturbation, childhood sexual trauma, fear of pregnancy or HIV/AIDS, a history of sexual humiliation or rejection, and a fundamentalist religious background or an antierotic value system.

The sexual history taking and processing of sexual exercises will help identify factors that inhibit desire. Common causes of secondary inhibited desire are disappointment or anger with the partner and negative sexual experiences (e.g., rape, unwanted pregnancy, painful intercourse, or being blamed for the partner's sexual dysfunction). Other possible causes include insufficient couple time, exhaustion due to child care, devaluing marital sexuality, a belief that only intercourse counts as "sex," feelings of pressure or coercion by her partner, feelings of being trapped in a boring sexual routine, fear of another pregnancy, and comparisons of present sexual experiences with earlier experiences.

Couple exercises can facilitate sexual desire (McCarthy & McCarthy, 2002). These include building comfort with nudity and body image, taking turns initiating, identifying characteristics of the partner that the woman finds attractive, making one to three requests for change that increase attraction, establishing a trust/vulnerability position, identifying and playing out an erotic scenario, initiating erotic touching on a weekly basis, identifying subjective and external stimuli as turn-ons, and using a veto to stop an uncomfortable sexual experience (this is a crucial technique for those with a history of sexual trauma). A focus of the therapy sessions is on the woman's learning to view the partner as an intimate friend who is aware of her needs and open to her requests.

A key concept in dealing with inhibited sexual desire is the woman's establishing her "sexual voice." Female sexuality groups (Barbach, 1975) originally focused on teaching women to be orgasmic. They now have been expanded to deal with desire and arousal issues. The successful resolution of sexual dysfunction (e.g., learning to be aroused, to be orgasmic, to eliminate pain, or to overcome vaginismus) is of great value, but is not enough. Orgasm alone does not build desire. Desire involves a complex interplay among cognitive, behavioral, emotional, and relational phenomena. Basson (2000) has introduced an integrative model to understand unique aspects of female sexual function and dysfunction, with a special emphasis on responsive sexual desire.

Orgasmic Dysfunction

A common sexual complaint is a woman's not being orgasmic during intercourse. Typically, the man is more upset than the woman. He wants her to function like him—to have one orgasm during intercourse, which is seen as the "right" way to be sexual. In fact, one in three women who are regularly orgasmic with couple sex are not orgasmic during intercourse. This is not a dysfunction, but a normal variation in female sexual expression. Female sexual response is more variable and complex than male sexual response. A woman may be nonorgasmic, singly orgasmic, or multiorgasmic. Orgasms can occur with pleasuring/foreplay, during intercourse, or in afterplay. Feminist sexologists (e.g., Tiefer, 1998) have noted that concepts of sexual function and dysfunction are heavily influenced by the traditional male model, with a phallocentrist obsession with intercourse as "real sex." The feminist sexual response model honors flexibility, variability, and individual differences in the meaning and experience of sexuality. Intimacy, pleasuring, playfulness, eroticism, manual–oral–rubbing stimulation, and variant sexual scenarios and techniques are in the normal range. Self-stimulation is encouraged during partner sex (Heiman & LoPiccolo, 1988). An example of the variability of female sexual response is that 15–20% of women have a multiorgasmic response pattern, most commonly with cunnilingus or erotic nonintercourse stimulation.

As noted, being nonorgasmic during intercourse is a normal variation, not a dysfunction. Not being orgasmic at each sexual experience is also a normal variation. The therapist can provide information and set positive, realistic expectations about orgasmic response. An unrealistic performance demand of simultaneous orgasm during intercourse is problematic, as is the goal of achieving orgasm during intercourse as the only "right" way to be sexual.

A positive, realistic expectation is that the woman develop a regular pattern of arousal and orgasm, with recognition of flexibility and variability. What is typically seen as dysfunctional is an absence of orgasm by any means (primary nonorgasmic response), orgasmic response with self-stimulation but not partner sex, or infrequent orgasmic response (orgasm in fewer than 25% of experiences). Since the 1970s, there has been a decrease in primary nonorgasmic response due to increased awareness of female sexuality, the availability of female sexuality therapy groups and self-help books, an increased use of vibrators, manual, and oral stimulation, and women's more active role in the sexual scenario. However, there has been an increase in secondary nonorgasmic response, partly due to performance demands and failure to incorporate the meaning and value of intimacy and sexuality in an ongoing relationship.

In assessing nonorgasmic response, several factors are crucial: the woman's attitudes toward sexuality and her body; awareness of her arousal–orgasm pattern; development of her "sexual voice"; awareness of what facilitates and inhibits desire and receptivity; inhibitions or resentments that interfere with responsivity and arousal; passivity; a history of sexual trauma; guilt over sexual secrets; and emotional and practical factors that block sexual expression. Orgasmic response is the natural culmination of comfort, pleasure, eroticism, and high arousal.

With secondary nonorgasmic response, it is crucial to carefully assess a range of personal, relational, physical, and situational factors that inhibit sexuality. Factors include side effects of medications (especially antidepressants); resentment toward or disappointment in the partner or the couple relationship; lack of time and energy due to competing demands from children, extended family, job, and house; feeling bored with a mechanical sexual pattern; or partner sexual dysfunction. Assessment continues in the treatment phase in response to exercises, processing during therapy, and exploring the meanings of sexuality and sexual dysfunction for the woman and relationship.

Therapeutic interventions for orgasmic dysfunction include encouraging the woman (and her partner) to develop her "sexual voice"; to make use of multiple stimulation during nonintercourse and intercourse sex; to identify "orgasm triggers" from masturbation experiences, and to generalize these to partner sex; to increase comfort, emotional intimacy, and trust; to identify and play out erotic scenarios; to request and guide stimulation; to make the transition to intercourse at her initiation; and to give herself permission to let go and be orgasmic with manual, oral, or rubbing stimulation. When a woman's orgasm is viewed as a sign of a man's expertise, this creates performance anxiety. Women are not autonomous sexual responders; both female socialization and physiology support intimate, interactive sexuality. The optimal prescription is intimacy, pleasuring, and eroticism.

Traditionally, eroticism has been underplayed in female sexuality. Without a solid base of receptivity and responsivity, erotic techniques cannot "force" orgasm. Orgasm is the natural culmination of pleasure, eroticism, arousal, and letting go. A man's attitudes, behavior, and feelings are integral to a woman's arousal. Often a man, under the guise of being a "sophisticated lover," is in fact manipulating the woman (i.e., her orgasm is to prove something for him). The woman is responsible for her orgasm. The man has to respect her sexual voice and autonomy. Sex is about awareness and sharing pleasure, not performing to an arbitrary criterion or goal. As noted, a crucial therapeutic strategy is to reinforce the one–two combination of each person taking responsibility for sexuality and the couple being an intimate team.

Sex therapy strategies and techniques are most effective with anxiety-based dysfunctions, lack of awareness, and inhibitions. Therapeutic techniques include self-stimulation (with or without a vibrator), increased awareness and guiding a receptive partner, using multiple erotic stimulation, gaining confidence in the arousal–orgasm pattern, and freedom to decide when and how to integrate intercourse into the couple's lovemaking style.

When dysfunction (especially secondary arousal dysfunction and/or nonorgasmic response) is confounded with negative emotions (disappointment, anger, alienation, distrust), treatment is more complex. Attention focuses on assessment/intervention at the systemic and meaning levels. An important technique is to help each person recognize the function of the sexual problem and do a cost–benefit assessment of the emotional and relational consequences of resolving the problem. Therapy sessions help clarify the functions and meaning of sexuality for the woman and the relationship.

Female Arousal Dysfunction

Although much attention has been given to male arousal dysfunction (erection), relatively little clinical or research attention has focused on female arousal dysfunction. The objective (physical) measures of arousal are ease and amount of vaginal lubrication. The subjective measure is feeling "turned on." Both are variable and difficult to quantify (Basson, 2000). The introduction of Viagra has caused renewed interest in female arousal for researchers and clinicians.

Often when a woman enters therapy with the complaint of painful intercourse or nonorgasmic response, a careful analysis reveals that the prime problem is lack of arousal. It is possible for a woman to have high desire and low arousal, or to be orgasmic but still have arousal dysfunction. The therapeutic focus is usually on desire or orgasm, but in fact arousal is a crucial component deserving assessment and intervention.

Key to understanding arousal is a careful assessment of the woman's receptivity–responsivity pattern. What pleasuring scenarios and techniques is she most receptive to? When is she open and responsive to erotic touch? What is the optimal timing and sequencing of erotic techniques? It is useful to think of sexual response on a 0–10 scale (10 is orgasm): 1–3 refers to comfort and sensuality, 3–5 to pleasure, 6–9 to eroticism/arousal.

Traditionally, it is the male who controls "foreplay," stimulates the woman until he judges she is ready for intercourse, and initiates intromission. In the treatment program for female arousal dysfunction, it is the woman who controls the type of stimulation and timing of transitions. For example, many women prefer prolonged nongenital pleasuring. Some women prefer taking turns in the pleasurer-recipient format, while others prefer mutual pleasuring. Attitudinally, the focus is on "pleasuring," not "foreplay." Intercourse is not necessarily the centerpiece of the pleasuring–eroticism process. In designing and processing exercises, she is encouraged to experiment with utilizing single versus multiple stimulation; being solely the recipient versus both actively giving and receiving; utilizing manual, oral, or rubbing stimulation versus intercourse; and using lubricants such as Astroglide, nonallergenic lotions, or K-Y Jelly. She is actively involved in the pleasuring-eroticism–arousal process.

For those women who feel subjectively aroused but do not lubricate sufficiently, the preferrred intervention is to use lubricants. This can be done in a comfortable, sensual manner. Being self-conscious or apologetic blocks erotic flow. A rhythm of comfort, pleasure, and eroticism is integral to overcoming female arousal dysfunction.

Painful Intercourse and Vaginismus

The problem of painful intercourse is paradoxical: Some cases are quite easy to resolve, while other cases require the coordinated efforts of a gynecologist and a sex therapist to confront complex physical conditions and couple dynamics. Goodwin and Agronin's (1997) self-help book emphasizes the importance of knowledge and comfort with the woman's genitalia, the use of general relaxation and specific vulva relaxation techniques, the woman's controlling the type and pacing of genital stimulation, the use of lubricants, her initiation and guidance of intromission, and the couple's finding intercourse positions and types of thrusting that

are pain-free. The assumption behind these techniques is that the woman is an active participant and values sexuality. Involvement and arousal are the antidotes to passivity, hypervigilance about pain, and viewing intercourse as the man's domain.

Clinicians and researchers who deal with sexual pain (e.g., Bergeron, Binik, Khalife, & Pogidas, 1997) recognize it as a complex biopsychosocial phenomenon that needs to be addressed in a multicausal, multidimensional manner. Assessment often requires the participation of a gynecologist with a subspecialty in pain to assess such syndromes as vulvadinia, vaginal tears, vulvar vestibulitis syndrome, infections, sexually transmitted diseases, poor vaginal tone, and medication side effects. Medical interventions include surgery, oral medications, and vaginal creams. A common therapeutic technique is exercising the pubococcygeal (PC) muscle, which increases awareness and strengthens the vaginal wall. Clinicians emphasize the efficacy of the PC muscle exercise, although empirical support is weak.

Couple sex therapy for pain again focuses on the one–two combination of the woman's being an active, responsible person, and the couple's functioning as an intimate team. The emphasis is on psychological and relational factors that facilitate comfort, pleasure, eroticism, and intercourse. This requires major attitudinal, behavioral, and emotional changes for both partners. It requires that she be assertive and he be open to her requests, her guidance, and especially the rhythm of the sexual scenario. Comfort is the underpinning of desire and arousal. Pain or fear of pain sabotages sexual pleasure.

Vaginismus is one of the most successfully treated dysfunctions, yet one of the most complex. A psychoeducational videotape on vaginismus (LoPiccolo, 1984) clearly outlines the preferred treatment program. Yet, as Donahey (1998) observed, many women have high anticipatory anxiety, are unaccepting of their bodies, and are intimidated by their partners' sexual desire and arousal. The change process for vaginismus may be slow, with a need for carefully crafted individual and couple interventions. Clinical guidelines for painful intercourse are applicable, with a special emphasis on comfort with vaginal insertion. Use of fingers (hers and then his), graduated sizes of dilators, and insertion of the lubricated penis are stepwise interventions. Insertion is easier when the woman is both subjectively and objectively aroused.

In summary, assessment and treatment of female sexual dysfunction require a broad-based approach to physical, psychological, relational, cultural, and sexual technique factors. The organizing concept is the woman's being an aware, comfortable, and responsible sexual person—speaking with a clear "sexual voice." Couple interventions center around feeling and functioning as an intimate team in which the woman is an equitable partner. Her anticipation, her feeling deserving, and both partners' respecting her conditions for healthy sexuality are important in facilitating desire. Integrating sensuality and eroticism, openness to requests and guidance, and focusing on erotic techniques (especially multiple stimulation and the woman's guiding of intercourse) are important for arousal. Awareness of her arousal–orgasm pattern, using self- or partner stimulation during intercourse, using multiple stimulation and orgasm triggers, and giving herself permission to be erotic and letting go are important for orgasm. Developing afterplay scenarios, sharing intimacy, acknowledging emotional and sexual connection, and feeling bonded are important for satisfaction.

Male Sexual Dysfunctions

With the exception of early ejaculation, the great majority of male sexual problems are secondary. Males are generally eager to be in sex therapy when the problem is female dysfunction, but reluctant and embarrassed when the problem is male dysfunction.

Male sexual socialization is antithetical to the strategies and techniques of couple sex therapy. In traditional socialization, the male is supposed to be the "sex expert" with no anxieties or inhibitions. Sexual performance is supposed to be totally predictable and perfect; sex is competitive, and no weaknesses or questions are tolerated; and masculinity and sexuality are highly related. The self-defeating concept is that a "real man" is willing and able to have sex with any woman, at any time, in any situation (McCarthy & McCarthy, 1998a). Males learn that desire, arousal, and orgasm are easy, predictable, and autonomous (i.e., a man needs nothing from a woman). Traditionally, males do not value intimate, interactive sexuality. This is a prime cause of secondary sexual dysfunction as men and their relationships age.

Sex therapy can help a man resolve a dysfunction; even more importantly, it can help him to learn healthy attitudes and skills, especially the value of intimate, interactive sex. These learnings set the stage for relapse prevention and inoculate him against sexual problems with aging.

Sex therapy concepts and techniques are more acceptable to women, but are just as beneficial for men. When a couple stops having sex, whether at 40 or 70, it is typically the man's decision—communicated nonverbally (Butler & Lewis, 1993). A major cause of such a process is feeling embarrassed and stigmatized because he has failed at the male sexual performance model. In therapy, the male learns to view sexuality as a pleasure, not a performance; to value the woman as his sexual friend, not someone to prove something to; to enjoy a variable, flexible couple sexual style, rather than a rigid intercourse pass–fail test; and to regard sexuality as intimate and interactive, not autonomous.

Early Ejaculation

Although early ejaculation is the most common male sexual dysfunction, it is not easy to measure objectivity. The most clinically useful assessment/definition of early ejaculation focuses on the couple's subjective evaluation of pleasure and satisfaction rather than a strict performance criterion (McCarthy, 1989). When the man ejaculates before intromission, at the point of intromission, with fewer than 10 thrusts, or within a minute of intercourse, almost all couples will identify this as early ejaculation. Most men begin their sexual careers with rapid ejaculation, and 30% of adult males complain of early ejaculation. Masters and Johnson (1970) and Kaplan (1974) reported treatment success rates higher than 90% for this disorder. Metz, Pryor, Nesvacil, Abuzzan, and Koznar (1997) and Strassberg, Brazao, Rowland, Tan, and Slob (1999) present evidence that for some men, there is a significant physiological component that makes it difficult to learn ejaculatory control, and a significant number of such men relapse. A new trend, mimicking the movement to medicalize erectile dysfunction, is to use medication for ejaculatory control. Elsewhere (McCarthy, 1994), I have noted that ejaculatory control can be facilitated by use of medication; however, medication should be regarded as an additional resource, not as a substitute for ejaculatory control exercises.

The essence of the assessment–intervention program is to help the man break the connection between high arousal and quick orgasm. Contrary to "do-it-yourself" techniques to reduce arousal, such as wearing two condoms, applying a desensitizing cream to the glans of the penis, or using nonerotic thoughts, the focus in learning ejaculatory control is maintaining arousal while heightening awareness and comfort. The strategy is counterintuitive—practicing increased stimulation and arousal while increasing awareness, comfort, and control.

For the majority of males, early ejaculation is a powerfully overlearned habit in both masturbation and intercourse. Relearning involves two processes. The first is the ability to discriminate the point of ejaculatory inevitability (after which ejaculation is no longer a voluntary function), and the second is to increase erotic stimulation while lengthening the time from arousal to orgasm. The major learning technique is the "stop–start" approach which is easier to apply and more acceptable to the partner than the traditional "squeeze" technique (McCarthy, 1989).

Identifying the point of ejaculatory inevitability occurs through masturbation or partner manual stimulation. When the man is approaching the point of inevitability, he signals (either verbally or nonverbally) for the woman to cease stimulation. The urge to ejaculate decreases after 15–60 seconds, and stimulation is resumed. At first the stop–start technique may be used three or four times, but it becomes less necessary over time as the couple makes the transition into slowing down and altering stimulation.

Men (and women) have unrealistic expectations about the time spent in intercourse. A typical pleasuring/sexual scenario might last 15–45 minutes, with average time spent in intercourse 2–7 minutes. Few intercourse experiences exceed 10 minutes. Men are intimidated by the fantasy goal of hour-long intercourse. Maintaining realistic expectations is crucial. Acceptance is difficult for the man whose expectations are based on male boasting and a competitive, performance-based norm.

A crucial concept is for the man to view the woman as his intimate sexual friend. A man typically emphasizes performance *for* the woman rather than sharing pleasure *with* her. The male hopes that if intercourse lasts longer, he will "give her an orgasm during intercourse." The man acts as if ejaculatory control is for her, not him. A significant number of women find it easier to be orgasmic with nonintercourse stimulation (manual, oral, or rubbing stimulation). The purpose of learning ejaculatory control is for the man to enhance comfort and pleasure. In addition, the sexual experience is more involving and satisfying for the couple.

Exercises are designed in a stepwise manner; the man learns ejaculatory control first with manual and oral stimulation, and then with intercourse. The "quiet vagina" exercise involves minimal movement controlled by the woman from the female on top position. The most difficult position is the man

on top using short, rapid thrusting. A man often does better with circular thrusting; longer, slower thrusting; or the woman controlling thrusting. The couple works collaboratively to develop sexual scenarios and techniques that enhance pleasure and satisfaction. Throughout the process, the woman's sexual feelings and needs are important. The partner being an intimate team who clearly and comfortably communicate sexual feelings, techniques, and requests is integral to maintaining therapeutic gains.

A common result of unsuccessful treatment or "do-it-yourself" techniques is the development of erectile dysfunction. When the focus is on heightening awareness and pleasure, erectile functioning is not subverted. When arousal is decreased or self-consciousness raised, erectile problems are a likely outcome.

Erectile Dysfunction

With the introduction of Viagra in 1998, there has been a paradigm shift in the assessment and treatment of erectile dysfunction (Segreaves, 1998a). The medical and lay public now view it as primarily a physical problem and consider the first level of intervention to be Viagra. Only if that is not successful is further assessment undertaken. Moreover, the prescription for Viagra is typically written by a family practitioner or internist, rather than a sexual specialist. What does this mean for couple therapy?

Viagra is the first user-friendly medical intervention; it is much easier to accept taking a pill than using an external pump, penile injection, Muse system, or penile prosthesis. It has heightened public awareness of the frequency of erectile dysfunction, especially for men over 50, and as a side effect of surgery, illness, and medications. However, Viagra poses the danger of medicalizing male sexuality.

Althof (1998) stressed the crucial role of the sex therapist in assessment, treatment, and motivating the partners to integrate Viagra into their lovemaking style. McCarthy (1999a) has discussed the therapeutic and iatrogenic uses of Viagra, and proposed an assessment–intervention approach that emphasizes couple sex therapy. Basson (1998) has proposed a model of integrating Viagra and other medical interventions into a holistic treatment program.

Erection is *not* solely a male concern separate from the couple's experience. Viagra promises a return to the autonomous male model, with predictable sex and a downplaying of the woman's sexual feelings and role. We (McCarthy & McCarthy, 1998b) and Schnarch (1997) have presented separate models that emphasize intimate, interactive sexuality with a focus on quality and satisfaction. Marital sex may not be as frequent or intense as premarital sex, but quality, pleasure, and satisfaction can increase with time and age. A major transition for middle-aged and older males is being open to partner involvement and erotic stimulation.

The frequency of erectile dysfunction for males over 50 is estimated to be more than 50%. Erectile dysfunction is a multicausal, multidimensional phenomenon, with wide individual and couple differences. The simplistic "organic versus psychological" dichotomy of causation is recognized as scientifically invalid and therapeutically nonproductive. The present folklore that 90% of erection problems are caused by physical factors is no more valid than the past folk wisdom that 90% of erection problems were caused by psychological factors. Prostate surgery, degenerative diabetes, and spinal cord injury usually cause organic deficits. But even in a couple affected by such a disorder, examination of psychological, relational, and motivational factors are important in successfully integrating Viagra or other medical interventions into the couple's lovemaking style. When the man gets firm erections during masturbation oral sex, sex with another partner, or a fetish arousal pattern, use of Viagra is unlikely to be successfully integrated into the couple's sexual style, and can even be iatrogenic because core psychological and relationship problems are ignored.

The recommended assessment–intervention strategy is couple sex therapy, with medical assessment as an important component in evaluating hormonal, vascular, and neurological functioning as well as side effects of medications. Other common physical factors interfering with erections are drinking, smoking, and drug abuse. In the sexual history, it is crucial to obtain an honest assessment of situations where the man is functional. Being able to flag sensitive or secret material encourages honest reporting. A common pattern is the one in which the man gets erections with masturbation, while viewing pornography or cybersex, or in an affair (whether with a man or a woman, or a variant scenario with a prostitute). This information is vital in constructing an intervention strategy. The man who gets no erections by any means requires a thorough medical assessment and appropriate intervention. The clinician assesses whether a desire problem preceded or followed the erection problem. Any sexual secret—whether an affair,

variant arousal, compulsive sexuality, or a sexual orientation issue—needs to be carefully explored both for function and meaning.

A question to explore during the woman's history is how she felt about sexuality before the erectile dysfunction began. How has the problem affected her sexual desire and arousal? In many cases, a woman blames herself for the problem (attributing it to her weight gain, her lack of erotic skills, or his boredom with the relationship) and/or sees it as a symbol of loss of love. In other cases, the women has resented the man's sexual attitudes and behavior for years and is secretly glad he is not able to have intercourse. In still other cases, the woman is hostile or verbally abusive about the erectile dysfunction. By contrast, a women may be pleased because the partner now devotes time and energy to pleasuring her. The woman's attitudes and feelings both before and since the erectile dysfunction are carefully assessed. Erectile dysfunction makes some men open to receiving and giving sensual and erotic stimulation. Unfortunately, many males avoid any affectionate or sexual contact so that they do not have to face "the embarrassment of erectile failure."

The list of guidelines in Figure 24.1 is given to the couple as a handout at the feedback session, is referred to throughout therapy, and serves as the basis for relapse prevention.

The paradigm shift in the conceptualization of erectile dysfunction is more than the medicalization of the penis. It views erections as primarily, if not solely, the male's domain. In contrast, as I have noted throughout this chapter, sex therapy emphasizes the one–two combination of personal responsibility and being an intimate team. In selected couples, Viagra is used during genital pleasuring exercises. A healthy cognition is that Viagra is an additional resource to increase arousal and erections. With genital pleasuring exercises, it is important to reinforce the necessity of erotic stimulation to facilitate erection (it does not automatically occur because of Viagra) and the wax-and-wane exercise (when erotic flow is interrupted, the erection decreases, and it recurs with stimulation). This reinforces for both partners that it is not just the pill that helps; intimacy, pleasuring, and eroticism matter. This experience facilitates integration of Viagra into the couple's lovemaking style.

Therapeutic gains with Viagra must be generalized and maintained. When erection occurs with manual and/or oral stimulation, the couple can use Viagra as a backup resource if there are a series of unsuccessful intercourse attempts. As in

1. By age 40, 90% of males experience at least one erectile failure. This is a normal occurrence, not a sign of erectile dysfunction.
2. The majority of erectile problems (especially for men under 50) are caused primarily by psychological or relationship factors, not medical or physiological malfunctions. To evaluate medical factors, consult a urologist with training in erectile function and dysfunction.
3. Erectile problems can be caused by a wide variety of factors, including alcohol, anxiety, depression, vascular or neurological deficits, distraction, anger, side effects of medication, frustration, hormonal deficiency, fatigue, and not feeling sexual at that time or with that partner.
4. Medical interventions—especially the oral medication Viagra—can be a valuable resource to facilitate erectile function, but is not a "magic pill." Partners need to integrate Viagra (or other medical interventions) into their lovemaking style.
5. Don't believe the myth of the "male machine," ready to have intercourse at any time, with any woman, in any situation. You and your penis are human. You are not a performance machine.
6. View the erectile difficulty as a situational problem. Do not overreact and label yourself "impotent" or put yourself down as a "failure."
7. A pervasive myth is that if a man loses his initial erection, it means he's sexually turned off. It is a natural physiological process for erections to wax and wane during prolonged pleasuring.
8. In a typical 45-minute pleasuring session, erection will wax and wane two to five times. Subsequent erections, intercourse, and orgasm are quite satisfying.
9. You don't need an erect penis to satisfy a woman. Orgasm can be achieved through manual, oral, or rubbing stimulation. If you have problems getting or maintaining an erection, don't stop the sexual interaction. A woman finds it arousing to have the partner's fingers, tongue, or penis (erect or flaccid) used for stimulation.
10. Actively involve yourself in giving and receiving pleasurable and erotic touching. Erection is a natural result of pleasure, eroticism, and feeling turned on.
11. You cannot will or force an erection. Don't be a passive "spectator" who is distracted by the state of his penis. Sex is not a spectator sport; it requires active involvement.
12. Allow the woman to initiate intercourse and guide your penis into her vagina. This reduces performance pressure and, since she is the expert on her vagina, is the most practical procedure.
13. Feel comfortable saying, "I want sex to be pleasurable and playful. When I feel pressure to perform, I get uptight, and sex is not good. Let's make sexuality enjoyable by taking it at a comfortable pace, enjoying playing and pleasuring, and being an intimate team."
14. Erectile problems do not affect the ability to ejaculate (men can ejaculate with a flaccid penis). The man relearns ejaculation to the cue of an erect penis.
15. One way to regain confidence is through masturbation. During masturbation you can practice gaining and losing erections, relearn ejaculating with an erection, and focus on fantasies and stimulation that can be transferred to partner sex.
16. Don't try to use the morning erection for quick intercourse. This erection is associated with REM sleep and results from dreaming and being close to the partner. Men try vainly to have intercourse with the morning erection before losing it. Remember: Arousal and erection are regainable. Morning is a good time to be sexual.
17. When sleeping, you get an erection every 90 minutes—three to five erections a night. Sex is a natural physiological function. Don't block it by anticipatory anxiety, performance anxiety, distraction, or putting yourself down. Give yourself (and your partner) permission to enjoy the pleasure of sexuality.
18. Make clear, direct, assertive requests (not demands) for stimulation you find most erotic. Verbally and nonverbally guide your partner in how to pleasure and arouse you.
19. Stimulating a flaccid penis is counterproductive, because you can become obsessed and distracted by the state of your penis. Engage in sensuous, playful, nondemand stimulation. Enjoy giving and receiving stimulation, rather than trying to "will an erection."
20. Your attitudes and thoughts affect arousal. The key is "sex and pleasure," not "sex and performance."
21. A sexual experience is best measured by pleasure and satisfaction, not whether you had an erection, how hard it was, or whether your partner was orgasmic. Some sexual experiences will be great for both partners, some better for one than the other, some mediocre, and others unsuccessful. Do not put your sexual self-esteem on the line at each sexual experience.

FIGURE 24.1. Arousal and erection guidelines: A handout for clients.

the treatment of female dysfunction, we encourage the male to use self-stimulation in conjunction with partner stimulation. Many males are embarrassed to touch themselves when a partner is present—an inhibition that can be successfully confronted.

Erection exercises (McCarthy & McCarthy, 2002) are assigned in conjunction with a psycho-educational videotape (Focus International, 1991) to provide permission, information, suggestions, and a successful model. The cognition of "intercourse as a special pleasuring technique" is a significant change. This flexible, variable conceptualization is often more easily accepted by the woman than by the man. Traditional male sexual socialization, cultural norms, urologists, and the media emphasize that "real sex is intercourse" and "intercourse is the only measure of treatment success." Intercourse as the rigid performance criterion is self-defeating.

A positive, realistic conceptualization is that intimacy, pleasure, and eroticism flow to erection and intercourse in well over 75% of experiences. When intercourse does not occur, the couple can comfortably make a transition to one of two alternative scenarios—a sensual, pleasuring scenario or an erotic, nonintercourse scenario resulting in orgasm for one or both partners. Whether erectile problems occur once a year, once a month, or once every 10 times, it is normal to have occasional mediocre or unsatisfying sexual experiences. If this fact is not accepted, a man is "one failure away from square one." Clinging to the adolescent expectation of easy, automatic, 100% predictable erections is self-defeating. Even when using Viagra each time, men cannot live up to such perfectionistic criteria.

Inhibited Sexual Desire

For the great majority of males, inhibited sexual desire is a secondary dysfunction. ISD affects approximately 15% of men, and increases with age. The most common cause is another sexual dysfunction (erectile dysfunction or ejaculatory inhibition), which worsens over time. He becomes stuck in the cycle of anticipatory anxiety, tense and failed intercourse experiences, and sexual avoidance. Sex becomes an embarrassment rather than a pleasure. Although some men stop being sexual, the majority continue masturbation, and some develop a secret life of pornography, cybersex, or prostitutes.

Primary inhibited sexual desire is rare because of the cultural link between masculinity and sexuality, as well as adolescent experiences with masturbation. Sex is viewed as a positive, integral part of being a male. Causes of primary inhibited sexual desire range from testosterone deficiency to rigid family or religious antisexual messages. The most common cause is a sexual secret, such as a variant arousal pattern, a paraphilia, or homosexual orientation. Arousal during masturbation with the idiosyncratic sexual script may be more powerful than partner sex. Approximately 2–5% of males have a paraphilia (Abel, Osborn, Anthony, & Gardos, 1992). Most are benign, involving fetishes, cross-dressing or cybersex. Noxious paraphilias—exhibitionism, voyeurism, pedophilia, obscene phone calls—are illegal, cause trauma to others, and must be vigorously treated.

Homosexuality is in a different category. The emotional and sexual commitment to men is an acceptable sexual variation, and in fact is optimal for gay men. The scientific and clinical data strongly support acceptance of homosexuality as a normal sexual variation, although this remains controversial (especially among political and religious organizations). There is also major disagreement regarding the frequency of homosexuality, although the best estimate is that 10% of males have had major sexual involvement with men and 25% have been orgasmic with a man in adolescence or young adulthood. Perhaps 4–6% of males have a homosexual orientation.

Another subgroup of men with primary inhibited sexual desire are afraid of sexual failure, have a history of sexual trauma, or are guilty or shameful. The majority of primary inhibited desire involves a substitute sexual outlet rather than an absence of desire.

A man with inhibited sexual desire who appears for couple therapy is usually coerced by his partner. His goal is to avoid self-disclosure and therapy. He wants to keep his sexual life secret from the woman as well as the therapist. Partner sex usually results in dysfunction, leaving him feeling embarrassed and defeated. It is crucial that the therapist be empathic, be nonjudgmental, and not coerce the man to be sexual. The man feels alone and deficient; his sexual dysfunction is his "shameful secret." The therapist's permission giving, empathy, and understanding of how the problem has developed and is maintained constitute a valuable intervention.

Such a man usually feels that his female partner is his worst critic rather than an intimate sexual friend. The woman's role in assessment and treatment is crucial. The woman feels bewildered and rejected as a result of the man's inhibited sexual desire and avoidance. Underneath the anger are a sense of hurt and feelings of abandonment. It is important to explore whether the woman has a sexual outlet—masturbation or an affair. Does the woman experience inhibited desire herself? If so, did her problem proceed or follow the man's? Is the woman motivated to be an active, involved partner? The woman's sexual desire and arousal can facilitate the man's desire and arousal.

Male inhibited sexual desire, whether secondary (often linked to a dysfunction) or primary (caused by a variant arousal), is one of the most difficult problems to treat. A common secret is an affair he is unwilling to give up. An active affair is a contraindication for couple sex therapy. Affairs take time and energy. Couple therapy usually fails when there is an active affair, because the man lacks motivation and focus to confront his inhibited desire in the marriage.

Because there is a sexual dysfunction, couple sex therapy is not necessarily the treatment of choice. Severe individual problems, such as untreated alcoholism, bipolar disorder, or panic disorder, can subvert sex therapy. In addition to an affair, severe relationship distress (including partner abuse, lack of respect or trust, or conflict over money or children) can sabotage couple sex therapy. Traditionally, individual and/or couple therapy for such problems was recommended before proceeding with sex therapy. This decision requires high levels of clinical judgment, because the danger, especially with male inhibited sexual desire, is that sexual avoidance becomes more severe and chronic.

In successful treatment, each person develops bridges to sexual desire. The woman's responsiveness serves to reignite the man's sexuality (McCarthy, 1995). The man usually has an unspoken wish to return to the "good old days" when he was the sexual initiator and expert, but this is self-defeating. Strategies and techniques for treating female inhibited sexual desire are similar to those for the male disorder, but with a different focus. For the male version, the permission-giving element is for the man to find a new "sexual voice" that emphasizes intimate, interactive sexuality. Males are encouraged to use both internal and external cues to enhance desire. These may include to use fantasies, erotic stimuli such as videotapes, elaborate and intricate pleasuring scenarios, multiple stimulation during intercourse, and erotic scenarios other than intercourse. The man is encouraged to be aware of the positive functions of sexuality for himself and his relationship.

Married males who have a secret life with prostitutes, affairs, cybersex, or pornography are asked to assess carefully whether any elements of those experiences can be generalized to marital sexuality. Traditionally, such a man's wife is kept in a circumscribed role. As one male said, "Since I pay the prostitute, it's her role to turn me on." His wife said, "I don't need your money, but I do need you to be there, open to my touch, and willing to share eroticism." The major aphrodisiac is an involved, aroused partner.

Ejaculatory Inhibition

Ejaculatory inhibition is the least common and most misunderstood male dysfunction. Males with this dysfunction ejaculate with masturbation, and some can ejaculate with manual or oral stimulation, but they do not ejaculate during intercourse (or only rarely). Among young males, ejaculatory inhibition is mistakenly envied, because such a man is thought to be a "stud" whose lasting power ensures the woman has an orgasm during intercourse. Ejaculatory inhibition is frustrating for both the man and woman. The typical pattern is that the man gets an erection and quickly proceeds to intercourse, but his level of subjective arousal is low and intercourse is not erotic. By thrusting mechanically, he hopes to finally "come." Most women find that after 10–15 minutes of thrusting, arousal and lubrication wane. Intercourse in such cases is emotionally frustrating and physically irritating. Nonerotic intercourse is not pleasurable for either partner.

Men over 40 may develop intermittent ejaculatory inhibition. This dysfunction is the result of reduced eroticism during intercourse. For males in their 20s, it is easy (often too easy) to reach orgasm; this is not true for males in their 40s or 50s. Thrusting alone is not enough. The man is stuck in the performance myth that a real man does not need additional erotic stimulation to reach orgasm. Once again, the key to successful treatment is for both partners to value intimate, interactive sexuality. More specifically, the man requests multiple stimulation before and during intercourse, and utilizes "orgasm triggers" (McCarthy & McCarthy, 1998a). Because ejaculation is a natural result of high arousal, the partners collaborate to increase subjective arousal. The woman's responsiveness and arousal reinforce the man's arousal. An important technique is delaying the onset of intercourse until the man is highly aroused. Traditionally, a man begins intercourse as soon as he achieves an erection, even if his subjective arousal is at 2 (on a 10-point scale). The man is advised not to make the transition into intercourse until his subjective arousal is at 7 or 8. Intercourse requires verbal and nonverbal communication, as well as emphasizing the reciprocal effect of partner arousal and multiple stimulation throughout the sexual experience.

CASE ILLUSTRATION

This was a second marriage for 31-year-old Lauren, and a first marriage for 32-year-old Roger. They had been married 4 years and had separated twice—once for 4 days, once for 3 weeks. Lauren was in individual therapy, and Roger had been in individual therapy. They had had two courses of unsuccessful marital therapy, one with a psychiatrist and the other with a couple therapist. The referral for couple sex therapy came from Lauren's individual therapist.

Lauren complained of secondary inhibited sexual desire, arousal dysfunction, and painful intercourse. Interestingly, these problems did not affect her ability to reach orgasm. Roger was frustrated and blaming. He had a primary early ejaculation dysfunction, but was open to afterplay and enthusiastic about a second intercourse, during which he usually had better ejaculatory control.

Both were motivated for couple therapy, and Roger was particularly enthusiastic about a sexual focus. Each partner wanted the marriage to work, but both felt ambivalence and frustration. The marital bond was weak and tenuous. They agreed to a 6-month "good-faith" commitment to focus on the marriage and marital sex, with no threats of separation.

Lauren and Roger agreed that their best sex had occurred premaritally, but that this period had ended 3 months before the marriage. They had had severe conflict with Roger's parents, who were opposed to his marrying a divorced woman. There was much stress over the ceremony and whom to invite. Although they could have high-quality, functional sex on occasion, their typical pattern was sex of low frequency and quality.

Lauren's individual history revealed that she viewed herself as attractive and sexual. She had been sexually active since age 16, and desire, arousal, and orgasm had been easy. Men pursued her. Lauren enjoyed giving fellatio, but preferred receiving manual stimulation. If a relationship lasted more than 2 years, or if there was disappointment or stress, Lauren used a new lover to reignite sexual desire and responsiveness. Her parents were alive and married, but it was a conflictual, unsatisfying relationship. Roger knew from conversations with Lauren's father that each parent had had ongoing affairs, but this information was kept secret from Lauren. In her first marriage, Lauren had had no affairs involving intercourse, but numerous flirtatious relationships that included kissing, caressing, and giving oral stimulation. A major reason for the divorce was the ex-husband's abuse of cocaine and having sex with the woman who supplied his drugs. Feelings of betrayal and loss of respect destroyed her sexual desire. The marriage continued another 8 months during the ex-husband's drug rehabilitation, but for Lauren the bond had been broken.

Lauren's sexuality was contingent on being treated like a "princess." She felt that Roger had broken his promises, which lowered her desire. She blamed Roger for her inhibited desire and took no personal responsibility. Lauren had a number of secrets from Roger: criticalness about his weight;

a history of nonintercourse affairs; a history of shutting down sexually; and a plan to become pregnant, so that even if they divorced, she would take a baby from this relationship. At the therapist's urging, Lauren agreed to stay on birth control pills during the course of therapy. She did not agree to share her secrets, because she felt this would give Roger ammunition to blame her.

The sexual history with Roger was challenging. He wanted to talk about his premarital experiences: first sex to orgasm at age 10, first intercourse at age 12. He bragged about having over 100 partners, although Lauren was the "best sex partner ever." He was the only child from his father's second marriage, and his father's fifth wife was a woman younger than Lauren. His mother was in a stable but nonsexual second marriage. Roger considered himself well educated sexually, possessing liberal sexual attitudes, with no anxieties or inhibitions. There was a general air of arrogance about Roger, and a contemptuous attitude toward Lauren. He denied the role of early ejaculation. Although he was sure Lauren would never have an affair, he had had seven high-opportunity/low-involvement affairs. He was frustrated and resentful at Lauren for pulling a "bait and switch": She had pretended to be sexual, but once he committed to marriage, she had shut down.

When the sex therapist discussed this couple with prior therapists, the major theme that emerged was that Lauren and Roger were narcissistic individuals caught in a power struggle. Neither the individual nor couple therapists were optimistic about the viability of their marriage.

The feedback session is the core assessment–intervention strategy in couple sex therapy, as noted earlier. What captured Lauren and Roger's attention was the sex therapist's telling them that each person's story about the relationship and marital sex was so different that the clinician would not have thought they were talking about the same marriage. There was a lack of respect, trust, and empathy. If sex was to be functional, both partners had to address broad intimacy and sexuality issues. Specifically, Lauren had to take responsibility for her behavior (especially her inhibited sexual desire), and Roger had to take responsibility for his early ejaculation and for his arrogant and contemptuous attitude toward Lauren, which poisoned intimacy. Either they would solve the sexual problem as an intimate team, or they would jointly fail.

The role of the therapist is to keep the couple motivated, focused, and dedicated to following through on a change program, especially sexual exercises. In this case, the therapist urged Lauren and Roger not to be distracted by fears that they would not succeed, threats of separation, or interest in other people. They committed themselves to a good-faith effort, with the expectation that they would succeed.

The first homework assignment was for both partners to process the feedback, for Lauren to initiate the comfort exercise, and for Roger to initiate the attraction exercise from a chapter on revitalizing sexual desire (McCarthy & McCarthy, 2002). Some therapists might believe that this would be too much to process and too much to ask for in the first week between therapy sessions. However, Lauren and Roger were energized and excited by the feedback and eager to try the exercises. The trap to avoid was the tit-for-tat approach, in which one person backs off his/her commitment if the other does not do what he/she promised. Each partner's commitment must be to the self and the therapy process, noncontingent upon the partner's behavior. Roger committed himself not to put Lauren down or engage in intimate coercion. Lauren committed herself to stay involved in the therapy process and not revert to the critical, avoidance mode. Each promised to initiate once during the week and ideally twice, so there would be a minimum of two exercises and a maximum of four.

The session after the feedback sets the tone for ongoing therapy. The therapist actively structures the session, asking the couple to report successful experiences and acknowledge positive learnings first. In dealing with anxiety and failed experiences, the focus is on what can be learned and what to try next. This format brings out the "traps" that subvert change. The therapist confronts each partner's traps. With increased awareness, each person monitors his/her trap and strives not to fall into self-defeating behavior. Each is encouraged to focus on his/her traps, and is discouraged from admonishing the partner.

Lauren's behavior was repetitive: She would enthusiastically report a good experience and new learning, be upset that Roger did not validate this, and switch to criticalness and distance. If this cascade continued, she would become hostile and swear at him, at which time Roger would take the role of the offended spouse and emotionally distance himself. When in the critical mode, Lauren found it almost impossible to control her bitterness and hostility, thus negating positive experiences and squelching sexual desire.

Roger's trap was to position himself on the "sexual high ground," where he initiated and was solicitous of Lauren's pleasure. However, behind Roger's "sexual good guy" were arrogance toward and punishment of Lauren for not living up to the promise of their premarital sex. Roger adamantly denied being judgmental. When Lauren became angry and screamed at him, he saw this as her problem, abdicating his responsibility in this destructive pattern.

In the seventh session, a very significant intervention occurred: As Lauren started her angry cascade, the therapist asked her to take a 10-minute time out. She left the room and took a walk around the block, with the instruction to soothe herself and refocus on positive requests. Roger was alone with the therapist, who confronted him with his provocative and destructive behavior. He needed to "get off his pedestal and deal with Lauren as his intimate sexual friend"—as a person with both strengths and vulnerabilities. Roger had to be fully involved in the intimacy process, not just eroticism and intercourse.

It was crucial for Roger and Lauren to engage in sexual exercises. Both, but especially Lauren, were reluctant. One thing they agreed on was that they knew how to be an erotic couple. Their romantic love and passionate sex in the premarital period were shared, bonding memories. Lauren and Roger had failed to make the transition to a marital couple sexual style of initiation, intimacy, sensual and sexual ways to connect, and erotic and intercourse scenarios. Especially important were afterplay scenarios to stay connected and acknowledge intimacy. Adopting Gottman's (1993) 5:1 ratio of positive versus negative interactions/feelings was crucial for Roger and Lauren. Roger had to implement this outside the context of sexuality. Lauren had to reduce her criticalness and not use sexuality as the negative contingency for couple conflict. Roger and Lauren learned to unhook conflict and sexual issues. When there was a conflict, Roger agreed to revisit the issue in a problem-solving manner outside the bedroom; Lauren initiated either a sensual or erotic experience, which had the effect of increasing motivation to address emotional issues and conflicts.

The therapeutic strategy of maintaining the focus on intimacy and sexuality issues is a prime difference between couple sex therapy and traditional marital/couple therapy. Of course, some sex therapists would take a temporary hiatus from the sexual exercises until the emotional conflicts were at least moderately resolved, but this risks resensitizing sexual anxiety and avoidance. Clinical judgment, in both assessment and treatment, needs to weigh each person's ability to modulate negative emotions and utilize positive emotions from sexuality to help resolve relational differences.

As therapy progresses, the clinician's role becomes less active and the exercises less structured. However, the format is *never* one of walking into a session and asking, "How are things going?" The therapist has a repertoire of attitudinal, behavioral, emotional, relational, and sexual interventions that can be flexibly integrated into therapy. The goal is the couple's development of a sexual style that will be maintained after therapy is terminated. Finally, the therapist helps the couple develop a relapse prevention program.

As Lauren and Roger got into a rhythm of sexual "dates," they became more open to spontaneous affectionate, sensual, and sexual experiences. Affectionate and erotic touch were means to connect and energize the marital bond. Intimacy and pleasuring served as bridges for desire. One bridge for Lauren was to dress up, go to a party or listen to music, and leave early so they were awake and energetic. Sexuality began with touching and flirting in the car. This change countered the antierotic pattern Lauren felt stuck in. Roger had to break the habit of being the last person to leave a party. For Lauren, good-quality sex did not occur after midnight.

The biggest change for Roger was his willingness to engage in a program to develop ejaculatory control, rather than insisting that the solution was a second intercourse. Roger was dependent on Lauren's help with the stop–start technique. These techniques introduced a new dynamic in the relationship and his view of Lauren. She received an "A+" for involvement in the exercises, and both were pleased by the gradual but significant improvement. Lauren found that with decreased arrogance, Roger was a more attractive, inviting partner. This contributed greatly to her sexual desire. Intimacy and sexuality reached a higher level than at any previous point in the marriage. Roger was pleased that giving and receiving oral sex were now an integral part of lovemaking, not an isolated erotic technique. This change facilitated Lauren's arousal and lubrication, eliminating the painful intercourse problem. Integrating erotic scenarios and techniques into their couple style was also critical. Lauren observed, "We are intimate sexual friends for the first time since we've been married."

Sex therapy is not terminated when everything is going well. Lauren and Roger needed to learn two additional strategies—how to be resilient when relational stress and conflict interfered with sexu-

ality, and how not to overreact to mediocre or poor sexual experiences. The former problem naturally occurred, but the latter was instigated by a specific exercise. Stress, disappointment, and conflict are natural parts of even the most satisfying marriage. Roger and Lauren were both ambitious, competitive, and opinionated people. The key was not to allow their sexuality to be held hostage to their nonsexual conflicts. Roger took the lead in scheduling time to deal with conflicts via a positive-influence, problem-solving approach. They were both committed to not falling into the arrogant/critical trap. Sexuality generated energy and motivation to address and resolve conflicts.

In any attempts to enhance a couple's sexual repertoire, some techniques may fail. Being able to shrug off or laugh about a negative experience is a valuable marital resource. Roger tried to use the lateral coital intercourse position, but during lovemaking Lauren developed a "Charley horse," and Roger could not regain his erection. Rather than panicking or feeling apologetic, Lauren said, "No more acrobatics," and initiated sex again the next day.

The least successful component of treatment was the "booster sessions." Lauren liked checking in every 6 months with the therapist to ensure that sexuality stayed on track. She also used the sessions to raise other issues, especially lobbying to have two children. Roger said, "Let's make the decision one child at a time."

OTHER CLINICAL ISSUES

Relapse Prevention Strategies and Techniques

Relapse prevention is often ignored in psychotherapy, including sex therapy. Elsewhere (McCarthy, 1993), I have argued that relapse prevention strategies and techniques should be an integral component of sex therapy. The best prevention strategy is comprehensive, high-quality therapy that helps a couple to develop a comfortable, functional sexual style, and motivates the partners to maintain and generalize therapeutic gains. A relapse prevention program, like a sex therapy program, must be individualized. Common relapse prevention techniques are to keep the time allotted to a therapy session open, but, rather than attend a session, have an intimacy date at home; to schedule a pleasuring session with a ban on intercourse every 4–8 weeks; to design a new sexual scenario every 6 months; and, when there is a negative experience, to initiate a sensual or erotic date within 2 days. If the couple has not been sexual for 2 weeks, the partner with higher desire initiates a sensual or sexual experience; if that does not occur, another attempt is made within a week; if such an experience still does not occur, the partners schedule a therapy session. At least once a year, the couple takes a weekend away without children. On occasion, the partners are sexual outside the bedroom. Sexuality cannot rest on its laurels; it needs time, attention, and energy.

Perhaps the most important relapse prevention technique is establishing positive, realistic expectations. People wish that all sex would flow smoothly, yet the reality is that sexuality has a natural variability. Among well-functioning, satisfied married couples, fewer than 50% of sexual encounters involve equal desire, arousal, orgasm, and satisfaction for both people. Even more important is the fact that it is normal for 5–10% of sexual experiences to be mediocre or dysfunctional (Frank et al., 1978). Rather than seeing this as a source of panic or embarrassment, the couple should accept this as normal variability. The best way to react to a negative, dysfunctional, or disappointing experience is to view it as a "lapse" and actively prevent it from turning into a "relapse." The strategy is to return to being sexual in a day or two, when both partners feel open, awake, and aware, anticipating a pleasure-oriented experience. There are specific "traps" to be aware of for each sexual dysfunction, so a relapse prevention program for erectile dysfunction (McCarthy, 2001) will have different components than a relapse prevention program for inhibited sexual desire (McCarthy, 1999b).

Sex Therapy with Gay and Lesbian Couples

The breakthrough book on assessment and treatment of sexual dysfunction in gay and lesbian couples (Masters & Johnson, 1979) was not accepted in the gay community because of the section on promoting heterosexual functioning for highly motivated individuals. Nevertheless, it contained important data and insights into functional and dysfunctional gay behavior. There are more data on, and clinical discussions of, gay than lesbian sexual dysfunction. Rosser, Metz, Bockting, and Buroker (1997) have presented data suggesting that more than 50% of gay men experience a sexual dysfunction or dissatisfaction. Rates of erectile dysfunction and ejaculatory inhibition appear to be the same or higher for gay versus straight men, with early ejaculation and inhibited sexual desire at lower rates.

Another chapter in this *Handbook* (Green & Mitchell, Chapter 21) discusses couple therapy with gay and lesbian clients. A particular issue for such couples is the relational context of sex. Is there a committed, monogamous relationship, or a loosely bonded, open relationship? Sexually open relationships were formerly widely accepted as healthy for gay couples (McWhirter & Mattison, 1984), but this concept has become questionable because of STD/HIV risks. Although there is no empirical evidence to support it, the clinical guideline is to require a commitment to monogamy during the course of sex therapy. The agreement for monogamy during therapy is not because of moral issues, but because couple sex therapy requires a time commitment and focus that would be subverted by extrarelationship sex.

An advantage gay men have is freedom to utilize a variety of erotic techniques—self-stimulation, erotic videos, one-way sexual scenarios, use of anal stimulation, and a proerotic value system. Issues that interfere with treatment are comparisons with other partners; comparison with the gay stereotype of hot, problem-free sex; lack of commitment to work through difficult relationship and intimacy issues; pressure to perform for the partner; the assumption that if chemistry is present, sex should be easy; and emotional or erotic inhibitions. A common issue involves high desire for nonrelational sex, but low desire for intimate, interactive sexuality. In the therapy session, it is important to explore initiation patterns, erotic scenarios, affection outside the bedroom, and the meaning of couple sexuality. A particularly difficult issue is that of HIV/AIDS and safer sex. Will the partners jointly do an STD screen and HIV test? Will they commit to monogamy? If there is an incident of extrarelationship sex, will the man involved tell the partner and use condoms for 6 months until retesting?

Sexual exercises need to be modified and individualized for gay male couples, but the basic format is transferable. Pleasuring concepts are sometimes not easily accepted. The combination of traditional male and traditional gay focus on goal-oriented sex (i.e., orgasm) has resulted in deemphasizing the importance of intimacy and pleasuring, but these can be of great value. Of particular importance are comfort with and responsiveness to manual, oral, anal, and rubbing stimulation. In being specific about behavior and feelings, a common inhibition is challenged— "Gay men do it, not talk about it." Being aware of the frequency of sexual dysfunction and dissatisfaction allows the partners to "normalize" their experience. The concept that being gay is optimal and that each partner deserves to feel desire, arousal, orgasm, and satisfaction is a powerful antidote to internalized heterosexism and the sense of gay sex as "bad, but exciting." There are few outcome data on the effectiveness of sex therapy with gay couples (MacDonald, 1998).

There is even less scientific and clinical information on sex therapy with lesbian couples. Typically, lesbian couples seek out a female therapist. The most common complaint is inhibited sexual desire. More lesbian than straight women have a multiorgasmic response pattern; this is hypothesized to be the result of greater awareness of female sexual response and use of cunnilingus. There is less fear of STDs and HIV, as well as freedom from fear of pregnancy. Some clinicians hypothesize that an overemphasis on togetherness at the expense of autonomy and initiation is a core factor in inhibited sexual desire. Others hypothesize that traditional female socialization dampens sexual initiation and eroticism. Being overly solicitous of the partner's feelings and caretaking can inhibit desire, initiation, and eroticism.

Sexual exercises encourage each partner to take responsibility for sexuality and work as an intimate team to develop a comfortable, functional couple sexual style. Lesbian sexuality is facilitated by the cognition that each partner has a right to her "sexual voice." Issues of initiation and "bridges to desire" (i.e., the internal and external cues that elicit sexual anticipation) are particularly important. Each partner is encouraged to develop her bridges; these need not be shared bridges. A special emphasis is placed on exploring a level of intimacy that promotes sexual desire and initiation, taking turns initiating, trying exercises that emphasize pleasuring and eroticism, and promoting an erotic flow where each person's arousal plays off the other's. The couple can experiment with focused stimulation versus multiple stimulation; pleasurer–recipient format versus mutual stimulation; one-way sex versus interactive sex; and manual, oral, rubbing, and vibrator stimulation. Traps of self-consciousness, not wanting to outperform the partner, tentativeness, and spectatoring are confronted.

Therapy with Nonmarried Couples

It has been said that the best way to break up a nonviable unmarried couple is to put them in sex therapy. That is, the focus on intimacy and sexuality will destroy a fragile relationship.

Rates of sexual dysfunction are higher in nonmarried couples (where the partners have been together more than 2 years) than in married couples. Nonmarried couples have a right to have their problems addressed. A therapeutic contract that focuses on mutually agreed-upon goals is crucial. For some, the assumption is that if the sex problem is resolved, this will result in marriage. For others, the sexual dysfunction is primary or chronic, and the man wants the partner to be a sexual friend with the expectation that the relationship will last at least until the problem is resolved. The meaning of intimacy and commitment needs to be carefully explored, as well as the motivation for addressing the problem. For example, a divorced couple came to therapy to address the man's erectile dysfunction. The woman's motivation for therapy was guilt because she had left him for another man. His motivation was to perform so well that she would return to the marriage. In that case (and others like it), couple sex therapy is not the intervention of choice.

Couple sex therapy is an appropriate intervention when a nonmarried couple experiences a sexual dysfunction that subverts satisfaction, and the partners are motivated to address the problem jointly. Sexual dysfunctions in such couples are similar to those of married couples. Rates of dysfunction are higher, especially inhibited sexual desire and nonsexual relationships. The couple therapy/"common-sense" hypothesis that the sex problem is caused by ambivalence and lack of commitment has received little empirical testing or support. Common causes are anticipatory anxiety, performance anxiety, lack of sexual awareness, poor erotic skills, unrealistic performance expectations, and low-quality sexual communication. The couple and therapist need to decide whether to focus on sexual dysfunction or to look broadly at attitudes, values, and emotional intimacy.

The couple are cautioned not to treat couple sex therapy as a test for a marriage. In other words, successful resolution of the sexual dysfunction does not mean that the members of this couple are viable marital partners. The person with the dysfunction does not owe the partner for his/her sexual help, nor is the opposite true. Moreover, an unresolved sexual problem does not mean a couple cannot marry; the sexual problem is but one area of the relationship.

There are no empirical data on therapy outcome and the decision to marry. My own clinical experience is that the majority of nonmarried couples receiving sex therapy do not marry. The successful resolution of the sexual dysfunction improves the relationship in some cases, but the partners' decision to commit to sharing their lives involves a very different dimension. In other cases, a breakdown in the sex therapy is often attributable to a relationship that is not viable. An example of the first type of outcome was a woman with primary nonorgasmic response who learned to engage in self-stimulation to orgasm and be orgasmic with partner sex. Although they had an intimate friendship and both partners enjoyed the relationship, religious, political, and life organization factors made it clear that this was a better dating relationship than a marriage. An example of the latter type of situation was a man with early ejaculation who was contemptuous of his depressed, professionally underfunctioning girlfriend, although she was a prosexual, responsive partner. Engaging in couple therapy and processing exercises was enough to highlight their incompatibilities and resulted in the termination of living together. He continued individual sex therapy with a focus on masturbation training, guided imagery, and discussion of choosing a woman as an intimate friend.

Women without partners can benefit from female sexuality groups. Sexuality groups for men without partners have been difficult to organize. Individuals with sexual dysfunction benefit from interventions including exploring sexual history; masturbatory training; relaxation and guided imagery; establishing conditions for good sex; dealing with sexual health and contraception; setting positive, realistic sexual expectations; and choosing an appropriate partner.

Couple Sex Therapy When There Is a History of Sexual Trauma

The conceptualization, assessment, and intervention of sexual trauma involve some of the most complex and controversial topics in mental health (see Compton & Follette, Chapter 17, this volume). The major forms of sexual trauma are childhood sexual abuse, incest, and rape. Negative sexual experiences can be broadly defined to include dealing with an unwanted pregnancy; having an STD; experiencing a sexual dysfunction; being sexually humiliated or rejected; guilt about masturbation; shame or confusion about sexual fantasies; being exhibited to or peeped at; receiv-

ing obscene phone calls; or being sexually harassed. Negative, confusing, guilt-inducing, or traumatic sexual experiences are almost universal phenomena for both women and men, whether they occur in children, adolescence, adulthood, or old age.

The model espoused by trauma theorists and therapists has emphasized dealing with the trauma and its aftereffects first, and then, when these are resolved, focusing on couple sexual issues. The problem with this "benign neglect" strategy is that the longer the sexual hiatus lasts, the stronger the cycle of anticipatory anxiety, tension-filled sex, and avoidance becomes. Sexual avoidance builds anxiety and self-consciousness.

An alternative strategy proposed by Maltz (2001), which I have supported (McCarthy, 1997b), is to challenge the couple to be "partners in healing." A traumatized person who is able to experience desire, arousal, and orgasm, and feel intimately bonded, has taken back control of his/her life and sexuality. The person is a proud survivor, not a passive or angry victim. He/she accepts the adage "Living well is the best revenge." The person's partner has an active role in the healing process; sexuality is voluntary, mutual, and pleasure-oriented. If the traumatized person vetoes something, the veto is respected and honored (i.e., the opposite of sexual abuse).

The PLISSIT Model and Prevention

Annon (1974) has suggested an intervention model with four levels of clinician involvement. "PLISSIT" stands for "permission giving, limited information, specific suggestions, and intensive therapy." Ideally, all couple therapists are aware of and comfortable with being permission givers, and provide accurate, prosexuality information to individuals and couples.

Permission giving entails an accepting attitude toward sexuality as a positive component in the individual's and couple's life. Affectionate, sensual, and erotic expression is valued as a shared pleasure, a means to develop and reinforce intimacy, and a tension reducer to deal with the stresses of marriage and life. The clinician is comfortable and encouraging so that the couple can explore and discuss sexual scenarios and techniques, as well as the meaning of intimacy and sexuality. The permission-giving therapist does not approach sexuality with benign neglect; sexuality is treated as a positive, integral component of the couple's life. The clinician takes a prosexuality stance, not a neutral, value-free stance. The therapist is aware of and respects individual and cultural differences while working within the couple's value system. The therapist acknowledges the integral role of sexuality in marriage.

In the limited-information component, the couple therapist provides accurate, scientifically valid information about biological, psychological, and relational aspects of sexual function and dysfunction. He/she helps the couple establish positive, realistic sexual expectations. Limited information includes referral to an appropriate subspecialist in dealing with such issues as infertility; diagnosis and treatment of an STD; hormone replacement therapy; or side effects of antidepressant or blood pressure medications. Providing limited information involves confronting sexual myths, including new myths of sexual performance and pressure to prove that a couple is "liberated." It also emphasizes the importance of developing a couple sexual style that is comfortable and functional for both people; this style includes acceptance that occasional mediocre or poor sexual experiences are part of normal sexual variability. Contraception and safe sex are other integral components of limited information. Issues of initiation, sexual frequency, scenarios and techniques, sexual experimentation, and variations are covered. Discussion of sexual dysfunction, issues of sexual orientation, and sexual compulsions and deviations are open to exploration, with a possible referral to a subspecialist. Couple therapists are comfortable with permission giving and limited information on a wide range of sexual topics.

The third component, specific sexual suggestions, is not necessarily in the repertoire of a couple therapist. Referrals can be made to a sex therapist, physician, or individual therapist. Specific suggestions include pleasuring exercises with a prohibition on intercourse; experience with initiation and saying "no"; stop–start ejaculatory control exercises; the use of lubricants to facilitate female arousal; the wax-and-wane erection exercise; the use of a vibrator or self-stimulation for female orgasm during partner sex; and experimentation with afterplay scenarios and techniques. Specific suggestions involve integrating sexual counseling into couple therapy. This assessment–intervention approach is diagnostic in determining whether couple sex therapy is warranted. Sometimes simply conducting a sexual history clarifies issues and helps resolve the problem; at other times, it becomes clear that a referral for sex therapy is necessary.

Some couple therapists are comfortable, skilled, and interested in integrating sex therapy into their therapeutic repertoires. The majority of couple therapists do not choose to adopt sex therapy as a subspecialty skill; they are more comfortable making a referral to a sex therapist, as they would to any subspecialist. Not every clinician can or should do sex therapy. The mental health clinician may choose to refer to a specialist because of a lack of interest, comfort, training, or skill.

Sexual issues and problems are frequent sources of concern for both married and unmarried couples, straight and gay. The couple therapist can promote healthy sexuality and act in a primary prevention manner by engaging in permission giving and providing information. The clinician can intervene in terms of secondary prevention by making specific suggestions to deal with a sexual problem in its acute stage. If a sexual dysfunction is chronic and severe, referral for sex therapy is usually the appropriate choice.

SUMMARY

Sex therapy is a subspecialty skill. Intimacy and sexuality play positive, integral roles when sex is functional and satisfying. However, when sex is dysfunctional or absent, there is an extramarital affair, or fertility problems are present, the difficulty can play an inordinately powerful negative role, draining the overall relationship of vitality. Sexuality is a major force in relationship disintegration and divorce.

Couple sex therapy strategies and techniques enhance desire, arousal, orgasm, and satisfaction. The prescription for healthy integrated sexuality is intimacy, pleasuring, and eroticism. Each person's being responsible for his/her own sexuality, and the couple's being an intimate team, are essential for the assessment, treatment, and prevention of sexual problems.

REFERENCES

Abel, G., Osborn, C., Anthony, D., & Gardos, D. (1992). Current treatment of paraphiliacs. *Annual Review of Sex Research, 3*, 255–290.

Althof, S. (1998). New roles for mental health clinicians in the treatment of erectile dysfunction. *Journal of Sex Education and Therapy, 23*, 229–231.

American Association of Sex Educators, Counselors, and Therapists. (1993). *Code of ethics.* Mount Vernon, IA: Author.

American Psychiatric Association. (1994). *Diagnostic and*

statistical manual of mental disorders (4th ed.). Washington, DC: Author.

Annon, J. (1974). *The behavioral treatment of sexual problems.* Honolulu, HI: Enabling Systems.

Balon, R. (1999). Silfenafil and sexual dysfunction associated with antidepressants. *Journal of Sex and Marital Therapy, 25,* 259–264.

Barbach, L. (1975). *For yourself.* New York: Doubleday.

Basson, R. (1998). Integrating new biomedical treatments into the assessment and management of erectile dysfunction. *Canadian Journal of Human Sexuality, 7, 2* 12–229.

Basson, R. (2000). The female sexual response. *Journal of Sex and Marital Therapy, 26,* 51–65.

Bergeron, S., Binik, Y., Khalife, S., & Pagidas, K. (1997). Vulvar vestibulitis syndrome. *Clinical Journal of Pain, 13,* 27–42.

Butler, R., & Lewis, M. (1993). *Love and sex after sixty.* New York: Ballantine Books.

Davis, C., Yarber, W., Bauserman, R., Schree, L., & Davis, S. (1998). *Handbook of sexuality related measures.* Thousand Oaks, CA: Sage.

Derogatis, L. (1975). *Derogatis Sexual Function Inventory.* Baltimore: Clinical Psychometrics Research.

Donahey, K. (1998). Review of treating vaginismus. *Journal of Sex Education and Therapy, 23,* 266–267.

Focus International (Producer). (1991). *Erection* [Videotape] Chapel Hill, NC: Producer.

Frank., E., Anderson, A., & Rubinstein, D. (1978). Frequency of sexual dysfunction in "normal" couples. *New England Journal of Medicine, 229,* 111–115.

Goodwin, A., & Agronin, M. (1997). *A woman's guide to overcoming fear and pain.* Oakland, CA: New Harbinger.

Goldstein, I., Lue, T., Padma-Nathan, H., Rosen, R., Steers, W., & Wicker, P. (1998). Oral sildenafil in the treatment of erectile dysfunction. *New England Journal of Medicine, 338,* 1397–1404.

Gottman, J. (1993). A theory of marital dissolution and stability. *Journal of Family Psychology, 17,* 3–7.

Heiman, J., Epps, P. H., & Ellis, B. (1995). Sexual desire disorders. In A. Gurman & N. Jacobson (Eds.), *Clinical handbook of couple therapy* (2nd ed., pp. 471–495). New York: Guilford Press.

Heiman, J., & LoPiccolo, J. (1988). *Becoming orgasmic.* Englewood Cliffs, NJ: Prentice-Hall.

Jacobson, N., & Addis, M. (1993). Research on couples and couples therapy. *Journal of Consulting and Clinical Psychology, 65,* 85–93.

Kaplan, H. (1974). *The new sex therapy.* New York: Brunner/Mazel.

Kaplan, H. (1995). *The sexual desire disorders.* New York: Brunner/Mazel.

Laumann, F., Gagnon, J., Michael, R., & Michaels, S. (1994). *The social organization of sexuality.* Chicago: University of Chicago Press.

Laumann, E., Rosen, R., & Paik, A. (1999). Sexual dysfunction in the United States. *Journal of the American Medical Association, 281*(6), 537–544.

Leiblum, S., & Rosen, R. (Eds.). (1988). *Sexual desire disorders.* New York: Guilford Press.

Leiblum, S., & Rosen, R. (Eds.). (1989). *Principles and practice of sex therapy* (2nd ed.). New York: Guilford Press.

Lobitz, W., & Lobitz, G. (1996). Resolving the sexual intimacy paradox. *Journal of Sex and Marital Therapy, 22,* 71–84.

LoPiccolo, J. (Producer). (1984). *Treating vaginismus* [Videotape]. Chapel Hill, NC: Focus International.

LoPiccolo, J., & Friedman, J. (1988). Broad-based treatment of low sexual desire. In S. Leiblum & R. Rosen (Eds.), *Sexual desire disorders* (pp. 107–144). New York: Guilford Press.

LoPiccolo, J., & Steger, J. (1974). The Sexual Interaction Inventory. *Archives of Sexual Behavior, 3,* 585–595.

MacDonald, B. (1998). Issues in therapy with gay and lesbian couples. *Journal of Sex and Marital Therapy, 24,* 165–190.

Maltz, W. (2001). *The sexual healing journey.* New York: Harper Collier.

Masters, W., & Johnson, V. (1970). *Human sexual inadequacy.* Boston: Little, Brown.

Masters, W., & Johnson, V. (1979). *Homosexuality in perspective.* Boston: Little, Brown.

McCarthy, B. (1989). Cognitive-behavioral strategies and techniques in the treatment of early ejaculation. In S. Leiblum & R. Rosen (Eds.), *Principles and practice of sex therapy* (2nd ed., pp. 141–167). New York: Guilford Press.

McCarthy, B. (1993). Relapse prevention strategies and techniques in sex therapy. *Journal of Sex and Marital Therapy, 19,* 142–146.

McCarthy, B. (1994). Etiology and treatment of early ejaculation. *Journal of Sex Education and Therapy, 20,* 5–6.

McCarthy, B. (1995). Bridges to sexual desire. *Journal of Sex Education and Therapy, 21,* 132–141.

McCarthy, B. (1997a). Strategies and techniques for revitalizing a non-sexual marriage. *Journal of Sex and Marital Therapy, 23,* 231–240.

McCarthy, B. (1997b). Therapeutic and iatrogenic interventions with adults who were sexually abused as children. *Journal of Sex and Marital Therapy, 23,* 118–125.

McCarthy, B. (1999a). Integrating Viagra into cognitive-behavioral sex therapy. *Journal of Sex Education and Therapy, 23,* 302–308.

McCarthy, B. (1999b). Relapse prevention strategies and techniques for inhibited sexual desire. *Journal of Sex and Marital Therapy, 25,* 297–303.

McCarthy, B. (2001). Relapse prevention strategies and techniques for erectile dysfunction. *Journal of Sex and Marital Therapy, 27,* 1–8.

McCarthy, B., & McCarthy, E. (1993). *Confronting the victim role.* New York: Carroll & Graf.

McCarthy, B., & McCarthy, E. (1998a). *Male sexual awareness.* New York: Carroll & Graf.

McCarthy, B., & McCarthy, E. (1998b). *Couple sexual awareness.* New York: Carroll & Graf.

McCarthy, B., & McCarthy, E. (2002). *Sexual awareness.* New York: Carroll & Graf.

McWhirter, D., & Mattison, A. (1984). *The male couple.* Englewood Cliffs, NJ: Prentice-Hall.

Metz, M., Pryor, J., Nesvacil, L., Abuzzan, F., & Koznar, J. (1997). Premature ejaculation: A psychophysiological review. *Journal of Sex and Marital Therapy, 23,* 3–23.

Michael, R., Gagnon, J., Laumann, E., & Kolata, G. (1994). *Sex in America.* Boston: Little, Brown.

Rosen, R., & Leiblum, S. (1995). *Case studies in sex therapy.* New York: Guilford Press.

Rosen, R., Philips, N., Gendrano, H., & Ferguson, D. (1999). Oral phenotalamine and female sexual arousal disorder. *Journal of Sex and Marital Therapy, 25*, 137–144.

Rosser, R., Metz, M., Bockting, W., & Buroker, T. (1997). Sexual difficulties, concerns, and satisfaction in homosexual men. *Lournal of Sex and Marital Therapy, 23*, 61–73.

Rust, J., & Golombok, 5. (1986). The Golombok–Rust Inventory of Sexual Satisfaction. *British Journal of Clinical Psychology, 24*, 63–64.

Schnarch, D. (1991). *Constructing the sexual crucible.* New York: Norton.

Schnarch, D. (1997). *Passionate marriage.* New York: Norton.

Segreaves, R. (1988). Drugs and desire. In S. Leiblum & R. Rosen (Eds.), *Sexual desire disorders* (pp. 313–347). New York: Guilford Press.

Segreaves, R. (1998a). Pharmacological era in the treatment of sexual disorders. *Journal of Sex and Marital Therapy, 24*, 67–68.

Segreaves, R. (1998b). Anti-depressant induced sexual dysfunction. *Journal of Clinical Psychiatry, 59*, 48–54.

Strassberg, D., Brazao, C., Rowland, D., Tan, R., & Slob, A. (1999). Clomipramine in the treatment of rapid ejaculation. *Journal of Sex and Marital Therapy, 25*, 89–101.

Tiefer, L. (1986). In pursuit of the perfect penis. *American Behavioral Scientist, 29* 579–599.

Tiefer, L. (1998). *Sex is not a natural act.* Boulder, CO: Westview Press.

Weeks, G., & Hof, L. (1987). *Integrating sex and marital therapy.* New York: Brunner/Mazel.

Wincze, J., & Barlow, D. (1996). *Enhancing sexuality: Client workbook.* Albany, NY: Graywind.

Chapter 25

Couple Therapy in the Treatment of Major Depression

JACKIE K. GOLLAN
MICHAEL A. FRIEDMAN
IVAN W. MILLER

Major depression, a devastating and recurrent disease, will emerge as the second leading cause of worldwide disability by 2020 (Murray & Lopez, 1996). Indeed, the proportion of individuals receiving outpatient treatment for depression has jumped significantly within the past 10 years (Olfson et al., 2002). And yet, despite indicators of an emerging public health crisis and an increased demand for psychiatric services, numerous depressed individuals who participate in psychosocial treatments for depression do not experience relief by the end of treatment. For example, between 30% and 40% of depressed adults do not completely respond to cognitive–behavioral therapy (CBT) (Thase et al., 1992). Moreover, relapse rates of depression are high. Among recovered outpatients treated with CBT, about half experience depression relapse within 2 years of completing treatment (Gortner, Gollan, Dobson, & Jacobson, 1998).

Relationship distress is one of the primary reasons for delayed or poor treatment response. Indeed, as many as half of depressed individuals report dissatisfaction and conflict in their intimate relationships. Likewise, more than half of couples who seek treatment for relationship distress report that one or both partners are depressed. Couple therapy is an effective treatment for adults who

present with depression and relationship distress (Beach, Fincham, & Katz, 1998; Kung, 2000). The aim of couple therapy for depression, as we discuss in this chapter, is to treat the depression by altering the cognitive and behavioral relationship patterns that perpetuate it (Halford, Bourma, Kelly, & Young, 1999).

This chapter begins with a discussion of the nature and impact of depression, since clinicians may have to educate partners about the influence of depression. Next we evaluate clinical research on couple distress and depression, to highlight the reciprocal influence of major depression and relationship distress, and to help clinicians think through the ways that depression and relationship problems intertwine. We also outline psychological theories that explain the development and maintenance of depression in distressed relationships, and we summarize approaches to couple therapy for depression. We then briefly review research on specific cognitive and behavioral factors that distinguish depressed/distressed couples from nondepressed/nondistressed couples. In addition, because family treatments target couple functioning, this chapter briefly refers to research on the influence of family functioning in perpetuating depression. Family therapy is not the same as couple therapy, but we include family treatments when the work elucidates effective interventions for distressed/depressed relationships. We conclude the chapter with a more detailed description of our preferred approach to couple therapy for depression, as well as a case illustration of selected clinical strategies.

THE NATURE AND IMPACT OF DEPRESSION

Up to 20% of persons in the general population are expected to experience major depression at least once during their lifetimes, with twice as many women as men reporting depression (American Psychiatric Association, 1994; Cross-National Collaborative Group, 1992; Nolen-Hoeksema, 1987; Wickramaratne, Weissman, Leaf, & Holford, 1989), even across different cultures (Dehle & Weiss, 1998; Frank, Carpenter, & Kupfer, 1988). These statistics may underestimate the true prevalence of depression, since symptom complaints are often disregarded or misdiagnosed, particularly among primary care and geriatric populations (Wells, Burnam, Rogers, Hays, & Camp, 1992). In addition to being a common mental health problem, depression recurs over the life span (Gortner et al., 1998; Thase et al., 1992). The Agency for Health Care Policy and Research has noted that risk of recurrence increases exponentially with each successive episode: about 50% of patients who become clinically depressed experience depression again. Indeed, even after treatment, 40% of patients with a history of three or more depressive episodes are likely to relapse within 7 weeks after recovery (Depression Guideline Panel, 1993). Given the prevalence and chronicity of depression, innumerable people face the prospect of a lifetime struggle with depression.

Beyond the emotional toll of depression, its social, economic, and health costs are devastating. Depression disrupts the lives of more than 19 million adults via job absenteeism, truncated education, and low earning potential, generating costs between $30 and $44 billion worldwide per year (Greenberg, Stiglin, Finlekstein, & Berndt, 1993). In addition, major depression is linked with the presence of costly medical illnesses, including cancer, coronary heart disease, Type 2 diabetes, and multiple sclerosis (Hays, Wells, Sherbourne, Rogers, & Spitzer, 1995), as well as increased morbidity associated with suicide (Johnson, Weissman, & Klerman, 1992). Although the proportion of the population receiving outpatient treatment for depression has increased significantly, from 0.73 per 100 persons in 1987 to 2.33 per 100 in 1997 (Olfson et al., 2002), it remains clear that numerous individuals do not seek or receive sufficient therapeutic assistance to cope with this disease. Developing effective treatments for this highly recurrent and costly disease has numerous implications for providing relief for what is projected to become a major cause of disability worldwide.

RESEARCH ON COUPLE THERAPY FOR DEPRESSION

The justification for using couple therapy to address depression is founded upon research showing that for some individuals, depression and relationship distress are linked. Because relationship distress delays or limits response to psychosocial treatments for depression, a key treatment target is to change the relational context. This section summarizes the ways in which relationship distress and depression are associated, as well as the efficacy of couple therapy for depression.

• *Relationship distress is concomitantly associated with depression.* Research relying upon treatment and community-based samples demonstrates a strong correlation between relationship distress and major depression (Beach, Smith, & Fincham, 1994; Fincham, Beach, Harold, & Osbourne, 1997; Gotlib & Hammen, 1992; Mundt, Goldstein, Hahlweg, & Fiedler, 1996; O'Leary, Christian, & Mendell, 1994). A summary of statistics from a recent meta-analysis of 26 treatment studies investigating the association between marital distress and depression indicated that lower marital satisfaction was associated with higher levels of depression (Whisman, 2001). Moreover, the association in this large sample (3,745 women and 2,700 men) was larger for women than for men. Specifically, Whisman calculated that marital dissatisfaction accounted for 18% of variance in wives' depression, as opposed to 14% of variance in husbands' depression. Furthermore, an average of 44% of the variance associated with depressive symptoms was explained by concurrent marital dissatisfaction. Consistent with the findings from this research, an association between relationship distress and depression among community samples has also been noted (Weissman, 1987; Whisman, 1999). This association remains steadfast even after the effects of demographic variables (e.g., age and gender) and length of marriage are controlled for (Bauserman, Arias, & Craighead, 1995; Stravynski, Tremblay, & Verrault, 1995).

The correlation between relationship distress and depression appears to hold true across the life span of relationships: Relationships in different phases of development, ranging from premarital couples to mature married couples over age 60, show a higher incidence of depression in the context of relationship distress (Beutel, Willner, Deekhardt, Von Rad, & Weiner, 1996; Kessler, Walters, & Forthofer, 1998; Sandberg & Harper, 1999; Steinberg & Bellavance, 1999). In addition, the incidence of depression is higher among adults who end their relationships, particularly for separating women, who report more intense depressive reactions than men (Bruce & Kim, 1992; Horowitz, White, & Howell-White, 1996).

• *Relationship distress is prospectively associated with depression.* The presence of relationship distress increases the risk of subsequent depression (Beach & O'Leary, 1993; Bradbury & Fincham, 1993; Brown & Moran, 1994; Dehle & Weiss, 1998; Fincham et al., 1997; Kurdek, 1998). Negative situations often preceding depression may threaten relationship stability, including discovery of an affair, experience of domestic violence, and severe couple conflict (Brown & Harris, 1978; Beach & O'Leary, 1993). Such situations raise the risk of depression by a factor of 3 to 10, particularly during the year following the event (Beach & Nelson, 1990; Burns, Sayer, & Moras, 1994; Whisman & Bruce, 1999). In addition, recovered depressed patients remain vulnerable to relapse when they experience relationship distress during their recovery (Beach & Nelson, 1990; Jacobson, Fruzzetti, Dobson, Whisman, & Hops, 1993; Lewinsohn, Hoberman, & Rosenbaum, 1988; Monroe, Bromet, Connell, & Steiner, 1986). In the family literature, recovered patients relapsed upon exposure to expressions of critical, hostile, and overinvolved attitudes from nondepressed spouses or other close family members (Hooley, Orley, & Teasdale, 1986; Hooley & Teasdale, 1989). Exposure to hostile and rejecting interactions may confirm a depressed individual's negative self-concept, thereby increasing the risk of depression (Gotlib & Whiffen, 1989).

• *Depression precedes, and is causal of, couple distress.* For some partners, depression precedes the onset of relationship distress. Research with premarital couples conducted by Smith, Vivian, and O'Leary (1990) revealed that depressed behavior during an interaction task predicted subsequent marital discord. Similarly, among a sample of married couples, Beach and O'Leary (1993) observed that marital distress increased after husbands reported depression. Research also indicates that partners are more likely to separate or divorce when depression appears before relationship distress among married couples (Prigerson, Maciejewski, & Rosenhack, 1999; Richards, Hardy, & Wadsworth, 1997). It is possible that once depression appears, relationship distress deepens the depressed partner's depressogenic state (e.g., anhedonia increases withdrawal, which generates partner criticism, which promotes hopelessness about change).

• *Research indicates the potential efficacy of couple therapy for depression.* Individual treatments for depression, for which compelling research demonstrates efficacy, include CBT (Beck, Rush, Shaw, & Emery, 1979), interpersonal psychotherapy (IPT; Klerman, Weissman, Rounsaville, & Chevron, 1984), and behavior therapy (Lewinsohn, Hoberman, Teri, & Hautzinger, 1985). All three approaches produce modest and equivalent short-term effects in reducing depression, helping between 50% and 70% of depressed adults who participate in treatment (Belsher & Costello, 1988; Elkin et al., 1989). One of the largest controlled clinical trials of depression, the National Institute of Mental Health Treatment of Depression Collaborative Research Program, reported that over half of patients treated with either CBT or IPT recovered by the end of treatment (55% and 51%, respectively) (Elkin et al., 1989). However, longitudinal follow-up studies, which examine outcome for a year or two after depressed adults leave treatment, report that recovered outpatients do not sustain treatment gains. Gortner et al. (1998) reported that among the 70% of depressed outpatients who received a component or the full package of CBT and recovered by the end of the 16-week acute treatment phase, about half experienced relapse within 2 years following treatment. Clearly, these results indicate that individual treatments have limited treatment efficacy. Moreover, in light of research showing that treatment response is lower among depressed individuals in distressed relationships, it is plausible that individual treatments for depression are unable to modify relational distress—a primary factor in perpetuating depression. Encouraging couple participation to modify the relational context of depression may offer greater therapeutic value than what individual psychotherapies offer currently.

As mentioned earlier, additional evidence for using couple therapy for depression is founded upon research findings that family therapy is more effective in treating depression than individual treatments (Clarkin, Haas, & Glick, 1988; Emanuels-Zuurveen & Emmelkamp, 1996; Foley, Rounsaville, Weissman, Sholmaskas, & Chevron, 1987; Jacobson, Dobson, Fruzzetti, Schmaling, & Salusky, 1991; O'Leary & Beach, 1990; Waring, Carver, Stalker, Fry, & Schaefer, 1990). This complements existing data showing that couple therapies treat depression as well as individual treatments for depression (Jacobson et al., 1992; Beach et al., 1990). It is likely that couple therapy has an added advantage in being able to directly improve relationship quality, compared to individual therapies for depression.

CURRENT THEORIES OF DEPRESSION

Several psychological theories provide compelling explanations about how relationship distress and depression interact (cf. Joiner, 2001). One theory proposes that relationship-derived stress and low partner support lead to depressive states. For example, Beach and O'Leary (1993) suggest that couple distress generates depression through both lost relationship cohesion and intimacy and manifestations of hostility and interpersonal tension. A second theory highlights the influence of relationship stress upon mood stability, focusing on the ways in which depressed individuals generate stress (Daley, Hammen, Burge, & Davila, 1997; Hammen, 1991). In contrast, other theories propose that depressed individuals behave, knowingly or unknowingly, in ways that perpetuate depression. For example, Swann, Wenzlaff, Krull, and Pelham (1992) propose that depressed persons selectively seek negative feedback that happens to map onto their own understanding of their faults. Asking for and receiving such criticism are used to confirm the depressed persons' self-concept of being unlovable, inadequate, or incompetent, which further perpetuates their depression. Finally, Coyne's (1976) interpersonal theory of depression, which is consistent with the explanation provided by Swann and colleagues, proposes that depressed persons behave in ways that family members and friends find aversive or tiring. Repeated interactions with a sad and withdrawn individual who has trouble functioning may burden nondepressed partners. According to this theory, with the passage of time, partners and friends express frustration and reject the depressed person. Negative social responses, if considered meaningful by the depressed person, are used to confirm depressogenic thinking.

COUPLE TREATMENTS FOR DEPRESSION

Couple therapy for depression is based on the premises that maladaptive relationship processes contribute to depression and that depression alters relationship health. Because depression and relationship distress reciprocally influence each other, the aim of treatment is to change relationship patterns to alleviate depression. This goal is similar to that used in an alternative therapeutic approach, referred to as "partner-involved therapy" (Emanuels-Zuurveen & Emmelkamp, 1997). Similarities include meeting with both partners and focusing on social support and adaptive coping. In contrast to couple therapy, however, which focuses on relationship change, partner-involved treatments consolidate existing relationship strengths in an effort to bolster the depressed person's capacity to change. In contrast, couple therapy attends almost exclusively to resolving relationship difficulties to reduce depression. We now describe the models of treatment change, along with efficacy research associated with current couple therapies for depression.

Behavioral Couple Therapy

Behavioral couple therapy (BCT), an empirically validated treatment for couple distress (Beach & Nelson, 1990; Beach et al., 1998), is based on principles of reinforcement, social learning, and behavior exchange (Bandura, 1974; Ferster, 1973; Mahoney, 1974; Skinner, 1969). Applying these principles to couple dynamics, BCT stipulates that depression is the result of ineffectual efforts to obtain positive reinforcement from the relationship. Specifically, partners influence each other's mood through a reciprocal series of punishing and reinforcing responses (Jacobson & Holtzworth-Munroe, 1986; Jacobson, Holtzworth-Munroe, & Schmaling, 1989). The therapy focuses on changing destructive relationship patterns to generate symptom relief for the depressed patient, and balancing each partner's psychological needs. BCT for depression initially emphasizes that partners support each other through mutually rewarding activities. Partners learn to track each other's positive behavior and evaluate their strengths increase cohesiveness, intimacy, and support. Treatment also aims to reduce defensiveness, hostility, and aggression. Once this is achieved, treatment then moves to a series of interventions that aim to improve skills in communication, conflict resolution, and problem solving. The final phase of treatment strengthens relapse prevention to encourage the couple's ability to maintain treatment effects.

Empirical support for treating depression with BCT is founded upon results from well-controlled psychotherapy outcome studies. O'Leary and Beach (1990) compared individual cognitive therapy (CT) with BCT, as well as with a 15-week waiting-list control group. The sample included 36 discordant married couples with depressed wives; the couples were randomly assigned to treatment groups and evaluated both at posttreatment and at a 1-year follow-up period. Results revealed that both active treatments (CT and BCT) outperformed the waiting-list control condition and reduced depression. In fact, there were no differences in overall efficacy between CT and BCT. With regard to relationship functioning, however, 83% of those receiving BCT experienced significant improvement in marital functioning (15 points or higher on a measure of relationship satisfaction), compared to 25% of those receiving CT. Both the BCT and CT groups maintained these treatment effects at 1-year follow-up; in particular, only 1 of the 17 patients who responded to BCT had relapsed (Beach, 1996). Moreover, relationship satisfaction continued to be higher among these patients, suggesting that BCT is uniquely effective in alleviating depression as well as couple distress. Similar conclusions came from a separate trial of BCT for depression (Jacobson et al., 1991, 1993). When CT and BCT conditions were compared for 60 married couples with and without depressed wives, findings indicated that, relative to individual therapy, couple treatment was particularly effective for depressed/distressed couples. It was less efficacious for depressed couples that reported relationship satisfaction (Jacobson et al., 1991, 1993). Furthermore, patients receiving BCT maintained gains 1 year following treatment (Jacobson et al., 1993).

Cognitive and Cognitive-Behavioral Marital Therapy

Cognitive marital therapy (CMT; Baucom, Sayers, & Sher, 1990; Dobson, Jacobson, & Victor, 1989), a time-limited and structured treatment, emphasizes changes in attitude, behavior, and affect. Treatment initially focuses on outlining problems, modifying negative expectancies about individual and relationship change, and changing explanatory style. The treatment then focuses on cognitive interventions to reduce unrealistic expectations and test beliefs for the purposes of promoting independence, self-efficacy, and social support (Addis & Jacobson, 1991; Jacobson, 1984).

Trials of CMT show successful treatment of couple distress and major depression (Emanuels-Zuurveen & Emmelkamp, 1996; Waring et al., 1990). In one study comparing CMT with individual CT and with a waiting-list control group, the CMT group reported significantly reduced depression by the end of therapy, compared to the CT group. The CT group showed no symptom reduction (Teichman, Bar-el, Shor, Sirota, & Elizur, 1995). Furthermore, the CMT group exhibited lower depressive symptoms at posttreatment, compared to the CT group and the waiting-list control group. These group differences, however, were no longer evident at the 6-month follow-up. In a subsequent study comparing CMT, CT, and a waiting-list control with pharmacotherapy (amitriptyline), the CMT group experienced significantly lower depression scores than the other groups. At the 6-month follow-up, there were no differences between CMT and CT groups, but they both demonstrated significantly lower depression scores than the pharmacotherapy group did (Teichman, 1997), Cognitive-behavioral marital treatment (CBMT), consisting of CMT and communication skills training (Emanuels-Zuurveen, & Emmelkamp, 1996; Emanuels-Zuurveen, Van Linden van der Heuvel, & Ruphan, 1988), and individual CBT were found to be equally effective in treating depression. Moreover, as in other controlled outcome studies, the couple-based treatment (CBMT) outperformed the individual treatment (CBT) in reducing relationship distress.

Strategic Couple Therapy

Coyne's (1988) strategic therapy for depression proposes that depression occurs as a consequence of ineffective coping and negative interpersonal feedback. Strategic couple therapy aims to help each partner develop coping skills to reduce the aversive behaviors and negative reactions associated with both depression and relationship distress. Treatment differs from other couple therapies, as the therapist works with each partner in individual sessions. Conjoint sessions are interspersed to provide practice opportunities. No studies to date have provided empirical support for this approach.

Conjoint Interpersonal Psychotherapy

Conjoint IPT for depressed patients with couple problems is an extension of the principles of individual IPT for depression (Klerman et al., 1984; Rounsaville & Chevron, 1982). The therapy focuses on relationship functioning to improve communication, intimacy expression, outlining relationship roles, and adaptive behavior. Specific to depression, conjoint IPT focuses on modifying the identified depressed person's symptoms of depression and resolving couple conflicts that arise from depression. Attention is given to elucidating the role disputes in such areas as responsibilities, finances, social and work activities, intimacy, and communication. A pilot study comparing conjoint IPT with individual IPT among 18 married couples provided preliminary data about efficacy in reducing depression, improving social functioning, and marital adjustment (Foley et al., 1989). Results showed that both treatments produced significant improvements in social functioning and depressive status. Furthermore, there was more improved marital functioning (increased affectional expression and sexual relations) among patients in the conjoint IPT condition than among those in the individual IPT condition (Foley et al., 1989). These promising results should be interpreted with caution, however, as the study lacked both a diverse sample and a control condition.

WHAT DO DEPRESSED/DISTRESSED COUPLES LOOK LIKE?

Depressed/distressed couples present with a constellation of clinical concerns—including problems with communication, problem solving, social behavior, and cognitive interpretations—that are different from those presented by both nondepressed/distressed and healthy couples. This section reviews studies that examine the emergence of differences and escalation of distress over time, the effects of exposure to distress and depression upon relationship health, and differences across multiple dimensions of relationship and individual functioning.

Communication

Depressed/distressed partners express greater tension, conflict, and negativity than do nondepressed/distressed couples (Hautzinger, Linden, & Hoffman,

1982; Johnson & Jacob, 2000; Ruscher & Gotlib, 1988). Partners tend to be reactive and hostile to each other (Jacobson, Follette, & Revenstorf, 1982). In addition, depressed couples present with depressive concerns that influence the relationship interaction. Not surprisingly, depressed women in nondistressed relationships express more dysphoria than their nondepressed male partners. However, nondepressed men, even if initially expressing support and concern, can also communicate condescension and criticism. Furthermore, female partners who care for depressed spouses for a long period of time face an increased risk for depression (Blumberg & Hokanson, 1983; Coyne et al., 1987). Explanations of this suggest that female depression among distressed couples may suppress male aggression (Biglan et al., 1985; Hautzinger et al., 1982; Hops et al., 1987; Linden et al., 1983; Nelson & Beach, 1990; O'Leary & Cano, 2001; Schmaling & Jacobson, 1990a, 1990b; Schmaling, Whisman, Fruzzetti, Truax, & Jacobson, 1991). Controversy continues with this explanation, because studies both support and refute the hypothesis that depression has a suppressive effect on husband aggression (Schmaling & Jacobson, 1990a, 1990b).

Problem Solving

The behavioral profile of distressed/depressed couples is further elucidated from research about conflict resolution. Distressed couples manifest problem-solving deficits as a matter of course; however, depressed/distressed couples manifest even greater difficulty in identifying how and when to implement resolution strategies (Christian, O'Leary, & Vivian, 1994). Furthermore, distressed/depressed couples demonstrate significant trouble defining their problems and coordinating a productive resolution process (McCabe & Gotlib, 1993; Whisman & Jacobson, 1989). Also, depressed women are less adept at identifying and summarizing relationship problems that are nondepressed women (Schmaling, Deklyen, & Jacobson, 1989). This finding dovetails with additional research showing that depressed individuals are inappropriately confrontive and avoidant in relationship interactions, making it harder to resolve problems agreeably (Gottman, 1993). It is not surprising that depressed/distressed couples report problem-solving troubles, as depressed individuals demonstrate depression-specific social deficits, including difficulty with time management (Epstein,

1985), seeking social support, and being assertive (Lewinsohn & Arconad, 1981).

Cognitive Factors

Research on cognitive models of depression (Abramson, Metalsky, & Alloy, 1989; Beach, Nelson, & O'Leary, 1988; Beck et al., 1979) offers important information about the cognitive styles of partners in depressed/distressed relationships. Compared to healthy couples, depressed/distressed couples tend to think more negatively and be more self-blaming (Kowalik & Gotlib, 1987). Research focused solely on depressed individuals indicates that they are less accurate in decoding and comprehending their partners' messages (Sher, Baucom, & Larus, 1990). They are also more likely to color their partners' negative comments with global and stable negative attributions (Camper, Jacobson, Holtzworth-Munroe, & Schmaling, 1988; Sher et al., 1990). Finally, depressed individuals have lower self-confidence and tend to think of themselves as being in inferior social positions, compared to their nondepressed partners (Hautzinger et al., 1982; Linden, Hautzinger, & Hoffman, 1983).

Intimacy

Compared to nondepressed/distressed couples, depressed/distressed partners report significantly more dissatisfaction about their degree of intimacy with each significant other (Coryell et al., 1993). Depressed/distressed couples also exhibit less interest in intimacy than do nondepressed/distressed couples (Crowe, 1997). Low intimacy may be normative among distressed couples, but depression generally flattens expressions of intimacy. Research indicates that low intimacy among married women is associated with higher risk for depression (Schweitzer, Logan, & Strassberg, 1992). Moreover, depression is more likely among couples reporting conflict about different preferences for relationship intimacy (Beach et al., 1988; Hickie, Parker, Wilhelm, & Tennant, 1991).

BEHAVIORAL COUPLE THERAPY FOR DEPRESSION

We now discuss BCT for depression to illustrate the structure and process of treatment and the role of the therapist. We focus on BCT because it has the most empirical support for its efficacy, in addition to the longest history of investigation and development of extant approaches (Beach, 2001). Moreover, BCT is transportable. It has been applied to cross-cultural populations (Hahlweg & Markman, 1988), translated into treatment manuals for mental health care providers (Markman, Stanley, & Blumberg, 1994), and successfully used in managed care settings (Ralthus & Sanderson, 1999).

Nature of Depression and Treatment Rationale

Behavioral models conceptualize depression as a result of both a lack of contingency between a patient's behavior and the ability to receive positive reinforcement and avoidance of aversive stimuli. As a result of the patient's inability to engage in operant behavior, he/she develops depression in response to low positive reinforcement, as well as negative mood in response to inability to escape adverse stimuli. These symptoms include anhedonia, low motivation, sadness, and hopelessness. Social learning models (Bandura, 1974) emphasize that the patient's emotional state is maintained by the patient's ongoing interaction with his/her environment. BCT conceptualizes the lack of contingent behavior as most notable within the context of the couple relationship. That is, the patient will be most affected by lack of positive experiences within the relationship, as well as conflict within it. Thus the goal of BCT is both to increase positive behaviors, and to reduce negative interactions, in the relationship. BCT treats the symptoms of depression indirectly by focusing on the causes of relationship distress.

BCT is best designed to be used in the following clinical scenarios: (1) The depressed individual and partner attribute the depression to relationship problems; (2) the depression is influencing relationship functioning; and (3) the partners report concurrent relationship distress with the depression (Beach, 2001). Referral to a psychiatrist for pharmacotherapy consultation may also be considered if a partner reports the presence of bipolar symptoms or psychotic features, diagnostic uncertainty, or severe suicidal ideation or plans (Whisman & Ubelacker, 1999). Pharmacotherapy may also be useful if the depressed patient reports a history of severe or recurrent depression (Thase et al., 1997), or if the patient demonstrates trouble managing negative emotions and reduces participation in couple therapy as a result. If emotional dysregulation or active suicidality emerges as a primary clinical problem, the therapist may consider delaying couple therapy and using a combination of individual therapy and pharmacotherapy focused specifically on symptom reduction and safety issues. The aim is to ensure clinical safety before delving into relationship issues. If a depressed patient does not exhibit symptom improvement in the first 4 to 8 weeks with couple therapy, should be considered an alternative treatment. The therapist should refer the patient for a pharmacotherapy evaluation.

Assessment of Relationship and Individual Functioning

Systematic assessment of couple and individual functioning is the primary goal in the initial stages of therapy. The aim is to identify why the couple is seeking treatment, to discern the scope and nature of the clinical problems, and to ascertain whether couple therapy will be useful. The assessment process, which spans several sessions, should rely upon a multimethod measurement approach to integrate information from clinical interviews, direct observation, and self-reports.

Assessment of Relationship Functioning

Initial questions should focus on the trajectory and development of stages of courtship. Focusing on this area is intentionally designed to evoke positive feelings and to recall situations and personal characteristics that each partner originally found to be attractive. It may also serve to remind both partners about some of the existing strengths of their relationship. Clinicians should expect that some adults will provide a generally negative appraisal of their courtship and refuse to discuss positive attributes of themselves or their partners. As discussed above, this is consistent with depressogenic thinking (i.e., depressed patients adopt a pessimistic view of themselves and others); as such, clinicians are cautioned against accepting these explanations as realistic evaluations. Rather, negative appraisals provide additional information regarding the cognitive patterns of each individual and areas of dissatisfaction. Once this is accomplished, the therapist reviews the developmental course of the relationship, focusing on each stage of commitment to determine how and when it tran-

spired. For a married couple, this might include a review of decisions to cohabit, marry, and have children. For a gay couple, this may focus on decisions to make relationship commitments, arrange cohabitation, and share finances. The evaluation should cover each individual's expectations, goals, and commitment to the relationship. Finally, the clinician should inquire about the reasons that each partner wants to participate in therapy, with attention to subtle and overt coercion (e.g., one partner has demanded therapy or he/she will leave the relationship). Clinicians should also assess for emotional and psychological abuse, as distressed couples are at risk for domestic violence, and partners may be reluctant to disclose such interactions. Since research indicates that depressed/distressed couples are at risk for domestic violence (O'Leary & Cano, 2001), we emphasize that screening for historical and current coercion (e.g., emotional, verbal, or physical violence) is a key part of the evaluation, because domestic violence cannot be effectively treated in a couple therapy format (Vivian & Malone, 1997).

Self-report measures of couple distress complement the clinical interview. In addition to being concise, reliable, and valid, they cover a realistic range of topics and evaluate behaviors that occur outside the treatment session. Self-report forms may also aid in developing accurate case conceptualization and treatment formulation. The disadvantages are that self-report forms evaluate possibly irrelevant items and disregard clinically relevant ones. Traditionally, self-reports are used throughout BCT to generate weekly (or monthly) status reports from which change can be accurately measured. Some self-report measures, considered standard fare in clinical research studies, may also be adapted for clinical work. Depending on the therapist's time and training, we recommend the Dyadic Adjustment Scale (DAS; Carey, Spector, Lantinga, & Krauss, 1993; Spanier, 1976), a 31-item self-report that assesses specific relationship dimensions, including satisfaction, cohesion, consensus, and affection. Other measures include the Marital Satisfaction Inventory (MSI; Snyder, Lachar, & Wills, 1988; Snyder, Willis, & Keiser, 1979); the Marital Status Inventory (Weiss & Cerreto, 1980); the Locke–Wallace Marital Adjustment Scale (Jouriles & O'Leary, 1986; Locke & Wallace, 1959), the Areas of Change Questionnaire (Margolin, Talovic, & Weinstein, 1983; Weiss, Hops, & Patterson, 1973), and the Spouse Observation Checklist (Broderick & O'Leary, 1986; Weiss & Margolin, 1977). It is not necessary to use all of these measures simultaneously;

however, because they evaluate specific dimensions of relationship functioning, three or more will provide relevant details for case conceptualization.

Therapists may also incorporate video or audio technology to capture couple interactions on tape, and thus to provide *in vivo* data regarding relationship functioning. These approaches are preferred, but not mandatory, for evaluation. Specialized observational coding protocols, designed specifically for research on relationship functioning, offer useful systems to identify microinteractions between partners. Videotapes of partners who are asked to talk about several problems areas in their relationship are watched carefully and coded for dimensions of affective responsivity, communication styles, and problem-solving behavior. Such observational coding systems include the Marital Interaction Coding System (Heyman, Weiss, & Eddy, 1995; Weiss et al., 1973) and the Specific Affect Coding System (Gottman, 1979). These marital coding systems were developed for research protocols and the expectations that the interaction would be videotaped in a laboratory, and thus require two video cameras, coding equipment, and trained coders. These are resources available to few clinicians. However, the basic principle of data collection may still be used through informal audio recording of couples' efforts to communicate and resolve conflict.

Throughout the assessment, the therapist should focus on the couple's positive expectations for improvement. Specifically, this means promoting hopefulness about the couple's collaborative potential, pointing out the relationship's strengths, and describing the benefits of therapy. In addition, the therapist should identify presenting problems, future plans, social support systems, and individual functioning. The therapist's confidence and attention to positive relationship attributes may give partners hope during their initial sessions.

Assessment of Individual Functioning

Assessment of individual functioning includes family development, past and current psychiatric status, cognitive and social functioning, and personal relationship history. Therapists should also examine treatment issues associated domestic violence, intention to divorce, and suicidality. For novice clinicians, semistructured assessments of depression are helpful in measuring the course and severity of depressive illness. Examples include the Structured Clinical Interview for DSM-IV (First, Spitzer, Gibbon, & Williams, 1997) and the Modified Hamilton Rating Scale for Depression (Miller, Bishop, Norman, & Maddover, 1985). With these instruments, clinicians can ascertain the temporal relationship between distress and depression. Self-report measures of depression symptoms include the Beck Depression Inventory II (BDI-II; Beck & Steer, 1987), an inventory that covers vegetative and cognitive symptoms of depression, and the Beck Hopelessness Scale (Beck, Weissman, Lester, & Trexler, 1974) a measure of state hopelessness. Measurement of historical and current status of suicide-related behaviors can be effectively accomplished with self-report scales and clinical interviews. The Beck Medical Damage Scale (Malone et al., 1995) evaluates severity of previous attempts; the Suicide Probability Scale (Cull & Gill, 1989) and the Scale for Suicide Ideation (Beck, Kovacs, & Weissman, 1979) measure dimensions of suicide ideation, preparation, and deterrents facilitating determinations of self-harm. In work with depressed individuals, it is our standard practice to assess regularly for suicide-related behaviors, as depressed individuals may avoid such issues in treatment. We also recommend following established protocols for evaluating and managing suicide to provide high-quality clinical care (cf. Jacobs, 1998).

Couple Feedback

During the third couple session, the therapist provides feedback about the presenting problems, specific dimensions of individual and collective strengths, and areas of disagreement and improvement. This discussion should also include a brief presentation of BCT, including the approach and areas of work, other possible treatment approaches that effectively treat depression, and the rationale for using BCT. The therapist should briefly describe the expectations for the couple during treatment participation. This explanation should indicate that each partner should attend all sessions, should refrain from pursuing separation or divorce, should provide honest feedback in sessions, and should try the assigned homework in earnest. During this feedback session, it is important that the therapist present his/her observations about couple functioning in a clear and nonblaming way. In addition, the therapist should explain how couple dynamics maintain depression, impressing upon the nondepressed partner that his/her participation is important. After this presentation, partners are told to take time to decide whether they want to participate, perhaps arranging to meet the therapist the following week to renew their decision.

Many couples decide during the feedback session that they want to continue. In this situation, the clinician may consider developing a homework assignment with the couple for the upcoming week.

Setting Treatment Goals

The first goal of treatment is to help partners identify how they reciprocally influence each other's relationship satisfaction and mood. The second treatment goal is to reestablish behavior that increases collaboration between the partners. The content of the treatment goals may be left to the couple and negotiated with the therapist.

Structure of Therapy

In a clinical setting, BCT can be extended for as long as necessary as it seems helpful; however, in the context of controlled clinical trials, BCT usually consists of 12–16 sessions lasting 50 minutes each. Given the focus on couple dynamics, other family members do not attend these sessions; such involvement distracts the focus on the couple, which is the primary target of change. BCT for depression also limits the number of individual sessions, to reduce the potential that the therapist will develop a conflict of interest. Specifically, individual meetings strengthen individual rapport, but may also increase the risk of developing conflicting allegiances that interfere with treatment (e.g., a husband asks his couple therapist not to tell his wife about his extramarital affair, or he will terminate therapy). Therapists are encouraged to have a policy of open communication between partners, so that individual disclosures will not be held confidential. It is important, therefore, to delineate with precision that confidences will be revealed in couple sessions.

Role of the Therapist

The therapist has multiple roles in couple therapy for depression, including fostering a collaborative relationship, developing a therapeutic alliance with each partner, and encouraging behavior exchange (BE), and skills development. The therapist is also charged with supervising the direction and pace of treatment in accordance with the couple's treatment goals. The therapist is usually more directive in early phases of treatment, guiding the assessment and treatment phases of therapy. When the couple

engages in prescribed couple behaviors independently, the partners assume greater direction of session content and homework. In addition to training and experience with treating depression and couple distress, we think that therapists need three clinical skills to present couple therapy competently. First, therapists should be able to communicate clearly. BCT is a structured and technical therapy, and it helps if therapists are skilled in presenting treatment strategies succinctly and in simple terms. Second, therapists should have strong clinical skills to help them structure sessions, maintain therapeutic neutrality, and bypass potentially awkward issues. Finally, therapists need to be interpersonally skilled to successfully challenge and validate patients, to infuse humor, and to defuse tension.

Techniques

Presentation of Treatment Rationale

Therapists should present compelling treatment rationales to establish patient expectations, to elucidate what therapy can and cannot achieve, and to help patients understand why couple therapy is appropriate. In addition, treatment rationales should match the varying needs of couples. To illustrate the different kinds of treatment rationales, Prince and Jacobson (1995) discuss four kinds of couples that usually benefit from treatment: "classic," "denial," "systemic," and "social support" couples (Dobson et al., 1988). In a "classic" couple, both partners are depressed and distressed. Because this type of couple is interested in reducing both depression and distress, the treatment rationale may focus on an explanation of the association between depression and relationship distress, and on details about the effects of improved relationships in reducing depression. In a "denial" couple, the female partner reports depression, but both partners deny relationship distress. Nonetheless, both partners unknowingly reveal relationship distress, either by self-report or by description of their relationship. This couple is interested in organizing treatment so that the depressed woman attends individual or partner-involved treatment, rather than in initiating couple therapy for depression. To address this, the therapist may provide psychoeducation about the influence of depression upon relationship health, and may note that the couple exhibits signs of relationship strain. Since both partners are experiencing some degree of relationship distress, the clinician may suggest that couple therapy is an effective way of improving both depression and the relationship.

The "systemic" couple is the third kind of depressed/distressed couple. Specifically, the partners report relationship distress with no accompanying depression, even though it becomes apparent that one or both partners are depressed. Although they are receptive to couple therapy for depression, these individuals are less interested in depression treatment. To respond to this, the therapist may highlight how couple therapy addresses distress and mood. This may include psychoeducation about the presentation and effect of depression upon relationships. A "social support" couple reports a good relationship, despite the female partner's depressed condition. These partners express no interest in couple therapy because they do not identify having relational problems. Although this is a valid explanation, the treatment rationale may focus on the benefits of shifting the partners' attention from managing the woman's depression to enhancing their relationship, which will indirectly reduce depression. With all of these kinds of couples, a carefully prepared treatment rationale, specifically tailored to each couple's needs, will provide a more compelling presentation of treatment.

Psychoeducation and Collaborative Empiricism

In the initial treatment sessions, the clinician begins with psychoeducation about the chronic nature of depression, factors that contribute to relapse, and associated disabilities. This explanation normalizes each partner's experience with depression, and it provides a map that helps the depressed individual avoid depressogenic situations and interactions. The therapist may also talk with the nondepressed partner about frustrations that arise while living with a depressed person. Such explanations provide reassurance to the nondepressed partner that depression can be treated successfully, and information about the unique stress that depression exerts on relationships. In addition, specific attention is given to explain and explore how the nondepressed person inadvertently reinforces the partner's depressive symptoms.

The therapist also aims to develop a stance of "collaborative empiricism." This refers to a strategy of helping partners to observe each other's behavior with objectivity or scientific neutrality. This strategy aims to reduce the valence associated with certain interactions, and to help each partner see how his/her behavior contributes to the interaction and influences the other partner's response. Each partner practices responding in exaggerated ways to see how the other partner responds. In treatment, partners report their observations to each other, with the aim of developing insight about the maladaptive patterns of couple interaction.

Behavior Exchange

Early phases of treatment focus on BE techniques in order to increase each partner's sense of relationship security (Jacobson, 1979; Jacobson & Margolin, 1984). BE strategies are designed to improve each individual's ability to offer positive feedback and support. Based on the model of relationship exchange, these exercises aim to shift partners from a defensive and critical stance to a more proactive and constructive approach toward each other. Partners learn to exchange positive behavior by providing each other with tokens of affection, positive communication, appreciations, and enjoyable activities. BE has two components. The first component consists of asking each person to identify a set of behaviors that the other partner considers desirable (e.g., paying compliments, helping around the house, initiating conversation). The second component requires that the partners engage in these desirable behaviors frequently. Instructing the couple to do more positive things aims to increase relationship satisfaction without relying on the couple's interest in changing broader interaction patterns.

When introducing BE, the therapist helps the couple select behaviors for the initial assignment that generate little or no disagreement. Such choices limit the potential for conflict. The selections should not include additional negotiations or quid pro quo arrangements. Instead, each partner focuses on what he/she can do for the other partner without looking for an equal offer in return. Finally, BE emphasizes positive behaviors, rather than eliminating negative behaviors, to offset each partner's tendency to attend to negative behaviors. Thus the therapist delineates that each partner is responsible for deciding when and how they please the other. The benefits of BE strategies are to produce positive behaviors and to demonstrate that partners can set up positive contingencies for each other, as well as to reduce depression symptoms. This intervention usually generates more positive perceptions that each partner is demonstrating more interest, attention, and commitment to the relationship.

BCT assumes that patients will practice these exercises outside treatment sessions to generate competence. The rationale and design of homework assignments should be presented clearly, with the explicit statement that the results will be reviewed at the following therapy session. In presenting reasons for homework, the therapist should emphasize the link between homework completion and the upcoming session. Partners are far more likely to remember to do homework when they understand that an incomplete homework assignment means that the next session relies on feedback from the homework exercise. If one or both partners do not complete homework, reasons for nonadherence should be discussed and resolved.

Communication Training

Communication training is a direct extension of traditional behavior therapy (Stuart, 1980; Weiss et al., 1973). The focus is on teaching partners how to improve their receptive and expressive listening skills so that they understand each other accurately. This component also aims to help the partners accept emotional expression. Generating perceived support within the relationship is a critical factor in alleviating depression. Therefore, it is an important goal to ensure that both partners learn clear self-expression and listening skills. To accomplish this, partners are taught enhanced communication in three ways. First, the therapist directly instructs each partner how to communicate, and the couple practices through role-playing different scenarios. To generalize new communication skills, the therapist then encourages the couple to practice skills outside treatment sessions and to report back. Finally, the therapist offers feedback to the partners about the competencies and deficits in their demonstration of the new behaviors (this is referred to as "reinforced practice"). With all three options, the therapist and each partner provide encouragement to the other partner as he/she tries new behaviors, to shape and reinforce their recurrence. Efforts are also made to target communication patterns that increase mood and relationship satisfaction—for example, increasing the expression of intimacy and confiding. Such communication can stir renewed affection and positive feelings.

Problem-Solving Training

Problem solving is a powerful treatment strategy that encourages partners to behave collaboratively in order to resolve difficulties productively. Creating guidelines for collaborative problem solving generates the sense that the couple is working together in ways that are productive, attentive, and calming. Conveying an active problem-solving attitude also increases optimism in the couple that problems will be addressed and that change will occur. Optimism and social support through conjoint problem solving are important in improving depressive symptoms. The premise of problem solving is that both partners acknowledge their contribution to the problems and actively assume responsibility for finding a solution. Problem-solving training involves two sequential steps: First, the couple attempts to define the parameters of the problem clearly; after consensus is reached, the partners move to the stage of generating possible solutions. Problem definition helps the partners divide a problem into its component parts, and allows the partners to sort out differences in their understanding. The solution phase begins only after the problem definition phase is complete, at which point the couple does not return to the problem definition phase until an agreeable solution is generated. To ensure that the problem-solving strategies are effective, partners are instructed to do the following: (1) discuss one problem at a time, (2) paraphrase each other, (3) avoid making negative inferences about each other's motivations, and (4) avoid contemptuous or critical exchanges. This is an effort to encourage partners to provide each other with self-esteem support and affirmation, in order to cultivate baseline positive interaction. Partners are also encouraged to begin their responses with a positive statement, and then to specify what they feel using "I" statements and to define the problem in brief terms (e.g., "I really appreciate your attempt to make me feel better, but I feel frustrated"). After the problem is defined, the rest of the conversation is focused on solutions and compromise.

Relapse Prevention

The last phases of therapy attempt to solidify new learning and maintain treatment effects through relapse prevention techniques. Patients learn how to recognize situations that increase risk of relationship conflict and depression. Through practicing their skills when things are going well, and walking themselves through the skills when they feel as if they are at risk, the partners aim to maintain adaptive relationship interaction and stable mood. Before ending therapy, the partners should have demonstrated that they are able to generalize their skills and manage their relationship difficulties independently. The depressed person should also have demonstrated considerable recovery of depressive symptoms.

Curative Factors/Mechanisms of Change

Research has identified a set of factors that enhance efficacy of treatment and can be considered integral for effective resolution of depression (Jacobson, 1989; O'Leary & Rathus, 1993). Though targeted research on mechanisms of change in couple therapy for depression is limited, initial data suggest that predictors of successful outcome in BCT for depression include the following changes: (1) the degree to which partners use adaptive relationship skills, (2) efforts to reduce aversive relationship behaviors, (3) mobilization of renewed social support, and (4) a shift in attributional style (Beach & O'Leary, 1992; Kung, 2000). The unique effects of BCT lie in changing the reinforcement contingencies of behavior to make it more pleasurable (e.g., reinforcing), so that each partner will actively invest in the relationship and cultivate the other's satisfaction (Beach et al., 1990; Jacobson et al., 1991). Consistent with this principle, collaborative efforts to reduce aversive behaviors and increase facilitative efforts maximize depression recovery (Emanuels-Zuurveen & Emmelkamp, 1996; Jacobson et al., 1993). In addition, increased self-efficacy while using better communication and BE skills are curative factors in treatment. Clearer communication reduces the likelihood of misunderstandings and opportunities for negotiation. Likewise, BE increases the level and variety of depressed partners' activities, thereby increasing the chances that depressed partners will expand their repertoire of enjoyable activities.

Mobilization of support and altering cognitive misattributions are also important curative factors. Partner support is among the primary predictors of successful response to treatment for depression (Barnett & Gotlib, 1988; Coyne & DeLongis, 1986). Even when partners have access to close friendships, not having or losing a confiding relationship with one's partner increases vulnerability to depression (Brown & Harris, 1978). Encouraging a distressed/depressed partner to cultivate relationship intimacy is consistent with the research findings that bolstering social connections reduces depression and buffers against future relapse. In addition, altering attributions of meaning increases the likelihood of therapeutic change in BCT (Fincham et al., 1997). Even though BCT does not directly aim to change cognitive style and information processing, BCT influences cognitive mechanisms (e.g., it increases optimism about living harmoniously with one's partner, reduces negative partner misattributions, and reduces self-blame).

Finally, nonspecific treatment factors (e.g., warmth, rapport, empathy, informality) are major facilitative factors in enhancing response to BCT for depression (Emanuels-Zuurveen & Emmelkamp, 1996; Jacobson et al., 1993; Zeiss, Lewinsohn, & Munoz, 1979). Such factors encourage independence, convey competence, and provide supportive encouragement. These critical ingredients are important in helping couples shift behaviors. In fact, researchers suggest that these factors may be more powerful curative agents than specific treatment strategies (Zeiss et al., 1979).

CASE ILLUSTRATION

This couple participated in BCT for 20 sessions over a period of 6 months. Susan, aged 28, and Tom, aged 30, were European American and college-educated. They met as college students and dated for 18 months before marriage. Both reported relationship satisfaction until a year before they sought treatment. Their relationship, which became strained soon after they moved from the Northwest to New England, was characterized by miscommunication and criticism. Their arguments usually focused on Susan's seeming passivity toward establishing employment and friendships, as well as on Tom's overinvolvement in his graduate studies. Tom reported that Susan was "trying to sabotage the relationship by staying depressed." In turn, Susan contended that Tom was overly critical and unsympathetic. With repeated arguments and recriminations, Susan started to feel depressed about 4 months before coming for treatment. Their mutual dissatisfaction was sufficiently high that both were considering separation. Tom set up treatment to avoid this possibility.

Initial Clinical Interview

The first two couple therapy sessions collected information about the relationship and Susan's depression. The therapist described the assessment process, and then reviewed the nature and course of their relationship problems. Both partners discussed their relationship and social histories, relationship strengths and weaknesses, and individual coping efforts. In this conversation, Tom expressed a willingness to try new things to make Susan feel better. Susan expressed anger with Tom and less interest in working on the relationship. Tom and

Susan both understood Susan's depression to be related to her difficulty in adjusting to their cross-country move and relationship distress. Susan had moved reluctantly to accommodate her husband's interest in graduate school. After the move, she was unable to find satisfying work and social opportunities. Tom knew that Susan was not enthusiastic about the move, but had stopped trying to convince her that it was a good decision for both of them. Both reported areas for improvement, with Tom reporting a greater willingness to change. Though neither partner had taken action toward divorce, they had agreed to separate if things did not improve in the next 6 months. They suggested that treatment focus on communicating better, doing more enjoyable activities together (including expressing more affection), and resolving their disagreements more quickly.

The following dialogue, from the second session, shows how a therapist collects information about depression and relationship distress, while investigating the partners' response to the suggestion of BE exercises.

THERAPIST: Susan, you've just described how depressed you feel these days, and it sounds like your depression is decreasing your self-esteem, confidence, and interest in the relationship. You mentioned that this is particularly so when you and Tom fight about your unemployment. Tom, what relationship problems are associated with Susan's depression?

TOM: It was primarily the move not the relationship. When we moved here, Susan got more depressed and had trouble dealing with things. This transition has been tough for her, but it has been really difficult for me as well. I resent that she won't do things to make her life more satisfying, and there seems to be nothing I can do to make her see it my point of view.

THERAPIST: (To Tom again) So you think that the move was the main reason that Susan got depressed? What happened to the relationship when you got here?

TOM: We spent less time together, and I kind of avoided her because she wasn't doing anything.

THERAPIST: Susan, do you think that was related to your depression? What do you think about what Tom said?

SUSAN: Well, he's right to some extent. The move was hard for me. I don't know anyone here, and because I cannot find work, I have a lot of spare time with nothing to do. I've tried to adjust, but I feel like I'm on my own. Tom is not supporting me. I don't see much of Tom, and I can't help thinking that he doesn't really care about my happiness here.

THERAPIST: So we've identified a couple of things that seem to be related to your depression. Susan, you mentioned that the move was hard and that you have few friendships here. We'll look more directly at each of these issues as we talk more, but for now, it is also possible that relationship problems are contributing to your depression. Now let's turn to what you each do to make the other feel more positive about life and your relationship. (To Susan) Are there things that Tom can do to make you feel less depressed?

SUSAN: He talks to me about his day, which makes me feel included in his world. He talks about doing fun things together, but they never happen, so I've come not to expect it.

THERAPIST: What specific behaviors occur too often, or not often enough, that you feel unhappy?

SUSAN: He can be critical, which makes me feel stupid. It makes me feel bad, which gets to be frustrating and makes me sad. He doesn't get it! I can't remember the last time we talked with each other about finances or my getting a job without either one of us getting upset. We end up saying things that are not really true about the other, but I don't think that either of us understands where the other is coming from.

TOM: Well, she won't socialize, she doesn't want to work, and she sits home and mopes. She doesn't seem interested in how I feel about all of this. She's not interested in sex, and that makes me wonder why I'm in this relationship. It was one of the things I really enjoyed with Susan, and I keep thinking that maybe if we had more sex, we'd enjoy being together more. But maybe more than that, I get annoyed when she's obviously mad at me, even though I am trying to help her, but then won't say it. It's like I have to play "Guess Susan's Mood." I'm fed up!

THERAPIST: So both of you are pointing out things that you want from the other, and saying that you have expectations to continue some of the relationship behaviors you enjoyed while in the Northwest. Tom, I hear you saying that you still find Susan attractive and would like to be close with her. Susan, you're saying that you hope that Tom describes his day to you. I know you are both expressing frustration, and we'll get to that in a minute, but do you see how you both hope for certain things from each other—that you still get something from each other that makes you feel less sad? In treatment, we might spend more time encouraging you both to offer these things to the other, in an effort to generate more positive feelings about your relationship. You have both worked hard at this relationship, but now things must change for you both.

The therapist attempted to reframe the partners' frustration and emphasize the expectations of positive BE. An important dynamic to be aware of is the "downward spiral" of depressogenic thinking and criticisms that can occur in a session. Susan and Tom outlined their concerns, but they began to itemize their frustrations and call upon the therapist to judge their complaints. The therapist reframed this interaction toward helping both partners understand that they were frustrated and critical because they were invested in their relationship.

Individual Interviews

The individual session with Susan focused on the onset and course of her depression, coping, social support, and daily routine. During this session, key descriptive information was collected about the function of depression. Susan presented with most of the classic depressive symptoms, except for suicide-related behaviors. Her low mood, anhedonia, and fatigue gave Tom the impression that she was unreasonably irritable with others. Her overeating and weight gain, in combination with low libido, contributed to her tendency to feel unattractive. She spent most of her days in bed, watching television and ruminating about moving back to the Northwest without Tom. Her lethargy prompted hopelessness and inactivity. Her depression had begun before their relationship problems, although they had always experienced difficulty ending their arguments. Susan reported jealousy about Tom's relatively smooth transition into school, and frustration about the prospect of accepting unexciting temporary jobs to support them both financially. Furthermore, Susan felt isolated, as Tom rarely returned home before 11 P.M. on weeknights. At home, she described an inactive day, comprised of sleeping up to 14 hours a day, engaging in fantasy, and watching cable television. She had not explored the neighborhood and was not engaging in a regular exercise routine, which was previously enjoyable.

Before her depression, Susan had been energetic and positive around her husband. She contended that in the past 6 months, Tom had become more critical and contemptuous, arguing about her job search and money expenditures. Finally, Susan confided that she was much more hopeless about reconciliation than she had indicated in the first session, partly because Tom was unrelentingly critical. She explained that she was scared to divulge this to her husband and the therapist. The therapist obtained Susan's permission to talk about her true sense of hopelessness in the upcoming conjoint sessions.

The individual interview with Tom focused on his occasional dysphoria and relationship distress. He was "fed up" with supporting Susan and thought that she was "lazy and passive toward life." He explained that Susan was unappreciative of his support. Despite his resentment, he continued to monitor Susan because he worried about her during the day. Furthermore, he worried about their financial situation and frequently urged Susan to watch her financial expenditures. Finally, he berated himself for not being able to comfort Susan. He reported that he had initially been able to contain his frustration; now, when they argued, he withdrew and stopped communicating.

Self-Report Assessment

Self-report information was completed after the first couple therapy session, including the BDI-II, the DAS, the MSI, and the Conflict Tactics Scale. Neither Susan nor Tom expressed concerns about suicidality or domestic violence. Both partners reported dissatisfaction about the communicative, affectional, and expressive aspects of their relationship, noting that money, socializing, and lifestyle choices were the areas of most disagreement. Susan obtained a score of 32 on the BDI-II, confirming depression of moderate severity. Tom obtained a score of 8 on the BDI-II, indicating some symptoms of depression that fluctuated through the course of the week.

Case Conceptualization

The couple's presenting problems were conceptualized according to the BCT model. Susan's depression was related to relocation and financial stresses, along with each partner's inability to exit from arguments. Once Susan was depressed, relationship deficits maintained her low mood. Integral to the BCT-based conceptualization was the linkage of Susan's depression with the couple's low mutual support and increased aversive contact. Furthermore, the partners were reactive and hostile because of misattributions about each other's intentions. Specifically, Susan expressed fatigue and low mood, which Tom attributed to laziness and poor motivation. Though he tried to suppress his criticisms, they leaked through in his irritated comments and his nonverbal behavior. Likewise, Susan misattributed Tom's monitoring behavior as domineering and insensitive. Both partners had few satisfying social friendships outside the relationship, contributing to a mutual sense of isolation.

Treatment Plan

The treatment plan focused on addressing Susan's depression through improving the quality of the couple relationship. The therapist aimed to accomplish five things: (1) psychoeducation about depression and how relationship processes were associated with Susan's depression and relationship distress; (2) working on a behavioral activation plan with Susan to alleviate depression; (3) increasing positive behaviors and support through BE techniques; (4) improving communication and problem-solving skills to generate spousal support and expression of intimacy; and (5) developing socially rewarding friendships outside the relationship. Susan's depressive status was measured weekly via the BDI-II form.

During the first five sessions, Susan and Tom learned more about the nature and influence of depression and about how they inadvertently influenced each other's moods. Specific attention was given to the ways in which Susan's depression fluctuated according to her perceptions of Tom's behavior. Susan and Tom spent time generating more benign interpretations of each other's behavior (e.g., making up three interpretations and selecting the most positive). Explicit attention was also given to the ways in which Susan could use coping skills to manage her low mood. Specific techniques included doing more enjoyable activities, making phone calls to her family and friends, and going to a neighborhood cafe. The rest of these sessions focused on teaching the partners to shift their focus from defensiveness and avoidance, to more positive and constructive approaches through BE.

Behavior Exchange

The therapist promoted the couple's collaborative set by increasing the repertoire of BE activities (e.g., offering positive compliments, tracking each other's efforts, and expressing appreciations for each other). Each partner arranged to practice at least three activities that the other would enjoy. When these behaviors occurred, the other partner took the opportunity to reinforce the partner's efforts. For example, consistent with her goal of being more active during the day, Susan offered to please Tom by cooking him dinner three times a week, and to meet him at school for lunch twice a week. Susan considered these activities to be fun and knew that Tom would appreciate them. In return, Tom offered to come home by 6 P.M. with takeout food on two evenings per week, to finish his homework by 11 P.M. each night, and to keep Friday night open for social activities. These exchanges went smoothly, although the therapist spent extra time to help Susan stop keeping a mental count of the number of times Tom offered an exchange.

In the following dialogue, the therapist introduced the idea of BE and then worked with the couple to collaborate during a BE exercise.

THERAPIST: Today I'm going to increase your attention to the pleasurable things that you can do for each other. We'll start by identifying three enjoyable things you can do for each other during the week; it's what we call "behavior exchange" or "BE." Remember that the aim of this exercise is to increase your awareness about what things you can still do for each other, and to increase the positive interactions in your relationship. Now, for this to work, I would like to you put aside the expectation that you will get something in return for your gesture. Rather, this exercise will show you and your partner that you are interested in contributing to your relationship. Of the list of things that you have made, what can you do before next session that would make the other person's life more enjoyable or easier?

TOM: Hmm, we haven't done anything fun for a long time. We could go out together.

THERAPIST: Good. Now how could you frame that to be something that you are doing for Susan, rather than something the two of you do together? Remember, BE is about each person doing for the other without requiring the other person to do likewise.

TOM: I could arrange to take Susan out for a night on the town—perhaps dinner, drinks, and dancing, like we used to do before our move. That would be three things! (*Laughs*)

THERAPIST: You've both not done these things for a while, which may reduce your confidence that this will work. So these behaviors may seem awkward initially, but as you both enjoyed them previously, it is likely that you would enjoy doing them again. Let's stay focused on the activities you plan to do for each other. (*Both patients nod*) Tom, do you think that dinner and dancing is something that Susan would enjoy?

TOM: Likely.

THERAPIST: OK, so we've identified something that Tom will do for Susan. Susan, what about something you can do for Tom?

SUSAN: Well, I haven't been too happy with him these days. I'm not in the giving mood.

THERAPIST: Yeah, you're right in the sense that you are giving something to Tom, but the key point is that you can do things that you like to do, so you don't feel pressured into this or feel like you are doing this for his sake. What do you think Tom desires that you would like to do?

SUSAN: Well, I like snuggling with him and giving him back rubs on the couch, but I don't any more, because unless it leads to sex he's disappointed.

TOM: Let me defend myself here. The thing is, she gets close and then says that she's not in the mood. I'm not interested in only hugs. I start wondering why we aren't having sex more often.

THERAPIST: So do you think that getting a back rub without necessarily having sex would be enjoyable?

TOM: I would probably get frustrated.

THERAPIST: OK, your honesty is helpful. We want to identify an activity that you find enjoyable, not frustrating. Susan, could you tell that Tom got frustrated?

SUSAN: Yes, I think so. I just thought that he might like the physical contact. I can try something else, like ironing Tom's shirts. He never has time in the morning, and I have time during the day to do some.

THERAPIST: Is that something you would appreciate, Tom?

TOM: I think that would be great.

Several weeks after practicing BE, Tom reported that they were significantly more active—meeting for dinner several times each week, and going in-line skating in the park together. According to Tom, Susan seemed significantly less irritated and withdrawn. Susan reported that Tom's efforts indicated that he cared about her, which increased her hope about the relationship (although her BDI-II score remained in the 20s). Both agreed to continue these activities and add some new ones, to remind each other that they were attending to the relationship.

Communication

With both partners demonstrating positive behaviors toward each other after 7 weeks, the middle phase of treatment moved to social skills training. Communication skills training helped the partners learn to paraphrase, with the therapist providing instructions about appropriate emotional expression, and role-playing with each partner in sessions. Specific attention was paid to the partners' skills in expressing desires clearly, as well as negative feelings. Tom worked on active listening without offering advice, while Susan tried to listen actively to Tom's suggestions without responding negatively. Through shaping and encouragement from the therapist, the couple became better able to implement active expression and receptive listening.

Over the next four sessions, each partner worked on communication. Susan reported that these exercises helped to slow down the typical negative communication pattern, and helped her to modify her negative predictions about Tom. As a result, her depression improved (her BDI-II score went from the 20s to 15), and she felt more interested in job hunting and daily activities. Tom reported that he felt that his communications skills improved. The most helpful aspects of the training was to be the therapist's role-playing efforts in sessions to generate new ideas about how to respond supportively to his depressed partner. As seen in the dialogue below, encouragement and validation offered by the therapist through this component increased the couple's ability to practice modified communication.

THERAPIST: In the last session, you mentioned that you get tripped up in situations when Susan talks about her depression. It seems like there is a recurring pattern of behavior that you cannot get out of, even when you identify that it is occurring when you are having it. Correct me if I'm wrong, but it seems that when Susan expresses negative feelings, Tom responds with a helpful suggestion. Susan, you see that Tom is not directly responding in the way that you'd like, and you withdraw. Tom, you see Susan withdrawing and then snap at Susan, who withdraws further. Does that sound right?

SUSAN: (*Laughs*) It sounds so simple when you say it.

THERAPIST: Communicating your emotions clearly to each other may help you both exit from the arguments. I am observing that your communication is not as effective as it could be, which means that each of you may not picking up the signals that the other is sending. I'd like to teach you how to do "reflective listening." Let's try an exercise: I would like each of you to say something and wait for the other to say it back as accurately as you can. The other person will repeat it back to see if it was correct. Try to express "softer" emotions, like sadness, concern, and love, as opposed to anger, blame, or frustration. I will stop you both periodically to ask questions. How does this sound? (*Both nod*) OK, Susan, why don't you start off talking about a recent time when you were feeling sad?

SUSAN: Well, yesterday I was sitting at home, alone, sad, and lonely. I didn't feel like things would ever get better. I just went to sleep because I was so tired and bored.

TOM: Why didn't you call me? You knew my number.

THERAPIST: That's a good question, but first, Tom, can you reflect back to Susan what you heard her say?

TOM: Well, I heard her say that she felt really sad, bored, tired. She was sitting at home alone and was wondering whether things would get better. She sounded like she was giving up.

THERAPIST: Great summary, Tom. As Susan was unclear about what she was giving up on, we should ask her to clarify, which we will do in a minute. Susan, did Tom catch the essence of what you were saying?

SUSAN: Yes, he caught it. I was feeling that way, yeah, but I don't think I was giving up. That's why I don't express my feelings to him, because he judges me, like I'm lazy.

THERAPIST: We'll focus on your reaction in a moment. Tom, what do you think Susan said just then?

TOM: I guess I thought she said giving up. Aren't you?

THERAPIST: Tom, let's try it again. Susan, could you repeat your feelings?

SUSAN: I was feeling really tired and upset and not feeling like going on with the way things are currently. I was thinking that something has to change. That there has to be something better than what I am doing each day.

TOM: I hear you saying that you were tired and upset and not feeling like going on about what you're doing each day.

THERAPIST: That sounds like an accurate rephrase. Tom, what's your reaction to what Susan thinks?

TOM: Frustration. She could have called me, and she didn't.

THERAPIST: What is under the feeling of being upset?

TOM: I'm disappointed because I don't want her to be unhappy and alone. I would have just listened to her and tried not to tell her what to do.

THERAPIST: Hold onto that idea for a second. Susan, can you paraphrase what Tom just said?

SUSAN: He said that he wished that I had called him, and he was disappointed that I am alone during the day.

THERAPIST: There was one other piece in there. I heard him say that he cares. What do you think or feel about that?

SUSAN: (*Eyes tearing*) That makes me feel better, knowing that he wants me to talk to him when I'm down.

As evidenced above, Susan and Tom initially had difficulty listening and rephrasing accurately. The therapist gradually shaped the couple's behavior toward reflective listening, and fostered expression of softer emotion as opposed to harder, more negative emotion. Note that it is important for a therapist not to be critical of each partner's thinking process; instead, the therapist should model a more accepting, understanding style of interaction between the partners.

Problem Solving

As distress and depression decrease, a couple gains the necessary energy and focus to tackle more difficult interaction patterns. In the next four sessions, Tom and Susan focused on improving skills for problem identification and resolution. The therapist also began to increase humor and creative brainstorming in these sessions as the couple appeared more playful. These efforts actively reduced tensions when the couple was not able to get through the problem-solving exercises in a session. Susan and Tom were able to identify their problems, but had difficulty working out mutually agreeable solutions. Their negotiation about structuring their finances often deterioriated into sarcastic statements from Tom and berating criticism from Susan. In their most heated argument, Tom revealed that he thought that Susan was being "passive–aggressive" about pursuing employment. In return, she expressed resentment that he had unreasonable expectations that she would pay for his schooling and support them both. Susan continued to identify that she was more depressed after these fights, but reported more effective coping with her mood by reminding herself that Tom was still in therapy with her, which meant he was committed. After several weeks of not being able to resolve how they might structure their finances, the therapist redirected their focus to the collaborative BE exercises to emphasize their mutual interest in working together.

As they continued to provide positive benefits for each other outside of treatment, and agreed to remain civil while negotiating with each other, they began to compromise and resolve their financial disagreement. For 4 weeks, they focused on the problem-solving component until they both said they could do it without the therapist's guidance. Susan's depression dropped notably at about the 16th session (her BDI-II score went from 12 to 5). While Susan no longer qualified for a diagnosis of major depression, she reported residual symptoms of fatigue and occasional dysphoria.

Termination

As Susan and Tom demonstrated an ability to generalize these skills independently to novel problems, attention turned to discussing how the couple could implement the strategies to prevent relapse of relationship problems. Each partner identified behaviors that signified that the relationship or mood needed attention. Awareness about preventing distress and depression was emphasized by the therapist as a way to reduce the likelihood of relapse. After these sessions, the couple decided to end treatment, but wanted to come back in 4 months for a checkup. The therapist agreed, and four treatment sessions were spread over the following 6 weeks. Susan ended treatment recovered from depression (BDI-II score of 3), and with renewed enthusiasm about her relationship with Tom.

SUMMARY AND CONCLUSIONS

In this chapter, we have presented the clinical and research literature on couple therapies for depression, with a focus on BCT. Our review suggests that there is significant evidence establishing the rationale for the clinical development and empirical study of couple therapy for depression. There is clear research evidence suggesting a bidirectional link between relationship distress and depression. In particular, there is evidence that the presence of couple distress, as measured across a range of constructs, is associated with higher severity of depressive symptoms and a poorer course of depression (particularly higher rates of relapse). This suggests that modifying couple interactions and associated level of distress may improve the clinical outcome of depressed individuals. Furthermore, there is evidence across a range of treatment modalities that couple interventions can be efficacious in the treatment of major depression. In particular, we feel that there is significant evidence supporting the use of BCT for major depression. BCT focuses on modifying specific behaviors, such as engagement in pleasant events, communication patterns, and problem solving, in order to improve the symptoms of a depressed partner.

Although considerable work has been conducted thus far, the development of couple therapy for depression is in its early childhood, particularly as compared to individual-based treatments. New developments in the theory and techniques of couple therapy need to be made, and continued empirical investigation must be undertaken, before couple therapy will be accepted as a treatment approach on a par with alternative therapeutic modalities. We believe, however, that this represents a promising new area in treating depression and may significantly improve the clinical care of this population.

REFERENCES

Abramson, L. Y., Metalsky, G. I., & Alloy, L. B. (1989). Hopelessness depression: A theory-based subtype of depression. *Psychological Review, 96,* 358–372.

Addis, M. E., & Jacobson, N. S. (1991). Integration of cognitive therapy and behavioral marital therapy for depression. *Journal of Psychotherapy Integration, 1,* 249–264.

American Psychiatric Association. (1994). *Diagnostic and statistical manual of mental disorders* (4th ed.). Washington, DC: Author.

Bandura, A. (1974). *Social learning theory.* Englewoods Cliffs, NJ: Prentice-Hall.

Barnett, P. A., & Gotlib, I. H. (1998). Psychosocial functioning and depression: Distinguishing among antecedents, concomitant, and consequences. *Psychological Bulletin, 104*, 97–126.

Baucom, D. H., Sayers, S. L., & Sher, T. G. (1990). Supplementing behavioral marital therapy with cognitive restructuring and emotional expressiveness training: An outcome investigation. *Journal of Consulting and Clinical Psychology, 58*, 636–645.

Bauserman, S. A. K., Arias, I., & Craighead, W. E. (1995). Marital attributions in spouses of depressed patients. *Journal of Psychopathology and Behavioral Assessment, 17*, 231–249.

Beach, S. R. H. (1996). Marital therapy in the treatment of depression. In C. Mundt, M. J. Goldstein, K. Hahlweg, & P. Fiedler (Eds.), *Interpersonal factors in the origin and course of affective disorders* (pp. 341–361). London: Gaskell/Royal College of Psychiatrists.

Beach, S. R. H. (Ed.). (2001). *Marital and family processes in depression: A scientific foundation for clinical practice.* Washington, DC: American Psychological Association.

Beach, S. R. H., Fincham, F. D., & Katz, J. (1998). Marital therapy in the treatment of depression: Toward a third generation of therapy and research. *Clinical Psychology Review, 18*, 635–661.

Beach, S. R. H., & Nelson, G. M. (1990). Pursuing research on major psychopathology from a contextual perspective: The example of depression and marital discord. In G. Brody & I. E. Sigel (Eds.), *Family research* (Vol. 2, pp. 227–259). Hillsdale, NJ: Erlbaum.

Beach, S. R. H., Nelson, G. M., & O'Leary, K. D. (1988). Cognitive and marital factors in depression. *Journal of Psychopathology and Behavioral Assessment, 10*, 93–105.

Beach, S. R. H., & Nelson, G. M. (1990). Pursuing research on major psychopathology from a contextual perspective: The example of depression and marital discord. In G. Brody & I. E. Sigel (Eds.), *Family research* (Vol. 2, pp. 227–259). Hillsdale, NJ: Erlbaum.

Beach, S. R. H., & O'Leary, K. D. (1986). The treatment of depression occurring in the context of marital discord. *Behavior Therapy, 17*, 43–49.

Beach, S. R. H., & O'Leary, K. D. (1992). Treating depression in the context of marital discord: Outcome and predictors of response for marital therapy vs. cognitive therapy. *Behavior Therapy, 23*, 507–528.

Beach, S. R. H., & O'Leary, K. D. (1993). Marital discord and dysphoria: For whom does the marital relationship predict depressive symptomatology? *Journal of Social and Personal Relationships, 10*, 405–420.

Beach, S. R. H., Smith, D. A., & Fincham, F. D. (1994). Marital interventions for depression: Empirical foundation and future prospects. *Applied and Preventive Psychology, 3*, 233–250.

Beach, S. R. H., Whisman, M. A., & O'Leary, K. D. (1994). Marital therapy for depression: Theoretical foundations, current status, and future directions. *Behavior Therapy, 25*, 345–371.

Beck, A. T., Kovacs, M., & Weissman, A. (1979). Assessment of suicide intention: The Scale for Suicide Ideation. *Journal of Consulting and Clinical Psychology, 47*, 343–352.

Beck, A. T., Rush, A. J., Shaw, B. F., & Emery, G. (1979). *Cognitive therapy of depression.* New York: Guilford Press.

Beck, A. T., & Steer, R. A. (1987). *Manual for the revised Beck Depression Inventory.* San Antonio, TX: Psychological Corporation.

Beck, A. T., Weissman, A., Lester, D., & Trexler, L. (1974). The measurement of pessimism: The Hopelessness Scale. *Journal of Consulting and Clinical Psychology, 42*, 861–865.

Belsher, G., & Costello, C. G. (1988). Relapse after recovery from unipolar depression: A critical review. *Psychological Bulletin, 104*, 84–96.

Beutel, M., Willner, H., Deekhardt, R., Von Rad, M., & Weiner, H. (1996). Similarities and differences in couples' grief reactions following a miscarriage: Results from a longitudinal study. *Journal of Psychosomatic Research, 40*, 245–253.

Biglan, A., Hops, H., Sherman, L., Friedman, L., Arthur, J., & Osteen, V. (1985). Problem-solving interactions of depressed women and their husbands. *Behavior Therapy, 16*, 431–451.

Blumberg, S. R., & Hokanson, J. E. (1983). The effects of another person's response style on interpersonal behavior in depression. *Journal of Abnormal Psychology, 92*, 196–209.

Bradbury, T. N., & Fincham, F. D. (1990). Attributions in marriage: Review and critique. *Psychological Bulletin, 107*, 3–33.

Broadhead, W. E., Blazer, D. G., George, L. K., & Tse, C. K. (1990). Depression, disability days, and days lost from work in a prospective epidemiologic survey. *Journal of the American Medical Association, 264*, 2524–2538.

Broderick, J. E., & O'Leary, K. D. (1986). Contributions of affect, attitudes, and behavior to marital satisfaction. *Journal of Consulting and Clinical Psychology, 54*, 514–517.

Brown, G. W., & Harris, T. O. (1978). *Social origins of depression: A study of psychiatric disorder in women.* New York: Free Press.

Brown, G. W., & Moran, P. (1994). Clinical and psychosocial origins of chronic depressive episodes: I: A community survey. *British Journal of Psychiatry, 165*, 447–456.

Bruce, M. L., & Kim, K. M. (1992). Differences in the effects of divorce on major depression in men and women. *American Journal of Psychiatry, 149*, 914–949.

Burns, D., Sayers, S., & Moras, K. (1994). Intimate relationships and depression: Is there a causal connection? *Journal of Consulting and Clinical Psychology, 62*, 1033–1043.

Camper, P. M., Jacobson, N. S., Holtzworth-Munroe, A., & Schmaling, K. B. (1988). Causal attributions for interactional behaviors in married couples. *Cognitive Therapy and Research, 12*, 195–209.

Carey, M. P., Spector, I. P., Lantinga, L. J., & Krauss, D. J. (1993). Reliability of the Dyadic Adjustment Scale. *Psychological Assessment, 5*, 238–240.

Christian, J., O'Leary, K. D., & Vivian, D. (1994). Depressive symptomatology in martially discordant women and men: The role of individual and relationship variables. *Journal of Family Psychology, 8*, 32–42.

Clarkin, J. F., Haas, G. L., & Glick, I. D. (1988). Inpatient family intervention. In J. F. Clarkin, G. L. Haas, & I. D. Glick (Eds.), *Affective disorders and the family: Assessment and treatment* (pp. 134–152). New York: Guilford Press.

Coryell, W., Scheftner, W., Keller, M., Endicott, J., et al. (1993). The enduring psychosocial consequences of mania and depression. *American Journal of Psychiatry, 150*, 720–727.

Coyne, J. C. (1976). Depression and the response of others. *Journal of Abnormal Psychology, 85,* 186–193.

Coyne, J. C. (1988). Strategic therapy. In J. F. Clarkin, G. L. Haas, & I. D. Glick (Eds.), *Affective disorders and the family: Assessment and treatment* (pp. 89–113). New York: Guilford Press.

Coyne, J. C., & DeLongis, A. (1986). Going beyond social support: The role of social relationships in adaptation. *Journal of Consulting and Clinical Psychology, 54,* 454–460.

Coyne, J. C., Kessler, R. C., Tal, M., Turnbull, J., Wortman, C. B., & Greden, J. F. (1987). Living with a depressed person. *Journal of Consulting and Clinical Psychology, 55,* 347–352.

Cross-National Collaborative Group. (1992). The changing rate of major depression: Cross-national comparisons. *Journal of the American Medical Association, 268,* 3098–3105.

Crowe, M. (1997). Intimacy in relation to couple therapy. *Sexual and Marital Therapy, 12,* 225–236.

Crowther, J. H. (1985). The relationship between depression and marital maladjustment. *Journal of Nervous and Mental Disease, 173,* 227–231.

Cull, J., & Gill, W. (1989). *The Suicide Probability Scale Manual.* Los Angeles: Western Psychological Services.

Daley, S. E., Hammen, C., Burge, D., & Davila, J. (1997). Predictors of the generation of episodic stress: A longitudinal study of late adolescent women. *Journal of Abnormal Psychology, 106,* 251–259.

Dehle, C., & Weiss, R. (1998). Sex differences in prospective associations between marital quality and depressed mood. *Journal of Marriage and the Family, 60,* 1002–1011.

Depression Guideline Panel. (1993). *Depression in primary care: Vol. 2. Treatment of major depression* (Clinical Practice Guideline No. 5, AHCPR Publication No. 93-0551). Rockville, MD: U.S. Department of Health and Human Services.

Dobson, K. S., Jacobson, N. S., & Victor, J. (1988). Integration of cognitive therapy and behavioral marital therapy. In J. F. Clarkin, G. L. Haas, & I. D. Glick (Eds.), *Affective disorders and the family: Assessment and treatment* (pp. 53–88). New York: Guilford Press.

Elkin, I., Shea, M. T., Watkins, J. T., Imber, S. C., Sotsky, S. M., Collins, J. F., Glass, D. R., Pilkonis, P. A., Leber, W. R., Fiester, S. J., Docherty, J., & Parloff, M. B. (1989). National Institute of Mental Health Treatment of Depression Collaborative Research Program: General effectiveness of treatments. *Archives of General Psychiatry, 46,* 971–982.

Emanuels-Zuurveen, L., & Emmelkamp, P. M. (1996). Individual behavioural-cognitive therapy v. marital therapy for depression in martially distressed couples. *British Journal of Psychiatry, 169,* 181–188.

Emanuels-Zuurveen, L., & Emmelkamp, P. M. (1997). Spouse-aided therapy with depressed patients. *Behavior Modification, 21,* 62–77.

Emanuels-Zurveen, L., & Emmelkamp, P. M. (1996). Individual behavioural–cognitive therapy v. marital therapy for depression in martially distressed couples. *British Journal of Psychiatry, 169,* 181–188.

Epstein, N. (1985). Depression and marital dysfunction: Cognitive and behavioral linkages. *International Journal of Mental Health, 13,* 86–104.

Ferster, C. B. (1973). A functional analysis of depression. *American Psychologist, 28,* 857–870.

Fincham, F. D., Beach, S. R. H., & Bradbury, T. N. (1989). Marital distress, depression, and attributions: Is the marital distress–attribution association an artifact of depression? *Journal of Consulting and Clinical Psychology, 57,* 768–771.

Fincham, F. D., Beach, S. R. H., Harold, G. T., & Osbourne, L. N. (1997). Marital satisfaction and depression: Different causal relationships for men and women? *Psychological Science, 8,* 351–357.

Fincham, F. D., Beach, S. R. H., & Nelson, G. M. (1987). Attribution processes in distressed and nondistressed couples: 4. Self-partner attribution differences. *Journal of Personality and Social Psychology, 52,* 739–748.

First, M. B., Spitzer, R. L., Gibbon, M., & Williams, J. B. W. (1997). *Structured Clinical Interview for DSM-IV Axis I disorders: Clinical version (SCID-I).* Washington, DC: American Psychiatric Association.

Foley, S. H., Rounsaville, B. J., Weissman, M. M., Sholmaskas, D., & Chevron, E. (1989). Individual versus conjoint interpersonal psychotherapy for depressed patients with marital disputes. *International Journal of Family Psychiatry, 10,* 29–42.

Frank, E., Carpenter, L. L., & Kupfer, D. J. (1988). Sex differences in recurrent depression: Are there any that are significant? *American Journal of Psychiatry, 145,* 41–45.

Gortner, E. T., Gollan, J. K., Dobson, K. S., Jacobson, N. S. (1998). Cognitive-behavioral treatment for depression: Relapse prevention. *Journal of Consulting and Clinical Psychology, 66,* 377–384.

Gotlib, I. H., & Hammen, C. L. (1992). *Psychological aspects of depression: Toward a cognitive–interpersonal integration.* Chichester, England: Wiley.

Gotlib, I. H., & Whiffen, V. E. (1989). Depression and marital functioning: An examination of specificity and gender differences. *Journal of Abnormal Psychology, 98,* 23–30.

Gottman, J. M. (1979). *Marital interaction: Experimental investigations.* New York: Academic Press.

Gottman, J. M. (1993). The roles of conflict engagement, escalation, and avoidance in marital interaction: A longitudinal view of five types of couples. *Journal of Consulting and Clinical Psychology, 61,* 6–15.

Greenberg, L., & Johnson, S. (1986). Emotionally focused couples treatment: An integrated affective systemic approach. In N. Jacobson, & A. Gurman (Eds.), *Clinical handbook of marital therapy.* New York: Guilford Press.

Hahlweg, K., & Markman, H. J. (1988). Effectiveness of behavioral marital therapy: Empirical status of behavioral techniques in preventing and alleviating marital distress. *Journal of Consulting and Clinical Psychology, 56,* 440–447.

Halford, W. K., Bourma, R., Kelly, A., & Young, R. (1999). Individual psychopathology and marital distress: Analyzing the association and implications for therapy. *Behavior Modification, 23,* 179–216.

Hammen, C. (1991). Generation of stress in the course of depression of unipolar depression. *Journal of Abnormal Psychology, 100,* 555–561.

Hautzinger, M., Linden, M., & Hoffman, N. (1982). Distressed couples with and without a depressed partner: An analysis of their verbal interaction. *Journal of Behavior Therapy and Experimental Psychiatry, 13,* 307–314.

Hays, R. D., Wells, K. B., Sherbourne, C. D., Rogers, W., & Spitzer, K. (1995). Functioning and well-being outcome of patients with depression compared with chronic general medical illnesses. *Archives of General Psychiatry, 52,* 11–19.

Heyman, R. E., Weiss, R. L., & Eddy, J. M. (1995). Marital Interaction Coding System: Revision and empirical evaluation. *Behaviour Research and Therapy, 33,* 737–746.

Hickie, I., Parker, G., Wilhelm, K., & Tennant, C. (1991). Perceived interpersonal risk factors of nonendogenous depression. *Psychological Medicine, 21,* 399–412.

Hinchliffe, M., Hooper, D., & Roberts, F. J. (1978). *The melancholy marriage: Depression in marriage and psychosocial approaches to therapy.* New York: Wiley.

Hooley, J. M., Orley, J., & Teasdale, J. D. (1986). Levels of expressed emotion and relapse in depressed patients. *British Journal of Psychiatry, 148,* 642–647.

Hooley, J. M., & Teasdale, J. D. (1989). Predictors of relapse in unipolar depressives: Expressed emotion, marital distress, and perceived criticism. *Journal of Abnormal Psychology, 98,* 229–237.

Horowitz, A. V., White, H. R., & Howell-White, S. (1996). The use of multiple outcomes in stress research: A case study of gender differences in responses to marital dissolution. *Journal of Health and Social Behavior, 37,* 278–291.

Hops, H., Biglan, A., Sherman, L., Arthur, J., Friedman, L., & Osteen, V. (1987). Home observations of family interactions of depressed women. *Journal of Consulting and Clinical Psychology, 55,* 341–346.

Jacobs, D. G. (1998). *The Harvard Medical School guide to suicide assessment and intervention.* San Francisco: Jossey-Bass.

Jacobson, N. S. (1979). Increasing positive behavior in severely distressed marital relationships: The effects of problem-solving training. *Behavior Therapy, 10,* 311–326.

Jacobson, N. S. (1984). The modification of cognitive processes in behavioral marital therapy: Integrating cognitive and behavioral strategies. In K. Hahlweg & N. S. Jacobson (Eds.), *Marital interaction: Analysis and modification* (pp. 285–308). New York: Guilford.

Jacobson, N. S. (1989). The maintenance of treatment gains following social learning-based marital therapy. *Behavior Therapy, 20,* 325–336.

Jacobson, N. S. (1992). Behavioral couple therapy: A new beginning. *Behavior Therapy, 23,* 493–506.

Jacobson, N. S., Dobson, K., Fruzzetti, A. E., Schmaling, K. B., & Salusky, S. (1991). Marital therapy as a treatment for depression. *Journal of Consulting and Clinical Psychology, 59,* 549–557.

Jacobson, N. S., Dobson, K. S., Truax, P. A., Addis, M. E., Koerner, K., Gollan, J. K., Gortner, E., & Prince, S. E. (1996). A component analysis of cognitive behavioral treatment for depression. *Journal of Consulting and Clinical Psychology, 64,* 295–304.

Jacobson, N. S., Follette, W. C., Revenstorf, D., Baucom, D. H., Hahlweg, K., & Margolin, G. (1984). Variability in outcome and clinical significance of behavioral marital therapy: A reanalysis of outcome data. *Journal of Consulting and Clinical Psychology, 52,* 497–504.

Jacobson, N. S., Fruzzetti, A. E., Dobson, K., Whisman, M., & Hops, H. (1993). Couple therapy as a treatment for depression: II. The effects of relationship quality and therapy on depressive relapse. *Journal of Consulting and Clinical Psychology, 61,* 516–519.

Jacobson, N. S., & Holtzworth-Munroe, A. (1986). Marital therapy: A social learning–cognitive perspective. In N. S. Jacobson & A. S. Gurman (Eds.), *Clinical handbook of marital therapy* (pp. 29–70). New York: Guilford Press.

Jacobson, N. S., Holtzworth-Munroe, A., & Schmaling, K. B. (1989). Marital therapy and spouse involvement in the treatment of depression, agoraphobia, and alcoholism. *Journal of Consulting and Clinical Psychology, 57,* 5–10.

Jacobson, N. S., & Margolin, G. (1979). *Marital therapy: Strategies based on social learning and behavioral exchange principles.* New York: Brunner/Mazel.

Johnson, S. L., & Jacob, T. (2000). Sequential interactions in the marital communication of depressed men and women. *Journal of Consulting and Clinical Psychology, 68,* 4–12.

Johnson, J., Weissman, M. M., & Klerman, G. L. (1992). Service utilization and social morbidity associated with depressive symptoms in the community. *Journal of the American Medical Association, 267,* 1478–1438.

Joiner, T. (2001). Nodes of consilience between interpersonal–psychological theories of depression. In S. R. H. Beach (Ed.), *Marital and family processes in depression: A scientific foundation for clinical practice* (pp. 129–138). Washington, DC: American Psychological Association.

Jouriles, E. N., & O'Leary, K. D. (1986). Interspousal reliability of reports of marital violence. *Journal of Consulting and Clinical Psychology, 53,* 419–421.

Kessler, R. C., Walters, E. E., & Forthofer, M. S. (1998). The social consequences of psychiatric disorders: III. Probability of marital stability. *American Journal of Psychiatry, 155,* 1092–1096.

Klerman, G. L., Weissman, M. M., Rounsaville, B. J., & Chevron, E. (1984). *Interpersonal psychotherapy of depression.* New York: Basic Books.

Kowalik, D. L., & Gotlib, I. H. (1987). Depression and marital interaction: Concordance between intent and perception of communication. *Journal of Abnormal Psychology, 96,* 127–134.

Kung, W. W. (2000). The intertwined relationship between depression and marital distress: Elements of marital therapy conducive to effective treatment outcome. *Journal of Marital and Family Therapy, 26,* 51–63.

Kurdek, L. A. (1998). Relationship outcomes and their predictors: Longitudinal evidence from heterosexual married, gay cohabiting, and lesbian cohabiting couples. *Journal of Marriage and the Family, 60,* 553–568.

Lewinsohn, P. M., & Arconad, M. (1981). Behavioral treatment of depression: A social learning approach. In J. F. Clarkin & H. I. Glazer (Eds.), *Depression: Behavioral and directive intervention strategies* (pp. 33–67). New York: Garland Press.

Lewinsohn, P. M., Hoberman, H., Teri, L., & Hautzinger, A. (1985). An integrative theory of depression. In S. Reiss & R. Bootzin (Eds.), *Theoretical issues in behavior therapy* (pp. 331–359). New York: Academic Press.

Lewinsohn, P. M., Hoberman, H., & Rosenbaum, M. (1988). A prospective study of risk factors for unipolar depression. *Journal of Abnormal Psychology, 97,* 251–264.

Linden, M., Hautzinger, M., & Hoffman, N. (1983). Discriminant analysis of depressive interactions. *Behavior Modification, 7,* 403–422.

Locke, H. J., & Wallace, K. M. (1959). Short-term marital adjustment and prediction tests: Their reliability and validity. *Marriage and Family Living, 21,* 251–255.

Mahoney, M. (1974). *Cognition and behavior modification.* Cambridge, MA: Ballinger.

Malone, K. M., Szanto, K., Corbitt, E. M., & Mann, J. J. (1995). Clinical assessment versus research methods in the assessment of suicidal behavior. *American Journal of Psychiatry, 152,* 1601–1607.

Margolin, G., Talovic, S., & Weinstein, C. D. (1983). Areas of Change Questionnaire: A practical approach to marital assessment. *Journal of Consulting and Clinical Psychology, 51,* 920–931.

Markman, H., Stanley, S., & Blumberg, S. L. (1994). *Fighting for your marriage.* San Francisco: Jossey-Bass.

McCabe, S. B., & Gotlib, I. H. (1993). Interactions of couples with and without a depressed spouse: Self-report and observations of problem-solving situations. *Journal of Social and Personal Relationships, 10,* 589–599.

Merikangas, K. R. (1984). Divorce and assortative mating among depressed patients. *American Journal of Psychiatry, 141,* 74–76.

Miller, I. W., Bishop, S., Norman, W. H., & Maddover, H. (1985). The Modified Hamilton Rating Scale for Depression: Reliability and validity. *Psychiatry Research, 14,* 131–142.

Mintz, J., Mintz, L. I., Arruda, M. J., & Hwang, S. S. (1992). Treatments of depression and the functional capacity to work. *Archives of General Psychiatry, 49,* 761–768.

Monroe, S. M., Bromet, E. J., Connell, M. M., & Steiner, S. C. (1986). Social support, life events, and depressive symptoms: A 1-year prospective study. *Journal of Consulting and Clinical Psychology, 54,* 424–431.

Mundt, C. C., Goldstein, M. J., Hahlweg, K., & Fiedler, P. (Eds.). (1996). *Interpersonal factors in the origin and course of affective disorders.* London: Gaskell/Royal College of Psychiatrists.

Murray, C. J., & Lopez, A. D. (1996). Evidence-based health policy lessons for the Global Burden of Disease Study. *Science, 274,* 740–743.

Nelson, G. M., & Beach, S. R. (1990). Sequential interaction in depression: Effects of depressive behavior on spousal aggression. *Behavior Therapy, 21,* 167–182.

Nolen-Hoeksema, S. (1987). Sex differences in unipolar depression: Evidence and theory. *Psychological Bulletin, 101,* 259–282.

O'Leary, K. D., & Beach, S. R. H. (1990). Marital therapy: A viable treatment for depression and marital discord. *American Journal of Psychiatry, 147,* 183–186.

O'Leary, K. D. (1999). Developmental and affective issues in treating partner aggression. *Clinical Psychology: Science and Practice, 6,* 400–414.

O'Leary, K. D., & Cano, A. (2001). Marital discord and partner abuse: Correlates and causes of depression. In S. R. H. Beach (Ed.), *Marital and family processes in depression: A scientific foundation for clinical practice* (pp. 163–182). Washington, DC: American Psychological Association.

O'Leary, K. D., Christian, J. L., & Mendell, N. R. (1994). A closer look at the link between marital discord and depressive symptomatology. *Journal of Social and Clinical Psychology, 13,* 33–41.

O'Leary, K. D., & Rathus, J. H. (1993). Clients' perceptions of therapeutic helpfulness in cognitive and marital therapy for depression. *Cognitive Therapy and Research, 17,* 225–233.

Olfson, M., Marcus, S. C., Druss, B., Elison, L., Tanielian, T., & Pincus, H. A. (2002). National trends in the outpatient treatment of depression. *Journal of the American Medical Association, 287,* 203–209.

Prigerson, H. G., Maciejewski, P. K., & Rosenhack, R. A. (1999). The effects of marital dissolution and marital quality of health and health service use among women. *Medical Care, 37,* 858–873.

Prince, S. E., & Jacobson, N. S. (1995). Couple and family therapy for depression. In E. E. Beckham & W. Leber (Eds.), *Handbook of depression* (2nd ed., pp. 404–424). New York: Guilford Press.

Ralthus, J. C., & Sanderson, W. C. (1999). *Marital distress: Cognitive and behavioral interventions for couples.* Northvale, NJ: Aronson.

Richards, M., Hardy, R., & Wadsworth, M. (1997). The effects of divorce and separation on mental health in a national U.K. cohort. *Psychological Medicine, 27,* 1121–1128.

Rounsaville, B. J., & Chevron, E. (1982). Interpersonal psychotherapy: Clinical applications. In A. J. Rush (Ed.), *Short-term psychotherapies for depression* (pp. 107–142). New York: Guilford Press.

Rounsaville, B. J., Weissman, M. M., Prusoff, B. A., & Herceg-Baron, R. L. (1979). Marital disputes and treatment outcome in depressed women. *Comprehensive Psychiatry, 20,* 483–490.

Ruscher, S. M., & Gotlib, I. H. (1988). Marital interaction patterns of couples with and without a depressed partner. *Behavior Therapy, 19,* 455–470.

Sandberg, J. G., & Harper, J. M. (1999). Depression in mature marriages: Impact and implications for marital therapy. *Journal of Marriage and the Family, 25,* 393–406.

Schmaling, K. B., DeKlyen, M., & Jacobson, N. S. (1989). Direct observational methods for studying family functioning. In C. N. Ramsey (Ed.), *Family systems in medicine* (pp. 215–226). New York: Guilford Press.

Schmaling, K. B., & Jacobson, N. S. (1990a). Marital interaction and depression. *Journal of Abnormal Psychology, 99,* 229–236.

Schmaling, K. B., & Jacobson, N. S. (1990b). Marital interaction and depression [Published erratum]. *Journal of Abnormal Psychology, 99,* 439.

Schmaling, K. B., Whisman, M. A., Fruzzetti, A. E., Truax, P., & Jacobson, N. S. (1991). Identifying areas of marital conflict: Interactional behaviors associated with depression. *Journal of Family Psychology, 5,* 145–157.

Schweitzer, R. D., Logan, G. L., & Strassberg, D. (1992). The relationship between marital intimacy and postnatal depression. *Australian Journal of Marriage and Family, 13,* 19–23.

Sher, T. G., Baucom, D. H., & Larus, J. M. (1990). Communication patterns and response to treatment among depressed and nondepressed maritally distressed couples. *Journal of Family Psychology, 4,* 63–79.

Simon, G., Ormel, J., Von Korff, M., & Barlow, W. (1995). Health care costs associated with depressive and anxiety disorders. *American Journal of Psychiatry, 152,* 352–357.

Skinner, B. F. (1969). *Contingencies of reinforcement: A theoretical analysis.* New York: Appleton-Century-Crofts.

Smith, D. A., Vivian, D., & O'Leary, K. D. (1990). Longitudinal prediction of marital discord from premarital expressions of affect. *Journal of Consulting and Clinical Psychology, 58,* 790–798.

Snyder, D. K., Lachar, D., & Wills, R. M. (1988). Computer-based interpretation of the Marital Satisfaction Inventory: Use in treatment planning. *Journal of Marital and Family Therapy*, 14, 397–409.

Snyder, D. K., Wills, R. M., & Keiser, T. W. (1979). Empirical validation of the Marital Satisfaction Inventory: An actuarial approach. *Journal of Consulting and Clinical Psychology*, 49, 262–268.

Spanier, G. B. (1976). Measuring dyadic adjustment: New scales for assessing the quality of marriage and similar dyads. *Journal of Marriage and the Family*, 38, 15–28.

Spitzer, R. L., Williams, J. B., Gibbon, M., & First, M. B. (1992). The Structured Clinical Interview for DSM-III-R (SCID): I. History, rationale and description. *Archives of General Psychiatry*, 49, 624–629.

Stravynski, A., Tremblay, M., & Verrault, R. (1995). Marital adjustment and depression. *Psychopathology*, 28, 112–117.

Steinberg, S. I., & Bellavance, F. (1999). Characteristics and treatment of women with antenatal and postpartum depression. *International Journal of Psychiatry and Medicine*, 29, 209–233.

Stuart, R. B. (1980). *Helping couples change: A social learning approach to marital therapy*. New York: Guilford Press.

Swann, W. B., Jr., Wenzlaff, R. M., Krull, D. S., & Pelham, B. W. (1992). Allure of negative feedback: Self-verification strivings among depressed persons. *Journal of Abnormal Psychology*, 101, 293–306.

Teichman, Y. (1997). Depression in a marital context. In S. Dreman (Ed.), *The family on the threshold of the 21st century: Trends and implications* (pp. 49–70). Mahwah, NJ: Erlbaum.

Teichman, Y., Bar-el, Z, Shor, H., Sirota, P., & Elizur, A. (1995). A comparison of two modalities of cognitive therapy (individual and marital) in treating depression. *Psychiatry*, 58, 138–142.

Thase, M. E., Greenhouse, J. B., Frank, E., Reynolds, C. F. R., Pilkonis, P. A., Hurley, K., Grochocinski, V., & Kupfer, D. J. (1997). Treatment of depression with psychotherapy or psychotherapy–pharmacotherapy combinations. *Archives of General Psychiatry*, 54, 989–991.

Thase, M. E., Simons, A. D., McGeary, J., Cahalane, J. F., Hughes, C., Harden, T., & Friedman, E. (1992). Relapse after cognitive behavior therapy of depression: Potential implications for longer course of treatment. *American Journal of Psychiatry*, 149, 1046–1052.

Vivian, D., & Malone, J. (1997). Relationship factors and depressive symptomatology associated with mild and severe husband-to-wife physical aggression. *Violence and Victims*, 12, 3–18.

Waring, E. M., Carver, C., Stalker, C. A., Fry, R., & Schaefer, B. (1990). A randomized clinical trial of cognitive marital therapy. *Journal of Sex and Marital Therapy*, 16, 165–180.

Weiss, R. L., & Cerreto, M. C. (1980). The Marital Status Inventory: Development of a measure of dissolution potential. *American Journal of Family Therapy*, 8, 80–85.

Weiss, R. L., Hops, H., & Patterson, G. R. (1973). A framework for conceptualizing marital conflict, technology for altering it, some data for evaluating. In L. A. Hamerlynck, L. C. Handy, & E. J. Mash (Eds.), *Behavior change: Methodology, concepts, and practice*. Champaign, IL: Research Press.

Weiss, R. L., & Margolin, G. (1977). Assessment of marital conflict and accord. In A. R. Ciminero, K. D. Calhoun, & H. E. Adams (Eds.), *Handbook of behavior assessment*. New York: Wiley.

Weissman, M. M. (1987). Advances in psychiatric epidemiology: Rates and risks for major depression. *American Journal of Public Health*, 77, 445–451.

Wells, K. B., Burnam, M. A., Rogers, W., Hays, R., & Camp, P. (1992). The course of depression in adult outpatients: Results from the Medical Outcomes Study. *Archives of General Psychiatry*, 49, 788–794.

Whisman, M. A. (1999). Marital dissatisfaction and psychiatric disorders: Results from the National Comorbidity Survey. *Journal of Abnormal Psychology*, 108, 710–706.

Whisman, M. A. (2001). The association between depression and marital dissatisfaction. In S. R. H. Beach (Ed.), *Marital and family processes in depression: A scientific foundation for clinical practice* (pp. 3–24). Washington, DC: American Psychological Association.

Whisman, M. A., & Bruce, M. L. (1999). Marital dissatisfaction and incidence of major depressive episode in a community sample. *Journal of Abnormal Psychology*, 108, 674–678.

Whisman, M. A., & Jacobson, N. S. (1989). Depression, marital satisfaction, and marital and personality measures of sex roles. *Journal of Marital and Family Therapy*, 15, 177–186.

Whisman, M. A., & Ubelacker, L.A. (1999). Integrating couple therapy with individual therapies and antidepressant medications in the treatment of depression. *Clinical Psychology: Science and Practice*, 6, 415–429.

Wickramaratne, P. J., Weissman, M. M., Leaf, P. J., & Holford, T. R. (1989). Age, period, and cohort effects on the risk of major depression: Results from five United States communities. *Journal of Clinical Epidemiology*, 42, 333–343.

Zeiss, A., Lewinsohn, P. M., & Munoz, R. F. (1979). Nonspecific improvement effects in depression using interpersonal skills training, pleasant activities schedules, or cognitive training. *Journal of Consulting and Clinical Psychology*, 47, 427–439.

Chapter 26

Couple Therapy Complicated by a Biologically Based Psychiatric Disorder

DAVID J. MIKLOWITZ
ELIZABETH L. GEORGE

BACKGROUND

"Psychoeducation" means, literally, psychological education. It is a type of therapy that provides information to a couple or family about coping with a biologically based illness. It also addresses the emotional reactions of members of the couple or family to this information, including their resistances to the illness notion and their painful apprehensions about what the illness means for their lives. Finally, psychoeducation involves teaching the couple or family skills for coping with the illness more effectively.

Psychoeducational approaches have a long history. The empirical, research-based application of these approaches began with the work on schizophrenia of Robert Liberman (Liberman, Wallace, Falloon, & Vaughn, 1981), Michael Goldstein (Goldstein, Rodnick, Evans, May, & Steinberg, 1978), Julian Leff (Leff, Kuipers, Berkowitz, Eberlein-Vries, & Sturgeon, 1982), Ian Falloon (Falloon, Boyd, & McGill, 1984; Falloon et al., 1985), Gerald Hogarty and Carol Anderson (Anderson, Reiss, & Hogarty, 1986; Hogarty, Anderson, & Reiss, 1986; Hogarty et al., 1991), and Nicholas Tarrier (Tarrier et al., 1988). These investigators developed programs consisting of education for the family about schizophrenia and the teaching of communication and problem-solving skills. Their work showed great innovation, in that the approaches included therapist manuals, randomized experimental trials, attention to adjunctive medication treatments, and careful assessment of clinical outcomes. Consistently, the addition of family-based psychoeducation to neuroleptic medication led to lower rates of relapse, longer "survivorship" (time spent in the community without a psychotic relapse), and better psychosocial functioning among schizophrenic patients than was evident in comparison groups. Across studies, these comparison groups have included individual supportive therapy (Falloon et al., 1985), individual social skills training (Hogarty et al., 1991), and routine care or medication maintenance (Goldstein et al., 1978; Leff et al., 1982; Tarrier et al., 1988). Reviews of psychoeducational approaches to schizophrenia are available (Goldstein & Miklowitz, 1995; Penn & Mueser, 1996).

Most of the psychoeducational approaches to schizophrenia have focused on patients living with parents rather than spouses or partners. Schizophrenic patients are less likely than patients with other disorders to marry or develop long-term relationships, in part because of their ongoing symptoms and deficits in social functioning. However, these approaches share basic similarities with be-havioral models of marital/couple therapy. For example, Jacobson and Margolin's (1979) land-mark book *Marital Therapy*, the first treatment manual for a couple-based approach, described communication and problem-solving skills train-ing using role playing and behavioral rehearsal—techniques central to Liberman and Falloon's be-havioral family therapy model.

The biggest difference in behavioral couple versus psychoeducational approaches is, of course, the assumption that a couple has presented for treatment because of a biologically based mental disorder in one partner. In psychoeducational models, the couple's distress is seen as a direct result of this biologically based illness, rather than as a primary cause of the individual disturbance. In other words, communication and problem-solv-ing skills are suppressed by the stress of a psychotic episode in one family member, so that the pre-existing skills give way to anger, resentment, nega-tive attributions, and blaming. This view is in con-trast to early views (e.g., Bateson, Jackson, Haley, & Weakland, 1956), which held families respon-sible for causing schizophrenia through poor or confusing communication. No assumption of blame is made in psychoeducational models; rather, an alliance is developed between the therapist and the caretaking spouse/partner or parents, who are viewed as people undergoing a difficult, stressful experience. Part of the "repair" of family or couple relationships, then, involves helping the patient and the spouse/partner or parents to gain a more thorough understanding of the disorder and its biological underpinnings; to make clear that much of the patient's behavior is beyond his/her con-trol; and to teach new skills for listening, request-ing changes in each other's behaviors, balancing praise against negative feedback, and taking a struc-tured approach to problem solving. Thus the func-tioning of the family or couple is seen as central to the patient's prognosis over time, though not necessarily relevant to the disorder's etiology.

This chapter describes a psychoeducational approach to couples coping with a specific biologi-cally based mental disorder, bipolar disorder (manic–depressive illness). (In this chapter, the term "bipo-lar disorder" refers to either bipolar I or bipolar II disorder as defined by DSM-IV; American Psychi-atric Association, 1994.) The model, referred to as "family-focused treatment" (FFT), was designed, manualized, and tested by Miklowitz and Goldstein (Miklowitz & Goldstein, 1997; Miklowitz et al., 2000; Goldstein, Rea, & Miklowitz, 1996; Rea et al.,

in press). The FFT model is designed for patients who (1) have had a recent episode of bipolar dis-order, which can take the form of mania, hypoma-nia (mild mania), depression, or mixed disorder (depression and mania simultaneously); and (2) re-cover from this episode in the context of a couple or parental family environment. The model is a descendent of the behavioral family therapy model of Falloon, Liberman, and their associates, but addresses the different needs of bipolar patients.

THE HEALTHY VERSUS THE DYSFUNCTIONAL COUPLE COPING WITH BIPOLAR DISORDER

Are bipolar couples "dysfunctional"? In this sec-tion, we review the empirical findings about couples or parental families with a bipolar member. How are these couples or families different from couples or families coping with other psychiatric disorders? Are attributes of the couple environment predic-tive of the course of bipolar disorder?

Early Studies of Couples

Many early studies of couples with a bipolar part-ner did not examine comparison groups, did not involve systematic methods of assessment, and failed to evaluate couples longitudinally. Nonethe-less, their clinical observations are worth noting.

Whereas relations within bipolar couples are notorious among clinicians for their high levels of conflict and lack of stability, there is disagreement about whether bipolar couple relationships are any more unstable than "normal" ones. Some studies have reported high divorce rates. For example, Brodie and Leff (1971) reported that 57% of bipo-lar individuals' marriages ended in divorce, versus only 8% of the marriages of persons with major depressive disorder. Of course, this rate of 57% is not substantially higher than the 50% popula-tion rate. Carlson, Kotin, Davenport, and Adland (1974) reported that after a 3-year follow-up, 19 of 47 bipolar individuals' marriages ended in divorce, and when divorce did not occur, the well spouses reported remaining in the marriages only out of a sense of duty. Targum, Dibble, Davenport, and Gershon (1981) found that 53% of well spouses, versus only 5% of the patient spouses, claimed they would not have originally married had they known more about the bipolar disorder prior to becom-ing engaged.

Coryell et al. (1993), in a 5-year follow-up of patients who were initially studied during a period of illness, found that patients with bipolar disorder or unipolar depression were more likely (32% for the bipolar group and 22% for the unipolar group, respectively) to have never married than matched comparison subjects (parents, siblings, and adult children with no lifetime history of mood disorder), for whom the corresponding rates were 15% and 11%. Among those subjects who had been married, the bipolar patients were more than twice as likely (45%) to have been separated or divorced as their comparison subjects (18%). The rates for unipolar patients and their comparison subjects were 26% and 16%, respectively. Interestingly, among the currently married subjects, bipolar patients and comparison subjects gave equal ratings to the quality of their marriages and their sexual relationships. In contrast, the married patients with unipolar depression were more likely to rate their marriages and sexual activity as dissatisfying than their comparison subjects.

Other studies have reported that marriages with a bipolar partner are better adjusted than marriages containing a depressed member (e.g., Ruestow, Dunner, Bleecker, & Fieve, 1978) and do not differ from "normal" marriages when the patients are asymptomatic (Hirschfeld & Klerman, 1979; Frank et al., 1981). Indeed, if one observes a couple during the midst of or immediately after a major mood episode in the bipolar member, the couple will almost certainly look more dysfunctional than if one observes the partners after a period of stability. The disparity in these findings suggests the importance of examining patterns of couple interaction during a patient's mood episodes and during clinical remissions.

Studies of Expressed Emotion

More recent studies of bipolar disorder and couple/family functioning have focused on the construct of "expressed emotion" (EE), a measure of whether the "caretaking" spouse/partner or parent expresses critical, hostile, and/or emotionally overinvolved attitudes regarding the patient. The EE measure is based on the Camberwell Family Interview (CFI; Vaughn & Leff, 1976), which lasts 1 to 1½ hours and is conducted by a clinical interviewer when the patient is in the midst of an episode of illness. The attitudes that caretaking family members express about patients in the CFI are correlated with these relatives' face-to-face interactions with the patients;

for example, high-EE relatives are more likely than low-EE relatives to be critical toward patients in face-to-face interactions. This attitude–behavior consistency has been observed among relatives coping with schizophrenia (Miklowitz, Goldstein, Falloon, & Doane, 1984; Miklowitz et al., 1989), depression (Hooley, 1986), and bipolar disorder (Simoneau, Miklowitz, & Saleem, 1998). However, the overlap between EE and a couple's or family's interactional behavior is not complete. Not surprisingly, the behavior of patients during face-to-face interactional assessments strongly influences whether the relatives express high-EE attitudes (Simoneau et al., 1998; Strachan, Feingold, Goldstein, Miklowitz, & Nuechterlein, 1989).

EE is a strong prognostic index. Across 27 studies of schizophrenia, 23 have replicated the basic finding that schizophrenic patients who return following hospitalization to high-EE homes (in which at least one parent is highly critical, hostile, or emotionally overprotective) are at a two to three times greater risk for relapse in 9-month to 1-year follow-ups than those who return to low-EE (less critical and more benign) home environments. A meta-analysis of this literature by Butzlaff and Hooley (1998) indicated that the effect size for the EE–relapse association in patients with schizophrenia was strong ($r = .31$), but it was even stronger ($r = .39$) in patients with a mood disorder (depression or bipolar disorder), most of whom were living in marital couples rather than parental families. For example, Hooley, Orley, and Teasdale (1986) found that patients with major depression who returned following hospitalization to spouses who were even moderately critical (i.e., showed only two or three criticisms in an hour-long interview) were at substantially higher relapse risk at a 9-month follow-up than those whose spouses expressed one or no criticisms.

The prognostic value of EE in bipolar disorder is less well studied than in schizophrenia, but the results have supported the view that patients with high-EE parents or spouses have poorer outcomes than those with low-EE parents or spouses (Honig, Hofman, Rozendaal, & Dingemanns, 1997; Miklowitz, Goldstein, Nuechterlein, Snyder, & Mintz, 1988; Priebe, Wildgrube, & Muller-Oerlinghausen, 1989; O'Connell, Mayo, Flatow, Cuthbertson, & O'Brien, 1991). The Miklowitz et al. (1988) study was a study of patients in parental families, whereas the remaining studies were of patients in spousal or parental families.

The recent treatment study by Miklowitz et al. (2000) casts some doubt on whether EE is predictive of outcomes among patients in couples, as opposed to parental families. First, spouses of bipolar patients in this study were less likely to be high-EE than parents of bipolar patients (Miklowitz, Simoneau, Sachs-Ericsson, Warner, & Suddath, 1996). Second, EE was only predictive of relapse rates in a 1-year treatment study among patients with parental, but not spousal, relatives. However, this study did not provide a true test of the EE–outcome relationship, because all participants received FFT or a comparison treatment-as-usual intervention. Possibly, either intervention could have blunted the prognostic effects of EE in the marital couples.

Interactional Behavior among Families and Couples Coping with Bipolar Disorder

The EE research has gone hand in hand with research that attempts to elucidate patterns of family interaction in bipolar, schizophrenic, and other family environments. One study compared bipolar and schizophrenic patients' families directly (Miklowitz, Goldstein, & Nuechterlein, 1995). This study was limited to persons who developed a psychotic or a manic episode for which they were hospitalized, and who returned to live with (or remained in close association with) their parents. Nonetheless, its results are relevant to designing treatments for couples, some proportion of which might be expected to show similar family dynamics.

All families came to a university laboratory for a series of directed problem-solving discussions, which were videotaped and coded using measures of parent verbal behavior (affective style; Doane, West, Goldstein, Rodnick, & Jones, 1981) and offspring verbal behavior (coping style; Strachan et al., 1989). Patients were in partial but not full remission from their manic episodes, having been discharged from the hospital an average of 2–3 weeks earlier. Parents of schizophrenic patients were characterized by high levels of negative affect during face-to-face interactions with the patients. Negative statements from parents (criticism and intrusive, "mind-reading" statements) tended to be correlated with self-critical statements by the patients (e.g., "I know I've messed up and caused you guys a lot of trouble"). Not surprisingly, the schizophrenic patients were more withdrawn during the interactions than the bipolar patients. In contrast, the bipolar patients were quite motorically and verbally activated, and frequently made counter-criticisms of their parents. Possibly the parents of

bipolar patients became inhibited when faced with the aggressiveness of their bipolar offspring. These patients frequently "ran the show" when their families were asked to discuss a problem topic. Of course, these dynamics could be attributed in part to the patients' unresolved manic symptoms. Different interactional patterns might have been observed if these assessments had been conducted after the patients had had a depressive episode or a lengthy period of remission.

More recent studies in our laboratory have elucidated the family and couple dynamics that accompany high-EE parental and spousal units (Simoneau et al., 1998; Wendel, Miklowitz, Richards, & George, 2000). These studies involved a sample of bipolar patients who participated in a randomized trial of FFT versus a comparison condition (Miklowitz et al., 2000). The outcome results from this trial are summarized later in the chapter.

Simoneau et al. (1998) found that families and couples who were rated high-EE when the patients were in an acute bipolar episode showed negative patterns of interaction during problem-solving tasks conducted 1 month later. Sequential analyses showed that members of high-EE couples and parental families had "reciprocal dependencies" between their behaviors: When one member (patient or relative) criticized another, the other reciprocated the criticism, which led to a further criticism from the first member, and so forth. Low-EE couples or families were more able to discourage conflict from escalating: When one member criticized another, the criticism was less likely to be reciprocated. Similar patterns of communication have been observed in the high-EE families of schizophrenic patients (Hahlweg et al., 1989) and in nonclinical distressed couples (for a review, see Robinson & Jacobson, 1987). Collectively, these findings suggest a target for psychoeducational treatment: interrupting destructive patterns of verbal communication and teaching effective conflict resolution skills.

Wendel et al. (2000) clarified what may be occurring within the minds of relatives rated high-EE versus low-EE. When interacting with the patients, high-EE parental and spousal relatives made more "controllability attributions" about the patients' negative behaviors or role in negative events than low-EE parental or spousal relatives did (e.g., "You try to do so many things at once that you can never stop and focus on one thing"). Hooley (1987) explains that high-EE relatives of schizophrenic and depressed patients are more likely than low-EE relatives to view the patient's behavior (including illness-related behaviors or symptoms) as intentional and under the patient's personal control. In contrast, low-EE relatives are more prone to attributing negative patient behaviors to uncontrollable factors, such as a biologically based illness. These notions echo early clinical observations that some spouses view their bipolar mates' manic behavior as willfully and spitefully produced (Ablon, Davenport, Gershon, & Adland, 1975; Janowsky, Leff, & Epstein, 1970).

Conclusions

Couples coping with bipolar disorder experience significant conflicts and distress during the acute episodes of the disorder and during the postepisode recovery periods. Whether families or couples coping with the disorder are fundamentally different from ordinary community couples is unclear. Examining this question requires observing couples at multiple time points in the course of the illness, particularly after extended periods of the patients' remission.

Issues of gender, race, and socioeconomic status (SES) have not been examined in couple research on bipolar disorder. For example, differences between bipolar and schizophrenic patients in interactional behavior may be in part a function of demographic attributes: The bipolar patients in the Miklowitz et al. (1995) study had more education and were more often female than the schizophrenic patients.

Regardless of the source of distress among bipolar couples, it appears that many would benefit from a psychoeducational program administered shortly after an acute episode of illness. Educating a couple about what behaviors of the ill partner can and cannot be attributed to the bipolar disorder, and enhancing the couple's communication and problem-solving behavior in the aftermath of the episode, have the potential to improve the postepisode functioning of the couple. These are some of the assumptions of FFT.

THE ASSESSMENT OF COUPLE FUNCTIONING AND DYSFUNCTION

FFT begins with a series of assessments of individual and couple/family functioning. These are usually initiated during the postepisode aftercare period, when the patient is still symptomatic. These early assessment sessions, including a standard diagnostic assessment, give structure and regularity to contact with clinicians during the stabilization and recovery period. In the past, we have initiated assessments during the hospitalization period. Nowadays, many patients referred for couple or family treatment are outpatients who have recently had an acute illness episode.

Clinicians at our laboratory at the University of Colorado–Boulder use the Structured Clinical Interview for DSM-IV (SCID; First, Spitzer, Gibbon, & Williams, 1995) to verify the diagnosis. The SCID systematically evaluates the presence or absence of manic, depressive, psychotic, and anxiety symptoms, and the role of substance abuse or dependence. The SCID is rather laborious to administer, but yields important information about the diagnosis that even the most skilled clinical interviewers can miss.

A thorough history of the psychiatric disorder is also taken. Examining all prior episodes can inform the clinician's treatment plan. A common method of collecting this information is through the life-charting method and its associated computer software (Leverich & Post, 1998), in which the clinician records, on a time line, all prior manic, mixed, hypomanic, or depressive episodes; their length and polarity; their psychosocial precipitants; and the medical and psychosocial treatments received prior to and during each episode. One may learn, for example, that a patient has had mixed episodes as well as manic or depressive episodes, which tend to be more treatment-refractory (Calabrese, Fatemi, Kujawa, & Woyshville, 1996). Or one may learn that all of the prior hypomanic or manic episodes were precipitated by the use of tricyclic antidepressants or selective serotonin reuptake inhibitors, or that episodes were usually accompanied by severe couple conflict or separations.

The assessment of the couple begins with the CFI (see above), which assesses the partner's perceptions of the history of the disorder, including when the most recent episode began, how the patient behaved during the prodromal period, and how the illness affected the partner's emotional state. Specific symptoms (e.g., irritability) are assessed, as are the partner's emotional reactions to these symptoms. In our research, CFI tapes have been sent to a coder who does not know the couple and who applies a specific system for coding EE. The coder makes note of critical comments (e.g., "I'm annoyed by his eating habits"), evidence of hostility (e.g., "I like nothing about her"), and emotional overinvolvement or overprotectiveness (e.g., "I'm scared to death about his trip to California. I don't think he should go on a plane by himself"). If the part-ner scores high on any of these dimensions (i.e., makes six or more critical comments, shows hostil-ity, or scores at a 4 or 5 on a 0–5 scale of emotional overinvolvement), the couple is designated as "high-EE." If the partner scores below these cutoffs, the couple is designated as "low-EE."

Equally or more informative are assessments of the couple's interaction patterns. The advantage of these assessments is that they give the clinician a firsthand view of the verbal and nonverbal behav-ior that will need to be addressed in the couple therapy. For example, do problems get solved? What are the frequencies of attack–counterattack cycles? Does the well partner play an equal role in prob-lem solving, or does he/she get "run over" by the bipolar partner? Is communication clear? Are re-quests for behavior change made directly and suc-cinctly? Does each partner listen (i.e., keep good eye contact, give nonverbal and verbal acknowledgment), or does one consistently interrupt the other? What are the couple's strengths? What skills need to be acquired or refined? The clinician must always keep in mind that the patient's clinical status will affect these interactions. Reviewing the couple's interac-tional behaviors during a period of remission will clarify whether these behaviors are best conceptual-ized as "state" or "trait." For example, a highly with-drawn, depressed patient who is being nagged by a well partner may become quite assertive during a manic or remitted phase.

The disadvantage of laboratory interactional assessments is that they can be costly to obtain. In our laboratory, these assessments are conducted by the therapist who will be working with the couple and a research assistant or cotherapist. First, these clinicians interview each member of the couple individually and ask him/her to define problem topics, speaking into a tape recorder. The clinicians then play the partner's tape-recorded definition of the problem to the other partner and ask him/her to respond on tape. These audiotaped "conversa-tions" become stimuli for generating the discus-sions. The couple is asked to listen to the recorded problem definition and response, and then to dis-cuss it and attempt to solve it together for 10 min-utes, with the clinical personnel out of the room (see Miklowitz et al., 1984, 1995). This method helps assure that the members of the couple choose a problem topic of importance to them. Clinicians who work in practice may be able to simplify this procedure by giving the couple a list of problems to discuss, and then leaving the room and observ-ing through a one-way mirror.

Consider the following case vignette:

During a problem-solving discussion with his wife, Carl, a 48-year-old man with bipolar I disorder, frequently used military language, even though he had never been in the military. He would talk about his medications "blowing his brain to pieces" and state that looking for a job was "like wandering through a mine field." His verbal style became particularly aggressive and angry when he was talking to his wife about the mental health establishment. His wife, Sheila, was quite concerned about his clinical state. She would carefully address ques-tions to him about his doctors and about his use of his time when he was at home and she was working at her volunteer job. He would angrily berate her for being controlling; yet he would ask her to make phone calls to his doctors, pick up his drug prescriptions, and make up daily plans of activity for him. She seemed unaware of this contradiction in his messages to her, and usu-ally would comply with whatever he asked. The more she stressed her role in taking care of him, the more he became willing to give up control to her, while simulta-neously expressing his resentment.

In this example, the FFT clinician identified certain dynamics of the couple as targets for the later communication and problem-solving training. How could Carl be more explicit in what he did and did not need from Sheila? How could Sheila encourage him to be more responsible for his own behavior? Were there behavior prescriptions that could be given (e.g., asking Carl to contact his own doctor when issues about medication came up)? An interactional assessment can elucidate such targets for treatment as these. Of course, one learns even more about the members of a couple and how they interact as the treatment progresses, and hypoth-eses about couple dynamics and interventions are modified accordingly.

GOAL SETTING

FFT begins with a discussion with the couple of goals and expectations, including the format of the treatment (weekly, biweekly, then monthly ses-sions); the fact that educational information about bipolar disorder will be provided; and the fact that the couple will be expected to partake in exercises designed to promote better communication and problem solving. A typical beginning statement from the clinician is the following:

"In bipolar disorder, when the person begins to re-cover from an episode of mania and depression, there is a 'getting reacquainted' period in which you have to get to know each other again, and when you try to make sense as a couple of what just happened. This is a tough time for any couple, and part of our purpose here is to make this reacquaintance period less disturbing to the two of you. I'd like to give you some tools for dealing with this recovery period."

Thus the goals of FFT are framed in terms of the demands of the postillness episode period (Miklowitz & Goldstein, 1997). No implication is made that the couple is "dysfunctional" or has requested standard couple therapy.

FFT has six interrelated goals that apply to most couples and families (Miklowitz & Goldstein, 1997). They are to assist the patient and partner in doing the following:

1. Integrating the experiences associated with episodes of bipolar disorder.
2. Accepting the notion of a vulnerability to future episodes.
3. Accepting a dependency on psychotropic medication for symptom control.
4. Distinguishing between the patient's personality and his/her bipolar disorder.
5. Recognizing and learning to cope with stressful life events that trigger recurrences of bipolar disorder.
6. Reestablishing a functional relationship after an episode.

Of course, the emphasis given to any particular goal will vary from couple to couple. Depending on the partners and their approach to the disorder (e.g., their level of denial about the illness), these goals may or may not be stated by the clinician at the outset. First, the couple is encouraged to make sense of the most recent episode of the bipolar illness, including what symptoms were present, what psychosocial stressors contributed to the episode, and how biological factors (including nonadherence to medications) contributed to its onset. The clinician then encourages the patient and partner to recognize that the patient is vulnerable to future episodes (Objective 2), and that long-term pharmacotherapy will be a necessary component of his/her treatment (Objective 3).

Some patients are not surprised to learn that the FFT clinician recommends medication. Older patients will generally not challenge this notion. Younger patients, in contrast, often hope that FFT will be a substitute for medications—a belief that the FFT clinician must dispel. (FFT is virtually always used in conjunction with medications.) For

these patients, accepting that the disorder is recurrent and requires drug treatment is a "hard pill to swallow." They may strongly object to this idea, and press the notion that the illness was a once-only occurrence, even if they have had earlier episodes. As clarified later, there are specific techniques for addressing objections to the diagnosis and the pharmacological treatment.

The fourth objective, distinguishing personality from the disorder, is a greater issue for some patients than others. Patients often complain that their partners (or parents) have confused these phenomena: "She wants me to take a pill every time I get angry or sad" is a common refrain. We suspect that this same confusion takes place less frequently in schizophrenia, in which the psychotic phases are in most cases a clear departure from a patient's baseline functioning. In bipolar disorder, the symptoms are not always so extreme, and a patient's claims sometimes have validity. FFT attempts to help a couple make these personality-disorder distinctions (e.g., distinguishing "manipulativeness" from "sudden increases in irritability"), and addresses the issues about identity, hopes and aspirations, and fears about the future that often underlie questions about this distinction.

The fifth issue, regarding coping with psychosocial stressors, must be individualized for couples. Some bipolar patients are strongly affected by even minor events that affect sleep–wake rhythms (e.g., a flight to a different time zone; Malkoff-Schwartz et al., 1998). Others experience cycling after events that promote goal-directedness (e.g., getting promoted; Johnson et al., 2000). Part of the educational work involves helping the couple to identify which stressors have affected the patient in the past, and which are likely to cause him/her trouble in the future.

Finally, the overarching goal of FFT is to restore functional couple relationships after the episode. Achieving this goal involves offering didactic information on coping strategies (e.g., how the patient's partner can help to keep the home environment "low-key"), cognitive strategies, and communication/problem-solving strategies.

Of course, these goals are not imposed upon the couple in a rote way. Both partners are encouraged to comment on the applicability of each goal to their particular situation. Some bipolar patients, for example, do not contest their need for medication and approach FFT as a relationship-repairing treatment. Other patients or their partners are not particularly concerned about the status of their relationships, but are very concerned about a recent increase in the patients' mood cycling. One way to establish a couple's objectives is to ask, "Where would you like things to be in, say, 3 or 6 months? What would be a good outcome, in terms of your relationship, your disorder, and your job situation?"

THE STRUCTURE OF THE THERAPY PROCESS

General Structure

FFT is typically administered once a patient's condition begins stabilizing from an acute episode of bipolar disorder (a manic, depressed, mixed, or hypomanic episode). Some patients begin FFT after a period of symptomatic worsening that may be "subsyndromal" but nonetheless has impaired his/ her functioning. Generally, a couple is not motivated for FFT if the patient has been stable for a lengthy period, unless significant relationship problems (usually those unrelated to the disorder) have arisen.

FFT involves 12 weekly sessions, followed by 6 biweekly sessions and then 3 monthly sessions (a total of 21 sessions over 9 months). This structure derives from the recommendations of Falloon et al. (1984) for schizophrenic patients. As indicated, treatment frequency is most intensive when the patient's condition is stabilizing after his/her index episode, but is tapered as the patient recovers. During the initial treatment phase, the patient is often symptomatic; the focus of FFT during this phase is on getting to know the patient and developing an alliance with him/her and the partner (and/or other family members). The "well" partner's level of EE and the couple's interactional behavior are also assessed during this preliminary phase, if the patient is not too symptomatic to tolerate a behavioral assessment of communication styles.

About 2–3 weeks after the program is first introduced to the patient, and once initial assessments have been completed, the psychoeducational module begins. At least 7 weekly sessions are required to cover the basic didactic material. About 2–3 months into the program, most patients will have achieved a degree of clinical stability, especially if they have been compliant with drug treatments. At this point, the communication enhancement training exercises begin. About 7–10 sessions are devoted to learning and rehearsing such skills as active listening, delivering positive or negative

feedback to another family member, and politely requesting changes in another family member's behavior. By 12 weeks, sessions are tapered to biweekly for the next 3 months.

The final module, problem solving, begins by about Sessions 14–15. Sessions are still biweekly at this point. Four to five sessions are devoted to defining specific couple or family problems, generating solutions, and developing plans for implementing these solutions (e.g., how to structure the weekend, how to manage finances). The last few sessions are held monthly and are devoted to reviewing the communication and problem-solving skills and issues relevant to termination.

Who Participates?

Participants in FFT can include a patient's marital or romantic partner, siblings, or parents. Occasionally, we have conducted treatments in which a patient's spouse/partner *and* parents were involved. With time, these arrangements usually evolve into couple treatment, depending on which relatives are the most active in the patient's care. Adolescent offspring of a patient have been included in certain circumstances, if in the patient's estimation their involvement would benefit them and hasten the patient's improvement. Adult offspring who are involved in the care of a bipolar parent are strongly encouraged to participate. We are currently developing a model for FFT that focuses on patients with childhood-onset bipolar disorder.

Pharmacotherapy

The patient enrolls in pharmacotherapy with a psychiatrist at the same time as enrolling in FFT. Nowadays, typical drug treatment regimens include lithium carbonate or anticonvulsants (divalproex sodium [Depakote], carbamazepine [Tegretol], oxcarbazepine [Trileptal], lamotrigine (Lamictal), or, most recently, topiramate [Topamax]), with adjunctive agents. These adjunctives can include antidepressants of the selective serotonin reuptake inhibitor class (e.g., paroxetine [Paxil], fluoxetine [Prozac], or sertraline [Zoloft]), the monoamine oxidase inhibitor class (e.g., tranylcypromine [Parnate]), or the "novel antidepressant" class (bupropion [Wellbutrin], nefazodone [Serzone], or venlafaxine [Effexor]). Atypical antipsychotics (e.g., olanzapine [Zyprexa] or risperidone [Risperdal]) are often added for agitation, sleep disturbance, or psychosis. Sometimes patients are given adjunctive anxiolytic medications (e.g., clonazepam [Klonopin]) for sleep disturbance or anxiety.

A good relationship between the FFT clinician and the treating psychiatrist is essential. Regular dialogue between these treatment personnel should occur regarding the patient's style of approaching treatment, adherence to medications, and clinical status. In addition to assuring continuity of care and appropriate management of emergencies, this ongoing collaboration can help unlock the patient's resistances to medications (or, for that matter, to couple therapy).

Cotherapy Teams

There are at least three reasons to consider having a cotherapy team conduct FFT. First, bipolar patients and their partners can be quite difficult to treat. A cotherapist provides an objectivity that a single therapist sometimes cannot maintain. Second, if one clinician is more experienced than the other, the cotherapy arrangement provides a learning opportunity for the novice clinician. Third, and on a more practical level, the role-playing/communication exercises often require that the therapists model certain communication styles for the couple; such modeling requires a speaker and a listener.

Unfortunately, cotherapy teams double the cost of the treatment, which in the era of health care cost containment can be prohibitive. Second, bipolar patients are notorious for "splitting" teams of clinicians (i.e., responding to cotherapists as if one were good and the other were bad). Cotherapists have to be aware of when splitting is occurring, and must address it both with each other, and with the patient and partner as a cohesive unit. If there are preexisting disagreements or dramatic differences in clinical style between the clinicians, the chances for splitting are higher.

We believe that the advantages of cotherapy teams outweigh their disadvantages, particularly when a clinician is first learning FFT. But in nonresearch settings, the decision to involve two clinicians is likely to be affected by what cost limitations exist, whether two clinicians are available and interested, whether time schedules coincide, and other factors. There are no data on whether patients with bipolar disorder or schizophrenia vary in their outcomes after family psychoeducational treatments conducted by one versus two therapists.

THE ROLE OF THE THERAPIST

The Therapeutic Stance

FFT must be done with a "psychotherapeutic attitude." We firmly believe that FFT, and most behaviorally oriented interventions, proceed more smoothly when the clinician is sensitive to the affective issues that are inevitably aroused by the educational materials and skill training. The clinician must address the patient's and/or partner's disbelief in the diagnosis, their mistrust of the therapist, or other impediments to skill acquisition.

As in any couple treatment, the clinician develops an alliance with both members of the couple from the outset. This alliance building can be as simple as joking with the partners, allowing a certain amount of chit-chat, or self-disclosing and admitting to a degree of vulnerability (e.g., "If I get under stress, I'm probably more likely to get a stomachache or a headache than to get depressed. . . . I guess how you react to stress differs from person to person"). It is important to the bipolar patient that the clinician express interest in him/her as a person rather than as a "clinical specimen."

Some clinicians like to self-disclose important facts about themselves, such as having mental illness in their own families, having gone through painful life events, or having had rocky times in their own marriages/relationships. Although we do not view these self-disclosures as damaging to patients, they have the potential for damaging therapists' credibility. Bipolar patients are effective at identifying the vulnerabilities of their caretakers and playing upon them (Janowsky et al., 1970). For example, if a clinician admits to having had a father with a psychiatric illness, a patient may bring this up at a time when he/she is angry with the therapist (e.g., "Maybe you have some stuff about your own father's illness you haven't worked through"). On the other hand, admitting to less personal vulnerabilities (e.g., feeling uncomfortable about having one's blood drawn for medication management purposes) may help the clinician to join with the patient and family.

When the psychoeducational material is being covered (see below), it is easy to fall into the trap of being a teacher and not a clinician. FFT involves a fair amount of teaching (e.g., familiarizing the couple with the prodromal symptoms of manic or depressive episodes). But even when one is covering didactic material, it is best to have a give-and-take dialogue with the couple (e.g., "Can you tell us more about what you understand to be 'rapid cycling'?"). Sometimes discussing material as seemingly nonthreatening as the patient's sleep disturbances or spending habits can generate strong emotions in the clients. When members of a couple are having affective reactions, the clinician stops and checks in with them (e.g., "I'm guessing you're getting upset talking about all of this symptom stuff. That's understandable—sometimes this material can be painful to talk about. Can you tell us what this stirs up in you?").

It is essential to communicate an upbeat, optimistic tone. The couple should receive the message that if the patient takes his/her medications and the two members of the couple implement stress management strategies on a regular basis, there is every reason to think the patient will have a positive outcome of his/her disorder. The clinician emphasizes the patient's (and partner's) strengths throughout the treatment (e.g., "You're a person who has always had a lot of friends. . . . My guess is that even in the worst of times you'll be able to connect with others").

How Is the Role of the Clinician Described to the Couple?

Couples benefit from knowing what to expect of the clinician. Thus the clinician usually shares information about his/her stance early in treatment. A common introduction is as follows:

> "We'll be active and directive with you at some times, and we'll sit on the sidelines at others. We may talk about ourselves from time to time. We'll coach you on some new skills that should help you in your day-to-day dealings with each other. We'll offer concrete suggestions about what you can *do* to make your situation better. Also, we're going to encourage you to tell us if these sessions are not meeting your needs—there may be things we can do to make them more useful." (Miklowitz & Goldstein, 1997, p. 96)

Structuring the FFT Sessions

Most couple treatments go better when the clinician adheres to a structure. But patients with bipolar disorder tend to be talkative and verbally aggressive—especially when they are manic or hypomanic, but often even when they are in remission. As mentioned above, Miklowitz et al. (1995) found that bipolar patients spoke almost twice as much as schizophrenic patients when interacting with their relatives during a posthospitalization

assessment. Some patients have a temperament characterized by exuberance, intrusiveness, optimism, loudness, and a flair for the dramatic—a style Akiskal (1996) refers to as "hyperthymic." Others are not so cheerful; rather, they have a negativistic, irritable style and little patience for things that move too slowly.

The FFT clinician must be aware that many bipolar patients react quite negatively to anything that smacks of control by others. They become defensive when they perceive that others are trying to squelch their behavior, emotions, or thought processes. However, they may also react negatively to a clinician who is too passive. Thus the clinician must walk a fine line between structuring the sessions and keeping a patient task-focused on the one hand, and being overly didactic and directive on the other. The clinician "never loses control of the show," but also allows the clients to have the stage once in a while.

The degree to which the clinician must be directive can change during various stages of the therapy. For example, if a patient seems very irritated by an agenda-focused therapist, it may make sense to give the patient more "air time" at the beginning and gradually take more control of the sessions as they progress. In contrast, some patient–partner pairs are quite passive at the beginning of treatment. These couples may benefit from an initial structure (the psychoeducation), followed by encouragement to speak up more and more as the treatment progresses into the communication training phase.

Therapists' Attributes

The clinicians who have done the best in implementing FFT have shared several abilities: (1) a willingness to stay task-focused, but an awareness of when to shift gears and explore subtle relational dynamics; (2) a thorough knowledge of bipolar disorder from a medical as well as a psychosocial standpoint; and (3) the ability to "think systemically" and keep the focus on two-person transactions rather than the intrapsychic dynamics of either the patient or the partner. Some clinicians we have supervised begin with an agenda (e.g., taking the couple through a relapse prevention drill), but then quickly abandon the agenda when an opportunity arises to explore a patient's or partner's childhood. Both the patient and the partner eventually complain that the sessions are aimless and that they are uncertain how the treatment will help them. Exploring only one person's dynamics can also carry the implication that this person is at fault for the resulting couple dynamics.

Clinicians must also be very patient. Often a bipolar patient will "take a dive" between sessions and symptomatically deteriorate. The couple will then challenge the goals of the treatment and become frustrated that there do not seem to be clear answers to the harder questions, such as whether the patient should return to a certain job or whether he/she will respond to a particular medication. Clinicians who are relatively unflappable and who stick with a couple through the rough spots in the treatment, without becoming defensive or frustrated, usually have the best outcomes.

TECHNIQUES OF COUPLE THERAPY

This section describes the material that is covered in the three FFT modules. It describes the ways that the FFT clinician conducts the educational and skill training procedures, and addresses couples' resistances to the material.

Psychoeducation

The goal of psychoeducation is to encourage the couple to develop a shared understanding of bipolar disorder. First, the couple is given a handout listing the symptoms of mania, hypomania, depression, and psychosis. A common introduction is the following:

> "One of the ways we want to help you is to look at the symptoms of bipolar disorder and show you how a diagnosis is made. We want to identify which of these symptoms you had so we can know what you went through during your episode, as well as when you were becoming ill. Some people find it easy to talk about their symptoms, and others find it hard— they feel embarrassed or ashamed, or sometimes they just can't remember. But let's give it a try." (Miklowitz & Goldstein, 1997, p. 101)

The patient is encouraged to describe his/her most recent symptoms of mania, hypomania, and/or depression. Likewise, the partner describes what the most recent episode looked like to him/her. The focus is on the *development* of the episode: How did the well partner know that the bipolar partner was becoming ill? Did the bipolar partner recognize that something was wrong? Gradually, the couple defines a "prodromal" phase of the patient's episodes, which usually consists of observations about changes in mood (irritable, depressed, giddy), sleep (increased or decreased), levels of sociability (extra friendly/intrusive vs. withdrawn), thought patterns (racing vs. slowed down), and sexual drive or activity (increased vs. decreased).

The clinician gives the partners a handout in which "psychobiological vulnerability" and "socio-environmental stress" are described as interactive processes. They are given information about risk factors for episodes of bipolar disorder (e.g., taking street drugs, using alcohol excessively, sleep disruption) and protective factors that mitigate the likelihood of episodes (e.g., keeping regular sleep-wake regimens, keeping the home atmosphere low in stress, taking medication).

This material does not fully come alive for the couple until it is personalized for them. This is done in two ways. First, a handout giving a list of possible life events is distributed (e.g., promotion to a new job, change in residence, personal illness or injury). Each partner is asked to review the list and discuss any stressors that accompanied the recent episode.

For example, Kara, aged 37, listed "excessive workload" as contributing to her most recent manic episode, whereas her husband Jim, aged 42, listed "problem with child" (increased conflict between Kara and her 13-year-old son). Both agreed that these two stressors had played a pivotal role in activating her symptoms during her latest manic episode.

Many couples do not put together the relation between significant stressors and the onset of mood episode symptoms, and recent examples help to acquaint them with this feature of the disorder.

Second, couples are asked to describe their family pedigrees. Identifying one or more persons with bipolar disorder, unipolar depression, or alcoholism clarifies the notion of a psychobiological vulnerability. The clinician then pulls this information together by describing the vulnerability-stress model:

> "We think you probably have a predisposition to developing bipolar episodes. A 'predisposition' means that you're more likely to develop manic or depressive symptoms because of some factor within yourself, like the genes you inherit or the particular chemistry of your brain. But predispositions don't mean you'll automatically get the illness. They're more likely to become activated if you encounter something stressful. Later we'll talk about some things you can do to cut down the likelihood that you'll develop episodes. Some of these things are medical,

and some involve your lifestyle, like keeping a regular sleep–wake cycle or keeping your relationship low-key and nonstressful."

The Relapse Drill

The psychoeducation module ends with a relapse drill. The couple first reviews and writes down the patient's prodromal symptoms (usually identified in the earlier discussions), and then problem-solves about what to do if these symptoms reappear. Interestingly, some patients or relatives describe prodromal symptoms that do not fit neatly into any diagnostic criterion. For example, the parents of one male patient reported that when he got manic or mixed, he would begin to "mutter stuff underneath his breath." A female patient described "seeing things out of the corner of my eye" when she was becoming manic.

Couples need coaching in developing a contract for "who will do what" should these symptoms appear. Often quid pro quo arrangements can be made.

For example, Kara and Jim agreed that Jim would first encourage Kara to contact her doctor to have her medications reevaluated. But if Kara refused, he was to calmly discuss with her his worries about her, hold her, tell her he loved her, and communicate his concerns. Kara, for her part, agreed that if she were noncooperative, he would have to call the physician himself. They agreed to keep emergency phone numbers in easily locatable places. Jim also agreed to spend more time at home with Kara if she showed the early warning signs of mania. They discussed different options for her emergent depression (e.g., having her schedule pleasurable or activating events, Jim's encouraging her to be out of bed by a certain time, Jim's agreeing to keep evaluative comments to a minimum).

At the end of the drill, the clinician reviews with the partners their agreements about how to deal with emergencies. The clinician gives suggestions along the way ("When you're feeling that way, that's a good time to stay away from alcohol," "Maybe your spending habits are a prodromal sign of mania"). However, the therapist generally encourages the couple to take the lead in developing the relapse prevention plan.

Psychoeducation: Dealing with Resistances

The psychoeducational sessions, although enlightening, sometimes engender resistances and resentments among patients and their partners. Feeling that they are being labeled as "mentally ill," or that their behavior is being too conveniently summarized under a heading like "bipolar disorder," can bring about uncooperativeness among patients. Alternatively, partners can feel that patients are being too easily "let off the hook" for their irritability, low functioning, or other negative behaviors.

The clinician must keep in mind the questions that patients and spouses are asking themselves when learning about the disorder. Patients have concerns such as "Am I only 'bipolar' now? Do my prior accomplishments mean nothing? How much mood variability am I 'allowed' before my partner thinks I'm getting manic/depressed again? Are my hopes and aspirations gone?" Partners ask themselves questions such as "Will he/she ever get better/live and work productively? Will I always be taking care of him or her? Should I leave? Did I marry the wrong person?"

When patients and their partners begin asking themselves these questions, they often cope by either underidentifying or overidentifying with the disorder. Patients who underidentify believe that the disorder is unreal and will not come back, that it is a misinterpretation of their behavior, or that "I can control it by myself." These patients are often paired with partners who overidentify, or classify all or most of the patients' behaviors as part of the bipolar disorder (including features that are probably best attributed to personality factors, such as shyness or an overbearing style). These partners can become overprotective and overcontrolling. For example, one wife of a bipolar man carefully monitored his medication taking, arranged his doctor appointments, and carefully observed his sleeping patterns. The husband took little responsibility for the disorder, saying, "This is sort of her thing."

We have also seen cases of the reverse, where patients identify too heavily with the bipolar diagnosis and severely limit their goals and responsibilities, presumably in the service of maintaining wellness. The partners in these circumstances often underidentify with the disorder, believing the reverse: The patients are "faking it" or relying too heavily on the diagnosis to avoid doing what they do not want to do anyway.

The pairing of an underidentifying patient with an overidentifying partner, or the reverse, can lead to the kinds of negatively escalating "point–counterpoint" arguments that we have described among high-EE couples earlier. These conflicts can be inadvertently exacerbated by the educational material, which brings to light a couple's disagreements about what is and what is not the disorder.

Among the various options for the clinician is to anticipate these resistances before they occur, and to reframe them as healthy and expectable. For example, the clinician can say,

"As we go through this educational material, you may have a lot of questions about how the bipolar diagnosis applies to you. After a couple has experienced a manic episode, it's completely understandable to be confused and to think that what happened didn't really happen—that it was just a fluke and won't happen again. It's healthy to have these questions and confusions. If these questions come up for you, let's talk about them."

This intervention makes it safe for the couple to express their disagreements about the reality of the diagnosis and their predictions about the future course of the illness.

Second, the clinician "spreads the affliction." A patient often feels that he/she is being labeled as the "sick" person, and that the partner is now off the hook. The clinician can help achieve a balance between members of the couple by asking the "well" partner whether he/she has had any experiences of mood problems, anxiety problems, or other issues. Given the high rate of psychiatric disorders in the biological and nonbiological relatives of bipolar patients (e.g., Kitamura, Takazawa, & Moridaira, 1989), it is probable that at some point the partner has had emotional dysregulation. Encouraging the partner to talk about these problems and how he/she worked with them (e.g., getting psychotherapy, relying on social supports) helps to take the patient off the hot seat.

Third, the clinician makes analogies to medical disorders that do not carry the same stigma as psychiatric illness. He/she recognizes that the bipolar label can unintentionally put the patient in a one-down position. The patient may have an easier time with the diagnostic label if it is described much like a medical disorder, such as diabetes or hypertension:

"People with diabetes also have a biochemical imbalance . . . as a result, they need to learn to manage their disorder over time—become educated about it and its treatment, and gradually come to accept it. Their families also have to come to terms with the fact that their loved one has a chronic illness that requires ongoing care. This can create a lot of tension and conflict in the family. Perhaps what they experience is a little bit like what you're experiencing." (Miklowitz & Goldstein, 1997, pp. 156–157)

Analogies like these help to "normalize" the experience of illness for the patient and partner. The clinician should be quick to acknowledge that bipolar disorder carries a stigma that medical illnesses do not. However, this stigma is blamed on the society at large rather than the person (e.g., "Most people in society don't understand what bipolar disorder is, so they're afraid of it"). Addressing the diagnosis in this manner does much to strengthen the therapeutic alliance with the couple and increase the partner's openness to learning more about the disorder.

Communication Enhancement Training

The transition to communication enhancement training is made easier by the fact that the couple now has a sense of what the disorder is, what the future may hold, and what the partners can each do in the case of emergencies. This opens the door to skill training exercises that are oriented more toward relational functioning than individual psychopathology.

Communication training is usually best done once the patient has achieved a degree of stability, which the psychoeducational sessions (generally Sessions 1–7) can help bring about. The couple, and especially the patient, may be relieved by moving from material that focuses on the disorder to interventions that focus on the dyad. Furthermore, by this time the clinician has gained a good sense of the couple's communication patterns, and has some ideas as to where to intervene. Between 7 and 10 sessions are devoted to communication training.

The couple is first given a rationale for communication enhancement training, with a specific linkage to the overall goal of learning to cope with the patient's bipolar disorder:

"A person can be at risk for another relapse of bipolar disorder if the home environment is tense and there is much conflict. In contrast, good communication and problem solving . . . can be among those 'protective factors' against stress that we talked about before. . . . We want to help you communicate in the most clear and the least stressful way possible, so that everyone's voice is heard and problems get solved." (Miklowitz & Goldstein, 1997, p. 191).

The clinician then proceeds in a systematic way to teach four communication skills: delivering positive feedback (i.e., compliments); active listening (paraphrasing, nodding, asking clarifying questions); requesting changes in others' behaviors (diplomatically asking the partner to do something differently); and delivering negative feedback (constructive criticisms paired with encouragement to problem-solve). This is best done in a role-playing/behavior rehearsal format, in which the clinician models a specific skill and then encourages the partners to rehearse it with each other, with coaching. The clinician then assigns homework, usually involving setting a time for a weekly couple "appointment" to practice the skills and record the efforts on a homework assignment sheet.

Couples coping with bipolar disorder can be somewhat resistant to this behavioral approach because of the value they place on spontaneity. They prefer unpredictable, affectively charged interchanges to the polite, mannered interchanges that communication training requires. This is in many ways the "yin and yang" of bipolar disorder: Patients (and often their partners) are attracted to chaos, spontaneity, and stimulation, and do not like to be bridled. Yet introducing structure into their lives is central to achieving mood stability. So, just as they must sleep and wake regularly (Frank et al., 1999), having structure imposed on their communication patterns helps contribute to their relational health.

The clinician must strike a balance between allowing the partners to vent and indulge their attraction to chaos on the one hand, and encouraging structure on the other. For example, a bipolar patient will often begin a speaking or listening exercise by talking loudly and rapidly. The clinician allows this for a time, but when the patient begins to become verbally aggressive with the partner, the clinician redirects the discussion by encouraging the patient to wait for his/her partner's response and then paraphrasing it. The clinician or partner may also self-disclose in a way that is nonthreatening to the patient (e.g., "Could you repeat that a little slower? I'm having a tough time keeping up with you today").

Communication training can also be used to restructure the negative point–counterpoint interchanges that characterize high-EE couples. For example, partners are taught to paraphrase each other in the middle of debates, or change the subject, or call for a time out. Often this requires in-session rehearsal with the clinician actively intervening (e.g., "I want you to continue this discussion, but let's just change one element. Every time the other person makes a point, your first job is to summarize it back to him/her. Then go ahead and make your own point. Let's see if that makes things more constructive").

Problem-Solving Training

Once the couple has developed a shared understanding of the disorder and a sense of collaboration through the communication training, they are more in a position to constructively solve problems related to the disorder. Four or five sessions of FFT are devoted to problem-solving training, in which couples are given a template for defining specific problems, generating solutions, evaluating the advantages/disadvantages of each, choosing viable solutions, and developing an implementation plan. Structured problem solving is a relatively well-established method for working with families (Liberman et al., 1981) and couples (Jacobson & Margolin, 1979), but has some unique elements when applied to the couple with a bipolar partner.

First, problem solving is focused on the conflicts associated with the postepisode recovery period. Miklowitz and Goldstein (1997) have summarized these problems as falling into one of four areas: medication usage and compliance; resumption of prior work and social roles; cleanup of "life trashing" (i.e., repairing the social, occupational, or financial fallout from the last illness episode); and relationship/living situation conflicts.

Problems are identified by the couple throughout FFT, and sometimes it makes sense to focus on these problems earlier rather than later in treatment. In other cases, the communication skills training should come first because it enhances the outcome of problem-solving training. Couples are given a handout summarizing the steps of problem solving, and are asked to go through these steps while the clinician acts as a coach. Generally, a clinician encourages a couple to choose a relatively straightforward, easily solvable problem first before moving on to larger, more affectively laden issues. Homework assignments, in which the partners practice going through one or more of the problem-solving steps and record their efforts, are given routinely.

An example from one of our couples will illustrate the problem-solving training.

Helen became overstimulated in situations involving her husband's family. Greg, her husband, was very attached to his family and was annoyed that she seemed unable to handle these gatherings, and often pressured her to go. She would usually go with him but would soon get irritable, experience racing thoughts, and become anxious. She often sought out alcohol to calm her nerves. The next day, she would feel more depressed and withdrawn. Thus planning related to social gatherings became a form of relapse prevention for this couple.

Problem solving focused on how the couple could interact with Greg's family without Helen's becoming overstimulated. They evaluated a number of possibilities, such as his agreeing to go home with her when she became anxious; their agreeing on when they would leave before arriving at the gathering; their driving in separate cars; Helen's full avoidance of alcohol; and Greg's being tolerant of her "disappearing" during the gatherings. They also considered doing something "light and more cheerful" before going (e.g., talking a walk, playing Ping-Pong). They finally settled on an agreement that combined several of these elements.

Helen reported feeling less anxiety because she knew that there was a plan in place for the next family gathering. As problem solving progressed, however, it became evident that the couple had trouble putting into place some of these elements (e.g., agreeing on when they would leave the gathering). Sessions of FFT then reverted to communication training, such that each partner clarified what issues were at stake in this problem (for Greg, that Helen would never become integrated into his family and friendships; for Helen, that there was pressure on her to perform and that she could not live up to Greg's expectations). Examining these underlying issues helped to unlock their mutual resistances to solving the problem, and eventually a workable plan was put into place.

Termination

The final three sessions of FFT are held monthly. Usually these sessions are devoted to additional problem solving and terminating the therapy. Termination involves examining the six objectives of FFT (see above) and determining which need additional coverage. Does the patient now understand the need for a continued medication regimen? Have the partners tried their relapse prevention plan? If so, has it worked, or does it need to be reformulated? Do the partners have a better understanding of the role of stress in eliciting the illness episodes? Has the stability of the marriage or partnership improved? Do the partners wish to have more traditional couple-oriented treatment? For some couples, the communication and problem-solving training does nothing more than help them realize that they need to continue working on their communication.

The clinician may decide to refer either partner to individual therapy. We also routinely refer couples and families to the National Alliance for the Mentally Ill (800-950-6264 or www.nami.org) or the National Depressive and Manic–Depressive Association (800-826-3632 or www.ndmda.org).

These organizations provide mutual support groups for relatives and patients coping with chronic psychiatric disorders. Lastly, the clinician makes sure that the patient intends to continue his/her drug treatment sessions. If he/she is toying with discontinuing medications in concert with terminating couple treatment, the clinician can invite the physician to attend the final sessions to discuss the patient's intentions. The patient and partner are given the consistent message that remaining adherent to the medication regimen is central to maintaining the stability they have achieved by this point.

MECHANISMS OF CHANGE IN COUPLE THERAPY

The primary assumption of the FFT model is that couples benefit from an increased knowledge and acceptance of the syndrome of bipolar disorder. Once they learn specific skills for coping with the disorder (e.g., recognizing the emergent signs of relapse and knowing when to implement relapse prevention plans) and for communicating and problem solving, the environment becomes lower-key and more facilitative of sustained remission of the disorder. However, the biological or psychosocial mechanisms by which better coping or stress management leads to improved outcomes of the disorder are unknown. Nonetheless, at least one empirical study of FFT has clarified some of its mechanisms of action.

A Randomized, Controlled Study of FFT

Do couples and families learn the skills that are taught in FFT? The Colorado Treatment/Outcome Project (CTOP; Miklowitz et al., 2000), a randomized trial, examined 101 patients assigned (via a 1:2 formula) to 21 sessions of FFT ($n = 31$) with standard medications, or to a comparison intervention known as "crisis management," also with medication maintenance ($n = 70$). All treatments were done in couples' or families' homes, as Falloon et al. (1984) had done with schizophrenic patients. Patients in crisis management received two sessions of family education (also done in their homes) plus crisis intervention sessions as needed for 9 months. At a minimum, patients in crisis management were telephoned every month by a case manager who offered support and assistance. Patients began the study in an acute, usually hospitalized bipolar I manic, mixed, or depressed episode. Outcome assessments focusing on symptoms and medication adherence were done every 3 months over a 2-year period (9 months of active treatment plus 15 months of follow-up).

At 1 year, patients in FFT plus medication had lower rates of relapse (29%) than patients in crisis management plus medication (53%). Patients in FFT remained well without relapsing for longer intervals during Year 1 than those in crisis management. Patients in FFT also had less severe depressive symptoms during the first study year (Miklowitz et al., 2000). Interestingly, FFT had little effect on manic symptoms or relapses. Data from the second year of the study are now being analyzed.

A close examination of 44 patients and their relatives who completed pretreatment and posttreatment laboratory interactional assessments clarified some of the mechanisms by which FFT achieved its clinical effects (Simoneau, Miklowitz, Richards, Saleem, & George, 1999). Levels of EE changed in both treatment groups: on average, relatives became less critical and hostile over the 1-year interval. However, patients and relatives in FFT showed increases from pretreatment to posttreatment in the frequency of *positive* interactional behaviors, as revealed in the interactional assessment sessions. They showed increases in verbal problem-solving statements, acceptance statements, and self-disclosures, as well as positive nonverbal behaviors. Patients and relatives in crisis management did not show the same level of improvement in positive communication. Improvements were seen both in spousal couples and in family units containing parents and patients. Paralleling the EE results, patients and relatives in FFT did not show greater changes in *negative* interactional behaviors (e.g., frequency of criticisms, negative looks, statements of disagreement, negative solutions to problems). Interestingly, improvements in the patients' interactional behaviors from before to after treatment were more closely associated with patients' symptomatic improvements over the first study year than were improvements in the relatives' interactional behaviors.

Could the clinical improvements of patients in FFT be attributed to improvements in the patients' adherence to medications? Patients in FFT and crisis management did not differ in *average* levels of drug adherence (rated on a scale from 1 [full adherence] to 3 [complete nonadherence] over the first year of treatment and follow-up. However, examining the *pattern* of drug adherence ratings

across time revealed a more complex relationship. Patients in FFT were more likely (55%) to be fully adherent during each 3-month follow-up interval of Year 1 than patients in crisis management (36%). Patients in crisis management were more likely to have one or more intervals in which they were partially or completely nonadherent. These results are preliminary and await replication.

The CTOP study could be criticized on the grounds that the FFT and crisis management comparison groups were not matched on the number of therapy sessions. Also, as noted above, treatments were done in the couples' or families' homes; although this perhaps increased treatment adherence, it raises the question of whether similar effects would be observed in a clinic setting. Several of these limitations were addressed in a randomized trial of FFT conducted in an outpatient clinic at the University of California–Los Angeles (Goldstein et al., 1996; Rea et al., in press). This study compared 21 sessions of FFT (with maintenance medication) to comparably paced individual case management with medication. The majority of these patients lived with their parents rather than with spouses or partners. Results again indicated that clinical outcomes—in terms of rates and timing of relapses and rehospitalizations—were better among FFT-treated patients than among those in case management. The group differences were not observed until the second year of follow-up (the year after the treatment protocols had been terminated), suggesting some delayed effect of FFT on the course of the disorder (Rea et al., in press). No pre–post examinations of family interactional behavior have been reported as yet.

Therapist Factors

No studies exist of clinician factors that predict response to FFT, but we have some impressions. As in any couple therapy, clinicians who develop a strong therapeutic alliance with their clients and nurture the alliance as they proceed are likely to see greater benefits. Furthermore, clinicians who stay agenda-focused, but who allow enough flexibility to address issues that do not fall within the FFT agenda (e.g., the problems of a nonbipolar partner in his/her job), also produce greater benefits. We have observed repeatedly that clinicians who begin with an agenda (e.g., communication training), but then quickly abandon it for a more "exploratory" approach, generally frustrate their clients. In this sense, FFT is probably no different from other structured, behaviorally or cognitively oriented couple approaches.

Commitment to a medical-model approach to bipolar disorder appears to be critical to the success of the intervention. Clinicians who imply that bipolar disorder has a primarily psychogenic basis and is rooted in childhood experiences, or who deemphasize the role of pharmacotherapy in recovery, often have trouble implementing the FFT modules. Couples being treated by clinicians who give this message become confused as to why communication training is essential, or why problem solving would help. This is not to say that exploring childhood experiences is irrelevant to the treatment of bipolar disorder. Rather, it is not given emphasis in this model of couple and family functioning.

TREATMENT APPLICABILITY

Are there specific kinds of couples for which FFT is intended? We examined within the CTOP study a number of predictors of response to FFT. The sample size of that study ($n = 101$) limited our power to identify predictors. Given this caveat, we found no evidence that the efficacy of FFT varied as a function of the patient's sex or of whether the family unit was a couple or a parental family. We also did not find that the efficacy of the treatment differed according to the chronicity of the patient's illness, the severity of the episode prior to treatment, or the patient's beginning treatment as an inpatient or outpatient. SES did not appear to predict whether patients benefited from FFT. However, lower-SES patients were less likely to adhere to and stay in the 2-year protocol than middle- to upper-SES patients, regardless of the treatment condition. This occurred even though both of the treatments involved aggressive outreach and were offered in the home. Clearly, future studies will need to do more to address the needs of lower-SES families coping with bipolar disorder.

The best predictor of response was a family's or couple's initial EE status. Patients in high-EE family units showed more dramatic improvements in their depression symptoms over the first year of treatment and follow-up than those in low-EE units. There were not enough patients to determine whether this treatment × EE interaction held true for couples as well as families. Nonetheless, patients in high-EE families, while difficult to treat, may be the most likely to benefit from FFT.

We also have some clinical impressions as to which couples are *not* likely to benefit from FFT. First, patients who refuse to comply with their medication regimens at the outset are unlikely to be stable enough to engage in or contribute productively to the educational or skill training tasks. Clinicians can have unproductive push–pull interactions with such patients about whether they really do have bipolar disorder, which will frustrate the patients, their partners, and certainly the clinicians. In contrast, many patients enter FFT uncertain as to whether they have bipolar disorder, often due to misunderstandings about what the diagnosis means. These patients may benefit a great deal from educational sessions to help them come to terms with the disorder. Generally, the clinician must make clear at the outset that FFT is not a substitute for medication, and that one of its goals is to help both members of a couple accept the need for medication in the disorder's long-term maintenance. We may admit a patient who is not taking medication into treatment, but we make it clear that the FFT will be time-limited (e.g., a few sessions) and proceed with the expressed goal of getting the patient to agree to a time-limited trial of medication.

Patients with active, severe substance abuse or dependence are not good candidates for FFT. First, an accurate diagnosis is a presumption of FFT. If the patient is actively using alcohol or other substances, it is often impossible to tell whether the real diagnosis is bipolar disorder or a substance-induced mood disorder. Educating the couple about bipolar disorder will be unproductive if the diagnosis is wrong. Second, a substance-misusing patient is likely to deny the reality of the disorder and the necessity of drug treatment. Third, mood-stabilizing medications are not as efficacious with patients who have comorbid substance use disorders. Substance abuse is associated with shorter intervals prior to relapse in longitudinal studies of bipolar patients (e.g., Tohen, Waternaux, & Tsuang, 1990).

In contrast, patients who have a prior history of substance abuse or dependence that is now in remission, or those who have milder substance use problems that may occasionally disturb their functioning, can be treated with FFT. For such patients, we emphasize that drug and alcohol abstinence is an important contributor to long-term mood stability. If the patients are unwilling to discontinue using a substance, we encourage them to track their usage and observe its relation to their cyclic mood states. Usually, such patients require ancillary substance use treatment programs in conjunction with FFT.

CASE ILLUSTRATION

Marsha and Bob, aged 50 and 51, were referred for FFT by Marsha's psychiatrist, Dr. Lee. Marsha had carried a diagnosis of bipolar II disorder for 7 years. Despite trying many medications, she experienced unremitting symptoms of hypomania and depression. She had been previously treated with an antidepressant medication alone (without a mood stabilizer) which had exacerbated her hypomanic symptoms, particularly her irritability. In addition, she experienced many side effects from the traditional anticonvulsant medications used to treat bipolar II disorder (Depakote, Tegretol). At the time she and Bob were referred to FFT, she was taking Lithobid (a form of lithium carbonate), Lamictal (lamotrigine, a mood-stabilizing anticonvulsant), and Zyprexa (olanzapine, an atypical antipsychotic). Although this combination of medications was more effective than those she had tried in the past, Marsha still experienced "breakthrough" symptoms of depression, anhedonia (lack of pleasure), and irritability. Bob had been diagnosed with generalized anxiety disorder and was taking Zoloft (sertraline), which he had found helpful.

The partners had been in a relationship for 4 years and had been living together for 18 months. Their self-stated goal was "to learn to manage our own problems but still have a good relationship." Marsha had experienced an episode of depression in the months before they began FFT; this episode had put a great deal of strain on their relationship. They described a "demand–withdrawal" pattern. When Marsha was depressed, she became very withdrawn and uncommunicative. This stance heightened Bob's anxiety and caused him to pursue Marsha, usually verbally (e.g., "Talk to me; tell me what's wrong"). His pursuit made Marsha feel vulnerable, and she withdrew even more. As a result, Bob began working long hours to "manage my anxiety," and Marsha's depression worsened. When Marsha was at her lowest, she began contemplating suicide; and in fact, prior to FFT, she had been hospitalized following a suicidal gesture.

The two therapists (both PhD clinical psychologists) began the treatment by conducting a life chart assessment to gather a chronological history of Marsha's episodes of hypomania and depression, and Bob's intense periods of anxiety. Interestingly, the life chart indicated that Marsha and Bob's past episodes of depression and anxiety were most often precipitated by conflict in romantic relationships. Bob stated that when things were not going well in his relationships, he would become anxious over a fear of abandonment. Although she acknowledged the biological basis of her mood disorder, Marsha also felt that her episodes of depression were precipitated by conflicts over her partners' expectations of her, which she felt unable to fill. As a result she would withdraw, which typically engendered conflict and, eventually, dissolution of the relationship. Her depression would then become fully syndromic, and she would take months to recover.

The therapists used a formal protocol for assessing Marsha's and Bob's communication and problem-solving skills, consisting of individual interviews of each member of the couple followed by two 10-minute problem-solving discussions. For one of the discussions, Marsha and Bob discussed Bob's career, which required him to travel often. They showed some communication strengths: They listened to each other's positions without interrupting and generally stayed on the topic. However, difficulties were also apparent. Perhaps due to her mild hypomanic symptoms, Marsha would communicate information in a hurried, disjointed style, presenting ideas or pieces of information incompletely. Bob would try to follow her, but eventually would respond to one specific item in Marsha's list, which made her feel that he was missing the "big picture."

The couple also had trouble defining problems. Typically, Marsha would present a problem as multifaceted, and Bob would again try to focus on one relatively minor aspect of the problem. Their discussions would lead to back-and-forth volleys of expansion and reduction, which would then lead them to abandon their attempts to solve the problem.

The education section of FFT began approximately 2 weeks after this pretreatment assessment. The therapists began by assessing each person's understanding of his/her own diagnosis. Bob's anxiety disorder diagnosis was rather recent, so neither he nor Marsha knew a great deal about it. Marsha had long been diagnosed with bipolar II disorder, and she had gathered a considerable amount of information from the literature. Bob, however, felt that he understood very little about Marsha's mood disorder.

The therapists guided Marsha and Bob through a discussion of the symptoms accompanying each partner's disorder, and helped them identify which behavior changes were most likely to appear at the beginning of new episodes. During this discussion of symptoms, it became clear that Marsha and Bob were very sensitive to each other's psychological state, and that one partner's symptoms precipitated symptoms in the other. For example, a large portion of Bob's anxiety was fueled by fears of Marsha's becoming deeply depressed again. When Bob became anxious, Marsha said she would become overstimulated, feel irritable, and then get depressed. Marsha's irritability and depression would then heighten Bob's anxiety. It was helpful for Bob to learn about the difference between "situational depression" and "bipolar depression," which had become merged in his mind. He came to realize that every instance in which Marsha's mood dipped did not necessarily signal that she was about to become deeply depressed.

Once the couple identified the subsyndromal symptoms of depression, the partners discussed how to keep these symptoms from worsening. Marsha's requests for Bob included maintaining contact with her without speaking directly (e.g., reading in the same room); refraining from asking a lot of questions; and accepting that Marsha might not be able to do a lot of planning (e.g., for social events or vacations) when in her depressed state. Bob identified some activities he could do on his own when Marsha was depressed (e.g., painting, working on his car, taking the dogs out, socializing with friends).

The psychoeducation progressed with weekly meetings for approximately 2 months. The therapists discussed with the couple the vulnerability–stress hypothesis, helped both partners identify risk and protective factors, and reviewed the causes of bipolar disorder. Toward the end of the education, Marsha and Bob reviewed the symptoms of her hypomania and apparent triggers for episodes of activation. Although the clinicians did not describe hypomania as dangerous to Marsha, they did point out that "hypomania often leaves a depression in its wake." They discussed with the couple the importance of regular sleep–wake monitoring as a way of preventing the prodromal symptoms of hypomania from spiraling further. Bob agreed to alert Marsha if he felt that her hypomanic or depressive symptoms were starting to emerge.

The therapists began communication training (Session 8) by modeling how to express positive feelings. It appeared that this skill would be very easy for the couple, given that the partners had already shared many positive emotions in previous sessions. However, Marsha was very resistant to the role-play exercises. She explained that she had been depressed

for so long that she was "not aware of having many positive feelings." She often thought very nice things about Bob, but did not know whether she could express these thoughts to him directly.

At this point the therapists returned to education and explained the effects of depression on emotions. They explained that Marsha's positive feelings toward Bob might be blunted or difficult to identify during depressions, but that they still existed. This observation helped alleviate Marsha's guilt related to her belief that she was not capable of giving as much as Bob deserved. Bob understood this explanation, but was still impatient that she was not willing to compliment him; he felt that her illness was "getting her off the hook." The therapists acknowledged this possibility, and assigned homework for each partner to find something the other person did each day that was pleasing to him/her, and to practice praising the partner outside of the session (Jacobson & Margolin, 1979; Falloon et al., 1984).

At the next session, Marsha and Bob appeared to be more relaxed with each other and emotionally connected. They reported that the "Catch a Person Pleasing You" assignment had made them feel closer. They were able to rehearse other communication skills, such as active listening and making positive requests for changes, over the next several sessions with minimal difficulty. The therapists continued to assign homework in which the partners practiced the skills between sessions, emphasizing the importance of integrating these techniques into their day-to-day life.

The treatment was titrated to biweekly sessions after 4 months. At about 6 months into the treatment, Marsha began having new symptoms of hypomania, with agitation, sleep loss, racing thoughts, and irritability. She attributed the symptoms to the change in the season, although it was not clear that her bipolar disorder was truly seasonal. She became discouraged with FFT because she felt that Bob had gone into an anxiety-driven style of responding, instead of remembering the communication strategies that they had been taught. One of the family clinicians contacted Dr. Lee, the physician, to see whether a change in medications was warranted. The physician opted to monitor Marsha more closely, but kept the regimen unchanged.

The therapists used this symptom crisis as a segue into teaching the couple problem-solving skills. They pointed out that the partners had not had problems in learning the communication skills, but were having difficulty in employing them in their day-to-day lives. Bob explained that when he was anxious, he was unable to remember to use the skills and fell back into old patterns of responding. The therapists normalized this trouble through educating the couple about how anxiety can interfere with memory and attention, both of which are essential to the use of effective communication skills.

Marsha and Bob generated a list of viable solutions to their self-identified problem of difficulty in using the communication skills when either partner was symptomatic. They evaluated the advantages and disadvantages of a number of solutions, and chose two solutions to employ. First, Marsha agreed to cue Bob with the word "anxiety" when she perceived that he was becoming anxious and forgetting to use the skills. Second, each of them wrote up a plan for using the skills when under stress. They posted the plans on the refrigerator. Specifically, if Marsha was not depressed, the couple agreed to use the skills as learned during FFT sessions. If Marsha was depressed, she agreed to tell Bob that she felt unable to listen actively or be direct in her requests, but that she still wanted to remain connected with him. He, in turn, was to try to rely more on his outside social supports when she cycled into depression. They returned the following week feeling more satisfied, although there were still signs of tension. Bob reported feeling more in control of his anxiety, and Marsha reported feeling less irritable but still somewhat depressed.

In the final months of treatment, the couple came in monthly and worked on solving specific problems. The therapists were directive during the problem-solving sessions, but gradually became less so as the couple began to use the skills spontaneously. FFT was terminated after Session 19, approximately 10 months after it had begun. Marsha's condition was stable and she did not want further therapy, although she agreed to continue taking her medications and attending maintenance pharmacotherapy sessions with Dr. Lee. Bob continued his Zoloft and was given a referral for individual therapy.

ACKNOWLEDGMENTS

Preparation of this chapter was supported by Grants No. MH 43931, No. MH 62555, and MH55101 from the National Institute of Mental Health, a Distinguished Investigator Award (2001 Callaghan Investigator) from the National Alliance for Research on Schizophrenia and Depression, and by a Grant-in-Aid From the University of Colorado's Council on Research and Creative Work.

REFERENCES

Ablon, S. L., Davenport, Y. B., Gershon, E. S., & Adland, M. L. (1975). The married manic. *American Journal of Orthopsychiatry, 45,* 854–866.

Akiskal, H. S. (1996). The prevalent clinical spectrum of bipolar disorders: Beyond DSM-IV. *Journal of Clinical Psychopharmacology, 16*(Suppl. 1), 4–14.

American Psychiatric Association. (1994). *Diagnostic and statistical manual of mental disorders* (4th ed.). Washington, DC: Author.

Anderson, C. M., Reiss, D. J., & Hogarty, G. E. (1986). *Schizophrenia and the family.* New York: Guilford Press.

Bateson, G., Jackson, D. D., Haley, J., & Weakland, J. (1956). Toward a theory of schizophrenia. *Behavioral Science, 1,* 251–264.

Brodie, H. K. H., & Leff, M. J. (1971). Bipolar depression: A comparative study of patient characteristics. *American Journal of Psychiatry, 127,* 1086–1090.

Butzlaff, R. L., & Hooley, J. M. (1998). Expressed emotion and psychiatric relapse: A meta-analysis. *Archives of General Psychiatry, 55,* 547–552.

Calabrese, J. R., Fatemi, S. H., Kujawa, M., & Woyshville, M. J. (1996). Predictors of response to mood stabilizers. *Journal of Clinical Psychopharmacology, 16*(Suppl. 1), 24–31.

Carlson, G. A., Kotin, J., Davenport, Y. B., & Adland, M. (1974). Follow-up of 53 bipolar manic-depressive patients. *British Journal of Psychiatry, 124,* 134–139.

Coryell, W., Scheftner, W., Keller, M., Endicott, J., Maser, J., & Klerman, G. L. (1993). The enduring psychosocial consequences of mania and depression. *American Journal of Psychiatry, 150,* 720–727.

Doane, J. A., West, K. L., Goldstein, M. J., Rodnick, E. H., & Jones, J. E. (1981). Parental communication deviance and affective style: Predictors of subsequent schizophrenia spectrum disorders in vulnerable adolescents. *Archives of General Psychiatry, 38,* 679–685.

Falloon, I. R. H., Boyd, J. L., & McGill, C. W. (1984). *Family care of schizophrenia: A problem-solving approach to the treatment of mental illness.* New York: Guilford Press.

Falloon, I. R. H., Boyd, J. L., McGill, C. W., Williamson, M., Razani, J., Moss, H. B., Gilderman, A. M., & Simpson, G. M. (1985). Family management in the prevention of morbidity of schizophrenia. *Archives of General Psychiatry, 42,* 887–896.

First, M. B., Spitzer, R. L., Gibbon, M., & Williams, J. B. W. (1995). *Structured Clinical Interview for DSM-IV Axis I disorders.* New York: Biometrics Research Department, New York State Psychiatric Institute.

Frank, E., Swartz, H. A., Mallinger, A. G., Thase, M. E., Weaver, E. V., & Kupfer, D. J. (1999). Adjunctive psychotherapy for bipolar disorder: Effects of changing treatment modality. *Journal of Abnormal Psychology, 108,* 579–587.

Frank, E., Targum, S. D., Gershon, E. S., Anderson, C., Stewart, B. D., Davenport, Y., Ketchum, K. L., & Kupfer, D. J. (1981). A comparison of nonpatient and bipolar patient–well spouse couples. *American Journal of Psychiatry, 138,* 764–767.

Goldstein, M. J., & Miklowitz, D. J. (1995). The effectiveness of psychoeducational family therapy in the treatment of schizophrenic disorders. *Journal of Marital and Family Therapy, 21,* 361–376.

Goldstein, M. J., Rea, M. M., & Miklowitz, D. J. (1996). Family factors related to the course and outcome of bipolar disorder. In C. Mundt, M. J. Goldstein, K. Hahlweg, & P. Fiedler (Eds.), *Interpersonal factors in the origin and course of affective disorders* (pp. 193–203). London: Gaskell.

Goldstein, M. J., Rodnick, E. H., Evans, J. R., May, P. R. A., & Steinberg, M. R. (1978). Drug and family therapy in the aftercare of acute schizophrenics. *Archives of General Psychiatry, 35,* 1169–1177.

Hahlweg, K., Goldstein, M. J., Nuechterlein, K. H., Magana, A. B., Mintz, J., Doane, J. A., Miklowitz, D. J., & Snyder, K. S. (1989). Expressed emotion and patient–relative interaction in families of recent-onset schizophrenics. *Journal of Consulting and Clinical Psychology, 57,* 11–18.

Hirschfeld, R. M. A., & Klerman, G. L. (1979). Personality attributes and affective disorders. *American Journal of Psychiatry, 136,* 67–70.

Hogarty, G. E., Anderson, C. M., & Reiss, D. J. (1986). Family psychoeducation, social skills training and maintenance chemotherapy in the aftercare treatment of schizophrenia: I. One-year effects of a controlled study on relapse and expressed emotion. *Archives of General Psychiatry, 43,* 633–642.

Hogarty, G. E., Anderson, C. M., Reiss, D. J., Kornblith, S. J., Greenwald, D. P., Ulrich, R. F., & Carter, M. (1991). Family psychoeducation, social skills training, and maintenance chemotherapy in the aftercare of schizophrenia. *Archives of General Psychiatry, 48,* 340–347.

Honig, A., Hofman, A., Rozendaal, N., & Dingemanns, P. (1997). Psychoeducation in bipolar disorder: Effect on expressed emotion. *Psychiatry Research, 72,* 17–22.

Hooley, J. M. (1986). Expressed emotion and depression: Interactions between patients and high- versus low-expressed-emotion spouses. *Journal of Abnormal Psychology, 95,* 237–246.

Hooley, J. M. (1987). The nature and origins of expressed emotion. In K. Hahlweg & M. J. Golstein (Eds.), *Understanding major mental disorder: The contribution of family interaction research* (pp. 176–194). New York: Family Process Press.

Hooley, J. M., Orley, J., & Teasdale, J. D. (1986). Levels of expressed emotion and relapse in depressed patients. *British Journal of Psychiatry, 148,* 642–647.

Jacobson, N., & Margolin, G. (1979). *Marital therapy.* New York: Brunner/Mazel.

Janowsky, D. S., Leff, M., & Epstein, R. S. (1970). Playing the manic game. *Archives of General Psychiatry, 22,* 252–261.

Johnson, S. L., Sandrow, D., Meyer, B., Winters, R., Miller, I., Solomon, D., & Keitner, G. (2000). Increases in manic symptoms after life events involving goal-attainment. *Journal of Abnormal Psychology, 109,* 721–727.

Kitamura, T., Takazawa, N., & Moridaira, J. (1989). Family history of major psychiatric disorders and syndromes. *International Journal of Social Psychiatry, 35,* 333–342.

Leff, J., Kuipers, L., Berkowitz, R., Eberlein-Vries, R., & Sturgeon, D. (1982). A controlled trial of social intervention in the families of schizophrenic patients. *British Journal of Psychiatry, 141,* 121–134.

Leverich, G. S., & Post, R. M. (1998). Life charting of affective disorders. *CNS Spectrums, 3,* 21–37.

Liberman, R. P., Wallace, C. J., Falloon, I. R. H., & Vaughn, C. E. (1981). Interpersonal problem-solving therapy for schizophrenics and their families. *Comprehensive Psychiatry, 22,* 627–629.

Malkoff-Schwartz, S., Frank, E., Anderson, B., Sherrill, J. T., Siegel, L., Patterson, D., & Kupfer, D. J. (1998). Stressful life events and social rhythm disruption in the onset of manic and depressive bipolar episodes: A preliminary investigation. *Archives of General Psychiatry, 55,* 702–707.

Miklowitz, D. J., & Goldstein, M. J. (1997). *Bipolar disorder: A family-focused treatment approach.* New York: Guilford Press.

Miklowitz, D. J., Goldstein, M. J., Doane, J. A., Nuechterlein, K. H., Strachan, A. M., Snyder, K. S., & Magana, A. (1989). Is expressed emotion an index of a transactional process?: I. Parents' affective style. *Family Process, 28,* 153–167.

Miklowitz, D. J., Goldstein, M. J., Falloon, I. R. H., & Doane, J. A. (1984). Interactional correlates of expressed emotion in the families of schizophrenics. *British Journal of Psychiatry, 144,* 482–487.

Miklowitz, D. J., Goldstein, M. J., & Nuechterlein, K. H. (1995). Verbal interactions in the families of schizophrenic and bipolar affective patients. *Journal of Abnormal Psychology, 104,* 268–276.

Miklowitz, D. J., Goldstein, M. J., Nuechterlein, K. H., Snyder, K. S., & Mintz, J. (1988). Family factors and the course of bipolar affective disorder. *Archives of General Psychiatry, 45,* 225–231.

Miklowitz, D. J., Simoneau, T. L., George, E. A., Richards, J. A., Kalbag, A., Sachs-Ericsson, N., & Suddath, R. (2000). Family-focused treatment of bipolar disorder: One-year effects of a psychoeducational program in conjunction with pharmacotherapy. *Biological Psychiatry, 48,* 582–592.

Miklowitz, D. J., Simoneau, T. L., Sachs-Ericsson, N., Warner, R., & Suddath, R. (1996). Family risk indicators in the course of bipolar affective disorder. In C. Mundt, M. J. Goldstein, K. Hahlweg, & P. Fiedler (Eds.), *Interpersonal factors in the origin and course of affective disorders* (pp. 204–217). London: Gaskell.

O'Connell, R. A., Mayo, J. A., Flatow, L., Cuthbertson, B., & O'Brien, B. E. (1991). Outcome of bipolar disorder on long-term treatment with lithium. *British Journal of Psychiatry, 159,* 132–129.

Penn, D. L., & Mueser, K. T. (1996). Research update on the psychosocial treatment of schizophrenia. *American Journal of Psychiatry, 153,* 607–617.

Priebe, S., Wildgrube, C., & Muller-Oerlinghausen, B. (1989). Lithium prophylaxis and expressed emotion. *British Journal of Psychiatry, 154,* 396–399.

Rea, M. M., Tompson, M., Miklowitz, D. J., & Goldstein, M. J., Hwang, S., & Mintz, J. (in press). Family focused treatment vs. individual treatment for bipolar disorder: Results of a randomized clinical trial. *Journal of Consulting and Clinical Psychology.*

Robinson, E. A., & Jacobson, N. S. (1987). Social learning theory and family psychopathology: A Kantian model in behaviorism? In T. Jacob (Ed.), *Family interaction and psychopathology: Theories, methods, and findings* (pp. 117–162). New York: Plenum Press.

Ruestow, P., Dunner, D. L., Bleecker, B., & Fieve, R. R. (1978). Marital adjustment in primary affective disorder. *Comprehensive Psychiatry, 19,* 565–571.

Simoneau, T. L., Miklowitz, D. J., Richards, J. A., Saleem,

R., & George, E. L. (1999). Bipolar disorder and family communication: Effects of a psychoeducational treatment program. *Journal of Abnormal Psychology, 108,* 588–597.

Simoneau, T. L., Miklowitz, D. J., & Saleem, R. (1998). Expressed emotion and interactional patterns in the families of bipolar patients. *Journal of Abnormal Psychology, 107,* 497–507.

Strachan, A. M., Feingold, D., Goldstein, M. J., Miklowitz, D. J., & Nuechterlein, K. H. (1989). Is expressed emotion an index of a transactional process?: II. Patient's coping style. *Family Process, 28,* 169–181.

Targum, S. D., Dibble, E. D., Davenport, Y. B., & Gershon, E. S. (1981). The Family Attitudes Questionnaire: Patients and spouses' views of bipolar illness. *Archives of General Psychiatry, 38,* 562–568.

Tarrier, N., Barrowclough, C., Vaughn, C., Bamrah, J. S., Porceddu, K., Watts, S., & Freeman, H. (1988). The community management of schizophrenia: A controlled trial of a behavioral intervention with families to reduce relapse. *British Journal of Psychiatry, 153,* 532–542.

Tohen, M., Waternaux, C. M., & Tsuang, M. T. (1990). Outcome in mania: A 4-year prospective follow-up of 75 patients utilizing survival analysis. *Archives of General Psychiatry, 47,* 1106–1111.

Vaughn, C. E., & Leff, J. P. (1976). The influence of family and social factors on the course of psychiatric illness: A comparison of schizophrenia and depressed neurotic patients. *British Journal of Psychiatry, 129,* 125–137.

Wendel, J. S., Miklowitz, D. J., Richards, J. A., & George, E. L. (2000). Expressed emotion and attributions in the relatives of bipolar patients: An analysis of problem-solving interactions. *Journal of Abnormal Psychology, 109,* 792–796.

Chapter 27

Couple Therapy and Medical Issues: Working with Couples Facing Illness

NANCY B. RUDDY
SUSAN H. McDANIEL

BACKGROUND OF THE MODEL/APPROACH

Medicine, like psychotherapy, has always been a hybrid of science and art. A health care professional can choose to attend to only some aspects of a patient's illness experience—perhaps an organ system, or interrelated symptoms. Since 1950, the medical community has increasingly attended to many levels of the patient's illness experience, and sought an understanding of the interplay of these levels in health and disease. Much of medicine (especially in primary care) has moved from a biomedical model, which emphasizes primarily biological processes, toward a "biopsychosocial model" (Engel, 1977) (see Figure 27.1). The biopsychosocial model emphasizes the interelatedness of biological, psychological, interelational, and community factors in health and disease. It applies systems theory to human functioning by recognizing how all of these levels simultaneously affect one another, and how health care intervention affects many levels of human experience.

The advent of the biopsychosocial model has facilitated the growth of two major movements that focus on helping couples cope with medical problems. Many in the family medicine movement have made the family, rather than the individual or an organ system, the unit of care (Bloch, 1983; Doherty & Baird, 1983; McDaniel, Campbell, & Seaburn, 1990). These family medicine practitioners acknowledge the reciprocal effects of family relationships and of health and disease. Although some physicians from all specialties recognize the importance of these relationships, family medicine clinicians were the first to integrate family systems thinking into day-to-day health care. This means including consideration of fathers in prenatal care, spouses/partners or adult children in geriatric care, parents in adolescent care, and so forth. When the family is the center of health care, communication and other issues that are typically the purview of family therapists become the purview of physicians as well. Family medicine's need for collaboration with specialists, and its emphasis on the family, gives family therapists a special inroad to treating families in a medical setting. This inroad provides family therapists with a "front-line" view of how couples cope with illness, and how psychotherapy can help couples face the challenges of illness (Rolland, 1994).

The second major movement has been the growth of interdisciplinary clinics that specialize in treating specific diseases (Blount, 1998; Seaburn, Lorenz, Gawinski, & Gunn, 1996). Providers in specialty clinics for such chronic illnesses as cystic fibrosis, cancer, and diabetes have noted the importance of family factors in achieving the best possible outcomes, and have noted the stresses

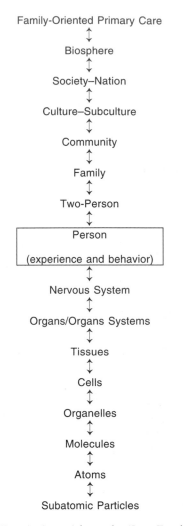

Family-Oriented Primary Care

Biosphere

Society–Nation

Culture–Subculture

Community

Family

Two-Person

Person

(experience and behavior)

Nervous System

Organs/Organs Systems

Tissues

Cells

Organelles

Molecules

Atoms

Subatomic Particles

FIGURE 27.1. Systems hierarchy. From Engel (1980). Copyright 1980 by the American Psychiatric Association. Reprinted by permission.

such illnesses placed on family members. They often harness the power of the family in treating illnesses, particularly when treatment involves lifestyle changes. They create space for dialogue about illness in the family, and learn from the families themselves about the impact of chronic illnesses and the best ways to help patients and families cope (McDaniel & Hepworth, in press; McDaniel & Campbell, 2000). In addition, such specialty clinics have been a natural spawning grounds for support groups focusing on specific illnesses. Although the evolution of these groups has not been documented, it seems likely that serendipitous waiting room chats and providers' noting themes across

families may have been precursors to the many groups and associations available to families today. Finally, behavioral medicine has grown out of clinics that specialize in pain management and treatment, broadening the role of mental health professionals. Noting the impact of behavioral interventions on physical symptoms has lent further credence to the idea that mind and body are not only connected, but also both necessary elements to healing (Belar & Deardorff, 1995).

Family medicine practices and specialty clinics have created rich environments for the development of family therapy theory and techniques specifically designed for families and couples facing illness. In 1990, Susan McDaniel, Thomas Campbell, and David Seaburn published a book for physicians in training, *Family Oriented Primary Care*, outlining a family systems approach to medical care. Two years later, McDaniel, Jeri Hepworth, and William Doherty (1992) applied knowledge gleaned from providing mental health services practicing in primary care medical settings to a book for family therapists—*Medical Family Therapy*, which described both how families often react and ultimately cope with illness, and how therapists can help them through this process. In 1994, John Rolland published *Families, Illness and Disability*, describing common patterns of family coping with different types of illnesses and situations. These last two books have become helpful guideposts for psychotherapists working with families facing illness.

HEALTHY/WELL-FUNCTIONING VERSUS PATHOLOGICAL/ DYSFUNCTIONAL RELATIONSHIPS

The Challenges of Chronic Illnesses

Although the poor and minorities are more likely to suffer from chronic illnesses (Lantz et al., 1998; Marmot et al., 1991; Sorlie, Backlund, & Keller, 1995), ill health knows no socioeconomic or racial bounds. Illness strikes both well-functioning and struggling couples. Illness stresses a couple system at all levels. The key to successful management of illness is adaptability.

The ways in which a couple must adapt, and the extent to which these necessary adaptations affect day-to-day life, differ across illnesses. Some illnesses, such as mild diabetes, require lifestyle changes but do not necessarily force the couple to face mortality or manage major role changes. Other illnesses can be more debilitating on a day-to-day basis, requiring major role changes and placing a larger caregiving burden on the healthy partner.

Bill and Mary Ann were referred by Bill's neurologist because of Bill's reluctance to accept help with his muscular dystrophy, and the stress that this was placing on their marriage. Mary Ann was threatening to leave her husband of 30 years; she was clearly very frustrated at his refusal to use a wheelchair or other appliances that would assist his movement. Because of his refusal, Mary Ann more often had to lift or guide him, and even pick him up because of frequent falls. Bill also refused to stop driving, and had hit and hurt a woman in a parking lot recently. Mary Ann, for her part, had serious diabetes. Bill had had to inject her with insulin on two occasions in the past year to bring her out of a diabetic coma. She seemed to be doing better since being put on a pump. The spouses had to delay their appointment for psychological assessment because of their annual vacation on a Caribbean island without any medical care.

Clearly, Bill and Mary Ann had resisted accepting the extent of their own illnesses, and had not yet adjusted their roles to fit the demands of these chronic illnesses.

The course of an illness also affects how a couple must learn to cope. Some illnesses, such as muscular dystrophy, challenge couples by being unpredictable; any given day could be a "good day" or a "bad day." In other cases, an illness starts as an acute episode that everyone expects to "go away;" only over time does it become clear that the illness is chronic, and that life is forever changed. Still other illnesses, such as Parkinson's disease, take a progressive downward course, and couples must cope with the knowledge that it is likely to get only worse. This inevitability requires pacing and a high tolerance for uncertainty that often taxes even emotionally healthy couples.

Gregory was diagnosed with Parkinson's disease after some of his medical colleagues asked the family whether he had Parkinson's. Gregory and Anna had always been dedicated to each other, through his active career and their raising five children. As Gregory's illness resulted in his slow deterioration, Anna cared for his every need. Their children and his fellow health care professionals suggested in-home care and respite, but Anna would allow it only when Gregory became psychotic and combative at night. When he improved, she would discharge the outside help. "I don't like strangers in my house," she said. Gregory agreed, and didn't like Anna to be out of his sight. As the years went by and Gregory's functioning worsened, Anna became more and more fatigued, and their children began to worry about her health. During one confrontation with their physician,

Anna admitted that for her, accepting outside help meant that Gregory was doing worse and would soon have to go to a nursing home, or even, die. The longer she could do without help, she thought, the longer he would be with her.

Couples' Adaptations' to Illness

Many types of adaptations may be necessary when a partner like Gregory becomes ill. First, roles need to shift. These shifts first may occur simply at the "daily chores" level. However, role changes are usually broader, including shifts in the emotional/interactional roles. If the ill partner has typically managed the emotional life of the couple, this role may need to shift to maintain relational emotional health. For example, role strain will take on a different form when a woman becomes seriously ill during the early years of child rearing if she has been the emotional center of the family than if she has been the major breadwinner of the family. The first scenario may result in behavioral and mental health problems; ideally, her partner will become much more attuned and responsive to the emotional needs of family members and the relationships. The second scenario will result in financial difficulties; ideally, her partner will be able to make an increased contribution to the family finances. Gender-related socialization may play a major role in a couple's ability to adapt. Couples that are not able to adapt easily may benefit from referral for counseling or psychotherapy.

Gene was at a loss when his wife of 10 years, Gretchen, developed breast cancer. She had been the primary parents to their 5- and 7-year-old boys and the link to their social life, while he had worked hard to become a partner in a law firm. The onset of her illness challenged the couple's division of labor and resulted in frequent fighting. Gene felt resentment about added duties, guilt about his resentment, and fear for his wife's health. Gretchen was overwhelmed with fear of dying, and was largely paralyzed by this fear. She sensed that Gene was struggling to manage everything, and felt guilty that she was not able to do more for her family. Gene and Gretchen avoided talking about her illness and its effects on their family. Occasionally, tempers would flare, resulting in terrible arguments. They had never discussed difficult issues until Gretchen's illness, and they were ill equipped to handle this challenge. Gretchen's primary care physician, sensing that she was struggling to cope with her illness, suggested she see a therapist. Her therapist asked directly about the effect of Gretchen's illness on her marriage. Gretchen acknowledged the difficulties and agreed to invite her husband to the next session. Although both were nervous about the appointment, they experienced a great deal of relief when they had a venue to discuss how difficult the illness had been, and to learn new means of coping. Just learning that other couples struggled in similar ways in the face of an illness was very helpful.

Role shift issues may be particularly difficult to resolve because other family members may not communicate about family issues with the ill person, out of fear of stressing him/her and exacerbating the illness. If the ill member has generally initiated conversations about family matters, the dialogue may not start because he/she does not now have the physical or emotional energy to corral the family for dialogue to ensure that issues are resolved.

Second, the couple may need to make major lifestyle changes. Often the medical management of an illness entails dietary changes, smoking cessation, activity level changes, schedule changes for administration of medicines, and/or other changes in daily routine. Clearly, these changes both affect and are affected by family members. It is often helpful to engender the assistance of family members in helping the ill person make lifestyle changes. Sometimes other family members are the ones who need to make changes. The couple's ability to adapt to these changes as a unit, and to discuss the issues these changes create, is one factor in determining overall coping (Doherty, 1988; Harkaway, 1983).

Third, the couple needs to find a way to communicate about all of the stresses the illness places on both partners, and to find support. This sense of "communion" (McDaniel et al., 1992) both mitigates the conflict that is bound to arise at a stressful time, and gives both partners a sense that they are there for each other. In addition, couples often need to reach out to other people who have experienced similar challenges—both to normalize their experiences, and to obtain means of coping that have worked for others.

Fourth, the couple must determine which aspects of the illness experience the partners can control, and which aspects they cannot. Clearly, there are many things the couple cannot change about the situation. This reality can lead to a sense of overall helplessness that can be debilitating, both emotionally and physically. Family members who generate a sense of "agency" by recognizing and managing those aspects of the illness they can control typically cope much better (McDaniel et al., 1992).

Fifth, the couple must find meaning in the illness. It is common for both the individual with the illness and the partner to ask, "Why me?" Like any challenge, illness is an opportunity for reflection and change. This process of reflection and change often provides the answer to this question. Finding meaning in the illness gives the couple a sense of peace and acceptance (Rolland, 1994; McDaniel et al., 1992).

Sixth, the couple must grieve for the many losses the illness causes. The most obvious loss is the anticipated loss of life associated with terminal illness (Rolland, 1994; McDaniel & Cole-Kelly, in press). Partners in many couples avoid discussing death out of a desire to protect themselves and each other from this grim reality. Even a well partner's mortality is threatened by watching a close loved one die. It seems likely that partners who are able to discuss the ultimate loss productively are better prepared to make critical decisions at the end of life, and that the surviving partner in such a couple may cope better after the death of the other partner. In addition, there are many other, less obvious losses. The partners need to grieve for the loss of their preillness life and the patient's loss of functioning. The ill person may lose the ability to work, to drive, to walk, or to live independently. His/her increasing dependence may limit sharply the activities of the partner as well. The couple may lose the ability to be sexually intimate. Partners need to grieve actively for the change in function they experience.

Seventh, the couple's interactions with the health care community affect overall coping. Most people have preconceived ideas about and experiences with medical care providers. These ideas can interfere with the establishment of a good, collaborative relationship between the couple and the health care team. Also, the couple will have variable experiences with different health care professionals, which can affect the quality of the relationship and the couple's expectations. The couple and the healthcare team must learn to work together with a shared mission to return the ill partner's health or maximize his/her quality of life.

Donald was diagnosed with prostate cancer at the age of 73. His family physician, Dr. Marks, had a difficult time telling him that cancer cells were found outside the prostate capsule, as Donald was the same age as Dr. Marks's father. At first Dr. Marks minimized the danger, but when Donald's wife pushed him for more information about prognosis and treatment, he acknowledged there was a significant risk that the cancer could eventually be terminal. Dr. Marks discussed the case with the psychologist on his team, who helped him see how he could use his attachment to Donald to do the best possible job of caring for him through this difficult time. At Christmas of that year, Donald and his wife wrote a card to Dr. Marks saying how much they appreciated his partnership with them in caring for Donald's illness.

Problematic Patterns

The development of maladaptive patterns is another source of difficulties for couples facing illness. Caregivers can become overwhelmed and resentful of their duties. In many families, caregivers experience difficulty obtaining support for themselves—either because they do not ask directly, or because other family members are unable or unwilling to help. Research indicates a high level of depression in caregiving partners (Schultz, O'Brien, Bookwala, & Fleissner, 1995).

The stress of illness can also exacerbate premorbid maladaptive patterns. Communication difficulties, old resentments, patterns of over- or underfunctioning, and other problems can become entrenched or intensified just when adaptability and support are most needed. Partners who have achieved a comfortable balance between closeness and distance suddenly must work closely together under unusually stressful conditions.

Paradoxically, given the need for caregiving, illness breeds isolation. The reduction in activities, the need for caregiving, and other factors often preclude socializing. In addition, friends and family members may withdraw because they do not know how to support the couple, or are overwhelmed by their own emotional reactions to the illness. Again, this emotional distancing occurs just when the couple (and each individual within the couple) most needs support. Even within a couple, the illness can increase emotional distance. Some partners find that an illness is like having "an elephant in the living room" they cannot discuss with each other. It is not uncommon for each member of the couple to avoid talking because he/she believes the other "can't handle" talking about the illness. Protecting oneself in the guise of protecting a loved one is a common dynamic. Also, as mentioned earlier, many illnesses and their treatments interfere with sexual intimacy, creating yet another way a couple cannot feel "normal" and emotionally close.

Each individual within the family will find his/her own way to cope with the illness. Sometimes levels of acceptance and different coping mechanisms clash, resulting in conflict. For example, one family member may withdraw in an attempt to shield self and others from his/her own pain, while others feel abandoned by the distance. Denial is another coping strategy that family members may use differently. Denial can be healthy, helping one to tolerate massive stressors. However, too much denial (i.e., denial that interferes with appropriate treatment) can be problematic. Differing levels of denial can create conflict: Some family members may feel that others are making too much of a small issue, while others feel that very real issues are not being dealt with. This tension is particularly challenging for family members facing an illness with an unclear prognosis or treatment plan.

Karl was diagnosed with a rare bone cancer at the age of 39. His family physician, Dr. Jackson, had a difficult time telling him that his cancer was likely to be fatal. She waited for the oncologist and the surgeon to tell this young patient about the implication of his illness. However, no one made this clear. Karl came to Dr. Jackson and seemed to indicate in a roundabout way that he wanted to know what his tests showed. Dr. Jackson thought about Karl; his wife, Debra; and his 2-year-old twins. She told Karl that it was important for them to talk about his illness, and to schedule an appointment when his wife could come along and they could get a babysitter. In the meantime, Dr. Jackson came to her psychologist collaborator (SHM), told her about the meeting, and asked whether she could join them because of the sensitivity and importance of what needed to be said. Dr. Jackson was concerned that Karl was not ready to hear his terminal diagnosis. She said that she knew little about the family, his wife, and the wife's understanding of Karl's illness. The psychologist encouraged her to start with a brief genogram (so they would know which family members were available, where they lived, and what the family's previous experience with illness was), and then ask the spouses what they knew about the illness.

Within a few days, Karl, Debra, and the two professionals met. The genogram was quite helpful in assessing the family's support network. When Dr. Jackson asked the spouses what they knew about the illness, Karl responded that he knew he was dying, although no one had told him this directly. He said that his wife refused to accept this. When Debra anxiously turned to Dr. Jackson for reassurance, Dr. Jackson told her the difficult news: "Karl is right. He has a cancer that's not curable." Debra began crying and said angrily, "Well, how much time does he have? Six years? Six months?" Dr. Jackson responded by saying, "We don't know for sure, but it's likely to be closer to 6 months." Debra began wailing, then turned to her husband: "But my plan was to grow old with you. You can't leave me now." The session lasted 45 minutes, with the psychologist encouraging the couple to ask questions of Dr. Jackson, to talk to each other, to begin planning how best to use the time they had left, and to think about how to communicate with the twins. In fact, Karl had already begun making a videotape, talking to the twins about his own life and his wishes for theirs. The session ended without a dry eye in the room.

Sometimes what appear to be different levels of denial may really reflect family members' differing levels of acceptance and understanding of the illness. Family members go through an acceptance process much like the stages of acceptance that patients go through in accepting a terminal diagnosis (McDaniel et al., 1992). Each family member progresses through this process at his/her own speed. Differing levels of acceptance can result in mismatched expectations, coping behaviors, and degrees of readiness to make decisions and take action. This discrepancy can create conflict, particularly when family members need to make treatment or end-of-life decisions collectively. The acceptance process can be facilitated or hampered by the characteristics of the illness. An illness that remits and returns may force the family to endure the acceptance process many times over. An illness that does not coincide with the course and prognosis predicted by health care providers also may confound the family.

As noted above, the roles played by members of a couple often need to shift in the context of illness. One common issue in couples facing illness is that the "illness role" becomes rigid and entrenched. The person with the illness begins to identify him-/herself as an "ill person" and to maximize his/her dependence on others. The healthy partner identifies with the caregiver role, and does not encourage greater independence on the part of the ill person. At extremes, this can result in the ill person's continuing to play the sick role even this is when no longer necessary, or the caregiver's actively creating illness (or the illusion of illness) in the formerly ill partner. The ill person may not take advantage of periods of improved health because of the entrenched dependent interactional pattern. Often people who have chronic illness need support and encouragement to "try out their wings" when feeling better. Partners whose illness-related roles are very entrenched cannot adapt to health or take advantage of "good times."

Some role rigidity can be rooted in gender issues (McDaniel & Cole-Kelly, in press). First, illness often pulls for couples to respond to "caregiver" and "ill person" roles in ways consistent with traditional gender roles. This can be problematic in a number of ways. Women's socialization to the caregiver role may make them vulnerable to rigidly assuming that role in the face of illness, and they may struggle to ask for or accept assistance when it is needed. Men's lack of socialization for caregiving may result in feelings of inadequacy or a lack of skills in this area. Second, traditional coping mechanisms of "female" emoting versus "male" action may may not meet the needs of each member of a couple, and can clash with the demands of an illness. If a man copes with his feelings only by taking action in caring for an ill wife, he may have difficulty when his wife wants to talk about her situation. It is not difficult to imagine that both members of this couple may feel frustrated or unsupported. The traditional gender roles mirror the concepts of "agency" and "communion," *both* of which are essential to coping with illness. The challenge is in helping the partners balance their needs for each and adapt this balance to the demands of the illness. Third, when partners have assumed nontraditional gender roles, these roles can be challenged by the health care system. Health care professionals may assume that the woman has been the caregiver and the man the primary wage earner, failing to recognize how a non-gender-stereotyped couple may have different concerns. Finally, how well the ill person adjusts to the illness may be affected by gender as well. Men have been socialized to avoid showing weakness. Although this may make acknowledging and managing the illness more challenging, it may also insulate men from taking on a rigid "sick role." Women may have less difficulty accepting the illness, but more difficulty adjusting to health once the illness is cured or managed more effectively.

The stress of an illness, like any major stressor, has ramifications for the family's development, and vice versa. Late-life illness is more consistent with normal development, and therefore may be somewhat less stressful. Illness that occurs out of the normal individual or family life cycle can have larger ramifications (e.g., the primary wage earner's becoming sick in middle age, the primary child care provider's becoming ill when children are young, etc.) A family may become "stuck" at the lifestyle stage at which the illness started or was most acute. The lack of continued development can result in a myriad of problematic patterns for the couple and family.

ASSESSMENT OF COUPLE FUNCTIONING AND DYSFUNCTION

Overall, therapists should be aware that illness may be a part of the context for any couple's presenting concern. Either patients or therapists can fail to make the connection between a history of illness and current need for treatment. Every couple presenting for couple therapy should be asked whether either partner is now suffering, or has previously suffered, from a significant illness.

Often when patients are referred for assistance in coping with an illness, they will present alone. In such a case, it is the therapist's job to broaden the focus to the couple and family. The first step in accomplishing this is to ask questions that bring others' perspectives and experiences into the dialogue, even if they are not physically present. We list questions that can facilitate this in Table 27.1.

Assessment of the family and relational levels is consistent with the biopsychosocial model. To remain true to this model, therapists must also assess the impact of the biological processes and social and community issues. Often a therapist must work together with other professionals to better understand the biological and social context of an illness. Therefore, collaboration with other health professionals is critical—both in gathering information about the illness, its treatment, and prognosis; and in understanding the patient's relationships with the health care system.

Helping the couple create a time line of the illness is very helpful. A time line should include family history with this or other illnesses, as scripts about illness are often part of a family's "lore." This is particularly true when an illness is common to many family members or has a significant genetic component. Beyond specific illnesses in the family, it is helpful to hear how the family has traditionally dealt with illness and its history with the health care system. Again, these can be sources of expectations, fears, and myths leading to seemingly "noncompliant" behavior, and thus relevant to adapting to the illness. Stretching the time line to include the family's expectations of the future is also useful. If the illness is terminal, it is helpful to assess the couple's (and each individual's) acceptance level. Even if the illness is not anticipated to result in death, it almost certainly has already caused and will cause numerous permanent and temporary losses. Assessing the couple's awareness of and anxiety about these losses, and their ability to tolerate overt conversation about them, is essential.

Maria was referred for psychotherapy with one of us (NBR) to help her cope with her declining health related to chronic obstructive pulmonary disorder. In addition, her physician was frustrated because she con-

TABLE 27.1. Questions to Elicit Patient's and Family Members' Illness Perceptions

For the patient

1. What do you think caused your problem?
2. Why do you think it started when it did?
3. What do you think your sickness does to you? How does it work?
4. How severe is your sickness? Will it have a long or short course?
5. What are the chief problems your sickness has caused for you?
6. What do you fear most about your sickness?
7. What kind of treatment do you think you should receive?
8. What are the most important results you hope to receive from this treatment
9. Should we expect complications?
10. What has been your extended family's experience with illness?
11. Has anyone else in your family faced an illness similar to the one you have now? If so, what was its course?
12. What is your and your family's past history of recuperation?
13. What might make healing now a struggle for you?
14. Do you see yourself as having much to live for?

For family members

15. What changes in family responsibilities do you think will be needed because of the patient's sickness?
16. If the patient needs care or special help, what family members are going to be responsible for providing it?
17. If the illness is already chronic or appears likely to become chronic, what are the patient's and family members' plans for taking care of the problem over the long term?

Note. The first eight questions are taken from Kleinman, Eisenberg, and Good (1978). Questions 9 and 10 are adapted from Seaburn, Lorenz, and Kaplan (1993). Questions 11 through 14 are adapted from Friedman (1991). Questions 15 through 17 are from Shields, Wynne, and Sirkin (1992).

tinued to smoke even as her lung functioning deteriorated. Her family was frustrated with her because they did not believe she was being honest with them about her illness, and did not trust that she was caring for herself in the best manner. In a family meeting with her husband and three of her four children, the therapist, and her physician, Dr. Grange, the children discussed their experience of Maria's surviving ovarian cancer a decade earlier. Maria, her husband, and the extended family had colluded to hide her cancer from the children, and had never told them directly that she was expected to die. The children had thus been confused by mixed messages about their mother's illness. Now, as they faced a new illness experience with their mother, they did not trust that their parents would be honest with them. Multiple family meetings and ongoing psychotherapy with Maria and her husband helped them begin to share more openly with their adult children, and helped the children understand the family's earlier behavior and trust their parents more. The family once again needed to process the likelihood that Maria's illness would ultimately be terminal, although they recognized that her downward course would take years.

The therapist should also investigate the couple's preillness level of functioning. As noted earlier, the stress of an illness can exacerbate preexisting problems; it can also disorganize an otherwise healthy couple relationship. Understanding the partners' lives before the illness provides a context for the current situation, and gives the therapist a sense of how much adaptation the couple has already made. Acknowledging the steps the partners have already taken to cope with the illness can help them recognize how they have taken control over what feels uncontrollable. When the ill person is incapacitated, this discussion can also shed light on his/her personality and functioning prior to the illness. While noting issues that might be exacerbated by the illness, the therapist should also note the strengths the couple brings to their struggle. Often these strengths form the basis of maximizing the couple's quality of life and adaptation.

George and Joanne sought couple therapy after George had a heart attack and could no longer work. George had always been a workaholic. Joanne had coped by developing an active social life that did not include George. Now that George wasn't working, Joanne experienced his presence as an interference. Their "comfortable distance" no longer worked. Couple therapy helped them to realize how their preillness pattern was now maladaptive, and to find a new balance. In addition, George developed more outside interests, and he respected Joanne's need for privacy and distance at times.

Hearing the couple's illness story also allows the therapist to understand the couple's interactions with the health care system. These interactions can be a source of great comfort and caring for the couple, or a source of enormous frustration, pain, and anger. Often the couple has had a mix of experiences with different providers and institutions. It is helpful to hear the illness story from the beginning; many families go through a long, arduous diagnostic process that also may have been a source of stress. If misdiagnosis or delayed diagnosis, occurred, this can set the stage for mistrust

of all health care professionals, including couple therapists.

Examining the couple's life cycle issues is another useful assessment tool (Carter & McGoldrick, 1999). Are illness and debilitation normal aspects of the couple's stage of development, or has the illness struck out of sequence? What challenges does the couple face as part of normal development that might be intensified by the illness? Understanding how the couple has navigated other life cycle challenges can help the therapist maximize the partners' natural coping strengths to manage this challenge as well. For example, the members of one couple had a lengthy discussion about how their division of labor when their children were young might be useful now as they cared for the husband's ailing mother.

Intrinsic in this discussion of assessing a couple is the assumption that the couple benefits from the assessment. Overt conversations about the losses and challenges the couple faces, time lines, life cycle discussions, collaboration with medical professionals, and genograms all help the therapist better understand the family. However, they also help the family members better understand themselves, and put their current situation in a coherent context. The process of telling one's illness narrative and hearing how other family members have experienced the illness are all therapeutic, in and of themselves.

GOAL SETTING

The primary goal for couples facing illness is to adapt to the changes illness has thrust upon their lives. Couples may need assistance in forming smaller goals that will enhance their overall adaptation. Common smaller goals include resolution of preexisting issues that block a couple's ability to adapt and work together as a team, finding meaning in the illness, taking control over the controllable aspects of the illness, accepting the uncontrollable aspects for what they are, and learning to live around the illness. Most couples need to improve their ability to communicate in general, as well as about the illness. In addition, many couples need assistance in communicating with the health care system.

Two general goals that underlie successful adaptation are "agency" and "communion" (McDaniel et al., 1992). Adapting Bakan's (1969) general usage of the term to an illness context, Totman (1979) used "agency" to describe active involvement in and commitment to one's own care. Couples can feel overwhelmed and powerless in the face of illness, resulting in increased passivity. This passivity can be reinforced by the health care system and the "patient" or "illness" roles. Patients who manage to take control over what is controllable, and accept what is not, tend to more easily adapt and accept. Second, patients need a sense of support and community around them as they struggle to cope with an illness. Because illness can be very isolating, and can fragment family and other social bonds, family or couple therapy can be beneficial by increasing social support. Psychotherapy facilitates communion by helping family members join together, by drawing in family members who may have distanced themselves, and by helping the family connect with other families facing similar challenges.

Alice had a history of seizures and depression. After hospitalization for seizure evaluation, her neurologist told her that she had nonelectrical seizures he felt were rooted in marital and family problems. He sent her and her family to a family psychologist (SHM). In the first session, Alice stated that her goal was "to have everyone in the family stop blaming her and stop being so dependent" on her for household chores. With her agreement, the psychologist suggested that Alice's goals were to stop being blamed and stop accepting blame for the family's problems, and to stop babying her adult children and her husband. Alice's husband, Bob, stated that his goal for therapy was to help his wife "in whatever time she had left on this earth." After comments by his wife and daughter about his needing antidepressant medication, Bob acknowledged that he himself suffered from serious mood swings, but said, "They have no effect on our family life." With his agreement, the psychologist suggested that Bob's goals were to help his wife physically and emotionally, and to evaluate the effect of his mood swings on the family.

As in many couples, Alice suffered from too much communion and not enough agency, while Bob suffered from too much agency and not enough communion. One therapeutic goal thus became achieving a balance between agency and communion for the individuals and the family. Hegelson (1994), in a review of the research on agency and communion, found that unmitigated agency or unmitigated communion is associated with negative health outcomes.

STRUCTURE OF THE THERAPY PROCESS

As noted earlier, patients who are referred for psychotherapy to assist them in coping with illness often present alone. Expanding the session attendance to include all who affect, or are affected by, the illness facilitates treatment. The patient and his/her partner may recognize more and more such people as treatment progresses. Therefore, it is helpful to have a fluid plan as to who should attend sessions and at what point. Clearly, people outside the biological family fall into this group. Including important nonfamily members can facilitate assessment and increase the family's sense of social support. Finally, members of the health care team obviously affect the illness, and (perhaps less obviously) may be affected by the illness as well. Including members of the health care team, even when the interface between the couple and the team is not problematic, can be very helpful. Family members may feel more comfortable asking questions about the illness in a therapy setting than during a medical appointment. Also, there is often fear among family members that someone is hiding critical information. Talking directly with treatment team members can mitigate these fears.

Dr. Giancomo, Alice's neurologist, attended the last 15 minutes of the first family session. In response to the psychologist's request, he described Alice's hospitalization, the tests she took, and the certainty of the health care team that she did not have epilepsy. Instead, he said, she was experiencing stress-induced, nonelectrical seizures. He praised the family for having the courage to come to psychotherapy, and said he was certain that Alice and Bob would benefit from their work with the psychologist.

Collaboration with health care providers also gives therapists who are unable to prescribe psychotropic medication built-in consultants regarding these issues. Psychotropic medication can be particularly helpful when a patient's level of functioning is significantly impaired. Deciding about psychotropic medication is another opportunity for the patient to be actively involved in his/her own care. When the interactions with the treatment team are problematic, it is an opportunity for the couple to experience agency when these problems are resolved in therapy sessions. Treatment team members also benefit from the dialogue; they can learn how the family is coping, as well as how the team contributes to issues or how this particular patient affects team members.

Alice and Bob's family physician, Dr. Romero, attended the sixth session with the spouses, after they had discussed Bob's mood swings and the possibility of antidepressant medication. After making records of his moods and their effect on his family life, Bob was more open to the possibility of medication as well as psychotherapy. Dr. Romero participated in the first part of a session to describe potential benefits and side effects. Soon thereafter, he prescribed medication for Bob, who benefited considerably.

Some therapists who work primarily with families facing illness choose to work in a health care setting. This context changes the structure of therapy in a number of ways. First, the therapy room may be an exam room or may be adjacent to medical office space, making it easier for physicians such as Drs. Giancomo and Romero to participate in a session. Second, the therapist may engage patients during medical appointments, or be part of the "medical treatment team." Third, patients and their partners who come to psychotherapy in a medical setting may be at a different level of "readiness for change" (Prochaska & DiClemente, 1983). They may attend psychotherapy because their doctor told them to, or because it is expected by the treatment team, rather than because they feel they have some emotional issue to resolve. The physician may be the "customer" for the psychotherapy, rather than the patient. In such a case, the therapist needs to "back up" and assess the couple's willingness to attend therapy. If the partners are not interested in psychotherapy, the therapist can consult with the health care provider about what the concerns behind the referral are, and how the health care professional can prepare the couple for referral. If the couple agrees to continue, the therapist may need to adjust expectations and pacing, and begin with basic psychoeducation about how therapy can help the couple cope.

Another result of practicing in a close alignment with medical professionals is a different pace of therapy than is often seen in other settings. Because patients usually go to their health care providers on an "as-needed" basis, they may seek psychotherapy only when they feel it is immediately necessary. This pattern can disrupt the typical "joining/assessment–midphase–termination" cycle of psychotherapy. However, it can parallel the course of an illness in ways that help the therapist understand the couple's different needs at different times. It is common that patients are seen one or two times a month, rather than every week.

Sometimes, especially with severely somatizing or otherwise complex patients, it can be helpful to have a physician serve as a cotherapist (McDaniel et al., 1990; McDaniel, 1997). The physician's biomedical expertise can facilitate discussion of the illness itself. Moreover, the physician's understanding of the dynamics of the health care team can help the therapist and couple understand any issues they have with the care or the professionals.

We also utilize family members or other social supports as "link therapists" (Landau, 1981). A "link therapist" is a social support who is able to connect with all factions of the family, and facilitate communication among them to create movement toward consensus and joint functioning. This technique is particularly helpful when a family or couple has fragmented in the context of the illness, or when some family members cannot or will not attend therapy sessions.

ROLE OF THE THERAPIST

One means of empowering the couple is to take a collaborative stance toward the therapy. Although the therapist may have expertise in helping couples cope with illness in general, the members of each couple are the experts on their own illness experience. The therapist can normalize reactions that patients sometimes find confusing or painful (e.g., anger), facilitate communication and dialogue, and help the couple find a sense of agency and communion. A collaborative stance minimizes the likelihood that the partners will experience psychotherapy as disempowering or imposed upon them, the way they may experience other aspects of the overall treatment plan.

In part because of the collaborative nature of this work, therapists tend to be quite active. Couples often need encouragement to discuss these challenging topics. Psychoeducation is a commonly used strategy, in that couples need the therapist to provide basic information about illness and how it affects couples and families.

Self-disclosure is generally limited. Personal anecdotes may be offered to make a specific point. If a therapist has personal experience with the couple's illness, he/she must be careful to allow this to inform the treatment while not hampering his/her understanding of this particular couple's illness experience. Therapists also need to be conscious in general of their own illness experiences and health beliefs, and of the ways these affect the therapy. In many ways, the use of the therapist's family-of-origin experiences concerning health and illness may inform the therapist, just as other family-of-origin experiences can be helpful or hindering in all types of psychotherapy (McDaniel et al., 1992).

Theresa was referred for psychotherapy because she was having difficulty coping with multiple family problems. It quickly became apparent that she had coped with stress somatically for much of her life. Her husband, Larry, agreed to attend psychotherapy with her, primarily out of frustration about how her many illnesses affected the family. One major issue both Theresa and Larry acknowledged was a rift between Theresa and their adult daughters. Larry frequently felt caught between "the girls" and his wife. Both were angry that their daughters were not more understanding of their mother's physical problems. The therapist (NBR), who was about the same age as their daughters, discussed her own experience with her mother's cardiac illness, which had resulted in heart transplant. The therapist noted that even though she understood her mother was not to blame for her illness, there were times it was difficult not to feel at least "cheated" that her mother was not healthy. This seemed to help Theresa and Larry look at the situation as their daughters might experience it. They began to recognize how this sense of loss might be particularly strong, given that their mother had often been unable to mother them when they were younger as well.

Some therapists are more likely than others to enjoy and thrive in the health care environment. First, therapists who understand and are drawn to the complex interplay of biological, psychological, and relational elements of the illness experience are more likely to enjoy helping couples cope with illness. Therapists who enjoy working as part of a team, and are willing to collaborate with other health care professionals, also may thrive in a more medicalized environment. Clearly, anyone who has very negative feelings about the medical profession or health care system will have to work hard to be open to recognize the positive experiences had by others. They may be less likely to enjoy the collaborative aspects of this work, less able to tolerate issues that press their "antimedicine" buttons, and perhaps more likely to become triangulated when a couple experiences difficulties with the medical system. Accessibility of peer consultation is important for all medical family therapists.

TECHNIQUES OF THERAPY WITH COUPLES FACING ILLNESS

McDaniel et al. (1992), in their work on medical family therapy, discuss a number of key concepts and techniques in helping families cope with serious illness. The first is of these to recognize the biological dimension of a couple's or family's problems. In some forms of family therapy, the family's labeling of one member as "sick" is seen as part of the problem. In medical family therapy, the therapist accepts the family's definition of the problem as a medical illness. We often include physicians in one of the initial encounters to give an explanation of the illness, its prognosis, and its probable course. This ensures that the therapist, patient, and family members all have the same information about the illness, and it demystifies the illness for the family.

In the context of an ambiguous diagnosis or course of illness, it is important to be open to many possible explanations for the patient's symptomatology. It is easy to "pigeonhole" a patient into a medical, psychological, or relational diagnosis. Both biomedical and psychosocial factors can be given too much weight. It is not uncommon to find that there are relational and intrapsychic issues exacerbating the illness in even the most biomedical of illnesses. Sometimes a patient is referred simply because the health care team has been unable to find a biomedical explanation for the patient's symptoms. Under these circumstances, it can be tempting to assume that the issues are primarily psychosocial, or at least "stress-related." Patients sometimes experience this stance as negating their illness experience, suggesting that their symptoms are "all in their head." Ambiguous diagnoses and ailments that do not fall easily into a diagnostic category (and may therefore not fall into a clear treatment plan category) can be particularly challenging for couples. They may feel blamed for the illness, or confused because they do not understand or frustrated because of the lack of a clear path back to health. Therefore, it is not difficult to understand how couples facing illness and ambiguity may struggle the most.

Theresa and Larry struggled to understand why Theresa so often experienced illnesses for which the medical community did not have ready diagnosis and treatment. Theresa vacillated between being angry with her medical team and feeling guilty that she kept getting sick. Only after a great deal of treatment did she and her husband begin to discuss the link between stress and illness in a productive, nonblaming way. Larry and their daughters tended to believe either that Theresa was "really sick" (e.g., the physicians had a diagnosis, prognosis, and treatment), or that "it was all in her head." Theresa felt she had to "prove" her illness with physicians' testimonials or medical test results, which pushed her utilization of medical care and diagnostic testing even higher. Slowly Larry came to accept that all illness is both biological and psychological, and stopped trying to categorize Theresa's illnesses. Removing this pressure enabled Theresa to begin to discuss and change her life-long pattern of avoiding conflict and emotional upset by channeling her difficulties to somatic symptoms.

The second tenet of medical family therapy is to solicit the illness story. Many partners have not had the opportunity to review their entire experience with an illness from its first symptoms to the present. Physicians who gather a biomedical history understandably focus on only certain aspects of the experience. Family members and friends may feel comfortable hearing only certain elements, or may have attempted to avoid hearing the story. The partners find just telling their story to an empathic listener very therapeutic. Giving them space to share their story facilitates the joining and assessment processes as well.

In addition to referring to Table 27.1 to assist in soliciting the illness story, therapists are encouraged to gather data for an illness time line, as noted earlier. In organizing the time line, the therapist should ask about the onset of the illness; illness symptoms; diagnostic process and diagnosis; treatments that have been suggested, have been tried, or are desired; the patient's and family members' emotional and practical responses to the illness; and the patient's current condition. Gathering genogram information allows the therapist to solicit the illness story that may have unfolded over generations, and better understand the family's general scripts about illness.

In one of the first couple sesssions Larry and Theresa attended, the therapist completed a genogram. Although Larry was aware that Theresa's father had died of gastrointestinal (GI) cancer, he did not know that six of the father's seven siblings had also died of GI cancer. Theresa recounted how horrifyingly painful her father's death had been, and her fear that she too would contract a GI cancer. She also stated that she had been told she should have her GI tract scoped whenever she "felt any kind of twinge," because of her strong family history. Hearing her story helped the therapist, Larry, and Theresa herself understand why she was quite focused on body sensations, particularly those from her abdomen, and why she immediately looked to her medical care providers to reassure her that she would not succumb to her father's dreadful fate. Given Theresa's script about cancer, the therapist also made sure that her physician reeducated her about what types of GI symptoms are worrisome versus benign, and about modern cancer treatment.

The third general technique is to respect defenses, remove blame, and accept unacceptable feelings. A couple facing an illness is facing a crisis. As in any crisis intervention treatment, the couple's current coping mechanisms need to be left intact until the partners develop new strategies. This is particularly true of the use of denial. Denial that gives a couple enough hope to face the next day, while not interfering with appropriate treatment or planning for the future, is adaptive. In addition, a couple facing illness can be particularly sensitive and vulnerable to perceived criticism, as there is often a latent sense of guilt about the illness. If family members feel they are being criticized, and they are ambivalent about the psychotherapy referral, it is highly unlikely they will engage in treatment. A strong dose of support, in the context of helping the couple examine and change maladaptive patterns, is generally much more likely to result in a positive outcome.

Much of the latent sense of guilt over illness stems from ideas about fairness and personal responsibility. People want to believe that bad things like illness just do not happen randomly; someone must have done something to cause this terrible thing. Add this general cognitive schema to the links between behavior and illness, and it is understandable why patients and their families often point to something they or their health care team did or did not do as the reason why an illness has occurred or continued. Facilitating a dialogue about these fears allows the family to accept the illness, relieve the patient or others of inappropriate blame, and use rituals to heal wounds from real relational or behavioral causes of the illness.

Mary Jane harbored the fear that she had miscarried in her third month because of a fall she had taken in her second month. Her therapist (SHM) convened a meeting among Mary Jane; her husband, John; and their obstetrician, Dr. Eisen, to discuss the cause of her miscarriage. Dr. Eisen reassured Mary Jane that it was unlikely that her fall was related to her miscarriage, and told her that one in five pregnancies end in miscarriage. Furthermore, he was able both to sympathize with the couple's loss and to reassure John and Mary Jane that any future pregnancies would have as good a chance at completion as those of any other couple.

The partners in any couple have negative feelings about each other. Many couples have a difficult time discussing and processing those feelings even under the best of circumstances. What was once difficult can seem impossible to couples facing illness. Although this avoidance of some issues can result in fewer squabbles over relatively unimportant issues, it can also result in avoidance of talking through important issues, and in increased emotional distance within a couple. Medical family therapy can help family members accept unacceptable emotions, particularly those that tend to emerge under the stress of illness. For example, the well partner may begin to resent the needs of the ill partner, and may feel guilty about this resentment. Both normalizing this process and helping the couple discuss their "unacceptable" feelings are therapeutic.

The fourth general technique of medical family therapy is to maintain and facilitate communication. The desire to protect one another can result in poor communication among family members, and thus in a general sense of loneliness or isolation. First, it is often helpful for the family to realize that any secretiveness is usually well intended. Also, each member of a couple must recognize and acknowledge his/her own secretive behavior. Often one partner notices when the other is secretive, but is not aware of how his or her own secretive behavior blocks communication. As the partners begin to discuss painful issues, the therapist can help them recognize how open communication fosters a sense of support and teamwork. Medical family therapy gives family members a venue in which to discuss these important issues safely, and it normalizes the desire to avoid difficult feelings so as to protect one another while under stress.

The medical family therapist can also work to improve communication between the couple and the health care system. The therapist can use his/ her expertise in collaborating with health care professionals to coach both members of the couple in preparing questions for medical appointments, and appropriately asserting themselves. When there are issues in the relationship between the couple and the medical professionals, the therapist can hold a joint meeting to facilitate communication in the moment. Meetings that include medical care providers are also helpful in reducing the likelihood that the medical family therapist will become triangulated between the couple and the other professionals. Also, the therapist should maintain open communication with other members of the health care team, both to provide a model for the couple and to avoid creating parallel processes of poor communication among the team, the couple, and the therapist.

Dr. Loren came to one of us (SHM) and said she felt caught because her 65-year-old patient, Jack Brown, told her that he did not want his wife, Jane, to know that he was dying. He feared "she could not handle it." Meanwhile, privately, Mrs. Brown told Dr. Loren that she did not want her to share her husband's terminal diagnosis with him, because he was "not yet ready to hear it." The therapist suggested a family conference, and met with the couple and Dr. Loren. At the therapist's suggestion, Dr. Loren opened the meeting by asking both spouses what they knew of Jack's illness and what questions they had about prognosis and treatment. Within a few minutes, Jack and Jane each reported what they knew (which was remarkably similar information) and moved on to discuss pain management and hospice care.

The fifth general approach of medical family therapy is to attend to developmental issues (Carter & McGoldrick, 1999; Rolland, 1994; McDaniel et al., 1990). The therapist and couple must attend to matters involving both individual and family development, development of the illness and its ramifications, and the interaction between the illness and developmental needs of the individual and family—while not allowing the illness to "take over." Gonzalez, Steinglass, and Reiss (1989) describe this as "putting illness in its place." Medical family therapists can help families keep "illness in its place" by encouraging the couple and family to maintain routines, rituals, and traditions, and to create space for each family member to get his/ her own needs met as much as possible.

Lorena and Joe Williams sought therapy to help them cope with Lorena's breast cancer. They had two children in their late teens. Their older child had planned to attend college out of state. However, with her mother's diagnosis, she announced to the family that she planned to attend the local community college; this would allow her to be closer to her mother and to help the family. Lorena and Joe did not want her to make this sacrifice, as they felt it might prevent her from living up to her potential. In therapy, they were able to discuss how they wanted to approach their daughter about this. This dialogue was an opportunity for them to discuss the sacrifices everyone was making because of the illness. Lorena acknowledged her guilt about this, and Joe discussed his sadness that there was nothing he could do to protect his wife from her ordeal.

The sixth general technique of medical family therapy is to increase a sense of agency in the patient and couple. As noted earlier, among the major challenges in adapting to illness are to differentiate controllable from uncontrollable factors, to take charge of the controllable issues, and to accept the uncontrollable issues. There are a number of ways therapists can facilitate this process. First, a couple can be encouraged to have input into treatment decisions. Second, when a couple or patient disagrees with or does not adhere to medical advice, the therapist can help the couple and the health care team understand this behavior as an attempt to gain control. The therapist can help the couple work through "resistance," or disagreement, by emphasizing the temporary nature of all decisions. This approach can help free the members of the couple (or the health care team) to "try out" a suggestion they are ambivalent about trying, or allow them to reconsider hard-line stances in the future. This situation is most challenging when a patient has an uncertain diagnosis.

Judith became more and more fatigued, until finally she went to her doctor for a physical. She told both her husband and her doctor that she was sure it was "nothing." However, her white blood cell count was very high. Unfortunately, this started a process that took almost a year before Judith was found to meet the criteria for non-Hodgkin's Lymphoma. During this time, Judith became active in searching the Internet and the library for information about her condition. She took lists of questions to her physician, trying to make the most efficient use of each appointment. She focused on what she could do to increase a sense of agency in a highly uncertain and stressful situation.

The therapist should avoid giving advice or pushing the couple in a specific direction. The most helpful strategies are encouraging the couple to gather information, discussing options, and facilitating decision making. First, putting the responsibility and power of decisions firmly in the couple's court facilitates a sense of agency. Second, taking a facilitative rather than an advising role avoids creating a parallel process, in which the couple is "nonadherent" with the therapist as well.

As their final general technique of medical family therapy, McDaniel et al. (1992) advise therapists to "keep the door open"—a principle in common with most time-effective brief psychotherapy (Budman & Gurman, 1988). Family members will consult with the therapist on an as-needed basis. Accepting the couple's time line for seeking psychotherapy supports the partners' decision-making skills and sense of agency. In addition, because the physician will continue to be involved, the couple does have a sounding board for issues, and may be referred back for further treatment if the physician and couple feel it may be helpful. Conducting follow-up—either by seeing the patient during a medical visit if the physician and therapist share space, or by placing a phone call or writing a letter 6–12 months after termination—can set the stage for the couple to return if needed.

John Bell and Gerry Sanders had been long-term partners when Gerry suffered a serious heart attack. Both men had difficulty with the lifestyle changes encouraged by Gerry's cardiologist and his family physician. Gerry's heart condition really required him to change his diet, decrease his stress, and increase his exercise regimen. Both physicians knew these changes were much more likely to happen if the partners worked on them together, and so all parties worked with a therapist (SHM) to develop a plan that was possible for the couple. These goals were accomplished in six sessions over a 3-month period. Because maintenance was of great importance, the couple agreed to return at 3-, 6-, and 12-month intervals for booster sessions.

Several additional techniques are worth describing here. Rolland (1994) has focused specifically on the effect of illness on intimacy. He notes that illness challenges the "intimacy homeostasis" a couple has evolved over time, both physically and emotionally. The first challenges to this homeostasis are the real and anticipated losses associated with illness. Rolland notes that loss is not always associated with negative emotions, and that a direct focus on the loss may not be most helpful. Rather, he suggests that a therapist help the couple see the threatened loss as an opportunity to live more fully in the present, and to broaden the partners' experience of intimacy. Rolland (1994) suggests that "In general, couples adapt best when they revise their closeness to include rather than avoid issues of incapacitation and threatened loss" (p. 237).

The second challenge to intimacy involves the changes the partners must make in how they communicate. Rolland notes that partners must find a "functional balance" in their communication. In other words, they must discern which fears, feelings, and thoughts need to be shared (no matter how difficult this may be), and which are best kept to themselves. Like McDaniel et al. (1992), Rolland 1994) notes that illness challenges communication in a couple because of the many new issues and adaptations that must be addressed; because so many of these issues are difficult to discuss; because the partners want to protect each other from stress; and because so many of the fears, feelings, and thoughts are overwhelming or shameful. A therapist can help a couple by normalizing these intense experiences, and by helping the partners share their experiences rather than allowing them to create distance. Rolland notes that the anger that accompanies illness can be particularly challenging for couples.

The second major element of Rolland's (1994) treatment plan for a couple facing illness is rebalancing relationship skews. If the illness is seen as only one person's problem, the relationship will be redefined around inequality in the couple. The inequality in health can generalize to inequalities in power and control, resulting in decreased intimacy, resentment, guilt, and emotional distance. To avoid this, Rolland suggests that the members of the couple redefine the illness as "our" problem. This acknowledges the very real changes that both partners experience as a result of the illness. Realizing how each of them must adapt allows them to discuss and challenge their preconceptions about "appropriate" roles of the ill and well partners. A couple may need assistance breaking out of roles and scripts about illness that are based on family-of-origin experiences with illness.

Karen and Joel had a very unstable marital relationship. Both partners attributed many of their difficulties to Karen's long-standing difficulty with a mood disorder. After much struggling, Karen started to take a mood stabilizer that was very helpful to her. However, the couple's dynamics in relating to her illness continued to be a problem. Joel harbored a great deal of resentment about old incidents, and particularly about some financial difficulties that were related to Karen's mood swings. He often stated that all of the problems had been "Karen's fault" and that there was nothing he could do to better their relationship. He refused to take any responsibility for difficulties, including the financial problems that were related to *his* behavior. He clearly had felt powerless to help Karen, and was torn between his love for her and his anger about how difficult their lives were. Even when Karen's condition stabilized, he had difficulty shifting out of this powerlessness. Ultimately, the couple separated and divorced. It was only with distance and individual therapy that Karen recognized how her illness was a large factor in her "lightning rod" position in many relationships. She acknowledged that her relationship with Joel had had been based on her being "the sick one" and Joel's being the "victim" of her illness. Joel began to recognize his own culpability in the problems, and worked to create a more balanced relationship with his next partner.

Furthermore, the couple needs assistance in drawing a boundary around the illness, so that the relationship does not ultimately become defined by the illness. The very real changes that illness can necessitate can make the partners feel that their entire lives and relationship are never to be the same, and will change only for the worse. They can become so focused on the illness and its effects that they see themselves as separate from the healthy world. As Rolland (1994) states, "Living a normal life is external to the relationship and illness that is within" (p. 242). To counteract these insidious assumptions and their effects, Rolland suggests some simple strategies for compartmentalizing the illness. The partners can agree upon times that the illness is the focus of their communication, and other times when it is "off limits." The boundary can be placed geographically, prohibiting discussion of the illness in certain places, such as the bedroom. The couple can be encouraged to maintain social contacts and continue preillness social routines as much as possible.

Rolland also notes that members of a couple need to be able to adapt their functioning to the level required by the illness. There will be crisis periods when the illness is central and all consuming. However, the partners often need assistance in recognizing when these phases have passed and they can return to a lifestyle more consistent with their preillness functioning. They may need specific information about the illness or the ill person's current level of health and ability to tolerate stress, in order to feel safe engaging in more emotionally or physically strenuous activities. An overt discussion of resuming the couple's sex life, for example, is particularly helpful, as many couples are embarrassed to ask about this and fear that physical intimacy is contraindicated.

Jerry and Marta came to therapy because they were having difficulty adjusting to life after Jerry's heart attack. Jerry had smoked heavily and was unable to stop until the day he was hospitalized with chest pain and an eventual myocardial infarction. Marta came to the hospital every day, and then, as Jerry said, "watched him like a hawk" thereafter. He had not had a cigarette since the hospitalization, and Marta was trying to learn to cook low-fat foods, but Jerry was complaining about the taste and threatening to start smoking again. Before taking the needed lifestyle changes, the therapist (SHM) spent two sessions talking about how scary the heart attack experience had been for both members of the couple. In the second session, for the first time, Jerry broke down and cried, admitting how worried he was about whether he would live to see his grandchildren. Marta, with support from the therapist, was able to listen and empathize with her husband's fears. Jerry had always been the strong, silent type, and so expressing his feelings was a new experience for both of them. In the fourth session, the therapist asked about when they planned to resume their sex life. Jerry was relieved that she brought the subject up, and said that both he and Marta were worried about the possibility of his "dying like Nelson Rockefeller." The therapist asked Jerry's family doctor to stop by during the next session to reassure them and answer any questions about sexual activity. The therapist also encouraged them to continue developing all aspects of their communication.

Illness can be like a new, unwanted family member. Like any other family member, the illness itself can be the third point in triangulation of conflicts, reducing the couple's ability to resolve issues as a dyad. Also, when the illness becomes the source of resolution of some problem (albeit an unhealthy resolution), the illness becomes necessary. This can interfere with restoring health, and can increase the likelihood that symptoms are supported by relational issues or secondary gain. When the illness becomes a central point in the couple's dynamics, the therapy must help the couple realign the relationship to make this the third point of the triangle less necessary. The demise of Karen and Joel's relationship after Karen improved illustrates what can happen when the illness is central in how the partners relate to each other.

A number of other general psychotherapy techniques can be usefully applied to therapy with couples facing illness. Many authors have discussed the role of psychoeducation in helping couples cope with illness (McDaniel et al., 1992; Rolland, 1994). Psychoeducation prepares couples for possible changes in mood, energy level, behavioral inhibition or disinhibition, and other areas that can be expected in an individual related to illness. Reviewing possible relational challenges helps the couple understand "normal" change, and recognize potentially unhealthy changes. Therefore, psychoeducation can set the stage for the couple to engage in preventive work before patterns become embedded, or the relationship becomes very damaged. When partners discuss the challenges ahead of time, they can "know the enemy," predict which issues are likely to be most challenging for them, and agree on a plan for preventing and managing these issues before they become too problematic. Because many patients and their partners are unfamiliar with psychotherapy, or may be seeking psychotherapy only because their physician suggested it, we begin by educating the couple about the process of psychotherapy. For example, we help the patient and partner understand how psychotherapy encounters will be different from medical encounters, and what skills psychotherapist have to assist them.

A couple therapist should actively assist the couple in developing and maintaining communication, especially a social and support network. The partners need assistance in recognizing family members and friends who can support them, and "permission" and encouragement to access these groups. Just as they do not want to burden each other with problems, partners may shut out possible sources of support because they fear that asking for help will alienate or overburden others, or

will be seen as a sign of weakness. Sometimes couples fear creating inequity in their social relationships, or feel that others do not understand how the illness is affecting them. Under these circumstances, they may be most comfortable reaching out to support groups that focus on their particular illness, or on couples facing illness in general. Finally, the therapist, through his/her collaboration with the medical professionals and other team members, can assist the family members in maximizing their benefit from the available professional supports.

CURATIVE FACTORS IN COUPLE THERAPY/MECHANISMS OF CHANGE

While not welcome, illness does create an opportunity for growth. Couples may be able to face intrapsychic and existential issues that they might otherwise have avoided. Clearly, different illnesses create different opportunities, but almost all increase a couple's awareness of the fragility of life, and of simple, daily pleasures that were previously taken for granted. Illness can make partners appreciate each other in new ways—both because it may force them to contemplate life without each other, and because they must work as a team and support each other. Illness also can force the partners to explore new ways of relating to each other, as old patterns become less functional. They must broaden their repertoire of interactional patterns to accommodate the illness. Therapy facilitates adaptation in interactional patterns and perceptions by making the adaptations overt and facilitating discussion of the elements of successful adaptation. Therapy empowers the couple to increase agency by taking control over the situation and making informed, planful decisions. Sometimes partners who learn to take a proactive stance toward the illness begin to take more a more proactive stance in other areas of life as well. When the partners begin to view these adaptations as a positive force in their lives, they find meaning in the illness and develop a greater sense of cohesion. The growth catalyzed by illness can result in a more satisfying relationship overall.

Therapists who attend to biological, psychological, and social context factors are more likely to facilitate positive change with couples facing illness than those who neglect any of these areas. Even when illness is not the presenting concern, it is critical that therapists attend to these factors, and to the role health and illness play in the lives of all couples.

Collaboration with health care professionals is very valuable in couple therapy, even in the absence of significant illness. Often such professionals have a long-term view of a couple, and understand the couple's current situation in the context of a much richer history that can be gathered only through a long-term relationship. In the context of illness, collaboration with health care professionals is essential. Broadening the "treatment team" to include the family and natural support systems also facilitates a sense of communion and positive outcome. Our model maintains a focus on healthy adaptation, and on the strengths couples bring to the challenging transitions imposed by illness. Together, these elements form the essential core of successful couple therapy related to illness. Clearly, this approach integrates many models, and applies them to the specific instance of relational difficulties related to illness. The metaframeworks of the biopsychosocial model and collaborative family health care can be layered over established couple treatments.

TREATMENT APPLICABILITY

Our model was developed through work with couples facing illness. However, much of what we have learned can be applied to couples facing any major life transition. Most couples presenting for psychotherapy are in transition. The stress of the transition may be the cause of the presenting problems, or may merely have exposed preexisting issues that must be resolved for a couple to progress successfully. Using the multiple lenses implicit in the biopsychosocial model allows therapists to assess and intervene sensitively, and to help create change.

Though all illnesses force transition and adaptation, some are particularly challenging for couples. For example, illnesses that have a genetic component can force a couple to make difficult decisions about childbearing. Genetic illnesses can also create a sense of guilt in the partner who "brought" the illness into the family. Survivor guilt may occur for family members who have been spared the genetic problem (McDaniel & Speice, in press). Other health problems directly related to developmental challenges (e.g., infertility) can clearly challenge couples as they attempt to make the transition to parenthood. Infertility assessment lends itself to blame and divisiveness, as the members of a couple seek to determine who has "the problem" that prevents them from bearing children (McDaniel et al., 1992).

It is not uncommon for illness to strike couples whose members have other significant issues. We augment our work with programs specifically designed to treat substance abuse/dependence or major mental illness when warranted. Further, our model can be helpful to families coping with these issues as well. There are many parallels between the adaptations families must make to chronic physical illness, and the adaptations families must make in the face of major psychiatric illness or substance abuse.

Working with couples facing medical illness does engender some ethical issues that are less likely to appear in other couple work (McDaniel et al., 1992). First, therapists working in a medical setting are likely to encounter different norms regarding confidentiality. They must navigate maintaining an appropriate level of confidentiality while collaborating with medical professionals, who are freer with information about patients than mental health professionals tend to be. Couple therapists may also become involved in treatment plan negotiations, particularly when a couple and medical care providers disagree on the best course of treatment. Therapists may encounter ethical issues about end-of-life decisions and advanced directives about treatment, should a patient become incapacitated. Many other medico-ethical issues may arise in treating couples coping with such controversial medical procedures as abortion, fertility treatments, transplantation, and genetic testing. Therapists themselves may need consultation to cope with these challenging issues, or at least a place to process their own reactions and feelings about them.

CONCLUSION

It is not accidental that marriage vows include the words "in sickness and in health." Illness is one of the most difficult challenges a couple can face. Couples coping with illness are often on an emotional roller coaster full of unexpected twists and turns. Couple therapists who take a biopsychosocial view of their work are in a unique position to help these couples cope. Although psychotherapy for couples facing illness uses many skills from more general crisis intervention and transition-oriented therapies (Seaburn, Landau-Stanton, & Horwitz, 1995)—including emphasizing strengths, noting patterns, facilitating communication and increasing social support—several important skills and intervention principles are specific to this work. When illness is even a part of a couple's situation (even when it is not the stated presenting problem), it is critical that the therapist address issues related to the illness. This may require collaborating with the medical community; learning about disease progression as it relates to functionality and behavior; providing specific psychoeducation; normalizing difficulties; and helping the couple find a sense of meaning, agency, and communion.

REFERENCES

Bakan, D. (1969). *The duality of human existence*. Chicago: Rand McNally.

Belar, C. D., & Deardorff, W. W. (1995). *Clinical health psychology in medical settings: A practitioner's guidebook*. Washington, DC: American Psychological Association.

Bloch, D. (1983). Family systems medicine: The field and the journal. *Family Systems Medicine, 1*, 3–11.

Blount, A. (1998). *Integrative primary care*. New York: Basic Books.

Budman, S. H., & Gurman, A. S. (1988). *Theory and practice of brief therapy*. New York: Guilford Press.

Carter E., & McGoldrick, M. (1999). *The expanded family life cycle*. Needham Heights, MA: Allyn & Bacon.

Doherty, W. J. (1988). Implications of chronic illness for family treatment. In C. Childman, E. Nunnally, & F. Cox (Eds.), *Chronic illness and disability* (pp. 193–210). Newbury Park, CA: Sage.

Doherty, W. J., & Baird, M. (1983). *Family therapy and family medicine: Toward the primary care of families*. New York: Guilford Press.

Engel, G. L. (1977). The need for a new medical model: A challenge for biomedicine. *Science, 196*, 129–136.

Engel, G. L. (1980). The clinical application of the biopsychosocial model. *American Journal of Psychiatry, 137*, 535–544.

Friedman, E. (1991, June). *Managing crisis: Bowen theory incarnate*. Audiotape of a presentation at a Family Systems Theory seminar, Bethesda, MD.

Gonzalez, S., Steinglass, P., & Reiss, D. (1989). Putting illness in its place: Discussion groups for families with chronic medical illness. *Family Process, 28*, 69–87.

Harkaway, J. (1983). Obesity: Reducing the larger system. *Journal of Strategic and Systemic Therapy, 2*, 2–16.

Hegelson, V. S. (1994). Relation of agency and communion to well-being: Evidence and potential explanations. *Psychological Bulletin, 116*, 412–428.

Kleinman, A., Eisenberg, M., & Good, B. (1978). Culture illness, and care: Clinical lessons from anthropological and cross-cultural research. *Annals of Internal Medicine, 88*, 251–258.

Landau, J. (1981). Link therapy as a family therapy technique for transitional extended families. *Psychotherapia, 7*(4), 1–15.

Lantz, P. M., House, J. S., Lepkowski, J. M., Williams, D. R., Mero, R. P., & Chen, J. (1998). Socioeconomic factors, health behaviors, and mortality: Results from a nationally representative prospective study of US adults. *Journal of the American Medical Association, 279*, 1703–1708.

Marmot, M. G., Smith, G. D., Stansfeld, S., Patel, C.,

North, F., & Head, J. (1991). Health inequalities among British civil servants: The Whitehall II study. *Lancet, 337*, 1387–1393.

McDaniel, S. H. (1997). Trapped inside a body without a voice: Two cases of somatic fixation. In S. H. McDaniel, J. Hepworth, & W. J. Doherty (Eds.), *The shared experience of illness: Stories of patients, families and their therapists* (pp. 274–290). New York: Basic Books.

McDaniel, S. H., & Campbell, T. L. (2000). Consumers and collaborative family healthcare. *Families, Systems and Health, 18*, 133–136.

McDaniel, S. H., Campbell, T. L., & Seaburn, D. (1990). *Family oriented primary care: A manual for providers*. New York: Springer-Verlag.

McDaniel, S. H., & Cole-Kelly, K. (in press). Gender, couples, and illness: A feminist analysis of medical family therapy. In T. Goodrich & L. Silverstein (Eds.), *Feminist family therapy*. Washington, DC: American Psychological Association.

McDaniel, S. H., & Hepworth, J. (in press). Family psychology in primary care: Managing issues of power and dependency through collaboration. In R. Frank, S. H. McDaniel, J. Bray, & M. Heldring (Eds.), *Primary care psychology*. Washington, DC: American Psychological Association Publications.

McDaniel, S. H., Hepworth, J., & Doherty, W. J. (1992). *Medical family therapy: A biopsychosocial approach to families with health problems*. New York: Basic Books.

McDaniel, S. H., & Speice, J. (2001). What family psychology has to offer women's health: The examples of conversion, somatization, infertility treatment, and genetic testing. *Professional Psychology: Research and Practice, 32*(1), 44–51.

Prochaska, J., & DiClemente, C. (1983). Stages and process of self-change of smoking: Toward an integrative model of change. *Journal of Consulting and Clinical Psychology, 51*, 390–395.

Rolland, J. (1994). *Families, illness and disability: An integrative treatment model*. New York: Basic Books

Schultz, R., O'Brien, T., Bookwala, J., & Fleissner, K. (1995). Psychiatric and physical morbidity effects of Alzheimer's disease caregiving: Prevalence, correlates and causes. *The Gerontologist, 35*, 771–791.

Seaburn, D. B., Lorenz, A., Gawinski, B. A., & Gunn, W. (1996). *Models of collaboration: A guide for family therapists practicing with health care professionals*. New York: Basic Books.

Seaburn, D., Lorenz, A., & Kaplan, D. (in press). The transgenerational development of chronic illness meanings. *Family Systems Medicine*.

Seaburn, D. B., Landau-Stanton, J., & Horwitz, S. (1995). Core techniques in family therapy. In D. Mikesell, D. D. Lusterman, & S. H. McDaniel (Eds.), *Integrating family therapy: Handbook of systems theory and family psychology* (pp. 5–26). Washington, DC: American Psychological Association.

Shields, C., Wynne, L., & Sirkin, M. (1992). Illness, family theory, and family therapy: I. Conceptual issues. II. The perception of physical illness in the family system. *Family Process, 31*, 3–18.

Sorlie, P. D., Backlund, E., & Keller, J. B. (1995). US mortality by economic, demographic, and social characteristics: The National Longitudinal Mortality Study. *American Journal of Public Health, 85*, 949–956.

Totman, R. (1979). *Social causes of illness*. New York: Pantheon Books.

Index